FIGURES OF SPEECH
USED IN THE BIBLE

FIGURES OF SPEECH

USED

IN THE BIBLE

EXPLAINED AND ILLUSTRATED

—

By E. W. Bullinger, D.D.

—

"How is it that ye do not understand? . . .
Then understood they."

MATT. xvi. 11, 12

BAKER BOOK HOUSE
Grand Rapids, Michigan

Reprinted 1968 by
Baker Book House Company

Originally published
in 1898 by
Messrs. Eyre and Spottiswoode,
in London

ISBN: 0-8010-0559-0

Sixteenth printing, March 1991

PHOTOLITHOPRINTED BY CUSHING - MALLOY, INC.
ANN ARBOR, MICHIGAN, UNITED STATES OF AMERICA

INTRODUCTION.

JEHOVAH has been pleased to give us the revelation of His mind and will in words. It is therefore absolutely necessary that we should understand not merely the meanings of the words themselves, but also the laws which govern their usage and combinations.

All language is governed by law; but, in order to increase the power of a word, or the force of an expression, these laws are designedly departed from, and words and sentences are thrown into, and used in, new forms, or *figures*.

The ancient Greeks reduced these new and peculiar forms to science, and gave names to more than two hundred of them.

The Romans carried forward this science: but with the decline of learning in the Middle Ages, it practically died out. A few writers have since then occasionally touched upon it briefly, and have given a few trivial examples: but the knowledge of this ancient science is so completely forgotten, that its very name to-day is used in a different sense and with almost an opposite meaning.

These manifold forms which words and sentences assume were called by the Greeks *Schema* (σχῆμα) and by the Romans, *Figura*. Both words have the same meaning, *viz., a shape* or *figure*. When we speak of a person as being "a figure" we mean one who is dressed in some peculiar style, and out of the ordinary manner. The Greek word *Schema* is found in 1 Cor. vii. 31, "*The fashion* of this world passeth away"; Phil. ii. 8, "being found *in fashion* as a man." The Latin word *Figura* is from the verb *fingere, to form*, and has passed into the English language in the words figure, transfigure, configuration, effigy, feint, feign, etc., etc.

We use the word *figure* now in various senses. Its primitive meaning applies to any marks, lines, or outlines, which make a form or shape. Arithmetical figures are certain marks or forms which represent numbers (1, 2, 3, etc.). All secondary and derived meanings of the word "figure" retain this primitive meaning.

Applied to words, a figure denotes some form which a word or sentence takes, different from its ordinary and natural form. This is always for the purpose of giving additional force, more life, intensified feeling, and greater emphasis. Whereas to-day "*Figurative language*" is ignorantly spoken of as though it made less of the meaning, and deprived the words of their power and force. A passage of God's Word is quoted; and it is met with the cry, "Oh, that is figurative"— implying that its meaning is weakened, or that it has quite a different meaning, or that it has no meaning at all. But the very opposite is the case. For an unusual form (*figura*) is never used except to *add* force to the truth conveyed, emphasis to the statement of it, and depth to the meaning of it. When we apply this science then to God's words and to Divine truths, we see at once that no branch of Bible study can be more important, or offer greater promise of substantial reward.

It lies at the very root of all translation; and it is the key to true interpretation . . . As the course of language moves smoothly along, according to the laws which govern it, there is nothing by which it can awaken or attract our attention. It is as when we are travelling by rail-way. As long as everything proceeds according to the regulations we notice nothing ; we sleep, or we read, or meditate as the case may be. But, let the train slacken its speed, or make an unexpected stop ;—we immediately hear the question asked, "What is the matter ?" "What are we stopping for ?" We hear one window go down and then another: attention is thoroughly aroused, and interest excited. So it is exactly with our reading. As long as all proceeds smoothly and according to law we notice nothing. But suddenly there is a departure from some law, a deviation from the even course—an unlooked for change—our attention is attracted, and we at once give our mind to discover why the words have been used in a new form, what the particular force of the passage is, and why we are to put special emphasis on the fact stated or on the truth conveyed. In fact, it is not too much to say that, in the use of these figures, we have, as it were, the Holy Spirit's own markings of our Bibles.

This is the most important point of all. For it is not by fleshly wisdom that the "words which the Holy Ghost teacheth" are to be understood. The natural man cannot understand the Word of God. It is foolishness unto him. A man may admire a sun-dial, he may marvel at its use, and appreciate the cleverness of its design; he may be interested in its carved-work, or wonder at the mosaics or other beauties which adorn its structure : but, if he holds a lamp in his hand or any other light emanating from himself or from this world, he can make it any hour he pleases, and he will never be able to tell the time of day. Nothing but the light from God's sun in the Heavens can tell him that. So it is with the Word of God. The natural man may admire its structure, or be interested in its statements ; he may study its geography, its history, yea, even its prophecy ; but none of these things will reveal to him his relation to time and eternity. Nothing but the light that cometh from Heaven. Nothing but the Sun of Righteousness can tell him that. It may be said of the Bible, therefore, as it is of the New Jerusalem—" The Lamb is the light thereof." The Holy Spirit's work in this world is to lead to Christ, to glorify Christ. The Scriptures are inspired by the Holy Spirit ; and the same Spirit that inspired the words in the Book must inspire its truths in our hearts, for they can and must be " Spiritually discerned " (1 Cor. ii. 1-16).

On this foundation, then, we have prosecuted this work. And on these lines we have sought to carry it out.

We are dealing with the words " which the Holy Ghost teacheth." All His works are perfect. " The words of the Lord are pure words "; human words, indeed, words pertaining to this world, but purified as silver is refined in a furnace. Therefore we must study every word, and in so doing we shall soon learn to say with Jeremiah (xv. 16), " Thy WORDS were found, and I did eat them ; and Thy WORD was unto me the joy and rejoicing of mine heart . . ."

It is clear, therefore, that no branch of Bible-study can be more important : and yet we may truly say that there is no branch of it which has been so utterly neglected.

John Vilant Macbeth (Professor of Rhetoric, etc., in the University of West Virginia) has said :—

" There is no even tolerably good treatise on Figures existing at present in our language—Is there in any other tongue ? There is no consecutive discussion of them of more than a few pages ; the examples brought forward by all others being trivial in the extreme and threadbare ; while the main conception of what constitutes the chief class of figures is altogether narrow, erroneous, and unphilosophical. Writers generally, even the ablest, are wholly in the dark as to the precise distinction between a *trope* and a *metonomy ;* and very few even of literary men have so much as heard of *Hypocatastasis* or Implication, one of the most important of figures, and one, too, that is constantly shedding its light upon us."*

---

* *The Might and Mirth of Literature*, by John Walker Vilant Macbeth, Professor of Rhetoric, etc., in the University of West Virginia, New York, 1875, page xxxviii. This work was published simultaneously in London, but the edition had to be sent back to New York, owing to the fact that there was no demand for it !

Solomon Glassius (1593-1656), a converted Jew, and a distinguished theologian, in Germany, two centuries and a half ago, published (in 1625) his important work *Philologia Sacra*, in which he includes an important treatise on Sacred Rhetoric. This is by far the fullest account of Biblical Figures ever published. But this work is written in Latin, and has never been translated into any language.

Benjamin Keach (1640-1704) published in 1682 his *Troposchema-logia : or, a Key to open the Scripture Metaphors and Types*. He does not hesitate to avail himself largely of Glassius's work, though he barely acknowledges it, or the extent to which he is indebted to it. There is much that is good and true and useful, with much that is fanciful, in Keach's volumes.

John Albert Bengel (1687-1752) is the only commentator who has ever taken Figures of Language seriously into account as a key to the interpretation and elucidation of the Scriptures. It is this fact which gives his commentary on the New Testament (which he calls a *Gnomon*) such great value, and imparts such excellence to it, making it unique among commentaries.

M. John Alb. Burk has drawn up an explanatory Index of over 100 of these "technical terms" occuring in Bengel's Commentary, and a Translation of it, by Canon Fausset, is added to T. and T. Clark's English Edition of Bengel, to serve as a key to that work.

Beyond this there is but little. Dr. McGill, in his *Lectures on Rhetoric and Criticism*, Glasgow, 1838, devotes one chapter to the subject of Figurative language, and describes about sixteen Figures. Alexander Carson in a Treatise on the Figures of Speech,* classifies and names about forty-three figures.

Archdeacon Farrar in *A brief Greek Syntax*, London, 1867, has one chapter on Figures, and describes a few, illustrating them from the classics.

Horne's *Introduction to the Bible* devotes one chapter out of his four volumes to "Figurative Language," but confines himself to describing only ten Figures.

There are one or two small works of more recent date. *The Rhetorical Speaker and Poetical Class-book*, by R. T. Linnington, 1844. He describes some 35 Figures, but uses them only as a study for rhetorical effect, and illustrates them from general literature for purposes of recitation.

---

* Bound up in a Vol., with *An Examination of the Principles of Biblical Interpretation*, New York, 1855.

The S.P.C.K. also published, in 1849, a course of lectures on the Figurative Language of the Holy Scriptures, delivered in the Parish Church of Nayland in Suffolk in 1786.

Thus we are justified in saying that Bible students can find no complete work on the subject of Figurative Language in its relation to the Bible.

There are several small works on Rhetoric. But Rhetoric is an adaptation of Figurative Language for the purposes of elocution ; and, treatises on Rhetoric hardly come within the scope of our present object.

Translators and commentators, as a rule, have entirely ignored the subject ; while by some it has been derided. There is great need, therefore, for a work which shall deal exhaustively with the great subject of Figurative Language ; and, if possible, reduce the Figures to some kind of system (which has never yet been completely done either by the Ancients or Moderns), and apply them to the elucidation of the Word of God. The gems and pearls which will be strung together will be exquisite, because they are Divine ; but the thread, though human, will be of no mean value. The mode of treatment is new and comprehensive. It is new ; for never before has Figurative Language been taken as a subject of Bible study : it is comphrensive, for it embraces the facts and truths which lie at the foundation of the Christian faith, and the principles which are the essence of Protestant truth.

It is moreover a difficult study for the general reader. For, besides the difficulty which naturally arises from the absence of any standard works upon the subject, there are three other difficulties of no mean magnitude which have doubtless tended much to deter students from taking up the subject, even where there may have been a desire to study it.

The *first* difficulty is their *nomenclature.* All the names of these figures are either in Greek or Latin. This difficulty can be, to a great extent, cleared away by a simple explanation, and by sub-stituting an English equivalent, which we have here attempted.

The *second* difficulty is their *number.* We have catalogued over 200 distinct figures, several of them with from 30 to 40 varieties. Many figures have duplicate names which brings up the total number of names to more than 500.

John Holmes, in his *Rhetoric made easy* (1755), gives a list of 250.

J. Vilant Macbeth, (in his work already referred to), deals with 220, which he illustrates only from English and American literature.

While G. W. Hervey's *System of Christian Rhetoric* (1873) defines 256 with 467 names.

The *third* difficulty is the utter absence of any *classification.* These figures do not seem to have ever been arranged in any satisfactory order. If the Greeks did this work, no record of it seems to have come down to us.

The three great Divisions into which they usually fall are :

I. Figures of ETYMOLOGY : which are departures from the ordinary *spelling* of words. These consist of some 18 Figures, such as

Aphær'esis, *front-cut,* 'ghast for aghast, 'fore for before, etc.

Syn'cope, *mid-cut,* e'er for ever, o'er for over.

Apoc'ope, *end-cut,* Lucrece for Lucretia, etc., etc.

II. Figures of SYNTAX or GRAMMAR : which are alterations of the ordinary *meaning* of words.

III. Figures of RHETORIC : which are deviations from the ordinary *application* of words.

With the first of these, we are not now concerned, as it has nothing to do with our present work.

It is only with the Figures of Syntax and Rhetoric that we have to deal.

These have been sometimes mixed together, and then divided into two classes :—

I. Figures that affect *words.*

II. Figures that affect *thought.*

But this is a very imperfect arrangement ; and, as Dr. Blair says, " Is of no great use ; as nothing can be built upon it in practice, neither is it always clear."

Another arrangement is (1) figures that are the result of *feeling,* and (2) those that are the result of *imagination.* But this also is defective and inadequate.

In the absence of any known authoritative arrangement of the Figures, we have grouped them in this work under three great natural divisions :—

I. Figures which depend for their peculiarity on any OMISSION : in which something is omitted in the words themselves or in the sense conveyed by them (Elliptical Figures).

II. Figures which depend on any ADDITION, by REPETITION of words or sense (Pleonastic Figures) : and

III. Figures which depend on CHANGE, or Alteration in the usage, order, or application of words.

We have fully set out this arrangement in a Summary of Classification, and, in an Analytical Table of Contents; where, for the first time, will be seen a complete classified list of Figures, with English equivalents, brief definitions, and alternative names.

A figure is, as we have before said, a departure from the natural and fixed laws of Grammar or Syntax; but it is a departure not arising from ignorance or accident. Figures are not mere mistakes of Grammar; on the contrary, they are *legitimate* departures from law, for a special purpose. They are permitted variations with a particular object. Therefore they are limited as to their number, and can be ascertained, named, and described.

No one is at liberty to exercise any arbitrary power in their use. All that art can do is to ascertain the laws to which nature has subjected them. There is no room for private opinion, neither can speculation concerning them have any authority.

It is not open to any one to say of this or that word or sentence, "This is a figure," according to his own fancy, or to suit his own purpose. We are dealing with a science whose laws and their workings are known. If a word or words be a figure, then that figure can be named, and described. It is used for a definite purpose and with a specific object. Man may use figures in ignorance, without any particular object. But when the Holy Spirit takes up human words and uses a figure (or peculiar form), it is for a special purpose, and that purpose must be observed and have due weight given to it.

Many misunderstood and perverted passages are difficult, only because we have not known the Lord's design in the difficulty.

Thomas Boys has well said (*Commentary*, 1 Pet. iii.), "There is much in the Holy Scriptures, which we find it hard to understand: nay, much that we seem to understand so fully as to imagine that we have discovered in it some difficulty or inconsistency. Yet the truth is, that passages of this kind are often the very parts of the Bible in which the greatest instruction is to be found: and, more than this, the instruction is to be obtained in the contemplation of the very difficulties by which at first we are startled. This is the *intention* of these apparent inconsistencies. The expressions are used, in order that we may mark them, dwell upon them, and draw instruction out of them. Things are put to us in a strange way, because, if they were put in a more ordinary way, we should not notice them."

This is true, not only of mere difficulties as such, but especially of all Figures: *i.e.*, of all new and unwonted forms of words and speech: and our design in this work is that we should learn to notice them and gain the instruction they were intended to give us.

The Word of God may, in one respect, be compared to the earth. All things necessary to life and sustenance may be obtained by scratching the surface of the earth: but there are treasures of beauty and wealth to be obtained by digging deeper into it. So it is with the Bible. "All things necessary to life and godliness" lie upon its surface for the humblest saint; but, beneath that surface are "great spoils" which are found only by those who seek after them as for "hid treasure."

_____

THE PLAN OF THE WORK IS AS FOLLOWS:—

1. To give in its proper order and place each one of two hundred and seventeen figures of speech, by name.

2. Then to give the proper pronunciation of its name.

3. Then its etymology, showing why the name was given to it, and what is its meaning.

4. And, after this, a number of passages of Scripture, in full, where the figure is used, ranging from two or three instances, to some hundreds under each figure, accompanied by a full explanation. These special passages amount, in all, to nearly eight thousand.

We repeat, and it must be borne in mind, that all these many forms are employed only to set forth the truth with greater vigour, and with a far greater meaning: and this, for the express purpose of indicating to us what is emphatic; and to call and attract our attention, so that it may be directed to, and fixed upon, the special truth which is to be conveyed to us.

Not every Figure is of equal importance, nor is every passage of equal interest.

But we advise all students of this great subject to go patiently forward, assuring them that from time to time they will be amply rewarded; and often when least expected.

_____

THE USE OF THE WORK.

This work may be used either for the direct study of this important subject; or it may be used simply as a constant companion to the Bible, and as a work of reference.

A copious index of Texts and Passages illustrated has been compiled for this purpose; and will be found, with six other Indexes, and five Appendixes, at the end of the volume.

ETHELBERT W. BULLINGER.

25 Connaught Street,
London.
November, 1899.

NOTE

ON

FIGURES IN GENERAL.

A FIGURE is simply a word or a sentence thrown into a peculiar *form*, different from its original or simplest meaning or use. These forms are constantly used by every speaker and writer. It is impossible to hold the simplest conversation, or to write a few sentences without, it may be unconsciously, making use of figures. We may say, " the ground needs rain " : that is a plain, cold, matter-of-fact statement; but if we say " the ground is thirsty," we immediately use a figure. It is not true to *fact*, and therefore it must be a figure. But how true to *feeling* it is ! how full of warmth and life ! Hence, we say, " the crops suffer " ; we speak of " a hard heart," " a rough man," " an iron will." In all these cases we take a word which has a certain, definite meaning, and apply the name, or the quality, or the act, to some other thing with which it is associated, by time or place, cause or effect, relation or resemblance.

Some figures are common to many languages; others are peculiar to some one language. There are figures used in the English language, which have nothing that answers to them in Hebrew or Greek; and there are Oriental figures which have no counterpart in English; while there are some figures in various languages, arising from human infirmity and folly, which find, of course, no place in the word of God.

It may be asked, " How are we to know, then, when words are to be taken in their simple, original form (*i.e.*, literally), and when they are to be taken in some other and peculiar form (*i.e.*, as a *Figure*) ? " The answer is that, whenever and wherever it is possible, the words of Scripture are to be understood *literally*, but when a statement appears to be contrary to our experience, or to known fact, or revealed truth; or seems to be at variance with the general teaching of the Scriptures, then we may reasonably expect that some figure is employed. And as it is employed only to call our attention to some specially designed emphasis, we are at once bound to diligently examine the figure for the purpose of discovering and learning the truth that is thus emphasized.

From non-attention to these Figures, translators have made blunders as serious as they are foolish. Sometimes they have translated the figure literally, totally ignoring its existence; sometimes they have taken it fully into account, and have translated, not according to the letter, but according to the spirit; sometimes they have taken literal words and translated them figuratively. Commentators and interpreters, from inattention to the figures, have been led astray from the real meaning of many important passages of God's Word; while ignorance of them has been the fruitful parent of error and false doctrine. It may be truly said that most of the gigantic errors of Rome, as well as the erroneous and conflicting views of the Lord's People, have their root and source, either in figuratively explaining away passages which should be taken literally, or in taking literally what has been thrown into a peculiar form or Figure of language: thus, not only falling into error, but losing the express teaching, and missing the special emphasis which the particular Figure was designed to impart to them.

This is an additional reason for using greater exactitude and care when we are dealing with the words of God. Man's words are scarcely worthy of such study. Man uses figures, but often at random and often in ignorance or in error. But "the words of the Lord are pure words." All His works are perfect, and when the Holy Spirit takes up and uses human words, He does so, we may be sure, with unerring accuracy, infinite wisdom, and perfect beauty.

We may well, therefore, give all our attention to "the words which the Holy Ghost teacheth."

SOME ERRATA.

PAGE	LINE	FOR	READ
5	20	nominative	accusative
21	3	Heroditus	Herodotus
—	note	ἐς	ἐς
36	15	*Are*	*Have*
49	last	.	?
53	note	בַּלְנֹוּר	בְּמֻּוֹר
—	—	*betsinnōr*	*batsinnor*
63	12	נָשָׁא	נָשָׁא
—	—	*nashah*	*nahsah*
64	2	*l'kikahm*	*l'vikam*
68	33	ἐργάτος	ἐργάτης
—	last	ἀντιδιαθεμένοι	ἀντιδιαθέμενοι
70	24	words	words,
77	6	nominative	accusative
92	12	τό	τὸ
103	23	δειλια	δειλίας
		deilia	*deilias*
104	note	Samuel	Samuel's
115	last	וַתָּהָם (*vattacham*)	וּתָהָם (*vattachas*)
116	4	transpose the letters λ and λ	
„			
„	5	תחם	תחם
„		אחם	אחם
120	28	בֵּן	בֵּן
122	37	*meen*	*mee*
131	35	προ	πρό
142	27	A and B	A and *A*
—	27, 28	B and *A*	B and *B*
144	2	be	be ye

146	... ...	19	... ...	furnish :	... ...	furnish
149	... ...	3	... ...	ἀπὸ	... ...	απο
159	... ...	10	... ...	ἐναντιος	... ...	ἐναντίος
160	... ...	2	... ...	were	... ...	were yet
161	... ...	34	... ...	*Synonimia*	... ...	*Synonymia*
172	... ...	8	... ...	settest	... ...	settedst
173	... ...	1	... ...	B˙	... ...	*B*
177	.. ...	18	... ...	μετα	... ...	μετα
„	... ...	„	... ...	κγαιόντων	... ...	κλαιοντων
180	....	15	... ...	παρα	... ...	παρά
181	... ...	4	... ...	verse 1	... ...	verses 1, 2
				verse 2	... ...	verse 3
187	... ...	19	... ...	ל	... ...	־ל
191	... ...	15	... ...	*oomizeh*	... ...	*oomizzeh*
—	... ...	last	... ...	Lord	... ...	LORD
206	... ...	11	... ...	*resume*	... ...	*resumes*
215	... ...	19	... ...	G	... ...	G
220	... ...	5	... ...		... ...	insert B

232 ... ... note, take out Rom. i. 27 where (in the Received Text) is ἄρρην (*arreen*), *male*, and should be ἄρσεν (*arsen*). neuter, as in Rev. xii. 5, 13, according to the authorities cited in Text.

241 ... ... — delete the example Deut. xxxii. 10.

711 ... ... 27 ... ... lived only 450 ... ... died some 500

SUMMARY OF CLASSIFICATION.

b

ANALYTICAL TABLE OF CONTENTS.

FIRST DIVISION.

FIGURES INVOLVING OMISSION.

I. *AFFECTING WORDS.*

II. *AFFECTING THE SENSE.*

SECOND DIVISION.

FIGURES INVOLVING ADDITION.

I. *AFFECTING WORDS.*

1. Repetition of Letters and Syllables.

(*a*) Of the same Letters.

(*b*) Of different Letters.

2. The Repetition of the Same Word.

(*a*) In the same Sense.

II. *AFFECTING THE SENSE (Figures of Rhetoric).*

1. REPETITIO.

By way of Repetition.

2. AMPLIFICATIO.

By way of Addition or Amplification.

3. DESCRIPTIO.

By way of Description.

4. CONCLUSIO.

By way of Conclusion.

5. Interpositio.

By way of Interposition.

6. Ratiocinatio.

By way of Reasoning.

THIRD DIVISION.

FIGURES INVOLVING CHANGE.*

I. *AFFECTING THE MEANING OF WORDS.*

*. See page 489 for Summary Classification of these.

c

II. AFFECTING THE ARRANGEMENT AND ORDER OF WORDS.

1. SEPARATE WORDS.

III. *AFFECTING THE APPLICATION OF WORDS.*

1. AS TO SENSE.

2. As to Persons.

3. AS TO SUBJECT-MATTER.

4. AS TO TIME.

5. As to Feeling.

6. As to Argumentation.

APPENDICES.

INDEXES.

LIST OF ABBREVIATIONS.

A. - - Alford and his critical Greek Text.

Acc. - The Accusative Case.

A.V. - The Authorized Version, or current Text of our English Bible, 1611.

G. - - Griesbach and his critical Greek Text.

Gen. - The Genitive Case.

Comp. Compare.

Cf. - - Compare (for Latin, *confer*).

Imp. - The Imperative Mood.

Ind. - The Indicative Mood.

Inf. - The Infinitive Mood.

L. - - Lachmann and his critical Greek Text.

LXX. - The Septuagint Version (325 B.C.).

Marg. - Margin.

Nom. - The Nominative Case.

P.B.V. The Prayer Book Version of the Psalms (from Coverdale's Bible).

Part. - Participle.

Pl. - - The Plural Number.

Q.v. - Which see.

R.V. - The Revised Version, 1881.

Sept. - The Septuagint Version.

Sing. - The Singular Number.

Sqq. - Following.

Tr. - - Tregelles and his critical Greek Text.

T. - - Tischendorf and his critical Greek Text.

WH. - Westcott and Hort, and their critical Greek Text.

(10) - A figure in brackets, immediately after a reference, denotes the number of the verse in the Hebrew or Greek where the versification differs from the A.V.

Denotes that one thing *equals* or is the same as the other.

FIGURES INVOLVING OMISSION.

I. *AFFECTING WORDS.*

ELLIPSIS.

El-lip'-sis. This is the Greek word ἔλλειψις, *a leaving in,* from ἐν (*en*) *in,* and λείπειν (*leipein*) *to leave.*

The figure is so called, because some gap is *left in* the sentence, which means that a word or words are *left out* or *omitted.* The English name of the figure would therefore be *Omission.*

The figure is a peculiar form given to a passage when a word or words are omitted ; words which are necessary for the grammar, but are not necessary for the sense.

The laws of geometry declare that there must be at least three straight lines to enclose a space. So the laws of syntax declare that there must be at least three words to make complete sense, or the simplest complete sentence. These three words are variously named by grammarians. In the sentence " Thy word is truth," " Thy word " is the subject spoken of, " truth " is what is said of it (the predicate), and the verb " is " (the copula) connects it.

But any of these three may be dispensed with ; and this law of syntax may be legitimately broken by Ellipsis.

The omission arises not from want of thought, or lack of care, or from accident, but from design, in order that we may not stop to think of, or lay stress on, the word omitted, but may dwell on the other words which are thus emphasised by the omission. For instance, in Matt. xiv. 19, we read that the Lord Jesus " gave the loaves to His disciples, and the disciples to the multitude."

There is no sense in the latter sentence, which is incomplete, " the disciples to the multitude," because there is no verb. The verb " gave " is omitted by the figure of Ellipsis for some purpose. If we read the last sentence as it stands, it reads as though *Jesus gave the disciples to the multitude !*

A

This at once serves to arrest our attention; it causes us to note the figure employed; we observe the emphasis; we learn the intended lesson. What is it? Why, this; we are asked to dwell on the fact that the disciples gave the bread, but only instrumentally, not really. The Lord Jesus Himself was the alone Giver of that bread. Our thoughts are thus, at once, centred on Him and not on the disciples.

These Ellipses are variously dealt with in the English Versions (both Authorized and Revised). In many cases they are correctly supplied by *italics*. In some cases the sentences are very erroneously completed. Sometimes an Ellipsis in the Text is not seen, and therefore is not taken into account in the Translation. Sometimes an Ellipsis is imagined and supplied where none really exists in the original.

Where an Ellipsis is wrongly supplied, or not supplied at all, the words of the Text have to be very freely translated in order to make sense, and their literal meaning is sometimes widely departed from.

But on the other hand, where we correctly supply the Ellipsis— one word, it may be—it at once enables us to take all the other words of the passage in their literal signification. This is in itself an enormous gain, to say nothing of the wonderful light that may be thus thrown upon the Scripture.

These Ellipses must not be arbitrarily supplied according to our own individual views; we are not at liberty to insert any words, according to our own fancies: but they are all scientifically arranged and classified, and each must therefore be filled up, according to definite principles which are well ascertained, and in obedience to laws which are carefully laid down.

Ellipsis is of three kinds :—

> *Absolute* Ellipsis,
> *Relative* Ellipsis, and the
> Ellipsis of *Repetition* :—

A. *Absolute*, where the omitted word or words are to be supplied from *the nature of the subject* alone.

B. *Relative*, where the omitted word or words are to be supplied from, and are suggested by the *context*.

C. The Ellipsis of *Repetition*, where the omitted word or words are to be supplied by repeating them from a clause which precedes or follows.

These three great divisions may be further set forth as follows :—

A. ABSOLUTE ELLIPSIS, where the omitted word or words are to be supplied from the *nature* of the subject.

  I. Nouns and Pronouns.

      1. The Nominative.

      2. The Accusative.

      3. Pronouns.

      4. Other connected words.

  II. Verbs and Participles :—

      1. When the verb finite is wanting :

          (*a*) especially the verb *to say*.

      2. When the verb infinitive is wanting :

          (*a*) after יָכֹל *to be able.*

          (*b*) after the verb *to finish*.

          (*c*) after another verb, personal or impersonal.

      3. When the verb substantive is wanting.

      4. When the participle is wanting.

  III. Certain connected words in the same member of a passage.

  IV. A whole clause in a connected passage :—

      1. The first clause.

      2. The latter clause or Apodosis (*Anantapodoton*).

      3. A comparison.

B. RELATIVE ELLIPSIS—

  I. Where the omitted word is to be supplied from a cognate word in the context.

      1. The noun from the verb.

      2. The verb from the noun.

  II. Where the omitted word is to be supplied from a contrary word.

  III. Where the omitted word is to be supplied from analogous or related words.

  IV. Where the omitted word is contained in another word : the one word comprising the two significations—(*Concisa Locutio, Syntheton* or *Compositio, Constructio Prægnans*).

C. ELLIPSIS OF REPETITION—

   I. Simple: where the Ellipsis is to be supplied from a preceding or a succeeding clause.

     1. From a preceding clause.

      (*a*) Nouns and Pronouns.

      (*b*) Verbs.

      (*c*) Particles.

        (i.) Negatives.

        (ii.) Interrogatives.

      (*d*) Sentences.

     2. From a succeeding clause.

  II. Complex: where the two clauses are mutually involved, and the Ellipsis in the former clause is to be supplied from the latter, and at the same time an Ellipsis in the latter clause is to be supplied from the former. (Called also *Semiduplex Oratio*).

     1. Single words.

     2. Sentences.

A. ABSOLUTE ELLIPSIS:

That is, the omission of words or terms which must be supplied only from *the nature of the subject*. The omitted word may be a noun, adjective, pronoun, verb, participle, adverb, preposition.

I. THE OMISSION OF NOUNS AND PRONOUNS.

1. The Omission of the NOMINATIVE.

Gen. xiv. 19, 20.—Melchizedek said to Abram, "Blessed be the most high God, which hath delivered thine enemies into thine hand. And he [*i.e., Abram*] gave him tithes of all."

From the context, as well as from Heb. vii. 4, it is clear that it was Abram who gave the tithes to Melchizedek, and not Melchizedek to Abram.

Gen. xxxix. 6.—"And he left all that he had in Joseph's hand; and he knew not ought he had, save the bread which he did eat. And Joseph was *a* goodly *person*, and well-favoured."

Here it is not at all clear which it was of the two who " knew not ought he had." If we understand Potiphar, it is difficult to see how he only knew the bread he ate: or if Joseph, it is difficult to understand how he knew not ought he had.

If the *Ellipsis*, however, is rightly supplied, it makes it all clear.

The verse may be rendered, and the Ellipsis supplied as follows :—
"And he [*Potiphar*] left all that he had in Joseph's hand : and he [*Potiphar*] knew not anything save the bread which he was eating. And Joseph was beautiful of figure, and beautiful of appearance." All difficulty is removed when we remember that "the Egyptians might not eat bread with the Hebrews, for that is an abomination unto the Egyptians " (xliii. 32). Everything, therefore, was committed by Potiphar to Joseph's care, except that which pertained to the matter of food.

2 Sam. iii. 7.—" And Saul had a concubine, whose name *was* Rizpah, the daughter of Aiah, and . . . said to Abner, Wherefore, etc."
Here it is clear from the sense of the next verse and 2 Sam. xxi. 8 that " *Ishbosheth* " is the word to be supplied, as is done in italics.

2 Sam. xxiii. 20.—" He slew two lionlike men of Moab."
The Massorah points out* that the word Ariel occurs three times, in this passage and Isa. xxix. 1. In Isa. the word is twice transliterated as a proper name, while in 2 Sam. xxiii. 20, margin, it is translated *lions of God :* the first part of the word אֲרִי (*aree*) *a lion*, and the second part אֵל (*ĕl*) *God*. But if we keep it uniformly and consistently as a proper name we have with the *Ellipsis* of the nominative (*sons*) the following sense : " He slew the two *sons of* Ariel of Moab."

2 Sam. xxiv. 1.—" And again the anger of the LORD was kindled against Israel, and he moved David against them to say, Go, number Israel and Judah."
Here the nominative to the verb "moved " is wanting. Someone moved, and who that was we learn from 1 Chron. xxi. 1, from which it is clear that the word *Satan* or *the Adversary* is to be supplied, as is done in the margin :—" And again the anger of the LORD was kindled against Israel, and [*the Adversary*] moved David against them to say, Go, number Israel and Judah."

1 Chron. vi. 28 (12).—" And the sons of Samuel ; the firstborn Vashni (marg., *called also Joel*, ver. 33 and 1 Sam. viii. 2) and Abiah."
Here there is an Ellipsis of the name of the firstborn : while the word וַשְׁנִי, *Vashni*, when otherwise pointed (וְשֵׁנִי) means "*and the second* " ! so that the verse reads,
"And the sons of Samuel ; the firstborn [*Joel*] and the second Abiah." This agrees with the Syriac Version. The R.V. correctly supplies the Ellipsis, and translates *vashni* " and the second."
" Joel " is supplied from ver. 33 (see also 1 Sam. viii. 2, and the note in Ginsburg's edition of the Hebrew Bible).

*Ginsburg's Edition, Vol. i., p. 106.

Ps. xxxiv. 17.—"*[They]* cry, and the Lord heareth, and delivereth them out of all their troubles."

The immediate subject in ver. 16 is *evildoers.* But it is not these who cry. It is the righteous. Hence the A.V. and the R.V. supply the words "*the righteous*" in italics. The nominative is omitted, in order that our attention may be fixed not on their persons or their characters, but upon their cry, and the Lord's gracious answer.

The same design is seen in all similar cases.

Ps. cv. 40.—"[They] asked, and he brought quails," *i.e.*, the *People* asked. The nominative is supplied in the A.V. But the R.V. translates it literally "They asked."

Prov. xxii. 27.—"If thou hast nothing to pay, why should one [*i.e.*, *the creditor*] take away thy bed from under thee?"

Isa. xxvi. 1.—"In that day shall this song be sung in the land of Judah; we have a strong city; salvation will one [*i.e.* *God*] appoint *for* walls and bulwarks."

The A.V. interprets by supplying the nominative. The R.V. translates it literally.

Jer. li. 19.—"He is the former of all things, and *Israel is* the rod of his inheritance."

Here both the A.V. and R.V. supply the *Ellipsis* from x. 16. Had it been supplied from the immediate context, it would have come under the head of Relative *Ellipsis*, or that of Repetition.

Ezek. xlvi. 12.—"Now when the Prince shall prepare a voluntary offering or peace offerings voluntarily unto the LORD, *one* shall then open him the gate that looketh toward the East, &c.," *i.e.*, הַשֹּׁעֵר *the gate-keeper* (supplied from the noun הַשַּׁעַר, *the gate*), which follows, shall open the gate.

Zech. vii. 2.—"When they (*Heb.* he) had sent unto the house of God, Sherezer and Regem-melech and their men, to pray before the LORD" [*i.e.*, when *the people who had returned to Judea* had sent].

Matt. xvi. 22.—"Be it far from Thee, Lord."

Here the Ellipsis in the Greek is destroyed by the translation. The Greek reads, "Ἵλεώς σοι, κύριε" (*hileōs soi, kyrie*), which is untranslatable literally, unless we supply the *Ellipsis* of the Nominative, thus: "[*God be*] merciful to Thee, Lord!" Thus it is in the Septuagint 1 Chron. xi. 19, where it is rendered "God forbid that I should do this thing," but it ought to be, "[*God*] be merciful to me [*to keep me from doing*] this thing."

Acts xiii. 29.—"And when they had fulfilled all that was written of him, they took *him* down from the tree, and laid *him* in a sepulchre," *i.e.,* Joseph of Arimathæa and Nicodemus took him down. But it is the *act* which we are to think of here rather than the *persons* who did it. Hence the *Ellipsis.*

1 Cor. xv. 25.—" For he must reign, till he hath put all enemies under his feet," *i.e.,* "he [*the Son*] must reign, until he [*the Son*] shall have put all things under his [*the Son's*] feet." Here the subjection refers to the period of Christ's personal reign.

This is one of the seven New Testament references to Ps. cx. 1, "Jehovah said unto Adon—Sit thou at my right hand, until I make thine enemies thy footstool." The English word "make" occurs 1,111 times in the Old Testament, as the rendering of 49 Hebrew words. The one so rendered here is שׁית (*Sheeth*) and means *to put, place, set,* or *appoint,* and is rendered *make* only 19 times out of 94. Its proper meaning is *put* or *appoint.* (See Gen. iii. 15; iv. 25; xxx. 40. Ps. cxl. 5. Isa. xxvi. 1, &c.)

The word in the N. T. is τίθημι (*titheemi*), and has the same meaning. It is rendered *make* only 10 times out of 91, but in these cases it means to *set* or *appoint* (Acts xx. 28. Rom. iv. 17, &c.). In every case the verb is in the second aorist subjunctive, and should be rendered "*shall have put.*"

Six of the seven references (Matt. xxii. 44. Mark xii. 36. Luke xx. 42. Acts ii. 34. Heb. i. 13; x. 13) refer to Christ's *session* on the Father's throne (not to His *reign* upon His own, Rev. iii. 21). And this session will continue until such time as the Father shall have placed Christ's enemies as a footstool for His feet. When that shall have been done, He will rise up from His seat and come forth into the air *for* His people, to receive them to Himself, and take them up to meet Him in the air so to be ever with the Lord. Then He will come unto the earth *with* them, and sit upon the throne of His glory, and reign until He shall have put all enemies under His feet. The other *six* passages refer to Christ's *session.* This *one* refers to His *reign* upon His own throne (not to His *session* on His Father's throne, Rev. iii. 21). And this reign will continue until He·(Christ) hath put all His enemies under His feet.

Note, that in the six passages His enemies are placed "as a footstool for His feet," and there is not a word about their being *under* His feet. In the one passage (1 Cor. xv. 25) there is not a word about being placed "as a footstool," but the word "under" His feet is used. We must distinguish between *placing* and *making,* and Christ's *session* and His *reign.* Then all these passages teach the Pre-Millennial and Pre-Tribulation coming of Christ *for* His people before His coming *with* them.*

---

* See *Things to Come* for October, 1898.

1 Cor. xv. 53.—" For this corruptible [*body*] must put on incorruption, and this mortal [*body*] must put on immortality."
The noun " body " must also be supplied in the next verse.

Eph. i. 8.—" Wherein he hath abounded towards us in all wisdom and prudence."
It is not "wherein," but ἧς (*hees*) *which, i.e.,* " [*the knowledge*] or *grace*, which he hath made to abound in us in all wisdom and prudence."

Titus i. 15.—" Unto the pure all things *are* pure."
The noun "meats" (*i.e.*, foods) must be supplied as in 1 Cor. vi. 12. "All [*meats*] indeed are clean to the clean." The word "clean " being used in its ceremonial or Levitical sense, for none can be otherwise either " pure " or " clean."

Heb. ix. 1.—" Then verily the first *covenant* had also ordinances of divine service." Here the word *covenant* is properly supplied in italics.

2 Pet. iii. 1.—" This second epistle, beloved, I now write unto you ; in *both* which I stir up your pure minds by way of remembrance," *i.e.*, " In *both* which [*epistles*] I stir up," etc.

1 John v. 16.—" If any man see his brother sin a sin *which is* not unto death, he shall ask, and he shall give him life, etc.," *i.e.*, " [*God*] shall give him life." See also Matt. v. 11, 15 ; Luke vi. 38, where *men* must be the word supplied.

2. The Omission of the OBJECT or ACCUSATIVE, etc., after the verb.

2 Sam. vi. 6.—" And when they came to Nachon's threshing-floor, Uzzah put forth *his hand* to the ark of God."
Here the omission is supplied. The *Ellipsis* is used, and the accusative is omitted, in order to call our attention to the *act*, rather than to the *manner* of it.

1 Chron. xvi. 7.—" Then on that day, David delivered first *this psalm* to thank the LORD, etc."
The *Ellipsis* might also be supplied thus : " David delivered first [*the following words*] to thank the LORD, etc."

Job. xxiv. 6.—" They reap *everyone* his corn in the field."
This hardly makes sense with the context, which describes the wicked doings of those who know not God.
The question is whether the word בְּלִילוֹ (*beleelō*) translated " his corn " is to be taken as one word, or whether it is to be read as two words בְּלִי לוֹ (*belee lō*) which mean *not their own*. In this case there

is the *Ellipsis* of the accusative, which must be supplied. The whole verse will then read,

" They reap [*their corn*] in a field not their own :
They glean the vintage of the wicked,"

which carries on the thought of the passage without a break in the argument.

If we read it as one word, then we must supply the Ellipsis differently:—" They reap their corn in a field [*not their own*]," so that it comes, in sense, to the same thing.

Ps. xxi. 12 (13).—" When thou shalt make ready *thine arrows* upon thy strings."

Ps. xliv. 10 (11).—" They which hate us spoil for themselves." The word spoil is שָׁסָה (*shahsah*), and means *to plunder*. And it is clear that the accusative, which is omitted, should be supplied:— " They which hate us plunder [*our goods*] for themselves." The emphasis being, of course, on the *act* and the *motive* in the verb " plunder," and " for themselves," rather than on the goods which they plunder.

In verse 12 (13), both the A.V. and R.V. have supplied the accusative, "*thy wealth*."

Ps. lvii. 2 (3).—" I will cry unto God most high ; unto God that performeth *all things* for me." Here the object is supplied in the words "*all things*." Other translators suggest " *His mercy*," " *His promises*," " *my desires*." Luther has " *my sorrow*," the Hebrew being גָּמַר (*gamar*), *to bring to an end, complete*, etc. The *Ellipsis* is left for emphasis. Nothing is particularised, so that we may supply everything. The mention of any one thing necessarily excludes others.

In Ps. cxxxviii. 8 we have the same verb (though with a different construction) and the same Ellipsis : but the former is translated " the LORD will perfect," and the latter is supplied " *that which* concerneth me ": *i.e.*, will consummate all *consummations* for me.

Ps. xciv. 10.—" He that chastiseth the heathen, shall not he correct [*you among the heathen*] ? " This is evidently the completion of the sense. The A.V. fills up the *Ellipsis* in the next sentence. This is of a different character, and comes under another division : " He that teacheth man knowledge, *shall not he know* ? "

Ps. ciii. 9.—" Neither will he keep *his anger* for ever." So in Nah. i. 2 ; Jer. iii. 5, 12.

Ps. cxxxvii. 5.—" If I forget thee, O Jerusalem, let my right nand forget *her cunning*."

Here both versions thus supply the accusative. But surely more is implied in the *Ellipsis* than mere skill of workmanship. Surely it means, " If I forget thee, O Jerusalem, let my right hand forget *me.*" Let it forget to work for me, to feed me and to defend me, if I forget to pray for thee and to defend thee.

Prov. xxiv. 24.—" He that saith unto the wicked, Thou art righteous; him shall the people curse, nations shall abhor him ; " *i.e.,* " He that saith to the wicked [*king*]." This is clear from the context.

Verses 21-25 read literally. " Fear the Lord, O my son, and the king. With men that make a difference (שָׁנָה, *shanah* see Est. i. 7; iii. 8), *between a king and an ordinary man* thou shalt not mingle thyself. For their calamity (whose? evidently that of two persons, viz., that of the king and also of the *common man*) shall rise suddenly ; and who knoweth the ruin of them both ? These *matters* also belong to the wise." To make no difference between man and man belongs to everyone alike, see Deut. i. 17.; but to make no difference between a man and a king is a matter that pertains only to the wise. " *It is* not good to have respect of persons in judgment. He that saith to the wicked [*king, as well as common man*], Thou art righteous ; him shall the people curse, nations shall abhor him ; but to them that rebuke him (*i.e., the wicked king*) shall be delight, and a good blessing shall come upon them."

Here there is accuracy of translation and consistency of interpretation. There is only one subject in verses 21-25.* Here it is the command not to flatter a wicked king ; and this explains the word " both " in verse 22, and the reference to " people " and " nations " in verse 24. Unless the *Ellipsis* is thus supplied, the meaning is not clear.

That which is a true admonition as to kingcraft, is also a solemn warning as to priestcraft. The " wise " makes no difference between a

---

* Each " proverb " or paragraph in the book of Proverbs is occupied with only one subject, even if it consists of several verses. This may sometimes throw light on a passage, *e.g.,* Prov. xxvi. 3-5, where verses 4 and 5 follow up the subject of verse 3, not changing the subject but enforcing it ; *i.e.,* " For the horse a whip, for the ass a bridle, and for the fool's back a rod." In other words you cannot reason with a horse or an ass, neither can you reason with a fool. Then follow two very finely stated *facts, not commands.* If you answer him according to his folly, he will think you are a fool like himself, and if you answer him not according to his folly, he will think that he is wise like yourself! So that we have a kind of hypothetical command:

Do this, and you will see that ;
Do that, and you will see, &c.

so-called priest and another man ; for he knows that all the people of God are made " priests unto God " (Rev. i. 6), and " an holy priest-hood " (1 Pet. ii. 5). Those who make a difference do so to their own loss, and to the dishonour of Christ.

Isa. liii. 12.—"Therefore will I divide him *a portion* with the great, and he shall divide the spoil with the strong " ; *i.e.,* " Therefore will I [Jehovah] divide (or apportion) to him a great multitude [*for booty*], and the strong ones will he (*i.e.,* Messiah) divide as spoil."

The structure shows that liii. 12 corresponds with, and is to be explained by lii. 15. The passage is concerning :—

Jehovah's Servant—the Sin Offering.

A. | lii. 13. His Presentation.
  B. | 14. His Affliction.
    C. | 15. His Reward.
A. | liii. 1-3. His Reception.
  B. | 4-10. His Affliction.
    C. | 10-12. His Reward.

Hence the " many nations " of lii. 15, answer to the " great multitudes " of liii. 12 ; and " the kings " of lii. 15 answer to " the strong ones " of liii. 12. Thus the two passages explain each other. The first line of verse 12 is what Jehovah divides to His Servant ; and the second line is what He divides as Victor for Himself and His host. Compare Ps. cx. 2-5, Rev. xix. 11-16.

The word נָזָה *(nazah)* in lii. 15, means *to leap, leap out:* of liquids, *to spurt out* as blood: of people, *to leap up* from joy or astonishment. So the astonishment of verse 15 answers to that of verse 14. Moreover the verb is in the *Hiphil,* and means *to cause* astonishment.*

Jer. xvi. 7.—" Neither shall *men* tear *themselves* for them in mourning." The word tear is פָּרַם *(paras) to* break, *cleave, divide.* So that the *Ellipsis* will be, " Neither shall men break [*bread*] for them in mourning " (as Ezek. xxiv. 17, Hos. ix. 4, etc., and A.V. marg. and R.V.).

See under *Idiom.*

Jer. viii. 4.—" Thus saith the LORD, Shall they fall, and not arise ? Shall he turn away and not return ? "

This is unintelligible, and the R.V. is no clearer :—" Shall one turn away and not turn again ? "

---

* See *Things to Come,* August, 1898.

The fact is that the Massorah[*] calls attention to this passage as one of several examples where two connected words are wrongly divided. Here, the first letter of the second of these two words should be the last letter of the preceding word. Then the sense comes out most beautifully :

> " Shall they return [*to the Lord*]
> And He not return [*to them*] ? "

Agreeing with Mal. iii. 7, and with the context; and bringing out the parallel between the two lines as well as exhibiting more clearly the figure of *Polyptoton* (*q.v.*)

Matt. xi. 18.—" John came neither eating nor drinking."

Clearly there must be an *Ellipsis* here; for John, being human, could not live without food. The sense is clear in the Hebrew idiom, which requires the *Ellipsis* to be thus supplied in the English :—

"John came neither eating [*with others*] nor drinking [*strong drink*]." · See Luke i. 15. Or, observing the force of the Greek negative : " John came [*declining invitations*] to eat and drink."

Luke ix. 52.—" And sent messengers before his face; and they went, and entered into a village of the Samaritans, to make ready . . for him," *i.e.*, to prepare *reception* for him.

John xv. 6.—" If a man abide not in me, he is cast forth as a branch, and is withered; and men gather them and cast *them* into the fire, and they are burned."

Here the accusative " them " is not repeated.

But the meaning of the verse is obscured, or rather a new meaning is read into it by inconsistency of rendering. Why, we ask, are the words ἐὰν μή (*ean mee*) translated " except " twice in verse 4, and here in verse 6 " if . . not " ? It is an expression that occurs fifty-two times, and more than thirty of these are rendered " except."[†] Here it should be rendered " Except anyone abide in me." In the preceding verses the Lord had been speaking of His disciples " you " and " ye." Here in verse 6 He makes a general proposition concerning anyone. Not, if anyone who is already in Him does not continue in Him, for He is not speaking of a real branch ; but except anyone is abiding in Him he is cast forth " AS a branch."

---

* See note on this passage in Ginsburg's Edition of the Hebrew Bible.

†See Matt. v. 20 ; xii. 29; xviii. 3; xxvi. 42. Mark iii. 27 ; vii. 3, 4. John iii. 2, 3, 5, 27 ; iv. 48; vi. 44, 53, 65 ; xii. 24 ; xv. 4 (twice) ; xx. 25. Acts viii. 31 ; xv. 1 ; xxvii. 31. Rom. x. 15. 1 Cor. xiv. 6, 7, 9 ; xv. 36. 2 Thess. ii. 3. 2 Tim. ii. 5. Rev. ii. 5, 22. εἰ μή (*ei mee*), *if not*, is also rendered " except " Matt. xix. 9 ; xxiv. 22. Mark xiii. 20. John xix. 11. Rom. vii. 7 ; ix. 29. 2 Cor. xii. 13.

Likewise, in verse 2, the verb is αἴρω (*airō*) *to lift up*,* *raise up.* "Every branch in me that beareth not fruit he lifteth up," *i.e.*, He raises it from the ground where it can bear no fruit, and tends it, that it may bring forth fruit, "and every *branch* that beareth fruit, he pruneth it, that it may bring forth more fruit."

Thus there are two conditions spoken of—two kinds of branches : one that bears no fruit, and one that does. The former He raises up that it may bear fruit, and the latter He prunes that it may bear more.

Acts ix. 34.—" Arise, and make thy bed."

Here both versions translate the figure. The Greek reads, "Arise, and spread for thyself," *i.e.*, spread [*a bed*] for thyself: in other words, "make thy bed."

Acts x. 10.—" But while they made ready, he fell into a trance," *i.e.*, while they made ready [*the food*].

Rom. xv. 28.—" When therefore I have performed this, and have sealed to them this fruit, I will come by you into Spain": *i.e.*, "When, therefore, I have performed this *business.*"

1 Cor. iii. 1.—" And I; brethren, could not speak unto you as unto spiritual [*men*], but as unto carnal [*men*]." (See under 1 Cor. ii. 2).

1 Cor. vii. 17.—" But as God hath distributed to every man." This is literally :—" Only as God hath apportioned [*the gift*] to each."

1 Cor. x. 24.—" Let no man seek his own [*advantage only*], but every man that of his neighbour [*also*]."

"Wealth," in the A.V. is the old English word for well-being generally. As we pray in the Litany, "In all time of our wealth "; and in the expression, "Commonwealth," *i.e.*, common weal. Compare verse 33, where the word "*profit* " is used. The R.V. supplies "*good.*"

2 Cor. v. 16.—" Wherefore henceforth know we no man after the flesh (κατὰ σάρκα, *kata sarka, according to flesh, i.e.*, according to natural standing): yea, though we have known Christ after the flesh, yet now, henceforth know we *him* [*thus*] no more."

Our standing is now a spiritual one, "in Christ " risen from the dead ; a standing on resurrection ground, as the members of the Mystical or Spiritual Body of Christ.

2 Cor. v. 20.—" Now then we are ambassadors for Christ, as though God did beseech *you* by us : we pray *you* in Christ's stead, be ye reconciled to God."

Here the word "*you* " is incorrectly supplied. Paul was not

---

*As in Luke xvii. 13.   John xi. 41.   Acts iv. 24.   Rev. x. 5.

beseeching the saints in Corinth to be reconciled to God.   They were reconciled as verse 18 declares, "Who hath reconciled us to himself by Jesus Christ."   Then in verse 19 he goes on to speak of "men"; and in verse 20 he says that he beseeches *them*, as though God did beseech *them* by us; we pray *them* in Christ's stead, *and say :*—" Be ye reconciled to God."   This was the tenor of his Gospel to the unconverted.

2 Cor. xi. 20.—" If a man take [*your goods*]."

Phil. iii. 13.—" Brethren, I count not myself to have apprehended [*the prize* (from verse 14)]."

1 Thess. iii. 1.—" When we could no longer forbear."   Here στέγω (*stegō*) means *to hold out, to bear, to endure,* and must have the accusative supplied :—" Wherefore, when we could no longer bear [*our anxiety*], etc."   The same *Ellipsis* occurs in verse 5, where it must be similarly supplied.

2 Thess. ii. 6, 7.—" And now ye know what withholdeth that he might be revealed in his time.   For the mystery of iniquity doth already work: only he who now letteth *will let*, until he be taken out of the way."

Here, there is an *Ellipsis.*   But the A.V. treats it as though it were the verb that is omitted, and repeats the verb "*will let.*"   The R.V. avoids this, by translating it thus :—" only *there is* one that restraineth now, until, etc."

Both the A.V. and R.V. fail to see that it is the *Ellipsis* of the *accusative* after the verb in both verses.   The verb is κατέχω (*katechō*), which is rendered "withhold" in verse 6 and "*let*" in verse 7 (and in R.V. "*restrain*" in both verses).   But this verb, being transitive, must have an *object* or accusative case after it; and, as it is omitted by *Ellipsis*, it has therefore to be supplied.

The verb κατέχω (*katechō*) means *to have and hold fast.*   The preposition κατά (*kata*), in composition, does not necessarily preserve its meaning of *down*, to hold down; but it may be *intensive*, and mean *to hold firmly, to hold fast, to hold in secure possession.*   This is proved by its usage; which clearly shows that restraining or withholding is no necessary part of its meaning.   It occurs nineteen times, and is nowhere else so rendered.   On the other hand there are four or five other words which might have been better used had "restrain" been the thought in this passage.

Indeed its true meaning is fixed by its use in these epistles.   In 1 Thess. v. 21 we read "hold fast that which is good," not restrain it or "withhold" that which is good!   But the idea is of keeping and retaining and holding on fast to that which is proved to be good. So it is in all the passages where the word occurs :—

Matt.	xxi.	38.	*Let us seize on* his inheritance.
Luke	iv.	42.	And *stayed* him, that he should not depart.
Luke	viii.	15.	Having heard the word, *keep* it.
Luke	xiv.	9.	Thou begin with shame *to take* the lowest room.
John	v.	4.	Of whatsoever disease *he had* (*i.e.*, was held).
Acts	xxvii.	40.	And *made* toward shore (*i.e.*, they *held* their course, or *kept* going for the shore).
Rom.	i.	18.	*Who hold* the truth in unrighteousness.
Rom.	vii.	6.	Being dead to that wherein we *were held* (margin and R.V.).
1 Cor.	vii.	30.	As though they *possessed* not.
1 Cor.	xi.	2.	And *keep* the ordinances.
1 Cor.	xv.	2.	If ye *keep in memory* what I preached.
2 Cor.	vi.	10.	And yet *possessing* all things.
1 Thess.	v.	21.	*Hold fast* that which is good.
Philem.		13.	Whom I would have *retained* with me.
Heb.	iii.	6.	If we *hold fast* the confidence.
Heb.	iii.	14.	If we *hold* the beginning.
Heb.	x.	23.	*Let* us *hold fast* the profession.

This fixes for us the meaning of the verb κατέχω. But WHAT is it that thus holds fast " the man of sin " ? and WHO is it that holds fast something which is not mentioned, and which has therefore to be supplied ? For, in verse 6, that which holds fast is neuter, τὸ κατέχον (*to katechon*), while in verse 7 it is masculine ὁ κατέχων (*ho katechōn*) : so that in verse 6 it is some*thing* (neuter) which holds the man of sin fast, while in verse 7 some *one* is holding fast to something.

We submit that in verse 6, that something is τὸ φρέαρ (*to phrear*) *the pit* (Rev. ix. 1, 2 and xi. 7) out of which he ascends, and in which he is now kept in sure possession until the season arrive when he is to be openly revealed : meanwhile, his secret counsels and plans are already working, preparing the way for his revelation.

The whole subject of the context is the revelation of two personages (not of one), viz., " the man of sin " (verse 3) and " the lawless one " (verse 8). These correspond with the two beasts of Rev. xiii.

This is clear from the structure of the first twelve verses of this chapter :—*

---

* See *The Structure of the Two Epistles to the Thessalonians* by the same author and publisher.

2 Thess. ii. 1-12.

A | 1-3-.   Exhortation not to be believing what the apostle did *not* say.
  B | -3, 4.   Reason.   " For, etc."
A | 5, 6.   Exhortation to believe what the apostle *did* say.
  B | 7-12.   Reason.   " For, etc."

Or more fully, thus :—

A | 1-3-.   Exhortation (negative).
  B | a | -3-.   The Apostasy (open).
       b | -3.   The Revelation of the "Man of Sin."   (The Beast
          from the *Sea*, Rev. xiii. 1-10).
       c | 4.   The character of his acts.   See Rev. xiii. 6-8.
A | 5-6.   Exhortation (positive).
  B | a | 7.   Lawlessness (secret working).
       b | 8.   The Revelation of the Lawless one.   (The Beast
          from the *Earth*, Rev. xiii. 11-18).
       c | 9-12.   The character of his acts.   See Rev. xiii. 13-15.

Thus the *open* working of the apostasy and the *secret* working of the counsels of the Lawless one are set in contrast. We must note that the word " mystery " means *a secret, a secret plan or purpose, secret counsel.**

Thus we have here two subjects : (1) "The Man of Sin" (the beast from the sea, Rev. xiii. 1-10), and the open apostasy which precedes and marks his revelation; (2) "The Lawless one" (the beast from the earth, Rev. xiii. 11-18), and the working of his secret counsels which precedes his revelation, and the ejection of the Devil from the heavens which brings it about.

An attempt has been made to translate the words, ἐκ μέσου γένηται (*ek mesou geneetai*) *be taken out of the way*, as meaning, "arise out of the midst." But this translates an idiomatic expression literally ; which cannot be done without introducing error. ἐκ μέσου γένηται is an idiom,† for *being gone away*, or *being absent* or *away*.

This is clear from the other places where the idiomatic expression occurs.‡

---

* See *The Mystery*, by the same author and publisher.

† See below under the figure *Idioma*.

‡ In Matt. xiii. 49, the wicked are severed *from among* the just " (*i.e.*, taken away).   In Acts xvii. 33, " Paul departed *from among* them " (*i.e.*, went away). In xxiii. 10, he was taken " by force *from among* them " (*i.e.*, taken out of the way).   1 Cor. v. 2 is very clear, where he complains that they had not mourned that " he that hath done this thing might be taken away from among you."   In 2 Cor. vi. 17, we are commanded, " Wherefore come out *from among* them and be ye separate."   In Col. ii. 14 we read of the handwriting of ordinances which was

Thus the lawless one is, at present, being held fast in the pit (while his secret counsels are at work) ; and the Devil is holding ón to his position in the heavenlies (Eph. ii. 2 ; vi. 12). But presently there will be "war in Heaven" (Rev. xii.), and Satan will be cast out into the earth. Then in Rev. xiii. 1, we read, "and he (Satan) stood upon the sand of the sea" (R.V.) Then it is that he will call up this lawless one, whom John immediately sees rising up out of the sea to run his brief career, and be destroyed by the glory of the Lord's appearing.

The complete rendering therefore of these two verses (1 Thess. ii. 6-7), will be as follows :—"And now ye know what holds him [*the lawless one*] fast, to the end that he may be revealed in his own appointed season. For the secret counsel of lawlessness doth already work; only, there is one [*Satan*] who at present holds fast [*to his possessions in the heavenlies*], until he be cast out [*into the earth*, Rev. xii. 9-12 ; *and "stand upon the sand of the sea*," Rev. xiii. 1, R.V.], and then shall be revealed that lawless one whom the Lord Jesus shall slay with the spirit of his mouth, and destroy with the brightness of his coming" (Isa. xi. 4).

Jas. v. 3.—"Ye have heaped treasure together for the last days." The R.V. is tame in comparison with this, "Ye have laid up your treasure in the last days." θησαυρίζω *(theesaurizo)* means simply *to treasure up.* In Rom. ii. 5, we have the expression "treasurest up wrath." So here, there is the *Ellipsis* of what is treasured up. We may supply "wrath" here. "Ye have treasured up [*wrath*] for the last days," or in last (or final) days, *i.e.*, days of extremity.

1 Pet. ii. 23.—"But committed *himself* to him that judgeth righteously."

Here the omitted accusative is supplied, but it is a question whether it ought to be "*himself*," or rather as in the margin both of A.V. and R.V. "*his cause*."

---

against us ; Christ "took it *out of the way*." We have the same in the Septuagint in Isa. lii. 11 : "Depart ye . . . . go ye *out of the midst* of her," and Isa. lvii. 1 : "the righteous is taken *away from* the evil to come."

The same usage is seen in Classical writers—Plutarch (*Timol.* p. 238, 3) : "He determined to live by himself, having *got himself out of the way*," *i.e.*, from the public ; Herodotus (3, 83 ; and 8, 22) : The speaker exhorts some to "be on our side ; but, if this is impossible, then sit down *out of the way*," *i.e.*, leave the coast clear as we should say, keep neutral and stand aside. The same idiom is seen in Latin—Terence (*Phorm.* v. 8, 30) : "She is dead, she is gone from among us" *(e medio abiit).* The opposite expression shows the same thing. In Xenophon (*Cyr.* 5, 2, 26), one asks, "What *stands in the way* of your joining us ?" (ἐν μέσῳ εἶναι).

B

3. The Omission of the PRONOUN.

Where there can be no doubt to whom or to what the noun refers, the pronoun is frequently omitted in the Greek, and in most cases is supplied in *italic* type in the A.V.

The omission of the pronoun makes it more emphatic, attention being called more prominently to it.

Matt. xix. 13.—"That He should put the hands [*of Him*] upon them," *i.e., His* hands.

Matt. xxi. 7.—"And put on them the clothes [*of them*] " *i.e., their* garments, " and he sat upon them." This is the reading of the critical editions.

Mark v. 23.—" Come and lay the hands [*of thee*] upon her" *i.e., thy* hands. Where the A.V. does not even put *thy* in italics. Compare Matt. ix. 18, where the pronoun (σον, *sou*) *thy* is used.

Mark vi. 5.—"And he laid the hands [*of him*] upon a few sick folk," *i.e., his* hands. So also viii. 25, xvi. 18 ; Acts ix. 17.

Luke xxiv. 40.—"And when He had thus spoken, He showed them the hands and the feet [*of Him*], *i.e.,* as in A.V., " *his* hands and *his* feet."

John xi. 41.—"And Jesus lifted up the eyes [of Him]," *i.e., his* eyes.

Acts xiii. 3.—"And when they had fasted and prayed, and laid the hands [*of them*] on them," *i.e., their* hands on them.

Acts xix. 6.—"And when Paul had laid the hands [*of him*] upon them," *i.e., his* hands.

Eph. iii. 17, 18.—" That ye, being rooted and grounded in love, may know what is the breadth [*of it*], and length [*of it*], and the depth [*of it*], and the height [*of it*]," *i.e.,* of love. " That ye may know what is [*its*] breadth, and length, and depth, and height, etc."

Heb. iv. 15.—" But was in all points tempted. according to the likeness [*of us*] apart from sin," *i.e.,* according to [*our*] likeness.

Rom. vi. 3, 4.—May be perhaps best explained by this figure. " Know ye not that so many of us as were baptized into Christ Jesus, unto his death we were baptized ? Therefore we were buried together with him by the baptism [*of him*] (*i.e.,* by *his* baptism) unto death." For He had " a cup " to drink of (His *death*), and " a baptism to be baptized with " (His *burial*), and when He died and was buried, His people died and were buried with Him, and, as the next verse goes on to say, rose again with Him.

So the passage reads : " Therefore we were buried with him by his baptism-unto-death [*i.e.*, his burial], in order that just as Christ was raised from among the dead by the glory of the Father, so we also, in newness of life should walk. For if we have become identified in the likeness of his death, certainly in that of his resurrection also we shall be : knowing this, that our old man was crucified together with [*him*] in order that the body of sin may be annulled, that we should no longer be in servitude to sin. For he that hath died hath been righteously acquitted from the sin [*of him*], *i.e., his* sin. Now if we died together with Christ, we believe that we shall live also together with him."

The whole argument lies in this that we are reckoned as having died with Him, and as having been buried with Him in His burial (or baptism-unto-death). (See Matt. xx. 23 ; Mark x. 38, 39 ; Luke xii. 50). Hence all such are free from the dominion and condemnation of sin, and stand in the newness of resurrection life. This is " the gospel of the glory " (2 Cor. iv. 4), for it was by the glory of the Father that Christ was raised, and it is glorious news indeed which tells us that all who are in Christ are " complete in Him " (Col. ii. 10), " accepted in the beloved " (Eph. i. 6), " perfect in Christ Jesus " (Col. i. 28).

With this agrees Col. ii. 10-12. " And ye are complete in him, which is the head of all principality and power. In whom (ἐν ᾧ, *en hō*) also ye are circumcised with the circumcision made without hands, in putting off the body of the sins of the flesh by the circumcision of Christ ; buried with him in the baptism [*of him*] *i.e.*, in *his* baptism-unto-death, in whom (ἐν ᾧ, not " wherein," but as it is rendered above) ye were raised together also through the faith of the operation of God, who raised him from among the dead," etc.

Here, again, the whole argument turns on the fact that the " circumcision " and the " baptism " spoken of are both " made without hands," and both are fulfilled in Christ. The whole context of these two passages must be studied in order to see the one point and the great truth which is revealed : viz., that in His *death* we are circumcised and cut off, " crucified with Him " (Rom. vi. 6): in His *burial* (or baptism-unto-death) we are baptized (Rom. vi. 4 ; Col. ii. 12): and in His *resurrection* we now have our true standing before God. We have all in Christ. Hence, our completeness and perfection in Him is such that nothing can be added to it. All who are baptized by Him with the Holy Spirit are identified with Him in His death, burial, and resurrection. Hence, those who are being baptized are baptized for the dead, if the dead rise not (1 Cor. xv. 29, see below), for they do not rise if

Christ be not raised. But, if Christ be raised, then we are raised in Him; and " Christ being raised from the dead dieth no more . . . for, in that he died, he died unto sin once for all; but in that he liveth, he liveth unto God. Likewise ye also reckon yourselves dead indeed unto sin, but alive unto God, IN CHRIST JESUS " (Rom. vi. 8-11).

Rom. ii. 18.—Thou " makest thy boast of God, and knowest the will [*of him*]," *i.e., his* will : the will of God.

1 Tim. vi. 1.—" That the name of God and *his* doctrine be not blasphemed." The R.V. reads " that the name of God and the doctrine be not blasphemed," but it is better " the doctrine [*of him*]," *i.e.,* his doctrine, as in the A.V.

4. The Omission of OTHER CONNECTED WORDS.

1 Kings iii. 22.—" Thus they spake before the king." It is not to be supposed that two women under these exciting circumstances would confine themselves to the few concise words of verse 22! Moreover, there is no " thus " in the Hebrew. Literally it reads— " and they talked before the king," *i.e.,* " they talked [*very much*] or *kept talking* before the king."

2 Kings vi. 25.—" An ass's head was *sold* for fourscore *pieces* of silver, and the fourth part of a cab of dove's dung for five *pieces* of silver." Here it is more correct to supply (with the R.V. margin) " *shekels* " instead of " *pieces*," and translate " was at eighty *shekels* of silver."

2 Kings xxv. 3.—" And on the ninth *day* of the *fourth* month the famine prevailed."

The Hebrew reads, " and on the ninth month." But the *Ellipsis* is correctly supplied from Jer. lii. 6.

Ps. cxix. 56.—" This I had, because I kept thy precepts; " *i e.,* this [*consolation*] I had. Luther supplies the word " *treasure*."

Jer. li. 31.—" One post shall run to meet another, and one messenger to meet another, to show the king of Babylon that his city is taken at *one* end."

The R.V. translates " *on every quarter* " ! Another version renders it " *to its utmost end.*" Another " *at the extremity.*" Thus it is clear that there is an *Ellipsis*, and much confusion in supplying it.

The Hebrew is " from the end ": or with the *Ellipsis* supplied " from [*each*] end." So in chap. l. 26 (A.V. and R.V.), " come against her from the utmost border." (Margin: " Hebrew, *from the end* "), *i.e.,* as we have suggested, " from [*each*] end."

And so the prophecy was *exactly* fulfilled. The Babylonians, after their first discomfiture by Cyrus in the field, retired to the city . . . and, as Heroditus says, "remained in their holds."*

The forces of Cyrus, having turned the waters of the Euphrates, entered the city by the bed of the river at each end; and the messengers who entered at the end where the waters quitted the city ran to meet those who had come in where the waters entered the city; so that they met one another. Herodotus expressly describes this in his history (book i. §191). Those who were at the extremities were at once slain, while those in the centre were feasting in utter ignorance of what was going on. See Daniel v. 3, 4, 23, 30. Thus the correct supply of the *Ellipsis* is furnished and established by the exact fulfilment of the prophecy, proving the wonderful accuracy of the Divine Word.

Ezek. xiii. 18.—"Woe to the women that sew pillows to all armholes."

This may be translated literally, "Woe to those who sew together coverings upon all joints of [*the people of*] my hands," *i.e., my people.* The context supplies the *Ellipsis*, for the subject is the deception of God's people by the false prophets; and the covering and veiling of verse 18 corresponds to the daubing and coating of verse 14, etc., *i.e.,* the making things easy for the people so that they should not attend to God's word.

The R.V. reads, "that sew pillows upon all elbows," margin, "Heb. *joints of the hands.*" A.V. margin, "elbows."

Matt. xix. 17.—"Keep the commandments," *i.e., of God.*

Mark vi. 14-16.—The parenthesis in verse 14 must be extended to the end of verse 15. What Herod said is stated in verse 16. The rumour of what others said is stated in the parenthesis:—"And king Herod heard [*of these mighty works*]; (for his name was spread abroad, and [*one*] † said that John the Baptist was risen from the dead, and therefore mighty works do show forth themselves in him. Others said, It is Elias; and others said, It is a prophet, or as one of the

---

* Οἱ βαβυλώνιοι. . . . ἐσσωθέντες τῇ μάχῃ κατειλήθησαν ἐς τὸ ἄστυ. HEROD. Hist. lib. i. §190. See also XENOPHON, Cyrop. lib. vii. Compare Jer. li. 30, "The mighty men of Babylon have forborne to fight, they have remained in *their* holds."

† The Greek reads ἔλεγεν (*elegen*), *one said.* The reading put by Tr. and R.V. in the margin, and by Lachmann, and Westcott and Hort in the Text is ἔλεγον (*elegon*) *some said.*

prophets). But when Herod heard* *thereof*,† he said, It is John whom I beheaded: he is risen from the dead."

Luke xiv. 18.—"They all with one *consent* began to make excuse."

ἀπὸ μιᾶς *(apo mias)* with one [*mind*], or with one [*declining*]: *i.e.*, they all *alike* began to decline the invitation.

John iii. 13.—"No man hath ascended up to heaven, but he that came down from heaven, *even* the Son of Man which is in heaven." The words translated "which is" are ὁ ὤν *(ho ōn)* the article, and the present participle of the verb "to be"—literally, the *one* being: *i.e.*, who *was* being, or simply *who was.* Compare John i. 18 "who was (ὁ ὤν) in the bosom of the Father." John ix. 25, "Whereas I was blind" (τυφλὸς ὤν). John xix. 38, "being a disciple," *i.e.*, who was a disciple. Luke xxiv. 44, "I spake whilst I was yet with you" (ἔτι ὤν, *eti ōn*). 2 Cor. viii. 9, "Though he was rich" (πλούσιος ὤν, *plousios ōn*).

Hence our verse reads, "Even the Son of Man who was in heaven." This agrees with John vi. 62, where we have the words, "What and if ye shall see the Son of Man ascend up where he was before?"

The fact taught us by this is, that the human body of the Lord Jesus cannot be in more than one place at the same time. This fact cuts at the roots of all errors that are based on any presence of Christ on earth during this present dispensation. The presence of the Holy Spirit is the witness to the absence of Christ. There can be no presence of Christ now except by the Holy Spirit. He will be present again bodily only at His personal return from Heaven. Now He is seated at the right hand of God, "henceforth expecting," until the moment arrives for God to place His enemies as a footstool for His feet, when He shall rise up to receive His people to Himself and come with and reign until He shall have put all enemies under His feet. (See above, page 7).

Any presence, therefore, of Christ in the Lord's Supper, other than by His Spirit in our hearts,‡ is a denial of His real human nature, and of His return from Heaven: and this is an error which affects both the first and second Advents. The Lord's Supper, therefore, is the witness of His *real absence;* for it is instituted only "till He come." And not until that glorious day will there be any "real presence" on earth. And then it will be a bodily presence,

---

* Repeated from verse 14.

† Or when Herod heard *these various opinions.*

‡ See the Rubrick at the end of the Communion Service of the Church of England.

for it is "on the Mount of Olives," that His feet will rest, and "on Mount Zion" that He shall reign.

Acts x. 36.—"The word which *God* sent unto the children of Israel preaching peace by Jesus Christ."

The *Ellipsis* here is caused by a Hebraism, as in Hag. ii. 5. "*According to* the word that I covenanted with you," etc. So this will read, "[*According to*] the word which God sent, etc."

Or it may be taken as parallel to Ps. cvii. 20. "He sent his word, and healed them." So Isa. ix. 8. God "sent" when His Son came, through whom God proclaimed the Gospel of peace. Hence "[*This is*] the word which God sent."

Acts xviii. 22.—"And when he had landed at Cæsarea, and gone up . . . and saluted the Church, he went down to Antioch," *i.e.,* "Gone up [*to Jerusalem*]." As is clear from verse 21, as well as from the circumstances of the case.

Rom. ii. 27.—"And shall not uncircumcision which is by nature, if it fulfil the law, judge thee, who by the letter and circumcision dost trangress the law?"

Here we have, first, to note the figure of *Hendiadys* (*q.v.*) "letter and circumcision" and translate it *literal circumcision*. And next we have to preserve the emphasis marked by the order of the words, which we can well do if we correctly supply the *Ellipsis*:—

"And shall not uncircumcision which by nature fulfilleth the law, condemn thee [*though thou art a Jew*], who, through the literal circumcision, art a trangressor of the law?"

Rom. xi. 11.—"I say then, Have they stumbled that they should fall [*for ever*]? God forbid: but *rather* through their fall salvation is come unto the Gentiles, for to provoke them to jealousy." The fall mentioned here must be interpreted by verse 1 "cast away," and verse 25 "until," and by the condition of verse 23. Is their fall the object or end of their stumbling? See John xi. 4.

Rom. xii. 19.—"Dearly beloved, avenge not yourselves, but *rather* give place unto wrath." This does not mean "yield to the wrath of your enemy," but "give place to the wrath* [*of God*], for (the reason is given) it is written, Vengeance is mine; I will repay, saith the Lord."

Rom. xiv. 2.—"For one believeth that he may eat all things; another, who is weak [*in the faith*], eateth herbs [*only*]."

Rom. xiv. 5.—"One man esteemeth one day above another,"

---

* τῇ ὀργῇ (*tee orgee*).

i.e., "one man indeed (μέν), esteemeth one day [*more holy*] than another; but (δέ) another esteemeth every day [*alike*]."

Rom. xiv. 20.—"All things indeed are pure," *i.e.,* "all [*meats*] indeed [*are*] clean; but [*it is*] evil to the man who eateth with offence [*to his weak brother*]." "Clean" here means ceremonially clean, and hence, allowed to be eaten.

Rom. xiv. 23.—"And he that doubteth is damned (or condemned) if he eat," *i.e.,* "and he that holdeth a difference [*between meats*] is condemned if he eat, because [*he eateth*] not from (ἐκ) faith; for whatsoever is not of faith is sin."

1 Cor. vii. 6.—"But I speak this [*which I have said*] by permission and not commandment."

1 Cor. ix. 9, 10.—"Doth God take care for oxen [*only*]? Or saith he it altogether for our sakes?"

1 Cor. xii. 6.—The expression "all in all" is elliptical: and the sense must be completed according to the nature of the subject and the context, both here, and in the other passages where it occurs.

Here, "it is the same God, which worketh all [*these gifts*] in all [*the members of Christ's body*]:" what these gifts are, and who these members are, is fully explained in the immediate context. See verses 4-31.

1 Cor. xv. 28.—"Then shall the Son also himself be subject unto him that put all things under him, that God may be all in all." The word πάντα occurs six times in the 27th and 28th verses and is in each case translated correctly "all things" except in this last occurrence. We have no liberty to change the translation here. It must be "all things," and to complete the sense we must render it "that God may be [*over*] all things, in all [*places*]; *i.e.,* over all beings in all parts of the universe.

Eph. i. 23.—"The church, which is His body, the fulness* of him that filleth all in all." Here, we must supply:—"that filleth all [*the members of His body*] with all [*spiritual gifts and graces*]." Compare chap. iv. 10-13.

Col. iii. 11.—"Christ *is* all, and in all." Here the Greek is slightly different from the other occurrences, but it is still elliptical; and the sense must be completed thus:—In the new creation "there is

---

* The termination of the word πλήρωμα denotes the result or product of the verb *to fill*, *i.e.,* of the act of the verb. Hence this fulness means a filling up in exchange for emptiness. His members fill up the Body of Christ, and He fills up the members with all spiritual gifts and graces.

neither Greek nor Jew, circumcision nor uncircumcision, Barbarian, Scythian, bond *nor* free : but, Christ is [*created in*] all [*who believe*] and in all [*places of the world*]," *i.e.*, no man is excluded on account of earthly considerations of condition or location from the blessings and benefits of the new creation. See Gal. iii. 28, where the same truth is expressed in different words.

1 Cor. xiv. 27.—" If any man speak in an *unknown* tongue, let it be by two, or at the most three [*sentences*, or perhaps, *persons*] and that by course (*i.e., separately*) ; and let one interpret."

2 Cor. i. 6.—" And whether we be afflicted, *it is* for your consolation and salvation, which is effectual [*in you*] in the enduring of the same sufferings which we also suffer, etc."

2 Cor. v. 5.—" Now he that hath wrought us for the self same [*desire*], is God."

Gal. v. 10.—" I have confidence in you through the Lord, that ye will be none otherwise minded."

The Greek reads " that you will think nothing differently [*from me*]."

Phil. i. 18.—" What then [*does it matter*] ? at any rate, in every way, whether in pretence or in truth, Christ is preached ; and I therein do rejoice, yea, and will rejoice."

1 Thess. iii. 7.—" Therefore, brethren, we were comforted over you in all our affliction and distress by your faith," *i.e.*, " by [*the news received of*] your faith."

1 Thess. iv. 1.—" As ye have received of us how ye ought to walk and to please God, so ye would abound more and more [*therein*]." See also verse 10.

Heb. xiii. 25.—" Grace *be* with you all," *i.e.*, " The grace [*of God be*] with you all."

1 John v. 15.—" And if we know that he hear us [*concerning*] whatsoever we ask, we know that we have the petitions that we desired of him."

1 John v. 19. — " The whole world lieth in wickedness : " R.V., " in the wicked one." But this is not English. The *Ellipsis* must be supplied thus :—" The whole world lieth in [*the power of*] the wicked one."

II. The Omission of Verbs and Participles.

A verb is a word which signifies *to be*, *to do*, or *to suffer*, and expresses the action, the suffering, or the being, or the doing.

When therefore the *verb* is omitted, it throws the emphasis on the thing that is done rather than on the doing of it.

On the other hand, when the *noun* is omitted, our thought is directed to the action of the verb, and is centred on that rather than on the object or the subject.

Bearing this in mind, we proceed to consider a few examples :—

1. When the VERB FINITE is wanting.

Gen. xxv. 28.—"And Isaac loved Esau, because he did eat of *his* venison." Or it may be that there is no *Ellipsis*, and it may mean " because hunting was in his [*Esau's*] mouth," *i.e.*, on his tongue.

The A.V. has given a very free translation. But here again, the correct supply of the words omitted enables us to retain a literal rendering of the words that are given : " because the food taken by him in hunting [*was sweet*, or *was pleasant*] in his mouth."

Num. xvi. 28.—" And Moses said, ' Hereby ye shall know that the LORD hath sent me to do all these works; for not of my own mind.' "

Here we may render it, " for not of mine own heart [*have I said these things*]. See verse 24.

1 Sam. xix. 3.—" I will commune with my father of thee; and what I see, that I will tell thee."

The R.V. translates " and if I see aught." But the Hebrew with the *Ellipsis* supplied, is : " and will see what [*he replies*], and will tell thee."

2 Sam. iv. 10.—" When one told me, saying, behold, Saul is dead, thinking to have brought good tidings, I took hold of him, and slew him in Ziklag, who *thought* that I would have given him a reward for his tidings."

Here the A.V. has supplied the verb " *thought*," but perhaps the verb " *had come* " is better, *i.e.*, " who [*had come*] that I should give him a reward for his tidings."

The R.V. translates, " which was the reward I gave him for his tidings."

2 Sam. xviii. 12.—" Beware that none *touch* the young man Absalom."

2 Sam. xxiii. 17.—This is a case in which the *Ellipsis* is wrongly supplied in the A.V. " And he said, Be it far from me, O LORD, that I should do this : *is not this* the blood of the men that went in jeopardy of their lives ? "

The R.V. rightly supplies from 1 Chron. xi. 19, " Be it far from me, O LORD, that I should do this : *shall I drink* the blood of the men, etc."

1 Kings xi. 25.—" And he was an adversary to Israel all the days of Solomon, beside the mischief that Hadad *did*," *i.e.*, that Hadad *wrought* or *brought upon him*.

1 Kings xiv. 6.—" I am sent to thee *with* heavy *tidings*." The Hebrew is, " I am sent to thee hard."

The *Ellipsis* may thus be supplied: " I am sent to thee [*to tell thee*, or *to bring thee*, or *to prophesy to thee*] hard [*things*]. See verse 5.

1 Kings xxii. 36.—" And there went a proclamation throughout the host about the going down of the sun, saying, " Every man to his city, and every man to his own country." Here the verb *return* is to be supplied. "*Let* every man *return* to his city, etc.," or " [*Return*] every man to his city, etc."

2 Kings xxv. 4.—The word "*fled*" is not in the Hebrew. The *Ellipsis* is thus supplied in the A.V. and R.V. correctly in italics.

Ezra x. 14.—" Let now our rulers of all the congregation stand, and let all them which have taken strange wives in our cities come at appointed times, and with them the elders of every city, and the judges thereof, until the fierce wrath of our God for this matter be turned away."

The Hebrew of the last clause reads, " Until (עַד) the fierce wrath of our God be turned back from us, until (עַד) this matter [*be carried out*]."

This filling up of the *Ellipsis* enables us to take the other words in the verse literally. The non-observance of the figure leads the A.V. to give two different meanings (viz., " until " and " for ") to the word עַד *until*, which is used twice in the same passage.

The R.V. reads, " Until the fierce wrath of our God be turned from us, until this matter be dispatched," and gives an alternative in the margin for the last clause " *as touching this matter*."

Ezra x. 19.—" And being guilty, *they offered* a ram of the flock for their trespass."

Here the *Ellipsis* of the verb is properly supplied.

Job. iii. 21.—" Which long for death, but it *cometh* not; and dig for it more than for hid treasures [*but find it not*]."

The A.V. supplies the first verb, but not the second.

Job iv. 6.—" *Is* not *this* thy fear, thy confidence, thy hope, and the uprightness of thy ways ? "

The R.V. renders it :—" Is not thy fear of *God* thy confidence, *and* thy hope the integrity of thy ways ? "

These two lines are arranged as an introversion in the Hebrew:—

> Is not thy fear
> thy confidence?
> And thy hope
> the integrity of thy ways?

Or by transposing the words they may be exhibited as an alternation:

> Is not thy fear thy confidence?
> And the integrity of thy ways, thy hope?

It should be noted that the A.V. of 1611 originally read, " *Is* not this thy feare thy confidence; the uprightness of thy wayes and thy hope?" The change first appears in the Cambridge edition of 1638. But by whom this and many similar unauthorised changes have been made in the text of the A.V: of 1611, is not known, and can only be conjectured! *

Job xxxix. 13 seems to have caused much trouble to the translators. The A.V. reads, " *Gavest thou* the goodly wings unto the peacocks? or wings and feathers unto the ostrich?" The R.V. and other versions which ignore the Ellipsis (which the A.V. correctly supplies) have to give a very unnatural translation, and miss the challenge which is connected with all the other wonders of God's works in these chapters.

The scanty featherless wing of the ostrich (רְנָנִים *renana*, not peacock) is contrasted with the warm full-feathered wing of the stork (חֲסִידָה *chaseedah*, not ostrich), and man is challenged, " *Didst thou give* either the one or the other?"

Ps. iv. 2.—"O ye sons of men, how long *will ye turn* my glory into shame?"

Ps. xxii. 16.—"They pierced my hands and my feet." Through not seeing the Ellipsis of the verb in this verse, the word in the Hebrew text כָּאֲרִי (*kāree*), *as a lion*, has been translated as though it were a verb כָּארוּ (*kāroo*) *they pierced.*† But we have no authority thus to ignore the printed text. On the contrary, verse 16 corresponds exactly with verse 12. In verse 12 we have two animals, "bulls" and "a lion" (the first plural, and the second singular). So also we have in verse 16, two animals, "dogs" and "a lion." If, however, we take *kāree* as a noun, there is an Ellipsis of the verb, which we may well supply from Isa. xxxviii. 13, and then we may translate

---

* See Appendix A.

† In the first case the *Kaph* כ is rendered "as" and is prefixed to אֲרִי (*aree*) *a lion*; in the latter case it forms part of the verb כָּרוּ (*kāroo*).

the rest literally: " As a lion [*they will break up*] my hands and my feet."*

The structure of the passage proves that this is the case. Verses 12-17 form the centre of this part of the Psalm :—

A | 12-13. They. Beasts surrounding: " bulls " (pl.), and " a lion " (sing.).
　　B | 14-15. I. The consequence. " I am poured out like water."
A | 16. They. Beasts surrounding: " dogs " (pl.), and " a lion " (sing.).
　　B | 17. I. The consequence. " I may tell all my bones."

Ps. xxv. 15.—" Mine eyes *are* ever towards the Lord," *i.e.*, " mine eyes are ever *lifted up* or *looking* toward the Lord." See Ps. cxxi. 1.   The verb is omitted, that we may not think of the act of looking, but at the object to which we look.

Ps. cxx. 7.—" I *am for* peace ; but when I speak, they *are* for war."   There are no verbs in the Hebrew, which is :—" I peace ; but when I speak, they for war."   The verbs to be supplied are doubtless, " I [*love*] peace ; but when I speak they [*cry out*] for war," or " they *break forth* into war."

Ecc. viii. 2.—" I *counsel thee* keep the king's commandment."

Isa. lx. 7.—" For your shame *ye shall have* double."   Here the Ellipsis is properly supplied. (See this passage under other Figures).

Isa. lxvi. 6.—" A voice of noise (tumult, R.V.) from the city, a voice from the temple, a voice of the Lord that rendereth recompense to his enemies " : *i.e.*, a voice of tumult *is heard* from the city, a voice *sounds forth* from the temple, etc.

Jer. xviii. 14.—" Will *a man* leave the snow of Lebanon *which cometh* from the rock of the field ? "

There is no sense whatever in this rendering, and the R.V. is but little better: " Shall the snow of Lebanon fail from the rock of the field ? "

The Ellipsis is not to be supplied by the verb " cometh."   But it should be :

" Will *a man* leave the snow of Lebanon for the rock of the field ?
Or shall the cold flowing waters *be forsaken* for strange waters? "

Jer. xix. 1.—" Go and get (R.V. buy) a potter's earthen vessel and *take* of the elders of the people, &c."

Hos. viii. 1.—" *He shall come* as an eagle against the house of the Lord : " *i.e.*, as an eagle *shall the enemy come* against the house of the Lord.

Amos iii. 11.—" Thus saith the Lord God (Adonai Jehovah): an adversary *there shall be*, etc."   So the R.V.   But " an adversary *shall come*," would be better."

---

* See Ginsburg's *Introduction to the Massoretico-Critical Hebrew Bible*, p. 969.

Matt. xxvi. 5.—" But they said, not on the feast *day*," *i.e.*, *Let us* not *do it* on the feast day (so also Mark xiv. 2).

Acts xv. 25.—" Certain which went out from us have troubled you with words, subverting your souls, saying, ye *must* be circumcised, and keep the law," *i.e.*, saying, ye *ought* to be circumcised, and to keep the law.

Rom. ii. 7-10.—There are several *ellipses* in these verses which may be thus supplied.

" To them who by patient continuance in well doing seek for glory and honour and immortality [*he will give*] eternal life. But unto them that are contentious and do not obey the truth, but obey unrighteousness, [*shall come*] indignation and wrath, tribulation and anguish upon every soul of man that doeth evil, of the Jew first and also of the Gentile* ; but glory, honour, and peace [*shall be rendered*] to every man that worketh good, to the Jew first and also to the Gentile."

Rom. iv. 9.—" *Cometh* this blessedness then on the circumcision *only*, or upon the uncircumcision also ? "

I.e., " This blessedness, then, [*cometh it only*] on the circumcision ? "

Rom. vi. 19.—" For as ye have yielded your members servants to uncleanness and to iniquity unto iniquity ; even so now yield your members servants to righteousness unto holiness."

I.e., " To [*work*] iniquity " : and " to [*work*] holiness."

Rom. xi. 18.—" Boast not against the branches. But if thou boast, thou bearest not the root, but the root thee," *i.e.*, but if thou boast, *I tell thee* (or *know thou*) thou bearest not the root, but the root *beareth* thee.

Rom. xiii. 11.—" And that, knowing the time, that now *it is* high time to awake out of sleep, etc."

The Greek is καὶ τοῦτο (*kai touto*), " and this [*I add* or *I exhort*] knowing the reason, that [*it is*] already the hour [*for us*] to awake out of sleep."

---

* In Deut. xxviii. 53, this is applied to *the Jew* (cf. Sept.). " In thy anguish and tribulation wherewith thine enemy shall afflict thee." (A.V., " In the siege and in the straitness wherewith thine enemies shall distress thee "). Cf. Isa. viii. 22.

While in Isa. xiii. 9, this is applied to *the Gentile*.

Thus these words are applied even in the Old Testament : " to the Jew first, and also to the Gentile."

1 Cor. ii. 12.—"Now we have received, not the spirit of the world, but the Spirit which is of God."

There is no verb in this latter clause, and the verb "is" which is supplied in the A.V. should be in italics. But "which [*cometh*] from God," is better; or "*is received*," repeated from the previous sentence.

1 Cor. iv. 20.—"For the kingdom of God *is* not in word but in power." There is no verb in the whole of this verse; consequently one *must* be supplied:—"For the kingdom of God [*is established* or *governed*] not by word (or speech as in verse 19) but by power."

1 Cor. xiv. 33.—"For God is not *the author* of confusion, but of peace, as in all churches of the saints." There is no verb in the latter clause, therefore one must be supplied. The word "God" may also be repeated as in the R.V.:—

"For God is not [*a God*] of confusion, but of peace, as [*He is*] in all churches of the saints." Or, "as in all the churches of the saints [*is well known*]."

2 Cor. ix. 14.—"And by their prayer for you, which long after you for the exceeding grace of God in you." The Greek is ἐφ᾽ ὑμῖν (*eph' humin*) *upon you*, and requires the verb to be supplied, "for the exceeding grace of God [*bestowed*] upon you."

2 Cor. xii. 18.—"I desired Titus [*to go to you*], etc."

Gal. v. 13.—"Only *use* not liberty for an occasion to the flesh."

Here the A.V. supplies "use." But it might well be "*misuse* or *abuse*."

Eph. iv. 9.—"Now that he ascended." The Greek reads as in R.V., "Now this, He ascended." But the *Ellipsis* must be supplied: "Now, this [*fact*]" or "Now, this [*expression*], He ascended, what is it unless that he also descended first into the lower parts of the earth?"

Eph. v. 9.—"For the fruit of the Spirit *is* in all goodness and righteousness and truth:" *i.e.*, [*consists*] in these things.

All the ancient MSS. and critical texts, and the R.V. agree in reading φωτός (*phōtos*) *of the light*, instead of πνεύματος (*pneumatos*) *of the Spirit*; and thus "the fruits of the light" are contrasted with "the unfruitful works of darkness."

Phil. iii. 15.—"Let us therefore, as many as be perfect, be thus minded:" *i.e.*, [*desire to be*] perfect. There is no verb, and the word "be" ought to have been put in italics.

1 Tim. ii. 6.—"Who gave himself a ransom for all, to be testified in due time." Here there is no verb in the latter clause. The Greek reads, "the testimony in due times" or in its own seasons. Hence the

A.V. has boldly substituted a verb for the noun "to be testified"; while the R.V. has rendered it : " the testimony *to be borne* in its own times." We may supply the Ellipsis more fully thus : " the testimony [*of which, was to be borne by us*] in his own appointed season."

The word " all " must be taken here in the sense of " all " *without distinction*, because before Christ's death the ransom was only for one nation—Israel. It cannot be " all " *without exception*, for in that case all would and must be saved. See under *Synecdoche.*

Philem. 6.—" [*I pray*] that the communication of thy faith may become effectual, etc."

1 Pet. iv. 11.—" If any man speak, *let him speak*, as the oracles of God [*require*].

2 Pet. ii. 3.—" Whose judgment now of a long time lingereth not." There is no " now " in the Greek. " Whose judgment [*threatened*] of old, lingereth not. See Jude 4.

1 John iii. 20.—" For if our heart condemn us, God is greater than our heart, and knoweth all things."

In the Greek, the word ὅτι *(hoti)*, *that*, occurs twice, and the construction is difficult. The A.V. avoids it by translating the first ὅτι " for," and ignoring the second occurrence altogether. The R.V. evades it by adopting for the first ὅτι the reading (ὅ τι for ὅτι), which, beyond the Alexandrian Codex, has scarcely any MS. support, and only that of one Textual critic (Lachmann). The R.V. connects verse 20 with verse 10, and translates " and shall assure our heart before him, whereinsoever our heart condemn us, because God is greater, &c." But this English is as difficult as the Greek.

The difficulty is met by supplying the ellipsis before the second ὅτι, and translating it "that," as it is rendered 613 times in the N.T. :—

" For if our heart condemn us [*we know*] that God is greater than our heart."

(*a*) THE VERB "*to say.*"

This is frequently omitted in the original, but is generally supplied in *italics* in the A.V.

Where it is omitted the emphasis is to be placed on *what* is said rather than on *the act* of saying it.

Gen. xxvi. 7.—" Lest, *said he*, the men of the place should kill me."

1 Kings xx. 34.—" Then *said* Ahab."

Ps. ii. 2.—" Why do . . . the rulers take counsel together against the Lord, and against his anointed, *saying*."

Ps. cix. 5.—The structure of this Psalm shows that the verb *saying* must be supplied at the end of verse 5.

A | 1-5.   David's prayer for himself: and complaint.

    B | 6-20. David's enemies' *words* against him: (ending " that speak evil against my soul.")

A | 21-28-. David's prayer for himself: and complaint.

    B | -28-31.   David's enemies' *acts* against him: (ending "that condemn his soul.")

Here in B and *B* we have David's enemies. In B (6-20) their words and in *B* (-28-31) their acts. So that verses 6-20 are not David's words at all, but the words of David's enemies, the evil which *they* speak against his soul. The evil which they speak is contrasted with the " good " which he prays for himself in the next verse (21). " Let them curse," he says in verse 28, " but bless Thou ! "   Let them say " let Satan stand at his right hand" (verse 6); but he is assured (verse 31) that not Satan but Jehovah shall " stand at the right hand of the poor to save him from them that condemn his soul."

Hence in verse 20 David prays, " Let this be the wages* of mine enemies from the Lord, and of them that speak evil against my soul."

So that verse 5 will now read :—

> " And they have rewarded me evil for good,
> And hatred for my good will [*saying*]."

Then the Psalm goes on (verses 6-19) to describe the " hatred."

Having said in verses 2 and 3 that

" The mouth of the wicked and the mouth of the deceitful are opened upon me.
They have spoken against me with a lying tongue.
They compassed me about also with words of hatred,"

it is only natural to supply the verb *saying* at the end of verse 5.

Ps. cxliv. 12 is similar. The structure shows that verses 12 to 15 contain the words of the " strange children," and not the words of David.

  A¹ | 1-7.   David's words (Thanksgiving and Prayer).

    B¹ | 8.   The words of the strange children (vanity and falsehood).

  A² | 9-11-.   David's words (Thanksgiving and Prayer).

    B² | -11-15-.   The words of the strange children (vanity and falsehood).

  A³ | -15.   David's words. The true conclusion as opposed to the " vanity."

---

* פְּעֻלָּה (*peullah*), *wages*, as in Lev. xix. 13.   Isa. xl. 10; xlix. 4; lxi. 8; lxii. 11.   Jer. xxii. 13.

C

The word *say* should be put in italics after the word "that" in verse 12, and then all the many italics inserted in verses 11-15 can be dispensed with. It is clearly suggested in verses 8 and 11. So clearly that there is hardly any necessity to use it or repeat it in verse 12. The pronoun אֲשֶׁר (*asher*), *who*, is clearer than "that." *Lit.*, "who [*say*]." Then the Psalm (B.11-15-) goes on to give the vanity and the falsehood as to what constitutes the true happiness of any people :—Who *say*

> "Our sons *are* as plants grown up in their youth ;
> Our daughters *are* as corner-stones, polished after the similitude of a palace ;
> Our garners are full, affording all manner of store ;
> Our sheep bring forth thousands and ten thousands in our streets ;
> Our oxen are strong to labour.
> There is no breaking in nor going out.
> There is no complaining in our streets.
> Happy people that are in such a case ! "

Then comes, in contrast, David's true estimate :

"NO! Happy is that people whose God is Jehovah."

This is the truth as to real happiness, as is so beautifully declared in Ps. iv. 6, 7 :—

> " There be many that say, Who will show us good?
> LORD, lift Thou up the light of Thy countenance upon us.
> Thou hast put gladness in my heart,
> More than in the time that their corn and their wine increased."

Yes, this is the only real "good." This is the only source of abiding happiness and gladness for any People. It is not the increase of corn and wine, but the light of God's countenance ; it is not the store which men put in their garners, but it is the "gladness" which God puts in our hearts. The structure of the whole Psalm agrees with this, and indeed necessitates this interpretation.

So, in Ps. cxlvi. 6, happiness is declared to consist in having the God of Jacob for our help, and our hope and help in the LORD our God : for there is "no help" in man (verse 3).

Isa. v. 9.—"In mine ears *said* the LORD of hosts."

Isa. xiv. 8.—"Yea, the fir trees rejoice at thee, *and* the cedars of Lebanon, *saying*."

Isa. xviii. 2.—"That sendeth ambassadors by the sea, even in vessels of bulrushes upon the waters, *saying*."

Isa. xxii. 13.—" And behold joy and gladness, slaying oxen, and killing sheep, eating flesh, and drinking wine : [*saying*] Let us eat and drink ; for to-morrow we shall die."

Isa. xxiv. 14, 15.—"They shall cry aloud from the sea, [*saying*], Wherefore," etc.

Isa. xxviii. 9.—"Whom shall he teach knowledge?" etc.

That is, "Whom [*say they*] shall he teach knowledge?" This verse and the following are the scornful words of "the scornful men" mentioned in verse 14. They ridicule the words of the prophet, saying, "for *it is* tsav upon tsav, tsav upon tsav, &c.,"* not "*must be*" but "*it is*."

Then, in verse 11, the prophet answers "For," or "Yea, verily, with stammerings of lip and another (or foreign) tongue will he speak to this people," and he tells them why "the word of the LORD was unto them precept upon precept;" viz. (verse 13), that they might fall and be broken.

Jer. ix. 19.—"For a voice of wailing is heard out of Zion, [*saying*], How are we spoiled!"

Jer. xi. 19.—"I knew not that they had devised devices against me, *saying*."

Jer. l. 5.—"They shall ask the way to Zion with their faces thitherward, *saying*."

Lam. iii. 41.—"Let us lift up our heart with *our* hands unto God in the heavens, [*saying*]."

Hos. xiv. 8.—"Ephraim *shall say*," etc.

Acts ix. 6.—"And the Lord *said* unto him," etc.

Acts x. 15.—"And the voice *spake* unto him again the second time."

Acts xiv. 22.—"Confirming the souls of the disciples, and exhorting them to continue in the faith, and *saying* that we must through much tribulation enter into the kingdom of God."

2 Cor. xii. 16.—"But be it so, I did not burden you : nevertheless [*you say that*] being crafty, I caught you with guile."

2. When the INFINITIVE of the verb is wanting:

(*a*) After the Hebrew יָכֹל *yahkōl*) *able*.

Ps. xxi. 11.—"They imagined a mischievous device, *which* they are not able *to perform*."

Ps. ci. 5.—"Him that hath an high look and a proud heart will not I suffer," *i.e.*, I am not able *to bear*.

---

*See under *Paronomasia*.

Isa. i. 13.—" The new moons and sabbaths, the calling of assemblies, I cannot away with," *i.e.*, I am not able *to endure.* See Jer. xliv. 22.

Ps. cxxxix. 6.—"*Such* knowledge *is* too wonderful for me; it is high, I cannot *attain* unto it." Here the *Ellipsis* is properly supplied: *i.e.*, I am not able *to attain* unto it.

Hos. viii. 5.—" How long *will it be* ere they attain to innocency ? " *i.e.*, how long ere they are able *to practise* innocency ?

1 Cor. iii. 2.—" I have fed you with milk, and not with meat : for hitherto ye were not able *to bear it*," *i.e.*, to *eat*, or *partake of it*, or, to *digest it.*

(*b*) After the verb *to finish.*

1 Sam. xvi. 11.—" Are here all *thy* children ? " Here the *Ellipsis* is avoided by a free and idiomatic translation. The Heb. reads, " Are the young men finished ? " *i.e.*, " *Are* the young men finished *passing by ?* " or done passing before me ?

Matt. x. 23.—" Ye shall not have gone over the cities of Israel till the Son of Man be come." Lit. " Ye will not have finished *going over* the cities," etc., referring to verses 6 and 7.

Matt. xiii. 53.—" When Jesus had finished these parables," *i.e.*, when Jesus had finished *speaking* these parables.

(*c*) When the INFINITIVE is wanting after *another* verb, personal or impersonal.

Gen. ix. 20.—" And Noah began *to be* an husbandman," or, " And Noah the husbandman began and planted, etc."

1 Kings vii. 47.—" And Solomon left all the vessels *unweighed* because they were exceeding many," *i.e.*, and Solomon omitted *to weigh*, etc.

Prov. xxi. 5.—" The thoughts of the diligent *tend* only to plenteousness : but of every one *that is* hasty only to want."

Here plenteousness is מוֹתָר (*mōthar*) *that which is over and above*, excess, (from יָתַר (*yahthar*) *to be superfluous*).

" The thoughts of the diligent tend only to excess, and [*the thoughts*] of every one that hasteth [*to get riches tend*] only to want."

The R.V. supplies the *Ellipses* thus. " But every one that is hasty *hasteth* only to want "; " *hasting* to want " is very obscure, but the " hasting to get riches " tending to want is clear.

Mark xv. 8.—" And the multitude crying aloud began to desire *him to do* as he had ever done unto them," *i.e.*, *that he should do.*

Luke xiii. 33.—" Nevertheless I must walk to-day, and to-morrow, and the *day* following," etc.

The R.V. has " Howbeit I must go on my way." But the Greek is " Howbeit it behoves me to-day, and to-morrow, and the *day* following, to go on [*to work*]," *i.e.*, to continue working.

Rom. iv. 25.—" Who was delivered [*to die*] for our offences."

3. When the VERB SUBSTANTIVE is omitted.

The Hebrew having no verb substantive, this is generally expressed in italics in the A.V. But inasmuch as it is absolutely necessary for the sense in English, the R.V. has printed it in roman type. (See preface to R.V.).

Gen. i. 2.—" Darkness *was* upon the face of the deep."

Gen. ii. 10.—Lit. " And *there was* a river going out of Eden."

Gen. iii. 6.—" And when the woman saw that the tree *was* good for food, and that it *was* pleasant to the eyes," etc.

Gen iv. 13.—" My punishment *is* greater than I can bear."

Gen. v. 1.—" This *is* the book of the generations of Adam."

Num. xiv. 9.—" Only rebel not ye against the LORD, neither fear ye the people of the land; for they *are* bread for us: their defence is departed from them, and the LORD *is* with us; fear them not."

These are the words of Joshua and Caleb to the people to encourage them to go up in spite of the false report of the other spies.

Note first the marginal rendering of the word "defence." It is given " Heb. *shadow*," *i.e.*, "Their shadow is departed." So in the R.V. the word "shadow" is treated as though it were a figure (*Metonymy*). The literal meaning of the word is departed from, as well as the literal rendering of the preceding sentence. This is בִּי לַחְמֵנוּ (*kee lachmenoo*) " for they *are* our bread."

The A.V. correctly supplies the *Ellipsis*, *i.e.*, our bread aptly represents their condition.

What was their "bread"? It was manna. What was the manna like? It was most marvellous bread, for it was so *hard* that it had to be ground in mills, or beaten in a mortar (Num. xi. 8); and yet its consistency was so peculiar that it melted in the sun! (Ex. xvi. 21). If it were not gathered every morning before the sun arose and the shadows departed, "when the sun waxed hot, it melted"!*

---

*Marvellous bread indeed! A standing miracle, both as to the manner in which it was given, and also as to its consistency. Bread indeed, hard, and yet melting like ice in the sun.

The wicked spies had just said (Num. xiii. 31) that Israel could not go up against the people of the land, for they are "stronger than we": they were strong and hard. No, replies Joshua, it may be they are strong, but so is our bread the manna—so strong that it needs grinding and crushing, and yet, when the shadow goes from off it, it melts away. Even so is it with them, as the words of Rahab testify (Josh. ii. 11). The two spies whom Joshua afterwards sent heard the very same truth from the lips of Rahab, which he, one of the two faithful spies whom Moses had sent, forty years before declared. She tells them:—"As soon as we had heard *these things*, our hearts did melt, neither did there remain any more courage in any man, because of you."

Thus, while the literal signification of the words gives no sense, they point to the true figure; and then, in turn, the figure explains the literal signification of the words, and the true meaning of the passage. So that we may render it thus:—" Only rebel not ye against Jehovah, neither fear ye the people of the land; for they [*are like*] our bread; their shadow hath turned aside from off them, and Jehovah is with us; fear them not," *i.e.*, as when the shadow turns aside from off our bread, it melts away and disappears, so these enemies, hard and strong as they might be, would surely melt away before the Lord God, the Sun and the Shield of His people. In no sense could Jehovah be the shadow or defence of the people of the land against whom Israel was about to fight.

1 Sam. xix. 11.—" To-morrow *thou shalt be* slain."

2 Kings vi. 33.—" Behold, this evil *is* of the LORD."

2 Chron. iii. 9.—"And the weight of the nails *was* fifty shekels of gold."

The verb is omitted to show that the emphasis is on the " nails " and their " weight." And what a wonderful emphasis it is! For in all the requirements for " the house of God," the fir-trees, the fine gold, the precious stones, the beams, the posts, the walls, etc., are mentioned; yet, the "nails" that held all together are not omitted. Though they were small, yet God used them: though out of sight, they were necessary.

Ps. xxxiii. 4.—" For the word of the LORD *is* right."

Ps. xcix. 9.—" For the LORD our God *is* holy."

It is worthy of note that there are three Psalms which begin with the words: " The LORD reigneth," viz., xciii., xcvii., and xcix. They each end with a reference to *holiness*.

Ps. xciii. " Holiness becometh Thine house, O LORD, for ever."

Ps. xcvii. " Give thanks at the remembrance of His holiness."

Ps. xcix. The third Psalm, three times :

> Verse 3. " It *is* holy."
>
> „ 5. " He *is* holy."
>
> „ 9. " The LORD our God *is* holy."

To those who have ears to hear, this plainly declares that when the Lord shall reign, all will be holy ; that when His kingdom comes, His name will be hallowed on earth as it is in heaven. " In that day shall there be upon the bells (or bridles) of the horses, HOLINESS UNTO THE LORD ; and the pots in the LORD's house shall be like the bowls before the altar. Yea, every pot in Jerusalem and Judah shall be HOLINESS unto the LORD of hosts " (Zech. xiv. 20, 21). " Her merchandise and her hire shall be holiness to the Lord " (Isa. xxiii. 18).

The cry of the living creatures (Rev. iv. 8, etc.) is " Holy, holy, holy," and their call is for the judgments which will issue in the Lord's reign, which is celebrated in these three Psalms. Those who teach that the Cherubim (or the Cherubs) are the Church fail to see that their chief function is to call for judgment !

Ps. cxix. 89.—" For ever, O LORD." The verb must here be supplied. The verb in the parallel line answers to the verb here :—

> " For ever [*art Thou*] O LORD ;
>
> Thy word is settled in heaven.
>
> Thy faithfulness *is* unto all generations ;
>
> Thou hast established the earth, and it abideth."

In the first and third lines, we have Jehovah. In the second and fourth lines, we have what He has settled and established.

Ecc. vii. 12.—" Wisdom *is* a defence."

Isa. xliii. 25.—" I, *even* I, *am* he that blotteth out thy transgressions for mine own sake, and will not remember thy sins."

We may take this in connection with Ps. ciii. 14. " For he knoweth our frame ; he remembereth that we *are* dust."

Here the verbs are omitted to throw the emphasis on the persons, rather than on the acts. This points us to Jehovah in the former passage, and ourselves in the latter—His Deity, and our vanity—and to contrast His thoughts with our thoughts, His ways with our ways. God remembers our infirmities ; but this is the very thing that man will not remember ! Man will make no allowance for our infirmities. On the other hand, man will remember our sins. Let any one of us fall into sin, and many will remember it after many years: but this is what God says He will not remember! "Their sins and their iniquities will I remember no more." He *is* Jehovah, we *are* dust! Hence our sins, which man remembers, God will forget; but our infirmities, which man forgets, God will remember.   Blessed be God!

Isa. xliv. 6.—"I *am* the first and I *am* the last, and beside me *there is* no God."

Ezek. xxxiv. 17.—"And *as for* you."

The *Ellipses* of this passage may be thus supplied: "And ye, O my flock, thus saith the Lord GOD (Adonai Jehovah): Behold, I judge between cattle and cattle, between the rams and the he goats.   [*Is it*] a small thing to you [*goats*] to have eaten up the good pasture, but ye must tread down with your feet the residue of your pastures? and to have drunk of the deep waters, but ye must foul the residue with your feet?   And [*is it a small thing that*] my flock [*i.e., my sheep*] eat [*or must eat*] that which ye [*goats*] have trodden with your feet; and drink that which ye have fouled with your feet?"

The contrast is between the sheep and the goats.   Sheep never become goats, and goats never become sheep, either in nature or in grace.   The Chief Shepherd knows His sheep here; He separates them now, and will eternally separate them from the goats in the coming day, when He shall "save his flock, and judge between cattle and cattle" (verses 20, 22, 23).

The characteristic of the goat alluded to here, is graphically set forth in a paper read before the Victoria Institute, Feb. 1, 1892, by J. W. Slater, Esq., P.C.S., F.E.S. He says, "The native *flora* and *fauna* of St. Helena have been practically extirpated by the goat.   These young seedlings were browsed down as fast as they sprung up, and when the old giants of the forest decayed there were no successors to take their place.   As a necessary consequence, the insects and birds disappeared in turn.   The same 'horned wretch'—fit type of evil— which, as Sir Joseph Hooker shows, has ravaged the earth to a greater extent than man has done by war, is now in the very same manner laying waste South Africa.   To such an extent has the mischief already been carried, that a troop of the Colonial Cavalry on the march actually gave three cheers on meeting a tree!"

Have we not here a fit illustration of Ezek. xxxiv.?   And may we not see in ecclesiastical affairs around us (through the unfaithfulness of the shepherds) the ravages of the "goats" in treading down and laying waste, and fouling the pastures of the flock of God?   The goats have turned our churches and chapels into places of amusement and of musical entertainment, where they may have " pleasant afternoons," and " make provision for the flesh " ; so much so that the. Lord's sheep are " pushed " and " scattered," and scarcely know where to find the " green pastures " and the " living waters " of the pure Word of God and the Gospel of His grace ! Thank God, the Chief Shepherd is coming : and, when He comes, though He will scarcely " find faith on the earth " (Luke xviii. 8), He will " save His flock " and separate them from the goats for ever, and be their One True Shepherd.

Luke ii. 14.—" Glory to God in the highest," *i.e.*, Glory *be* to God in the highest.

Luke xxii. 21.—" The hand of him that betrayeth me *is* with me on the table."

John iv. 24.—" God *is* a Spirit."
See under *Hendiadys and Hyperbaton.*

Acts ii. 29.—" Men *and* brethren, let me freely speak unto you of the patriarch David."

Here the verb " speak " is the infinitive : *lit.*, " to speak," and " let me " is the present participle (ἐξόν, *exon*),* *permitted* or *allowed.* So that we must supply the verb substantive (ἔστω, *esto*), let me be :—" [*let me be*] permitted to speak freely unto you, or *I am*, or *may be*, permitted, etc."

1 Cor. vi. 13.—" Meats [*are*] for the belly, and the belly [*is*] for meats."

1 Cor. xv. 29.—" Else what shall they do which are baptized for the dead, if the dead rise not at all ? "

This passage has been supposed to refer to a practice which obtained even in those apostolic days of persons being baptized on behalf of and for the spiritual benefit of those who were already dead. As this practice thus receives a tacit approval, and yet is destitute of any historical evidence as to its existence, apart from this passage, various methods have been proposed of meeting the difficulty which is thus raised. Some have erroneously suggested that " the dead " refers to Christ : but they have done so in ignorance of the fact that the word is plural, as is clearly shown by the verb " rise." Others (with Macknight) suggest the supply of the words "*resurrection of* "—" What shall they do which are baptized for the [*resurrection of*] the dead ? " But

---

* ἐξόν (*exon*) occurs only three times, of these the first (Matt. xii. 4) has ἦν (*een*), *was*, after it ; while in the other two places (here, and 2 Cor. xii. 4) it stands alone. In 2 Cor. xii. 4 it seems plain that we must supply ἐστίν (*estin*), *is ;* and so probably we should do here.

this implies the omission of the very word which is most essential to the argument; and would be a form of Ellipsis seldom, if ever, found. There are a multitude of other explanations; but the true solution of the difficulty is (we submit) to be sought in punctuation, and in the correct supply of the *Ellipsis*.

We must bear in mind that there is no punctuation in the ancient manuscripts, beyond the greater pauses. All interpunctuation is purely human in its origin, and we may be thankful that it is so seldom necessary to question its accuracy. We have also to note the *structure* of the whole context, for this, like all other texts, must be interpreted in harmony with the scope of the whole passage, and with the design of the whole argument.

The following is the structure of 1 Cor. xv. 12-58.*

> A | 12. The difficulty stated (as to the *fact*). " How ? "
> > B | 13-32. The difficulty met.
> > > C | 33, 34. Practical application.
> *A* | 35. The difficulty stated (as to the *manner*). " How?"
> > *B* | 36-57. The difficulty met.
> > > *C* | 58. Practical application.

The structure of " B " (verses 13-32). *The difficulty met.*

> B | a | 13-18. Negative hypothesis and its consequences.
> > b | 19. Conclusion (*positive*) as to Christ's in this life.
> a | 20-28. Positive assertion and its consequences.
> > b | 29-32. Conclusion (*negative*) as to Christ's in this life.

The structure of " a " (verses 13-18). *Negative hypothesis.*

> a | c | 13. If no resurrection : Consequence—then Christ is not risen.
> > d | 14,15. If Christ not risen.
> > Consequences : { Our preaching vain. / Your faith vain. / We false witnesses.
> c | 16. If no resurrection : Consequence—then Christ is not risen.
> > d | 17, 18. If Christ not risen.
> > Consequences : { Your faith vain. / Ye yet in sins. / The dead perished.

---

*The first eleven verses are constructed as follows :—

> D | 1-. The apostle's declaration.
> > E | -1, 2. The Gospel he preached.
> D | 3-. The apostle's declaration.
> > E | 3-11. The Gospel he received.

The structure of " *A* " and " *B*" (verses 35-57). *The difficulty stated.*

A | e | 35. Question: How are the dead raised up ?
      f | 35. Question : With what body do they come ?
B | *f* | 36-49. Answer to "f."
  e | 50-57. Answer to " e."

The structure therefore of this chapter shows that verses 20-28 ("*a* ") are placed, practically, in a parenthesis, so that this 29th verse reads on from the 19th verse, and continues the argument thus :—" 17. If Christ be not raised, your faith is vain ; ye are yet in your sins. 18. Then they also which are fallen asleep in Christ are perished. 19. If in this life only we have hope in Christ, we are of all men most miserable. 29. Else what shall they do which are being baptized ?"*

But here comes in the matter of punctuation. In Rom. viii. 34 we have a very similar construction, which, if we treat it as 1 Cor. xv. 29 is treated in the A.V. and R.V., would read thus, " Who is he that condemneth Christ that died ? " But the question is made to end at the word " condemneth," and the *Ellipsis* of the verb substantive is supplied thus:—" Who is he that condemneth ? *It is* Christ that died " (or better, " *Is it* Christ who died ?" See below). Now if we treat 1 Cor. xv. 29 in the same manner, it will read, " What shall they do which are being baptized ? *It is* on behalf of the dead if the dead rise not at all ! "

From Rom. vi. we learn that our circumcision is in Christ's death, our baptism is in Christ's burial. " Buried with Him by the baptism of Him, (*i.e.*, by His baptism-unto-death)" ; and if He is not raised, we cannot be raised, Rom. vi. 4. (See above, pages 18, 19). " Buried with Him in the baptism *of him*," *i.e.*, His baptism (Col. ii. 11, 12).

Therefore if Christ be not raised, we are not raised in Him, and our baptism is for the dead.

Whenever we have the word νεκρός (*nekros*), *dead*, with the article (as it is here in 1 Cor. xv. 29), it always denotes *dead bodies, corpses.* (See Gen. xxiii. 3, 4, 5, 6, 8, 13, 15. Deut. xxviii. 26. Jer. xii. 33. Ezek. xxxvii. 19. Luke xxiv. 5.) On the contrary, when it is *without* the article it denotes the *persons who are dead, dead people.* (See Deut. xiv. 1. Matt. xxii. 33. Mark ix. 10. Luke xvi. 30, 31 ; xxiv. 46. John xx. 9. Acts x. 41; xxvi. 23. Rom. vi. 13; x. 7 ; xi. 15. Heb. xi. 19; xiii. 20).

---

*Alford (who arrives at a very different conclusion) points out that οἱ βαπτιζόμενοι (*hoi baptizomenoi*) is the *present* participle and not the *past, i.e., those who are being baptized.* He observes : " The distinction is important as affecting the interpretation."

So that this is an additional argument why, if Christ be not raised, and we are buried with Him, then baptism is in the interest of those who are to remain dead corpses, and not of risen ones, raised with Christ.

This is the force of the word ὑπέρ (*hyper*). Like the English " for," it denotes the *object of interest*, not merely the subject, and ranges from mere reference to actual substitution, *e.g.*, 2 Cor. viii. 23, " Whether any enquire *about* Titus "; Matt. v. 44, " Pray *for* those who persecute you "; Mark ix. 40, " He who is not against us is *for* us "; 2 Cor. i. 6, " Whether we be afflicted, it is *for* your consolation "; Philem. 13, " That he might minister to me *instead of* thee."*

If Christ be not raised, well may those who are being baptized into Christ's burial be asked, " What shall they do ? " Truly, " *It is* for the dead." For they will remain dead, as corpses. In this life they " die daily " (verse 31); in death they perish (verse 18); and are thus " of all men most miserable " (verse 19).

" What shall they do who are being baptized ? *It is* for the dead if the dead rise not at all ! " It is to remain dead, as corpses, without hope of resurrection.

Thus, the expression, " baptized for the dead," vanishes from the Scripture, and is banished from theology; for the assumed practice is gathered only from this passage, and is unknown to history apart from it.

1 Cor. xv. 48.—" As *is* the earthy [*man, Adam*] such [*shall be*] also they that are earthy ; and as *is* the heavenly [*man, the Lord*] such [*shall be*] they also that are heavenly."

This is clear from the verse that follows :—" And as we have borne the image of the earthy [*man, Adam*] we shall also bear the image of the heavenly [*man, the Lord*]." See Phil. iii. 21.

2 Cor. xi. 22.—" Are they Hebrews ? So *am* I," etc.

Eph. iii. 1.—" For this cause I Paul, the prisoner of Jesus Christ for you Gentiles," *i.e.*, " I Paul [*am*] the prisoner," etc.

Phil. iv. 16.—" For even [*when I was*] in Thessalonica ye sent once and again unto my necessity."

2 Tim. iii. 16.—" All Scripture *is* given by inspiration of God, and *is* profitable."†

With this we may take eight other passages, where we have the same construction: viz., Rom. vii. 12. 1 Cor. xi. 30. 2 Cor. x. 10. 1 Tim. i. 15; ii. 3; iv. 4; iv. 9. and Heb. iv. 13.

---

*See also Rom. ix. 27. 2 Cor. i. 11 ; viii. 23, 24. 2 Thess. ii. 1. Col. i. 7.

† See this passage also under the figures of *Asyndeton* and *Paregmenon*.

These nine passages may be taken together, and considered in their bearing on the translation of 2 Tim. iii. 16 in the Revised Version, which is as follows:—

" Every scripture inspired of God is also profitable," etc.

In each of these passages we have the very *same Greek construction*, and four of them are in the Epistles to Timothy. The A.V. translates all these nine passages in precisely the same way, and on the same principles. But the R.V. translates eight of them in one way (*i.e.*, like the A.V.), while it renders one on quite a different principle.

Here are the passages, and the rendering as in the Authorized Version :—

ROM. vii. 12.

| ἡ ἐντολὴ | | ἀγία | καὶ | δικαία |
| The commandment | is | holy | and | just. |

1 COR. xi. 30.

| πολλοὶ | | ἀσθενεῖς | καὶ | ἄῤῥωστοι |
| many | are | weak | and | sickly. |

2 COR. x. 10.

| ἐπιστολαί | | βαρεῖαι | καὶ | ἰσχυραί |
| *his* letters | are | weighty | and | powerful. |

1 TIM. i. 15 and iv. 9.

| πιστὸς | | ὁ λόγος | καὶ | πάσης ἀποδοχῆς ἄξιος |
| faithful | is | the saying | and | worthy of all accepta-tion. |

1 TIM. ii. 3.

| τοῦτο | | καλόν | καὶ | ἀπόδεκτον |
| this | is | good | and | acceptable. |

1 TIM. iv. 4.

| πᾶν κτίσμα Θεου | | καλόν | καὶ | οὐδὲν ἀπόβλητον |
| Every creature of God | is | good | and | nothing to be refused. |

2 TIM. iii. 16.

| πᾶσα γραφὴ | | Θεόπνευστος | καὶ | ὠφέλιμος |
| All Scripture | is | given by inspira-tion of God | and | *is* profitable. |

HEB. iv. 13.

| πάντα | | γυμνὰ | καὶ | τετραχηλισμένα |
| All things | are | naked | and | opened. |

Now the case stands thus. The Revisers have translated eight of these passages, which we have cited, on the same principles as the A.V., *i.e.*, supplying in italics the verb substantive "*is*" and "*are*" respectively, and taking the copulative καὶ, "and," as joining together the two predicates. But when the Revisers come to the *ninth* passage (2 Tim. iii. 16), they separate the two conjoined predicates, making the first a part of the subject, and then are obliged to translate the καὶ in the sense of "also," when there is nothing antecedent to it. Thus:—

"Every scripture inspired of God *is* also profitable."

Now, if the Revisers had translated the other eight passages in the same way, the renderings would have been *consistent*, whatever else they might not have been.

Rom. vii. 12 would have been—

"The holy commandment *is* also just."

1 Cor. xi. 30 would have been—

"Many weak *ones are* also sickly."

2 Cor. x. 10 would have been—

"His weighty letters *are* also powerful."

1 Tim. i. 15 and iv. 9 would have been—

"The faithful saying *is* also worthy of all acceptation."

Tim. ii. 3 would have been—

"This good thing *is* also acceptable."

1 Tim. iv. 4 would have been—

"Every good creature of God *is* also nothing to be refused."

Heb. iv. 13 would have been—

"All naked things *are* also opened," etc.

But the Revisers do not translate them thus! And the fact that they render the whole of these eight passages as in the A.V., and single out 2 Tim. iii. 16 for different treatment, forbids us to accept the inconsistent rendering, and deprives it of all authority. Without inquiring as to what the motives of the Revisers may have been, we are justified in regretting that this should be the passage singled out for this inconsistent and exceptional treatment, reducing it to a mere platitude. It is only fair to add that the correct rendering of the A.V. is given in the margin.

Philem, 11.—"Which in time past was to thee unprofitable, but now [*is*] profitable to thee and to me."

4. When the PARTICIPLE is wanting.

Num. xxiv. 19.—"Out of Jacob shall come he that shall have dominion."

The R.V. is more literal:—"And out of Jacob shall one have dominion."

The Heb. is simply:—"And one shall rule (or have dominion) out of Jacob."

The *Ellipsis* of the participle being supplied, it reads :—" And *one* shall rule [*being born*] out of Jacob."

1 Sam. xv. 7.—" And Saul smote the Amalekites [*dwelling*] from Havilah *unto* Shur."

This refers to the region occupied by the Amalekites, and not to the people smitten, as is clear from chap. xxx.

Isa. lvii. 8.—" Thou hast discovered *thyself to another* than me," *i.e.,* " thou hast discovered thyself, *departing* from me," מֵאִתִּי (*meïttee*).

Ezek. xi. 11.—" This *city* shall not be your caldron, neither shall ye be the flesh in the midst thereof ; *but* I will judge you [*scattered*] in the border of Israel."

Mark vii. 4.—" And [*on coming*] from the market, they eat not except they wash."

Mark vii. 17.—" And when he was entered into the house [*getting away*] from the people."

Acts xiii. 20.—" And after that he gave *unto them* judges about the space of 450 years." Lit., " After these things [*were done*]," *i.e.,* after the division of the land by Joshua.*

2 Thess. i. 9.—" Who shall be punished with everlasting destruction [*driven out*] from the presence of the Lord."

Heb. ii. 3.—" Which at the first began to be spoken by the Lord, and was confirmed unto us by them that heard *him*," *i.e.,* " which at the first began to be spoken by the Lord, and, [*being brought*] unto us by them that heard him, was confirmed," etc.

III. When Certain Connected Words are omitted in the same Member of a Passage.

This particular form of *Ellipsis* has a distinct name, BRACHY-LOGIA (βραχυλογία from βραχύς, *brachus*, short, and λόγος, *logos*, discourse), English, *Bra-chyl'-o-gy.* Or from the Latin, BRÈVILO-QUENCE, it means brevity of speech or writing, and is used of an *Ellipsis*, in which words are omitted chiefly for the sake of brevity ; which words may easily be supplied from the nature of the subject.

Gen. xxv. 32.—" And Esau said, Behold, I *am* at the point to die ; and what profit shall this birthright do to me ? " There must be supplied, the *thought*, if not the *words* :—" *I will sell it.*" So with the next verse. " And Jacob said, Swear to me this day [*that thou wilt*

---

* For the question as to the Chronology involved in this difficulty, see *Number in Scripture*, by the same author and publisher, page 5.

sell it me]; and he sware unto him: and he sold his birthright unto Jacob."

Gen. xlv. 12.—"And behold, your eyes see, and the eyes of my brother Benjamin, that *it is* my mouth that speaketh unto you." Lit., it is, "because my mouth (כִּי־פִי, *kee phee*) is speaking unto you." If we supply the *Ellipsis*, we may retain this literal rendering.

Joseph had been speaking of his glory (verse 8): but, on the principle of Prov. xxvii. 2: "Let another man praise thee, and not thine own mouth," he breaks off and says, "Now, behold, your eyes are seeing, and the eyes of my brother Benjamin; because my own mouth is speaking unto you [*I cannot speak of all my glory*], but ye shall declare to my father all my glory in Egypt, and all that ye have seen," *i.e.*, THEY were to describe what HE could not well say of himself.

2 Kings xix. 9.—"And when he had heard say of Tirhakah king of Ethiopia, Behold, he is come out to fight against thee: [*he turned his army against him; and, having conquered him, he returned to Jerusalem, and*] he sent messengers again unto Hezekiah."

2 Kings xxii. 18.—"Thus saith the LORD God of Israel, *As touching* the words which thou hast heard."

So the R.V. but without italics. But surely the sense is:—"Thus saith the LORD God of Israel: The words which thou (Josiah) hast heard [*shall surely come to pass, but*] because thine heart was tender, and thou hast humbled thyself," etc. . . . "thou shalt be gathered into thy grave in peace; and thine eyes shall not see all the evil which I will bring upon this place."

1 Chron. xviii. 10.—"He sent Hadoram his son to king David, to enquire of his welfare, and to congratulate him, because he had fought against Hadarezer, and smitten him; (for Hadarezer had war with Tou;) and *with him* all manner of vessels of gold and silver and brass."

The R.V. supplies "and *he had with him*." But the *Ellipsis* is to be supplied from 2 Sam. viii. 10, thus, "And all manner of vessels of gold and silver and brass *were in his hand*" (בְּיָדוֹ הָיוּ).

Ezek. xlvii. 13.—"Joseph *shall have two* portions," *i.e.*, *shall inherit.*

Matt. xxi. 22.—"All things, whatsoever ye shall ask in prayer, believing, ye shall receive," *i.e.*, add "*if it be His will.*" Compare Matt. xxvi. 39-44; Jas. v. 14, 15; 1 John v. 14, 15. This is the one abiding condition of all real prayer, and the *Ellipsis* must be thus supplied wherever it is found.

In Mark v. we have by way of illustration *three* prayers—

1. In verses 12, 13. " The devils besought him," and " Jesus gave them leave."
2. In verse 17. The Gadarenes " began to pray him to depart out of their coasts." And Jesus left them.
3. In verses 18, 19. " He that had been possessed with the devil prayed him that he might be with him. Howbeit Jesus suffered him not."

"No!" is an answer to prayer! and often, very often, a most gracious and loving answer too. No greater calamity could come upon us than for God to answer " Yes " to all our ignorant requests. Better to have our prayers refused with this man who had been the subject of His grace and love and power, than to have them answered with Devils and Gadarenes.

Matt. xxv. 9.—" But the wise answered, saying, *Not so;* lest there be not enough for us and you ;" *i.e.,* " But the wise answered, *By no means, for look,* there will not be enough, &c., or *we cannot give to you,* lest, &c."

Mark xiv. 49.—" But the Scriptures must be fulfilled." The Greek is, " But that the Scriptures may be fulfilled." The R.V. correctly supplies the *Ellipsis,* " But *this is done* that the Scriptures should be fulfilled." (Compare Matt. xxvi. 56.)

Luke vii. 43.—" Simon answered and said, I suppose that *he* to whom he forgave most [*will love him most*]."

John ii. 18.—" What sign showest thou unto us [*that thou art the Messiah*], seeing that thou doest these things ? " As in Judges vi. 17, Gideon says, " Show me a sign that thou [*art Jehovah that*] talkest with me."

John vii. 38.—" He that believeth on me, as the Scripture hath said, out of his belly shall flow rivers of living water."

The difficulties of this verse are great, as may be seen by a reference to the commentators. It will be noted that a comparison is suggested by the word καθώς (*kathōs*), *like as,* and that there is an *Ellipsis* which must be supplied. Bengel suggests "as the Scripture hath said *so it shall be,*" or "*so shall it be.*" But something more is evidently required. Is there not a reference to the *Haphtarah, i.e.,* the portion selected (from the Prophets) as the lesson to be read on the *first* day of the Feast of Tabernacles, which was Zech. xiv. 1-21.* The

---

* The portion from the Law (Acts xiii. 15) read in conjunction with this was Lev. xxii. 26—xxiii. 44 ; with Num. xxix. 12-16.   D ˎ

Lord was not present then, for it was not until " the midst of the feast " that He went up (verse 14). But in " the last day, that great day of the feast, Jesus stood and cried," with evident reference to the Scripture which had been read, " He that believeth on me (as the Scripture hath said [*concerning Jerusalem: so shall it be*]) out of his heart rivers of living water shall flow." What the Scripture had said concerning Jerusalem in Zech. xiv. 8 was this :—" And it shall be in that day, *that* living waters shall go out from Jerusalem ; half of them toward the former sea, and half of them toward the hinder sea," &c. To this agree the words of the prophecy in Ezek. xlvii. 1-11. These prophecies shall yet be literally fulfilled with regard to Jerusalem : and what will then actually take place illustrates what takes place now in the experience of every one who believes in Jesus. Even as those rivers will flow forth from Jerusalem in that day, so now the Holy Spirit, in all His wondrous powers, and gifts, and graces, flows forth from the inward parts—the new nature of the believer.

John xiii. 18.—" I speak not of you all : I know whom I have chosen : but [*I have done this*] that the Scripture may be fulfilled, He that eateth bread with me hath lifted up his heel against me." Compare verses 26-30.

John xv. 25.—" But *this cometh to pass*, that the word might be fulfilled that is written in their law, They hated me without a cause." The abbreviated expression emphasizes the statement to which we are thus hastened on. And our attention is called to the fact that δωρεάν (*dōrean*) here rendered " without a cause " is in Rom. iii. 24 rendered " freely."—" Being justified freely by his grace ": *i.e.*, there was no more *cause* why we should be " justified " than there was why Jesus should be " hated " !

John xv. 27.—" Ye have been with me from the beginning [*and are still with me*]." Compare xvi. 4, and see 1 John iii. 8 below.

Rom. ix. 16.—Here the reference is to Esau and Jacob, spoken of in verses 10-13, and to the history as recorded in Gen. xxvii. 3, 4.

" So then [*election is*] not of him who willeth [as *Isaac wished to bless Esau* according to " the will of the flesh "*], nor of him that runneth [*as Esau ran for venison that his father might eat, and bless him*], but of God who showeth mercy."

---

*As Jacob was asked to bless Ephraim and Manasseh according to " the will of man " (Joseph) (Gen. xlviii. 5-14). Both cases are instanced in Heb. xi. 20, 21 as acts of " *Faith*," *i.e.*, *faith's* exercise of gifts contrary to " the will of the flesh," as in the case of Isaac ; and contrary to " the will of man " in the case of Jacob.

1 Cor. ix. 4.—" Have we not power to eat and to drink [*at the expense of our converts or of the Church*] ? " Without this there is no sequence in the apostle's argument. Or we may supply [*without working with our own hands*], see verses 6 and 7.

2 Cor. v. 3.—" If so be that being clothed we shall not be found naked."

Here the blessed hope of Resurrection is described as being clothed upon with the heavenly body. This is the subject which commences at 2 Cor. iv. 14. In chap. v. 3 the καί is ignored in both A.V. and R.V. The Greek is, " If indeed BEING CLOTHED also, we shall not be found naked [*as some among you say*]." There were some among the Corinthians who said " there is no resurrection of the dead " (1 Cor. xv. 12, 35), and here those assertions are thus referred to.

Gal. ii. 9.—" They gave to me and Barnabas the right hands of fellowship; that we unto the heathen, and they unto the circumcision, [*should carry the apostolic message and decrees*]."

Eph. iv. 29.—Here the word εἰ (*ei*) *if* is omitted in the translation both in the A.V. and R.V. Not observing the *Ellipsis*, the word " if " was omitted to make sense.

With the " if " retained, the *Ellipsis* is properly supplied thus :—

" Let no corrupt communication proceed out of your mouth, but, if any [*speech be*] good to the use of edifying, [*let it be spoken*] that it may minister grace unto the hearers."

Phil. iv. 11.—" I have learned in whatsoever state I am, *therewith* to be content."

The R.V. reads " therein to be content," without italics. But what is he to be content with ? Surely not content with the circumstances, but with *the will of God*. So that the verse will read, " I have learned, in whatsoever state I am, to be content with [*the will of God*]."

1 John iii. 8.—" The devil sinneth from the beginning [*and still sinneth*]."

IV. When a Whole Clause is omitted in a Connected Passage.

1. When the FIRST MEMBER of a clause is omitted.

Matt. xvi. 7.—" And they reasoned among themselves, saying, *It is* because we have taken no bread."

Here the first member of the latter clause is wanting. It is supplied in the A.V. by the words " *It is*." The R.V., not seeing this Ellipsis, has boldly omitted the ὅτι (*hoti*) *because*, and translated :—

"And they reasoned among themselves, saying, We took no bread" (giving the A.V. in the margin).

The *Ellipsis* of the first member is properly filled up thus:—"And they reasoned among themselves, saying [*Jesus spoke thus*, verse 6], because we have taken no bread."

See further under *Hypocatastasis*.

Mark iii. 30.—"Because they said, He hath an unclean spirit." Here the first clause is omitted:—"[*Jesus said this unto them*], because they said, He hath an unclean spirit."

Luke ix. 13.—"He said unto them, Give ye them to eat. And they said, We have no more but five loaves and two fishes; except we should go and buy meat for all this people."

There is something wanting here, which may be thus supplied:—"We have no more than five loaves and two fishes; [*therefore we are not able to give to them to eat*] except we should go and buy meat for all this people."

John v. 7.—"The impotent man answered him, Sir, [*I am indeed willing, but*], I have no man, when the water is troubled, to put me into the pool," etc.

2 Thess. ii. 3.—"Let no man deceive you by any means: for *that day shall not come*, except there come a falling away first." (Lit., the apostasy.) The R.V. fills up the *Ellipsis* of the prior member, by the words "*it will not be*," which is weak and tame compared with the A.V.

What is referred to is the day of the Lord,[*] mentioned in the preceding verse. "Let no man deceive you by any means: for [*the day of the Lord shall not come*] except there come the falling away first:" *i.e.*, the great apostasy, which is the subject of many prophecies, must precede the *day of the Lord*. But it does not precede *the day of Christ*. Hence the saints in Thessalonica might well be troubled if the day of the Lord had set in, and they had not been previously gathered together to meet the Lord in the air in the day of Christ, as had been promised (1 Thess. iv. 16, 17; 2 Thess. ii. 1).[†]

This is not the popular teaching, but it is the truth of God. Popular theology is very different. It says, "That day cannot come until the world's conversion comes." The Scripture says it cannot come until the apostasy shall have come. Popular theology says the world is not good enough yet for Christ to come. The Scripture teaches that the world is not yet bad enough! The Thessalonian

---

[*] Not "the day of Christ," as in A.V. The R.V. and the Ancient MSS. and Critical Texts read correctly "the day of the Lord."

[†] See *Four Prophetic Periods*, by the same author and publisher.

saints believed their teachers, and are an example for all time for holiness of walk and for missionary zeal. People to-day believe their teachers, and all men see their works!

2. The Ellipsis of a LATTER CLAUSE, called *Anantapodoton, i.e.,* without *apodosis.**

It is a hypothetical proposition without the consequent clause.

Gen. xxx. 27.—" And Laban said unto him, I pray thee, if I have found favour in thine eyes [*remain with me : for*] I have learned by experience that the LORD hath blessed me for thy sake."

2 Sam. ii. 27.—" And Joab said [*to Abner*], *As* God liveth, unless thou hadst spoken [*the words which gave the provocation* (see verse 14)], surely then in the morning the people had gone up (marg. *gone away*) every one from following his brother."

2 Sam. v. 6-8.—The Ellipsis here involves a retranslation of this difficult passage :—" And the king and his men went to Jerusalem, unto the Jebusites, the inhabitants of the land : which spake unto David, saying,† Thou shalt not come in hither, for (or *but,* כִּי אִם, *kee eem,* see Ps. i. 3, 4 ; ' for,' Prov. xxiii. 18 ; Lam. v. 22) the blind and lame shall drive thee away (so Coverdale) by saying (לֵאמֹר, *laimōr, saying,* margin), David shall not come in hither. Nevertheless, David took the stronghold of Zion ; the same is the city of David. And David said on that day, Whosoever getteth up by the Tsinnor,‡ and smiteth the Jebusites, and the lame and the blind, who hate David's soul (R.V. margin), *he shall be chief or captain,* because they (the blind and the lame) had said, He shall not come into the house (A.V. margin)," or citadel.

The Ellipsis is supplied from 1 Chron. xi. 6 ; and thus, with one or two simple emendations, the whole passage is made clear.

It would seem that the citadel was so strong that the Jebusites put their blind and lame there, who defended it by merely crying out, " David shall not come in hither."

Matt. vi. 25.—" Is not the life more than meat, and the body than raiment ? [and if *God vouchsafes the greater, how much more that which is less*]."

---

* *Apodosis,* Greek ἀπόδοσις, *a giving back again :* hence, it is the *consequent* clause. The former clause is called the *Protasis* (πρότασις, *to stretch before*).

†Both the A.V. and the R.V. transpose the following two sentences.

‡ בַּלְּנוֹר (*betsinnōr*) *in,* or *by the Tsinnor,* which was an underground watercourse, recently discovered by Sir Charles Warren. See his *Recovery of Jerusalem,* pp. 107, 109, 124.

Matt. viii. 9.—" For I am a man under authority, having soldiers under me : and I say to this man, Go, and he goeth ; and to another, Come, and he cometh ; and to my servant, Do this, and he doeth it [*how much more art Thou, who art God, able to command, or to speak the word only that my servant may recover*]."

Mark xi. 32.—" But if we shall say, Of men : [*what will happen to us ?*] for, they feared the people." Or we may supply, " *it will not be wise.*"

Luke ii. 21.—" And when eight days were accomplished for the circumcising of the child [*then they circumcised him, and*] his name was called JESUS."

John iii. 2.—" Rabbi, we know that thou art a teacher come from God : for no man can do these miracles which thou doest, except God be with him : [*therefore am I come to thee, that thou mayest teach me the way of salvation*]."

John vi. 62.—" *What* and if ye shall see the Son of man ascend up where he was before ? "

Here the *Apodosis* is entirely wanting. The Greek reads simply " If then ye should see the Son of man ascending up where he was before ? " The thought is the same as in John iii. 12 : " If I have told you earthly things and ye believe not, how shall ye believe if I tell you of heavenly things ? " So that the apodosis may be supplied thus, " *will ye believe then ?*" or, " *ye will not be offended then,*" *i.e.*, ye will marvel then not at My doctrine but at your own unbelief of it. Compare viii. 28 and iii. 13. (But see further under the figure of *Aposiopesis*).

Rom. ix. 22-24.—Here we have a remarkable *anantapodoton.* The conclusion of the argument is omitted. It begins with " if " (verse 22), and the *apodosis* must be supplied at the end of verse 24 from verse 20, *i.e.*, if God chooses to do this or that " *who art thou that repliest against God ?*" What have you to say ?

Or, indeed, we may treat it as the *Ellipsis* of a prior member, in which case verse 22 would commence " [*what reply hast thou to make*], if God, willing to show his wrath," etc.

Jas. ii. 13.—" For he shall have judgment without mercy, that hath showed no mercy ; and mercy rejoiceth against judgment [*to him that hath showed mercy*]."

2 Pet. ii. 4.—The *apodosis* is wanting here, but it is difficult to supply it without breaking the argument ; which is, " If God spared not the angels that sinned," *neither will he spare the false prophets and teachers*, mentioned in verse 1.

It is deferred till verse 12, where we have it :—they " shall utterly perish in their own corruption."

3. When the COMPARISON is wanting.   This is a kind of *anantapodoton*.

Rom. vii. 3.—In verses 2 and 3 the hypothesis is given in which the husband dies, while in verse 4 the fact to be illustrated is the case in which the wife dies.   Death ending the power of the marriage-law in each case.

At the end of verse 3, therefore, the other hypothesis must be supplied (mentally if not actually) :—

" If her husband be dead, she is free from that law ; so that she is no adulteress, though she be married to another man [*and I need not say that if she be dead, she is, of course, free from that law*].   Wherefore, my brethren, ye also have died to the law through the body of Christ ; that ye should be joined to another, even to him who is raised from the dead," *i.e.*, God's people have died in Christ ; and, on the other side of death, have risen with Christ, and are united to Him.   Thus being dead with Christ, the Law has no longer any dominion over them, and they are free to be united to another, " being dead to that wherein we were held " (verse 6, margin, and, R.V.).   Compare the following Scriptures on this important doctrine :—Rom. viii. 2 ; vi. 1-11 ; Gal. ii. 19 ; v. 18 ; vi. 14 ; Col. ii. 14 ; iii. 3 ; 1 Pet. ii. 24.   This figure comes under the head of Rhetoric, and is then called *Enthymema* (*q.v.*).

1 Tim. i. 3, 4.—" As I besought thee to abide still at Ephesus, when I went into Macedonia, that thou mightest charge some that they teach no other doctrine, Neither give heed to fables and endless genealogies, which minister questions, rather than godly edifying which is in faith [*so I repeat my charge, that thou remain at Ephesus, etc.*]"

2 Tim. ii. 20.—" In a great house there are not only vessels of gold and of silver, but also of wood and of earth, and, some to honour ; and some to dishonour : [*so in the great house of the church there are not only the elect saints, which are the vessels of honour, but there are the impious and reprobate, who are the vessels of dishonour*]." Therefore the admonition follows, in verse 21, to purge ourselves from these ; *i.e.*, not from the vessels of gold and silver, or wood and earth, but from *persons*. Still less does it say we are to purge the persons or the assembly ! Each one is to " purge himself," not the others.

We now come to the second great division.

B. Relative Ellipsis:

Where the omitted word must be supplied from the words actually related to it and employed in the context itself.

I. Where the omitted Word is supplied from a COGNATE Word occurring in the Immediate Context.

1. Where the Noun is suggested by the Verb.

Lev. iv. 2.—" If a soul shall sin through ignorance against any of the commandments of the Lord *concerning things* which ought not to be done."

Here the verb " shall sin " supplies the noun " sins," *i.e.,* " *concerning sins* which ought not to be done."

The R.V. evades the difficulty by a freer translation. But the correct supply of the *Ellipsis* enables us to retain the literal translation.

Num. xi. 14.—" I am not able to bear all this people alone, because *it is* too heavy for me."

Here the noun is latent in the verb, and is naturally supplied by it thus :—" I am not able to bear *the burden of* all this people alone, because *it is* too heavy for me." The word " it " does not refer to the People, but to the burden of them.

In verse 17 it is translated fully.

2 Kings xvii. 14.—" Notwithstanding they would not hear, but hardened their necks, like to the neck of their fathers," *i.e.,* like to the *hardness of* the necks of their fathers.

Ps. xiii. 3 (4).—" Lighten mine eyes, lest I sleep the death," *i.e.,* the *sleep of* death.

Ps. lxxvi. 11.—" Vow, and pay unto the Lord your God," *i.e.,* pay *your vows.*

Ps. cvii. 41.—" And maketh *him* families like a flock."

Lit., maketh like a flock the families.

The two parallel lines are thus completed by supplying the *Ellipsis* :—

" Yet setteth he the poor on high from (or, after) affliction,
And maketh like a flock the families [*of the afflicted*]."

Hos. ix. 4.—" They shall not offer wine to the Lord," *i.e.,* wine *offerings.* As in A.V.

Gal. iv. 24.—" Which things are an allegory: for these [*two women*] are the two covenants; the one, indeed, from the mount Sinai, which bringeth forth [*children*] into bondage, which is Hagar." The *apodosis* or conclusion is suspended till verse 26. " But Jerusalem which is above is the free [*woman*], who is the mother of us all." In verse 25, it must be noted that the word "this" is the article τό, which is neuter, while " Hagar" is feminine. Τό, therefore, must agree with some neuter word, which must be supplied, such as ὄνομα (*onoma*) name :—" For this [*name*] Hagar is (or, denotes) Mount Sinai in Arabia." It is a fact that in Arabia the word Hagar (which means *a stone*) is the name for Mount Sinai.

2. Where the VERB is to be supplied from the NOUN.

1 Sam. xiii. 8.—" And he tarried seven days, according to the time that Samuel [*had appointed*]."

1 Chron. xvii. 18.—" What can David *speak* more to thee for the honour of thy servant ? " *i.e.*, the honour *put upon* thy servant.

Ps. xciv. 10.—" He that chastiseth the heathen, shall not he correct ? he that teacheth man knowledge, *shall not he know ?* "

Compare verse 9, where we have similar questions.

Hos. i. 2.—" Go, take thee a wife of whoredoms and children of whoredoms."

The sense, as we see from verses 3, 6, and 8, must be " and [*beget*] children," etc.

Micah vii. 3.—" The prince asketh, and the judge *asketh* for a reward."

Here the A.V. supplies the *Ellipsis* by repeating the previous verb. The R.V. supplies it with the verb " *is ready*," *i.e.*, " the judge *is ready* for a reward."

But the verb is latent in the noun (" judge ") and is to be supplied from it, thus :—

" The prince asketh, and the judge *judgeth* for a reward."

The subject of the former sentence must be supplied from the latter, and then the two lines will read thus :—

"The prince asketh for [*a reward*],
And the judge [*judgeth*] for a reward."

Rom. xii. 6-8.—" Having then gifts differing according to the grace given to us, whether prophecy, *let us prophesy* according to the proportion of the faith [*given* or *dealt to us*, verse 3]." The verbs must also be supplied in the following exhortations :—" Or ministry, [*let us be diligent*] in the ministry : or he that teacheth, [*let him be faithful*] in teaching ; or he who exhorteth, [*let him employ himself*] in exhortation : he who distributeth, [*let him distribute*] with simplicity ; he who presideth, [*let him preside*] with care ; he that showeth mercy, [*let him show it*] with cheerfulness."

In the A.V. and R.V., some are supplied and some are not.

Rom. xiii. 7.—" Render therefore to all their dues ; tribute to whom tribute *is due*, etc."

Here the verb *to be due* is latent in the noun *dues*.

I Cor. i. 26.—" For ye see your calling, brethren, how that not many wise men after the flesh, not many mighty, not many noble, *are called*."

Here the thought or subject is the " calling "—*the act of calling*, *i.e.*, not the persons who are called, but the persons who call. The following verses go on to explain the manner in which God calls : viz., by choosing the weak and the base to confound the wise and the mighty. So in like manner He had chosen weak instruments like Paul, Apollos and Cephas to call the saints in Corinth, and to produce such wondrous results, in order " that no flesh should glory in His presence."

The *Ellipsis* would in this case be better supplied thus :—" Not many wise men after the flesh, not many mighty, not many noble *call you*."

2 Cor. v. 17.—" Therefore if any man *be* in Christ, *he is* a new creature."

Here the verb substantive is supplied twice, but the verb *created* must be supplied from the noun " creature " :—" If any man be in Christ, [*he is created*] a new creature."

Or else there is only one Ellipsis, and the sentence reads on, thus : " If any man *be* in Christ a new creation, old things have passed away ; behold, all things are become new."

Eph. iii. 16.—" [*Praying*] that he would grant you," from " bowing my knees " in verse 14.

II. Where the omitted Word is to be supplied from a CONTRARY Word.

Gen. xxxiii. 10.—" And Jacob [*refused and*] said, etc."
This word is latent in the contrary words which follow.

Gen. xxxiii. 15.—" And Esau said, Let me now leave with thee *some* of the folk that *are* with me. And he [*Jacob*] said, What needeth it ? [*Thou shalt not leave any*]," etc.

Gen. xlix. 4.—" Unstable as water, thou shalt not excel."

R.V. marg., " Bubbling over as water, thou shalt not have the excellency."

The word rendered " unstable " is פַּחַז (*pachaz*), *to bubble up and overflow, to flow down* like water. (So Sam. and Syr.). The *Ellipsis* is supplied from the contrary words, " Flowing down like water [*it shall pass away*], thou shalt not have the excellency."

This follows on verse 3. " Reuben, thou art my firstborn, my might, and the beginning of my strength, the excellency of dignity, and the excellency of power, with rapidity, like water, [*all this shall pass away*], thou shalt not have the excellency ! "

And so it came to pass. See 1 Chron. v. 1.

Judges v. 6.—Here, because the *Ellipsis* has not been observed, liberties have been taken in the translation. The Heb. is literally " In the days of Jael the high-ways ceased " (as in verse 7).

The A.V. and R.V. both render, " The high-ways were unoccupied." The R.V. tries to preserve the correctness of translation by giving in the margin " *the caravans ceased*."

But the Ellipsis when supplied by the contrary words which follow makes all clear :—" In the days of Jael, the highways ceased [*to be safe*], and the travellers walked through by-ways."

Ps. vii. 11.—" God judgeth the righteous, and God is angry *with the wicked* every day."

Ps. lxv. 8.—" Thou makest the outgoings of the morning and of the evening to rejoice."

This does not mean the outgoings of the evening as well as the morning. The contrary word must be supplied, viz., " [*the incomings or return*] of the evening."

Ps. lxvi. 20.—" Blessed *be* God, which hath not turned away my prayer, nor his mercy from me." This is not " my prayer from me," but " my prayer [*from himself*]."

Ps. lxxxiv. 10.—" For a day in thy courts *is* better than a thousand [*elsewhere*, or *in any other place*]."

Prov. xix. 1.—" Better *is* the poor that walketh in his integrity, than [*the rich, that is*] perverse in his lips, and is a fool."

Here the A.V. has supplied " *he that is*." It is necessary merely to define the person as *rich* to complete the contrast which is clearly implied.

Prov. xxiv. 17, 18.—" Rejoice not when thine enemy falleth, and let not thine heart be glad when he stumbleth : lest the LORD see *it*, and it displease him, and he turn away his wrath from him [*to thee*]."

Without the supply of this Ellipsis "*to thee*," there is no sense in the words.

Prov. xxviii. 16.—"The prince that lacketh understanding [*and*] also a great oppressor [*shall cut off his days*], *but* he that hateth covetousness, shall prolong *his* days."

Jer. xviii. 15.—"My people hath forgotten me, they have burned incense to vanity, and they have caused them to stumble in their ways [*so that they forsake*] the ancient paths," etc.

Dan. iii. 15.—Here the *Ellipsis* is so patent that it is supplied. "Now if ye be ready that at what time ye hear the sound of the cornet, flute, harp, sackbut, psaltery, and dulcimer, and all kinds of music, ye fall down and worship the image which I have made; [*well and good*]." Compare Luke xiii. 9.

Luke xiii. 9.—"And if it bear fruit, *well ;* and if not, *then,* after that thou shalt cut it down."

Here the omitted verb is suggested by the contrary verb that is given. Thus: "If it bear fruit [*thou shalt leave it to stand,* or *shalt not cut it down*], and if not, after that, thou shalt cut it down."

See further under the figure of *Aposiopesis.*

Rom. vi. 17.—"But God be thanked, that ye were the servants of sin, but ye have obeyed," etc.

Here the word δέ (*de*), *but,* in the latter clause implies and points us to the word μέν (*men*) which is omitted in the former clause. The two go together in a sentence of this character, and the employment of the one reveals the omission of the other. It should be rendered:—"But God be thanked that [*although*] ye were the servants of sin, yet ye have obeyed from the heart that form of doctrine which was delivered unto you."

This is clearly the sense, for we are not to thank God that we were the servants of sin, but that, *though* we were, we are so no longer.*

---

* For the importance of this word μέν (*men*), *although,* compare 1 Pet. iv. 6, where both the A.V. and R.V. ignore it, though it is there in the Greek, thus translating the words:—"For this cause was the gospel preached to them that are dead also, that they might be judged according to men in the flesh, but live according to God in the spirit." Surely, it cannot be that the gospel was preached in order that men might be judged ! And it is unaccountable why the A.V. and R.V. should both altogether ignore the important word μέν (*men*), *although,* and leave it untranslated !

They have both created an *Ellipsis* in the English, though there is none in the Greek, which reads ἵνα κριθῶσι μέν (*hina krithōsi men*), "in order that, though

1 Cor. vii. 19.—" Circumcision is nothing, and uncircumcision is nothing, but the keeping of the commandments of God [*is everything*]," *i.e.*, alone avails.

2 Cor. viii. 14.—" But by an equality, *that* now at this time your abundance *may be a supply* for their want, that [*at another time*] their abundance also may be *a supply* for your want, that there may be equality."

1 Tim. iv. 3.—" Forbidding to marry [*and commanding*] to abstain from meats." (See under *Zeugma*.)

III. WHERE THE OMITTED WORD IS TO BE SUPPLIED FROM ANALOGOUS, OR RELATED WORDS.

Gen. l. 23.—" The children also of Machir the son of Manasseh were brought up upon Joseph's knees." Margin, *borne*. R.V., *born*. But the *Ellipsis* of relation is :—" [*and educated*] at Joseph's knees."

Exod. xiii. 15.—" Therefore I sacrifice to the LORD all [*beasts*]," etc.

Lev. xxi. 4.—" But he being a chief man [*a priest*] among his people, shall not defile himself [*for his wife*] to profane himself." See verse 14 ; and Ezek. xxiv. 16, 17.

Deut. xv. 12.—" And if thy brother, [*or thy sister*], an Hebrew man, or an Hebrew woman, be sold unto thee," etc.

Ps. cxlii. 4.—" I looked on *my* right hand, and beheld [*on my left hand*]."

Isa. xxx. 17.—" One thousand *shall flee* at the rebuke of one ; at the rebuke of five shall ye [*all*] flee."

Isa. xxxviii. 12.—" I have cut off as a weaver my life," *i.e.*, I have cut off my life as a weaver [*his thread*].

Matt. iii. 4.—" And a leathern girdle [*was bound*] about his loins." In John vii. 39, the verb *given* is rightly supplied in the A.V. : " For the Holy Spirit was not yet *given*."

---

they might be condemned according to the will of men[a] as to the flesh, yet they might live (ζῶσι δὲ, *zōsi de*) according to the will of God, as to the spirit." That is to say, the gospel was preached to those who had since died, not "that they might be judged " thus, but " that THOUGH they might be judged." (See a pamphlet on *The Spirits in Prison*, by the same author and publisher.)

---

[a] Greek κατὰ ἀνθρώπους (*kata anthrōpous*), just like Rom. viii. 27, where the A.V. and R.V. both supply the words " *the will of* " in italics :—κατὰ θεόν (*kata theon*) according to *the will of* God.

Rom. xiv. 21.—"*It is* good neither to eat flesh, nor to drink wine, nor *any thing* whereby thy brother stumbleth," *i.e.*, nor *to do any thing* whereby, etc.

The point is not merely abstaining from the use of anything that other people abuse, but from that which is a cause of stumbling to the weak conscience of the brother in Christ, who thought it wrong to eat or drink that which has been offered to an idol.

Rom. xvi. 16.—" Salute one another with an holy kiss."

Here, the fact that ἀλλήλους (*alleelous*) is masculine, and the undoubted and overwhelming testimony of the Primitive Church, necessitate an *Ellipsis*; which must certainly be understood, if not actually supplied. It was, and is, contrary to all Eastern usage for women (who were always covered, 1 Cor. xi. 5) and men to kiss each other indiscriminately. The *Ellipsis* understood is:—" Salute one another [*men and women respectively*] with a holy kiss."

The *Apostolical Constitutions* (Cent. III.) say:—" Let the men salute one another (masc.), and the women one another (fem.), with a kiss."

In this sense are to be understood also 1 Cor. xvi. 20; 2 Cor. xiii. 12; 1 Thess. v. 26; 1 Pet. v. 14.*

IV. Where the omitted Word is contained in another Word, the One combining the two Significations.

This has been called METALEPSIS: but this is hardly correct; for *Metalepsis* (*q.v.*) is a compound *Metonomy*, and a *Metonomy* has to do only with *nouns*. It has also been called SYNTHETON, or SYNTHESIS (Latin, COMPOSITIO), which signifies the placing of two things together. (See under the Figure of *Metonymy*). It has also a Latin name: " CONCISA LOCUTIO," *i.e.*, a concise form of speech, or abbreviated expression.

It is also called CONSTRUCTIO PRÆGNANS, when the verb thus derives an additional force.

Gen. xii. 15.—"And the woman was taken into Pharaoh's house."

Here the figure is translated, for לָקַח (*laqach*) signifies *to catch*, or *capture*. (Gen. xiv. 12. Num. xxi. 25. Deut. iii. 14; xxix. 7. 1 Sam. xix. 14, 20. Isa. lii. 5. Jer. xlviii. 46). And here the two senses are combined (take, in the sense of *catch*, and take, in the sense of *lead*), to

---

* For an exhaustive treatment of the whole subject, see a work, entitled *Salute One Another*, by the Rev. Jas. Neil, M.A. Lond.: Simpkin and Marshall.

take possession of, and *lead into*, *i.e.*, "The woman was taken [*and brought*] into Pharaoh's house."

See for a similar use, *seized*, or *caught* and *led*, or *taken* and *brought*, etc., Gen. xv. 9, 10. Ex. xviii. 2 ; xxv. 2 ; xxvii. 20. Num. xix. 2. Est. ii. 16.

Gen. xliii. 33.—"And the men marvelled one at another." They did not marvel one at another, but, marvelling at what Joseph did, they looked one at another. The two senses are contained in the one verb, thus :—"And the men marvelled [*and looked*] one at another."

In verse 34, the two senses are translated both in A.V. and R.V., "and he took *and sent* messes unto them from before him." For this use of the verb נָשָׂא (*nashah*) *to take*, see also Ex. xviii. 12 ; xxv. 2 ; xxviii. 20, etc.

Ex. xxiii. 18, and xxxiv. 25.—Here the Hebrew זָבַח (*zavach*) *to sacrifice*, or *slay*, is not literally translated, but the two senses, *slay* and *pour out* (the blood) are combined in the one word " offer."

The Heb. עַל (*al*) is also in consequence translated *with*, instead of *upon*. The result is that there is no sense in the translation. The filling up of the *Ellipsis* preserves the literal signification of the other words as well as the sense of the verse, thus :—" Thou shalt not slay [*and pour out*] the blood of my sacrifice upon leavened bread."

Lev. xvii. 3.—" What man soever *there be* of the house of Israel that killeth an ox, or lamb, or goat, in the camp, or that killeth *it* out of the camp, and bringeth it not unto the door of the tabernacle of the congregation . . blood shall be imputed unto that man . . that man shall be cut off from among his people."

This appears to be quite at variance with Deut. xii. 15, 21, which expressly declares, "Thou mayest kill and eat flesh in all thy gates, whatsoever thy soul lusteth after."

The difficulty is at once removed by supplying the second sense which is included in the same word, " that killeth [*in sacrifice*]."

Num. xxv. 1.—Here, through not seeing the *Ellipsis*, אֶל (*el*) which means *to*, is translated *with*.

"And the people began to commit whoredom with the daughters of Moab," *i.e.*, they " began to commit whoredom [*and to join them-selves*] to the daughters of Moab."

Josh. viii. 29.—"Joshua commanded that they should raise thereon a great heap of stones *that remaineth* unto this day."

Here, as well as in x. 27, the *Ellipsis* is supplied.

2 Chron. xxxii. 1.—" And thought to win them for himself." ——
Here לִבְקָעָם אֵלָיו (*l'kikahm eylaiv*) means (as given in the margin)
to break them up, but this being "for himself," conveyed no sense; so
the translation of the verb, which means "*break up*," was modified
to "*win*," in order to agree with the preposition "*for*." But the
correct supply of the *Ellipsis* makes the meaning clear, and enables us
to retain the literal sense of the verb:—He "encamped against the
fenced cities, and thought to break them up [*and annex them*] to himself," or "thought to rend them [*from the kingdom of Judah, and annex
them*] to himself."

Ezra ii. 62.—Here the figure is translated. The Heb., as given
in the margin, reads literally, " Therefore they were polluted from the
priesthood." This is translated, " Therefore were they, as polluted,
put from the priesthood." But a more correct translation of the
figure would be: " Therefore they were polluted [*and put*] from the
priesthood."

Ps. xxi. 12.—We have already noted the *Ellipsis* of the accusative
in this verse, "*thine arrows*." Now we have the *Ellipsis*, in the same
verse, of the second signification of the verb:—" When thou shalt make
ready *thine arrows* upon thy bowstrings [*and shoot them*] against their
face."

Ps. xxii. 21.—" Thou hast heard me [*and delivered me*], from the
horns of the unicorns."

So Ps. cxviii. 5, where the *Ellipsis* is correctly supplied. See also
Heb. verse 7, below.

Ps. lv. 18.—" He hath delivered my soul in peace." R.V.: " He
hath redeemed my soul in peace."

The sense is obtained by supplying the *Ellipsis*—" He hath
redeemed my soul [*and set it*] in peace."

Ps. lxiii. 8.—" My soul followeth hard after thee."
Here to get the sense, the Heb. דָּבְקָה (*dahvqah*), which means
to cleave, to stick (see Gen. ii. 24. Deut. xxviii. 60. Ps. cxix. 31.
Lam. iv. 4), is translated *followeth hard*, in order to combine it with
אַחֲרֶיךָ (*achareyach*) *after thee.* " My soul followeth hard after thee."
The supply of the *Ellipsis* makes the sense clear and retains the literal
meaning of the words, thus:—" My soul cleaveth to [*and followeth*]
after thee."

Ps. lxvi. 14.—The Heb. is:—" Which my lips have opened."
See margin. The A.V. translates freely, " Which my lips have uttered."
But the sense is:—" Which (*vows*) my lips have opened [*and vowed*]."

Ps. lxviii. 18.—" Thou hast received gifts for men." The Heb. is :—" Thou hast received gifts among men," *i.e.*, " Thou hast received [*and given*] gifts among men " ; compare Eph. iv. 8.

Ps. lxxiii. 27.—" Thou hast destroyed all them that go a whoring from thee."

To make sense we must read :—" Thou hast destroyed all them that go a whoring, [*departing*] from thee," *i.e.*, " Thou hast destroyed all them that practise idolatry, departing from thee."

Ps. lxxxix. 39.—Here the *Ellipsis* is supplied. " Thou hast profaned his crown [*by casting it*] to the ground.'

Ps. civ. 22.—" The sun ariseth, they gather themselves together, and lay them down in their dens." The Heb. is :—" And unto their dens (וְאֶל־מְעוֹנֹתָם) they lie down," *i.e.*, " The sun ariseth, they gather themselves together, [*depart, and*] lay themselves down in their dens."

Prov. xxv. 22.—The Heb. reads :—" For coals of fire thou shalt receive upon his head," *i.e.*, " for coals of fire thou shalt receive [*and place*] upon his head."

The verb חָתָה (*chathah*) means *to take hold of, to seize*, spoken once of a person, Isa. lii. 5 (7), and elsewhere always of taking up fire or burning coals. See Isa. xxx. 14. Prov. vi. 27. *I.e.*, the coals of fire which thine enemy casts at thee, thou shalt take them and put them upon his head : he will thus get what he intended for thee.

The " burning coals " are put by *Metonymy* (*q.v.*) for cruel words and hard speeches (see Prov. xvi. 27 ; xxvi. 23).

Ps. cxl. 9, 10. But if thou doest good to him who uses cruel words of you, that will burn him as coals of fire.

Matt. iv. 5.—" Then the Devil taketh him up into the holy city." Παραλαμβάνω (*paralambanō*) means *to take and bring with one's self, to join one's self*. There is no equivalent for " up." The double sense of the verse must be supplied in the *Ellipsis* :—" Then the Devil taketh him with himself [*and leadeth*] him," etc. So verse 8 and xxvii. 27. The sense is sometimes completed by a second verb, Matt. ii. 13, 20. John xix. 16. Acts xxiii. 18.

Matt. v. 23.—" Therefore if thou bring thy gift to the altar, and there rememberest that thy brother hath ought against thee " ; *i.e.*, " if thou bring thy gift [*even thy sacrifice*] to the altar." An offering was the only gift that could be brought to an altar. In Lev. ii. 1, 2, the Septuagint translates, " If a soul bring a gift, a sacrifice, to the LORD, his gift shall be," etc., and thus supplies the explanatory words. To

E

apply these words to the placing money on the Lord's Table is a perverse use of language.

Luke iv. 1, 2.—"And Jesus being full of the Holy Ghost returned from Jordan, and was led by the Spirit into the wilderness, being forty days tempted of the devil."

The A.V. connects the forty days with the temptation: but we learn from Matt. iv. 3 that it was not till after the forty days that the tempter came to Him, when He was hungry. The words are elliptical, and are a *concisa locutio, i.e.*, an abbreviated expression, in order that our thought may dwell on the fact of the *leading*, rather than on the fact of His being there.

The Greek is:—" He was being led by the Spirit into the wilderness, [*and was in the wilderness*] forty days."

Luke iv. 38.—"And he arose out of the synagogue," *i.e.*, " And rising up [*he departed*] out* of the synagogue, *and* entered into the house of Simon." By this figure our attention is directed to the fact which is important, viz., His rising up, and thus preventing any comment on the miracle; rather than to the mere act of going out of the synagogue.

Luke xviii. 14.—" I tell you, this man went down to his house justified *rather* than the other."

The Greek reads, "This man went down to his house justified than the other," but the A.V. correctly supplies the *disjunction* contained in the comparative ἤ (*ee*), when following a positive assertion. The thought lies in the Heb. use of the word מִן (*min*), Ps. cxviii. 8, 9 : " *It is* better to trust in the LORD than [*i.e., and not*] to put confidence in man. *It is* better to trust in the LORD than [*i.e., and not*] to put confidence in princes." So Jonah iv. 3. "Now, O Lord, take, I beseech thee, my life from me; for *it is* better for me to die than [*i.e., and not*] to live."

So in the N.T., Heb. xi. 25 : " Choosing rather to suffer affliction with the People of God, than [*i.e., and not*] to enjoy the pleasures of sin for a season."

So here the doctrine is that the Publican was justified *and not* the Pharisee. Not that the Pharisee was justified a little, and the Publican was justified a little more! The parable is wholly concern-

---

* The ancient reading was ἀπὸ, *from*, supported by the Critical Texts of Tischendorf, Tregelles, Alford, and Westcott and Hort. It was altered later by some copyist who did not see the force of the figure, so as to make it agree better with the single verb employed.

ing *justification* (verse 9), and not a parable about the nature of prayer. The manner of the prayer is merely the vehicle for the illustration of the truth.*

Luke xix. 44.—"And shall lay thee even with the ground." ἐδαφίζειν (*edaphizein*) signifies both *to level to the ground*, and *to dash to the ground*. In this last sense it occurs in Ps. cxxxvii. 9. Hos. x. 14; LXX.

Luke xx. 9.—"A certain man planted a vineyard, and let it forth to husbandmen, and went into a far country for a long time," *i.e.*, "he went into a far country, [*and remained there*] a long time"; or, we may supply, "*and was absent* for a long time."

Luke xxi. 38.—"And all the people came early in the morning to him in the temple, for to hear him."

But ὀρθρίζω (*orthrizō*) does not mean to come early, but *to rise up early*, and the sense is :—"And all the people rising early in the morning, [*came*] to him in the temple."

John i. 23.—"He said, I *am* the voice of one crying in the wilderness," etc. : *i.e.*, "I [*am he of whom it is written*] the voice of one crying in the wilderness."

John vi. 21.—"Then they willingly received him into the ship." Here the figure is hidden by a free translation. The Greek is :—"They were willing, then, to receive him into the ship, [*and they did receive him*]."

Acts vii. 9.—"And the patriarchs, moved with envy, sold Joseph into Egypt," *i.e.*, "And the patriarchs, moved with envy, sold Joseph [*and sent him away*] into Egypt.

Ἀποδίδωμι (*apodidōmi*) does not mean merely *to sell*, but *to put away by giving over*, whether for money or for any other return.

Acts xx. 30.—"Also of your own selves shall men arise, speaking perverse things, to draw away disciples after them," *i.e.*, "speaking perverse things [*and seeking*] to draw away."

Acts xxiii. 24.—"And provide *them* beasts, that they may set Paul on, and bring *him* safe unto Felix the governor." The Greek

---

* Ignorance of the doctrine of justification, it may have been, or oversight as to the point of the parable, that gave rise to the difficulties presented by the Text, which was altered and glossed in various ways in order to make sense. The *Textus Receptus* has ἢ ἐκεῖνος, the MSS. APQ, &c. have ἢ γὰρ ἐκεῖνος, with T.Tr. marg. (*i.e.*, "This man went down to his house justified . . . or was it then the other, &c."). The MSS. BLℵ have παρ' ἐκεῖνον, with L.Tr.WH.Alf. (*i.e.*, passing over the other).

is, lit., :—" διασώζω (*diasōzō*) *to save through*," *i.e.*, "and keep him in safety [*and bring him*] unto Felix."

Here, by the omission of the verb *to bring*, which is required by the preposition, our attention is called to the fact which is of greater importance, *viz.*, the preservation of Paul from his enemies.

Gal. v. 4.—" Christ is become of no effect unto you, whosoever of you are justified by the law ; ye are fallen from grace."

The Greek is :—κατηργήθητε ἀπὸ τοῦ Χριστοῦ (*kateergeetheete apo tou Christou*) ; and the R.V. translates it :—" Ye are severed from Christ," and puts in the margin, Greek "*brought to nought.*" But we may take the Greek literally, if we put the margin in the Text and supply the *Ellipsis* correctly :—

" Ye are made void [*and cut off*] from Christ."

Eph. iv. 8.—" When he ascended up on high, he led captivity captive and, [*receiving*] gifts, gave them to men." See Ps. lxviii. 18 above.

2 Tim. i. 10.—" And hath brought life and immortality to light through the gospel."

Here, following the order of the Greek, we may read :—" And brought to light, [*and procured for us*] life and immortality through the gospel." By the Figure of *Hendiadys* (*q.v.*), that which is procured is immortal life, showing us that the emphasis is on the word "*immortal.*"

2 Tim. ii. 26.—" And *that* they may recover themselves out of the snare of the devil, who are taken captive by him at his will."

Here both the figure and the sense are lost by defective translation. The margin tells us that the words "*recover themselves*" are used to render the Greek "*awake*," *i.e.*, " lest they may awake [*and be delivered*] out of the snare of the devil."

The structure of this Scripture makes the whole passage clear :—

Subversion.

A | 14. The aim of the enemy " Subversion " (καταστροφῇ).
   B | 15. The workman (ἐργάτος).
      C | 16. Exhortation. "Shun."
         D | 17, 18-. Illustration. "Canker."
            E | -18. Effect on others. "Overthrown."
            E | 19. Effect on Foundation. "Standeth sure."
         D | 20, 21. Illustration. "Vessels."
      C | 22, 23. Exhortation. "Flee . . Avoid."
   B | 24, 25-. The Servant (δοῦλος).
A | -25, 26. The aim of the enemy. " Opposition " (ἀντιδιατιθεμένοι).

Then by expanding this last member *A*, we see the meaning of verses -25, 26 :—

A. *The aim of the enemy.*

A | a | -25-. " Lest God should give them repentance "
      b | -25. " Unto (εἰς) the knowledge of the truth,"
   a | 26-. " And lest, being taken alive by him, [*by God*, as in " a "] they may awake [*and be delivered*] from the devil's snare "
      b | -26. " Unto (εἰς) his [*God's*] will (*i.e.*, to *do* the will *of God*)."

Here in " a " and " *a* " we have the action of Gōd in delivering, while in " b " and " *b* " we have the object for which the captive is delivered.

2 Tim. iv. 18.—" And the Lord shall deliver me from every evil work, and will preserve *me* unto his heavenly kingdom : " *i.e.*, " preserve *me*, [*and bring me*] ." Thus fixing our thought rather on the wondrous *preservation* than on the act of *bringing*.

Heb. v. 3.—" And by reason hereof he ought, as for the people, so also for himself, to offer [*sacrifices*] for sins."

Heb. v. 7.—" And was heard [*and delivered*] from his fear." ἀπὸ τῆς εὐλαβείας (*apo tees eulabeias*). (Only here and Heb. xii. 28). See Ps. xxii. 21, above.

Heb. ix. 16, 17.—" For where a testament *is*, there must also of necessity be the death of the testator. For a testament is of force after men are dead : otherwise it is of no strength at all whilst the testator liveth."

It is clear that it is a " covenant " to which these words refer, and not a testamentary document. The reference to the " first " covenant at Sinai mentioned in the verses which immediately follow, decides this for us. See Ex. xxiv. 5-8.

And the mention also of the sprinkling of the blood shows that sacrifices are referred to.

The word translated " testator " is the participle :—διαθέμενος (*diathemenos*), and means *appointed*.* Its use shows that the sacrifice

---

* Participle of διατίθημι (*diatitheemi*), *to appoint* (see Luke xxii. 29). " And I *appoint* unto you a kingdom, as my Father hath *appointed* unto me." Acts iii. 25 : "The covenant which God *made* with our fathers." Heb. viii. 10 : "This is the covenant which I will *make* with the house of Israel after those days, saith the Lord." So also Heb. x. 16. These are the only places where the verb occurs, except this passage.

by which the covenant was made is really contained in the word.

And the word διαθήκη (*diatheekee*) everywhere means *covenant*.

So that, in accordance with these Scriptures and facts, we may translate verses 16-18, as follows :—

"For where a covenant *is*, there must also of necessity be the death of him (or that) which makes [*the sacrifice*]. For a covenant is of force over* dead [*victims or sacrifices*] ; otherwise it is never held to be of force while he who is the appointed [*sacrifice*] is alive. Whereupon neither the first [*covenant*] was dedicated without blood," etc.

Heb. x. 23.—"Having our hearts sprinkled from an evil conscience," *i.e.*, "Having our hearts sprinkled [*and so being delivered*] from an evil conscience."

1 Pet. iii. 20.—"Were saved by water," *i.e.*, "Were preserved [*and delivered*] by water."

Rev. xiii. 3.—"And all the world wondered after the beast." ὀπίσω (*opisō*) is an adverb of *place* or time, and means *back, behind, after* (see Rev. i. 10 ; xii. 15). It cannot, therefore, be taken in connection simply with wondered. But the following is the sense :—

"And all the world wondered [*and followed*] after the beast."

Rev. xx. 2.—"And bound him a thousand years," *i.e.*, "And bound him [*and kept him bound*] a thousand years."

C. THE ELLIPSIS OF REPETITION:

Where the omitted word or words is, or are to be supplied out of the *preceding* or *following* clause, in order to complete the sense.

This Ellipsis is either simple or complex.

Simple, when anything is to be repeated separately, either out of what precedes or follows.

Complex, when two things are to be repeated ; one out of a preceding clause into the following clause ; and at *the same time* another out of the following into the preceding clause.

---

* ἐπί means *over*, as marking the ground or foundation of the action. See Matt. xxiv. 47. Luke xii. 44 ; xv. 7 (7), 10 ; xix. 41 ; xxiii. 38. Acts viii. 2. 1 Thess. iii. 7. Rev. xi. 10 ; xviii. 11. It is translated, " upon " and " on," etc., many times ; but " after " only here and Luke i. 59.

I. Simple.

1. Where the Omission is to be supplied by REPEATING a word or words out of the Preceding Clause.

(a) Nouns and Pronouns.

Ex. xii. 4.—"Let him and his neighbour next unto his house take *it*," *i.e., the lamb* from verse 3.

1 Kings i. 6.—"And [*Haggith*] bare him after Absalom."

2 Kings iii. 25.—"Only in Kir-haraseth left they the stones thereof."

The Heb. reads (see margin):—"Until he left the stones thereof in Kir-haraseth."

The *Ellipsis* is to be supplied from verse 24. "Until in Kir-haraseth [*only*] they left the stones thereof [*to the Moabites*]."

Ps. xii. 6, (7).—"The words of the Lord *are* pure words: *as* silver tried in a furnace of earth, purified seven times."

Here there is an important *Ellipsis*. It has been a great difficulty with many to think that the Lord's words should require purifying, especially after the declaration in the first part of the verse, that they are "pure." What increases the difficulty is the fact that the word for earth is אֶרֶץ (*eretz*), *the earth*: *i.e.*, the dry land or the world as created, as in Gen. i. 1: "In the beginning God created the heaven and the earth" (אֶרֶץ, *eretz*). It is generally taken as though it were used of a crucible made of earth or clay; but in this case it would be אֲדָמָה (*adamah*), *ground, soil, clay*; and not *eretz*, the whole earth. Moreover, the *Lamed* prefixed (לְ) means *to* or *pertaining to*. It is the sign of the dative case and not of the genitive. The Revisers note this and render it:—"As silver tried in a furnace on the earth," as though it was important for us to note that it is not in or under the earth! But this does not touch the real difficulty. This is removed only by correctly supplying the *Ellipsis*, and repeating the noun "words" from the beginning of the verse.

Then, all is clear, and we not only may, but must then take the rest of the words in their literal sense. Thus:—"The words of the Lord are pure words, *as* silver tried in a furnace; [*words*] of the earth: (or pertaining to the earth), purified seven times."

That is to say the words in which Jehovah has been pleased to make His revelation, are not the words of angels (1 Cor. xiii. 1), nor the "unspeakable words of Paradise" (2 Cor. xii. 4), but they were words pertaining to man in this world—human words—but refined and purified as silver.   Hence, in taking human language, there are many words which the Holy Spirit has not chosen, and which cannot be found in the Scriptures:

Some are exalted to an altogether *higher* meaning as

ἀρετή (*aretee*), as man had used it, meant merely *excellence* of any kind, *manhood, nobility, valour, prowess*.   But, in the Scriptures, it is used in the higher sense of *glory* (Hab. iii. 3), *praise* (Isa. xlii. 8, 12; xliii. 21; lxiii. 7).   And so in the New Testament, Phil. iv. 8; 1 Pet. ii. 9; 2 Pet. i. 3, 5.

ἦθος (*eethos*) was only the *haunt* of an animal, but it became *custom, morals, character*.

Some are used in a totally *different* sense from that in which they had ever been used before.

χορηγέω (*choreegeō*) was simply *to furnish or lead a chorus*, but it was changed *to furnish* or *supply*.   1 Pet. iv. 11: "My God shall supply all your need."

εὐαγγέλιον (*euangelion*) was merely *the dispatch* containing the news, but it was used in the new sense of *the gospel* of God.

ἐκκλησία (*ekkleesia*) was used by the Greeks of any *assembly*, but especially of citizens, or as we should say of a selection from them, "burgesses."   The word means *an assembly of those called out, an elect assembly*.

Hence it is used in the Septuagint of Israel as called out from and as being an election from the nations.

Then, it was used of the congregation worshipping at the Tabernacle as distinguished from the rest of the people.

In this sense it is used in the Old Testament, the Gospels, and partly in the Acts.   But in the Pauline Epistles the Holy Spirit uses the word and exalts it to a far higher meaning; *viz.*, of the special election from both Jews and Gentiles, forming them as members of Christ's Mystical Body into a new *ecclesia* or assembly.   This is a sense in which it had never before been used.*

σωτηρία (*sōteeria*) was merely *preservation* or *deliverance* from danger, but in the Scriptures it is "the salvation of God."

παράκλητος (*paracleetos*) was merely the *legal assistant* or *helper*. In the New Testament there is one *Paracleetos* within us that we may not sin (John xiv. 16, 26; xv. 26; xvi. 7); and another *Paracleetos* with the Father if we do sin (1 John ii. 1).

---

* See *The Mystery*, by the same author and publisher.

σκάνδαλον (*skandalon*) was used only of *the trigger* of a trap to catch animals; but in the New Testament it is used in a new and moral sense, of that which causes any one to be caught or made to trip.

Other words were coined by the Holy Spirit Himself, and cannot be found in any human writings.

σκανδαλίζω (*skandalizō*) is a new word altogether. It is never used in Classical Greek, it means *to cause to stumble or fall, to give cause of offence.*

ἐπιούσιος (*epiousios*) is a word used only by our Lord (Matt. vi. 11 and Luke xi. 3) in the Lord's Prayer, where it is rendered "daily."

Hence the difficulty in interpreting it, as there is no usage to help us. It is a question, therefore, of etymology. It is the preposition ἐπὶ (*epi*), *upon*, prefixed to the participle of a verb. But what verb? It cannot be the participle of the verb εἰμί (*eimi*), *to be*, for its participle is οὖσα (*ousa*), and the combination of οὖσα with ἐπὶ would be ἐποῦσα. It must be εἶμι (*eimi*), *to go or come*, for its participle is ἰοῦσα (*iousa*), and the combination of ἰοῦσα with ἐπί will be ἐπιοῦσα, as used by our Lord. The word means, therefore, *coming upon* or *going upon*, and would refer either to bread for our *going* or *journeying upon*, or to the bread *coming* or *descending upon* us from heaven, as the manna descended and came down upon Israel (John vi. 32, 33).

Hence it combines the two ideas of *heavenly* and *daily*, inasmuch as the manna not only came down from heaven, but did so every day, and on the strength of this they journeyed. It is a word therefore of great fulness of meaning.

That the Ellipsis exists in Psalm xii. 6 (which verse we are considering), and may be thus supplied, is shown further from the structure of the Psalm :—

A | 1. Decrease of good.
    B | a | 2. Man's words (Falsehood).
        | b | 3, 4. Their end : "cut off."
            C | 5-. Oppression.
               D | -5-. Sighing.
               D | -5-. I will arise (for sighing).
            C | -5. I will deliver (from oppression).
    B | a | 6. Jehovah's words (Truth).
        | b | 7. Their end : (preserved).
A | 8. Increase of bad.

Here in *B*, Jehovah's words are placed in contrast with man's words in B: in a and *a*, their *character* respectively: and in b and *b* their *end*.

Finally, we may expand a (verse 6) as follows:—

> *a* | c | The words of Jehovah are pure words.
>
>   d | *As* silver tried in a furnace:
>
> *c* | [*Words*] pertaining to the earth.
>
>   *d* | Purified seven times.

Here in c and *c* we have "words," and in d and *d* we have the *purifying* of the silver.

Ps. lxviii. 18.—"Thou hast ascended on high, thou hast led captivity captive: thou hast received gifts for men; yea, *for* the rebellious also, that the LORD God might dwell *among them*," *i.e.*, among or with those rebels who have been taken captives.

Ecc. xii. 11.—"The words of the wise *are* as goads, and as nails fastened *by* the masters of assemblies, *which* are given from one shepherd."

Here, instead of repeating "the words" from the first clause, the A.V. inserts the word "*by*," thus producing incoherence in the passage. The structure shows us at once how the Ellipsis should be filled up.

> a | The words of the wise
>
>   b | *are* as goads,
>
>   *b* | and as tent-pegs well fixed,
>
> *a* | are [*the words*] of the masters of the assemblies.

Here, in a and *a*, we have "*words*," and in b and *b*, what they are compared to.

In "a" we have the words of those which act like goads, inciting to action, or probing the conscience; while in *a* we have the words of those who are the leaders of assemblies, propounding firmly established principles and settled teaching. "*Both* of these (not "*which*") are given by the same shepherd."

That is, as a chief shepherd gives to one servant a goad for his use, and to another a stake, or "tent-peg," to fix firmly in the ground, so the God of all wisdom, by the Chief Shepherd in glory, gives to His servants "words," different in their tendency and action, but conducing to the same end, showing the one source from which the various gifts are received. He gives to some of His under-shepherds "words" which act as goads; while He gives to others "words" which "stablish, strengthen and settle."

Isa. xl. 13.—" Who hath directed the Spirit of the LORD, or *being* his counsellor hath taught him ? "

Here the *Ellipsis* is arbitrarily supplied by the word " *being*," which necessitates a departure from the Heb., which is given in the margin, " *made him understand.*"

The *Ellipsis* is correctly supplied thus :—" Who hath directed the Spirit of the LORD ; or [*who*] as His counsellor hath made him *to* understand ? "

Amos iii. 12.—" As the shepherd taketh out of the mouth of the lion two legs, or a piece of an ear ; so shall the children of Israel be taken out that dwell in Samaria in the corner of a bed, and in Damascus *in* a couch," *i.e.,* " and [*in the corner of*] a couch."

Mal. ii. 14.—" Yet ye say, Wherefore ? " *i.e.,* from verse 13, wherefore [*does He not regard our offering, etc.*] ?

Acts vii. 15, 16.—" So Jacob went down into Egypt, and died, he, and our fathers, and were carried over into Sychem, and laid in the sepulchre that Abraham bought for a sum of money of the sons of Emmor *the father* of Sychem."

Here the article τοῦ (*tou*), *of the*, rendered " *the father*," should be ἐν (*en*), *in*, according to Tischendorf, Tregelles, Westcott and Hort, and the R.V.

There must have been three purchases altogether, of which two are recorded in Genesis, and one in Acts vii.

(1) According to Acts vii. 16, Abraham bought a sepulchre from the sons of Hamor.

There is no record of this purchase in Genesis. But Stephen, " full of the Holy Ghost," supplies the information. It was purchased of Hamor, *the son* of Shechem, for " a sum of money." Shechem was the place where God first appeared to Abraham in Canaan (Gen. xii. 6), and where he first built an altar (verse 7). Here it was that (according to Acts vii. 16) he bought " a sepulchre."

The original Shechem must have been an important person to have given his name to a place ; and it was of his son that Abraham bought it.

(2) According to Gen. xxiii., Abraham purchased a field with trees in it and round it ; and a cave called Machpelah at the end of it. It was situated at Hebron (Mamre), and was purchased of Ephron the Hittite, the son of Zohar, for 400 shekels of silver. Here Abraham buried Sarah, and here he himself was buried. Here also were buried Isaac, Rebekah and Jacob (Gen. xlix. 29-32 ; l. 13).

(3) Jacob's purchase in Gen. xxxiii. 19, was years afterward, of another Hamor, another descendant of the former Shechem. What

Jacob bought was "a parcel of a field," of Hamor, a Hivite, perhaps the very field which surrounded the "sepulchre" which Abraham had before bought of an ancestor of this Hamor. Jacob gave 100 pieces of money (or *lambs*, margin) for it. Here Joseph was buried (Josh. xxiv. 32), and here Jacob's sons were " carried over," or *transferred*, as Joseph was.

Now Acts vii. 15 speaks of two parties, as well as of three purchases :—" he " (*i.e.*, Jacob), and " our fathers." In verse 16 the verb is plural and must necessarily refer not to " he " (Jacob), who was buried in Machpelah, but to " our fathers." They were carried over and laid in the sepulchre that Abraham bought, not of " Ephron the Hittite " (Gen. xxiii.), but of Hamor the Hivite.

In the abbreviated rehearsal of facts well known to all to whom Stephen spoke, and who would gladly have caught at the least slip, if he had made one, Stephen condensed the history, and presented it elliptically thus :—

" So Jacob went down into Egypt, and died, he and our fathers, and [*our fathers*] were carried over into Sychem, and laid in the sepulchre :—[*he, i.e., Jacob*] in that which (ᾧ, *ho**) Abraham bought for a sum of money, [*and they in that which was bought*] from the sons of Hamor in Sychem."

It is probable that the rest of the " fathers " who died in Egypt were gathered to both of these burial places, for Josephus says (*Ant.* lib. ii. 4) that they were buried at Hebron ; while Jerome (*Ep. ad Pammach.*) declares that in his day their sepulchres were at Shechem, and were visited by strangers.

Rom. vi. 5.—" For if we have been planted together in the likeness of his death, we shall be also *in the likeness* of *his* resurrection." Here it is, " We shall be *raised* [*in the likeness*] of his resurrection also." (See above, pages 18, 19).

Rom. xii. 11.—" Not slothful in business." Lit., " not slothful in earnest care [*i.e.*, earnest care for *others* (from verse 10)]."

1 Cor. ii. 11.—" For what man knoweth the things of a man ? " *i.e.*, the [*deep*] things (or *depths*), from verse 10—the secret thoughts and purposes of the spirit of man. " So the [*deep*] things (or *depths*) of God, knoweth no man but the Spirit of God."

1 Cor. ii. 13.—" Which things also we speak, not in the words which man's wisdom teacheth, but which the Holy Ghost teacheth ; comparing spiritual things with spiritual."

---

* Griesbach, Lachmann, Tischendorf, Tregelles, Alford, Wordsworth, Westcott and Hort, read ᾧ (*hō*) *in that which*, instead of ὅ (*ho*) *which*.

Here we have, first, to repeat in the second clause the expression " in the words " from the first clause:—" Not in the words which man's wisdom teacheth, but [*in the words*] which the Holy Ghost teacheth." This prepares the way for the supply of the important *Ellipses* of the last sentence. The two adjectives " spiritual " (one neuter nominative plural and the other masculine dative plural) must have nouns which they respectively qualify, and the question is, What are these nouns to be ? The A.V. suggests " things " (which ought to have been in italics). The R.V. suggests, in the margin, two different nouns :— "*interpreting spiritual things to spiritual* men." Much depends on the meaning of the verb συγκρίνω (*sunkrinō*) which occurs only here, and in 2 Cor. x. 12, in the New Testament. Its etymological meaning is clear, being a compound of κρίνω (*krinō*), *to separate* or *sift* (hence, *to judge*) and σύν (*sun*), *together with*, so that it means literally *to separate or take to pieces and then to put together*. When we do this with *things*, we compare them by judging them, or we judge them by comparing them ; hence, συγκρίνω (*sunkrino*), is translated " *compare* " in 2 Cor. x. 12, and is used of the foolishness of those who " measuring themselves by themselves, and comparing themselves among themselves, are not wise " (margin, " understand *it* not "). Here the force of the idea of *judging* is clearly seen. So also the verb is used in Wisdom vii. 29, where wisdom " being compared with the light is found before it." In Wisdom xv. 18 :—" They worshipped those beasts also that are most hateful : for being compared together, some are worse than others."

In 1 Macc. x. 71, the idea of judging is very clear, being translated " *try.*" Apollonius says to Jonathan, " Now therefore, if thou trustest in thine own strength, come down to us into the plain field, and there let us try the matter together;" *i.e.*, let us judge or determine the matter together.

In Gen. xl. 8, 16, 22 ; xli. 12, 15, it is used for פָּתַר (*pahthar*), *to open*, hence, *to interpret;* and in Dan. v. 13, 17 for the Chald. פְּשַׁר (*p'shar*), *to explain, interpret ;* also in Num. xv. 34 for פָּרַשׁ (*pahrash*), *to separate* or *divide*, hence (in Pual), *to declare distinctly.**

> " And they put him in ward, because it was not declared what should be done to him " (*i.e.*, to the man who had gathered sticks on the Sabbath).

Hence, for these are all the occurrences of the verb συγκρίνω (*sunkrinō*), the general meaning of the verb is *to communicate distinctly so as to expound* or *interpret* or *make anything clear and plain : i.e., to*

---

* See also Neh. viii. 8, " distinctly," and Ezra iv. 18, " plainly."

separate or take anything to pieces and put it together again so as to make its nature or construction known. This meaning—*to make known* or *declare*—thus seems to combine all the various ideas included in the verb. For we cannot become known to ourselves by measuring ourselves with others (2 Cor. x. 12). Hence the dreams were interpreted or *made known* (Gen. xl. 8, etc.), and it was not *made known* what was to be done to the Sabbath-breaker (Num. xv. 34). This meaning, too, agrees with 1 Cor. ii. 13, where it is used in connection with *persons.*

Some propose to supply the *Ellipsis* with the word "words" from the former part of the verse. But though it is true, in fact, that the apostle declared spiritual things with spiritual words, it is not in harmony with what is said in the larger context here.

In verse 1 he explains that when he came to them he could not declare unto them "the mystery of God." For so the words must be read, as in the R.V., and all the critical Greek Texts.*

He was obliged to confine his teaching to truths connected with "Christ crucified," and could not go on to those glorious truths connected with Christ risen (as in Eph. and Col.) Howbeit (he adds) we do "teach wisdom among them that are initiated" (verse 5), even the mystery (verse 6) which had been hidden, but which God had now revealed (verse 10) to him and to the Church through him : *viz.,* the hitherto profound and absolute secret of the Body of Christ, consisting of Christ the glorious Head in heaven, and His people the members of that body here upon earth ; Jews and Gentiles forming "one new man" in Christ.

But these Corinthians (when he went to them) were all taken up with their own "Bodies." One said, "I am of Paul"; and another, "I am of Apollos." How, then, could they be prepared to hear, and be initiated into, the wondrous secret concerning the One Body ?

No! These "spiritual *things*" could be declared and made known only (verse 13) to "spiritual *persons,*" and the apostle says (iii. 1-6): "I could not speak unto you as unto spiritual, but as unto carnal."

This, then, is evidently the scope of the whole context, and it shows us that to receive these "spiritual things" we must be "spiritual persons": members of the One Body of Christ, rather than of one of the many "bodies" of men. Then we shall be prepared to learn the "deep things of God," which were afterwards taught to these Corinthian saints by epistle in 1 Cor. xii.†

---

* Μυστήριον (*musteerion*), *mystery,* and not μαρτύριον (*marturion*), *testimony.*

† See further on this subject in a pamphlet on *The Mystery,* by the same author and publisher.

1 Cor. iv. 4.—" For I know nothing by myself, yet am I not hereby justified."

I.e., " For I am not conscious to myself of any [*unfaithful,* from verse 2] thing, yet I am not justified by this ; but he that judgeth me is the Lord," and He is able to bring all such hidden and secret things to light. The R.V. has " against myself."

2 Cor. iii. 16.—" Nevertheless when [*their heart,* from verse 15] shall turn to the Lord, the veil shall be taken away [*from it*]" : *i.e.,* " is taken away " (R.V.), for it is the *present* tense, and is very emphatic because it explains why their heart shall turn to the Lord ! We might almost read it " When the veil is taken away from [*their heart*], it shall turn to the Lord." See Mal. iv. 6.

2 Cor. vi. 16.—" And what agreement hath the temple of God with [*the temple of*] idols ? "

2 Cor. xi. 14, 15.—" And no marvel ; for Satan himself transformeth himself into an angel of light. Therefore *it is* no great [*marvel*] if his ministers also transform themselves as ministers of righteousness ; whose end shall be according to their works:" whatever may be their present appearance or " reward."

This is the most dangerous of all Satan's " devices." (1) He goes about as " a roaring lion " (1 Pet. v. 8), and we know that we must flee from him. (2) He beguiles through his subtilty, as " the old serpent " (2 Cor. xi. 3), and there is great fear, lest we be " corrupted." But (3), most dangerous of all, he transforms himself into "an angel of light." Here it is that God's servants are deceived and " join affinity " with Ahabs and Jezebels to " do (so-called) good " !

Eph. iii. 17-19.—" That Christ may dwell in your hearts by faith ; that ye being rooted and grounded in love, may be able to comprehend with all saints what *is* the breadth and length and depth and height ; and to know the love of Christ, which passeth knowledge, that ye might be filled with all the fulness of God."

We following the R.V. rendering and supplying the Ellipsis from the preceding clause :—

" That Christ may dwell in your hearts through faith ; to the end that (ἵνα) ye, being rooted and grounded in love, may be strong to apprehend with all the saints what the breadth and length and height and depth [*of love is*] even (τε) to know the love of Christ which passeth knowledge," etc.

We are to be rooted as a tree, in love ; we are to be founded as a building in love; but we can never know what it is in all its length and breadth and height and depth until we know Christ's love for us, for that surpasses all knowledge.

Bengel beautifully explains the four terms: the "length" extending through all ages from everlasting to everlasting; the "breadth" extending to people from all nations; the "height" to which no man can reach or attain, and from which no creature can pluck us; its "depth," so deep that it cannot be fathomed or exhausted. (See on this verse above, page 18.)

1 Tim. i. 16.—" Howbeit, for this cause I obtained mercy that in me first Jesus Christ might show forth all long suffering, for a pattern to them which should hereafter believe on him to life everlasting."

Here πρῶτος (*prōtos*), translated " first," is the same word which is translated "chief" in the preceding verse. If we retain this rendering, we may also supply the Ellipsis from the same context, thus:—" That in me the chief [*of sinners*], Jesus Christ might show forth all long suffering."

The R.V. renders "that in me as chief," etc.

Heb. ii. 11.—" For both he that sanctifieth and they who are sanctified *are* all [*sons*] of one [*father*] : for which cause he is not ashamed to call them brethren."

Heb. vii. 4.—" Now consider how great this man *was*, unto whom even the patriarch Abraham gave the tenth of the spoils."

There is here no word for " man " in the Greek, and we may better supply the word "priest" from verse 3. " Now consider how great this [*priest*] was."

Titus iii. 8.—" *This is* a faithful saying, and these things I will that thou affirm constantly." The Greek reads, as in the R.V., "concerning these." The A.V. and R.V. supply "*things*." But we may repeat the word " heirs " from the preceding verse:—" That being justified by his grace, we should be made heirs according to the hope of eternal life. *This is* a faithful saying, and concerning these [*heirs*] I will that thou affirm constantly (R.V., confidently), that they which have believed in God might be careful to maintain good works."

1 John ii. 2.—" He is the propitiation for our sins : and not for ours only, but also for *the sins of* the whole world."

The words here are correctly repeated from the preceding clause. The contrast is between " ours " and " the world." A very emphatic word is here used for " ours," not the genitive case of the ordinary pronoun ἡμῶν (*heemōn*) " our," which is used in the first clause, but a special possessive pronoun, which is very emphatic, ἡμέτερος (*heemeteros*), *our own.*   It is used of that which is peculiarly *ours* as distinct from that which belongs to others, *e.g.* :—

Acts	ii.	11.	We do hear them speak in *our* tongues.
Acts	xxiv.	6.	According to *our* law.
Acts	xxvi.	5.	Sect of *our* religion.
Rom.	xv.	4.	Were written for *our* learning.
2 Tim.	iv.	15.	He hath greatly withstood *our* words.
Tit.	iii.	14.	And let *ours* also learn.
1 John	i.	3.	And truly *our* fellowship is with the Father and his Son, Jesus Christ.

So that "our sins" refers to the writer and his People, as Jews, as distinct from the rest of the world.   Before this, propitiation was only for the sins of Israel; but now, and henceforth, Christ's propitiation was for all without distinction, "out of every kindred, and tongue, and people, and nation" : not for all *without exception*, for then all must be saved, which is not the case.

See further on this verse under *Synecdoche.*

(*b*) Where the omitted VERB is to be REPEATED from

a PRECEDING clause.

Gen. i. 30.—The verb "*I have given*" is correctly repeated in the A.V. from verse 29.

Gen. iv. 24.—"If Cain shall be avenged sevenfold, truly Lamech seventy and sevenfold," *i.e.*, "Lamech [*shall be avenged*] seventy and sevenfold."

This is spoken with reference to what is stated in the preceding verse, which is very obscure both in the A.V. and R.V.   The A.V. renders it "I have slain," and margin "*I would slay*," while the R.V. renders it "I have slain a man for wounding me," etc., and margin "*I will slay*."   But we must note that these words of Lamech were called forth by the fact that through his son, who was "an instructor of every artificer in brass and iron," Lamech was in possession of superior weapons.

This is the earliest form of poetry in the Bible.   It is significant that it should be in praise of that violence which was soon to overspread the earth.   It is in praise of the new weapons of war which Lamech had now obtained ; and so proud is he of his newly-acquired power, that if anyone injured him he declares that he would be so avenged that he would outdo Jehovah in His punishment of Cain. See further for the poetical form, under *Parallelism.*

F

Deut. i. 4.—"And Og, the king of Bashan, which dwelt at Astaroth [*he* (*i.e.*, *Moses*) *slew*] in Edrei." See Num. xxi. 33. Deut. iii. 1.

1 Kings xx. 34.—"Then *said Ahab.*" The verb must be repeated from the preceding clause.

Ps. i. 5.—"Therefore the ungodly shall not stand in the judgment, and sinners [*shall not stand*] in the congregation of the righteous."

Thus, the blessing of the righteous is, that they do not stand among "sinners" (verse 1) now; and the punishment of the ungodly will be that they shall not stand among the righteous in the judgment (verse 5).

Ps. xlv. 3.—"Gird thy sword upon *thy* thigh, O *most* mighty: [*gird thyself*] with thy glory and thy majesty."

Ps. cxxvi. 4.—"Turn again our captivity, O Lord, as the streams in the south."

There must be a figure employed here, as the grammatical construction is not complete. There is neither subject nor verb in the second clause, as will be apparent if we set them forth, thus :—

Subject.	Verb.	Object.
O Lord	turn again	our captivity,
as . . .	. . .	the streams of the south.

Consequently, it is clear that a figure is employed, and that this figure is *Ellipsis*.

The correct supply of the *Ellipsis* will enable us to give a literal translation of the other words. The comparison employed shows us that the verb required in the second sentence must be repeated from the first.

"Turn again our captivity, O Lord, as [*thou turnest*] the streams in the south." But this does not yield the whole sense, unless we see the correct and literal meaning of the words.

The word "streams" is אֲפִיקִים (*apheekeem*). It is from the root אָפַק (*aphak*) *to put a force, constraint or restraint upon* (Gen. xliii. 30; xlv. 1. Est. v. 19).

It is the proper name for a narrow and practically inaccessible water-course, either natural (in a gorge, or underground); or artificial (in an aqueduct), in which the water is *forced*, *restrained*, and *turned about* by its strong barriers in various directions. It occurs eighteen

times.* Six times with the word " sea " or " waters." Thus in
Ps. xlii. 1 and Joel i. 20, the hart is pictured עַל־אֲפִיקֵי־מָיִם (*al apheekai
mayim*), *over* (not "*for*," see Gen. i. 2, " darkness was *upon* the face of
the deep "; i. 20, " fowl that may fly *above* the earth," etc.), *above* the
apheekai mayim. The hart hears the rushing of the waters far below
in their rocky bed, and she " crieth out " עָרַג (*arag*) *to cry, to long
for*, only here and Joel i. 20) for the waters she cannot reach.

Then as to the word rendered " south " (נֶגֶב, *Negeb*). This is the
proper name of a certain district in Canaan. It was " south " relatively
to Canaan, but not absolutely. This is clear from Gen. xii. 9, where
we read, " Abram journeyed [*from Bethel*] going on still toward the
south " (הַנֶּגְבָּה, *the Negeb*). Afterwards we read (xiii. 1): " And Abram
went up (north) out of Egypt . . . into the south " (הַנֶּגְבָּה, *the Negeb*).†

---

   * 2 Sam. xxii. 16. "The *channels* of the sea appeared."

      Job vi. 15. " As *the stream* of brooks they pass away."

      Job xii. 21. "He weakeneth the strength of *the mighty* " (*i.e., the apheekeem*).

      Job xl. 18. " His [Behemoth's] bones are as *strong pieces* of brass " (*i.e.,*
            like *apheekeem* or *aqueducts* of brass).

      Job xli. 15. " His [Leviathan's] *scales* are his pride " (marg., *strong pieces
            of shields*).

      Ps. xviii. 15. " Then the *channels* of waters were seen."

      Ps. xlii. 1. " As the hart panteth (marg., *brayeth*) after the *water*-brooks:"
            i.e., the apheekeem. So also Joel i. 20.

      Ps. cxxvi. 4. " Turn our captivity, O Lord, as the *streams* in the south."

      Song Sol. v. 12. " His eyes are as the eyes of doves by the *rivers* of waters "
            (*i.e.,* inhabiting the rocky cliffs of the *apheekeem*).

      Isa. viii. 7. " He [the king of Assyria] shall come up over all his *channels*
            (*i.e.,* over the rocky barriers of the *apheekeem*).

      Ezek. vi. 3. " Thus saith the Lord GOD to the mountains, and to the
            hills, to the *rivers*, and to the valleys " (*i.e.,* to *the
            gorges* and the valleys, answering to the mountains
            and hills of the first line). So also xxxvi. 4, 6.

      Ezek. xxxi. 12. " His boughs are broken by all *the rivers* of the land."

      Ezek. xxxii. 6. " *The rivers* shall be full of thee."

      Ezek. xxxiv. 13. " And feed them upon the mountains of Israel by *the* rivers."

      Ezek. xxxv. 8. " And in all *thy rivers*, shall they fall that are slain with the

      Joel iii. 18. " All *the rivers* of Judah shall flow with waters."   [sword."

   † It is still more clear from Deut. i. 7, where we have four distinct topo-
graphical names :—" in the plain (*i.e.,* in ARABAH, the Jordan Valley), in the hills
(*i.e.,* the HILL COUNTRY of Judah), and in the vale (*i.e.,* in SHEPHELAH, the
plain of Philistia), in the south " (*i.e.,* in the NEGEB, the region south of the hill
country of Judah).

   For other passages, see Num. xiii. 17, 29 ; xxi. 1. Deut. xxxiv. 3. Josh. x. 40:
xii. 8; xv. 21. Judges i. 9. 1 Sam. xxx. 1. Jer. xvii. 6.

   Noting these words, several passages are greatly elucidated, such as Jer.
xxxii. 44: xxxiii. 13. Zech. vii. 7. Gen. xiii. 1, etc.

The *Negeb* is intersected by deep and rocky gorges, or wadis, called "*apheekeem*." Springs and wells are almost unknown in that region.

We can now take the literal signification of these words, and supply the *Ellipsis* by repeating the verb of the first clause, in the second, and thus learn the meaning of the passage :—" Turn again our captivity, O LORD, as [*thou turnest*] the *apheekeem* in the Negeb," *i.e.*, as those rushing waters are turned hither and thither by their mighty, rocky barriers, so Thou canst put forth Thy might, and restrain the violence of our enemies, and turn us again (as the rocky cliffs and walls turn about the *apheekeem*) into our own land.

Prov. x. 23.—"*It is* as sport to a fool to do mischief : but a man of understanding, hath wisdom," *i.e.*, "*It is* as sport to a fool to do mischief, but [*to exercise*] wisdom [*is as sport*] to a man of understanding."

Prov. xvii. 21.—" He that begetteth a fool *doeth it* to his sorrow," *i.e.*, *begetteth him* to his sorrow.

1 Kings xiv. 14.—" The LORD shall raise him up a king over Israel who shall cut off the house of Jeroboam that day : but what ? even now," *i.e.*, " but what [*do I say*] ? even now [*has he raised him up*] : " for Baasha, who was to cut off the house of Jeroboam, had even then been born. Chap. xv. 27, etc. See under *Aposiopesis.*

2 Kings ix. 27.—" And Jehu . . . said, Smite him also in the chariot, *and they did so*," *i.e.*, " And [*they smote him*] at the going up to Gur."

1 Chron. ii. 23.—" All these *belonged to* the sons of Machir, the father of Gilead."

Here the *Ellipsis* is arbitrarily supplied in the A.V. by introducing a new word into the text. The verb "*took*" must be repeated from the preceding clause, and not the verb " belonged " brought in from nowhere :—" And he took Geshur, and Aram, with the towns of Jair, from them, with Kenath, and the towns thereof, *even* threescore cities. All these [*took*] the sons of Machir the father of Gilead."

Neh. v. 4.—" There were also that said, We have borrowed money for the king's tribute, *and that upon* our lands and vineyards."

Here the words "*we have mortgaged*" must be repeated from verse 3. Thus :—" There were also *some* that said, We have borrowed money for the king's tribute, [*we have mortgaged*] our lands and vineyards."

Ecc. x. 1.—Here the *Ellipsis* is supplied by the words " *so doth.*" But it is better to repeat the verb, thus:—" As dead flies cause the ointment of the apothecary to send forth a stinking savour: so a little folly [*causeth*] him that is in reputation for wisdom and honour [*to send forth an offensive odour*]."

Isa. viii. 19, 20.—"And when they shall say unto' you, Seek unto them that have familiar spirits, and unto wizards that peep, and that mutter: should not a people seek unto their God? for [*should*] the living [*seek unto*] to the dead? To the Law and to the Testimony: if they speak not according to this word, *it is* because *there is* no light in them."

Amos vi. 12.—" Shall horses run upon a rock? will *one* plow there with oxen?" *i.e.,* " Shall horses run upon a rock? will *a husbandman* plow [*a rock*] with oxen?"

Mark xii. 5.—" And again he sent another; and him they killed, and many others [*whom he sent, and they used them shamefully*, from verse 4], beating some, and killing some."

Mark xiv. 29.—" Although all shall be offended, yet *will* not I [*be offended*]."

Luke xxii. 37.—" For I say unto you, that this that is written must yet be accomplished in me, And he was reckoned amongst the transgressors: for the things [*written*] concerning me have an end."

This was the last prophecy written of Him which was to be fulfilled before His betrayal, so He now abrogated a precept, necessary at the presentation of Himself, but no longer necessary now that He had been rejected, and was about to die. Now, therefore, they might not only carry a sword, but buy one. So that He was only "reckoned" by man among the transgressors.

John xv. 4.—" No more can ye, except ye abide in me," *i.e.,* " No more can ye [*bear fruit*] except ye abide in me" (see above, pages 12, 13).

Rom. i. 12.—" That is, that I may be comforted together with you." The verse begins in the Greek, τοῦτο δέ ἐστι (*touto de esti*), *but this is.* The verse reads, " But this [*imparting to you some spiritual gift*] is (or means) our being jointly comforted by our mutual faith." He refers to his desire to see these saints in Rome, and the verb is repeated from verse 11, " For I long to see you."

Rom. vii. 24, 25.—"O wretched man that I am! who shall deliver me from the body of this death? I thank God through Jesus Christ our Lord."

The sense in this last clause is manifestly incomplete as an answer to the previous question. Following the most approved reading, instead of "I thank God," we take the more ancient words, "Thanks be to God,"* and repeat the words from verse 24, thus:—"Who shall deliver me from the body of this death? Thanks be to God, [*He will deliver me*] through Jesus Christ our Lord."

The deliverance here desired is from the conflict between the old nature and the new, the flesh and the spirit.†

But as the flesh is bound up with this "body of death," *i.e.*, this dying body, this mortal body, there is no deliverance except either through death and resurrection, or through that "change" which shall take place at the coming of Christ.

The old heart is not changed or taken away, but a new heart is given, and these two are contrary the one to the other. They remain together, and must remain until God shall "deliver" us from the burden of this sinful flesh—this mortal body—by a glorious resurrection like unto Christ's. This deliverance is further described in viii. 11 and 23; and it is "through Jesus" that our mortal bodies shall be raised again. See 1 Thess. iv. 14, διὰ Ἰησοῦ (*dia Ieesou*), "by means of Jesus," and 1 Thess. v. 9: "God hath not appointed us to wrath, but to obtain salvation (*i.e.*, full deliverance from this body of sin and death) by (*i.e.*, by means of, or through) our Lord Jesus Christ."

See this passage under the Figures of *Metonymy*, *Hypallage*, *Ecphonesis*, and *Erotesis*.

---

* Through not noticing the *Ellipsis*, attempts have been made from the earliest times to get sense by altering the text. The T.R. has εὐχαριστῶ τῷ θεῷ, with Griesbach, Scholz, and A K L P ℵ. But χάρις τῷ θεῷ Griesbach, Lachmann, Tischendorf, Tregelles, Alford, Westcott and Hort, and R.V. Also the Vatican MS. Others read, "But thanks be to God," and others, "It is the grace of God" (DE), and others, "It is the grace of the Lord" (FG).

† It is to be noted that "spirit" with a small "s" is one of the names given to the new nature which is implanted in every believer who is born again of the Holy Spirit; and this term "spirit" is to be distinguished from the Person of the Holy Spirit, from the context as well as from the absence of the article. Even in Rom. viii. 1-15, the Person of the Holy Spirit is not mentioned. Not until verse 16, "spirit of God" in viii. 9 and 14 is *divine spirit*, *i.e.*, "divine nature" (2 Pet. i. 4), "spirit of Christ" (viii. 9) is *Pueuma-Christou*, *Christ-Spirit*, another term for the new nature. So, "spirit of adoption" (verse 15) is "*sonship-spirit*," and "the spirit of Him" (verse 11) is "the new nature [*given by*] Him who raised up," &c.

Rom. viii. 19-21 may be explained thus:—

A | 19. For the earnest expectation of the creature waiteth for the manifestation of the sons of God. } Expectation.

   B | 20-. For the creature was made subject to vanity, not willingly, but by reason of him who hath subjected *the same :* } The Reason.

A | -20. [*Waiteth, I say* (from verse 19)] in hope, } Expectation.

   B | 21. Because the creature itself shall be delivered from the bondage of corruption into the glorious liberty of the children of God. } The Reason.

Here, A, corresponding with *A*, shows us that we are to repeat in the latter member, *A*, the verb used in the former, A ; the subject of each member being the same.

Rom. viii. 33.—"Who shall lay anything to the charge of God's elect ? *It is* God that justifieth. Who *is* he that condemneth ? *It is* Christ that died."

We have to remember that, while only the greater pauses are indicated in the ancient manuscripts, there is no authority for the minor interpunctuation. This can generally be accurately gathered by the devout student of the context. Here it is probable that the questions ought to be repeated :—" Who shall lay anything to the charge of God's elect ? [*Shall*] God who justifieth [*them*] ? Who is he that condemneth [*them*] ? [*Is it*] Christ who died [*for them*] ? Yea, rather ; that is risen again, etc."

1 Cor. iv. 15.—" For though ye have ten thousand instructors in Christ, yet *have ye* not many fathers."

Here the verb " ye have " is correctly repeated in the A.V.

1 Cor. xv. 23.—" But every man [*shall be made alive* (from verse 22)] in his own order : Christ the firstfruits ; afterward they that are Christ's at his coming. Then the end," *i.e.*, not " then *cometh* the end," for τὸ τέλος (*to telos*) is used of the last company of a body of soldiers.* τὸ τέλος (*to telos*) is the end : but of what, or what end, can be determined only by the context. Here the subject is the various bodies τάγματα (*tagmata*) *ranks*, *i.e.*, every man in his own proper band. Of these bands or ranks Christ is first ; then they that are

---

* Hom. *Il.* 7, 380 ; 10, 470, etc.

Christ's at His coming ; then the last of these bands at the end of the thousand years (Rev. xx. 5), when Christ shall deliver up the kingdom.

The second of these is not the resurrection foretold in 1 Thess. iv. 16, as the privilege of those who are " in Christ," but the " first " of the two resurrections referred to in the Old Testament, the Gospels, and the Apocalypse.

2 Cor. i. 6.—" And whether we be afflicted, *it is* for your consolation."

Here the A.V. supplies the verb substantive. It is better to repeat the verb " [*we are afflicted*] for your consolation."

2 Cor. iii. 11.—" For if that which is done away *was* glorious, much more that which remaineth *is* glorious."

Here the two words διὰ δόξης (*dia doxees*), *by means of glory*, and ἐν δόξῃ (*en doxee*), *in glory*, are both translated by the same word, " glorious," while the verb substantive (" *was* " and " *is* ") is thus necessarily, though incorrectly, supplied. The R.V. renders the verse, " For if that which passeth away (margin, *is being done away*) *was* with glory, much more that which remaineth *is* in glory."

But, if we repeat the verbs already used by the Holy Spirit, we can take the Greek literally :—" For if that which is done away [*is done away*] by glory (see verse 10), much more that which remaineth, [*remaineth*] in glory."

2 Cor. xii. 2.—" Such an one [*I knew*] caught up, etc."

The verb ἁρπάζω (*harpazo*) does not necessarily mean that the catching is " up," but rather "*away*." In Matt. xi. 12. John vi. 15. Acts xxiii. 10 it is rendered *take by force*. In Matt. xiii. 19. Acts viii. 39 it is *catch away*. In John x. 12 it is rendered " catch " ; in John x. 28, 29, it is " pluck " ; while in Jude 23 it is *pull*.

See also Ezek. viii. 3. Rev. i. 10. " Such an one [*I knew*] caught away :" and this either with reference to place or time, *i.e.*, caught away to some present place (Acts viii. 39, 40), or to a vision of some future time (as in Ezek. viii. 3. Rev. i. 10 ; iv. 2, etc.).

Gal. ii. 7.—" The gospel of the uncircumcision was committed unto me, as *the gospel* of the circumcision *was* [*committed*] unto Peter."

Gal. v. 17.—" For the flesh lusteth against the Spirit, and the Spirit against the flesh : and these are contrary the one to the other, so that ye cannot do the things that ye would."

Here the word ἐπιθυμέω (*epithumeo*) is connected with κατά (*kata*), against, *i.e.*, *to desire that which is against*, or *contrary to*. The same verb is used both of the flesh and of the spirit (*i.e.*, the new nature), and the *Ellipsis* of the verb with reference to the latter enables it to be used in its bad sense with regard to the flesh and in a good sense with regard to the spirit :—" For the flesh desires *that which is* against the spirit, and the spirit *desires that which is* against the flesh ; and these *desires* are contrary to one another, so that ye cannot do the things that ye would," *i.e.*, so that your new nature is hindered ofttimes in doing those good things that ye would, and, thank God, your old nature is also hindered from doing the things which it lusts after.

Eph. i. 13.—" In whom ye also *trusted.*" Here the verb is repeated from verse 12 : but it seems rather that another verb should be repeated, from verse 11 : " In whom ye also were allotted as *God's own inheritance,*" for it is the inheritance which is the subject of the context and not the matter of trusting.

The R.V. neither sees, nor supplies the *Ellipsis*, treating it as an *Anacoluthon* (*q.v.*).

Eph. iv. 22.—We must repeat from verse 17, " [*I say also*] that ye put off concerning the former conversation the old man, which is corrupt according to the deceitful lusts."

1 Thess. ii. 11.—" Ye know how we exhorted and comforted and charged every one of you, as a father *doth* his children."

Here all three verbs are to be understood, *i.e.*, " as a father [*exhorteth*, and *comforteth*, and *chargeth*] his children." (See under *Polysyndeton*).

The R.V. better preserves the order of the Greek, supplying and treating the *Ellipsis* as absolute. " As ye know how we *dealt with* each one of you, as a father with his own children, exhorting you, and encouraging *you*, and testifying, etc."

1 Thess. iv. 14.—" For if we believe that Jesus died and rose again, even so them also which sleep in Jesus will God bring with him."

R.V. :—" Even so them also that are fallen asleep in Jesus will God bring with him."

The two clauses of this verse, as they are thus translated, are so inconsequent that the passage has been a source of difficulty to many, and is practically unintelligible. When this is the case we must ask whether there is a figure employed, and, if so, what it is. Here it can be only the figure *Ellipsis*. But what are the omitted words, which if supplied will cause the passage to yield sense as to teaching, and completeness as to structure ?

Before we can answer this question we must institute an enquiry into the usage of the word translated "even : " as this is the key that will open this lock, besides explaining and throwing light on many other passages. The word " even " here is καί (*kai*), and καί (*kai*) is the ordinary conjunction, *and*, which has two distinct senses, (1) *and*, (2) *also* or *even*. It is the latter of these with which we are now concerned. It is a matter of great importance that we should always know what is the word which it emphasizes. In the Greek, this is never in doubt.* But in English literature, including both the A.V. and the R.V., its usage is very inconsistent and defective. In the Greek, καί, when it means *also*, is always placed immediately BEFORE the word which it emphasizes; while in English usage it may be placed either before or after the word. When we add to this that both in the A.V. and R.V. it is often dissociated altogether from this word, the confusion and ambiguity can be imagined.

The word καί is used in the sense of *also* some 636 times in the New Testament.†

In 258 of these it is placed (in the A.V.) *after* the word.

In 275 it is placed *before* the word, or in connection with another word to which it does not belong.

In 60 places it is not translated at all.

In 43 places it is rendered *even*, and placed before the word.

Sometimes the A.V. and R.V. agree in this, and sometimes they differ.

Now, remembering that the English word " also " must immediately follow the word which it emphasizes, we ask what is that word here (1 Thess. iv. 14) ? As the Greek stands, it reads, " If we believe that Jesus died and rose again, even so them which sleep in Jesus, GOD also will bring with him." But this yields no intelligible meaning. The hope that is mentioned in the second clause cannot be conditioned on our belief of the fact stated in the former clause.

But notice, before we proceed, that the preposition διά (*dia*), when it governs the genitive case, as it does here, denotes agency, and is rendered " by " 235 times, " through " 87 times, etc. ; but " in " only 8 times. See its use in the very next chapter (1 Thess. v. 9), " We are appointed to obtain salvation by our Lord Jesus Christ " (διὰ τοῦ κυρίου ἡμῶν Ἰησοῦ Χριστοῦ); Rom. vii. 25, " I thank God through Jesus Christ

---

* Nor is it in the Hebrew, as the ‍ו is always joined to and forms part of the word with which it is connected.

† See a pamphlet on the usage of the word " Also " in the New Testament, by the same author and publisher.

our Lord " (διὰ ’Ιησοῦ Χριστοῦ) ; Rom. v. 9, " We shall be saved from wrath through him " (δι ’ αὐτοῦ). No wonder therefore that the R.V., while translating it here " in Jesus," says in the margin, " Greek, *through*," and adds the alternative rendering, " *Will God through Jesus bring*."

The one thought and subject is Resurrection, as the great and blessed hope of the Lord's people. The three clauses are perfectly balanced, as will be seen in the following structure of verse 14 :—

```
a |  If we believe   (Belief )
   b |  that Jesus died   (Death)
      c |  and rose again,   (Resurrection)
a |  In like manner [we believe] also   (Belief )
   b |  That them which are asleep   (Death)
      c |  will God (by Jesus) bring with Him
          [from the dead].   (Resurrection).
```

Here in a and a we have the statement of our *belief*, in b and b we have *death* (in b the death of Jesus, and in b the death of His saints), while in c and c we have *resurrection* (in c the resurrection of Jesus by God, and in c the resurrection of His people by God), but in an explanatory parenthesis it is explained that the Lord Jesus will be the agent, as the context goes on to show (see John v. 21 : xi. 25, 43). It was God who brought Jesus from the dead (Heb. xiii. 20). In like manner will He—by Jesus—bring His people from the dead.

Hence, we must repeat the verb " *we believe* " from the first clause : " If we believe that Jesus died and rose again, in like manner [*we believe*] also *that* God will, through Jesus, bring, with Him, them that are fallen asleep."

This is the scope of the passage, which immediately goes on to explain how this will be accomplished. We have the same hope presented in the same manner in Rom. vi. 5; viii. 11. 2 Cor. iv. 14, *viz.*, that Resurrection and Advent are the only hope of mourning saints.

Heb. iii. 15.—" While it is said, To-day, etc." (So R.V.). The Greek is " ἐν τῷ λέγεσθαι, Σήμερον," " in (or by) its being said, To-day."

The simplest solution of this confessedly difficult passage is to repeat the exhortation from verse 13 : " [*As ye are exhorted*] by the saying, To-day, etc."

Heb. iv. 7.—" Again [*seeing*] he limiteth," from verse 6.

Heb. iv. 10.—" For he that hath entered into his rest, he himself also hath rested from his works, as God [*rested*] from his."

Heb. vii. 8.—"And here men that die receive tithes; but there he *receiveth them*, of whom it is witnessed that he liveth."

The reference is clearly to Melchisedec, and it is not testified of him that he now liveth. In Ps. cx. 4 it is testified of Christ, "Thou art a priest for ever after the order of Melchisedec." That which marked "the order of Melchisedec" as being different from "the order of Aaron" was the fact that the days of Aaron's order of priesthood began at 30 years of age, and ended at the age of 50 years, whereas the days of Melchisedec's had neither such a beginning nor such a limitation: his priesthood had "neither beginning of days nor end of life," but he remained a priest continually, *i.e.*, all his life (vii. 3). εἰς τό διηνεκές (*eis to dieenekes*) means *for a continuance*, the duration being determined by the nature of the context.

In chap. vii. 1 it must mean that Melchisedec remained a priest all his life; in chap. x. 1 it must mean that the sacrifices were continually offered until the end of the Mosaic dispensation; in x. 12 it means that the one sacrifice of Christ is efficacious in perpetuity (or, with Macknight, that Christ offered only one sacrifice during His whole life); while in chap. x. 14 it means that the perfection arising from this sacrifice is limited only by the life of those who are sanctified.

Hence, here in vii. 8 the *Ellipsis* may be thus supplied:—"And here men that die receive tithes; but there [*a man received them*] of whom it is testified that he lived [*a priest all his life.*]"*

As Melchisedec was a priest all the days of his life, and his was a mortal life; so Christ was a Priest after the same order; and therefore, as His life is eternal, and has no limit, His priesthood (unlike that of Aaron's) must also be without limit, and He is "a priest for ever."

Heb. xii. 25.—"See that ye refuse not him that speaketh. For if they escaped not who refused 'him that spake on earth, much more *shall not* we *escape*, if we turn away from him that *speaketh* from heaven." Here the words are correctly repeated from what precedes.

2 Pet. i. 19.—"We have also a more sure word of prophecy; whereunto ye do well that ye take heed, as unto a light that shineth in

---

* The present tense is here (as is often the case) put (by the figure of *Enallage* (*q.v.*), or "Exchange") for the preterite as in Acts ix. 26), not believing that he *is* a disciple (*i.e.*, was); Heb. vii. 3, he remaineth (*i.e.*, remained); Mark v. 15, they come and see (*i.e.*, came and saw); John i. 29, John seeth (*i.e.*, saw), John i. 46, Philip findeth and saith (*i.e.*, found and said); John ix. 13, they bring him (*i.e.*, they brought), etc., etc. In all such cases the figure of Enallage marks the action which is thus emphasized.

a dark place, until the day dawn, and the day star arise; [*taking heed, I say*] in your hearts."

It cannot be that we are to take heed until we are illuminated by God's Spirit, or until we are converted! but that we are to take heed to the word of prophecy in our hearts; for it is like a light shining in a dark place. A light is for our eyes to see, and for our feet to use, but the prophetic word is for our hearts to be exercised with. This is contrary to popular theology. This word declares that the world is the "dark place," and prophecy is the only light we have in it, to which we do well that we take heed. Popular theology says that prophecy is the "dark place," and we "do well" to avoid it!

1 John iii. 10.—"Whosoever doeth not righteousness is not [*born*] of God," from verse 9. So also verse 12, "Not as Cain, *who* was [*born*] of that wicked one." Also verse 19, "We know that we are [*born*] of the truth."

2 John 2.—"[*Loving you*] for the truth's sake," from verse 1.

2 John 12.—"Having many things to write unto you, I would not *write* with paper and ink."

Rev. xix. 10.—"And I fell at his feet to worship him. And he said unto me, See *thou do it* not," *i.e.*, "See [*thou worship me*] not."

(*c*) Where an omitted PARTICLE is to be repeated from the preceding clause.

(i.) Negatives.

The negative is frequently omitted; and is generally supplied in the A.V. and R.V.

Deut. xxxiii. 6.—"Let Reuben live, and not die; and let *not* his men be few."

1 Sam. ii. 3.—"Talk no more so exceeding proudly; let *not* arrogancy come out of your mouth."

1 Kings ii. 9.—"Now therefore hold him not guiltless: for thou *art* a wise man, and knowest what thou oughtest to do unto him; but his hoar head bring thou down to the grave with blood."

This has been a favourite text with "those that oppose them-selves" (2 Tim. ii. 25). Misunderstanding the phrase, where David is called "a man after God's own heart" (as though it referred to David's *character*, instead of to David's *calling*, being *chosen* by God and not, as Saul was, by *man*), infidels have pointed to 1 Kings ii. 9 to show David's faithless and bloodthirsty character! But if, as in so many other cases, we repeat the negative from the preceding clause, there is no such difficulty: " but his hoar head bring thou [*not*] down to the grave with blood."

True, Solomon did put Shimei to death, but this was for quite another reason, and as Solomon said, Shimei's blood was upon his own head (verse 37).

Thus the passage is brought into agreement with David's oath to Shimei, which is repeated in immediate connection with this verse (verse 8 from 2 Sam. xix. 23).

Ps. ix. 18.—" For the needy shall not alway be forgotten : the expectation of the poor shall *not* perish for ever."

Here the negative is supplied by the A.V. in italics.

Ps. xxxviii. 1.—" O LORD, rebuke me not in thy wrath : and chasten me [*not*] in thy hot displeasure."

Ps. lxxv. 5.—"Lift not up your horn on high : speak *not with* a stiff neck."

Here the negative is supplied, as it is in many passages.

Prov. xxv. 27.—" *It is* not good to eat much honey: so *for men* to search their own glory *is not* glory."

Isa. xxxviii. 18.—" For the grave cannot praise thee, death can *not* celebrate thee."

It is open to question whether

Gen. ii. 6 is one of these cases. The three verses 4-6 describe the condition of the earth before the creation of man (verse 7), and before the plants and herbs of the field grew. (Compare verses 4 and 9). Then three negative reasons are given why these did not grow :— (1) " For (כִּי) the LORD God had not (לֹא) caused it to rain upon the earth, (2) and (ו) there was a man nowhere (אַיִן) to till the ground, (3) and (ו) [*no*] mist went up to water the whole face of the ground."

(ii.) Interrogatives.

לָמֶּה (*lammah*). *Why ?*

Ps. ii. 1, 2.—" Why do the heathen rage, and [*why do*] the people imagine a vain thing ? [*Why do*] the kings of the earth set themselves, and [*why do*] the rulers take counsel together ? "

Ps. x. 1.—Here the A.V. repeats it: " Why (לָמֶּה) standest thou afar off, O LORD ? *why* hidest thou *thyself* in times of trouble ? "

כַּמֶּה (*kammah*). *How oft ?*

Job xxi. 17.—" How oft is the candle of the wicked put out ! and *how oft* cometh their destruction upon them ! " Here the words " *how* *oft"* are correctly repeated in the A.V. But why not repeat them also in the following sentences, instead of supplying the word " *God*," and translate thus: " [*How oft*] He distributeth sorrows in His anger! [*How oft*] are they as stubble before the wind, and as chaff that the storm carrieth away! [*How oft*] God layeth up calamity for his (*i.e.*, the wicked man's) children.* He recompenseth him and he shall know it; his eyes shall see his destruction, and he shall drink the wrath of the Almighty."

אֵיךְ (*eykh*). *How ?*

Ps. lxxiii. 19.—" How are they *brought* into desolation, as in a moment! they are utterly consumed with terrors." But it is better to repeat the word " how " :—" *How* are they utterly consumed with terror ! "

אֵיכָה (*eykah*). *How !*

An exclamation of pain and grief " How !" This gives its title to the book of Lamentations in the Hebrew Canon† "*Eykah.*"

Three prophets use this word of Israel:—Moses uses it of Israel in his glory and *pride* (Deut. i. 12) : Isaiah, of Jerusalem in her *dissipation* (Isa. i. 21) : and Jeremiah, of Jerusalem in her *desolation* (Lam. i. 1, etc.).

Hence, the word very frequently occurs in the book of Lamentations; and its *Ellipsis* or omission is frequently to be supplied by repetition. In many cases this is done in the A.V. Note, for example :—

Lam. i. 1, 2.—" How doth the city sit solitary, *that was* full of people ! *how* is she become as a widow! she *that was* great among the nations, *and* princess among the provinces, *how* is she become tributary! 2. [*How*] she weepeth sore in the night," etc. 3. [*How*] is Judah gone into captivity . . . 4. [*How*] the ways of Zion do mourn."

See also ii. 1, 2, etc.; iv. 1, 4, 8, 10.

מָה (*mah*). *How !*

Joel i. 18.—" How (מָה) do the beasts groan ! [*How*] are the herds of cattle perplexed ! "

עַד־מֶה (*ad-meh*). *How long ?*

Ps. iv. 3.—" O ye sons of men, how long *will ye turn* my glory into shame ? *how long* will ye love vanity ? "

---

* The R.V., missing the proper *Ellipsis*, arbitrarily introduces the words " *Ye say*, God layeth up iniquity for his children," taking the words as the words of the wicked man instead of the children !

† The title in the English Version is from the Latin Vulgate. See *The Names and Order of the Books of the Old Testament*, by the same author and publisher.

Here the interrogative is repeated, but why not repeat it again instead of supplying the word "*and*"?   Thus:—" [*How long*] will ye seek after leasing?"

Ps. lxxxix. 46.—" How long, LORD? wilt thou hide thyself for ever?   [*How long, Lord*] shall thy wrath burn like fire?"

עַד־מָתַי (*ad-mahthai*).   How long?

Ps. xciv. 3, 4.—" Lord, how long shall the wicked, how long shall the wicked triumph?   *How long* shall they utter *and* speak hard things?   [*How long*] shall all the workers of iniquity boast themselves?"

(*d*) Where the omission of CONNECTED WORDS is to be supplied by repeating them out of a preceding clause.

This form of Ellipsis, though it is very clear, is not always supplied in the A.V.

Num. xxvi. 3, 4.—"And Moses . . spake . . saying, *Take the sum of the people*, from twenty years old and upward," which words are correctly repeated from verse 2.

Josh. xxiv. 19.—"And Joshua said unto the people, Ye cannot serve the LORD: for he *is* an holy God," etc.

The words must be supplied from verses 14-16 : see also verses 20, 23.   Thus:—" Ye cannot serve the LORD [*unless ye put away your idols*], for he *is* a holy God," etc.

Ps. lxxxiv. 3.—"Yea, the sparrow hath found an house, and the swallow a nest for herself, where she may lay her young, *even* thine altars, O LORD of hosts, my King and my God."

There is evidently a figure here : for in what way could birds build nests and lay young in the altars of God?   The one was covered over with brazen plates, with fires perpetually burning and sacrifices continually being offered upon it ; the other was overlaid with gold, and was within the Holy Place!   The question therefore is, What is the kind of figure here?   It is the figure of *Ellipsis*, which the A.V. and R.V. have made worse by inserting the word " *even* " (the A.V. in italic type, the R.V. in Roman).   It must be correctly supplied by repeating the words from the preceding clause : " *so hath my soul found* thy altars, O LORD of hosts," *i.e.*, as the birds find, and love, and use their house, *so I find* and love Thy house, my King and my God.

If we observe the *structure* of the passage,* we see how this supply of the Ellipsis is necessitated :—

a | 1. How amiable *are* thy tabernacles, O LORD of hosts !

    b | 2. My soul longeth, yea, even fainteth for the courts of the LORD : my heart and my flesh crieth out for the living God.

        c | 3. Yea, the sparrow hath found an house,

         c | and the swallow a nest for herself, where she may lay her young,

    b | *even* thine altars, O LORD of hosts, my King and my God.

a | 4. Blessed *are* they that dwell in thy house : they will be still praising thee. Selah.

This structure at once puts c and *c* practically in a parenthesis, and b and *b* may be read on literally and connectedly without a break, and without any apparent Ellipsis ; thus :—

    b | 2. My soul longeth, yea, even fainteth for the courts of the LORD : my heart and my flesh crieth out for the living God,

    b | *even* thine altars, O LORD of hosts, my King and my God.

But *b* read after *c* must have the Ellipsis supplied :—" The sparrow hath found an house, and the swallow a nest for herself . . . [*so have I found*] thine altars, O LORD of hosts."

Prov. xxi. 1.—" The king's heart *is* in the hand of the LORD, as the rivers of water : he turneth it whithersoever he will."

Here the second sentence is manifestly incomplete. There is a subject, but there is no verb, and no object, as will be seen if we present it in this way :—

Subject.	*Verb.*	*Object.*
The King's heart	is	in the hand of the LORD.
as the rivers of water	. .	. . . . . .

It is clear from this that we have to supply both the verb and the predicate in the latter sentence. What they are to be will be seen more clearly when we translate the other words more correctly.

The expression " rivers of water " is in the Hebrew פַּלְגֵי־מָיִם (*pal-gey mayim*). *Palgey* means *divisions of,* and is the plural construct of פֶּלַג (*palag*), *to divide.*† The name of the Patriarch *Peleg* (*i.e., division*) was so called " because in his days was the earth

---

* See *Key to the Psalms,* p. 79. Edited by the same author.

† פֶּלַג (*palag*), *to divide,* occurs only in Gen. x. 25. 1 Chron. i. 19. " In his days was the earth divided." Job xxxviii. 25, " Who hath divided a watercourse," and Ps. lv. 9. " Destroy their tongues and divide them."

G

divided" (Gen. x. 25). The term *palgey mayim*[*] is the technical term for the little channels, or gullies, of water which *divide* the Eastern garden into small squares of about 12 feet each, for purposes of irrigation. Hence the word is used for any little channel by which the water is distributed or *divided*, especially the channels which divide-up a garden. It is used also of the trickling of tears. In Ps. i. 3, the man who meditates in the law of God is like a tree planted by the *palgey mayim, i.e.*, in a garden, where it will have a sure supply of water and the constant care of the gardener! Not left out in the plain to shift for itself; to thrive if it gets water, and to die if it does not!

These little channels were filled by the gardener with water from the spring, or well, or fountain, which every Eastern garden must possess; and then the water was sent first into one channel, then into another, by the simple movement of his foot: "the land whither thou goest in to possess it, is not as the land of Egypt from whence ye came out, where thou sowedst thy seed, and wateredst it with thy foot, as a garden of herbs" (Deut. xi. 10). The gardener did not deign to use a tool, or to stoop down and use his hands. By simply moving the foot he dammed up one little stream, or by a similar movement he released the water in another.

Now we are able to supply the *Ellipsis* correctly in this verse :—

" The king's heart is in the hand of the LORD as the palgey mayim [*are in the hand of the gardener*]: He turneth it whithersoever He will."

To an Eastern mind this would be perfectly clear without the supply of the Ellipsis. Just as in England the expression, " A coach and four" is perfectly clear, and the supply of the *Ellipsis* "horses" is wholly unnecessary. But an Esquimaux or a South Sea Islander, or an Arab, would ask, " A coach and four what?" It would be unintelligible to him, while with us it needs no explanation.

---

[*] The word is used of any very small artificial channel. The following are all the occurrences :—

Job xxix.	6.	The rock poured me out *rivers* of oil.
Ps. i.	3.	Like a tree planted by *the rivers of water*.
Ps. xlvi.	4.	A river *the streams whereof* shall make glad.
Ps. lxv.	9.	Enrichest it with *the river* of God.
Ps. cxix.	136.	*Rivers* of waters run down mine eyes.
Prov. v.	16.	(And) *rivers* of waters in the streets.
Isa. xxx.	25.	*Rivers* and streams of waters.
Isa. xxxii.	2.	As *rivers* of water in a dry place.
Lam. iii.	48.	Mine eye runneth down with *rivers* of water.

So when we learn and understand the customs and peculiarities of the East we can often supply the *Ellipsis* from such knowledge, as Easterns would supply it naturally.

The teaching of the passage then is that just as the little channels of water in a garden are turned about by the gardener by the simple movement of his foot, so the king's heart is as easily turned about by the LORD, "whithersoever He wills."

Oh how full of comfort for ourselves, for our friends, for our children, to know this, and to be assured of it ! "On that night could not the king sleep" (Est. vi. 1). A sleepless night ! The king's heart turned—the law of the Medes and Persians reversed—and Israel delivered. Oh how simple ! Let us never again limit His almighty power—for it is almighty power that is required to turn the heart of man. We know how difficult it is to convince even a friend on the simplest matter of fact. But let us remember that the heart of even an Eastern despot is as easily turned by the LORD's mighty hand as the *palgai mayim* are turned by the simple movement of a gardener's foot.

Job iii. 23.—" *Why is light given* to a man whose way is hid, and whom God hath hedged in ? "

Here the words, "*why is light given,*" are correctly repeated from verse 20. This expression about giving light is similar to that of "seeing the sun" (vi. 5, and vii. 5). Both are idioms (*q.v.*) for living or being alive, as is clear from verses 20, 21. "Wherefore is light given," *i.e.*, why is life prolonged, in the case of those who are in misery and long for death ?

The latter part of the verse may be cleared by noting that the word "hid," as applied to "a way," differs from that in Ps. ii. 12. In Ps. ii. 12 אָבַד (*avad*) is *to lose a way* which is already known. Here, it is סָתַר (*sathar*) which implies that the way is not known at all. It hides itself. In this case God has hidden it and it cannot be found.

What good is life, Job complains, to a man if God has completely covered up the way ? The word סָכַךְ (*sakak*), rendered "hedged in," refers to the way, not to the man, and means, not "hedged in," but *covered up* (see xxxviii. 8). It is not the same word as i. 10 (which is שׂוּךְ (*sook*), *to hedge in*), nor as xix. 8, as indicated in the margin (which is גָּדַר (*gadar*) *to fence up*).

Ecc. vii. 11, 12 has evidently given some trouble, as is clear from the italics in Text and margin both of A.V. and R.V.

" Wisdom *is* good with an inheritance : and *by it there is* profit to them that see the sun." Margin, " *as good as an inheritance, yea, better too.*"

The R.V. reads:—" Wisdom is as good as an inheritance: yea, more excellent is it for them that see the sun." Margin, " *is good together with an inheritance : and profitable unto them,*" etc.

We must take עִם (*im*), *with*, in its idea of accompaniment, *in common with, i.e., like* or *as* (see Gen. xviii. 23, 25. Job iii. 14, 15; ix. 26; xxi. 8; xl. 15. Ps. lxxiii. 5, 25; cxliii. 7. Ecc. ii. 16), and translate :—

"Wisdom *is* good, as an inheritance *is good*, and more excellent to them that see the sun" (*i.e.,* for living men, see above under Job iii. 23). For *to be* in (בְּ, *b*, which is ignored by A.V. and R.V.) the shelter (צֵל, *tzel,* Gen. xix. 8; Num. xiv. 9; Ps. xvii. 9) of wisdom [*is more excellent than to be*] under the shelter (בְּ) of money ; and the advantage of wisdom *is* that wisdom preserveth the life of them that possess it."

That is to say, briefly, wisdom is good: and money is good, but wisdom has this advantage over money; it can preserve life, while an inheritance or money cannot.

Zech. xiv. 18.—The verse reads in the Hebrew (see margin) :— " And if the family of Egypt go not up, and come not, not upon them there shall be the plague wherewith the Lord will smite the heathen that come not up to keep the feast of tabernacles."

Here, there is evidently a figure: because, read with verse 17, there is not only no sense, but quite an opposite sense to that which is clearly intended. Our duty is to ask, What is the figure ? For we are not at liberty to suggest an alteration of the Text, or to make even a free translation of it. The R.V. resorts to the easy method of suggesting in the margin : " The text is probably corrupt." This is a very common practice of commentators! It never seems to enter their heads that the difficulty lies with themselves. It would have been more becoming to have said, " Our understandings are probably at fault" ! The R.V. arbitrarily inserts words, as does the A.V., and even then both Versions fail to make sense.

The A.V. says : " That *have* no *rain* " (marg., " *upon whom* there is *not*").

The R.V. : " Neither *shall it be* upon them " (marg., " *shall there not be upon them the plague ?* " etc.).

The Ellipsis is correctly and simply supplied by repeating " there shall be no rain " from the preceding clause : which, describing millennial days, says :—

" Whoso will not come up of *all* the families of the earth unto Jerusalem to worship the King, the Lord of hosts, even upon them shall be no rain. And if the family of Egypt go not up, and come not, not upon them [*shall there be no rain*];* there shall be the plague, [*aforesaid*, verse 12] wherewith the LORD will smite the heathen that come not up to the feast of tabernacles."

Matt. ii. 10.—" When they saw the star, they rejoiced with exceeding great joy:" *i.e.,* "When they saw the star [*standing over where the young child was*], they rejoiced." The words are to be repeated from verse 9.

Matt. xiii. 32.—" Which indeed is the least of all seeds [*which a man takes and sows in a field*];" from verse 31 ; *i.e.,* not the least, absolutely, but relatively, as to those seeds which are usually sown in the field.

Mark v. 23.—" And besought him greatly, saying, My little daughter lieth at the point of death : *I pray thee*, come and lay thy hands on her, that she may be healed."

Here the A.V. adds : "*I pray thee*," but it is better to repeat the verb from the beginning of the verse, and then we may take the other words literally : — "*I beseech thee earnestly* that having come thou wouldest lay on her thy hands," etc.

John i. 18.—" No man hath seen God at any time ; the only begotten Son, which is in the bosom of the Father, he hath declared *him*." Here the sense is to be completed by repeating the words from the preceding clause, thus : " No man hath seen God at any time ; the only begotten Son, which is in the bosom of the Father, he hath [*seen God, and*] declared [*the Father*] ."

John ix. 3.—Here the *Ellipsis* is to be supplied from verse 2. " Neither hath this man sinned, nor his parents [*that he should be born blind*]: but that the works of God should be made manifest in him." See below (page 107).

Rom. iv. 12.—" And the father of circumcision to them who are not of the circumcision," etc.

Here the words are to be repeated from the preceding clause :— " And the father of the circumcision [*that righteousness might be imputed*] to them who are not of the circumcision only, but also walk in the steps of that faith of our father Abraham, which *he had* being yet uncircumcised."

---

* Because Egypt has no rain, as it is, and is therefore thus excepted here.

Rom. v. 3.—" And not only *so*, but we glory in tribulations also,"
i.e., " And not only do we [*rejoice in hope of the glory of God*], but we
glory also in tribulations."*

Rom. v. 11.—" And not only *so* : " *i.e.*, " And not only [*are we
saved from wrath through him*], but we also† joy in God [*as our
God*] through our Lord Jesus Christ, by whom we have now received
the reconciliation."

It is at this point that the great doctrinal portion of Romans
divides into two portions.   It runs from i. 16 to viii. 39.   Up to v. 11
the subject is " sins " : from verse 12 it is " sin."   Up to this point the
subject is the products of the old nature : from this point it is the old
nature itself.   Up to v. 11 it is the fruits of the old tree: from v. 12
it is the old tree itself.   Up to this point we are considered as " in the
flesh " : from this point we are considered as " not in the flesh," but
the flesh is in us.‡

Rom. vii. 7.—" What shall we say then? [*that*] the law [*is*] sin ?
God forbid !   Nay, I had not known sin but by (or through) the law ;
for I had not known lust [*to be sin*] except the law had said, Thou
shalt not covet.   But [*I say that*] (from verse 7) sin taking occasion
by the commandment, wrought in me all manner of concupiscence (*or
desire*).   For without the law sin [*is*] dead."

Rom. viii. 23.—" And not only *they*," *i.e.*, " And not only [*every
creature groaneth*], but ourselves also," etc.

Rom. ix. 10.—" And not only *this*," *i.e.*, " And not only [*was there
that limitation of the promise to this son*], but when Rebecca also had
conceived [*twins*] by one, *even* by our father Isaac . . . . it was
said unto her, The elder shall serve the younger."

Rom. x. 8.—" But what saith it ?   The word is nigh thee, *even*
in thy mouth and in thy heart: that is, the word of faith, which we
preach [*is nigh thee*]."

1 Cor. xv. 42.—" So also *is* the resurrection of the dead."   Here
instead of using the verb substantive we must repeat the words from

---

* In the Greek the emphasis is on the verb " glory."   " We GLORY also in
tribulations," *i.e.*, we not only have them like all other people, but by grace we are
able to glory in them.   For the usage of the word " also " see page 90.

† In the Greek the emphasis is on the word " joy."   " We JOY also in God."
See a pamphlet on the biblical usage of the word *Also*, by the same author and
publisher.

‡ See further, on this, a series of articles in *Things to Come* commencing
September, 1898.

verses 37 and 41, and then we can preserve the proper emphasis shown by the position of καί "also " :—" So the RESURRECTION also of the dead [*is with a different body*]." This preserves the harmony of the whole argument.

2 Cor. viii. 19.—" And not *that* only," *i.e.*, " And not only [*is his praise throughout all the churches*], but he was chosen* also of the churches to travel with us with this grace (or gift)," etc.

Col. iii. 4.—" When Christ, *who is* our life, shall appear." It is a question whether this *Ellipsis* should be supplied (as in A.V. and R.V.) by the verb substantive, or whether the words should be repeated from the preceding verse, " When Christ, [*with whom*] our life [*is hid*], shall appear, then shall ye also appear with him in glory." Many ancient MSS., with Lachmann (margin), Tischendorf, Tregelles, R.V. margin, read "your life."

2 Tim. i. 7.—" For God hath not given us the spirit of fear; but of power, and of love, and of a sound mind."

Here, by way of contrast, the words are to be repeated in the second clause: " but [*God hath given to us the spirit*] of power, and of love, and of a sound mind."

More properly it should be " a " spirit, not " the spirit," and the fact that a noun is used (by the figure of *Enallage*, *q.v.*) instead of an adjective, shows us that the emphasis is to be placed on the adjective. " a COWARDLY spirit," πνεῦμα δειλίας (*pneuma deilias*) ; δειλιά (*deilia*), means *timidity, fearfulness, cowardice,* and always in a bad sense (see the verb δειλιάω (*deiliaō*), John xiv. 27. The adjective, Matt. viii. 26. Mark iv. 40. Rev. xxi. 8).

1 John ii. 19.—Here the *Ellipsis* is correctly supplied in the A.V., "*they went out.*"

1 John v. 15.—" And if we know that he hear us, whatsoever we ask [*according to his will*], we know that we have the petitions that we desired of him."

Here the words, "*according to His will*," are to be supplied from the preceding verse.

2.   Where the omitted word is to be supplied out of a Succeeding Clause.

Josh. iii. 3.—" When ye see the ark of the covenant of the Lord your God, and the priests the Levites bearing it [*going before*], then ye shall remove from your place, and go after it."

---

* In the Greek the emphasis is on the word " chosen " :—" CHOSEN also."

Here the words *"going before"* are necessitated, and are to be supplied from the words that follow—*"go after."*

Judges xvi. 13, 14.—" If thou weavest the seven locks of my head with the web, [*and fastenest them with a pin in the beam* (from verse 14), *then shall I be weak and be as another man* (from verses 7 and 11)] : and she fastened *it* with the pin, etc." The Arabic and Vulgate Versions supply these words to complete the sense. See Appendix C. *Homœoteleuton*, where it is shown that this is not really an *Ellipsis*, but an ancient omission on the part of some scribe.

1 Sam. xvi. 7.—" The LORD said unto Samuel, Look not on his countenance, or on the height of his stature ; because I have refused him : for *the LORD seeth* not as man seeth ; for man looketh on the outward appearance (Heb. *on the eyes*), but the LORD looketh on the heart."

Here the verb *"seeth"* is correctly repeated from the succeeding clause. It is not necessary to repeat "the LORD," though it is true, and greatly beautifies the English. It may be simply "for *it is* not as man seeth," or, "for *I see* not as man seeth," which comes to the same thing.

1 Kings iii. 12.—"Lo, I have given thee a wise and understanding heart ; so that there was none like thee before thee, neither after thee shall any arise like unto thee," *i.e., among the kings*, which words follow in verse 13. See also x. 23.

1 Kings xiv. 15.—"For the LORD shall smite Israel, [*shaking him*] as a reed is shaken in the water."

1 Chron. iv. 7.—"And the sons of Helah *were*, Zereth, and Jezoar, and Ethnan, [*and Coz*]" : supply from verse 8.

So, at the end of verse 13 supply " *Meonothai*" from verse 14.

Also, in chap. vi., at end of verse 27, supply " *Samuel his son* " from verse 28.*

In chap. vii. at end of verse 18 supply "*and Shemidah*" from verse 19.

In chap. viii. at end of verse 7 add "*and Shaharaim*" from verse 8.

---

* In this verse there is a strange confusion. Samuel or Shemuel's firstborn was Joel, see verse 33. Vashni (וַשְׁנִי) is not a proper name, but means "the second." And the verse reads, "And the sons of Samuel, the firstborn [*Joel*, verse 33], the second Abiah." See 1 Sam. viii. 2, and see also above, page 5.

In chap. xxv. at end of verse 3 add "*and Shimei*" from verse 17, where he is named. In verse 3 only five out of the six are named. In the A.V. and R.V. Shimei's name is supplied in the margin.

Neh. v. 2.—"For there were that said, We, our sons, and our daughters, [*being*] many, [*are mortgaged*]," supply from verses 3, 4, 5.

Job xx. 17.—Here the word "floods" means, as in the margin and R.V., streaming or flowing, and belongs to the word "brooks." But it must be repeated also before the word rivers, thus :—" He shall not see the flowing rivers, the flowing brooks of honey and butter."

Job xxxviii. 19.—The *Ellipsis* is to be supplied thus :—" Where is the way [*to the place where*] light dwelleth? and *as for* darkness, where *is* the place thereof?"

Ps. xxxv. 16.—"With hypocritical mockers in feasts," *i.e.*, repeating the latter words of the former sentence.

"With hypocrites [*at feasts*], mocking at the feast," *i.e.*, like parasites who, for the sake of their belly, flatter others.

Prov. xiii. 1.—"A wise son *heareth* his father's instruction : but a scorner heareth not rebuke." Here the *Ellipsis* is plain, and is correctly supplied in the A.V.

Isa. xix. 11.—"How say ye unto [*the wise*] Pharaoh, I am the son of the wise?" etc.

Isa. xxxi. 5.—"As birds flying, so will the LORD of hosts defend Jerusalem."

Here the word "birds" is feminine. It refers therefore to female birds, and to maternal love : "As mother-birds fluttering (see Deut. xxxii. 11), or as fluttering birds [*defend their young* (from the next clause)] so will the LORD of hosts defend Jerusalem."

One of the words for defend is פָּסוֹחַ, (*pahsōk*), from פָּסַח (*pasak*), *Passover.* פָּסַח (*pasak*) means primarily to halt (see Isa. xxxv. 6. Lev. xxi. 18. 2 Sam. iv. 4). So 1 Kings xviii. 21, " How long halt ye (פֹּסְחִים) between two opinions?" Heb., as birds hop backwards and forwards *on two boughs.* Hence in Ex. xii. 13, it is not " when I see the blood, I will pass over you ; " but, it is פָסַחְתִּי עֲלֵכֶם, " I will halt or stop at you, and the plague shall not be upon you," *i.e.*, Jehovah will stop or halt at (עַל) the door and not suffer the destroyer to enter. So the precious blood of Christ stops the hand of justice, and is a perfect defence to the sinner who is sheltered by it.

Hab. ii. 3.—" For the vision [*is deferred*] for an appointed time," which word is clearly implied in the following sentence. See also Mal. i. 10.

Luke i. 17.—" And [*the hearts of the*] disobedient to the wisdom of the just."

Luke xxii. 36.—The Greek reads, "He that hath not, let him sell his garment and buy a sword." Here the A.V. boldly, correctly, and idiomatically supplies the *Ellipsis* in the first member from the following sentence :—" He that hath no sword, let him sell his garment and buy one " (see on Luke xxii. 37 above).

John vi. 32.—" Moses gave you not that bread from heaven," *i.e.*, " that [*true*] bread," from the succeeding clause: " But my Father giveth you the true bread from heaven."

John vi. 35.—" I am the bread of life : he that cometh to me shall never hunger; and he that believeth on me shall never thirst." The exquisite English of this can never be improved. As an idiomatic version it is perfect. The R.V. in attempting a more literal translation is very lame : " not hunger " and " never thirst." If we are to be literal, we must supply the *Ellipsis* by repeating the word πώποτε (*pōpote*), *at any time*, from the end of the verse. Both Versions practically ignore it by including it in the word " never."

" He that cometh to me shall in no wise hunger [*at any time*]; and he that believeth on me shall in no wise thirst at any time," *i.e.*, " never," as expressed thus in both sentences in the A.V.

It is very instructive to note that the negative here is most emphatic, a doubled negative, which signifies, *by no means, in no wise, in no case ;* and it is very solemn to notice that whenever it was used by man, man was never able to make good his asseveration, *e.g.*, *Peter*, in Matt. xvi. 22, said, " This shall not be unto thee," but it was. Again in xxvi. 35 he said, " Yet will I not deny thee," and in Mark xiv. 31, " I will not deny thee in any wise," but Peter did deny the Lord Jesus! *His enemies*, in John xi. 56, declared, " He will not come to the feast," but He did ! *Peter*, in John xiii. 8, declared, " Thou shalt never wash my feet," but Jesus did ! *Thomas*, in John xx. 25, declared, " I will not believe," but he did, and that without fulfilling his condition !* On the other hand, how sure, how true, how certain are the declarations of the Lord Jesus when made with this same positiveness. Among others note :—

---

* In all this we have a solemn warning to let our yea be yea, and our nay nay (Matt. v. 37).

Matt. v. 18. "One jot or one tittle shall *in no wise* pass from the law till all be fulfilled."

Matt. v. 20. "Except your righteousness exceed the righteousness of the scribes and Pharisees, ye shall *in no case* enter into the kingdom of heaven."

Luke xxii. 34. "The cock shall *not* crow this day."   John xiii. 38.

John vi. 37. "Him that cometh unto me, I will *in no wise* cast out," *i.e.*, no never, no never cast out.

Heb. viii. 12. "Their sins and their iniquities will I remember *no more*," *i.e.*, in no wise will I remember any more.

Heb. xiii. 5. "I will *never* leave thee nor forsake thee."

1 Pet. ii. 6. "He that believeth on him shall *not* be confounded."*

John ix. 2.—"And his disciples asked him, saying, Master, who did sin, this man [*that he is blind*], or his parents, that he was born blind?" (See above, page 101).

John xii. 25.—"He that loveth his life shall lose it; and he that hateth his life in this world shall keep it unto life eternal."

Here two expressions are to be repeated from the latter clause, in the former:—"He that loveth his life [*in this world*] shall lose it [*unto eternity*]."

Acts ii. 3.—"And there appeared unto them cloven tongues like as of fire, and it sat upon each of them," *i.e.*, *the Holy Spirit*, as is clear from the next verse.

The verse may be rendered:—"And there appeared unto them, distributed, tongues like as of fire; and he [*the Holy Ghost*] sat (or dwelt) upon each of them." The tongues were not divided into two parts, as suggested by the popular term "cloven tongues," but they were divided, or distributed, among the Twelve.

Acts vii. 59.—"And they stoned Stephen, calling upon *God*, and saying, Lord Jesus, receive my spirit."

The Greek reads, "calling upon and saying." There is evidently an *Ellipsis* after the verb "calling upon," which the A.V. supplies with the word "*God*." The R.V. supplies the word "*Lord*."

The meaning is clear, that Stephen being full of the Holy Ghost addressed his prayer to Christ, and his words were "Lord Jesus, receive my spirit." Both words must therefore be repeated thus:—"calling

---

* For other examples see John iv. 14; viii. 12; x. 28. Rom. iv. 8. 1 Thess. iv. 15; v. 3. Heb. x. 17. 2 Pet. i. 10. Rev. iii. 12, etc.

All these are the immutable promises and purposes of the living God, and though we are to "cease from man, whose breath is in his nostrils," the word of the Lord endureth for ever. See further under the figure called *Repeated Negation*, below.

upon the Lord Jesus and saying [*Lord Jesus*] receive my spirit." By
this *Ellipsis* the emphasis is thrown on the act of invocation and
shows that this act of prayer was addressed to the Lord Jesus, *i.e.*,
Lord, *who art* Jesus: or, Jesus *who art* the Lord.

Where two substantives are placed together in the same gender,
number and case, the latter is in apposition to, and is explanatory of
the former; or, there is an *Ellipsis* of the words of explanation, "that
is to say," or "that is." Sometimes this is supplied by the A.V. and
sometimes it is not. See Deut. xxii. 28, "a damsel *that is* a virgin."
Judges xi. 1, margin, "*a woman an harlot.*" Gen. xiii. 8, margin, "*men
brethren.*" Num. xxxii. 14, "an increase of sinful men," the Hebrew
reads:—" an increase of men *who are* sinners." Matt. xviii. 23, "a
certain King"; Greek, "a man *that is* a King," as in xx. 1, where the
Ellipsis is supplied, "a man *that is* an householder." Luke ii. 15,
margin, xxiv. 19, "a prophet"; Greek, "a man *that is* a prophet."
Acts ii. 29, "men *and* brethren"; Greek, "Men *who are* brethren,"
and verse 22, "men of Israel"; Greek, "men who are Israelites."
So here, Acts vii. 59, "Lord, *who art* Jesus"—compare Rev. xxii. 20.

Rom. ii. 12.—" For as many as have sinned without law, shall
perish also without [*being judged by*] law: and as many as have sinned
in the law (or under law) shall be judged by the law."

Rom. ii. 28, 29 is an elliptical passage in the Greek, which the
A.V. covers by a free translation.

Adhering to the order and literal meaning of the words in the
original, we must translate and supply as follows :—

" For not he that [*is a Jew*] outwardly, is a Jew, neither that
which [*is circumcision*] outwardly in the flesh, is circumcision; but he
that [*is a Jew*] inwardly, is a Jew, and circumcision of heart in the
spirit and not in the letter [*is circumcision*]."

Rom. iv. 13.—This verse is translated very freely in the A.V.
Following the R.V., we may supply the *Ellipsis* from the end of the
verse, which it has missed :—"For not through [*righteousness of*]
law was the promise [*made*] to Abraham, or to his seed, that he
should be the heir of the world, but through righteousness of
faith."

Rom. v. 16.—"Also not as [*the judgment* or *sentence came*]
through one that sinned [*is*] the free gift: for the judgment (κρῖμα)
[*was*] after one [*transgression*] unto condemnation (κατάκριμα); but
the free gift is after many offences unto δικαίωμα (*i.e.*, a righteous
acquittal)." (See below, page 111).

N.B.—It is not δικαιοσύνη (*dikaiosunee*) which is the attribute of *righteousness;* nor is it δικαίωσις (*dikaiösis*) which is the act of the Judge in *justifying;* but it is δικαίωμα (*dikaiōma*) which is the outcome of the act, the just thing done.

1 Cor. i. 26, 27.—" For ye see your calling, brethren, how that not many wise men after the flesh, not many mighty, not many noble *are called*, but God hath chosen the foolish things of the world to confound the wise," etc.

Here the words *"are called"* are repeated from the preceding clause, but *" are chosen,"* i.e., *to confound*, etc., might be supplied from the succeeding clause. (See above page 58).

1 Cor. v. 4, 5.—We must supply in verse 4 the verb "to deliver" from verse 5:—

" [*To deliver*] in the name of our Lord Jesus Christ (ye, and my spirit, being gathered together, with the power of our Lord Jesus Christ), to deliver [*I say*] such an one unto Satan for the destruction of the flesh, that the spirit may be saved in the day of the Lord Jesus."

1 Cor. vi. 12.—"All [*meats* (from verse 13)] are lawful unto me [*to eat*], but all are not profitable; (see x. 33) all [*meats*] are lawful for me [*to eat*], but I will not be brought under the power of any [*meat*]. Compare x. 23.

1 Cor. xiv. 22.—" But prophesying [*is for a sign* (from previous sentence)] not for them that believe not, but for them which believe."

1 Cor. xv. 47.—" The first man *is* of the earth, earthy: the second man, the Lord from heaven, [*is heavenly* (from verse 48).*" See above on Acts vii. 59, as to these two nouns, "the second man [*who is*] the Lord."

2 Cor. v. 10.—" That every one may receive the things *done* in *his* body, according to that he hath done, whether good or bad."

Here the verb " *done* " is correctly supplied from the succeeding clause.

Eph. ii. 1.—There is evidently an *Ellipsis* in this verse; which has been variously supplied by translators; the usual mode being to supply the words from a succeeding clause (verse 5) as in the A.V. So in the R.V., " did he quicken." But it is worth consideration whether it may not be supplied from i. 19, 20, " the exceeding greatness of his power to us-ward who believe, according to the working of his mighty power, which he wrought in Christ when he raised him from the dead . . . . and you [*when you were raised in Him, and quickened with Him*] were dead in trespasses and sins," etc.

It may also be supplied by repeating the verb from i. 23, "Which is his body, the fulness of him which filleth all [*his saints*] with all [*spiritual gifts*]. And you [*hath he thus filled*] who were dead in trespasses and sins "(chap. ii. 1): καὶ ὑμᾶς ὄντας, "and you when ye were," must be compared with verse 5, καὶ ὄντας ἡμᾶς, "and we when we were." This points to the use of the verb "quickened" in each case.

Phil. iii. 13.—" Brethren, I count not myself to have apprehended [*the prize* (from verse 14)] : but *this* one thing *I do*, forgetting those things which are behind [*me*], and reaching forth unto those things which are before [*me*], etc."

2 Tim. i. 5.—" When I call to remembrance the unfeigned faith that is in thee."

There is no verb in the Greek, and the words *that is* should have been placed in *italics*. The Greek reads, "Taking remembrance of the unfeigned faith [*dwelling in thee* (from the succeeding clause)], which dwelt first in thy grandmother Lois, and thy mother Eunice, and I am persuaded that [*it dwelleth*] in thee also." Here it is repeated from the preceding clause.

Tit. ii. 2.—"That the aged men be sober, grave, etc." Supply the verb " exhort " from verse 6 here, and also in verses 4 and 9 :— "[*Exhort*] that the aged men be sober, etc."

Heb. viii. 1.—" We have such an high priest, who is set on the right hand of the throne of the Majesty in the heavens," *i.e.*, " such a high priest [*as became us*]" (from vii. 26).

II. Complex: Where both Clauses are Involved.

An abbreviated form of expression, in which an Ellipsis in the first of two members has to be supplied from the second, and *at the same time* an Ellipsis in the second member has to be supplied from the first.

Simple Ellipsis puts one member, and leaves the other to be inferred.

Complex Ellipsis puts two members, and implies two others, and these two are interchanged. Hence this figure has been called " *Semi-duplex Oratio*," *i.e.*, semi-double discourse.

1. Where single words are involved.

Prov. x. 1.—" A wise son maketh a glad father : but a foolish son *is* the heaviness of his mother."

Here the word " father " in the former clause is to be understood in the latter; and the word " mother " in the latter clause is to be understood in the former. For a wise son is a joy to a mother as well as to a father, and a foolish son is a heaviness to a father as well as to a mother.

See also chaps. xv. 20 ; xvii. 25 ; xxiii. 24 ; xxx. 17.

Matt. xxiii. 29.—" Woe unto you, scribes and Pharisees, hypocrites ! because ye build the tombs of the prophets, and garnish the sepulchres of the righteous."

Here the word " build " refers also to the " sepulchres " of the latter clause ; and the word " garnish " refers also to the word " tombs " of the former clause.

I.e., ye not only build the tombs of the prophets, but ye garnish them : ye not only garnish the sepulchres of the righteous, but ye build them.

Rom. v. 16.—"And not as *it was* by one that sinned *so is* the gift : for the judgment *was* by one to condemnation, but the free gift is of many offences unto justification."

There is evidently an *Ellipsis* here, as is shown by the italics employed in the A.V. and the R.V. But the question is, Is the omission correctly supplied ? We submit the following, treating the first clause as a complex Ellipsis :—

" And not, as [*the judgment came*] by one that sinned, [*does*] the free gift [*come by one who was righteous*]: for the judgment [*was death*] after one [*offence*] to condemnation, but the free gift [*is pardon*] after many offences, unto justification ; " *i.e.,* Adam brought the judgment of death by one sin, Christ by bearing that judgment, brought life and pardon for many sins. (See above, page 108).

Rom. x. 10.—" With the heart man believeth unto righteousness ; and with the mouth confession is made unto salvation."

Here " righteousness " is to be understood in the latter clause, as well as " salvation " ; and " salvation " is to be understood in the former clause, as well as " righteousness." Moreover " confession " must be made with the heart as well as with the mouth ; and righteousness includes salvation. The full completion of the sense is:— " With the heart man believeth unto righteousness [*and salvation*] and with [*the heart and*] the mouth confession is made unto [*righteousness and*] salvation."

2. Where SENTENCES are involved.

Ps. i. 6.—" For the LORD knoweth the way of the righteous ; but the way of the ungodly shall perish."

In the former sentence we have the *cause*, in the latter the *effect*. But both effect and cause are latent in each statement: "The LORD knoweth the way of the righteous [*and it shall not perish*], but [*the LORD knoweth*] the way of the ungodly [*and it*] shall perish."

Ps. xlii. 8.—"The LORD will command his loving kindness in the daytime and in the night his song *shall be* with me."

Here the *Ellipsis* is insufficiently supplied by the words, "*shall be*." The *Ellipsis* is complex, and to be understood thus:—The LORD will command his loving kindness [*and his song with me*] in the daytime, and in the night also [*he will command his loving kindness and*] his song.

Isa. xxxii. 3.—"And the eyes of them that see shall no,t be dim, [*and they shall see*] : and the ears of them that hear shall [*not be dull, but*] hearken."

John v. 21.—"For like as the Father raiseth up the dead, and quickeneth *them ;* even so the Son quickeneth whom he will."

Here the *Ellipsis* is treated as being Simple, instead of Complex, and is supplied by the word "*them*." But the words "raiseth up the dead" in the former clause are latent in the latter, while the words "whom he will" in the latter clause are latent in the former, thus:—

"For as the Father raiseth up the dead, and quickeneth [*whom he will*] ; even so the Son [*raiseth up the dead, and*] quickeneth whom he will]."

Or according to the Greek, "So THE SON also."

John viii. 28.—"I do nothing of myself; but as my Father hath taught me, I speak these things;" *i.e.*, "Of myself I do nothing [*nor speak*] ; but I speak these things as the Father hath taught me, [*and I do them*]."

See a similar illustration in verse 38.

John xiv. 10.—"The words that I speak unto you I speak not of myself : but the Father that dwelleth in me, he doeth the works."

This complex *Ellipsis* must be understood as follows:—"The words which I speak unto you, I speak not of myself, [*but the Father that dwelleth in me, he speaketh them*]: and [*the works which I do, I do not of myself*], but the Father that dwelleth in me, he doeth the works."

John xvii. 26.—"And I have declared unto them thy name, and will declare *it :* that the love wherewith thou hast loved me may be in them, and I in them," *i.e.*, "And I have declared to them thy name, and will declare [*thy love*]: that the love wherewith thou hast loved me may be in them, and I [*and my love*] may be in them."

Rom. vi. 4.—" Therefore we are buried with him by baptism into death : that like as Christ was raised up from the dead by the glory of the Father," etc.

The complex *Ellipsis* here may be thus worked out : " Therefore we are buried with him by *His* baptism-unto-death [*and raised again from the dead*], that' like as Christ wás [*buried and*] raised again from the dead by the glory of the Father, even so we also should walk in newness of life." (See pages 18, 19, on the context of this passage).

Heb. xii. 20.—" And if so much as a beast touch the mountain, it shall be stoned, or thrust through with a dart." In Ex. xix. 13, the text is, " There shall not a hand touch it, for he shall surely be stoned or shot through with a dart ; whether it be man or beast, he shall not live."

Here the man was to be stoned and the beast shot. In the MSS. words have been gratuitously inserted by transcribers to make sense, in ignorance of the complex Ellipsis. The sense is made clear thus:—

" And if so much as [*a man or*] a beast touch the mountain—[*if a man touch*] it, he shall be stoned [*and if a beast touch it, it shall be*] thrust through with a dart."

H

FALSE ELLIPSIS.

THERE are not only many instances where the *Ellipses* which exist in the original have been incorrectly supplied in the translation : but there are cases also of italics being inserted, where there is really *no Ellipsis* in the original.

In these cases the italics have been necessitated by the faulty translation, and not by the Text.

We give a few examples, arising from various causes :

Gen xxxvii. 12, 13.—"And his brethren went to feed their father's flock in Shechem. And Israel said unto Joseph, Do not thy brethren feed *the flock* in Shechem?"

The Massorah gives the words rendered "their father's flock" as one of the fifteen dotted words,* *i.e.*, words which ought to be cancelled in reading, though they have not been removed from the Text. If these words are removed, then the inference is that they had gone to feed themselves and make merry, and the words "*the flock*" in verse 13 need not be inserted in italics.

Num. xvi. 1.—The last word "*men*" is necessitated by having put the verb "took" out of its place. There is no Ellipsis. The verse reads that "Korah . . . and Dathan and Abiram . . . and On took the sons of Reuben." Or that Korah . . . took Dathan . . . and Abiram . . . and On, the son of Peleth, the son† of Reuben.

Deut. xxix. 29.—" The secret *things belong* unto the Lord our God, but those *things which are* revealed *belong* unto us and to our children for ever, that *we* may do all the words of this law."

The italics thus supplied make excellent sense in English, but this is not the sense of the Hebrew.

The Massorah gives the words, "to the LORD our God," as being one of fifteen examples in which the words are dotted and which are therefore to be cancelled in reading.‡ If these words be removed the sense will be, "The secret things and the revealed things *are* for us and for our children for ever, that we may do all the words of this law,"

---

* See Ginsburg's *Introduction*, pp. 320, 325. Also *The Massorah*, by the same author and publisher.

† According to the Samaritan Pentateuch and the Septuagint Version and a few MSS.

‡ See Ginsburg's *Introduction*, pp. 370, 572.

i.e., the secret things which have not been, but will yet be revealed. Compare chap. xxx. 11-14.

Deut. xxxii. 34, 35.—Here, in verse 35, the word " *belongeth* " is inserted in italic type through reading the Hebrew לִּי (*lee*) as being the preposition and pronoun " *to me.*" But the י (*yod*) is really the abbreviation of the word יוֹם (*yōm*) *day*,* as is clear from the Targum of Onkelos, the Samaritan Pentateuch, and the Septuagint translation Taking, then, לִּי (*lee*) as being an abbreviation of לְיוֹם (*l'yom*) *for the day*, the four lines form an alternate correspondence : the first line reading on consecutively with the third, and the second with the fourth, thus :—

> a | Is not this laid up in store with me,
> b | Sealed up in my treasuries
> *a* | For the day of vengeance and recompense,
> *b* | For the time when their foot shall slip ?

Here, b is in a parenthesis with respect to a and *a*, while *a* is in a parenthesis with respect to b and *b* ; and the passage really reads thus as regards the actual sense ; " Is not this laid up in store with me for the day of vengeance and recompense :

" Sealed up in my treasuries for the time when their foot shall slide ? "

The word לְיוֹם (*l'yōm*), *for the day*, corresponds with לְעֵת (*l'ath*), *for the time.*

The R.V. renders the last two lines, " Vengeance is mine and recompense, at the time when their foot shall slide."

Josh. xxiv. 17.—" For the LORD our God, He *it is* that brought us up and our fathers out of the land of Egypt." Here the two words " *it is* " are supplied in italics, because it is not observed that there is an *Homœoteleuton*† (*q.v.*) in the Hebrew Text ; *i.e.,* the Scribe having written the word " He " omitted the next word " *is* God," his eye going back to a second " He " which follows it. This is clear from the fact that the words " *is* God " are preserved in the Septuagint translation.

The passage therefore reads, " For the LORD our God, He is God, He brought us up, etc.," thus emphasizing the pronoun " He " by *Repetition* (*q.v.*).

1 Sam. xxiv. 9, 10.—" David said to Saul . . . *some* bade *me* kill thee, but *mine eye* spared thee." The Hebrew Text as it now stands is וַתָּחָם (*vattacham*) *but she spared thee.* This yields no sense, so the

---

* See Ginsburg's *Introduction*, Part II., chap. v., pp. 165-170.

† See Ginsburg's *Introduction*, Part II. chap. vi. pp. 171-182.

A.V. and R.V. have followed the Vulgate and inserted "*mine eye*" in italics. But Dr. Ginsburg points out* that in all probability in the transcription of the Text from the ancient Phœnician characters into the square characters, Ж (which is א) was mistaken for Ж (which is ת) and so תחם, *she spared*, was written instead of אחם, *I spared*. There can be no question that this was the primitive reading as it is preserved in the LXX. Chaldee, and Syriac.

2 Sam. i. 18.—"He bade them teach the children of Judah *the use of* the bow : behold, *it is* written in the book of Jasher."

Here the words supplied are manifestly incorrect. It should be, "He commanded them to teach the children of Judah 'The Bow,' or [*this Song of*] 'The Bow,' behold, it is written in the book of Jashar," *i.e., the upright*, a book of national songs, probably, but of which nothing is known. It is clear that this song of David's had not already been written in that book, but he gave directions that it should be there written. See also Josh. x. 13.

2 Sam. i. 21.—"For there the shield of the mighty is vilely cast away, the shield of Saul, *as though he had* not *been* anointed with oil."

The italics are wrongly supplied through not knowing that בְּלִי (*b'lee*) *not* should be כְּלִי †(*k'lee*) *weapons*.

With this emendation the verse reads:—
"For there the shield of the mighty is vilely cast away,
The shield of Saul, the weapons anointed with oil,"
or, "The weapons *of him* anointed with oil."

1 Kings xx. 33.—"Now the men did diligently observe *whether anything would come* from him, and did hastily catch it."

The A.V. is a loose paraphrase. The R.V. indicates the difficulty. In the Eastern Recension the words are divided differently from the *Textus Receptus*,‡ and should be rendered,

"Now the men divined and hasted [*i.e.*, by *Hendiadys* (*q.v.*) quickly divined (*his drift*)] and they pressed whether it was from him, and they said, etc."

---

* *Introduction*, pp. 291, 292.

† This is the reading of the first Edition of the Hebrew Bible, Soncino, 1488 ; also of the Syriac and Arabic Versions, and the Chaldee paraphrase. The mistake of ב for כ could be easily made. See Ginsburg's *Introduction*, p. 144.

‡ See Ginsburg's *Introduction*, p. 438.

Neh. iv. 12.—"They said unto us ten times, from all places whence ye shall return unto us, [*they will be upon you*]," margin, "*that from all places ye must return to us.*"

The R.V. puts the margin of A.V. in the Text, and the Text in the margin.

It appears that it is not a case in which the *apodosis* is to be supplied, but it may be taken literally. "They said unto us ten times, From all places ye shall return unto us."

Ps. i. 4.—"The ungodly *are* not so." Lit., "Not so the ungodly." The structure of the Psalm shows that

Verse 1 corresponds with verse 5.
   ,, 2   ,,   ,,   ,, 4-.
   ,, 3   ,,   ,,   ,, -4.

Verses 1-3 concerning the godly.
Verses 4 and 5 the ungodly.

Thus :—

A | 1-3. The godly ⎫
   B | 4, 5. The ungodly ⎬ present.
A | 6-. The godly ⎫
   B | -6. The ungodly ⎬ future.

The first two may be expanded thus :—

A | a | 1. Their blessing (not standing with the ungodly now) ⎫
      b | 2. Their character ⎱ Their way. ⎬ The godly.
      c | 3. Comparison ⎰ ⎭

B | b | 4-. Their character ⎱ Their way. ⎫
      c | -4. Comparison ⎰ ⎬ The ungodly.
    a | 5. Their punishment (not standing witn the godly in the judgment) ⎭

Therefore verse 4 corresponds with verse 2; and verse 2 must be *understood*, if not supplied, thus :—" Not so the ungodly: their delight is not in the law of the LORD, neither do they meditate in His law, etc."

For the Ellipsis in verse 5 see page 82.

Ps. ii. 12.—"And ye perish *from* the way." R.V. "and ye perish in the way."

There is no "*in*" or "*from*" in the Hebrew: it is literally, "and ye lose the way." *To lose the way* is a Hebrew idiom for *perishing*, or *being lost*. It ought either to be translated literally, "and ye lose the way," or idiomatically, "*and ye be lost*," or, "*and ye perish*." Psalm i. ends with the perishing of "*the way*," and Psalm ii. ends with the perishing *of those who refuse to walk in it,* by submitting themselves to the Son. "*Kiss,*" Ps. ii. 12, is the same as "*be ruled by*" in Gen. xli. 40, margin.

Ps. x. 3.—"For the wicked boasteth of his heart's desire, and blesseth the covetous *whom* the Lord abhorreth." Margin, "and *the covetous* blesseth *himself, he abhorreth the Lord.*"

The struggles of the Revisers to make sense of the present Hebrew Text may be seen in their rendering:

"For the wicked boasteth of his heart's desire, and the covetous renounceth, *yea,* contemneth the Lord." Margin, "and blesseth the covetous, but revileth the Lord."

The simple fact is that this is one of the passages altered by the Sopherim through a mistaken reverence, in order to avoid the uttering of the words involving a curse on Jehovah. But in this case, having altered "he blasphemeth" into "he blesseth," the word "blesseth" they did not remove it from the text. Hence both words now stand in the printed text, which is as follows:

"For the wicked boasteth of his heart's desire; and the robber blesseth, blasphemeth the Lord."*

If we simply remove the word "blesseth," we have the primitive text without more ado, and have no need to supply any *Ellipsis.*

Ps. xix. 3.—"*There is* no speech nor language, *where* their voice is not heard."

Here the word "*where*" seems to be unnecessarily supplied. The R.V. omits it. The sense appears to be, as expressed in the margin, "*without these* their voice is heard." That is to say, with regard to the heavens "[*they have*] no speech nor language; their voice is not heard," and yet they do utter speech, they do declare knowledge; and their words go forth through all the earth.†

Ps. xxvii. 13.—"*I had fainted* unless I had believed to see the goodness of the Lord in the land of the living."

The words, "*I had fainted,*" both in the A.V. and R.V., are an arbitrary addition in order to make sense.

The difficulty arises from disregarding the fact that the word "unless" is dotted in the printed text, and should be cancelled in reading. It is cancelled in the LXX. Syriac and Vulgate, and the clause should be rendered:

---

* See Ginsburg's *Introduction*, p. 365.

† See *The Witness of the Stars* (by the same author and publisher), pp. 4-6.

" I believe that I shall see the goodness of the LORD in the land of the living." *

Ps. lxviii. 16.—" Why leap ye, ye high hills? *This is* the hill *which* God desireth to dwell in."

Here, by taking רָצַד (*ratzad*) as meaning *to leap*, the sense has been obscured, and then the attempt is made to clear it by the use of the italics.

רָצַד occurs only here, and is an Arabic word, which means *to look askance at*, or *to envy*, and the verse reads naturally : " Why do ye envy, O ye high hills, the hill God desired for His seat ? " *i.e.*, Sinai, see verse 17. The R.V. agrees with this.

Ps. lxix. 4.—" They that would destroy me, *being* mine enemies wrongfully."

The Syriac supplies a letter (ע), thus giving the reading, " *more than my bones*," instead of " they that would destroy me *being*," etc. So that the verse reads :

" They that hate me without a cause are more than the hairs of
 my head ;

" They that are mine enemies falsely *are* more than my bones."

Ps. lxix. 20 (21).—" I looked *for some* to take pity, but *there was* none ; and for comforters, but I found none."

Translated more closely with the Chaldee, Septuagint, Syriac, and Vulgate, we may dispense with the italics :—

" I looked for a sympathizer, but *there was* none. And for comforters, but I found none."

Ps. lxxv. 5 (6).—" Lift not up your horn on high : speak *not with* a stiff neck."

Here, owing to the fact that quiescent letters are sometimes inserted and sometimes omitted in the Heb. text, the א (*aleph*) is inserted in the word בְּצוּר (*b'tzur*) *rock*, making it בְּצַוָּאר (*b'tzavvahr*) *neck*. The LXX. evidently read it as *rock*, without the *aleph*, and the passage ought to read without the italics :—

" Do not exalt your horn toward heaven, nor speak arrogantly of the Rock."

Ps. cxviii. 5.—" I called upon JAH in distress : Jehovah answered me, *and set me* in a large place." According to the Western Recension of the Heb. text (which the *Textus Receptus* follows) בַּמֶּרְחַבְיָה (*Bammerchavyah*) is one word, and means *in a large place*, and hence, *with freedom* or *with deliverance* (compare Hos. iv. 16,

---

* See Ginsburg's *Introduction*, p. 333.

Ps. xxxi. 8). But according to the Eastern Recension the reading is presented in two words בְּמֶרְחָב יָהּ,* and the verse should be rendered:

"I called upon JAH in my distress. He answered me with the deliverance of JAH."

It will be noted that both the A.V. and R.V. ignore the *Textus Receptus*, and not only divide the word into two, but remove it from the end to the beginning of the line. Consequently they have to supply the sense with the italics, "*and set me.*"

Ps. cxxvi. 3.—"*Whereof* we are glad." Here the word "*whereof*" is unnecessary.

The structure gives:—

> a | 2-. Our gladness.
> > b | -2. The LORD's great things.
> > b | 3-. The LORD's great things.
> a | -3. Our gladness.

Or fully thus :—

> a | 2-. Then was our mouth filled with laughter and our tongue with singing.
> > b | -2. Then said they among the heathen, The LORD hath done great things for them.
> > b | 3-. The LORD hath done great things for us :
> a | -3. We are glad.

It will be seen how *a* answers to a, and *b* to b.

Ps. cxxvii. 2.—"*It is* vain for you to rise up early, to sit up late, to eat the bread of sorrows ; *for* so he giveth his beloved sleep."

Here the word "*for*" is unnecessarily introduced, creating a confusion of thought and hiding the meaning. Translated correctly, the sense is perfect without any human addition. The word "so," is כֵּן *thus, in this manner.* It refers to what follows, *viz.*, to the Lord's way of giving in contrast to man's way of "works." God's spiritual blessings are not obtained by incessant labour—rising early and sitting up late, nor by painful and sorrowful effort. "Thus He giveth "—this is the way He giveth to His beloved—How ? "sleeping" or while they sleep· שֵׁנָא (*sheynah*) is an adverbial accusative, meaning "*in sleep.*"

It was in this way He gave His wondrous gifts to Solomon. His name was (יְדִידְיָה) "*Yedidiah*," *i.e., beloved of Jehovah* (2 Sam. xii. 25). The word here is also יְדִיד *Yedeed, i.e., beloved.* And this Psalm relates to Solomon, as we learn from the Title. Solomon knew by a blessed experience how God gave to him His richest blessings while he was

---

*See Ginsburg's *Introduction*, pp. 385, 386.

"sleeping" (1 Kings iii. 3-15). Even so He gave to Adam a Bride (Gen. ii. 21, 22); to Abram, the everlasting Covenant (Gen. xv. 12-16), and to Jedidiah "His beloved," wisdom, riches and honour. "Thus He giveth to His beloved while they sleep"; when they are helpless and are unable to put forth any effort of works, by which to earn the blessing, and in which the flesh might glory before God. (1 Cor. i. 29.)

> How wondrously He gives! E'en while we sleep—
>   When we from all our "works" have ceased, and rest ;
> And He our life doth mercifully keep,
>   Then, without works, are His beloved blest.*
> Yes! "His beloved"! lovèd not because
>   Of any work which we have ever done; †
> But loved in perfect grace, "without a cause ": ‡
>   This is the source whence all our blessings come.
>
> He gives in sleep! In vain we toil and strive—
>   And rise up early and so late take rest :
> But, while our powers in sweetest sleep revive,
>   And we abandon all our anxious quest—
> Then He bestows His gifts of grace on us,
>   And where we've never sown, He makes us reap
> A harvest, full of richest blessing. "Thus
>   He gives to His belovèd while they sleep."

Song Sol. viii. 6.—" For love *is* strong as death: jealousy *is* cruel as the grave : the coals thereof are coals of fire, *which hath* a most vehement flame." This last sentence is the rendering of one word in the *Textus Receptus* שַׁלְהֶבֶתְיָה (*Shalhebethyah*), but, according to the Eastern Recension, and several early editions, it is divided into two words, "*the flames of Jah.*" Hence the sense is :

> " Love is strong as death.
>   Affection is inexorable as Hades.
> Its flames are flames of fire.
>   The flames of Jah."§

The second and fourth lines are the intensification of the first and third.

The R.V. renders the last line, " A very flame of the LORD."

---

* Rom. xi. 6.

† Tit. iii. 5.

‡ Rom. iii. 24. "Being justified freely by His grace." The word "freely" here is the same word (δωρεάν) *dōrean* as in John xv. 25, where it is rendered "without a cause." (" They hated me without a cause "). There was absolutely no cause why our blessed Lord Jesus was " hated." Even so it is with regard to our justification :—" Being justified without a cause by His grace."

§ See Ginsburg's *Introduction*, p. 386.

Ezek. xxii. 20.—" As they gather silver, and brass, and iron, and lead, and tin, into the midst of the furnace, to blow the fire upon it, to melt it: so will I gather *you* in mine anger and in my fury, and I will leave *you there* and melt you."

It will be noticed that this last sentence is a *non sequitur*, both as to rhythm and parallelism. The R.V. is no clearer: " And I will lay you there."

The fact is that the letter פ (*Pe*) in וְהִפַּחְתִּי (*v'hippachtee*), in the ancient and primitive text was mistaken for נ (*nun*), (owing to the similarity of the Phœnician characters, when transcribed into the more modern square characters); and thus *I will blow* became *I will leave*, and then the two words, "*you there*," had to be supplied in order to make sense.* The parallelism is thus beautifully perfect:

a | As they gather . . .
b | to blow . . .
c | to melt it:
a | So will I gather . . .
b | and I will blow
c | and melt you.

It will be seen how the words, " I will leave," mar this structure.

Hos. iv. 7.—" As they were increased, so they sinned against me : *therefore* will I change their glory into shame."

The word " therefore " is inserted by the translators; who did not know that this is one of the eighteen emendations of the Sopherim† by which the primitive text, " my glory," by the change of one letter (י *for* ם) became " their glory," and the first person became the third. The original text stood :—

" As they increased, so they sinned against me :
They have changed my glory into shame ;
They eat up," etc.

A like alteration was made in Jer. ii. 11, and very anciently; for it is followed by the LXX., the ancient versions, and A.V. and R.V. It should be " my glory," not " their glory."

Jonah iii. 9.—" Who can tell *if* God will turn and repent, and turn away from his fierce anger, that we perish not ? "

Here it is not necessary to put the word " *if* " in italics. The Hebrew idiom, in the formula or expression מִי־יוֹדֵעַ (*meen yōdeah*) means *who knoweth ?* in the sense of *no one knows whether, or no one*

---

* See Ginsburg's *Introduction*, p. 294.

† See Appendix E : and Ginsburg's *Introduction*, p. 357.

knows but that (see Ps. xc. 11. Ecc. ii. 19 ; iii. 21 ; vi. 12 ; viii. 1. Joel ii. 14). The R.V. translates Jonah iii. 9 as the A.V. renders Ecc. ii. 19, " who knoweth whether " (without italics).

Ralph Venning* beautifully expresses the , theology of this and similar passages† in the following lines :—

> " But stay! Is God like one of us ? Can He,
> When He hath said it, alter His decree ?
> Denouncèd judgment God doth oft prevent,
> But neither changeth counsel nor intent ;
> The voice of heaven doth seldom threat perdition,
> But with express or an implied condition :
> So that, if Nineveh return from ill,
> God turns His hand : He doth not turn His will."

Mal. iii. 9.—"Ye *are* cursed with a curse : for ye have robbed me, even this whole nation." This must be added to the eighteen emendations of the Sopherim.‡

The primitive text was, " Ye have cursed me with a curse." The active was changed into the passive by putting נ for מ.

Matt. xx. 23.—" To sit on my right hand, and on my left, is not mine to give, but *it shall be given to them* for whom it is prepared of my Father."

This supply of the Ellipsis has caused much confusion. The R.V. also unnecessarily inserts " but *it is for them* for whom it is prepared of my Father."

The passage reads :—" To sit on my right hand, and on my left, is not mine to give but [*it is already given*] to them for whom it is prepared of my Father."

Mark xi. 13.—"And seeing a fig-tree afar off having leaves, he came, if haply he might find anything thereon : and when he came to it, he found nothing but leaves ; for the time of figs was not *yet*."

Here, want of accuracy in the translation has created a difficulty, and the word "*yet*" has been added, in order to meet it. Want of attention to the full meaning of the Greek has led to alterations of the Text itself by various copyists : for man is always ready to assume anything to be at fault, except his own understanding.

The last clause, by the figure of HYPERBATON (*q.v.*), is put out of its grammatical order ; for the purpose of calling attention to it, and to complete the structure (see below). Naturally, it would follow the

---

* *Orthodox Paradoxes*, 1650-1660 A.D.

† Such as 2 Chron. xxxiv. 19-21. Isa. xxxix. 5, 8.

‡ See Appendix E : and Ginsburg's *Introduction*, p. 363.

word "thereon." The word "for" introduces the explanation of "if haply." It does not give the reason why He found nothing, but the reason why it was doubtful.

The R.V. translates literally, "for it was not-the season of figs:" but still leaves the difficulty of Jesus going to find figs when it was not the fig-season.

There are two or three points to be noted:

The word καιρός (*kairos*) means not "time," which is χρόνος (*chronos*), but *a limited portion of time*, and always with the idea of *suitability ;* hence, *the right time, proper season, stated season,* when the thing referred to comes to a head, or crisis. Hence, applied to a tree, it denotes the ordinary and regular fruit-season of that tree.* The Passover did not occur at the proper fig-season; but figs remained on the trees (dried) right through the winter. These, which could generally be found, were called פַּג (*pag*). The name is preserved in the word Bethphage (βηθφαγή, for בֵּית־פָּאגֵי, *house of figs*). At the time of the Passover, such figs might well have been looked for.

The Lord went to see "if consequently (εἰ ἄρα) he might find anything thereon." It was "if consequently," because "it was not the proper season of figs" (σῦκα, *suka :* not ὄλυνθοι, *olunthoi,* as the others were called, and for which He sought).

We must also remember that in the East all fruit trees were enclosed in gardens, and had an owner. This tree, though, by the roadside (Matt. xxi. 19) must have been enclosed, and as it grew over the wall, passers by might partake of the fruit. But the owner had probably shaken the fruit off, or gathered it himself, and hence deserved the judgment which came upon him (see Lev. xix. 9, 10 ; xxiii. 22. Deut. xxiv. 19-21). This is one of the two miracles of destruction wrought by Jesus : and we know that in the other case the owners of the swine were justly punished.

The miracle has its prophetic teaching for us. In the preceding verse we read how Jesus went into the temple, and "looked round about upon all things," and went out to Bethany. In the morning He destroyed this tree on His way to the cleansing of the Temple ; after which (verse 17) He taught them, saying, "Is it not written, My house shall be called a house of prayer for all the nations? but ye have made it a den of robbers" (R.V.). The fruit of such a tree was for all who passed by (Deut. xxiii. 24) : but it did not answer its end, and it was

---

* It is interesting to note that in modern Greek, the word καιρός (*kairos*), *season,* has come to mean "*weather*"; while χρόνος (*chronos*), *time,* is now used not merely of time, but "*year.*"

destroyed. In like manner that House, which through the greed of man had failed to fulfil its purpose, would be destroyed as that fig-tree had been.

The verse then reads thus: "And seeing a fig-tree afar off, having leaves, he went if consequently anything [*i.e.*, any ὄλυνθοι (*olunthoi*), *dried figs*] he should find on it: for it was not the time of figs (σῦκα, *suka*): and on coming up to it, nothing found he save leaves." The explanatory clause (though it belongs to the former clause, as here rendered) is put last to complete the structure which is as follows:—

Structure of the passage (Mark xi. 13).

```
A | And seeing a fig-tree afar off
  B | having leaves,
      C | a | he came,
          |   b | if haply he might find anything thereon :
      C | a | and when he came to it,
          |   b | he found nothing
  B | but leaves only,
A | for it was not the proper season of figs.
```

The subjects correspond thus :—

```
A | Fig-tree.
  B | Leaves.
      C | a | Coming.
          |   b | Finding.
      C | a | Coming.
          |   b | Finding.
  B | Leaves.
A | Figs.
```

John viii. 6.—Here the A.V. has given an addition which pertains rather to the expositor than to the Translator :

"But Jesus stooped down, and with his finger wrote on the ground *as though he heard them not.*"

It is impossible to know all the motives of the Lord Jesus in this act; but, judging from Eastern habits of to-day, there was a silent contempt and an impressive rebuke implied in this inattention to their insincere charge.

Rom. i. 7.
1 Cor. i. 2. } "Called *to be* saints," and

Rom. i. 1, and 1 Cor. i. 1.—" Called *to be* an apostle."

It is a question whether there is any ellipsis here, or whether it is correctly supplied. The Greek is κλητοῖς ἁγίοις (*kleetois hagiois*).

But we have these same words in the Septuagint translation of Lev. xxiii. 2, which throws light upon the expression. " Speak unto the children of Israel, and say unto them, *Concerning* the feasts of the LORD, which ye shall proclaim *to be* holy convocations, *even* these *are* my feasts." The LXX. translates the words " holy convocations," κλητὰς ἁγίας (*kleetas hagias*), *i.e.*, assemblies *by special calling as holy* to the Lord. Hence, in the New Testament expressions the meaning is the same, *i.e.*, *saints by the calling* of God, or by Divine calling : *viz.*, those who have been Divinely selected and appointed as saints. So also of an apostle it denotes one who has by a special calling of God been made an apostle. In other words, " by Divine calling, saints ; " or " by Divine calling, an apostle."

Rom. xii. 3.—" For I say, through the grace given unto me, to every man that is among you, not to think *of himself* more highly than he ought to think."

It is a question here, whether the thinking ought to be limited by the insertion of the words "*of himself*," as there is no limitation in the Greek. The verb ὑπερφρονέω (*hyperphroneō*) occurs only in this passage, and it means *to think more than one ought*, not merely of one's self, but of anything. It denotes especially a highmindedness about *any subject*, which makes one proud, arrogant, boastful or insolent. Indeed, there is in this verse another figure, or peculiar form of words, called PAREGMENON (*q.v.*), where several words of a common origin are used in the same sentence. This figure is used for the purpose of calling our attention to the statement so as to emphasize it. The words can be only inadequately expressed in translation : " For I say, through the grace given unto me, to every man that is among you, not to THINK - more - highly (ὑπερφονεῖν *hyperphronein*) than he ought to THINK (φρονεῖν *phronein*), but to THINK (φρονεῖν, *phronein*) so as to THINK - soberly (σωφρονεῖν *sōphronein*), according as to each one [*of you*] God hath distributed [*his*] measure of faith."

The verses which follow show that God has dealt out spiritual gifts in different measures (verse 6), and that he who has a larger measure than another is not on that account to be proud, or to think on any subject beyond his own measure of faith.

2 Cor. vi. 1.—" We then, *as* workers together *with him*, beseech *you* also, &c."

The insertion of the words, "*with him*," here, and in the R V. also, gives a totally false view of our position as workers. The sense is quite complete without any addition whatever. We are not fellow-workers with God, but with our brethren ; *with you*, not *with him*, should be the words supplied, if any. The verse reads : " But working together (or as fellow-workers *with you*), we exhort also that ye receive not the grace of God in vain."

Gal. iii. 24.—" The law was our schoolmaster *to bring us* unto Christ."

Here there is no need to introduce the words, " to *bring us*," the sense being complete without them : εἰς (*eis*), *unto*, is used in its well-known sense of *up to*, or *until*. See Phil. i. 10, " That ye may be sincere and without offence till the day of Christ." Eph. i. 14, " Which is the earnest of our inheritance until the redemption of the purchased possession."

That is to say, until Christ came and brought justification by free, pure, and true grace, the Law, like a tutor, kept them under restraint ; and is here in entire contrast to that liberty wherewith Christ hath made His people free (see chap. v. 1, and John viii. 36. Rom. viii. 2).

Gal. iii. 20.—" Now a mediator is not *a mediator* of one ; but God is one."

Here the A.V. and R.V. both repeat the noun mediator, which only introduces confusion. The sense is clear without it.

" Now a mediator is not of one [*party*] : " *i.e.*, there must be two parties where there is a mediator ; for he is a person who stands between the two others. Now when God gave the promise to Abram (Gen. xv. 9-21), there was only one party ; for God caused Abram to fall into a deep sleep, and He Himself " was one "—the One who, alone, was thus the one party to this glorious covenant ; which is therefore unconditional, and must stand for ever.

Heb. ii. 16.—" For verily he took not on *him the nature of* angels." The Greek is, " For verily he taketh not hold of angels, but of the seed of Abraham he taketh hold," *i.e.*, to redeem them, hence he had to partake of *the nature of* Abraham's seed ; but this is in verse 17, not 16.

Heb. iv. 15.—" But was in all points tempted like as *we are, yet* without sin," *i.e.*, " but was tried according to all things, according to *our* likeness, apart from sin."

Heb. xii. 2.—" Looking unto Jesus, the author and finisher of *our* faith." There is no Ellipsis here, but both the A.V. and R.V. have supplied the word " our," which introduces quite a different thought into the passage.

It is evident that it is not our faith, but faith itself.

In the preceding chapter we have many examples of faith. Each one exhibits some particular aspect of faith in its perfection. For example; in Abel, we have the most perfect example of faith in connection with *worship :* in Enoch the most perfect example of faith's *walk :* while in Noah, we have the most perfect example of faith's *witness,* and so on through the chapter ; the historical order corresponding with the theological and experimental order. Each is like a portrait in which some particular feature is perfect : while the chapter concludes with two groups of portraits ; the one illustrating faith's power to *conquer* (verses 32-35), and the other illustrating faith's power to *suffer* (verses 36-38). Then chap. xii. continues, "Wherefore seeing we also are compassed about with so great a cloud of witnesses* let us lay aside every weight, and the sin which doth so easily beset us, and let us run with patience the race that is set before us, looking (*i.e.,* ἀφορῶντες, *aphorōntes, looking away from*) unto."

Unlike these examples, which each had only one aspect of faith in perfection, Jesus had every aspect perfect. His was a portrait in which every feature was perfect, for He is the Beginner and Ender of faith. He leads the van and brings up the rear ; He is the Sum and the Substance of faith. It is not "*our*" faith of which Jesus is here the Author and Finisher, but faith itself. The Greek goes on to say, " looking off unto the author and finisher of faith—Jesus."

Looking off from all these human examples, each of which after all exhibited only one feature of faith, unto Him who is the perfect Prince† and Leader of all faithful ones and the Author of faith itself— even Jesus, "who for the joy that was set before him endured the cross, despising the shame, and is set down at the right hand of the throne of God."

---

* *I.e.,* those who gave testimony or evidence by their words, their life or death. There is no idea of eye-witnesses in this word, as though they were beholding or looking upon us. The witnesses referred to are the examples of faith cited in chap. xi.

† The word translated "author " is ἀρχηγός *(archeegos)* really an adjective, *leading, furnishing the first cause ;* then it means *a leader,* but it is more *a chief leader ;* hence it is sometimes rendered *Prince. Originator, beginner, and author* are all parts of its meaning. It occurs only in Acts iii. 15, " killed *the Prince* of life," *i.e.,* the author and giver of life; Acts v. 31, " exalted to be *a Prince* and a Saviour " ; Heb. ii. 10, " to make *the Captain* of their salvation perfect," *i.e.* the author of their salvation. Hence, *princely-leader* is a meaning which embraces all the others.

1 John iii. 16.—" Hereby perceive we the love *of God*, because he laid down his life for us: and we ought to lay down *our* lives for the brethren."

This passage read without the italics is perfectly clear and beautiful:—" Hereby perceive we love," *i.e., what* love *really is !* or " Hereby have we got to know love " (perfect tense). For it was never known what love was, until HE—Jesus—laid down His life for us. The only *Ellipsis* here is in the definition of the subject " he." It is ἐκεῖνος (*ekeinos*), *that one*, that blessed One, the Lord Jesus. All the more emphatic from its being presupposed that He is so wonderful that there can be no possible doubt as to His identity. Just as in 2 Tim. i. 12: " For I know whom (he does not say, in whom) I have believed, and I am persuaded that he is able to keep that (he does not say what) which He has committed unto me against that day " (R.V. margin), (he does not say what day)! That which God had committed unto Paul was "that goodly deposit"—the revelation. of the mystery concerning the Body of Christ. The word παραθήκη (*paratheeke*) occurs only here (verse 14) and 1 Tim. vi. 20 (according to the best texts). It was committed to Timothy also, and he was to guard it by the Holy Spirit dwelling within him. And though all might turn away from him and his teaching concerning it (verse 15), yet God would guard it and care for it, and preserve it against that day.

2 Pet. i. 20, 21.—" Knowing this first, that no prophecy of the Scripture is of any private interpretation. For the prophecy came not in old time (marg:, *at any time*) by the will of man: but holy men of God spake *as they were* moved by the Holy Ghost."

Here, there is no Ellipsis. The words " *as they were* moved " merely represent the participle " being moved," as in the R.V.

The confessed difficulty of this passage arises partly from the peculiar words employed. (1) The noun translated " interpretation " (ἐπίλυσις, *epilusis*) occurs nowhere else in the whole Bible, and only once or twice in secular Greek writings. Even the verb (ἐπιλύω, *epiluō*) occurs only twice, *viz.*, Mark iv. 34, " He *expounded* all things to his disciples," and Acts xix. 39, " It *shall be determined* in a lawful assembly," *i.e., made known* in such an assembly. The verb means to *untie, unloose*, and hence *to unfold* or *disclose*. This is its meaning in the only place where it occurs in the LXX., Gen. xli. 12, of Joseph *interpreting* the dreams of Pharaoh's servants. Here it is used as the translation of the Heb. פָּתַר (*pathar*), *to open, unfold*, or *disclose*. Hence, the noun can mean only an *unfolding*, or *disclosure :* just as when one unties a parcel or bundle, and discloses what is contained within it.

I

(2) The word " private " is the translation of the word ἴδιος (*idios*), which occurs 113 times.   It is never translated " private," except here. Seventy-seven times it is rendered " his own " (*e.g.*, " his own servants," Matt. xxv. 14; " his own country," John iv. 44; " his own name," John v. 43; " his own sheep," John x. 3, 4, etc.).

Then the verb " is " is not the equivalent for the verb " *to be*," but it is quite a different verb—(γίνομαι, *ginomai*), which means *to begin to be, come into existence, to originate, arise, become, come to pass,* etc.

Now, putting these facts together and observing the order of the words in the original, we read the passage thus:—

" Knowing this first, that all prophecy of Scripture came (or originated) not of his or its own [*i.e., the prophet's own*] unfolding (or sending forth) ; for not by the will of man was prophecy at any time brought in, but borne along by the Holy Spirit spake the holy men of God."

Or keeping to the A.V. as far as possible :—" Knowing this first, that no prophecy of the Scripture came of [*the prophet's,* or *of its own*] unfolding ; for prophecy came not in old time by the will of man ; but the holy men of God spake as they were moved by the Holy Ghost."

Or taking the last clause as in the R.V., " But holy men spake from God, [*not from themselves*], moved by the Holy Ghost."

The whole scope of this passage is, not the interpretation of Scripture, but its origin : it does not speak of what the Scripture *means*, but of whence it comes.

ZEUGMA : or, UNEQUAL YOKE.

Zeug'-ma. Greek ζεῦγμα, *a yoke ;* from ζεύγνυμι *(zeugnumi),* *to join* or *yoke together.*

This name is given to the figure, because one verb is yoked on to two subjects while grammatically it strictly refers only to one of them : The two subjects properly require two different verbs. This figure, therefore, differs from one of the ordinary forms of Ellipsis, where one of the two verbs is omitted which belongs to only one clause. (See under Relative Ellipsis, page 62.)

The second verb is omitted, and the grammatical law is broken, in order that our attention may be attracted to the passage, and that we may thus discover that the emphasis is to be placed on the verb that is used, and not be distracted from it by the verb that is omitted. Though the law of grammar is violated, it is not " bad grammar "; for it is broken with design, legitimately broken, under the special form, usage, or figure, called ZEUGMA.

So perfectly was this figure studied and used by the Greeks, that they gave different names to its various forms, according to the position of the verb or *yoke* in the sentence. There are four forms of *Zeugma :*—

1. PROTOZEUGMA, *ante-yoke.* Latin, INJUNCTUM, *joined together.*

2. MESOZEUGMA, *middle-yoke.* Latin, CONJUNCTUM, *joined with.*

3. HYPOZEUGMA, *end-yoke ;* or *subjoined.*

4. SYNEZEUGMENON, *connected-yoke.* Latin, ADJUNC-TUM, *joined together.*

1. PROTOZEUGMA : or, ANTE-YOKE.

Pro'-to-zeug'-ma, from πρῶτον *(prō'-ton),* *the first,* or *the beginning,* and *Zeugma :* meaning *yoked at the beginning ;* because the verb, which is thus unequally yoked, is placed at the beginning of the sentence. Hence, it was called also ANTEZEUGMENON, *i.e.,* yoked before (from the Latin, *ante, before),* or *ante-yoked.* Another name was PROEPIZEUXIS *(pró-ep'-i-zeux'-is),* *yoked upon before* (from προ *(pro),* *before,* and ἐπί *(epi),* *upon).*

The Latins called it INJUNCTUM, *i.e., joined,* or *yoked to,* from *in,* and *jugum,* a yoke (from *jungo, to join).*

Gen. iv. 20.—"And Adah bare Jabal : he was the father of such as dwell in tents and cattle."

Here the verb "dwell" is placed before "tents" and "cattle," with both of which it is yoked, though it is accurately appropriate only to "tents," and not to "cattle." The verb "possess" would be more suitable for cattle. And this is why the figure is a kind of *Ellipsis*, for the verse if completed would read, "he was the father of such as dwell in tents [*and possess*] cattle." But how stilted and tame compared with the figure which bids us throw the emphasis on the fact that he was a *nomade* (יָבָל, *a wanderer* or *nomade*), and cared more for wandering about than for the shepherd part of his life !

The A.V. has supplied the verb in italics :—"[*such as have*] cattle," as though it were a case of ordinary Ellipsis. The R.V. supplies the second verb "*have*."

It may be, however, that the sense is better completed by taking the words וְאָהֳלֵי מִקְנֶה (*vahaley michneh*), *tents of cattle*, as in 2 Chron. xiv. 14, *i.e.*, cattle-tents, *i.e.*, herdsmen. Or, as in Gen. xlvi. 32, 34, by supplying the Ellipsis :—"Such as dwell in tents and [*men of*] cattle," *i.e.*, herdsmen. So that the sense would be much the same.

Ex. iii. 16.—" I have surely visited you, and that which is done to you in Egypt." We are thus reminded that it was not merely that Jehovah had *seen* that which they had suffered, but rather had *visited* because of His covenant with their fathers.

The A.V. and R.V. both supply the second verb : "[*seen*] that which is done to you, etc."

It may be that the verb פָּקַד (*pachad*), though used only *once*, should be repeated (by implication) in another sense, which it has, *viz.* : " I have surely visited (*i.e.*, *looked after* or *cared for*) you, and [*visited*] (*i.e.*, *punished for*) that which is done to you in Egypt)." The two senses being to *go to* with the view of helping ; and to *go for* or *against* with the view of punishing, which would be the figure of *Syllepsis* (*q.v.*).

Deut. iv. 12.—"And the LORD spake unto you out of the midst of the fire : ye heard the voice of words, but saw no similitude, only a voice."

The A.V. and R.V. supply the second verb " [*heard*] only *a voice*." The figure shows us that all the emphasis is to be placed on the fact that no similitude was seen ; thus idolatry was specially condemned.

The word " idol " means, literally, something that is seen, and thus all worship that involves the use of sight, and indeed, of any of the *senses* (hence called *sensuous worship*), rather than the *heart*, partakes of the nature of *idolatry*, and is abomination in the sight of God.

2 Kings xi. 12.—"And he brought forth the king's son, and put the crown upon him, and the testimony." (2 Chron. xxiii. 11).

Here the A.V. and R.V. supply the second verb, "*gave him* the testimony." If it were a simple *Ellipsis*, we might instead supply *in his hand* after the word "testimony." But it is rather the figure of *Zeugma*, by which our attention is called to the importance of the "testimony" under such circumstances (see Deut. xvii. 19) rather than to the mere act of the giving it.

Isa. ii. 3.—"Come ye, and let us go up to the mountain of the LORD, to the house of the God of Jacob," *i.e.*, [*and let us enter into*] the house of the God of Jacob.

Luke xxiv. 27.—"And beginning at Moses and all the prophets, he expounded unto them in all the Scriptures the things concerning himself."

Here the verb "beginning" suits, of course, only "Moses"; and some such verb as *going through* would be more appropriate; as he could not begin at all the "prophets."

This figure tells us that it is not the *act* which we are to think of, but the *books* and the Scripture that we are to emphasize as being the subject of the Risen Lord's exposition.

1 Cor. iii. 2.—"I have fed you with milk, and not with meat."

Here the verb is ποτίζω, *to give drink*, and it suits the subject, "milk," but not "meat." Hence the emphasis is not so much on the feeding as on the food, and on the contrast between the "milk" and the "meat." The A.V. avoids the figure by giving the verb a neutral meaning. See how tame the passage would have been had it read: "I have given you milk to drink and not meat to eat"! All the fire and force and emphasis would have been lost, and we might have mistakenly put the emphasis on the verbs instead of on the subjects: while the figure would have been a *Pleonasm* (*q.v.*) instead of a *Zeugma*.

1 Cor. vii. 10.—"And unto the married I command, *yet* not I, but the Lord."

Here the one verb is connected with the two objects: but we are, by this figure, shown that it is connected affirmatively with the Lord, and only negatively with the apostle.

1 Cor. xiv. 34.—"For it is not permitted them to speak; but to be under authority."

This has been treated as a simple *Ellipsis:* but the unequal yoke (*Zeugma*) is seen, the one verb being used for the two opposite things;

thus emphasizing the fact that it is not so much the *permitting*, or *the commanding*, which is important, but the act of *speaking*, and the condition of *being under authority*.

1 Tim. iv. 3.—"Forbidding to marry and to abstain from meats."

This has been classed already under *Ellipsis ;* but the *Zeugma* is also seen; emphasizing the fact that it is *celibacy* and *abstinence* which are to be noted as the marks of the latter times rather than the mere acts of "forbidding" or commanding. The latter verb, which is omitted, is supplied by *Paronomasia* (*q.v.*), "forbidding (κωλυόντων, kōluontōn), to marry, and [*commanding* (κελευόντων, keleuontōn)] , etc."

2. MESOZEUGMA ; or, MIDDLE-YOKE.

Mes̨-o-zeug´-ma, i.e., middle-yoke, from μέσος (*mesos*), *middle*. The *Zeugma* is so-called when the verb or adjective occurs in the middle of the sentence.

The Latins called it CONJUNCTUM, *joined-together-with.*

Mark xiii. 26.—"Then shall they see the Son of Man coming in the clouds with great power and glory."

Here in the Greek the adjective is put between the two nouns, thus : "Power, great, and glory," and it applies to both in a peculiar manner. This *Zeugma* calls our attention to the fact that the power will be great and the glory will be great: and this more effectually emphasizes the greatness of both, than if it had been stated in so many words.

So also v. 40, "The father of the child and the mother"; (verse 42) "Arose the damsel and walked."

Luke i. 64.—"And his mouth was opened immediately and his tongue, and he spake and praised God."

Here it is not the act of the opening and loosing that we are to think of, but the fact that through this predicted miracle he praised God with his mouth and his tongue in spite of all the months of his enforced silence.

3. HYPOZEUGMA ; or, END-YOKE.

Hy´-po-zeug´ma, i.e., end-yoke, from ὑπό (*hupo* or *hypo*), *underneath.* Hence ὑποζεύγνυμι (*hypozeugnumi*), *to yoke under.* The figure of *Zeugma* is so called when the verb is at the end of the sentence, and so underneath, the two objects.

Acts iv. 27, 28.—"They were gathered together, to do whatsoever thy hand and thy counsel determined before to be done."

Here the verb "determined" relates only to "counsel" and not to "hand" : and shows us that we are to place the emphasis on the fact that, though the power of God's hand was felt sooner than His counsel (as Bengel puts it), yet even this was only in consequence of His own determinate counsel and foreknowledge. Compare chap. ii. 23, and iii. 18.

4. SYNEZEUGMENON ; or, JOINT-YOKE.

Syn'-e-zeug'-men-on, i.e., yoked together with, or *yoked connectedly,* from σύν (*sun* or *syn*), *together with,* and ζεύγνυμι, *to yoke.*

This name is given to the *Zeugma* when the verb is joined to more than two clauses, each of which would require its own proper verb in order to complete the sense.* By the Latins it was called ADJUNC-TUM, *i.e., joined together.*

Ex. xx. 18.—"And all the people saw the thunderings, and the lightnings, and the noise of the trumpet, and the mountain smoking." How tame this would be if the proper verbs had been expressed in each case! The verb "saw" is appropriate to the "lightnings" and "mountain." And by the omission of the second verb "heard" we are informed that the people were impressed by what they saw, rather than by what they heard.

Ps. xv.—Here the whole of the objects in verses 2-5 are connected with one verb which occurs in the last verse (repeated from first verse). All the sentences in verses 2-5 are incomplete. There is the *Ellipsis of* the verb, *e.g.,* verse 2 : " He that walketh uprightly [*shall abide in thy tabernacle and shall never be moved*], he that worketh righteousness [*shall never be moved*]," etc.

This gives rise to, or is the consequence of the structure of the Psalm :—

A | 1. Who shall abide ? (stability).
    B | a | 2. Positive
       | b | 3. Negative   } qualities.
    B | a | 4- Positive
       | b | -4-5- Negative
  A | -5. Who shall abide ? (stability).

---

* On the other hand, when in a succession of clauses each subject has its own proper verb, expressed instead of being understood, then it is called HYPOZEUXIS (*Hy'-po-zeux'-is*), *i.e., sub-connection with.* See Ps. cxlv. 5-7. 1 Cor. xiii. 8. Where several members, which at first form one sentence, are unyoked and separated into two or more clauses, the figure is called DIEZEUG-MENON, *Di'-e-zeug'-men-on, i.e., yoked-through,* from διά (*dia*), through. This was called by the Latins DISJUNCTIO. See under *Prosapodosis.*

Eph. iv. 31.—" Let all bitterness, and wrath, and anger, and clamour, and evil speaking, be put away from you."

Here the one verb " put away," αἴρω (*airō*), is used of all these various subjects, though it does not apply equally to each: *e.g.*, " bitterness," πικρία (*pikria*), the opposite of "kindness," verse 32; " wrath," θυμός (*thumos*), harshness, the opposite of " tender-hearted," verse 32; " anger," ὀργή (*orgee*), the opposite of "forgiving," verse 32; " clamour," κραυγή (*kraugee*), " evil-speaking," βλασφημία (*blasphemia*), " malice," κακία (*kakia*), *wickedness*.

It is the thing we are not to be, that is important, rather than the act of giving it up. (See the same passage under *Polysyndeton*).

Phil. iii. 10.—" That I may know him, and the power of his resurrection, and the fellowship of his sufferings, being made conformable unto his death."

Here the one verb "know" properly refers to " Him." The verbs suited to the other subjects are not expressed, in order that we may not be diverted by other action from the one great fact of our knowledge of Him. "That I may know Him (is the one great object, but to know Him I must experience) the power of His resurrection, and (to feel this I must first share) the fellowship of His sufferings (How? by) being made like Him in His death," *i.e.*, by reckoning myself as having died with Christ (Rom. vi. 11), and been planted together in the likeness of His death (verse 5). So only can I know the power of that new resurrection life which I have as "risen with Christ," enabling me to " walk in newness of life," and thus to "know Him."

The order of thought is introverted in verses 10 and 11.

Resurrection.

Suffering.

Death.

Resurrection.

And resurrection, though mentioned first, cannot be known until fellowship with His sufferings and conformity to His death have been experienced by faith. Then the power of His resurrection which it exercises on the new life can be known; and we can know Him only in what God has made Christ to be to His people, and what He has made His people to be in Christ.

ASYNDETON ; or, NO-ANDS.

THIS figure should not be studied apart from the opposite figure *POLYSYNDETON* (*q.v.*), as they form a pair, and mutually throw light upon and illustrate each other.

It is pronounced *a-syn'-de-ton*, and means simply *without conjunctions;* or it may be Englished by the term NO-ANDS.

It is from the Greek α, negative, and σύνδετον (*sundeton*), *bound together with* (from δεῖν, *dein*, to bind).

Hence, in grammar, asyndeton means *without any conjunctions.*

It is called also ASYNTHETON, from τίθημι (*titheemi*), *to put* or *place.* Hence, *Asyntheton* means *no placings* or *puttings* (*i.e.*, of the conjunction " and ").

Other names for this figure are :—

DIALYSIS (*Di-al'-y-sis*), from διά (*dia*), *through*, and λύειν (*luein*), *to loosen ; a loosening through.*

DIALYTON (*Di-al'-y-ton*), *a separation of the parts.*

SOLUTUM (*So-lu-tum*), from the Latin *solvo*, *to dissolve.*

DISSOLUTIO (*Dis-so-lu'-ti-o*), *a dissolving.*

EPITROCHASMOS (*Ep'-i-tro-chas'-mos*), from ἐπί (*epi*), *upon*, and τροχαῖος (*trochaios*), *a running along, tripping along.* This name is given also to a certain kind of *Parenthesis* (*q.v.*).

PERCURSIO (*Per-cur'-si-o*), *a running through.*

All these names are given, because, without any "*ands*" the items are soon run over.

When the figure *Asyndeton* is used, we are not detained over the separate statements, and asked to consider each in detail, but we are hurried on over the various matters that are mentioned, as though they were of no account, in comparison with the great climax to which they lead up, and which alone we are thus asked by this figure to emphasize.

The beauties of *Asyndeton* cannot be fully seen or appreciated without comparing with it the figure of *Polysyndeton.* They should be studied together, in order to bring out, by the wonderful contrast, the object and importance of both.

Asyndeta have been divided into four classes :—

> *Conjunctive* or *copulative*, when the words or propositions are to be joined together.
>
> *Disjunctive*, when they are to be separated from each other.
>
> *Explanatory*, when they explain each other.
>
> *Causal*, when a reason is subjoined.

For the sake of more easy reference, the following examples have not been thus classified, but are given in the order in which they occur in the Bible :

Ex. xv. 9, 10.—" The enemy said,
—I will pursue,
—I will overtake,
—I will divide the spoil ;
—My lust shall be satisfied upon them ;
—I will draw my sword,
—My hand shall destroy them.
—Thou didst blow with thy wind,
—The sea covered them :
They sank as lead in the mighty waters."

Here we are hurried over what " the enemy said," because it was not of the least importance what he said or what he did. The great fact is recorded in the climax: on which all the emphasis is to be placed both in thought and in public reading.

Judges v. 27.—" At her feet he bowed,
—he fell,
—he lay down ;
—at her feet he bowed,
—he fell :
—where he bowed,
there he fell down dead."

1 Sam. xv. 6.—" And Saul said unto the Kenites,
—Go,
—depart,
—get you down from among the Amalekites,
—lest I destroy you with them."

Isa. xxxiii. 7-12.—Here the figure is used to hasten us on through the details which describe the judgment on Assyria, in order

that we may dwell on the important fact that the hour of Judah's
deliverance has come:—

" Behold, their valiant ones shall cry without ;
—the ambassadors of peace shall weep bitterly:
—the highways lie waste,
—the wayfaring man ceaseth :
—he hath broken the covenant,
—he hath despised the cities,
—he regardeth no man :
—the earth mourneth (the "and" here (in A.V.) is incorrectly inserted),
—languisheth :
—Lebanon is ashamed,
—hewn down (here again the "and" is introduced and mars the figure).
—Sharon is like a wilderness ;
—And Bashan and Carmel shake [*their leaves*] (or, are all astir).

" Now will I arise, saith the Lord :
—now will I be exalted ;
—now will I lift up myself.

" Ye shall conceive chaff (חֲשַׁשׁ, *dried grass*, or *tinder*).
—Ye shall bring forth stubble ;
—your breath *as* fire shall devour you.
—And the people shall be as the burnings of lime ;
—As thorns cut up shall they be burned in the fire."

Ezek. xxxiii. 15, 16.—" If the wicked restore the pledge,
—give again that he had robbed,
—walk in the statutes of life, without committing iniquity ;
—he shall surely live
—he shall not die."*
—" None of his sins that he hath committed shall be mentioned unto
       him :
—he hath done that which is lawful and right ;
—he shall surely live."

Mark ii. 27, 28.—In the *Textus Receptus* the "and " is
omitted, but it is inserted both in the A.V. and R.V. with T. Tr.
A., WH.

It reads, in spite of this, as though the "and " were an addition to
the text. Without it there is an *Asyndeton*, and a forcible conclusion
flowing from it.

---

* Here, in the climax, we have the figure of *Pleonasm* (*q.v.*).

"The Sabbath was made for man,
—not man for the Sabbath;
**therefore the Son of Man is Lord of the Sabbath
also.**"*

Mark vii. 21-23.—"For from within, out of the heart of men,
proceed
evil thoughts,
—adulteries,
—fornications,
—murders,
—thefts,
—covetousness,
—wickedness,
—deceit,
—lasciviousness,
—an evil eye,
—blasphemy,
—pride,
—foolishness :
—**all these evil things come from within, and defile the
man.**"

This weighty truth, thus emphasized, writes folly on all modern
attempts to *improve human nature ;* because they all proceed on the
false assumption that it is what goes into the man that defiles him, and
ignore the solemn fact that in the natural heart there is " no good thing "
(Rom. vii. 18). Until, therefore, a new heart has been given by God, all
attempts to make black white will be labour in vain. Compare Matt.
xv. 18-20.

Luke xvii. 27-30.—"They did eat,
—they drank,
—they married wives,
—they were given in marriage, until the day that Noah entered into
the ark,
and the Flood came, and destroyed them all.

---

* A.V., wrongly, "Lord also." R.V., "even of the Sabbath." See
"*Also,*" *a Bible Study on the Use of the Word,* by the same author and
publisher.

" Likewise also as it was in the days of Lot ; they did eat,
—they drank,
—they bought,
—they sold,
—they planted,
—they builded ; but the same day that Lot went out of Sodom
it rained fire and brimstone from heaven, and destroyed
them all. Even thus shall it be in the day when the Son
of Man is revealed."

Rom. i. 29-31.—A long list is given of the marks of the " reprobate mind," and we are taken through the awful catalogue, and
hastened on to the climax in verse 32, that the righteous sentence of
God has been passed, and only judgment now awaits them that " not
only do the same, but have pleasure" in them that do
them.

1 Cor. iii. 12, 13.—" Now if any man build upon this foundation
gold,
—silver,
—precious stones,
—wood,
—hay,
—stubble ;
every man's work shall be made manifest ; for the day shall
declare it," etc.

Here it is the consequence which is emphasized by the climax
thus led up to. The builder here is the minister, and the work is
ministerial.

Those who have been reformed or apparently converted by human
persuasion or other influences working and acting on the flesh, are like
" *wood, hay, stubble ;*" and will be burnt up in that day ; for, as the Lord
Jesus declared (using the work of a husbandman as the illustration,
instead of, as here, the work of the builder), " every plant which
my heavenly Father hath not planted shall be rooted up " (Matt.
xv. 13).

But those who have been converted *by God* (and not merely as
the popular phrase goes " to God ") shall be as " gold, silver, precious
stones," for whom the fire shall have " no hurt."

1 Cor. xii. 28-31.—" And God hath set some in the church,
—first apostles,
—secondarily prophets,
—thirdly teachers,
—after that miracles,
—then gifts of. healings,
—helps,
—governments,
—diversities of tongues.
  Are all apostles ?
—*are* all prophets ?
—*are* all teachers ?
—*are* all workers of miracles ?
—Have all the gifts of healing ?
—Do all speak with tongues ?
—Do all interpret ?
**But covet earnestly the best gifts : and yet show I unto you
a more excellent way.**"

Here we have part of the revelation concerning the Mystical body
of Christ.

It commences at verse 1 :—

A | xii. 1-11. Nine gifts which God has given to His Church.

  B | 12-17. The unity of the Body. Nine enumerations.

  B | 18-27. What God hath set in the Body. Eight enumerations.

A | 28-31. What God hath set in the Church. Eight gifts.

Thus in A and *A* we have the Church. And in B and *B* we have
the Body. In A and B we have seventeen* enumerations, and in *B* and
A we have seventeen also. These arrangements bind all four together
in a remarkable way to show that " the Body is one."

1 Cor. xiii. 13.—" And now abideth faith,
—hope,
—charity,
these three," etc.

---

* For the significance of this number, see *Number in Scripture*, by the same
author and publisher. Also *The Mystery*.

2 Cor. vii. 5, 6.—" For, when we were come into Macedonia, our flesh had no rest, but
—we were troubled on every side ;
—without *were* fightings,
—within *were* fears.

Nevertheless God, that comforteth those that are cast down, comforted us by the coming of Titus."

Gal. v. 19-21.—" Now the works of the flesh are manifest, which are *these*,
   Adultery,
—fornication,
—uncleanness,
—lasciviousness,
—idolatry,
—witchcraft,
—hatred,
—variance,
—emulations,
—wrath,
—strife,
—seditions,
—heresies,
—envyings,
—murders,
—drunkenness,
—revellings, and such like: of the which I tell you before, as I have also told *you* in time past,

that they which do such things shall not inherit the kingdom of God."

See also under *Merismus* and *Synonymia*.

Gal. v. 22.—" But the fruit of the Spirit is love,
—joy,
—peace,
—longsuffering,
—gentleness,
—goodness,
—faith,
—meekness,
—temperance :

against such there is no law."

Contrast this with the *Polysyndeton* in 2 Pet. i. 5-7.

Eph. iv. 32.—Contrast this with the *Polysyndeton* in verse 31.

" And be kind one to another,

—tenderhearted,

—forgiving one another,

even as God for Christ's sake hath forgiven you." (Lit. " like as GOD also ").

Phil. iii. 5-7.—" Though I might also have confidence in the flesh (Greek :—' Though I might have confidence IN THE FLESH also '). If any other man thinketh that he hath whereof he might boast in the flesh, I more :

" Circumcised the eighth day,

—of the stock of Israel,

—*of* the tribe of Benjamin,

—an Hebrew of the Hebrews ;

—as touching the Law, a Pharisee ;

—concerning zeal, persecuting the Church ;

—touching the righteousness which is in the law, blameless.

But what things were gain to me, those I counted loss for Christ."

Paul is speaking not of his sins, but of his gains. As to his standing in the flesh we hear his words, " I more," so we need not strive to gain it. As to his guilt as a sinner we hear his words, " I am chief," so we need not despair. For God has set him forth as a pattern showing how all sinners must be converted (1 Tim. i. 16).

1 Thess. v. 14-18.—" Now we exhort you, brethren, warn them that are unruly,

—comfort the feeble minded,

—support the weak,

—be patient toward all *men*.

—See that none render evil for evil unto any *man ;* but

—ever follow that which is good both among yourselves and to all *men*.

—Rejoice evermore.

—Pray without ceasing.

—In every thing give thanks :

for this is the will of God in Christ Jesus concerning you."

1 Tim. i. 17.—" Now unto the King

eternal,

—immortal,

—invisible;

—the only wise God,

be **honour and glory for ever and ever. Amen.**"

1 Tim. iv. 13-16.—" Till I come,
give attendance to reading,
>—to exhortation,
>—to doctrine.

—Neglect not the gift that is in thee, which was given thee by prophecy,
with the laying on of the hands of the presbytery.
—Meditate upon these things ;
—give thyself wholly to them ; that thy profiting may appear to all.
—Take heed unto thyself, and unto the doctrine ;
—continue in them :
**for in doing this thou shalt save both thyself, and them that
hear thee.**"

2 Tim. iii. 1-5.—" This know also, that in the last days perilous
times shall come.   For men shall be lovers of their own selves,
—covetous,
—boasters,
—proud,
—blasphemers,
—disobedient to parents,
—unthankful,
—unholy,
—without natural affection,
—trucebreakers,
—false accusers,
—incontinent,
—fierce,
—despisers of those that are good,
—traitors,
—heady,
—highminded,
—lovers of pleasures more than lovers of God ;
from such turn away."

2 Tim. iii. 10, 11.—" But thou hast fully known my doctrine,
—manner of life,
—purpose,
—faith,
—longsuffering,
—charity,
—patience,
—persecutions,

K

—afflictions, which came unto me at Antioch,

                    —at Iconium,

                    —at Lystra: what persecutions I endured;

but out of *them* **all the Lord delivered me."**[*]

As much as to say, " It does not matter what my troubles may have been: the great and blessed fact is that out of them all the Lord hath delivered me."

2 Tim. iii. 16, 17.—" All Scripture is given by inspiration of God,[†] and *is* profitable

—for doctrine,

—for reproof,

—for correction,

—for instruction in righteousness:

that the man of God may be perfect, throughly furnished unto all good works."

Here we are hurried on, and not asked to stop and consider each of the four things for which all Scripture is profitable: but we are asked especially to dwell on the *object* of it : *viz.*, thoroughly to furnish : the man of God for all the circumstances in which he may be placed.

The words "perfect" and "throughly furnished" are cognate in the Greek, and should be similarly rendered.[‡] If the former ἄρτιος (*artios*) is rendered "perfect," the latter ἐξηρτισμένος (*exeertismenos*) should be "perfected" (as in the margin). If the former is translated *fitted*, the latter should be *fitted* out-and-out. If the latter is rendered "furnished completely," then the former should be furnished. Perhaps the best rendering would be "fitted" . . . "fitted out," *i.e.*, "that the man of God may be fitted, fitted out unto all good works."

The adjective ἄρτιος (*artios*) is from the Ancient Aryan root AR, which means *to fit*. In the Greek it implies *perfect adaptation* and *suitability*. The Greeks used it of *time*, as denoting the *exact* or right moment ; and of numbers as denoting a perfect or *even* number as opposed to an odd number.

The verb ἐξαρτίζω (*exartizo*) means *to fit out ;* and is used of *furnishing* a house, making full preparation for war, or especially of *fitting out* a vessel for sea, in doing which every emergency must be provided for—heat and cold, calm and storm, peace and war, fire and

---

[*] Compare and contrast with this the *Polysyndeton* of 2 Tim. iv. 17, 18.

[†] See under the figure of *Ellipsis*, page 44.

[‡] See under the figure of *Paregmenon*.

accident. Hence, he who studies God's word, will be a "man of God," *fitted out* and *provided* for all the circumstances and emergencies of life. But he who neglects this, and studies man's books, will become at best a *man of men;* he will be only what man's wisdom can make him, a prey for every enemy, exposed to every danger.*

The adjective ἄρτιος occurs only here : and the verb ἐξαρτίζω only here, and in Acts xxi. 5. The importance of this passage is shown by the perfection of its structure :—

A | a | All Scripture is given by inspiration of God ;
   | b | and is profitable
     B | for doctrine,
       C | for reproof,
       C | for correction,
     B | for instruction in righteousness :
A | a | that the man of God may be perfect;
   | b | throughly furnished unto all good works.

Here in A and *A* we have that which is connected with "*God*"; while in B, C and *B, C,* we have that which is connected with His "*Word.*" Thus:—

A | a | God's divinely inspired word.
   | b | Its profit to God's man.
     B | Positive : Teaching what is true.
       C | Negative : Convicting of what is wrong in practice.
       C | Negative : Correcting what is wrong in doctrine.
     B | Positive : Instructing in what is right.
A | a | God's divinely-fitted man.
   | b | His profit in God's word.

There is a further reference to this verse (2 Tim. iii. 16) in verses 2 and 3 of the next chapter, which may be compared thus :—

The God-breathed Word is profitable

2 Tim. iii. 16.		2 Tim. iv. 2, 3.
for doctrine :	therefore	Preach the word; be instant in season, out of season ;
for reproof :	„	reprove,
for correction :	„	rebuke,
for instruction in righteousness :	„	exhort with all longsuffering and doctrine.

---

* See *The Man of God,* a pamphlet by the same author and publisher.

Thus we have the same figure in both of these corresponding members:

2 Tim. iv. 2, 3.—" Preach the word ;
—be instant in season, out of season ;
—reprove,
—rebuke,
—exhort with all longsuffering and doctrine.
For the time will come when they will not endure sound doctrine.''

This important conclusion is pressed upon us and thus emphasized in order to show us that, when men " will not endure sound doctrine,'' we are not to search for something to preach that they will endure, but all the more earnestly and persistently we are to "preach the word!'' Nothing else is given us to preach, whether men will hear or whether they will forbear.

Jas. i. 19, 20.—"Wherefore, my beloved brethren, let every man (ἄνθρωπος, *anthrōpos*) be
swift to hear,
—slow to speak,
—slow to wrath :
for the wrath of man (ἀνδρός, *andros*) **worketh not the righteousness of God.''**

Jas. v. 6.—Here the translators have inserted "*and*" twice in italics, utterly destroying the figure and hiding the conclusion.
" Ye have condemned,
—ye have killed the just [*One*];
—He doth not resist you.
Be patient therefore, brethren, unto the coming of the Lord.''

Rev. iii. 7, 8.—"These things saith
He that is holy,
—he that is true,
—he that hath the key of David,
—he that openeth, and no man shutteth; and shutteth, and no man
    openeth ;
I know thy works.''

Contrast the *Polysyndeton* in verses 8, 12, 17, 18.

Among other examples may be noted :—

Isa. xxi. 11.   Mark xvi. 6, 17, 18.   Luke i. 17.   Rom. ii. 19-23.
1 Cor. iv. 8; xiii. 4-7; xv. 41-44.   2 Cor. vii. 2-4.   Heb. xi. 32-38.
Rev. vii. 5-8; xxi. 18-20.

APHÆRESIS: or, FRONT-CUT,

pronounced *Aph-cer'-e-sis*, is the Greek word ἀφαίρεσις, and means *a taking away from*, from ἀφαιρεῖν (*aphairein*), *to take away*, from ἀπὸ (*apo*), *away*, αἱρεῖν (*hairein*), *to take*. It is a figure of etymology which relates to the *spelling* of words, and is used of the cutting off of a letter or syllable from the *beginning* of a word. We may, therefore, give it the English name of FRONT-CUT. We see it in such words as *'neath* for beneath; *mazed* for amazed. In the Scripture we have an example in *Coniah* for *Jeconiah*. He is called Jeconiah in his genealogy (1 Chron. iii. 16); but, in Jer. xxii. 24, where Jehovah declares that He will cut him off, his name corresponds with the act, for the front part is *cut off*, and he is called " Coniah."*

Jeconiah means *Let Jehovah establish*. Cutting off the first syllable may intimate the disappointment (for the time) of the hope.

Josiah, who justified the hope expressed in his name (*Let Jehovah heal*) that Jehovah would establish the kingdom, gave his son the name of Eliakim, afterwards called Jehoiakim, which means *God will establish* (as does his grandson's, Jehoiachin—this Jeconiah). But his hopes were vain. Josiah's family is remarkable for the manner in which the names are broken up and their kingdom overtaken by disaster.

See Jer. xxii. 24. "*As* I live, saith the LORD, though CONIAH, the son of Jehoiakim king of Judah were the signet upon my right hand, yet would I pluck thee thence"; and read on to the end of the chapter.

In verse 30, " Write ye this man childless " is explained to mean that not one of his seven sons (1 Chron. iii. 17, 18) sat upon his throne, but Zerubbabel, his grandson, became governor after Coniah had died in Babylon (2 Kings xxv. 29, 30).

---

* Only here, and in xxxvii. 1.

APOCOPE ; or, END-CUT.

A-pŏc'-o-pe is the Greek word ἀποκοπή, *a cutting off*, from ἀποκόπτειν (*apokoptein*), to cut off, and this from ἀπό (*apo*), *away from*, and κόπτειν (*koptein*), *to cut*. It is a figure of etymology which relates to the spelling of words, and is used of cutting off a letter or syllable from the *end* of a word. We may give it the name of END-CUT. We have examples in such words as *yon* for yonder, *after* for afterward.

In the Scripture we have an example in the name of Jude for Judas.

There is no Apocope in the Greek ; and therefore there is no teaching in the use of the figure ; which exists only in the translation.

II. *AFFECTING THE SENSE.*

APOSIOPESIS; or, SUDDEN-SILENCE.

THIS is a rhetorical figure, and not a figure of grammar, but it may be placed under the figures depending on *omission*, because in it something is omitted.

Apo-si-o-pee'-sis is the Greek word ἀποσιώπησις (*a becoming silent*), *from* ἀποσιωπάω (*aposiōpaō*), *to be silent after speaking, to keep silence, observe a deliberate silence.*

The name of this figure may be represented in English by SUDDEN-SILENCE. The Latins named it RETICENTIA, which means the same thing. It is the sudden breaking off of what is being said (or written), so that the mind may be the more impressed by what is too wonderful, or solemn, or awful for words : or when a thing may be, as we sometimes say, "better imagined than described."

Its use is to call our attention to what is being said, for the purpose of impressing us with its importance.

It has been divided under four heads, according to the character of the subject :—

      1. Promise.
      2. Anger and Threatening.
      3. Grief and Complaint.
      4. Enquiry and Deprecation.

    1. PROMISE : where some great thing is promised, too great
              to be conveyed in words.

Ex. xxxii. 31, 32.—"And Moses returned unto the LORD, and said, Oh, this people have sinned a great sin, and have made them gods of gold. Yet now, if thou wilt forgive their sin——; and if not, blot me, I pray thee, out of thy book which thou hast written."

Here it seems that Moses was about to promise something on behalf of the people; but neither knew what promise he could make for them, nor how far he could answer for its fulfilment by them. His sudden silence is solemnly eloquent.

2 Sam. v. 8.—"And David said on that day, Whosoever getteth up to the gutter——."

We learn from 1 Chron. xi. 6 that the promise was fulfilled in Joab, who was made chief or captain. Hence these words have been supplied in the A.V., as we have explained above, under the figure of Absolute *Ellipsis*, page 53.

1 Chron. iv. 10.—"And Jabez called on the God of Israel, saying, Oh that thou wouldest bless me indeed, and enlarge my coast, and that thine hand might be with me, and that thou wouldest keep *me* from evil, that it may not grieve me——"

Then there is a sudden silence, as though it were impossible for Jabez to express the manner in which he would give God thanks and declare his praise for His great mercies. But the words that immediately follow seem to show that God was so much more ready to hear than Jabez was to pray, that without waiting for him to finish his prayer it is added, "And God granted him that which he requested."

Dan. iii. 15.—" Now if ye be ready that at what time ye hear the sound of the cornet, flute, harp, sackbut, psaltery and dulcimer, and all kinds of music, ye fall down and worship the image which I have made —— but if ye worship not," etc.

Here Nebuchadnezzar was ready with his threat of the punishment, but he was careful not to commit himself to any promise.

Luke xiii. 9 has already been treated under the figure of *Ellipsis :* but beside the grammatical ellipsis, there is also the rhetorical: " And if it bear fruit——," as though the vine-dresser would say, " I cannot say what I will not do for it : not only will I not cut it down, but I will continue to care for it and tend it !" The A.V. has supplied the word, " *well !* "

2. Anger and Threatening.

Gen. iii. 22.—"And now, lest he put forth his hand, and take also of the tree of life, and eat, and live for ever——Therefore the LORD God sent him forth from the garden of Eden," etc.

Here the exact consequences of eating of the tree of life in his fallen condition are left unrevealed, as though they were too awful to be contemplated : and the sudden silence leaves us in the darkness in which the Fall involved us. But we may at least understand that whatever might be involved in this unspoken threatening, it included this fact :—*I will drive him away from the tree of life !*

Gen. xx. 3.—" Behold, thou *art* but a dead man——for the woman which thou hast taken ; for she is a man's wife."

Here, we must supply *if thou dost not restore her ;* or, *her husband will slay thee.* This is clear from verse 7.

Jas. iii. 1.—" My brethren, be not many masters, knowing that we shall receive the greater condemnation——."

He does not stop to specify what the many things are, in which those who occupy such positions may give cause of condemnation. This is also to be understood as if it continued " unless we give a right judgment," etc. (Matt. vii. 2).

3. Grief and Complaint.

Gen. xxv. 22.—" If *it be* so, why *am* I thus—— ? "

Rebekah's words of grief and complaint are not completed. She could not understand why, if Jehovah was intreated and answered Isaac's prayer, she should so suffer that the answer was almost as hard to be borne as her former condition.

Judges v. 29, 30.—There is a wonderful *Aposiopesis* here, where the mother of Sisera looks out of her lattice and wonders where Sisera is, and why he does not return. Her wise ladies answered her, " But she repeated her words to herself." Her soliloquy ends in a sudden silence. Everything is left to the imagination as to how she bears it. All is lost in the sudden outburst of the song " So perish all thy foes, O Jehovah"! See under *Homœopropheron*.

Ps. vi. 3.—" My soul is also sore vexed; but thou, O Lord, how long—— ? "

The words are drowned in grief: " How long shall I be sore vexed ? How long [*before thou wilt arise ?*]" Thus his prayer is submitted to the will of God.

Luke xv. 21.—" Father, I have sinned against heaven, and in thy sight, and am no more worthy to be called thy son——."

It is as though, broken down by the grief which the utterance of these words brought into his heart, he could not continue, and say the rest of what, we are told, he had resolved to say in verse 19.

Or it is also to show us as well, that the father's joy to receive is so great that he would not wait for the son to finish, but anticipated him with his seven-fold blessing.

See under *Polysyndeton*.

Luke xix. 42.—" If thou hadst known, even thou, at least in this thy day, the things *which belong* unto thy peace——! but now they are hid from thine eyes."

The blessedness involved in this knowledge is overwhelmed by the tribulation which is to come upon the nation.

The continuation of the sense would probably be " How happy thou wouldest have been ! How blessed ! How safe ! How secure ! but now they are hid from thine eyes."

4. ENQUIRY and DEPRECATION.

Hos. ix. 14.—"Give them, O LORD : what wilt thou give——? " As though unable to conceive the punishment deserved, the Prophet breaks off and goes back to the thought of verse 11.

John vi. 62.—" And if ye shall see the Son of Man ascend up where he was before—— ? "

This has already been referred to under *Ellipsis* (see p. 54).   But something more is implied; more than can be supplied by any specific words, such as, " *Will ye believe then ?* "   For He did afterwards ascend up, but they still refused to believe !

Acts xxiii. 9.—According to some ancient MSS. all the critical Greek texts read the verse, "We find no evil in this man: but, if a spirit or an angel hath spoken to him——."

Either the Pharisees were afraid to express their thoughts, or their words were drowned in the "great dissension" (verse 10) which immediately "arose."   For there is a sudden silence, which some copyists have attempted to fill up by adding the words μὴ θεομαχῶμεν (*mee theomachōmen*), "*let us not fight against God.*"

MEIOSIS: or, A BE-LITTLEING.

(A be-littleing of one thing to magnify another).

Mei-ō'-sis. Greek μείωσις, *a lessening,* or *diminution: from* μειόω (*mei-o-ō*), *to make smaller.*

It is known also by the name LITOTES, *li'-to-tees:* Greek λιτότης, *plainness, simplicity.*

The Latins called it DIMINUTIO (*Di-mi-nu'-ti-o*) and EX-TENUATIO (*Ex-ten'-u-a'-ti-o*).

By this figure one thing is diminished in order to increase *another* thing. It thus differs from *Tapeinosis* (*q.v.*), in which a thing is lessened in order to emphasize *its own* greatness or importance.

In *Meiosis* there is an omission therefore, not of words, but of sense.. One thing is lowered in order to magnify and intensify something else by way of contrast.

It is used for the purpose of emphasis; to call our attention, not to the smallness of the thing thus lessened, but to the importance of that which is put in contrast with it.

Gen. xviii. 27.—" And Abraham answered and said, Behold now, I have taken upon me to speak unto the Lord, which *am but* dust and ashes."

Here Abraham humbles himself; and, alluding to the creation of man out of the dust of the ground (Gen. ii. 7), he implies much more than he expresses. In calling himself " dust and ashes," he contrasts himself with the high and holy God whom he is addressing, and takes the place of a man most vile and a creature most abject. So Jehovah uses the same figure in 1 Kings xvi. 2. Ps. cxiii. 7, &c. See under *Synecdoche.*

Num. xiii. 33.—" And we were in our own sight as grasshoppers, and so we were in their sight." This is the *Meiosis* of unbelief. To gain credence for their words they exaggerated the size of the Anakim by lessening their own stature. On the other hand, the language of faith used a very different figure. Compare xiv. 9, under the Figure of *Ellipsis*, page 37.

1 Sam. xxiv. 14.—" After whom is the king of Israel come out ? After whom dost thou pursue ? After a dead dog, after a flea," *i.e.,* you do that which is altogether unworthy of a king, in pursuing one who is as harmless as a dead dog (compare xvii. 43 ; 2 Sam. iii. 8 ; ix. 8 ; xvi. 9) and as worthless as a flea, which is poor game for a royal hunter (1 Sam. xxvi. 20).

Ezra ix. 8.—" And now for a little space (Heb. *moment*) grace hath been *shewed* from the LORD our God." To magnify the greatness of the grace the Holy Spirit, by Ezra, speaks of the "little space." The comparison is not to the greatness of their transgressions, which are stated in verses 6 and 7, etc., but to their length and the length of the previous chastisement, which had been begun by the kings of Assyria. See Neh. ix. 32, and Ezra vi. 22, where Cyrus, "the king of Babylon" (v. 13), is called the king of Assyria, having absorbed the kingdoms of Media, Persia, and Assyria, and thus the oppressor, by God's grace, had become the friend.

Ps. xxii. 6.—" I *am* a worm, and no man." Here, as elsewhere, this figure is used to denote a much greater depth of humility and affliction than words can express. So Job xxv. 6. Isa. xli. 14. The greater the humiliation, the greater the contrast with His glorification: for He who is "a worm and no man" in Ps. xxii. is "Jehovah my shepherd" of Ps. xxiii., and "the King of glory" of Ps. xxiv. In these three Psalms we thus have in xxii. "the Good Shepherd" in death (John x. 11); "the Great Shepherd" in resurrection (Heb. xiii. 20; and "the Chief Shepherd" in glory (1 Pet. v. 4).

Isa. xl. 15.—" Behold, the nations *are* as a drop of a bucket, and are counted as the small dust of the balance: behold, he taketh up the isles as a very little thing."

And even this fails to convey to our minds the wondrous gulf between the finite and the infinite.

Verse 17 : "All nations before him *are* as nothing: and they are counted to him less than nothing and vanity."

Matt. xv. 26.—" It is not meet to take the children's bread, and to cast it to dogs." It is not only not fair, but it is cruel to one's children thus to deprive them of their food.

See further under the figure of *Hypocatastasis.*

Matt. xviii. 14.—" Even so it is not the will of your Father which is in heaven, that one of these little ones should perish."

No! It is contrary to His wish. His will embraces much more than this, it includes :—

Predestination (Eph. i. 5).

Regeneration (John i. 13 ; Jas. i. 18).

Deliverance from the world (Gal. i. 4).

Sanctification (1 Thess. iv. 3 ; Heb. x. 10).

Final Preservation, Resurrection, and Eternal Life (John vi. 39, 40).

Matt. xxii. 3.—" And they would not come." The Greek is :— οὐκ ἤθελον ἐλθεῖν (*ouk eethelon elthein*), *they did not wish to come*, this is enhancing, by *Meiosis*, the fact that they not only absolutely refused, but in doing so they acted only on the wish of their heart.

Luke xvii. 9.—" Doth he thank that servant because he did the things that were commanded him? I trow not." *i.e.*, I think not. More is to be understood than is expressed: *i.e.*, I know very well he doth not thank him. So far from that, he scarcely notices the matter.

John xv. 20.—" If they have kept my saying, they will keep yours also," *i.e.*, as surely as they have NOT kept my saying, they will not keep yours. The whole context shows that this must be the figure of *Meiosis*.

Rom. x. 19.—" I will provoke you to jealousy by *them that are* no people." οὐκ ἔθνος (*ouk ethnos*), *a non-people*. So 1 Pet. ii. 10 : " Which in time past *were* not a people," οὐ λαός* (*ou laos*). Owing to the reversive power of the negative our own word "*nothing*" is literally a *non-thing*, *i.e.*, a thing which has no existence at all.†

Such were we Gentiles. But through grace, " a people" is now being taken out from among all nations (Acts xv. 14. Rev. v. 9 ; vii. 9), which shall have an existence for ever and ever.

1 Cor. ix. 17.—" For if I do this thing willingly, I have a reward." He means *gratuitously ;* but lessens the wording, so as to increase his meaning. See also under *Oxymoron*.

1 Cor. xv. 9.—" I am the least of the apostles." This is said to magnify the grace of God (verse 10). Whereas, when magnifying his claims, he could say to these same Corinthians, " I suppose I was not a whit behind the very chiefest apostles" (2 Cor. xi. 5, and xii. 11, 12).

Eph. iii. 8.—" Who am less than the least of all saints." This marks the apostle's growth in grace, who a year after could say he was " the chief of sinners" (1 Tim. i. 15). See also under *Oxymoron*.

Philem. 11.—" Which in time past was to thee unprofitable." This is a *Meiosis*, for Onesimus was guilty of injury.

Heb. ix. 12.—" The blood of goats and calves," (13) " the blood of bulls and of goats." Here the figure lessens the importance of the sacrifices which were offered under the Law, in order to increase by contrast the great sacrifice to which they all pointed.

---

* This is not the same as Rom. ix. 26, where the pronoun " my " is used.

† In Amos vi. 13, " a thing of naught " is the same, a *non-existent-thing*

Heb. xiii. 17.—" For that *is* unprofitable for you." It is really much more than that ! It is disastrous and ruinous.

1 John iii. 17.—" But whoso hath this world's good," etc.

Here the Greek is τὸν βίον τοῦ κόσμου (*ton bion tou kosmou*), the life of the world, *i.e.*, the means of life or of living which the world gives. Whoso has this, and will not give it up for his brother, how dwelleth the Love of God in him ? The force of the *Meiosis* is seen when we compare this with verse 16, " We ought to lay down *our* lives for the brethren." But here is a man who will not only not lay down his life (ψυχή), *psyche*, but will not even part with the means of supporting it. What a contrast to true *love !* Hereby know we LOVE, because HE laid down His life for us.

TAPEINOSIS ; or, DEMEANING

(A lessening of a thing in order to increase it).

Ta-pei-nō'-sis. Greek ταπείνωσις, a *demeaning* or *humbling*.

This differs from *Meiosis* in that in *Meiosis* one thing is diminished in order, by contrast, to increase the greatness of *another*, or something else.

Whereas, in *Tapeinosis* the thing that is lessened is the *same* thing which is increased and intensified.

The figure was also called ANTENANTIOSIS. *Ant'-en-an-ti-o'-sis* from ἀντί (*anti*), *over against*, or *instead of*, and ἐναντιος (*enantios*), *opposite*.

When the figure is used parenthetically, it is called ANÆRESIS. See below under *Parenthesis*.

The figure is used in connection with nouns, verbs, and adverbs,

        (1) Positively.
        (2) Negatively.

1. POSITIVELY.

ONE (אֶחָד) in the plural (in Heb.) is used for a few or some :—

Gen. xxvii. 44.—" Tarry with him a few days, until thy brother's fury turn away."

We learn from xxix. 20 that the love which he bore to Rachel is emphasized by speaking of the seven years in which he served for her as " a few days."

SOME (τις) in plural (in Greek) is used for the greater number:—

Rom. iii. 3.—" For what if some did not believe?" Our attention is by this at once pointed to the fact that it was in reality the very opposite. It was only " some " who believed, while the nation as a whole did not believe.

1 Tim. iv. 1.—" Now the Spirit speaketh expressly, that in the latter times some shall depart from the faith, giving heed to seducing spirits (πνεύμασιν πλάνοις, *wandering* or *deceiving spirits* or *angels*), and teachings of demons:" *i.e.*, a vast number of people will be deceived by evil angels and demons in these last days.

Acts v. 36.—" Theudas, boasting himself to be somebody " (τινα) *i.e.*, some great person; as is explained in Acts viii. 9.

Gal. ii. 6.—" But of these who seemed to be somewhat (τι)." They seemed to be something, really they were nothing (vi. 3).

SICK, for those who were dead in sins:

Rom. v. 6.—" For when we were without strength " (ἀσθενῶν, *usthenōn, sick*).　We were really " dead in sin," but are spoken of as infirm, because called " ungodly," " sinners " (verses 6-8), "enemies " (verse 10).

REBUKE, for the great punishment of excommunication.

2 Cor. ii. 6.—" Sufficient to such a man *is* this punishment " (ἐπιτιμία, *epitimia*), *rebuke.*　See further under *Idiom.*

2. NEGATIVELY.

When the emphasis is made by the use of the negative in order to express the positive in a very high degree, this is the figure of *Antenantiosis* (see above).

When we say of a man that " he is no fool," we mean that he is very wise ; or when we say of a thing, " it is not a hundred miles from here," we mean that it is quite close at hand.　We thus emphasize that which we seem to lessen : *e.g.*, when it is written, " I praise you not," it means I greatly blame you!

Ex. xx. 7.—" The LORD will not hold him guiltless:" *i.e.*, He will hold him guilty of breaking the whole law.

Lev. x. 1.—They " offered strange fire before the LORD, which he had commanded them not."　Here, the figure is translated.　The Heb. is literally, " which the Lord had not commanded them," *i.e.*, He had very solemnly prohibited it ; see Ex. xxx. 9.

Num. xxi. 23.—" And Sihon would not suffer Israel to pass through his border."　Heb. : " would not give permission," *i.e.*, he did more, he prohibited them, as the verse goes on to explain, and opposed them even to the extent of using force.

Ps. xliii. 1.—" Plead my cause against an ungodly (margin, Heb., ' unmerciful ') nation."　Heb. לֹא חָסִיד (*lō chahseed*), *not merciful, i.e.*, *cruel* and *malignant.*

Ps. li. 17.—" A broken and a contrite heart, O God, thou wilt not despise:" *i.e.*, Thou wilt graciously accept and welcome and bless.

Ps. lxxviii. 50.—" He spared not their soul from death," *i.e.*, He gave their life over to the pestilence.

Ps. lxxxiii. 1 (2).—" Keep not thou silence, O God : hold not thy peace, and be not still, O God:" *i.e.*, Arise, O God; and speak; vindicate and deliver me from mine enemies.

Ps. lxxxiv. 11.—" No good *thing* will he withhold from them that walk uprightly : " *i.e.,* he will give them every good thing, and preserve them from all evil.

Ps. cvii. 38.—" And suffereth not their cattle to decrease : " *i.e.,* will abundantly multiply their cattle.

Prov. xii. 3.—" A man shall not be established by wickedness : " *i.e.,* he shall be overthrown.

Prov. xvii. 21.—" The father of a fool hath no joy : " *i.e.,* he hath plenty of sorrow.

Prov. xviii. 5.—" It is not good to accept the person of the wicked," *i.e.,* it is a very hateful thing in God's sight to do so.

Prov. xxx. 25.—" The ants are a people not strong," *i.e.,* very weak.

Isa. xiv. 6.—" And none hindereth," *i.e.,* all help.

Isa. xlii. 3.—" A bruised reed shall he not break, and the smoking flax shall he not quench : " *i.e.,* He will strengthen the bruised reed and kindle to a flame the smouldering wick.

Jer. ii. 8.—" The prophets prophesied by Baal, and walked after *things that* do not profit : " *i.e.,* that led to their ruin.   So verse 11.

Zech. viii. 17.—" Love no false oath," *i.e.,* hate every such oath.

Matt. ii. 6.—And thou Bethlehem, *in* the land of Juda, art not the least among the princes of Juda : " *i.e.,* thou art the greatest !

Matt. xii. 32.—" It shall not be forgiven him : " *i.e.,* he shall have the gravest punishment in this life and in the life to come (Mark iii. 29). Just as those, on the other hand, whose sins are forgiven are " blessed " (Rom. iv. 7).

John vi. 37.—" Him that cometh to me, I will in no wise cast out."

Here, there is very much more implied than is expressed in the literal words.   Not only will I not cast him out, but I will by all means receive him and preserve him, and defend him : he shall never perish, neither shall any man pluck him out of My hand. Compare x. 28, and see further under *Ellipsis* (page 106) and *Repeated Negation* and *Synonimia* below.

John xiv. 18.—" I will not leave you comfortless," *i.e.,* I will certainly come to you by My Holy Spirit and be your ever present help and defence. Moreover, I will come again and receive you to Mine own self.

Acts xx. 12.—" And they brought the young man alive, and were not a little comforted : " *i.e.*, they were very greatly comforted.

Acts xxi. 39.—"A citizen of no mean city : " *i.e.*, a very important city.

Tarsus was celebrated as a distinguished seat of Greek Philosophy and Literature. According to Strabo it ranked with Athens and Alexandria in the number of its schools and learned men.

Acts xxii. 18.—" Make haste, and get thee quickly out of Jerusalem : for they will not receive thy testimony concerning me : " *i.e.*, they will not only reject it, oppose it to the uttermost, but will seek to kill thee.

Acts xxvi. 19.—" I was not disobedient unto the heavenly vision " : *i.e.*, I was immediately and altogether obedient. He thus makes his own obedience more emphatic ; while by stating it negatively he denies what his enemies implied. They implied that he ought to have been disobedient; but he meets this by asserting that he was " not disobedient," *i.e.*, most obedient.

Rom. i. 13.—" I would not have you ignorant, brethren."

This means very much more than a mere negative wish. It is a strong positive and earnest desire that they might assuredly know and be well instructed.

Ignorance is man's special human infirmity. Animals know more than man (Isa. i. 3). No animal is so helpless as man in the years of infancy.

It is remarkable, therefore, that in connection with the Church of God, and the epistles addressed to churches as such, containing the special instruction necessary in consequence of man's ignorance concerning the church as the mystery of God, there are six different occasions on which it is written : " I would not have you ignorant, brethren."

" SIX " is the number specially significant of *man*. Man was created on the *sixth* day ; and, wherever in Scripture we have this number or any multiple of it, it always stamps the subject as having to do with Man.*

The significance of these six occurrences of this weighty expression will be seen by those who have patience to work them out in the order in which they are given to us by the Holy Spirit.

---

* Many illustrations of this will be found in *Number in Scripture*, by the same author and publisher.

Rom. i. 13.   Of Paul's purpose to prosecute his great mission and ministry to the saints in Rome.   So chap. xv. 23.

Rom. xi. 25.   That blindness in part is happened to Israel.

1 Cor. x. 1-11.   That the camp in the wilderness was the type of the baptized assembly under the preaching of the kingdom.

1 Cc xii. 1. Concerning spiritual things connected with the Church as the Body of Christ by the baptism with the Holy Spirit.

2 Cor. i. 8.   Of the trouble at Ephesus, at the close of his ministry there (Acts xix.), when his preaching the kingdom ends and the revelation of the Mystery begins.

1 Thess. iv. 13.   Concerning those that are asleep.   Their resurrection and translation with the saints that are alive at the coming of the Lord, to be for ever with Him, when the Mystery is completed.

Rom. i. 16.—" I am not ashamed of the gospel of Christ:" *i.e.,* I count it my highest honour and glory to proclaim it, and to suffer for it, while I have full confidence in its power to accomplish all God's purposes of grace.

Rom. iv. 19.—"And being not weak in faith ": *i.e.,* Abraham being very strong in faith.

Rom. v. 5.—" Hope maketh not ashamed ": *i.e.,* it enables us to " rejoice in hope of the glory of God " (verse 2), and to " joy in God through our Lord Jesus Christ." This hope, therefore, is no false hope, but will prove a great and eternal reality.

Rom. x. 2.—"They have a zeal of God, but not according to knowledge."

By lessening the terms of the expression, the truth is more strongly stated ; and the emphasis is thrown on their blindness and ignorance, which is enlarged upon in the next verse, while zeal and ignorance are combined in verse 19.   Hence the expression, " not according to knowledge," by the figure of *Tapeinosis* means really *with great blindness.*

Rom. xiii. 10.—" Love worketh no ill to his neighbour ": *i.e.,* it refuses to work ill, and not only so, but it works good for his neighbour.

1 Cor. ii. 14.—"The natural man receiveth not the things of the Spirit of God ": *i.e.,* he does more than this, he rejects them, he will not have them : why ? " For they are foolishness unto him." This on the one hand constitutes the guilt of man in the invariable result of the exercise of his "free-will": while on the other hand it is equally true as to God's sovereignty ; " neither can he know *them* (lit., *get to know* them), because they are spiritually discerned."

1 Cor. xi. 22.—" I praise you not ": *i.e.*, I condemn you in this thing.

2 Cor. ii. 11.—" We are not ignorant of his devices," *i.e.*, we are very well aware of them.

Gal. v. 21.—" They which do such things, shall not inherit the kingdom of God ": *i.e.*, they shall not only not inherit the kingdom, but shall be cast out into outer darkness and destroyed without remedy.

Heb. xi. 16.—" Wherefore God is not ashamed to be called their God ": *i.e.*, God is well-pleased to be their God, and to own them as His chosen people.

Heb. xiii. 2.—" Be not forgetful to entertain strangers ": *i.e.*, make it your business to remember to show hospitality.

Rev. xii. 11.—" They loved not their lives unto the death." The fact implied is that they disregarded their life to the point of death, and that because there was One whom they loved more than life and for whose sake they willingly gave it up.

Rev. xviii. 7.—" I am no widow ": *i.e.*, I am well-husbanded and prosperous.

CATABASIS (See *Anabasis*).

SYLLOGISMUS ; or, OMISSION OF THE CONCLUSION.

Syl'-lo-gis'-mus. Greek, συλλογισμός, *a reckoning altogether*, a bringing of all the premisses; and, the conclusion before the mind. From σύν (*sun*), *together*, and λογίζεσθαι (*logizesthai*), *to reckon.* (Hence the word " logic ").

The regular form of every argument consists of three pro-positions of which the first two are called "*premisses*" (the first being the *major*, and the latter the *minor*), while the last, which necessarily follows from them, is called the "*conclusion.*"

But the term *Syllogismus* is given to this figure because it is a departure from this rule, the law of logic being legitimately broken for the sake of emphasis.

It falls into this division because it is a figure of Rhetoric, in which something is *omitted* for the sake of emphasis. It is not the omission of *words*, as such, as in *Ellipsis ;* or of *sense*, as in *Meiosis* or *Tapeinosis ;* but it is a figure in which the premisses are stated, but the conclusion is omitted, and left to the imagination to enhance and heighten the effect ; as when we say, " it can be better imagined than described." Indeed, so great is the emphasis which is thus acquired that the Latins gave it other names.

They called it SIGNIFICATIO, because something is *signified* which is not expressed :

RATIOCINATIO, or *Reasoning*, because only the Reasons (and not the conclusion) are stated ; or, special importance is given to the *reasons*, even though the conclusion may be given (See Rom. iii.)

And it is called EMPHASIS, because of the emphasis thus given to the argument which is omitted.

1 Sam. xvii. 4-7.—The description of Goliath's armour and weapons is given ; and it is left for us to conclude how great his strength must have been.

Isa. ii. 3, 4.—" Out of Zion shall go forth the law, and the word of the LORD from Jerusalem. And he shall judge among the nations, and shall rebuke many people : and they shall beat their swords into plowshares, and their spears into pruninghooks."

Here the facts, or premises, are stated, but it is left for us to draw the conclusion as to the marvellous results of this wonder-working word, which going out of Zion shall bring them about. That "Word of the Lord" by which the heavens and earth were created shall presently be spoken and bring peace and prosperity to the nations.

Isa. iv. 1.—"And in that day seven women shall take hold of one man, saying, We will eat our own bread, and wear our own apparel : only let us be called by thy name, to take away our reproach."

This is the continuation and conclusion of chap. iii. : in which, from verse 18, the punishment of the pride of the "daughters of Zion" is set forth : but it is left for us to draw the solemn conclusion, How great must be the desolation :—the gates, where the husbands of the daughters of Zion used to assemble, now mourn and are deserted ; (iii. 26. Jer. xiv. 2. Lam. i. 4)—and the women whom many men did woo now come and offer themselves to one man, renouncing the legal claim of the wife (Ex. xxi. 10).

Isa. xlix. 20. — Here the greatness of Zion's blessing and prosperity is shown by the statement of the facts in verses 18-21. It is left for us to draw this conclusion which is left unstated.

Matt. x. 30.—"But the very hairs of your head are all numbered," *i.e.*, therefore how infinite must be the knowledge of our "Father"! how should I not therefore fear Him !

Matt. xxiv. 20.—"But pray ye that your flight be not in the winter, neither on the sabbath day." The conclusion is implied :—for then would your troubles and distress be increased and intensified beyond the power of tongue to tell.

Luke vii. 44.—"Thou gavest me no water for my feet : but she hath washed my feet with tears, and wiped *them* with the hairs of her head." What is implied is—How much greater therefore is her love than yours ! So verses 45 and 46.

1 Cor. xi. 6.—"If the woman be not covered, let her be shorn also."

But she is not shorn, therefore the conclusion is, let her be covered.

2 Thess. iii. 10.—"If any would not work, neither should he eat."

Here the conclusion is to be supplied : *Every man must eat ; therefore every man must work :* for it is not meant that a man's food is to be withdrawn from him.

ENTHYMEMA ; or, OMISSION OF PREMISS.

En'-thy-mee-ma.   Greek ἐνθύμημα, *a thought* or *a consideration*.

This is the opposite of SYLLOGISMUS.

In Syllogismus, the *premisses* are stated, but the conclusion is omitted ; while, in *Enthymema*, the conclusion is stated and one or both of the premisses omitted.

Both are alike, therefore, in being an abbreviated Syllogism.

It is also related to *Hypocatastasis* (*q.v.*), in that it is an implication. But in *Hypocatastasis* it is an ordinary statement or word which is to be implied ; while, in *Enthymema* it is the premiss of an argument which is left to be supplied.

The Latins call it COMMENTUM, *a thought* or *a contrivance*, and CONCEPTIO, *the wording* or *drawing up of a statement*.

It may be illustrated thus :—" We are dependent ; we should, therefore, be humble."   Here the major premiss is omitted— " dependent persons should be humble."

A Biblical example occurs in

Rom. vii. 1-6.—Here the fact is asserted that law has dominion over a man only while he is alive (verse 1), and this fact is applied to those who died (*i.e.*, were judicially reckoned as having died) when Christ died.   So that all the members of the body of Christ died, and therefore the law has no longer dominion over them (verses 5, 6).

In proof of this, an illustrative argument is used, as to the case of a husband and wife.   Both are bound to each other by law : and, while both are alive the union of one of them with another person is unlawful ; but, if one be dead, then such a union on the part of the survivor is legitimate.

But only one of the cases is given : *viz.*, the death of the husband.

The death of the wife is there, but only *in thought ;* and this other premiss has to be supplied by the mind in the course of the argument.

So that after the third verse we must add the other premiss in some such words as these :—

" *And if the wife die, I need not say that she is free* " ; or, " *but it goes without saying that if the wife die, of course she is free.*"

Wherefore (as the conclusion is given in verse 6) we died in Christ, and are therefore free from that law wherein we were held ; for " he that has once so died stands justified (the penalty having been paid) from' his sin.

Now if we died with Christ we have been raised also with Him (vi. 8. Col. ii. 12). Thus we were planted together with Him in His death, and raised with Him (vi. 4) to newness of life. And be it noted that this is no mere marriage union. To prevent this conclusion the verb *to marry* is not used in verses 3 and 4. There, instead of the usual verb *marry*, which we should expect to find, we have the verb *to become*, with the dative case; and must in each instance supply the *Ellipsis.* In the case of the woman, she "becomes" joined, "becomes" bound under the law to a husband; but, in the case of those who died with Christ, they "*become*" united to Him as members of His body and "become" His property. Their union with Him is not in Incarnation, but in death, burial, and resurrection; and having died with Him are freed from the Law, instead of being bound to it.

Matt. xxvii. 19.—" Have thou nothing to do with that just man."

Here the fire, and feeling, and urgency of Pilate's wife is all the more forcible, in that she does not stop to formulate a tame, cold argument, but she omits the major premiss; which is greatly emphasized by being left for Pilate to supply. The complete Syllogism would have been:

1. It is very wicked to punish a just or innocent man.

2. Jesus is a just man.

3. Have therefore nothing to do with punishing him.

The conclusion thus contains the proof of each of the premisses on which it rests.

Thus is emphasized one of the four testimonies borne to the innocence of the Lord Jesus by Gentiles at the time of His condemnation.

1. Pilate's wife (Matt. xxvii. 19).

2. Pilate himself, " I am innocent of the blood of this just person " (Matt. xxvii. 24).

3. The dying malefactor, " This man hath done nothing amiss " (Luke xxiii. 41).

4. The Centurion, " Certainly this was a righteous man " (Luke xxiii. 47).

SECOND DIVISION.

———

FIGURES INVOLVING ADDITION.

———

We now come to the second great division of our subject, *viz.*, figures which depend, for their new form, on some *addition*, either of words or of sense.

In the one case, only the words are affected, by their repetition in various forms and ways. In the other, the addition is made to the sense by the use of other words.

These all come under the head of Pleonastic Figures; just as the first division included all Elliptical Figures.

All these various forms of repetition and addition are used for the purpose of attracting our attention, and of emphasizing what is said, which might otherwise be passed by unnoticed.

When we reflect that no error in composition is more readily made than the undue repetition of words, called *Tautology*, it is remarkable that there are more than forty different ways of repeating words used by the Holy Spirit: over forty *legitimate* modes of breaking the law which governs the use of language; and of repeating words, in such a way that not only is there no tautology, but beauty is added to the composition and emphasis given to the sense.

Under this division come all the forms of repetition, either of letters, words, sentences, or subjects; which may be thus classified:—

Figures involving Repetition and Addition.

I. Affecting Words.

1. Repetition of letters and syllables.

    (*a*) The same letters.

    (*b*) Different letters.

2. Repetition of the same word.

    (*a*) In the same sense.

    (*b*) In a different sense.

3. Repetition of different words.

    (*a*) In a similar order (but same sense).

    (*b*) In a different order (but same sense).

    (*c*) With a similar sound (but different sense).

    (*d*) With a different sound (but similar sense).

4. Repetition of sentences and phrases.

5. Repetition of subjects (*Correspondence*).

II. AFFECTING THE SENSE.

1. By way of Repetition.

2. By way of Amplification.

3. By way of Description.

4. By way of Conclusion.

5. By way of Interposition.

6. By way of Argumentation.

We will now consider the various Figures which come under these various heads :

I. *AFFECTING WORDS.*

1. Of Letters and Syllables.

(*a*) Of the same Letters.

HOMŒOPROPHERON; or, ALLITERATION.

The Repetition of the same Letter or Syllable at the commencement of Successive Words.

Ho-mœ-o-proph'-e-ron, from ὅμοιος (*homoios*), *like*, and προφέρω (*propherō*), *to carry*, or *place before*: *i.e.*, Successive words which carry the same letter or the same syllable *before*, or at the beginning.

This figure, therefore, is the repetition of the same letter or syllable at the beginning of two or more words in close succession. Its English name is ALLITERATION (from *ad*, *to*, and *litera*, *letter*). Churchill speaks of "Apt Alliteration's Artful Aid."

This figure is seen, of course, only in the Hebrew and the Greek. It is difficult to reproduce it in a translation. And where it occurs in the English it may be only accidental, and carry no weight or emphasis.

The song of Deborah, in Judges v., abounds with examples of *Homœopropheron*, which add great fire and force and beauty to the original. It is impossible to accurately and literally reproduce it in English, but with a little liberty we can give the English reader some idea of the use of this Figure.

We may as well, at the same time, do so according to its structure (see under *Correspondence*) and we present the structure first in outline, before setting it out in full.

The structure of Judges v. in outline:

A | 2-. Praise to Jehovah for the avenging of Israel.

    B | a | -2, 3. Israel. The people's voluntary service.
          b | 4-8. Contrasted states of the country.
        a | 9. Israel. The leaders' voluntary service.
          b | 10, 11. Contrasted states of the country.

    B | b | 12-18. Contrasted conduct.
        a | 19-22. The Enemy. Assault and defeat.
          b | 23-27. Contrasted conduct.
        a | 28-30. The Enemy. Presumption and disappointment.

A | 31. Praise to Jehovah for the avenging of Israel.

Adhering to this form, we may set the song forth thus :—

A | 2. Bless ye Jehovah,

B   a | That the Leaders in Israel took the lead ;
           That the people willingly offered themselves.
           Hear, O ye kings ; Hearken, O ye princes ;
           I, even I, will sing to Jehovah,
           Will strike the strings unto Jehovah, Israel's God.

        b | Jehovah, when thou settest forth from Seir,
           When thou wentest forth from Edom's field,
           The earth trembled, yea, the heavens dropped ;
           Yea, the clouds dropped down water,
           The mountains melted away before Jehovah,
           Even yon, Sinai, before Jehovah, God of Israel.*
           In the days of Shamgar, son of Anath,
           In Jael's days,
           The highways were effaced ;
           The travellers had to walk in tortuous ways,
           Effaced were Israel's hamlets—effaced
           Till I, Deborah, rose up—rose up a mother in Israel
           New gods had they got them,
           Therefore the press of war approached their gates.
           Was there found shield or spear among forty
               thousand in Israel ?

     a | My heart is with the leaders of Israel,
         Who willingly offered themselves among the People :
         Bless ye Jehovah.

        b | Ye who ride upon white asses,
           Ye who recline upon rich rugs,
           Who walk by the way—Speak !
           Instead of the shouting of the archers among the
               water-drawers.
           They praise there the righteous acts of Jehovah,
           His righteous acts in His villages in Israel.
           Then the People of Jehovah hastened down to the
               gates.

B

b Awake, awake,† Deborah!
Awake, awake, speak the song!
Barak, arise! conquer thy conquest,
Thou son of Abinoam.
Then down against the robust rushed a remnant;
Jehovah's Host rushed with me against the
    powerful,
From Ephraim's stock—the victors over Amalek:
After thee *marched* Benjamin among thy peoples;
From Machir came the Masters,
Men that wield the Marshall's staff out of
    Zebulun.
But the princes of Issachar were with Deborah,
Yea, Issachar was like Barak,
When into the valley his men threw themselves at
    his feet,
While by the brooks abode Reuben,
With great resolutions of heart.
Why sittest thou among the folds listening to the
    shepherd's flute?
By the brooks Reuben has great searchings of
    heart.
Gilead stays beyond Jordan,
And Dan—Why does he abide in his ships?
Asher stays still on the shore of the sea,
Staying still in its bays,
But Zebulun hazarded his soul unto death
With Naphthali, upon the heights of the field.

a Kings came to fight—then the Kings of Canaan fought
At Taanach and by Megiddo's Meres;
Silver gained they none.
From heaven they strove; the stars in their courses
They strove against Sisera:
Kishon's stream swept them away—
A stream of succours was Kishon's stream.
Tread strongly on, my Soul!
When struck the sounding hoof of the rushing steed—
Of the rushing‡ strong ones.

---

* *Hyperbole* (*q.v.*).　† *Geminatio.*　‡ *·Epizeuxis* (*q.v.*).

b | Curse ye Meroz, commands Jehovah's Angel,
Curse ye, curse ye her inhabitants,
Because they came not to Jehovah's help,
To Jehovah's help* amid the mighty.
Blessed above women be Jael,
Heber the Kenite's wife,
Blessed above women† of the tents!
He'asks for water, she gives him milk;
In a beauteous bowl she carries him cream:
With her left hand she takes the tent-peg,
With her right the heavy hammer,
She swings it over Sisera, smites his head,
Crashes through and transfixes his temples,
At her feet he falls—he lies,
At her feet† he lies, writhes again, and falls,
As he writhes himself again he falls—dead! ‡

a | Sisera's mother looks from the window-edge,
She looks from the lattice-ledge and laments:
" Why lingers his car so long?
Why stop his chariots' steps? "
Her wise ladies answer her,
But she repeats her words to herself:
" Will they not find booty and share it?
Two maidens for each man ;‖
Booty of purple robes for Sisera,
Yea, booty of purple robes!
Two for each neck 'of the captors? "§

A | So fall all thy foes, O Jehovah,
But let them that love Him shine forth as the sun in his strength.

---

* *Epizeuxis* (*q.v.*).

† Anaphora (*q.v.*).

‡ Asyndeton (*q.v.*).

‖ Some critics have quoted this as a specimen of the low moral standard of theScriptures, not seeing that it is merely telling us what the heathen woman (Sisera's mother) said! And in that woman's language we have the key to the victory which one woman won; and to the vengeance which another woman wrought.

§ *Aposiopesis* (*q.v.*).

Rom. xi. 33.—" How unsearchable (ἀνεξερεύνητα, **anex***ereuneeta*) *are* his judgments, and his ways past finding out (ἀνεξιχνίαστοι, **anex***ichniastoi*) ! "

Here, the two important words are rendered still more emphatic by commencing with the same syllables.

His judgments are **anex***ereuneeta* (unsearchable), and His ways **anex***ichniastoi* (untrackable).

This means that His judgments are incomprehensible, and His ways untrackable. The former word occurs nowhere else in the N.T.; the latter only here, and in Eph. iii. 8, where it is rendered "unsearchable" :— " The unsearchable riches of Christ." This does not merely vaguely express that Christ's riches are uncountable or untold, but that they *cannot be traced out.* The context shows that this present interval between "the sufferings of Christ" and "the glory that should follow," had been kept a secret (μυστήριον, *musteerion*, or *mystery*), and had not been revealed, until it was made known by the Spirit through Paul (Rom. xvi. 25, 26. Eph. iii. 2-11. Col. i. 26, 27). The prophets sought to know the secret as to " what or what manner of time " the Spirit of Christ which was in them did signify : but, it was *untrackable ;* they could not follow it : His ways were " past finding out."*

1 Thess. i. 2.—"We give thanks to God always for you all." The last words are emphasized by being put as a beautiful Homœo-propheron. The Greek is πάντοτε περὶ πάντων (**P***antote* **P***eri* **P***antōn*), *i.e.*, always concerning you all.

1 Thess. v. 23.—We give our own rendering: " And may the God of peace Himself sanctify you wholly (ὁλοτελεῖς, **holo***teleis*), and may your whole being (ὁλόκληρον, **holo***kleeron*), the spirit, and the soul, and the body, be preserved (*i.e.*, reserved, see 1 Pet. i. 4. 2 Pet. ii. 4, 9, 17 ; iii. 7. Jude 6, 13), unblamable at (ἐν) the parousia (presence or coming) of our Lord Jesus Christ."

Here the two words are " **holo***teleis kai* **holo***kleeron*."

Heb. i. 1.—" God who at sundry times and in divers manners, etc." πολυμερῶς καὶ πολυτρόπως πάλαι (pol*ymerōs* και pol*ytropōs* pala*i*), " *in many parts* and *many ways of old.*"

Here, there is both *Homœopropheron* and *Homœteleuton* : the two words both beginning with *poly*- and ending with -*ōs*.

---

* See *The Mystery*, by the same author and publisher.

HOMŒOTELEUTON; or, LIKE ENDINGS.

The Repetition of the same Letters or Syllables at the end of Successive Words.

Hō'-mœ-o-tel-eu'-ton. From ὅμοιος (*homoios*), *like*, and τελευτή (*teleutee*), *an ending*, *i.e.*, words with *like endings*.

This is the opposite Figure to *Homœopropheron;* and is used when successive words end with the same or similar letters or syllables.

These two figures are for the most part involved in others which affect the whole of the connected words; and therefore we shall meet with other examples as we proceed.

Mark xii. 30.—"This is the first commandment." In the Greek this sentence consists of three words, each ending with the same syllable: αὕτη πρώτη ἐντολή (*haut*ee *prōt*ee *entol*ee); and thus our attention is called to this weighty saying.

1 Pet. i. 3, 4.—"Blessed *be* the God and Father of our Lord Jesus Christ, which according to his abundant mercy hath begotten us again unto a lively hope by the resurrection of Jesus Christ from the dead, to an inheritance incorruptible, and undefiled, and that fadeth not away."

Here, the *Homœoteleuton* emphasizes the wondrous character of this inheritance :—

ἄφθαρτον, ἀμίαντον, ἀμάραντον (*aphthar*ton, *amian*ton, *amaran*ton), *uncorruptible, undefiled, unfading*. It is difficult accurately to reproduce the sound of this in English; except in marking it by the voice in reading aloud.

We might say, *incorruptible, indefilable, indestructible,* but this would be at the expense of exact accuracy in translating.

HOMŒOPTOTON: or, LIKE INFLECTIONS.

The Repetition of Inflections.

Ho-me-op¹-to-ton, from ὅμοιος (*homoios*), *like*, and πτῶσις (*ptōsis*), *a falling*, which in grammar means an *inflection* : *i.e.*, *a case* formed by the declining of a noun, or *tenses*, *etc.*, in the conjugation of a verb : as in the Latin message of Julius Cæsar, "*veni, vidi, vici*," *i.e.*, "I came, I saw, I conquered."

This figure differs from the two former, in that the endings are not only similar, but the similarity arises from the same inflections of verbs or nouns, etc.

It will be seen, therefore, that this figure belongs peculiarly to the Original languages, and cannot always be transferred in translation.

Rom. xii. 15.—" Rejoice with them that do rejoice, and weep with them that weep." Here the inflections of the infinitive and participles necessarily go together in the Greek, though, of course, not in the English.

χαίρειν μετὰ χαιρόντων.   Chairein meta chairontōn.

κλαίειν μετα κγαιόντων.   Klaiein meta klaiontōn.

The two lines likewise each exhibit an example of *Polyptōton* (*q.v.*), and also of *Homœopropheron* (*q.v.*):

The figure may be reproduced in English thus :—

> Be cheerful with those that are glad,
>
> Be tearful with those that are sad.

2 Cor. xi. 3.—Lest your minds "be corrupted from the simplicity (ἁπλότητος, *haplo***teetos**) and purity (ἁγνότητος, *hagno***teetos**), that is towards (*i.e.*, with reference to) Christ."

This is the reading of the R.V., and is according to all the critical Greek Texts.

In English the words may be rendered "simpleness and singleness."

2 Tim. iii. 2, 3.—In these two verses nearly all the words end in -οι (-*oi*), the masculine plural case-termination.

These similar *endings* may arise, as above, where the *words* are quite different. But when the two words are derived from the same root ; or when they occur, not in the language in which they appear, but in the language from which they are translated (either written or spoken), then the figure is called—

M

PAROMŒOSIS: or, LIKE-SOUNDING INFLECTIONS.

The Repetition of Inflections similar in Sound.

Par'-o-mœ-o'-sis. Greek, παρομοίωσις, *assimilation*, especially of words; *assonance.* It is from παρά (*para*), *beside*, and ὁμοίωσις (*homoiōsis*), *likeness.*

It is called also PAROMŒON, παρόμοιον, *nearly like.*

Sometimes it is wrongly called PARECHESIS, παρήχησις, *likeness of sound* or *tone*, from παρά, *beside*, and ἦχος (*eechos*), *a sound*, or ἤχησις (*eecheesis*), *a sounding.* But *Parechesis* properly describes the figure when one of the two words belongs to another language, or when the similarity is seen only in the original language and not in the translation. See *Parechesis.*

Matt. xi. 17.—"We have piped unto you, and ye have not danced (*ōrchee*sasthe); we have mourned unto you, and ye have not lamented (*ekop*sasthe)."

Here the two words have the same ending, *sasthe*, which greatly emphasizes the sense. It is as though we could render it, "We have piped for you, and ye never **stept**; we dirged for you, and ye never **wept**." Though this would emphasize it, it would be by another figure (*Paronomasia, q.v.*), because the words are similar, only vaguely in *sound*, but are not spelt with the same letters.

And, though the similar ending is caused by the inflection of the verb, it is not the figure of *Homœoptoton*, because the two words are derived from the same root, which lends an additional force and emphasis.

In the language of Syria, which Christ probably used, the words would be רְקָדָתוּן, *ra-ked-toon*, and אֲרְקָדָתוּן, *ar-ked-toon*, both verbs being from the same root and differing only in the conjugation: רקד, meaning in one, *to leap* or *spring up*, from joy (Ecc. iii. 4) and in the other *to leap* or *start up* from fear (Ps. xxix. 6 ; cxiv. 4, 6).*

John i. 5.—"And the light shineth in darkness; and the darkness comprehended it not."

---

* This figure is not preserved in the Hebrew translation of the New Testament; the word being רְקָדְתֶּם, rekadtem, and סְפַדְתֶּם, sephadtem, which is *Homœoteleuton* pure and simple.

The figure does not appear either in the English or the Greek: but in the Chaldee or Syriac language " darkness " is קְבַל, k'vel and " comprehended " is קְבַל, kabel.

John x. 1.—" He that entereth not in by the door into the sheep fold." Is beautifully expressed in the Syriac מִן תַּרעָא לְטִירָא, min tharô leteero.

1 Cor. i. 23, 24.—In these verses there is a beautiful combination of four different words from the same root in order to emphasize the solemnity of the passage :

" We preach Christ crucified (מִשׁכָל, mishkal, *a cross*, see Gen. xlviii. 14), unto the Jews a stumbling-block (מכשׁול, mikshol), and unto the Greeks foolishness (סכל, sekel), but unto them that are called, both Jews and Greeks, Christ the power (הַשׂכּיל, hishkeel) of God and the wisdom (שׂכל, sekel) of God."

ACROSTICHION : or, ACROSTIC.

Repetition of the same or successive Letters at the beginnings of Words or Clauses.

The English name of this figure is *Ac-ros'-tic,* and comes from the Greek, ἄκρος (*akros*), *at the point* (*i.e.,* at *the beginning* or *the end*) and στίχος (*stichos*), *a row* or *order.* It is a figure of repetition, not of the same letter, but of different letters at the beginning or end of words arranged in *lines.*

These letters may be thus repeated at the beginning or end of lines, either in the same *order* in which they occur in the Alphabet (in which case they are called ABECEDARIAN), or in some other certain or particular order, making the letters at the beginning or end of successive lines or words spell another word.

The Greeks gave it another name, PARASTICHIS (παραστιχίς) from παρα (*para*), *beside,* and στίχος (*stichos*), *a row,* meaning that the letters are placed at *the side.*

By the use of this peculiar figure, our attention is attracted to the special importance of certain passages. There are thirteen such passages in the Scriptures, and whenever we meet with them, we are asked to give great attention to them, and to put marked emphasis upon them.

The following are all the Acrostic or Abecedarian passages in the Bible, in which the order of the Alphabet is followed :—

Pss. ix. and x.—These two Psalms are linked together by an irregular alphabet running through, and thus combining the two. Ps. ix. beginning with א and Ps. x. with ל, which begins the last half of the alphabet.

The figure tells us that we are to connect these two Psalms together, and shows us that we are to read them together, and that their subject is one : *viz.:* "the man of the earth" (x. 18), the Antichrist ; whose days, character, and end they give. While " the Great Tribulation " is referred to twice (ix. 9 and x. 1). לְעִתּוֹת בַּצָּרָה, "*times of trouble.*" A phrase which occurs only in these two places.

Other significant expressions also occur in each of the two Psalms :

"Arise," ix. 19, x. 12 ; " the oppressed," ix. 9, x. 18 ; " forget not the poor," ix. 12, x. 12 ; "the heathen," ix. 5, 15, 17, 19, 20, and x. 16.

Ps. ix. is "the expectation of the poor" (18). Ps. x. is "the desire of the meek" (17).

The acrostic alphabet is incomplete and irregular, like the "times" which these Psalms describe. We cannot reproduce the two Psalms here, but can only indicate the Acrostic in them :—

א commences each of the four lines of verse 1 ; ב, verse 2 ; ג, verse 5 ; ד is wanting ; ה, verse 6 ; ו, verses 7, 8, 9, 10 ; ז, verse 11 ; ח, verse 13; ט, verse 15; י, verse 17; כ, verse 18. ל, x. 1 ; מ, verse 5; y, verse 8; נ, ס, פ, צ are wanting; ק, verse 12, is repeated from ix. 19 in order to call our attention to the same words of the same prayer ; ר is found in verse 14 ; ש, twice in verse 15; ת, in verse 17.

We must believe that the Acrostic is purposely incomplete, but what the design and the lesson may be must be left to the patient students of God's word. It may be that it is to correspond with these "times of trouble," for they also will be broken up and incomplete.

Ps. xxv.—Here again the Acrostic is designedly irregular, proving its genuineness rather than suggesting its corruption.

This design is shown by the fact that, in Ps. xxxiv., the same letter ו is omitted, and the same letter פ is duplicated by being added for the last verse. Ps. xxv. 22 and xxxiv. 22 commence with the same word פָּדָה (*pahdah*), "*redeem*," and both verses thus marked contain a similar sentiment: Ps. xxiv. 22, "Redeem Israel, O God, out of all his troubles": and xxxiv. 22, "The LORD redeemeth the soul of his servants." These two verses are thus made to stand out by themselves.

The Acrostic letters are thus distributed :—א, verses 1 and 2 ; ב, verse 2 (second word) ; ג, verse 3 ; ד, verse 4 ; ה, verse 5 ; ו omitted ; , verse 6 ; ח, verse 7 ; ט, verse 8 ; י, verse 9 ; כ, verse 10 ; ל, verse 11 ; מ, verse 12 ; נ, verse 13 ; ס, verse 14 ; y, verse 15 ; פ, verse 16 ; צ, verse 17 ; ק omitted ; ר, verse 18, 19 ; ש, verse 20 : ת, verse 21 ; (repeated), verse 22.

Ps. xxxiv.—Here, as in Ps. xxv., the sixth letter ו is omitted, the alphabet ending at verse 21; and the פ repeated thus puts verse 22 outside the alphabetical series.

Thus far the two Psalms (xxv. and xxxiv.) are framed on the same model.

In this Psalm, with the above exception, there is one letter left for each verse in its order.

Ps. xxxvii.—Here the series is complete. The y being masked behind the preposition ל (in the word לעולם, *for ever*, verse 28), and the ת behind the conjunction ו "*but*," in verse 39.

Every letter has two verses of two lines each, except three : ‫ר‬, verse 7 ; ‫כ‬, verse 20, and ‫ק‬, verse 34, which have but one verse of three lines each.*

The Acrostic is as follows :—‫א‬ commences verse 1 ; ‫ב‬, verse 3 ; ‫ג‬, verse 5 ; ‫ד‬, verse 7 ; ‫ה‬, verse 8 ; ‫ו‬, verse 10 ; ‫ז‬, verse 12 ; ‫ח‬, verse 14 ; ‫ט‬, verse 16 ; ‫י‬, verse 18 ; ‫כ‬, verse 20 ; ‫ל‬, verse 21 ; ‫מ‬, verse 23 ; ‫נ‬, verse 25 ; ‫ס‬, verse 27 ; ‫לע‬, verse 28, third line ("they are pre-served for ever ") ; ‫פ‬, verse 30 ; ‫צ‬, verse 32 ; ‫ק‬, verse 34 ; ‫ר‬, verse 35 ; ‫ש‬, 37 ; ‫ות‬,† verse 39.

Ps. cxi.—The acrostic here is perfect. The Psalm has twenty-two lines, which commence successively with the twenty-two letters of the Hebrew alphabet.

Ps. cxii. is formed on precisely the same model, and the two Psalms form a pair, Ps. cxi. being occupied with Jehovah and Ps. cxii. with the man that feareth Jehovah. They may be thus compared—the letters marking the *Correspondence* (*q.v.*).

Ps. cxi.

cxi. | *a* | 1-3.—‫א‬ His righteousness for ever.

           b | 4-8.—‫ו‬ Gracious and full of compassion; ever mind-ful of His covenant.

           c | 9, 10.—‫פ‬ His covenant and praise for ever.

Ps. cxii.

cxii. | *a* | 1-3.—‫א‬ His righteousness for ever.

           b | 4-8.—‫ו‬ Gracious and full of compassion ; in ever-lasting remembrance.

           c | 9, 10.—‫פ‬ His exaltation for ever.

Ps. cxix.—This Acrostic Psalm differs from every other. It consists of 176 verses, divided into 22 groups of eight verses each : $(8 \times 22 = 176)$. The eight verses of each group begin with the same letter. For example : the first eight verses each begin with *Aleph* ‫א‬ (A), the second eight with *Beth* ‫ב‬ (B) ; and so on through the whole Psalm.

It is very difficult to preserve this in a translation, and impossible where the letters of one language are not the same either in power or number or order.

It so happens, however, that the *ninth* portion (verses 65-72), in which each verse begins with *Teth* ‫ט‬ (T), begins also with T in the Authorized Version in all the verses except two (67 and 71). These

---

* It is noteworthy that the first of these (‫ד‬) occurs seven verses from the beginning ; the last (‫ק‬), seven verses from the end ; while the middle letter (‫כ‬) is the middle of the whole Psalm.

† Ginsburg's Hebrew Bible omits the Vau (‫ו‬).

can be easily made to begin with T also, by changing the word
"Before" in verse 67 to *Till;* and the words "It is" in verse 71 to
'Tis. Then it will exactly correspond to the Hebrew original.

Attempts have been made to render other portions in a similar
manner, but with little success. What comes naturally in an Original
Text, must be somewhat forced in translating it into another language.
We offer the following as an example:—

A.

Ah! the happinesses of the perfect in the way,
　　Such as walk in the law of Jehovah.
Ah! the happinesses of the keepers of His testimonies,
　　Who seek Him with their whole heart.
Assuredly they have not worked iniquity :
　　In His ways they ever walked.
As to Thy commandments—Thou hast commanded us,
　　That we should diligently keep them.
Ah! *Lord*, that my ways were prepared
　　To keep Thy statutes.
Ashamed, then, I shall never be,
　　While I have respect unto all Thy commandments.
All my heart shall praise Thee in uprightness,
　　While I learn the judgments of Thy righteousness.
All Thy statutes also I will keep :
　　Leave me not utterly.

B.

By what means shall a young man cleanse his way ?
　　By taking heed thereto according to Thy word.
By every means my heart hath sought Thee :
　　Let me not err from Thy commandments.
Besides, I have laid up Thy word in my heart,
　　That I might not sin against Thee.
Blessed art Thou, O Jehovah,
　　Teach me Thy statutes.
By my lips have I recounted
　　All the judgments of Thy mouth.
By walking in Thy Mandate's way,
　　I found joy beyond all wealth.
By Thy precepts shall I guide my musings,
　　And shall pore o'er Thy paths,
By thy statutes shall I be delighted ;
　　Thy word I shall not forget.

Ps. cxlv.—Here the Acrostic is perfect, with the exception of the letter *Nun*, נ (N), which comes between verses 13 and 14.

It has evidently dropped out through the carelessness of some scribe; for it must have been in the manuscripts from which the Septuagint, Vulgate, Syriac, Arabic and Æthiopic Versions were made, as they contain the verse. One Hebrew MS. has been found by Dr. Ginsburg containing the verse; which reads, "The Lord is faithful in all His words, and holy in all His works."

Moreover, it falls in with the structure of the Psalm, for the member, in which verse *nun* (נ) occurs, consists of verses 13-20 and is as follows:—

> a | 13. "Thou," second person.
>
>   b | 14. "He," third person.
>
> *a* | 15, 16. "Thou," second person.
>
>   *b* | 17-20. "He," third person.

The members b and *b* thus commence with similar words.

The Psalm is "David's Psalm of praise." It is the only Psalm that is dignified by this title. It is a special Psalm, therefore, and the Acrostic marks it as such, there being exactly 22 verses, one letter for each verse, and each verse consisting of two lines.

The structure (see under *Correspondence*) shows that it consists of seven members, arranged alternately, the subject of the first being *Praise promised*, and that of the second, *Praise offered* in fulfilment of that promise.

It is as follows:—

Psalm cxlv.

A¹ | 1, 2. Praise promised (first person) for Jehovah Himself.

  B¹ | 3. Praise offered (third person) to Jehovah.

A² | 4-7. Praise promised (first and third persons alternately) for Jehovah's works.

  B² | 8, 9. Praise offered (third person) for Jehovah's works.

A³ | 10-12. Praise promised (third person only) for Jehovah's kingdom.

  B³ | 13-20. Praise offered (third person) for Jehovah's kingdom.

A⁴ | 21. Praise promised (first and third persons) (יברך, *shall bless*, as in verse 10).

Prov. xxxi. 10-31 is a perfect alphabetical Acrostic, marking and calling our attention to this song in praise of a virtuous woman.

Döderlein calls it "*a golden A B C for women*." It follows here, the words of a faithful mother. The following is the structure of the passage :—

> A | 10. The woman and her worth.
> B¹ | 11, 12. Her husband.
> C | 13-22. Her work.
> B² | 23. Her husband.
> C | 24-27. Her work.
> B³ | 28, 29. Her children and her husband.
> A | 30, 31. The woman and her worth.

Like Ps. cxlv. it consists of twenty-two verses, and each verse contains two lines.

Lam. i. is an acrostic chapter. It consists of 22 verses, each of which commences with a successive letter of the alphabet, and each consists of three lines, except verse 7 (ז, *Zayin*) which contains four lines.

Lam. ii. is the same, except that in this case it is verse 19 (ק, *Koph*) which contains four lines. ע and פ (verses 16 and 17) are transposed.

Lam. iii. is different. It consists of 66 verses ; the first three each commencing with א (A) ; the second three each commencing with (B), and so on. Here, also as in chap. ii., ע and פ (verses 46-48 and 49-51) are transposed.

Lam. iv.—Here, there are 22 verses, each verse commencing successively with the letters of the alphabet, and consisting of two lines. Here, also as in chaps. ii. and iii., the ע and פ (verses 16 and 17) are designedly transposed.

These are all the Alphabetical Acrostics.

There are, however, others, to which our attention is called by the Massorah, as well as by their being written in larger characters in certain Manuscripts.

In these cases the Acrostic letters spell certain words. But these are no more accidental than those which are alphabetical. Other acrostics have been found ; but, as they are without Massoretic or Manuscript authority (and, therefore, probably are undesigned) we do not notice them.

Ps. xcvi. 11.—The Massorah has a rubric calling attention to the name of Jehovah here in a complete sentence of four words :—*

---

* Reading the English words backwards.

ישמחו השמים ותגל הארץ

earth-the   glad-be-let-and   heavens-the   rejoice-Let.

" Let the heavens rejoice, and let the earth be glad " (lit., " *Let-rejoice the-heavens and-let-be-glad the-earth*).

This is the great truth and the grand climax of God's purposes, which the Psalms as a whole set forth and declare. Especially so in this fourth book of the Psalms, which reveals those purposes in relation to the earth.

Ps. xcvi. is a call to "all the earth" (verse 1) to sing the " new song," and Ps. xcvii. is, or rather will yet be, the earth's glad answer to that call.*

Esther.—In the Book of Esther four times the name of Jehovah occurs in the form of an Acrostic.†

Jehovah had declared (Deut. xxxi. 16-18) that if His people forsook Him He would hide His face from them. Here this threatening was fulfilled. But, though He was hidden from them, He was present, working for them, to deliver them. Hence the outward form of the book is in harmony with the circumstances of the people : Jehovah was not *with* them, but He was *for them;* and therefore, though His name does not occur so that it may be sounded and pronounced by the voice, it appears, so that it may be visible to the opened eyes.

Further, the four Acrostics are all different from each other.

THE FIRST

occurs in i. 20. It is formed by the *initial* letters, for the event was initial. It is formed by spelling the word *backwards*, for Jehovah was *overruling* and turning back the wisdom of man. The four Hebrew words are

היא וכל הנשים יתנו

i.e., " *All the wives shall give,*" or exhibiting a similar Acrostic in English—

" **D**ue **R**espect **O**ur **L**adies

shall give to their husbands, etc."

This counsel resulted in bringing Esther to the throne; so that when Haman's plot had been made, it might be thwarted (iv. 14).

THE SECOND

(v. 4) is formed, as before, by the *initial* letters; for Jehovah was

---

* See *A Key to the Psalms,*

† See a separate pamphlet on this subject by the same author and publisher, *The Name of Jehovah in the Book of Esther.*

initiating His plans: but it is spelt *forwards* (as in our common form of Acrostics), for Jehovah was *ruling* rather than overruling. The four Hebrew words are—

יבוא המלד והמן היום

"*Let the King and Haman come this day,*" or,

"Let Our Royal Dinner

be graced this day by the King and Haman." The name of Jehovah appears in the invitation; for He was to be there in order to bring the counsels of man to nought and "take the wise in their own craftiness."

Nothing happens at the dinner beyond an invitation to Haman to dine at the royal table the next day. "Then went Haman forth that day joyful and with a glad heart" (v. 9). Yes, "that day," for it was his last!

THE THIRD ACROSTIC

(v. 13) is the beginning of the end. Hence it is formed by the *final* letters, for the end was approaching. It is read *backwards,* for the Lord was *turning back* all the proud purposes of Haman. Haman goes home to his wife and says:

זה איננו שוה ל

"*This availeth me nothing,*" or "Yet am I

saD, foR nO avaiL

is all this to me."

This sadness was a precursor of, and foreboded, his coming execution. Haman dines on the morrow with the king and queen; and events soon reached their climax; which comes in

THE FOURTH ACROSTIC

(vii. 7). It is again in the *final* letters, for Haman's *end* had come. It is spelt *forwards*; for Jehovah was *ruling,* and had determined the event:—

כי כלתה אליו הרעה

Haman saw "*that evil was determined against him,*" or, "For he saw that there was

eviL tO feaR determineD

against him by the King."

There was indeed evil to fear: for that evil had been determined not by King Ahasuerus, but by Jehovah: and the evil came swiftly upon him, for he was at once taken out and hanged.

Thus these four Acrostics at once conceal and reveal the Name of Jehovah, and emphasize the four pivots on which the whole history turns.

Est. vii. 5.—This is another Acrostic for which there is Massoretic authority; the letters being written in larger characters in certain MSS.

It is that name by which God revealed himself to Moses and to Israel, the " I AM," who had come down to deliver them. He who came down to deliver them in Egypt now comes down to deliver them in Persia : and, though He was not revealed, nor His name written, yet He has caused it to be emblazoned on the pages of the history.

When Ahasuerus learned from Esther, that "the Jews' enemy" had laid his plot to destroy the whole nation, he cries out in his ignorance,

"WHO IS HE, AND WHERE IS HE

that durst presume in his heart to do so?" He uses the words of which the *final* letters spell the name EHJHE (pronounced *E-he-yhe* both backwards and forwards).

הוּא זֶה וְאֵי זֶה הוּא

EHEYEH knew who Haman was and where he was. He who is the great " I am," sees the end from the beginning; and both rules and over-rules all events for the accomplishment of His purposes, and for the deliverance of His People. (See Ex. ii. 23-25 ; iii. 14, 15).

Acrostics, like many other figures, occur only in the Originals, and cannot be reproduced in a translation.

It is possible also for figures to occur in a translation which are not in the Hebrew or Greek! In such cases they are, of course, either accidental or designed. In either case they are of no value or weight.

An Acrostic can be made, for example, in the English of John iii. 16, which is accidental. But as it may be useful to some in teaching others, we note it here—

John iii. 16.

G od so loved the world, that he gave his

O nly begotten

S on, that whosoever believeth in him should not

P erish, but have

E verlasting

L ife.

This verse contains the good news of the Gospel, which, by a singular coincidence, is the very word which may thus be written as an Acrostic.

2. OF THE SAME WORD.

(a) In the Same Sense.

There are no less than twelve ways in which the *same word* may be repeated in the *same sense* in the same sentence. The first is called

EPIZEUXIS: or, DUPLICATION.

The Repetition of the Same Word in the Same Sense.

When the word is repeated in close and immediate succession, no other word or words coming between, it is called GEMINATIO, pronounced *Gem-i-nā'-tio*, which means *a doubling, duplication, a re-doubling.* It is also called ITERATIO (*It'-er-ā-ti-o*), *iteration;* CONDUPLICATIO (*con-dū-pli-ca'-tio*), *conduplication,* or *full doubling.*

When the words do not immediately succeed each other, but are separated by one or more intervening words, the figure is then called EPIZEUXIS, pronounced *Ep'-i-zeux'-is.* It is the Greek word ἐπίζευξις, from ἐπὶ (*epi*), *upon,* and ζεύγνυμί (*zeugnumi*), *to yoke,* or *join closely together.* The intervening words thus form the yoke which joins the repeated words.

The Latins give this figure the name of SUBJUNCTIO (*Sub-junc'-tio*), which is derived from the Greek and has exactly the same meaning, *subjoining* (from *jugum, a yoke*).

We may give the figure the English name of " Duplication," " Gemination," " Iteration," or " Repetition."

It is a common and powerful way of emphasizing a particular word, by thus marking it and calling attention to it.

In writing, one might accomplish this by putting the word in larger letters, or by underlining it two or three times. In speaking, it is easy to mark it by expressing it with increased emphasis or vehemence.

How important for us to notice, in the Scriptures, the words and expressions which the Holy Spirit has thus marked and emphasized in order to impress us with their importance !

Gen. vi. 17.—" And, behold, I, even, I, do bring a flood of waters. upon the earth."

Gen. vii. 19.—" And the waters prevailed exceedingly."

Here, as in other passages, the doubled adverb is used for a superlative. מְאֹד מְאֹד (*meōd, meōd*), **greatly, greatly.** We have the same words in xvii. 2, "And I will multiply thee **exceed-ingly** (*meōd, meōd*). So also verse 6, **exceeding**; and verse 20, **exceedingly**; xxx. 43, "And the man increased **exceedingly** (*meōd, meōd*)"; Ex. i. 7, "*Waxed* **exceeding**"; Num. xiv. 7, "It is an **exceeding** (*meōd, meōd*) good land"; 1 Kings vii. 47, "Because they were **exceeding** (*meōd, meōd*) many"; 2 Kings x. 4, "But they were **exceedingly** (*meōd, meōd*) afraid"; Ezek. ix. 9, "And Judah is **exceeding** (*meōd, meōd*) great"; xvi. 13, "And thou wast **exceeding** (*meōd, meōd*) beautiful"; xxxvii. 10, "An **exceeding** (*meōd, meōd*) great army."

Gen. xxii. 11.—"And the angel of the LORD called unto him out of heaven, and said, **Abraham, Abraham**."

This is the first occurrence of this figure, used of names. There are *ten* such in the Scriptures (the number *ten* completing the cycle of Divine order).*

Seven of these are used by God to man (four of which are in the Old Testament, and three in the New), the other three being used under other circumstances. When thus used, the figure calls special attention to the occasion or to the person, and to some solemn moment of importance in the action, or of significance in the words.

1. Abraham, Abraham (Gen. xxii. 11). ⎫ Old ⎫ Used
2. Jacob, Jacob (Gen. xlvi. 2). ⎬ Test. ⎬ by
3. Moses, Moses (Ex. iii. 4). ⎪ (4) ⎪ God
4. Samuel, Samuel (1 Sam. iii. 10). ⎭ ⎪ to
5. Martha, Martha (Luke x. 41). ⎫ New ⎬ men.
6. Simon, Simon† (Luke xxii. 31). ⎬ Test. ⎪ (7)
7. Saul, Saul (Acts ix. 4). ⎭ (3) ⎭
8. Lord, Lord (Matt. vii. 21, 22. Luke ⎫ Used
   vi. 46; xiii. 25). ⎪ under
9. Jerusalem, Jerusalem (Matt. xxiii. 37. ⎬ other
   Luke xiii. 34). ⎪ circum-
10. Eloi, Eloi (Mark xv. 34. Matt. xxvii. 46. ⎪ stances.‡
    Ps. xxii. 1). ⎭ (3)

---

* See *Number in Scripture*, by the same author and publisher.

† "Satan hath desired to have you (ὑμᾶς, *plural*) that he may sift you (ὑμᾶς, *plural*) as wheat: but I have prayed for thee (σοῦ *singular*) that thy faith fail not."

Satan "sifts" to get rid of the wheat! Christ "fans" to get rid of the chaff (Matt. iii. 12).

‡ Each of these three examples is unique. In No. 8 it is the name of the Lord used by man. In No. 9 it is used of God's city and people by Christ. In No. 10 it is used of God by Christ.

It is to be noted that in raising the dead the Lord Jesus never used this figure! As much as to say it needed no emphasis whatever to make the dead hear His voice (see Mark v. 41).

The disciples may cry, "**Master, Master,** we perish!" (Luke viii. 24), but He calmly rebukes the winds and the waves.

Gen. xxv. 30.—"And Esau said to Jacob, "Feed me, I pray thee, with that same red *pottage*."

The Hebrew having no superlative, doubles the adjective (see under *Idiom*), הָאָדֹם הָאָדֹם (*hah-ahdom, hah-ahdom*), red, red, *i.e.,* this very red [*food*] ; or, this deliciously red *food*.

Ex. ii. 12.—"And he looked this way and that way."

Here the Hebrew כֹּה וָכֹה (*kōh vahkōh*), this and this, is well translated, The repetition emphasizes the fact that he looked in every direction. See also Josh. viii. 20, *i.e.,* in any direction. 2 Kings ii. 8. Also Josh. viii. 33, מִזֶּה וּמִזֶּה (*mizzeh oomizeh*), *i.e.,* on all sides. 1 Kings ii. 36, "Go not forth thence any-whither" אָנֶה וָאָנָה (*ahneh vah-ah-nah*), this and this. 2 Kings iv. 35, see margin.

Ex. iv. 16.—"And he shall be, even he shall be to thee instead of a mouth :" *i.e.,* he shall surely be, etc.

Ex. xv. 16.—"Till thy people pass over, O Lord, till the people pass over, which thou hast purchased:" *i.e.,* till thy people have completely passed over and are safe on the other side.

Ex. xxiii. 30.—"By little and little I will drive them out from before thee," מְעַט מְעַט (*me-at, me-at*), "little, little, I will drive, etc. :" *i.e.,* I will drive them out by very slow degrees. There s no "by" or "and" in the Hebrew of this passage. These words should be in italics. The figure is beautifully rendered in English idiom, where two adverbs are used to express the superlative.

Ex. xxviii. 34.—"A golden bell and a pomegranate, a golden bell and a pomegranate upon the hem of the robe round about:" *i.e.,* alternately.

Ex. xxxiv. 6.—"And the Lord passed by before him, and proclaimed, **JEHOVAH, JEHOVAH.**"

Here, if we were to translate the figure idiomatically, it means that He proclaimed *the wonderful name, Jehovah!* (which He did in the sixth and seventh verses).

Lev. vi. 12 (5).—"And the priest shall burn wood on it every morning." בַּבֹּקֶר בַּבֹּקֶר (*babbōker, babbōker*), **morning, morning:** *i.e.,* every morning, regularly, and without intermission.

Lev xxiv. 8.—"Every sabbath he shall set it in order before the Lord continually."

Hebrew בְּיוֹם הַשַּׁבָּת בְּיוֹם הַשַּׁבָּת (*Beyōm hashabbath beyom hashabbath*), on-the-day-of the-Sabbath, on-the-day-of the-Sabbath: *i.e.*, every Sabbath, with emphasis on the word "every," *i.e.*, every Sabbath without fail.

Num. xvii. 12, 13 (27, 28).—After Aaron's rod had been brought forth, the people were frightened and cried to Moses, " Behold, we die, **we perish, we all perish.** Whosoever **cometh near, cometh near** unto the tabernacle of the LORD shall die: shall we be consumed with dying?"

Here the figure is הַקָּרֵב הַקָּרֵב (*hakkahrev hakkahrev*), *cometh near, cometh near.* It is idiomatically translated by the A.V., but literally by the R.V.

There is also the repetition of the word אָבָדְנוּ (*ahvadnoo*), "we perish, we all perish."

Deut. xxviii. 43.—Here the figure is really translated idiomatically, and not literally. " The stranger that *is* within thee shall get up above thee very high," *i.e.*, מַעְלָה מָּעְלָה (*mahlah, mahalah*), high, high ; " and thou shalt come down very low " (*i.e.*, מַטָּה מָטָּה (*mattah, mattah*), low, low).

Thus the figure emphasizes the depth of the misery into which Israel should be brought if they would not hearken to the voice of Jehovah (verse 15).

Judges v. 22.—

> " Then did the horsehoofs stamp:
>> By reason of **the pransings, the pransings** of his
>> mighty ones."

מִדַּהֲרוֹת דַּהֲרוֹת (*middaharoth daharoth*), *i.e.*, the violent pransings, if translated idiomatically. See under *Idiom*.

1 Sam. ii. 3.—" Talk no more exceeding proudly."

גְּבֹהָה גְבֹהָה (*gevohah, gevohah*), **proudly, proudly,** *i.e.*, arrogantly or haughtily.

Here the repeated adjective is idiomatically translated as a superlative.

2 Sam. vii. 5.—" Go and tell my servant David (Heb., to my servant, to David), Thus saith the LORD, Shalt thou build, **me** a house for **me** to dwell in ? "

Here there is great emphasis to be placed on the repeated pronoun, " me," in order to rebuke the popular and universal thought of the natural heart, which ever says, " See now, I dwell in a house of cedar, but the ark of God dwelleth within curtains."

2 Sam. xviii. 33.—" O my son Absalom, my son, my son Absalom ! Would God I had died for thee, O Absalom, my son, my son ! "

Here the figure emphasizes the vehemence of David's grief.

2 Kings iv. 19.—" And he said unto his father, My head, my head." (רֹאשִׁי רֹאשִׁי, *roshee, roshee.*)

How eloquent : and what a volume is contained in this simple figure, so naturally used by the child; as an English child would say, " My poor head."

2 Chron. iv. 3.—" Compassing the sea round about." סָבִיב סָבִיב (*sahveev, sahveev*), around, around: *i.e.*, completely round, all around. The same repetition is used, to express complete surrounding, in Ezek. xxxvii. 2 ; xl. 5, 14, 16 (twice), 17, 25, 29, 30, 33, 36, 43 ; xli. 5, 6, 7, 8, 10, 11, 12, 16 (the second " round about "), 17, 19 ; xlii. 15, 20 ; xliii. 12. In all these descriptions of the new and future Temple, the repetition of סָבִיב סָבִיב (*sahveev, sahveev*) emphasizes the completeness of the measurements.

Ps. xxii. 1.—" My God, my God (אֵלִי אֵלִי, *Elee, Elee*), why hast thou forsaken me ? "

Who can tell the depth of meaning and of feeling, which this figure here reveals ? It is thus impressed upon us, because it cannot be expressed by words. See Mark xv. 34.

Ps. lxvii. 6, 7 (7, 8).—

" God shall bless us,
God shall bless us : "

i.e., God shall really and truly bless us in very deed.

Ps. lxxvii. 16 (17).—

" The waters saw thee, O God,
The waters saw thee."

(See under *Prosopopœia.*) Thus emphatically describing Ex. xiv.

Ps. xcvi. 13.—

" For He cometh, for He cometh : "

i.e., for He shall surely come.

Ps. cxviii. 11.—Twice " They compassed me about "; and in verses 15 and 16, we have three times " The right hand of the Lord."

Ps. cxxxvii. 7.—" Remember, O LORD, the children of Edom in the day of Jerusalem ; who said, Rase *it*, rase *it*, *even* to the foundation thereof," *i.e.*, עָרוּ עָרוּ (*ahroo, ahroo*), " Down-with-it, down-with-it," or we might render the figure, *utterly overthrow it.*

N

Prov. xx. 14.—"*It is* naught, *it is* naught, saith the buyer : but when he is gone his way, then he boasteth."

Heb. is רַע רָע (*ra, ra*), *i.e.*, "very bad," or "worth nothing." What a picture of Eastern bargaining!

Ecc. iii. 18.—Lit., I said in my heart respecting the estate of the sons of men that . . . they, even they are like beasts."

Here the figure of *Pleonasm* (*q.v.*) first emphasizes the word "men," and then the *Epizeuxis* again increases that emphasis.

Ecc. vii. 24.—"That which is far off and exceeding deep, who can find it out ?"

עָמֹק עָמֹק (*ahmok, ahmok*), deep, deep : *i.e.*, as it is translated, "exceeding deep."

Isa. vi. 3.—The holiness of Jehovah is emphasized beyond measure, and the three persons in one God are indicated by the thrice repeated "Holy, holy, holy *is* the Lord of hosts." Here the highest degree of holiness is ascribed to Jehovah.

Isa. xxi. 9.—"Babylon is fallen, is fallen": to emphasize the certainty and the greatness of the fall of that great city, and the completeness of its final overthrow. See also Rev. xviii. 2.

Isa. xxvi. 3.—"Thou wilt keep him in perfect peace."

Here the figure is idiomatically *translated*. The Hebrew reads (see margin) שָׁלוֹם שָׁלוֹם (*shalom, shalom*), peace, peace, thus emphasizing the word and denoting *much peace, great peace;* or, as in A.V., "perfect peace." In lvii. 19 and Jer. vi. 14 it is not thus translated.

Professor Driver mentions this duplication of words as being a post-Isaian feature of literary style (*Introduction to the Literature of the Old Testament*, pp. 233, 234). He says, " The literary style of chapters xl.-lxvi. is very different from that of Isaiah ": one of the " literary features " being the repetition of words. It is remarkable, as being characteristic of the wisdom and acumen assumed by the higher critics, that though Professor Driver mentions the repetition of שלום שלום, *peace, peace*, in Isa. lvii. 19, he does not mention the very same repetition in xxvi. 3 : which is an evidence of the very unity of the two parts of Isaiah which he is seeking to disprove.*

* The same applies to other arguments : *e.g.*, Dr. Driver says (p. 227) that certain words " occurring in chapters xl.-lxvi. point to a later period of language than Isaiah's age . . . A remarkable instance is afforded by lxv. 25 . . . where יחד, the common Hebrew word for *together*, is replaced by כאחד, an expression modelled upon the Aramaic כחדא, and occurring besides only in the latest books of the Old Testament." But Professor Driver does not mention the fact that the word

Isa. xxviii. 10.—This is probably the ironical language of the
" scornful men" (verse 14), introduced by the Ellipsis of verse 9:
" Whom [*say they*] shall he teach knowledge ? . . . for [*it is*] precept
upon **precept**; **precept** upon **precept**; **line** upon **line**; **line** upon
line; **here a little**, *and* **there a little**." And, then, the Prophet
retorts: " For (or Yea, verily) with stammering lips (marg., *stammerings of lips*) and another tongue will he speak (marg., *he hath spoken*) to
this people."

In the English the *Epizeuxis* is not perfect, because the word
" upon " comes between, but in the Hebrew the words follow each other
closely.

$$\text{צַו לָצָו צַו לָצָו קַו לָקָו קַו לָקָו}$$
$$\text{זְעֵיר שָׁם זְעֵיר שָׁם}$$

i.e., " For it is *tzav latzav; tzav latzav; kav lakav, kav lakav; zēhr
shāhm, zēhr shāhm.*"

See also verse 13.

Isa. xl. 1.—" **Comfort ye, comfort ye** my people, saith your
God." Here the *Epizeuxis* consists of one word in the Hebrew,
נַחֲמוּ נַחֲמוּ (*nachmoo, nachmoo*) : and calls our attention to the passage ;
while it emphasizes the plenitude of that comfort wherewith Jehovah
has determined to comfort His People Israel at no distant date.

Isa. li.—In this Scripture we have three calls emphasized by this
figure.

A¹ | li. 9-11. A call to the arm of Jehovah :—" **Awake, awake,** put on
strength, O arm of the LORD."

B¹ | 12-16. Followed by comfort.

A² | 17-20. A call to Jerusalem :—" **Awake, awake,** stand up,
O Jerusalem."

B² | 21-23. Followed by comfort.

A³ | lii. 1, 2. A call to Zion :—" **Awake, awake,** put on strength,
O Zion."

B³ | 3-12. Followed by comfort.

Isa. lvii. 19.—" I create the fruit of the lips :—**Peace, peace** to
him that is far off and to *him that is* near," etc. : *i.e.,* great peace,
perfect peace as in xxvi. 3 (*q.v.*).

---

occurs in the earlier books of the Bible : so early indeed as Gen. iii. 22; xlix. 16.
1 Sam. xvii. 36, and elsewhere. True, in these passages it is in the construct
state : but that makes no difference so far as the argument is concerned. Moreover, as this very word יַרְדֵּן occurs in chap. i. 28, 31, and xi. 6, 7, as well as in
lxvi. 17, it is an argument against Dr. Driver's division of Isaiah into two halves.

Jer. iv. 19.—" My bowels, my bowels ! " to emphasize the great distress experienced.

Jer. vi. 14.—" They have healed also the hurt *of the daughter** of my people slightly, saying **Peace, peace**; when there is no peace." Here the figure contrasts with the fact that there was no peace for Jerusalem the fact that her false prophets continually promised plenty of peace, much peace.

Jer. xxii. 29.—" O **earth, earth, earth**, hear the word of the LORD."

Ezek. xxi. 9-13 (Heb. 14-18).—" A **sword, a sword** is sharpened, and also furbished."

This is to call our attention to "the sword of the LORD," *viz.*, Babylon, and to show that His sword is a sword for *war*, and not a sword worn for *honour*. This is the key to this difficult passage. That there are difficulties is seen the moment we observe the italics, note the marginal alternatives, and consult the commentators !

Jehovah's sword was not like the sword of His son Judah, not like his " rod " or " sceptre " (verse 10), which was merely for honour, and was no use against a tree. But this sword (verse 10) " contemneth the rod (or sceptre) of my son, *as [it despiseth]* every tree (or wood)." Verse 12 should be, " Cry and howl, son of man : for it shall be upon my people, it *shall be* upon all the princes of Israel : my people shall be delivered to the sword : smite therefore upon *thy* thigh " (which was the symbol of fear in man, as beating the breast was in woman). Verse 13. " Because *it was* proved, and what? (*i.e., what will happen ? what will be the result ?*) if *the sword* shall not despise the wood, saith the Lord ! It will not be, saith Adonai Jehovah ! " (*i.e., it will not despise it ! it will destroy it !*)

Thus we have the sword of Jehovah emphasized : and the structure of these verses explains their meaning.

A | 8-10. The sword of Jehovah (Babylon).   Its sharpness and brightness.

    B | -10. Its contempt for the rod or sceptre of His son Judah.

A | 11, 12. The sword of Jehovah.   Its destroying power.

    B | 13. Its contempt for the wooden rod or sceptre of Judah.

The point is that the sword of the Lord is a sword of war, not of honour ; and its power is so great that the sceptre of Judah (which was of *wood*) will not withstand it.

---

* These words are supplied, apparently from chap. viii. 11, 21.

Ezek. xxi. 27.—"I will **overturn, overturn, overturn** it; and it shall be no *more* until he come whose right it is; and I will give it him": *i.e.*, I will completely and thoroughly overturn it.

The threefold *Epizeuxis* emphasizes the completeness of the overthrow of the throne of David; hence, by implication, the certainty of the promised fulfilment of the prophecy that He who is David's Son and David's Lord, shall surely reign upon that same throne according to Luke i. 32, 33, and many other Scriptures.

Ezek. xxii. 2.—"**Wilt thou judge, wilt thou judge?**": *i.e.*, Wilt thou really and truly judge? See under *Heterosis*.

Ezek. xxxiii. 11.—"**Turn ye, turn ye** from your evil ways."

Ezek. xxxiv. 11.—"**Behold, I, even I,** will both search my sheep and seek them out."

And verse 20: "**Behold I, even, I,** will judge between the fat cattle and between the lean cattle."

Thus does Adonai Jehovah emphasize what He will do in consequence of the unfaithfulness of the shepherds, who fed not His flock, but fed themselves. (See under *Ellipsis*, page   ).

Ezek. xxxiv. 17.—"I judge between **cattle** and **cattle**." (שֶׂה לָשֶׂה.)

For the emphasis in this passage, see the notes on it under the figure of *Ellipsis* (page 40).

Dan. v. 11.—"Whom **the king** Nebuchadnezzar **thy father, the king,** *I say*, **thy father,** made master of the magicians": *i.e.*, thy father the great and mighty king Nebuchadnezzar.

Dan. x. 19.—"**Be strong,** yea, **be strong:**" *i.e.*, be very strong.

Zeph. i. 14.—"The great day of the LORD is **near, is near,** and hasteth greatly": *i.e.*, is very near.

Matt. v. 37.—"But let your communication (R.V., speech) be, **Yea, yea; Nay, nay:** for whatsoever is more than these cometh of evil."

Here the figure emphasizes the fact, not that we are forbidden to *say*, "Yea" or "nay" *twice;* but that we are merely to say, "Yes" or "no," and not to indulge in vehement asseverations and oaths; "for whatsoever is more than these cometh of evil."

Matt. xxiii. 37.—"O **Jerusalem, Jerusalem,** thou that killest the prophets," etc.: emphasizing the pathetic appeal by the exceeding guilt of the city in killing the prophets of Jehovah.

Luke xxiii. 21.—"Crucify *him*, crucify him," emphasizing the vehemence of the cry, and the determination of the priest-led people.

John i. 51.—" Verily, verily, I say unto you." ἀμὴν, ἀμήν (*ameen ameen*). Twenty-five solemn sayings of the Lord Jesus are thus emphatically marked in John's Gospel: *viz.*, i. 51; iii. 3, 5, 11; v. 19, 24, 25; vi. 26, 32, 47, 53; viii. 34, 51, 58; x. 1, 7; xii. 24; xiii. 16, 20, 21, 38; xiv. 12; xvi. 20, 23; xxi. 18. It might prove a useful study to trace the sequence of truth in these successive statements.

Apart from the Repetition, which occurs only in the fourth Gospel, there is something to be learnt from the number of times the word occurs.*

Heb. x. 37.—"Yet a little while." Lit., how little, how little." Greek: ἔτι γὰρ μικρὸν ὅσον ὅσον (*eti gar mikron* hoson hoson).

Eph. iii. 9.—Lit. " And to enlighten all [*as to*] what [*is*] the dispensation of the Mystery which has been hidden away, away, from the ages in [or by] God." Showing the completeness with which the secret was hidden in former times. Compare Rom. xvi. 25, and Col. i. 26.

---

* See *Number in Scripture*, by the same author and publisher.

ANAPHORA ; or, LIKE SENTENCE-BEGINNINGS.

The Repetition of the same Word at the beginning of successive Sentences.

A-naph'-o-ra, from two Greek words, ἀνά (*ana*), *again*, and φέρω (*pherō*), *to bring* or *carry*. It means *a carrying back*, *reference*, or *repeating over again*.

This figure is also sometimes called EPANAPHORA : which is the same word with ἐπί (*epi*), *upon*, prefixed. In Latin it is called RELATIO.

This figure is so-called because it is the repeating of the same word at the beginning of successive clauses : thus adding weight and emphasis to statements and arguments by calling special attention to them.

Anaphora differs from *Epibole* (*q.v.*). In the case of *Epibole* several words are repeated, consisting of a sentence or phrase ; whereas, in *Anaphora* only one word is thus repeated.

Scripture abounds with this figure, which adds great importance to many of its solemn statements. We give a few examples :—

Deut. xxviii. 3-6.—
" **Blessed** shalt thou be in the city, and
blessed shalt thou be in the field :
blessed shall be the fruit of the body,
    and* the fruit of thy ground,
    and the fruit of thy cattle,
      the increase of thy kine,
    and the flocks of thy sheep.
blessed shall be thy basket and thy store,
blessed shalt thou be when thou comest in,
blessed shalt thou be when thou goest out."

See the same figure in verses 16-19 with the word " **cursed** " repeated at the beginning of successive sentences.

2 Sam. xxiii. 5.—According to the Hebrew, each line begins with the word כִּי (*kee*), *For*.

---

* See *Polysyndeton*.

" For is not my house thus with God ?
　　For He hath made with me an everlasting covenant, ordered
　　　　in all things and sure,
　　For this is all my salvation, and all my desire.
　　For shall He not make it to prosper ? "

These four lines are in the form of an introversion :—

　　a | Question.

　　　　b | Answer and Reason.

　　　　b | Answer and Reason.

　　a | Question.

In a and *a* the question is concerning David's house ; while in b
and *b* the subject is Jehovah's covenant.　See under *Correspondence.*

Ps. iii. 1, 2 (2, 3).—

" Many are they that rise up against me,
　　Many there be which say of my soul," etc.

Ps. xciv. 3, 4.—" How long ? "　In verse 4 it should be
repeated by *Ellipsis* and put in italics twice.　In the A.V. it is thus
put only once ; in the R.V. not at all, the figure not being seen.

Ps. cxv. 12, 13.—

" He will bless us.
　　He will bless the house of Israel.
　　He will bless the house of Aaron.
　　He will bless them that fear the LORD."

This figure stands here in immediate contrast with the figure of
Epistrophe (*q.v.*) in verses 9-11, where the same phrase *ends* successive
clauses.

See also in the Songs of Degrees, Ps. cxxi. 7, 8 ; cxxii. 6, 7 ; cxxiii.
2, 3 ; cxxiv. 1, 2, and 3, 4, 5 ; cxxvi. 2 ; cxxvii. 1 ; cxxviii. 5, 6 ; cxxix. 1, 2.

Ps. cxlviii. 1-4.—" Praise " is seven times repeated at the
beginning of successive sentences.　So also in the whole of Ps. cl.

Isa. li. 1, 4, 7.—*Three* times we have the Divine call " Hearken
unto me."

Jer. i. 18.—" Behold, I have made thee this day a defenced city,
　　and an iron pillar,
　　and brazen walls—
　　against the whole land,
　　against the kings of Judah,
　　against the princes thereof,
　　against the priests thereof, and
　　against the people of the land."

The figure, here, emphasizes the fact that the prophet in being God's spokesman was recognised as the " man of God,"* but also (and therefore) as necessarily " against " man. For, inasmuch as man's thoughts and man's ways are always the opposite of God's, he who is for God cannot help being opposed to man.

Jer. iv. 23-26.—We have " I beheld " four times repeated; to enchance the solemnity of the desolation of Jehovah's judgments.

Jer. v. 17.—" **They shall eat up** " is three times repeated; to emphasize the complete devouring of the land by the enemy.

Jer. l. 35, 36.—" **A sword** " is four times repeated; to emphasize the slaughter in the destruction of Babylon.

Jer. li. 20-23.—*Ten* times we have the words " **with thee** " repeated to amplify the statement in verse 20. "Thou art my battle ax," spoken of Israel.

Hos. iii. 4.—" For the children of Israel shall abide many days
    without a king,
    and **without** a prince,
    and **without** a sacrifice,
    and **without** an image,
    and **without** an ephod,
    and **without** teraphim."

Here there is something more than a simple *Polysyndeton* (q.v.), as another word is joined with the conjunction.

The employment of this figure emphasizes the present desolation of Israel.

Micah v. 9-13.—"**I will cut off**" is repeated *four* times; to amplify and extend the prophecy in verse 9.

Micah vii. 11, 12.—Here we have " **In that day** " repeated to emphasize the time; and " **from** " to amplify the places whence they shall come.

Zeph. . 2, 3.—"**I will consume**," *three* times repeated, indicates the solemnity of the threatening and the certainty of its execution.

Matt. v. 3-11.—The word " **Blessed** " nine times repeated.

Matt. v. 22.—
    " **Whosoever** is angry, etc.
    Whosoever shall say, etc."

---

* See *The Man of God*, by the same author and publisher ; price one penny.

Matt. xi. 7, 8, 9.—" What went ye out . . . to see ? "

This question is three times repeated ; to emphasize and call attention to the fact that, though they were all attracted to John, yet they rejected him, and his ministry, and his testimony. See under *Erotesis.*

Matt. xi. 18, 19.—This is lost in the English Version: as in the Greek the verb " came " is put out of its natural place (by the figure of *Hyperbaton*, *q.v.*), and is made to commence the two successive sentences.

It is a very remarkable *Anaphora.*

Rom. viii. 33, 34, 35.—Here we have the three questions, each beginning with " **Who shall ?** "   (See page 87).

The first two questions should be answered like the third.

> " **Who shall** lay anything to the charge of God's elect ?
>> **Shall** God that justifieth ?
> **Who** is he that condemneth ?
>> **Shall** Christ that died, . . . ?
> **Who** shall separate us . . . ?
>> **Shall** tribulation ? etc."

1 Cor. iii. 9.—This, too, is hidden in the translation.   In the Greek the figure is clearly seen.

> " **God's** fellow-labourers we are :
> **God's** husbandry,
> **God's** building, ye are."

Note, that the fellow-labourers are ourselves with one another ; and not we who are fellow-labourers with God. We are not to dishonour God by bringing Him down and making Him one of ourselves. The popular explanation is only another instance of man's nature, which made him so easy a prey to Satan's temptation-promise, " Ye shall be as gods " (Gen. iii. 5).

Herein lies the difference between the First Adam and the Last, between the First man and the Second. The first man thought equality with God was a thing to be grasped at : but the Second Man did not so consider it (Phil. ii. 6, R.V.). Equality with God was not a thing to be obtained, but a thing to be either inherently possessed (as He possessed it as the Son of God), or to be received as the gift of God (as He received it as the Son of Man).

1 Cor. vi. 11.—" And such were some of you,

> **but** ye are washed,
> **but** ye are sanctified,
> **but** ye are justified in the name of the Lord Jesus and by the Spirit of our God."

1 Cor. vi. 12.

    " **All** things [or rather *meats*] are lawful unto me, but

    All things [to *eat*] are not expedient:

    All things [or *meats*] are lawful for me [*to eat*], but I will
        not be brought under the power of any."

Here the figure is combined with another called *Mesarchia* (*q.v.*).

1 Cor. xi. 3.—" But I would have you know that

    the head of every man is Christ: and

    the head of the woman is the man: and

    the head of Christ is God."

We have here *Polysyndeton* (*q.v.*), as well as an irregular
Climax (*q.v.*).

1 Cor. xii. 8-11.—We have the repetition of the words, "**to
another**." In the Greek the word is not exactly the same in each
case. It is ἄλλος (*allos*), **another** (of the same kind), six times, and
ἕτερος (*heteros*), **another** (of a different kind), *twice*, in connection
with "faith" and "kinds of tongues."*

    " **To one** is given by the Spirit the word of wisdom,

    to another (*allos*) the word of knowledge by the same Spirit.

    To another (*heteros*) faith by the same Spirit;

    to another (*allos*) the gifts of healing by the same Spirit.

    To another (*allos*) the working of miracles;

    to another (*allos*) prophecy;

    to another (*allos*) discerning of spirits;

    to another (*heteros*) divers kinds of tongues;

    to another (*allos*) the interpretation of tongues:

but all these worketh that one and the selfsame Spirit, dividing to
every man severally AS HE WILL," and not as we may will or
" claim."

1 Cor. xiii. 4.—In the first three verses we have the figure of
Polysyndeton (*q.v.*), or "many ands." In verses 4-7, we have a com-
bination of two figures:—*Asyndeton* (*q.v.*), or "no-ands"; and
Anaphora in the repetition of the word "Charity" (verse 4).

In verse 7, the Greek order of the words is: Charity

    " **all things** beareth,

    all things believeth,

    all things hopeth,

    all things endureth.'

---

* It is probable that *Heteros* marks a new class; while *Allos* refers to subdivisions of the same class.

In verse 8 :
>   " Whether there be prophecies, they shall fail ;
>   whether there be tongues, they shall cease ;
>   whether there be knowledge, it shall vanish away."

In verse 9 :
>   " In part we know, and
>   in part we prophesy."

In verse 11.   " When I was a child,
>   as a child I spake,
>   as a child I understood,
>   as a child I thought."

2 Cor. xi. 26.—Here we have the repetition of "in perils" eight times.

2 Cor. vii. 11.—We have the repetition of the word "yea" to increase the effects and results of true godly sorrow for sin in *seven* particulars.   Referring to *six* different aspects of their sorrow as manifested in three different directions.

The word rendered "yea" really means *but ;* and it may be preserved by supplying the *Ellipsis :*—what carefulness (or rather earnestness) it wrought in you, but not earnestness merely—that is saying too little—

>   but self-defence, ⎱
>   but indignation, ⎰ in respect of themselves.
>   but fear,   ⎱
>   but vehement desire, ⎰ in respect of Paul.
>   but zeal,   ⎱
>   but revenge, ⎰ in respect of him who had done the wrong.

The first "but" combines the additional figure of *Epitasis* (*q.v.*), which is here an emphatic addition to a statement or argument of six particulars.

Eph. vi. 12.—" For we wrestle not
>   against flesh and blood, but
>   against principalities,
>   against powers,
>   against the rulers of the darkness of this world,
>   against spiritual wickedness in high places."

This is to emphasize the fact that our conflict is *spiritual,* and that Satan's sphere of operations is not immorality or crime, but religion.   See all the references to him in Scripture, and note how opposed they are to popular Satan-myth of the world and of Christendom.

Phil. iii. 2.—Note the repetition of the word " **beware.**"

Phil. iv. 2.—" I **beseech** Euodias, and **beseech** Syntyche."

Phil. iv. 8.—We have here the repetition of the word " **what-**soever things" with which the figure of *Asyndeton* (*q.v.*) is combined, in order to emphasize the important conclusion " **Think on these things:**" and these things, in eight nouns are arranged in the figure of *Chiasmus* (*q.v.*).

1 John i. 1-3.—

> " **That which** was from the beginning,
> **which** we have heard,
> **which** we have seen with our eyes,
> **which** we have looked upon . . .
> **That which** we have seen and heard declare we unto you."

This five-fold repetition of the pronoun ὃ (*ho*), *which*, emphasizes with great solemnity the subject of the epistle which is opened thus in so stately a manner.

Jas. v. 7, 8.—Three times we have " **Be patient** " with reference to the coming of the Lord.

Jas. v. 13, 14.—*Twice* we have the question " **Is any ?** "

> " **Is any** among you afflicted ?
> Let him pray.
> **Is any** merry ?
> Let him sing psalms.
> **Is any** sick among you?
> Let him call," etc.

Here are contrasted *prayer* and *praise;* and praying with singing. Teaching us that prayer is not to be sung.*

1 John iii. 5, 8.—" **He was manifested** to take away our sins; . . . the Son of God was manifested** that he might destroy the works of the devil."

Here the two great purposes of Christ's manifestation are declared : the one present, and the other future ; the one in grace now, and the other in power hereafter ; the one in sufferings, and the other in glory.

Other examples of *Anaphora* may be seen in Gal. i. 8, 9. Rev. vii. 5-8 (with *Epistrophe*), and elsewhere : for these examples are given only as specimens.

---

* See *Intoned Prayers and Musical Services*, by the same author and publisher.

EPANALEPSIS; or, RESUMPTION.

The repetition of the same word after a break, or parenthesis.

Ep'-an-a-lep'-sis. It is from the Greek ἐπί (*epi*), *upon*, ἀνά (*ana*), *again*, and λῆψις (*leepsis*), *a taking ;* and means *a taking up upon again.*

In Latin it is called RESUMPTIO (*Re-sump'-tio*).

In this figure the word is *resumed*, rather than repeated, from the beginning of another sentence : and when the word is resumed after a parenthesis it is called APOSTASIS, and the parenthesis is closed by the *apostasis.*

A-pos'-ta-sis is from the Greek ἀπόστασις, which means *a standing away* or *off from, distance, interval ;* the repeated word which *resume* the statement or argument, standing away at a distance from the first word.

Moreover, the word so taken up and resumed may not be necessarily from the beginning of the sentence, bnt it may be *taken up again* from the middle or from any other part, as in this sentence :—

"The persecutions undergone by the Apostles were a trial to their faith, and a confirmation to ours ; a trial to them," etc.

It differs from *Anaphora* (*q.v.*) in that the repeated words are not immediately successive, but are separated by a break or parenthesis : the repetition being a *resumption* of what the writer or speaker had already before begun to say.

Rom. iii. 25, 26.—" Whom God hath set forth *to be* a propitiation through faith in his blood, to declare [his righteousness for the remission of sins that are past, through the forbearance of God ; to declare, *I say*], at this time his righteousness : " etc.

1 Cor. iv. 11, 13, where the words in verse 11, "unto this present hour," are taken up again at the end of verse 13, " unto this day."

1 Cor. x. 25, 29.—Here, after a parenthesis (verses 26-28) the word " conscience " is repeated from the end of verse 25, and the argument is resumed in verse 29.

Eph. iii. 1, 14.—" For this cause I, Paul, [the prisoner of Jesus Christ . . . (then after a parenthesis of thirteen verses he *resumes* in verse 14), For this cause] I bow my knees," etc.

Phil. i. 22, 24.—In verse 20, the apostle had been speaking of glorifying God " by life, or by death." For, if he lived, it would be

"Christ," and if he died, it would be "gain" to him, and would release him and give him rest from all his labours. The real conclusion is that if he continued to abide in the flesh it would be better for them. But this conclusion is interrupted by the mention, parenthetically, of a third thing, which made him unable to say which of the two (living or dying) he would really prefer, because this third thing was so much better than either of the other two; for it was—the return of Christ. Then, having mentioned this, he takes up the statement again, repeating the beginning of verse 22 (" in the flesh ") and continuing it in verse 24.

Verse 23 :—" But if I live **in the flesh**, [this is the fruit of my labour (yet what I shall choose I wot not, for I am being pressed* out of† these two, having a strong desire unto the return,‡ and to be with Christ, which is a far, far better thing) : but to remain **in the flesh**] is more needful for you " [*i.e.*, than dying—not better than Christ's return].

He had told the Thessalonian saints that " we which are alive and remain shall not precede those who are asleep. For the Lord Himself shall descend from heaven with a shout, with the voice of the archangel and with the trump of God; and the dead in Christ shall first rise. Then we which are alive and remain shall be caught up together with them in clouds to meet the Lord in the air, and SO (οὕτω, *houtō*, *thus, in this manner*) shall we ever be with the Lord." There, is therefore, no other way of being with the Lord." The Spirit of God would not have written one thing to the Thessalonians and a different thing to the Philippians.

---

* συνέχομαι, I am being pressed.

† ἐκ occurs 857 times, and is never translated "betwixt" anywhere else, But it is 165 times rendered "out of."

‡ This is not the infinitive mood of the verb depart, but three distinct words. εἰς (*eis*), *unto*, τὸ (*to*) *the*, ἀναλῦσαι (*analusai*), *return*. This verb occurs in N.T. only in Luke xii. 36, " when he shall return from the wedding." It does mean, to depart, but from thence to here, not from hence to there. See Tobit. ii. 1. Judith xiii. 1. 1 Esd. iii. 3. Wisd. ii. 1 ; v. 12. Ecclus. iii. 15. 2 Mac. viii. 25 ; ix. 1 ; xii. 7 ; xv. 28. Josephus *Ant.* vi., 4, 1.

POLYSYNDETON ; or, MANY-ANDS.

The repetition of the word " and " at the beginning of successive clauses.

Pol'-y-syn'-de-ton. Greek, πολυσύνδετον, from πολύς (*polūs*), *many*, and συνδετόν (*syndeton*), *bound together;* hence, in grammar, it means *a conjunction* (from σύν (*syn*) and δεῖν (*dein*), *to bind*). The word, therefore, means *much bound together* or *many conjunctions.*

It is called also POLYSYNTHETON, from τίθημι (*titheemi*), *to put* or *place.* Hence *many puttings: i.e.,* of the same word—in this case of the word " and."

The English name for the Figure will, therefore, be MANY-ANDS. *Polysyndeton* is merely one special form of *Anaphora (q.v.) : i.e.,* it is a repetition of the same word at the beginning of successive sentences : but this is always one special word " and."

To understand the full significance and use of *Polysyndeton,* the student must consider along with it the opposite Figure *A-syndeton* (the same word *syndeton* with " a " prefixed, meaning *no,* instead of " poly," meaning *many*). See *A-syn'-de-ton, i.e.,* NO-ANDS (page 137).

The two Figures form a pair, and should be - studied together.

The Laws of Grammar decide for us how the conjunction "and" should be used. If we are enumerating a number of things, we (by usage) place the conjunction immediately before the last. This is the cold law, which leaves what we say without any special emphasis. But this law may be legitimately broken in two different ways for the sake of emphasis. In order to attract the attention of the hearer or reader, we may either use NO ANDS, or we may use MANY ANDS. Man may use these figures, however, without sufficient reason, and unwisely : but the Holy Spirit ever uses words in all perfection, and it behoves us carefully to note whatever He thus calls our attention to.

When He uses " No-ands," He does not ask us to stop and consider the various particulars which are enumerated, but to hasten on to some grand climax. In this case that climax which we read at the end, is the all-important matter on which the greatest emphasis is to be placed.

When He uses " many-ands," there is never any climax at the end. Instead of hurrying us on, breathlessly, to reach the important conclusion; we are asked to stop at each point, to weigh each matter that is presented to us, and to consider each particular that is thus added and emphasized.

One illustration of each will make this quite clear. We have an example of both in one chapter (Luke xiv.), and, strange to say, in connection with precisely the same four words.

In verse 13, we have *Asyndeton* (no-ands) : and in verse 21, *Polysyndeton* (many-ands).

In the former case (*Asyndeton*), we are not asked to consider the various classes of persons mentioned, but we are hastened on to the important and weighty conclusion :—

Verse 13, 14. " When thou makest a feast, call the poor,
—the maimed,
—the lame,
—the blind :

and thou shalt be blessed.''

In other words, we are taught that, though we are not obliged to make a feast at all, yet, even if we do, we can call whom we please : but, if we call such persons as are here described, there is a great blessing attached : hence, we are hurried over the enumeration of these classes to be told of this blessing. And, even then, it really does not matter much whether they are actually blind or lame, etc. The point is they must not be able to return it.

On the other hand, the Master's servant is commanded to " bring in " such persons to the Lord's feast, as a matter of simple obedience : and when he has done this, he has done no more than his duty, and is at the best, but an " unprofitable servant.'' Hence, by the use of this figure of *Polysyndeton* in verse 21, we are not hurried on to any climax at the end, but we are detained at each step, and are thus asked to consider carefully what is taught us by the mention of each of these various classes :—

" Go out quickly into the streets and lanes of the city,
and bring in hither the poor (*i.e.*, those whom no one would think of inviting, but who would welcome the invitation (xv. 1. Matt. xx 31) :—" the poor " who could not afford to buy " a piece of ground " (verse 18), or " five yoke of oxen " (verse 19).
and the maimed (*i.e.*, those who would be most unlikely to be able to say, " I have married a wife " (verse 20),
and the halt (χωλούς, as in verse 13, where it is translated " lame " : *i.e.*, those who could not " go " to use the oxen, or to " prove them,'' at the plough, verse 19),
and the blind (*i.e.*, those who could not say, " I must needs go and see " the piece of land which I have bought, verse 18).

Here, by this figure, instead of being hurried forward to a weighty conclusion we are led gently *backward* by each " and " to think of

o

these four classes, and to contrast them with those whom the Lord had just described in the preceding parable as making excuses.

These two illustrations will prepare us for the consideration of the two figures separately, and enable us to understand them.

We consider here only the illustrations of *Polysyndeton.* The examples of *Asyndeton* will be found under that figure (pages 137-148), which being *Elliptical, i.e.,* characterised by the omission of the word "and" has been placed under the First Division, Figures of Omission.

Gen. viii. 22.—Here the completeness of the covenant and the fulness of the blessing, and the certainty of the Divine promise, is set forth in a double four-fold description :—

" While the earth remaineth,
seedtime and harvest,
and cold and heat,
and summer and winter,
and day and night, shall not cease."

Gen. xix. 12.—" And the men said unto Lot
Hast thou here any beside ?
son-in-law,
and thy sons,
and thy daughters,
and whatsoever thou hast in the city, and bring them out of this place.'
See also verses 16, 19 ; and verse 17 for *Asyndeton.*

Gen. xxii. 9, 11.—The solemnity and deliberation of Abraham's actions is emphasised, and each is marked off from the other by this figure:—
and they came to the place which God had told him of;
and Abraham built an altar there,
and laid the wood in order,
and bound Isaac his son,
and laid him on the altar upon the wood :
and Abraham stretched forth his hand :
and took the knife to slay his son :
and the angel of the Lord," etc.

Gen. xxv. 34.—"Then Jacob gave Esau bread and pottage of lentiles ;
and he did eat
and drink,
and rose up,
and went his way :
And Esau despised his birthright."

Here our attention is drawn to the deliberateness of Esau's action. There is no haste in the words, as there was none in Esau's deed. Each part of it is minutely pointed out, and dwelt upon, as showing that Esau did not fall under some sudden temptation, but that he deliberately and wilfully " despised his birthright." (See Heb. xii. 16, 17.)

Gen. xliii. 8.—This is shown more clearly in the Hebrew; it is partly hidden in the A.V., to suit the English idiom. Here, the *Polysyndeton* is used to heighten the effect of Judah's appeal to his father to let them all depart and procure the food they so greatly needed. The Hebrew reads :—

" **And** Judah said unto Israel, his father, Send the lad with me,
and we will get up,
and we will go,
and we shall live,
and so we shall not die ;
also we,
also thou,
also our households."

Ex. i. 7.—Here the figure is employed in order to impress us with the marvellous increase of Israel by the Divine blessing (See Ps. cv. 24 ; cvii. 33).
" and the children of Israel were fruitful,
and increased abundantly,
and multiplied,
and waxed exceeding great,
and the land was filled with them,"

Josh. vii. 11.—Jehovah shows to Joshua (and to us) the greatness of Achan's sin, by bringing out emphatically all the acts which formed part of it. The Hebrew reads :—
" Israel hath sinned,
and they have also transgressed my covenant, which I commanded them ;
and (וְגַם), *vegam*, they have also taken of the accursed thing,
and have also stolen,
and have dissembled also,
and they have also put it among their own stuff."
Five times we have וְגַם (*vegam*), *and also*, in this verse.

Josh. vii. 24.—Here, to show the awful solemnity of the judgment executed upon Achan, and the magnitude of his sin,

twelve times we have the conjunction, eleven of the times with
וְאֶת (אֶת).
" And Joshua,
and all Israel with him, took Achan the son of Zerah,
and the silver,
and the garment,
and the wedge of gold,
and his sons,
and his daughters,
and his oxen,
and his asses,
and his sheep,
and his tent,
and all that he had :
and they brought them unto the valley of Achor."

1 Sam. xvii. 34-36.—Here David enhances the importance of
what he tells King Saul, by bringing out graphically each detail of that
which makes him a type of the Good Shepherd :—

" And David said unto Saul, Thy servant kept his father's sheep
and there came a lion
and a bear,
and took a lamb out of the flock :
and I went out after him
and smote him,
and delivered *it* out of his mouth :
and when he arose against me, I caught *him* by his beard,
and smote him,
and slew him.   Thy servant slew
both (גַּם) the lion,
and (גַּם) the bear.
and this uncircumcised Philistine shall be as one of them, etc."

2 Kings ii. 12, 14.—" And he took hold of his own clothes,
and rent them in two pieces :
and he took up (he took up also) the mantle of Elijah that fell from
him,
and went back,
and stood by the bank of Jordan ;
and he took the mantle of Elijah that fell from him,
and smote the waters,
and said, Where is the Lord God of Elijah ?

and when he also had smitten the waters, they parted hither and
    thither,
and Elisha went over."

All this to show us the importance, not of any great climax, but of
each part of that wondrous miracle.

2 Kings v. 26.—In the words of Elisha to Gehazi on his return
from Naaman, he brings out by the use of this figure all that was in
Gehazi's heart ; showing that he knew how Gehazi had already planned
and arranged how he should spend and lay out the money which he
had asked of Naaman.

"*Is it* a time to receive money,
and to receive garments,
and oliveyards,
and vineyards,
and sheep,
and oxen,
and menservants,
and maidservants ? "

1 Chron. xxix. 11-13.—Here the greatness and the goodness of
Jehovah is set forth in *David's Thanksgiving*. The whole structure* of
this thanksgiving is as follows :—

Praise.

A | a | 10-. David blessing Jehovah
   | b | -10. Jehovah's eternity.

      B | 11. Jehovah's greatness "above all."

      B | 12. Jehovah's goodness "unto all."

A | *a* | 13. David blessing Jehovah,
   | *b* | 14, 15. David's mortality.

Prayer.

C | 16. The House and its provision,

    D | 17. " I give " " mine heart." (Time past and present).

    D | 17-19. Prepare their heart to give. (Time to come).

C | 19. The house and its provision.

The figure occurs in B and *B* :—

" Thine, O LORD, is the greatness (Ps. cxlv. 3),
and the power (verse 12 and Ps. xxi. 14),

---

* For these *structures* see under *Correspondence* below.

and the glory (*beauty*, verse 13. Ps. xcvi. 6),
and the victory (*lustre*, 1 Sam, xv. 29),
and the majesty (Ps. xxi. 6) ; for all *that is* in the heaven
and in the earth (*is thine*):*

> Thine is the Kingdom, O LORD,
and thou art exalted as head above all,
and the riches ⎰ (The figure is lost by saying "both riches and
and the .honour ⎱   honour.)
> come of thee,
and thou reignest over all ;
and in thine hand *is* power
and might ;
and in thine hand *it is* to make great,
and to give strength unto all :
and now, our God, (not " Now therefore ") we thank thee,
and praise thy glorious name ! "

Ps. cvii. 35-37.—Here, to enhance the blessings which Jehovah bestows upon His people they are set forth with such distinctness that we are asked to dwell upon each one that goes to make up the whole :

> " He turneth the wilderness into a standing water,
and dry ground into watersprings,
and there he maketh the hungry to dwell, that they may prepare a
>   city for habitation;
and sow the fields,
and plant vineyards, which may yield fruits of increase."

Isa. ii. 11-19.—Here the figure is employed to set forth the completeness of the manner in which Jehovah will shake terribly the earth " (19, 21). There is another figure employed (see under *Synonymia*) : and this, with the structure, shows us the importance and solemnity of the whole passage. It commences with chap. ii., and ends with chap. iv.   Thus :—

> A | ii. 1-5. Promise.

> B | ii. 6-22. Threatening of judgment (general).

> B | iii.-iv. 1. Threatening of punishment (particular).

> A | iv. 2-6. Promise.

---

* Or, omitting the italics " because of all in the heavens and in the earth."

Then these members may be expanded thus :—

A. *The Promise*, ii. 1-5.

A | C | ii. 1, 2. Zion, its exaltation. All people flowing unto it.
  | D | 3-. What they say : " Come ye, . . we will walk, etc."
  | C | -3, 4. Zion, its rule. The word going out from it.
  | D | 5. What the people say : " Come ye, . . let us walk, etc."

Then the second member B, with which we have to do (the figure o *Polysyndeton* marking it and stamping it as a whole), may be expanded, thus :—

B. *Threatening of judgment (general)*, ii. 6-22.
*(With special reference to men.)**

E | F | 6-. Jehovah ceasing from His People.
  | G | -6-9. Reason. Because they exalt themselves before God, and humble themselves before their idols.
  | G | 10-21. Judgment. The People humbled, and Jehovah alone exalted. Idols abolished.
 | F | 22. " Cease ye from man," &c.

Once more, the member G may be expanded, thus :—

G. *The Judgment* (ii. 10-21).

G | H¹ | a | 10-. Concealment. " Go to the rock," etc.
   | b | -10. Reason : " For fear of the Lord," etc.
     | J | c | 11. Man abased. Jehovah exalted ⎫
       | d | 12-16. High things brought low ⎪   by
      | c | 17. Man abased. Jehovah exalted ⎬ Jehovah.
       | d | 18. Idols utterly abolished ⎭
 | H² | a | 19-. Concealment. " They shall go to the rocks," etc.
   | b | -19. Reason : " For fear of the Lord," etc.
    | J | 20-. Idols cast away by man.
 | H³ | a | 21-. Concealment, " to go into the clefts of the rocks."
   | β | -21. Reason : " For fear of the Lord," etc.

---

* In *B* (iii.-iv. 1) the reference is specially to women.
In *A* (iv. 2-6) the reference is :—

   a | 2. General.
    b | 3. To men.
     b | 4. To women.
   a | 6. General.

We may note in passing that in J we have Jehovah and Idols: while in *J* we have Man and his Idols.

Now, we are prepared to see how the judgment executed by Jehovah in J (verses 11-18) is further emphasized by the figure of *Polysyndeton;* as it is still further marked and emphasized by the figure of Synonymia (*q.v.*):—

J | c | 11. The lofty looks of man shall be humbled,
and the haughtiness of men shall be bowed down,
and the LORD alone shall be exalted in that day.
} MAN

d | 12-16. For the day of the LORD* of hosts *shall be* upon every *one* [or *thing*] *that is* proud and lofty,
and upon every *one* [*thing*] *that is* lifted up;
and he shall be brought low:
and upon all the cedars of Lebanon *that are* high and lifted up,
and upon all the oaks of Bashan,
and upon all the high mountains,
and upon all the hills *that are* lifted up,
} Jehovah's judgment on GOD'S WORKS (*seven members*).

and upon every high tower,
and upon every fenced wall,
and upon all the ships of Tarshish,
and upon all pleasant pictures.
} Jehovah's judgment on MAN'S WORKS (*four*).

c | 17. And the loftiness of man shall be bowed down,
and the haughtiness of men shall be made low;
and the LORD alone shall be exalted in that day.
} MAN.

d | 18. And the Idols, he shall utterly abolish.
} Jehovah's judgment on man's works.

This is the first mention of "the Day of the Lord." For the significance of this, see *Number in Scripture* by the same author and publisher.

Isa. iii. 17-iv. 1.—Here, we have, in these few verses, the "many ands" marking the minuteness of the Lord's judgment on the daughters of Zion.

These verses form one member (*B*) of the larger structure (see above), which may be expanded, as follows:—

B. iii.-iv. 1.   *Threatening of judgment* (*Particular*).

B | e | iii. 1-7. Threatening. What Jehovah will "take away" from Jerusalem and from Judah.
  f | 8-9-. Sin. Tongue, doings, countenance.
  e | -9-11. Threatening. "Woe, woe."
    f | 12. Sin. Weak and oppressive rulers (4, 4).
  ε | 13-15. Threatening. Jehovah will judge and rule.
    φ | 16. Sin. Feminine haughtiness.
  η | 17-iv. 1. Threatening. What Jehovah will "take away" from the daughters of Zion.

Here, in the last member η (iii. 17-iv. 1), we have *twenty-six* "ands," which the reader can notice for himself.

Isa. xxxvii. 37.—Here, to enhance the overthrow of Sennacherib's army, and to show how completely Jerusalem was delivered from the siege which he made against it, we read:—

" So Sennacherib king of Assyria departed,
and went,
and returned,
and dwelt at Ninevah."

Jer. xxxi. 28.—Here the figure emphasises both the "scattering" and the " gathering " of Israel:—

" And it shall come to pass, that, like as I have watched over them
  to pluck up,
and to break down,
and to throw down,
and to destroy,
and to afflict; so will I watch over them, to build
and to plant, saith the LORD."

Hag. i. 11.—To enhance the description of the troubles which had fallen upon Israel, a nine-fold " and " is employed (nine being the number of *judgment*)* :—

---

* See *Number in Scripture*, by the same author and publisher.

"**And** I called for a drought upon the land,
and upon the mountains,
and upon the corn,
and upon the new wine,
and upon the oil,
and upon *that* which the ground bringeth forth,
and upon men,
and upon cattle,
and upon all the labour of the hands."

Matt. vii. 25.—Here the perfect security of the "wise man," who hears the sayings of Jesus, and is likened unto a man who built his house upon a rock, is emphasized by a five-fold "*and*" (five being the number of *grace*).

"**And** the rain descended (on the roof),
and the floods came (at the foundations),
and the winds blew (at the sides),
and beat upon that house :
and it fell not."

While, on the other hand, in verse 27, the insecurity of the "foolish man," who hears, but does not, the sayings of Jesus, is set forth by a six-fold "and" (six being the number of *man* and of *human independence and imperfection* :—

"**And** the rain descended,
and the floods came,
and the winds blew,
and beat upon that house ;
and it fell :
and great was the fall of it."

Matt. xxiv. 29-31.—Here, to emphasize the wondrous events of the day of the Lord, and the order of them, the figure is used.

" Immediately after the tribulation of those days
　　The sun shall be darkened,
and the moon shall not give her light,
and the stars shall fall from heaven,
and the powers* of the heavens shall be shaken,
and then shall appear the sign of the Son of Man† in heaven :
and then shall all the tribes of the earth mourn,
and they shall see the Son of Man† coming in the clouds of heaven
　　with power and ‡great glory.
and he shall send his angels with a trumpet and ‡a great sound (marg.),

---

* See under *Catachreesis*.　† See under *Idiom* and *Synecdoche*.　‡ See under *Hendiadys*.

and they shall gather together his elect from the four winds,* from one end of heaven to the other."

This important passage describes the events which shall succeed "immediately after" the great tribulation (which was the subject of Old Testament prophecy. See Ps. ix. 9; x. 1. Jer. xxx. 7. Joel ii. 11, 31. Amos v. 18. Zeph. i. 14, etc. Rev. vi. 17) : so that there is, therefore, no interval for a millennium of peace and blessedness before the coming of the Lord.

This is the coming of the Lord *with* His saints (the Church), not His coming *for* what will already have previously taken place before the Great Tribulation begins. The Second coming corresponds with the First Coming (so-called) in that the first part of it answers to His "coming forth" at Bethlehem (Micah v. ii.), and the second part answers to the "cometh unto" at Jerusalem (Zech. ix. 9), the latter being referred to in 2 Thess. ii. 2, R.V., and the former revealed in 1 Thess. iv. 16, 17.

Consequently his title, "The Son of Man," agrees with the scope of the passage; which has to do with dominion on the earth. While the *elect* can only be the elect of Israel (see Deut. xxx. 4 (lxx.) Zech. ii. 6, etc.).

Mark iii. 31-35.—Here each part of the instructive scene is emphasized to attract our attention :—

"There came then his brethren,
and his mother,
and standing without, sent unto him, calling him :
and the multitude sat about him,
and they said unto him, Behold thy mother
and thy brethren without seek for thee :
and he answered them, saying, Who is my mother, or my brethren ?
and he looked round about on them which sat about him,
and said, Behold my mother,
and my brethren !   For whosoever shall do the will of God, the same
    is my brother,
and my sister,
and mother."

The scene which is thus emphasized is connected with verse 21 as appears *from the structure*† of this whole passage.

---

* See under *Metonomy* (of the adjunct).

† For what is meant by Structure see below under *Correspondence.*

Mark iii. 21-35.

A | a | 21-. Jesus's kindred (margin),
   | b | -21-. Their interference with him.
   | c | -21. Their disparagement of him.
   | | d | 22-. The Scribes' first charge: " He hath a devil."
   | | e | -22. The Scribes' second charge : " By the prince of the devil scasteth he out devils."
   | B | e | 23-27. His answer to the second charge.
   | | d | 28, 29. His denunciation of the first charge.

A | a | 31-. Jesus's kindred,
   | b | -31, 32. Their interference with Him,
   | c | 33-35. His disparagement of them.

From this structure we learn that (1) the object of the visit, is explained in verses 21-31, and that (2) the reference of verse 28 is to the first charge of the Scribes—explaining what is called "the unpardonable sin ": and (3) that the " kindred " of verse 31 included his mother in the design and conspiracy.

Luke i. 31, 32.—Here the birth of the Lord Jesus is presented as it is in Isa. ix. 6, 7, with the " sufferings " overleaped, and the present season of His rejection not noticed. Our attention is called to all the wondrous details and separate parts of His glory, which, though thus linked together and connected with His birth, are not *immediately* consecutive.

" **And**, behold, thou shalt conceive in thy womb,
and bring forth a son,
and shalt call his name JESUS.   He shall be great,
and shall be called the Son of the Highest:
and the Lord God shall give unto him the throne of his father David :
and he shall reign over the house of Jacob for ever ;
and of his kingdom there shall be no end."

It is Matt. i. 21, 23, which refers to Isa. vii., and thus connects the King with the " sufferings ": while it is Luke, which refers to Isa. ix., and thus connects "the Man " with the glory that shall follow.†

Luke vii. 11-18.—Here, there is no climax, but we are asked to stop and dwell upon each additional circumstance, and see why it is mentioned, and what is its peculiar lesson for us :—

---

* For these structures see below under *Correspondence.*

† See below under Rev. xii.

And it came to pass the day after, that he went into a city called Nain :
and many of his disciples went with him,
and much people.   Now, when he came nigh to the gate of the city,
    behold, there was a dead man carried out, the only son of his mother,
and she was a widow :
and much people of the city was with her :
and when the Lord saw her, he had compassion on her,
and said unto her, Weep not.
and he came
and touched the bier :
and they that bare *him* stood still.
and he said, Young man, I say unto thee, Arise.
and he that was dead sat up,
and began to speak ;
and he delivered him to his mother ;
and there came a fear on all :
and they glorified God, saying, That a great prophet is risen up
        among us ;
and, That God hath visited his people,
and this rumour of him went forth throughout all Judæa,
and throughout all the region round about ;
and the disciples of John showed him of all these things."

Here in these eight verses we have no less than twenty " ands,"
each introducing a fact and a statement for our earnest consideration ;
each fraught with truth and teaching. The last, for example, is the
reason why John sent his disciples to Jesus.   This reason is not given
in Matt. xi. 2 : which is thus explained. John was languishing in
prison; and, when he heard that Jesus was raising the dead, he
naturally wondered, if Jesus were " He that should come," why he
should be suffering in prison.

See also Mark iii. 1-6, the miracle of the man with the withered
hand.

Luke vii. 38.—Here the woman's devotion to the Lord is set
forth in a gracious five-fold enumeration of the parts of which it was
made up :—

" **And** stood at his feet behind *him* weeping,
and began to wash his feet with tears,
and did wipe them with the hairs of her head,
and kissed his feet,
and anointed *them* with the ointment."

Five " ands " in one verse !

Luke x. 27.—Here a five-fold description is given in order to set forth that love which is "the fulfilling of the Law " :—

" Thou shalt love the Lord thy God with all thy heart,
and with all thy soul,
and with all thy strength,
and with all thy mind :
and thy neighbour as thyself."

It is sometimes said that we are never commanded to do that which is impossible. But the truth is, the Law is given, and the perfection of this command is thus emphasized, in order to reveal and bring to light our own *impotence*, that we may thankfully cast ourselves on God's *omnipotence* in that Saviour whom He has provided and anointed.

Luke xii. 45, 46.—Here, the sin of the wicked servant, who said, "My lord delayeth his coming," is set forth in a fourfold description:—
" **And** shall begin to beat the menservants and maidens,
and to eat
and drink,
and to be drunken."

Likewise his punishment is described in a fourfold manner :—

" The lord of that servant will come in a day when he looketh not for *him*,
and at an hour when he is not aware,
and will cut him in sunder,
and will appoint him his portion with the unbelievers."

What a solemn fact it is that those who put off the hope of the Lord's Coming till after the Tribulation are the ones who "smite" their fellow-servants; and this merely because they hope to be taken away before it comes!

Luke xv. 20.—Here, five particulars give the fulness of Divine grace in receiving the lost sinner :—
" When he was yet a great way off,
his father saw him (eyes),
and had compassion (heart),
and ran (feet),
and fell on his neck (arms),
and kissed him " (lips).

There is no climax; but we are asked to dwell separately on these five aspects of grace, *five* (4 + 1) being the number which is symbolical of grace.*

---

* See *Number in Scripture*, by the same author and publisher.

Luke xv. 22, 23.—Here, we have an eight-fold enumeration of the gifts: showing the completeness of the blessings poured upon accepted one :—

" The father said to his servants, Bring forth the best robe (but do more than that) ;
and put it on him ;
and put a ring on his hand,
and shoes on his feet :
and bring hither the fatted calf,
and kill *it ;*
and let us eat
and be merry."

John x. 27, 28.—The riches of the grace bestowed upon the Lord's people are thus enumerated and emphasized by the five-fold *Polysyndeton :*—

" My sheep hear my voice,
and I know them,
and they follow me ;
and I give unto them eternal life ;
and they shall never* perish,
and not anyone shall pluck them out of my hand " (so Greek).

Acts. i. 8.—" But ye shall receive power, after that the Holy Ghost is come upon you :
and ye shall be witnesses unto me
both in Jerusalem,
and in all Judea,
and in Samaria,
and unto the uttermost part of the earth."

Thus is emphasized for us the fact that there is one message, for all places and for all times. " Preach the Gospel to every creature." Not " adapt the Gospel to every century."

There are, here, three concentric circles. (1) The innermost " Jerusalem and in all Judea," the place of *Religiousness* where they professed to worship God and to read His word. (2) " And in Samaria " which was the place of *corrupt* religion, for it is written of Samaria, " they feared the LORD, and served their own gods " (2 Kings xvii. 33). (3) " And unto the uttermost part of the earth," which was the place of *no religion.*

---

* See under *Repeated Negation.*

The witness for each was to be, not concerning Doctrines or Sacraments, or Rites and Ceremonies; but, concerning a PERSON! "Ye shall be witnesses unto ME"—a crucified, risen, and coming Saviour. This is to be the witness : and this is the Gospel.

Rom. viii. 29, 30.—Here there is no climax or conclusion, but each great fact is to be weighed and duly considered. We emend the A.V. only by putting the word "also" in the correct place[*]

" For whom he did foreknow, he did predestinate also . .
Moreover whom he did predestinate, them he called also :
and whom he called, them he justified also :
and whom he justified, them he glorified also."

Rom ix. 4.—Here the figure is used to impress us with the wonderful possessions and privileges of Israel,

"Who are Israelites ; to whom *pertaineth* the adoption (υἱοθεσία *sonship*, Deut. iv. 7, 33, 34),
and the glory (1 Sam. iv. 21),
and the covenants (which precede the Law, Gal. iii. 17),
and the giving of the Law,
and the service of God (ἡ λατρεία, *hee latreia, the* [tabernacle] *worship*),
and the promises."

1 Cor. i. 30.—"But of him are ye in Christ Jesus, who of God is made unto us wisdom,
and righteousness,
and sanctification,
and redemption."

The R.V. rendering does not alter the fact that these four wondrous things are distinctly separated, so that we are to study them, each one by itself, and to learn the weighty lessons and the equal importance of each. It is Christ Jesus who is our righteousness ; and He is equally our sanctification, and in Him we are perfect and complete as to our *standing* before God ; and in Him we now wait for Resurrection : *i.e.*, the redemption of our bodies from the power of the grave (Rom. viii. 23. Eph. iv. 30).

Eph. iv. 31.—" Let all bitterness (πικρία, *pikria*, the opposite of χρηστοί, *chreestoi*, verse 32, *kind*).
and wrath (θυμός, *thumos*, the opposite of εὔσπλαγχνοι, *eusplangchnoi tender-hearted*),

---

[*] See a pamphlet, entitled, *Also : a Bible-Study on the use of the Word*, by the same author and publisher.

and anger (ὀργή, *orgee*, the opposite of χαριζόμενοι, *charizomenoi*, *forgiving*),
and clamour,
and evil-speaking be put away from you with all malice."

Here there is no climax; but in the next verse we have the opposite figure of *Asyndeton*, in which there are no "ands," because there is a weighty conclusion at the end, to which we are hastened on.

* "Be ye kind (χρηστοί, *chreestoi*, the opposite of πικρία, *pikria bitterness*, verse 31),
—tender-hearted (εὔσπλαγχνοι, *eusplangchnoi*, the opposite of θυμός, *thumos, wrath*),
—forgiving one another (χαριζόμενοι, *charizomenoi*, the opposite of ὀργη, *orgee, anger*),
even as God for Christ's sake hath forgiven you."†

Phil. iii. 3.—" For we are the circumcision, which worship God in the spirit,
and rejoice in Christ Jesus,
and have no confidence in the flesh."

Thus the Spirit emphasises these three great fundamental prin-ciples of Christianity, and asks us to dwell upon each, noting the necessity of making all our worship wholly *spiritual* (John iv. 23, 24); making the Lord Jesus the source of all our jōy; and renouncing all attempts to work out a righteousness of our own.

1 Thess. ii. 11.—" Ye know how we exhorted
and comforted
and charged every one of you, as a father *doth* his children." (See under *Ellipsis*, page 89).

1 Tim. i. 5.—Here, the figure points us to the true genealogy of charity, or love.

"Now the end of the commandment is charity out of a pure heart,
and *of* a good conscience,
and of faith unfeigned."

If the faith be not right and unfeigned, then the " conscience " cannot be " good." Conscience is the result of faith. It will condemn us in the doing of what we believe to be wrong. It will approve the

---

* There is an " and " here in the A.V., but the Greek is δέ (*de*), *but*. This is omitted by Lachmann, and put in the margin by Tregelles, Westcott and Hort.

† Lachmann has ὑμῖν (*humin*), *us*, which is put in the margin by Tr. W.H. and R.V.

doing of what we believe to be right.   Hence, the importance of a true " faith."

If the conscience be not " good," the heart cannot be pure ; and if the heart be not pure, there can be no true, divine love.

2 Tim. iv. 17, 18.—Contrast this passage with the example of *Asyndeton* in 2 Tim iii. 10, 11.   In that passage we are not detained over the manner of the Lord's deliverance, but pointed to the great fact that He did deliver out of all.   But here we have no such climax, and are asked to stop and consider each part of the wondrous deliverance.

" Notwithstanding, the Lord stood with me,
and strengthened me ; that by me the preaching might be fully known,
and that all the Gentiles might hear :
and I was delivered* out of the mouth of the lion.
and the Lord shall deliver me from every evil work,
and will preserve me† unto his heavenly kingdom, to whom be glory for ever and ever.   Amen."

Heb. xiii. 8.—" Jesus Christ the same yesterday,
and to-day,
and for ever."

Jas. i. 24.—Here the repeated " and " greatly emphasises what Bengel calls the " hastiness joined with levity " of the natural man.

" For he beholdeth himself,
and goeth his way,
and straightway forgeteth what manner of man he was."

Jas. iv. 13.—The *Polysyndeton* here, Bengel says, expresses the caprice of a mind secure and indifferent—the will of a mind at ease.

" Go to now, ye that say, To-day or to-morrow we will go into such a city,
and continue there a year,
and buy
and sell,
and get gain."

2 Pet. i. 5-7.—Here the sevenfold " and " points to all that is included in and follows the greatest gift of God (verse 3).   Faith itself is God's gift (Eph. ii. 8), and therefore it is not added to any-

---

* See under the figures of *Ellipsis and Polyptoton.*

† See under the figure of *Paregmenon.*

thing. It is the "precious faith" which is "obtained" through the righteousness of God (verse 1).

"**And** besides this (καὶ αὐτό τοῦτο, *kai auto touto, and for this very reason : i.e.*, because we have "precious faith" (verse 1), and are "partakers of the Divine nature" (verse 4), giving all diligence (see verse 15 and iii. 14), add to your faith, virtue (τὴν ἀρετήν, *teen areteen, courage*) ;

and to virtue, knowledge ;

and to knowledge, temperance (ἐγκράτεια, *engkrateia, self-control*, which is the fruit of knowledge. It means having self well reined in, the government of *all* the passions of the flesh) ;

and to temperance, patience˙ (under afflictions or the sufferance of evil, as courage is used in encountering and averting evil) ;

and to patience, godliness (which is the only foundation of true patience or endurance. Apart from godliness it is stoicism, or mere indifference),

and to godliness, brotherly kindness (the love of your Christian brethren) ;

and to brotherly kindness, charity " (the love of all). (1 Pet. i. 22).

Thus " faith " is the source out of which all virtues must spring, and " love " is the point to which all such virtues tend. Hence, " Whatsoever is not of faith is sin " (Rom. xiv. 23,), and " the end of the commandment is love " (1 Tim. i. 5).

Another important figure is combined here with *Polysyndeton* (see under *Climax* (which is repeated *Anadiplosis*).

Rev. i. 11.—Here the seven churches are to be separated as being equal in importance, and distinct in their position :—

"What thou seest write in a book

and send *it* unto the seven churches which are in Asia ; unto Ephesus,

and unto Smyrna,

and unto Pergamos,

and unto Thyatira,

and unto Sardis,

and unto Philadelphia,

and unto Laodicea"

Rev. iii. 17.—Here, the figure is used to bring out the Laodicean condition of soul.

" Because thou sayest, I am rich
and increased with goods,
and have need of nothing;
and knowest not that thou art wretched,
and miserable,
and poor,
and blind,
and naked."

Rev. vi. 15.—Here, to show the universality of the fear which will be manifested when "the great day of his wrath is come"—all classes of society are named and stated with all formality in order to impress our minds :—
and the kings of the earth,
and the great men,
and the rich men,
and the chief captains,
and the mighty men,
and every bondmen,
and every free man, hid themselves in the dens and in the rocks of the mountains."

Rev. xii.—This chapter is rendered remarkable by the figure of *Polysyndeton*. *Forty-four* times the word " and" is repeated, bringing before us a variety of details connected with matters which are thus shown to be of the greatest possible importance. In chap. v., we have the book written " within and without " (ἔσωθεν καὶ ὄπισθεν, *esōthen kai opisthen*), pointing to its *esoteric* (or *inner*) and *exoteric* (or *outer*) meaning. What follows in chaps. vi.-xi., describes the *exoteric* or outside manifestations—events which will be seen by all ; for chap. xi. carries us right on to the end, to the sounding of the " seventh " or last trumpet, and thus covers the whole ground, even including Resurrection and Judgment, and the setting up of the kingdom of the Messiah. See xi. 15-18, which is coterminous with Rev. xx.

Chapter xii. does not, therefore, go forward, but takes us *back* to the time, even before chap. v., and gives us the *esoteric* or inner meaning, and reveals to us the sources, springs, and secrets of all that leads up to the judgments recorded in chaps. vi.-xi. Chapters xiii.-xix. introduce supplementary information which must be read into those earlier preceding chapters (vi.-xi.), showing the part that the Dragon and his agent the Antichrist will have in them.

Chapter xii. is constructed as follows :.—

Rev. xii.

A | a | 1-5. The woman, the dragon, and the child.
     b | 6. The woman's flight, and its duration (1,260 days).

     B | 7-13. War in heaven (ἐγένετο, *came to pass*).

A | *b* | 14. The woman's flight and its duration three years and a half.
   a | 15, 16. The woman, the dragon, and the rest of her seed.

     B | 17. War on earth.

Each of these members can, of course, be expanded. For example :—

    a : (1-5). *The woman, the dragon, and the child.*

a | c | 1-. A great sign in heaven.
    d | -1. A woman. Her description ("crown," σтέφανος, a victor's crown).
       e | 2. Her action : and the child.
                     The woman.
  c | 3-. Another great sign in heaven.
    d | -3. The dragon. His description ("crowns," διάδηματα, royal fillets) (see only here, and xiii. 1 and xix. 12).
       e | 4, 5. His action: and the child (Dan. viii. 10).
                     The dragon.

    b : (verse 6) may be expanded thus : as may be also *b* (verse 14).

b | f | 6-. The woman : her flight.
    g | -6-. Her place—the wilderness.
  f | -6-. The woman : her nourishment.
    g | -6. Her continuance—1,260 days.

The larger member B: (7-13) may be thus shown :—

    B : (7-13) *War in heaven.*

B | h | 7, 8. Heaven. War in heaven.
    i | 9. Earth. The dragon cast into the earth.
  h | 10-12. Heaven. Rejoicing in heaven.
    i | 13. Earth. The dragon cast into the earth.

i (verse 9) thus :—

> *The dragon cast out on earth.*

i | j | 9-. The Dragon.
         k | -9-. Place ; cast out into the earth.
    j | -9-. His angels.
       k | -9. Place.   Cast out with him.

h (verses 10-12) thus :—

> *Rejoicing in heaven.*

h | l | 10. Heaven.   Rejoicing.
       m | -10-.   Earth.   Salvation come for it.
          n | -10, 11. Reason.   " For the accuser, etc."
    l | 12. Heaven.   Rejoicing.
       m | -12-.   Earth.   Woe to the inhabiters.
          n | -12. Reason.   " For the devil is come down," etc.

The woman and her seed and the dragon takes us back to Gen. iii., where we see the " enmity " placed between them. Thence we are taken to the woman (Israel), through whom the child was to come, as seen in the call of Abraham, and in the establishment of " Israel," and his twelve sons, of which the twelve stars (the Zodiacal signs*) were the symbols. (See Gen. xxxvii.).

The Zodiac is a certain zone of the heavens extending about 9° each side of the Ecliptic. This is divided into twelve parts, each of which has its own peculiar " sign." The word " Zodiac " is not to be derived from ζάω, or ζήν, to live, or ζώδιον, a little animal (for not all the signs are animals), but from a more ancient root through the Hebrew צעד, to go, to go. by steps, to step, to move slowly in a regular and stately manner. (See 2 Sam. vi. 13. Jer. x. 5. Judges v. 4. Ps. lxviii. 8. Hab. iii. 12). The noun means a step. So that the Zodiac is literally a way with steps. Its later Biblical name is Mazzaroth (מַזָּרוֹת), Job xxxviii. 32 (see margin) ; or Mazzaloth (מַזָּלוֹת), 2 Kings xxiii. 5 (see margin), from the root אָזַל (azal), to go or revolve, divided, as the Zodiac is divided into signs. Gesenius points out that the Mazzaroth (from אזר) has another sense, and means to admonish, premonish, presage. See Gen. xxxvii. 9, 10, where in Joseph's prophetic dream he sees the

---

* Just as the seven stars in chap. i. are the symbols of the Churches.

whole family represented as "The sun, and the moon, and the eleven stars," (himself being the twelfth.*

The birth of the seed of this woman is set forth in the Old Testament in two distinct prophecies, showing its two-fold character, one answering to "the sufferings of Christ"; the other, to "the glory that should follow."

In Isa. vii. 14, we have the Incarnation of "Emmanuel—God with us" (Matt. i. 23).

While, in Isa. ix. 6, 7, we have the birth presented, with the scene of humiliation overleaped.

The former is the "suffering" aspect: the latter is the "glory" aspect of the birth of this Child.

It is remarkable that in Matthew—(the gospel of the kingdom)—we have the suffering aspect from Isa. vii. 14; while in Luke—the gospel of Christ as man—we have the glory aspect from Isa. ix. 6, 7. See and compare Luke i. 31-33.

---

* Ancient Jewish authorities hold that these twelve stars were the signs of the Zodiac. This is, without doubt, the case. These "stars" have been well called "signs," for in them is written in the very heavens the history of redemption. Each of the symbolical figures is pictured performing some typical action. From the earliest times, also, one was appropriated to each of the twelve sons of Jacob. Josephus informs us that the tribes carried these signs on the tribal standards. The Chaldee paraphrase, of a still earlier date, says the same. The Targums also add their testimony. As the order of encampment is described in Num. i. and ii., the four tribes: Judah, Ephraim, Dan and Reuben are equidistant. The sign of Judah was "Leo," the lion; Ephraim's was "Taurus," the bull; Dan's was "Scorpio," the scorpion (afterwards changed to the "Aquila," the eagle); and Reuben's was "Aquarius," the man. These four signs are at the four cardinal points of the Zodiac, exactly corresponding with the position of the four tribes. It is interesting to note that the sign now known as "Libra," or, the scales, is not found in the more ancient Zodiacs, its place being occupied by "Ara," the altar, the top of which the sign or hieroglyphic ♎ much more resembles. The idea contained in Libra, the scales, or Justice, is the altar on which justice was satisfied. Libra or Ara was not borne on any of the standards, Simeon and Levi being included under one (Pisces). Hence the place of Libra, or rather of Ara, the altar, was the place occupied by the Tabernacle, and by the altar of burnt offering itself. It is remarkable that the three decans, or constellations of Libra, or Ara, are the Cross, the Victim, and the Crown.

The evidence is altogether too overwhelming for us to take these "twelve stars" as representing anything but Israel. It is a "woman" that is seen, but her surroundings (of sun and moon, and the twelve signs of the Zodiac) show that she personifies emblematically the whole nation of Israel.

See The Witness of the Stars by the same author and publisher.

In Rev. xii. 5, it is this latter, or the glory aspect of Messiah's birth that is presented, as referred to in Pss. ii. and lxxxvii. It leaps over the " sufferings of Christ," and over the whole of the interval of this present dispensation, and goes forward at once to the time when He shall reign over and rule all nations. " Who was to rule " (verse 5) is μέλλει (mellei), and means " who is to rule all nations." It passes from the birth of the man-child, and goes on at once to " the glory which should follow, when the government shall be upon his shoulder."

It is Christ Personal therefore, in the first instance, who is the subject of this prophecy. He was the " man-child " " caught up to God and His throne."

But this does not exhaust the prophecy. The word rendered " man-child " in verse 5 is a peculiar word.* The R.V. renders it "a son, a man child." Here it is, according to all the critical texts (including the Revisers' Text) and Ancient MSS, ἄρσεν (arsen). Now ἄρσεν here is neuter, and therefore cannot possibly refer to any one individual. It cannot apply to either a man or a woman. The mother of this child is not an individual ! but is collective and composite. So also is the child.†

Some see in this " man-child " the Church of God. But the Church is neither " woman " nor " child," " neither male nor female " (Gal. iii. 28). The Church is " one new man " in Christ (Eph. ii. 15). The Church was before creation, " before the foundation of the world " (Eph. i. 4), and is not, therefore, the subject of prophecy, as is the kingdom and dominion in the earth, which was "from the foundation of the world " (Matt. xiii. 35 ; xxv. 34, etc.).

On the other hand, we have such distinct prophecies in the Old Testament of this woman and her child that it surprising any should fail to connect them.

A time is coming when a new nation is to be brought forth in Israel ; a nation bringing forth the fruits which Israel should have brought forth ; the nation referred to in Matt. xxi. 43.

Concerning that day Jehovah bids Zion to " sing " (Isa. liv. 1-10).

Of that day Jehovah has said, " Before she travailed, she brought forth ; before her pain came, she was delivered of a MAN-CHILD.

---

* The masculine form, ἄρσην (arseen), occurs only in Matt. xix. 4. Mark x. 6. Luke ii. 23. Rom. i. 27. Gal. iii. 28, where in each case the sex is emphatic.

† We have a similar example of a neuter word including both sexes in the word γυναικάρια (gunaikaria), in 2 Tim. iii. 6, where it is rendered " silly women." But it occurs only here, and is neuter. It therefore includes silly women of both sexes !

Who hath heard such a thing? who hath seen such things? Shall the earth be made to bring forth in one day? or shall a nation be born at once? for as soon as Zion travailed she brought forth her children" (Isa. lxvi. 5-14).

Again Micah iv. 9, 10 distinctly foretells this travail of Zion; while chap. v. 2, 3 connects together this composite man-child. In verse 3, we have the birth of Him, who shall be "ruler in Israel." His rejection by His people is not named, but the consequent rejection of His people by Him both implies it and contains it; for, in the next verse, we read, "Therefore will He give them up, until the time that she which travaileth hath brought forth; then the remnant of his brethren shall return unto the children of Israel. And He shall stand and rule (marg.) in the strength of the LORD, in the majesty of the name of the LORD his God; and they shall abide: for now shall he be great unto the ends of the earth."

Surely, if there is any connection whatever between prophecy and its fulfilment, we have it in Rev. xii., where we see in this woman, Zion, "travailing in birth, and pained to be delivered" (verse 2), and the dragon standing "before the woman which was ready to be delivered, for to devour her child as soon as it was born."

This was true of Messiah, and it will be true of the servant (the composite "child"), as the rest of the chapter goes on to explain.

It is this birth of a nation "in one day," which will lead to the "war in heaven,"* (see Dan. x. 20; xii. 1), and lead to the Dragon's being cast out into the earth. This will bring on the crisis described in this chapter and chapter xiii. (See 2 Thess. ii. 6, under *Ellipsis.*

The chapter is too long to quote here in full, but if all the many "ands" be noted and marked, the importance of all these details will be at once noticed. See the next example.

Rev. xiii. 1-9.—Here the figure is used to mark, to emphasize, and to call our attention to the solemn events, which will follow upon Satan's being cast out into the earth, to find no more place in heaven (xii. 8). Forty-five times the word "and" is repeated in this chapter!

Rev. xii. is the key to the Apocalypse for the events recorded in it are preliminary to the events recorded in the earlier part of the book.

First of all comes the taking up of the Body of Christ (xii. 5) which causes the "war in heaven (xii. 7-12), and ends in the casting

---

* See a small pamphlet, *Things to Come*, by the same author and publisher.

out of Satan. This is the great event which is the beginning of the end, and which ushers in the Apocalyptic scenes and judgments.*

Consequent on this follows a great persecution of Israel; which will be to those who are left, the first *exoteric* or visible sign of the Devil's "great wrath" (xii. 12). But this persecution will for a time be thwarted. "The earth" will "help the woman" (xii. 16). That is to say, the settled state of the peoples of the earth will stop this persecution.

Then the Dragon at once proceeds to organise his great rebellion. In the Greek the twelfth chapter ends with the first sentence of chap. xiii.: where, as in the R.V., the true reading is—"And HE stood upon the sand of the sea." The best MSS., with Lachmann, Tregelles, Alford, and Westcott and Hort, read ἐστάθη (*estathee*), *he stood*, not ἐστάθην (*estatheen*), *I stood*.

That is to say, the settled state of "the earth" preventing the destruction of Israel, the Dragon takes his post upon the sand of "the sea" and out of the waters and the earth (of the peoples) he calls up the two Beasts of chap. xiii.—his last two great instruments,—the "Antichrist" and the "False Prophet,"—by which he will seek to carry out his purposes.

John sees them "rising up." The word is ἀναβαῖνον (*anabainon*, present participle), *rising* or *mounting up*, not "rise up" as in A.V. The R.V. has "coming up." John sees the first Beast "rising up out of the sea" (implying a gradual rather than a sudden act): and the second Beast out of "the earth" (verse 11).

And then he proceeds to describe their characters and their deeds. The figure of *Polysyndeton* (a remarkable example) calls our attention to the many important details, each one of which is to be dwelt upon by us as being full of meaning and instruction :—

And he stood upon the sand of the sea (*i.e.*, the dragon, when cast out from heaven),

and I saw a beast rising up out of the sea having seven heads,

and ten horns,

and upon his horns ten crowns,

and upon his heads the names of blasphemy;

and the beast which I saw was like a leopard (a combination of Daniel's beasts in one, Dan. vii.) (a leopard is Greece),

---

† Chap. ix. 1, though coming before chap. xii., records a vision subsequent to it. John says, "I saw a star lying fallen πεπτωκότα (*peptōkota*) from heaven." not "fall," as in A.V. R.V. has "fallen."

and his feet were as *the feet* of a bear (Persia),

and his mouth as the mouth of a lion (Babylon),

and the dragon gave him his power (six times we have in this chapter
"it was given him "),

and his seat (or throne, ii. 13 ; xvi. 10),

and great authority (Luke iv. 6. 2 Thess. ii. 9, 10).

and I saw one of his heads, as it were, wounded to death (similar to
verses 6, 12, 14),

and his deadly wound was healed ;

and all the world wondered [*and followed*] after the beast (iii. 10.
2 Thess. ii. 11, 12),

and they worshipped the dragon (this is the one great object, aim, and
end of Satan, Matt. iv. 9) which gave power unto the beast ;

and they worshiped the beast, saying, Who is like unto the beast ?
who is able to make war with him ? (Compare Ex. xv. 3, 11,
for the blasphemy.)

and there was given to him a mouth, speaking great things and
blasphemies (2 Thess. ii. 4),

and authority was given him to continue forty *and* two months
(Dan. vii. 25),

and he opened his mouth in blasphemy against God, to blaspheme his
name (Dan. vii. 8, 11, 20, 25 ; xi. 36. Ps. lii. 2 Thess. ii. 4),

and his tabernacle (whither the saints have been previously taken),

and them that dwell in heaven (*i.e.,* the body of Christ which shall
have been caught up, when the accuser has been cast down).

and it was given him to make war with the saints (Dan. vii. 21, 25 ;
xi. 40-44),

and to overcome them (Dan. viii. 12, 24 ; xi. 28, 30-33 ; xii. 7) :

and power was given him (John xix. 11) over all kindreds,

and tongues,

and nations (as with Nebuchadnezzar, Dan. iii. 7) ;

and all that dwell upon the earth shall worship him (2 Thess. ii. 11, 12),
whose names are not written in the book of life (Matt.
xxiv. 24. Dan. xii. 1. These are they who " *overcome* " him
ii. 7, 11, 17, 26 ; iii. 5, 12, 21 ; xii. 11) of the Lamb slain from
the foundation of the world. If any man have an ear to hear,
let him hear."*

This chapter contains two visions relating to two Beasts*: the
first, the Antichrist; the second, the "False Prophet." The first is the

---

* See 2 Thess ii., under *Ellipsis* and *Correspondence.*

false Christ, and the second is the false—and satanic counterfeit of the Holy Ghost. The second is marked, like the first, by the figure of *Polysyndeton.*

The structure of this chapter is very remarkable. In the Greek the first sentence forms the end of chap. xii. So we commence with the second " And I saw " :—

The Vision of the Two Beasts (Rev. xiii.).

A | 1-. The vision (καὶ εἶδον), " And I saw."

   B | -1-. The first Beast (Antichrist).

      C | -1-. His origin. The sea (ἀναβαῖνον, *rising*).

         D | -1, 2-. His description.

            E | -2. His power (δύναμις) derived from the dragon.

            F | 3-8. His deeds.

               G | a | 9. The Spirit's call : " Let him hear."

                     b | 10. The lesson : " Here is patience and faith."

A | 11-. The vision (καὶ εἶδον), " And I saw."

   B | -11-. The second Beast. " The False Prophet " (xvi. 13; xix. 20).

      C | -11-. His origin. The earth (ἀναβαῖνον, *rising*).

         D | -11. His description.

           E | 12-. His authority (ἐξουσία) derived from the first Beast.

           F | -12-17. His deeds.

              G | b | 18-. The lesson : " Here is wisdom."

                  a | -18. The Spirit's call : " Let him count."

Here A to F and *A* to *F* relate to the Beasts, while G and *G* relate to the saints. The order of the two members of G and *G* is an introversion, to make them off from the rest.

Rev. xviii. 12, 13.—Here the figure heaps up and amasses the wealth of Babylon. Each item is to be dwelt upon : there is no climax :—

" The merchandise of gold,
and silver,
and precious stones,
and of pearls,

and fine linen (merchandise, nót the gift of grace as with the Bride,
    xix. 8, " granted " to her : her *righteous award*),
and purple,
and silk,
and scarlet,
and all thyine wood,
and all manner of vessels of ivory,
and all manner of vessels of most precious wood,
and of brass,
and iron,
and marble,
and cinnamon (*amomum,* an Italian shrub of sweet odour),
and odours,
and ointments,
and frankincense,
and wine,
and oil,
and fine flour,
and wheat,
and beasts (of burden),
and sheep,
and horses,
and chariots,
and slaves,*
and souls of men.

Many other examples of *Polysyndeton* are to be found, *e.g.*, Num.
xx. 2 Chron. xxxii. 27, 28, 29, 30. Isa. iii. 18-24. Zeph, i. 15, 16. Mark
iv. 1-9. Eph. i. 21. Phil. iv. 9. Rev. xi. 17, 18 ; xx. 9-15 ; xxi. 8 and
22-27 ; xxii. 1-6, 17.

---

* (Greek σώματα *somata, bódies,* was used by the Figure of *Syneċdoche as*
a term for *slaves,* as we use " hands " for labourers. See lxx. Gen. xxxvi. 6.
Hebrew נפשׁ in both passages, used of the dead body (Num. ix. 6; xix. 11-13)
and for the living (Lev. xxiv. 17), but especially for slaves or captives (Num.
xxxi. 35, 40, 46. The " bodies " carry the merchandise, and the " souls " *are*
counted as merchandise. See under *Synecdoche.*)

PARADIASTOLE ; or, NEITHERS and NORS.

The Repetition of the Disjunctives Neither and Nor, or, Either and Or.

Par'-a-di-as'-to-lee. Greek, παραδιαστολή, from παρά (*para*), *beside* or *along*, and στολή (*stolee*), *a sending* (from στέλλω (*stello*), *to send*). Hence *a sending beside* or *along*. It is a form of *Anaphora*, by which one word is repeated at the beginning of successive sentences. It differs from *Polysyndeton*, in that instead of a *conjunction*, the repeated word is a *disjunctive*, because it denotes a sending along, *i.e.*, it separates and distinguishes. The words NEITHER and NOR, or EITHER and OR, are the words which are repeated in the figure of *Paradiastole*, causing the various items to be put together *disjunctively* instead of conjunctively.

Hence the Latins called it DISJUNCTIO, *Disjunction*.

Its use is to call our attention to, and to emphasize, that which is thus written for our learning.

Ex. xxxiv. 4.—" The diseased have ye not strengthened,
neither have ye healed that which was sick,
neither have ye bound up that which was broken,
neither have ye brought again that which was driven away,
neither have ye sought that which was lost."

Thus are the false shepherds indicted for their unfaithfulness and neglect.

Luke xviii. 29.—" And he said unto them, Verily I say unto you there is no man that hath left home,
or parents,
or brethren,
or wife,
or children, for the kingdom of God's sake, who shall not receive manifold more in this present time, and in the world to come, life everlasting."

John i. 13.—" Which were born
not of blood,
nor of the will of the flesh,
nor of the will of man, but of God."

Thus is emphasized the important doctrine that the new birth is entirely the work of the sovereign grace of God.

Rom. viii. 35.—" Who shall separate us from the love of Christ ?
Shall tribulation,
or distress,
or persecution,
or famine,
or nakedness,
or peril,
or sword ? "

Thus is emphasized the blessed fact that our eternal security
depends not on human " *perseverance*," but on Divine *preservation*, as the
Lord Jesus said " This is *the* FATHER'S WILL which hath sent me,
that of all which He hath given me I should lose nothing (John vi. 39).

This is followed up by the wondrous answer to the question in
verses 38 and 39. " I am persuaded that
neither death,
nor life,
nor angels,
nor principalities,
nor powers,
nor things present,
nor things to come,
nor height,
nor depth,
nor any other creature, shall be able to separate us from the love of
    God, which is in Christ Jesus our Lord."

1 Cor. iii. 21, 22.—" All things are yours ; whether Paul,
or Apollos,
or Cephas,
or the world,
or life,
or death,
or things present,
or things to come ;
    all are yours ; and ye are Christ's ; and Christ is God's.

Thus the riches of the glory of our inheritance in Christ is
revealed and set forth and displayed before our eyes.

2 Thess. ii. 2.—" That ye be
not quickly shaken from your mind,
nor yet be troubled,
neither by spirit,
nor by word,

nor by Epistle as from us as [*though we had said*] that the day of the
    Lord has set in."

Thus does the apostle emphasize his strong desire that nothing
might loosen them (as a ship is loosed from its moorings) from the
blessed hope of "our gathering together unto Him" when He shall
"come forth" into the air "for" His people, who then shall be
"caught up to meet Him," and thus be for ever with Him.

This he had taught them in the first epistle (iv. 13-18) for their
comfort, but now some person or persons must have deceived them by
asserting that the apostle had said, or written to say, that "the Day of
the Lord had set in." If this were so, they might well be troubled,
for he was proved to have deceived them and to have given them a
false hope, for they had not been "gathered" to Christ to meet Him
in the air before the day of the Lord. So he writes ὑπέρ (*hyper*), *on
behalf of*, or *in the interest of* that blessed hope, in order to thus assure
them that he had never said or written any such thing.

Nothing stands between the day of Christ and our ascension to
meet Him in the air. Many things stand between that event and our
coming "with" Him in "the Day of the Lord." The teaching of Paul
by the Holy Ghost is very different from popular Christian teaching
to-day. The popular teaching is that that shall not come till the
world's conversion comes: the truth here stated is that it cannot
come till the apostasy shall have come!

Popular teaching is that the world is not yet good enough! The
figure here points us to the fact that the world is not bad enough!
There yet lacks the coming of the Apostasy and of Antichrist. See
further under Ellipsis, page 14-17.

EPISTROPHE; or, LIKE SENTENCE-ENDINGS.

The Repetition of the same Word or Words at the end of successive Sentences.

E-pis'-tro-phee. Greek ἐπιστροφή, *a turning upon* or *wheeling about*, from ἐπί (*epi*), *upon*, and στρέφω (*strepho*), *to turn.*

It is a figure in which the same word or words are repeated at *the end* of successive sentences or clauses, instead of (as in *Anaphora*) at the beginning.

It is sometimes called ANTISTROPHE (*an-tis'-tro-phee*), *a turning against;* also EPIPHORA (*e-piph'-o-ra*), *a bringing to* or *upon.*

The Latin name is CONVERSIO (*con-ver'-si-o*), *a turning round.*

All these titles express the character of the figure, which is thus the opposite of *Anaphora.*

Gen. xiii. 5.—"And the land was not able to bear them that they might **dwell together**: for their substance was so great that they could not **dwell together**."

Deut. xxvii. 15-26, where each clause ends with the word "**Amen.**"

Deut. xxxii. 10.—It is beautifully expressed in the Hebrew by the repetition of the pronoun הוּ (*hū*), *him*, at the end of each sentence. It in hidden in the translation, both in the A.V. and R.V., on account of not being in accordance with the English idiom. It reads:—

> "In a desert land He found **him**
> And in the waste howling wilderness, about, he led **him**.
> He instructed **him**.
> As the apple of His eye He kept **him**."

So also in verse 12 :—

> "So the Lord alone did lead **him**,
> And there was no strange god with **him**."

Ps. xxiv. 10.—

> "Who is this **King of glory**?
> The Lord of hosts, He is the **King of glory**."

Ω

Ps. cxv. 9-11.—

> "O Israel, trust thou in **Jehovah,**
> > he is their help and their shield.
> O house of Aaron trust in **Jehovah,**
> > he is their help and their shield.
> Ye that fear the Lord, trust in **Jehovah,**
> > he is their help and their shield."

Thus is emphasized by *Epistrophe* the strength and security of Jehovah's people.

Ps. cxviii. 18, 19.—Twice we have the *Epistrophe* :—

"Than to put any confidence in man."

And three times (verses 10-11) :—

"But in the name of the Lord I will destroy them."

We have also *Anaphora* in verses 8, 9, and 10-12.

See also in the Psalms called the "Songs of degrees":

> cxx. 2, 3, "false or deceitful tongue";
> cxxi. 3, 4, "not slumber";
> cxxiii. 4, 5, "contempt";
> cxxv. 1, 2, "for ever";
> cxxxi. 2, "a weaned child";
> cxxxii. 2, 5, "the mighty God of Jacob."

Ps. cxxxvi. is a notable example of this figure, for every clause ends with the well-known words, "for his mercy endureth for ever."

Ezek. xxxiii. 25, 26.—The words are twice repeated to emphasize their solemnity. "And shall ye possess the land."

Joel ii. 26, 27.—Twice are the words repeated and thus solemnly emphasized. "And my people shall never be ashamed."

Rom. vii.. 31.—

> "If God be for **us**
> Who can be against **us?**"

Rev. vii. 5-8, which have the repetition of the sealing and the **number,** as we have *Anaphora* at the beginning in the words "**of the tribe.**"

Rev. xxii. 11.—We have here the word "still" repeated at the end of *four* successive sentences. The figure of *Polysyndeton* is also seen in the repetition of the word "and" at the beginning of these sentences (verse 17).

The repetition of the verb "come."

This figure may not only exist in the originals, and be hidden in the translation, but there may apparently be a repetition in the English when there may be none in the original. For example, Acts xix. 15, " Jesus I know, and Paul I know." But, in the Greek, the two words for " know " are quite different. Jesus I know (γινώσκω (ginōskō), *to perceive*, or *know*, and *to be influenced by the knowledge*), and Paul I know (ἐπίσταμαι (epistamai), *to have knowledge of*).

EPIPHOZA; or, EPISTROPHE IN ARGUMENT.

The Repetition of the same Word or Words at the end of successive Sentences: used in Argument.

Ep-i-pho'-za, from the Greek ἐπί (*epi*), *upon*, and φερείν (*pherein*) to *bear* or *bring*. Hence in a bad sense *to attack* or *assault*, especially with words. *Epiphoza* is the figure of *Epistrophe*, when used rhetorically in attack or in strong argument. We have an example in

2 Cor xi. 22.—

"Are they Hebrew ? so am I ;
Are they Israelites ? so am I ;
Are they the seed of Abraham ? so am I."

The repetition here greatly emphasizes and displays the feeling.

———

EPANADIPLOSIS; or, ENCIRCLING.

The Repetition of the same Word or Words at the beginning and end of a Sentence.

Ep'-an-a-di-plō'-sĭs. Greek ἐπαναδίπλωσις, from ἐπί (*epi*), *upon,* ἀνα (*ana*), *again,* and διπλοῦς *(diplous), a doubling.*

It means *a doubling upon again,* and the Figure is so called because the same word is repeated both at the beginning and at the end of a sentence.

The Latins called it INCLUSIO, *inclusion :* either because the first word of the sentence is included at the end, or because of the importance of the matter which is thus included between the two words.

They called it also CYCLUS, from the Greek κύκλος (*kyklos*), *a circle,* because the repetition concluded what is said, as in a circle.

When this figure is used, it marks what is said as being comprised in one complete circle, thus calling our attention to its solemnity ; giving completeness of the statement that is made, or to the truth enumerated, thus marking and emphasizing its importance.

The Massorah gives two lists of this peculiar form of repetition,* which we have incorporated in our examples marking them with an asterisk.

The Figure is frequently hidden or lost in translation (both in A.V. and R.V.), so that in these cases we shall be obliged to vary the rendering in order to properly exhibit it. Some are very difficult to reproduce, as in our first example.

* Gen. ix. 3.—" **Everything** (כל) moving that liveth shall be meat for you ; even as the green herb have I given you **everything.**"

Here the first, according to our English idiom, is *every,* while the last means the whole.

Ex. xxxii. 16.—"**The tables** were the work of God, and the writing the writing of God, graven upon **the tables.**" See also under *Anadiplosis.*

* Lev. vii. 19.—" **The flesh** that toucheth any unclean thing shall not be eaten : it shall be burnt with fire ; and as for the flesh, all that be clean shall eat of **the flesh.**"

---

* See Ginsburg's *Massorah,* Rubrics, 424, Vol. II., letter מ ; and 98, Vol.I., letter ו.

* **Lev. xxiii. 42.**—" In booths shall ye dwell seven days; all that are Israelites born shall dwell in booths."

* **Num. iii. 33.**—" Of **Merari** was the family of the Mahlites, and the family of the Mushites: these are the families of **Merari**."

* **Num. viii. 12.**—" The Levites shall lay their hand upon the bullocks: and thou shalt offer the one for a sin-offering and the other for a burnt-offering, unto the LORD, to make an atonement for **the Levites**."

* **Num. xxxi. 40.**—" And the **persons** (Hebrew, *souls*) were sixteen thousand: of which the LORD's tribute was thirty-and-two **persons** (Hebrew, *souls*)."

* **Num. xxxii. 1.**—" And **cattle,** a very great multitude, had the sons of Reuben and the sons of Gad; and when they saw the land of Jazer, and the land of Gilead, behold the place was a place for **cattle**."

* **Num. xxxii. 41.**—" And Jair, the son of Manasseh, went and took the small towns thereof, and called them Havoth-Jair."

* **Deut. xxxi. 3.**—" **Jehovah** thy God, he will go over before thee, and he will destroy these nations from before thee, and thou shalt possess them: and Joshua, he shall go over before thee, as hath said **Jehovah**." See also under *Anadiplosis.*

* **Josh. xv. 25.**—" And **Hazor,** Hadattah, and Kerioth, and Hezron, which is **Hazor**."

* **Judges xi. 1.**—Now **Jephthah** the Gileadite was a mighty man of valour, and he was the son of an harlot, and Gilead begat **Jephthah**."

* **1 Sam. xxvi. 23.**—" **Jehovah** render to every man his righteousness and his faithfulness: for the Jehovah delivered thee into my hand to-day, but I would not stretch forth mine hand against the anointed of **Jehovah**."

* **2 Sam. ix. 12.**—" **Mephibosheth** had a young son whose name was Micha. And all that dwelt in the house of Ziba were servants unto **Mephibosheth**." See also under *Anadiplosis.*

* **2 Sam. xix. 8.**—" **Now** (עַתָּה, *attah*) therefore, arise, go forth, and speak comfortably unto thy servants; for I swear by the LORD, if thou go not forth, there will not tarry one with thee this night; and that will be worse unto thee than all the evil that befel thee from thy youth until **now** (עַתָּה, *attah*).

* **1 Kings xxii. 47.**—" A king there was not in Edom; a deputy was king."

* **2 Kings xxiii. 25.**—" And like **him** there was no king before him; that turneth to the LORD with all his heart, and with all his soul, and with all his might, according to all the law of Moses: neither after him arose there any like **him.**"

* **1 Chron. ix. 8.**—The verse begins and ends with " **Ibneiah.**"

* **Neh. xi. 21.**—" The Nethinims dwelt in Ophel: and Ziha and Gispa were over the **Nethinims.**"

* **Est vii. 7.**—" The king, arising from the banquet of wine in his wrath, went into the palace garden. And Haman stood up to make request for his life to Esther the queen: for he saw that there was evil determined against him by the king."

Ps. xxvii. 14.—" Wait on the LORD; be of good courage, and He shall strengthen thine heart, wait (I say) on the LORD."
See also under *Apostrophe.*

Ps. liii. 2.—" God looked down from heaven upon the children of men, to see if there were any that did understand, that did seek God."

Ps. cxxii. 7, 8.—

" Peace be within thy walls
And prosperity within thy palaces.
For my brethren and companion's sake,
I will now say, Peace be within thee."

Ecc. i. 2.—" Vanity of vanities, saith the preacher, vanity of vanities; all is vanity."
There is also the figure in this verse of *Mesadiplosis (q.v.).*

Ecc. vii. 2.—" A good name is better than ointment that is good."
The figure is lost by the translation both in the A.V. and the R.V. There is another figure in this verse: *Paronomasia (q.v.).*

Mark vii. 14-16.—Hearken (ἀκούετε, *akouete*) unto me every one of you and understand: there is nothing from without a man, that entering into him can defile him: but the things which come out of him those are they that defile the man. If any man have ears to hear, let him hearken (ἀκουέτω, *akouetō*)."
See under *Polyptoton,* for the figure employed in the last sentence.

Mark xiii. 35-37.—" Watch ye, therefore: for ye know not when the master of the house cometh, at even, or at midnight, or at the cock-crowing, or in the morning: lest coming suddenly he find you sleeping. And what I say unto you I say unto all, Watch."

---

* See *The Name of Jehovah in the Book of Esther,* in four acrostics, by the same author and publisher.

Luke xii. 5.—"Fear him, which after he hath killed hath power to cast into hell: yea, I say unto you, **Fear him.**"

John iii. 8.—In this verse the figure is hidden both in the A.V. and R.V. The word is τὸ πνεῦμα (*to pneuma*), **the Spirit**, which is used both at the beginning and the end of the passage in the original. But at the beginning it is translated "the wind," and at the end "the Spirit." The R.V. has "the Spirit breathed, etc." in the margin.

Now the word πνεῦμα (*pneuma*), *spirit*, occurs 385 times in the New Testament, and is never translated "wind," except in this one place. There is a proper word for "wind," which is ἄνεμος (*anemos*). It occurs 31 times, and is always translated *wind*. So that it would have been much clearer to have used this word, if "wind" had really been meant.

If then we keep here the translation "spirit," which is used everywhere else, the verse will read and the figure appear as follows:—

"**The Spirit** breatheth where He willeth, and thou hearest His voice, but thou knowest not whence He cometh or whither He goeth; so is every one that is born of **the Spirit.**"

The wind has no will, but the Spirit has a will and a voice, and it is of Him that we are born.

The verb θελεῖν (*thelein*), *to will*, occurs 213 times, and always expresses a mental act of desire or determination proceeding from one capable of wishing, willing, or determining. See the nearly synonymous expression in 1 Cor. xii. 11. "But all these worketh that one and the selfsame Spirit, dividing to every man severally AS He will."

Moreover, it is not correct to assert this of the "wind." We *do* know whence it comes and whither it goes, and the Scriptures themthemselves assert that the comings and goings of the wind can be easily known and traced. See Job. i. 19. Ps. xviii. 10. Ecc. i. 6, Ezek. xxxvii. 9. Luke viii. 23. But not so of the Spirit (see Ecc. xi. 5), where "spirit" is placed in direct contrast with "wind" in the previous verse.

The things opposed in the immediate context are flesh and spirit, earthly things and heavenly things, nature and grace, and AS the Spirit in His movements is contrary to nature and above nature, SO is every one who is born of the Spirit. Those who are thus born are "sons of God, therefore the world knoweth us not, because it knew Him not" (1 John iii. 1). As the world knoweth not and understands not the motions and working of the Spirit of God, so the new breathings, and new will, and new desires, and new motions of the new nature in those who are born of the Spirit are also unknown.

Rom. viii. 24.—" Hope that is seen is not hope."

Gal. ii. 20.—In this verse the figure, which is in the Greek, is lost in the translation owing to the difference of idiom. In the Greek it reads :—

" **Christ**, I have been crucified-together-with, yet I live : and yet it is no longer I that live, but, in me, **Christ.**"

See also under *Hyperbaton.*

Phil. iv. 4.—" **Rejoice** in the LORD alway: and again I say **Rejoice.**"

James ii. 14-16.—The passage begins and ends with the words, " **What doth it profit.**"

The repetitions at the beginning and end of distinct portions, or independent passages (such as Pss. viii., ciii., etc.), belong rather to the subject-matter and are classed under *Correspondence (q.v.).*

EPADIPLOSIS; or, DOUBLE ENCIRCLING.

Repeated Epanadiplosis.

WHEN *Epanadiplosis* occurs at the beginning and end of *successive* sentences, it is called EPADIPLOSIS (*Ep-a-dip'-lo-sis*), *a doubling upon*.

Ps. xlvii. 6.—

"Sing praises to God, sing praises :
Sing praises unto our King, sing praises."

Rom. xiv. 8.—"For whether **we live**, to the Lord **we live** ; and whether **we die**, to the Lord **we die**."

ANADIPLOSIS ; or, LIKE SENTENCE ENDINGS AND BEGINNINGS.

The Repetition of the same Word or Words at the end of one Sentence and at the beginning of another.

An'-a-di-plo'-sis. Greek, ἀναδίπλωσις, ἀνά (*ana*), *again*, and διπλοῦν (*diploun*), *to double*, or διπλοῦς (*diplous*), *double*.

It is also called EPANASTROPHE (*Ep'-a-nas'-tro-phe*), from ἐπί (*epi*), *upon*, ἀνά (*ana*), *again*, and στρέφειν (*strephein, to turn*), and means, *a turning upon again.*

Also PALILLOGIA (*pa-lil-log'-i-a*), from πάλιν (*palin*), *again*, and λόγος (*logos*), *a word.*

In Latin it is called REVERSIO, *a turning back;* and RE-DUPLICATIO, *a reduplication.* The figure is so-called because the word which ends one sentence is repeated at the beginning of the next.

The words so repeated are thus emphasised as being the most important words in the sentence, which we are to mark and consider in translation and exposition.

The Massorah* gives two lists of such words; which we have included in our examples, marking them with an asterisk.

The figure is frequently missed in the English translation, both in the A.V. and R.V. In these cases we have given our own translation of the original, so as to bring out and exhibit the words which are thus affected by the figure of *Anadiplosis.*

Gen. i. 1, 2.—" In the beginning God created the heaven and **the earth**. And **the earth** became without form and void."

Thus *Anadiplosis* is the very first Figure employed in the Bible. And it is used to call our attention to, and emphasize, the fact that, while the first statement refers to two things, " the heaven and the earth"; the following statement proceeds to speak of only one of them, leaving the other entirely out of consideration.

Both were created " in the beginning." But the earth, at some time, and by some means, and from some cause (not stated) became a ruin :—empty, waste, and desolate; or, as it is expressed by another Figure (*Paronomasia, q.v.*), **tohoo** and **bohoo**. Now, whatever may be the meaning of *tohoo* (תֹהוּ), it is expressly stated, in Isa. xlv. 18, by Him who created the earth that " He created it not *tohoo* (תֹהוּ)."

---

* See Ginsburg's *Massorah*, Rubrics *422* and *423*, Vol. II. מ.

Therefore it must at, and after some subsequent period of unknown duration, have fallen into the ruin which the second verse declares and describes.

The repetition of the word " earth " here, directs our attention to this fact; and proceeds to describe the process by which the earth was restored and peopled.

The whole chapter exhibits a parallel between this work, and that " new creation "* which takes place in the case of every one who is born again of the Holy Ghost, and has the new man created within him.

* **Gen. vii. 18, 19.**—"And the ark went upon the face of the waters : and the waters prevailed exceedingly." (See under *Epizeuxis*).

* **Gen. xxxi. 6, 7.**—" Ye know that with all my power I have served your father: and your father hath deceived me, and changed my wages ten times; but God suffered him not to hurt me." (See under *Hysterologia* and *Idiom*.

* **Gen. xxxi. 33, 34.**—"Then went he out of Leah's tent and entered into the tent of Rachel. Now Rachel had taken the images," etc. Here, by rendering it " Rachel's tent " the figure is hidden, and the emphasis on Rachel is lost.

* **Ex. vii. 16, 17.**—Here the figure is entirely hidden in the English. The words כֹּה‎, כֹּה‎ being translated *hitherto* and *this*. To preserve the figure we must render it, " And, behold, thou wouldest not hear until now. Now saith Jehovah."

* **Ex. xii. 4, 5.**—" Every man, according to his eating shall make your count for the lamb. The lamb shall be without blemish."

* **Ex. xxxii. 16.**—"And the tables were the work of God, and the writing, the writing of God, graven upon the tables." Here we have not only the figure of *Anadiplosis* in the repetition of the word *writing* (מִכְתָּב‎, *miktav*), in the middle of the verse, but we have *Epanadiplosis* in the repetition of the words, *the tables* (הַלֻּחֹת‎, *halluchoth*). See also under *Anthopopatheia*.

* **Num. xxxiii. 3, 4.**—" Israel went out with an high hand in the sight of all the Egyptians. For the Egyptians buried all their firstborn, etc."

---

* Compare 2 Cor. iv. 6; v. 17, etc.; and see a pamphlet on " *The New Creation and the Old*," by the same author and publisher.

* **Deut. xxxi. 3, 4.**—" And Joshua, he shall go over before thee, as hath said **Jehovah**, and **Jehovah** shall do unto them as he did to Sihon and Og, etc."

* **2 Sam. ix. 12, 13.**—" All that dwelt in the house of Ziba were servants unto **Mephibosheth**. So **Mephibosheth** dwelt in Jerusalem."

* **2 Sam xix. 10, 11.**——" Now, therefore, why speak ye not a word of bringing back **the King**? And **the King** David sent to Zadok," etc. This emphasis on the word *king* is lost in the English.

* **Est. vi. 5, 6.**—" And the king said, Let him **come in**. Then **came in** Haman."

* **Est. vii. 7, 8.**—" He saw that there was evil determined against him by **the king**. Then **the king** returned out of the palace garden."

Thus the fourth acrostic containing the name of Jehovah is emphasised.*

Ps. xcviii. 4, 5.—The Hebrew figure is lost in the A.V., but is preserved in the R.V. In the Hebrew, verse 4 ends with the word זַמְּרוּ (*zammeroo*), and verse 5 begins with the same word.

" Make a joyful noise unto the LORD, all the earth:
Break forth and sing for joy, yea, **sing praises**.
Sing praises unto the LORD with the harp."

Ps. cxiii. 8.—
" He lifteth the needy out of the dunghill,
That He may set him **with princes**;
The princes of His People."

Ps. cxv. 12.—
" The Lord hath been mindful of us, and **He will bless**:
He will bless the house of Israel.
He will bless the house of Aaron.
He will bless them that fear the LORD," etc.

Here, the figure of *Anadiplosis* passes on into *Anaphora*.

* **Ps. cxxi. 1, 2.**—
" I will lift up mine eyes unto the hills from whence cometh **my help**.
My help cometh from the LORD which made heaven and earth."

* **Ps. cxxii. 2, 3.**—
"Our feet shall stand within thy gates, O **Jerusalem**,
Jerusalem is builded as a city that is compacted together."

---

* See under *Acrostichion* (page 186), also a pamphlet on these four acrostics by the same author and publisher.

The difference between this figure and that of *Epizeuxis* will be seen by comparing Matt. xxiii. 37 ; when the same word is repeated, but in quite a different manner ; for another purpose and with another emphasis.

Ps. cxxvi. 2, 3.—
" Then said they among the heathen,
The Lord **hath done great things for them,**
The Lord **hath done great things** for us, whereof we are glad."

Ps. cxxvii. 1, 2.—
" Except the Lord keep the city,
The watchman waketh **in vain.**
In vain ye rise up early," etc.

Ps. cxlv. 18.—
" The Lord is nigh **unto all them that call upon him** ;
To all that call upon him in truth"

* **Prov. xiii. 21, 22.—**
" To the righteous shall be repayed **good.**
A **good** man leaveth an inheritance," etc.

* **Isa. xxiv. 4, 5.**—" Languish do the haughty people of **the land.**
The land also is defiled under the inhabitants thereof."
These four lines form an *Epanodos* (*q.v.*).

* **Hos. ii. 21, 22 (Heb. 23, 24).**—" And they shall hear **the land :**
and **the land** shall hear the corn," etc.

See also under *Anaphora, Polysyndeton, Climax* and *Prosopopœia* : so richly emphasized is the wondrous prophecy.

Matt. vii. 22.—" Lord, Lord, have we not prophesied **in thy name?** and **in thy name** have cast out devils ? and in thy name done many wonderful works ? Here the *Anadiplosis* develops into *Anaphora* by the repetition of the words at the beginning of the last sentence. See under *Erotesis.*

Hab. iii. 2.—" Revive thy work **in the midst of the years, in the midst of the years** make known." See also under *Pleonasm.*

Matt x. 40.—" He that receiveth you **receiveth me,** and he that **receiveth me** receiveth him that sent me." The figure is clearer in the Greek than in the English.

John xiv. 11.—" Believe me that I am in **the Father,** and **the Father** in me."

John xviii. 37.—It is difficult to express the figure in this verse in English. The " I " is repeated thus:

" Thou sayest that a King am **I**. **I** to this end was born."

Rom. viii. 17.—" If children, then **heirs** : **heirs** of God, etc."

Rom. ix. 30.—" What shall we say then? That the Gentiles which followed not after righteousness have attained to **righteousness** ; **righteousness** which is of faith."

Rom. x. 17.—" So then, faith cometh by **hearing**, and **hearing** by the word of God."

2 Cor. v. 17, 18.—To see the figure, which is in the Greek, we must translate " Behold, become new are **all things**, and **all things** are of God."

2 Cor. ix. 6.—" He that soweth **sparingly**, **sparingly** shall reap also : he that soweth **bountifully**, **bountifully** shall reap also."

Here is combined also the figure of *Symploce* (*q.v.*) in the repetition of the words " sow " and " reap." There is also a double *Epanodos* in the arrangement of the lines.

Gal. iv. 31, and v. 1.—So then, brethren, we are not children of a bondwoman, but of **the free** (ἐλευθέρας, *eleutheras*). **In the freedom** (ἐλευθερία, *eleutheria*) wherewith Christ hath made us free, stand fast."

Phil. ii. 8.—" And being found in fashion as a man, he became obedient unto **death**, the **death** of the cross."

Jas. i. 3.—" The trying of your faith worketh **patience**, but **patience**—let it have its perfect work, etc." See below, under Climax.

CLIMAX ; or, GRADATION.

Repeated Anadiplosis.

WHEN *Anadiplosis* is repeated in successive sentences, it is called *Climax*, from κλῖμαξ (*klimax*), *a ladder, a gradual ascent, a going up by steps.*

Hence, in Latin, it is called SCALA, *a ladder ;* GRADUS, *a step ;* or, GRADATIO, *a gradation.*

By some, it is called EPIPLOCE (*e-pip'-lo-ce*), *a folding upon.*

There are two figures to which this name is sometimes given. There is a *climax* where only *words* are concerned, and a *climax* where the *sense* is concerned. A *climax* of *words* is a figure of Grammar ; and a *climax* of *sense* is a figure of Rhetoric. We have confined our use of the word *climax* to the former ; as there are other names appropriated to the latter. A Climax in Rhetoric is known as *Anabasis* (*q.v.*), where the gradation is upward ; and *Catabasis* (*q.v.*), where it is downward : and these have other alternative titles. See below under figures of sense.

Climax relates to words ; and is, as we have said, a repeated *Anadiplosis*, or a combination of successive *Anadiplosis* and *Epanadiplosis :* where the *last* word of one sentence is repeated as the *first* word of the next, and the last of this next sentence is repeated as the first word of the sentence following, and so on.

Sometimes there may be two or three words, only one of which is repeated ; or the repeated noun may be represented by a pronoun.

It is a beautiful figure, very expressive ; and at once attracts our attention to the importance of a passage.

Hos. ii. 21.—"And it shall come to pass in that day, I will hear, saith the LORD, I will hear

   the heavens, and

   they shall hear

     the earth ; and

     the earth shall hear

       the corn, and the wine, and the oil, and

       they shall hear Jezreel."

Thus does the Spirit emphasize the blessing wherewith Jehovah will bless His People—when they shall obtain mercy, and He will betroth them unto Himself for ever.

Jezreel (*i.e.*, Israel, by the figure of *Metonymy, q.v.*) shall cry out for and expect the corn and wine and oil; and these, by the beautiful figure of *Prosopopœïa* (*q. v.*), are represented as hearing, and in their turn, crying out to the Earth to bring them forth: the Earth, in its turn, is represented as hearing them, and crying out to the heavens to send rain and heat and light and air; and these in their turn hear, and cry out to Jehovah, the giver of all, who in judgment had made the heaven as brass, the earth as iron, and the rain as powder and dust (Deut. xxviii. 23, 24), but who in that day will first give repentance to Israel, and then their cry reaches to Jehovah, who will open the heavens, and give rain, and the Earth shall bring forth her fruit (Jer. xiv. 22).

Thus the figures *Epizeuxis* (" I will hear"), *Polysyndeton, Climax,* and *Prosopopœïa* are heaped together to express the coming fulness of Israel's blessing.

Joel i. 3, 4.—The prophecy of Joel opens with the solemnity which this figure always gives. "Tell ye
    your children of it, and let
    your children tell
        their children, and
        their children another generation.
That which the palmerworm hath left hath
    the locust eaten; and that which
    the locust hath left hath
        the cankerworm eaten; and that which
        the cankerworm hath left hath
            the caterpiller eaten."

John i. 1, 2.—" In the beginning was
    the Word: and
    the Word was with
        God: and
        God
            the Word was, and
            the same [*word*] was in the beginning with God."

The order of the words as thus placed in the Greek exhibits, by the figure of *Climax*, a great solemnity in the measured rising of the sense, and emphasizes the fact that " the word was God," for the use of the article in the third proposition preserves the actual sense from being mistaken or hidden by the *Climax*, which is obtained by the inversion of the words from their natural order.

Thus beautifully is the true Deity of the Lord Jesus affirmed.

His attributes and their effect are similarly marked in verses 4 and 5 :—

John i. 4, 5.—" In Him was
  life ; and the
  life was the
    light of men. And the
    light shineth in
      darkness ; and the
      darkness comprehended it not."

Rom. v. 3,-4,-5.—" And not only so, but we glory also* in
  tribulations : knowing that
  tribulation worketh
    patience ; and
    patience [*worketh*]
      experience ; and
      experience worketh
        hope ; and
        hope maketh not ashamed."

Rom. viii. 29, 30.—" For whom he did foreknow, he did
  predestinate also to be conformed to the image of his Son,
        that he might be the firstborn among many
        brethren. Moreover, whom He did
  predestinate, them he
    called also ; and whom he
    called, them He
      justified also ; but whom he
      justified, them he glorified also."

Rom. x. 14,-15.—"Whosoever shall
  call upon the name of LORD shall be saved.
    How then shall they
  call on him in whom they have not
  believed ? and how shall they
  believe in him of whom they have not
    heard ? And how shall they
    hear without a
      preacher ? And how shall they
      preach, except they may be sent."

---

* See " *Also* " : *a Biblical Study*, by the same author and publisher.

Jas. i. 3, 4.—" Knowing this that the trying of your faith worketh
  patience.   But let
  patience have her
      perfect work, that ye may be
      perfect and entire, wanting nothing."

Jas. i. 14, 15.—" But every man is tempted when he is drawn
away of his own
    lust, and enticed.   Then when
    lust hath conceived, it bringeth forth
      sin : and
      sin when it is finished, bringeth forth death."

2 Peter i. 5-7.—" We have already considered this verse under
the figure of *Polysyndeton*, which is almost inseparable from the figure
of *Climax*.   It is there very differently exhibited, however, to show
that figure.

We need not further explain the passage here, but merely exhibit
it to show the sevenfold Climax.

" Add to your faith
    virtue : and to
    virtue
        knowledge : and to
        knowledge
            temperance : and to
            temperance
                patience : and to
                patience
                    godliness : and to
                    godliness
                        brotherly kindness : and to
                        brotherly kindness, charity.

MESARCHIA; or, BEGINNING AND MIDDLE REPETITION.

The Repetition of the same Word or Words at the beginning and middle of successive Sentences.

Mes-ar'-chi-a, from the Greek μέσος (*mesos*), *middle*, and ἀρχή (*archee*), *beginning*, because the same word or words are repeated at the *beginning* and *middle* of successive sentences.

It differs little from *Anaphora*, where the sentences are independent.

It resembles also *Epizeuxis*, when the repetition comes very close together.

Num. ix. 20.—"**According to the commandment of the** LORD they abode in their tents, and **according to the commandment of the** LORD they journeyed."

Here, the repetition is at the beginning and the middle of the passage.

Ecc. i. 2.—"**Vanity of vanities**, saith the Preacher, **vanity of vanities**, all is vanity."

This may be regarded also as combined with *Epanadiplosis* (*q.v.*).

Jer. xxii. 10.—"**Weep** ye not for the dead, . . . but **weep** sore for him that goeth away." (See also *Polyptoton*).

Ezek. xxxvii. 25.—"**And they shall dwell** in the land that I have given unto Jacob my servant, wherein your fathers have dwelt, **and they shall dwell** therein, even they and their children and their children's children for ever."

Zeph. i. 15, 16.—"**That day** is a day of wrath, **a day** of trouble and distress, **a day** of wasteness and desolation, **a day** of darkness and gloominess, **a day** of clouds and thick darkness, **a day** of the trumpet and alarm," etc.

This is the figure of *Mesarchia*, for it occurs in the beginning and middle of the first sentence. Afterwards it becomes the figure of *Mesodiplosis*, inasmuch as the word "day" occurs in the middle of successive sentences, the first part of which consists of the repetition of the *Ellipsis*: "That day is . . ."

Matt. x. 40, 41.—Here the verb "receive" is repeated several times at the beginning and middle of several sentences.

MESODIPLOSIS; or, MIDDLE REPETITION.

The Repetition of the same Word or Words in the middle of successive Sentences.

Mes-o-dip-lo'sis, from the Greek μέσος (*mesos*), *middle,* and δίπλωσις (*diplōsis*), *a doubling.* The doubling or repetition of a word or words in the middle of successive sentences.

Sometimes called MESOPHONIA (*Mes-o-pho'-ni-a*), from μέσος (*mesos*), *middle,* and φωνή (*phōnee*), *a sound, tone, speech,* or *voice.*

2 Cor. iv. 8, 9.—

"We are troubled on every side, yet not distressed ;
We are perplexed, but not in despair :
Persecuted, but not forsaken ;
Cast down, but not destroyed."

MESOTELEUTON; or, MIDDLE AND END REPETITION.

The Repetition of the same Word or Words in the middle and at the end of successive Sentences.

Mes-o-tel-eu-ton, from μέσος (*mesos*), *middle*, and τελευτή (*teleutee*), a finish, or end, *i.e.*, the same word or words repeated in the *middle* and at the end of successive sentences.

2 Kings xix. 7.—"Behold I will send a blast upon him, and he shall hear a rumour, and shall return to **his own land**: aud I will cause him to fall by the sword in **his own land**."

The repetition greatly emphasizes the fact stated.

Isa. viii. 12.—"Say ye not **a confederacy** to all them to whom this people shall say **a confederacy**."

There is the figure also of *Polyptoton* (*q.v.*) in "say ye" and "shall say."

Mark v. 2, 3.—"And when he was come out of the ship, immediately there met him out of **the tombs** a man with an unclean spirit, who had his dwelling among **the tombs**."

See also *Polyptoton*.

REPETITIO ; or, REPETITION.

Repetition of the same Word or Words irregularly in the same Passage.

THIS name is generally given as an alternative to the figure of *Geminatio* or *Epizeuxis*. But as that figure already has several names, and there is another form of repetition which seems to be without a name, we have appropriated *Repetitio* (*i.e.*, *Repetition*), to that form which comes under none of the figures already enumerated.

A word or words are repeated, not in immediate succession, as in *Epizeuxis*; not at the beginning, middle, or end of sentences (as in those just treated); not at definite intervals; but frequently in the same passage and *irregularly* for the sake of emphasizing and calling attention to it.

The name clearly defines the nature of the figure, which may frequently be met with. We append a few examples :—

Ezek. xxxvi. 23-29.—Here the words "**you**" and "**your**" are very frequently thus repeated, giving great emphasis to the whole of this precious promise for Israel in the latter day. The use of this figure strongly forbids the interpretation of this passage to any but Israel (verses 22, 32).

John xiv. 1-4.—The repetition of the pronouns "**I**" and "**you**" emphasizes the fact that nothing is to come between the Lord and the hearts of His people, so that His promised return may be the object ever before them.

John xvi. 12-15.—Here, the verbs "shall" and "will" are repeated eleven times in these four verses, in order to impress us with the importance of the promise and the absolute certainty of its performance.

" I have yet many things to say unto you, but ye cannot bear them now. Howbeit, when He, the Spirit of truth, is (**shall** have) come, He **will** guide you into all truth (" all the truth," R.V.): for He **shall** not speak of (*i.e.*, from) Himself ; but whatsoever He **shall** hear, that **shall** He speak : and He **will** show you things to come. He **shall** glorify me : for He **shall** receive of mine, and **shall** show it unto you. All things that the Father hath are mine : therefore said I, that He **shall** take of mine, and **shall** show it unto you."

Thus is emphasized the solemn promise of the Lord Jesus that the Holy Spirit should give a further revelation of Truth, which could not be made known at that time. We have it in the seven Epistles addressed to churches by the Holy Spirit, through Paul.* That great promise cannot find its fulfilment subjectively or individually, giving " truths " to different persons, so different (not to say opposite) that fierce controversies rage concerning them. It cannot have been fulfilled in the inspiration of any one church. It can have been fulfilled only by the provision of those text-books of Christian doctrine, which we have in the " Pauline" Epistles addressed to churches, beginning with Romans and ending with Thessalonians. Here, we have " all the truth " into which the Spirit was to guide. Truth which glorifies Christ and instructs the Christian as to his standing before God and his walk with God. No other part of God's Word contains such a body of Christian Theology. Every Scripture is written *for* us, " for our learning "; but these are written specially *about* the Church of God.

Gal. iv. 9.—" How turn ye **again** to the weak and beggarly elements whereunto ye desire **again** to be in bondage."

By this repetition we are pointed to the key to this whole passage, as well as to the explanation of an obscure word and a difficult expression. All turns on the meaning of the word, which is rendered " elements " (στοιχεῖα, *stoicheia*). "The elements of the world" (verse 3), and " weak and beggarly elements " (verse 10). The word "again," twice used, connects these two together, and emphasizes them.

Verse 3 reads:—

" Even so we, when we were children, were in bondage under the στοιχεῖα τοῦ κόσμου " (*stoicheia tou kosmou*): *i.e.*, the *stoicheia* pertaining to the world.

It is clear what the *cosmos* is, for it is the world with reference to its creation, and embraces the whole world. But what are the *stoicheia*? The answer is given in verse 8, " When ye knew not God ye did service (or ' were in bondage,' the same word as in verses 3 and 10) unto them which by nature are no gods." The *stoicheia* were the rites and ceremonies of heathen idolatry.

In Greece to-day every mountain, tree, and grove and fountain has its *stoicheion* or god, who has to be appeased and propitiated.

These Galatians had been such idolators (verse 8), but they had abandoned these rites and ceremonies for Christianity, and yet wanted to bring in the *stoicheia*, or the rites and ceremonies of Judaism into the Church.

---

* See *Things to Come* for 1898 and 1899.

The same term is thus applied both to Paganism and Judaism, and from the stand-point of being " all one in Christ Jesus " (iii. 28).

The Jewish rites of circumcision, purification, and the observance of " days and months and times and years," etc., are put upon the same level as the worship and propitiation of spirits in trees and mountains, etc. And the Holy Spirit asks by the apostle, " When ye knew not God ye were in bondage unto them which by nature are no gods. But now having known God . . . how turn ye **again** unto the weak and beggarly *stoicheia* whereto ye desire **again** to be in bondage ? Ye observe days and months and times and years. I am afraid of you, lest I have bestowed upon you labour in vain " (Gal. iv. 8-11. Compare Col. ii. 16-18).

Hence, *stoicheiolatry* consists of introducing that which belongs to the world (κόσμος, *cosmos*) into Christian worship and practice. Romanism has given the *stoicheia* of paganism and Judaism a very large place in its creeds and ritual ; while the Protestant Churches show that they have not wholly purged themselves from them when they adopt worldly methods and adapt Jewish rites and ceremonies to Christian faith and practice.

1 Thess. v. 1, 2, 4, 5.—The repetition of the pronoun " **you** " and " **ye** " in these verses stands in marked contrast to the repetition of the pronouns " **they** " and " **them** " in verse 3, thus pointing out to us the significant lesson that those who are " waiting for God's Son from Heaven " are not concerned with " times and seasons " which have to do with " the day of the Lord," and His coming as " a thief " on the ungodly. The day of the Lord is His coming *with* His saints unto the world. But, before this can happen, He will have come forth into the air to receive them to Himself (1 Thess. iv.) Therefore, though " times and seasons " have to do with " the day of the Lord," they have nothing to do with those who look for " the day of Christ."

2 Tim. iii. 14, 15.—" But continue **thou** in the things which **thou** hast learned and hast been assured of, knowing of whom **thou** hast learned them : and that from a child **thou** hast known the holy Scriptures, which are able to make **thee** wise unto salvation."

This is in harmony with the whole of this second epistle to Timothy, which is thus marked as being so different from the first epistle.

In the first epistle we see the Church in its *rule ;* and in the second, we see it in its *ruin.* In the first, Timothy is instructed as to how he is to conduct himself in the Church in its corporate capacity ; whom he is to appoint to its various offices; and what are to be their qualifications, etc., etc.

But when we pass to the second epistle we find all changed. The corporate position and testimony of the Church is gone, and all now is individual—intensely individual, as may be seen all through. In the four chapters we have the four stages of the " Down-grade movement."

In i. 15 all turn away from Paul's teaching: but " **I** am not ashamed : for **I** know whom **I** have believed " (verse 12) : " Be not **thou** ashamed " (verse 8), " I call to remembrance the unfeigned faith that is in **thee** " (verse 5).

In chap. ii. 18, 19, others err " concerning the truth. Nevertheless, the foundation of God standeth sure, having this seal, the Lord knoweth them that are his. And let **everyone** that nameth the name of Christ depart from iniquity."

In chap. iii. 8 there are those who " resist the truth," but the only hope is for the individual believer to cling fast to the God-breathed word, and to use this sword of the Spirit.

In chap. iv. 4 there are and shall be those who turn away their ears from the truth, and shall be turned unto fables." The immediate injunction follows: " but watch **thou** in all things . . make full proof of **thy** ministry, etc."

All this is emphasized and forced upon our notice by the repetition of the pronouns in this epistle.

Rev. viii. 7-12.—*Eleven* times are the words, the " **third part** " repeated (τὸ τρίτον, *to triton*).

POLYPTOTON ; or, MANY INFLECTIONS.

The Repetition of the same Part of Speech in different Inflections.

Po-lyp'-tō-ton.   Greek, πολύπτωτον ; from πολύς (*polūs*), *many*, and πτῶσις (*ptōsis*), *a falling :* in grammar, *a case* (from an assumed form πτόω, *ptoō, to fall*).   Hence, *Polyptoton* means *with many cases, i.e.,* a repetition of the same noun in several cases, or of the same verb in several moods or tenses.   *With many inflections* is a definition which covers both nouns and verbs.

It is called also METAGOGE (*met-a-gō-gee*).   Greek μεταγωγή, from μετά (*meta*), *a change,* and ἄγω (*agō*), *to lead.*   It means *a change of course ; a different arrangement* of the same word, a leading of the same word through different inflections.

In Latin it is called CASUUM VARIETAS, *a variety of cases.*

This figure, therefore, is a repetition of the same word in the same sense, but not in the same form : from the same root, but in some other termination ; as that of case, mood, tense, person, degree, number, gender, etc.

By " case," etc., is to be understood not merely the case of nouns, but inflections of all kinds.

We have arranged the different forms of *Polyptoton*, as follows :—

I. Verbs.

1. Verbs repeated in different moods and tenses.
2. Verbs with their imperatives, or participles (HOMOGENE).
    (*a*) In strong affirmation.
    (*b*) In strong negation.
3. Verbs with cognate noun.
4. Verbs with other parts of speech (combined *Polyptoton*).

II. Nouns and Pronouns.

1. Nouns repeated in different cases.
2. Nouns repeated in different numbers.
    (*a*) In singular and plural.
    (*b*) In singular and dependent genitive plural.

III. Adjectives.

I. Verbs.

1. Verbs repeated in different moods and tenses.

Gen. l. 24.—Here, the Hebrew is : " God, when **He visiteth,** or in **visiting, will visit** you."

And this, in order to emphasize the certainty of Joseph's belief in the promise of God, as is stated in Heb. xi. 22. " By faith Joseph, when he died made mention of (margin, *remembered*) the departing of the children of Israel ; and gave commandment concerning his bones : " *i.e.,* Joseph remembered the promise of God made to his fathers and had such faith in it that he expressed his certainty s to its fulfilment by the use of this figure.

It is translated : " God will surely visit you " : but to give effect to the figure we might render it : " God will most certainly visit you," putting great emphasis on the words " most certainly."

Ex. xxiii. 5.—" If thou wouldest forbear to **help** him, **helping** thou shalt **help** with him " : *i.e.,* as A.V., " thou shalt surely help with him " (See Appendix D, *Homonyms*).

2 Kings xxi. 13.—" And I will **wipe** Jerusalem as a man **wipeth** a dish, **wiping** it and turning it upside down."

The figure is thus used to emphasise the completeness with which the Lord would empty Jerusalem.

Jer. viii. 4.—
> " Shall they fall and not arise ?
> Shall he turn away and not return ? "

As these words stand they are unintelligible and the figure is obscured. The R.V. is no improvement :—
> " Shall men fall, and not rise up again ?
> Shall one turn away and not return ? "

The Massorah* calls attention to the fact that of the two words " turn and," the first letter of the second word should be the last letter of the first word, this being one of the examples where words are wrongly divided.

Thus read the sense comes out in agreement with the context of which Israel is the subject :—
> " Shall they fall and not arise ?
> Shall **they return** [*to Him*] and **He** not **return** [*to them*].

---

* Ginsburg's Edition, Vol. II, page 54.

This agrees also with Mal. iii. 7, and it brings out the correspondence between the two lines, as well as exhibits more clearly the *Polyptoton.*

Matt. xi. 15.—"·He that hath ears to hear, let him hear," ὦτα ἀκούειν, ἀκουέτω (*ōta akouein akouetō*).

On· *fourteen* occasions in the New Testament does the Lord use this expression (thus, or in similar words), and we place them all together here under the first occurrence so that we may see the fulness of the cumulative effect.

In the English we have a *Paronomasia* (*q.v.*) as well, "ears *to* hear," but not in the Greek, except in the case of the eight in Revelations, where we have οὖς ακουσάτω (ous *ak*ous*ato*). The real figure lies in the emphatic *polyptoton* in each case.

This solemn injunction was never· used by mere human lips. No mortal man could demand the attention to which this emphatic command lays claim None but the Lord ever used these words. They are (unlike many other of the examples) translated literally, but they mean : He whose ears are opened, let him surely hear, or let him take heed to give the most earnest attention !

This attention and obedience the Lord claimed on fourteen separate occasions.

The fourteen are not divided into two sevens, but into six and eight (two fours and two threes).

Six being the number of *man*, He spoke the words six times as "the Son of Man" on earth : and *eight* being the number of *resurrection*), He spoke the words eight times as the Risen Lord from heaven.

Though the occasions were *fourteen* (7×2) on which the words were used, the actual number of times the words are written down by the Holy Spirit is *sixteen* (4×4, or 4^2), two being in the parallel passages in the Gospels.*

These fourteen occasions are connected with different parts of one great subject, which is *dispensational* in its character : and this figure being used only of this one subject, points us to the significant fac that it requires the Divinely opened ear to understand the great dispensational change which was about to take place.

It had been foretold in Isa. vi. 9 (see above) that it should come about in consequence of the ears being closed to the divine announcement : and seven times this solemn infliction of judicial blindness is written down in the Scriptures of Truth.

---

* For the significance of these numbers see *Number in Scripture* (pp 20-47). bythe same author and publisher.

When the great change was announced in consequence and
fulfilment of this! then, fourteen times did the Lord Himself emphasize
the important fact that only the opened ear would be able to understand it; implying that it referred to secret things, and that only
those to whom that secret was revealed would be able to understand it
or receive it.

For the interpretation of these fourteen occurrences, see *Things
to Come* (July to Dec., 1896; Jan. and Feb., 1897; Sept. and Oct.,
1898, etc.)*　We here give merely their order.

1. Elijah and John the Baptist (Matt. xi. 15).
2. The parable of the sower (Matt. xiii. 9; Mark iv. 9; Luke viii. 8).
3. The candlestick (Mark iv. 21-23).
4. The parable of the tares (Matt. xiii. 43).
5. The two dispensations (Mark vii. 16).
6. The tower; the king and the salt: or, the great supper and its
   lessons (Luke xiv. 16-35).
7-13. The epistles to the seven churches (Rev. ii., iii.).
14. The beast from the sea (Rev. xiii. 9).

Matt. xiii. 9, 43.—See xi. 15.

Matt. xix. 12.—" He that is able to receive it, let him receive
it." (χωρεῖν χωρείτω, *chōrein chōreitō*).

Mark iv. 12.—See Matt. xiii. 13.

Mark iv. 23.—See Matt. xi. 15.

Mark vii. 16.—See Matt. xi. 15.

Luke viii. 8.—See Matt. xiii. 13.

Luke xiv. 35.—See Matt. xi. 15.

John xii. 40.—See Matt. xiii. 13.

John xiii. 7.—Here there is apparently a *Polyptoton* of the verb
" to know," but it is only in the English, not in the Greek.　" What I
do thou knowest not now, but thou shalt know hereafter."

In the Greek the two verbs are different.　The first is οὐκ οἶδας
(*ouk oidas*), *thou knowest not* as a matter of fact.　The second is γνώσῃ
(*gnōsee*) *thou shalt learn, i.e., get to know* hereafter."　It is this latter
verb which is used in 1 Cor. ii. 14, for the natural man not only cannot
receive, or discern, them, but he cannot even *learn* them, or get to know
them, not having the necessary spiritual capacity.

---

* G. Stoneman, 39 Warwick Lane, London, E.C.

John xiii. 10.—Here again there is no *Polyptoton* of the verb *to wash*, as appears in the English, for in the Greek the two words are quite different. " He that is washed (λελουμένος, *leloumenos*, *i.e.*, *bathed*) needeth not save to wash (νίψασθαι, *nipsasthai*, *i.e.*, *to wash* a part of the body) his feet." The teaching is that he who is purged by the offering on the brazen altar, needeth only the water of the brazen laver, which was for " the priests to wash in." So those who are regenerated by the Holy Ghost and have their *standing* in Christ need only the washing of the hands and the feet, *i.e.*, the cleansing of their works and ways by " the washing of water by the word."

John xvii. 26.—" And **I** have declared unto them thy name and **will** declare it."

John xvii. 25.—" O righteous Father, the world **hath** not **known** (ἔγνω, *egnō*) thee : but **I** have **known** (ἔγνων, *egnōn*) thee, and **these** have **known** (ἔγνωσαν, *egnosan*) that thou hast sent me."

Rom. ii. 21-23.—" Thou therefore that **teachest** (ὁ διδάσκων *ho didaskōn*) another, **teachest** (διδάσκεις, *didaskeis*) thou not thyself ?

Thou that preachest a man should not **steal**, dost thou **steal** (μὴ κλέπτειν, κλέπτεις, *mee kleptein, klepteis*) ?

Thou that sayest a man should not **commit adultery**, dost thou **commit adultery** (μὴ μοιχεύειν, μοιχεύεις, *mee moicheuein, moicheueis*) ?

Thou that makest thy boast of **the law** (νόμῳ, *nomō*) through breaking **the law** (νόμου, *nomou*), dishonourest thou God ? "

1 Cor. vi. 2.—" Do ye not know that the saints **shall judge** (κρινοῦσιν, *krinousin*) the world ? and if the world shall **be judged** (κρίνεται, *krinetai*) by you, are ye unworthy [*to judge*] (Ellipsis of the verb) the smallest matters (κριτηρίων, *kriteeriōn*), *i.e.*, " are you unworthy [*to judge*] the smallest judgments ? "

2 Cor. i. 10.—" Who **delivered** us from so great a death, and **doth deliver**: in whom we trust that He **will** yet **deliver** us."

Gal. i. 8, 9.—" But though we, or an angel from heaven, **preach any other gospel** (εὐαγγελίζηται, *euangelizeetai*) unto you than that which we **have preached** (εὐηγγελισάμεθα, *eueengelisametha*) unto you, let him be accursed. As we said before, so say I now again, If any man **preach any other gospel** (εὐαγγελίζεται, *euangelizetai*) unto you . . . . let him be accursed.'

See also under *Anaphora*.

2 Tim. iii. 13.—" But evil men and seducers shall wax worse and worse, **deceiving** and **being deceived**."

2 Tim. iv. 17, 18.—"And I was delivered out of the mouth of the lion.　And the Lord shall deliver me from every evil work."

There is also the figure of *Polysyndeton* in this verse (*q.v.*).

1 John iii. 7.—" Little children, let no man deceive you ; he that doeth righteousness is righteous, even as He is righteous."

See also this verse under the figure of *Tapeinosis*.

Heb. x. 37.—"He who cometh will come": *i.e.*, He will surely come.

See also under the figure of *Epizeuxis*.

Rev. ii. 7, 11, 17, 29 ; iii. 6, 13, 22 ; xiii. 9.—See Matt. xi. 15, and, under *Correspondence*, " The seven epistles to the churches" by the Holy Spirit through St. Paul.

2. Verbs with their Infinitives or Participles.

In this case a verb and its participle are used in combination in order to add an intensity to the sense ; or to give the verb, as it were, a superlative degree.

This form of the figure is sometimes called *Ho-mog′-e-nee* (from ὁμός (*homos*), *the same*, and γένος, *genos*, *kindred*).

HOMOGENE means therefore *of the same kindred*, *akin*, because the two verbs are akin.

It is used in two ways :—

 (*a*) In strong and emphatic affirmation.

 (*b*) In strong negation.

(*a*) In strong affirmation or exhortation.

Gen. ii. 16.—' Of every tree of the garden thou mayest freely eat."　Hebrew, eating thou shalt eat.

The conjugated verb is strengthened and emphasized by the infinitive preceding it.　This infinitive Eve omitted in iii. 2, and thus " diminished " from the word of God.

Gen. ii. 17.—"Thou shalt surely die."　Hebrew, dying thou shalt die.

Here again Eve (iii. 3) alters the Word of God by saying " Lest ye die "!* מות תמות (*moth tahmuth*) *thou shalt most certainly die*, were the words of the LORD God.

---

 * Not only does she thus *diminish* from and *alter* the Word of God but she *adds* to it the words " neither shall ye touch it," which the LORD God had not spoken !

Thus she changes a certainty into a contingency.

See this verse under the figure of *Synecdoche*.

Gen. iii. 16.—" Unto the woman He said **multiplying, I will multiply** thy sorrow, etc.," *i.e.*, as in A.V., " I will greatly multiply."

Gen. xxviii. 22.—Hebrew, " Tithing, will I tithe for thee," *i.e.*, as in A.V., " I will surely give the tenth unto thee."

Gen. xxxvii. 33.—" Joseph is without doubt torn in pieces."
The Heb. is טָרֹף טֹרַף (*taroph, toraph*), **tearing, he is torn.** The figure employed shows the intensity of Jacob's feelings. He exclaims:

" The tunic of my son !
A wild beast hath devoured him !
Tearing—Joseph is **torn.**"

I.e., he hath been certainly killed or cruelly mangled.

Ex. iii. 16.—" I have surely visited you." Hebrew, **visiting I have visited** you.

Ex. xix. 12.—Here the figure is translated : " He . . . shall be surely put to death." Lit., **stoning, he shall be stoned.**
So verse 13 : " He shall surely be stoned."

Josh. xxiv. 10.—" But I would not hearken unto Balaam : therefore he blessed you still." Hebrew, **blessing, he blessed you** : *i.e.*, he kept blessing you, or he surely blessed you, or he did nothing but bless you, or he blessed you exceedingly.

2 Kings iii. 23.—" The kings are surely slain." Hebrew, **destroying they are destroyed.**

Ps. cxviii. 18.—" The LORD hath chastened me sore." Hebrew, *Jah* **chastening hast chastened** *me.*

Isa. vi. 9.—" Hear ye indeed." Hebrew, *Hear ye in hearing.* " And see ye indeed." Hebrew, " See ye in seeing," etc.

On four occasions is this great dispensational prophecy repeated in the New Testament in order to emphasise and call attention to the great change which was about to take place.

(1)   Matt. xiii. 14.   Mark iv. 12.   Luke viii. 4.
(2)   John xii. 39, 40.
(3)   Acts xxviii. 25-27,
(4)   Rom. xi. 8.

Thus, *seven* times in all, this great prophecy is written down by the Holy Spirit in the Scriptures of Truth.

See Matt. xi. 15 above (page 269).

s

Jer. xxii. 10.—"Weep sore for him that goeth away." Hebrew, **weeping weep.**

Jer. xxiii. 17.—"They say still unto them that despise me," etc. Hebrew, **saying they say** : *i.e., they maintain,* or *they keep saying,* etc.

Dan. xi. 13.—"He shall certainly come." Hebrew, **coming he shall come.**

Zech. viii. 21.—"Let us go speedily." Hebrew, **going let us go.**

Matt. xiii. 13.—"Because they **seeing see** not, and **hearing they hear** not" : *i.e.,* they are determined not to hear and not to see. See also Mark iv. 12. Luke viii. 10. John xii. 40. Acts xxviii. 26; and Rom. xi. 8 : where Isa. vi. 9 is quoted.

Acts vii. 34.—Here the figure of *Polyptoton* is translated as though it were *Epizeuxis* (*q.v.*). Lit. it is "**Seeing I have seen**" : *i.e.,* I have surely seen.

Acts xxviii. 26, 27.—See Matt. xiii. 13.

Rom. xi. 8.—See Matt. xiii. 13.

Rom. xii. 15.—In this verse we have two examples of the repetition of the infinitive and participle.

"**Rejoice** with them that **do rejoice** (χαίρειν μετὰ χαιρόντων, *chairein meta chairontōn*), and **weep** with them **that weep** (κλαίειν μετὰ κλαιόντων, *klaiain meta klaiontōn*)."

Two other figures are combined here—*Homœopropheron* and *Homœoptoton* (*q.v.*).

Heb. vi. 14.—"**Surely blessing I will bless** thee, and **multiplying I will multiply** thee" : *i.e.,* Surely in blessing I will most certainly bless thee, etc.

(*a*) In strong negation.

Gen. iii. 4.—"And the serpent said unto the woman, Ye shall not surely die."

Here the serpent emphatically denies Jehovah's words, and says, **dying thou shalt not die.**

He is thus introduced to us in his special sphere—denying the Word of God. For he is the god of this world's *religion* and not of its *crimes* and *immoralities.* And his sphere is in the corruption of the truth rather than in the degradation of the flesh.*

Ex. v. 23.—"Thou hast not delivered them at all."

---

* See *The Silence of God,* by Robert Anderson, LL.D., C.B., published by Hodder and Stoughton.

Thus beautifully is the figure rendered. Hebrew, **delivering thou hast not delivered** them.

Ex. xxxiv. 7.—"And wilt by no means clear the guilty." Hebrew, **clearing thou wilt not clear.** Even so the Substitute of the Lord's people was not cleared. When he bore their sins he bore the punishment also that was due to them.

Ps. xlix. 7 (8).—"None of them can by any means redeem his brother."

Thus beautifully is the figure rendered, which the R.V. has not attempted to improve.

Hebrew, *a brother* **redeeming doth not redeem** *a man : i.e.,* even though he pay down the price there is no redemption.

3. Verbs with cognate noun.

A verb and a cognate noun are used together, when great emphasis is placed upon the assertion or expression. It is a kind of superlative degree in verbs to declare the magnitude and gravity of an action or the greatness and importance of its results.

Gen. i. 11.—"Let the earth bring forth grass, the herb yielding seed." Lit., **seeding seed.** Thus emphasizing the fact that trees, etc., were created bearing the seeds : and not the seeds producing the trees. The hen was created producing the egg, and not the egg producing the hen. Thus, at the very outset of the Word of God, the modern figment of "evolution" is exploded.

Gen. viii. 21.—"And the LORD smelled a sweet savour." Lit., **smelled the sweet smell,** or **the savour of rest:** *i.e.,* Jehovah accepted the sacrifice, and was satisfied with the atonement made by Noah.

The figure of *Anthrōpopatheia* (*q.v.*) is involved.

Gen. xxvii. 3.—"Take me some venison." Lit., **hunt** me some hunting, *i.e.,* fetch me some game.

The lxx. similarly expresses it θήρευσόν μοι θήραν.

Venison, so called from the Latin *venatio*, to hunt.

Gen. xxvii. 33.—"And Isaac trembled very exceedingly."

Thus beautifully is the Hebrew figure turned into an English idiom.

The Hebrew is: "And Isaac **trembled** with a great **trembling** greatly." (See margin).

Gen. xxvii. 34.—"And . . . Esau . . . **cried** with a great and exceeding bitter **cry**."

Gen. xxviii. 20.—"And Jacob **vowed** a **vow**," *i.e.*, solemnly vowed.

Gen. xxx. 8.—"And Rachel said, With great wrestlings have I wrestled with my sister." Lit., "with **wrestlings** of God, **have I wrestled** with my sister"; where we have another figure, *Enallage*, by which the Noun "of God" is used instead of the adjective "great," denoting therefore "with very great and super-human wrestlings have I wrestled." (See *Enallage*).

Gen. xxxv. 14.—"And Jacob set up a pillar וַיַּצֵּב מַצֵּבָה (*vaya-tzev matzevah*), lit., and he **pillared** a **pillar**. So verse 20.*

Num. iv. 23.—"All that enter in **to serve the service** to **work the work** in the Tabernacle of the congregation."

Num. xi. 4.—"And the mixt multitude that was among them fell a lusting." Hebrew, **lusted a lust**: *i.e.*, lusted exceedi

Num. xvi. 30.—"But if the LORD make a new thing." Hebrew, **create a creation**: *i.e.*, do something wonderful.

1 Sam iv. 5.—"All Israel **shouted** with **a great shout**": *i.e.*, with a very loud and prolonged or sustained cry.

2 Sam. xii. 16.—"And David fasted," *lit.*, **fasted a fast**: *i.e.*, completely or truly fasted.

2 Sam. xiii. 36.—"And all his servants wept very sore." In Hebrew the figure is "**wept** a great **weeping** greatly."

1 Kings i. 40.—"The people **piped** with **pipes**, and **rejoiced** with great **joy**": *i.e.*, their joy scarcely knew bounds.

2 Kings iv. 13.—"Thou hast been **careful** for us with all this **care**": *i.e.*, exceedingly careful.

2 Kings xiii. 14.—"Now Elisha was **fallen sick** of his **sickness**": *i.e.*, was exceeding sick so that he died.

---

* It seems clear that this should be the reading also in Gen. xxxiii. 20, where we have the same verb וַיַּצֶּב (*vayatzev*), which means *to stand* or *rear up*, as one lifts and sets up a (single) memorial stone which we now call a "*menhir.*" But the noun is different מִזְבֵּחַ (*mizbeach*), which means *an altar*. Some ancient scribe either mistook *matzevah* (*a pillar*) and wrote *mizbeach* (*an altar*), or the noun was originally abbreviated by the use of the initial letter מ (*mem*) and was after-wards filled out incorrectly. Because the verb that always goes with *altar* is בָּנָה (*banah*), *to build*, as with bricks, etc. (except in Gen. xxxv. 1, 3 and Ex. xxx. 1, where it is עָשָׂה (*asah*), *to make*; and 1 Kings xvi. 32, where it is קוּם (*kum*), *to raise* or *set up* as a building, and not נָצַב (*natzav*), *to stand up* as a pillar).

2 Kings. xix. 7.—"He shall hear a rumour," lit., **hear a hearing,*** *i.e.*, he shall hear important news, something that will upset his plans.

Ps. xiv. 5 and liii. 5.—"There were they in great fear." The Figure is "they **feared a fear.**"

Ps. cxliv. 6.—" Cast forth lightning." Heb., **lighten lightning,** *i.e.*, lighten exceedingly, and destroy them.

Prov. xxx. 24.—"**Wise,** made **wise.**" Here, the emphasis created by the repetition in the form of *Polyptoton*, makes a superlative adjective and is beautifully and idiomatically rendered "exceeding wise."

Man is by nature ignorant. He is born more ignorant than the beasts. He has, therefore, to be "made wise"; and, in spiritual things, this can be done only by the Holy Spirit of God.

Isa. viii. 12.—"Neither **fear** ye their **fear,** nor be afraid (*i.e.*, fearful). Sanctify the LORD of hosts Himself, and let Him be your fear."

Isa. xxii. 17.—" Behold, the LORD will carry thee away with a mighty captivity." This verse and the next are very difficult, as is attested by a comparison of the A.V. and R.V. with their marginal readings. The above words are literally, " Behold, Jehovah will **hurl** thee **with the hurling** of a [strong] man." The R.V. expresses it: " The LORD will hurl thee away violently."

Jer. xxii. 16.—"He judged the cause." Lit., He **judged** the **judgment**; *i.e.*, righteously judged.

So Lam. iii. 59.

Jer. li. 2.—"And will send unto Babylon **fanners** (זָרִים, *zareem*) that shall **fan** her זֵרוּהָ, *v'zerŭaha*)."

Ezek. xviii. 2.—" What mean ye that ye use this proverb? Heb. : מֹשְׁלִים אֶת־הַמָּשָׁל (*mishleem eth-hammahshal*). Lit., **ye proverb** this **proverb**, *i.e.*, ye have this proverb in constant use.

Ezek. xxxviii. 12.—" To take a spoil, and to take a prey." Lit., **to spoil spoil** and **to prey prey**; *i.e.*, to take great spoil and a great prey.

Dan. xi. 3.—" A mighty King shall stand up that shall **rule** with a great **rule** "; *i.e.*, have a vast dominion.

Jonah i. 10.—" Then were the men exceedingly afraid." Lit., **feared with great fear.**

---

* See *Metonymy* (of adjunct).

Micah ii. 4.—" In that day shall one take up a parable against you, and lament with a **lamentation of lamentations** " : *i.e.*, shall exceedingly lament. Or, as in A.V. " lament with a doleful lamentation." See below, page 284.

Nah. i. 15 (ii. 1.).—" Keep thy solemn feasts." Hebrew, **Feast** thy solemn **feasts.**

The figure gives a superlative degree, as it were, to the verb, implying that, before this, feasts had only been formally observed : henceforth they are to be truly celebrated.

Hab. iii. 2.—"O LORD, I have heard thy speech, and was afraid." Hebrew, I have **heard hearing** of thee, *i.e.*, I have heard thy fame.

Zech. i. 2.—" The LORD hath been sore displeased with your fathers." The figure is thus beautifully rendered. Lit., it is " Jehovah hath been **displeased** with **displeasure** with your fathers."

Verse 14. " I am **jealous** for Jerusalem and for Zion with a great **jealousy,**" *i.e.*, I am exceedingly jealous.

Verse 15. " I am very sore displeased with the heathen that are at ease." Lit., " with a great **wrath** am I **wroth.**"

Zech. vii. 9.—" Execute true judgment." Thus elegantly is the figure expressed : " **Judge judgment** of truth." See John vii. 24.

This Hebrew idiom appears in the New Testament, showing that though the words are Greek the thoughts and idioms are Hebrew. (See under *Idioma*).

Matt. ii. 10.—" They **rejoiced** with exceeding great **joy.**" (ἐχάρησαν χαράν, *echareesan charan*).

See this verse under *Ellipsis.*

Mark iv. 41.—" They feared exceedingly " (ἐφοβήθησαν φόβον, *ephobeetheesan phobon*). *Lit.*, they **feared a fear.**

Luke xxii. 15.—" With **desire I have desired** to eat this passover with you."

Having translated the figure literally in the Text, the A.V. half repents it, and gives the English idiom in the margin, " *I have heartily desired.*"

John vi. 28.—" What shall we do that we might **work the works** of God ? " *i.e.*, might really do what God wills us to do.

John vii. 24.—" **Judge** righteous **judgment** " (τὴν δικαίαν κρίσιν κρίνατε, *teen dikaian krisin krinate*). See Zech. vii. 9.

Acts. xxiii. 12.—"Certain of the Jews banded together, and bound themselves under a curse." (Marg., or, *with an oath of execration*).

And then, in verse 14, to emphasize this, they say, "We have bound ourselves under a great curse." ἀναθέματι ἀνεθεματίσαμεν (*anathemati anethematisamen.*) Lit., we have **vowed a great vow.**

Anathematizo means *to devote*, and so to separate from ; especially to devote to destruction.

Eph. vi. 18.—"**Praying** always with all **prayer**," *i.e.*, earnestly praying.

Col. ii. 19.—"**Increaseth** with the **increase** of God " (αὔξει τὴν αὔξησιν, *auxei teen auxeesin*). *Lit.*, **increaseth the increase**, *i.e.*, receives abundant increase from God, or *worthy* of God : or, receives Divine increase.

1 Tim. i. 18.—"That thou . . . mightest **war** a good **warfare** " (στρατεύῃ στρατείαν, *strateuee strateian*). This comes also under the figure of *Paronomasia (q.v.).*

2 Tim. iv. 7.—" I have **fought** a good **fight** " (τὸν ἀγῶνα τὸν καλὸν ἠγώνισμαι, *ton agōna ton kalon eegōnismai*) : *i.e.*, I have earnestly fought the good fight.

Jas. v. 17.—"He prayed earnestly." This is the beautiful rendering of the figure προσευχῇ προσηύξατο (*proseuchee proseeuxato*) **with prayer he prayed.** See *Paronomasia.*

Rev. xvi. 9.—"And men were scorched with great heat." Lit., **burnt with great burning,** *i.e.*, exceedingly burnt.

Rev. xvii. 6.—" I **wondered** with great **wonder** " (A.V., admiration), *i.e.*, I wondered exceedingly.

This figure exists even when the noun is absent through the figure of *Ellipsis* :

Num. xi. 14.—" I am not able to bear [*the burden of*] all this people alone, because it, [*i.e., the burden*] is too heavy for me."

Verse 17 shows that the word *burden* is implied ; and that Moses means, I am not able to bear the heavy burden of all this People alone. (See under *Ellipsis*, page 56).

Ps. xiii. 3.—Here the noun is actually supplied in the A.V. " Sleep *the sleep of* death," *i.e*, sleep the last solemn sleep of death.

4. Verbs with other parts of speech.   (Combined
Polyptoton).

Isa. xxiv. 16.—" My leanness, my leanness,* woe unto me ! the
treacherous dealers have **dealt treacherously**; yea, the
treacherous dealers have **dealt very treacherously.**"

Here, from the two roots " deal " and " treachery " is heaped
together this variety of inflections, to enhance the result of the
enemy's treatment.

Hos. x. 1 (R.V.).—" Israel is a luxuriant vine, which **putteth
forth** his **fruit**: according to the **multitude** of his **fruit** he hath
multiplied his altars, according to the **goodness** of his land they
have made **goodly** pillars " (*i.e.*, images).

Here, in the repetition of the various inflections of the words
" fruit," " multiply," and " good," and in the repetition of " according
to " (*Anaphora*), and in the repetition of sense in " altars " and
" images," our attention is arrested and drawn to the fact that
prosperity only led the People astray into idolatry.

2 Cor. x. 12.—" For we dare not make **ourselves** of the number,
or **compare ourselves** with some that commend **themselves**: but
they measuring **themselves** by **themselves**, and **comparing themselves** among **themselves**, are not wise.

This is still more emphatic when we see the structure of this
verse.

a | For we are not bold (οὐ)

    b | to number (ἐγκρῖναι) or **compare** (συγκρῖναι) **ourselves**

       c | with certain of them that **commend themselves** :

       c | but they themselves, **measuring themselves by them-
selves,**

    b | and **comparing** (συγκρίνοντες) **themselves with themselves**

a | are without understanding (οὐ).

Here in " a " and " a " we have the declaration, in " a " as to
what *we* are not, and in " a " as to what *they* are not.

In " b " and " b " we have comparison (συγκρίνω).

In " c " and " c " we have commending and measuring.

Note also that in " b " and " c " the pronoun occurs once, while in
the corresponding members it is answered by a double occurrence.

For the meaning of the verb " compare," see below under
adjectives (page 284), and also under *Ellipsis*, page 77.

---

* This is the figure of *Epizeuxis* (*q.v.*).

Gal. v. 7, 8-10.—"Ye did run well: who did hinder you that ye should not **obey** (πείθεσθαι, *peithesthai*) the truth ? This **persuasion** (πεισμονή, *peismonee*) *cometh* not of him that calleth you . . A little eaven leaveneth* the whole lump. I have **confidence** (πέποιθα, *pepoitha*) in you through the LORD, that ye will be none otherwise minded.

Here we have three forms of the same word, or three words from the same root. This is lost in the translation. Πείθω (*peithō*) is more than *to believe*, it is *to be persuaded*, *to hold* or *hold on* to a belief. Hence, πεῖσμα (*peisma*) denotes *a ship's cable*, by which it *holds on*, and in which it *trusts*, while πεισμονή is *a holding on*, here (in verse 8) evidently a holding on to one's own views with obstinacy.

Perhaps the word "confidence" may best be repeated : "who did hinder you that ye should not have **confidence** in the truth ? This self-confidence cometh not of him that calleth you . . . but I have confidence in you," etc.

Eph. i. 3.—"Blessed (εὐλογητός, *eulogeetos*) be the God and Father of our Lord Jesus Christ, who hath **blessed** (ὁ εὐλογήσας, *ho eulogeesas*) us with all spiritual **blessings** (εὐλογία, *eulogia*) in heavenly *places* (or *spheres*) in Christ" : *i.e.*, who hath richly blessed us with all, etc.

II. NOUNS AND PRONOUNS.

1. Nouns repeated in different cases.

Ezek. xxviii. 2.—"Son of man, say unto the prince of Tyrus, Thus saith the Lord GOD (Adonai Jehovah) : Because thine **heart** (לִבְּךָ) is lifted up, and thou hast said I am a God, I sit in the seat of God (2 Thess. ii. 4) in the **heart** (בְּלֵב, *i.e., in the heart*) of the seas ; yet thou art a man and not God, though thou set thine **heart** (לִבְּךָ) as the **heart** (כְּלֵב) of God."

John iii. 13.—"And no man hath ascended up to **heaven** (εἰς τὸν οὐρανόν, *eis ton ouranon*), but He that came down from **heaven** (ἐκ τοῦ οὐρανοῦ, *ek tou ouranou*), even the Son of Man which is (or was) in **heaven** (ὁ ὢν ἐν τῷ οὐρανῷ, *ho ōn en tō ouranō*)."

It is to be remembered that the last clause is doubtful. " Many ancient authorities omit it," as the R.V. remarks in the margin.

But, taking it as it stands, we have the three inflections of the word "heaven," calling our attention to a great fact that no one has

---

* Another example of *Polyptoton*.

ever gone up to heaven that is by his own act (see Prov. xxx. 4), for the verb "ascended" is *active*: and the *tense* is the Perfect, meaning no one hath ascended up, and is in heaven. The verb, too, is πορευθείς (*poreutheis*), intimating a leisurely journey, not an instantaneous rapture.

It does not deny that men like Enoch and Elijah had been *taken up* by God, which is a very different thing.

And then the expression ὁ ὤν (*ho ōn*) is difficult to express in English. It is *lit., the one being*, but it means here not "who is," but *who was in heaven, i.e.*, before He came down as stated in chap. i. 1, and who shall again "ascend up where He was before" (chap. vi. 62).

So in chap. i. 18, it should be rendered "which was in the bosom of the Father."

Compare, for this sense, chaps. ix. 25 ; xix. 38. Luke xxiv. 44. 2 Cor. viii. 9. And see above, under *Ellipsis* (page 22), and *Heterosis*.

Rom. iv. 18.—"Who against **hope** believed in hope (παρ ἐλπίδα ἐπ ἐλπίδι, *par elpida ep elpidi*).

Rom. xi. 36.—"For **of Him**, and **through Him**, and **to Him** are all things."

Gal. ii. 19, 20.—"For I **through the law** am dead (died) **to the law** (ἐγὼ γὰρ διὰ νόμου νόμῳ ἀπέθανον, *egō gar dia nomou nomō apethanon*), that I **might live** (ζήσω, *zeesō*) unto God. I am crucified with Christ: nevertheless I **live** (ζῶ, *zō*) ; yet not I but Christ **liveth** (ζῇ, *zee*) in me, and that [*life*] which I now **live** (ζῶ, *zō*) in the flesh I **live** (ζῶ, *zō*) by the faith of the Son of God."

See further on this verse under the figure of *Epanadiplosis*.

2. Nouns repeated in different numbers.

(*a*) In singular and plural.

Ps. lxviii. 15, 16 (16, 17).—In the Hebrew it is clearer than in the English, because what in English requires two or more words, in Hebrew is only one word, or a compound word.

"**A mountain** of God is **the mountain** of Bashan.
A mountain of **mountain peaks** is **the mountain** of Bashan.
Why look ye askance (or envy) **ye mountain peaks**.
At **the mountain** which God hath desired for His abode?
Yea, the LORD will dwell in it for ever."

Thus, is the Hill of Zion specially marked out as the place which Jehovah chose for His House.

Isa. ii. 11.—The lofty looks of **man** shall be humbled, and the haughtiness of **men** shall be bowed down.

So also in verse 17, where the singular and plural are used together (as here) to emphasize the far reaching effects of the day of the Lord, here (verse 12) mentioned for the first time in the Bible.

In other places also we have the same figure: and it tells us that God makes a distinction between " man " and " men," opposite to that which the world makes.

As for " man " God has condemned him root and branch, while the world would deify him.

As for " men " God saves and blesses them with an everlasting salvation, while the world makes very little of " men " as individuals, and indeed pursues them with persecutions, and fights against them with " wars and hatreds."

See further on this whole passage, under the figures of *Polysyndeton* and *Synonymia*.

Jer. xv. 16.—" **Thy words** were found, and I did eat them ; and **thy word** was unto me the joy and rejoicing of mine heart."

Here the two numbers (sing. and pl.) in close conjunction, bring out the contrast between the separate " words " and the " word " of God as a whole.

Compare John xvii. 8, 14, 17.

(*b*) In singular and genitive plural.

A noun is repeated in the genitive plural in order to express very emphatically the superlative degree which does not exist in Hebrew. See under *Idiom*.

Thus this figure is a kind of *Enallage* (*q.v.*), or exchange, by which a noun in the genitive plural, is used instead of a superlative adjective.

Gen. ix. 25.—" **A servant** of **servants** shall [Canaan] be " : *i.e.*, the lowest and most degraded of servants, or the most abject slave.

Ex. xxvi. 33, etc.—" **Holy of holies.**" In A.V.: " the most holy."

Num. iii. 32.—" **Chief of the chief.**" In A.V.: " chief over the chief."

Deut. x. 17.—" For Jehovah your Elohim is **Elohai of** the **Elohim**, and **Adonai of** the **Adonim**, a great El."*

---

* See in *Divine Names and Titles*, by the same author and publisher.

In A.V. and R.V. this is rendered, "The Lord your God is God of Gods, and Lord of Lords, a great God," etc.

1 **Kings viii. 27.**—**The heaven** and **heaven of heavens** cannot contain thee " : *i.e.*, the highest heaven."

Ecc. i. 2, etc.—"**Vanity of vanities** ": *i.e.*, the greatest vanity.

Song Sol. i. 1.—"**The song of songs**," *i.e.*, the most beautiful or excellent song.

Dan. ii. 37. Ezek. xxvi. 17.—"**A king of kings** ": *i.e.*, the most mighty king.

Dan. ii. 47.—"**God of gods** ": *i.e.*, the great, living, or true God. The most mighty God.

Dan. viii. 25.—"**The Prince of princes** ": *i.e.*, the most powerful Prince.

Hos. x. 15.—" So shall Bethel do unto you because of your great wickedness.' The figure is here translated, and given in the margin " Hebrew, **the evil of your evil**."

Micah ii. 4.—"**A lamentation of lamentations**," *i.e.*, a great lamentation. See above, page 278.

Phil. iii. 5.—"**A Hebrew of the Hebrews**," *i.e.*, a thorough Hebrew. See this verse under *Asyndeton*.

1 **Tim. vi. 15.**—"**The King of kings, and Lord of lords**." Compare Rev. xvii. 14 and xix. 16.

Rev. i. 6.—"**The ages of the ages**," *i.e.*, to the remotest age, for ever and ever.

III. Adjectives.

John i. 11.—" He came unto **His own**, (τὰ ἴδια, *ta idea ; i.e.*, his own possessions, *neuter*) and **His own** (οἱ ἴδιοι, *hoi idioi, i.e.*, His own people, *masculine*), received Him not."

1 **Cor. ii. 13.**—"Comparing **spiritual** things with **spiritual**." In the Greek it is πνευματικοῖς πνευματικὰ συγκρίνοντες (*pneumatikois pneumatika sunkrinontes*), *i.e.*, *to spiritual persons spiritual things declaring*.

Or, as in the English order, "declaring (*sunkrinontes*, see Num. xv. 34) spiritual things (*pneumatika, neuter plural*) to spiritual persons (*pneumatikois, masculine gender dative plural*).*

2 **Cor. ix. 8.**—" And God is able to make **all** (πᾶσαν, *pāsan*), grace abound toward you; that ye always having **all** sufficiency in **all** things (παντὶ πάντοτε πᾶσαν, *panti pantote pāsan*) may abound to **every** (all) (πᾶν, *pān*) good work."

---

* Compare chap. iii. 1 ; and see *The Mystery*, by the same author and publisher. And see under *Ellipsis*, page 77.

(b) Repetition of the same word: in a Different Sense.

ANTANACLASIS: or, WORD-CLASHING.

Repetition of the same Word in the same Sentence,
with Different Meanings.

Ant'-an-a-cla'-sis, from ἀντί (*anti*), *against* or *back*, ἀνά (*ana*), *up*, and
κλάσις (*klasis*), *a breaking* from κλάω (*klaō*), *to break*. Hence, *a breaking up against.* This name is given to this figure; because, when
a word has been used once in a sentence in its plain and natural sense,
it is used again in the same sentence in another sense which *breaks up
against it.* It is the use of the same word in the same sentence in two
different senses. It is essential to this figure that the two words must
be *the same* in spelling.* When they are *similar* in spelling but alike in
sound, the figure is known by another name, *Paronomasia (q.v.).*

It is in frequent use in all languages: *e.g.,* " while we **live**, let us
live " : or " learn some **craft** while you are young that when you are
old you may live without **craft.**"

When the Declaration of American Independence was being
signed, Hancock said, " We must be unanimous; there must be no
pulling different ways." " Yes," said Franklin, " we must all **hang**
together, or most assuredly we shall all **hang** separately."

A correspondent recently wrote concerning a certain subject:
" The more I **think** of it the less I **think** of it," where the meaning is
obvious.

With this figure we combine in our references the figure of

PLOCE: or, WORD-FOLDING,

pronounced *plo'-kee.* Greek πλοκή (*plokee*), *a fold* or *plait*, from πλέκω
(*plekō*), *to twine, twist, weave,* or *braid.*

As in *Antanaclasis,* the same word is repeated in a different sense.
Only with *Ploce* that sense implies more than the first use of it. It
often expresses a property or attribute of it. " His **wife** is a **wife**
indeed." In that great victory " **Cæsar** was **Cæsar**." Lord Chatham
says, speaking of Oliver Cromwell, " He astonished mankind by

---

* This differs from a *Homonym* (see Appendix D), which is a different word
though spelt in the same way.

his intelligence, yet did not derive it from spies in the **cabinet** of every prince in Europe ; he drew it from the **cabinet** of his own sagacious mind. He observed facts, and traced them forward to their consequences."

In our examples from Scripture, we will not give two separate lists of these figures, as it is often very difficult to classify them. In many of the examples the reader will have, however, little difficulty in distinguishing them. Other names are also used for this figure, either synonymous, or referring to some special variation, or shade of meaning. It is sometimes called HOMOGENE (ὁμογενής), *hō 'mo-genes*, from ὁμός, *the same*, and γένος, *kind : i.e., of the same family :* in the case of words from the same root or origin : and is thus more appropriately confined to the figure *Polyptoton (q.v.).*

ANACLASIS, *an'-a-clas'-is, a breaking back.*

ANTISTASIS (ἀντίστασις), *an-tis'-ta-sis, a standing against*, or *opposition.* So called because the one word stands against the other in an opposite sense. In Rhetoric, the figure is used where an action is defended by showing that something worse would have happened if it had not been done.

DIALOGIA (*di-a-log'-i-a*), the interchange of words or of their meanings.

In Latin the figure is called

REFRACTIO (*re-frac'-ti-o*), *a breaking back ;* similar in meaning to *Antanaclasis.*

RECIPROCATIO (*re-cip'-ro-ca'-ti-o*), *interchange* of words or meanings.

There are instances of two words being spelt exactly alike, and yet having different meanings. These are called HOMONYMS. We can hardly class them with Figures of Speech, because they are not used as such, and are not used in Repetitions. We have, however, given a list of the most important in Appendix D.

The following are examples of *Antanaclasis*, or Ploce :—

Judges xi. 40.—"The daughters of Israel went from **days to days** to talk with the daughter of Jephthah the Gileadite four **days** in a year."

Here, " days " is first used by *Syncedoche* for a year (*i.e.*, year to year), and afterwards literally for days of twenty-four hours ("four days "). See under *Synecdoche*.

Judges xv. 16.—The word חֲמוֹר (*hamōr*) means not only an *ass*, but a *mass* (or *heaps* as the word is rendered) to imply that the Philistines were to be no more regarded than asses:—

> "With the jaw-bone of an ass (hamōr),
>
> 　A mass (hamōr), yea, masses ; *
>
> With the jaw-bone of an ass,
>
> 　I slew a thousand men."

1 Sam. i. 24.—"And the child was young." Hebrew: And the child (נַעַר, *naar*) was a child (נַעַר, *naar*). In English idiom we should put the emphasis on "WAS."

In the former case the word is used of the child Samuel; and in the latter case, a child of tender age, (by the figure *Synechdoche*, *q.v.*, the word "child" is used to denote the kind).

Ps. cxli. 5.—" It shall be an excellent oil (oil of the **head**) (רֹאשׁ, *rosh*) : let not my **head** (רֹאשִׁי, *roshee*) reject it.

The first time it means the head, or head of hair; and the second time it is put by *Synecdoche* (*q.v.*) for the whole body or person, *i.e.*, let me not refuse it.

Isa. xxxvii. 18.—" Of a truth, Lord, the kings of Assyria have laid waste all the nations (הָאֲרָצוֹת, *ha-aratzoth*, **lands**) and their countries (אַרְצָם, *artzam*, **land**)." Here, the repeated word is אֶרֶץ, land.

As the Text now stands, the word *lands* is put by *Metonomy* (*q.v.*) for the inhabitants (but according to an alternative reading in some MSS. it is actually *nations*, as it is the parallel passage 2 Kings xix. 17) ; and in the second, for their country which they inhabited. Hence, the A.V. has translated the figure by giving two different renderings (" nations " and " countries ") of the one repeated word " land."

Isa. lviii. 10.—" If thou draw out thy **soul** to the hungry and satisfy the afflicted **soul**."

Here, the word " soul " is first put (by *Metonymy*) for the feelings of kindness, liberality, and charity ; and then (by *Synecdoche*) for the person himself who is in trouble.

Isa. lxvi. 3, 4.—Here, the words of Jehovah are emphasized and solemnised by the structure of the passage which exhibits *Epanodos* or

---

* According to another pointing of the same consonants (as exhibited in the lxx.), this line would read, " *I have utterly destroyed them.*" In this case the Figure would be (not *Antanaclasis*) but *Polyptoton* (*q.v.*) : viz., lxx., ἐξαλείφων ἐξήλειψα *exaleiphon exeeleipsa*), or Hebrew, הַחֲמוֹר הַמַרְתִּים (*chamōr chamarteem*). Thus preserving the correspondence between the second and fourth lines.

Chiasmos (*q.v.*); and the words when repeated are used in another sense, the first time of the natural acts of men, and the second by *Anthropopatheia* (*q.v.*), of God.

a | Their soul **delighteth** in their abominations.

   b | I also will **choose** their delusions and will bring their fears
     | upon them:

      c | Because when I called, none did answer:

      c | When I spake, they did not hear;

   b | But they did evil before mine eyes, and **chose** that

a | In which I **delighted** not.

Here, in "a" and "*a*," we have delighting: in "b" and "*b*," the choosing: while, in "c" and "*c*," we have the reason given for each.

Jer. vii. 18, 19.—"That they may **provoke** me to anger. Do they **provoke** me to anger? saith the LORD."

In the first place, it is used of the act of the people in provoking God: in the latter, it is used of the punishments inflicted. Do they provoke me? No; they bring upon themselves the anger and fury of Jehovah, as the next verse goes on to explain.

Jer. viii. 14.—"Let us be **silent** there." Thus the People propose to rest in quietness and security in their sin. But the prophet answers them with the same word in a different sense: "The LORD our God hath put us to **silence**;" *i.e.*, the silence of Divine punishment—the silence of death.

Jer. xxxiv. 17.—"Ye have not hearkened unto me, in proclaiming **liberty** . . behold, I proclaim a **liberty** for you, saith the LORD."

The people had refused to give "liberty" to the oppressed, which He had commanded in verse 9. Therefore He will proclaim another kind of liberty—liberty for the sword, and pestilence, and famine to destroy them; as the context shows.

Ezek. xx. 24-26.—Here the figure is heightened by the structure of the passage.

A | a | Because they had not executed my **judgments**,
   | b | but had despised my **statutes**,
        B | and had **polluted** my sabbaths . .
A | *b* | Wherefore I gave them **statutes** that were not good,
  | *a* | and **judgments** whereby they should not live:
       B | and I **polluted** them in their own gifts, etc."

T

Matt. viii. 22.—" Let the **dead** bury their **dead**."

In the former place, the word refers to the spiritually dead, " dead in sin "; in the latter, to those who have departed this mortal life.

John i. 10.—" The **world** was made by Him (the Word), and the **world** knew Him not."

The former place refers to the created world, the latter to unbelieving men.

John. 1. 11.—" He came unto **His own**, and **His own** received Him not."

In the former place, it refers to His own possessions (*neuter plural*); in the latter, to His own people (*masculine plural*). See under *Polyptoton.*

John ii. 23, 24.—" Many believed ($\pi\iota\sigma\tau\epsilon\acute{\nu}\epsilon\iota\nu$, *pisteuein*) in His name, when they saw the miracles which He did. But Jesus did not commit himself ($\pi\iota\sigma\tau\epsilon\acute{\nu}\epsilon\iota\nu$, *pisteuein*) unto them."

In the former place, the word " believed " means to assent to His doctrines by a confession of faith; in the latter place, to trust as a friend, to place confidence in. The words read therefore : " Many **believed** in His name when they saw the miracles which He did. But Jesus did not himself **believe in** them."

John iii. 31.—" He that is **of the earth** ($\dot{\epsilon}\kappa$ $\tau\hat{\eta}s$ $\gamma\hat{\eta}s$, *ek tees gees*) is **of the earth** ($\dot{\epsilon}\kappa$ $\tau\hat{\eta}s$ $\gamma\hat{\eta}s$, *ek tees gees*), and speaketh **of the earth** ($\dot{\epsilon}\kappa$ $\tau\hat{\eta}s$ $\gamma\hat{\eta}s$, *ek tees gees*); " *i.e.*, he that is of the earth (in respect to his natural birth and origin) is of the earth (in respect to his nature) and speaketh according (to his nature).

John iv. 31, 32.—" His disciples prayed him, saying, Master, **eat**. But He said unto them, I have meat to **eat** that ye know not of."

In the former place, the word is used naturally of eating food; in the latter, spiritually, of doing the Father's will. See verse 34.

John xix. 22.—" What I have **written**, I have **written**."

In the former place, it refers to the act of writing; in the latter, to the writing which standeth written.

Rom. ii. 12.—" As many as have sinned **without law** ($\dot{a}\nu\acute{o}\mu\omega s$, *anomōs*) shall also perish **without law** ($\dot{a}\nu\acute{o}\mu\omega s$, *anomōs*). Here, in the former case, it means not under the Law; in the latter, it means without the judgment of the Law.

Rom. ii. 26.—" If the **uncircumcision** keep the righteousness of the law, shall not his **uncircumcision** be counted for circumcision."

In the former place, the word " uncircumcision " denotes the Gentiles ; and in the latter, their condition as fulfilling the requirements of the Law. For this is the force of δικαίωμα (*dikaiōma*), which is not righteousness as a state or condition, but the *righteous requirements* of the Law.

Rom. iii. 21.—" But now the righteousness of God without the law is manifested, being witnessed by the **Law** and the Prophets."

In the former case, the word denotes moral law (*no article*) without the works of the law, as opposed to faith; in the latter case, the word denotes the Mosaic Law (*with article*).

N.B.—There is no article before the word righteousness, so that it means a Divine righteousness: the same as in chap. i. 17.

Rom. iii. 27.—" Where is boasting then? It is excluded. By what **law**? of works? Nay; but by the **law** of faith."

In the first place it refers to divine law; and in the second not to law at all but to faith itself by the genitive of apposition, " the law, *i.e.*, faith," as in i. 17. (See Appendix B).

Rom. vii. 13.—" But sin, that it might appear **sin**."

In the former place, sin is used of the old nature; while, in the latter it is used of its real sinful nature and character.

Rom. vii. 23.—" But I see another **law** in my members, warring against the **law** of my mind, and bringing me into captivity to the **law** of sin which is in my members."

In the first and third places, the word " law " refers to the old nature, which is indwelling sin, because it once lorded it over him, though now it only struggles to usurp again; in the second it refers to the divine law (*i.e.*, the new nature) implanted in him, which is contrary to the former, and contests its claims.

Rom. ix. 6.—" They are not all **Israel** which are of **Israel**."

Here the former place refers to the true spiritual seed of Israel; the latter denotes Israel according to the flesh, the natural descendants from Israel's loins.

Rom. xii. 13, 14.—" Given (διώκοντες, *diōkontes*) to hospitality. Bless them that **persecute** (διώκοντας, *diōkontas*) you."

The word διώκειν (*diōkein*) is used in the former place, and means *to pursue* or *follow closely* in a friendly sense; but, in the latter place, it means the same in a hostile sense, to follow closely so as to persecute.

In the A.V., the figure is lost by translation. Literally, it is " **Follow up** hospitality. Bless them that **follow you up** [*to injure you*].

1 Cor. xi. 24.—" And when He had given thanks, he **brake** it, and said, Take, eat: this is my body, which is **broken** for you."

Here the verb *to break* is used, in the former case, in its proper signification: while, in the second place, it is used spiritually for the sufferings and crucifixion of Christ; as is clear from Luke xxii. 19, where the word is "given."

1 Cor. xv. 28.—"And when all things shall be subdued (ὑποτάσσειν, *hupotassein*) unto him, then shall the Son also himself be subject (ὑποτάσσειν, *hupotassein*) unto Him that put all things under Him."

The verb means *to arrange in order*, but also *to reduce to order*. The former sense is used of Christ, the latter of all others (as explained on Ps. cx. 1).*

1 Cor. xv. 28.—"That put all things under him, that God may be all in all."

In the first place "all" refers to all created things and beings; in the second, to all universal power, "that God may be *over* all things; and, in the third, it refers to all places.

"All," being an adjective, must be associated with some noun (expressed or implied) which it qualifies. Here the nouns are implied, and the omission (see under *Ellipsis*) produces the figure of *Antanaclasis*.

2 Cor. v. 21.—"For He hath made Him to be sin for us, who knew no sin."

The order of the Greek is not ambiguous as is the English:—

"For He who knew no sin was made sin for us." Here, in the former place, it means "sin" in the ordinary acceptation of the word; while in the latter place, it is put by *Metonymy* (*q.v.*) for a sin-offering.

Eph. i. 3.—"Blessed (εὐλογητός, *eulogeetos*) be the God and Father of our Lord Jesus Christ who hath blessed us (ὁ εὐλογήσας, *ho eulogeesas*)," etc.

This is really *Polyptoton*. But here we repeat it in order to point out that the word "blessed" is used in two different senses. We do not bless God in the same way that He blesses us. The former word is always used of God, the latter may be used of men. The former word means the Being who is to be spoken well of, the latter means the being of whom good has been lastingly spoken—especially by God Himself.

1 Tim. vi. 5, 6.—"Supposing that godliness is to be a way of making gain . . . but godliness with contentment is a great way of making gain."

---

* See *Things to Come* for October, 1898.

Here the word πορισμός (*porismos*) is used in two opposite associations. In the former case of what a false Christianity supposes it to be; and in the second, what it really is.

Heb. ii. 14.—"That through **death** he might destroy him that had the power of **death**, that is, the devil." Here, the first "death" is put by *Synecdoche*, for the atoning results of Christ's death: while the second means the act and article of natural or physical death.

I Pet. iii. 1.—"That, if any obey not **the word** [τῷ λόγῳ, *tō logō*: *i.e.*, the Gospel], they also may without **the word** [λόγου, *logou*: *i.e.*, speaking or talking] be won by the conversation of the wives."

SYNŒCEIOSIS; or, COHABITATION.

The Repetition of the same Word in the same Sentence with an Extended Meaning.

Syn'-œ-cei-o'-sis from σύν (*sun*), *together with*, and οἰκείωσις (*oikeiōsis*), *dwelling in the same house.*

This figure is so called because two words are used, and in the general sense, but with a different and more extended signification. They *dwell together* as it were *in the same house;* and yet, while one speaker takes up the word and uses it in the same sense, he yet means a different thing.

The Latins called it COHABITATIO, cohabitation, *a dwelling together.*

Matt. v. 19.—"Whosoever ... shall break one of these **least** commandments, and shall teach men so, he shall be called the **least** in the kingdom of heaven."

In the former place, the allusion is to the distinction which the Pharisees made between different commandments (just as Rome has since made the distinction between "venial" and "mortal" sins). There is no such distinction, and therefore, when in the latter place Christ says "he shall be called the least," He means that he will not be there at all, for there will be no such distinction there. There is no least in either case.

Matt. xviii. 1.—"Who, in that case, is the **greatest** in the kingdom of heaven?" In verse 4 Christ answers, "Whosoever shall humble himself as this little child, the same is **greatest** in the kingdom of heaven."

In the former place the disciples use the word in its ordinary sense of pre-eminence. But in the latter place Christ (alluding to the former sense) means that no one except Himself has ever humbled Himself thus: and who is to dispute that He must be greatest in that kingdom. The occasion also is important; compare verse 1 with xvii. 24-27.

Matt. xix. 16, 17.—"And behold one came and said unto him, **Good** Master, what **good** thing shall I do that I may have eternal life? And He said unto him, Why callest thou me **good**? There is none **good** but one, *that is* God."

In the former case, the young man uses the word "good" of mere creature goodness, such as he supposed Christ to have ; while in the latter case, the Lord alludes to the first, using the word in the same sense, but not in the same way ; thus teaching that there is no real "good" apart from God—no "good" except that which comes from God and returns to Him.

John vi. 28, 29.—"What shall we do that we might work the **works*** of God ?   Jesus answered . . . them, This is the **work** of God, that ye believe on Him whom He hath sent."

In the former case, the word "works" is used by the Jews in its proper acceptation : it is repeated by Christ in the same sense, but with another meaning altogether, as He goes on to explain.

Acts xxvi. 28, 29.—Here the apostle repeats the word "**almost**" (or "with little" R.V.) in the same sense, but with a far higher and more extended meaning.

---

* See *Polyptoton.*

SYLLEPSIS ; or, COMBINATION.

The Repetition of the Sense without the Repetition of the Word.

Syl-lep'-sis, from σύν *(sun), together with,* and λῆψις *(leepsis) a taking.*

This name is given to the figure when only *one* word is used, and yet it takes on *two* meanings at the same time.

The word itself is used only once ; and ought to be, but is *not repeated* in the next clause, being omitted by *Ellipsis (q.v.),* but the two meanings are *taken together with* the one word.

It is called SYNESIS *(Syn'-e-sis),* a joining or *meeting together,* and SYNTHESIS *(Syn'-the-sis), a putting together, compounding,* from σύν *(sun), together,* and τίθημι *(titheemi), to put* or *place.*

The *Syllepsis* here considered is rhetorical rather than grammatical *(q.v.).* There is a form of *Syllepsis* which involves *change* rather than addition. It will be found therefore under those figures in our third division.

2 Chron. xxxi. 8.—" They blessed the LORD and his people Israel."

Here there is a duplex statement. They blessed the LORD, that is they gave Him thanks and celebrated His praises ; and they blessed His People Israel ; but in a different way ; they prayed for all spiritual and temporal blessings for them in the name of the Lord.

Two meanings are thus given to the word, which is used only once. The sense is repeated, but not the word, and the sense is not the same in each case.

Joel ii. 13.—" Rend your heart, and not your garments."

Here the word " rend " is used only once, but with two significations : in the former sentence it is used figuratively ; in the latter literally—the heart not being rent in the same sense in which garments are rent.

2. Of Different Words.

(*a*) In a similar order (and in the same sense).

SYMPLOCE ; or, INTERTWINING.

The Repetition of different Words in successive Sentences in the same Order and the same Sense.

Sym¹-plo-kee¹, from σύν (*sun*), *together with,* and πλοκή (*plokee*), *a folding.* An *intertwining* of two different words in a similar order : one at the beginning and the other at the end of successive sentences.

It is a combination of *Anaphora* (*q.v.*) and *Epistrophe* (*q.v.*).

The Latins called it COMPLEXIO, *combination,* and COMPLI-CATIO, *a folding together.*

When phrases or sentences are thus repeated, instead of single words, it is called *Cænotes* (*q.v.*).

Though there may be more than one word in the English, it does not follow that there is more than one in the original.

Isa. ii. 7, 8.—We have it in alternate lines :
" **Their land** also is full of silver and gold,
Neither is there any end of their treasures;
Their land is also full of horses.
Neither is there any end of their chariots;
Their land also is full of idols, etc."

Isa. lxv. 13, 14.—"Thus saith the Lord God,
" **Behold my servants** shall eat,
But ye shall be hungry.
Behold my servants shall drink,
But ye shall be thirsty.
Behold my servants shall rejoice,
But ye shall be ashamed.
Behold my servants shall sing for joy of heart,
But ye shall cry for sorrow of heart."

In the last two lines we have *Epistrophe* in the word heart.

Jer. ix. 23 (22).—Here, in the Hebrew, the three sentences begin, " **Let him not glory** " (אַל־יִתְהַלֵּל, *al-yithhalleyl*), and each ends with the pronominal suffix וֹ, *his.*

1 Cor. xii. 4, 5, 6.—Here in the Greek each verse begins with "**diversities**" or differences (διαιρέσεις, *diaireseis*), and ends with "**the same**" (αὐτός, *autos*).

1 Cor. xiv. 15.—Here the two words repeated and emphasized by *Symploce* are "**the spirit**" and "**the understanding.**"

1 Cor. xv. 42-44.—Here we have four pairs, a kind of double *Anaphora.*

> "**It is sown** in corruption ;
>   **It is raised** in incorruption.
> **It is sown** in dishonour ;
>   **It is raised** in glory.
> **It is sown** in weakness ;
>   **It is raised** in power.
> **It is sown** a natural body ;
>   **It is raised** a spiritual body."

2 Cor. ix. 6.—Here the Greek exhibits a beautiful example of this figure.

> " He that **soweth** sparingly, sparingly shall **reap also** :
> He that **soweth** bountifully, bountifully shall **reap also.**"

With this is combined the figure of *Anadiplosis* (*q.v.*), in the repetition of the words " sparingly " and " bountifully."

Rev. xviii. 21-23.—To emphasize the complete overthrow of Babylon *six* times we have the repeated words " no more."

Babylon . . . shall be found **no more at all,**
and the voice of harpers, and musicians, and of pipers, and trumpeters shall be heard **in thee no more at all.**
and no craftsman, of whatsoever craft he be, shall be found **in thee any more at all :**
and the sound of a millstone shall be heard **in thee no more at all.**
and the light of a candle shall shine **in thee no more at all :**
and the voice of the bridegroom and of the bride shall be heard **in thee no more at all.**"

Here we have *Anastrophe* (*i.e., Polysyndeton*) combined with *Epistrophe.*

(*b*) In a different order (but the same sense).

EPANODOS ; or, INVERSION.

The Repetition of the same Words in an inverse Order (but same Sense).

E-pan¹-o-dos is from ἐπί (*epi*), *upon*, ἀνά (*ana*), *back*, and ὁδός (*hodos*), *a way*, and means *a way back again*, or more simply *a return*.

After two, three, or more words have been mentioned, they are repeated, not in the same order again, but backward.

The Latins called it REGRESSIO, *i.e.*, *regression*, and INVERSIO, *i.e.*, *inversion*.

When *propositions* are inverted and thus contrasted, and not merely the words, the figure is called ANTIMETABOLE (see the next figure).

When only the *subject* matter is thus related it is called CHIASMUS (*q.v.*), though this may also be called an *Epanodos*. This we have given under *Correspondence*. When *words or phrases* are repeated in this inverse order it is called SYNANTESIS, *a meeting together*.

Gen x. 1-31.—
    a | 1-. **Shem**,
        b | -1-. **Ham**,
            c | -1. and **Japheth**.
            c | 2-5. The sons of **Japheth**.
        b | 6-20. The sons of **Ham**.
    a | 21-31. The sons of **Shem**.

Ex. ix. 31.—
    a | " And **the flax**
        b | and **the barley** was smitten,
        b | for **the barley** was in the ear,
    a | and **the flax** was bolled."

Isa. vi. 10.—
    a | " Make the **heart** of this people fat,
        b | and make their **ears** heavy,
            c | and shut their **eyes** ;
            c | lest they see with their **eyes**,
        b | and hear with their **ears**,
    a | and understand with their **heart**."

Rom. ii. 14.—" Which have not the law (μὴ νόμον, *mee nomon*) . .
these having not the law (νόμον μὴ, *nomon mee*)." The figure, which does
not appear in the English, shows us that in the former sentence we
are to place the emphasis on the word " *not,*" and in the latter on the
word " law."

N.B.—The words " by nature " must be read with " who have not
the law," and not with the verb " do." Gentiles by nature are not
under the Law of Moses, yet they do many things unconsciously in
accordance with it ; and so far, they endorse it, and condemn themselves.
The keeping of this law can no more save them than the law of Moses
can save the Jews. All are under sin (iii. 9), the Gentile (chap. i.), the
Jew (chap. ii), and all alike guilty before God (iii. 19).

2 Cor. i. 3.—
    a | " Blessed be **God,**
        b | even the **Father** of our Lord Jesus Christ,
        b | the **Father** of mercies,
    a | and the **God** of all comfort."

3 John 11.—
    a | " Follow not that which is **evil,**
        b | but that which is **good.**
        b | He that doeth **good** is of God ;
    a | But he that doeth **evil** hath not seen God."

For further illustration see under *Correspondence.*

ANTIMETABOLE ; or, COUNTERCHANGE.

Epanodos, with Contrast or Opposition.

An'-ti-me-tab'-o-lee, from ἀντί (*anti*), *against*, μετά (*meta*), *reversely*, and βάλλειν (*ballein*), *to throw*.

This figure repeats the word or words in a reverse order, for the purpose of *opposing* one thing to another, or of contrasting two or more things. It is the figure of *Epanodos* with this special added object of opposing words against one another.

It is also called DIALLELON, from διά (*dia*), *through*, and λαλέω (*laleo*), *to speak, to say* (or place by speaking) *one thing against another*. Also METATHESIS, *Me-tath'-e-sis*, *i.e.*, *transposition*, from μετά (*meta*), *beyond*, or *over*, and τίθημι (*titheemi*), *to place*. This name is also given in Etymology, where *letters* are transposed. The Latins called it COMMUTATIO, commutation, *i.e.*, *changing about*.

Gen. iv. 4, 5.—
    a | And the LORD had respect
        b | unto Abel and to his offering:
        b | But unto Cain, and his offering
    a | he had not respect.

2 Chron. xxxii. 7, 8.—
    a | There be more with us
        b | than with him ;
        b | With him is an arm of flesh,
    a | but with us is the LORD our God.

Isa. v. 20.—" Woe unto them that call
evil
    good, and
    good
evil ;
that put darkness
    for light,
    and light for
darkness ;
that put bitter
    for sweet,
    and sweet for
bitter."

Isa. lv. 8.—

    a | " For **my** thoughts

        b | are not **your** thoughts,

        b | neither are **your** ways

    a | **my** ways, saith the Lord."

In verse 9 these words are in their natural order.

In verses 8 and 9 taken together, the figure is a simple *Epanodos*:

a | " For **my thoughts** are not **your thoughts**,

    b | Neither are **your ways my ways**, saith the Lord.

    b | For as the heavens are higher than the earth, so are **my
ways** higher than **your ways**,

a | and **my thoughts** than **your thoughts**."

Here in a and *a* we have " thoughts "; while in b and *b* we have
" ways."

Further, there is another involved *Epanodos* in b and *b*, between
the " my " and " your "; as there is between a and b.

Mark ii. 27.—

    a | " The **sabbath**

        b | was made for **man,**

        b | and not **man** for

    a | the **sabbath**."

John viii. 47.—

    a | " He that is of **God,**

        b | heareth God's **words,**

        b | ye therefore hear **them** not (*i.e.*, the words)

    a | because ye are not of **God**."

John xv. 16.—

    a | " **Ye** have not chosen

        b | **me,**

        b | but **I**

    a | have chosen **you**."

John xiv. 17.—" Even the Spirit of Truth ;

    a | whom the world cannot **receive,**

        b | because it **seeth** him not,

            c | neither **knoweth** him :

            c | but ye **know** him ;

        b | for he **dwelleth** with you,

    a | and shall **be in** you."

Here the words are not repeated in *b* and *c*, but the fact is stated
as to seeing and receiving

1 Cor. xi. 8, 9.—

    a | " For the màn

        b | is not of the **woman** ;

        b | but the **woman**

    a | of the **man**.

            c | Neither was the **man** created

                d | for the **woman**,

                d | but the **woman**

            c | for the **man**."

Gal. v. 17.—

    a | " **The flesh** lusteth

        b | against **the spirit,**

        b | and **the spirit**

    a | against **the flesh**."

1 John ii. 18.—

    a | **Last time** (little children)

        b | **Antichrist to come** (and as)

        b | many **come** (even now)

    a | **last time** (whereby).

2 John 6.—

    a | " This is love, that we **walk**

        b | after his **commandments.**

        b | This is the **commandment,**

    a | that . . ye should **walk** in it."

3 John 11.—

    a | " Follow not that which is **evil,**

        b | but that which is **good** ;

        b | He that doeth **good** is of God,

    a | but he that doeth **evil** hath not seen God."

Other examples of introverted parallelism (of lines) may be studied in Gen. xii. 16. Deut. xvi. 5, 6: xxviii. 1, 2. 1 Sam. i. 2; xxv. 3; 2 Sam. iii. 1. 1 Kings xvi. 22. Prov. xxx. 8, 9. Isa. lvi. 3-7. Joel ii. 18-21, 30, 31. Micah iii. 12-iv. 2. Zech. ix. 5. But they are to be found everywhere, and they abound in the Psalms.

These examples will be sufficient to explain and illustrate the figure and show its importance.

See further under *Parallelism* and *Correspondence*.

(*a*) Similar in sound (but different in sense).

PAREGMENON ; or, DERIVATION.

The Repetition of Words derived from the same Root.

Pa-reg'-me-non, from παρά (*para*), *beside* or *along*, ἄγειν (*agein*), *to lead.*

In this figure the repeated words are derived from the same root. Hence, the name *Paregmenon* is used of the Figure when the words are similar in origin and sound, but not similar in sense.

The Latins called it DERIVATIO.

This is one of the Figures common to all languages, but is generally very difficult to translate from one tongue into another.

Ps. lxviii. 28 (29).—" Thy God hath commanded thy **strength** (עֻזֶּךָ, *uzzechah*) : strengthen (עֻזָּה, *uzzah*) O God that which thou hast wrought for us."

Matt. xvi. 18.—" Thou art Peter (πέτρος, **petros**) and upon this rock (πέτρα, **petra**) I will build my assembly."

Here note (1) that *Petros* is not merely Simon's name given by our Lord, but given because of its meaning. " *Petros* " means *a stone, a piece of a rock, a moving stone* which can be thrown by the hand. While " *petra* " means *a rock* or *cliff* or *crag*, immovable, firm, and sure. Both words are from the same root, both have the same derivation, but though similar in origin and sound they are thus different in meaning. This difference is preserved in the Latin, in which *petros* is *saxum*, while *petra* is *rupes* or *scopulus*.

(2) In the case of *petros*, we have another figure : *viz.*, *Syllepsis*, for the word is used in two senses, though used only once. There is a repetition, not of the word but of the thought which is not expressed : " Thou art πέτρος," where it is used as a proper name *Peter*, and there is no figure : but the sense of the word is there as well, though not repeated in words : " Thou art (πέτρος), *a stone*." Thus there is a *metaphor* implied, *i.e.*, *Hypocatastasis* (*q.v.*).

(3) While *petros* is used of Peter, *petra* is used of Christ : for so Peter himself understood it (see 1 Pet. ii. 4, 5, 6, and Acts iv. 11, 12 ; and so the Holy Spirit asserts in 1 Cor. x. 4. " And that rock (πέτρα) was Christ," where we have a pure *metaphor* (*q.v.*). So that *petros* represents Peter's instability and uselessness as a foundation, while

petra represents Christ's stability as the foundation which God Himself has laid (1 Cor. iii. 11. Isa. xxviii. 16).

John xiii. 7 appears to be the Figure of *Paregmenon* in the English. But there is no figure in the Greek. "What I do thou knowest not now; but thou shalt know hereafter."

Here, the two words "know" are different in the Greek. The first is οἶδα (*oida*), *to know*, as a matter of absolute knowledge, but the latter is γινώσκω (*ginōskō*), *to get to know, learn.*

John xv. 2.—"Every branch in me that beareth not fruit he taketh away (αἴρει, **airei***): and every *branch* that beareth fruit he purgeth it† (καθαίρει, **kathairei**)."

Acts viii. 31.—"Understandest thou what thou readest" (γινώσκεις ἃ ἀναγινώσκεις, **ginōskeis ha anaginōskeis**).

Here, the former verb means *to know by learning, to get to know;* and the latter (which is the same verb compounded with ἀνά (*and*), *again*, means *to read*, especially, *to read out loud.*

Rom. ii. 1.—"Thou art inexcusable, O man, whosoever thou art that judgest (ὁ κρίνων, **ho krinōn**), for wherein thou judgest (κρίνεις, **krineis**) another thou condemnest (κατακρίνεις, **katakrineis**) thyself; for thou that judgest (ὁ κρίνων, **ho krinōn**) doest the same things."

Rom. v. 19.—"For as by one man's disobedience (παρακοῆς, **parakoees**) many were made sinners, so by the obedience (ὑπακοῆς, **hypakoees**) of one shall many be made righteous."

Rom. xii. 3.—"Not to think *of himself* more highly (ὑπερφρονεῖν, **hyperphronein**) than he ought to think (φρονεῖν, **phronein**); but to think (φρονεῖν, **phronein**) soberly (σωφρονεῖν, **sōphronein**)," etc.; *i.e.*, "but so to think that he may think soberly."

1 Cor. xi. 29.—"For he that eateth and drinketh unworthily, eateth and drinketh damnation (κρίμα, **krima**) to himself, not discerning (διακρίνων, **diakrinōn**) the body [*of the Lord*]."

Here the last words "of the Lord" go out (according to L.T.Tr. W.H. and R.V.). And the former word **krima** means not damnation, but *a matter for judgment, an accusation;* while the latter word *diakrinōn* means *to distinguish, to make a distinction;* though, by the act of communion, they professed to belong to the Body of Christ, yet if they did not discern the truth connected with that Body (*i.e.*, Christ Mystical) and distinguish their fellow-members of that Body from all

---

* *I.e., he lifteth up*, as in Luke xvii. 13. John xi. 41. Acts iv. 24. Rev. x. 5, and especially Dan. vii. 4 (Theodotian's Version). See under *Ellipsis*, page 13.

† *I.e., he pruneth it.*

U

others, they condemned themselves, they accused themselves. For, while they ate and drank thus, they did so unworthily: and by that very act they condemned themselves.

1 Cor. xi. 31, 32.—" For if we would judge (διεκρίνομεν, **diekrinomen**) ourselves, we should not be judged (ἐκρινόμεθα, **ekrinometha**). But when we are judged (κρινόμενοι, **krinomenoi**) we are chastened of the Lord, that we should not be condemned (κατακριθῶμεν, **katakrithō-men**) with the world."

2 Cor. iv. 8.—" Perplexed (ἀπορούμενοι, **aporoumenoi**), but not in despair (ἐξαπορούμενοι, **exàporoumenoi**)," *i.e., at a loss to know what to do, but not utterly at a loss.*

2 Cor. v. 4.—" Not for that we would be un.clothed (ἐκδύσασθαι, **ekdusasthai**), but clothed upon (ἐπενδύσασθαι, **ependusasthai**) ": *i.e., that we would not be found naked in the grave, but be clothed with our resurrection body.*

The figure belongs also to *Paregmenon (q.v.).*

2 Cor. x. 6.—" Having in a readiness to revenge all disobedience (παρακοήν, **parakoeen**) when your obedience (ὑπακοή, **hupakoee**) is fulfilled." So Rom. v. 19.

2 Thess. iii. 11.—" Working (ἐργαζομένους, **ergazomenous**) not at all, but are busybodies (περιεργαζομένους, **periergazomenous**)."

It is difficult to express the thought in English. The latter word means *to overdo anything ;* to do with pains what is not worth doing. We might say *doing nothing, yet over-doing ;* or, *not as official, but officious ;* or, *not busy, but fussy ;* or, *not doing their own business, but the business of others.*

Heb. x. 34.—" Ye . . . took joyfully the spoiling of your goods (ὑπαρχόντων, **huparchontōn**), knowing in yourselves that ye have in heaven a better and an enduring substance (ὕπαρξιν, **huparxin**)."

Jas. ii. 4.—" Are ye not then partial in yourselves, and are become judges of evil thoughts ? " There the two words διεκρίθητε (**diekritheete**) and κρίται (**kritai**) are from the same root: the former means *to make a distinction,* and the latter *judges.*

1 John iii. 20.—" For if our heart condemn (καταγινώσκῃ, **kataginōskee**) us, God is greater than our heart, and knoweth (γινώσκει, **ginōskei**) all things."

Both words are from the same root, and mean *to know,* but the former *to know something against ;* and the latter, simply *to know,* or rather *get to know, learn.* For nothing can be hidden from God. Man cannot get to know our hearts by any means which he may try. God can ; and does.

PARONOMASIA ; or, RHYMING-WORDS.

The Repetition of Words similar in Sound, but not necessarily in Sense.

Par-o-no-ma¹-si-a, from παρά (*para*) *beside*, and ὀνομάζειν (*onomazein*) *to name, make a name*, or *a word*. The figure is so-called because one word is *placed alongside of another*, which sounds and seems like a repetition of it. But it is not the same; it is only similar. The meaning may be similar or not, the point is that two (or more) words are different in origin and meaning, but are similar in sound or appearance.

Some rhetoricians misname this figure *Prosonomasia*, others include it in *Antanaclasis* or *Parechesis*.

The Latins called it ANNOMINATIO, or AGNOMINATIO, from *ad, to*, and *nominatio, a naming* (from *nominare, to name*). The word thus has the same meaning as the Greek name.

This figure is not by any means what we call a pun. Far from it. But two things are emphasized, and our attention is called to this emphasis by the similarity of sound. Otherwise, we might read the passage, and pass it by unnoticed; but the eye or the ear is at once attracted by the similarity of sound or appearance, and our attention is thus drawn to a solemn or important statement which would otherwise have been unheeded. Sometimes a great lesson is taught us by this figure; an interpretation is put upon the one word by the use of the other; or a reason is given in the one for what is referred to by the other. Sometimes a contrast is made; sometimes a thought is added.

The figure is very frequently used and is never to be disregarded.

This figure is common to all languages, but the instances cannot readily be translated from one language into another. In some cases we have attempted to express the Hebrew or Greek words by the use of similar words in English; but this is generally at the sacrifice of exact translation. Only by a very free translation of the sentence can the two words be thus represented.

Sometimes we have found even this to be impossible: but in each case we have given the original words in English characters, so that the similarity of sound may be perceived. We have not in each case stopped to point the lesson taught by the figure, as it is generally sufficiently plain and clear.

Neither have we made any classification of the passages, otherwise they might well be divided into those which are connected with
proper names, or prophetic denunciations, etc. Or we might have
classified them as (1) *synonymous* ; (2) *antithetic* ; and (3) *of varied
signification.*

Gen. i. 2.—"And the earth had become **tohū** (תֹהוּ) and **bohū**
(בֹהוּ)." For the lesson taught by this (the second Figure used in the
Bible), see under *Anadiplosis.*

Gen. iv. 25.—" She called his name Seth (שֵׁת, **Sheth**). For God,
said she, hath appointed (שָׁת, **shāth**, *set*) me a seed instead of Abel,
whom Cain slew."

Gen. ix. 27.—" God shall enlarge (יַפְתְּ, **yapht**) Japhet (לְיֶפֶת,
l'yephet)."

Gen. xi. 9.—"Therefore is the name of it called Babel (בָּבֶל,
Babel), because the Lord did there confound (בָּלַל, **balal**, or
turn to babble) the language of all the earth."

Gen. xviii. 27.—Abraham says, " Behold now, I have taken upon
me to speak unto the Lord, which am but dust (עָפָר, **aphar**) and ashes
(וָאֵפֶר, **v'epher**)." See also Job xxx. 19.

Gen. xxix. 34.—" Now this time will my husband be joined
(יִלָּוֶה, **yillaveh**) . . . therefore was his name called Levi (לֵוִי, **Levi**,
or *joiner*)."

Gen. xxix. 35.—" Now will I praise (אוֹדֶה, **ōdeh**) the Lord :
therefore she called his name Judah (יְהוּדָה, y'hudah)."

Gen. xli. 51.—" And Joseph called the name of the firstborn
Manasseh (מְנַשֶּׁה, **M'nasheh**) : For God, said he, hath made me forget
(נַשַּׁנִי, nasshanee)."

Gen. xli. 52.—" And the name of the second called he Ephraim
(אֶפְרַיִם, **Ephrayim**) : for God hath caused me to be fruitful (הִפְרַנִי,
hiphranee) in the land of my affliction."

Gen. xlix. 8.—"Thou Judah (יְהוּדָה, y'hudah), thy brethren
shall praise thee (יוֹדוּךָ, **yoducha**)."

Gen. xlix. 16.—" Dan (דָּן, **Dan**) shall judge (יָדִין, yadeen) his
People as one of the tribes of Israel."*

Gen. xlix. 19.—" Gad (גָּד, **Gad**), a troop (גְּדוּד, g'dūd) shall overcome him (יְגוּדֶנּוּ, y'gūdennū); but he shall overcome (יָגֻד, yagud)
at the last."

---

* *Compare* Gen. xxx. 6: "And Rachel said, God hath judged me (דְּנַנִּי,
dananni) . . . therefore she called his name Dan (דָּן, **Dan**)."

Ex. xxxii. 18.—"And he said, *It is* not the voice of *them that* shout (עֲנוֹת, anōth) for mastery, neither *is it* the voice of *them that* cry (עֲנוֹת, anōth) for being overcome: *but* the noise of *them that* sing (עַנּוֹת, annōth) do I hear."

It may be Englished thus: "It is not the sound of those who **strike**, neither the sound of those who are **stricken**: but the sound of those who **strike up** (musically) do I hear."

Num. v. 18.—"And the priest shall have in his hand the bitter water (מֵי הַמָּרִים, mey hammarīm) that causeth the curse (הַמְאָרְדִים, hamarrim)."

Num. xviii. 2.—"And thy brethren also of the tribe of Levi (לוִי, Levee), the tribe of thy father bring thou with thee, that they may be joined (וְיִלָּווּ, v'yillavu) unto thee to minister unto thee."

Num. xxiv. 21.—"And he looked on the Kenites (הַקֵּינִי, hakeynī), and took up his parable, and said, Strong is thy dwellingplace, and thou puttest thy nest (קִנֶּךָ, kinnecha) in a rock."

Deut. xxx. 3.—And in all the passages where Jehovah says, "I will turn or bring again (וְשַׁבְתִּי, v'shavtī) the captivity (אֶת־שְׁבוּת, eth-sh'vūth) of my people," there is this use of two similar words. See 2 Chron. xxviii. 11. Neh. viii. 17. Job xlii. 10. Ps. xiv. 7; liii. 6 (7); lxxxv. 1 (2); cxxvi. 1, 4. Jer. xxx. 3, 18; xxxi. 23; xxxii. 44; xxxiii. 7, 11, 26; xlviii. 47; xlix. 6, 39. Lam. ii. 14. Ezek. xvi. 53; xxix. 14; xxxix. 25. Amos ix. 14. Zeph. ii. 7; iii. 20.

1 Sam. i. 27, 28.—"For this child I prayed; and the Lord hath given me my petition (שְׁאֵלָתִי, sh'alāthī), which I asked of him (שָׁאַלְתִּי, shāaltee): therefore also I have lent him (הִשְׁאִלְתִּיהוּ, hishiltīhū) to the Lord; as long as he liveth he shall be lent (שָׁאוּל, shaūl)."

1 Sam. xiii. 7.—"And some of the Hebrews (וְעִבְרִים, v'ivrīm) went over (עָבְרוּ, avrū) Jordan."

N.B.—"Abram the Hebrew" was so called to describe him as the man who had come from the other side of the Euphrates and had *crossed over* into Canaan. They are so called by Saul in this chapter, verse 3. See also xiv. 11, 21, where the Philistines call them so.

2 Sam. xxii. 42.—"They looked (יִשְׁעוּ, yishū), but there was none to save (מוֹשִׁיעַ, mōshia)." Or, they might **crave**, but there was none to **save**.

See also Ps. xviii. 41 (42).

From the two similar roots שָׁעָה (shaah), *to look*, and יָשַׁע (yasha), *to save.*

1 Kings ii. 36.—"And the king sent and called for Shimei, and said unto him, Build thee an house in Jerusalem, and dwell there, and go not forth thence any whither" (אָנֶה וָאָנָה, aneh veanah), *i.e.,* as in English, hither and thither. So verse 42; and 2 Kings v. 25: Gehazi said "Thy servant went no whither," *i.e.,* **aneh veanah,** hither and thither.

1 Chron. xxii. 9.—"For his name shall be Solomon (שְׁלֹמֹה, Shelōmōh), and I will give peace (שָׁלוֹם, shalōm) and quietness unto Israel in his days."

2 Chron. xxviii. 11; Neh. viii. 17. See Deut. xxx. 3.

Job. xi. 12.—"For vain (נָבוּב, navūv) man would be wise (יִלָּבֵב, yillavev), though man be born like a wild ass's colt." Or, For man, in his **vanity,** will vaunt of **sanity;** though **humanity** be born as a wild ass's colt.

From the two verbs of like origin.

Job xlii. 10.—See Deut. xxx. 3.

Ps. xiv. 7 (8).—See Deut. xxx. 3.

Ps. xviii. 7.—"The earth shook (וַתִּגְעַשׁ, vattigash) and trembled (וַתִּרְעַשׁ, vattirash)." Or, The earth **shaked** and **quaked.**

Ps. xxii. 16 (17).—Every important Massorah gives a list of words which occur twice in different senses. The word כָּאֲרִי (kaarī) is one of these words, and the two places are Isa. xxxviii. 13 and Ps. xxii. 16. There can be no doubt also that some Codices read כארו (ka-arū) as a rival reading. Dr. Ginsburg concludes from the Chaldee translation that both these readings were at one time in the text, and it is not improbable that one of the words of this pair dropped out.* If this was the case then there was originally not only a beautiful completeness as to the sense, but also a forcible *Paronomasia* as well.

"They tore (כארו, kaarū) like a lion (כארי, kaari) my hands and my feet." Or

"Like a lion they tore my hands and my feet."

This is borne out by the *structure* of the passage (verses 12-17).†

The reading is shown to require the two words, which thus make the beautiful *Paronomasia :*

"Like a lion they tore my hands and feet."

Exactly as in Isa. xxxviii. 13.

---

* See his *Introduction to the Hebrew Bible,* pp. 968-972.

† See under *Ellipsis,* pp. 28, 29.

Ps. xxv. 16.—" Turn thee unto me, and have mercy upon me ; for I am desolate and afflicted " (וְעָנִי אָנִי, v'ahnī ahnī, lit. " *afflicted am I* ").

Ps. xxxix. 11 (12).—" When thou with rebukes dost correct man (אִישׁ, īsh) for iniquity, thou makest his beauty to consume away like a moth (עָשׁ, āsh)."

Ps. xl. 3 (4).—" Many shall see it (יִרְאוּ, yirū) and fear (וְיִירָאוּ, v'yiraū)." Or, Many will **peer** and **fear**.

See also Ps. lii. 6.

Ps. liii. 6 (8).—See Deut. xxx. 3.

Ps. lvi. 8 (9).—" Thou tellest my wanderings (נֹדִי, nōdee) ; put thou my tears into thy bottle (בְנֹאדֶךָ, b'nodecha)." The similarity of sound is intended to call our attention to the fact that the tears caused by our wanderings are noted and noticed by God.

Ps. lxiv. 4 (5).—"Suddenly do they shoot at him (יֹרֻהוּ, yoruhū) and fear (יִירָאוּ, yīrakū) not."

Ps. lxix. 30, 31 (31, 32).—" I will praise the name of God with a song (בְּשִׁיר, b'shīr). . . . This also shall please the LORD better than an ox (מִשּׁוֹר, mishōr) or bullock that hath horns and hoofs."

Ps. lxxxv. 1. See Deut. xxx. 3.

Ps. xcvi. 5.—" For all the gods (כָּל־אֱלֹהֵי, kol-elohay) of the nations are idols (אֱלִילִים, elilim)." This latter word means *nothings*, or things of *naught ;* so that we might render it, " The gods of the **nations** are **imaginations**."

Ps. cxix. 13.—" With my lips (בִּשְׂפָתַי, bispatai) have I declared (סִפַּרְתִּי, sipparti)."

Ps. cxxii. 6.—" Pray for (שַׁאֲלוּ, shaalū) the peace of (שְׁלוֹם, sh'lom) Jerusalem (יְרוּשָׁלָיִם, Y'rūshalayim) : they shall prosper (יִשְׁלָיוּ, yishlahyū) that love thee."

Ps. cxxvi. 1, 4.—See Deut. xxx. 3.

Ps. cxxxvii. 5.—" If I forget thee, O Jerusalem, let my right hand forget *her cunning*." This is how the passage stands in the A.V. and R.V. It has also been treated as an *Ellipsis* (see pp. 9, 10) ; where we have supplied " *me* " after the verb, *i.e.*, let my " right hand forget *me*."

The first verb is אֶשְׁכָּחֵךְ (eshkachech), *if I forget thee*. And the second is תִּשְׁכַּח (tishkach), *let it forget* (third pers. sing. Kal. fut. from שָׁכַח, shachach).

Dr. Ginsburg suggests that in the transcription from the ancient Phœnician characters to the present square Hebrew characters, the *aleph* (Λ = א) which originally commenced the latter word, was mistaken for *Tau* (Λ = ת), which it closely resembles, and thus the verb was changed from the first person to the third in the second clause. If we restore the *Aleph* (א) we have the following sense and a beautiful *Paronomasia* :—

"If I forget thee (אֶשְׁכָּחֵךְ, eshkachech), O Jerusalem, may I forget (אֶשְׁכַּח, eshkach) my right hand."

Prov. vi. 23.—"For the commandment is a lamp, and the law (וְתוֹרָה, v'tōrah) is light (אוֹר, ōr); and reproofs of instruction are the way of life."

Prov. xviii. 24.—The *Paronomasia* here lies in the word "friends," רֵעִים, reyim, and לְהִתְרוֹעֵעַ, lehitrōēa (*i.e., reye* and *rōēa :* the "*m*" of the former, and "*lehith*" of the latter belonging to the inflections). The latter is from רָעָה (*raah*), *to break* (and not from רָעָה (*raah*), *to feed*), and means *to our own detriment*, and not *to make friends.* Then further, אֵשׁ (*ish*) is not a peculiar spelling of אִישׁ (*ïsh*), *man*, but stands for יֵשׁ, *there is.* So that the verse reads:

"There are friends to our own detriment (or ruin);
But there is a friend that sticketh closer than a brother."

Or, as we might put it :

"There are friends that **break** us,
But there is a friend that **makes** us."

Or :—

"There are friends that give us broken **hearts**,
But there is a friend who ne'er **departs**."

Ecc. vii. 1.—"A good (טוֹב, tōv) name (שֵׁם, shem) is better than ointment (מִשֶּׁמֶן, mishshemen) that is good (טוֹב, tov).
See under *Epanadiplosis.*

Ecc. vii. 6.—"As the crackling (marg. *sound*) of thorns (הַסִּירִים, hassirim) under the pot (הַסִּיר, hassir) so is the laughter of fools."

Here the figure attracts the attention to the fact that the burning of the thorns makes a noise, but it lasts only for a moment and it is all over. So it is with the laughter of fools. See further and compare Ps. lviii. 9 ; cxviii. 12, and Ecc. ii. 2.

It may be Englished thus: "As the sound of the **nettle** under the **kettle**;" or, "as the flaming of **whin*** neath a caldron of **tin**;" or, "as the blazing of **grass** neath a caldron of **brass**."

---

* Furze or gorse.

Isa. ii. 19, 21.—"When He ariseth to shake terribly (לַעֲרֹץ, laarōtz) the earth (הָאָרֶץ, haaretz)."

Isa. v. 7.—"He looked for judgment (מִשְׁפָּט, mishpat), but behold oppression (מִשְׂפָּח, mishpach); for righteousness (צְדָקָה, tzdakah), but behold 'a cry (צְעָקָה, tzeākāh)."

We might English this by rendering it, "He looked for **equity**, but behold **iniquity**; for a righteous **nation**, but behold lamentation."

Isa. vii. 9.—"If ye will not believe (אִם לֹא תַאֲמִינוּ, im lo taaminū), surely ye shall not be established (כִּי לֹא תֵאָמֵנוּ, ki lo teamenū.

We may English it thus:—"If ye will not **understand**, ye shall not **surely stand**." Or,

"If ye have no **belief**, surely ye shall have no **relief**."

Or, "no **confiding**, no **abiding**."

Isa. x. 16.—"And under his glory he shall kindle (יֵקַד, yekad) a burning (יְקֹד, yekōd) like the burning (כִּיקוֹד, kikōd) of a fire."

Isa. xiii. 4.—"The LORD of hosts (צְבָאוֹת, tzevaōth) mustereth the host (צָבָא, tzeva) of the battle," or a host for the battle.

Isa. xiii. 6.—"Howl ye; for the day of the LORD is at hand; it shall come as a destruction (כְּשֹׁד, k'shōd) from the Almighty (מִשַּׁדַּי, mish-shaddai)." The awful nature of that day is emphasized by this figure, and our attention is directed to the fact that Destruction comes from the all-bountiful One! It is like "the wrath of the Lamb," of which we read in Rev. vi. 16, 17. We have the same figure again in Joel. i. 15.

Isa. xv. 9.—"For the waters of Dimon (דִּימוֹן, Dimōn) shall be full of blood (דָּם, dam)."

Isa. xvii. 1.—"Behold, Damascus is taken away from being a city מֵעִיר, meyeer) and it shall be a ruinous heap (מְעִי, me-ī)." The latter word is put for מַעֲוִי, ma-avee, so that by an unusual form of the word it may allude to the word "city."

Isa. xvii. 2.—"The cities (עָרֵי, araye) of Aroer" (עֲרֹעֵר, Aroer).

Isa. xxi. 2.—"Go up (עֲלִי, alee), O Elam (עֵילָם, eylam)."

Isa. xxii. 18.—"He will surely (צָנוֹף, tzanōph) violently turn (יִצְנָפְךָ, yitznaphcha) and toss thee (צְנֵפָה, tzenepha)."

Isa. xxiv. 3.—"The land shall be utterly (הִבּוֹק, hibbōk) emptied (תִּבּוֹק, tibbōk), and utterly (וְהִבּוֹז, v'hibbōz) spoiled (תִּבּוֹז, tibbōz): for the LORD hath spoken this word."

Isa. xxiv. 4.—"The earth mourneth (אָבְלָה, avelah) and fadeth away (נָבְלָה, navlah), the world (תֵּבֵל, tevel) languisheth (אֻמְלְלָה, umlelah), and fadeth away (נָבְלָה, navlah), the haughty people of the earth do languish (אֻמְלָלוּ, umlalū).

Isa. xxiv. 17, 18.—" Fear (פַּחַד, pachad), and the pit (וָפַחַת, v'phachat), and the snare (וָפָח, vapach) are upon thee, O, inhabitant of the earth. And it shall come to pass, that he who fleeth from the noise of the fear (הַפַּחַד, happachad) shall fall into the pit (הַפַּחַת, happachat): and he that cometh up out of the midst of the pit (הַפַּחַת, happachat) shall be taken in the snare (בַּפָּח, bappach).

See also Jer. xlviii. 43, 44.

Isa. xxv. 1.—" O LORD, thou art my GOD: I will exalt thee (אֲרוֹמִמְךָ, arōmimcha), I will praise thy name (אוֹדֶה שִׁמְךָ, ōdeh shimcha)."

Isa. xxv. 6.—" And in this mountain shall the LORD of hosts make unto all people a feast (מִשְׁתֵּה, mishteh) of fat things (שְׁמָנִים, sh'maneem) a feast (מִשְׁתֵּה, mishteyh) of wines on the lees (שְׁמָרִים, sh'marim), of fat things (שְׁמָנִים, sh'manim) full of marrow (מְמֻחָיִם, m'muchayeem), of wines on the lees (שְׁמָרִים, sh'marim) well refined.

Isa. xxx. 16.—" But ye said, No; for we will flee (נָנוּס, nanūs) upon horses (סוּס, sūs): therefore shall ye flee (תְּנוּסוּן, t'nūsūn): and, We will ride upon the swift (קַל, kal); therefore shall they that pursue you be swift (יִקַּלּוּ, yikkallū)."

Isa. xxxii. 6.—" For the vile person (נָבָל, naval) will speak villainy (נְבָלָה, n'valah)," where the A.V. preserves the figure very well.

Isa. xxxii. 7.—" The instruments also of the churl (וְכֵלַי כֵּלָיו, vechelei kelav) are evil."

Isa. xxxii. 19.—" When it shall hail (וּבָרָד, ūvarad) coming down on (בְּרֶדֶת, b'redeth) the forest."

Isa. xli. 5.—" The isles saw it (רָאוּ, raū), and feared (וַיִּרָאוּ, v'yiraū): the ends of the earth were afraid (יֶחֱרָדוּ, yecheradū) drew near (קָרְבוּ, karvū) and came.

Isa. liv. 8.—" In a little (בְּשֶׁצֶף, b'shetzeph) wrath (קֶצֶף, ketzeph) I hid my face from thee for a moment."

Isa. lvii. 6.—" Among the smooth stones (בְּחַלְּקֵי, bechalkai) of the stream is thy portion (חֶלְקֵךְ, chelkech)."

Isa. lxi. 3.—" To appoint unto them that mourn in Zion, to give unto them beauty (פְּאֵר, p'eyr) for ashes (אֵפֶר, epher).''

Jer. i. 11, 12 (R.V.)—" The word of the LORD came unto me, saying, Jeremiah, What seest thou? And I said, I see a rod of an almond tree (שָׁקֵד, shaked). Then said the LORD unto me, Thou hast well seen ; for I will watch over it (שֹׁקֵד, shoked). So, A.V. margin.

Our attention is thus called to the fact that the almond tree has to do with judgment deferred, but finally executed. This is just what we have in Jeremiah: and hence it is the truth set forth in the opening chapter.

The times of the Gentiles are passed over to show that their judgment is deferred till that foretold shall have been executed on Babylon (chap. xxv).

Chapters l. and li. give us the day of reckoning with Babylon for the plunder and destruction of the temple. Jer. l. 4, 5 tells us when it shall take place. So again l. 20. If we compare the following passages, it is clear that all this is yet future. Compare:

Jer. li. 13	with	Rev. xvii. 1, 15 ;
,, li. 8	,,	,, xviii. 2 ;
,, li. 45	,,	,, xviii. 4 ;
,, l. 13	,,	,, xviii. 19;
,, li. 48	,,	,, xviii. 20;
,, l. 15, xxv. 10	,,	,, xviii. 22, 23 ;

and we shall see that the judgment is indeed deferred; but, it will surely come. God will " watch over " it to bring it to pass, and this is emphasized and marked by the three words :

Shaked—shoked—sheshach.*

For the Figure involved in these three words, see under *Ænigma*.

Jer. i. 17.—Here there are two *Paronomasias* which are alternated :—

" Be not dismayed (תֵּחַת, techath) at their faces (מִפְּנֵיהֶם, mipnehem),

Lest I confound thee (אַחִתְּךָ, achitcha) before them (לִפְנֵיהֶם, liphnehem).''

Jer. vi. 1.—" Blow (תִּקְעוּ, tiku) in Tekoa (בִּתְקוֹעַ), the trumpet.''

Jer. viii. 13.—"I will surely (אָסֹף, ahsōph) consume them (אֲסִיפֵם, asiphem).''

---

* See Jer. xxv. 26 ; li. 41.

Jer. x. 11.—"The gods that have not made (עֲבַדוּ, avadū) the heavens and the earth, even they shall perish (יֵאבַדוּ, yevadū) from the earth, and from under these heavens."

Thus is the verse emphasized, and our attention called to it. And when we look at it we find that, unlike the rest of the prophecies of Jeremiah, this verse is not written in Hebrew but in Chaldee! It is a message sent to the Gentiles and their gods by the God of Israel; and, like parts of the book of Daniel which specially relate to the Gentiles, and their times, it is in the Gentile and not in the Hebrew tongue.

See Dan. ii. 4-vii. 28. Ezra iv. 8-vi. 18; vii. 12-26, where Israel is under Gentile power. Jer. xxx. 3, 18; xxxi. 23; xxxii. 44; xxxiii. 7, 10, 11, 25, 26. See Deut. xxx. 3.

Jer. xlviii. 2.—"In Heshbon (בְּחֶשְׁבּוֹן, b'cheshbōn) they have devised (חָשְׁבוּ, chashvū) evil against it: come, and let us cut it off from being a nation. Also thou shalt be cut down (תִּדֹּמִּי, tiddōmmi), O Madmen (מַדְמֵן, madmen)."

Jer. xlviii. 9.—"Give wings unto Moab, that it may flee (נֵצָא, natzo) and get away (תֵּצֵא, tetze)." Or, may fly and flee away.

Jer. xlviii. 43, 44.—See Isa. xxiv. 17, 18.

Jer. xlviii. 47; xlix. 6, 39.—See Deut. xxx. 3.

Lam. ii. 5.—"And hath increased in the daughter of Judah mourning (תַּאֲנִיָּה, ta'aniyah) and lamentation (וַאֲנִיָּה, v'aniyah)."

Lam. ii. 14.—See Deut. xxx. 3.

Lam. iii. 47.—"Fear (פַּחַד, pachad) and a snare (וָפַחַת, vaphachath) is come upon us." Or, scare and a snare.

Ezek. vii. 6.—"An end (קֵץ, ketz) is come, the end (הַקֵּץ, haketz): it watcheth (הֵקִיץ, hekitz) for thee: behold, it is come."

Ezek, xii. 10.—"Say thou unto them, Thus saith the Lord God: This burden (הַמַּשָּׂא, hammassa) concerneth the prince (הַנָּשִׂיא, hannasi)." Or, this grief concerns a chief.

Ezek. xvi. 53.—See Deut. xxx. 3.

Ezek. xxiv. 21.—"I will profane my sanctuary, the excellency of your strength, the desire (מַחְמַד, machmad) of your eyes, and that which your soul pitieth (וּמַחְמַל, umachmal)." Lit., *the pity of your soul*. Or, your eyes' admiration and your soul's commiseration.

Ezek. xxv. 16.—"Behold I will stretch out mine hand upon the Philistines, and I will cut off (וְהִכְרַתִּי, v'hichratti) the Cherethims (כְּרֵתִים, k'rethim)."

Ezek. xxix. 14; xxxix. 25.—See Deut. xxx. 3.

Dan. v. 26-28.—" This is the interpretation of the thing :

MENE (מְנֵא, m'ney) : God hath numbered (מְנָה, m'nah) thy kingdom and finished it.

TEKEL (תְּקֵל, t'kel) : thou art weighed (תְּקִלְתָּא, t'kilta) in the balances and art found wanting.

PERES (פְּרֵס, p'res) : thy kingdom is divided (פְּרִיסַת, p'risath) and given to the Medes and Persians (וּפָרָס, upharas).

Hos. viii. 7.—" The bud (צֶמַח, tzemach) shall yield no (קֶמַח, kemach) meal." Or, the flower shall yield no flour.

Hos. ix. 15.—" Their princes (שָׂרֵיהֶם, sarehem) are revolters (סוֹרְרִים, sōrrim)."

Hos. xii. 11.—" Is there iniquity in Gilead (גִּלְעָד, gilad, i.e., heap of testimony) ? surely they are vanity : they sacrifice bullocks in Gilgal (בַּגִּלְגָּל, baggilgal, i.e., heap of heap) : yea, their altars are as heaps (כְּגַלִּים, k'gallim) in the furrows of the field."

Joel. i. 15.—See Isa. xiii. 6.

Amos. viii. 1, 2.—" And he said, Amos, what seest thou ? And I said, a basket of summer fruit (קָיִץ, kayitz*). Then said the LORD unto me. The end (הַקֵּץ, haketz) is come upon my people Israel; I will not again pass by them any more."

I.e., they are now like the ripe fig, ready to be cut off, or ripe for judgment.

Amos. ix. 14.—See Deut. xxx. 3.

Jonah iv. 6.—" And the LORD God prepared a gourd, and made it to come up over Jonah, that it might be a shadow (צֵל, tzel) over his head, to deliver (לְהַצִּיל, l'hatzil) him from his grief." Or, a shield to shelter his head.

Micah i. 10.—" In the house of Aphrah (לְעַפְרָה, l'aphrah) roll thyself in the dust (עָפָר, aphar)."

The names of all these places (10-15) are significant and connected with the prophecy associated with them.

" Declare ye it not at Gath, weep not at Accho "† (**Water Town**).

" In the house of Aphra (**Dust** *town*) roll thyself in the **dust**."

---

* From קוּץ (kutz), to cut off, pick or gather ripe fruits.

† For so it should read, בָּכוֹ (bacho) rendered " at all," being the primitive form of the word and standing for the later and fuller spelling בְּעַכּוֹ. Accho was connected with water, being a maritime town, and in the neighbourhood of inland swamps. Now called Akka (French St. Jean d'Acre).

" Pass ye away thou inhabitant of Saphir (**Fair** *town*) in nakedness and shame " (R.V. and see margin A.V.).

" The inhabitant of Zaanan (**Flock**-town) is not come forth " (R.V.).

" The wailing of Beth-ezel (House-of-**sloth**) shall take from you the stay thereof" (R.V.).

" For the inhabitant of Maroth (**Bitter**-town) waiteth anxiously for good (R.V. marg., " *is in travail* "), because evil is come down from the LORD into the gate of Jerusalem."

" Bind the chariot to the swift steed, O inhabitant of Lachish (**Horse**-town) : she was the beginning of sin to the daughter of Zion : for the trangressions of Israel were found in thee."

" Therefore shalt thou give a parting gift to Moresheth-gath (Gath's **possession**)."

" The houses of Ackzib (**Lie**-town or **False**-town) shall be a lie to the kings of Israel."

" Yet will I bring an heir unto thee, O inhabitant of Mareshah (**Heritage**-town)."

" He shall come unto Adullam (**Rest**-town) the glory of Israel."

Nah. ii. 10.—" She is empty (בּוּקָה, b'ukah), and void וּמְבוּקָה, ūmbooquah), and waste (וּמְבֻלָּקָה, umbullakah)."

Hab. ii. 18.—" What profiteth the graven image that the maker thereof hath graven it : the molten image, and a teacher of lies, that the maker of his work trusteth therein, to make dumb (אֱלִמִים, illimim) idols (אֱלִילִם, elilim)."

Zeph. i. 2.—" I will utterly (אָסֹף, ahsoph) consume (אָסֵף, aseph) all things from off the land, saith the LORD." Lit., אָסֹף, אָסֵף (*asoph, aseph*), *to end, I end*, *i.e.*, by taking away I will make an end of.

Zeph. ii. 4.—" For Gaza (עַזָּה, Aazzah) shall be forsaken (עֲזוּבָה, aazuvah) . . and Ekron (וְעֶקְרוֹן, v'ekrōn) shall be rooted out (תֵּעָקֵר, teaker).

Zeph. ii. 7 and iii. 20.—See Deut. xxx. 3.

Zech. ix. 3.—" And Tyrus (צֹר, Tzōr) did build herself a stronghold (מָצוֹר, matzōr)."

Zech. ix. 5.—" Ashkelon shall see it (תֵּרֶא, tere) and fear (וְתִירָא, v'thira).

Matt. xxi. 41.—" He will miserably (κακῶς, kakōs) destroy those wicked (κακούς, kakous) wicked men."

In the Greek the two words come together, thus: κακοὺς κακῶς (kakous kakōs).

Matt. xxii. 3.—"They would not come." οὐκ ἤθελον ἐλθεῖν (ouk eethelon elthein). See under *Meiosis*.

Matt. xxiv. 7.—"There shall be famines (λιμοί, limoi), and pestilences (λοιμοί, loimoi)." So Luke xxi. 11.

Rom. i. 29.—" Fornication (πορνείᾳ, *porneia**), wickedness (πονηρίᾳ, *poneeria*) . . . full of envy (φθόνου, phthonou), murder (φόνου, phonou)," etc.

Rom. i. 31.—"Without understanding (ἀσυνέτους, asunetous) covenant-breakers (ἀσυνθέτους, asunthetous)."

Rom. ix. 18.—"Therefore hath He mercy on whom He will have mercy." Lit., so then on whom he will θελει (thelei) he shews mercy ἐλεεῖ (eleei).

1 Cor. ix. 17.—" For if I do this thing willingly (ἑκών, hekōn), I have (ἔχω, echō) a reward." See under *Oxymoron*.

2 Cor. viii. 22.—"And we have sent with them our brother, whom we have oftentimes (πολλάκις, pollakis) proved diligent in many things (πολλοῖς, pollois)."

In the Greek the words come together, and in a different order:— πολλοῖς πολλάκις (pollois pollakis).

2 Cor. ix. 8.—" Having all sufficiency in all things," παντὶ πάντοτε πᾶσαν (panti pantote pasan).

Phil. iii. 2.—" Beware of the katatomee (κατατομή): for we are the peritomee (περιτομή).

Thus are contrasted the false and the true circumcision. True circumcision is " to worship God in the spirit, to rejoice in Christ Jesus, and to have no confidence in the flesh " (Phil. iii. 3). It is " of the heart in spirit, and not in letter " (Rom. ii. 25, 29).

To go back therefore to ordinances, and to this ordinance, after having been made free in Christ is *mutilation*, not true circumcision. The verb κατατέμνειν (*katatemnein*) is always connected with *mutilation*, see Lev. xxi. 5. 1 Kings xviii. 28. Isa. xv. 2. Hos. vii. 14.

1 Tim. i. 18.—" War a good warfare," **strateian strateuein.**

1 Tim. iv. 3.—This passage has been referred to under *Ellipsis* and *Zeugma;* but there is a latent *Paronomasia* in one word that is omitted. The Greek is κωλυόντων (kōleuontōn), *forbidding*. This word suggests the other word which is omitted, but is obviously to

---

*This word should go out according to the Texts of L.T.Tr. W.H., and R.V.

be understood :—κελευόντων (**keleuontōn**), *commanding.* There is the difference of only one letter between the two words. This is not, of course, a pure *paronomasia* as only one of the words is expressed.

1 Tim. vi. 5, 6.—Where the word **porismos**, *gain,* is connected with **peirasmos**, temptation, in verse 9.

Heb. v. 8.—" Though he were a Son yet learned he (ἔμαθεν, **emathen**) obedience by the things which he suffered (ἔποθεν, **epathen**)."

Jas. v. 17.—" With prayer (προσευχῇ, **proseuchee**) he prayed (προσηύξατο, **proseeuxato**) " : *i.e.*, as in A.V., " He prayed earnestly." See *Polyptoton.*

PARECHESIS;
or, FOREIGN PARONOMASIA.

The Repetition of Words similar in Sound, but different in Language.

Par-ee-che'-sis. Greek, παρήχησις: from παρά (*para*), *beside*, and ἠχή (*eechee*), *a sound, a sounding of one word beside another.*

Parechesis is a *Paronomasia*, when the repeated words of similar sound are *in another tongue.*

The examples of *Paronomasia* which we have given are such only in the Hebrew and the Greek, not in the English rendering of them There is no figure in the English Translation; except when it may be possible to reproduce the similar words in translation (as is done in Rom. x. 19, *disobedience* and *obedience*, etc.). So far as the English is concerned, and as related to it, all the examples of *Paronomasia* are really *Parechesis*, because they exist in another language and not in the translation of it.

Similarly, as the New Testament (if not originally written in Hebrew, and then at a very early date translated into Greek) is at least full of Hebrew thought and idiom. (See under *Idiom.*) So that, though there may be no *Paronomasia* in the Greek words, there may be in the Hebrew thought, or in the Hebrew words which the Greek words represent. In these cases, where the *Paronomasia* is in the Hebrew thought, it is called *Parechesis* so far as the Greek is concerned. And it is only when we go to the Hebrew thought that we can hear the Hebrew words *sounding beside* the Greek words.

To put the difference in a simpler form: Two words similar in sound are a *Paronomasia* with regard to their particular language, both words being in the same language. But a *Parechesis* is found when the two words are not in the same language.

The Greeks also called this figure

PAROMŒOSIS, from παρόμοιος, *very much alike ;* and

PARISON or PARISOSIS, from παρά (*para*), *beside*, and ἴσος (*isos*), *equal to.*

So that words equal to other words in one language are seen to be similar to those in another language when placed beside them.

It follows, from what we have said, that all the examples of *Parechesis* must occur in the New Testament:

x

Matt. iii. 9.—"God is able of these *stones* to raise up children unto Abraham."

Here, there is no *Paronomasia* either in the Greek or the English, but there is in the Hebrew thought. Hence, these would be this *Parechesis* :—

אֲבָנִים (abanim), *stones*.   בָּנִים (banim), *children*.

"God is able of these **abanim** to raise up **banim** unto Abraham."

Matt. x. 30.—"The very *hairs* of your head are all *numbered*." מְנֵא, mene, and מִנְיָן, manyan.

Matt. xi. 17.—"We have piped unto you, and ye have not danced (ὠρχήσασθε, **ōrcheesasthe**): we have mourned unto you, and ye have not lamented (ἐκόψασθε, **ekopsasthe**).

There is a *Homœoteleuton* in these two Greek words but no *Paronomasia*. The *Parechesis* is seen by the Syriac, referring to which the Lord doubtless used. There we see, a beautiful example of *Paronomasia*, for the word "danced" would be רְקֶדְתּוּן, rakedton, and the word "lamented" would be אַרְקֶדוּוּן, arkedton.

In the English it would be :—"We have piped unto you and ye did not **leap**: we have mourned unto you, and ye do not **weep**."

Matt. xi. 29.—"I am *meek*, and ye shall find *rest*."

In the Peshito we have נִיח (nich), and נְיָחָא (n'yacha), and better still in the Lewis-Codex וְאֲנִיחכוּן (v'enichkon), *i.e., I shall give you rest*," *i.e.,* I am **neech** and v'**eneechkōn**.

Mark viii. 32.—The words of Peter to Jesus are rendered in the Lewis-Codex :—"As if he *pitied* him: be it *far* from thee." This is הָאֵס, haes ; חָס, chas.

Luke vii. 41, 42.—See Rom. xiii. 8.

John i. 5.—"The light shineth in darkness, and the darkness comprehended it not."

In Syriac the word "darkness" would be קְבַל, keval, and "comprehend" would be קַבֵּל, kabbel.

John x. 1.—"He that entereth not by the door into the sheepfold" would be מִן תַּרְעָא לְטִירָא, min tara letira.

Rom. xiii. 8.—"*Owe* no man anything but to *love* one another."

In the Greek (as in the English) these words are very different: but, to a Hebrew, the two words would immediately be, in the mind, (א)חב, achāb and חוב, chab. "**Chāv**, be debtor to no man, but **achāb** one another." The same is seen in Luke vii. 41, 42.

Rom. xv. 4.—"That we through *patience* . . . might have *hope*."
This would be סַבַּר, sabbar and סוּבַר, subar (from the same root).
"That we through **sabbar** might have **saubar**."

1 Cor. i. 23, 24.—"We preach Christ crucified, unto the Jews a stumbling-block, and unto the Greeks foolishness; but unto them which are called, both Jews and Greeks, Christ the power of God, and the wisdom of God."

Here, there is a beautiful combination of words. By a simple change of letters, the words signify *cross, stumbling-block, foolishness, power,* and *wisdom* :—

מַשְׂכַּל (maskal) is cross.

מִכְשׁוֹל (michshōl) is stumbling-block.

סֶכֶל (sechel) is foolishness.

הִשְׂכִּיל (haschil) is power: *i.e.*, prosperity or success resulting
     from power in doing anything.

שֶׂכֶל (sechel) is wisdom (1 Chron. xxii. 12 ; xxvi. 14. Prov. xii. 8).

So that the whole passage would sound, in reading, thus:—"We preach Christ, **maskal**, to the Jews **michshōl**, and to the Greeks **sekel**, but to them that are called both Jews and Greeks, Christ the **haschil** of God and the **sechel** of God."

2 Cor. xi. 17.—"But as it were *foolishly*, in this confidence of *boasting*."

Here, foolishness and boasting are (from the same root)—

הִתְהַלֵּל (hithallel) and

הִתְהוֹלֵל (hithōlel).

(*d*) With a different sound (but similar sense).

SYNONYMIA ; or, SYNONYMOUS WORDS.

The Repetition of Words similar in Sense, but different in Sound and Origin.

Syn-o-nym'-i-a, from σύν (*sun*), *together with*, and ὄνομα (*onoma*), *a name.* A Synonym is so called when the sense of two or more words is similar, though the sound and appearance and derivation may be quite different. Synonyms do not make the figure called *Synonymia* unless they are used for the purpose of enhancing the force and fire of the passage.

The Figure of *Synonymia* is a repetition of words different in sound and origin, but similar in shades of meaning. When used rhetorically—repeating the same sentence in other words—it has a variety of uses, to which distinct names have been given according to the nature of the subject, or the object of the speaker. See below under the next section (Section II., Repetition, affecting the sense).

Synonymia, when employed by man, is often an unnecessary and vain repetition of empty words; but, when used by the Holy Spirit, it causes the mind to look again and again at the subject. Man may use it to expose his unhappy vanity: but God uses it to emphasize His wisdom, power, or purpose, when words of similar meaning are heaped together to attract the attention, and impress the mind.

We have not, except in a few important instances, attempted to define the various Synonyms employed. This is a work by itself, and will well repay the most patient and careful study.

Ex. i. 7.—"And the children of Israel were **fruitful,** and **increased,** and **multiplied.**"

Here, we are impressed with the extraordinary great and rapid increase of Israel in Egypt, on which the Divine Comment in Ps. cv. 24 is, "He increased His People exceedingly." See also Gen. xlvi. 3; Deut. xxvi. 5; Acts vii. 17.

The figure of *Polysyndeton* (*q.v.*) is combined, here, with *Synonymia.*

Ex. ii. 23-25.—"And the children of Israel **sighed** by reason of the bondage, and they **cried,** and their **cry** came up unto God by reason of the bondage."

Here the distress of the People is emphasized; as in the next verses the faithfulness of God to His covenant is impressed upon us:

"And God **heard** their groaning, and God **remembered** his covenant
>   **with** Abraham,
>   **with** Isaac, and
>   **with** Jacob:

and God **looked** upon the children of Israel,
and God had **respect** unto them."

Here we have *Anaphora* (*q.v.*), in the repetition of the word "with": *Polysyndeton* (*q.v.*), in the repetition of the word "with," combined with *Synonymia*, and all this in order to emphasize this remarkable crisis and turning-point of Israel's history.

Ex. xii. 2.—"This **month** shall be unto you the beginning of **months**: it shall be the first **month** of the year to you."

Thus the important fact of the change of the beginning of the year is emphasized. It was no ordinary event; and it is thus impressed upon the People.

Ex. xv. 16.—"**Fear** and **dread** shall fall upon them."

Ex. xxxiv. 6, 7.—The import of the name "Jehovah" is revealed by a nine-fold synonymous description, which may be thus exhibited:

"Jehovah passed by before him (Moses) and proclaimed Jehovah, Jehovah, El
>   **merciful,**
> and **gracious,**
>   **longsuffering,**
> and abundant in **goodness**
>   and **truth,**
>   keeping **mercy** for thousands,
>   forgiving **iniquity,**
>   and **transgression,**
>   and **sin.**"

Deut. xiii. 4.—"Ye shall **walk** after the LORD your God,
and **fear** him,
and **keep** his commandments,
and **obey** his voice;
and ye shall **serve** him,
and **cleave** unto him."

Here the synonyms are heaped together in order to emphasize the steadfastness with which the people were to follow Jehovah, and to impress them with the perfection demanded by the Law.

With this is combined *Polysyndeton* (*q.v.*).

Deut. xx. 3.—" Hear, O Israel, ye approach this day unto battle against your enemies : let not your hearts faint,

> fear not, and
> do not tremble,
> neither be ye terrified

because of them."

Ps. v. 1, 2 (2, 3).—

> " Give ear to my words, O Lord,
> Consider my meditation ;
> Hearken unto the voice of my cry, my King and my God."

So David's words and meditation and cry and prayer and voice are thus emphasized.

Ps. vi. 8, 9 (9, 10).—

> " The Lord hath heard the voice of my weeping,
> The Lord hath heard my supplication,
> The Lord will receive my prayer."

Here we have *Anaphora* (*q.v.*) and *Synonymia* in David's prayer, as well as in Jehovah's hearkening thereto, in order to emphasize the great truth conveyed in these two verses.

Ps. vii. 14, (15).—

> " Behold he travaileth with iniquity,
> and hath conceived mischief,
> and brought forth falsehood."

Here we have a double series of synonyms: in the nouns, as well as the verbs.

Ps. vii. 15 (16).—

> " He made a pit and digged it,
> And he is fallen into the ditch which he made."

Ps. viii. 4 (5).—

> " What is man that thou art mindful of him ?
> And the son of man that thou visitest him ?

Ps. x. 17.—

> " Lord, thou hast heard the desire of the humble :
> Thou wilt prepare their heart,
> Thou wilt cause Thine ear to hear."

Here *Synonymia* is enforced in the last line by *Polyptoton* (*q.v.*).

Ps. xxix. 1, 2.—

" Give the LORD, O ye sons of GOD (*i.e.*, Angels; A.V., " mighty")
Give the LORD **glory** and **strength**.
Give the LORD the **glory** due unto His name;
Worship the LORD in the **beauty** of holiness."

Ps. xxxii. 1, 2.—

" Blessed is he whose **trangression** is forgiven,
Whose **sin** is covered.
Blessed is the man unto whom the LORD imputeth not
iniquity."

These three synonyms must be understood, in order to receive the
blessing which the figure here announces.

(1) **Trangression** is פֶּשַׁע (*pesha*), from the root, *to break*, *to
break with;* hence, *to break covenant with*, *revolt*, *rebel* (see 1 Kings
xii. 19; 2 Kings viii. 20). When Jehovah says (Isa. xliii. 27) : " Thy
teachers have transgressed." He means they have *revolted* from
Him. So with Isa. i. 2.

(2) **Sin** is הַטָּאת (*chattath*), *a missing, not hitting the mark* (Judges
xx. 16) ; also of the feet, *to miss the step* or *footing ;* and hence,
stumble ; then, *to err*, *go astray*, *trespass*. Every departure from God
is, therefore, a missing of the mark, and trespass against Him.

(3) **Iniquity** is עָוֹן (*aven*), *a bending* or *curving ;* then, of actions,
acting crookedly or *perversely*. It is generally rendered *perverseness*. See
Isa. liii. 5 (where it is rendered *iniquities*), 6, 11 ; Jer. xxxiii. 8.

The first of these three words refers specially to *thought*, the
second to *deed*, and the third to *word*.

The first is " forgiven " : *i.e.*, taken up and carried away (Gen.
xxvii. 3 (*take*); Isa. liii. 4 (*borne*), 12 (*bare*).

The second is " covered " by atonement.

The third is " not imputed " : *i.e.*, not reckoned or counted. Gen.
l. 20 : " Ye thought (or **meant**) evil against me ; but God **meant** it
for good. (Here, we have the same word twice).

" Oh! the blessednessess!
Rebellion forgiven ;
Errings atoned for ;
Perverseness not imputed (or remembered)."

Compare Ps. ciii. 14 and Isa. xliii. 25, where our infirmities which
man will not remember or make allowance for, God remembers, but our
sins and iniquities which man always remembers, God will remember
no more for ever.

Ps. lxxxix. 30, 31 (31, 32).—

" If his children **forsake** my law,
　　And **walk not** in my judgments ;
　If they **break** my statutes,
　　And **keep not** my commandments."

Here the *Synonymia* is alternated (positive and negative); together
with alternated *Anaphora*.

Prov. iv. 14, 15.—Here, the synonyms are heaped together to
emphasize the necessity of avoiding all evil and evil persons.

" **Enter not** into the path of the wicked,
　　And **go not** in the way of evil *men ;*
　Avoid it,
　Pass not by it,
　Turn from it,
　　And **pass away**."

Isa. i. 4.—Here, four synonymous descriptions are used to give
some estimate of Israel's condition.　See under *Anabasis* and
Eiphonesis.

Isa. ii. 11-17.—We have already seen under the figure of
Polysyndeton (*q.v.*), how this passage is emphasised both by that
figure and by its structure.

We have now to note the bearing of another figure upon it : *viz.*,
Synonymia.　But the use of this figure, the Synonyms are heaped
together in order still further to attract our attention ; and to impress
us with the importance and emphasis, which the Holy Spirit would
have us give to this Scripture ; in which " the Day of the LORD " is
first mentioned, and in which the essence of its meaning and character
is given.

There are two classes of words—a kind of double *Synonymia*
—going on at the same time : one marking the pride of man and the
true exaltation of the LORD, which shall mark that Day, and the other
the abasement of man which shall then take place.

Verse 11.　The **lofty** (גָּבַהּ, *gavah*) looks of man shall be **humbled**
　　　　　　(שָׁפֵל, *shaphel*),
　　　　And the **haughtiness** (רוּם, *rum*) of men shall be **bowed
　　　　　　down** (שָׁחָה, *shachach*),
　　　　And the LORD alone shall be **exalted** (שָׂגַב, *sagav*) in that
　　　　　　day.

Verse 12. For the Day of the LORD of hosts *shall be* upon every *one
that is* proud (גֵּאָה, *gaach*) and **lofty** (רוּם, *rum*),

And upon every one (or thing) that is **lifted up** (נָשָׂא,
nahsah);

And he shall be **brought low** (שָׁפֵל, *shaphel*):

Verse 13. And upon all the cedars of Lebanon that are **high** (רוּם
rum) and **lifted up** (נָשָׂא, *nasa*),

And upon all the oaks of Bashan,

Verse 14. And upon all the **high** (רוּם, *rum*) mountains,

And upon all the hills that are **lifted up** (נָשָׂא, *nasa*),

Verse 15. And upon every **high** (גָּבַהּ, *gavah*) tower,

And upon every fenced wall,

Verse 16. And upon all the ships of Tarshish,

And upon all pleasant pictures.

Verse 17. And the **loftiness** (גָבַהּ, *navah*) of man shall be **bowed
down** (שָׁחַח, *shachah*),

And the **haughtiness** (רוּם, *rum*) of men shall be **made
low** (שָׁפֵל, *shaphel*):

And the LORD alone shall be **exalted** (שָׂגַב, *sagav*) in that
day."

Here we have five words for *high* repeated fourteen times; and
two words for *low* repeated five times.

The five :—

גָבַהּ (*gavah*). *Three* times: lofty, verse 11; high, verse 15;
loftiness, verse 17 (in R.V., verses 11 and 15, lofty; in
verse 17, loftiness),

רוּם (*rum*). *Five* times: haughtiness, verses 11, 17; lofty,
verse 12 (R.V., haughty); high, verses 13, 14 (R.V., high).

שָׂגַב (*sagav*). *Twice* : exalted, verses 11, 17 (so R.V.).

גֵּאָה (*gaah*). *Once* : proud, verse 12 (so R.V.).

נָשָׂא (*nasa*). *Three* times: lifted up, verses 12, 13, 14 (so
R.V.).

The two :—

שָׁפֵל (*shaphel*). *Three* times: humbled, verse 11; brought
low, verse 12; made low, verse 17 (R.V., brought low).

שָׁחַח (*shachach*). *Twice* : bowed down, verses 11, 17 (so
R.V.).

These two words occur also in verse 9.

It will be seen that the A.V. has quite destroyed the figure by
its variety of rendering. The R.V. has evidently aimed at more

uniformity, and has preserved one English word for each Hebrew word, except in two cases, where in verses 13 and 14 they have rendered רוּם (*rum*), *high*, and in 11, 17, *haughtiness*, and 12, *haughty*. "Haughty" could hardly be used of trees and mountains, but "high" could have been used of men, and thus have made the translation uniform.

This is the first occurrence of the expression "the day of the LORD," and hence its definition is thus given and thus emphasized by the figure of *Synonymia*.

The structure of the definition lends weight and solemnity to the description :

> A | 11. Definition of the Day. "Man" and "Men" brought
> low, and God alone exalted.
>
>   B | 12. Persons (every one).
>
>   *B* | 13-16. Things (every thing).
>
> *A* | 17. Definition of the Day. "Man" and "Men" brought
> low, and God alone exalted.

The order of the words too in A and *A* is remarkable. In connection with the loftiness of man they are arranged alternately.

$$A \left| a \mid גָּבַהּ \; (gavah), \atop b \mid רוּם \; (rum), \right\} \text{verse 11.}$$

$$A \left| a \mid גָּבַהּ \; (gavah), \atop {}^{\prime}b \mid רוּם \; (rum), \right\} \text{verse 17.}$$

While in the humbling of man they are arranged in an *Epanodos* (*q.v.*)

$$A \left| c \mid שָׁפֵל \; (shaphel), \atop d \mid שָׁחַח \; (shachach), \right\} \text{verse 11.}$$

$$A \left| d \mid שָׁחַח \; (shachach), \atop c \mid שָׁפֵל \; (shuphel), \right\} \text{verse 17.}$$

Isa. lii. 13.—" Behold my servant . . . shall be **exalted**, and **extolled**, and be **very high**."

Thus the future exaltation of the Messiah is emphasized.

Jer. xiii. 17.—" But if ye will not hear it, my soul shall **weep** in secret places for your pride ; and mine eye shall **weep sore**, and **run down with tears**, because the LORD's flock is carried away captive."

This sorrow of the prophet thus emphasized was seen in greater solemnity when the Saviour in later days wept over Jerusalem (Luke xix. 41).

Jer. xlviii. 29.—" We have heard the **pride** of Moab,
 (he is exceeding **proud**),
 his **loftiness,**
 and his **arrogancy,**
 and his **pride,**
 and the **haughtiness** of his heart."

Here is a six-fold *Synonymia* combined with *Parenthesis* (*q.v.*) and *Polysyndeton.* And all to exhibit the terrible pride of Moab which was to be punished. Compare Isa. xvi. 6.

Nah. ii. 11, 12 (12, 13).—
 " Where is the dwelling of the **lions,**
 And the feeding place of the **young lions,**
 Where the **lion,** even the **old lion,** walked, and the **lion's whelp,**
 And none made them afraid ?
 The **lion** did tear them in pieces enough for his **whelps,**
 And strangled for his **lionesses,**" etc.

Zeph. i. 15.—" That day is
 a day of **wrath,**
 a day of **trouble**
  and **distress,**
 a day of **wasteness**
  and **desolation,**
 a day of **darkness,**
  and **gloominess,**
 a day of **clouds**
  and **thick darkness.**"

Here these Synonyms are heaped up to impress the wicked with the terrors of "that day." This is further heightened by being combined with the figures: *Epizeuxis* (*q.v.*), verse 14, *Mesarchia* (*q.v.*), *Mesadiplosis* (*q.v.*), *Paronomasia* (*q.v.*), and *Asyndeton* (*q.v.*).

Zeph. ii. 9.—Moab and Ammon shall be as Sodom and Gomorrah,
 " even the breeding of **nettles,**
 and **saltpits,**
 and a perpetual **desolation.**"

Mark xii. 30.—" And thou shalt love the Lord thy God
 with all thy **heart,**
 and with all thy **soul,**
 and with all thy **mind,**
 and with all thy **strength.**"

Thus is the first and great commandment emphasized by the combined figures of *Homœteleuton* (*q.v.*), *Polysyndeton* (*q.v.*), and *Synonymia*, in order to convict us of the impossibility of keeping this law and to bring us to the feet of Christ, who alone could keep it : that so we might be impressed with a sense of our own impotence, and cause us thankfully to cast ourselves on His omnipotence (see Luke x. 27).

Luke x. 27.—See Mark xii. 30.

Acts ii. 23.—" Counsel and **foreknowledge,**
Crucified and **slain.**"

Rom. ii. 4.—" Or despisest thou the riches of His
goodness,
and **forbearance,**
and **longsuffering** ? "
Here *Polysyndeton* (*q.v.*) is combined with *Synonymia*.

Rom. ii. 7.—" To them who by patient continuation in well-doing seek for
glory,
and **honour,**
and **immortality,**
[*He will give*] **eternal life.**"
See under *Ellipsis.*

Rom. ii. 8, 9.—" But unto them that are contentious, and do not obey the truth, but obey unrighteousness, [*will be rendered*]
indignation and
wrath,
tribulation, and
anguish."
See under *Ellipsis.*

Rom. ii. 10.—" But **glory, honour,** and **peace** [*will be rendered*] to every man that worketh good, etc."
See under *Ellipsis.*

Rom. ii. 18, 19, 20.—In these verses the synonyms are heaped together to describe the Jew who causes the Name of God to be blasphemed among the Gentiles (verse 24).

Rom. vi. 6.—" Knowing this that our **old man** is (was) crucified with him (Christ), that the **body of sin** might be destroyed, that henceforth we should not serve **sin.**"
Here all three terms refer, by the figure of *Synonymia*, to different aspects of the same thing:

The " old man" expresses the origin in Adam.

By reason of its powers and operations it is called " the body of sin," or sinful body.

And, lastly, its very nature and character is expressed by the name of " sin."

Rom. ix. 33.—" Stumbling-stone and **rock of offence.**"

Rom. x. 15.—" **Gospel** of peace, and . . . **glad tidings** of good things."

1 Cor. xiv. 21.—" With men of other **tongues** and other **lips,** etc."

Gal. i. 12.—" For I neither **received** it of man, neither was I **taught** it, but by the revelation of Jesus Christ."

Thus is emphasized the special commission which Paul received direct from God; and thus is it distinguished from that commission which had been given to the Twelve.

Gal. v. 19-21.—The works of the flesh are emphasized by sixteen synonyms, and by the figure of *Asyndeton (q.v.).*

Eph. i. 20, 21.—To describe the exaltation of Christ we are told how He has been set " Far above all

principality,
and power,
and might,
and dominion,
and every name that is named," etc.

Eph. v. 19.—Here the three synonyms, " **Psalms, and hymns,** and spiritual songs,**" are used to emphasize the true inward and spiritual occupation of the heart with Christ, which is at once the result of being " filled with the Spirit " (verse 18), and the test or the measure of being so filled.

It may be well to define these synonyms : ψαλμός *(psalmos)* means *a touching,* then a *touching* of an instrument with a " plectrum." ψάλλω *(psallō)*, the verb, means *to sweep the strings.* So that the noun was used first of the instrument, and then of the song accompanied by it. It is used *seven* times in the New Testament, and four times of the Book of Psalms (Luke xx. 42 ; xxiv. 44. Acts i. 20 ; xiii. 33), and *three* times of psalms generally (1 Cor. xiv. 26. Eph. v. 19. Col. iii. 16). This points to the conclusion that the psalms referred to here are the inspired Psalms of the Old Testament.

ὕμνος *(hymnos)*, whence our word " hymn," which was originally a heathen word used of a song in praise of a god or hero after death.　The word was so steeped in profane and idolatrous associations that the early Christians hesitated to use it, and it was not till the fourth century that it came to be generally adopted.　But then it was studiously confined to *a direct address of praise and glory to the true and living God ;* whereas the Psalm might commemorate the mercies and blessings He bestowed.　It occurs only here and Col. iii. 16.　The verb ὑμνέω *(hymneō)* occurs four times (Matt. xxvi. 30. Mark xiv. 26. Acts xvi. 25, and Heb. ii. 12).　The latter two passages fully confirm the limited use of the word : " And sang praises unto God " (Acts xvi. 25).　" Will I sing praise unto Thee " (Heb. ii. 12), while the former two would refer to the Old Testament Psalms always sung at the Passover.

ᾠδή *(ōdee),* whence our word " ode," occurs *seven* times,* *five* in the Apocalypse, and *two* in the Epistles (Eph. v. 19, and Col. iii. 16), where it is specially combined with πνευματική *(pneumatikee) spiritual,* implying very strongly that they were composed by spiritual persons, and had to do only with the things pertaining to the Spirit of God. The heathen used it of any kind of song : harvest, festal, wedding, or battle, etc.　Hence the limitation suggested by the word " *spiritual,*" as distinct from these.

Although the first word, *psalmos,* implies musical instruments, it was only in Old Testament worship that these were used : not in the New Testament, nor in the Primitive Church.　Basil, Ambrose, and Chrysostom all speak in panegyrics on music, but do not mention *instrumental* music.　Indeed, Clement of Alexandria, forbade the use of the flute in the *Agape,* though he permitted the harp.　Basil condemns it, and Justin Martyr expressly says that it was not used in the Christian Church.

There is no gift of God which fallen man has not misused, and indeed *diverted,* or rather *per*verted from its original design.　The great enemy uses it for the destruction of *spiritual* worship, under the guise of aiding it ; and few discern the meshes of his marvellously clever snare.†

Music and singing are clearly defined in these two passages Eph. v. 19 and Col. iii. 16.　The three verbs are " speaking," " teaching," and " admonishing."　This is to be done " to yourselves," " in you," " in your hearts," " admonishing yourselves " (ἑαυτούς, *heautous),*

---

* The verb ᾄδω *(adō)* occurs *five* times (Eph. v. 19. Col. iii. 16. Rev. v. 9 ; xiv. 3 ; xv. 3).

† See *Intoned Prayers and Musical Services,* by the same author and publisher.　One penny.

not " one another " (see R.V. margin). The great requirement for this is " the Spirit " and " all wisdom " and " grace."

The words " be filled with the Spirit* " are usually quoted as though they were followed by a full stop, and formed a complete sentence. This is not the case. How is any one to know whether he is filled with the Spirit ? The answer is given :—

"The word of Christ" will dwell in him richly: *i.e.*, the word spoken by Christ and the word relating to Christ: the word which has Christ for its object and Christ for its subject, or Christ Himself " by " (ἐν, *en*) the Spirit.

This indwelling of Christ will be the evidence of the Holy Spirit's presence and operation. For the Spirit and the Word can never be separated. He gives it ; and He uses it, and operates through it. It is His work to take of the things of Christ and show them unto us, and thus to " glorify " Christ; never calling our attention to His work *in* us, but to Christ's work *for* us.

When this word thus dwells in us, we shall be full of its wondrous *Psalms ;* we shall be speaking in ourselves to God, by our *hymns :* and our *songs* will be spiritual, because they will be *sung in our hearts. There* will be the melody which ascends and reaches up to the Presence of God : because it will be a " singing by grace and with grace unto God."

This occupation of the heart with Christ and His Word will be the measure in which we are filled with the Spirit (*i.e.*, with spiritual gifts).

It will be the singing of the " heart," and not of the throat : and it will be " to the praise and glory of God " (as it used to be) and not to the praise and glory of the choir or of the performers. The heart which is indwelt by the Spirit, can sing to God. It will need no "" soloist " to do it by proxy. For we are not commanded to *listen* to the singing of another or others, however exquisite it may be, but to sing ourselves as worshippers. This singing requires no " ear for music," but it needs a " heart " for Christ. For this music comes from God and returns to God.

In the Word of God, prayer is always spoken, and never sung :—

" Moses besought the Lord, *saying* " (Deut. iii. 23 ; Ex. xxxii. 11, etc.).

" Manoah intreated the Lord, and *said* " (Judges xiii. 8).

" Hannah prayed, and *said* " (1 Sam. ii. 1).

---

* It will be seen, under the Figure of *Metonymy*, that the word " Spirit " here (as in several other passages) is put for the *gifts of the Spirit.*

" Elisha prayed, and *said* " (2 Kings vi. 17).

" Daniel prayed, and made confession, and *said* " (Dan. ix. 4, 20).

Indeed prayer is *contrasted* with praise, for " Solomon spread forth his hands towards heaven, and *said* " (1 Kings viii. 22, 23, 54). But when it is a question of praise then we read that it was made with music and singing. (2 Chron. v. 12, 13).

In the upper room the Lord and His apostles "*sang* a hymn " (Matt. xxvi. 30) ; but when in Gethsemane " He fell on his face and prayed, *saying* " (verse 39).

In Jas. v. 13 they are again set in contrast : " Is any among you afflicted ? let him *pray*. Is any merry ? let him *sing psalms*."

This universal testimony of Scripture settles for us the question as to the distinction between prayer embodied in hymns and prayer sung instead of said. That testimony of Scripture is dead against the singing of prayers in any form or manner. It draws no distinction between intoning prayers and singing them. Intoning is singing, and nothing else : it is merely singing on one note instead of many. It is art and artificial ; it is unnatural and unreal—neither pleasing to God nor edifying for man.

Public worship is that in which the Word of God should be *read*, prayers *prayed*, and praise *sung*. God's Word we read, not as our own, but as His, for our instruction. In prayer and praise we say and sing our own words, *as our own*. It is therefore no argument to urge that the Psalms were sung and they contain prayers. For

(1) We do not admit the first premises. Too little is known to justify the assertion that all the Psalms were sung. Some were, undoubtedly ; and these may be sung by us to-day, if we can adopt the words *as our own ;* but not otherwise.

(2) We cannot adopt the words of all the Psalms as our own, but only so far as they are in harmony with the New Testament teaching as to our standing in Christ. The language of those which were under the Old Covenant of Works cannot be adopted as the language of those who are under the New Covenant of Grace.

We may read them as we read the other Scriptures for our instruction, but we might just as well sing the Lessons as sing some of the Psalms.

Again we repeat, therefore, the other New Testament Rubrick— " Is any afflicted ? let him pray. Is any merry ? let him sing Psalms " (Jas. v. 13) ; and we conclude that *prayer* is to be said, and *praise* is to be sung. Praise may even be *said* ; for three times are songs said to be *spoken*. The Song of Moses (Deut. xxxi. 30) ; the Song of Deborah

(Judges v. 12); and the Song of David (2 Sam. xxii. 1 ; Ps. xviii. Title). But, while praise may be spoken, prayer is never said to be sung.

Instead, therefore, of flying in the face of the universal testimony of Scripture, simply because prayer is embodied by human poets in our hymns, we ought rather to question whether the prayer in hymns should not be *said*, and only our hymns of praise sung. But habits once formed are too strong for us to entertain the hope of making so radical a reformation ; though it would be better, if not easier, to alter a wrong habit than to alter the testimony of the Word of God.

Phil. iv. 9.—" Those things which ye have both **learned,**
> and **received,**
> and **heard,**
> and **seen** in me, do."

Col. i. 16.—" For by him were all things created, that are in heaven, and that are in earth, visible and invisible, whether they be **thrones,** or **dominions,** or **principalities,** or **powers** : all things were created by him, and for him."

Here we are impressed with the wonders of the invisible world, of which so little is revealed.

Col. iii. 16.—See Eph. v. 19.

1 Tim. i. 2.—" **Grace, mercy, and peace.**"

So also in the other two so-called " Pastoral Epistles," 2 Tim. i. 2, and Tit. ii. 4.

In all the other epistles it is only " grace," or " grace and peace." In these three epistles " mercy " is added : as though to imply that with the many responsibilities of the pastoral office, God's " mercy " would be specially needed by those who exercised pastoral duties in the Church of God.

1 Tim. iii. 15.—" That thou mayest know how thou oughtest (R.V., how men ought) to behave thyself [or what conduct is incumbent on us] in

> the **house of God,**
> which is the **Church of the living God,**
> the **pillar** and **ground** of the truth."

What this is is shown in the next verse, *viz.,* the " great secret " concerning Christ Mystical and not Christ Personal.*

---

* See *The Mystery,* by the same author and publisher.
See also under *Hendiadys.*

This great Mystery is the Body of Christ, the House in which God dwells by His Spirit; the assembly of the saints peculiarly belonging to the living God, as purchased with the blood of the everlasting covenant; and this is the pillar and ground—the great foundation pillar of the truth, so specially revealed to Paul to make known among the Gentiles.

2 Tim. i. 2.—See 1 Tim. i. 2.

2 Tim. iii. 14, 15.—" But continue thou in the things which thou
hast **learned** and
hast been **assured** of, knowing of whom thou
hast **learned** them.   And that from a child thou
hast **known** the holy scriptures, which are able to make thee wise, etc."

Here the importance of personal knowledge and study of the word of God is enforced: not a mere acquaintance with the letter, but an assurance of the truth.

Tit. i. 4.—See 1 Tim. i. 2.

REPEATED NEGATION; or,
MANY NOES.

The Repetition of divers Negatives.

THIS seems to deserve a place by itself, though the Greeks did not classify it, or name it. They *used* it, however, and this is the all-important point.

It is a special form of *Synonymia*, the synonyms being negatives of different kinds heaped together for a special purpose.

Negatives are repeated even in English to strengthen and increase the emphasis: just as we say " No, no," " No, I will not." But in the Greek this is done much more emphatically. Two or more negatives are used to strengthen the assertion.

These negatives are οὐ (*ou*) and μή (*mee*), which both equally mean *no* or *not*.

As we are now considering their combined use we need not too closely define their separate use. Otherwise we might enlarge on the fact that the one, οὐ (*ou*), denies absolutely what is a matter of fact, and negatives an affirmation: the other μή (*mee*) denies hypothetically what is implied, and negatives a supposition.

This difference may be seen in such passages as 1 Cor. ii. 14 (οὐ). John iii. 18, where we have οὐ in the first sentence, and μή (both times) in the second.

Matt. xxii. 29.—"Ye do err not (μή, *mee*), knowing the Scriptures." Here the μή (*mee*) denies *subjectively*, not absolutely, implying that though they did actually know the letter, they did not wish to know their truth.

When however they and their compounds, οὐδὲ μή (*oude mee*), and οὐδὲ οὐ μή (*oude ou mee*), are used together, this difference is sunk, and the combination produces a most solemn and emphatic asseveration.

Indeed, so strong is it, that whenever man used it *the result always belied it.* See:—

Matt. xvi. 22: where Peter says "This shall *not* be unto thee." *But it was.*

John xiii. 8: Peter says again, "Thou shalt *never* wash my feet." *But Christ did.*

Matt. xxvi. 35 : where Peter affirms " I will *not* deny thee." *But he did.*

John xx. 25 : Thomas says, " Except I shall see, etc., I will *not* believe." *But he did.*

On the other hand, our Lord often used this figure: and, whenever He did so, He always made it good :—

Matt. v. 18.—" Till heaven and earth pass, one jot or one tittle* shall *in no wise* pass from the law, etc." Here we have the certainty of Divine Truth.

Matt. v. 20.—" Except your righteousness shall exceed *the righteousness* of the scribes and Pharisees, ye shall *in no case* enter into the kingdom of heaven." Here we have the absolute necessity of Divine righteousness.

Matt. v. 26.—" Thou shalt *by no means* come out thence till thou hast paid the uttermost farthing." Here we have the inflexibility of Divine justice.

Matt. xiii. 14.—As in Acts xxviii. 26, we have here the solemn announcement concerning Israel's judicial blindness, emphasising and strengthening its certainty.

Matt. xvi. 28.—The certainty of His promise as to the manifestation of His coming glory (see xvii. 1-5, and 2 Pet. i. 16-18).

Matt. xviii. 3.—The absolute necessity of conversion.

Matt. xxiii. 39.—The certainty of His words concerning the conditions as to His return.

Matt. xxiv. 2.—Completeness of the overthrow and dismemberment of the Temple.

Matt. xxiv. 21.—The greatness of the tribulation.

Matt. xxiv. 34.—The fact that when once these things begin to come to pass (γένηται, not πληρόω, compare Luke xxi. 24 and 32), *that* generation which sees the abomination of desolation set up (verse 15) shall see " all these things " come to pass.

Matt. xxiv. 35.—The inviolability of Christ's words.

---

* This is a little ornament $\sqrt{}$ something like a *fleur-de-lis* over certain letters. The Hebrew name for this is *Taag*, or little crown (plural *Taagim*). The Greek is κεραία (*keraia*), *a little horn*, which is exactly what the *Taag* is. See *The Massorah*, by the same author and publisher, One Shilling. The jot or yod is the smallest letter of the alphabet. For full information on this subject see Dr. Ginsburg's *Introduction to the Hebrew Bible*, published by the Trinitarian Bible Society.

Matt. xxvi. 29.—The certitude of Christ's pledge (Mark xiv. 25. Luke xxii. 18).

Luke vi. 37.—The certainty of divers promises.   So Luke x. 19.

Luke xviii. 7.—The speediness of the Divine avenging.

Luke xviii. 30.—The certainty of the future recompense.

Luke xxi. 18.—The perfectness of Divine protection.

Luke xxii. 67, 68.—The accuracy of the Lord's foreknowledge.

John iv. 14.—The satisfying power of the Divine gifts.

John iv. 48.—The obstinacy of unbelief.

John vi. 35.—The satisfying power of " the bread of life."

John viii. 12.—The perfection of the Divine light.

John viii. 51, 52.—Eternal security for the keepers of Christ's sayings.

John x. 5.—The miraculous power of His sheep's spiritual instinct.

John x. 28.—The Divine preservation of Christ's sheep.

John xi. 26.—The certainty of being " changed in a moment " for those who are " alive and remain " till His coming.

Once this repeated negation was used by an angel—Gabriel, in Luke i. 15, of John the Baptist, that " he shall *neither* drink wine *nor* strong drink."   And this was perfectly fulfilled (Matt. xi. 18).

But there is one more use of the figure by Christ, so blessed and so important that we have reserved it to the last :—

John vi. 37.—" All ($\pi\hat{a}\nu$ $\acute{o}$, *pan ho*, *everything*) that the Father giveth me shall come to ($\acute{\eta}\xi\epsilon\iota$, *heexei*, *will reach*) me ; and him that cometh ($\tau\acute{o}\nu$ $\acute{\epsilon}\rho\chi\acute{o}\mu\epsilon\nu o\nu$, *ton erchomenon*, *he who is on his way to*) to me I will *in no wise* cast out."

The repeated " not " in the Greek is thus beautifully rendered, and George Keith effectively sums it up in his hymn on Heb. xiii. 5 : " I will never leave thee nor forsake thee," where we have the $o\grave{v}$ $\mu\acute{\eta}$ in both clauses :—

> " The soul that on Jesus has fled for repose,
> He cannot, He will not desert to his foes ;
> That soul, though all hell should endeavour to shake,
> He'll never, no never, no never forsake."

4. REPETITION OF SENTENCES AND PHRASES.

CYCLOIDES ; or, CIRCULAR REPETITION.

The Repetition of the same Phrase at regular Intervals.

Cy-clo-id'-es means *having the form of a circle ;* from κύκλος (*kuklos*). *a circle, and* εἶδος (*eidos*), *form.*

The figure is so called because the sentence or phrase is repeated at intervals, as though in regular circles.

When this repetition occurs at *the end* of successive passages, as in poetry, in the form of a *Refrain* or *Burden*, it is called AMŒBÆON (*q.v.*). But when it occurs at the beginning or middle or any other part of the passage it is called *Cycloides.*

2 Sam. i. 19, 25, 27.—Where we have the burden of the lamentation three times, " How are the mighty fallen."

Ps. xlii. 5, 11 (6, 12) and xliii. 5.—We have the three-fold emphasis on the great question : " Why art thou cast down, O my soul ? and the blessed answer, " Hope thou in God ! "

Ps. xlvi. 7, 11.—Here, the phrase occurs twice, " The LORD of hosts is with us : the God of Jacob is our refuge."

Ps. lvi. 4, 10 (5, 11).—Where we have the sentence repeated, to emphasize the fact that when our enemies seem mightiest, we can say, " In God will I praise His word."

Ps. lxxx. 3, 7, 19 (4, 8, 20).—Three times we have the prayer : " Turn us again, O God, and cause thy face to shine, and we shall be saved."

Jer. iii. 12, 22.—Where we have the twice repeated command to the backsliding People to " return."

Ezek. xxxii. 20, 21, 22, 23, 24, 25, 26, 28, 29, 30, 31, 32,—Twelve times we have the expression repeated " **Slain with the sword**," at intervals, irregularly, but *twelve* times to denote the judgment as being executed by Divine *government.**

---

* See *Number in Scripture*, by the same author and publisher.

AMŒBÆON; or, REFRAIN.

The Repetition of the same Phrase at the End of successive Paragraphs.

Am-œ-bæ'-on. It is from the Greek ἀμοιβή (*amoibee*), *change, alteration* (from ἀμείβειν (*ameibein*), *to change.* It is used of the repetition of the same phrase or sentence, where it occurs in poetry *at the end* of successive periods.

Cycloides may occur at the beginning, or middle, or any part of the circle, but *Amœbæon* only at the end.

This burden, therefore, thus emphasized is the main point for us to notice in what is being said.

Ps. cxviii. 1, 2, 3, 4.—Where, we have the refrain "For His mercy endureth for ever." (See under *Symploce*).

Ps. cxxxvi.—Where at the end of every verse, we have the refrain, "For His mercy endureth for ever."

Isa. ix. 12, 17, 21 and x. 4.—Where we have the four-fold burden, to emphasize the solemn warning, "For all this his anger is not turned away, but his hand is stretched out still."

Amos. iv. 6, 8, 9, 10, 11.—Here we have the solemn refrain five times repeated "Yet have ye not returned unto me saith the LORD."

Matt. vi. 2, 5, 16.—Where we have the thrice repeated lesson, "Verily . . . they have their reward." See under *Idiom.*

Luke xiii. 3 and 5.—Where, twice, we have the solemn words, "I tell you, Nay; but except ye repent ye shall all likewise perish."

John vi. 39, 40, 44, 54.—Four times we have the glorious fact repeated for our assurance, I will raise him up at the last day."

This, of course, is the Resurrection which was the subject of Old Test ment prophecy, and the one referred to in Rev. xx. (the first or former of the two there named). But not the one which was the subject of a special revelation to the Church of God in 1 Thess. iv. 16.

Rev. ii. 7, 11, 17, 29; iii. 6, 13, 22.—Seven times, at the end of each of these Epistles is the solemn burden repeated "He that hath an ear, let him hear what the Spirit saith unto the Churches."

These words are in the figure called *Polyptoton* (*q.v.,*) but this seven-fold repetition, is the figure of *Amœbæon*. See under *Polyptoton* for the significance of this phrase, as here used.*

Rev. xviii. 21, 22, 23.—Here, the figure *Epistrophe* in the repetition of the words "no more at all" becomes the figure *Amœbæon* in that the words are a solemn burden or refrain in announcing the judgment on Babylon.

---

* Also the series of articles in *Things to Come*, commencing September, 1898.

CŒNOTES; or, COMBINED REPETITION.

The Repetition of two different Phrases: one at the Beginning and the Other at the End of successive Paragraphs.

Cee¹-no-tees. Greek, κοινότης (*koinotees*), *sharing in common.* The figure is so called when two separate *phrases* are repeated, one at the beginning and the other at the end of successive sentences or paragraphs.

When only *words* are thus repeated, the figure is called *Symploce* (*q.v.*), which is repeated *Epanadiplosis.*

It is a combination of *Anaphora* and *Epistrophe*; but, affecting phrases rather than single words.

The Latins sometimes called this figure (as well as *Symploce*) COMPLEXIO, *combination.*

Ps. cxviii. 2, 3, 4.—This is clearer in the Hebrew, where the three verses begin successively with the words, "Let say," and end with the words, "for his mercy endureth for ever."

Ps. cxviii. 8, 9.—

"It is better to trust in the LORD
        than to put confidence in man:
    It is better to trust in the LORD
        than to put confidence in princes."

See also verses 15, 16.—

    "The right hand of the LORD doeth valiantly,
    The right hand of the LORD is exalted:
    The right hand of the LORD doeth valiantly."

In verses 10-12 there are three figures combined: There is *Anaphora*, in the repetition of "They compassed me" at the beginning of several clauses; *Epistrophe*, in the repetition of "In the name of the LORD I will destroy them" at the end; and in verse 11 we have *Epizeuxis* in "they compassed me" being repeated in immediate succession.

Ps. cxxxvi. 1, 2, 3.—Where the three successive verses begin with the words, "O, give thanks," and end with the words "for his mercy endureth for ever."

EPIBOLE ; or, OVERLAID REPETITION.

The Repetition of the same Phrase at irregular Intervals.

E-pi'-bo-lee is from ἐπιβάλλειν (*epiballein*), *to cast upon.* The figure is so named, because the same sentence or phrase is *cast upon* or *laid upon* (like layers or courses of bricks) several successive paragraphs.

It thus differs from *Anaphora* (*q.v.*) in that it consists of the repetition of several words, whereas in *Anaphora* only one word is repeated.

Ex. xvi. 35.—"And the children of Israel **did eat manna** forty years, until they came to a land inhabited ; they **did eat manna,** until they came unto the borders of the land of Canaan."

Num. ix. 18.—"At the commandment of the Lord the children of Israel journeyed, and **at the commandment of the Lord** they pitched."

Judges v. 27.—
" At her feet he bowed, he fell, he lay down :
At her feet he bowed, he fell : where he bowed, there he
fell down dead."
See under *Anaphora*, and *Asyndeton.*

Ps. xxix. 3, 4 (twice), 5, 7, 8, 9.—Where *seven* times we have the words, " **The voice of the Lord,**" commencing seven successive clauses. The number of spiritual perfection.

Isa. ii. 7, 8.—"**Their land also is full** of silver and gold. . . **Their land also is full** of idols."

Isa. v. 8, 11, 18, 20, 21, 22.—*Six* times we have paragraphs beginning "**Woe unto them.**"

Matt. vi. 19, 20.—We cannot forbear to quote these verses according to their structure.

A | **Lay not up for yourselves**
   B | Treasures upon earth,
      C | Where moth and rust doth corrupt,
         D | And where thieves break through and steal :
A | **But lay up for yourselves**
   B | Treasures in heaven,
      C | Where neither moth nor rust doth corrupt,
         D | And where thieves do not break through nor steal.

It will be seen how in each member there is the *Correspondence* (*q.v.*) of the same words, or thought, by way of comparison or contrast.

Acts xx. 22 and 25.—Where two solemn statements are emphasized by commencing

" And now, behold, I go . . .
And now, behold, I know."

SYNANTESIS; or, INTROVERTED REPETITION.

The Repetition of the same Sentences or Phrases in Inverse Order.

Syn-an-tee'-sis, from συναντάω (*sunantaō*), to meet *face to face*, means *a meeting*.

It is similar to *Epanodos* and *Antimetabole* (*q.v.*), but differs from them in that it relates to the inverse repetition of sentences and phrases rather than of single words.

See, for examples, under *Parallelism* and *Correspondence*, below.

---

5. REPETITION OF SUBJECTS.

PARALLELISM; or, PARALLEL LINES.

The Repetition of similar, synonymous, or opposite Thoughts or Words in parallel or successive Lines.

THIS form of sacred writing has been noted from the earliest times. De Rossi,* a learned Jew of the sixteenth century, first published a mass of information on the subject in a remarkable work, *Meor Enajim* (*i.e.*, *The Light of the Eyes*). Bishop Lowth translated chapter lx.†, which deals with the construction of *lines* : and Bishop Jebb in his *Sacred Literature* extended the study. But none of these got beyond *Parallelism* as it is applied to *lines*. This has universally gone under the name of, and been treated as, *Poetry*.

It is a form of the figure *Synonymiá*, by which the subject of one line is repeated in the next line in different, but so-called, synonymous terms.

Parallelism is of seven kinds : three simple and four complex :—

I. SIMPLE.

1. Synonymous or Gradational.
2. Antithetic or Opposite.
3. Synthetic or Constructive.

II. COMPLEX.

1. Alternate.   Two lines repeated only once (four lines in all).
2. Repeated Alternation.   Two lines repeated more than once.
3. Extended Alternation.   Three or more lines repeated.
4. Introverted.

I. SIMPLE.

1. Synonymous or Gradational.

This is when the lines are parallel in thought, and in the use of synonymous words.

---

* Kitto. *Bib. Cyc.* III. 702.

† Lowth's Translation of Isaiah, Prel. Dis. p. xxviii. (15th Ed. 1857).

The oldest example, and the first in the Bible, is in

Gen. iv. 23, 24.—In these oldest human poetic lines Lamech celebrates the invention of weapons of war: and it is significant that this should be the first subject of poetry! Lamech's son was "an instructor of every artificer in brass and iron," and the injury of others was the earliest application of the art.

Lamech is so elated with that which would give him power among men that he at once breaks out in eulogy; and boasts that if any one injures him, he would outdo even Jehovah in His punishment of those who should injure Cain.

There are three pairs of lines, and the synonymous words will be at once seen, as we have exhibited them :—

> " Adah and Zillah **hearken** to my **voice**;
> Ye wives of Lamech **listen** to my **speech**.
>
> For I can slay a **man**, if he **injures** me,
> And a **young man**, if he **hurts** me.
>
> If Cain shall be **avenged seven**-fold,
> Truly Lamech [*shall be* **avenged**]* seventy-**seven**-fold."

Luke i. 46, 47.—
> " My **soul** doth **magnify** the Lord,
> And my **spirit** hath **rejoiced** in God my Saviour."

Ps. i. 1.—" Blessed is the man
> that **walketh** not in the **counsel** of the **ungodly**,
> nor **standeth** in the **way** of **sinners**,
> nor **sitteth** in the **seat** of the **scornful**."

Here, we have three series of gradation :—

> Walketh, standeth, sitteth,
> Counsel, way, seat.
> Ungodly, sinners, scornful.

These gradations point us to the fact that there is a mine of truth contained in the verse, on which a volume might be written.

The *tenses* also have their lessons for us too, for they imply "that *never did* walk . . . stand . . . sit": and so help to teach us that in this first Psalm David speaketh " concerning ": *i.e.*, " with *an ultimate* reference to" (εἰς, *eis*), "CHRIST" (see Acts ii. 25). In fact, this *first* Psalm speaks of Christ as the one perfect *Man ;* while the *second* speaks of Him as the one perfect *King:* (" the *model* Shepherd," He Himself says He is: ὁ ποιμὴν ὁ καλός (*ho poimeen ho kalos*), not simply

---

* See under *Ellipsis.*

ὁ καλὸς ποιμήν (*ho kalos poimeen*) : and then twice over at least (see John x. 11 and 14) ; and so, too, is He the "model" *Man* and the "model" *King*.

2. Antithetic, or Opposite.

This is when the words are contrasted in the two or more lines, being *opposed in sense* the one to the other.

Prov. x. 1.—
> "A wise son maketh a glad father;
> But a foolish son is the heaviness of his mother"

Prov. xxvii. 6.—
> "Faithful are the wounds of a friend,
> But deceitful are the kisses of an enemy"

3. Synthetic, or Constructive.

This is where the parallelism consists only in the similar form of construction :—

Ps. xix. 7-9.—
> "The law of the Lord is perfect, converting the soul:
> The testimony of the Lord is sure, making wise the simple.
> The statutes of the Lord are right, rejoicing the heart:
> The commandment of the Lord is pure, enlightening the eyes.
> The fear of the Lord is clean, enduring for ever:
> The judgments of the Lord are true, and righteous altogether"

Here, there is neither gradation nor opposition of words in the several lines; which are independent, and depend for their parallelism on their construction.

In all the above cases the lines are simply parallel, and are chiefly in pairs.

When the parallelism appears in four or more lines, then it may be called

II. Complex.

1. Alternate.

This is when the lines are placed alternately. In this case, the first and third lines, and the second and fourth lines, may, as a rule, be read continuously, while the intervening line is thus placed in a parenthesis.

These alternate lines may be either synonymous or antithetic.

Gen. xix. 25.—

      a | " The **cities** (and He overthrew)
        b | The **plain** (and all the plain),
    a | The inhabitants of the **cities**,
      b | The produce of the **plain**."

Deut. xxxii. 21.—

      a | " They have moved me to **jealousy**
        b | with that which is not God:
    a | They have provoked me to **anger**
      b | with their vanities :

      c | And I will move them to **jealousy**
        d | with those which are not a people :
    c | I will provoke them to **anger**
      d | with a foolish nation."

Deut. xxxii. 42.—Here a and *a* are continuous, and likewise b and *b*. They must be so read, thus dispensing with the italics. The line *b* we give from the R.V.

      a | " I will make mine arrows drunk **with blood,**
        b | and my sword shall devour much flesh ;
      a | **with the blood** of the slain and of the captives,
        b | from the head of the leaders of the enemy."

Here a and *a* relate to the arrows, while b and *b* refer to the sword.

1 Chron. xxi. 22.—

a | Request. "**Grant me** the place of this threshingfloor."
    b | Design. "**That** I may build an altar therein unto the Lᴏʀᴅ."
a | Request. "Thou shalt **grant it me** for the full price."
    b | Design. "**That** the plague may be stayed from the people."

Here a and *a* are continuous, likewise b and *b*. We must read on from b to *b*, placing *a* in a parenthesis. This shows that the plague was stayed, not because David paid the full price for the place, but because of the atoning sacrifice which he offered.

Est. viii. 5.—

a | The king. "If it please **the king**."
    b | Esther's personal influence. "And if **I** have found favour."
a | The king. "And **the thing** seem right before the king."
    b | Esther's personal influence. "And **I** be pleasing in his eyes."

Prov. xviii. 24,—The parallel here is lost owing to an obscurity in the Hebrew. The Massorah records that the word אִישׁ (*īsh*) (which

has been taken by translators as another spelling of אִישׁ (*eesh*), *a man*)
is put three times* for יֵשׁ (*yesh*), *there is.*

The R.V. avoids the *italics* of the A.V. which are put in to make
some sort of sense owing to the A.V. having taken לְהִתְרֹעֵעַ from the
wrong root (רָעָה, *to feed*), instead of רָעָה, *to break*). So that instead of
meaning *to make friends*, it means (as in the R.V.) *to be broken in pieces.*
Hence, *to ruin oneself.*

The point and the parallel, therefore, lies in the plural "friends":
i.e., or many friends in contrast with the faithfulness of the one
"friend":—

  a | "There are "**friends**
   b | to our own detriment :
  a | But there is a **friend**
   b | that sticketh closer than a brother."

See under *Paronomasia.*

Prov. xxiv. 19, 20.—

  a | "Fret not thyself because of **evil men,**
   b | neither be thou envious at the **wicked**;
  a | For there shall be no reward to the **evil man**;
   b | The candle of the **wicked** shall be put out."

Isa. i. 29, 30.—

  a | "For they shall be ashamed of **the oaks** which ye have
    desired,
   b | And ye shall be confounded for **the gardens** that
    ye have chosen.
  a | For ye shall be as **an oak** whose leaf fadeth,
   b | And as **a garden** that hath no water."

Isa. ix. 10.—

  a | "The bricks are **fallen down,**
   b | but we will **build** with hewn stones :
  a | The sycamores are **cut down,**
   b | But we will **change** them into cedars."

---

* The other two passages are 2 Sam. xiv. 19 (where the sense is unaffected,
"If there is any that turn" meaning "none can turn"), and Micah vi. 10, where
the reading called *Sevir* which is equal in authority to the *Keri*, is boldly adopted
into the Text by both the A.V. and the R.V. "Are there yet the treasures of
wickedness in the house of the wicked," etc.

z

Isa. xiv. 26, 27.—

    a | " This is the **purpose** that is purposed upon the whole earth :

        b | And this is the **hand** that is stretched out upon all the nations,

    a | For the Lord of hosts hath **purposed**, and who shall disannul it ?

        b | And his **hand** is stretched out, and who shall turn it back ? "

Isa. xvii. 7, 8.—

    a | " At that day shall a man **look to** his Maker,

        b | and his eyes shall **have respect** to the Holy One of Israel,

    a | And he shall not **look to** the altars, the work of his hands,

        b | neither shall respect that which his fingers have made : "

Isa. xviii. 6.—

    a | **Fowls.** " They shall be left, etc."

        b | **Beasts.** " And to the beasts, etc."

    a | **Fowls.** " And the fowls, etc."

        b | **Beasts.** " And all the beasts, etc."

Isa. xxxi. 3.—

    a | " The Egyptians are **men**,

        b | and not **God** :

    a | And their horses **flesh**,

        b | and not **spirit**."

See under *Pleonasm.*

Isa. xxxiv. 6.—Here the first and third lines are continuous, as are also the second and fourth lines.

    a | " The sword of the Lord is filled **with blood**,

        b | it is **made fat** with fatness,

    a | and **with the blood** of lambs and goats,

        b | **with the fat** of the kidneys of rams."

Isa. li. 20 (R.V..).—Here a and *a*, and b and *b* must be read together in order to catch the sense.

    a | " Thy sons have fainted,

        b | they lie [*i.e.*, are cast down]

    a | at the top of all the streets,

        b | as an antelope in a net."

Isa. lix. 5, 6.—

> a | " They hatch cockatrice' **eggs**,
>> b | and weave the spider's **web** ;
> *a* | He that eateth of their **eggs** dieth. . .
>> *b* | Their **webs** shall not become garments."

Isa. lxi. 4.—

> a | "And they shall **build** the old wastes,
>> b | They shall raise up the former **desolations**,
> *a* | and they shall **repair** the waste cities,
>> *b* | The **desolations** of many generations."

See also under *Epanodos, Antimetabole,* and *Chiasmos.*

2. Repeated Alternation.

This is not confined to two alternate lines repeated, making four lines in all, as in the preceding examples; but in the repetition of the two parallel subjects in *several* lines.

Isa. lxv. 21, 22.—

> a^1 | "And they shall **build** houses,
>> b^1 | and **inhabit** them ;
> a^2 | And they shall **plant** vineyards,
>> b^2 | and **eat** the fruit of them.
> a^3 | They shall not **build**,
>> b^3 | and another **inhabit** ;
> a^4 | They shall not **plant**,
>> b^4 | and another **eat**."

Or, these may be arranged in four longer alternate lines, thus :—

> a | **Houses** (they shall **build**),
>> b | **Vineyards** (they shall **plant**). } Positive.
> *a* | **Houses** (they shall not **build**),
>> *b* | **Vineyards** (they shall not **plant**). } Negative.

Where the first two lines are positive and the last negative.

1 John ii. 15, 16.—

> a^1 | " If any man love the **world**,
>> b^1 | the love of the **Father** is not in him,
> a^2 | For all that is in the **world** . .
>> b^2 | is not of the **Father**,
> a^3 | but is of the **world**."

3. Extended Alternation.

The Scriptures abound with other illustrations of the arrangement of *alternate* parallel lines.

But these alternate lines may consist not merely of two pairs, or of four lines; or, of *repeated* alternations: the alternation may be *extended*. That is to say, the alternation may be extended so as to consist of *three* or *more* lines.

Judges x. 17.—

> a | "Then the **children** of Ammon
> > b | were **gathered** together,
> > > c | and **encamped** in Gilead.
>
> *a* | And the **children** of Israel
> > *b* | **assembled** themselves together,
> > > *c* | and **encamped** in Mizpeh."

Matt. vi. 19, 20.—

> a | " Lay not up for yourselves **treasures** upon earth,
> > b | where **moth and rust** doth corrupt,
> > > c | and where **thieves** break through and steal :
>
> *a* | But lay up for yourselves **treasures** in heaven,
> > *b* | where neither **moth nor rust** doth corrupt,
> > > *c* | and where **thieves** do not break through nor steal."

See under *Epibole*.

4. Introverted Parallelisms.

This is when the parallel lines are so placed that if there be six lines, the first corresponds with the sixth, the second with the fifth, and the third with the fourth.

When this *Introversion* consists only of words and of the same words, it is called *Epanodos* (*q.v.*).

When *Propositions* are introverted, it is called *Antimetabole* (*q.v.*).

When *Subjects* are introverted, it is called *Chiasmus* (see under *Correspondence*).

Gen. iii. 19.—

> a | End. " Till thou **return** unto the ground."
> > b | Origin. " For out of it was thou taken."
> > *b* | Origin. " For **dust** thou art."
> *a* | End. " And unto dust shalt thou **return**."

Ex. ix. 31.—

a | " And the **flax**
   b | and the **barley** was smitten :
   b | For the **barley** was in the ear,
a | and the **flax** was bolled."

Num. xv. 35, 36.—

a | " And the LORD said unto **Moses,**
   b | The man shall be surely **put to death** :
      c | they shall **stone him with stones,**
         d | **all the congregation without the camp.**
         d | And they brought him forth, **all the congregation**
            without the camp,
      c | and **stoned him with stones,**
   b | and **he died** ;
a | as the LORD commanded **Moses."**

Deut. xxxii. 16.—

a | " They **provoked** Him to jealousy
   b | **with** strange gods :
   b | **with** abominations
a | **provoked** they Him to anger."

This shows that when " abominations " are spoken of, *idols* are meant.

1 Sam. i. 2.—

a | " The name of the one was **Hannah,**
   b | and the name of the other was **Peninnah** :
   b | And **Peninnah** had children,
a | but **Hannah** had no children."

2 Sam. iii. 1.—

a | " Now there was long war between **the house of Saul**
   b | and the house of **David** :
   b | but [*the house of*] **David** waxed stronger and stronger,
a | And **the house of Saul** waxed weaker and weaker."

1 Kings xvi. 22.—

a | " But the people that followed **Omri** prevailed
   b | against the people that followed **Tibni** the son of Ginath :
   b | So **Tibni** died,
a | and **Omri** reigned."

2 Chron. xxxii. 7, 8.—

a | Our resource.   " There be more with us."

   b | His resource.   " Than with him."

   b | His resource.   " With him is an arm of flesh."

a | Our resource.   " But with us is the LORD our God."

Ps. lxxvi. 1.—

a | " In Judah

   b | is God known :

   b | His name is great

a | In Israel."

This shows how " the Name " of God stands, and is put for God Himself.   See under *Metonomy.*

Ps. cxv. 4-8.—

a | 4-. The idols.

   b | -4. Their fabrication.

      c | 5-. Mouth without speech (singular in Heb.).

         d | -5. Eyes without sight (plural).

            e | 6-. Ears without hearing (pl.)

               f | -6. Nose without smell (sing.)

            e | 7-. Hands without handling (pl.)

         d | -7. Feet without walking (pl.)

      c | -7. Throat without voice (sing.)

   b | 8-. The fabricators.

a | -8. The idolators.

Ps. cxxxv. 15-18.—

a | The idols of the heathen.

   b | Their fabrication.

      c | Mouths without speech.

         d | Eyes without sight.

         d | Ears without hearing.

      c | Mouths without breath.

   b | The fabricators.

a | The idolatrous heathen.

Prov. i. 26, 27.—

a | " I also will laugh at your destruction,

   b | I will mock when your fear cometh ;

   b | When your fear cometh as desolation,

a | and your destruction cometh as a whirlwind.'

Prov. iii. 16.—

a | Blessings. "**Length of days.**"
  b | Hand. "Is in her **right hand.**"
  b | Hand. "And in her **left hand.**"
a | Blessings. "**Riches and honour.**"

Isa. v. 7.—

a | "For the **vineyard** of the LORD of hosts
  b | is the house of **Israel,**
  b | and the men of **Judah**
a | His pleasant **plant.**"

Isa. vi. 10.—

a | "Make the **heart** of this people fat,
  b | and make their **ears** heavy,
    c | and shut their **eyes**;
    c | lest they see with their **eyes,**
  b | and hear with their **ears,**
a | and understand with their **heart.**"

See under *Polyptoton*, page 299.

Isa. xi. 4.—

a | "He shall **smite** the oppressor,
  b | with the **rod of his mouth,**
  b | and with the **breath of his lips**
a | Shall He **slay** the wicked."

The current Hebrew Text reads אֶרֶץ (*eretz*), *the earth*, but this is manifestly a scribal error for עָרִיץ (*aritz*), *the oppressor*. The *Aleph* (א) being similar in sound with *Ayin* (ע) was easily exchanged by transcribers. And the Parallelism shows beyond doubt that this is the case here.*

Isa. l. 1.—

a | "Where is the bill of your mother's divorcement, whom I have put away?
  b | or which of my creditors is it to whom I have **sold** you?
  b | Behold, for your iniquities have ye **sold** yourselves,
a | And for your transgressions is your mother **put away.**"

---

* This is from the MS. notes for the second edition of Dr. Ginsburg's Hebrew Bible.

Isa. li. 8, 9.—

a | " For my **thoughts** are not your **thoughts,**

　　b | Neither are your **ways** my **ways,** saith the Lord,

　　b | For as the heavens are higher than the earth, so are my **ways**
　　　　higher than your **ways,**

a | and my **thoughts** than your **thoughts."**

Here the whole paragraph is introverted. In a and *a* we have
" thoughts," in b and *b* we have " ways." But the pronouns in a and
a are alternate as to the " thoughts ":—

　　　c | My thoughts.

　　　　d | Your thoughts.

　　　c | My thoughts.

　　　　d | Your thoughts.

While they are introverted in b and *b* as to the " ways ":—

　　　　e | Your ways.

　　　　　f | My ways.

　　　　　f | My ways.

　　　　e | Your ways.

Further we may note that a and b are negative ; and *b* and *a* are
positive.

Isa. lx. 1-3.—

a | " **Arise,**

　　b | Shine; for **thy light** is come,

　　　c | and the **glory of the Lord** is risen **upon thee.**

　　　　d | For behold **darkness** shall cover the earth,

　　　　d | and gross **darkness** the people :

　　　c | but **the Lord** shall arise upon thee and **His glory**
　　　　　shall be seen **upon thee.**

　　b | And the Gentiles shall come to thy light,

a | and kings to the brightness of thy rising."

All these structures may be *described*, as well as set forth in full.
Thus :—

a | The rising of Israel. (" Rising up.")

　　b | The Light received.

　　　c | The glory of the Lord.

　　　　d | The darkness of the earth.

　　　　d | The darkness of the peoples.

　　　c | The glory of the Lord.

　　b | The Light reflected.

a—The rising of Israel. (Dawning : " Thy sunrise.")

Dan. v. 19.—

a | Severity (" Whom he would **he slew** ").

  b | Favour (" and whom he would **kept alive** ").

  b | Favour (" and whom he would **he set up** ").

a | Severity (" and whom he would he **put down** ").

Matt vi. 24.—

a | " No man can **serve** two masters :

  b | For either he will **hate** the one

    c | and **love** the other :

    c | or else he will **hold** to the one

  b | and **despise** the other.

a | Ye cannot **serve** God and mammon."

Matt. vii. 6.—

a | " Give not that which is holy unto the dogs,

  b | neither cast ye your pearls before swine,

  b | lest they trample them under their feet,

a | and turn again and rend you."

Here, the introversion shows that it is the swine who tread the pearls under foot, and the dogs which rend.

Rom. xi. 21-23.—

a | " If God spared not the **natural** branches,

  b | take heed lest He also spare not **thee.**

   -c | Behold therefore the **goodness**

    d | and **severity** of God :

    d | on them which fell, **severity** ;

   c | but toward thee, **goodness**, . . .

  b | otherwise **thou** also shalt be cut off.

a | And **they** also (the natural branches), if they abide not still in unbelief, shall be graffed in."

This passage occurs in the Dispensational part of the Epistle to the Romans (ix.-xi.). See under *Correspondence*. Hence, it relates to Jew and *Gentile* as *such ;* and consequently it is not to be interpreted of the Church, the standing of which is so clearly set forth in chapter viii. So that the statement in line *b* can have no reference to those who are in Christ, for whom there is no condemnation and no separation.

1 Cor. i. 24, 25.—

a | Power. " Christ the **power** of God."
   b | Wisdom. " And the **wisdom** of God."
   b | Wisdom. " Because the foolishness of God is **wiser** than men."
a | Power. " And the weakness of God is **stronger** than men."

2 Cor. i. 3.—

a | Deity. " Blessed be **God**."
   b | Paternity. " Even the **Father**."
   b | Paternity. " The **Father** of mercies."
a | Deity. " And the **God** of all comfort."

2 Cor. viii. 14.—

a | Equality. " By an equality."
   b | Liberality. " That now . . . at this time your abundance may be a supply for their want."
   b | Liberality. " That their abundance also may be a supply for your want.
a | Equality. " That there may be . . . equality."

Gal. ii. 7, 8.—

a | Paul's commission. " When they saw that the Gospel of the uncircumcision was committed **unto me**."
   b | Peter's. " As the Gospel of circumcision was **unto Peter**."
   b | Peter's. " For he that wrought effectually **in Peter** to the apostleship of the circumcision."
a | Paul's commission. " The same was mighty **in me** toward the Gentiles."

CORRESPONDENCE.

It was reserved for Thomas Boys to extend and develope the study of *Parallelism*. What others before him had thought to be confined to *lines*, or only to short passages, he discerned to be true also of whole paragraphs; yea, of whole sections and even of books. He therefore discarded the term *Parallelism* as being altogether inadequate when used of paragraphs and subjects. He adopted the term CORRESPONDENCE as applying to and covering all the Phenomena connected with the structure of the sacred text. In 1824 he gave the world his *Tactica Sacra*, and in the following year he gave his *Key to the Book of Psalms*, which opened out the whole subject, and gave some examples from the Psalms. In 1890, Dr. Bullinger edited from Mr. Boys's Interleaved Hebrew Bible, and other of his papers,* a complete edition of the whole 150 Psalms, which he called, "*A Key to the Psalms*," thus connecting it with the work published in 1825.

This law of Correspondence is seen in the *Repetition of Subjects*, rather than of *Lines*, or *Propositions*.

These subjects may be repeated in three different ways, or rather in two, for the third is only a combination of the other two. They may be repeated *alternately*; or they may be *introverted*, when it is called *Chiasmus* (and sometimes *Epanodos*); or these two may be combined in innumerable ways.

Each of the subjects occupies a separate paragraph, and these we call *members*. These members may be of any length; one may be very short, the other quite long. A longer member may be again divided up and expanded, as each member possesses its own separate structure, and this again may be part of one still larger.

For the sake of convenience, we arbitrarily place letters against each member for the purpose of distinguishing it from the others and of linking it to its corresponding member, as well as for easy reference. Using *Roman* and *Italic* type we are enabled to mark the different subjects which correspond, or are set in contrast, the one with the other.

Thus the subject of the *member* marked " A " (*Roman type*) will be the same subject which is repeated in A (*Italic type*). The same with B and *B*, a and *a*, b and *b*.

---

* These were most kindly placed at his service by the Rev. Sydney Thelwall (Vicar of Radford), in whose possession they are. See Mr. Thelwall's preface to the *Key to Psalms*.

In whatever form we may have this figure, it is always of the greatest possible use and importance. It enables us not merely to perceive the symmetrical perfection of the passage, but to understand its true sense; to see its scope and thus be guided to a sound interpretation.

What may be obscure in one member may be clear in its corresponding member.

The subject, which may not be mentioned in one member may be named in the other. We are thus helped to a correct interpretation. For example, in the structure of 1 Pet. iii. 18-22 it is not clear who or what may be " the in-prison-spirits " of verse 19. But in the corresponding member (verse 22) they are mentioned by name as " angels." We thus learn that the subject of the former member (verse 19) is the *disobedience* of angels in the days of Noah (Gen. vi.), while the subject of the latter (verse 22) is the *subjection* of angels and authorities and powers. Having thus got the scope of the passage, we get the meaning of " spirits," and remember how it is written, " He maketh His angels spirits " (Ps. civ. 4. Heb. i. 7). We at once connect their sin in the days of Noah and their prison with Gen. vi. 1. 2 Pet. ii. 4, and Jude 6. We thus have the clue to the true interpretation of this passage, which if followed out will lead to a correct exegesis.*

For another example see Ps. cxliv. (page 33), where the structure (an extended alternation) clearly shows that verses 12-15 consist of the " vanity " which the " strange children " speak, and the " falsehood " which they utter. The Psalm ends with a solemn conclusion (-15), which stands out apart from the structure by itself in all its solemnity.

Ps. cxliv.—

A | 1-4. Thanksgiving.

    B | 5-7. Prayer (" Bow thy heavens," etc.).

        C | 8. Description of the strange children and their vain words : " Whose mouth," etc.

A | 9, 10. Thanksgiving.

    B | 11-. Prayer (" Rid me ").

        C | -11-15. Description of the strange children. After אֲשֶׁר, " *who* " in verse 12 supply " *say*," in italics,† corresponding with " whose mouth " in verse 8.

Then we have, in the concluding sentence, the true estimate of happiness, and in what it consists, as opposed to the vain and false estimate of the strange children :—

---

* See a pamphlet on *The Spirits in Prison*, by the same author and publisher.

† See under *Ellipsis* (page 33).

" Blessed the people whose God is Jehovah," as is further set forth in Ps. iv. 6, 7 and cxlvi. 5.

The correspondence, here, corrects the common and popular interpretation of this Psalm, and rescues it for the glory of God.

It is clear, therefore, from this, that the subject of *Correspondence* cannot be too diligently studied, if we would discover some of the wondrous perfections of the Word of God, or arrive at its proper interpretation.

Correspondence may be thus arranged :—

I. ALTERNATE.

1. SIMPLE : where there are only two series, each consisting of two members.
2. EXTENDED : where there are two series, but each consisting of several members.
3. REPEATED : where there are more than two series :
   (*a*) consisting of two members each.
   (*b*) consisting of more than two members each.

II. INTROVERTED.

III. COMPLEX, or COMBINED, where there is a combination of the other two.

I. ALTERNATE Correspondence of Subjects.

This is when the subjects of the alternate members correspond with each other, either by way of similiarity or contrast.

We now give a few examples selected from all parts of Scripture.

1. SIMPLE ALTERNATION.

We so call it when it consists of only *four* members: *i.e.*, two series with two members each. In this case the first member of the first series corresponds with the first member of the second, while the second member of the first series corresponds with the second member of the second series.

In other words, it is alternate when, of the four members, the first corresponds with the third, and the second with the fourth.

Josh. ix. 22-25.—

A | 22. The question of Joshua. " And Joshua called."

  B | 23. The sentence of Joshua. " Now therefore" (וְעַתָּה, *veattah*).

A | 24. The reply of the Gibeonites. " And they answered."

  B | 25. Submission to Joshua's sentence. " Now, behold " (וְעַתָּה, *veattah*),

Ps. xix.—

> A | 1-4-. The heavens.
>> B | -4-6. The sun in them (בָּהֶם, *bahem, in them*).
> *A* | 7-10. The Scriptures.
>> *B* | 11-14. Thy servant in them (בָּהֶם, *bahem, in them*).

Prov. i. 8-19.—

A | 8. Two-fold exhortation. " My son, hear . . . forsake not."
> B | 9. Reason. " For they shall be," etc.
A | 10-15. Two-fold exhortation. " My son, if . . . my son walk not."
> *B* | 16-19. Reason. " For their feet," etc.

Isa. xxxii. 5-7.—

A | The vile person shall be no more called liberal,
> B | Nor the churl said to be bountiful.

A | For the vile person will speak villany and his heart will work iniquity to practise hypocrisy, and to utter error against the LORD, to make empty the soul of the hungry, and he will cause the drink of the thirsty to fail.
> *B* | The instruments of the churl are evil; he deviseth wicked devices to destroy the poor with lying words, even when the needy speaketh right."

Here, in A, and *A*, we have the vile person; while in B and *B* we have the churl.   A and B are negative; and *A* and *B* are positive.

Jer. xvii. 5-8.—

A | 5. Cursed is the man (גֶּבֶר, *gever*)* that trusteth in man (אָדָם, *adam*)† and maketh flesh his arm, and whose heart departeth from the LORD.
> B | 6. For he shall be like the heath in the desert, and shall not see when good cometh, but shall inhabit the parched places in the wilderness, in a salt land and not inhabited.
A | 7. Blessed is the man (גֶּבֶר, *gever*) that trusteth in the LORD, and whose hope the LORD is.
> *B* | 8. For he shall be as a tree planted by the waters, and that spreadeth out her roots by the river, and shall not see when heat cometh, but her leaf shall be green; and shall not be careful in the year of drought, neither shall cease from yielding fruit.

---

* *Gever* is *vir*, a strong man.

† *Adam* is *homo*, a *created* man, and is thus put in contrast with Jehovah in *A*.

Ezek. xxxvi. 26, 27.—

A | "A new **heart** also will I give you,

   B | And a new **spirit** will I put within you:

A | And I will take away the stony **heart** out of your flesh, and I will give you an **heart** of flesh.

   B | And I will put my **Spirit** within you.

Here, in this prophecy concerning Israel in the day of their coming glory, there are four members and two subjects. In the first and third it is the "heart," while in the second and fourth it is the "spirit."

These words cannot be applied to the Christian now, inasmuch as the old nature is not taken away, but a new nature is imparted. This is the teaching of Rom. i. 16-viii. 39, where in i. 16-v. 11, *sins* are first dealt with, as the fruit of the old nature, and then, from v. 12-viii. 39, *sin* is dealt with, as the tree which produces the fruit: and we are taught that, though the evil *fruits* are still produced, God reckons the *tree* itself as dead. So, though *sin* itself no longer reigns, yet *sins* are still committed by the old nature; but the saved sinner is to reckon that old nature, *i.e.*, himself, as having died with Christ, and he has now a new nature.

The old nature is not taken away, as it will be in the case of Israel in that day: so the believer has in himself one nature that cannot but sin, and another that cannot sin (1 John iii. 9; v. 18).

The old nature can never be improved, and the new nature needs no improvement.

Until the believer recognises this truth he can never know peace with God.

Heb. i. ii.—

   A | i. 1, 2-. God speaking.

      B | -2-14. The Son of God: "better than the angels."

   A | ii. 1-4. God speaking.

      B | 5-18. The Son of Man: "lower than the angels."

Here the two subjects are arranged alternately. And note that B is in a parenthesis with respect to A and *A*; while *A* is in a parenthesis with respect to B and *B*. In other words, A and *A* read on continuously, without reference to B, while B and *B* likewise read on without reference to *A*, which is thus practically in a parenthesis.

Hence the word "therefore," ii. 1, is not consequent on i. 14, but on i. 2-. And the "for" in ii. 5 is consequent, not on ii. 4, but on i. 14. The respective members therefore read on

Thus: (i. 1) "God, who at sundry times and in divers manners spake in time past unto the fathers by the prophets, hath in these last days spoken unto us by his Son . . . (ii. i.) therefore we ought to give the more earnest heed to the the things which we have heard, etc."

And: (i. 14) "Are they not all ministering (worshipping) spirits, sent forth to minister for (to serve) them who shall be heirs of salvation ? . . (ii. 5) for unto the angels hath he not put into subjection the world to come, etc."

2. EXTENDED Alternation.

This is when there are still only *two* series, but each series consists of more than two members.

And these are so arranged that the first of the one series corresponds with the first of the other ; and likewise the second of the former corresponds with the second in the latter.

This has been called by some Direct *Chiasmus*, reserving the term "Indirect *Chiasmus*" for what we have called Introverted Correspondence, or *Chiasmus* proper.

Bengel calls this "Direct Chiasmus": but this is contrary to the very name of the figure: *viz.*, the letter *Chi* (X.), which he says, is, as it were, the type or mould according to which the sentence or words is or are arranged.

We prefer to consider it merely as Alternate Correspondence in an *extended* form, reserving the term *Chiasmus* for Introverted Correspondence.

Ps. lxvi.—

A | I, 2. Exhortation to praise.

   B | 3. Address. God's works in the world.

      C | 4. Address. Promise for the world.

         D | 5-7. Invitation: "Come and see."

A | 8, 9. Exhortation to praise.

   B | 10-12. Address. God's dealings with His People.

      C | 13-15. Address. Promise for himself.

         D | 16-20. Invitation: "Come and hear."

Ps. lxxii.—

> A | 2-4. Messiah's goodness to the poor.
>
> > B | 5-10. Other attributes.
> >
> > > C | 11. General adoration.
>
> *A* | 12-14. Messiah's goodness to the poor.
>
> > *B* | 15-17-. Other attributes.
> >
> > > *C* | -17. General adoration.

The two members B and *B* form together a wonderful introverted Correspondence.*

Ps. cxxxii.—This Psalm affords a beautiful example of an extended Alternation of subjects. We cannot, here, print the whole Psalm in full, but give the following key to it :—

> A | 1, 2. David swears to Jehovah.
>
> > B | 3-5. What David sware.
> >
> > > C | 6, 7. Search for and discovery of the dwelling-place.
> > >
> > > > D | 8. Prayer to enter into rest.
> > > >
> > > > > E | 9-. Prayer for priests.
> > > > >
> > > > > > F | -9. Prayer for saints.
> > > > > >
> > > > > > > G | 10. Prayer for Messiah.
>
> *A* | 11-. Jehovah swears to David.
>
> > *B* | -11, 12. What Jehovah sware.
> >
> > > *C* | 13. Designation of the dwelling-place.
> > >
> > > > *D* | 14, 15. Answer to prayer in D.
> > > >
> > > > > *E* | 16-. Answer to prayer in E.
> > > > >
> > > > > > *F* | -16. Answer to prayer in F.
> > > > > >
> > > > > > > *G* | 17, 18. Answer to prayer in G.

---

* See *The Key to the Psalms.* Edited by the same author, and published by Eyre & Spottiswood.

Acts vii. 1-53.—

  A | 2. Mesopotamia.
   B | 3-8. Abraham.
    C | 9-19. Joseph.
     D | 20-38. Moses.
      E | 39-43. Resistance.
 A | 44. The wilderness.
  B | 45-. Joshua.
   C | -45, 46. David.
    D | 47-50. Solomon.
     E | 51-53. Resistance.

Rom. ii. 17-20.—

A | " Restest in the law,
 B | and makest thy boast of God,
  C | and knowest His will,
   D | and approvest the things that are more excellent
    E | being instructed out of the law ;
A | and art confident that thou thyself art a guide of the blind,
 B | a light of them which are in darkness,
  C | an instructor of the foolish,
   D | a teacher of babes,
    E | which hast the form of knowledge and of the
     | truth of the law."

In the first series, we have what the Jew considers as to himself.
In the second series, how he uses it in relation to others.

1 Thess. i. 2-10, and ii. 13-16.—

A | i. 2-4. The thanksgiving of Paul and his brethren.
 B | 5. Reason : Reception of the Gospel in the power of God.
  C | 6-9. The effect of the Gospel thus received.
   D | 10-. Believing. Thessalonians " wait " for God's Son.
    E | -10. Deliverance *from* the wrath to come.
A | ii. 13-. The thanksgiving of Paul and his brethren.
 B | -13. Reason : Reception of the Gospel in the power of God.
  C | 14. The effect of the Gospel thus received.
   D | 15, 16-. Unbelieving Jews " killed " God's Son.
    E | -16. Delivered *to* the wrath to come.

1 Thess. iv. 13-v. 11.—

A | iv. 13. Instruction *necessary* as to " them which are asleep " (κεκοιμημένων.* The R.V. reads κοιμωμένων, *are falling asleep*).

　　B | 14. *First* reason (γάρ) : For, those who have fallen asleep (κοιμηθέντας) God (by Jesus) will bring again from the dead.

　　　　C | 15. *Second* reason (γάρ): For, those who " are alive and remain " (οἱ ζῶντες οἱ περιλειπόμενοι) shall not precede them.

　　　　　　D | 16, 17. *Third* reason (ὅτι): Because both will be caught up together (ἅμα) at the Descent of the Lord into the air.

　　　　　　　　E | 18. Encouragement : " Wherefore comfort one another with these words."

A | v. 1. Instruction *not* necessary as to " the times and the seasons " of this Resurrection and Ascension, which will take place *before* the Day of the Lord.

　　B | 2-6. *First* reason (γάρ) : For they already knew that the destruction of the wicked will mark the coming of the Day of the Lord. Contrast (verses 4, 5) and Exhortation (verse 6) : " Therefore let us not sleep (καθεύδωμεν) ;† but " let us watch " (γρηγορῶμεν).‡ (See note on page 372).

　　　　C | 7, 8. *Second* reason (γάρ) : " For they that sleep (καθεύδοντες) sleep (καθεύδουσι) in the night." Contrast and Exhortation (verse 8).

　　　　　　D | 9, 10. *Third* reason (ὅτι): Because God hath not appointed us to wrath, but to obtain salvation (*viz.*, that of the body in Resurrection) through our Lord Jesus Christ, that whether we watch(γρηγορῶμεν)‡ or sleep (καθεύδωμεν), we should together (ἅμα) live with Him (as in D, above).

　　　　　　　　E | 11. Encouragement : " Wherefore comfort yourselves together," etc.

---

* κοιμάομαι, *to fall asleep*, involuntarily : hence used (in nearly every place) of *death*, but only of saints.　Matt. xxvii. 52 ; xxviii. 13. Luke xxii. 45. John xi. 11, 12. Acts vii. 60 ; xii. 6; xiii. 36. 1 Cor. vii. 39 ; xi. 30 ; xv. 6, 18, 20, 51. 1 Thess. iv. 13, 14, 15. 2 Pet. iii. 4.

† καθεύδω, *to go to sleep*, voluntarily : hence not used of death, but either of taking rest in sleep, or of the opposite of watchfulness.　Matt. viii. 24 ; ix. 42 ;

2 Tim. iii. 16 and iv. 2.—There is a beautiful extended alternation between the subjects of these two verses. See pages 146 and 148.

The Word of God is God-breathed and profitable for

    A | " doctrine,
        B | for reproof (or conviction),
           C | for correction,
                D | for instruction."

              Therefore.

    A | " Preach the word,
        B | reprove (or convict),
           C | rebuke,
                D | exhort," etc.

3. REPEATED ALTERNATION.

Alternate correspondence is *repeated* when there are more than two series.

    (*a*) Two members in each series.

In this case the first member of the first series corresponds with the first member of the second, third, fourth series, etc.; while the second member of the first series corresponds with the second member of the other series. These we have indicated as A¹, A², A³ and B¹, B², B³ respectively, A corresponding with A², A³, etc.: and B¹ with B², B³, etc.

Ps. xxvi.—

        A¹ | 1-. Prayer.
           B¹ | -1. Profession.
        A² | 2. Prayer.
           B² | 3-8. Profession.
        A³ | 9, 10. Prayer.
           B³ | 11-. Profession.
        A⁴ | -11. Prayer.
           B⁴ | 12. Profession.

---

xiii. 25 ; xxv. 5 ; xxvi. 40, 43, 45. Mark iv. 27, 38 ; v. 39 ; xiii. 36 ; xiv. 37, 37, 40, 41. Luke viii. 52 ; xxii. 46. Eph. v. 14. 1 Thess. v. 6, 7, 7, 10.

   ‡ γρηγορέω is translated "wake" only in verse 10, above. Elsewhere it is always "watch," "be watchful," or "be vigilant."

Thus the marked use of κοιμάομαι in the *first* series, and of καθεύδω in the *second* series teaches us that the hope of Resurrection and Ascension before the Day of the Lord is for *all* who are Christ's, whether they are *dead* or *alive ;* whether they are *watchful* or *unwatchful.*

Ps. lxxx.—

      A^1 | 1-3. Prayer (People).
         B^1 | 4-6. Representation (People).
      A^2 | 7. Prayer (People).
         B^2 | 8-13. Representation (Vine).
      A^3 | 14, 15. Prayer (Vine and Vineyard).
         B^3 | 16. Representation (Vine and People).
      A^4 | 17-19. Prayer (People).

Ps. cxlv.—

A^1 | 1, 2. Praise promised; from me (to Jehovah).

  B^1 | 3. Praise offered.

A^2 | 4-7. Praise promised; from others and me (to Jehovah for His works).

  B^2 | 8, 9. Praise offered.

A^3 | 10-12. Praise promised; from others and works (to Jehovah for His kingdom).

  B^3 | 13-20. Praise offered.

A^4 | 21. Praise promised; from me and others.

Here, in "David's Psalm of Praise" we have seven members, with two subjects in an *extended* alternation.

(b) More than two members in each series.

This is a combination of *Extended* with *Repeated* Correspondence.

In this case, the first members of each series correspond with each other; while the second member corresponds with the second, the third with the third, etc.

Ps. xxiv. — Here, we have an alternation of three members repeated in three series:

      A^1 | 1, 2. Right to the earth.
         B^1 | 3. Questions.
            C^1 | 4-6. Answer.
      A^2 | 7. Right to heaven.
         B^2 | 8-. Question.
            C^2 | -8. Answer.
      A^3 | 9. Right to heaven.
         B^3 | 10-. Question.
            C^3 | -10. Answer.

Ps. cxlvii.—

A¹ | 1-3. Praise, and reason. (Kindness to Israel).

  B¹ | 4, 5. General operations. (Kingdom of nature).

    C¹ | 6. Contrast. (What the Lord does).

A² | 7. Praise.

  B² | 8, 9. General operations. (Kingdom of nature).

    C² | 10, 11. Contrast. (What the Lord delights in).

A³ | 12-14. Praise, and reason. (Kindness to Israel).

  B³ | 15-18. General operations. (Kingdom of nature).

    C³ | 19, 20-. Contrast. (What the Lord has shown).

A⁴ | -20. Praise.

II. INTROVERTED Correspondence.

This is where there are two series, and the *first* of the one series of members corresponds with the *last* of the second ; the *second* of the first corresponds with the *penultimate* (or the last but one) of the second : and the *third* of the first corresponds with the *antepenultimate* of the second. That is to say, if there are *six* members, the *first* corresponds with the *sixth*, the *second* with the *fifth*, and the *third* with the *fourth*. And so on.

The Greeks called it CHIASMOS or CHIASTON from its likeness in form to the letter *Chi* (X.). For the same reason the Latins called it CHIASMUS, as well as DECUSSATA ORATIO from *decusso, to divide cross-wise* (*i.e.*, in the shape of an X). The Greeks called it also ALLELOUCHIA (from ἀλλήλους (*alleelous*), *together* and ἔχειν (*echein*), *to have* or *hold, a holding or hanging together.*

This is by far the most stately and dignified presentation of a subject; and is always used in the most solemn and important portions of the Scriptures.

Bengel observes with regard to this form of the Figure, that "its employment is never without some use : *viz.*, in perceiving the ornament and in observing the force of the language ; in understanding the true and full sense ; in making clear the sound Interpretation ; in demonstrating the true and neat analysis of the sacred text."[*]

Gen. xliii. 3-5.—

A | Judah's words : " The man did solemnly protest unto us, etc."

  B | Jacob's act : " If thou wilt send."

  B | Jacob's act : " But if thou wilt not send him."

A | Joseph's words : " For the man said unto us, etc."

In A and *A*, we have Joseph's words; and in B and *B*, Jacob's action.

---

[*] See *The Structure of the Books of the Bible*, by the same author and publisher.

Lev. xiv. 51, 52.—

A | " And he shall take the cedar wood, and the hyssop, and the scarlet,

  B | and the living bird,

    C | and dip them in the blood of the slain bird, and in the running water,

      D | and sprinkle the house seven times :

      D | And he shall cleanse the house

    C | with the blood of the bird, and with the running water,

  B | and with the living bird,

A | and with the cedar wood, and with the hyssop, and with the scarlet."

Note also the figure of *Polysyndeton* (*q.v.*) emphasizing each particular item in this ordinance.

Deut. xxxii. 1-43 (the Song of Moses).—

A | 1-6. Call to hear ; and the reason. The publishing of Jehovah's Name, His perfect work and righteous ways.

  B | 7-14. The goodness and bounty of Jehovah to Israel. (Period of the Pentateuch).

    C | 15-19. Israel's evil return for the good. Their pride ; forsaking of God : despising the Rock of their salvation. Moving Him to anger. (Period of past history).

      D | 20. Divine reflections on the period while Israel is " *Lo-ammi.*"* God's hiding from them (Hosea).

        E | 21. Jehovah's provocation of Israel. (Period of Acts and present dispensation).

        E | 22-25. Jehovah's threatening of judgment. (The great tribulation).

      D | 26-33. Divine reflections on the period while Israel is "*Lo-ammi.*"* Their scattering from God (Hosea).

    C | 34-38. Israel's evil return for Jehovah's goodness. Their helpless condition moving Him to pity. He not forsaking them. Their rock useless. (Period of present history).

  B | 39-42. The vengeance of Jehovah. (The period of the Apocalypse).

A | 43. Call to rejoice ; and the reason. The publishing of Jehovah's kingdom. Vengeance on Israel's enemies. Mercy on His land and His people. (Fulfilment of the Prophets).

---

* Hebrew : *not my people.*

Ps. xxiii. is a simple introversion, which is marked by the use of the persons.

> A | 1-3. First and *third* persons : " I " and " He."
>
> > B | 4. First and *second :* " I " and " Thou."
> >
> > *B* | 5. First and *second :* " I " and " Thou."
>
> *A* | 6. First and *third :* " I " and His.

Ps. ciii. is a beautiful example of a large introversion of ten members :—

> A | 1-5. Exhortation to bless.
>
> > B | 6, 7. Gracious goodness. (Kingdom of Grace).
> >
> > > C | 8. Merciful goodness.
> > >
> > > > D | 9. Sparing goodness.
> > > >
> > > > > E | 10. Pardoning goodness.
> > > > >
> > > > > *E* | 11-13. Pardoning goodness
> > > >
> > > > *D* | 14-16. Sparing goodness.
> > >
> > > *C* | 17, 18. Merciful goodness.
> >
> > *B* | 19. Glorious goodness.　(Kingdom of Glory).
>
> *A* | 20-22. Exhortation to bless.

The Visions of Zechariah.—

A | i. 1-17. *False* peace under the kingdom of the Gentiles.

> B | i. 18-21. Providential workings to break up the empires of Daniel ii., and restore Judah, Israel and Jerusalem.
>
> > C | ii. 1-13. Deliverance of the *true* Jerusalem *out of* Babylon.
> >
> > > D | iii. 1-10. Priesthood and Royalty remodelled. Jerusalem changed before *God* after the pattern of Messiah.
> > >
> > > *D* | iv. I-14. Royalty and Priesthood remodelled. Jerusalem changed before *men* after the pattern of Messiah.
> >
> > *C* | v. 1-11. The evil of the *false* Jerusalem sent *into* Babylon.
>
> *B* | vi. 1-8. Providential workings to break up the kingdoms of Daniel vii., and restore Judah, Israel, and Jerusalem.

A | vi. 9-15. *True* peace under the kingdom of Messiah.

Matt. iii. 10-12.—

A | " And now also the ax is laid unto the root of the trees : there-
fore every tree which bringeth not forth good fruit is hewn down,
and cast into the **fire.**

  B | I indeed **baptize** you with water unto repentance :

    C | but **he** that cometh after me is mightier than **I,**

    C | **whose** shoes I am not worthy to bear :

  B | He shall **baptize** you with the Holy Ghost and with fire.

A | Whose **fan** is in his hand, and he will throughly purge his floor,
and gather His wheat into the garner ; but He will burn up the
chaff with unquenchable fire."

Mark v. 2-6.—

A | " And when he was come out of the ship, immediately there **met
him** out of the tombs a man with an unclean spirit,

  B | who had his dwelling among the **tombs ;**

    C | and no man could **bind him** . . . no, not with chains :

      D | because that he had been often bound with **fetters**

        E | and **chains,**

        E | and the **chains** had been plucked asunder by him,

      D | and the **fetters** broken in pieces :

    C | neither could any man **tame him.**

  B | And always, night and day, he was in the mountains and in
the **tombs** crying and cutting himself with stones.

A | But when he **saw Jesus** afar off, he ran and worshipped Him."

John v. 8-11.—

A | " Jesus saith unto him, Rise, **take up thy bed, and walk.**

  B | And immediately the man was **made whole,**

    C | And took his **bed** and walked ;

      D | And on the same day was the **sabbath.**

      D | The Jews therefore said unto him that was cured, It
is the **sabbath** day.

    C | It is not lawful for thee to carry thy **bed.**

  B | He answered them, He that **made me whole,**

A | The same said unto me, **Take up thy bed and walk.**"

Here in A and *A* we have the words of Christ; in B and *B* the man made whole; in C and *C* the bed he carried; and in D and *D* the Sabbath.

John v. 21-29.—We have a combined series of introverted and alternate correspondence in these verses:—

> A | 21. Concerning quickening and resurrection.
>
>   B | 22, 23. Concerning judgment.
>
>   *B* | 24. Concerning judgment.
>
> *A* | 25-29. Concerning quickening and resurrection.

The last member *A* is alternate, and may be thus extended:—

> *A* | c | 25, 26. Concerning life and resurrection.
>
>   d | 27. Concerning judgment.
>
>   *c* | 28, 29-. Concerning resurrection.
>
>   *d* | -29. Concerning judgment.

These complex structures are not confined to Psalms or selected passages, but pervade the whole Bible, affecting the order of the books themselves, and the separate structure of each.

Gal. ii. 16.—

> A | " Knowing that a man is not **justified**
>
>   B | by the **works of the law,**
>
>   C | but by the **faith of Jesus Christ,**
>
>   *C* | even we have believed in Jesus Christ, that we might be justified by the **faith of Christ,**
>
>   *B* | and not by the **works of the law**: for by the **works of the law**
>
> *A* | shall no flesh be justified."

The Epistle to Philemon.—

A | 1-3. Epistolary ⎰ a | 1, 2. Names of those with Philemon.
　　　　　　　　　　⎱ b | 3. Benediction.

　B | 4-7. Prayers of St. Paul for Philemon. Philemon's hospitality.

　　C | 8. Authority.

　　　D | 9, 10-. Supplication.

　　　　E | -10. Onesimus, a convert of St. Paul's.

　　　　　F | 11, 12-. Wrong done by Onesimus. Amends made by St. Paul.

　　　　　　G | -12. To receive Onesimus the same as receiving Paul.

　　　　　　　H | 13, 14. Paul and Philemon.

　　　　　　　　I | 15. Onesimus.

　　　　　　　　I | 16-. Onesimus.

　　　　　　　H | -16. Paul and Philemon.

　　　　　　G | 17. To receive Onesimus the same as receiving Paul.

　　　　　F | 18, 19-. Wrong done by Onesimus. Amends made by St. Paul.

　　　　E | -19. Philemon a convert of St. Paul's.

　　　D | 20. Supplication.

　　C | 21. Authority.

　B | 22. Philemon's hospitality. Prayers of Philemon for Paul.

A | 23-25. Epistolary. ⎰ *a* | 23, 24. Names of those with Paul.
　　　　　　　　　　　⎱ *b* | 25. Benediction.

It will be observed that the first and last members are *alternate*.

III. COMPLEX Correspondence.

This is where the members of a structure are arranged both in *alternation* (simple or extended) and in *introversion*, combined together in various ways, giving the greatest possible variety and beauty to the presentation.

Not only is this complex arrangement of a passage complete in itself; but very often there is a double arrangement, the one within the other, and consistent with it, though differing from it.

And further, the longer members of any particular structure generally contain and have their own special arrangement, and may be severally expanded.

In some of the following examples, we have given first the general structure of a whole book or passage and then the expansion of some of the larger members of which it is composed.

The Ten Commandments as a whole, as well as separately, are beautiful examples of complex structure. Take the fourth as a specimen (Ex. xx. 8-11) :—

A | 8. The Sabbath-day to be kept in remembrance by man.

   B | a | 9. The six days for man's work.

         b | 10. The seventh day for man's rest.

   B | *a* | 11-. The six days for Jehovah's work.

         b | -11-. The seventh day for Jehovah's rest.

A | -11. The Sabbath-day blessed and hallowed by Jehovah."

Here, it will be noted that the first half (A and B) is concerning *man's* side and duty, and the latter half (*A* and *B*) is concerning *God's* side.

Ps. lxxxiv.—

A | a | 1-4. Blessedness of the dwellers.

      b | 5-7. Blessedness of the approachers.

        B | 8. Prayer.

        B | 9. Prayer.

A | *a* | 10. Blessedness of the dwellers. (" For.")

      b | 11, 12. Blessedness of the approachers. (" For.")

This Psalm is a simple introversion of four members, but the first member, " a," while it thus forms part of a larger member is itself constructed as an extended introversion, which helps to the understanding of verses 1-4.

a | c | 1. " Thy tabernacles."

     d | 2. Desire for the courts of the Lord.

        e | 3-. As the sparrow.

        e | -3-. As the swallow.

     d | -3. Desire for the altars of the Lord.

  c | 4. " Thy house."

The two members d and *d* read on connectedly thus: "My soul longeth, yea, even fainteth for the courts of the LORD: my heart and my flesh crieth out for the living God . . . *even* thine altars, O LORD of hosts, my King and my God."

Thus we are prevented from supposing that birds could build nests in the altar of burnt offerings, on which fires were always burning, and which was overlaid with brass; or in the altar of incense, which was within the Holy Place, and overlaid with gold! (see page 96).

Ps. xlix. is perhaps one of the most striking examples of Complex Correspondence which the Scriptures afford. The Psalm, as a whole, is *alternate*, with a *Thema*, or general subject. The first and third members are arranged as an introversion; while in each of the four members of which it is composed, a couplet is answered by a quatrain, and a quatrain by a couplet.

The THEMA, or SUBJECT, anticipates the double form of the Psalm itself. It is in two quatrains: (1) All people to hear (2) I will speak. The first two lines of each quatrain are broken up and arranged alternately, while the second two lines of each quatrain are introverted:

(1) *All People to hear.*

s | 1-. "**Hear** this
    t | -1-. All ye **people,**
s | -1-. **Give ear,**
    t | -1. All ye **inhabitants** of the world.
u | 2-. **Low**
    v | -2-. and **high.**
    v | -2-. **rich**
u | -2. and **poor.**"

(2) *I will speak.*

w | 3-. "**My mouth** shall speak
    x | -3-. of **wisdom,**
w | -3-. and the meditation of **my heart** shall be
    x | -3. of **understanding.**
y | 4-. I will incline mine **ear**
    z | -4-. to a **parable** ;
    z | -4-. I will open my **dark saying**
y | -4. upon the **harp.**"

Then comes the Psalm proper :

The Psalm itself.

A | a | 5. Why fear ? (couplet).
    b | 6-9. No redemption for the worldly (quatrain, alternate).
     c | 10-. Death (couplet).
      d | -10, 11. Worldly wisdom (quatrain, introverted).

      B | 12. Man compared to beasts (couplet).

A
      d | 13. Worldly wisdom (couplet).
     c | 14. Death (quatrain, introverted).
    b | 15. Redemption for me (couplet).
  a | 16-19. Fear not (quatrain, alternate).

      B | 20. Man compared to beasts (couplet).

Here note that, as in other cases, the corresponding members (which are marked by the same letters) may be read on, the one being explanatory of the other : the question in " a " (" Why fear ? ") being answered in *a* (" Fear not, etc.")

Ps. cv. affords another beautiful example, but we can give only the key to it.

A | 1-7. Exhortation to praise the LORD (second person, plural).

  B | 8-12. Basis of praise, God's covenant with Abraham, in promise.

   C | a | 13. The journeyings of the Patriarchs.
     b | 14, 15. Their favour and protection.
      c | 16. Their affliction.
       d | 17-22. Mission of Joseph to deliver.

   C | a | 23. The journeyings of the People.
     b | 24. Their favour and protection.
      c | 25. Their affliction.
       d | 26-41. Mission of Moses to deliver.

  B | 42-45-. Basis of praise. God's covenant with Abraham, in performance.

A | -45. Exhortation to praise the LORD (second person, plural).

Here, the Psalm as a whole is an *introversion*, while the two central members are placed in strong correspondence by an extended *alternate* arrangement; in which we have in the first (C) the history of the Patriarchs (Genesis), and in the second (C) the history of the Nation (Exodus).

Note also that while A and *A* are in the second person plural, all the rest of the Psalm is in the third person.

Note further that the two longer members B and *B* are similarly constructed, and the subjects repeated by extended alternation (as in C and C), thus:—

> B | e | 8-10. The Covenant remembered.
>   f | 11. The Land promised.
>   g | 12. The People described.
>
> *B* | *e* | 42, 43. The Covenant remembered.
>   *f* | 44. The Land inherited.
>   *g* | 45. The People described.

In like manner the two longer members d and *d* may be shown to have the same wonderful structure.

> d | h | 17. The sending of the deliverer.
>   i | 18, 19. His trial by the word.
>   k | 20-22. The deliverance.
>
> *d* | *h* | 26. The sending of the deliverers.
>   *i* | 27-36. Egypt's trial by the word (see verse 27, margin).
>   *k* | 37-41. The deliverance.

Ps. cxlvi.—This Psalm affords another beautiful example of the combined correspondence. As a whole the Psalm is an Introversion; while the inner members consist of an extended alternation :—

> A | 1, 2. Praise. Hallelujah.
>
> B | a | 3-. Wrong trust, in man.
>   b | -3. Man powerless.
>   c | 4. Man perishable.
>
> *B* | *a* | 5. Right trust, in God.
>   *b* | 6-9. God all-powerful,
>   *c* | 10-. God eternal.
>
> *A* | -10. Praise. Hallelujah.

Ps. cxlviii.—

A | 1-. Hallelujah.

    B | a | -1. Praise from the heavens (second person).

          b | 2-4. Enumeration of heavenly things.

            c | 5-. Injunction to praise (third person).

              d | -5, 6. Inducements : ("for ").

    B | a | 7-. Praise from the earth (second person'.

          b | -7-12. Enumeration of earthly things.

            c | 13-. Injunction to praise (third person).

              d | -13, 14-. Inducements: ("for").

A | -14. Hallelujah.

Here, again, while the whole Psalm is introverted, the two centre members are arranged as an extended alternation.

Mark iii. 21-35.—

A | a | 21-. His kindred. " His friends " (marg. *kinsmen*).

      b | -21-. Their interference. " Went out."

        c | -21. Their disparagement of Him. " For they said, etc."

          B | d | 22-. The Scribes : Their first charge, " He hath."

            e | -22. Their second charge, " He casteth out."

          B | *e* | 23-27. His answer to the second charge.

            d | 28-30. His denunciation of the first charge.

A | *a* | 31-. His kindred. " There came then his, etc."

      b | -31, 32. Their interference. " Sent, calling."

        c | 33-35. His disparagement of them.

From this beautiful complex structure, we learn that, as "*d*" corresponds with " d," the sin against the Holy Ghost is the saying that *Christ was possessed by a devil !* And also, from the correspondence of "*b*," with " b " we learn that the interference of the mother and brethren of Christ was because they said He was " beside Himself." No wonder then that their disparagement of Him (in " c ") is answered by His disparagement of them (in "*c* ").

We give examples of the Seven Epistles addressed by the Holy Spirit through St. Paul to the Churches: but for the fuller development of them we must refer the reader to our larger work on this great and important subject.*

---

* *What is the Spirit saying to the Churches?* See a series of articles commenced in *Things to Come*, Sept., 1898.

THE PAULINE EPISTLES TO THE SEVEN CHURCHES.

Epistle to the Romans.—

Introversion.

A | i. 1-6. The Gospel. Always revealed : never hidden.

   B | 7-15. Epistolary.

      C | a | i. 16-viii. 39. Doctrinal.
            b | ix.-xi. Dispensational.

      C | *a* | xii. 1-xv. 7. Practical.
            b | 8-13. Dispensational.

   B | xv. 14-xvi. 24. Epistolary.

A | xvi. 25-27. The Mystery. Always hidden : never before revealed.

THE EXPANSION OF B AND *B* (i. 7-15, and xv. 14-xvi. 24).

Epistolary.

B | c | i. 7. Salutation.
      d | 8, 9. Prayer, etc. (his for them).
        e | 10-13. His journey.
          f | 14, 15. His ministry.

B |
          f | xv. 15-21. His ministry.
        e | 22-29. His journey.
      d | 30-33. Prayer, etc. (theirs for him).
   c | xvi. 1-24. Salutation.

The whole of this epistle is marvellously constructed, and the construction is absolutely essential to its correct interpretation.

It is hardly the design of this work to go too deeply into these structures ; but the doctrinal portion (a | i. 16-viii. 39) is too important to be passed over.

It is divided into two parts. The first deals with the old nature, and with the fruits of the old tree. The second deals with the tree itself, and the conflict between the two natures in the believer.

B 1

C. Romans i. 16-viii. 39.

Doctrine.

It is of the greatest importance to note that the break occurs at the end of chapter v. 11.

Up to that point the question dealt with is "sins." From that point it is "sin." And, unless this great distinction be made the doctrine cannot be understood. The two parts, then, stand, as follows :—

> a | D | i. 16-v. 11. SINS. The products of old nature. The fruits of the old tree.
>   E | v. 12-viii. 39. SIN. The old nature. The old tree itself

The First Division, D (i. 16-v. 11). SINS.

The old nature and its fruits.

D | g | i. 16, 17. The power of God unto salvation to every one that believeth God's Gospel revealing a righteousness from God.
     h | i. 18. The wrath of God revealed against all ungodliness and unrighteousness.
     h | i. 19-iii. 20. The wrath of God revealed against all ungodliness and unrighteousness.
  g | iii. 21-v. 11. The power of God unto salvation to every one that believeth God's Gospel revealing a righteousness from God.

The Second Division, E (v. 12-viii. 39). SIN.

The old nature itself, and its conflict with the new nature.

E | i | v. 12-21. Condemnation to death through a single sin of one man (τὸ παράπτωμα): but justification of life through a single righteous act of one man (τὸ δικαίωμα).
     k | vi. 1-vii. 6. We are not in sin, having died in Christ.
     k | vii. 7-25. Sin is in us, though we are alive in Christ.
  i | viii. 1-39. Condemnation of sin in the flesh, but now "NO condemnation" to us who are alive unto God in Christ Jesus and in whom is Christ.

THE EXPANSION OF b (ROM. ix.-xi.).

Dispensational.

A | ix. 1-5. Paul's sorrow regarding Israel's failure.

　　B | 1 | 6-13. God's purpose regarded only a portion.

　　　　　m | 14-29. God's purpose regarded only a remnant.

　　　　　　　C | n^1 | ix. 30-33. Israel's failure in spite of the *Prophets.*

　　　　　　　　　n^2 | x. 1-13. Israel's failure in spite of the *Law.*

　　　　　　　　　n^3 | 14-21. Israel's failure in spite of the *Gospel.*

　　B | 　m | xi. 1-10. God's purpose regarding the remnant accomplished.

　　　　| l | 11-32. God's purpose will ultimately embrace the whole.

A | 33-36. Paul's joy regarding God's purpose.

EXPANSION OF *a* (ROM. xii. 1-xv. 7).

Practical.

　a | o | xii. 1, 2. Personal and individual.

　　　p | 3-8. Ecclesiastical.

　　　　q | 9-18. Social.

　　　　　r | 19-21. Civil.

　　　　　r | xiii. 1-7. Civil.

　　　　q | 8-14. Social.

　　p | xiv. 1-23. Ecclesiastical.

　o | xv. 1-7. Personal and individual.

The First Epistle to the Corinthians.—

A | i. 1-9. Epistolary. Salutation. Introduction.

　B | a | 10-iv. 16. Ministerial, ecclesiastical and corporal.

　　　b | c | 17. Mission of Timothy.

　　　　　d | 18-21. Visit of Paul.

　　　　　　C | v., vi. Things reported to Paul.

　　　　　　C | vii., viii. Things enquired of by Paul.

　B | a | ix.-xv. Ministerial, ecclesiastical and corporal.

　　　b | 　　d | xvi. 1-9. Visit of Paul.

　　　　　c | 10-18. Mission of Timothy.

A | 19-24. Epistolary. Salutation. Conclusion.

The Second Epistle to the Corinthians.—
Extended Alternation.

A | i. 1, 2. Salutation.
  B | a | 3-11. Thanksgiving.
  | | b | 12. His ministry.
  | | C | i. 13-ii. 13. Epistolary.
  B | a | 14-17. Thanksgiving.
  | | b | iii.-vii. 4. His ministry.
  | | C | 5-xiii. 10. Epistolary.
  A | 11-14. Salutations.

EXPANSION OF C (i. 13-ii. 13) and C (vii. 5-xiii. 10).
Epistolary.

C | D | c | 13, 14. Present Epistle.
  | | d | 15-ii. 2. Visit. { g | 15, 16. Purpose.
  | | | { h | 17-ii. 2. Vindication.
  | | E | e | i | ii. 3-11. Former Epistle.
  | | | | | k | 12, 13-. No rest in spirit.
  | | | | f | -13. Macedonia. Journey.
C | | E | e | | k | vii. 5-7. No rest in flesh.
  | | | | i | 8-16. Former Epistle.
  | | | | f | viii., ix. Macedonia. Journey.
  | D | | d | x.-xiii. 1. Visit. { h | x. 1-xii. 13. Vindication.
  | | | { g | 14- xiii. 1. Purpose.
  | | c | 2-10. Present Epistle.

The Epistle to the Galatians.—
Complex.   Repeated Alternation.

A | i. 1-5. Epistolary and Salutation.
  B¹ | a | 6-ii. 14. Apostleship.
  | | b | 15-iv. 11. Doctrine.
  B² | a | 12-20. Apostleship.
  | | b | 21-vi. 10. Doctrine.
  B³ | a | 11-13. Apostleship.
  | | β | 14-15. Doctrine.
  A | 16-18. Epistolary and Salutation.

The Epistle to the Ephesians.—
Introversion.

A | i. 1, 2. Epistolary. Salutation.
  B | i. 3-iii. 21. Doctrinal.
  B | iv. 1-vi. 22. Practical.
  A | 23, 24. Epistolary. Salutation.

The Expansion of B (i. 3-iii. 21).

Doctrinal.

B | a | c | 1. 3-14. The purpose of God in Himself (i. 9) concerning Christ Personal. " The Mystery of God."

   d | i. 15-23. Prayer to " the God of our Lord Jesus Christ," as to " c."

    b | ii. Ourselves the objects of these purposes and prayers.

 a | c | iii. 1-13. The purpose of God in Christ (iii. 11) concerning Christ Mystical. " The Mystery of Christ (iii. 4)."

   d | iii. 14-21. Prayer to " the Father of our Lord Jesus Christ," as to " *c*."

The Expansion of " b " (chap. ii.). *Alternation.*

Ourselves.

b | e | ii. 1-3. Past.

  f | 4-10. Present.

 e | 11, 12. Past.

  f | 13-22. Present.

Expansion of *B* (iv. 1-vi. 22). *Alternation.*

Practical.

B | g | iv. 1-16. Their walk among themselves as worthy of their calling being members of the One Body. (*Ecclesiastical*).

  h | iv. 17-v. 21. Their walk among others. (*Spiritual*).

 g | v. 22-vi. 9. Their walk among themselves. (*Domestic*).

  h | vi. 10-20. Their walk among others. (*Spiritual*).

The Epistle to the Philippians.—

Introversion.

A | i. 1, 2. Epistolary. Salutation.

 B | 3-26. Paul's concern for the Philippians.

  C | 27-ii. 18. The first example : Christ.

   D | 19-24. The second example : Timothy.

   D | 25-30. The third example : Epaphroditus.

  C | iii.-iv. 9. The fourth example : Paul.

 B | 10-20. The Philippians' care of Paul.

A | 21-23. Epistolary and salutation.

The Epistle to the Colossians.—

Introversion.

A | i. 1, 2. Epistolary, and Salutation.

    B | 3-8. Mutual reports and messages by Epaphras; our dear fellow-servant and your faithful minister.

        C | 9-ii. 7. Paul's prayer and concern for the Colossian saints. We "pray for you": and that concerning his preaching of the Mystery.

            D | ii. 8-23. Doctrine and Instruction consequent on having died with Christ. Correctional.

            D | iii. 1-iv. 1. Doctrine and Instruction consequent on being risen with Christ. Correctional.

        C | iv. 2-6. The Colossians' prayer and concern for Paul: "praying alway for us": and that concerning his preaching of the Mystery.

    B | iv. 7-9. Mutual reports and messages by Tychicus and Onesimus, "beloved brethren."

A | 10-18. Epistolary and salutations.

All these may be severally expanded according to their respective structures. We give three such expansions :—

THE EXPANSION OF C (i. 9-ii. 7).

Paul's prayer and concern for the Colossians.

C | a^1 | i. 9-11. Solicitude that they might be filled with wisdom concerning Christ.

    b^1 | 12-22. The Mystery revealed. (The wisdom and fulness of Christ).

  a^2 | 23-25. Solicitude that they might stand fast in "the faith."

    b^2 | 26, 27. The Mystery declared.

  a^3 | 28-ii. 2-. Solicitude and conflict.

    b^3 | -2, 3. The Mystery acknowledged.

  a^4 | 4-7. Solicitude that they might be established in "the faith."

THE EXPANSION OF D (ii. 8-23).   *Extended Alternation.*

Doctrine and Instruction consequent on having died with Christ.

D | c | 8. Caution.
    d | 9, 10. Christ the Head, and His People complete in Him.
      e | 11-15. Ordinances, therefore, done away in Christ.
  c | 16-18. Caution.
    d | 19. Christ the Head, and His People nourished by Him.
      e | 20-23. Ordinances, therefore, done away in Christ.

THE EXPANSION OF *D* (iii. 1-iv. 1).   *Extended Alternation.*

Doctrine and Instruction consequent on being risen with Christ.

D | f | iii. 1-9.   The rule of the old man over.   Died and risen with Christ.
    g | 10, 11. The new man put on.
      h | 12-14.   Effects seen in the exercise of love as the bond of perfectness.
  f | 15.   The peace of God ruling our hearts.   The peace of His presence enjoyed by us as seated with Christ.
    g | 16. The word of Christ indwelling.
      h | 17-iv. 1.   Effects manifested in the exercise of love the bond of all domestic relations.

The First Epistle to the Thessalonians.—

Complex Introversion.

A | i. 1. EPISTOLARY (Introduction).
  B | a | i. 2-iii. 10. NARRATION. Thanksgiving and appeal.   In four members (alternate).
    b | iii. 11-13. PRAYER, in view of "the coming of our Lord Jesus Christ."
  B | *a* | iv. 1-v. 22. EXHORTATION and Instruction. In four members (introverted).
    b | v. 23-25. PRAYER, in view of "the coming of our Lord Jesus Christ."
A | v. 26-28. EPISTOLARY (Conclusion).*

---

* For the further structure of all these various members see pages 370, 371. Also *The Structure of the Two Epistles to the Thessalonians* by the same author and publisher.

The Second Epistle to the Thessalonians.—

Complex Introversion.

A | i. 1, 2. Epistolary (shorter).

  B | a | 3-10. Thanksgiving (longer).

    b | 11, 12. Prayer (shorter).

      c | ii. 1-12.   Admonition (longer, prophetic and general).

  B | a | ii. 13-15. Thanksgiving (shorter).

    b | 16-iii. 5. Prayer (longer).

      c | 6-15. Admonition (shorter, more immediate and personal.

A | iii. 16-18. Epistolary (longer).

Here, note that most of these members may be expanded. Also that, while they are alternated throughout, shorter and longer, yet these are so arranged that the shorter prayer corresponds with the longer prayer, and the longer thanksgiving with the shorter thanksgiving, and so with the other members.*

We add the structure of the two Epistles of St. Peter :—

The First Epistle of Peter.—†

Complex Introversion.

A | i. 1, 2. EPISTOLARY.

  B | i. 3-12. INTRODUCTION. Thanksgiving; foreshadowing the subject of the Epistle.

    C | a | i. 13-ii. 10. EXHORTATIONS (GENERAL) in view of "THE END," as to Hope in the Fiery Trial.

      b | ii. 11-iv. 6. EXHORTATIONS (PARTICULAR) AS TO SUFFERINGS AND GLORY.

    C | a | iv. 7-19. EXHORTATIONS (GENERAL) in view of "THE END," as to Joy in the Fiery Trial.

      b | v. 1-9. EXHORTATIONS (PARTICULAR) AS TO SUFFERINGS AND GLORY.

  B | v. 10, 11. CONCLUSION. Prayer; embodying the object of the Epistle.

A | v. 12-14. EPISTOLARY.

---

* For the structure of particular portions of these Epistles, and expansions of the various members, see the series of articles commencing in *Things to Come* for Sept., 1898.

† For the expansion of these various members, see *The Spirits in Prison*, by the same author and publisher.

The Second Epistle of Peter.—

Complex Introversion.

A | i. 1-4. EPISTOLARY. Grace and knowledge to be increased. Divine gift (3-). God and Saviour (-1).

   B | a | i. 5-7. EXHORTATION (second person, plural imperative, with participle preceding). Diligence. Positive, to acquire every grace.

     b | i. 8, 9. TWO REASONS. ταῦτα γαρ ὧ γαρ. Ample supply, ample fruit. Wilful ignorance and spiritual darkness.

   a | i. 10-. EXHORTATION. "Wherefore . . . brethren." Διό : Diligence, " sure."

     b | i. -10, 11. TWO REASONS. ταῦτα γαρ οὕτω γαρ. " These things."

       C | c | i. 12-15. Peter.

          d | f | i. 16-18. Apostles.

              g | 19-21. Prophets.

              e | ii. 1-22. The wicked.

       C | c | iii. 1. Peter.

          d | g | iii. 2-. Prophets.

            | f | -2. Apostles.

              e | iii. 3-13. The wicked.

  B | h | iii. 14-16. EXHORTATION. "Wherefore (Διό) beloved."

     i | And REASON. " Seeing . . . ye look, etc."

   h | iii. 17. EXHORTATION. "Therefore . . . beloved."

     i | And REASON. "Seeing . . . ye know . . . etc."

A | iii. 18. EPISTOLARY. Grace and knowledge to be increased. Traced to Divine glory. " Lord and Saviour."

It will be noted that the Epistle as a whole is an introversion of six members. While B and *B* are a simple alternation, and C and *C* an extended alternation, with which another inner introversion is combined.

II. AFFECTING THE SENSE.

(Figures of Rhetoric).

WE now pass from figures more closely affecting Grammar and Syntax to those which relate to Rhetoric. Figures, which not merely affect the *meaning* of words, but the use and *application* of words.

These are figures of repetition and addition of *sense* rather than of words: and are used in reasoning.

Sometimes the same sense is repeated in other words.

Sometimes the words themselves are repeated, but always by way of amplifying the sense for purposes of definition, emphasis, or explanation.

We have endeavoured to embrace them all under six great divisions, where the sense is added to by way of:

1. Repetition for Definition, REPETITIO.
2. Amplification, AMPLIFICATIO.
3. Description, DESCRIPTIO.
4. Conclusion, CONCLUSIO.
5. Parenthesis, INTERPOSITIO.
6. Reasoning, RATIOCINATIO.

1. REPETITIO.

Addition by way of Repetition for various reasons as follows:

PROSAPODOSIS ; or, DETAILING.

A Returning for Repetition and Explanation.

Pros-a-pod'-o-sis, a giving back to, or *return.* It is from πρός (*pros*), *to,* and ἀπόδοσις (*apodosis*), *a giving back ;* (from ἀποδίδωμι (*apodidomi*), *to give back, return*).

The figure is so called because after the mention of two or three words or subjects together, there is *a return* to them again, and they are repeated separately for purposes of definition or explanation.

The Latins called it REDITIO (from *redire*), which means the same thing, *a going* or *returning back ;* or REDDITIO (from *reddire*), *a giving back.* They called it also SEJUGATIO, *a disjunction* or *separation,* from *sejungo, to unyoke* (*jugum,* a yoke), or *disjoin,* because of the separation of the words or subjects which takes place : first being mentioned or yoked together, and then unyoked and mentioned separately.

For the same reason they called it DISJUNCTIO, *disjunction.*

The Greeks used a similar descriptive word when they called the figure DIEZEUGMENON (*Di-e-zeug¹-me-non*), from *zeugma, a yoke,* *i.e., an unyoking,* or *disjunction.*

John xvi. 8-11.—" And when he is come, he will reprove (marg., *convince*) the world of sin, and of righteousness, and of judgment :—

" Of **sin,** because they believe not on me ;

" Of **righteousness,** because I go to my Father, and ye see me no more ;

" Of **judgment,** because the prince of this world is judged."

Here, after the mention of the three words together, " sin," " righteousness," and " judgment," the Lord *returns to* them again, and repeats them separately, for the purpose of explaining and more particularly defining them.   Thus we learn that the mission and work of the Holy Ghost with regard to the world was to *bring it in guilty* (for that is the meaning of the word) concerning these three important facts.

(1) " *Sin* " is not, as man regards it, some mere yielding to the lusts of the flesh, but a refusal to believe God's Gospel concerning His Son, the Lord Jesus Christ.   *That* is sin in God's sight.

(2) " Righteousness."   Seeing they rejected Christ, and would not believe on Him, He was, in righteousness, removed from the earth, and is returned to the Father, until He comes again in

(3) " Judgment."   For the prince of this world has been judged, sentence has been passed upon him, and ere long it will be put into execution.

Rom. xi. 22.—" Behold therefore, the goodness and severity of God : on them which fell, **severity** ; but toward thee, **goodness,** if thou continue in his goodness ; otherwise thou also shalt be cut off."

Here, the return to the two words is not *direct,* as in John xvi. 8-11, but in an *Epanodos* (*q.v.*).

> a | Goodness.
>   b | Severity.
>   *b* | Severity.
> *a* | Goodness.

The statement refers to the Gentiles as such (see verse 13, " I speak to you, Gentiles "), and cannot refer to the Church of God; for, of the members of Christ's Body it has been already stated and declared in chapter viii., that there is no condemnation, and no separation.

To interpret Rom. xi. of the Church, and not of the Gentiles *as* Gentiles is not only to miss the whole teaching conveyed by the structure (see page 385) as to the separate Doctrinal and Dispensational sections of the Epistle, but it is to make the grace of God of no effect, and to destroy the standing of the Christian, and his eternal preservation in Christ.

Phil. i. 15-17.—" Some indeed preach Christ even of envy and strife ; and some also of good will :

The one preach Christ of **contention**, not sincerely, supposing to add affliction to my bonds :

But the other of **love**, knowing that I am set for the defence of the Gospel."

Here, after having first stated the two classes, he *returns to* them to explain his meaning further.

EPIDIEGESIS; or, RE-STATEMENT.

A Repetition in order to restate in full.

Ep'-i-di'-e-ge'-sis, a repetition of the statement of a case or narration of facts: from ἐπί (*epi*), *upon*, and διήγησις (*dieegesis*), *the statement of a case* (from διηγέομαι, *dieegeomai*, *to describe* or *narrate in detail*).

This is a kind of *Prosapodosis*: and it is so called when the repetition is for the purpose not of explanation, but of kindling emotion, provoking indignation, or evoking comparison.

EPEXEGESIS; or, FULLER EXPLAINING.

A Repetition for the purpose of explaining more fully.

Ep-ex'-e-gee'-sis, a returning to explain. It is from ἐπί (*epi*), *upon*, ἐξ (*ex*), *out*, and ἡγεῖσθαι (*heegeisthai*), *to lead* or *guide*.

The figure is so called because the repetition is for purposes of *explanation*.

It has several names. It is called EXEGESIS (*ex'-e-gee'sis*), *an explanation*.

ECPHRASIS (*ec'-phra-sis*), from ἐκ (*ek*), *out*, and φράζω (*phrazo*), *to give to know, cause to understand, intimate, point out.* Hence the figure is called *Ecphrasis*, which means *an explaining, recounting*.

It is also called EPICHREMA (*epi-chree'-ma*), from ἐπί (*epi*), *upon*, and χρῆμα (*chreema*), *a furnishing*, from χράομαι (*chra'-o-mai*), *to furnish what is needful*. The figure is thus called because *upon* what has been said less clearly *the needful information* is added or furnished.

This figure *Epexegesis* may be divided into three parts: (1) where what is added is a working out and *developing* what has been previously said (*Exergasia*); (2) where what has been said is dwelt upon to deepen the *impression* (*Epimone*); and (3) where what is added is by way of *interpretation* (*Hermeneia*).

For these three Figures see the following :

EXERGASIA: or, WORKING OUT.

A Repetition, so as to work out or illustrate what has already been said.

Ex-er-ga'-si-a. Greek, ἐξεργασία, which means *a working out* (from ἐξ (*ex*), *out*, and ἐργάζομαι (*ergazomai*), *to work*.

In this figure the same thought, idea, or subject is repeated in other words, and thus *worked out* and developed. It, therefore, resembles *Synonymia*; but differs from it in that not merely synonymous *words* are repeated, but synonymous *expressions* or *sense*.

It is sometimes called EPEXERGASIA, *i.e.*, the addition of the preposition ἐπί (*epi*), *upon*, to the word *exergasia* and implies *a working out upon*. Words of the same signification are repeated to make plainer the previous statement: or to illustrate the sense of what has been mentioned before.

The Latins called it EXPOLITIO, *a polishing up;* because by such repetition the meaning is embellished as well as strengthened and not merely explained or interpreted as in other repetitions.

This figure necessarily implies that the separate repetitions must be placed in parallel lines.

It is of frequent occurrence, and therefore we can give only a few examples.

Ps. xvii. 1.—

> " Hear the right, O LORD,
> Attend unto my cry,
> Give ear unto my prayer."

Ps. xviii. 1, 2.—

> " I will love thee O LORD, my strength.
> The LORD is my rock, and my fortress, and my deliverer:
> My God (El), my strength, in whom I will trust;
> My buckler, the horn of my salvation, and my high tower."

Ps. xxxv. 1-3.—

a¹ | " Plead my cause, O LORD, with them that strive with me;
　　b¹ | Fight against them that fight against me.
a² | Take hold of shield and buckler, and stand up for my help.
　　b² | Draw out also the spear, and stop the way against them that persecute me:
a³ | Say unto my soul, I am thy salvation.
　　b³ | 4-8. Let them, etc."

And so the Psalm goes on. In a¹, a², and a³, we have prayer for himself (*Defensive*), and in b¹, b², and b³, prayer against his enemies (*Offensive*). In each case the meaning is further developed.

Ps. xxxv. 4.—

" Let them be confounded and put to shame that seek after my soul :
Let them be turned back and brought to confusion that devise my hurt.
Let them be as the chaff before the wind :
And let the angel of the LORD chase them, etc."

In verses 4-8 we have :

     c | 4. Prayer against those who devise evil.
          d | 5. The angel of the LORD.
          d | 6. The angel of the LORD.
     c | 7, 8. Prayer against those who devise evil.

Jonah ii. 2 (3).—

     a | " I cried by reason of mine affliction unto the LORD,
          b | and he heard me :
     a | Out of the belly of hell (Sheol) cried I,
          b | and thou heardest my voice."

Jonah ii. 3 (4).—

     c | For thou hadst cast me into the deep,
          d | in the midst of the seas;
          d | and the floods compassed me about :
     c | all thy billows and thy waves passed over me."

Here, in a and *a* we have Jonah's affliction : and in b and *b* Jehovah's respect to him. In c and *c* we have the deep as a whole, and in d and *d* the waters which make it up.

Zech. vi. 12, 13.—

" Thus speaketh the LORD of hosts, saying :
Behold, the man whose name is the BRANCH ;
And He shall grow up out of His place,
And He shall build the temple of the LORD :
Even He shall build the temple of the LORD :
And He shall bear the glory,
And shall sit and rule upon His throne ;
And He shall be a priest upon His throne :.
And the counsel of peace shall be between them."

Here, the figure is enhanced by *Polysyndeton* (*q.v.*).

EPIMONE ; or, LINGERING.

Repetition in order to dwell upon for the sake of Impressing.

E-pim¹-o-nee. Greek, ἐπιμονή, *a staying on,* or *dwelling upon,* from ἐπί (*epi*), *upon,* and μένω (*menō*), *to remain,* or *dwell.* In Latin COMMORATIO.

This figure is so called because the repetition is not of words, but of sense, by way of *dwelling upon* the principal point of a subject, so that it may be well understood, and remain with due weight upon the mind of the hearer or reader.

Zech. i. 3-6 is referred to *Epimone;* because the solemn fact is *dwelt upon* and emphasized that the people had brought all this trouble upon themselves, because they had neglected to hear the words of Jehovah.

Matt. vii. 21-23.—Here, the one thought is *dwelt upon* by being expressed in several different ways.

Matt. xii. 31, 32.—Here, the one truth in verse 31 is *dwelt upon* by a further statement of it, in another form, in verse 32. It is clear from verse 24 that the sin against the Holy Ghost was the attributing of the Lord's work to Beelzebub, or the Evil Spirit. See verse 28, and page 384.

Matt. xv. 18-20.—Here, after the statement that "those things which proceed out of the mouth come forth from the heart; and they defile the man," the Lord goes on to impress the important fact by dwelling upon it, and explaining that "out of the heart proceed evil thoughts, etc. . . ." and adding "these are the things that defile a man. And not to eat with unwashed hands. He shows that it is "not that which goeth into the mouth" (verse 11): these things do not defile a man.

Mark vii. 20-23.—The solemn fact of verse 20 as to what really defiles is *dwelt upon* in the following verses, in order to impress its truth upon the mind.

John xxi. 15-17.—Peter's threefold restoration is *dwelt upon* in these verses, to assure him that his threefold denial had not cut him off; and that though *he* failed, the prayer of his great Advocate was heard and answered, so that his *faith* did not fail.

Col. ii. 14, 15.—Here the blessed effect of Christ's death is *dwelt upon* in the enumeration of some of its triumphant results.

HERMENEIA ; or, INTERPRETATION.

Repetition for the Purpose of Interpreting what has been already said.

Her-mee'-neia, ἑρμηνεία, *interpretation, explanation.* This figure is so-called because, after a particular statement the explanation follows immediately to make more clear what has been said less clearly.

The Latins consequently called it INTERPRETATIO, or *Interpretation.*

Ps. vii., where verse 13 (14) explains verse 12 (13).

Ps. lxxvii. 19.—After saying
      " Thy way is in the sea,
          And thy path in the great waters,"
the interpretation is added :
      " And thy footsteps are not known."

Isa. i. 23.—After the words
      " Thy silver is become dross,
          Thy wine mixed with water,"
the interpretation is added :
      " Thy princes are rebellious, etc."

Isa. xxxiv. 6.—Here the statement about the sword of the LORD in the former part of the verse is explained in the latter part.

Isa. xliv. 3.—
      " I will pour water upon him that is thirsty,
          And floods upon the dry ground."
This is immediately explained to mean :
      " I will pour my spirit upon thy seed,
          And my blessing upon thine offspring."

Isa. li., where verse 2 explains verse 1.

Hos. vii. 8, 9.—Here verse 9 is the interpretation of verse 8.

Amos iii. 8.—Here we have first
      " The lion hath roared,
          Who will not fear ? "
and then the interpretation :
      " Adonai Jehovah hath spoken,
          Who can but prophesy ? "

Matt. vi. 24 and Luke xvi. 13.—Here the last clause interprets the first. This is on account of, and is shown by the structure :

   A | " No servant can serve two masters,

      B | a | For either he will hate the one,

           b | and love the other ;

      B | *b* | or else he will hold to the one,

         a | and despise the other.

   A | Ye cannot serve God and Mammon.

Here *A* interprets A, showing that the two masters meant are God and Mammon ; while, in B and *B*, the two-fold reason is given in the form of an *Epanodos* (*q.v.*).

John vii. 39 is added in order to interpret what had been said in said in verse 38.

2 Tim. iv. 6.—" I am now ready to be offered " is explained by what follows : " the time of my departure is at hand."

All the passages which commence, " which being interpreted means, etc.," come under this figure *Hermeneia.*

BATTOLOGIA; or, VAIN REPETITION.

Bat-to-log'-i-a, βαττολογία, *vain repetitions.* These are repetitions, of course, which are vain, meaningless, and senseless.

None of these is to be found in the word of God. Indeed, we are exhorted not to use them as the heathen do, who think that by using them in their prayers they shall be "heard for their much speaking." The verb in Matt. vi. 7 is βαττολογήσητε (*battologee'-seete*) *use not vain repetitions.* The Holy Spirit therefore does not use them : so that we have no examples to give for this figure which man has named and so frequently uses.

Examples of man's use of *Battologia* may easily be found, *e.g.*, 1 Kings xviii. 26. Acts xix. 34, etc. Also in the Prayer Book.

2. AMPLIFICATIO.

By way of addition or amplification (Pleonastic figures).

———

PLEONASM; or, REDUNDANCY.

When more Words are used than the Grammar requires.

Ple'-o-nasm. Greek, πλεονασμός (*pleonasmos*): from πλεονάζειν (*pleonazein*), *to be more than enough.* This is from πλέον (*pleon*), or πλεῖον (*pleion*), *more,* and πλέος (*pleos*), full. We have it in our words com*plete,* *pleni*tude, re*plete,* etc.

The figure is so called when there appears to be a redundancy of words in a sentence; and the sense is grammatically complete without them. Sometimes the substantive appears to be redundant when its idea is already implied in the adjective; or when two nouns are used where one appears to be sufficient.

But this redundancy is only apparent. These words are not really superfluous when used by the Holy Spirit, nor are they idle or useless. They are necessary to fill up the sense, which without them would be incomplete and imperfect.

This figure is used to set forth the subject more fully by repeating it in other, sometimes in opposite, terms. What is first expressed affirmatively is sometimes repeated negatively, and *vice versa.* It is also used for the purpose of marking the emphasis; or, for intensifying the feeling; or, for enhancing in some way what has been already said. The term *pleonastic* may therefore be applied to all similar figures of repetition or addition. But we have endeavoured to classify them according to the object in view in the repetition; whether it be definition, or interpretation, or for mere emphasis by amplification, etc.

We have reserved the term *pleonasm* for this latter class, where what is said is immediately after put in another or opposite way to make it impossible for the sense to be missed; and thus to emphasize it.

The figure may affect words, or sentences.   We have therefore
arranged the examples as follows :—

I. Words.

1. Certain idiomatic words.

2. Other words.

II. Sentences.

1. Affirmative.

2. Negative.

I. Words.

1. Certain idiomatic words.

According to the Hebrew idiom (see under *Idiom*), two nouns are
often used together, one of which appears to be redundant.   Glassius*
gives a list of certain words, which are thus commonly used to
enhance and emphasize the force of the other noun.   Not as an
adjective; for in that case the figure would be *Enallage* instead of
Pleonasm.   Some of these come under the figures *Synecdoche* and
Idiom (q.v.)

The ten words are as follows :—

1. פָּנִים *(Pahneem)*, faces.

The word is always in the plural on account of the various
features of the face.

Gen. i. 2.—" And darkness was upon the faces of the deep," *i.e.,*
upon the deep.   But how much more forcible and emphatic the
expression becomes by the pleonasm.

Gen. xi. 8.—" So the LORD scattered them abroad from thence
upon the face of all the earth : " *i.e.,* all over the earth.

Gen. xvi. 8.—" I flee from the face of my mistress Sarai,"
instead of " from my mistress."

Gen. xxiii. 3.—" And Abraham stood up from before his dead."
Lit., from the face of his dead, *i.e.,* from the presence of his dead wife.

Sometimes the word is omitted in translation :

Ex. vii. 10.—" And Aaron cast down his rod before Pharaoh,"
Lit., before *the face of* Pharaoh, *i.e.,* before his very eyes.

Philol. Sac., Lib. i., Tract 1, Can. xxxviii.

Lev. xxiii. 40.—"And ye shall rejoice before the Lord your God." Lit., before the face of the Lord your God, *i.e.*, in His very presence.

Judges xi. 3.—"Then Jephthah fled from his brethren." Here the A.V. has again omitted the word "face," but in this case has put it in the margin.

1 Sam. xiv. 25.—"And there was honey upon the ground." Lit., upon *the face of* the ground, *i.e.*, spread out.

Isa. xiv. 21.—"That they do not rise, nor possess the land, nor fill the face of the earth with cities."

Isa. xix. 8.—"And they that spread nets upon the waters." Lit., upon the face of the waters.

Hos. x. 7.—"As the foam upon the water." See margin, "*the face of the water.*"

Amos. v. 8.—"And poureth them out upon the face of the earth." In the N.T., though we have Greek words, we have the same Hebrew idiom.

Luke xxi. 35.—"As a snare shall it come on all them that dwell on the face of the whole earth." Here the *Pleonasm* emphasizes the universal character of the events connected with "the great Tribulation."

Acts iii. 19.—"That so there may come (R.V.) times of refreshing from the presence (face) of the Lord."

Acts v. 41.—"And they departed from the presence of the council." Lit., *the face of.*

Acts xvii. 26.—"For to dwell on all the face of the earth."

Rev. xii. 14.—"From the face of the serpent," *i.e.*, a great way off from the serpent.

2. פֶּה (*Peh*), mouth.

This word seems to be redundant when used with the word "sword": "the mouth of the sword." But this use of the Figure is to emphasize the fact that it is not a mere sword, but a sword with its sharp devouring edge, which is thus compared to a mouth.

Gen. xxxiv. 26.—"And they slew Hamor and Shechem his son with the edge (marg., Heb., mouth) of the sword."

So also Ex. xvii. 13. Deut. xiii. 15. Ezek. vi. 11. Amos vii. 11. Luke xxi. 24. Heb. xi. 34.

A sword with two mouths is a sword which devoured exceedingly and slew large numbers; Judges iii. 16. Rev. i. 16 ; ii. 13. Heb. iv. 12.

Other uses of the word are seen in

Gen. xliii. 7.—" We told him according to the tenor (Heb., the mouth) of all these words " : *i.e.*, all those things concerning which they had been interrogated.

Num. xxvi. 56.—" According to the (mouth of the) lot " : *i.e.*, according to what the lot shall say or determine.

Prov. xxii. 6.—" Train up a child in the way he should go."

Heb., in the mouth of his way : *i.e.*, at the very mouth or entrance on life, so that it may be determined in a direction of justice and honesty, etc.

3. בָּנִים (*Bahneem*), sons or children.

Gen. xi. 5.—" The LORD came down to see the city and the tower, which the children of men builded " : *i.e.*, men viewed as the descendants of Adam ; the human race.

1 Kings viii. 39.—" Thou . . . knowest the hearts of all the children of men " : *i.e.*, *of all men*, with emphasis on the " all."

Ecc. iii. 18.—" I said in mine heart concerning the estate of the sons of men."

R.V. : " I said in mine heart, *It is* because of the sons of men, that God may prove them, etc."

Here, the figure shows that the emphasis is on " men " in contrast to " beasts." " Yet I said in my heart respecting MEN, God hath chosen them to show that they, even they, are like beasts."

Ps. xxxvi. 7.—" How excellent is thy lovingkindness, O God ! therefore the children of men put their trust under the shadow of thy wings," *i.e.*, men in all ages—not merely men, as such, but men in all their successive generations.

So also in the New Testament we find the same usage :

Mark iii. 28.—" All sins shall be forgiven unto the sons of men," *i.e.*, men in all ages, as in Matt. xii. 31.

Eph. iii. 5.—" Which (*i.e.*, the Mystery) in other ages was not made known unto the sons of men : " *i.e.*, to any human being.

It is according to this Figure or Hebraism that Christ is called " the Son of Man," as *the* man, the representative man, the man who had been long promised as the seed of the woman; the man prophesied. Therefore this title used of Christ usually has reference to that aspect of His work as the appointed Judge of men (Acts xvii. 31). "The Son of Man" is therefore an emphatic dispensational title of Christ. It means merely "man," but with emphasis on all that the word means as used of Christ and his dominion in the earth. See Matt. x. 23; xvi. 13, 27, 28. Mark ii. 28. Luke vi. 5. John iii. 14. etc., etc.

Ezekiel is often thus addressed by God (chap. ii., 1, 11, etc.), as "son of man," but in his case without the article.

See also Ps. viii. 4 (the first occurrence); cxliv. 3, etc.

In Ps. cxxvii. 4 (5) we have "children of the youth," *i.e.*, young children.

Joel iii. 6.—"The sons of Greece," *i.e.*, Greeks.

Deut. ix. 2.—"Sons of the Anakim": *i.e.*, Anakim.

The word in the plural means simply the name of the nation viewed as descended from some progenitor: *e.g.*, "children of Israel": *i.e.*, Israelites, "children of Ammon, Moab, etc."

4. םֵשׁ (*Shem*), name.

(*a*) This word appears to be redundant in the phrase "the name of God." It means *God Himself*, and has greater emphasis than if the simple word God were used.

Isa. xxx. 27.—"Behold, the name of the LORD cometh from far": *i.e.*, Jehovah Himself.

Jer. xliv. 26.—"Behold, I have sworn by my great name, saith the LORD": *i.e.*, by myself, by my own majesty, by all that my name implies.

Micah v. 4.—"And he shall stand and feed in the strength of the LORD, in the majesty of the name of the LORD his God"; *i.e.*, in the majesty of Jehovah Himself.

Ps. xx. 1 (2).—"The LORD hear thee in the day of trouble: the name of the God of Jacob defend thee:" *i.e.*, Jacob's God Himself.

So also verse 7 (8), etc.

Ps. cxiii. 1.—"Praise the name of the LORD": *i.e.*, "Praise Jehovah Himself."

(*b*) When used with the verb קָרָא (*karah*), to call, it means emphatically *to name*.

See Gen. xi. 9; xix. 22; xxvii. 36; xli. 51.

(c) The worship and profession of God is indicated by the phrases "call upon the name of the LORD : " *i.e.*, to worship Jehovah himself (Gen. iv. 26. Jer. x. 25).

"To love the name of the LORD ; "
"To walk in the name of the LORD ; "
"To praise the name of the LORD."

All these expressions mean, by the figure of *Pleonasm*, to worship and fear Jehovah Himself as opposed to self, and all other gods.

We have the same figure in the New Testament :—

Matt. vi. 9 and Luke xi. 2.—"Hallowed be thy name ": *i.e.,* "Let thy holy majesty—thyself alone—be worshipped."

Rev. xv. 4.—"Who shall not fear Thee, O Lord, and glorify thy name ? ": *i.e.*, fear and worship Thee Thyself.

Matt. i. 21.—"Thou shalt call his name JESUS ": *i.e.*, shall call *Him* that holy one Himself.

So Luke i. 13; ii. 21.

Rom. x. 13.—"Whosoever shall call upon the name of the Lord shall be saved ": *i.e.*, not whosoever shall utter the name, but whosoever shall be a true worshipper of God in Christ shall be saved.

So Heb. xiii. 15. John i. 12; ii. 23; iii. 18, etc.

5. יָד (*yad*), hand.

The word "hand" is used in various ways (both idiomatically and by *Metonymy*, *q.v.*) to express the instrument by which a thing is done ; and this in order to put the emphasis on the fact that the power did not lie in the instrument, but in him who used it.

Gen. ix. 5.—It seems superfluous, but it is not. It emphasizes the fact that it is God who requires punishment for shedding man's blood, and that he will use all and every instrument to accomplish His will.

Ex. iv. 13.—"And he (Moses) said, O Lord (Adonai), send I pray thee by the hand thou wilt send ": *i.e.*, by any agency except me !

1 Sam. xvii. 37.—"The LORD that delivered me out of the paw (hand) of the lion, and out of the paw (hand) of the bear, he will deliver me out of the hand of this Philistine ": *i.e.*, the power of the lion, and the bear, and Goliath. See Ps. xxii. 20 (21) (= the dog); xlix. 15 (16); cvii. 2. 1 Kings xi. 12.

1 Kings viii. 53.—" Thou spakest by the hand of Moses thy servant " : *i.e.*, by Moses. Jehovah was the speaker, Moses was only the instrument.

So also 2 Kings xvii. 13, and many other passages in which Jehovah speaks by *the hand of* his prophets.

1 Chron. vi. 31 (16).—" And these are they whom David set over the service of song in the house of the LORD." Lit., " over the hands of song," *i.e.*, over the instruments of song, so as to minister music. So 2 Chron. xxix. 27, " the hands of the instruments (marg.).

Isa. lxiv. 6 (5).—" And our iniquities." Lit., " the hand of our iniquities " : *i.e.*, the power of our iniquities.

To this belongs Ps. vii. 3 (4), " If there be any iniquity in my hands." Lit., in the hands of me : *i.e.*, in me. A kind of *Metonymy* (*q.v.*), or *Synecdoche*, by which a part of a person is put for the whole.

In the New Testament we have the same use of the word χείρ (*cheir*), **hand.**

Mark vi. 2.—" That even such mighty works are wrought by his hands." Lit., " by the hands of him " : *i.e.*, by Him.

Luke i. 71.—" From the hand of all that hate us" : *i.e.*, not merely from our enemies, but from the power of those enemies who hate us and cause us to serve them.

So also Acts v. 12 ; vii. 25, 35.

In Acts xv. 23, the A.V. omits " by the hands of them," and substitutes the word " *letters* " in italics. The R.V. says, " They wrote *thus* by them " (Gal. iii. 19 and Rev. xix. 2).

6. תָּוֶךְ (*tavech*) and קֶרֶב (*kerev*), **midst.**

The phrase " in the midst " is used phonastically when it is not to be taken literally as being equidistant from the extremes, or when it only adds emphasis to the sense.

Gen. xlv. 6.—" These two years hath the famine been in the land." Lit., " in the midst of the land" : *i.e.*, all over it. Here it is not translated at all.

Num. xiv. 13.—" Thou broughtest up this people in (or by) thy might from among them." Lit., " out of the midst of them " : out of Egypt. See also

Josh. iii. 17. 2 Kings iv. 13. Ps. xxii. 14 (15).—" My heart is like wax ; it is melted in the midst of my bowels " : *i.e.*, within me. So Ps. xl. 8, 10 (9, 11).

Ps. xxii. 22 (23).—"In the midst of the congregation will I praise thee": *i.e.*, in the assembly of the People; not of the "church," which was afterwards revealed to Paul in the New Testament Scriptures as the "Mystery."* But wherever God's People are assembled, there is He "in the midst of (*i.e.*, with) them."

Ps. xl. 8, 10 (9, 11).—"In the midst of my heart": *i.e.*, in me.

Ps. xlviii. 9 (10).—"In the midst of thy temple": *i.e.*, in thy temple.

Isa. x. 23.—"In the midst of all the land."

Hab. iii. 2.—"Revive thy work in the midst of the years, in the midst of the years make known": *i.e.*, within or during that time of Tribulation. (See also under *Anadiplosis*).

Zech. ii. 5, 10, 11 (9, 14, 15).—"In the midst of thee": *i.e.*, in thee.

Matt. xiii. 49.—"And sever the wicked from among the just": *i.e.*, from. So Acts xvii. 33. 2 Cor. vi. 17.

For other illustrations see Matt. xiii. 25. Luke xvii. 11. Heb. ii. 12. (Compare Ps. xxii. 22 (23), above).

7. לֵב (*lev*), לֵבָב (*levav*), heart.

The word "heart" is sometimes used pleonastically by *Metonymy* (*q.v.*) for *the midst*, when it does not mean literally the precise middle point.

Ex. xv. 8.—"In the heart of the sea." So Ps. xlvi. 2. Prov. xxiii. 34; xxx. 19. Ezek. xxvii. 4.

Matt. xii. 40.—"In the heart of the earth": *i.e.*, in the earth.

8. דָּבָר (*Davar*), word,

is very frequently used in the same way.

Ps. xxxv. 20.—"Deceitful matters." Lit., "words of frauds": *i.e.*, frauds.

Ps. lxv. 3 (4).—"Iniquities prevail against me." Here the A.V. puts the literal meaning in the margin, "the words or matters of iniquity": *i.e.*, my iniquitous matters. So with

Ps. cv. 27.—"The words of his signs."

Ps. cxlv. 5.—"The words of thy wonders": *i.e.*, as rendered "thy wondrous works."

---

* See *The Mystery*, by the same author and publisher.

9. קוֹל (*Kōl*), voice.

Gen. iii. 8.—" They heard the voice of the LORD God walking, etc." : *i.e.*, the sound, or merely Jehovah Elohim.

Ps. xcviii. 5.—" The voice of a psalm " : *i.e.*, with a psalm.

Ps. cii. 5 (6).—" The voice of my groaning " : *i.e.*, my groaning.

Isa. xxiv. 18.—" The noise (voice) of the fear. (See also under *Paronomasia*).

Jer. xvi. 9.—" I will cause to cease out of this place in your eyes, and in your days,

the voice of mirth, and
the voice of gladness,
the voice of the bridgeroom, and
the voice of the bride."

This does not mean that there shall be any bridegrooms and brides without voices, but that marriage itself shall cease.

Jer. li. 54.—" A sound of a cry." Lit., the voice of a cry: *i.e.*, a great clamour. So Zeph. i. 10, etc.

10. יָמִים (*yahmeem*), days.

The word *days* joined with *years*, etc., is used pleonastically. See Gen. xlvii. 8, (9). Ex. xiii. 10. Judges xix. 2 (marg.). 2 Sam. xix. 34 (marg.). Ps. xc. 10.

Gen. xxix. 14.—" And he abode with him the space of a month." Marg.: " Heb., a month of days." This, by the figure of *Hypallage* (*q.v.*), stands for the days of a month : *i.e.*, a full month. So Num. xi. 20, 21.

11. וַיְהִי (*vayehee*), and it came to pass.

Sometimes this word appears to be redundant ; as well as the Greek καὶ ἐγένετο (*kai egeneto*). That is to say, as the sense is complete without it, it is added for the sake of emphasis.

See the *preterite*. Gen. xxxviii. 1, 7, 24, 28 ; xxxix. 10, 13, 15, etc. Matt. vii. 28 ; ix. 10 ; xi. 1 ; xiii. 53 ; xix. 1 ; xxvi. 1. Mark i. 9 ; ii. 15. Luke i. 24, 41 ; ii. 1, 6 ; v. 1.

So with the *future ;* Deut. xviii. 19. Josh. ii. 14. 1 Kings xviii. 24 ; xx. 7. Isa. vii. 23. Hos. ii. 23. Joel iii. 15. Acts ii. 6 ; iii. 23. Rom. ix. 26.

2. Other Words.

Deut. xxxiii. 19.—"Treasures hid in the sand."

Here the figure is very freely rendered. Lit., it is "*hidden-things hidden of the sand*" : *i.e.*, the hidden things of the earth, in contrast with the treasures of the sea.

Ps. xl. 7.—"Then said I, Lo, I come : in the **volume** of the **book** it is written of me " *i.e.*, *in the book*, namely, Holy Scripture. (See under *Synecdoche*). The second noun (*in regimen*) being as the genitive of apposition. See Appendix B.

Isa. xxxiii. 23.—" Then is the **prey** of a great **spoil** divided. Heb., עַד שָׁלָל (*ad shalal*), a prey of a spoil: *i.e.*, a great spoil.

Dan. xii. 2.—" And some to **shame** and everlasting **contempt.**"

Rom. i. 23.—" Unto an image made like." Lit., " unto a likeness of an image."

By this figure the meaning is enhanced, so that it is as though it said, " They changed the glory of the incorruptible God actually into an image of corruptible man !

2 Cor. v. 1.—" The earthly **house** of this **tabernacle**," emphasizing this mortal body as being so different from the heavenly body.

Eph. iv. 23.—" And be renewed in the **spirit** of your **mind**" : *i.e.*, that your whole new nature or inner man being a new creation, Divine in its origin and impeccable in its character now causes the whole course of life to flow in a different direction.

1 Thess. ii. 23.—" When ye received the **word** of God, which ye **heard** of us." Lit., *the word of hearing.* λόγος ἀκοῆς (*logos akoees*). ἀκοή (*akoee*) which means *hearing*, is often used by the figure of *Metonymy* (*q.v.*), for *what is heard.* See John xii. 38. Rom. x. 16. " Who hath believed our hearing " : *i.e.*, what they have heard ; our preaching or testimony.

So here, the figure cannot be rendered literally, but the whole sense is enchanced by the fact that it was the word of God, which they heard, and not only heard but received it into their hearts.

Compare Heb. iv. 2 ; and see under *Metonymy.*

Rev. xvi. 19.—" The fierceness of His wrath."

Here, the figure is seen and beautifully translated : not literally, but according to the enhanced sense.

The Greek is θυμὸς ὀργῆς (*thumos orgees*), *the anger of His wrath,* the two words being synonymous. Both refer to the working of the passions of the mind, but ὀργή (*orgee*) is *the heat of the fire,* while θυμός (*thumos*) is *the bursting forth of the flame.* ὀργή (*orgee*), there-fore, is the more lasting feeling of anger and wrath. θυμός (*thumos*) is the more sudden manifestation of it, so that " fierceness of His wrath beautifully expresses the figure.

II. Sentences.

Another kind of *Pleonasm* is when the sense or whole sentence is repeated in another form, and thus put in another way. This may be done either affirmatively or negatively.

1. Affirmatively.

When the same sense is repeated affirmatively, it is hardly to be distinguished from *Synonymia* (*q.v.*), which it much resembles. See Ps. xxix. 1, 2 ; lxxxix. 31, 32. Isa. lii. 13, etc.

Gen. i. 20.—" And fowl that may fly **above the earth,** in the **open firmament of heaven."**

Instead of saying simply *in the air*, it first says " above the earth," and then it is further emphasized by " the open firmament of heaven," in order to make the distinction between these and what had been created to be in the waters, and on the earth.

Num. xix. 2.—" This is the **ordinance** of the **law** which Jehovah hath **commanded** " : *i.e.*, the law or statute, but it is put thus to impress upon the people the importance of the special truth connected with " the red heifer."

Deut. xxxii. 6.—" Is not he thy father that hath bought thee ? **Hath he not made thee ? and established thee ? "**

John i. 22.—" Who art thou ? . . . **What sayest thou of thyself ? "**

John v. 24.—" He that heareth my words, and believeth on him that sent me, hath everlasting life, and shall not come into condemna-tion (judgment), but **is passed from death unto life."**

Acts xiii. 45.—" But when the Jews saw the multitudes, hey were filled with envy, and **spake against** those things which were spoken by Paul, **contradicting,** and **blaspheming."**

Phil. i. 23.—" Which is far better."

Here, the return of Christ is declared to be πολλῷ (*pollō*), **much** ; μᾶλλον (*mallon*), **more** ; κρεῖσσον (*kreisson*), **better**, than either living or dying; *out of* (ἐκ) which two he was being pressed by that third thing: *viz.*, the great desire εἰς τὸ ἀναλῦσαι (*eis to analusai*) unto the return (see under *Antimeria, Epanalepsis, Resumptio,* and *Apostasis*).

Ἀναλύω means *to return from thence* hither (not from hence thither). See Luke xii. 36. Job ii. 1. Judith xiii. 1. 1 Esd. iii. 3. Wisd. ii. 1; v. 12. Eccles. iii. 15. Macc. viii. 25; ix. 1: xii. 7; xv. 28. Josephus Aut. vi. 41.

There is no other way of being "with Christ," as the Thessalonian saints are told 1 Thess. iv. 17, οὕτως (*houtōs*), *thus in this matter,* shall we ever be with the Lord: *i.e.*, by being "caught up to meet the Lord in the air": the sleeping saints not preceding those who are alive, and the living ones not preceding those who have fallen asleep (verse 15), but both sleeping and living saints raised and changed, together (ἅμα *hama*) caught away.

See under *Epanalepsis* (pp. 206, 207), where it is shown that for him to abide in the flesh is better for them—better than dying—but not better than the coming of Christ.

2. Negatively.

Here the sense is first put positively and then negatively, or *vice versa*. This of course greatly emphasizes the original statement, and calls very special attention to it.

Gen. xl. 23.—"Yet did not the chief butler remember Joseph, **but forgat him.**"

Here the simple statement that the chief butler did not remember Joseph, would have expressed the fact simply and clearly; but in order to emphasize and forcibly mark it, it is repeated negatively:—"but forgat him," as though to remind us that he acted after the manner of man. In this character of man lies the justification of that definition of "gratitude" which the world has given in condemnation of itself:— that it is "a lively sense of favours to come"!

Gen xlii. 2.—"That we may live **and not die.**" So xliii. 8, etc.

Ex. ix. 19.—"Every man and beast which shall be found in the field, and shall **not be brought home.**"

Ex. xii. 20.—"Ye shall eat nothing leavened: in all your habitations ye shall eat **unleavened bread.**"

Deut. xxviii. 13.—"And the LORD shall make thee the head and **not the tail**: and thou shalt be above only, and thou **shalt not be beneath.**"

Deut. xxxii. 6.—"O foolish people, and **unwise.**"

Deut. xxxiii. 6.—" Let Reuben live **and not die.**"
Thus this figure simply but emphatically reverses the pronounce-
ment of Jacob in Gen. xlix. 3, 4.

1 Sam. i. 11.—"And remember me, and **not forget thine
handmaid.**"

1 Kings vi. 18.—The stones within the Temple-walls were overlaid
with cedar (verses 15, 16), and this cedar was further overlaid with
gold (verse 21). It is not, therefore, necessary to the *description* to add
verse 18 : " **There was no stone seen** ": but it was necessary to
emphasize the fact, because of the important truth which these stones
were afterwards to be used to typify : *viz.*, that the " living stones "
(1 Pet. ii. 5), who are built up a spiritual house, are as completely
covered with the Divine and the glorious righteousness of Christ, in
which they appear in the presence of God, " perfect in Christ Jesus,"
" complete in Him." Nothing whatever in or of themselves being
seen.

2 Kings xx. 1.—" Set thine house in order ; for thou shalt die,
and not live ": *i.e.*, thou shalt surely die.

Isa. iii. 9.—" They declare their sin as Sodom, **they hide it
not.**"

Isa. xxxi. 3.—" Now the Egyptians are men, **and not God** (El) ;
and their horses are flesh **and not spirit.**" The figure is thus used
to show the people how easily Jehovah could destroy them.

Isa. xxxviii. 1.—" Thou shalt die, **and not live** ": to emphasize
the certainty of his death.

Isa. xlv. 22.—" I am God, **and there is none else.**" This to
show that there is none that save like Him.
So Isa. xlvi. 9 and xliv. 8.

Jer. xx. 14.—" Cursed be the day wherein I was born : **let not
the day wherein my mother bare me be blessed.**"

Ezek. xviii. 13.—" He shall not live : he hath done all these
abominations ; **he shall surely die.**" Here, the negative is put first,
and then repeated in the positive form.

Ezek. xxviii. 2.—" Thou art a man, **and not God.**"

Ezek. xxxiii. 15.—" He shall surely live : **he shall not die.***

Hos. v. 3.—" I know Ephraim, and **Israel is not hid from me.**"

Hos. xi. 9.—" I am God, **and not man.**"

---

* See also under *Asyndeton.*

Amos v. 20.—" Shall not the day of the LORD be darkness, and not light ? "

See this passage also under *Erotesis* and *Metonymy*.

Hab. ii. 3.—" It will surely come, it will not tarry."

Luke xviii. 34.—

> " And they understood none of these things :
> And this saying was hid from them,
> **Neither knew they** the things which were spoken."

All this to enhance the fact of the utter ignorance of the disciples.

John i. 3.—" All things were made by Him, and **without Him was not anything made that was made.**"

John i. 20.—" And he confessed, and **denied not** ; but confessed, I am not the Christ."

John iii. 15.—" That whosoever believeth in him should not perish, **but have eternal life.**"

Acts xviii. 9.—" Be not afraid, but speak, **and hold not thy peace.**"

Rom. iv. 20.—" He staggered not at the promise of God through unbelief; **but was strong in faith.**"

Rom. xii. 11.—" Not slothful in business." Lit., *in diligence*, **not slothful.** See under *Ellipsis* and *Idiom.*

Rom xii. 14.—" Bless, and **curse not.**"

1 Cor. i. 10.—" That there be no divisions among you ; but that ye be **perfectly joined together** in the same mind and in the same judgment."

Gal. v. 1.—" Stand fast therefore in the liberty wherewith Christ hath made us free, **and be not entangled again** with the yoke of bondage."

1 John i. 5.—" God is light, and in Him is **no darkness at all.**"

1 John i. 8.—" If we say that we have no sin, we deceive ourselves, and **the truth is not in us.**" So ii. 4, etc.

PERIPHRASIS; or, CIRCUMLOCUTION.

When a Description is used instead of the Name.

Pe-riph'-ra-sis, περίφρασις, from περί (*peri*), *around* or *about*, and φράζειν (*phrazein*), *to speak*.

The figure is so called because more words than are necessary are used to describe anything : as when a thing is spoken of by a description of it, instead of simply using its name : and this for the sake of calling attention to it; and in order to emphasize and increase the effect. Or, when a person or thing is spoken of by some attribute, instead of by its proper simple name : as when, instead of saying Luther, we say "the monk that shook the world," or "the miner's son."

When this is done for emphasis, and to enhance the meaning, it is called Periphrasis, and by the Latins CIRCUMLOCUTIO, or CIRCUITIO : *i.e.*, *a speaking* or *going round about a thing.*

When this is done to avoid what may be indelicate or unseemly, or to hide what might in some way give offence, then it is called *Euphemism* (*q.v.*) or smooth-speech, *i.e.*, an elegant or refined expression for a distasteful or coarse one, or a gentle and beautiful expression instead of the strictly literal one, which might offend the ear or the persons addressed. But as this, though a kind of Periphrasis, is the *change* or substitution of one word or term for another, we have described and illustrated *Euphemism* under our third great division, *viz.*, Figures involving Change.

Gen. xx. 16.—Abimelech said unto Sarah concerning Abraham, "Behold, I have given thy brother a thousand pieces of silver; behold, he is to thee a covering of the eyes unto all that are with thee, and with all *other :* thus she was reproved."

"A covering of the eyes" is a *periphrasis* for a husband. Having said "thy brother," Abimelech avoids calling him directly thy husband, and thus rebukes her by using this beautiful periphrasis. See Gen. xxiv. 65. 1 Cor. xi. 5, etc.

Gen. xlvi. 26.—Those that "came out of his loins": *i.e.*, his direct descendants—his children and grandchildren. Hence, the number of these differs from (and is smaller than) the number spoken of in Acts vii. 14, which embraces "all his kindred": *i.e.*, all his other relations who are specifically excepted in Gen. xlvi. 26.

Judges v. 10.—"Speak, ye that ride on white asses (*i.e.*, princes), ye that sit in judgment (*i.e.*, rulers), and walk by the way (*i.e.*, merchants)."

These periphrases mean simply, "Speak, ye princes, ye rulers, and ye merchants"; but their description, instead of their names, emphasizes the classes of persons so described.

2 Sam. iii. 29.—"That falleth on the sword": *i.e.*, is put to death by the public executioner.

2 Chron. xxvi. 5.—Uzziah "sought God in the days of Zechariah who had understanding in the visions of God": *i.e.*, who was a Prophet.

2 Chron. xxxii. 21.—"They that came forth of his own bowels (*i.e.*, his own sons) slew him," who ought to have been the very last to commit such a crime.

Prov. xxx. 31.—The *Periphrasis*, here, in the Heb. (see marg.) is *well girt in the loins*, which both the A.V. and R.V. have rendered "greyhound"! But the figure is used of a war-horse caparisoned, mail-clad, and adorned for war.

Eccles. xii. is full of the most beautiful examples. See under *Euphemism* and *Metalepsis*.

Ps. iv. 7.—"Thou hast put gladness in my heart, more than in the time that their corn and their wine increased": *i.e.*, more than in the joy of their abundant harvest and vintage.

Ps. cv. 18 is a *Periphrasis* for Joseph's captivity, referring to Gen. xxxix. 20-23; xli. 12.

Ps. cxxxii. 3, 4.—The *Periphrasis* is used in order to emphasize David's determination not to rest until he had done it.

Isa. xiv. 15.—"Yet thou shalt be brought down to hell (Sheol), to the sides of the pit": *i.e.*, be dead and buried.

Jer xxi. 13.—"Inhabitress of the valley and rock of the plain": *i.e.*, Zion is spoken of by this description on account of its situation. Compare Josh. xv. 8.

Ezek. i. 22.—"The likeness of the firmament upon (or over) the heads of the living creature was as a species of ice exceedingly strong (*i.e.*, crystal), etc."

Ezek. xxiv. 16.—"The desire of thine eyes": *i.e.*, thy wife, as is clear from verse 18. So verses 21 and 25.

Ezek. xxiv. 25.—"The lifting up of their soul": marg., their beloved sons and daughters.

Ezek. xxvi. 9.—" Engines of war " : battering-rams.

Ezek. xxxi. 14.—" The trees by the waters." Lit., " trees drinking water." The *Periphrasis* is used for trees that are watered by irrigation. Hence, trees planted in a garden.

Micah vii. 5.—Here we have a double *Periphrasis.* " The doors of thy mouth," by *Metonymy* for *words*, or what is said, and " her that lieth in thy bosom " for thy wife.

Zeph. i. 9.—" Those that leap on the threshold ": *i.e.*, the servants of the rulers and others who were sent to enter the houses of others and take away the good things that were therein. The words that follow show this to be the correct interpretation ; for such are said to fill their Masters' homes with what they have taken by violence and deceit. It does not, as many suppose, refer to idolatrous worship, for the word דָּלַג (*dalag*) is not so used. On the contrary : compare 2 Sam. xxii. 30. Ps. xviii. 29 (30). Song ii. 8. Isa. xxxv. 6.

Matt. xi. 11.—" Born of women " ; *i.e.*, born by natural process. See Luke vii. 28. Job xiv. 1 ; xv. 14 ; xxv. 4. Luke ii. 23.

Matt. xxvi. 29.—" This fruit of the vine " for wine. See *Metonymy.*

Matt. xxvii. 62.—" The next day, that followed the day of the preparation " : *i.e.*, the Sabbath. This seems to be one of the most striking instances in the New Testament, especially when we compare Luke xxiii. 56. The selfsame day is meant. But mark the difference. To the holy and devout women that day was still the Sabbath. But in the case of those who had rejected " the Lord of the Sabbath," what happens ? It has been observed that, when He is on the point of leaving the Temple for the last time, our Lord, who formerly, even in that same week, before He had been finally rejected in that House, than which He was greater, had spoken of it as " My Father's House," now calls it "*your* house." So, here again. From these rejectors of the Sabbath's Lord, the very *name* of their sacred day is taken away. And the Spirit uses this long, round-about, depreciatory phrase : " the next day, that followed the day of the preparation."

Luke ii. 11.—" In the city of David " : *i.e.*, Bethlehem.

Luke xxi. 35.—" All them that dwell on the face of the whole earth ": *i.e.*, everyone. See under *Pleonasm.*

John i. 9.—" That was the true Light, which lighteth every man that cometh into the world."

This rendering is obtained by disregarding the figure, taking the participle "coming" as though it were the present tense, and referring it to "every man," instead of to "the True Light." The common Hebrew *Periphrasis* for man was הבא בעולם, *the comer into the world.** But this expression (the Coming One) in the New Testament (and especially in John's writings) is used exclusively of Christ alone, and this in an exalted sense as *the Coming One.* Thus the verse reads, "The True Light is he who, coming into the world, lighteneth every man " (*i.e.,* of course, every man *without distinction,* not without exception! which would not be true).

Thus the verse teaches : (1) that no longer was the Light to be confined to one nation or to one People, but was to enlighten all *without distinction* of race ; and (2) that no man can be enlightened except by Christ.

2 Cor. v. 1.—" Our earthly house of this tabernacle " : *i.e.,* this body.

1 Thess. iv.—In this chapter there are three examples of *Periphrasis,* all used for *the Gentiles :*—

Verse 5, " which know not God."

„ 12, " them that are without."

„ 13, " others which have no hope."

The description, by which the Gentiles are thus spoken of, is so much more expressive than the mere mention of the word " Gentiles."

Heb. i. 14.—" Heirs of salvation " is a beautiful *Periphrasis* for the elect.

2 Pet. i. 13.—" As long as I am in this tabernacle " : *i.e.,* am alive.

Verse 14, " Shortly I must put off this my tabernacle " : *i.e.,* must die. This is strictly speaking *Euphemy (q.v.) : viz.,* a pleasant *periphrasis* to describe an unpleasant fact, instead of naming it plainly.

---

* In accordance with Luke ii. 23.

HYPERBOLE ; or, EXAGGERATION.

When more is said than is literally meant.

Hy-per'-bo-le is from ὑπέρ (*huper* or *hyper*), *over and above*, or *beyond* (like Lat., *super*), and βολή (*bolee*), *a casting*, from βάλλειν (*ballein*), *to throw*. Hence, *a casting* or *going beyond, overshooting, excess*.

The figure is so called because the expression adds to the sense so much that it exaggerates it, and enlarges or diminishes it more than is really meant in fact. Or, when more is said than is meant to be literally understood, in order to heighten the sense.

It is the superlative degree applied to verbs and sentences and expressions or descriptions, rather than to mere adjectives.

The figure is known by several names. It is called EPAUXESIS (*Ep'-aux-ee'-sis*), *growth* or *increase upon.* HYPEROCHE (*hy-per'-o-ché*), *excess, superabundance.* HYPERTHESIS (*hy-per'-the-sis*), *a placing* or *passing beyond, superlative.* It was called by the Latins SUPERLATIO (*su-per-la'ti-o*), *a carrying beyond, an exaggerating*.

Gen. ii. 24.—" Therefore shall a man leave his father and his mother, and shall cleave unto his wife." This does not mean that he is to forsake and no longer to love or care for his parents. So Matt. xix. 5.

Gen. xli. 47.—"And in the seven plenteous years the earth brought forth by handfuls ": *i.e.*, one grain produced a handful of grains, which is *hyperbolical* of a prolific increase.

So verse 49.

Gen xlii. 28.—" Their heart failed them." Here the *Hyperbole* " their heart went out," is thus beautifully rendered.

Ex. viii. 17.—" All the dust of the land became lice throughout all the land of Egypt ": *i.e.*, wherever in all the land there was dust, it became lice.

Deut. i. 28.—" The cities are great, and walled up to heaven," to express their great height. So Deut. ix. 1, etc.

Judges v. 4, 5, beautifully sets forth the Divine Majesty manifested in Jehovah's leading the People into the Promised Land.

Judges xx. 16.—" Every one could sling stones at an hair and not miss ": to describe the wonderful proficiency which the Benjamites had attained in slinging stones. The A.V. has added *breadth* in italics, so as to lessen the boldness of the *Hyperbole*, " an hair *breadth.*"

1 Sam. v. 12.—"The cry of the city went up to heaven," to describe the greatness of the cry.

1 Sam. vii. 6.—"And they gathered together to Mizpeh, and drew water, and poured it out before the LORD, and fasted, etc." This is an *hyperbolical* description of the intensity of their weeping and lamentation. Similar descriptions occur Ps. vi. 6; cxix. 136. Jer. ix. 1. Lam. iii. 48, 49.

1 Sam. xxv. 37.—Nabal's "heart died within him, and he became as a stone": *i.e.*, he was terribly frightened and collapsed or fainted away.

1 Kings i. 40.—"So that the earth rent with the sound of them." A *hyperbolical* description of their jumping and leaping for joy.

1 Kings x. 5.—"There was no more spirit in her": *i.e.*, she was dazed or stupefied, as we say, with astonishment.

2 Chron. xxviii. 9.—"A rage that reacheth up unto heaven," to express the intensity of the rage.

Ezra ix. 6.—"Our trespass is grown up unto the heavens," to express the enormity of their sin.

Neh. viii. 4.—"And Ezra the Scribe stood upon a tower (marg.) of wood": *i.e.*, a high wooden structure; or, as we should say, a platform or pulpit.

Job xxix. 6.—"The rock poured me out rivers of oil": *i.e.*, I had abundance of all good things. So chap. xx. 17 and Micah vi. 7.

Job xxxix. 19.—"Hast thou clothed his neck with thunder?"

Glassius gives this as an *Hyperbole* for the neighing of the horse, but it seems better to take רַעְמָה (*ra'mah*), *of a flowing mane*, from רָעַם (*ra'am*), *to tremble, shake, wave*, as in verse 25.

The word denotes *a shaking*, as well as the noise caused by the shaking. See Ps. civ. 7. Isa. xxix. 6. The lxx. has φόβον (*phobon*), *fear*, perhaps a mistake for φόβην (*phobeen*), *a mane :*—"Thou hast clothed his neck with a flowing mane."

Ps. cvii. 26.—"They mount up to the heaven, they go down again to the depths": to express the violence of a storm; and waves, as we say, "mountain-high."

Prov. xxiii. 8.—"The morsel which thou hast eaten shalt thou vomit up": to express the suffering of regrets at having received benefits from such a host.

Isa. v. 25 and xlii. 15.—These are *hyperbolical* descriptions to set forth the excessive anger and judgments of Jehovah in making the Land desolate.

Isa. xiv. 13.—" I will ascend into heaven " : to express the pride of Lucifer.

Isa. lvii. 9.—" Thou . . . didst debase thyself even unto hell (Sheol) " ; to emphasize the indignity of Ahaz, king of Judah in sending to Tiglath-Pileser, king of Assyria, to help him against Israel, saying, " I am thy servant ! " (2 Kings xvi. 7, etc.).

Jer. i. 19 ; xv. 20.—" They shall fight against thee " (see below, Jas. iv. 1).

The verb, which means to wage war, is *Hyperbole* when used of a single individual ; but it told Jeremiah how bitter the opposition of man would be to his Divine message.

Jer. iv. 29.—" The whole city shall flee . . . they shall go into thickets." Lit., into the clouds ; to express the inaccessible places.

Jer. li. 9.—" Her judgment reacheth unto heaven, and is lifted up even to the skies " : to express the magnitude of Babylon's sin which called for such a judgment (Rev. xviii. 5).

Jer. li. 53.—" Though Babylon should mount up to heaven " ; to express the pride of Babylon.

Lam. ii. 1.—" How hath the Lord . . . cast down from heaven unto the earth the beauty of Israel " : to express the degradation of Zion and the height of glory from which she had fallen.

Lam. ii. 11.—" My liver is poured upon the earth, etc " : to express the depth of the Prophet's grief and sorrow at the desolations of Zion.

Ezek. xxvii. 28.—" The suburbs shall shake at the sound of the cry of thy pilots."

So R.V., but both margins say *waves*. The root גָּרַשׁ (*garash*) means to *drive out, drive about*. When used of a city, it refers to the suburbs which are driven out from the city : but, used of the sea, it means the driving and casting about of its waves. See Isa. lvii. 20.

The figure here expresses the greatness of the terror of the defenders of Tyre in the day of its overthrow : " the waves of the sea shall lash themselves at the sound of the cry of thy pilots."

Dan. ix. 21.—" Gabriel . . . being caused to fly swiftly." Lit. (see marg.), with weariness : *i.e.*, with such swiftness as to cause weariness.

Matt. xi. 23.—" And thou, Capernaum, which art exalted unto heaven, shall be brought down to hell." Or, as in the R.V., " And thou Capernaum, shalt thou be exalted unto heaven ? thou shalt go down (or be brought down) unto Hades."

Matt. xxi. 13.—" My house shall be called a house of prayer, but ye have made it a den of thieves." The Lord thus emphasizes the fact which is plainly stated in Mal. iii. 8 : " Ye have robbed me."

Luke xiv. 26.—" If any man come to me and hate not his father and mother " : *i.e.*, does not esteem them less than me. So the verb *to hate* is used (Gen. xxix. 31. Rom. ix. 13).

" *Anger* " is used for displeasure (Deut. iii. 26).

" *Save* " is used for preserve (Job ii. 6. Ezek. xviii. 17).

" *Lose* the life " is used of esteeming it as a small matter (Matt. x. 39 ; xvi. 25. Mark viii. 35. Luke ix. 24 ; xvii. 33, as is clear from Rev. xii. 11).

To *mar* is used for hurting (Ruth iv. 6) : *i.e.*, for his heirs.

To *rob* is used of receiving wages (2 Cor. xi. 8).*

Luke xviii. 5.—" Lest by her continual coming she weary me." True of man—but an *Hyperbole* as applied to God.

See *Anthropopatheia.*

John iii. 26.—" All men come to him." Thus his disciples said to John, to show their sense of the many people who followed the Lord.

John xii. 19.—" Behold, the world is gone after him." The enemies of the Lord thus expressed their indignation at the vast multitudes which followed Him.

Jas. iii. 6.—" The tongue is a fire, a world of iniquity." It is a question here, whethor κόσμος (*kosmos*) does not mean *ornament* or *adorning*, as in 1 Pet. iii. 3 : *i.e.*, the decking or adorning of iniquity, glozing it over and making that which is sinful, appear to be innocent, etc.

Jas. iv. 1.—" From whence come wars and fightings among you." The word " war " is used *hyperbolically* when applied to the quarrels of social life. So Jer. i. 19 ; xv. 20 (*q.v.*). See above.

Other examples of *Hyperbole* may be seen in 2 Sam. xvii. 13. 2 Kings xix. 24. Job. xl. 18. Isa. xiv. 14 ; xxxiv. 3, 4, 7. Ezek. xxvi. 4 ; xxxii. 5, 6, 7, 8. Amos ix. 13. Nah. ii. 3. Gal. iv. 15.

Examples pertaining to

COMPARISONS

are frequent, where one thing is compared with another, when there is nothing common between them :—

The *sand of the sea* and the *dust of the earth* are constantly used to express a vast number. (See under *Idiom*).

---

* As we often say, in declining a favour, " I have no wish to rob you."

Gen. xiii. 16; xxii. 17; xxviii. 14. 1 Kings iv. 20. 2 Chron. i. 9. Heb. xi. 12 : of Abraham's seed.

Judges vii. 12 : of the Midianites.

1 Sam. xiii. 5 : of the Philistines.

1 Kings iv. 29 : of Solomon's largeness of heart.

Job. xxix. 18 : of the days of a man's life.

Ps. lxxviii. 27 : of the feathered fowl in the wilderness.

Isa. xxix. 5 : of other peoples.

Jer. xv. 8 : of Judah's widows.

Other comparisons may be seen.

2 Sam i. 23.—Saul and Jonathan " swifter than eagles," " stronger than lions."

So Jer. iv. 13, and Lam. iv. 19, to express great velocity.

1 Kings x. 27.—Silver and gold as stones. So 2 Chron. i. 15 ; ix. 20.

Job vi. 3.—Job's grief heavier than the sand.

Job xli. 18.—Leviathan's sneezings causing light to shine.

Hab. ii. 5.—To express great rapacity.

Lam. iv. 7, 8.—To express and contrast the dignity and indignity of the sons of Zion.

HYPOTHESES.

Sometimes we have Hyperbolical *Hypotheses*, which are impossible in themselves, but are used to express the greatness of the subject spoken of.

Ps. cxxxix. 8, 10.—To show the wondrous omnipresence of God.

Prov. xxvii 22.—To show the folly and incorrigibility of the fool.

Obad. 4.—To emphasize the certainty of the coming judgment of Edom.   Compare Jer. xlix. 16, and Matt. xi. 23 as quoted above.

Mark viii. 36.   Luke ix. 25.—To express the utmost gain and make the strongest contrast.

1 Cor. iv. 15.—To express the difference between pedagogues and parents.

1 Cor. xiii. 1-3.—There are many hyperbolical *hypotheses* in these verses, to show the all-importance of the love of God shed abroad in the heart by the Holy Ghost.

Gal. i. 8.—An angel from heaven preaching a different gospel is inconceivable.   The *hypothesis* is used in order to show the importance of the Gospel of God.

1 Kings xx. 10.—" The boasting of Benhadad."

Matt. v. 29.—" If thy right eye offend thee, pluck it out . . ."

Matt. v. 30.—" If thy right hand offend thee, etc."

It is perfectly clear that Christ does not wish us to mutilate our bodies : so that this must be an hyperbolical or emphatic exhortation to avoid and remove everything and anything that causes us to stumble.

Luke x. 4 is an hyperbolical command not to loiter or delay in ceremonious salutations (such as are common even to the present day).

John xxi. 25 is also *Hyperbole.*   The verb χωρῆσαι (*chōreesai*) is to be taken in the same sense, as it is in Matt. xix. 11, where the Lord says, " All men cannot *receive* this saying; " and in verse 12, " He that is able to receive it, let him receive it."   The " world " is also put by *Metonymy* for mankind.

Hence, Thophylact expounds χωρῆσαι (*chōreesai*), *to receive, by* νοῆσαι (*noeesai*), *to understand.*

Rom. ix. 3.—" For I could wish that myself were accursed from Christ " is an hyperbolical supposition.

Or we may take this sentence as being in a parenthesis, and render the *imperfect* tense ηὐχόμην (*eeuchomeen*) in the sense of *I used to wish.*

The passage would then read, " I have great heaviness and continual sorrow in my heart for my brethren, my kinsmen according to the flesh, (for I used to wish myself to be a cursed thing from Christ)."

Jude 23.—" Hating even the garment spotted by the flesh."   This is an *hyperbolical* prohibition as to avoiding all contact with defilement.

In the statements of the Lord Jesus there often seems to be an *Hyperbole* when there is really none : *e.g.,* Mark xvi. 15.   John iii. 32.

ANABASIS; or, GRADUAL ASCENT.

An Increase of Sense in successive Sentences.

A-năb'-a-sĭs. Greek, ἀνάβασις, from ἀνά (*ana*), *up*, and βαίνειν (*bainein*), to go; βάσις (*basis*) means *a stepping*, or *a step*. So that *Anabasis* means *a going up** or *ascent*. The Figure is so called when a writing, speech, or discourse, *ascends up* step by step, each with an increase of emphasis or sense.

This figure was called by the Latins INCREMENTUM (*In'-crē-men'-tum*), *growth* or *increase*, from *incresco, to grow on* or *upon*. Hence our words "increase" and "increment."

When this increase or ascent is from weaker to stronger expression, and is confined to *words*, it is called *Climax* (*q.v.*).

[N.B.—When the sense or gradation is downward instead of upward, it is called *Catabasis*, see below.]

The figure was also called AUXESIS (*aux-ee'-sis*), *growth* or *increase*.

This increase is often connected with *Parallelism* (*q.v.*).

When the increase is not a mere increase of vehemence, or of evil, but leads up from things inferior to things superior; from things terrestial to things celestial; from things mundane to things spiritual; the figure is called ANAGOGE (*an'-a-gō-gee*), from ἀνά (*ana*), *again* or *up*, and ἄγειν (*agein*), *to lead*, *a leading up*.

Ps. i. 1.—" Blessed is the man
    that walketh not in the counsel of the ungodly,
    nor standeth in the way of sinners,
    nor sitteth in the seat of the scornful."
Here is a triple *Anabasis* depending on *Parallelism* (*q.v.*).
    The first are *impious*, as to their mind.
    The second are *sinners*, who not only think, but carry out the
        workings of their evil minds.
    The third are *scorners*, glorying in their wickedness and
        scoffing at righteousness.
Again, the first continue in that mind, taking evil counsel.
    The second carry it out, as the principle of their walk.
    The third settle down in their evil, as on a seat.

---

* Hence, the journey or expedition of Cyrus up from the coast into Central Asia is called his *Anabasis*, by Xenophon.

These three are exemplified in the first three verses of the next Psalm, where a corresponding *Anabasis* is seen :—

Ps. ii. 1, 2, 3.—First, we have the " heathen" : *i.e.*, the Gentile nations ; then "the peoples " : *i.e.*, the Tribes of God, Israel imagining vain things ; and in the third, we have "kings" and " rulers," all conspiring together.

Acts iv. 27 gives us the fulfilment:—(1) we have the kings and rulers taking counsel ; (2) we have the rage and vain imaginations ; and (3) the open and actual rebellion.   On Ps. i. 1, see page 350.

Ps. vii. 5.—
> " Let the enemy persecute my soul, and take it ;
> Yea, let him tread down my life upon the earth.
> And lay mine honour in the dust."

Ps. xviii. 37, 38.—
> " I have pursued mine enemies,
> And overtaken them :
> Neither did I turn again till they were consumed.
> I have wounded them that they were not able to rise :
> They are fallen under my feet."

Isa. i. 4.—
> " Ah sinful nation,
> A people laden with iniquity,
> A seed of evildoers,
> Children that are corrupters."

Ezek. ii. 6.—" And thou son of man,
> be not afraid of them,
> neither be afraid of their words,
> though briers and thorns be with thee,
> and thou dost dwell among scorpions :
> Be not afraid of the words,
> nor be dismayed at their looks,
> though they be a rebellious house."

And why this *Anabasis ?* To impress upon us that whatever opposition we may encounter, we are to speak and give forth the word of God, whether men will hear or whether they will forbear (verses 5 and 7), and not to corrupt it or alter it to please the people: to distribute versions of it, not "the best that people will take," but the best that we can make.

Dan. ix. 5.—

" We have sinned,
  and have committed iniquity,
  and have done wickedly,
  and have rebelled, even by departing from thy precepts and
    from thy judgments."

Hab. i. 5.—

" Behold ye among the heathen,
  and regard,
  and wonder marvellously :
For I will work a work in your days, which ye will not believe,
though it be told you."

Zech. vii. 11.—

" But they refused to hearken,
  And pulled away the shoulder,
  And stopped their ears that they should not hear.
  Yea, they made their hearts as an adamant stone, lest they
    should hear the law, etc."

Thus the *Anabasis* powerfully and emphatically sets forth the
secret cause of Israel's trouble.

Zech. viii. 12.—

" For the seed shall be prosperous,
  The vine shall give her fruit,
  And the ground shall give her increase,
  And the heavens shall give their dew,
  And I will cause the remnant of this people to possess all
    these things."

1 Cor. iv. 8.—

" Now ye are full,
  Now ye are rich,
  Ye have reigned as kings without us."
See under *Asyndeton.*

1 John i. 1.—

" That which was from the beginning,
  which we have heard,
  which we have seen with our eyes,
  which we have looked upon,
  and our hands have handled, of the Word of life."

As contrasted with *Anabasis*, we here introduce *Catabasis*, instead
of including it under Figures involving Omission, in order that the
contrast may be more clearly seen :—

CATABASIS; or, GRADUAL DESCENT.

The Opposite of Anabasis.

Cat-ab'-a-sis, a going down: from κατά (*kata*), *down,* and βάσις (*basis*), *a going.* This is the opposite of *Anabasis,* and is used to emphasize humiliation, degradation, sorrow, etc.

The Latins called it DECREMENTUM, *i.e., decrease*—an increase in the opposite direction, an increase of depreciation.

Isa. xl. 31.—"They that wait upon the LORD shall renew their strength;

> they shall mount up with wings as eagles,
> they shall run, and not be weary,
> they shall walk, and not faint."

The figure *Catabasis* here illustrates the effect of growth in grace. At first the believer *flies;* but as his experience increases, he *runs,* and at the end of his course he *walks.* Like Paul, who first said "I suppose I was not a whit behind the very chiefest *apostles*" (2 Cor. xi. 5; xii. 11). Later he writes, I "am less than the least of all *saints*" (Eph. iii. 8); while at the end of his life he says, I am the chief of *sinners!* (1 Tim. i. 15).

Jer. ix. 1.—

> "Oh that my head were waters,
> and mine eyes a fountain of tears,
> that I might weep day and night for the slain of the daughter
> of my people!" (See above.)

Lam. iv. 1, 2.—"How is the most fine gold changed!

> The stones of the sanctuary are poured out in the top of
> every street.
> The precious sons of Zion, comparable to fine gold,
> How are they esteemed as earthen pitchers,
> the work of the hands of the potter!"

Ezek. xxii. 18.—"Son of man, the house of Israel is to me become dross: all they

> are brass,
> and tin,
> and iron,
> and lead, in the midst of the furnace; they are even the dross
> of silver."

Dan. ii.—The Figure *Catabasis* is seen in the four successive world-powers, showing a deterioration and a growing inferiority. Gold, silver, brass, iron and clay. Not only is this deterioration in power and authority shown in the decrease of value, but in the decrease of specific gravity:—Gold is equivalent to 19·3; silver, 10·51; brass, 8·5; iron, 7·6; and clay, 1·9. Down from 19·3 to 1·9.*

Amos ix. 2, 3.—

" Though they climb up to heaven, thence will I bring them down :

And though they hide themselves in the top of Carmel, I will search and take them out thence :

And though they be hid from my sight in the bottom of the sea, thence will I command the serpent, and he shall bite them."

Thus powerfully is shown the impossibility of escaping from the judgments of God.

Phil. ii. 6-8.—" Who, being in the form of God,

1. Thought it not robbery to be equal with God :
2. But made himself of no reputation.
3. And took upon him the form of a servant,
4. And was made in the likeness of men,
5. And being found in fashion as a man, he humbled himself,
6. And became obedient unto death,
7. Even the death of the cross."

These seven downward steps in the Saviour's humiliation, are followed in verses 9-11 by *seven* steps upward in His glorification.

The word "robbery" is ἁρπαγμός (*harpagmos*), and means, not the thing grasped or seized, but the act of seizing. The contrast is between the first man and the second : the first Adam and the last. The Tempter promised our first parents that they should " be as gods " (*i.e.*, as God Himself), and they grasped at equality with God.

The second man, on the contrary, did not yield to the temptation, but humbled himself, and reached the highest position in glory through suffering and death, even the death of the cross.

There is also probably a reference to John vi. 15. Our Lord was perfectly aware that He was " a born King " (Matt. ii. 2). And Herod and all Jerusalem knew it too. Hence the consequent alarm. But the Lord knew also that Cæsar had, for the time, been allowed of God

---

* See *Ten Sermons on the Second Advent*, by the same author and publisher.

E 1

to lord it over His people, for their sins, and the fulfilment of His designs. He would therefore countenance no unauthorized attempt on the part of those who did not believingly own Him either as to His Divine or His human nature and rights.

Note also as to the words used: "Thought." The verb ἡγεῖσθαι (*heegeisthai*), *to bring one's self to think.* Adam and his wife may have "brought themselves to think," at the serpent's instigation, that the thing he suggested was *something to grasp at,* and therefore worth the *grasping effort.* Eve, at any rate, would seem to have thought so. Adam we cannot, perhaps, say the same of, for "Adam," we are expressly told, "was not deceived." Hence, apparently, his deeper guilt. But no "subtil serpent" could for a moment—(notice the Aor. ἡγήσατο, He *never once admitted the thought*)—induce the "second Man," "the Lord from heaven," to think it possible to *become* equal with God, any more than he could induce Him to deny or forget that essentially He *was* so in His Divine nature: Son of God, as truly as Son of Man. Hence we may suggest such a rendering as this: "Who, being originally in the form of God, never considered the being on an equality with God a usurping (or usurper's) business." To be what one is is no usurping business. Nor is it so, either, to know and assert that one is so.

MERISMOS ; or, DISTRIBUTION.

An Enumeration of the Parts of a Whole which has been mentioned.

Mĕ-ris'-mos. Greek, μερισμός (*merismos*), *division*, from μέρος (*meros*), *a part.* The figure is so called because, after mentioning a thing as a whole, the parts are afterwards enumerated.

Also EPIMERISMOS, which is *merismos* with ἐπί (*epi*), upon, prefixed (*Ep'-i-mĕ-ris'-mus*).

It was called also DIALLAGE (*Dĭ-al'-la-gee*), διαλλαγή, *interchange*, from διά (*dia*), *through*, or *asunder*, and ἀλλάσσειν (*allassein*), *to make other than it is*, *to change throughout*.

The Latins called it DISTRIBUTIO (*Dis-tri-bu'-ti-o*), and DISCRIMINATIO (*Dis-crim'-i-na-ti-o*). Also DIGESTIO (*Di-ges'-ti-o*), *i.e.*, *reduction to order, classification.*

Though these names express, in the first instance, division, we have classed the figure under figures of addition ; because, after the thing has been named and mentioned, it is divided up, and the various parts are *added* together to enhance the effect, increase the emphasis, and amplify the sense.

Isa. xxiv. 1-3: where, after stating the fact, "Behold, the Lord maketh the earth empty," the statement is amplified, and the way in which God will do this and scatter the People is afterwards enumerated.

Ezek. xxxvi. 4.—After saying " Ye mountains of Israel, hear the word of the Lord God (Adonai Jehovah)," the word is spoken, not only to the mountains, but to the hills and rivers, and valleys, and desolate wastes, and the cities that are forsaken.

And all this to show how complete shall be the blessing for the land of Israel.

Rom. ii. 6-8.—Here, after stating that God " will render to every man according to his deeds " in verse 6, verses 7 and 8 go on to enumerate the particulars of the two great classes of deeds.

Gal. v. 19-21.—"The works of the flesh " are first mentioned as a whole, and then the whole sixteen are named and enumerated.

Gal. v. 22, 23.—" The fruit of the Spirit " is first mentioned, and then the nine manifestations of it are enumerated. It is " fruit " in the singular, though made up of many parts like a cluster of grapes.

SYNATHRŒSMOS; or, ENUMERATION.

The Enumeration of the Parts of a Whole which has not been mentioned.

Syn¹-ath-rœs¹-mos. Greek, συναθροίσμος (*syn-ath-rois-mos*), *gathering together, assembling.* It is used of an assemblage of terms or species brought together without being first mentioned as a whole, and not being necessarily the distribution of the parts of any one thing.

The figure is also called APARITHMESIS (*ap-a-rith¹-mee-sis*), from ἀπό (*apo*), *from* or *off*, and ἀριθμεῖν (*arithmein*), *to count.* Hence, *to count off, enumerate.* The Latins, from this, called it ENUMERATIO, which has the same meaning. The Latin term for *Synathrœsmus* is CONGERIES (*con-ge¹-ri-ees*), from *con*, *together*, and *gerere*, *to bear, carry* or *bring*; and denotes *a heap*, or *combination.*

From the fact that such enumeration or combination sometimes made the argument or statement *drag*, the figure was called SYRMOS, which is the Greek συρμός (*syrmos*), *a trailing*, from σύρειν (*surein*), *to drag, trail along.* And, because a number of different words were thus united, it was also called EIRMOS (*eir¹-mos*), from εἴρω (*eirō*), *to string together.*

It differs from *Merismus* in that the things enumerated are not first briefly mentioned under one head: and it differs from *Synonymia*, in that they are not synonymous, but may be of many kinds and descriptions.

It also differs from *Symperasma*, in that they do not occur at the *conclusion*, but in the course of what is said.

The use of the figure is to enrich a discourse, or part of it, by enumerating particulars, or by multiplying epithets.

All the figures which we are grouping under this head are figures of *Amplification*; otherwise *this* is called by some *Amplificatio.* But we have used this as a general term for the whole group and have not restricted it to any one particular figure.

Isa. i. 11, 13.—"To what purpose is the multitude of your sacrifices unto me ? saith the Lord: I am full of the burnt offerings of rams, and the fat of fed beasts; and I delight not in the blood of bullocks, or of lambs, or of he-goats . . . Bring no more vain oblations; incense is an abomination unto me."

One sentence would have expressed the whole, " your sacrifices are not pleasing to me." But, by the figure *Synathrœsmos*, all kinds of sacrifices are enumerated, and the sense is thus amplified and emphasized to show that, with all their outward show of "religion," there was no true worship of the spirit and heart.

So with the feasts, in verse 14, and with prayers, in verse 15.

The figure is used here to emphasize the fact that religious ordinances and services are nothing in themselves.

In the days of our Lord there was plenty of "religion": Isa. i. describes the abundance of it; but there was no heart in it. It was all form! and it was these very religious people (and not the rabble) who crucified the Lord!

Isa. iii. 16-23.—Here, the various ornaments of women are heaped together, to heighten the effect, and to emphasize the awful judgment of verses 24-iv. 1.

Rom. i. 29-31.—Here, many abominations of the heathen are enumerated to show what is the outcome of the "reprobate mind."

There are other figures in this passage. See under *Paronomasia*, *Ellipsis*, and *Asyndeton*.

It will be easy to recognize this figure whenever it is met with.

1 Tim. iv. 1-3.—Here, is an enumeration of the characters which will make the "latter times" so perilous. Also in

2 Tim. iii. 1-7, we have another enumeration.

1 Pet. iv. 3.—Here, are enumerated the things which characterize the condition of the Gentiles.

———————

EPITROCHASMOS; or, SUMMARISING.

A running lightly over by way of Summary.

When the enumeration called *Synathrœsmus* is made, not for the sake of amplifying, but only for the sake of abbreviating, by summarising, so as to hurry over what is being said (rather than for the sake of dwelling upon it), so as to pass on quickly to another subject, it is then called EPITROCHASMOS (*Ep'-i-tro-chas'-mos*), from ἐπί (*epi*), *upon* or *over,* and τροχάζειν (*trochazein*), *to run along quickly.* Hence *Epitrochasmus* means *a running lightly over.*

The Latins called it PERCURSIO, which means *a running through.*

In this connection, it is practically the same as *Asyndeton* (*q.v.*), where examples may be found. See Ex. xv. 9, 10.

Epitrochasmus is therefore a figure of *Omission ;* in that the conjunction " and " is omitted for the sake of running quickly through the enumeration ; and an omission of sense also, in that it abbreviates and summarises.

On the other hand it comes under the head of figures involving *addition* in that it at the same time certainly *amplifies* by a copious pouring forth of words.

Thus, while there is an actual addition of words, that very addition is for the purpose of avoiding a longer statement.

We have therefore mentioned this figure here in this division.

Heb. xi. 32 is an example ; where a number of persons are named or alluded to, but not dwelt upon.

DIEXODOS; or, EXPANSION.

A lengthening out by copious Exposition of Facts.

WHEN *Synathræsmos* is used of facts, etc., instead of single words or things, it is called DIEXODOS (*Di-ex'-od-os*), *a way out through*, from διά (*dia*), *through;* ἐξ (*ex*), *out of;* and ὁδός (*hodos*), *a way*.

The figure is employed when there is a copious statement or exposition of facts, not so much for the purpose of amplification, or of abbreviation, as of *digression*. Indeed, it is the opposite of *Syntomia :* which means a *cutting off short, abridgment :* whereas *Diexodos* is *a lengthening out* by a digression in order to expand.

See 2 Pet. ii. 13, 15, 17. Jude 12, 13, 16, etc.

EPITHETON ; or, EPITHET.

A Naming of a Thing by describing it.

E-pith¹-e-ton. Greek, ἐπίθετον, from ἐπίθετος (*epithetos*), *placed upon*, or *added*. The figure is so-called when an adjective or noun is used, which adds to the sense of the thing spoken of by simply holding forth some attribute, character, or quality descriptive of it. The adjective or the noun used for it by *Enallage* (*q.v.*) is thus placed in *apposition* to it for the purpose of amplification by way of distinction, explanation, or description.

Hence it was called by the Latins APPOSITUM, and is so put by *apposition*.

When the *epithet* is continued and used, after the reason for its being given has ceased, it is then called *Ampliatio* (*q.v.*). Most of the examples will be found under that name. An *Ampliatio* is a *change* ; an *Epitheton* is an *addition*.

Gen. xxi. 16.—" And she (Hagar) went, and sat her down over against him, a good way off, as it were a bowshot " : the bowshot being an *Epithet* for a certain distance.

Ex. xxv. 25 ; xxxvii. 12. 1 Kings vii. 26. 2 Chron. iv. 5. Ps. xxxix. 5. Ezek. xl. 5.—An hand-breadth is used as an *Epithet* for a certain thickness.

Num. xxiv. 20.—" And when he looked on Amalek, he took up his parable, and said,

> Amalek was the first of the nations,
> But his latter end *shall be* that he perish for ever."

The last phrase " he perish " is an *epithet*, the result of the war which Jehovah would wage with him. The marginal reading shows the difficulty felt by the translators. Literally it is

> " The first of the nations is Amalek,
> And his end—for ever he perisheth" : *i.e.*,

> " The first of the nations is Amalek,
> And his end is destruction."

For Amalek was the first who fought against Israel (Ex. xvii. 8), and Jehovah will fight against Amalek to the end (Ex. xvii. 16).

We may compare Amos vi. 1.

Judges xx. 16.—A " hair-breadth " is used as an *epithet* of a minute width. See *Hyperbole*.

John xvii. 3.—" That they might know thee, the only true God."
Here " true " is not a mere adjective qualifying God, but is an epithet :
" That they might know Thee—God, the only God, the true (or very)
God." So 1 John v. 20. 1 Thess. i. 9.

Such epithets are used of God, not to qualify but to distinguish
Him from them who are no gods. See Gal. iv. 8. 1 Cor. viii. 5, 6.

Luke xxii. 41.—A " stone's-throw " is used as an epithet of a
certain distance.

1 Pet. iv. 3.—" Abominable idolatries "—abominable things : *i.e.*,
the worship of idols.

SYNTHETON; or, COMBINATION.

A placing together of two Words by Usage.

Syn'-the-ton. Greek, σύνθετον, from σύν (*sun*), *together*, and τιθέναι (*tithenai*), *to place.* Hence, σύνθετος (*synthetos*) means *put together*.

It is used of this Figure because two words are by common usage joined by a conjunction for the sake of emphasis, as when we say "time and tide," "end and aim," "rank and fortune."

It differs from *Synthesis* (*q.v.*). And also from *Hendiadys*, where only *one* thing is meant, though two are used (see *Hendiadys*).

Gen. xviii. 27.—"Dust and ashes."

Ps. cxv. 13.—"Small and great."

Acts vii. 22.—Moses was "mighty in words and in deeds."

There are many examples where certain words thus become linked together by usage : *e.g.*, "rich and poor," "old and young," "bread and wine," "meat and drink," "babes and sucklings," "sins and iniquities," "faith and works," "God and man," "thoughts and deeds," etc., etc.

The opposite of this Figure is *Hendiadys* (*q.v.*), by which, though two words are used, only one thing is meant.

Here, in *Syntheton*, much more is meant than is expressed and embraced by the conjunction of the two words.

HORISMOS; or, DEFINITION.

A Definition of Terms.

Hor-is'-mos. Greek, ὁρισμός (*horismos*), *a boundary*, from ὁρίζω (*horizo*), to *divide, mark out, settle, define.* Hence, it is called DEFINITIO, *definition.*

It is the figure by which the meaning of terms is defined and fixed, briefly and precisely: *the definition of terms,* so important in all kinds of argumentation.

3. DESCRIPTIO.

By way of Description.

In this division the addition to the sense is made by giving a description of a person, place, time, thing, or action. Hence, the term *Descriptio* is applied to some eleven different forms which the Description takes according to its nature or character. The first is

HYPOTYPOSIS ; or, WORD-PICTURE.

Visible Representation of Objects or Actions by Words.

Hy¹-po-ty-po¹-sis. Greek, ὑποτύπωσις, from ὑποτυποῦν (*hypotypoun*), *to sketch out ;* from ὑπό (*hypo*), *under*, and τυποῦν (*typoun*), *to impress ;* and this from τύπος (*typos*), *impression.* It occurs twice in the New Testament (1 Tim. i. 16 and 2 Tim. i. 13). In the plural it would express what we call " outlines."

The name is given to this figure because it describes an action, event, person, condition, passion, etc., in a lively and forcible manner, giving a vivid representation of it.

In Latin, therefore, the name is REPRÆSENTATIO, *representation*, and ADUMBRATIO, *a shadowing out* or *a sketching out* in words.

Other Greek names of this figure are DIATYPOSIS (*di¹-a-ty-po¹-sis*), from διά (*dia*), *through*, and τυποῦν (*typoun*), *to impress.* The verb meaning *to form thoroughly, to give a thorough form.*

ENARGEIA, ἐνάργεια (*en-ar-gei-a*), *vivid description, visible representation* (*in words*).

PHANTASIA, φαντασία (*phan-ta¹-si-a*), *a making visible, a presentation of objects to the mind.*

ICON (εἰκών, *eikōn*), *an image, figure, likeness ;* and Latin IMAGO, *an imitation, copy,* or *picture*, but especially *a statue*, visibly presenting the object to the eye or mind.

EICASIA. Greek, εἰκασία (*ei-ca¹-si-a*), *a likeness,* or *image*, from εἰκάζω (*eikazo*), *to make like to, represent by a likeness.*

Thus the nature of this figure is quite clear from the various names given to it. *Hypotyposis* is employed whenever anything is so described as to present it forcibly and vividly to the mind.

There are many examples in Scripture : but it is not necessary to transcribe whole passages, and in some cases whole chapters, in full.

Examples may be classified, in which things are thus vividly presented to the eye, and so described as to seem very real.

(1) The blessings on the obedience of Israel (Deut. xxviii. 1-14).

(2) The curses and the judgments (Deut. xxviii. 15-45. Isa. i. 6-9; xxxiv. Jer. iv. 19-31). The greater part of Lamentations (esp., iv. 4-8).

(3) The captivity and scattering of Israel (Deut. xxviii. 49-68).

(4) The executioners of God's judgments (Isa. v. 26-30).

(5) The hollowness of mere religion, such as existed when Christ was on earth (Isa. i. 11-15).

(6) The folly of idolators and idols and idolatry (Isa. xliv. 9-17; xlvi. 6, 7).

(7) The sufferings of Christ (Ps. xxii.; lix. Isa. liii).

(8) The glory and triumph of Christ (Col. ii. 14, 15, etc.).

(9) Certain similitudes: as when the blessings of Christ's coming are compared to the rising sun (Mal. iv. 2), or a warrior (Rev. xix. 11-16); or when God is compared to a wine-refreshed giant when He arises to avenge His people (Ps. lxxviii. 65, 66); or when the godly remnant of Israel is compared to a Bride (Ps. xlv.); or when the prosperity of the wicked is likened to a green bay-tree (Ps. xxxvii. 35); and that of the righteous to the palm and the cedar (Ps. xcii. 12-14).

PROSOPOGRAPHIA ; or, DESCRIPTION OF PERSONS.

Pros'-ō-po-graph'-i-a, from πρόσωπον (*pros'-ō-pon*), *a face, one's look*, or *countenance*, and later, *a person*; and γράφειν (*graphein*), *to write*, or *describe*. Hence *Prosopographia* is a vivid description of a person by delineating the general mien, dress manners, etc.

Called by the Latins PERSONÆ DESCRIPTIO, *description of a person*.

See Matt. iii. 4, where John's appearance, etc., is described.

See also the graphic description of the Lord, after the execution of His judgments in the day of His vengeance (Isa. lxiii. 1-6). (Compare, for the interpretation of the passage, Isa. xxxiv. 8 ; lxi. 2).

Also the description of Jerusalem compared with a person when she was caused "to know her abominations" (Ezek. xvi. 4-26).

When the description is confined to the *personal appearance*, or features, it is called

EFFICTIO; or, WORD-PORTRAIT.

Ef-fic'-ti-o, from Latin, *effingo, to form, fashion artistically, to portray.* Hence, the name is given to the figure when a portrait is given in words, and the features, etc., are delineated and described.

When the description is confined to the *character*, morals, of a person, it is called

CHARACTERISMOS; or, DESCRIPTION OF CHARACTER.

Char'-ac-ter-is'-mos.   Greek, χαρακτηρισμός (*characteerismos*), *designation by a characteristic mark.*   Hence, the name is given to the figure which gives a description of the character or morals of a person.

When the description is confined to *manners*, it is called

ETHOPŒIA ; or, DESCRIPTION OF MANNERS.

Ēth'-o-pœ'-i-a. Greek, ἠθοποιΐα (*eethopœïa*), *expression of manner or custom;* hence, used of a description of a person's peculiarities as to manners, caprices, habits, whether in voice, gestures, or otherwise.

Called by the Latins NOTATIO, *a marking* or *noting.* Hence, a description of any manner or custom, etc., that a person is peculiarly noted for.

Called also MORUM EXPRESSIO.

Isa. iii. 16.—"The daughters of Zion are haughty, and walk with stretched forth necks, and wanton eyes, walking and mincing as they go, and making a tinkling with their feet."

See also Jer. xlviii. 3-46; and Luke xviii. 9-14, where the Pharisee and the Publican are described by their manner, gesture, etc.

In 1 Pet. iii. 3, where women are exhorted to show the disposition of mind by avoiding the outward costume which is described.

When the description or expression is confined to the *feelings* it is called

PATHOPŒIA; or, DESCRIPTION OF FEELINGS.

Path'-o-pœ'-i-a. Greek, παθοποιΐα, from πάθος, *feeling*, and ποιεῖν (*poiein*), *to make.* Hence, the figure is so named, when the feelings and affections are described or expressed.

For examples, see Isa. xxii. 4; xlix. 15. Jer. ix. 1, 2; xxiii. 9; xxxi. 20. Hos. xi. 7-9. Mark iii. 5; vi. 32; vii. 34; x. 14, 21. Luke xix. 41. 2 Cor. ii. 4. Gal. iv. 19, 20.

We have included this figure here, and also under those involving change, because sometimes this description is given by way of additional information, and sometimes it is given instead of naming or otherwise indicating the person or thing spoken of.

The reader must distinguish these examples himself.

When the description is confined to *sayings*, it is called

MIMESIS; or, DESCRIPTION OF SAYINGS.

Mi-mee-sis, from the Greek μίμησις (*mi-mee-sis*), *imitation,* from μιμεῖσθαι (*mimeisthai*), *to imitate.*

The name is used when the *sayings* (and sometimes motions and thoughts) of another are described or imitated by way of emphasis.

Hence called by the Latins IMITATIO, *imitation.*

See Ex. xv. 9 (see *Asyndeton*). Ps. cxxxvii. 7; cxliv. 12-15 (see *Ellipsis*). Isa. xiv. 13, 14; xxviii. 15. Hos. xiv. 2, 3. Ezek. xxxvi. 2. Micah ii. 11; iii. 11.

So also 1 Cor. xv. 35, and Phil. iii. 4, 5.

Sometimes there is a use of a word which another is wont to use, and which is repeated so as delicately, but yet acutely, to direct him aright. As in 2 Cor. x. 1, 10; and Gal. vi. 2.

———

PRAGMATOGRAPHIA ; or, DESCRIPTION OF ACTIONS.

Prag'-mat-o-graph'-i-a, from πρᾶγμα (*pragma*), *an action* or *event*, and γράφειν (*graphein*), *to write* : *i.e.*, *a description of an action or event*. Hence, called by the Latins, REI AUT ACTIONIS DESCRIPTIO.

See Joel ii. 1-11, where the description of the actions connected with the great people and strong which should come upon Zion is minutely and graphically given.

Matt. xxiv. and Mark xiii. describe the events of the Great Tribulation ; and Luke xxi. 12, etc., the events which should long precede it.

See also some minute touches, especially in the Gospel of Mark : *e.g.*, viii. 33 ; and Acts vi. 15 ; vii. 55, 56.

When the description is confined to *places*, it is called

TOPOGRAPHIA ; or, DESCRIPTION OF PLACE.

Top'-o-graph'i-a, from τόπος (*top'-os*), *a place*, and γράφειν (*graphein*), *to write* or *describe*.

Hence it is used of the figure which adds something to what is said by describing a place; or any peculiarity which marks the place, and throws light on what is being treated of.

Called by the Latins LOCI DESCRIPTIO.

Topographia is such a description of a place as exhibits it to our view ; as the description of *Sheol*, Isa. xiv. 9-12 ; xxx. 33 :

The new Heaven and Earth, Isa. lxv. 17, etc.; Rev. xxi. 1, etc.:

The future glory of Jerusalem and the Land, Isa. xxxiii. 20, 21; xxxv. 6-10. Ps. xlvi. 5, 6 ; lx. 6-9.

In Ps. lxxxix. 12, the description shows that the points of the compass are always* reckoned with reference to Jerusalem, " The north and the south thou hast created them : Tabor (in the west) and Hermon (in the east) shall rejoice in thy name."

Thus the description of these places completes the four points of the compass.

The names of the places in Isa. x. 28-32 give us the course of the invasion of the land by the King of Assyria.

The " Sea " is frequently mentioned by way of description to show that the *West* is intended : the Mediterranean being on the West of the Land. See Num. ii. 18 (Heb.). Josh. xvi. 5, 6. Ezek. xlii. 19 (Heb.).

In Ps. cvii. 3, however, the Sea evidently denotes the Red Sea, and though the word " sea" is in the Hebrew, it is rendered " South." The emphasis put upon the wonderful Exodus is thus quietly but very powerfully introduced : " And gathered them out of the lands, from the east, and from the west, from the north, and from the sea ! " because the deliverance from Egypt was through the sea.

In Ps. lxxii. 8, "from sea to sea " means from the Mediterranean to the Red Sea and the Persian Gulf. Compare Ex. xxiii. 31.

Sometimes a description of place is added and thrown in to convey a lesson, *e.g.*, John vi. 10, " Now there was much grass in the place." Acts viii. 26, "Which is desert," to show that it mattered

---

* Excepting perhaps parts of Ezekiel written in Babylon.

not to the true servant whether he ministered in a city (verse 5), and gave joy to crowds of people (verse 8), or whether he ministered to one soul in the desert (verse 26).

See also Isa. lxv. 17-25. Joel ii. 3. Luke xvi. 24-26. John xi. 18.

When the description is confined to *time*, it is called

CHRONOGRAPHIA ; or, DESCRIPTION OF TIME.

Chron'-o-graph'-i-a, from χρόνος (*chronos*), *time*, and γράφειν (*graphein*), *to write*. It is called by the Latins, TEMPORIS DESCRIPTIO, a description of the time.

The Figure is used, when, by the addition of the time, something explanatory is given which helps to the understanding of what is said; or, supplies some important fact; or, implies some extra lesson.

All such expressions, as "then" or "at that time," should be noticed; and attention should be directed to the time to see when it was, and why the particular time should have been thus described or referred to. See'

Matt. xi. 25, 26.—"At that time Jesus answered and said, I thank thee, O Father, Lord of heaven and earth, because thou hast hid these things from the wise and prudent, and hast revealed them unto babes. Even so Father: for so it seemed good in thy sight."

Why is this specially marked by the words "at that time"? Because it was the time when John the Baptist questioned Him (xi. 2-6); when the people are rebuked for having said that John had a devil, and Christ was a glutton and drunkard (16-19); when the cities, in which most of His mighty works were done, repented not, and had their "woe" pronounced (20-24). "At that time," Jesus said, "Even so, Father: for so it seemed good in thy sight." In other words, He found *rest* "at that time," in the hour of what man would call disappointment and failure, in the Father's will. And then, He turns to His weary and heavy-laden servants, and invites them to come and find their rest where He found His; and thus to wear His yoke, and find His rest. (See this passage under other Figures: *viz.*, *Synecdoche, Catachresis, Idiom*, and *Parechesis*.)

John x. 22.—"And it was winter." This brief description of time, is intended to convey to us a sense of the humiliation and rejection of the Lord Jesus. The next verse tells how He "walked in Solomon's porch," on the bleak summit of Mount Moriah, to keep Himself warm; no one asking Him to house or inviting Him even into such of the Temple chambers as had fires in them.

We may compare John xviii. 18.

See also Mark vi. 48. Acts ii. 15; x. 3, 9, etc.

When the description is confined to the *circumstances*, it is called

PERISTASIS ; or, DESCRIPTION OF CIRCUMSTANCES.

Per-is'-ta-sis', from the Greek περίστασις, *anything that is round about, circumstances*; and this from περι (*peri*), *around*, and στάσις (*stasis*), *a standing, setting,* or *placing*.

Peristasis is the name of the figure which describes the circumstances ; and hence, it was called by the Latins, CIRCUMSTANTIÆ DESCRIPTIO.

See John iv. 6 ; xviii. 18, etc.

When this figure is used for the purpose of moving the passions by a graphic description of circumstances, it is·called

DIASKEUE.

Di-as-keu'-ee' (διασκευή), from διασκευάζεσθαι (*diaskeuazesthai*), *to arm, equip,* or *prepare oneself*: the argument being made out of the particular circumstances of a case.

When the description is confined to the *order* of certain persons, things, events, or circumstances, it is called

PROTIMESIS; or, DESCRIPTION OF ORDER.

Pro'-ti-mee'-sis (προτίμησις), *a putting of one thing before another :* from πρό (*pro*), *before*, and τιμή (*timee*), *honour*. Hence, the figure is employed when things are enumerated according to their places of honour or importance, using the particles "*first,*" "*again,*" "*then,*" or "*firstly,*" "*secondly,*" "*thirdly,*" etc.

This figure, therefore, increases the emphasis of a particular statement by setting forth the *order* in which the things treated of stand, or take place.

I Cor. xv. 5-8.—Speaking of the resurrection of Christ, it is written : ".He was seen of Cephas ; **then** of the twelve: **after that,** he was seen of above five hundred brethren at once: . . . **after that,** he was seen of James ; **then** of all the apostles : and, **last of all** he was seen of me also, as of one born out of due time."

In like manner we have the same words employed of the resurrection of "those who are Christ's " :

I Cor. xv. 22-24, where, after saying that, as all who are in Adam die, even so all who are in (*the*) Christ will be made alive (see *Synecdoche*), "but every man in his own order (or rank).

"Christ the **first-fruits** ;

"**Afterward** they that are Christ's at His coming.

"**Then** *cometh* the end"; or, "then, τὸ τέλος, the end" or the last final rank of this great army of raised people. So that there is no such thing as what is called a "general resurrection"; for as nearly nineteen hundred years have elapsed between the "first-fruits" and "them that are Christ's," so there will be a thousand years between then and the last or second resurrection (Rev. xx. 1-6). See page 87, under *Ellipsis*.

I Thess. iv. 15-17.—Here, we have the order of events at the coming forth of Christ into the air to receive His people unto Himself, before His coming unto the earth with them.

This new revelation was given to the apostle "by the word of the Lord," and contains facts not before made known.

The resurrection, here revealed, is altogether different in time and order from the "first" and "second" resurrections in 1 Cor. xv. 22-24 and Rev. xx. 1-6. These were never a secret, but known, and referred to in the Old Testament Scriptures (Dan. xii. 1, 2. Ps. xlix. 14 (15), etc.), as well as in the Gospels (John v. 28, 29, etc.). This resurrection takes its place with that which is told as a secret in 1 Cor. xv. 51-57 : "Behold, I show you a mystery" : *i.e.*, "Behold, I tell you a secret."

So, here, it is revealed that " we which are alive and remain unto the coming of the Lord shall not prevent (*i.e.*, precede) them which are asleep. For the Lord Himself shall descend from heaven with a shout, with the voice of the archangel, and with the trump of God ; and the dead in Christ shall rise *first*: then, we which are alive and remain shall be caught up together with them in the clouds, to meet the Lord in the air: and so (*i.e.*, thus, in this manner) shall we ever be with the Lord."

4. CONCLUSIO.

By way of Conclusion.

THIS figure is the addition of a short sentence at the end of a paragraph or statement, for various purposes: either by way of moral, deduction, approbation, apology, or reflection, etc. Different names are given to it, according to the purpose for which it is employed.

The sense being complete without it, the figure comes under the head of an *addition*.

EPICRISIS; or, JUDGMENT.

Addition of Conclusion by way of Deduction.

Ep'-i-cri'-sis, from the Greek ἐπὶ (*epi*), *upon*, and κρίσις (*krisis*), *a judgment sentence*. Hence *Epicrisis* is used as an *adjudication*.

It is a short sentence added at the end by way of an additional conclusion, other and more than has been already stated: not necessary to the sense of it, but as showing that there is something more and something deeper than what lies on the surface.

It notes a cause or a consequence arising from the place, occasion, end, or effect, of things, actions, or speeches.

A few examples will explain better the use of this figure.

John i. 24.—The sentence, "And they which were sent were of the Pharisees," is added to remind us of the fact that the Pharisees made a great point of Baptism; which compelled them therefore to acknowledge the baptism of John to be a matter of great importance.

John i. 28.—"These things were done in Bethabara beyond Jordan, where John was baptizing."

This is to explain that the people had come a long way.

John iii. 24.—"For John was not yet cast into prison."

This is why John had not ceased to baptize.

John v. 39, 40.—Here we have in two verses a double *Epicrisis*, the first approving, and the second condemning, but both adding a solemn truth, independent of the statement that goes before.

A | "Search the Scriptures;
    B | For in them ye think ye have eternal life.
A | And they are they which testify of me:
    B | And ye will not come to me, that ye might have life."

The structure agrees also with this. It is thus exhibited in four members.

In the first and third members (A and *A*), we have the Scriptures; while in the second and fourth (B and *B*, the *Epicrisis*), we have the action and the conduct of those who possessed them.

Note that the verb "search" is imperative, and not indicative, as we never find the verb in the indicative commencing a sentence without the pronoun or some other word; while the imperative is frequently so used. See John xiv. 11; xv. 20. The Jews *read*, but they did not "search."

The verb "think" also means *to hold as an opinion, believe* (see Acts xv. 28. 1 Cor. iv. 9; vii. 40, etc.).

John vi. 4.—"And the passover, a feast of the Jews, was nigh." This is added to explain how it was that so many were going out of the country up to Jerusalem before the Passover in order to purify themselves.

John vii. 5.—"For neither did his brethren believe in him." This solemn addition explains a great deal: especially Mark iii.; from which it is clear, by comparing verses 21 and 31, that His mother and brethren set out to lay hands on Him, bringing on themselves the rebuke of verses 32-35. See under *Correspondence* (page 384).

John viii. 20. – "These words spake Jesus in the treasury, as he taught in the Temple: and no man laid hands on him; for his hour was not yet come."

This *Epicrisis* is used to show how easily (humanly speaking) He might have been taken where there were so many people assembled.

John viii. 27.—"They understood not that he spake unto them of the Father."

By means of this additional explanatory conclusion, we are made astonished at the unbelief and blindness of the Jews. See xii. 37.

John ix. 14.—"And it was the sabbath day when Jesus made the clay, and opened his eyes."

The *Epicrisis* here explains much concerning the events recorded in this chapter.

John ix. 22.—"These words spake his parents, because they feared the Jews:" etc.

This is added to explain the action of the parents of the man born blind.

John x. 22, 23.—" And it was at Jerusalem the feast of the dedication, and it was. winter, and Jesus walked in the temple, in Solomon's Porch."

This is added to show that Christ happened to be at that feast, and that he had not gone up to it as to the other feasts. After He had accomplished His journey to the feast of Tabernacles (vii. 8), He made a delay there, so as to remain over the feast of Dedication. (For this feast, see 1 Macc. iv. 59). See page 455.

John xi. 13.—" Howbeit Jesus spake of his death : but they thought that he had spoken of taking of rest in sleep."

This *Epicrisis* is used to explain the meaning of what the Lord Jesus had said.

John xi. 30.—" Now Jesus was not yet come into the town, but was in that place where Martha met him."

This explanation is needed to enable us to understand the course of events.

John xii. 33.—" This he said, signifying what death he should die."

John xii. 37.—" But though he had done so many miracles before them, yet they believed not on him."

Acts xix. 20. — " So mightily grew the word of God and prevailed."

1 John iii. 1.—After the words " sons of God," the best Texts with R.V. add καὶ ἐσμεν (*kai esmen*), *and we are ;* or, *and such we are.* This is a short parenthetical reflective comment. Compare i. 2.

EPITASIS; or, AMPLIFICATION.

Addition of Conclusion by way of Emphasis.

E-pit'-a-sis (ἐπίτασις), *a stretching,* from ἐπί (*epi*), *upon,* and τείνειν (*teinein*), *to stretch* or *extend.*

The Figure is used when a concluding sentence is added by way of increasing the emphasis. It is not independent of what has gone before, but it is some emphatic increase added to it by way of conclusion.

The Latins called it INTENTIO, which means the same thing, *a straining,* or *tension ; increase,* or *augmentation.*

The difference between this figure and the figure of *Amplification* is that it comes by way of *Conclusion.*

Ex. iii. 19.—"And I am sure that the king of Egypt will not let you go, no, not by a mighty hand."

Mark x. 43, 44.—In verse 43, "Whosoever will be great among you, shall be your minister (or servant)."

And in the next verse the meaning is the same, but the *Epitasis* is added, " of all ":—"Whosoever will be the chiefest, shall be the servant of all."

John xiii. 34.—"A new commandment I give unto you, That ye love one another—(then the *Epitasis* is added)—as I have loved you, that ye also love one another."

Acts vii. 5.—"And he gave him none inheritance in it, no, not so much as to set his foot on."

Rom. xiii. 1.—"The powers that be are ordained of God." This is an *Epitasis* to explain and augment the force of the previous enunciation.

2 Cor. iii. : where verse 6 is an *Epitasis* to verse 5, explaining and emphasizing what has been before said.

ANESIS; or, ABATING.

Addition of Conclusion by way of lessening the Effect.

An'-e-sis (ἄνεσις), *a loosening, relaxing, abating.* This is the opposite of *Epitasis;* the addition of a concluding sentence which *diminishes* the effect of what has been said.

2 Kings v. 1.—"Now Naaman, captain of the host of the king of Syria, was a great man with his master, and honourable, because by him the Lord had given deliverance unto Syria : he was also a mighty man of valour, **but he was a leper**": and therefore all his grandeur and importance counted for nothing.

EPIPHONEMA; or, EXCLAMATION.

Addition of Conclusion by way of Exclamation.

Ep'-i-phō-nee'-ma (ἐπιφώνημα), from ἐπί (*epi*), *upon*, and φωνεῖν (*phōnein*), *to speak*. Hence, *something uttered besides;* an *exclamation* at the *conclusion of a sentence*.

When the exclamation occurs as an independent separate passage, then it is called *Ecphonesis* or *Exclamatio* (*q.v.*), and does not come under this division as a mere *addition* of words; but rather under their *application* as an expression of feeling. See *Ecphonesis*.

And note, further, that, when the exclamation is thrown in parenthetically, it is called *Interjectio* (*q.v.*).

Epiphonema is called also DEINOSIS when it is very brief and emphatic, from δείνωσις, an *enhancing, exaggerating*.

Judges v. 31.—" So let all thine enemies perish, O LORD."

Ps. ii. 12.—"Blessed are all they that put their trust in him."

Ps. iii. 8.—"Salvation belongeth unto the LORD. Thy blessing is upon Thy people."

Ps. xiv. 7.—At the conclusion of the Psalm, this exclamation is added: " Oh, that the salvation of Israel were come out of Zion!" etc. See under *Paronomasia* and *Metonomy*.

Ps. cxxxiv. 21.—" Praise ye the LORD " : *i.e.*, Hallelujah, coming at the end of this and other Psalms, is an *Epiphonema*.

Jonah ii. 9.—"Salvation is of the LORD."

Matt. xi. 15.—" He that hath ears to hear, let him hear." Also in all the sixteen occurrences of this *Epiphonema*. (See under *Polyptoton*).

Matt. xvii. 5.—"This is my beloved Son, in whom I am well pleased." And, then, the beautiful *Epiphonema* is added, " Hear ye Him" as an appended exhortation.

Matt. xx. 16.—" For many are called, but few are chosen." See also xxii. 14.

Matt. xxiv. 28.—" For wheresoever the carcase is, there will the eagles be gathered together." See under *Parœmia*.

Rev. xxii. 20 is a beautiful *Epiphonema*, not only to the chapter and the book, but to the whole Bible : " Even so, come, Lord Jesus."

PROECTHESIS; or, JUSTIFICATION.

Addition of Conclusion by way of Justification.

Pro-ec¹-the-sis (προέκθεσις), from πρό (*pro*), *before*, and ἔκθεσις (*ekthesis*), *a setting out by way of conclusion*, from ἐκτίθημι (*ektitheemi*), *to set out.* A conclusion from what has been before set out or put forth.

The figure is employed when a sentence is added at the end by way of justification. It is a conclusion by way of adding a justifying reason for what has been said.

Matt. ix. 13.—" I will have mercy, and not sacrifice : for I am not come to call the righteous, but sinners to repentance."

Matt. xii. 12.—" How much then is a man better than a sheep ? Wherefore it is lawful to do well on the sabbath days."

EPITHERAPEIA; or, QUALIFICATION.

Addition of Conclusion by way of Modification.

Ep¹-i-ther-a-pei¹a, from ἐπί (*epi*), *upon*, and θεραπεία (*therapei¹-a*), *a waiting on*, especially of medical *attendance*, from θεραπεύειν (*therapeuein*), *to serve as an attendant, to tend*, especially medically.

Hence, the compound *Epitherapeia* is used of *applying an additional remedy.* And the figure is employed when a sentence is added at the end, *to heal, soften, mitigate,* or *modify* what has been before said, so that modesty or other feeling might not be offended or injured. It may be added by way of apology.

But where this is added *beforehand*, to secure indulgence, it is called *Protherapeia* (*q.v.*); and where this is done to prepare for a shock it is called *Prodiorthosis* (*q.v.*).

Matt. xxvi. 40, 41.—" What, could not ye watch with me one hour ? Watch and pray, that ye enter not into temptation : **the spirit indeed is willing, but the flesh is weak."**

Phil. iv. 10.—" I rejoiced in the Lord greatly, that now, at the last, your care of me hath flourished again ; wherein ye were careful also, **but ye lacked opportunity."**

When what has been said concludes with an *example*, it is called

EXEMPLUM; or, EXAMPLE.

Addition of Conclusion by way of Example.

THIS is not the same as using examples in the course of argument. We do this latter when in any reasoning we adduce one known object or thing as a sample of another in respect to some particular point.

Exemplum, on the other hand, is when we conclude a sentence by employing an *example* as a precedent to be followed or avoided :—

Luke xvii. 31, 32.—"In that day, he which shall be upon the house top, and his stuff in the house, let him not come down to take it away; and he that is in the field, let him likewise not return back. **Remember Lot's wife.**"

SYMPERASMA; or,
CONCLUDING SUMMARY.

Addition of Conclusion by way of a brief Summary.

Sym¹-per-as¹-ma (συμπέρασμα), *a finishing* or *end.* In logic it is the conclusion of a syllogism. It is from σύν (*sun*), *together with*, and περαιόω (*peraioō*), *to carry over* or *across*.

Hence, *Symperasma* means *to conclude along with, to end together*, and is used when what has been said is briefly summed up, and when certain foregoing enumerations are given in a brief epitome.

It is called also ATHRŒSMOS (*a-thrœs¹-mos*), from ἀθροίζω (*athroizō*), *to collect* or *gather together*.

It differs from *Synathrœsmus* (*q.v.*) in that it is used at the end and as the conclusion of what has been before said, and not in the course, and as part of the statement.

Matt. i. 17.—Here, in this one verse, is given a brief summary of the preceding sixteen verses.

John xx. 30.—Here is a brief reference to much that is not contained in the whole Gospel.

Heb. xi. 39.—Here, after having enumerated a number of persons, and of facts concerning them, one brief sentence includes and is true of them all: "And these all, having obtained a good report through faith, received not the promise."

5. INTERPOSITIO.

By way of Interposition.

THIS figure is the addition of a sentence, not at the end, but in the midst of another sentence, which has no *grammatical* connection with what precedes or follows. It has a close connection with it, but it may or may not be necessary to the *sense*.

The current of the language is interrupted by the interposition of another sentence, which requires to be considered separately. There may, however, be more than one such sentence interposed.

These interpositions are of various kinds, according to their nature, and to the object in view.

Sometimes the interposition requires the leading word to be repeated after it : such repetition is called *Apostasis* (see under *Epanalepsis*).

Sometimes it is not put down at all till after the interposition.

In the structure of a passage, (see under *Correspondence*), the various members are more or less parenthetical with relation to those that precede and follow.

For example, in an alternate structure such as the first and second chapters of the Epistle to the Hebrews :—

> A | Heb. i. 1, 2.
> B | Heb. i. 2-14.
> *A* | Heb. ii. 1-4.
> *B* | Heb. ii. 5-18.

B is parenthetical with reference to A and *A*, while *A* is parenthetical with reference to B and *B* : *A* reading on in continuation of A ; and *B* the same with reference to B.

So also in an introverted structure :

> A | ——
> B | ——
> C | ——
> *C* | ——
> *B* | ——
> *A* | ——

The whole of B, C, *C*, and *B* are parenthetical with relation to A and *A* ; while C and *C* are the same with reference to B and *B*.

The observation of this is often necessary to the true understanding and indeed the interpretation of many passages of Scripture.

But these are not true interpositions, and do not come under the class of figures called INTERPOSITIO.

They are not always marked, either in the Greek Text or in the translations. Modern editors of the Greek Text mark them sometimes by commas, and sometimes by colons.

The translators have sometimes indicated them by the use of the curved lines (——), or by dashes — and —, or simply by commas. But there are many more beside those that are thus pointed out.

PARENTHESIS.

Parenthetic Addition, by way of Explanation : Complete in Itself.

Pa-ren¹-the-sis, παρένθεσις, from παρά (*para*), *beside,* and ἐντιθέναι (*entithenai*), *to put* or *place in.*

The figure is used when a word or sentence is inserted which is necessary to explain the context. As to grammar, the context is complete without it, but not as to clearness and sense.

A true Parenthesis is not complete without the context. When it is, it is called *Parembole.* (See below.)

Parentheses are for the most part indicated ; but there are others which are not marked.

Heb. ii. 9.—" But we see Jesus, who was made a little lower than the angels

(for the suffering of death crowned with glory and honour);

that He, by the grace of God, should taste death for every* man."

This shows that the Lord was made a little lower than the angels in order that He might die. And that he was crowned with glory and honour on account of His sufferings. †

2 Pet. i. 19.—" We have also a more sure word of prophecy ; whereunto ye do well that ye take heed (as unto a light that shineth in a dark place, until the day dawn, and the day-star arise) in your hearts."

Here, it is clear that there must be a *parenthesis,* for it is prophecy that is the light that shines, and Christ and His appearing are the Day-star and the Day-dawn. Surely, the meaning cannot be that we are exhorted to take heed to the prophetic word until Christ is revealed

-----

* *I.e.,* without *distinction,* not without exception.

† See *Christ's Prophetic Teaching,* by the same author and publisher.

in our hearts! No; but we are to take heed in our hearts to this prophetic word, until the fulfilment comes in the appearing of Christ—the rising of Him who is called "the Morning Star." See under *Ellipsis*, page 92.

When the interposed sentence is thrown in by way of remark, it is called

EPITRECHON ; or, RUNNING ALONG.

Parenthetic Addition by way of Statement thrown in, not complete in itself.

Ep'-i-tre-chon, from ἐπί (*epi*), upon, and τρέχειν (*trechein*), to run : *to run over* or *along, to overrun*.

The figure is so-called because the sentence, more or less short, is rapidly thrown in as an explanatory remark.

SUBCONTINUATIO is the name given to it by the Latins; because sentences thus thrown in, by the way, as a kind of undercurrent, continue one thought or statement underneath another, or follow another immediately after.

Gen. xv. 13.—" Know of a surety that thy seed* shall be a stranger in a land that is not theirs
    (and shall serve them ; and they shall afflict them ;)
four hundred years."

The *Epitrechon*, like a true Parenthesis, is the result of Structure, or Correspondence :

  a | " Know of a surety that thy seed shall be a stranger in a
     | land that is not theirs :

    b | and shall serve them ;

    b | and they shall afflict them ;

  a | four hundred years."

Here in " a " and " a " we have the whole sojourn, while in ' b " and " b " we have the servitude in Egypt.

Gen. xlvi. 26.—" All the souls that came with Jacob into Egypt
    (which came out of his loins)
besides Jacob's sons wives, all the souls were three-score and six.

This *Epitrechon* points us to the difference between the enumeration here (66) and Acts vii. 14, where it is 75 souls, because it there includes " all his kindred."

Ex. xii. 40.—" Now the sojourning of the children of Israel
    (who dwelt in Egypt)
was four hundred and thirty years."

---

* *I.e.*, from the birth of Isaac, Abraham's " seed," not from the call of Abraham, as Ex. xii. 40.

It does not say (as most commentators read it) that they were or had been in Egypt 430 years. It was "the sojourning of the children of Israel" which continued during that time, while the *Epitrechon*, "who dwelt in Egypt," is a parenthetical interposition thrown in as a further explanation as to these children of Israel.

1 Kings viii. 39, 42.

Ps. lxviii. 18 (19) is a beautiful *Epitrechon.*

"Thou hast ascended on high,
Thou hast led captivity captive :
Thou hast received [*and given**] gifts for men,
(Yea, for the rebellious also),
That the LORD God might dwell among them."

How blessed and full of precious truth and teaching is the fact thus thrown in. Reaching out and stooping down to the most unworthy recipients of such divine gifts.

Matt. ix. 6.—" But that ye may know that the Son of Man hath power on earth to forgive sins,
(then saith he to the sick of the palsy)
Arise, take up thy bed, and go unto thine house."

John ii. 9.—" (but the servants which drew the water knew)."

John iv. 7-9.—" Jesus saith unto her, Give me to drink
(For his disciples were gone away into the city to buy meat).
Then saith the woman," etc.

Acts i. 15.—" And in those days Peter stood up in the midst of the disciples, and said
(the number of names together were about an hundred and twenty) :
Men and brethren," etc.

Rom. iii. 7, 8.—" Why yet am I also judged as a sinner ? And [*why*] not [*say*]
(as we be slanderously reported, and some affirm that we say) :
Let us do evil that good may come ? "

Rom. viii. 19-21.—This parenthesis is better shown by exhibiting the four alternate members :—

A | 19. Expectation.
   B | 20-. Reason. (Creation made subject).
A | -20. Expectation.
   B | 21. Reason. (Creation delivered).

---

* See *Ellipsis*, page 74.

See under *Ellipsis* (page 87), and note that the words "not willingly, but by reason of Him who hath subjected the same" are an *Epitrechon*, and the previous statement requires to be taken up— "[*waiteth, I say*] in hope."

Rom. ix. 2, 3.—"I have great heaviness and continual sorrow in my heart
  (for I used to wish, even I myself, to be accursed from Christ) for my brethren, my kinsmen according to the flesh."

The word ηὐχόμην (*eeuchomeen*) is by *Hyperbaton* (*q.v.*) put (out of its usual place) at the beginning of the sentence in order to attract our attention ; and, when we look further at it, we notice that it is in the imperfect tense, and is best as well as most correctly rendered : "I used to wish."

See under *Euche*, a figure so called on account of this very word, *eeuchomeen*.

Rom. x. 6, 7.—"Say not in thine heart, Who shall ascend into heaven ?
  (that is, to bring Christ down from above) ;
or, Who shall descend into the deep ?
  (that is, to bring up Christ again from the dead)."

Eph. ii. 5 "(by grace ye are saved)."

Col. ii. 21, 22 is an important *Epitrechon*, which writes folly on all the attempts to improve the old nature, by vows and pledges and badges.

Heb. xii. 20, 21.

CATAPLOCE ; or,
SUDDEN EXCLAMATION.

Parenthetic Addition by Way of Exclamation.

Cat¹-a-plok¹-ee (καταπλοκή), *from* κατά (*kata*), *down*, and πλοκή (*plokee*), *a twining* or *plaiting.* The figure is so called because the short sentence so interposed is intertwined with another. This name is given to a parenthesis when it takes the form of a sudden exclamation.

Ezek. xvi. 23, 24.— "And it came to pass after all thy wickedness

(woe, woe unto thee ! saith Adonai-Jehovah)

That thou hast also built unto thee," etc.

Rom. ix. 2, 3.—This is a kind of *Cataploce* as well as *Epitrechon* (see page 428), and *Euche.*

PAREMBOLE; or, INSERTION.

Parenthetic Independent Addition.

Par-em¹-bol-ee¹ (παρεμβολή), from παρά (*para*), *beside*, ἐν (*en*), *in*, and βολή (*bolee*), *a throwing* or *casting* (from βάλλω, *ballō, to throw*).

Hence, a *Parembole* is an insertion beside, between, or among others; and the name is used when the sentence interposed is independent and complete in itself; and would make complete sense if it were separated from the sentence which it divides.

It is called also EPEMBOLE (*Ep-em¹-bol-ee*, ἐπεμβολή), from ἐπί (*epi*), *upon*, ἐν (*en*), *in*, and βολή (*bolee*), *a casting*. *A casting in upon.*

And PAREMPTOSIS (*Par-emp-tò¹-sis*, παρέμπτωσις), from παρά (*para*), *beside*, ἐν (*en*), *in*, and πτῶσις (*ptōsis*), *a falling* (from πίπτω, *to fall*), *a falling in beside.*

Isa. lx. 12 is a *Parembole*, complete in itself.

Mark vii. 3, 4.—These two verses are interposed, and are independent of the context.

Luke xvii. 9 is an independent question and answer thrown in, in the midst of the argument.

Acts ii. 8-11 form a *Parembole.*

See also Rom. iii. 27-31 ; vi. 13-17.

Rom. viii. 2-15 is a long *Parembole* setting forth the further relation between flesh and spirit : *i.e.*, the Old man and the New man, the Old nature and the New divine and spiritual nature, the πνεῦμα (*pneuma*), or πνεῦμα χριστοῦ (*pneuma-Christou*) which is given to all who are in Christ. Consequently the " s " in spirit should be a small " s," and not a capital letter, in all these verses: the Holy Spirit Himself not being mentioned, or referred to, as a Person until verse 16.

The whole of the interpretation of this important passage depends on this *Parembole.**

1 Cor. xv. 20-28 is an independent digression : and the sense reads on from verse 19 to 29. Thus :—

(19). " If in this life only we have hope in Christ, we are of all men most miserable . . .

(29). Else, what shall they do who are being baptized ? *It is* for the dead, if the dead rise not all ? " etc. (see under *Ellipsis*, page 41).

---

* See article on Romans viii., *Things to Come*, May, 1899.

2 Cor. iii. 7-16.

Phil. iii. 18, 19.—These verses are an independent *Parembole*.

Eph. i. -19-23 is a *Parembole*, and the sense reads on from i. 19 to chap. ii. 1: " And what is the exceeding greatness of his power to us-ward who believe (. . .), even you who were dead in trespasses and sins," etc. But see under *Ellipsis* (page 109).

Eph. iii. 2-13 is a *Parembole*, and a digression explaining Paul's special ministry in connection with the Gentiles.

1 Tim. v. -22, 23.—" Keep thyself . . . infirmities " forms a *Parembole*.

Heb. xii. 18-29.

1 Pet. iii. 19-21.*

1 John i. 2.

---

* See *The Spirits in Prison*, by the same author and publisher.

INTERJECTIO ; or, INTERJECTION.

Parenthetic Addition by Way of Feeling.

In'-ter-jec'-ti-o, from the Latin, *inter*, between, and *jacio*, *to throw :* *something thrown in between*. While, therefore, the word is similar in meaning to the former figure, this term is confined to an *exclamation* which is *thrown in* by way of parenthesis.

But note that, when the exclamation is added at the *end* of a passage, it is called *Epiphonema* (*q.v.*).

And when it is quite independent of the context, and forms a definite part of it, it is called *Ecphonesis* (*q.v.*).

Ps. xlii. 2 (3).—" My soul is athirst for God, for the living God ; " and then is thrown in, parenthetically, the exclamation, " When shall I come and appear before God ? "

Ezek. xvi. 23, 24.—" And it came to pass after all thy wickedness (woe, woe unto thee ! saith Adonai Jehovah), That thou hast also built thee a brothel-house in every street " (*i.e.*, an idol's temple).

See also under *Cataploce.*

EJACULATIO; or, EJACULATION.

Parenthetic Addition by way of Wish or Prayer.

E-jac '-u-la '-ti-o, from the Latin *e, out ;* and *jaculari, jaculatus, the throwing of a javelin,* from *jaculum, a javelin* (from *jacére, to throw*).

This name is confined to a parenthesis which consists of a short prayer, such as " God forbid," "God be praised," "Thank God."

Hosea ix. 14.—Here, the prayer is in the form of a question:— " Give them, O LORD: what wilt thou give ? give them," etc. See under *Aposiopesis.*

HYPOTIMESIS; or, UNDER-ESTIMATING.

Parenthetic Addition by way of Apology or Excuse.

Hy-po-ti-mee'-sis (ὑποτίμησις), from ὑπό (*hypo*), *under*, and τίμησις (*timeesis*), *a valuing*, or *estimating*, from τιμάω (*timaō*), *to deem*, or *hold worthy*. Hence, *an under-estimating, under-valuing*.

A parenthetical remark is so called when it is apologetic, in order to excuse some bold or extravagant use of language, such as " If I may so say," or " So to speak," or, " As it were."

The name MEILIGMATA is given to the words so used, from μείλιγμα (*meiligma*), *anything that serves to soothe*. And this from μειλίσσω (*meilissō*), *to soothe, propitiate*.

Rom. iii. 5.—" I speak as a man."

2 Cor. xi. 23.—" I speak as a fool."

ANÆRESIS ; or, DETRACTION.

A Parenthetic Addition by way of Detraction.

(Parenthetic Tapeinōsis).

An æ'-re-sis (ἀναίρεσις), from ἀνά (*ana*), *up*, and αἱρέω (*haireō*), *to take away.* Hence *Anæresis* means *a taking up* or *carrying off.*

The parenthesis is so called, when, by a negative expression, we appear to take something away from the sense, but really add to it, and thus emphasize it.

Anæresis is the figure *Tapeinōsis* (or *Antenantiōsis*) used parenthetically.

---

6. RATIOCINATIO.

By way of Reasoning.

THIS class of additions to what is said does not relate to the sense, description, conclusion, or parenthesis, but to *argumentation*, or *reasoning*.

These figures are not often used in Scripture, and are artifices of argument invented for human reasoning.

We give them, in order to make our subject complete.

PARADIEGESIS; or, A BYE-LEADING.

Addition of Outside Facts by way of Reasoning.

Par-a-di-ee-gee¹-sis, from the Greek παρά (*para*), *beside*, διά (*dia*), *through*, or *by means of*, and ἡγεῖσθαι (*heegeisthai*), *to lead*, or *guide*. Hence the figure is used when there is an addition of facts which are beside the case, yet help to establish it.

SUSTENTATIO; or, SUSPENSE.

Addition suspending the Conclusion, by way of Reasoning.

Sus-ten-ta '-ti-ō : i.e., suspension. The figure is used when additions to the argument are made by which the conclusion is kept in suspense.

It is called also CREMAN from κρεμάννυμι (*kre-man-nu '-mi*), *to hang up, suspend.*

Also EXARTESIS (ἐξάρτησις), *ex-ar-tee '-sis, a hanging from, connection of parts with one another,* from ἐξαρτάω (*exartaō*), *to hang upon, suspend.*

PARALEIPSIS; or, A PASSING BY.

Addition (brief) of that which is professedly ignored.

Par-a-leips'-is, παράλειψις, *a passing over, omitting*, from παρά (*para*), *beside*, and λείπω (*leipō*), *to leave behind.* Sometimes spelt PARA-LEPSIS.

Called also PARASIOPESIS, παρασιώπησις, *a passing over in silence*, from παρά (*para*), *beside*, and σιώπησις (*siōpeesis*), *a being silent*, from σιωπάω (*siōpaō*), *to be silent.*

The Latins called it PRÆTERMISSIO, *a leaving aside, præter-mission, a passing over*, and PRÆTERITIO, *a going past, passing by.*

This figure is used when the speaker professes a wish to pass something by in silence, which he nevertheless adds by a brief allusion to it.

Heb. xi. 32.—"And what shall I more say? for the time would fail me to tell of Gedeon and of Barak," etc., and then proceeds to allude briefly to them all in verses 33-38.

PROSLEPSIS; or, ASSUMPTION.

Addition (full) of what is professed to be ignored.

Pros'-leeps'-is (πρόσληψις), *a taking* or *assuming besides.* From πρός (*pros*), *to, toward,* or *beside,* and λῆψις (*leepsis*), *a taking,* from λαμβάνω (*lambanō*), *to take.*

By the Latins it was called ASSUMPTIO, *an assuming,* or *taking to,* and CIRCUMDUCTIO, *a leading round.*

This name is given to the preceding figure of *Paraleipsis,* when it is expanded beyond its proper limits; and the speaker or writer, after having professed to omit it, proceeds actually to add and describe the particulars.

APOPHASIS; or, INSINUATION.

Addition of Insinuation (implied) by way of Reasoning.

A-*poph¹-a-sis* (ἀπόφασις), *denial, negation,* from ἀποφάναι (*apophanai*), *to speak off,* and this from ἀπό (*apo*), *off,* and φάναι (*phanai*), *to speak* or *say.*

The figure is used whĕn, professing to suppress certain matters or ideas, the speaker proceeds to add the insinuation, negatively: *e.g.,* "I will not mention the matter, but," etc.; or, "I will not mention another argument, which, however, if I should, you could not refute."

Philem. 19.—"I Paul have written it with mine own hand, I will repay it (albeit I do not say to thee how thou owest unto me even thine own self besides)."

When the matter or argument is actually added, the figure is then called

CATAPHASIS; or, AFFIRMATION.

Addition of Insinuation (stated) by way of Reasoning.

Cat-aph^¹-a-sis, Greek, κατάφασις, *an affirmation*, or *affirmative proposition*, from κατά (*kata*), *down*, and φασις (*phasis*), *a speaking*, from φάναι (*phanai*), *to say.*

In this case the insinuation is added, not negatively, but positively : *e.g.:* " I pass by his deceit," etc., and thus adds the insinuation as to his deception.

———————

ASTEISMOS; or, POLITENESS.

Addition by graceful disclosure of what is professedly concealed.

As-te-is'-mos. Greek, ἀστεϊσμός, *clever talk*, from ἀστεῖος (*asteios*), *of the city, polite*, from ἄστυ (*astu*), *city*.

The figure is used when, by pretending to conceal something, the speaker adds some graceful language which discloses it.

It comes in here when it is used as an *addition* by way of reasoning. We have included it also in Figures involving *change*, where the application of words is affected by way of *feeling*. (See below).

FIGURES INVOLVING CHANGE.

WE now come to the third and last great division of figures of language, *viz.*, *change*, *i.e.*, where the figure consists of a change affecting the *meaning, use, arrangement,* and *order,* of words, phrases, and sentences: also changes affecting the *application* of words.

Under this division come all the figures of *change* as to both Syntax and Rhetoric.

The figures involving change we have divided as follows:—

I. AFFECTING THE *Meaning* OF WORDS.

II. AFFECTING THE *Arrangement* AND ORDER OF WORDS.

      1. Separate words.

      2. Sentences and phrases.

III. AFFECTING THE *Application* OF WORDS.

      1. As to Sense.

      2. As to Persons.

      3. As to Subject-matter.

      4. As to Feeling.

      5. As to Argumentation.

I. *AFFECTING THE MEANING OF WORDS.*

ENALLAGE; or, EXCHANGE.

Exchange of one Word for another.

E-nal'-la-gee, ἐναλλαγή, *an exchange*, from ἐναλλάσσειν (*enallassein*), *to exchange*, from ἐν (*en*), *in*, and ἀλλάσσειν (*allassein*), *to change*.

Enallage is a figure of grammar; and consists of an exchange of words, or a substitution of one word for another. It differs from *Metonymy* (*q.v.*) in that *Metonymy* is the exchange or substitution of one *noun* for another noun: while *Enallage* is a change of one *part of speech* for another (*Antiméria*); or one *tense, mood, person,* or *number* for another (*Heterosis*); or one *case* for another (*Antiptosis*), but never of one noun for another.

It is also called ENALLAXIS (ἐνάλλαξις, *e-nal-lax'-is*), from another part of the same verb as *Enallage*, and with the same meaning, *an exchange.*

Also ALLŒOSIS (ἀλλοίωσις, *al-loi-ō'-sis*), a *change*, or *alteration*, from ἀλλοιόω (*alloioō*), to *make different*, to *change.*

Enallage consists of the following forms:

Antimereia,
Antiptosis,
Heterōsis, and
Hypallage', which will be considered in order :—

ANTIMEREIA : or, EXCHANGE OF PARTS OF SPEECH.

The Exchange of one part of Speech for another.

An'-ti-me'-rei-a, from ἀντί (*anti*), *over against* or *instead of*, and μέρεια (*mereia*) (for μερός), *a part*. It means that one *part of speech* is used instead of another :—as a noun for a verb or a verb for a noun, etc.

The following are the several kinds of *Antimereia* :—

ANTIMEREIA. Exchange of Parts of Speech.

I. Of the VERB.

    1. Infinitive for Noun.

    2. Participle (active) for Noun.

    3. Participle (passive) for Adjective.

II. Of the ADVERB.

    1. Adverb for Noun.

    2. Adverb for Adjective.

III. Of the ADJECTIVE.

    1. Adjective for Adverb.

    2. Adjective for Noun.

IV. Of the NOUN.

    1. Noun for Verb.

    2. Noun for Adverb.

    3. Noun for Adjective.

    4. Noun (repeated) for Adjective (*Epizeuxis*).

    5. Noun (*in regimen*) for Adjective.

    6. Noun (governing) for Adjective (*Hypallage*).

    7. The former of two (both *in regimen*) for Adjective.

    8. The latter of two (both *in regimen*) for Adjective.

    9. One of two in same case for Adjective (*Hendiadys*).

    10. Noun (*in regimen*) for Superlative Adjective.

HYPALLAGE. Interchange. The *Antimereia* of the governing Noun.

I. Antimereia of the Verb.

1. The Infinitive for a Noun.

Gen. xxxii. 24 (25).—Heb.: " Until the go-up of the dawn ": *i.e.*, until the rise or break of dawn.

1 Kings viii. 52.—"To hearken unto them in all their crying unto Thee ": *i.e.*, in all their prayer.

1 Chron. xvi. 36.—"And all the People said, 'Amen,' and be there praising Jehovah ": *i.e.*, and said, "Amen! and praise Jehovah!"

2 Chron. iii. 3.—" Now these [*are the things wherein*] Solomon was instructed (marg., *founded*) for the building of the house of God ": *i.e.*, these are the instructions or fundamentals [*given to*] Solomon for the building, etc.

Ps. ci. 3.—"I hate the doing of those turning aside ": *i.e.*, I hate the work of sinners.

Ps. cxxxii. 1.—"LORD, remember David and all his being afflicted ": *i.e.*, all the things in which he has been afflicted, or simply the noun as in A.V., " his afflictions."

Isa. iv. 4.—" By the spirit of judgment and the spirit of burning (or consuming) ": *i.e.*, by the spirit of burning or consuming.

Dan. x. 1.—"And the word to understand ": *i.e.*, "and he had a comprehension of the word, and an understanding of the vision."

Luke vii. 21.—" He granted to see ": *i.e.*, as in A.V., " he gave sight."

Phil. i. 23.—"Having a desire unto the return ": *i.e.*, (*lit.*) unto the to return (*i.e.*, the returning of Christ). Ἀναλύω (*analuō*), *to loosen back again*, but always from there to here; hence, *to return* (not from here to there, which would be to depart). See the only occurrences of the verb:—Luke xii. 36. Tobit ii. 1. Judith xiii. 1. 1 Esd. iii. 3. Wisd. ii. 1 ; v. 12. Ecclus. iii. 15. 2 Macc. viii. 25; ix. 1 ; xii. 7 ; xv. 28 ; and Josephus Ant. vi. 4, 1.

The meaning is that the Apostle knew not which to choose, whether to live or to die. His living would be better for them than his dying, but not better than a third thing which pressed him out of the other two, *viz.*, the return of Christ, which was " far better " than either. See further under *Epanalepsis, Resumptio, Pleonasm*, etc.

Heb. ii. 15.—"Through fear of death were all their living, subject to bondage ": *i.e.*, " all their lifetime," as in A.V.

Heb. iv. 1.—" A promise being left us to enter in " : *i.e.*, of entering in.

2. The Participle (active) for a Noun.

Gen. xxiii. 16.—" Current money of purchasing " : *i.e.*, " silver (or money) which passes with the merchant."

Job xiii. 4.—" Ye are all healing-ones of no value " : *i.e.*, as in A.V., physicians.

Prov. xiv. 20.—" The poor is hated even of his own neighbour : but many are loving the rich " : *i.e.*, the friends of the rich.

Jer. xxiii. 2. — " Against the shepherding-ones feeding my people " : *i.e.*, the feeders of my People. Compare Gen. iv. 2, where the term " shepherds " refers more to the *keeping* of the sheep. Hence the addition, here, of the *feeders.*

Ps. xvii. 14.—" Whose belly thou fillest with thy hid " : *i.e.*, thy treasure or secret thing.

Joel i. 17.—" Rotted have scattered *things* " : *i.e.*, rotted have the seeds.

Matt. iv. 3.   1 Thess. iii. 5.—" He the tempting-one " : *i.e.*, he who tempteth, *i.e.*, the tempter.

Matt. xi. 3 and elsewhere, " the One Coming " : *i.e.*, the Coming One.

Mark vi. 14, etc.—" John the baptizing-one " : *i.e.*, John the baptizer.

Mark xv. 29.—" The destroying-one " : *i.e.*, thou destroyer.   And " building it in three days " : *i.e.*, the builder of it.

1 Cor. ix. 25.—" He the striving-one " : *i.e.*, the one that strives— the competitor.

Heb. i. 6, etc.—" The world " : οἰκουμένη (*oikoumenee*), *inhabited,* hence used for the world as *inhabited.*

Heb. ix. 17.—" The maker of the covenant," (ὁ διαθέμενος) : *i.e.*, the sacrifice.   As long as the sacrifice was alive, the covenant was not made.   It was only ἐπὶ νεκροῖς (*epi nekrois*) over dead sacrifices that the covenant could have force.   See further under *Ellipsis* (page 69).

Heb. xii. 18.—" Ye are not come to a mount being touched " : *i.e.*, a touchable, palpable or literal mount.

Rev. ix. 11.—" The destroying-one " : *i.e.*, the Destroyer.

3. The Participle (Passive) for Adjective.

2 Kings xviii. 21.—"The staff of this bruised reed ": *i.e.*, this broken reed.

Ps. xii. 6 (7).—"Silver tried in a furnace ": *i.e.*, pure silver. See under *Ellipsis*, page 71.

Ps. xviii. 3 (4).—"I will call upon the LORD, the praised One " *i.e.*, laudable one, or as in A.V. worthy to be praised.

Prov. xxi. 20.—"There is treasure to be desired ": *i.e.*, a most desirable treasure.

Isạ. xxxiii. 19.—"Of a scorned tongue that thou canst not understand ": *i.e.*, a foreign tongue, which is often despised. The A.V. renders it "stammering " (but puts *ridiculing* in the margin); and the R.V. "strange " (with *stammering* in the margin).

Zeph. ii. 1.—"O nation not desired ": *i.e.*, not desirable. or better, incapable of shame.

Gal. ii. 11.—"Because he was to be blamed ": *i.e.*, blameworthy, or better, because he stood self-condemned.

Heb. xii. 27.—"That those things which cannot be shaken may remain ": *i.e.*, the unshakable things; the things that know no shaking.

II. ANTIMERIA OF THE ADVERB.

1. Adverb for Noun.

Luke x. 29.—"And who is near to me ": *i.e.*, my neighbour. The meaning is seen from Matt. xxii. 39; and Rom. xiii. 10.

John i. 25.—"He that cometh behind me (*i.e.*, after, as to position) is preferred before me ": *i.e.*, has precedence of me. The adverbs, ὀπίσω (*opisō*) *behind*, and ἔμπροσθεν (*emprosthen*) *before*, never refer to *time*, but to *position* or *grade*.

The verbs *to become* and *to be*, with an *adverb* or *adverbial phrase* often change the signification of the adverb into that of a noun. See 2 Sam. xi. 23. John vi. 25. Mark iv. 10. Acts v. 34; xiii. 5. Rom. vii. 3; xvi. 7. Eph. ii. 13. 2 Thess. ii. 7. 2 Tim. i. 17.

2. Adverb for Adjective.

Gen. xxx. 33.—"So shall my righteousness answer for me to-morrow ": *i.e.*, some future day.

1 Sam. xxv. 31.—"That thou hast shed blood causelessly ": *i.e.*, innocent blood. A.V. and R.V. render it "causeless."

Neh. ii. 12.—" I, and not enough men with me " : *i.e.*, as in A.V. " some few men."

Prov. iii. 25.—" Be not afraid of fear suddenly " : *i.e.*, sudden fear.

Prov. xv. 24.—" The way of life is above, to the wise, that he may depart from sheol beneath " : *i.e.*, the lower Sheol.

Prov. xxiv. 28.—" Be not a witness against thy neighbour heedlessly " : a rash, and hence likely to be, a false witness.

Prov. xxvii. 1.—" Boast not thyself of to-morrow " : *i.e.*, of any future day.

Matt. vi. 34.—" Be not full of care for to-morrow " : *i.e.*, have, then, no anxiety for any future day.

John xv. 5.—" Without (or apart from) me ye can do nothing " : *i.e.*, severed from me.

2 Cor. iv. 16.—" Though our without (*i.e.*, external or outward) man perish, yet the within (*i.e.*, internal or inward) man is renewed day by day."

2 Cor. iv. 17.—" For our momentary lightness of tribulation (*i.e.*, light tribulation) worketh for us exceedingly excessively an eternal weight of glory " : *i.e.*, an excessively surpassing eternal weight of glory." R.V. " more and more exceedingly."

III. Antimereia of the Adjective.

1. Adjective for Adverb.

Acts. xvi. 37.—" They have beaten us in public " : *i.e.*, publicly.

1 Cor. xii. 11.—" Dividing to each one personally " : *i.e.*, severally.

2. Adjective for Noun.

Gen. i. 9, 10.—" Let the dry appear " : *i.e.*, the land. So Ps. xcv. 5 ; and, in the Greek, Matt. xxiii. 15.

Isa. xxiv. 23.—" Then the pale shall be confounded " : *i.e.*, the moon, because pale.

Rom. i. 15.—" τὸ κατ᾽ ἐμὲ πρόθυμον " (*to kat' eme prothumon*), according to my ready [*mind*], *i.e.*, my readiness.

Rom. i. 19.—" The known (*i.e.*, knowable or discoverable) of God " : *i.e.*, that which may be learnt even by the natural man.

Rom. ii. 4.—" Not knowing the kind [*thing* or *gift*] of God " : *i.e.*, the kindness of God.

1 Cor. i. 27, 28.—" Foolish," " weak," " base," "despised " : *i.e.,* as in A.V., " the foolish things," etc.

2 Cor. viii. 8.—" To prove the genuine of your love ": *i.e.,* the genuineness (or genuine character of).

Eph. vi. 12.—" The spiritual [*powers, bands, hosts*] of wickedness " : *i.e., wicked spirits.*

Phil. ii. 6.—" Equal with God " : *i.e.,* on an equality with God.

This is what the first man grasped at, tempted and deceived by the Old Serpent. But Christ, the second man, the last Adam, did not think it a matter to be grasped at in this way, " but humbled Himself," and through suffering and death reached His exaltation. (See pages 202, 433).

Phil. iv. 5.—" Let your moderate be known unto all men " : *i.e.,* your moderation.

Heb. vi. 17.—" The unchangeable of his counsel" : *i.e.,* the unchangeableness of His counsel, or the unchangeable [*character*] of His counsel.

IV. ANTIMEREIA OF THE NOUN.

1. A Noun for a Verb.

This is called " *Antimereia* of the Noun."

Judges xvi. 23.—" Then the lords of the Philistines gathered them together for to offer a great sacrifice unto Dagon their God, and to rejoice." *Lit.,* for a great rejoicing.

Isa. vii. 1.—" Rezin . . . and Pekah . . . went up toward Jerusalem to war against it."

Lit., for the war. *Fig.,* to make war.

Mark xii. 38.—" And he said unto them in his doctrine." Here, the noun " doctrine " is put instead of the verb, " during his teaching " or, " while he taught."

2. A Noun for an Adverb.

Isa. xxi. 7.—" And he hearkened diligently with much heed " : *i.e.,* most attentively.

Ps. lxxv. 2 (3). — " I will judge upright [*judgments*]" : *i.e.,* righteously. So Prov. xxxi. 9.

Ps. cxxxix. 14.—" I will praise thee, for I am made with fears and wonder " : *i.e.,* fearfully and wonderfully.

Lam. i. 8.—"Jerusalem hath sinned a sin ": *i.e.*, grievously.

Mark vii. 3.—"Except they wash their hands with the fist":
i.e., carefully or assiduously.

Mark viii. 32.—"And he spake the word with boldness": *i.e.*,
boldly, openly, or publicly. So John vii. 26 ; x. 24 ; xi. 14 ; xvi. 25, 29 ;
xviii. 20 ; xi. 54.

3. A Noun for an Adjective.

Thus "circumcision " and "uncircumcision " are used instead of
circumcised or uncircumcised persons.

Anathema, which means accursed, is an accursed or excommuni-
cated person or thing.

1 Cor. xiv. 12.—" So also ye, forasmuch as ye are zealous of
spirits." Here, the noun is used instead of an adjective·($\pi\nu\epsilon\nu\mu\acute{a}\tau\omega\nu$ for
$\pi\nu\epsilon\nu\mu\alpha\tau\iota\kappa\hat{\omega}\nu$). Both the A.V. and R.V. insert *"gifts"* in italics.

1 Cor. xiv. 32.—" And the spirits of the prophets are subject to
the prophets." Here, the noun " spirits " is again used for the
adjective *spiritual gifts.* See under *Metonymy.*

Gal. i. 14.—" Being more exceedingly a zealot": *i.e.*, zealous, as
in A.V.

Heb. xii. 11.—"Any discipline for the present (*time*) seems not
to be of joy" ($\chi\alpha\rho\hat{a}s$, *charas*): *i.e.*, joyous, "but of grief" ($\lambda\acute{v}\pi\eta s$,
lupees): *i.e.*, grievous, as in A.V.

1 John v. 6.—" Because the Spirit is truth." Here the noun is
rendered literally: but it is used by the figure *Antimereia* for the
adjective *true ;* and the meaning is that the witness of the Holy Spirit
concerning Christ is *true* in every place and in every particular.

If this figure were not *Enallage,* then it would be a *Metaphor,*
which is quite out of the question.

4. A Noun (repeated) for an Adjective.

A noun is sometimes repeated in order to express the adjective in
the highest or superlative degree. This is called *Geminatio* or
Epizeuxis (q.v.).

Isa. xxvi. 3.—" Thou wilt keep him in peace, peace": *i.e.*, *perfect
peace.* See under *Epizeuxis,* where many examples are given.

5. A. Noun (*in regimen*) for an Adjective.

When, of two nouns, one noun is placed *in regimen :* *i.e.*, when
one governs the other in the genitive case : the latter word (sometimes
two words) becomes an adjective.

The natural and ordinary way of qualifying a noun is by using an adjective. But, if it is wished to emphasize the adjective, then this rule is departed from ; in order to attract the attention of the reader, and to tell him that the adjective is very emphatic, and is to be read as if it were underlined or under-scored in ordinary writing. For example : suppose we are speaking of Angels, and our thought is simply of *them* and their being, we should use the word "mighty" as an adjective, and say " Mighty ANGELS," but if we wished to emphasize the adjective " mighty," and call attention to the fact that we are not referring to angels as such, but to their wondrous power, and we should say "MIGHTY Angels." How is this to be done? By *Antimereia*. By using a *noun* instead of an adjective, and saying " Angels of might."

It is difficult to say how this should be dealt with in translation so as to render it idiomatically, and yet apprise the reader of the correct emphasis.

Neither the Authorized nor the Revised Version follows any fixed rule. Sometimes the noun is translated literally, and sometimes it is rendered as an adjective.

It is important, however, that the reader (especially the public reader) should know where the emphasis is required.

It should be observed, however, that the second noun (*i.e.*, the noun in the genitive case) is not always used instead of an adjective.

The word " of " takes many different meanings ; and it is important that each should be accurately defined and determined.

As this, however, does not belong strictly to the figure *Antimereia*, we have given an outline of the whole subject in the Appendix. (See Appendix B " On the usuage of the Genitive case.")

The following are examples of *Antimereia*, where a noun *in regimen* is used instead of an adjective :—

Ex. xxxiv. 7.—" The iniquity of the fathers " : *i.e.*, when the iniquity wrought by the children is the same in character, it will be punished in the same way.

2 Kings xxiv. 3.—" The sins of Manasseh " : *i.e.*, the sins like Manasseh's, as is explained by the next sentence, " according to all that he did."

2 Chron. xxiv. 6, 9.—" The collection of Moses " : *i.e.*, like that ordered by Moses. The italics of the A.V. are put in to fill out the sense.

Job. viii. 6.—" The home of thy righteousness " : *i.e.*, thy righteous home.

Ps. ii. 6.—" Upon Zion, the mount of my holiness " : *i.e.*, my holy mountain. See A.V. marg.

Ps. lx. 9 (11).—" Who will bring me into the city of strength " : *i.e.*, the strong city, with emphasis on strong. See 2 Sam. xi. 1, and xii. 26. See also under *Irony*.

Ezra viii. 18.—" A man of understanding " : *i.e.*, a wise and prudent man.

Ps. xxiii. 2.—" Pastures of tender grass " : *i.e.*, green pastures.

Ps. xxiii. 2.—" Waters of quietness " : *i.e.*, peaceful streams.

Ps. xxxi. 2 (3).—" Be to me for a rock of strength, for a house of bulwarks to save me " : *i.e.*, a strong rock, and a fortified house, or fortress.

Ps. cxl. 11 (12).—" Will not a man of tongue (*i.e.*, a braggart ; P.B.V., a man full of words ; A.V., an evil speaker) be established in the earth : evil will hunt the man of violence (*i.e.*, the violent man) to overthrow him."

Ps. cl. 1.—" The firmament of his power " : *i.e.*, his strong firmament.

Prov. x. 15.—" City of his strength " : *i.e.*, his strong city.

Prov. xxix. 8.—" Men of scorning " : *i.e.*, scoffers (A.V., " scornful men ").

Isa. i. 10.—" Ye rulers of Sodom . . . ye people of Gomorrah " : *i.e.*, rulers and a people who acted as those of Sodom and Gomorrah did.

Isa. xxviii. 1 (2).—" Crown of pride " : *i.e.*, Pride's crown.

Isa. xxx. 21.—" The graven images of thy silver " : *i.e.*, thy silver graven images.

Isa. xxxiii. 21.—" Broad of spaces " : *i.e.*, spacious or broad streams. (See A.V. margin).

Isa. li. 20.—" Like a wild bull of a net " : *i.e.*, a netted wild oryx.

Isa. lii. 1.—" The city of holiness " : *i.e.*, the holy city.

Isa. liv. 9.—" For this is the waters of Noah unto me " : *i.e.*, Noah's flood, as we call it. The times and circumstances referred to are to be like the days of Noah. The A.V. and R.V. supply " *as*."

Jer. xii. 10.—" My portion of desire " : *i.e.*, my desired portion.

Jer. xxii. 19.—" The burial of an ass " : *i.e.*, an ass's funeral !

Jer. li. 3.—" A sleep of perpetuity " : *i.e.*, a perpetual sleep.

Hab. i. 8.—"The wolves of evening": *i.e.*, evening wolves. See also Jer. v. 6; Zeph. iii. 3; and the explanation in Ps. civ. 20, 21.

Matt. v. 22.—"The gehenna of the fire": the fiery or burning Gehenna: or, the fiery Hinnom-vale.

Matt. xv. 26.—"The bread of the children": *i.e.*,-the children's own bread, with emphasis on the children.

Matt. xix. 28.—"The throne of His glory": *i.e.*, His glorious throne, with emphasis on glorious. There are no articles in the Greek.

Mark xi. 22.—"Have faith of God": *i.e.*, Divine or strong faith. Compare Jas. ii. 1 and 1 Pet. ii. 19.

Luke i. 17.—"The spirit and power of Elias": *i.e.*, with Elijah's spirit and power.

Luke vi. 12.—"Continued all night in the prayer of God": *i.e.*, in instant earnest prayer.

Luke xvi. 8.—"The steward of injustice": *i.e.*, the unjust steward.

Luke xviii. 6.—"Hear what the judge of injustice saith": *i.e.*, the unjust judge, as in A.V.

John x. 23.—"And Jesus walked in the porch of Solomon": *i.e.*, in the porch built like that of Solomon, and in the same place, etc. For Solomon's porch was burnt with the Temple by Nebuchadnezzar.

Rom. i. 26.—"Lusts of dishonour": *i e*, A.V., "vile passions."

Rom. vi. 4.—"In newness of life": *i.e.*, a life-long newness.

Rom. vii. 5.—"Motions (or passions, *margin*) of sins": *i.e.*, sinful passions: or, sins' passions; *i.e.*, the passions of the various sins set in motion by the Law.

Rom. vii. 24.—"Who shall deliver me from the body of this death?": *i.e.*, this dying body or this mortal body.

Rom. viii. 6, 7.—"Mind of the spirit" and "mind of the flesh" rendered "spiritually minded" and "carnally minded." This is almost stronger than the mere characterizing of the spirit or the flesh. It denotes the *ruling principle* which governs and controls the mind: the one being the old nature; and the other, the new.

2 Cor. iv. 2.—"The hidden things of dishonesty": *i.e.*, the shameful secret things.

Eph. ii. 3.—"Fulfilling the desires of the flesh and of the mind": *i.e.*, coarse fleshly lusts, and refined mental lusts; for there is "no difference" between these in God's sight, though there may be in man's.

Eph. iv. 22.—" Lusts of deceit ": *i.e.*, deceitful lusts ; or lusts which deceive, and are the instruments of deceit.

Verse 24 : " Righteousness and holiness of truth": *i.e.*, true righteousness and holiness, as contrasted with Adam (Gen. i. 27) with the emphasis on *true.*

Eph. vi. 12.—"Against the spiritual things of wickedness": *i.e.*, wicked spirits. Here we have two forms of *Antimereia, viz.*, the *Ant.* of the adjective " *spiritual* " for spiritual powers, or spirits, and the *Ant.* of the noun, " *of wickedness*," for their origin or character.

Phil. iii. 21.—" Who shall change the body of our humiliation (*i.e.*, our corruptible body) that it may be fashioned like unto His body of glory (*i.e.*, his glorious body) : with emphasis on corruptible and glorious.

Col. i. 11.—"According to the power of his glory": *i.e.*, His glorious power.

Col. i. 13.—" Who hath translated us into the Kingdom of the Son of His love ": *i.e.*, of His beloved Son.

Col. i. 22.—" The body of his flesh " : *i.e.*, his fleshly body.

Col. ii. 18.—" The mind of his flesh ": *i.e.*, as in A.V., his fleshly mind.

Col. iii. 14.—" Bond of perfectness ": *i.e.*, a perfect bond.

2 Thess. i. 7.—"The angels of His power ": *i.e.*, His mighty angels, with great emphasis on " mighty." (See margin).

2 Thess. ii. 3.—" The man of sin ": *i.e.*, the man characterized by sin, the sinful or wicked man, with the emphasis on " sinful." " The son of perdition." (See under *Metonomy*, for the use of the word " son.")

Heb. ix. 10.—" Which stood only in meats and drinks and divers washings (βαπτισμοῖς, *baptisms*) and (or even) ordinances of the flesh, put upon them until the time of setting things right " : *i.e.*, Baptisms whose character was fleshly, having effect only on the flesh, and thus opposite to that baptism of the Spirit with which Christ baptises the members of His Body.

Heb. xii. 9.—" Fathers of our flesh ": *i.e.*, human or natural fathers, in contrast with the Heavenly Father and giver of our spirits.

James i. 25.—"A hearer of forgetfulness": *i.e.*, as in A.V., a forgetful hearer : with emphasis on "forgetful."

Jas. ii. 4.—"Judges of evil thoughts": *i.e.*, evil-thinking judges.

Jas. iii. 13.—" Meekness of wisdom " : *i.e.*, wise meekness.

1 Pet. i. 2.—"Sanctification of [the] Spirit": *i.e.*, spiritual sanctification, or perhaps it may be the Genitive of *Origin*, and mean that sanctification of which the Spirit is the author and source.

2 Pet. ii. 1.—"Heresies of perdition": *i.e.*, destructive heresies or sects. The A.V. renders it "damnable heresies."

2 Pet. ii. 16.—" With the voice of a man": which the A.V. correctly renders man's voice; *i.e.*, a human being's voice in contrast to animal.

1 John i. 1.—"The Word of life": *i.e.*, the living Word. Accordingly, it is added in the next verse, "and the life (*viz.*, of the Word) was manifested."

Jude 11.—" The way of Cain . . . the error of Balaam . . . the gainsaying of Korah": *i.e.*, the way, the error, and gainsaying characterized like those of Cain, Balaam, and Korah.

Jude 18.—Walking "after their own lusts of ungodliness": *i.e.*, as in A.V., "ungodly lusts."

The Divine Names form a special class by themselves.

The Names of God (*El*), God (*Elohim*), Lord (*Jehovah*) are sometimes used, *in regimen*, as adjectives, denoting Divine; or that which is the greatest, highest, mightiest, most glorious, or beautiful.

Gen. vi. 1.—"The sons of God": *i.e.*, wondrous, mighty, supernatural beings. Hence, used always of *angels* in the Old Testament.

See every other occurrence:—Job i. 2; ii. 6; xxxviii. 7. Ps. xxix. 1; lxxxix. 6. Dan. iii. 25. In Gen. vi. 2, Codex A of the Septuagint reads ἄγγελοι τοῦ θεοῦ, *angels of God*. These are the fallen angels referred to as "in-prison" (2 Pet. ii. 4-9. Jude 6, 7, and 1 Peter iii. 18-20.

Gen. xxiii. 6.—" A prince of God" : *i.e.*, a mighty prince.

Gen. xxx. 8.—"Wrestlings of God": *i.e.*, great wrestlings.

Ex. ix. 28.—"Voices of God": *i.e.*, loud and powerful voices, or thunderings. Compare 1 Sam. xiv. 15.

2 Chron. xx. 29.—" A fear of God" : *i.e.*, a great fear.

2 Chron. xxviii. 13.—" A trespass of Jehovah " : *i.e.*, a terrible sin. The A.V. entirely loses the sense of this verse, which should be thus rendered : "Ye shall not bring in the captives hither; for ye propose that which will bring upon us a trespass of Jehovah (*i.e.*, a trespass of the greatest magnitude) to add to our sin and to our guilt; for abundant is the guilt we have and the fierceness of anger on Israel."

Job iv. 9.—"A blast of Eloah " : a vehement blast.

Ps. xxxvi. 6 (7) ; lxviii. 15 (16), etc.—" Mountains of God " : *i.e.*, the loftiest mountains.

Ps. lxxx. 10 (11).—" Cedars of God " : *i.e.*, the loftiest cedars.

Ps. civ. 16.—" Trees of Jehovah " : *i.e.*, the loftiest trees.

Song viii. 6.—" Flames of Jehovah " : *i.e.*, vehement flames. The verse should be rendered :

" For love is strong as death :
Affection is inexorable as Sheol :
Its flames are flames of fire :
The flames of Jehovah."*

Jer. ii. 31.—Here the last syllable of the word " darkness," יָהּ, is an abbreviation of Jehovah ; and the words should be rendered :

" Have I been a wilderness to Israel.
Is the land the darkness of Jah ? " *i.e.*, utter darkness. †

Ezek. xxviii. 13 ; xxxi. 8, 9.—" Garden of God " : *i.e.*, the Divine, beautiful or wonderful garden.

The Name of God is used in the same way in the DATIVE *case.*

Ruth ii. 20.—" Blessed be he to the LORD " : *i.e.*, divinely blessed with all things.   So iii. 10, " Blessed be thou to the LORD."

Isa. xxviii. 2.   Here, it is literally :

" Behold, a mighty and strong one to Adonai " : *i.e.*,
" Behold, a mighty one, immensely strong—
As a storm of hail, a destructive storm ;
As a flood of mighty waters overflowing
Hath he cast [*Ephraim*] down to the earth with his hand."

Jonah iii. 3.—" A city great to God " : *i.e.*, as in A.V., an exceeding great city.

Acts vii. 20.—Moses was " fair to God " : *i.e.*, Divinely beautiful.

2 Cor. x. 4.—" For the weapons of our warfare are not carnal, but mighty to God " (so A.V. margin) : *i.e.*, immensely powerful.

The word " SONS" or " CHILDREN " with a noun (in regimen)
is used idiomatically :—

The word " son," when qualified by another noun, denotes the *nature* and character of the person or persons so named, and even their source and origin : *e.g.*, " sons of Belial " (margin, *naughty men*).   Deut. xiii. 13.   Judges xix. 22.

---

* See Ginsburg's *Introduction*, page 386.   † Ditto, page 384.

"Sons of valour" (2 Sam. ii. 7.   1 Kings i. 52.   Deut. iii. 18) :
    i.e., brave men.

"Sons of the pledges" : *i.e.*, hostages (2 Kings xiv. 14).

"Son of oil" (Isa. v. 1, marg.) beautifully rendered "in a very
    fruitful hill."

"Sons of light" (Luke xvi. 8) : *i.e.*, men illuminated from above
    (John xii. 36.   1 Thess. v. 5.   Eph. v. 8).

"Children of the devil" (1 John iii. 10.   Acts xiii. 10).

"Children of wrath" (Eph. ii. 2).

"Children of this world" (Luke xx. 34) : *i.e.*, men who are
    characterized by living for this present age or life.

"Children of the resurrection" (Luke xx. 36) : *i.e.*, raised from
    the dead.

"Children of disobedience" : *i.e.*, disobedient children (Eph ii. 2).

"Children of obedience" : *i.e.*, obedient children (1 Pet. i. 14).

Heb. x. **39** must be explained by this usage, if sense is to be
made of the words, the difficulty of which is seen in the R V. margin :
"But we are not [*children of unbelief*] of drawing back unto
destruction of the soul (*i.e.*, unbelievers), but [*children*] of faith (*i.e.*,
believers) unto the gaining of it."

So the expression "son of man," "sons of men," "children of
men" is a Hebrew idiom for *a human being* as distinct from a beast on
the one hand and from God or angelic beings on the other (Gen. xi. 5,
etc.).

In like manner the "sons of God" in the New Testament are
those who partake of the New, Divine, or spiritual nature (2 Pet. i. 4),
whether angels or men, as distinct from the beasts and from mere
human beings.

Beni Ha-Elohim, the sons of God, is used seven times in the
Old Testament for angels (see above).

Once it is used of Restored Israel (Hos. i. 10) in Heb. ii. 1, but
here the expression is different, *Beni El-hai*.

In the singular with both articles it is used of Christ.

"The Son of God" is that blessed one who is perfect man and
perfect God, perfectly human as "the Son of man" (also with
both articles) and perfectly Divine as "the Son of God."

6. Noun (governing) for Adjective.

When the *first* noun (instead of the second noun, *in regimen*) is
changed, and used instead of the adjective, the figure is called
Hypallage.   See below.

7. The *former* of Two Nouns (both *in regimen*) used for an Adjective.

When two nouns are both of them *in regimen*, and only one of them is used for the adjective, sometimes it is the former*:

(*a*) Where the *former* of the two nouns (both *in regimen*) is used for an adjective, and is to receive the emphasis.

Gen. xvii. 5.—"A father of a multitude of nations ": *i.e.*, of many nations (as in the A.V.), with the emphasis on *many*, as is explained in Rom. iv. 17.

Gen. xlv. 22.—"Changes of raiment."

Acts vii. 30.—"In a flame of a fire of a bush ": *i.e.*, in a flame of a burning bush.

Rom. v. 2.—"And rejoice in hope of the glory of God ": *i.e.*, and rejoice in God's glorious hope.

Rom. viii. 2.—"The law of the spirit of life ": *i.e.*, the spiritual law of life.

2 Cor. iv. 6.—"The knowledge of the glory of God": *i.e.*, the knowledge of the glorious God.

Eph. i. 6.—"To the praise of the glory of His grace ": *i.e.*, of His glorious grace.

Tit. ii. 13.—"The appearing of the glory of our great God and Saviour ": *i.e.*, the glorious appearing of the great God, even our Saviour Jesus Christ.

Rev. xviii. 3.—"The wine of the wrath of her fornication ": *i.e.*, the furious wine, etc.

8. The *latter* of Two Nouns (both *in regimen*) used for an Adjective.

Gen. ix. 5.—"At the hand of a man of his brother ": *i.e.*, at the hand of his fellow or brother man. There is no " every " expressed in the Hebrew.

Rom. iii. 23.—"For all have sinned, and come short of the glory of God ": *i.e.*, of God's glory.

---

* Sometimes it is the latter that is put for the adjective. (See No. 8 below). Sometimes they are both of them different forms of the genitive case, and one of them is *in regimen* to the other : *i.e.*, depends upon the other. For examples of this, see Appendix B.

Rom. viii. 3.—" In likeness of flesh of sin " : *i.e.*, sinful flesh's likeness.

Col. i. 11.—" According to the power of the glory of Him " : *i.e.*, according to His glorious power.

Col. i. 13.—" And hath translated us into the kingdom of the son of His love " : *i.e.*, His beloved Son's kingdom. See Matt. iii. 17.

9. One of two Nouns in *the same* case (and not *in regimen*) used for an Adjective.

When two nouns in the same case are united by a conjunction, one of them (generally the latter) is used as a very emphatic adjective, *e.g.*, Acts xiv. 13 : " They brought oxen and garlands," means " They brought oxen, yes, and they were *garlanded* too ! " This figure is called *Hendiadys*, under which the reader will find many examples.

10. Noun (*in regimen*) for superlative of Adjective.

When the latter noun is the genitive plural of the former noun *e.g.*, King of Kings, Holy of Holies, it is put instead of, and to emphasise, the superlative degree of the adjective. As this is a species of *Polyptoton*, we have put the examples under that figure (*q.v.*).

ANTIPTOSIS ; or, EXCHANGE OF CASES.

Exchange of one case for another.

An'-tip-tō'-sis (ἀντίπτωσις), from ἀντί (*anti*), *against* or *instead of ;* and πτῶσις (*ptōsis*), *a falling ;* in grammar *an inflection* or *a case* of a noun in *declension ;* from πίπτειν (*piptein*), *to fall.*

The figure is so called, because one case is put instead of another case. Especially when the absolute is put for the construct: *i.e.,* where the governing noun is changed for the noun *in regimen*

Antiptosis is to be distinguished from *Hypallage.* In *Hypallage,* the two words and cases are interchanged, and the sense and relation of the two reversed; while in *Antiptosis* the governing noun becomes the adjective instead of the noun *in regimen.*

N.B.—When the noun *in regimen* is used instead of an adjective, it is a form of *Antimereia* (see above).

Ex. xix. 6.—"A kingdom of priests": *i.e.,* a royal priesthood. In 1 Pet. ii. 9, this is put literally, instead of (as here) by *Antiptosis.*

Ps. i. 1.—"O the blessedness or happinesses of the man ": *i.e.,* the happy or blessed man.

Matt. xiii. 5.—"No depth of earth ": *i.e.,* no deep earth.

Luke i. 48.—"The low estate of his handmaiden ": *i.e.,* his humiliated bondmaid: referring to the humiliation to which she had to be subject. If even Joseph could suspect her, however sorrowfully and sadly, what would others do? What, in fact, in Jewish teaching still !

Luke v. 9.—"At the haul of the fish": *i.e.,* the fish of the capture ; or, the captured fishes.

Rom. ii. 4.—"The good thing (τὸ χρηστόν, *to chreeston*) of God " : *i.e.,* the goodness of God. See under *Antimereia* of the adjective.

Rom. v. 17.—"The abundance of the grace " : *i.e.,* the abounding grace.

1 Cor. i. 17.—"Not with wisdom of speech": *i.e.,* not with learned or eloquent language.

1 Cor. i. 21.—"The folly of preaching " : *i.e.,* foolish (as the wise Gentiles ironically called it) preaching.

1 Cor. xiv. 12.—"So do ye also, since as ye are zealous of spirits." Here, the noun " spirits " is used for the adjective *spiritual* (πνευμάτων, *pneumatōn* for πνευματικῶν, *pneumatikōn*). Both the A.V. and R.V. insert the word "*gifts*" in italics. See under *Metonymy.*

2 Cor. viii. 8.—"The genuineness of your love": *i.e.*, your genuine love.

Gal. iii. 14.—"The promise of the Spirit": *i.e.*, the promised Spirit.

Gal. iv. 4.—"The fulness of the time": *i.e.*, the full or completed time.

Eph. i. 7.—"The riches of his grace." By *Enallage* this would be *gracious riches,* but it means more than this. Grace is the subject, and it is the exceeding wealth of this wondrous grace which has abounded toward those who are "accepted in the Beloved."

By *Antiptosis* the one is put for the other, and the noun "riches" is put for the adjective: *i.e.*, His exceeding rich grace. So also

Eph. i. 18.—"The riches of his glory" denotes the exceeding rich glory of His inheritance in the saints.

Eph. iv. 29.—"Building up or edifying of the need." The A.V. renders this—"Use of edifying;" but it is the word "use" (or need) which is in the genitive case, and not the word "edifying." The R.V. renders it "Edifying as the need may be."

But by the figure of *Antiptosis* (which neither Version perceived), the former noun is used for the adjective, instead of the latter in the genitive case.

The meaning, therefore, is "that which is good for edifying use."

Phil. iv. 5.—"The immutability of his counsel": *i.e.*, his immutable counsel.

Col. i. 27.—"The riches of the glory": *i.e.*, His wondrously rich glory, in the mystery revealed to and through Paul.

1 Thess. i. 3.—"Work of faith," "labour of love," and "patience of hope."

We have given these under the genitive of origin (see Appendix B): *i.e.*, work which proceeds from faith, labour which proceeds from love, and patience that proceeds from hope.

The genitive, however, may be, by *Antimereia,* faithful service, loving labour, and hopeful patience.

But, if the figure is *Antiptosis,* then it means a working faith (*i.e.*, a faith which is manifested by its works), a laborious love, and patient hope. Probably all three interpretations are correct!

Heb. vi. 17.—"The immutability of his counsel": *i.e.*, His unchangeable counsel."

Heb. ix. 15.—" The promise of the eternal inheritance ": *i.e.*, the promised eternal inheritance.

1 Pet. iii. 20.—" The longsuffering of God ": *i.e.*, the long-suffering God.

There are other exchanges of case beside that of the absolute for the construct. But these are for the most part peculiar to Greek usage.

Luke i. 55.—"As he spake to (πρός) our fathers, to Abraham (τῷ Ἀβραάμ), and to his seed (τῷ)." Here, the fathers is in the Accusative because more general; while Abraham, etc, is in the Dative, because more personal.

Heb. x. 5.—" A body hast thou prepared me (*Dat.* μοί (*moi*), *for me*)."

It is a question whether the *Dative* is used, by *Antiptosis*, for the *Accusative ;* to show that, while Christ's human body was prepared for Him, yet He was also constituted a servant for ever according to Ex. xxi. 6 and Deut. xv. 17. This is the sense in Ps. xl. 6 (7), and σῶμα (*sōma*), *body*, was used of slaves (Rev. xviii. 13), just as we use " hands " of labourers.

Rev. i. 5, 6.—" And from Jesus Christ (*Gen.*), the faithful witness (*Nom.*), and the first begotten (Nom.) from the dead . . to him (*Dat.*) that loved us . . and made us (Nom.) kings, etc., to him (Dat.)." All this change of cases seems to overwhelm us with the idea of the impossibility of expressing the praise and glory which should be ascribed to Jesus Christ.

See also (in the Greek) Rev. iii. 12, and xviii. 13.

HETEROSIS; or, EXCHANGE OF ACCIDENCE.

Exchange of one Voice, Mood, Tense, Person, Number, Degree, or Gender, for another.

Het'-e-rō'-sis, ἕτερος (*heteros*), *another, different*. It is the name given to that form of *Enallage* which consists of an exchange, not of actual parts of speech, but of the *accidence* of a part of speech.

It includes an exchange of one *Form of the Verb* for another (*e.g.*, intransitive for transitive); one *Mood* or *Tense* for another; one *Person* for another; one *Degree* of comparison for another; one *Number* or *Gender* for another.

When the exchange is of one *Case* for another, it has a separate name—*Antiptōsis* (see above), and when the exchange is of one *Part of Speech* for another, it is called *Antimereia* (see above).

The following are the various forms of *Heterosis* :—

HETEROSIS.

I. Of FORMS and VOICES.

    1. Intransitive for Transitive.

    2. Active for Passive.

    3. Middle for Passive.

II. Of MOODS.

    1. Indicative for Subjunctive.

    2. Subjunctive for Indicative.

    3. Imperative for Indicative.

    4. Imperative for Subjunctive.

    5. Infinitive for Indicative.

    6. Infinitive for Imperative.

III. Of Tenses.

    1. Past for Present.

    2.   „   „ Future.

    3. Aorist (Indefinite) for Past.

    4.   „   „ Present.

    5. Present for Past.

    6.   „   „ Future.

    7.   „   „ Paulo post futurum (*i.e.*, a little after

    8. Future for Past.   [Future).

    9.   „   „ Present.

    10.   „   „ Imperative.

IV. Of Persons.

    1. First Person for Third.

    2. Second for Third.

    3. Third for First or Second.

    4. Plural for Singular.

    5. Singular for Plural.

V. Of Adjectives (Degree) and Adverbs.

    1. Positive for Comparative.

    2.   „   „ Superlative.

    3. Comparative for Positive.

    4.   „   „ Superlative.

    5. Superlative for Comparative.

VI. Of Nouns (Number), Adjectives, and Pronouns.

    1. Singular for Plural.

    2. Plural for Singular.

    3. Plural for Indefinite Number or one of many.

VII. Of Gender.

    1. Masculine for Feminine.

    2. Masculine for Neuter.

    3. Feminine for Neuter.

    4. Neuter for Masculine or Feminine.

HETEROSIS OF THE VERB.

I. Of Forms and Voices.

1. Intransitive for Transitive.

Matt. v. 29.—" If thy right eye offend thee ": (σκανδαλίζω, *skandalizō*), *to make to stumble : i.e.*, make thee stumble. So xviii. 6. 1 Cor. viii. 13.

Matt. v. 45.—" He maketh his sun to rise " (ἀνατέλλω, *anatellō*), *to rise up.*

1 Cor. ii. 2.—" I determined not to know anything among you ": *i.e.*, to make known, preach.

1 Cor. iii. 6.—" God gave the increase," and verse 7 : " God that giveth the increase." So 2 Cor. ix. 10. In all other places the verb αὐξάνω (*auxanō*), *to increase,* is intransitive.

1 Cor. xiii. 12.—" Then shall I know, even as I also am known ": *i.e.*, I shall be made to know or taught.

2 Cor. ii. 14.—" Now, thanks be to the God that always causeth us to triumph." Here the A.V. recognises the figure of exchange ; as also in

2 Cor. ix. 8.—" God is able to make all grace abound in you."

Gal. iv. 9.—" But now after that ye have known God, or rather are known of God ": *i.e.*, been made to know, or been instructed by God.

Eph. i. 8.—" According to the riches (or wealth) of His grace which (grace) he hath made to overflow into us."

2 Tim. ii. 19.—" The Lord knoweth them that are his ": *i.e.*, the Lord maketh known who are His ; as in Num. xvi. 5.

2. Active for Passive.

1 Pet. ii. 6.—" Wherefore also it is contained in the Scriptures," *lit.*, it contains : *i.e.*, there is a passage in the Scripture.

3. Middle for Passive.

Luke ii. 5.—" To be taxed with Mary ": *lit.*, to enrol himself.

1 Cor. x. 2.—" And were all baptized into Moses ": *lit.*, baptized themselves.

II. Heterosis of Moods.

1. Indicative for Subjunctive.

As the Hebrew language has no subjunctive mood, the indicative is often put instead of that mood; and this is done in the New Testament, as well as in the Old Testament, inasmuch as, though the language is Greek, the thoughts and idioms are Hebrew.

1 Cor. xv. 12.—" Now if Christ be preached that he rose from the dead, how say some among you," etc.: *i.e.*, how is it that some among you say.

Verse 35. " But some men will say": *i.e.*, may say.

Verse 50. "Neither doth corruption inherit incorruption": *i.e.*, neither *can* corruption, etc.

2. Subjunctive for Indicative.

Matt. xi. 6.—" Blessed is he who may not be made to stumble": *i.e.*, who is not made to stumble or seeth nothing to stumble at in me.

John xv. 8.—" By this is my Father glorified, that ye may bear much fruit": *i.e.*, that ye bear or when ye bear, etc.

1 Cor. vi. 4.—" If, then, ye may have matters of judgment" (cases for the judge): *i.e.*, if ye have.

Jas. iv. 13.—" To-day or to-morrow we may go into such a city": *i.e.*, we will go.

Verse 15: " If the Lord should will, and we should live": *i.e.*, if He willeth, and we live.

Some Christians say, " If the Lord should tarry:" not perceiving that He may tarry, and yet not will that we should live, or do this or that. Tarrying and willing are two very different things.

3. Imperative for Indicative.

Gen. xx. 7.—" For he (Abraham) is a prophet, and let him pray for thee": *i.e.*, (as in A.V.), he shall pray for thee.

Gen. xlii. 18.—" This do ye and live": *i.e.*, and ye shall live.

Gen. xlv. 18.—" I will give you the good of the land of Egypt, and eat ye the fat of the land": *i.e.*, ye shall eat (as in A.V.).

Deut. xxxii. 50.—And be gathered unto thy people": *i.e.*, thou shalt be gathered.

Ps. xxii. 8 (9).—" Roll thyself on, or trust thou in the Lord."

Whatever part of the verb גֹּל (*gōl*) may be, it must be put for the indicative, for it is so rendered in the Septuagint (" He trusted in the Lord "), and is so quoted in the New Testament (Matt. xxvii. 43).

Ps. xxxvii. 27.—" Depart from evil and do good : and dwell for evermore " : *i.e.*, thou shalt dwell.

Prov. iii. 4.—" So shalt thou find favour."

Here the A.V. recognizes the figure, for the Heb. is imperative, " find." But the A.V. misses it in iv. 4. " Keep my commandments and live " : *i.e.*, and thou shalt live.

Rom. v. 1.—" Therefore, being justified by faith, we have peace with God."

Here the reading, according to the R.V. and the Textual critics, should be ἔχωμεν (imperative), instead of ἔχομεν (indicative), as in the T.R. and A.V. Alford, though he recognizes the reading, and puts it in the text, yet bows to the overwhelming evidence of the sense, and the context, and contends for the *Indicative*. The simple solution is that this is one of the instances, if the critics are right, in which the Imperative is used for the Indicative, and though the text may say " let us have," the meaning is " we have."

1 Cor. xvi. 22.—" If any man love not the Lord Jesus Christ, let him be Anathema Maran-atha " : *i.e.*, he is or will be Anathema (or accursed) when the Lord shall come.

In prophetic utterances the future indicative is very often declared by the imperative ; for " Whatsoever the LORD willeth, that doeth he."

Isa. viii. 10.—" Take counsel together . . . speak the word " : *i.e.*, ye shall take counsel together, and it will come to naught : and ye shall speak the word, but it will not stand." So also xxix. 9 ; xxxvii. 30 ; liv. 1, etc.

John ii. 19.—" Destroy this temple." This was not a command for the Jews to destroy Him, but a prophesy that they would do so. When they perverted His words, they did not do so by taking the figure literally, but by declaring that He said " I will destroy this temple."

Gal. vi. 2.—" And so fulfil (*i.e.*, so ye will fulfil) the law of Christ."

Jas. v. 1.—" Weep and howl : " *i.e.*, ye shall weep and howl.

4. Imperative for Subjunctive.

Num. xxiv. 21.—"Strong be thy dwelling place, and build in the flint-rock thy nest. Nevertheless": *i.e.*, thou mayest put, but," etc. A.V.: "Thou puttest" (Ind.), but the sense is subjunctive.

Ps. iv. 4 (5).—"Stand in awe, and sin not": *i.e.*, if ye stand in awe ye will not sin.

Nah. iii. 14.—Here, all the imperative commands are conditional declarations, as is shown by verse 15: *i.e.*, the people might do all these things, nevertheless, it would be all in vain.

Luke x. 28.—"This do, and thou shalt live": *i.e.*, if thou do this. Hence the Imperative very often implies only *permission* :—

2 Sam. xviii. 23.—"Run": *i.e.*, thou mayest run.

1 Kings xxii. 22.—"Go forth, and do so": *i.e.*, thou mayest go, and do it.

2 Kings ii. 17.—"Send": *i.e.*, ye may send.

Matt. viii. 32.—"Go": *i.e.*, ye may go.

1 Cor. vii. 15.—"Let him depart": *i.e.*, he may depart.

1 Cor. xi. 6.—"Let her also be shorn": *i.e.*, she may be shorn.

5. Infinitive for Indicative.

Gen. viii. 5.—"And the waters were in going and returning": *i.e.*, as in A.V., decreased continually.

Ex. viii. 15 (11).—"But when Pharaoh saw that there was respite, and to harden his heart, and hearkened not unto them": *i.e.*, hardening of his heart followed, or took place.

2 Sam. iii. 18.—"By the hand of my servant David to save my people Israel": *i.e.*, I shall save.

1 Kings xxii. 30 and 2 Chron. xviii. 29.—"And the king of Israel said unto Jehoshaphat: To disguise myself and to enter into the battle": I will disguise myself; or as in margin [*when he was*] to disguise, etc.

2 Chron. xxxi. 10.—"Since the People began to bring the offerings into the House of the Lord, to eat, to be satisfied, and to have left plenty": *i.e.*, we have eaten, and had enough, and have left plenty.

Ps. viii. 1 (2).—"Who to set thy glory above the heavens": who hast set. The Targum and the Syriac have the Indicative (Num. xxvii. 20).*

---

*See the note in Dr. Ginsburg's edition of the Hebrew Bible.

P.x xsxii. 9.—" Not to understand " : *i.e.*, having no understanding.

Ps. lxxvii. 1 (2).—" Even unto God with my voice, and to hear me " : *i.e.*, and He gave ear to me, or He will hear me ; or, by *Ellipsis*, and He [*will condescend*] to hear me.

Prov. xii. 6.—" The words of the wicked *are* to lie in wait for blood " : *i.e.*, lie in wait.

Isa. v. 5.—Here, the Infinitive is correctly rendered by the Indicative future : " I will take away, and break down," etc.

Isa. xxxviii. 16.—" So wilt thou recover me, and to make me to live " : *i.e.*, and vivify me, or preserve my life.

Isa. xlix. 7.—" To him to despise in soul " : *i.e.*, to him who is despised by man.

Jer. vii. 9.—" Will ye to steal, to murder," etc. Some interpret the letter ה (*He*) as interogative, but others as intensive, Will ye steal, etc. (with emphasis on the verbs).

Jer. xiv. 5.—" Yea, the hind also calved in the field, and to forsake it " : *i.e.*, and forsook it, because there was no grass ; or, the sense may be supplied by *Ellipsis*, and [*was obliged*] to forsake it, etc.

Ezek. i. 14.—" And the living creatures to run and to return " : *i.e.*, ran and returned.

Ezek. xi. 7.—" To bring you forth " : *i.e.*, I will bring you forth. " I shall bring " is actually the reading according to the *Sevir*, and indeed it is the Textual reading in some MSS., as well as the *Editio princeps* of the Hebrew Bible (Soncino, 1488), and the marginal reading of the first edition of the Rabbinic Bible by Felix Pratensis (Venice, 1517), as may be seen from the note in Dr. Ginsburg's Edition of the Hebrew Bible.

Hab. ii. 15.—" To make him drunk " : *i.e.*, and makest him drunken also (as in A.V.).

6. Infinitive for Imperative.

Ex. xx. 8.—" To remember the sabbath day, to keep it holy " : *i.e.*, remember thou. So Deut. v. 12.

Luke ix 3.—" Neither to have two coats " : *i.e.*, neither have ye.

Rom. xii. 15.—" To rejoice with them that rejoice " : *i.e.*, rejoice ye. See under *Homœoteleuton*.

Phil. iii. 16.—" To walk by the same rule ": *i.e.*, let us walk, or walk ye.

Other examples may be seen in Josh. i. 13. Job. xxxii. 10 (11). Ps. xvii. 5 ; xxii. 8 (9). Isa. xxxii. 11. Jer. ii. 2.

III. Heterosis of the Tenses.

As the Hebrew verb has only two principal tenses, the past and the future, these two with the participles supply all the other tenses. Hence, in the New Testament, where the thought and idiom are Hebrew, though the tenses are Greek they consequently have all the variety which these tenses have in Hebrew.

1. The Past for the Present.

The Past not only serves to express what is finished or past, but what is present : regarding it, and also the future, as actually done. The past tense expresses what is either imperfect or perfect, or what is a gentle imperative, or a fixed determination, or a continuation of the action or state. The exact sense can be known only from the context.

Gen. iv. 1.—" I have gotten a man from the Lord ": *i.e.*, I have got, or, possess.

Verse 9 : " I have not known ": *i.e.* (as in A.V.), I know not, or, I do not know.

Gen. xxiii. 11, 13.—" I have given thee the field ": *i.e.*, I give to thee the field.

Gen. xxxii. 10 (11).—" I have been unworthy of all the mercies ": *i.e.*, I am unworthy.

2 Sam. i. 5.—" How hast thou known (*i.e.*, how dost thou know) that Saul and Jonathan his son are dead ? "

2 Kings iii. 11.—" Here is Elisha, son of Shaphat, who hath poured (*i.e.*, poureth) water on the hands of Elijah." Elijah's servant is described by part of his service (this is by the figure of *Synecdoche* (*q.v.*).

Ps. i. 1.—" O the happiness of that one who hath not walked (*i.e.*, doth not (and never did) walk)," etc.

Ps. xiv. 1.—" The fool hath said (*i.e.*, sayeth) in his heart, There is no God." If this Psalm refers to Nabal (*a fool*), we may render it : " Nabal said " or " A fool sayeth."

Ps. xxv. 2.—" My God, in thee I have trusted : " *i.e.*, do I trust. So Ps. xxxi. 1 (2). Prov. xvii. 5 ; and in many other places : the sense being, " I have trusted, and still do trust, in Thee."

Ps. xxxi. 6.—" Thou hast delivered (*i.e.*, thou deliverest) me, O Jehovah."

Isa. ix. 2 (1).—" The People who walk in darkness have seen (*i.e.*, see) a great light."

John i. 4.—" In him was (*i.e.*, is) life, and the life was (*i.e.*, is) the light of men."

Verse 15 : " This was (*i.e.*, is) he of whom I spake."

John iii. 16.—" God so loved (*i.e.*, loveth) the world, that he gave (*i.e.*, giveth) his only begotten Son."

John ix. 36.—" Who is he, Lord, that I shall have believed (*i.e.*, may believe) on him."

John xx. 17.—" Hold me not, for I have not yet ascended " : *i.e.*, I do not yet ascend, or am not yet ascended.

Acts xii. 14.—Rhoda " told Peter to be standing before the porch " : *i.e.*, how Peter is standing.

Rom. v. 2.—" This grace wherein ye have stood " : *i.e.*, and continue to stand.

1 Cor. i. 10.—" In whom we have hoped (and continue to hope)."

Heb. x. 11.—" And every high priest stood (*i.e.*, standeth) daily " (as in A.V.).

Jas. i. 24.—" He beheld himself, and has gone away " : *i.e.*, he beholdeth himself, and goeth his way.

1 John iii. 6.—" Whosoever sinneth hath not seen him, neither known him " : *i.e.*, seeth Him not, neither knoweth Him.

Other examples may be seen in John v. 45 ; xi. 27 ; xvi. 27. 1 Tim. iv. 10 ; v. 5.

2. The Past for the Future.

This is put when the speaker views the action as being as good as done. This is very common in the Divine prophetic utterances : where, though the sense is literally future, it is regarded and spoken of as though it were already accomplished in the Divine purpose and determination : the figure is to show the absolute certainty of the things spoken of.

Gen. xlv. 9, 10.—" Haste ye and go up to my father, then ye have said (*i.e.*, will say) to him . . . and thou hast dwelt (*i.e.*, wilt dwell) in the land of Goshen."

Ex. xvii. 4.—" They have stoned me ": *i.e.*, they will stone me.

1 Sam. ii. 31.—" Lo, the days are coming, and I have cut off thine arm": *i.e.*, shall cut off, etc.

1 Sam. x. 2.—" Thou hast found ": *i.e.*, wilt find.

1 Sam. vi. 7, 8.—" And ye have bound (*i.e.*, will bind)," etc.

Job xix. 27.—" And mine eyes have beheld " (*i.e.*, will have seen).

Ps. xxiii. 5.—" Thou hast anointed ": *i.e.*, wilt anoint.

Ps. cvii. 42.—" And all iniquity hath shut (*i.e.*, will have shut) her mouth."

Prov. i. 22.—" The scorners have delighted (*i.e.*, will delight) in their scorning."

Prov. xi. 7, 21.—" The hope of the unjust men hath perished ": *i.e.*, will perish : but just one's seed hath escaped : *i.e.*, will escape.

Prov. xii. 21.—" And the wicked have been (*i.e.*, will be) full of evil."

Jer. xxi. 9.—" Whosoever goeth forth and hath fallen unto the Chaldeans ": *i.e.*, shall fall, etc.

As we have said above, nearly all the prophecies are thus written. See Isa. xi. : "And a rod hath come out of the stock of Jesse," and often through the chapter.

John iii. 13.—" No man hath ascended up into the heaven ": *i.e.* ascend up, or can ascend.

John iv. 38.—" Other men laboured, and ye have entered (*i.e.* shall enter, or are entered) into their labours."

Rom. viii. 30.—The called are spoken of as already (in the Divine purpose) in Christ, justified, yea, even glorified.

Eph. ii. 6.—Believers are regarded as already raised from the dead and seated in the heavenly places.

Heb. ii. 7.—" Thou hast made (*i.e.*, Thou wilt make) Him for a little while less than the angels." For this was a prophecy spoken of Christ long before, in Ps. viii.

Heb. iii. 14.—" We have been made (*i.e.*, we shall become) partakers of Christ, if we hold," etc.

Heb. xii. 22.—" But ye have come (*i.e.*, shall come) unto Mount Zion," etc.

3. The Aorist for the Past.

The Aorist, or *indefinite* past tense, is used to denote an action definitely past and completed some time ago.

Matt. xiv. 3.—" Now Herod, having laid hold of John, bound him ": *i.e.*, had bound him.

John xviii. 24.—" Now Annas sent him (*i.e.*, had sent him) bound unto Caiaphas."

4. The Aorist for the Present.

The Aorist is sometimes put for a past action or state continued up to the present time.

Matt. iii. 17.—" This is my beloved son, in whom I was (*i.e.*, was and am) well pleased."   So Mark i. 11, and Luke iii. 22.

Matt. xxiii. 2.—" The Scribes and Pharisees sat (*i.e.*, and continue to sit) in Moses' seat."

Mark xvi. 19.—" Was taken up into heaven, and sat (*i.e.*, sat and continues to sit) on the right hand of God."

Luke i. 47.—" My spirit rejoiced ": *i.e.*, hath rejoiced and doth rejoice.   A.V., " hath rejoiced."

Luke xv. 16.—" And he was longing to have filled ": *i.e.*, to fill."

John i. 12.—" To them gave he authority to have become (*i.e.*, to become, or that they might be) sons of God."

1 John iv. 8.—" He that loveth not, knew not (*i.e.*, knoweth not, or never knew) God."

John xi. 56.—" What think ye, that he will not have come (*i.e.*, there is no hope of his coming) to the feast ? "

John xv. 6.—" Except anyone abide in me he was cast out (*i.e.*, will be cast out), and was (*i.e.*, will be) burned."   See under *Ellipsis.*

5. The Present for the Past.

Matt. ii. 13.—" And when they were departed, behold, the angel of the Lord appeareth (*i.e.*, appeared)."

Mark ii. 4.—" They are letting down the bed " : *i.e.*, they did let down. See also chaps. iii. 19, 20, 31 and xvi. 2.

John iii. 13.—" No man hath ascended into heaven, but the Son of man who is (*i.e.*, who was) in heaven." Note that the perfect of the first verb is used for the future, as already observed above.

Acts ix. 26.—" They were all afraid of him, not believing (or refusing to believe) that he is (*i.e.*, was. So the A.V.) a disciple."

Gal. ii. 14.—" But when I saw that they do (*i.e.*, did) not walk uprightly."

Heb. ii. 16.—" For not, indeed, of angels' nature He taketh (*i.e.*, took) hold, but of Abraham's seed He taketh (*i.e*, took) hold."

Heb. vii. 3.—" He remaineth (*i.e.*, remained) a priest all his life."

Heb. vii. 8.—" One testified of that he liveth" (*i.e.*, that he lived, viz., a priest) all his life.   See above.

6. The Present for the Future.

This is put when the design is to show that some thing will certainly come to pass, and is spoken of as though it were already present.

Matt. ii. 4.—" Demanded of then where Christ should be (*i.e.*, is to be) born."

Matt. iii. 10.—" Every tree which bringeth not forth good fruit is hewn down " : *i.e.*, will be hewn down.

Matt. v. 46.—" What reward have ye ? " *i.e.*, will ye have ?

Matt. xvii. 11.—" Elias indeed cometh (*i.e.*, will come) first."

Matt. xxvi. 29.—" Until the day when I drink (*i.e.*, shall be drinking) it with you new," etc.

Mark ix. 31.—" The Son of man is delivered (*i.e.*, will be delivered) unto the hands of men."

Luke xiii. 32.—" And the third day I am (*i.e.*, shall be) perfected."

1 Cor. xv. 2.—" By which also ye are (*i.e.*, will be) saved."

1 Cor. xv. 12.—" How say some among you that there is (*i.e.*, will or can be) no resurrection of the dead ? "

2 Pet. iii. 11.—" Seeing that all these things are (*i.e.*, shall be) dissolved."

2 Pet. iii. 12.—" And the elements are (*i.e.*, shall be) melted."

Other examples may be seen in Matt. xi. 3. John vii. 27, 33, 34 ; viii. 58 ; x. 17, 18 ; xii. 26, 34 ; xiii. 6, 27 ; xvi. 16. Acts i. 6. 1 Cor. xv. 35 ; xvi. 5. Rev. xi. 5, etc., etc.

7. The Present for the Paulo post futurum.*

Matt. xxvi. 24.—" The Son of man indeed goeth (*i.e.*, will soon be gone, or given over), as it is written of Him."

So verse 45. Mark xiv. 41. Luke xxii. 22, 37. John xiii. 3 ; xiv. 3, 18, 19 ; xvii. 11, etc.

Luke xxii. 19.—" Which is given (*i.e.*, which will soon have been given) for you."

So also Matt. xxvi. 28. Mark xiv. 24. 1 Cor. xi. 24.

Luke xxiv. 49.—" Behold, I send (*i.e.*, I shall soon have sent) the promise of my Father," etc. So also John xx. 17.

2 Tim. iv. 6.—" For I already am being poured (or offered) " : *i.e.*, I shall soon have been offered up.

8. The Future for the Past.

The future is used for the past when it is understood that the thing or matter was future at the time of writing or speaking.

Ex. xv. 5.—" The depths will cover (*i.e.*, have covered and will continue to cover) them."

Judges ii. 1.—" I shall make (*i.e.*, I made) you to go up out of Egypt and shall bring (*i.e.*, have brought) you into the land which I sware unto your fathers." When the angel spake this it was past : when Jehovah said it, it was future.

Judges v. 8.—" He (*i.e.*, Israel) will choose (*i.e.*, he chose) new Gods." For Deborah is speaking of the cause of the affliction which had fallen upon the People : *viz.*, idolatry.

Judges xxi. 25.—" Each man will do (*i.e.*, did) what was right in his own eyes."

2 Sam. iii. 33.—" And the king lamented over Abner, and said, Will Abner die as a fool dieth ? " (*i.e.*, as in A.V., Died Abner, etc.).

2 Sam. xii. 3.—" She will (*i.e.*, did) eat of his own meat, and will drink (*i.e.*, drank) of his own cup, and will lie (*i.e.*, lay) in his bosom, and so she became unto him as a daughter."

---

* This tense differs from the simple or perfect future by denoting and referring to something which *will soon be past.*

Isa. lxiii. 3.—" I shall tread (*i.e.*, I have trodden) . . ." as in the rest of the verse.

9. The Future for the Present.

This is a case in which what was then future at the time of speaking, remained, or remains, as a present fact. The *present* in this case is often in the subjunctive or reflexive mood.

Gen. ii. 10.—" And thence it will part (*i.e.*, gets parted, or parts itself) and becomes four heads."

Num. xviii. 7.—" I shall give (*i.e.*, I do give) your priest's office unto you as a service of gift " : *i.e.*, the gift at the time of speaking was future; but, ministry remains an ever present gift.

Job iii. 20.—" Wherefore will light be given to him that is in misery ? " (*i e.*, is light given).

Ps. i. 2.—" And in His Law he will (*i.e.*, doth) meditate." So Ps. iii. 5 (6); xxii. 2 (3); xxv. 1; xxxi. 5 (6). Hos. i. 2, etc.

Matt. xii. 31.—" Every sin and blasphemy will be (*i.e.*, may be) forgiven to men.

Luke vi. 7.—" Whether he will heal (*i.e.*, whether he does heal) on the sabbath day." Here the Critical Texts actually read the present tense, as in the next passage (Luke xxiii. 46).

Luke xxiii. 46.—" Father, into thy hands I shall commend (*i.e.*, I commend) my spirit."

Rom. iii. 30.—" Seeing it is one God which shall (*i.e.*, doth) justify."

10. The Future for the Imperative.

The Future of the Indicative is by Hebrew idiom frequently used for the Imperative. When this is the case, the Imperative is very forcible and emphatic ; not being so much a mere command as the assertion of a fact which could hardly be otherwise. All the ten commandments are in this form.

" *Thou wilt not* " not merely " shalt not."

Judges v. 21.—" O my soul, thou wilt tread down strength " : *i.e.*, tread thou down (not, as in A.V., " hast trodden down "); or, R.V. : " march on."

So Ps. v. 11 (12).

1 Cor. v. 13.—" Ye will put away (*i.e.*, put away) from among yourselves that wicked person.

1 Tim. vi. 8.—" We shall be content " : *i.e.*, let us be content.

IV. HETEROSIS OF PERSON AND NUMBER (VERBS).

In order to make what is said more emphatic, Hebrew idiom sometimes changes the number and person of the verb. In most of these cases the figure is correctly rendered in the A.V., so that we need only give a few examples which are there passed over.

1. The First Person for the Third.

Ecc. iii. 18.—" I said in my heart according to the reasoning of the sons of men ": *i.e.*, according to the reasoning of man, or human reasoning : *i.e.*, man says in his heart.

In Rom. vii., Paul, though speaking in the first person, is saying what is true of all who share his experience : and not merely speaking of his own case as being peculiar or different from others.

Rom. x. 18.—" But I say." Who says it ? David ! But by the Holy Spirit what David said is now repeated by Paul in the first person.

2. The Second Person for the Third.

Isa. i. 29.—" They shall be ashamed for the oaks which ye (*i.e.*, they) have desired," etc.

For they desired them, of course : yet the persons addressed were equally guilty and are thus by the sudden change of persons charged with the same sin.

Isa. xlii. 20.—" Seeing many things, but thou observest not ": (*i.e.*, he observes not) as in the rest of the verse.

Jer. xxix. 19.—" But ye (*i.e.*, they) would not hear."

Gal. vi. 1.—"Ye that are spiritual restore such an one, in the spirit of meekness, considering thyself (instead of yourselves)." This is in order to emphasize the fact that those who are thus addressed stand each in the same individual danger.

3. The Third person for the First or Second.

Gen. xlix. 4.—" Because thou wentest up to thy father's bed ; then defiledst thou it : he went (*i.e.*, thou wentest) up to my couch."

Isa. liv. 1.—Here the third person is rendered correctly in A.V. by the second.

Lam. iii. 1.—" I am the man, he hath (*i.e.*, I have) seen affliction."

Micah vii. 18.—Here we have " his " inheritance, after the address " like thee."

4. The Plural for the Singular.

Gen. xxix. 27.—" Fulfil her week, and we (*i.e.*, I) will give thee this also for thy service."

Num. xxii. 6.—" Peradventure I shall prevail, that we (*i.e.*, I) may smite them."

2 Sam. xvi. 20.—" Then said Absalom to Ahithophel, Give counsel among you What shall we (*i.e.*, I) do ? "

Job xviii. 2.—" How long will it be ere ye (*i.e.*, thou) make an end of words ? mark, and afterwards we (*i.e.*, I) will speak."

Dan. ii. 36.—" This is the dream; and we (*i.e.*, I) will tell the interpretation thereof."

Mark iv. 30.—" Whereunto shall we (*i.e.*, I) liken the kingdom of God ? "

John iii. 11.—" We (*i.e.*, I) speak that we (*i.e.*, I) know, and testify that we (*i.e.*, I) have seen ; and ye receive not our (*i.e.*, my) witness."

John xxi. 24.—" And we (*i.e.*, I) know that his testimony is true."

Rom. i. 5.—" By whom we (*i.e.*, I, Paul) have received grace and apostleship."   (See also *Hendiadys*).

1 Tim. ii. 15.—" She will be saved through `the child-bearing if they (*i.e.*, Eve and all her daughters) abide in faith," etc.

5. The Singular for the Plural.

Num. xxxii. 25.—" Spake " is (sing) " he spake ": *i.e., the tribe* as composed of the children of Gad," etc. It is put for the plural, " they spake" ; and it should really be "they spake " (*viz.*, the children of Gad and the children of Reuben), according to the *Sevir*. This extra-official reading is the Textual reading in several MSS.; in the Samaritan Text, in the Targums of Jonathan and Onkelos, the Septuagint, the Syriac, and the Vulgate. See the note in Dr. Ginsburg's Hebrew Bible. So 1 Sam. xvi. 4 : *i.e.*, one particular elder spoke for all. But the sing. is put for the plural : for here, again, according to the note in Dr. Ginsburg's Text, the verb should be in the plural. This is not only the reading according to the *Sevir*, but it is in the Text of many MSS., the *Editio princeps* of the Prophets (Soncino, 1485-6), the first edition of the Hebrew Bible (1488), the Targum, the LXX. Syriac, and the Vulgate.

See also Est. ix. 23. Job xii. 7. Ps. lxxiii. 7. Prov. xiv. 1, 9.

V. Heterosis of Degree.

The Hebrew has no degrees of comparison in the Adjective: hence other methods are adopted to express them.

In the New Testament, while the language is Greek, the thoughts and idioms are Hebrew; so that the Hebrew methods of comparison are frequently adopted; and thus we have, by the use of *Enallage*, several examples of exchange in the expression of Degree. (See under *Idiom*).

1. The Positive for the Comparative.

Where the positive is used with the comparative particle ἤ (*ee*), *than*, it implies that, though there may be in one sense a comparison, yet, in another and true sense, there is really no comparison at all; for the use of the positive declares that the one case is so, rather than the other, which is not so.

Ps. cxviii. 8, 9.—" It is good to trust in the LORD, *rather* than to put confidence in man ": *i.e.*, the one is good, the other is not; yea, it is accursed (see Jer. xvii. 5, 7).

Matt. xii. 7.—" I will have mercy, and not sacrifice ": *i.e.*, rather than sacrifice.

Matt. xviii. 8.—" It is good for thee ": *i.e.*, (as in A.V.) it is better for thee, etc. But the meaning is that the one condition is good, and not the other. Hence it is expressed " rather than the other."

Mark iii. 4.—" Is it lawful to do good on the sabbath-days or to do evil ? ": *i.e.*, more lawful to do good than to do evil. The evil His enemies did on the sabbath was in watching Him.

Luke xviii. 14.—" I tell you, this man went down to his house justified *rather* than the other."

Here, the A.V. has translated it not as a comparative, but as positive; supplying the word " *rather*," which is quite correct. The thought being that, while there must be a comparison between the two men, the one was justified and the other was not.

The whole parable is concerning justification and not about prayer. See verse 9.

John vi. 27.—" Labour not for the meat which perisheth, but for the meat that endureth to eternal life ": *i.e.*, *labour more* for the latter than for the former, or *rather than*.

John xv. 22.—"If I had not come and spoken to them, they had not had sin": *i.e.*, *so much sin.*

1 Cor. iii. 7.—"So neither is the planter anything, nor the waterer; but God that maketh grow": *i.e.*, they were nothing in comparison with God.

2. The Positive for the Superlative.

1 Sam. xvii. 14.—"And David was the small *one* (*i.e.*, the smallest) : and the three great *ones* (*i.e.*, the greater or greatest three) followed Saul."

2 Chron. xxi. 17.—"The small one (*i.e.*, the smallest) of his sons."

Jonah iii. 5.—"From their great one (*i.e.*, the greatest one among them) to their small (*i.e.*, smallest) one."

Matt. v. 19.—"Whosoever therefore shall break one of these shortest commandments and shall teach men so, he shall be called least in the kingdom of heaven, but whosoever shall do and teach them, the same shall be called great in the kingdom of heaven." See under *Synœceiosis*.

Heb. x. 21.—"And having a great (*i.e.*, highest) priest over the house of God." So xiii. 20.

3. The Comparative for the Positive.

1 Tim. iii. 14.—"Hoping to come unto thee more quickly": *i.e.*, soon; or, as in A.V., shortly.

2 Tim. i. 18.—"And in how many things he ministered to me in Ephesus thou knowest better": *i.e.*, well; or (as in A.V.), very well : *i.e.*, to well to need reminding of.

4. The Comparative for the Superlative.

Matt. xiii. 32.—"Which indeed is less than (or least of) all the seeds (which men sow in the fields)."

Matt. xviii. 1.—"Who then is greater in the kingdom of heaven": or (as in A.V.), greatest.

John x. 29.—"My Father, which gave them me, is greater than (*i.e.*, greatest of) all."

1 Cor. xiii. 13.—"But the greater (*i.e.*, the greatest) of these is charity."

1 Cor. xv. 19.—"If in this life only we have hope in Christ, we are of all men more (*i.e.*, most, as in A.V.) miserable."

5. The Superlative for the Comparative.

John i. 15.—"For he was first of me": *i.e.*, prior to me (A.V. before me). So the word first is used in Mark vi. 21; Luke xix. 47; Acts xxv. 2; Rev. xiii. 12; and perhaps Rev. xxi. 1: "the *former* heaven and earth"; and Rev. xx. 6: the *former* resurrection of the two foretold in the Old Testament and in the Gospels. Not necessarily the special resurrection of the Church of God revealed in 1 Thess. iv. 16.

John xv. 18.—"If the world hate you, ye know that it hated me first of you": *i.e.*, before you. So 1 Cor. xiv. 30. 1 Tim. v. 12.

2 Thess. ii. 3.—"Except there come the apostacy first": *i.e.*, before it.

1 John iv. 19.—"We love Him because He first loved us": *i.e.*, before we loved Him.

VI. HETEROSIS OF NUMBER.

1. The Singular for the Plural.

Gen. iii. 8.—"Hid themselves from the presence of the LORD God amongst the tree (*i.e.*, trees) of the garden"; or, perhaps, tree in the sense of tree-growth or "a wood" as we speak of a collection of trees.

Gen. xlix. 6.—"In their anger they slew a man (*i.e.*, men) and in their self-will they houghed an ox (*i.e.*, oxen)."

Ex. xiv. 17.—Here, the A.V. has taken the singular "chariot" as though put for the plural. But it is a question whether it be so in this case, owing to the alternate structure.

> a | Pharaoh.
>   b | His host.
> *a* | Pharaoh's chariot.
>   *b* | His horsemen.

Ex. xv. 1, 21.—"The horse and his rider": *i.e.*, horses and their riders."

Ex. xxiii. 28.—"I shall send the hornet before thee": *i.e.*, hornets (without the article).

Lev. xi. 2.—"This is the beast which ye shall eat": *i.e., these are the beasts*, as in A.V.

2 Cor. xi. 26.—"Dangers in the city (*i.e.*, cities, or city-dangers), dangers in the wilderness (*i.e.*, wildernesses, or wilderness-dangers)."

1 Cor. vi. 5.—" One who shall be able to judge between his brother ": *i.e.*, his brethren.

See also Num. xxi. 7, 31. Deut. xx. 19. 2 Sam. xix. 41 (42). Prov. xvii. 22; Hos. v. 6. Jonah ii. 3 (4), etc. And in New Testament, Rev. xxi. 21, " street " for streets. Also often " demon " and " wicked ones " means all the demons and evil spirits. See John viii. 44, and Eph. vi. 16.

In Pronouns the singular is frequently put for the plural. See Deut. xxi. 10. Josh. ii. 4. 2 Kings iii. 3. Ps. xxxv. 8. Phil. iii. 20.

2. The Plural for the Singular.

This is so put when great excellence or magnitude is denoted.

Our attention is thus called to the importance of the thing or matter concerning which the statement is made.

Gen. iv. 10.—" Bloods ": *i.e.*, much blood.

Lev. xix. 24.—" It shall be holy to praise the LORD withal." Heb. (margin), it shall be " holiness of praises to the LORD ": *i.e.*, the fruit of a young tree was not to be eaten for three years, but in the fourth year it was to be counted as holy to the great praise and glory of Jehovah. See under *Prosopopœia*.

Gen. xix. 11.—" And they smote the men that were at the door of the house with the blindnesses ": *i.e.*, with intense blindness (as in 2 Kings vi. 18, the only occurrences of this word).

2 Sam. iii. 28.—" Bloods ": *i.e.*, much blood.

1 Chron. xxviii. 3.—" Bloods ": *i.e.*, much blood.

Ps. xxii. 3 (4).—" O Thou that inhabitest the praises of Israel ": *i.e.*, the loud or perfect praise.

Ps. xxviii. 8.—" The LORD is their strength, and he is the strength of salvations ": *i.e.*, great saving strength or strength of great and mighty salvation. The margin has " his strength," but למו stands for לעמו written defective for plene, as is shown and preserved in some ancient versions and noted in R.V. margin.* The meaning thus is :—

> " Jehovah is the strength of his people,
> And He is the strength of great salvation of His anointed."

Ps. xlii. 5 (6), 11 (12) ; xliii. 5.—" I shall yet praise him for the helps or healths ": *i.e.*, the wonderful help, great deliverance, or great salvation.

---

* See Dr. Ginsburg's edition of the Hebrew Bible.

Ps. xlv. 15 (16).—" With gladnesses and rejoicing shall they be brought ": *i.e.*, with great gladness and rejoicing.

Ps. xlvii. 6 (7).—" Praises " : *i.e.*, great or loudest praise.

Ps. xlix. 3 (4).—" My mouth shall speak wise things " : *i.e.*, great wisdom.

Ps. li. 17 (19).—" The sacrifices of God " : the great sacrifice of God is a broken spirit.

Ps. lxxxix. 1 (2).—" I will sing of the mercies " : *i.e.*, the great and wondrous mercy. So often in N.T., Rom. xii. 1. 2 Cor. i. 3.

Ps. xc. 10.—" And if by reason of strengths (or excellencies) " : *i.e.*, of *great strength.*

Ps. cxxxix. 14.—" I will confess thee, because that (with) wonders (*i.e.*, with great wonder) I have been distinguished, and wonderful are thy works."

Ps. cxliv. 7.—" Send thine hands from above ; rid me and deliver me " : *i.e.*, send thy gracious protection and great delivering power.

The singular is actually the Textual reading, not only in some Manuscripts, but in the *Editio princeps* of the Hagiographa (Naples, 1486-7), the Targum, the LXX, the Syriac, and the Vulgate. See Dr. Ginsburg's note on this passage in his edition of the Hebrew Bible.

See under *Anthropopatheia.*

Ecc. v. 6 (7).—" Vanities " : *i.e.*, great vanity.

Isa. xxvi. 2.—" Which keepeth truths " : *i.e.*, the great and important truth of God.

Isa. lviii. 11.—" In droughts " : *i.e.*, in *great drought.*

Jer. xxii. 21.—" I spake unto thee in thy prosperities (*i.e.*, in thy great prosperity), but thou saidst, I will not hear."

Lam. i. 9.—" Wonders " : *i.e.*, a great wonder.

Lam. iii. 22.—" It is of the LORD'S mercies " : *i.e.*, great mercy.

Ezek. xxii. 2.—" The city of the bloods " : *i.e.*, the city where so much blood has been shed.

Ezek. xxv. 17.—" Vengeances " : *i.e.*, great or terrible vengeance. See A.V. margin and Ps. xciv. 1.

Ezek. xxviii. 10.—" Deaths " : *i.e.*, the awful death.

Dan. ii. 18.—" Mercies " : *i.e.*, great mercy.

Matt. xxvi. 65.—" Then the High Priest rent his clothes " : *i.e.*, his great robe of office.

John i. 13.—" Not of bloods " : *i.e.*, not of the best or purest blood ; or not of the very best of human parents.

Acts i. 7.—" Times or seasons " : *i.e.*, the great and important time and season. So 1 Thess. v. 1.   1 Tim. vi. 15.   Tit. i. 3.

Rom. xii. 1.—" Mercies " : *i.e.*, great mercy.

1 Cor. xv. 29.—It has been suggested that in this passage we have the plural for the singular.   " What shall they do which are baptized for the dead ? " (plural) *i.e., for Christ*, who was put to death. But see this passage under *Ellipsis* (page 41).

2 Cor. i. 3.—" Mercies " : *i.e.*, great mercy.

Heb. ix. 12.—" Into the holies " : *i.e.*, the most holy place.

Heb. ix. 23.—" With better sacrifices than these " : *i.e.*, one better and greater sacrifice ; for Christ offered only one sacrifice.

Heb. x. 28.—" Without mercies " : *i.e.*, without the least mercy.

Jas. i. 17.—" Father of lights " : *i.e.*, true light.   Hence, the Father who is the source of all true light (being the genitive of *origin*).

1 Pet. v. 3.—" Not as being lords over *God's* heritages " : *i.e.*, great heritage.   The word " *God* " is repeated, by *Ellipsis*, from verse 2, and presents the same truth as Acts xx. 28.

The R.V. is a gloss and not a translation :—" Neither as lording it over the charge allotted to you."   The great point is that God's People are His *great inheritance ;* and that no man has a right to assume lordship or headship over it.   It is Peter who says this by the Holy Spirit.   The Greek is τῶν κλήρων (*tōn kleerōn*), the word from which we have the term " *clergy*."   So that man's thought is just the opposite of God's.   Man's thought is that the people are not to lord it over the clergy ; but that the clergy are to lord it over them.   This is just the opposite of what is taught us and impressed upon us by the use of this figure in 1 Pet. v. 3, where the truth is that the clergy are not to lord it over the laity.

2 Pet. iii. 11.—" In holy conversations and godlinesses " : *i.e.*, holy, weighty, and solemn conduct and piety.

Certain words are generally plural : *e.g.*, αἰῶνες (*aiōnes*), *ages*.   This may be to mark the fact that eternity is made up of successive ages : the singular referring either to one such age ; or including all, as a whole.   Hence we have εἰς τὸν αἰῶνα (*eis ton aiōna*), *unto the age* or *for ever* (Matt. xxi. 19.   John vi. 51, 58.   1 Pet. i. 25 from Isa. xl. 8, etc.). And εἰς τοὺς αἰῶνας (*eis tous aiōnas*), *unto the ages* (Luke i. 33.   Rom. i. 25 ; ix. 5.   Heb. xiii. 8, etc.).

Oὐρανοί (*ouranoi*), *heavens*, is generally plural; a usage arising from the Hebrew idiom where the word is dual. It is always plural in the phrase "kingdom of heaven," where "heaven" is used by *Metonymy* (*q.v.*) for God. The Hebrew idiom is sometimes rendered thus, literally, and sometimes idiomatically, "kingdom of God." See under *Idiom*.

3. Sometimes the PLURAL is put for an indefinite number, or for one of many.

In this latter case the word "one" is to be supplied by *Ellipsis*.

Gen. viii. 4.—"The mountains": *i.e.*, one of the mountains, or the great mountain.

Gen. xix. 29.—"The cities in which Lot dwelt": *i.e.*, in one of which cities.

Judges xii. 7.—Here the words "*one of*" are supplied in italics.

Neh. iii. 8.—"Uzziel the son of Harhaiah, of the goldsmiths": *i.e.*, of *one of* the goldsmiths.

Job xxi. 32.—"Yet shall he (the wicked) be brought to the graves": *i.e.*, to *one of* the graves: *i.e.*, his grave.

Matt. ii. 20.—"They are dead who seek," etc.: only Herod is meant (see Ex. iv. 19).

Matt. ix. 8.—"Which gave such power to men (pl.)." Only one is meant, *viz.*, Christ.

Transition or Change from the Singular to the Plural.

In these cases, it is not so much that one number or person is exchanged for another as that there is a sudden change from one to the other, calling our attention to the truth taught by this change. See under *Anacoluthon*.

Ex. x. 2.—"And that thou mayest tell in the ears of thy son . . . that ye may know how that I am the LORD."

Ps. xiv. 1.—"The fool hath said in his heart, 'There is no God.' They are corrupt," etc.

Isa. ii. 20.—"In that day shall a man cast his idols . . . which they have made each one for himself to worship."

Gal. iv. 6-8.—"Because ye are sons, God hath sent forth the spirit of His Son into your hearts . . . Wherefore thou art no more a servant, but a son . . . Howbeit, then, when ye knew not God," etc.

Gal. vi. 1.—" Ye which are spiritual restore such an one in the spirit of meekness; considering thyself."

See also 1 Thess. v. 1-10. 1 Tim. ii. 15. Rev. i. 3, etc.

VII. Heterosis of Gender.

As the Hebrew (like French) has no neuter gender, sometimes the masculine is used, and sometimes the feminine.

And this is seen in the Greek of the New Testament, notwithstanding that the Greek has the neuter gender.

There are, however, other exchanges of gender besides this.

1. The Masculine for the Feminine.

Acts ix. 37.—" Whom when they had washed." Here, though (in the Greek) the masculine " they " is put, women are meant.

Heb. ix. 16, 17.—"The testator," ὁ διαθέμενος (*ho diatheminos*): *i.e.*, the covenant-maker, is masculine; but the word for sacrifice, to which it refers, is feminine: yet the masculine is used, because the sacrifice was Christ Himself; otherwise it would have been feminine to agree with sacrifice (ἡ θύσια, *hee thusia*). Thus, though the Greek word is feminine, the Heb. בְּרִית is masculine, and ὁ διαθέμινος agrees with the Heb. *thought*, rather than with the Greek *word*. (See pages 69 and 493).

2. The Masculine for the Neuter.

Gen. ii. 18.—" He is not good ": *i.e.*, it is not a good thing for him (man) to be alone. See also Ps. cxix. 65. Isa. v. 20; vii. 15.

John xvi. 13.—"When HE—the Spirit of truth—is come, HE will guide you into all truth, for HE shall not speak of Himself; but whatsoever HE shall hear that shall HE speak, and HE will show you things to come." Here, though the word " Spirit " is neuter, the pronouns are masculine, and this is so put in order to show and impress upon us that the Holy Spirit is a *Person*.

3. The Feminine for the Neuter.

Gen. 1. 20.—" Ye thought evil (fem.) against me, but God meant it unto good (fem.)." While the masc. רָע is generally used for *moral* evil, its feminine רָעָה is used for the consequence of that—*viz.*, *physical* evil. So here, the feminine denotes *mischief, hurt:* " Ye meant me harm; but God meant it (masc.) for good ": *i.e.*, meant to turn it to good. So also Job v. 9. Ps. xii. 3; xxvii. 4.

Also for the use of pronouns (see Gen. xv. 6 ; xliii. 32.   Ex. x. 11. Num. xxiii. 23.   Ps. cxviii. 23.   Matt. xxi. 42.   Mark xii. 11.

4. The Neuter for the Masculine or Feminine.

Matt. i. 20.—"For that (neut.) which is conceived (or begotten) in her."   So Luke i. 35 : "that holy thing."

Matt. xviii. 11.—"For the Son of Man is come to save that (neut.) which was lost " : *i.e.*, lost sinners, of both sexes.

John i. 46 (47).—"Can there any good thing (neut.) come out of Nazareth?"   The words were spoken with reference to Christ.

John iii. 6.—"That (neut.) which is born of the flesh is flesh ; and that (neut.) which is born of the Spirit is spirit."   The neuter is used to agree with the word "thing," though person is meant : because that which is born of the flesh or spirit is rather the fleshly or spiritual nature, than the man as an individual : but also, because it includes men and women.

Heb. vii. 7.—"And without all contradiction the less (neut.) is blessed of the better."

See also Luke xvi. 15.   John vi. 39 (compare verse 40).   1 Cor. i. 27, 28.

1 John i. 1.—"That which was from the beginning," etc.: *i.e.*, Him who was.   Compare John i. 1, 14.

1 John v. 4.—"For whatsoever (neut.) is begotten of God."   That this refers to *persons* is clear from verses 1-5 : but it is put neuter both on account of the spiritual or new nature which is referred to (spirit being neuter), as well as from the fact that both men and women are included.

1 John v. 8.—"There are three that bear witness in earth, the spirit (neut.), and the water (neut.), and the blood (neut.), and these (masc.) three are one."   Because persons are meant, the pronoun is masculine, though the other words are neuter.

HYPALLAGE; or, INTERCHANGE.

Interchange of Construction.

Hy-pal'-la-gee, ὑπαλλαγή, from ὑπό (*hypo*), *under*, and ἀλλάσσειν (*allassein*), *to change*. *An underchange* or *interchange*.

Hypallage differs from *Antiptosis* in that it relates to an interchange of construction whereby an adjective or other word, which *logically* belongs to one connexion, is grammatically united with another, so that what is said of or attributed to one thing ought to be said of or attributed to the other.

In the case of two nouns (the latter *in regimen*), they are *interchanged* in sense, not as in *Antiptosis* (where the former becomes an adjective instead of the latter), but they are *reversed* in order or construction without regard to the purely adjectival sense.

Shakespeare makes Cassius say of Julius Cæsar:

"His coward lips did from their colour fly."

Instead of "the colour did fly from his coward lips."

This interchange attracts attraction to what is said, and thus emphasizes the true and real meaning.

Gen. x. 9.—"A strong man of hunting": *i.e.*, a mighty hunter, as in A.V. and R.V.

Here, according to the ordinary usage, the word "hunting" would be (by *Enallage*) the qualifying word: a hunting man of strength; but, by *Hypallage*, there is an Interchange, by which the noun becomes the adjective: a mighty hunter.

Gen. xxix. 14.—"And he abode with him a month of days": *i.e.*, the days of a month; a calendar month. A.V.: "The space of a month."

Lev. xii. 4.—"The blood of her purifying" or "purgation": *i.e.*, in the purgation or cleansing from her blood.

Deut. xii. 3.—"The graven images of their gods": *i.e.*, their gods consisting of graven images.

Josh. ii. 6.—"She hid them with the flax of stalks": *i.e.*, with the stalks of flax (as in A.V.), or *flax-stalks*.

2 Sam. xii. 27.—"I have fought against Rabbah and have taken the city of waters": *i.e.*, taken or cut off the waters of the city. Verse 28 shows he had not taken the city, for Joab says to David, come "lest I take the city."

When, therefore, in verse 26, it is said he "took the royal city," it must mean the royal part of the city, where the king resided.

1 Kings xvii. 14.—"Thus saith the LORD God of Israel : The barrel of meal (*i.e.*, the meal in the barrel) shall not waste, neither shall the cruse of oil (*i.e.*, the oil in the cruse) fail."

Neh. x. 34.—"For the offering of wood ": *i.e.*, the wood for the offering, unless it mean the free supply of wood.

Est. ix. 19.—"That dwelt in the cities of the villages": *i.e.*, in the villages belonging to the cities.

Job. xxxi. 27.—"Or my hand hath kissed my mouth ": *i.e.* (as A.V. renders it), my mouth hath kissed my hand.

Ps. xix. 13 (14).—"Keep back also thy servant from presumptious sins ": *i.e.*, keep back presumptuous sins from thy servant, "let them not," etc.

Ps. cxxxix. 23, 24.—"Search me, O God (El) . . and see if there be any wicked way in me, and lead me in the way everlasting": *i.e.*, see if I be in any wicked way. The Heb. is "a way of grief:" where grief (the effect of a wicked way) is put (by *Metonymy*) for the wicked way which causes it. See *Metonymy*.

Prov. xxvi. 23.—"Burning lips and a wicked heart are like a potsherd covered with silver of dross": *i.e.*, dross of silver.

Jer. xi. 19.—"I knew not that they had devised devices against me, saying, Let us destroy his dish in his food ": *i.e.*, the food in his dish.

Ezek. xxi. 29 (34).—"In the time of the iniquity of the end ": *i.e.*, in the time of the end of their iniquity ; or, as in A.V., "when their iniquity shall have an end."

Matt. viii. 3.—"His leprosy was cleansed ": *i.e.*, he was cleansed from his leprosy. Or perhaps leprosy is put (by *Metonymy* of the adjunct) for the person diseased with it. See under *Metonymy*.

Acts v. 20.—"All the words of this life ": *i.e.*, all these words of life.

Rom. v. 17.—"Abundance of grace": *i.e.*, abounding grace (not gracious abounding).

Rom. vii. 24.—"Who shall deliver me from the body of this death ?" *i.e.*, this body of death (as in A.V. margin) ; or, this mortal, dying body. Not until this mortal body shall die, or be changed and glorified, shall the saints be delivered from their conflict between the old and the new natures. It cannot be accomplished by vows or resolutions, or by discipline, which is the fond idea and aim of all who are ignorant of this teaching, from Rome to Keswick.

Rom. ix. 31.—" But Israel, which followed after the law of righteousness, hath not attained to the law of righteousness ": *i.e.*, to the righteousness of the law.

Rom. xv. 19.—" So that from Jerusalem, and round about unto Illyricum, I have fully preached the gospel of Christ ": *i.e.*, I have filled, with the gospel of Christ, Jerusalem and round about, etc.

2 Cor. iii. 7.—" If the ministration (or ministry) of death written and engraven in stones." It was the *letters*, not the ministry, which were engraven on stones.

Gal. vi. 1.—" The spirit of meekness ": *i.e.*, meekness of spirit.

Eph. i. 9.—" The mystery of His will."

The word μυστήριον (*musteerion*) rendered *mystery* always means a *secret*. And here it is the Secret pertaining to God's purpose: *i.e.*, the Secret which He hath purposed; or, by the figure *Hypallage*, His Secret purpose, because the noun *in regimen* is the word qualified instead of the word which qualifies.

In Judith ii. 2 we have the remarkable expression: Nebuchadnezzar " called together all his servants, and all his great men, and communicated with them his *secret* counsel ": *i.e.*, the secret of his will. The word μυστήριον is the same in each case, but in the case of Nebuchadnezzar it was the secret of his βουλή (*boulee*): *i.e.*, his will, because he had *determined* it: while in Eph. i. 9, it is the secret of God's θέλημα (*theleema*): *i.e.*, His will, because He *desired* it. Hence the meaning is " God's secret purpose or counsel."

Heb. ix. 15.—" That . . . they which are called might receive the promise of eternal inheritance ": *i.e.*, the eternal inheritance which had been promised.

Heb. ix. 23.—Here, the purification attributed to the heavenly things really applies to those who shall enter; as is clear from the former part of the verse.

Jas. ii. 17.—" Faith . . . is dead ": *i.e.*, the man who says he has such faith is dead.

Jas. iii. 4.—" Wherever the impulse of the steersman may will ": *i.e.*, as in A.V., whithersoever the governor (*i.e.*, pilot) listeth.

Rev. xxi. 24.—" And the nations of them that are saved ": *i.e.*, them that are saved of the nations. Compare vii. 9 and xix. 14.

METONYMY; or, CHANGE OF NOUN.

The Change of one Noun for another Related Noun.

Me-ton'-y-my. Sometimes pronounced *Met'-o-nym-y*. Greek, Μετωνυμία, from μετά (*meta*), indicating *change*, and ὄνομα (*onoma*), *a name*; or, in grammar, *a noun*.

Metonymy is a figure by which one name or noun is used instead of another, to which it stands in a certain relation.

The change is in the noun, and only in a verb as connected with the action proceeding from it.

The names of persons are put by *Metonymy* for something which stands in a special relation to them. Thus we speak of " a stanhope " (carriage), from the Hon. Mr. Stanhope; " a brougham," from Lord Brougham; " boycotting," from Capt. Boycott; a " blanket," " negus," a " spencer," a " d'oyley," etc., from the respective inventors.

Thus it will be seen that *Metonymy* is not founded on resemblance, but on *relation*.

When we say that a person writes " a bad hand," we do not mean a hand, but we use the noun " hand " for the characters which it writes.

Metonymy is of four kinds : *viz.*, of the *Cause*, of the *Effect*, of the *Subject*, and of the *Adjunct*.

I. Metonymy of the *Cause* is when the cause is put for the effect : *i.e.*, when the doer is put for the thing done; or, the instrument for that which is effected ; or, where the action is put for the effect produced by the action.

II. Metonymy of the *Effect* is the opposite of the above : when the effect is put for the cause.

III. Metonymy of the *Subject* is when the subject is put for something pertaining to it: as the possessor for the possessed ; the thing signified for the sign.

IV. Metonymy of the *Adjunct*, on the contrary, is when that which *pertains* to anything is put for the thing itself.

Some grammarians have added a fifth Metonymy, where the antecedent is put for the consequent; but it really belongs to Metonymy of the Cause.

The following is the complete outline of the figure now to be treated of :—

METONYMY

I. OF THE CAUSE.

    i.   The person acting for the thing done.

    ii. The instrument for the thing effected.

    iii. The thing or action for the thing produced by it.

    iv. The material for the thing made from or of it.

II. OF THE EFFECT.

    i.   The action or effect for the person producing it.

    ii. The thing effected for the instrument or organic cause of it.

    iii. The effect for the thing or action causing it.

    iv. The thing made for the material from which it is made or produced.

III. OF THE SUBJECT.

    i.   The subject receiving for the thing received.

    ii. The container for the contents.

    iii. The possessor for the thing possessed.

    iv. The object for that which pertains or relates to it.

    v.   The thing signified for the sign.

IV. OF THE ADJUNCT.

    i.   The accident for the subject.

    ii. The contents for the container.

    iii. The time for the things done or existing in it.

    iv. The appearance of a thing for its nature ; or, the opinion about it for the thing itself.

    v.   The action or affection for the object of it.

    vi. The sign for the thing signified.

    vii. The name of a person for the person himself, or the thing.

I. METONYMY OF THE CAUSE.

This is when the cause is put for the effect ; and it is of four kinds : (i.) The person for the action ; (ii.) The instrument for the effect ;

(iii.) The thing or the action for its product; and (iv.) The material cause for the matter made. We will consider these in their order: and the examples themselves will explain the meaning and use of the figure.

i. *The person acting for the thing done.*

1. The SPIRIT for the gifts and operations of the Spirit.

John iii. 34.—" For God giveth not the Spirit by measure to Him": *i.e.,* the gifts and operations produced by the Spirit. The Holy Spirit is a person, and cannot, therefore, be measured out or given by measure. The "measure" must consequently mean the measure of His power or gifts bestowed.

John vi. 63.—" The words that I speak unto you, they, are spirit (*i.e.,* the gift and operation of the Spirit of God), and they are life (*i.e.,* they give and produce divine, spiritual and eternal life)."

Acts xix. 2.—" Did ye on believing receive the Holy Ghost?" Here, this must mean the wondrous gifts of the Spirit, because they had already received Him, or they could not have believed at all. Verse 6 also shows that this must be so, for the very gifts and powers are named and exercised.

I Cor. xiv. 12.—" Forasmuch as ye also are zealous of spirits": *i.e.,* of spiritual powers and gifts and revelations. Here, the A.V. has actually so rendered the figure, and put the literal Greek in the margin! So verses 26 and 32.

I Cor. xiv. 32.—" The spirits (*i.e.,* the spiritual gifts) of prophets are subject to prophets": *i.e.,* they are able to use them to edification according to the instructions given in Scripture.

Gal. iii. 2.—" Received ye the Spirit (*i.e.,* the gifts of the Spirit) by the works of the law, or by the hearing of faith?"

Verse 5: " He, therefore, that ministereth to you the Spirit (*i.e.,* the gifts of the Spirit) and worketh miracles among you," etc.

Eph. v. 18.—" Be filled with the Spirit": *i.e.,* not with the Person of the Holy Spirit surely! but with His operations: *i.e.,* with the gifts which come through the ministry of the Word; as is clear from Col. iii. 16, where this effect is produced by the same cause: *viz.,* occupation of the heart with God—the Word of Christ dwelling richly within us.

I Thess. v. 19.—" Quench not the Spirit": *i.e.,* do not hinder in yourself or in others the use of spiritual gifts.

The verb *to quench* is σβέννυμι (*sbennumi*), *to put out*, and always of extinguishing a light or fire ; hence, *to extinguish*.* It is impossible for mortal man to extinguish the Holy Spirit of God : so that there must be a figure here. That figure lies not in the word "quench," but in the word "spirit," which is put for *the gifts of the Spirit.* These are quenched, when any, assuming and usurping authority, forbid the use of them by a brother, or hinder him in the exercise of them.

This is clearly the subject of the exhortation ; for the very next sentence goes on to speak of the manner in which it is to be obeyed : "Despise not prophesyings" : do not *treat them with contempt or scorn ;* do not *neglect or disregard them.* This is the meaning of ἐξουθενέω (*exoutheneō*) (see Luke xxiii. 11. Acts iv. 11. Rom. xiv. 10, where it is rendered *set at nought ;* and Luke xviii. 9. Rom. xiv. 3. 1 Cor. i. 28 ; xvi. 11. Gal. iv. 14, where it is rendered *despise :* and 1 Cor. vi. 4, *to be least esteemed ;* and 2 Cor. x. 10, *contemptible*).

2. The SPIRIT is put also for His quickening, regenerating and sanctifying work in man, in creating the new nature with its spiritual desires and powers.

Ps. li. 10 (12).—"Renew a right spirit within me " : *i.e.*, the Divine workings of the Spirit by which alone true obedience is rendered to God. See Ezek. xi. 19. Eph. iv. 23. Rom. xii. 2.

John iii. 6.—"That which is born of the Spirit is spirit."

Here, the second time the word "spirit" is used, it is in a different sense, by the figure of *Antanaclasis* (*q.v.*, page 286) ; and by *Metonymy* it is put for the effect of the Spirit's operation : *i.e.*, the New man, the New nature, in all its manifestations. This New nature is constantly spoken of as "spirit" (see Rom. viii. 1-15), just as the Old nature is spoken of as "flesh."

For examples of the word "spirit" being put for the work of the Holy Spirit within man, see Ps. li. 17 (19). Isa. xxvi. 9. Ezek. xviii. 31. Matt. v. 3 ; xxvi. 41. Acts xvii. 16 ; xix. 21 ; xx. 22. Rom. i. 9. 1 Cor. v. 3, 4, 5 ; vi. 20. 1 Pet. iii. 4, etc.

Rom. viii. 2.—"For the law of the spirit of life (*i.e.*, not the Holy Spirit, but His life-giving work in the New nature created within us) hath made me free from the law of sin and death."

---

* See its occurrences : Matt. xxii. 20. Mark ix. 44, 46, 48. Eph. vi. 16. Heb. xi. 34, where it is rendered "quench" ; and Matt. xxv. 8, where it is "gone out, or *going out*" (marg.).

The Law brought the knowledge of sin; and its wages—death. But the work of the Holy Spirit has freed me from that Law, and has given me a new nature, by which I serve and obey Him from a totally different motive.

3. The SPIRIT is put for special and extraordinary operations of the Spirit acting externally in various ways, publicly or privately.

Num. xi. 17.—"I will take of the spirit which is upon thee and will put it upon them": *i.e.,* not the Person of the Holy Spirit, but His operations, enabling Moses, and afterwards the seventy elders, to rule the People.

The history goes on to tell how Joshua would have had two of them forbidden! True specimen of official religion to-day, and through all time; ever ready to forbid the use of spiritual powers and gifts that come out of the ordinary course!

Eldad and Medad are types of what has been true from that time till the present day.

2 Kings ii. 9.—"Let a double portion of thy spirit be upon me": *i.e.,* of thy miraculous gifts, spiritual powers. It was so: and it was so shown; for while Elijah's miracles were *eight* in number, Elisha's were *sixteen.**

Dan. v. 12 and vi. 3.—"Because an excellent spirit . . was in him": *i.e.,* the wonderful and extraordinary operations of the Spirit were manifest in him.

John vii. 39.—"This spake he of the Spirit": *i.e.,* this outflow of spiritual power mentioned in verse 38. A person could not flow out from another person.

Luke i. 17.—"And he shall go before him in the spirit and power of Elijah": *i.e.,* the same wonderful spiritual power should be in John as was in Elijah. See under *Hendiadys.*

Luke i. 80.—"And the child grew and waxed strong in spirit": *i.e.,* in the special and peculiar manifestations of the Spirit. So ii. 40.

Acts i. 5.—"Ye shall be baptized with the Holy Ghost": *i.e.,* ye shall be immersed in spiritual "power" (see verse 8), which shall cover you as well as fill you and flow out from you.

Acts vii. 51.—"Ye do always resist the Holy Ghost": *i.e.,* the testimony of the Holy Spirit as given by the prophets. Their fathers resisted the prophets, and would not hear the Spirit's voice in them

---

* See *Number in Scripture,* by the same author and publisher, page 202.

and now they, like their fathers, were resisting the same testimony as given at Pentecost, and since then culminating in Stephen.

The Holy Ghost in His testimony is always resisted by the natural man : *i.e.*, opposed by him. He cannot, of course, be resisted in the sense of being successfully repelled. The Greek word here is ἀντιπίπτω (*antipiptō*), *to fall against, oppose.* It occurs only here, but the context clearly shows the nature and character of the opposition, the reference to the " ears " indicating that they refused to listen to His testimony. The natural ear is always closed against the Divine testimony, until it is " opened " by One who is stronger than the strong man armed.

2 Cor. iii. 6.—" Who hath made us competent ministers also of the New Covenant : not of letter (*i.e.*, the Divine Law of the Old Covenant), but of spirit (*i.e.*, the ministration of the Spirit, verse 8 : the New Covenant as contained in the Gospel)."

4. The SPIRIT is put also for special revelations and visions communicated by Him.

Ezek. xxxvii. 1.—" The hand of the LORD was upon me, and carried me out in the Spirit of the LORD " : *i.e*, in a vision.

2 Thess. ii. 2.—" That ye be not soon shaken in mind, or be troubled, neither by spirit (*i.e.*, *by a revelation professed to have been received by the Spirit*), nor by word (*professed to be spoken by us*), nor by letter as from us (*said to be written by us*), as that the Day of the Lord has set in." For the meaning of this last statement, see the next verse under *Ellipsis*, pages 52 and 53.

1 John iv. 1-3.—" Beloved, believe not every spirit (*i.e.*, *every doctrine that is put forth as the teaching of the Spirit*), but try the spirits (*i.e.*, *their teaching and doctrines*, Acts xvii. 11), whether they are of God (or of demons and evil spirits) : because many false prophets are gone out into the world. Hereby know ye the spirit (or *doctrine and teaching*) of God. Every spirit (*i.e.*, *doctrine*) which confesseth (or *teacheth*) that Jesus Christ is come in the flesh is of God : and every spirit (or *doctrine*) that confesseth not (*i.e.*, *that does not teach*) that Jesus Christ is come in the flesh is not of God ; and this is that spirit (*i.e.*, *teaching*) of Antichrist whereof ye have heard that it should come ; and even now is it in the world."

As Antichrist himself has not yet come, it must mean his *teaching* which is already here. The confusion of the small and capital letters (s and S) in this passage shows that the translators did not perceive the *Metonymy* here used.

Rev. i. 10.—"I was in spirit." Here the A.V. uses a capital S, and not a small one as in chap. iv. 2; xvii. 3, and Ezek. xxxvii. 1, etc., but, the meaning is the same. "I became in a spiritual vision or ecstasy; or, I received a spiritual revelation;" which was afterwards written down. See also Acts x. 10 and xxii. 17, and 2 Cor. xii. 2, where similar visions and revelations are called a "trance." There is great divergence of the use of small and capital letters in all different versions.

5. PARENTS and ANCESTORS are frequently put for their posterity, and for children : and the name of the stock or race is put for the patronymic.

Japhet and *Shem* are put for their posterity (Gen. ix. 27).

Jacob and *Israel* for the Israelitish people (Ex. v. 2. Num. xxv. 21 ; xxiv. 5, 17. Deut. xxxiii. 28. 1 Kings xviii. 17, 18. Ps. xiv. 7 ; cxxxv. 4. Amos vii. 9).

Isaac for the people of Israel (Amos vii. 9).

Esau for the people descended from Esau (Rom ix. 13).

David is put for him who is descended from David; and therefore especially of the Messiah, who was of the seed of David according to the flesh (Ezek. xxxiv. 23). Compare Rom. i. 3 ; ix. 5.

Abraham is put for Christ by the same figure of *Metonymy*. "In thee shall all families of the earth be blessed" : *i.e.*, in Christ (Gen. xii. 3 ; xviii. 18). So Isaac, xxvi. 4; and Jacob, xxviii. 14. This is explained in Gal. iii. 8, 14, 16. Gen. xxii. 18. Ps. lxxii. 17. Acts iii. 25, 26.

6. The WRITER is put for his writing or book.

Luke xvi. 29.—"They have Moses (*i.e.*, his writings) and the prophets (*i.e.*, their writings); let them hear them."

See Luke xxiv. 27. Acts xv. 21 ; xxi. 21. 2 Cor. iii. 15.

7. To this first species of *Metonymy* must be referred the use of the word SOUL for life, which is the effect of it.

Indeed, when so used, the Hebrew נֶפֶשׁ (*nephesh*) and the Greek ψυχή (*pseuchee*) are often so translated.

See Gen. ix. 5 ; xxxvii. 21. Ex. iv. 19. Lev. xvii. 11. Judges ix. 17. 1 Sam. xxvi. 21. 1 Kings ii. 23. Est. viii. 11. Ps. xxxiii. 19; xxxviii. 12 (13) ; lvi. 13 (14). Jer. xl. 14; xlv. 5. Lam. v. 9. Jonah ii. 6. Matt. ii. 20 ; x. 39 ; xvi. 25; xx. 28. John x. 17; xii. 25 ; xiii. 37, 38; xv. 13, etc.

8. The SOUL is also put for the *person*, as when we say a city contains so many thousand souls.

We have examples in such phrases as " Praise the LORD, O my soul" (*i.e.*, O myself) (Ps. ciii. 1, etc.); or, " My soul doth (*i.e.*, I myself do) magnify the Lord" (Luke i. 46); or, " Thou wilt not leave my soul (*i.e.*, me) in Sheol " (Ps. xvi. 10. Acts ii. 27, 31. See Ps. xlix. 15. Heb. 16). Rev. vi. 9: " I saw the souls of them that were beheaded": *i.e.*, I saw them (*i.e.*, the persons of them) that were slain." Compare xx. 4.

9. The SOUL is also put for the *will, affection,* or *desire,* which are its operations and effects :—

Gen. xxiii. 8. Ex. xxiii. 9. Deut. xxiii. 24. 1 Kings xix. 3. Prov. xxiii. 2. Jer. xxxiv. 16. John x. 24.

10. The word SPIRIT is sometimes so used for the soul or life in its manifestations :—

Gen. xlv. 27. Num. xiv. 24. Judges viii. 3. 2 Chron. xxi. 16; xxxvi. 22. Ezra i. 1. Ps. lxxvi. 12 (13); lxxvii. 3 (4), 6 (7). Prov. i. 23; xviii. 14; xxix. 11. Ecc. vii. 9. Isa. xxix. 10. Jer. li. 11. Ezek. xiii. 3. Dan. ii. 1, 3. Hag. i. 14. Rom. xi. 8. 1 Cor. ii. 12.

ii. *The ORGANIC CAUSE or instrument is put for the thing effected by it.*

1. The ORGANS OF SPEECH are put for the testimony borne.

The MOUTH is put for the *witness* or testimony borne by it.

Deut. xvii. 6.—"At the mouth (*i.e.*, on the testimony) of two witnesses or three shall he . . . be put to death." So Deut. xix. 15, and Matt. xviii. 16.

The Mouth is put for the *command* or *precept* given.

Gen. xlv. 21.—" And Joseph gave them wagons, according to the mouth (*i.e., commandment,* as in A.V.) of Pharaoh."

Ex. xvii. 1.—Israel journeyed " according to the mouth (*i.e., commandment,* as in A.V.) of Jehovah." So Num. iii. 16, 39; xx. 24; xxvii. 14. Deut. i. 26, 43.

Deut. xxxiv. 5.—" So Moses . . . died there according to the mouth (*i.e., the word*) of Jehovah."

The Targum of Jonathan takes this literally (or as *Anthropopathpœia, q.v.*), and interprets it as a kiss!

The Tongue is put for what is *spoken* by it.

Ps. v. 9 (10).—"They flatter with their tongue": *i.e.*, with what it says.

Prov. xxv. 15.—"A soft tongue (*i.e.*, gentle speech) breaketh the bone" (*i.e.*, overcomes obstinacy).

Prov. x. 20.—"The tongue (*i.e.*, *the words* or *speech*) of the just is as choice silver."

Jer. xviii. 18.—"Let us smite him with the tongue": *i.e.*, with hard words.

The Tongue is also put for the language peculiar to any people or nation.

Acts ii. 4.—"They . . . began to speak with other tongues": *i.e.*, *in other languages*). So verse 11. Mark xvi. 17. 1 Cor. xiv. 18.

The Lip is put for the language.

Gen. xi. 1.—"And the whole earth was of one lip (*i.e.*, *language*) and of one speech."

Prov. xii. 19.—"The lip (*i.e.*, speech) of truth shall be established for ever."

Verse 22: "Lying lips (*i.e.*, liars or lies) are abomination to the Lord."

Prov. xiv. 8.—"The lips of knowledge": *i.e.*, the words of wisdom, or wise words.

Prov. xvii. 7.—"Excellent lip (*i.e.*, speech) becometh not a fool; much less does a lip of lying a prince": *i.e.*, lying words. So xviii. 6, 7.

Isa. xxxiii. 19.—"A people deeper of lip (*i.e.*, speech) than to be understood."

The Palate is put for the words spoken.

Prov. v. 3.—"Her palate is smoother than oil": *i.e.*, her speech.

The Throat also is put for the words spoken.

Ps. v. 9 (10).—"Their throat (*i.e.*, their speech) is an open sepulchre." So Rom. iii. 13, explained by Luke xi. 44.

2. The Hand is put for the actions performed by it.

These are many and various; as finding, counselling, thought, purpose, impulse, effort, attempt, or care. The "hand" is put by *Metonymy* for all these and similar things.

Deut. xxxii. 36.—" When he seeth that their hand was gone." This is rightly rendered " power "; for which the " hand " is put by *Metonymy*.

1 Sam. xxii. 17.—Saul said, " Turn, and slay the priests of the LORD ; because their hand (*i.e.*, help) is with David, and because they knew him when he fled, and did not show it to me " : *i.e.*, the priests helped David with their counsel, and with food ; and by silence, in not betraying him. All this is contained in, and expressed by, the word " hand."

2 Sam. iii. 12.—" My hand (*i.e.*, my help) shall be with thee."

2 Sam. xiv. 19.—" Is not the hand (*i.e.*, the counsel) of Joab with thee in all this ? "

1 Kings x. 29.—" And so for all the kings of the Hittites, and for the kings of Syria, did they bring them out by their hand " (*i.e.*, as in A.V., by their means).

Ps. vii. 3 (4).—" O Jehovah my Elohim, if I have done this : if there be iniquity in my hands " : *i.e.*, if I have done iniquity. So Isa. i. 15.

The Hand is also put for instrumentality or agency, especially in connection with *Inspiration*.

Ezra. ix. 10, 11.—" Thy commandments which thou hast commanded by the hand (*i.e*, the agency) of thy servants the prophets."

In all these cases there is an implied reference to testimony preserved *in writing*.

Neh. ix. 30.—" Thou testifiedst against them by thy Spirit in (or by) the hand (*i.e.*, the agency) of thy prophets."

Zech. vii. 12.—" The words which the LORD of hosts hath sent in (or by) His Spirit by the hand of the former prophets " : *i.e.*, by their agency.

This is the testimony of one of the latter prophets to the Inspiration of the " former " : *viz.*, Joshua, Judges, Samuel, and Kings.

The Hand is also put for the writing done by it or hand-writing.
As we say of one " he writes a good hand."

See 1 Cor. xvi. 21. Col. iv. 18.

The Hand is also put for a gift given to anyone.

Ps. lxviii. 31 (32).—" Ethiopia shall soon stretch out her hands unto God " : *i.e.*, shall bring presents, as in verse 29, of which this is the continuation. As further explained in Ps. lxxii. 10. Isa. xlix. 7 ; lx. 6, 9. Ps. xxii. 27 (28).

3. The SWORD is put for war or for slaughter.

Ex. v. 3.—" Lest he fall upon us with pestilence, or with sword " : *i.e.*, with slaughter.

Lev. xxvi. 6.—" Neither shall the sword (*i.e* , war) go through your land."

So Isa. i. 20. Jer. xiv. 12, 13, 15, 16; xliii. 11. Ps. cxliv. 10. Rom. viii. 35, and many other passages.

Matt. x. 34.—" I came not to send peace, but a sword" (*i.e.*, but for war). That is to say, the *object* of His coming was peace, but the *effect* of it was war.

4. A LINE is used for the territory divided up or marked out by it.

Amos vii. 17.—" Thy land shall be divided by line " : *i.e.*, divided up among others.

Micah ii. 5.—" Thou wilt have none that shall cast a cord by lot in the congregation of Jehovah."

The land in Palestine round each village was divided by lot for the year, for each family to sow and reap. Referring to this, David says, "The lines are fallen unto me in pleasant places," and then he goes on to explain it, " Yea, I have a goodly heritage " (Ps. xvi. 6).

Hence the word " line " is used of an inheritance measured out. See Deut. iii. 4 (where it is rendered " region "). Joshua xvii. 14. Ps. cv. 11 (the lot of your inheritance).

In this sense Israel was (among the other nations) the line or lot of Jehovah's inheritance. Deut. xxxii. 8, 9.

2 Cor. x. 16.—" In another man's line " : *i.e.*, in another man's inheritance or sphere of labour.

Ps. xix. 4 (5).—" Their line is gone out through all the earth." The A.V. interprets the *Metonymy* incorrectly in the margin, " *their rule* or *direction*." It is their *inheritance* : *i.e.*, the whole earth was the sphere through which their words and speech went forth, and where the knowledge imparted by the stars was made known. See Rom. x. 18.*

5. SILVER is put for the thing procured by it.

Ex. xxi. 21.—Where a servant is said to be the money of the master.

---

* And *The Witness of the Stars*, by the same author and publisher.

6. HYSSOP is put for the sprinkling which was effected by it.

Hyssop (אֵזוֹב) a small humble moss-like shrub (1 Kings iv. 33; v. 13) used in ceremonial sprinklings. See Lev. xiv. 4. Num. xix. 18, etc.

Ps. li. 7 (9).—" Purge me with hyssop, and I shall be clean " : *i.e.*, purge me with the atoning blood; not with the herb.

iii. *The THING or ACTION is put for that which is the effect or product of it.*

Some Rhetorists confine *Metonymy* only to nouns, and deny its application to verbs. But there seem to be certain words, even verbs, the use of which cannot otherwise be classed except under the figure *Metonymy* : words which, if not actually changed for or strictly used instead of others, are yet *analagous*, and have the meaning of another word taken conventionally with them; so that a thing or action is put for some effect which is understood as being consequent upon it.

1. In certain NOUNS, where the FEELING or AFFECTION is put for the effects resulting or proceeding from the feeling.

LOVE is put for the benefits and blessings flowing from it.

I John iii. I.—" Behold, what manner of love the Father hath bestowed upon us " : *i.e.*, not merely the *feeling* of love, but the manifestation of it in all that it has done for us : one thing here being the calling and making lost sinners the sons of God, and blessing them with all spiritual blessings in Christ.

MERCY is put for the offices and benefits which are the outcome of it.

Gen. xx. 13.—" This is thy kindness which thou shalt show, etc."

Gen. xxxii. 10.—" I am not worthy of the least of all the mercies and of all the truth, which thou hast showed unto thy servant": *i.e.*, all the material and spiritual benefits bestowed in kindness and faithfulness.

2 Chron. xxxv. 26.—" Now the rest of the acts of Josiah, and his goodness " (marg. Heb. *kindnesses*) : *i.e.*, his acts of kindness.

By the same figure the Greek ἐλεημοσύνη (pity, or mercy) is put for benefits bestowed upon the poor.

Matt. vi. I.—" Take heed that ye do not your alms." The R.V. and Critical Texts (G.L.T.Tr.A.) have δικαιοσύνη (*dikaiosunee*), *righteousness*, instead of ἐλεημοσύνη (*eleēmosunee*), *mercy*. The reading doubtless arose from some scribe's not seeing the *Metonymy*, and trying to explain it.

In either case the feeling is put for the acts which manifest it. So Luke xi. 41. Acts x. 2, 4.

ANGER and WRATH are put for punishment, and various acts which flow from them.

Ps. lxxix. 6.—" Pour out thy wrath upon the heathen that have not known thee ": *i.e.*, thy judgments.　So 1 Sam. xxviii. 18.

Micah vii. 9.—" I will bear the indignation of Jehovah ": *i.e.*, the chastisements which it inflicts.

Rom. ii. 5.—Thou " treasurest up unto thyself wrath ": *i.e.*, the judgments produced by it.

Rom. iv. 15.—" The law worketh wrath ": *i.e.*, inflicts or executes punishments and penalties.　The word " *execute* " is actually supplied in Rom. xiii. 4.

Rom. xiii. 5.—" Wherefore ye must needs be subject, not only for wrath ": *i.e.*, on account of the effects of the anger, etc., of those who govern, " but also for conscience sake ": *i.e.*, because ye believe it to be right according to the will of God.

Eph. v. 6.—" For because of these things cometh the wrath of God upon the children of disobedience ": *i.e.*, the punishments inflicted by God on account of His wrath.

JUSTICE is put for the judgment or punishment which manifests it.

Ex. vi. 6.—" I will redeem you with a stretched-out arm and with great justice ": *i.e.*, as in A.V., judgments.　As rendered in Prov. xix. 29.　Ezek. xiv. 21, etc.

It is put also for the actual sentence and condemnation.

Jer. xxvi. 11.—" The judgment (*i.e.*, the sentence) of death is for this man."　This Metonymy is idiomatically rendered in A.V.　So John iii. 19 (κρίσις, *krisis*, the *act* or *process* of *judging*).

SIN and its synonyms are put for the effects or punishment of sin.

Gen. xix. 15.—" Lest thou be condemned in the iniquity ": *i.e.*, punishment, as in margin of A.V.　So Ps. vii. 16 (17).

Jer. xiv. 16.—" I will pour their wickedness upon them ": *i.e.*, the punishment on account of their wickedness.

Zech. xiv. 19.—" This shall be the sin (marg.) of Egypt ": *i.e.*, the punishment for Egypt's sin.

When joined with the verb *to bear* (*i.e.*, to bear iniquity), it means to bear the *punishment* or judgment for iniquity, etc. See Ex. xxviii. 43. Lev. v. 1 ; xx. 20 ; xxii. 9. Num. xiv. 33. Isa. liii. 4. Ezek. xxiii. 35, 49 ; xviii. 20.

When Christ is said to bear our sins, it means that He bore the punishment (*i.e.*, death) which was due to them. Heb. ix. 28. 1 Pet. ii. 24, etc.

WORK is put for the wages paid for it.

Lev. xix. 13.—Heb. *work* ; A.V., *wages*.

Jer. xxii. 13.—" And doth not give him his work ": *i.e.*, Heb. his wage. A.V. : " for his work."

Rom. xi. 6.—" If by grace, then is it no more of works": *i.e.*, of wages or merit.

Rev. xiv. 13.—" And their works (*i.e.*, their rewards) do follow with them."

DIVINATION is put for the money received for it.

Num. xxii. 7.—" So the elders departed with divinations in their hands." Here, both A.V. and R.V. do not scruple to boldly translate the Metonymy and put " the rewards of divination."

LABOUR is put for that which is produced by it.

Deut. xxviii. 33.—" All thy labours shall a nation which thou knowest not eat up " : *i.e.*, all the fruit of thy labours.

Ps. lxxviii. 46.—" He gave . . . their labour unto the locust " : *i.e.*, the fruit of their labour.

Ps. cv. 44.—" They inherited the labour of the people."

Ps. cxxviii. 2.—" Thou shalt eat the labour of thine hands " : *i.e.*, that which the labour of thy hands has produced.

Prov. v. 10.—" Lest . . . thy labours be in the house of a stranger " : *i.e.*, that which thou hast made or produced.

So Ecc. ii. 19. Isa. xlv. 14. Jer. iii. 24. Ezek. xxiii. 29.

STRENGTH is put for that which it effects or produces.

Gen. iv. 12.—" When thou tillest the ground, it shall not henceforth yield unto thee her strength " : *i.e.*, her fruits shall not be brought forth freely and liberally to thee.

Prov. v. 10.—" Lest strangers be filled with thy strength " : *i.e.*, that which thy strength brings forth. A.V. : wealth.

HUNTING is put for the flesh of the animal that is caught.

Gen. xxv. 28.—" And Isaac loved Esau because hunting was in his mouth." Here, the mouth is put for the eating which it performed, and hunting for the venison which it caught.   See also under *Ellipsis*, page 26.

Gen. xxvii. 3.—" Hunt me a hunting ": *i.e.*, catch or take for me some venison (as in A.V.).   See *Polyptoton*, page 275.

2. In certain VERBS.

The same Metonymy is seen in certain verbs, but it is confined to verbs of (*a*) Knowing, (*b*) Remembering, (*c*) Loving and Hating, and (*d*) Operation.

(*a*) Verbs of KNOWING

are used of the *effect of knowing : i.e.*, understanding, caring for, approving, etc.

Job xix. 25.—" I know that my redeemer liveth ": *i.e.*, I believe, or have a saving knowledge of the fact. .

Ps. i. 6.—" The LORD knoweth (*i.e.*, approveth) the way of the righteous."   So Rev. ii. 24.

Ps. ix. 10 (11).—" They that know thy name will put their trust in thee ": *i.e.*, they that understand Thee as their God and Saviour.

Ps. xxxv. 11.—" False witnesses did rise up; they laid to my charge things that I knew not ": *i.e.*, things which I was not conscious of, or did not acknowledge as true.   So Ps. li. 3 (5). 2 Cor. v. 21.

Ps. xc. 11.—" Who knoweth (*i.e.*, Who rightly considers) the power of thine anger ? "   Many may hear of it and know of it in the ordinary sense of the verb, but who rightly estimates it and understands it ?

Prov. xxiv. 23.—" It is not good to know (or discern) faces in (*giving*) the judgment ": *i.e.*, to have respect or show favour to them. See Deut. i. 17 (marg.) and xvi. 19. Job. xxxiv. 19.

Isa. i. 3.—" Israel doth not know."   The next parallel line goes on to explain it:—" My people doth not consider."   So Jer. viii. 7. Luke xix. 42 (cf. Ps. ci. 4).   This comes also under the figure *Exergasia* (*q.v.*)

Jer. ix. 24.—" Let him that glorieth glory in this, that he understandeth and knoweth me ": *i.e.*, loves me and believes me.   Compare verses 3 and 6.

Jer. xxxi. 34.—" They shall all know me ": *i.e.*, believe in me with a saving faith.

John viii. 43.—" Ye cannot hear (*i.e.*, receive, and understand, and approve) my word." See verse 44.

John x. 27.—" My sheep hear my voice, and I know them " : *i.e.*, I love them with all a shepherd's fondness.

John xvii. 3.—" This is life eternal that they might know (*i.e.*, believe on) thee—the only true God, and Jesus Christ, whom thou hast sent."

Acts x. 34.—" I perceive (*i.e.*, I now understand and am made to know from what has taken place) that God is no respecter of persons."

Rom. vii. 15.—" For that which I do I know not." Here, the A.V. translates the *Metonymy*, " that which I do I *allow* not ": *i.e.*, I do not approve. The old Eng. of the verb *allow* is *allaud, to praise* or *approve*, as in Ps xi. 5. Prayer Book (*i.e.*, Coverdale's) Version : " The Lord *alloweth* the righteous ": *i.e.*, approveth him.

1 Cor. viii. 3.—" If any man love God, the same is known of him ": *i.e.*, is loved and cared for by Him (see *Heterosis* of the verb).

Verbs of Knowing are sometimes put for *caring for* or manifesting affection to.

Gen. xxxix. 6.—" He (Potiphar) knew not ought he had " : *i.e.*, had no anxiety about it.

Ex. ii. 25.—" And God knew them ": *i.e.*, as in A.V., had respect unto them.

Deut. xxxiii. 9.—" Neither did he acknowledge his brethren, nor knew (*i.e.*, cared for) his own children."
So Ruth ii. 10, 19.

Judges ii. 10.—" There arose another generation after them, which knew not the LORD ": *i.e.*, which did not care for Him.

1 Chron. xvii. 18.—" Thou knowest (*i.e.*, hast respect to) thy servant."

Ps. xxxvii. 18.—" The LORD knoweth the days of the upright ": *i.e.*, has respect to them and acts accordingly.

Ps. cxlii. 4 (5).—" There was no man that would know me " : *i.e.*, that would care for me. See under *Ellipsis*.

Prov. xii. 10.—" A righteous man knoweth the life of his beast " : *i.e.*, he regardeth and careth for it.

Prov. xxix. 7.—" The righteous knoweth (A.V., considereth) the cause of the poor."

Jer. i. 5.—" Before I formed thee in the belly I knew thee ": *i.e.*, cared for and loved thee.

Jer. xxiv. 5.—" So shall I know (A.V., acknowledge) them that are carried away captive."

Amos iii. 2.—" You only have I known of all the families of the earth " : *i.e.*, loved and cared for. Cf. Deut. iv. 20.

1 Thess. v. 12.—" We beseech you, brethren, to know them which labour among you " : *i.e.*, to consider and care for them.

2 Tim. ii. 19.—" The Lord knoweth (*i.e.*, loves and cares for) them that are his." See also under *Heterosis*.

Verbs of Knowing are used also of *experiencing*, either by saving faith or by personal dealing.

Isa. liii. 11.—" By his knowledge shall my righteous servant justify many ": *i.e.*, knowledge of Him and the salvation which He gives. See Luke i. 77. " To give knowledge of salvation."

Matt. vii. 11.—" If ye then, being evil, know how to give good gifts unto your children," etc. : *i.e.*, are able, notwithstanding all your innate blindness, to understand enough, in spite of your selfishness, to give good gifts, etc.

Mark v. 29.—" And she knew (ἔγνω) by her body (*i.e.*, by the sensations of it) that she was healed of that plague " : *i.e.* (as in A.V.), " she felt." She experienced, just as the Lord Himself did in verse 30, where we have the same verb used of Him: " knowing in Himself" (ἐπιγνούς).

1 Cor. iv. 19.—" But I will come to you shortly, if the Lord will, and will know (*i.e.*, will find out and expose) not the speech of them which are puffed up, but the power."

2 Cor. i. 9.—" We had the sentence of death in ourselves " : *i.e.*, we experienced the feelings of those who have had the sentence of death pronounced upon them.

(*b*) Verbs of REMEMBERING

are used of a strong desire or wish for *the thing mentioned* or *remembered*.

Isa. xliv. 21.—" Remember these, O Jacob and Israel . . . thou shalt not be forgotten of me " : *i.e.*, desire the things which make for your peace, etc.

Ezek. xxiii. 19.—" Yet she multiplied her whoredoms, in calling to remembrance the days of her youth, wherein she had played the harlot in the land of Egypt ": *i.e.*, in desiring again the former sins.

Jonah ii. 7 (8).—" When my soul fainted within me, I remembered the LORD " (and therefore desired Him, and called upon Him).

2 Tim. ii. 8.—" Remember that Jesus Christ of the seed of David was raised from the dead according to my Gospel ": *i.e.*, Believe and enjoy, and rest in, the blessed knowledge of the fact.

Heb. xi. 15.—" If they had been mindful of that country from whence they came out ": *i.e.*, if they had longed for it, or desired to return to it, they could have done so. This is clear from the verb to " desire " in verse 16.

So the noun is used of the Lord's Supper, " in remembrance of Me ": *i.e.*, not a mere calling to mind, but that which is produced by such remembrance : *viz.*, faith, love, hope, which are all bound up in that acknowledgment of Christ's death (Luke xxii. 19. 1 Cor. xi. 24, 25). Hitherto they had celebrated their deliverance from Egypt. Henceforth they were to remember Christ, and the exodus which He accomplished, and to desire His return, looking for it with loving hope.

On the other hand, the verb TO FORGET is used of *unfaithfulness*, and *rejection*.

Hos. iv. 6.—" Seeing thou hast forgotten the law of thy God, I will also forget thy children ": *i.e.*, seeing thou hast been unfaithful to me, and will reject thy children.

(c) Verbs of LOVING and HATING

are put for the actions consequent upon them.

To LOVE is put for *to expect*, or *desire*, or *take*.

Ps. xi. 5.—" Him that loveth violence (*i.e.*, and hence practises it) his soul hateth."

Prov. xxi. 17.—" He that loveth (and therefore liveth in) pleasure shall be a poor man," etc. He would not be poor unless he gratified his love of pleasure by spending his substance.

Matt. vi. 5.—" They love to pray standing in the synagogues and in the corners of the streets," and they do it because they love it.

Luke xi. 43.—" Ye love the uppermost seats in the synagogues ": *i.e.*, ye not only love them, but take them because ye love them.

John iii. 19.—" Men loved darkness rather than light ": (and practised, and lived, and acted, accordingly).

2 Tim. iv. 8.—" All them also that love His appearing " (and act, and live, accordingly).

2 Tim. iv. 10.—" Demas hath forsaken me, having loved this present world " : (and returned to it).

To Love is used of the exercise of the greatest possible care for
whatever is the object of the love.   While *to hate* is used in
the opposite sense, of exercising less care, or of neglect.

Gen. xxix. 31.—" And when the LORD saw that Leah was hated " :
i.e., neglected, and the other more esteemed. See verse 30.

By some this is called *Hyperbole* (*q.v.*).

John xii. 25.—" He that loveth his life shall lose it " : *i.e.*, that cares more for his life than for Christ.   See under *Ellipsis* and *Hyperbole*.

This is the explanation of Matt. xvi. 25, where it reads, " whosoever shall save his life " : *i.e.*, shall care more for it, and preserve it, instead of giving it up for Christ.   Compare Luke xiv. 26.

To Love is used not merely for the act itself, but for the *effect* of it.

Ps. cix. 17.—" As he loved cursing " : *i.e.*, not merely loved to do it, but did it.

Prov. xiii. 24.—" He that spareth his rod hateth his son : but he that loveth him chasteneth him betimes " : *i.e.*, his love takes effect, and is seen, in the chastening.

Prov. xviii. 19.—" He loveth trangression that loveth strife " : *i.e.*, he trangresses who strives, for He does it because he loves to do it.

Prov. viii. 36.—" All they that hate me love death " : *i.e.*, so live and act as to injure life and accelerate death.

(*d*) Verbs of OPERATION.

The verb TO DO often denotes *the effect* rather than the act.

Gen. xii. 5.—" The souls that they had gotten (Heb., *made*) in Haran " : *i.e.*, the servants which they had acquired in Haran.   Thus the *Metonymy* is here translated by the word " gotten."

Gen. xxx. 30.—" And now when shall I do for my house also ? " The A.V. translates the *Metonymy* by the verb " provide " : " when shall I provide ? " etc.

Matt. xxv. 16.—" He that had received the five talents went and traded with the same and made them (*i.e.*, gained) other five talents," as explained in verse 20.

Certain Verbs have not their own proper signification, but are used of ›the actions or effects consequent upon them :

To JUDGE is put for *punish* or *condemn*.

Gen. xv. 14.—" That nation whom they serve shall I judge " : *i.e.*, punish with judgments, not simply rule. Acts vii. 7.

2 Chron. xx. 12.—" O our God, wilt thou not judge them ? " *i.e.*, punish them.

Ps. ix. 19 (20).—" Let the heathen be judged in thy sight."

Heb. xiii. 4.—" Whoremongers and adulterers God will judge " : *i.e.*, punish. See also John iii. 18 and Rom. xiv. 3.

To Judge is also used in the sense of *acquit*, which is also an effect of judging. See

Ps. xxxv. 24.—" Judge me, O Lord my God " : *i.e.*, acquit me.

To HURT or even TO INJURE is put for the *hurt* or *injury* done.

Luke x. 19.—" Nothing shall by any means hurt you " : *i.e.*, have any injurious effect upon you.

Rom. viii. 31.—" If God be for us, who *can be* against us ? " *i.e.*, who can hurt us or bring any evils upon us ? They can, of course, be " against us," but not have any hurtful effect.

iv. *The MATERIAL is put for the thing made of or from it.*

1. TREES are put for *arms* or *instruments* made from them.

Nah. ii. 3 (4).—" The fir-trees shall be terribly shaken." The context shows that " trees " are put for the spears, etc., which men make from them.

2 Sam. vi. 5.—" And David and all the house of Israel played before the LORD on all fir-woods." The A.V. and R.V. both treat this as though it were an *Ellipsis :* " on all manner of *instruments made of* firwood," instead of seeing the *Metonymy* and saying simply, " On all manner of instruments," which are immediately mentioned : *viz.*, harps and psalteries. But according to a note in Dr. Ginsburg's Hebrew Bible, the Septuagint reads *with all might and with songs* instead of " on all manner of fir-woods." Compare verse 14 and 1 Chron. xiii. 8.

2. Brass is put for *fetters*, etc

Lam. iii. 7.—" He hath made my brass heavy " : *i.e.*, my fetters, or bonds, or chains.

Judges xvi. 21.—" And bound him with two brasses " : *i.e.*, two brazen fetters.

2 Sam. iii. 34.—" Thy hands were not bound, nor thy feet put into brasses " : *i.e.*, fetters, as in A.V.

3. Curtains are put for *tents*.

2 Sam. vii. 2.—" The ark of God dwelleth within curtains " : *i.e.*, in the curtain or tent.

Jer. iv. 20.—" Suddenly are my tents spoiled, and my curtain (*i.e.*, my tabernacle or dwelling) in a moment."

Hab. iii. 7.—" And the curtains (*i.e.*, tents) of Midian's land did tremble."

4. Corn is put for *bread* or food generally.

Lam. ii. 12.—" They say to their mothers, Where is corn (*i.e.*, bread) and wine ? "

5. Gold and Silver and other metals and similar substances are put for what is made with them.

Gen. xxiii. 9.—" That he may give me the cave of Machpelah, which he hath, which is in the end of his field, for silver (*i.e.*, money made from silver) full (*i.e.*, of full value) he shall give it to me in your midst (*i.e.*, within your boundaries), for a possession of (*i.e.*, hereditary) sepulchre."

Gen. xxiv. 22.—" Of ten gold was their weight " : *i.e.*, bracelets made of gold, ten shekels in weight.

2 Kings v. 5.—" Six thousand of gold " : *i.e.*, pieces of money.

2 Kings xii. 4 (5), where it is rendered " money."

1 Chron. xxi. 22, 24.—" Full silver " : for full money value.   In A.V. rendered " full price."

1 Chron. xxix. 2.—Here, the figure is translated by the words " *things of* " in *italics*.   " I have prepared . . . the gold for gold (things), and the silver for silver (things), and the brass for brass (things)," etc.

Ps. cxv. 4.—" Their idols are silver and gold " : *i.e.*, made of silver and gold.

Matt. x. 9.—"Provide neither gold, nor silver, nor brass (*i.e.*, money made from these) in your purses."

Acts iii. 6.—"Silver and gold (*i.e.*, money, like the Scottish "siller" and French *l'argent*) have I none."

6. IRON is put for things made of it.

2 Kings vi. 5.—"As one was felling a beam the iron (*i.e.*, the axhead, as the A.V. renders it) fell into the water."

Ps. cv. 18.—"Whose foot they hurt with the gyve, his soul came into iron": *i.e.*, he was fast bound with iron chains.

7. STONES are put for things made of them.

Ex. vii. 19.—"Both in woods and in stones": *i.e.*, both in wooden vessels and stone vessels.

Deut. xxv. 13.—"Thou shalt not have in thy bag divers stones": *i.e.*, weights. Heb., a stone and a stone.

Prov. xi. 1.—"A perfect stone (*i.e.*, a just weight) is his delight."

Isa. xxxiv. 11.—"The stones of emptiness": *i.e.*, the stones which characterize waste land.

Jer. ii. 27.—"Saying . . . to a stone (*i.e.*, to an idol), Thou hast brought me forth" So iii. 9.

Zech. iv. 10.—"They shall see the stone of tin (*i.e*, the plummet) in Zerubbabel's hand."

8. WOOD is put for things made of wood.

See above Ex. vii. 19 (for vessels). Isa. xliv. 19. Jer. ii. 27; iii. 9; and x. 8. Hos. iv. 12 (for idols).

Ezek. xxxvii. 16.—"Take thee one wood and write upon it, 'For Judah and for the children of Israel his companions': then take another wood, and write upon it, 'For Joseph, the stick of Ephraim, and for all the house of Israel his companions' ": *i.e.*, take a tablet or stick made out of wood.

Gen. xl. 19.—"Shall hang thee on a tree": *i.e.*, a gallows. So Josh. viii. 29. Deut. xxi. 22, 23. Est. vii. 9, 10. Gal. iii. 13. 1 Pet. ii. 24.

2 Sam. xxi. 19.—"The wood (*i.e.*, as in A.V., "staff") of whose spear was like a weaver's beam."

Acts xvi. 24.—"And made their feet fast in the wood": *i.e* "in the stocks," as in A.V.

9. FLAX is put for the *wick* made of it.

Isa. xlii. 3.—" The smoking flax (*i.e.*, wicks) shall he not quench."
See under *Tapeinosis*.

Isa. xliii. 17.—" They are quenched as the flax ": *i.e.*, as a wick.
(A.V., tow).

10. DUST AND ASHES for *man*, who is made of dust.

Gen. iii. 19.—" Dust thou art ": *i.e.*, made of dust.

Gen. xviii. 27.—" Dust and ashes." See under *Paronomasia*.

Ps. ciii. 14.—" He remembereth that we are dust ": *i.e.*, made of
dust.

Ecc. xii. 7.—" Then shall the dust (*i.e.*, man) return to the earth
as it was."

11. SEED is put for *son* or posterity.

Gen. iv. 25.—" God ... hath appointed me another seed ": *i.e.*, son.

Gen. xv. 13.—" Thy seed shall be a stranger," etc. So Acts vii. 6 ;
where the period of sojourning is stated to be 400 years. Whereas,
in Ex. xii. 40, and Gal. iii. 17, where the period refers not to the
sojourning of Abraham's seed (which could not commence till Isaac
was born, thirty years after the promise), but includes that of Abraham
himself, the sum is given as 430 years.

12. FOREST or WOOD is put for the *houses*, etc., made of its trees.

Jer. xxi. 14 ; xxii. 7 : compare these with Jer. lii. 13. 2 Kings
xxv. 9 and 2 Chron. xxxvi. 19, and the figures in the last two passages
will be explained.

II. METONYMY OF THE EFFECT.

This is when the effect is put for the cause producing it. It is of
four kinds : (i.) The action for the actor. (ii.) The thing for the
organic cause of it. (iii.) The effect for the producer of it. (iv.) The
matter made for the material cause of it. We will consider these in
their order :—

i. *The ACTION or the EFFECT for the person producing the effect,
or for the author of it.*

1. NOUNS.

Gen. xxv. 23.—" Two nations are in thy womb " : *i.e.*, two infants
whose progeny should become two different nations.

Gen. xxvi. 35.—" Which were a grief of mind unto Isaac and to Rebekah": *i.e.*, the source of much sorrow to them.

Gen. xlix. 18.—" I have waited for thy salvation (*i.e.*, for Him who shall bring and work salvation), O LORD."

Neh. xii. 31, 38, 40.—" Two great celebrations." The A.V. and R.V. have supplied the words implied by the *Metonymy* (the former in italics, the latter in roman type), by rendering " two great *companies of them that gave* thanks." The effect of the praises or thanks, is put for the people who rendered them.

Ps. xviii. 1 (2).—" I will love thee, O Jehovah my strength ": *i.e.*, the author and source of my strength. So Ps. xxii. 19 (20). Jer. xvi. 19.

Ps. xxvii. 1.—" The LORD is my light and my salvation." This is not a *Metaphor* but a *Metonymy* : *i.e.*, Jehovah is the source of my light, and the author of my salvation. Compare Heb. v. 9.

Ps. cvi. 20.—" Thus they changed their glory (*i.e.*, God) into the similitude of an ox that eateth grass."

The Massorah records this as one of the passages in which the Sopherim changed the pronoun " my" into "their." It was thought to be too gross an anthropomorphism to say " my," Jehovah being the speaker. See Appendix E.

Isa. xlix. 6.—" That thou mayest be my salvation (*i.e.*, the Saviour whom I have sent) unto the end of the earth."

Jer. xxiii. 6.—" Jehovah our Righteousness ": *i.e.*, the Author of our righteousness : our Justifier.

Mark ix. 17, 25.—" A dumb spirit " : *i.e.*, a spirit which produced the effect of dumbness in the person possessed.

Luke xi. 14.—" And he was casting out a devil, and it was dumb": *i.e.*, it produced dumbness in the man possessed. Compare Matt. ix. 32, 33. Mark ix. 17, 25.

Luke ii. 30.—"Mine eyes have seen thy salvation ": *i.e.*, Christ the Saviour: the Worker and Author of Salvation. So iii. 6 and Isa. xlix. 6.

Luke xiii. 11.—"And, behold, there was a woman which had a spirit of infirmity." The negative μή (*mee*) implies that she felt unable to straighten herself up,* and indicates some *nervous* disorder. So the Lord uses the remarkable language about Satan as *binding* her.

---

* The Greek of this is εἰς τὸ παντελες (*eis to panteles*), which occurs only here and Heb. vii. 25. Here, to her *full height ;* there, to their *full need.*

This is not *Enallage*, "an infirm spirit," but it is *Metonymy*, by which the effect is put for the cause. The woman was troubled by a spirit which caused or produced this infirmity.

John xi. 25.—"I am the resurrection and the life": *i.e.*, the Worker of resurrection, and the Giver of resurrection life.

Rom. xiii. 3.—"Rulers are not a terror": *i.e.*, a source of terror.

2 Cor. i. 14.—"We are your rejoicing (*i.e.*, cause of rejoicing), even as ye also are ours in the day of the Lord Jesus." So 1 Thess. ii. 19, 20.

Rev. i. 12.—"And I turned to see the voice (*i.e.*, Him) that spake with me." So John i. 23.

2. VERBS.

Gen. xlii. 38.—"Shall ye bring down," etc.: *i.e.*, shall be the cause of my death. See under *Periphrasis*.

Gen. xliii. 6.—"Why have ye done evil to me, to disclose to the man that ye had yet another brother?" *i.e.*, why have you brought or caused all this evil to be brought upon me.

Ex. xxiii. 8.—"The gift blindeth the wise, and perverteth the words of the righteous": *i.e.*, is an occasion by which these effects are produced.

1 Kings xviii. 9.—"What have I sinned, that thou wouldest deliver thy servant (*i.e.*, cause to be delivered) into the hand of Ahab to slay me?"

Ps. lxxvi. 10 (11).—"Surely the wrath of man shall praise thee": *i.e.*, shall be the occasion of praise to thee.

Isa. xliii. 24.—"Thou hast made me to serve with thy sins": *i.e.*, thy sins have caused the hard service and Passion which I endured on account of them.

Jer. xxxviii. 23.—"Thou shalt burn this city with fire": *i.e.*, thou shalt cause it to be burnt. See A.V. margin.

Ezek. xix. 7.—"He laid waste their cities": *i.e.*, their sins caused them to be destroyed.

Acts i. 18.—"Now this man purchased (*i.e.*, caused to be purchased) a field."

Rom. xiv. 15.—"Destroy not him with thy meat for whom Christ died": *i.e.*, do not be a cause of destruction.

1 **Cor. vii. 16.**—" For what knowest thou, O wife, whether thou shalt save (*i.e.*, be the means of salvation or the occasion of much blessing to) thy husband ? " etc.   See 1 Pet. iii. 1.

ii. *The THING EFFECTED by an instrument for the instrument or organic cause of it.*

Gen. xlix. 6.—Lit., " My soul (*i.e.*, myself, I) will not come into their secret (*counsel*), mine honour shall not be with them in their assembly."

Here, " honour " is put for the tongue which gives it ; and it means that he would not honour them by speaking or taking part in their assembly.   Compare Ps. lvii. 8, and cviii. 1.

Deut. xxiv. 6.—" No man shall take the nether or the upper millstone to pledge : for he taketh *a man's* life to pledge."   Here " life," the effect, is put for the means of livelihood by which the life is preserved.

Ps. vii. 5 (6).—" Let him . . . lay mine honour in the dust " : *i.e.*, myself who gives honour.

Ps. xvi. 9.—" Therefore my heart is glad, and my glory rejoiceth " : *i.e.*, my tongue gives glory, as is explained in Acts ii. 26.

Ps. xxx. 12 (13).—" To the end that my glory may sing praise to thee and not be silent."

Here, the word " glory " may be put for the tongue which gives it : but the structure of the Psalm suggests another explanation of the *Metonymy*.   This verse corresponds, in the structure, with verse 4 : " Sing to Jehovah, O ye saints of His."   Compare 2 Cor. viii. 23.

So that verse 12 would be " To the end that Thy saints may sing praise to Thee " : " glory " being put for the saints who give the glory.

Ps. lvii. 8 (9).—" Awake up, my glory " : *i.e.*, my tongue, wake up and glorify God.

Prov. xxvii. 27.—" And *thou shalt have* goats' milk enough for thy food, for the food of thy household, and for the life (*marg.*) of thy maidens " : *i.e.*, as the A.V. renders it, " for the maintenance of thy maidens."

Mark xii. 44.—" She of her want did cast in all that she had, even all her living (or life) " : *i.e.*, all her means of supporting herself in life.

Luke xv. 12.—" And he divided unto them his living (or life) " : *i.e.*, his means or property, by which life is sustained.   So Mark xii. 44.

Acts xvii. 31.—Lit., "Whereof he hath given faith to all men." Here faith, the effect, is put for the proofs or evidence on which it rests. "Whereof He hath afforded evidence unto all men": and then the evidence or proof is stated, "in that he hath raised him from the dead." The A.V. and R.V. well render it "hath given *assurance.*"

The Resurrection of Christ is the evidence God affords of His purpose to judge the world by Him.

Rom. i. 16.—"For it [the gospel] is the power of God unto salvation to every one that believeth": *i.e.,* the belief is the effect of the power of God through the preaching of the gospel.

1 John v. 4.—"This is the victory that overcometh the world, even our faith." "Victory," the effect, is put for "our faith," which accomplishes it. From Eph. vi. 16 we learn that it is through Christ; who is the shield which faith uses.

iii. *The EFFECT for the thing or action causing or producing it.*

(a) In Nouns.

Ex. x. 17.—"Intreat the LORD your God, that he may take away from me this death only": *i.e.,* this plague which is causing death.

Deut. xxx. 15.—"I have set before thee this day life and good, and death and evil": *i.e.,* good things which end in life, and evil things which end in death. So in Deut. xxxii. 47, and Jer. xxi. 8, etc.

2 Kings iv. 40.—"There is death in the pot": *i.e.,* there is that which produces death as the effect of eating it. How forcible is this *Metonymy,* by the use of which time is saved, and perhaps life too.

Prov. x. 2.—"Righteousness delivereth from death": *i.e.,* from the things that end in death.

Prov. xix. 13.—"A foolish son is the calamity of his father": *i.e.,* does that which brings or produces calamity.

Prov. xx. 1.—"Wine is a mocker, strong drink is raging."

Here, wine, etc., is put for its effects. It brings him who drinks to excess into derision, and causes tumults.

Ecc. xi. 1.—"Cast thy bread (*i.e.,* the seed which produces it) upon the waters."

Isa. xxviii. 12.—"This is the rest": *i.e.,* this is what gives rest.

Jer. iii. 24.—"For shame hath devoured the labour of our fathers": *i.e.,* the worship of Baal, which brought upon them shame and sorrow. Shame is put for an idol or for idolatry in Jer. xi. 13 (see margin). Hos. ix. 10. See also Jer. xlviii. 13, etc.

Lam. ii. 14.—"Thy prophets have seen vain things for thee and expulsions": *i.e.*, the things which led to expulsion from the land and captivity.

Ezek. xliv. 18.—"They shall not gird themselves with sweat": *i.e.*, as in A.V., with anything that causeth sweat. The effect "sweat" being put for the garments which cause it.

Hos. iv. 18.—"Their drink is rebellious, or turned aside": *i.e.*, has caused them to turn aside from God. Through not seeing the *Metonymy*, the translators try to find other meanings for סָר (see text and margin). The verse refers to Isa. xxviii. 1 and v. 11.

Micah i. 5.—"What is the transgression of Jacob? Is it not Samaria? And what are the high places of Judah? Are they not Jerusalem?" *i.e.*, Samaria and Jerusalem were the cause of the transgression of Israel:—"What is *the cause of* Jacob's trangression?"

Hab. ii. 5.—"Yea, also because the wine transgresseth": *i.e.*, the effects of the wine was transgression; or, "Yea, so surely as wine causeth trangression."

John iii. 19.—"And this is the judgment": *i.e.*, the cause of which judgment or condemnation was the effect: *viz.*, "that light is come into the world, and men loved darkness rather than light," etc.

John xii. 50.—"And I know that his commandment is life everlasting": *i.e.*, the effect of it is eternal life.

John xvii. 3.—"This is life eternal": *i.e.*, the effect of it is life eternal.

Rom. vi. 6.—"The body of sin" is more than "sinful body." It is more than mere character. The effect is put for the cause; which is the old nature, that, through the body, works out sin; and sin is the effect; which is thus used, here and in other parts of this epistle (chap. v. 12-viii. 39), for the old nature itself.

Whereas, in chaps. i. 16-v. 11, we have "sins," as the product of the Old nature, and the fruit of the old tree, we have, in v. 11-viii. 39, "sin," or the Old nature, which causes and commits the "sins"; and the old tree itself which produces the fruits.

Rom. vii. 7.—"Is the law sin? (*i.e.*, Is sin the effect of the law?) God forbid. But *yet* I knew not sin except through the law!" There is no "nay" in the Greek. The word "but" brings out the meaning: "God forbid that sin should be the effect of the law. But nevertheless." So it is.

Rom. vii. 24.—"The body of this death"; or, by *Hypallage* (*q.v.*), as in A.V. margin, "this body of death": in which case, "of death " is either, by *Enallage*, put for the adjective " *dying*," or it may be the *Metonymy* of the effect, and the result "death " put for the cause—*viz.*, all that leads up to, and ends in, death.

Rom. viii. 6.—" To be carnally minded is death (*i.e.*, the cause of death), but to be spiritually minded is life and peace (*i.e.*, ends in life and peace or peaceful life)." So verse 10.

1 Cor. xii. 6.—" And there are diversities of operations " : *i.e.*, of faculties and gifts effected by the Divine operations.

1 Cor. xiv. 3.—" He that prophesieth speaketh unto men edification, and exhortation, and comfort " : *i.e.*, words which build up, exhort, and comfort.

The A.V. obtains this meaning by supplying the word " *to*."

2 Cor. i. 10.—" Who delivered us from so great a death " : *i.e.*, from the persecution or trouble which threatened to kill them, and end in death.

2 Cor. xi. 23.—" In deaths oft." This cannot, of course, mean that he had died more than once ; but that he had often been at death's door, and in troubles which cause or bring about death.

Phil. i. 13.—" My bonds in Christ are manifest in all the palace " : *i.e.*, the effect of his preaching made it manifest that his bonds were on account of his service for Christ, and not for any crimes.

Heb. vi. 1.—" Dead works " : *i.e.*, works wrought by the Old nature. So ix. 14, according to Rom. vi. 23.

Rev. vi. 8.—" And power was given unto them . . . to kill with the sword, and with hunger, and with death " : *i.e.*, with pestilence which produced death.

(*b*) In Verbs.

Ps. xxv. 2.—" O my God, I trust in thee : let me not be ashamed, let not mine enemies triumph over me " (and thus be a cause of my being put to shame). So verse 20. Ps. xxxi. 1 (2) ; cxix. 116, etc.

Ps. lxx. 4 (5).—" Let them rejoice and be glad in Thee, all that seek thee " : *i.e.*, let there be a cause of rejoicing and gladness to all seeking thee. Through not seeing the *Metonymy* the A.V. and R.V. render it : " Let all those that seek thee rejoice and be glad in thee."

The cause and effect are joined together in Ps. v. 11 (12), 12 (13).

Isa. xxviii. 16.—" He that believeth shall not make haste."

Here, hastening away or flight is put as the effect for the confusion and shame which is the cause of it. See Rom. ix. 33 ; x. 11. 1 Pet.

ii. 6, where the cause is put. The sense is that he that believeth will have no need of hurried flight, he will wait God's time.

iv. *The THING MADE, for the material from which it is made or produced.*

Ps. lxxiv. 15.—"Thou didst cleave the fountain and the flood": *i.e.*, the rock from which the fountain flowed.

Isa. xxviii. 28.—"Bread is bruised": *i.e.*, the corn of which it is made. The A.V. supplies "*corn.*" The sense is clear from verse 27 and Job. xxviii. 5. In Ps. civ. 14, we have the opposite of this in the *Metonymy* of the cause.

Isa. xxxiii. 12.—"And the people shall be as the burnings of lime": *i.e.*, as fuel for lime-kilns.

Isa. xlvii. 2.—"Take the millstones and grind meal": *i.e.*, grind corn, from which meal is made.

III. Metonymy of the SUBJECT.

The third division of *Metonymy* is when the subject is put for the adjunct: *i.e.*, for some circumstance pertaining to (or joined to) the subject: *e.g.*, as when the place, or thing *containing* it, is put for that which is contained: the *possessor* for the thing possessed, etc. It is divided into the five following heads:—

i. *The SUBJECT (i.e., the Thing or Action) for that which is connected with it (i.e., the adjunct).*

1. Nouns.

Gen. iii. 7.—"And the eyes of them both were opened, and they knew that they were naked." They knew this fact before: but they did not know all that was connected with it. Their nakedness, after the fall, received a new meaning.

1 Sam. i. 15—"I . . . have poured out my soul before the Lord": *i.e.*, my desires and longings.

1 Chron. xii. 38.—"All these . . . came with a perfect heart": *i.e.*, affections and desires.

Ps. vii. 9.—"God trieth the hearts and reins": *i.e.*, the thoughts and affections and desires. This is clear from Ps. li. 6 (8); lxxiii. 11. Prov. xxiii 7.

Ps. xvi. 7.—"My reins (*i.e.*, my thoughts) also instruct me in the night season."

Ps. xxvi. 2.—" Examine me, O Lord, and prove me: try my reins (*i.e.*, my thoughts) and my heart."

See also Jer. xi. 20 ; xvii. 10 ; xx. 12. Rev. ii. 23.

Ps. xxxviii. 8 (9).—" I have roared by reason of the disquietness of my heart" (*i.e.*, my thoughts).

Ps. lxii. 9.—" Pour out your heart before Him ": *i.e.*, your thoughts and desires. So Lam. ii. 19.

Ps. lxii. 10 (11).—" Set not your heart (*i.e.*, your affections) upon them."

Prov. vi. 32.—" Whoso committeth adultery with a woman lacketh heart." (So Heb., see A.V. margin). Here heart is put for " understanding," as in A.V.; because it is spoken of as the seat of wisdom and understanding. See Prov. ii. 10 ; viii. 5 ; xi. 29 ; xv. 14 ; xvi. 21.

Prov. vii. 7.—" A young man void of heart " : *i.e.*, of understanding. It is so used in Prov. ix. 4, 16 ; x. 13, 21.

Prov. xv. 32.—" He that heareth reproof possesseth an heart " : *i.e.*, as in A.V. margin, *getteth understanding*.

Prov. xvi. 23.—" The heart (*i.e.*, the desires and thoughts) of the wise maketh wise his mouth " : *i.e.*, *his words*, by *Metonymy* of the cause. See A.V. margin.

Prov. xxii. 17.—" Apply thine heart (*i.e.*, thy thoughts and powers) unto my knowledge."

Prov. xxvi. 7.—" The legs of the lame are not equal: so is a parable in the mouth of fools." So A.V.

R.V. : " The legs of the lame hang loose ! " The Heb. is : " The legs of the lame are lifted up " (see A.V. margin). Here " legs " are put for the clothes which being lifted up expose the lameness. So when a fool attempts to utter a parable, he soon exposes himself.

Prov. xxviii. 26.—" He that trusteth in his own heart (*i.e.*, understanding) is a fool."

Isa. v. 21.—" Woe unto them that are . . . prudent before their face " : *i.e.*, in themselves or in their own view of matters. See A.V. margin.

Isa. xlix. 16.—" I have graven thee upon the palms of my hands " : *i.e.*, as indelible as the lines graven in the palms of the hands, (with which we are born) will be My remembrance of thee.

Jer. xii. 2.—" Thou art near in their mouth (*i.e.*, their words, *Met.* of cause), and far from their reins " (*i.e.*, their affections, *Met.* of subject). See Isa. xxix. 13.

Hos. iv. 11.—" Whoredom and wine and new wine take away the heart ": *i.e.*, the understanding. That this is meant is clear from chap. v. 11.

Hos. vii. 11.—" Ephraim also is like a silly dove without heart " : *i.e.*, without understanding.

Matt. vi. 21.—" Where your treasure is, there will your heart (*i.e.*, your thoughts and affections) be also."

Matt. xvi. 19.—" Whatsoever thou (*i.e.*, by the word which thou shalt minister) shalt bind (see *Met.* of Adjunct below) on earth." So xviii. 18. Whatever this refers to, Peter had neither the power nor the authority to pass it on to any one else.

Matt. xxiv. 45.—" Who then (*i.e.*, how great and blessed and happy) is a faithful and wise servant ? "

John xx. 23.—" Whose soever sins ye (*i.e.*, by the word which ye minister) remit." See below under *verbs*. Whatever this may mean, it was spoken to the apostles : and it is certain that they had no commission, authority, or power to pass on that gift to others.

Acts i. 11.—" This same Jesus, which is taken up from you " : *i.e.*, from your presence and company. So verse 22.

Acts i. 24.—" Thou, Lord, which knowest the hearts (*i.e.*, the thoughts) of all men," etc. See Ps. cxxxix. 2, 4.

Rom. vi. 6.—" Our old man is (Gr., was) crucified with him " : *i.e.*, not a man really, but our Old nature derived from Adam : our old self with its desires and qualities and conditions. So Eph. iv. 22. Compare Rom. vi. 12 ; vii. 5, 7, 8. 2 Cor. vii. 1. Heb. xii. 1.

Rom. xv. 24.—" If first I be somewhat filled with you " : *i.e.*, your company, etc., as expressed in A.V. margin and verse 32.

Rom. xvi. 3, 7.—" My helpers in Christ Jesus " : *i.e.*, in the service of Christ.

2 Cor. v. 17.—" If any man be in Christ he is a new creature " : *i.e.*, he has a new nature created within him. Thus a new standing is given to him, with new thoughts and desires, etc. So Eph. iv. 24. Compare Rom. xii. 2 ; viii. 2, 5. 1 Pet. iii. 4 and Rom. vii. 22. 2 Cor. iv. 16.

Gal. iv. 15.—" Where is then the blessedness ye spake of" : *i.e.*, how great was that blessedness ye spake of! for, etc.

Phil. i. 21.—" To me to live is Christ " : *i.e.*, to serve Christ, to work and labour for Him.

2. Verbs.

Where the action is put for the declaration concerning it : or where what is said *to be done* is put for what is declared, or permitted, or foretold as *to be* done : or where an action, said *to be done*, is put for *the giving occasion* for such action.

Gen. ii. 7.—See below, under Deut. ix. 1.

Gen. xxvii. 37.—" Behold, I have made him (Jacob) thy lord " : *i.e.*, I have blessed him ; and this was part of the blessing.

Gen. xxx. 13.—" The daughters will call me blessed " : *i.e.*, I am now a mother.   For the parallels to this see Ps. lxxii. 17. Luke i. 48.

Gen. xxxiv. 12.—"Ask me never so much dowry and gift " : *i.e.*, ask me to give never so much, etc.

Gen. xxxv. 12.—" And the land which I gave Abraham and Isaac " : *i.e.*, which I promised to give, or gave in promise.

Gen. xli. 13.—" Me he restored (*i.e.*, declared that I should be restored) unto mine office, and him he hanged (*i.e.*, declared he should be hanged)."

Ex. xiii. 2.—" Sanctify unto me all the first-born " : *i.e.*, declare in My name to the People that I sanctify (*i.e.*, separate) them, etc. Which Moses did in verses 11 and 12.

Ex. xx. 7.—" The LORD will not make him guiltless" : *i.e.*, will not declare or pronounce.   Or " hold," as in A.V.

Lev. xiii. 3.—" And the priest shall look on him, and he shall be unclean (or " uncleanse him," for the verb is in the *Piel*)" : *i.e.*, " he shall pronounce him unclean," as in A.V.

Deut. ix. 1.—" Hear, O Israel : Thou art to pass over Jordan this day " : *i.e.*, it is declared this day that thou art to pass over Jordan.

With this passage compare Gen. ii. 17 : " In the day that thou eatest thereof thou shalt surely die " : *i.e.*, not that he should die in that day, but it should be declared " in that day " : *i.e.*, thou shalt be sentenced to die.

2 Sam. vii. 22.—" Wherefore thou art great" : *i.e.*, I will declare and praise Thee as great : or, Thou shalt be known as great.

See other examples in Isa. viii. 13. Jer. i. 5, 10. Ezek. xiii. 19; xx. 26.

Isa. vi. 10.—" Make the heart of this people fat " : *i.e.*, declare that it shall become so. (Isaiah could not make it fat, etc.) So Matt. xiii. 14. Mark iv. 12. Luke viii. 10. John xii. 40. Acts xxviii. 26, 27. Rom. xi. 8.

Jer. i. 10.—" I have this day set thee over the nations and over the kingdoms, to root out (*i.e.*, to declare that they shall be rooted out), and to pull down (*i.e.*, to prophesy that they shall be pulled down), and to destroy (*i.e.*, to declare that they shall be destroyed), and to throw down (*i.e.*, to foretell that they shall be thrown down)," etc.

Jer. iv. 10.—" Then said I, Ah, Lord GOD (Adonai-Jehovah) ! surely thou hast vehemently (or verily) deceived this people (*i.e.*, prophesied that this People shall be deceived), saying, Ye shall have peace ; whereas the sword reacheth unto the soul."

The people deceived themselves, assuring themselves that they should have peace (see chap. v. 12). The Lord had declared by his prophet that they would so deceive themselves, and so it came to pass that they were permitted to be deceived by their false prophets.

Jer. xxxviii. 23.—" Thou shalt burn this city with fire " : *i.e.*, thou shalt declare that it shalt be burnt. A.V. renders it cause it to be burnt, as though it were the *Metonymy* of the effect. It is clearly the *Metonymy* of the subject : for Zedekiah was not personally to set light to the city !

E zek. xiii. 19.—" And will ye pollute me among my people for handfuls of barley and for pieces of bread, to slay the souls that should not die and to save the souls alive that should not live " : to prophesy (falsely) that they should die, and to promise life to those who should not live.

Ezek. xiii. 22.—" Ye have . . . strengthened the hands of the wicked, that he should not return from his wicked way, by quickening him " : *i.e.*, by promising him life. See A.V. margin.

Ezek. xx. 25, 26.—" Wherefore I gave them also statutes that were not good, and judgments whereby they should not live (*i.e.*, I permitted them to receive such statutes from the heathen) ; And I polluted them in their own gifts," etc. : *i.e.*, I suffered them to pollute themselves in those gifts which, by the Law, they ought to have dedicated to Me.

See under *Antanaclasis.*

Hos. vi. 5.—" Therefore have I hewed them by the prophets (*i.e.*, I have declared by the prophets that they shall be hewed) ; I have slain them by the words of my mouth (*i.e.*, I have foretold by the words of my mouth that they shall be slain)."

Matt. vi. 13.—"And lead us not into temptation": *i.e.*, suffer us not to be led.

Matt. xvi. 19.—"Whatsoever thou shalt bind on earth (*i.e.*, declare to be binding as a precept, etc.), shall be bound in heaven; and whatsoever thou shalt loose on earth (*i.e.*, declare to be not bind‐ing) shall be loosed in heaven." But note that, whatsoever this may mean, it is nowhere stated that the apostle had either authority or power to transmit the gift to others; still less to transmit the power to others to give this gift! And in any case it refers to the "king‐dom" and not to the "Church." See also chap. xviii. 18.

Luke vii. 29.—"And all the people that heard him, and the Publicans justified God, being baptized with the baptism of John": *i.e.*, declared God to be just, and praised him for His justice and goodness; in that they humbled themselves in confession of sin and were baptized by John. So the word is used again in verse 35 and chaps. x. 29; xvi. 15, etc.

John xx. 23.—"Whose soever sins ye remit (*i.e.*, declare to be remitted) they are remitted unto them: and whose soever sins ye retain (*i.e.*, declare to be retained) they are retained."

Here note that the apostles had neither the authority nor the power to transmit this gift; still less to transmit the power to others to give it.

Acts x. 15.—"What God hath cleansed": *i.e.*, declared to be (ceremonially) clean: as is clear from verse 28.

Rom. vii. 9.—"But when the commandment came": *i.e.*, when its power was declared in revealing my impotence to obey it, I, in my experience, suffered its penalty—death. See Gal. iii. 23, below.

2 Cor. iii. 6.—"The letter killeth": *i.e.*, the Law of God manifests its power, in convincing of sin, and causing the sinner to condemn him‐self to death, which is the wages of sin. Compare Rom. vii. 10, and Hos. vi. 5.

Gal. iii. 23.—"Before faith came": *i.e.*, before the Gospel was declared, and brought a new object for faith.

Jas. ii. 21.—"Was not Abraham our father justified by works?" *i.e.*, declared to be justified. See verse 23 and Gen. xxii. 12. So also verses 24, 25.

Jas. ii. 22.—"By works was faith made (*i.e.*, declared to be, or manifested to be) perfect": *i.e.*, true and sincere.

ii. *The CONTAINER for the contents : and the PLACE for the thing placed in it.*

1. CIRCUIT is so put in all these cases for what is contained within it.

Num. xxii. 4.—" Now shall all this company lick up all our circuit " : *i.e.,* " all that are round about us " (as in A.V.).

Ezra i. 6.—" And all their circuit " : *i.e.,* all that were about them.

2. BASKET is put for its contents.

Deut. xxviii. 5.—" Blessed shall be thy basket and thy kneading-trough " (and verse 17 contra). Here the A.V. has translated the latter *Metonymy,* but not the former. The R.V. has translated neither. The container is put for the contents. Here, probably, the " basket " is put for the *seed,* and " kneading-trough " for the *meal ;* the beginning and the end of their labours.

3. WILDERNESS is put for the wild beasts in it.

Ps. xxix. 8.—" The voice of the LORD shaketh the wilderness " : *i.e.,* the people and animals or inhabitants of the wilderness, as is clear from the next verse, and Deut. viii. 15.

4. HOUSE is put for household.

Gen. vii. 1.—" Come thou and all thy house (*i.e.,* thy family) into the ark."

Gen. xxx. 30.—" When shall I provide for mine own house (*i.e.,* family) also ? "

Gen. xliii. 16.—Joseph . . " said to the ruler of his house " : *i.e.,* of his servants. We use the word " establishment " in the same way : as the French also use " *ménage.*"

Ex. i. 21.—God " made them houses " : *i.e.,* families, or progeny.

Ex. ii. 1.—" And there went a man of the house (*i.e.,* lineage) of Levi."

2 Sam. vii. 11.—" Jehovah telleth thee that make thee an house will Jehovah " : *i.e.,* a posterity, especially referring to Christ, Who should be of " the seed of David," and sit on His throne for ever. Luke i. 31-33. Observe the Figure *Epanadiplosis* in the above rendering of the Hebrew.

1 Chron. x. 6.—" So Saul died, and his three sons, and all his house died together " (*i.e.,* all his family), as explained in 1 Sam. xxxi. 6.

Ps. xlix. 11 (12).—" Their inward thought is that their houses (*i.e.*, their families) shall continue for ever."

Isa. xxxvi. 3.—" Then came forth unto him Eliakim, Hilkiah's son, which was over the house ": *i.e.*, the servants, or household.

Ezek. iii. 1.—" Go speak unto the house (*i.e.*, the descendants) of Israel." The margin of Ginsburg's Hebrew Bible gives another reading : " sons."

Ezek. xxvii. 14.—" They of the house of Togarmah ": *i.e.*, of Togarmah's descendants. See Gen. x. 3.

Luke xix. 9.—" This day is salvation come to this house": *i.e.*, to Zacchæus and his family.

Acts x. 2.—Cornelius . . " feared God with all his house ": *i.e.*, all his family or household.

1 Cor. i. 16.—Here the Greek word " house " is rendered " household " : *i.e.*, family.

1 Tim. iii. 4.—" One that ruleth well his own house ": *i.e.*, his own family.

2 Tim. iii. 6.—" For of this sort are they that creep into houses " : *i.e.*, families.

2 Tim. iv. 19.—Here the Greek, " house," is rendered " household " : *i.e.*, family.

Tit. i. 11.—" Who subvert whole houses " : *i.e.*, families.

Heb. xi. 7.—" Noah . . . prepared an ark to the saving of his house " : *i.e.*, of his family.

5. ISLANDS are put for their inhabitants.

Isa. xli. 1.—" Keep silence before me, O islands ": *i.e.*, the inhabitants of the islands. So xlii. 4 ; and li. 5.

6. TABLE is put for the things on it.

Ps. xxiii. 5.—" Thou preparest a table before me " : *i.e.*, the good things upon it. As, when we say that such an one " keeps a good table," we mean that it is spread bountifully.

Ps. lxxviii. 19.—" Can God (אל, the name of concentrated power) furnish (Heb., order, see A.V. marg.) a table in the wilderness ? ": *i.e.*, set the things upon it.

Under this head comes also

Hos. xiv. 2 (3).—" So will we render the calves of our lips."

Here, note first, that the word "render" is שִׁלֵּם (*shilem*), *to offer* or *pay a vow*. Next, that the word "calves" means *oxen*; *i.e.*, the animals used in sacrifice.

Then we have two *Metonymies*. First, *oxen* are put (by *Metonymy* of the subject) for the *sacrifices* offered; and then *the lips* are put (by *Metonymy* of the cause) for the *confession* made by them. So that the verse really should read: "So shall we offer our sacrifices of confession and prayer"; being exactly what is expressed in Ps. li. 17 (19). "The sacrifices of God are a broken spirit, etc.," and Heb. xiii. 15: "By him . . . let us offer the sacrifice of praise to God continually, that is, the fruit of our lips, giving thanks to his name." See also Ps. lxix. 30 (31), 31 (32); cxvi. 17; cxli. 2.

The R.V., while trying to improve the translation, misses both *Metonymies*: "So will we render as bullocks *the offering* of our lips"—retaining the "letter" ("bullocks" and "lips") and missing the "spirit" (sacrifices and confession).

Heb. xiii. 10.—"We have an altar": *i.e.*, a sacrifice, referring to the sin-offering which was burned without the camp including the skin and the dung, no soul having a right to eat of it. So Christ is our sin-offering offered without the gate. That it is a figure is clear, for the verse reads on: "We have an altar, whereof (ἐξ οὗ, *ex hou, of which*) they have no right to eat which serve the Tabernacle." People do not eat "altars"! The word "altar" must, therefore, be used by *Metonymy* for the sacrifices offered upon it, which were eaten.

But, here, it is the sin-offering which is referred to, which no one might eat; and therefore those who continued still "served the tabernacle" could have no part in Christ as the sin-offering.

7. MOUNTAIN is put for mountainous region.

Josh. xiii. 6.—"Mountain" is put for a mountainous region, translated here "hill country." See Judges vii. 24.

Judges iii. 27; vii. 24. — "Mountain of Ephraim": Mount Ephraim is put for the mountainous region of Ephraim.

Mountains are also put for idols worshipped there; or for their inhabitants.

Jer. iii. 23.—"Truly in vain is salvation hoped for from the hills, and from the multitude of mountains." Here, "mountains" and "hills" are put for the idols which were worshipped there. See Ezek. xviii. 6, 11, 15.

Micah i. 4.—"And the mountains shall be molten under him, and the valleys shall be cleft, as wax before the fire, and as the waters that are poured down a steep place." From a comparison with Ps. lxviii. 2 and 1 Chron. xii. 15 (16) it seems that "mountains" and "valleys" are here put for their *inhabitants.* So Ps. xcvii. 5.

8. The WORLD is put for its inhabitants.

John iii. 16.—"God so loved the world": *i.e.,* the inhabitants of the world, now *without distinction.* Before it was only Israel *without exception.*

See further under *Synecdoche.*

2 Cor. v. 19.—"Reconciling the world (*i.e.,* the inhabitants of the world) unto himself."

1 John ii. 2.—"He is the propitiation for our sins: and not for ours only, but also for the whole world": *i.e.,* for all the inhabitants of the world without *distinction;* as shown by the use of the word for "ours" (which is ἡμέτερος (*heemeteros*) and not ἡμῶν (*heemōn*), *of us : i.e.,* "our," as in the previous clause).

Heemeteros denotes that which is peculiarly *ours* as distinct from *others'.* See Acts ii. 11 ; xxiv. 6; xxvi. 5. Rom. xv. 4. 2 Tim. iv. 15. Tit. iii. 14. 1 John i. 3.

See also under *Synecdoche* and *Ellipsis.*

1 John v. 19.—"The whole world (*i.e.,* all the inhabitants of the world) lieth in [*the power of*] the wicked one." See under *Ellipsis.*

9. The WORLD is put for a portion of its inhabitants.

John i. 10.—"The world knew him not": *i.e.,* people of the world.

John iii. 17.—"That the world through him might be saved": *i.e.,* people in the world without distinction.

John vi. 33.—"The bread of God is he which cometh down from heaven, and giveth life unto the world": *i.e.,* to God's People in the world.

Compare verse 51. Hence John i. 9 and iii. 17.

John vii. 7.—"The world cannot hate you, but me it hateth" : *i.e.,* the inhabitants of the world, as without God.

John xiv. 17.—"The Spirit of truth ; whom the world (*i.e.,* men) cannot receive." So xv. 19 ; xvi. 20, 33 ; xvii. 9, 14, etc.

John xiv. 31.—"But that the world may know that I love the Father": *i.e.,* that the godly in the world. Hence John i. 9: "That was the true light, which, coming into the world (*i.e.*, among men), lighteth every man,"·without distinction of race or language, etc.; as heretofore only Israel, not *without exception*, for that is not the fact. See under *Periphrasis*.

John xvii. 21.—" That the world may believe " : *i.e.*, many in the world, without distinction.

1 Cor. xi. 32.—" That we should not be condemned with the world " : *i.e.*, with the ungodly.

1 John iii. 1.—" Therefore the world (*i.e.*, those who are without God) knoweth us not."   So iv. 5, and v. 4, 5, etc.

So the DEVIL is the Prince (or god) of this world : *i.e.*, the ungodly inhabitants of it.

John xii. 31 ; xiv. 30 ; xvi. 11. 2 Cor. iv. 4. Eph. ii. 2 ; vi. 12.

And conversely, the world may be put for God's people.

10.   SHIPS are put for the souls in them.

Isa. xxiii. 1.—" Howl, ye ships of Tarshish."   Here " ships " are put for the people in them.   So verse 14.

11.   NESTS are put for the birds in them.

Deut. xxxii. 11.—" As an eagle stirreth up her (Heb., masc.) nest " : *i.e.*, her young in the nest, as is clear from the rest of the verse.

12.   OPHIR is put for the gold of Ophir.

Job xxii. 24.—" Then shalt thou lay up gold as dust ; and Ophir (*i.e.*, the gold of Ophir) as the stones of the brooks."

13.   CUP is put for the wine in it.

Jer. xlix. 12.—" Cup " is put for the contents : *i.e.*, for the wine in it.

Ezek. xxiii. 32.—" Cup " is put for what is in it.

Luke xxii. 17, 20.—" Cup " is put for its contents, as is clear from verse 20, and Mark xiv. 24 and Matt. xxvi. 28.

1 Cor. x. 16, 21 ; xi. 25, 26, 27, 28.—In these and other places " cup " is put for the contents of it.

14.   REGION is put for its inhabitants.

Gen. xlvii. 15.—" All Egypt came unto Joseph " : *i.e.*, all the Egyptians, as in A.V.

Ps. cv. 38.—" Egypt was glad when they departed ": *i.e.*, the Egyptians were glad.

Ps. lxviii. 31 (32).—" Ethiopia shall soon stretch out her hands unto God ": *i.e.*, the Ethiopians.

Job i. 15.—" Sheba fell upon them ": *i.e.*, the Sabeans, as in A.V. See vi. 19 and Isa. xliii. 3.

Matt. iii. 5.—" Then went out to him Jerusalem (*i.e.*, the inhabitants of Jerusalem) and all Judæa (*i.e.*, the dwellers in Judæa)," etc.

Rom. xv. 26.—" For it pleased Macedonia and Achaia to make a certain contribution ": *i.e.*, the saints in Macedones and Achaia.

15. Grave is put for the dead buried in it.

Isa. xxxviii. 18.—" The grave (*i.e.*, those who are buried in it) cannot praise thee." This is clear from verse 19 and Ps. cxv. 17.

16. Tents, etc., are put for the dwellers therein.

Gen. xiii. 5.—" Tents " are put for the many servants, etc., who dwelt in them.

Ps. lxxviii. 67.—" He refused the tabernacle (or tent: *i.e.*, the tribe) of Joseph, and chose not the tribe of Ephraim."

Ps. lxxxvii. 2.—" The Lord loveth the gates of Zion more than all the dwellings (*i.e.*, tribes) of Jacob."

Ps. xci. 10.—" Neither shall any plague come nigh thy dwelling ": *i.e.*, those who dwell in it.

Prov. xiv. 11.—Here " house " and " tabernacle " are put for those who dwell in them.

17. The land or earth are put for its inhabitants.

Gen. vi. 11.—" The earth also was corrupt before God ": *i.e.*, the inhabitants of the earth, as is clear from the next verse.

Gen. xi. 1.—" And the whole earth was of one language, and of one speech ": *i.e.*, the people on the earth.

Gen. xviii. 25.—" Shall not the Judge of all the earth (*i.e.*, the people on the earth) do right ? "

Gen. xli. 30.—" The famine shall consume the land ": *i.e.*, the people in the land.

Gen. xli. 57.—" And all countries came into Egypt to Joseph to buy ": *i.e.*, people from all countries.

Judges v. 7.—" The villages ceased " : *i.e.*, the inhabitants of the villages, or the Peasantry. So also v. 11. See under *Ellipsis* and *Homœopropheron.*

1 Sam. xiv. 29.—" Then said Jonathan, My father hath troubled the land " : *i.e.*, the People.

2 Sam. xv. 23.—" And all the country (*i.e.*, the people) wept with a loud voice."

Prov. xxviii. 2.—" For the trangression of a land (*i.e.*, of the people of a country) many are the princes thereof."

Ps. ix. 8 (9).—" And he shall judge the world in righteousness " : *i.e.*, the inhabitants of the world.

Ps. xxii. 27 (28).—" All the ends of the world (*i.e.*, the people living in the uttermost parts of the world) shall remember and turn unto the LORD." So Ps. lxvii. 7 (8).

Ps. lxvi. 1.—" Make a joyful noise unto God, all ye lands " : *i.e.*, ye nations.

Ps. lxvi. 4.—" All the earth (*i.e.*, the peoples) shall worship thee." So Ps. lxxxii. 8; xcvi. 1. Ezek. xiv. 13.

Matt. v. 13.—" Ye are the salt of the earth " : *i.e.*, the peoples. " Salt " also is used by *Metaphor* (*q.v.*) for its preserving effects.

Land is also put for its spoils.

Isa. xliii. 3.—" Egypt " is put for the spoils of Egypt.

18. THEATRE is put for its spectacle.

1 Cor. iv. 9.—" For we are made a theatre to the world " : *i.e.*, a spectacle, as in A.V.

19. CITY, etc., put for its inhabitants.

1 Sam. xxii. 19.—" And Nob, the city of the priests, smote he " : *i.e.*, its inhabitants.

Jer. iv. 29.—" The whole city shall flee " : *i.e.*, all the inhabitants of the city.

Isa. xiv. 31.—" Cry, O city " : *i.e.*, ye inhabitants of the city.

Jer. xxvi. 2.—" Speak unto all the cities of Judah " : *i.e.*, to their representatives.

Jer. xlviii. 8.—" Here " city," valley," and " plain " are put for their respective inhabitants.

Jer. xlix. 23.—" Hamath " is put for its inhabitants. So Arpad too in verse 24, Damascus.

Micah vi. 9.—" The LORD's voice crieth unto the city " : *i.e.*, to the inhabitants.

Matt. xi. 21, 23.—" Chorazin," " Bethsaida," and " Capernaum," are put for their inhabitants.

Matt. xxiii. 37.—" O Jerusalem, Jerusalem " : *i.e.*, the people that dwelt there.

Mark i. 5. — " Judæa " is put for its inhabitants.

Mark i. 33.—" And all the city was gathered " : *i.e.*, all its inhabitants.

Acts viii. 25.—They " preached the gospel to many villages of the Samaritans " : *i.e.*, to their inhabitants. The A.V. evades and hides the *Metonymy* by rendering it " in many," etc.

20. HEAVEN is put for God, Who dwells there.

Ps. lxxiii. 9.—" They set their mouth against the heavens " : *i.e.*, against God, Who dwells there.

The rest of the verse confirms this :—" Their tongue (*Met.* for words) walketh through the earth." Here " earth " is put for the people who dwell upon it ; and so " heaven " is put for Him who dwells there.

So Dan. iv. 26, 29. 2 Chron. xxxii. 20.

Matt. iii. 2.—" The kingdom of heaven " : *i.e.*, of God ; the sphere in which God rules and reigns. For the word βασιλεία means *dominion* rather than *territory*.

The expression occurs only in Matthew, and in this gospel we have it 35 times. Whether the Lord spoke in Hebrew or Aramaic is open to question : but it is certain He did not speak in Greek.

It is also certain that several passages, which are exactly parallel in every other respect, are unlike in this : *e.g.*, Matt. xi. 11 : " He that is least in the kingdom of heaven is greater than he (*i.e.*, John the Baptist)," and Luke vii. 28 : " He that is least in the kingdom of God is greater than he."

How is this difference to be explained ? Only by the assumption that the Lord speaking in Aramaic, or Hebrew, used the words " kingdom of heaven." Then, in putting this into Greek, in Matthew the figure was *preserved*, literally ; while in Luke it was *translated*, " kingdom of God."

" Heaven " is frequently put for " God," who dwells there. We say " Heaven forbid," " Heaven protect us," etc. So the lost son says, " I have sinned against heaven." He means, against God !

This does not at all affect the truths concerning the kingdom, as contrasted with the Church.

While the kingdom or reign is *God's*, yet it has different aspects. In Matthew, the expression " Kingdom of heaven " corresponds with the aspect of the kingdom as presented in that Gospel.

Our suggestion is that in each case the words " kingdom of heaven " were the words spoken in Aramaic; but that, in presenting them in Greek, the figure is translated, and given idiomatically in Mark and Luke.

The effect of this figure, then, here, is that, by the figure of *Enallage*, the emphasis is placed on the words " heaven " and " God," and not on the word " kingdom "; and by the figure of *Heterosis*, the plural, " heavens " (as it is in the Greek) is put for the singular to still more emphasize the expression.

Hence the phrase means that this reign is the *Divine* or *Heavenly Dominion*, in contrast with all the kingdoms which are of or from this world.

In Matthew, the aspect of it is Old Testament and Jewish; while in the other gospels the aspect is larger and wider in its sphere.

The reign and rule of God comprises all in time and space, and many are the spheres and departments embraced within it. Thus, while the Church of God is embraced in it, the church is not the kingdom. While Israel is embraced in it, Israel does not exhaust the reign and dominion of God. While the Gentiles come within the reach of that dominion, they are neither the kingdom itself nor the church. All these are distinct from each other; and yet all are embraced in the universal reign of heaven; the church occupying its own unique position as the Body of Christ, in whom all things are to be headed-up (Eph. i. 10, 20-23).

Matt. xxi. 25.—" The baptism of John, whence was it? from heaven (*i.e.*, from God), or of men?" So Luke xx. 4.

Luke xv. 18.—" Father, I have sinned against heaven (*i.e.*, against God), and before thee."

John iii. 27.—" A man can receive nothing, except it be given him from heaven ": *i.e.*, from God (who dwells there).

21. HEART is put for nature and character.

Ps. xxiv. 4.—" He that hath clean hands, and a pure heart."
Here " hands " are put for the works done by them ; while
" heart " is not the muscular organ of the body, but is put for the
inward character.

Ps. lxxxiv. 2 (3).—" My soul longeth (*i.e.*, I long), yea, even fainteth
for the courts of the LORD : my heart and my flesh crieth out for the
living God " : *i.e.*, my soul and my body, my whole being.   See also
under *Synecdoche.*

1 Pet. iii. 4.—" Let it be the hidden man of the heart " : *i.e.*, the
new nature implanted within.

22. BELLY is put for heart or thoughts.

Job xv. 35.—"Their belly prepareth deceit " : *i.e.*, their thoughts
and desires.

Prov. xviii. 8.—" The words of a talebearer are as wounds, and
they go down into the chambers of the belly " : *i.e.*, the innermost
thoughts and feelings, moving them as the belly is actually moved by
excitement.   See Hab. iii. 16.   So xxvi. 22.

Prov. xx. 27.—" The spirit of man is the candle (or lamp : *i.e.*,
light) of the LORD, searching all the inward parts of the belly " : *i.e.*,
moving and influencing the thoughts and feelings, as the belly itself is
moved.

John vii. 38.—" He that believeth on me, as the Scripture hath
said, out of his belly shall flow rivers of living water."   Here, " belly "
is put for the innermost thoughts and feelings, and what the Scripture
hath said of this is written in Prov. xviii. 4.

iii.   *The possessor is put for the thing possessed.*

1. NATIONS are put for countries.

Deut. ix. 1.—" To possess nations " : *i.e.*, their countries, and all
that they contained.

2 Sam. viii. 2.—" And he smote Moab, and measured them (*i.e.*,
the territory of the Moabites) with a line, casting them (*i.e.*, the cities
within it) to the ground."

Ps. lxxix. 7.—" They have devoured Jacob " : *i.e.*, the riches and
good things of the descendents of Jacob.

Mark v. 35.—"While he yet spake, there came from the ruler of the synagogue": *i.e.,* from his house: *i.e.,* his servants, whom he employed.

2. PERSON is put for possessions.

Gen. xv. 3.—" And, lo, one born in my house inherits me ": *i.e.,* my possessions or property.

2 Cor. xi. 20.—" For ye suffer . . . if a man devour you ": *i.e.,* your goods or property, as expressed in Ps. xiv. 4.

3. PRINCES are put for the thousands whom they led.

Matt. ii. 6.—" Art not the least among the princes of Judah." Here the princes who led - men by the thousand are put for the thousands or families whom they led. See 1 Sam. x. 19.

In Micah v. 2 (1), we have the word " thousands " literally instead of the figure *Metonymy.* So Judges vi. 15, and 1 Sam. x. 19. Our English " hundreds," as applied to a territorial division, has the same origin.

4. GOD is put for the sacrifices offered to Him.

Josh. xiii. 33.—" The LORD God of Israel was their (the Levites') inheritance, as he said unto them ": see verse 14. From which it is clear that the name of Jehovah is put for the sacrifices which were offered to him, and which He accepted: *i.e.,* their priesthood, as stated in xviii. 7. Deut. x. 9. Ezek. xliv. 28. Num. xviii. 8, 20. Deut. xviii. 1-3.

5. CHRIST is put for His people.

Acts ix. 4.—" Saul, Saul, why persecutest thou me? " *i.e.,* My People who belong to Me. See verse 5; and compare verses 1 and 2.

I Cor. xii. 12.—" For as the body is one, and hath many members and all the members of that one body, being many, are one body ; so also is Christ " or the Christ: *i.e.,* Christ mystical; not personal; as is clear from verse 13 and what follows.

Col. i. 24.—"Who now rejoice in my sufferings for you, and fill up that which is behind of the afflictions of Christ in my flesh ": *i.e.,* Christ mystical; not personal; as is clear from what follows : " for His body's sake, which is the Church."

6. GOD is put for the power manifested by Him.

Luke i. 35.—" The power of the Highest shall overshadow thee ": *i.e.,* the Highest shall overshadow thee ; and His power, which is infinite, shall be put forth upon or manifested in thee.

iv. *The object is put for that which pertains or relates to it.*

1. JESUS is put for His doctrine.

2 Cor. xi. 4.—" For if he that cometh (*i.e.*, the one who is coming, perhaps from Jerusalem or the Twelve) preacheth another Jesus ": *i.e.*, a different doctrine or teaching concerning Jesus. See Gal. i. 8.

2. A GOD is put for his worship.

Ex. xxxii. 1.—" Make us a god which shall go before us " : *i.e.*, whom we may worship and honour. Compare 1 Kings xii. 28.

3. ATTRIBUTES are put for the praise and celebration of them.

Ps. xxix. 1.—" Give unto the LORD glory and strength " : How can we give these to God ? We can praise Him for these, but we cannot give them. They are thus put, by *Metonymy*, for the praise given to Him for his glory and strength. So also Ps. xcvi. 7.

Ps. viii. 2 (3).—" Out of the mouth of babes and sucklings hast thou ordained strength ": *i.e.*, praise for the manifestation and putting forth of God's strength, as is clear from Matt. xxi. 16, where it is rendered " Out of the mouth of babes and sucklings thou hast perfected praise."

4. BURDEN is put for the prophecy.

Isa. xxi. 1.—" The burden of the desert of the sea." Here, " burden " is put for the prophecy of Divine punishment which follows. So xiii. 1 ; xxiii. 1, etc., etc. Mal. i. 1 The burden might be in words, or by a vision.

5. SIN is put for the offering for sin.

Gen. iv. 7.—" Sin (*i.e.*, a sin offering) lieth at the door." So the word " sin " is frequently used for a sin offering. See Ex. xxx. 10. Lev. iv. 3 ; vi. 25. Num. viii. 8. Ps. xl. 6 (7), etc. Lev. vii. 5, 7. 1 Sam. vi. 3, 4, and 2 Cor. v. 21.

Ex. xxix. 14.—" It is a sin " : *i.e.*, an offering which atones for sin.

Hos. iv. 8.—" They eat up the sin, (*i.e.*, the sin-offering) of my people."

2 Cor. v. 21.—" He hath made him to be sin (*i.e.*, a sin-offering) for us." See Isa. liii. 10. Eph. v. 2.

6. PROMISE is put for the faith which receives it.

Rom. ix. 8.—"The children of the promise are counted for the seed": *i.e.*, who believe and receive the promise of God, as is clear from iv. 12, 16. Gal. iii. 7, 29; iv. 28.

7. COVENANT is put for the two tables of stone.

I Kings viii. 21.—"I have set there a place for the ark, wherein is the covenant of the LORD (*i.e*, the two tables of stone) which he made with our fathers," etc., as is clear from Ex. xxxiv. 28 Rom. ix. 4. See especially Deut. ix. 9, 11, 15, 17.

8. BLOOD is put for blood-shedding.

Isa. xxxiii. 15.—"That stoppeth his ears from hearing of blood": from listening to those who shed blood, according to Prov. i 10, 11.

9. DOUBLE is used for that which is complete, thorough, or ample; and of full compensation, whether of judgment or of blessing.

This *Metonymy* arose out of the literal use of the word. See
Gen. xliii. 12, where the "double money" was to pay for the corn taken that time as well as for that which was taken the time before.

Ex. xvi. 5.—The "double" manna was "twice as much," so as to be enough for two days instead of one.

Ex. xxii. 7, 9, where the thief was to restore "double": *i.e.*, to make compensation in full.

Deut. xv. 18, where the liberated bond-servant was worth the "double" of an hireling in serving six years instead of three (compare Isa. xvi. 14; xxi. 16).

From this literal use of the words *mishneh* (מִשְׁנֶה) and *kiphlayim* (כִּפְלַיִם), the word "*double*" is used by *Metonymy*, as follows:—

Job xi. 6.—"The secrets of wisdom are double to that which is": *i.e.*, far beyond, or much more.

Job xli. 13.—"Who can come to him (leviathan) with his double (*i.e.*, strong) bridle." Here it is כֶּפֶל (*kephel*) in the singular.

Isa. xl. 2.—"For she hath received of the LORD's hand double for all her sins": *i.e.*, full punishment.

Isa. lxi. 7.—"For your shame ye shall have double, and for confusion they shall rejoice in their portion: therefore, in their land they shall possess the double: everlasting joy shall be unto them."

Here, we have the "double" denoting not full punishment (as in xl. 2), but complete compensation. And this is marked in the alternation of the four lines : where we have this completeness in the first and third lines; and the consequent joy and rejoicing in the second and fourth lines :—

a | For your shame ye shall have complete compensation or full acquittal.

b | And for confusion they shall rejoice in their portion.

a | Therefore in their land they shall possess the complete pardon.

b | Everlasting joy shall be unto them.

Jer. xvii. 18.—"Destroy them with double destruction ": *i.e.,* with a complete destruction.

Jer. xvi. 18.—"And first I will recompense their iniquity and their sin double ": *i.e.,* with a complete and thorough punishment. Not literally double, but completely.

Zech. ix. 12.—"Turn you to the stronghold, ye prisoners of hope : even to-day do I declare that I will render double unto thee ": *i.e.,* I will completely pardon you and give you full compensation for all your troubles.

1 Tim. v. 17.—"Let the elders that rule be counted worthy of double (*i.e.,* liberal) honour (*i.e.,* maintenance)." See under *Idiom.*

v. *The thing signified is put for the sign.*

Ex. viii. 23 (19).—"And I will put a redemption between my people and thy people (*i.e.,* the judgment, which would be the sign of the redemption) : for to-morrow will this sign be."

Num. vi. 7.—"Because the consecration (Heb. *separation,* see margin) of his God is upon his head ": *i.e.,* the hair, which was the sign and symbol of his separation.

Deut. xvi. 3.—"Unleavened bread . . . even the bread of affliction ": *i.e.,* the bread which was the sign and symbol of their affliction in Egypt.

Deut. xxii. 15, 17.—Here the *Metonymy* is supplied in italics, the letter of the passage being so obviously figurative.

2 Kings xiii. 17.—"The arrow of the LORD's deliverance ": *i.e.,* the sign of the future deliverance which the Lord would work for His People.

1 Chron. xvi. 11.—"Seek the LORD and his strength ": *i.e.*, the Ark of the Covenant, which was the sign and symbol of His Presence and strength. So Ps. cv. 4, according to Ps. cxxxii. 8.

Ps. lxxviii. 6.—"And delivered his strength into captivity" *i.e.*, the Ark of the Covenant, referring to 1 Sam. iv. 11, etc. See Ps· cxxxii. 8.

Isa. xlix. 61.—"It is a light thing that thou shouldest be my servant to raise up the tribes of Jacob and to restore the desolations of Israel": *i.e.*, the land and the cities of Israel which have been reduced to desolation.

The A.V. renders it "preserved," not seeing the figure, but it puts "*desolations*" in the margin.

Ezek. vii. 27.—"The prince shall be clothed with desolation": *i.e.*, with his garments rent, which was the sign of his mourning.

IV. METONYMY OF THE ADJUNCT.

The fourth division of Metonymy is called the *Metonymy* of the Adjunct (or Relation), and is the opposite of *Metonymy* of the Subject.

It is so called because some circumstance pertaining to the subject is put for the subject itself; *e.g.*, the contents for the container, the possession for the possessor, etc. It is divided into the seven following parts:—

i. *The adjunct or accident is put for the subject.*

That which is an accident, or belongs to anything, is put for the subject or the thing itself to which it belongs.

1. The abstract is put for the concrete; or, the attribute is put for that to which anything is attributed.

Gen. xxxi. 54.—"Then Jacob killed beasts upon the mount": *i.e.*, he offered sacrifices, as the A.V. renders it. Here, by *Metonymy*, the abstract is put for its concrete.

Gen. xlii. 38.—"Then shall ye bring down my grey hairs (*i.e.*, me, in my old age) with sorrow to the grave."

Gen. xlvi. 34.—"For every shepherd is an abomination (*i.e.*, an abominable person) unto the Egyptians."

1 Sam. xv. 29.—"And also the eternity of Israel will not lie nor repent." Here, the A.V. renders it "Strength," but the attribute "Eternity" is put for Him to whom it is attributed: *i.e.*, the eternal One: *i.e.*, God. See A.V. margin.

2 Sam. xxiii. 23.—" And David set him over his listeners " : *i.e.*, those who stood at David's door and listened for his command. Hence his bodyguard. See xx. 23. 1 Kings i. 38.

N eh. v. 9.—" Because of the reproach (*i.e.*, the reproachful deeds) of the heathen our enemies."

Job v. 16.—" So the poor hath hope, and iniquity (*i e.*, the iniquitous man) stoppeth his mouth."

Job xxxi. 21.—" If I have lifted up my hand against the father-less, when I saw my help (*i.e.*, those who helped me or would be on my side) in the gate."

Job. xxxii. 7.—" I said, Days (*i.e.*, men of days, or men of full age) should speak, and multitude of years (*i.e.*, aged men) should teach wisdom."

Ps. xii. 1 (2).—" Help, LORD, for the godly man ceaseth : for the faithful from the sons of men fail " : *i.e.*, faithful men fail. So Ps. xxxi. 23 (24). 2 Sam. xx. 19.

Ps. lxv. 8 (9).—" They also that dwell in the uttermost parts are afraid at thy tokens : thou makest the outgoings of the morning and evening to rejoice " : *i.e.*, thou makest those who go out in the morning and return in the evening to sing. See under *Ellipsis.*

Ps. lxviii. 18 (19).—"Thou hast led captivity (*i.e.*, captives) captive." Isa. xlix. 24. Jer. xxix. 14.

Ps. cx. 3.—" From the womb of the morning : thou hast (or shall be) the dew of thy youth " : *i.e.*, thy young men shall be born to thee as dew is born in the morning.

Prov. xxiii. 21.—" For the drunkard and the glutton shall come to poverty : and drowsiness (*i.e.*, the sluggard) shall clothe a man (*i.e.*, himself) with rags."

Isa. lvii. 13.—" Vanity (*i.e.*, vain men) shall take them." So Ps. cxliv. 4. Jas. iv. 14.

Jer. ii. 5.—They " have walked after vanity (*i.e.*, vain things, or idols), and are become vain." See under *Paronomasia.* So Deut. xxxii. 21. Jer. xiv. 22, and compare Acts xiv. 15.

Ezek. xliv. 6.—" And thou shalt say unto rebellion " : *i.e.*, to the rebellious People.

Amos viii. 3.—" And the songs of the temple shall be howlings in that day."

Here, through missing the *Metonymy* in the first part of this sentence, the A.V. has been obliged to alter the latter part, and put in the margin, " Heb., *shall howl*." But if we note that " songs " are put for singers, then we have perfect sense :—" And the singers of the temple shall howl in that day."

Luke i. 78.—" Whereby the dayspring from on high hath visited us ": *i.e.*, the morning star which precedes the day. So John the Baptist, as the " morning star," preceded Christ, Who is " the Sun of Righteousness." See Isa. ix. 2 (1) ; lx. 1, 2. Mal. iv. 2 (iii. 20), etc.

John xi. 40.—" Said I not unto thee, that, if thou wouldest believe, thou shouldest see the glory (*i.e.*, the glorious work) of God ? "

Rom. iii. 30.—" Seeing it is one God, which shall justify the circumcision by faith and uncircumcision through faith." Here, " circumcision " is put for those who are circumcised ; and uncircumcision for uncircumcised persons, as in xv. 8 and Gal. ii. 9, 12.

Rom. viii. 19.—" The earnest expectation of the creation (*i.e.*, created things or creatures) waiteth."

Rom. xi. 7.—" But the election (*i.e.*, elect persons) hath obtained it."

Eph. i. 21.—Here, the attributes are put for the beings who possess them :—" Far above all princes, and powerful beings, and mighty ones, and lords ": *i.e.*, all spiritual beings in heavenly places. See also under *Synonymia* and *Polysyndeton*.

Phil. i. 16.—" Supposing to add affliction to my bonds ": *i.e.*, my captivity. See also under *Prosapodosis*.

1 Pet. ii. 17.—" Love the brotherhood ": *i.e.*, the brethren. Compare v. 9.

2. Other adjuncts also are put for the subjects to which they pertain : as LIGHT for the sun, OIL for anointing, etc.

Gen. xxxiv. 29.—" And all their strength ": *i.e.*, wealth, as in A.V.

Ex. xiv. 4.—" And I will be honoured upon Pharaoh and upon all his power." Heb. is חֵילוֹ: *i.e.*, his power, which is put by *Metonymy* for his army, which was the expression of his power. See below 1 Sám. xiv. 48.

Lev. xiii. 4.—" Then the priest shall shut up the plague seven days ": *i.e.*, as in A.V., " him that hath the plague." See verses 13, 31, 50.

Deut. viii. 17.—" And thou say in thine heart, My power and the might of mine hand hath gotten me this strength " : *i.e.*, wealth, as in A.V.

1 Sam. xiv. 48.—" And he gathered a power " (Heb. חַיִל, *i.e.*, an host), as in A.V.   See Ex. xiv. 4.

1 Kings vii. 9.—" From the foundation unto the coping."   Heb. מְפָחוֹת (*tephachoth*), *spans*, put by *Metonymy* for the height: *i.e.*, from the foundation to the summit.

Job vi. 22.—" Give a reward (or perhaps " bribe ") for me of your strength " : *i.e.*, " of your substance," as in A.V. ; *i.e.*, that which your strength has procured.

Job xxxi. 26.—" If I beheld the light when it shined."
Here " the light " is put for the sun, as in A.V. (see margin).   So also xxxvii. 21 and Hab. iii. 4.

Prov. v. 10.—" Lest strangers be filled with thy strength " : *i.e.*, thy wealth, as in A.V.

Prov. xv. 6.—" In the house of the righteous is much strength " : *i.e.*, treasure, as in A.V.

Isa. i. 18.—" Though your sins be as scarlet."   It is a question whether here " sins " be not put for *sinners*.   Certainly persons are spoken of, and it is not easy to think of " sins," as such, becoming white !   It is the sinner himself who is thus made " whiter than snow." Ps. li. 7.

Isa. x. 14.—" And my hand hath found (or found means to reach) as a nest the strength of the peoples " : *i.e.*, their riches, gotten by their strength, as in A.V.

Isa. x. 27.—" Because of the oil " : *i.e.*, the anointing, as in A.V. But, from the reference to Gideon's exploits which we have in verse 26, the sense may be: " And yoke snapt at sight of oil " : *i.e.*, as Midian's yoke *was distended till it snapt* before the *oil* (or *resin*) *burning in Gideon's lamps*, so will Asshur's yoke, again, recoil (יָסוּר, verse 26) from thy neck, before the hot " blast " (see xxxvii. 7, and compare Ps. xviii. 15 (16) ; see, too, 2 Thess. ii. 8).

Isa. xxx. 6.—" They will carry their strength (*i.e.*, riches) upon the shoulders of young asses."   Here " strength " is put for the riches and presents which Israel's ambassadors were taking down to Egypt, to induce Egypt to help Israel against Assyria.   In verses 2 and 3, " strength " is used literally.   But in the next verse (7), it is put by *Metonymy* for " Egypt," in whose strength they trusted.

Isa. xxx. 7.—" Their strength is to sit still."

These words are usually taken as an exhortation to the Lord's people to sit still and do nothing. But the fact is just the opposite. They are spoken of Egypt, on whom Israel was relying for help against the Assyrians. See verses 1, 3: "The strength of Pharaoh" was what they trusted in. But Jehovah declared that that would be a vain trust, for

> " The Egyptians shall help in vain, and to no purpose :
> Therefore have I cried concerning this,
> Their strength is to sit still : "

i.e., Egypt, when Israel's ambassadors arrived there (verses 4-6), would sit still, and not help them at all. "Strength" is put by *Metonymy* for Egypt, in the strength of which Israel trusted.

Jer. xx. 5.—"Moreover I will deliver all the strength (*i.e.*, all the riches which are procured by strength) of this city . . . into the hand of their enemies."

Jer. xl. 7.—"And of the poverty of the Land": *i.e.*, the poor people of the country.

Ezek. xxxviii. 4.—" And all thy power ": *i.e.*, " all thine army," as in A.V.

Matt. viii. 3.—" His leprosy was cleansed ": *i.e.*, the leper. See verses 2, 3, and compare Mark i. 42.

Mark xiv. 54.—And Peter " warmed himself at the light " : *i.e.*, at the fire, as in A.V. See John xviii. 18.

Acts xiv. 15.—" We . . . preach unto you that ye should turn from these vanities (*i.e.*, idols) unto the living God."

Note that the term " Living God " is generally used when idols are mentioned or implied in the context (See 1 Thess. i. 9, 10, etc.).

Gal. iii. 13.—" Being made a curse for us " : *i.e.*, accursed, one under the curse of the Law.

Eph. v. 8.—" For ye were sometimes darkness (*i.e.*, dark and ignorant), but now are ye light (*i.e.*, enlightened ones) in the Lord."

ii. *The CONTENTS, for that which contains them : and what is placed, for the place where it is located.*

Gen. xxviii. 22.—" And this stone, which I have set for a pillar, shall be God's house ": *i.e.*, this place, of which the stone formed a part.

Josh. xv. 19.—" Give me also springs of water ": *i.e.*, land containing them as well as the south land.

1 Chron. ix. 24.—" In four winds were the porters ": *i.e.*, in the four quarters, as in A.V. But see Jer. xlix. 32 below.

Ps. cxxxv. 7.—" Bringing the wind out of His treasures ": *i.e.*, treasuries, as the A.V. here properly renders the figure.

Isa. xxiii. 3.—" The harvest of the river ": *i.e.*, the country through which the river flows.

Jer. xlix. 32.—" I will scatter into all winds ": *i.e.*, all quarters (Heb., every wind).

Ezek. v. 12.—" I will scatter a third part into all the winds ": *i.e.*, into all quarters.

Ezek. xxvi. 5.—" It shall be the spreading of nets ": *i.e.*, a place for the spreading of nets, as in A.V.

Hos. ix. 6.—" Thorns shall be in their tabernacles ": *i.e.*, in the places where their tents were formerly pitched.

Amos viii. 5.—" Saying, When will the new moon be gone, that we may sell corn ? and the sabbath that we may open wheat (*i.e.*, granaries)." Not " set forth wheat," as in the A.V.. The translators have stumbled over the verb (see margin) through not seeing the *Metonymy* of the noun.

Matt. ii. 11.—" And when they had opened their treasures ": *i.e.*, their treasuries or caskets containing them; good and precious presents. So Ps. cxxxv. 7. Matt. xii. 35, etc.

Matt. xii. 35.—" A good man out of the good treasure ": *i.e.*, treasury. The words " of the heart " go out of the Text with the Textual Critics and R.V.

Matt. xiii. 52.—" Which bringeth forth out of his treasure (*i.e.*, treasury) things new and old."

Matt. xxiv. 31.—" They shall gather his elect from the four winds ": *i.e.*, from the four quarters of the earth. The elect Nation of Israel is referred to.

Matt. xxv. 10.—" They that were ready went in with him to the marriage ": *i.e.*, to the place where the marriage was to be celebrated.

Matt. xxv. 21, 23.—" Enter thou into the joy of the lord ": *i.e.*, into the place where the lord manifested his joy.

Luke xxi. 4.—" All these have of their abundance cast in unto the offerings of God ": *i.e.*, into the chest or receptacle which received those offerings made to God.   Compare Matt. xv. 5 ; xxvii. 6.

Acts xvi. 13.—" Where we supposed was prayer ": *i.e.*, a place of prayer.   See verse 16.   The word rendered " supposed " means that they looked for and expected to find a place of prayer as lawfully and legally allowed.   Compare Luke iii. 23.

1 Cor. ix. 24.—" Know ye not that they which run in a race-course (or stadium) ": *i.e.*, a race which is run there.

Gal. ii. 12.—" For before that certain came from James ": *i.e.*, from Jerusalem, where James presided.   See Acts xii. 17 ; xxi. 18.

Heb. xii. 1.—" Let us run the race-course (or stadium) " : *i.e.*, the race which is run there.   So 1 Cor. ix. 24.

Rev. viii. 3.—" And another angel came, having golden frankincense ": *i.e.*, a censer.   See verse 5.

iii. *TIME is put for the things done in it, or existing in it.*

1. The word TIME or TIMES.

1 Chron. xii. 32 (33).—" And of the children of Issachar, which were men that had understanding of the times ": *i.e.*, who understood what was going on and being done, and needful to be done.

Est. i. 13.—" Then the king said to the wise men which knew the times ": *i.e.*, what was best to be done in connection with present and future events.

Job xi. 17.—" And above the noonday shall be thy time ": *i.e.*, thy prosperity shall be brighter and clearer than noon.

Ps. xxxi. 15 (16).—" My times (*i.e.*, my affairs, and all that I do or that can be done to me) are in thy hand."   All are known to Thee, according to Ps. cxxxix. 1.

2 Tim. iii. 1.—" This know also that in the last days difficult times will come ": *i.e.*, difficult things will be done : which things are described in verses 2-5.

2. AGE (αἰών, *aiōn*), a period of time, is put for what takes place in it.

Matt. xiii. 22.—" The cares of this world ": lit., " of this age " : *i.e.*, the things of this life.   So Mark iv. 19.

Luke xvi. 8.—" The children of this world (*i.e.*, of this age) ": those who are living for the present things of this world.

Rom. xii. 2.—" Be not conformed to this age " : *i.e.*, to the passing fashions, practices, and maxims of this world.

2 Cor. iv. 4.—" The god of this age " : *i.e.*, of the things done in, and of the people who live in and for, this world.

Eph. ii. 2.—" Wherein in time past ye walked according to the age of this world " : *i.e.*, according to the practices, and customs, and follies of the world,

Eph. vi. 12.—" The rulers of the darkness of this age " : *i.e.*, of all the dark things done in this world ; the word " age " pointing to a time coming when that rule will be done away.

See under *Anaphora* and *Antimereia*.

2 Tim. iv. 10.—" For Demas hath forsaken me, having loved this present age " : *i.e.*, the course and life of this world.

Heb. i. 2.—" By whom also he made (or constituted) the ages " : *i.e.*, the world, and all that pertains to it.   So xi. 3, where the verb is καταρτίζω (*katartizō*), *to adjust*, *prepare*, *or restore*.

3. YEARS is put for what happens in them.

Prov. v. 9.—" Lest thou give thine honour unto others, and thy years (*i.e.*, thy strength and labours and life) unto the cruel."

4. DAY, or DAYS, is put for what transpires in them, the context showing what it is.

Deut. iv. 32.—" For ask now of the days that are past " : *i.e.*, of what has been done in them, past history.

Job xviii. 20.—" They that come after him shall be astonied at his day " : *i.e.*, at his fate.

Job xxiv. 1.—" Why, seeing times are not hidden from the Almighty, do not they that know him see his days ? " *i.e.*, understand His dealings with them.

Ps. xxxvii. 13.—" The Lord shall laugh at him : for he seeth that his day (*i.e.*, his punishment) is coming."

Ps. cxxxvii. 7.—" Remember, O LORD, the children of Edom in the day (*i.e.*, calamities) of Jeruṣalem ; who said, Rase it, rase it, even to the foundations thereof."

Isa. xiii. 6.—" Howl ye ; for the day (*i.e.*, the judgment) of the LORD is at hand."

Ezek. xxi. 29.—" The wicked, whose day is come " : *i.e.*, whose calamity or judgment shall haye an end.   Compare verse 25.

Ezek. xxii. 4.—" Thou hast caused thy days (*i.e.*, thy judgments) to draw near."

Hos. i. 11 (ii. 2).—" Great shall be the day of Jezreel ": *i.e.*, great shall be the day of Israel's restoration, and recovery of " life from the dead."

Joel i. 15.—" Alas for the day ! for the day (*i.e.*, the judgment) of the LORD is at hand." So ii. 1, 31 (iii. 4). Amos v. 20. Zeph. i. 14, 15, 16, 18; ii. 2.

Obad. 12.—" Thou shouldest not have looked on the day (*i.e.*, the calamity) of thy brother."

Micah vii. 4.—" The day of thy watchmen ": *i.e.*, the calamity which the watchmen will see coming.

Luke xvii. 22, 26.—" The days of the Son of man ": *i.e.*, the day when Christ, as the second man, the Lord from heaven, shall assume universal dominion over the earth and execute the judgments necessary to secure it.

Luke xix. 42.—" If thou hadst known, even thou, at least in this thy day " : *i.e.*, in this time of grace, and of all the wonderful blessings which have been brought to thee. See verse 44.

1 Cor. iv. 3.—" It is a very small thing that I should be judged of you, or of man's day ":* *i.e.*, by human judgment. For now is the time when man is judging; but the Lord's day is coming, when He will judge.

Eph. v. 16.—" Redeeming the time, because the days are evil ": *i.e.*, because of the evil deeds that are done. See Dan. ii. 8 (margin) and lxx. (both Versions: lxx. and Theodotian).

5. HOUR is put for what is done at the time.

Mark xiv. 35.—" And prayed that, if it were possible, the hour might pass from him " : *i.e.*, the suffering, etc.

John xii. 27.—" Now is my soul troubled ; and what shall I say ? Father, save me from this hour (*i.e.*, this time of trial) : but for this cause came I unto this hour (*i.e.*, these sufferings)."

6. END is put for that which takes place at the end.

Prov. xxiii. 18.—" For surely there is an end ; and thine expectation shall not be cut off." Here, " end " is put for the *reward* which comes at the end. See margin, and xxiv. 14, 20.

---

* See *Four Prophetic Periods*, by the same author and publisher. Price one penny.

Jer. xxix. 11.—"To give you an expected end": *i.e.*, reward. See under *Hendiadys*.

Jas. v. 11.—"Ye have heard of the patience of Job, and have seen the end (*i.e.*, the reward) of the Lord."

1 Pet. i. 9.—"Receiving the end (*i.e.*, reward) of your faith."

7. FEAST-DAY is put for the sacrifices offered at the Festival.

Ex. xxiii. 18.—"Neither shall the fat of my feast remain until the morning." Here, feast is put by *Metonymy* for the sacrifice offered on the day. See margin.

Ps. cxviii. 27.—"Bind the feast (*i.e.*, sacrifice) with cords."

Isa. xxix. 1.—"Woe to Ariel, to Ariel, the city where David dwelt! add ye year to year; let them kill sacrifices." Here, the A.V. translates the *Metonymy* "sacrifices," for which in the Hebrew is put "feasts"; lit., "kill the feasts": *i.e.*, the sacrifices.

In Mal. ii. 3, where it is so very clear, the A.V. leaves the word "feasts" and does not render it, as in Isa. xxix. 1.

Mal. ii. 3.—"Spread dung upon your faces, even the dung of your solemn feasts": *i.e.*, of your sacrifices.

8. PASSOVER is put for the Lamb slain at the Passover.

Ex. xii. 21.—"Kill the Passover": *i.e.*, the lamb.

2 Chron. xxx. 17.—"Killing of the Passovers": *i.e.*, the lambs.

Matt. xxvi. 17.—"To eat the Passover": *i.e.*, the lamb.

Mark xiv. 12.—"Killed the Passover": *i.e.*, the lamb.

Mark xiv. 14.—"Where I shall eat the Passover": *i.e.*, the paschal lamb.

Luke xxii. 8.—"Prepare us the Passover (*i.e.*, the lamb), that we may eat."

Luke xxii. 11.—"Where I shall eat the Passover": *i.e.*, the lamb.

Luke xxii. 15.—"With desire I have desired to eat this Passover": *i.e.*, this lamb.

9. SUMMER is put for the fruits gathered in it.

Isa. xvi. 9.—"For the shouting for thy summer." Here, "summer" is put for the *fruits* of the summer, and is so rendered. So 2 Sam. xvi. 1. Jer. xl. 10, and Amos viii. 1. So the word "harvest" in the next clause is put for the corn and fruits of the harvest.

10. HARVEST is put for the fruits of the harvest.

Deut. xxiv. 19.—" When thou cuttest down thine harvest ": *i.e.*, thy corn, etc.

Isa. xvii. 5.—" And it shall be as when the harvestman gathereth the harvest (*i.e.*, the corn, as in A.V.), and reapeth the ears with his arm."

Joel iii. 13 (iv. 13).—" Put ye in the sickle, for the harvest (*i.e.*, the corn) is ripe."

11. FAST is used for the time of year at which the Fast fell.

Acts xxvii. 9.—" Because the fast was now already past " : *i.e.*, the time appointed for fasting, viz., the tenth day of the seventh month. Lev. xxiii. 27, 29 (about our Oct. 1, when sailing in those seas is specially dangerous).

iv. *The APPEARANCE of a thing, or an opinion about it, is put for the thing itself.*

1. In NOUNS.

Jer. xxviii. 5, 10.—Hananiah is probably called a prophet, because he was reputed to be one. See verse 1.

Ezek. xxi. 4 (9).—" Seeing then that I will cut off from the righteous and the wicked." Here it is probably *Metonymy*, *i.e.*, those who were reputed as righteous, but were not so. See verse 3 (8).

Matt. viii. 12.—" The children of the kingdom shall be cast out into outer darkness " : *i.e.*, those who were considered to be such as by outward privilege and inheritance were so.

Matt. ix. 13.—" I am not come to call the righteous (*i.e.*, righteous in their own eyes)."

Luke ii. 48.—" Behold, thy father and I have sought thee sorrowing " : *i.e.*, reputed father. See iii. 23, and compare John vi. 42.

1 Cor. i. 21.—" The foolishness of preaching." The preaching of the gospel is not foolishness, but man thinks it is, and hence it is here so-called.

1 Cor. i. 25.—" The foolishness of God " : *i.e.*, that which man thinks foolishness. Compare verse 18.

2 Cor. iv. 4.—" The god of this world." Not that the Devil is really the God, but that the world takes him for such. See above, and compare Matt. iv. 9. Luke iv. 6, 7.

Gal. i. 6.—" Another gospel " : it was not the Gospel, though it was so called.

Tit. i. 12.—" A prophet of their own." Epiminedes was not a prophet except in the opinion of the Cretans. See under *Gnome*.

Jas. ii. 14, 17, 20, 24, 26.—The " faith " here is not real faith, but that which passed for such ; being only the external profession.

2. VERBS.

Matt. xiv. 9.—" And the king was sorry " (or appeared to be sorry).

Mark vi. 48.—" And would have passed by them," at least, so they thought.

3. CONNECTED WORDS or sentences.

2 Sam. xxii. 8.—" The foundations of heaven moved and shook " : *i.e.*, the mountains on which the heavens appear to rest. So also

Job xxvi. 11.—" The pillars of heaven tremble."

Ps. lxxii. 9.—" His enemies shall lick the dust " : *i.e.*, shall be so humbled and prostrate as though they were licking the dust.

Isa. xiii. 5.—" From the end of heaven " : *i.e.*, from where the earth seems to touch the heaven. So Deut. iv. 32 ; xxx. 4. Neh. i. 9. Matt. xxiv. 31.

v. *The ACTION or AFFECTION relating to an object is put for the object itself.*

1. The SENSES are put for the object of them, or for the things which are perceived by the senses.

Lev. xiii. 55.—" And if the plague have not changed his eye " : *i.e.*, his colour.

Num. xi. 7.—" And the eye of it as the eye of bdellium." (See A.V. margin).

Here " eye " is put for *colour*, because it is the eye which sees and distinguishes colour.

Ps. cxii. 7.—" He will not be afraid of evil hearing " : *i.e.*, of what he may hear ; rumour, common talk, or, as A.V., evil tidings.

Prov. xxiii. 31.—" When it giveth his eye (*i.e.*, colour) in the cup."

Isa. xxviii. 9.—"Whom shall he make to understand the hearing ? " *i.e.*, as in A.V., the doctrine. (See A.V. margin).

Isa. xxviii. 19.—"And it shall be a vexation only to understand the hearing ": *i.e.*, the rumour.

Isa. liii. 1.—"Who hath believed our hearing ": *i.e.*, what they have heard: *i.e.*, our report, as in A.V. So John xii. 38. Rom. x. 16. Gal. iii. 2, 5.

Ezek. i. 4.—"As the eye (*i.e.*, colour) of amber." So viii. 2 ; x. 9.

Ezek. vii. 26.—Here, the *Metonymy* is boldly translated " rumour upon rumour." Lit., " hearing upon hearing."

Hab. iii. 2.—"O Lord, I have heard thy hearing ": *i.e.*, thy words, what thou hast said for me to hear. A.V.: " speech " (but see margin). See under *Polyptoton*.

Obad. 1.—"We have heard a hearing from the Lord ": *i.e.*, a rumour, as in A.V.

Matt. iv. 24.—"And his hearing went throughout all Syria ": *i.e.*, his fame ; what was heard ; as A.V. So xiv. 1. Mark i. 28.

Matt. xxiv. 6.—"And hearing (*i.e.*, rumours) of wars." So Mark xiii. 7.

John xii. 38.—See Isa. liii. 1.

2. Faith is put for the thing believed.

Acts vi. 7.—"And a great company of the Priests were obedient to the faith ": *i.e.*, to the doctrine believed.

Gal. i. 23.—"He . . . now preacheth the faith which once be destroyed ": *i.e.*, the doctrine which he had now believed.

Gal. iii. 23.—"Before faith came ": *i.e.*, before the true doctrine of the Gospel was revealed.

Gal. v. 5.—"We through the Spirit wait for the hope of righteousness by faith ": *i.e.*, life eternal, which is promised to the righteous by faith : " The just shall live (*i.e.*, have eternal life) by faith."

Eph. iv. 5. — "One Lord, one faith (*i.e.*, doctrine), one baptism."

1 Tim. iv. 1.—"Some shall depart from the faith ": *i.e.*, from the doctrine of Christ. See under *Tapeinosis* and *Synathrœsmus*.

Tit. i. 13.—"That they may be sound in the faith ": *i.e.*, the doctrine of the Gospel.

Jude 3.—"Earnestly contend for the faith": *i.e.*, the true doctrine of Christ.

Rev. ii. 13.—"And hast not denied my faith": *i e.*, the doctrine believed concerning me.

3. HOPE is put for God, or for the object on which it is set.

Ps. lxxi. 5.—"Thou art my hope": *i.e.*, the One in whom I hope.

Isa. xx. 5.—"They shall be afraid and ashamed of Ethiopia their expectation (*i.e.*, the help they expected from the Ethiopians) and of Egypt their glory (*i.e.*, the Egyptians in whom they gloried)." See verse 6.

Prov. xiii. 12.—"Hope deferred maketh the heart sick." Here, it is not hope that is deferred, but the object hoped for.

Jer. xiv. 8.—"O the hope of Israel, the saviour thereof in time of trouble": *i.e.*, the God in Whom Israel hopes.

Jer. xvii. 7.—"Whose hope the LORD is."

Jer. xvii. 13.—"The hope of Israel": the God in Whom Israel hoped.

Jer. l. 7.—"The hope of their fathers": *i.e.*, the God in Whom their fathers hoped.

Acts xxviii. 20.—"For the hope of Israel I am bound with this chain": *i.e.*, for the Messiah's sake, Whom Israel hoped for. See xxvi. 6-8.

Rom. viii. 24.—"Hope (*i.e.*, the object hoped for) that is seen is not hope." See *Epanadiplosis*.

I Tim. i. 1.—"The Lord Jesus Christ, our hope": *i.e.*, Who is the object of our hope.

Tit. ii. 13.—"Looking for that blessed hope": *i.e.*, that blessed object of hope, the coming of Christ.

4. LOVE is put for the person or object loved.

Jer. ii. 33.—"Why trimmest thou thy way to seek love?" *i.e.*, an object to love.

Jer. xii. 7.—"I have given the love of my soul into the hand of her enemies": *i.e.*, the dearly beloved, as in A.V. See margin.

Hos. ix. 10.—"Their abominations were according to their love": *i.e.*, to their idols, which were the objects of their love. Not "as they loved," as in the A.V.

5. Desire is put for the person or thing desired.

Gen. xxvii. 15.—" And Rebekah took desirable of her eldest son Esau": *i.e.,* the coveted raiment which perhaps Jacob had desired.

Isa. xxxii. 12.—" They shall lament for the teats, for the fields of desire": *i.e.,* which they desired. The A.V. has treated it as *Enallage,* and rendered it " pleasant fields." See margin.

Isa. xliv. 9.—" Their delectable things shall not profit": *i.e.,* their things which they have desired.

Jer. iii. 19.—" How shall I give thee a land of desire": *i.e.,* a land to be desired. See A.V. margin.

Lam. i. 7.—" Jerusalem remembered . . . all her things of desire": *i.e.,* all the things she had desired. The A.V. renders it by *Enallage,* " pleasant," and, in margin, *desirable.* So verse 10.

Lam. ii. 4.—" He stood with his right hand as an adversary, and slew all the desires of the eye": *i.e.,* all the objects that the eye desired.

Ezek. xxiv. 16.—" The desire of thine eyes ": *i.e.,* thy wife, who is the object of thy desire. See under *Periphrasis,* and compare verses 18, 21 and 25.

Dan. ix. 23.—" Thou art a man of desires": *i.e.,* a man greatly to be desired. Or, as A.V., " greatly beloved." See x. 11, 19.

Hos. ix. 16.—" Yet will I slay the desires of their womb ": *i.e.,* that which the womb had desired and brought forth.

Amos v. 11.—" Ye have planted vineyards of desire ": *i.e.,* vine-yards which ye had desired. See A.V. margin.

Hag. ii. 7.—" The desire of all nations shall come ": *i.e.,* Christ, who shall be the object desired by all nations.

1 John ii. 16.—" The lust of the eyes": *i.e.,* that which the eyes desire.

6. Fear is put for God who is feared, or for any object of fear.

Gen. xxxi. 42.—" The fear of Isaac ": *i.e.,* the God whom Isaac feared. So verse 53.

Ps. liii. 5 (6).—" There were they in great fear." Heb.: " There they feared a fear ": *i.e.,* there was something that they were greatly afraid of. See under *Polyptoton.*

Isa. viii. 13.—" Sanctify the Lord of hosts himself ; and let him be your fear ": *i.e.,* the God Whom ye shall fear.

Prov. i. 26.—" I will mock when your fear cometh ": *i.e.*, when that which you fear shall come.   So verse 27.

Prov. iii. 25.—" Be not afraid of sudden fear ": *i.e.*, of a sudden thing to be feared.   See under *Antimereia*.

2 Cor. v. 11.—" Knowing, then, the fear of the Lord ": *i.e.*, knowing, therefore, the Lord as one who is to be feared.

7. OTHER ACTIONS are put for the object connected with, or related to them ; which object is shown by the context.

Gen. xliii. 11.—" Take of the praise of the earth ": *i.e.*, the fruits which adorn and beautify the earth.   The Chaldee has " which is praised in the earth "; and the Heb. : זָמֹר (*zahmor*) means *to adorn*. See the first occurrence in Judges v. 3 (in *Piel*), where it is used in connection with *a song in praise of God*.   But זָמַר does not mean primarily *to praise*, but *to embellish* or *adorn* or *trim* the song.

Ex. xv. 2.—" The LORD is my strength and song ": *i.e.*, He whom I praise in my song.   So Ps. cxviii. 14, and compare verses 15, 16.

Here, " strength " is the *Metonymy* of effect : *i.e*, producing strength in me.   So that the whole verse means : " Jah maketh me strong, and is the subject of my song."

Deut. xxviii. 8.—" And in every sending forth of thy hand ": *i.e.*, all things which thy hand accomplishes.   So xii. 7.

1 Sam. i. 27.—" And the LORD hath given me my petition (*i.e.*, Samuel) which I asked Him for ": *i.e.*, the object of my prayer.   See under *Paronomasia*.

Job vi. 8.—" Oh that I might have my request; and that God would grant me my expectation ": *i.e.*, the object of my prayer and desire.   See A.V. margin.

Isa. lx. 1.—" Arise, shine ; for thy light (*i.e.*, He who is thy light) is come."

Luke xvi. 15.—" That which is highly esteemed among men is abomination in the sight of God ": *i.e.*, a thing abominated by God.

Acts i. 4.—" They should not depart from Jerusalem, but wait for the promise of the Father ": *i.e.*, that which the Father had promised.

Gal. iii. 2, 5.—" The hearing of faith ": *i.e.*, the report which faith believed.

2 Thess. i. 11.—" We pray . . . that our God would count you worthy of this calling ": *i.e.*, of that for which He has called you : *viz.*, to deliver you out of the tribulation; so that He may be glorified in His saints before He comes forth " in flaming fire," etc. (verses 8 and 9). For that coming forth in judgment will not take place until He shall have come. (ἔλθῃ, *elthee*), thus to be glorified: ἔλθῃ is the 2nd Aor. Subj. Compare its use in Matt. xxi. 40. Luke xvii. 10. Mark viii. 38. John iv. 25; xvi. 13. Acts xxiii. 35. Rom. xi. 27. 1 Cor. xvi. 3. 2 Cor. iii. 16, etc.

Heb. xi. 13.—"These all died in faith, not having received the promises": *i.e.*, the things which had been promised. The promises were what they had received, but not the things promised.

vi. *The SIGN is put for the thing signified.*

1. NOUNS.

Gen. xlix. 10.—"The sceptre shall not depart from Judah . . . until Shiloh come." Here the sceptre (*i.e.*, the Rod of tribal supremacy) is put for Him who is entitled to hold it. So Isa xiv. 5. Zech. x. 11, etc.

Ex. xviii. 10.—"Blessed be the LORD, who hath delivered you out of the hand of the Egyptians, and out of the hand of Pharaoh, who hath delivered the people out of the hand of the Egyptians." Here, the " hand " is put for power, of which it is the sign; and it is repeated three times in order to emphasize the greatness of the power and the wonderful deliverance from it.

Num. xviii. 8.—"By reason of the anointing." Here, the anointing is put for the Priesthood, of which it was the sign.

2 Sam. xii. 10.—"The sword shall never depart from thy house": *i.e.*, manifested hostility.

1 Kings xix. 10.—"Thrown down thy altars": *i.e.*, given up thy worship (of which the altars were the sign and symbol).

Job v. 21.—"Thou shalt be hid from the scourge (*i.e.*, power) of the tongue."

Ps. xxiii. 4.—"Thy rod and thy staff they comfort me": *i.e.*, Thy care and Thy defence, of which these were the signs. The Shepherd carried two implements: *viz.*, the " rod," to help the sheep, and the " club," to destroy the sheep's enemies.

Ps. lxxxix. 4 (5).—"Thy seed will I establish for ever, and build up thy throne to all generations": *i.e.*, will raise up those (esp. One) who shall sit upon it.

Ps. lxxxix. 39 (40).—" Thou hast profound his crown by casting it to the ground": *i.e.,* thou hast removed him from his kingly position.

Ps. xliv. 6 (7).—" I will not trust in my bow, neither shall my sword save me": *i.e.,* military science, of which the bow and sword were the signs.

Isa. ii. 4.—Here, swords and plowshares, etc., are used for war and peace, of which they were the signs and symbols. See also under *Polysyndeton* and *Syllogismus.*

Jer. xlvii. 5.—" Baldness is come upon Gaza": *i.e.,* grief, from the practice of shaving the head in grief.

Lam. v. 9.—" We gat our bread with our lives (*i.e.,* with peril of our lives, as in A.V.), because of the sword (*i.e.,* the fightings) of the wilderness." So Ezek. xxi. 3, 4 (8, 9).

Ezek. vii. 15.—" The sword (*i.e.,* war, or destruction) is without."

Ezek. xxi. 26.—" Remove the diadem, and take off the crown." Here the diadem and crown are put for the symbols of royalty of him who wears them.

Matt. xxiii. 2.—" The Scribes and Pharisees sit in Moses' seat."

Here " sit " is put for public teaching (Matt. xxvi. 55. Luke iv. 20. John viii. 2. Acts xxii. 3), or for judgment (Ex. xviii. 13. Judg. v. 10. Matt. xxvii. 19. Ps. xxix. 10 ; cx. 1).

" Moses" is put for the Law and precepts and authority of Moses. " Seat" is put for right, authority or rule.

Rom. xiii. 4.—" He weareth not the sword in vain": *i.e.,* he does not wear merely the sign, but he has the power which it signifies.

Luke xi. 52.—" Ye have taken away the key of knowledge": *i.e.,* the means or power of entering into, or the right of attaining knowledge.

Acts xv. 10.—" Now therefore why tempt ye God, to put a yoke (*i.e ,* a burden) on the neck of the disciples."

Rev. iii. 7.—" The key of David." The key is put for governmental authority, of which it is the sign.

2. VERBS.

Gen. xxi. 6.—" And Sarah said, God hath made me to laugh (*i.e.,* to rejoice), so that all that hear will laugh (*i.e.,* rejoice) with me."

Gen. xxxi. 49.—"The LORD protect us when we are hidden (*i.e.*, absent) from one another." The *Metonymy* is used so as to imply that though hidden from one another, they were not hidden from God.

Gen. xli. 40.—"Thou (Joseph) shalt be over my house, and according unto thy word shall all my people kiss ": *i.e.*, be ruled or in subjection. See Ps. ii. 12 below, and A.V. margin.

Deut. x. 8.—"To stand (*i.e.*, to minister) before the LORD."

Deut. xxii. 1.—"Thou shalt not see thy brother's ox or his sheep go astray, and hide thyself from them ": *i.e.*, go away and leave them.

1 Kings xix. 18.—"Yet I have left me seven thousand in Israel, all the knees which have not bowed unto Baal, and every mouth which hath not kissed him": *i.e.*, have not obeyed or worshipped him.

Job v. 22.—"At destruction and famine thou shalt laugh " : *i.e.*, thou shalt be secure against them.

Job viii. 21.—"Till he fill thy mouth with laughing (*i.e.*, rejoicing), and thy lips with shouting for joy." See A.V. margin.

Job xxxi. 27.—"And my heart hath been secretly enticed, or my mouth hath kissed my hand": *i.e.*, I have made the outward sign of worship or homage.

Ps. ii. 12.—"Kiss the Son": *i.e.*, submit to the Son, be ruled by Him. See Gen. xli. 40 above ; and see under *Ellipsis* and *Epiphonema*.

Ps. iii. 5 (6).—"I laid me down and slept ": *i.e.*, was secure.

Ps. iv. 8 (9).—"I will both lay me down in peace, and sleep (*i.e.*, be perfectly secure): for thou, LORD, only makest me dwell in safety."

Ps. x. 5.—"As for all his enemies he bloweth upon them ": *i.e.*, he despiseth them. A.V.: puffeth at them.

Ps. xii. 5 (6).—"For the oppression of the poor, for the sighing of the needy, now will I arise, saith Jehovah; I will set him (*i.e.*, each one) in safety : he bloweth upon (*i.e.*, he despiseth) it (*i.e.*, the oppression)." The poor and needy being set in safety by Jehovah, despise the oppression of the enemy. Such have the sure words of Jehovah, and can despise the vain words of man.

Ps. xxvii. 5.—"In the time of trouble he shall hide (*i.e.*, protect) me in his pavilion : in the secret of his tabernacle shall he hide (*i.e.*, protect) me."

Ps. xxxi. 20 (21).—"Thou shalt hide them (*i.e.*, protect them) in the secret of thy presence from the pride of man."

Ps. lxiv. 2 (3).—"Hide (*i.e.*, protect) me from the secret counsel of the wicked."

Ps. cxxvi. 2.—"Then was our mouth filled with laughter (*i.e.*, with rejoicing), and our tongue with singing."

Ezek. viii. 11.—"And there stood (*i.e.*, ministered) before them seventy men," etc.

Zech. iii. 1.—"And he showed me Joshua the high priest standing (*i.e.*, ministering) before the angel of the LORD."

Matt. v. 47.—"If ye embrace (*i.e.*, salute or welcome) your brethren only, what do ye more than others?" Compare Heb. xi. 13.

Luke vi. 21.—"For ye shall laugh": *i.e.*, rejoice; and verse 25: "Ye that laugh (*i.e.*, rejoice) now."

Heb. xi. 13.—"And embraced them": *i.e.*, welcomed, believed, and hoped for them: *i.e.*, the promises.

3. Connected WORDS and PHRASES.

To bind and loose put for exercising of authority. Matt. xvi. 19; xviii. 18.

To open and shut is put for power of administration. Job xii. 14: Isa. xxii. 22. Rev. iii. 7.

To be stiff-necked is put for pride and obstinacy. Ps. lxxv. 5 (6). Here it is a question whether the letter *Aleph* (א) was not wrongly inserted in the text. If so, it alters the whole sense, and the verse should read: "Lift not up your horn on high, nor speak arrogantly of the Rock:" where the Rock is put by *Metonymy* of adjunct for God. See also 2 Chron. xxx. 8.

Cleanness of teeth put for famine. Amos iv. 6.

To lift up the eyes is put for implore or pray. Ps. cxxi. 1; cxxiii. 1. Ezek. xviii. 6, 15.

To lift up the head is put for lifting up the soul, or taking courage, or rejoicing. Judges viii. 28. Ps. lxxxiii. 2. Luke xxi. 28.

To lift up the face is put for boldness and courage. Deut. xxviii. 50 (margin). Num. vi. 26. Ecc. viii. 1. Dan. viii. 23.

To strengthen the face is put for boldness or impudence. Prov. vii. 13.

To cover the face or *head* is put for self condemnation, or condemnation. 2 Sam. xv. 30; xix. 4. Job ix. 24. Est. vii. 8. Jer. xiv. 4.

The face to wax pale is put for being afraid. Isa. xxix. 22.

To have a whore's forehead is put for impudence. Jer. iii. 3.

To bow the knee is put for compulsory submission. Isa. xlv. 23. Rom. xiv. 11. Phil. ii. 10.

To give the hand is put for voluntary submission. 1 Chron. xxix. 24. 2 Chron. xxx. 8. Also put for fellowship or confederacy. Lam. v. 6. Jer. l. 15. Ezek. xvii. 18. Gal. ii. 9.

To place the hand on is put for association. Lev. vi. 2.

To lift up the hand, or *hands* is put for swearing an oath, or making a promise. Gen. xiv. 22. Ex. vi. 8. Ps. cvi. 26. Isa. iii. 7 (marg.). Put also for praying. Ps. xxviii. 2; lxviii. 31 (32). 1 Tim. ii. 8.

To strike hands is put for making a promise, or bargain. Job. xvii. 3.

To put hands on the head is put for grief. Jer. ii. 37. 2 Sam. xiii. 19.

To put the hand or *hands on the mouth* is put for silence, or for having no answer. Judges xviii. 19. Job xxi. 5; xxix. 9; xl. 4. Micah vii. 16.

To pour water on the hands is put for serving. 2 Kings iii. 11.

To fill the hand or *hands* is put for consecrating anyone to a sacred office, because the person so appointed received the sign or symbol of the office in his hands. Ex. xxviii. 41; xxix. 9, 33, 35; xxxii. 29 (marg.). Lev. viii. 33; xvi. 32. Num. iii. 3. Judges xvii. 5, 12, etc.

To cover the feet is put for performing a duty of nature, because when stooping the garments fell over the feet. This is a beautiful example of *Euphemy* (*q.v.*). Judges iii. 24. 1 Sam. xxiv. 3.

Eating and drinking is put for living or being alive. Ex. xxiv. 11. Similarly *looking* is used in Gen. xvi. 13, because Hagar had seen God and yet lived. Compare Gen. xxxii. 30 and Judges xiii. 22.

The breaking of bonds (of various kinds) is put for liberating from servitude. Ps. ii. 3.

The clothing in sackcloth put for sorrowing. Job xvi. 15. Ps. xxxv. 13; lxix. 11 (12); Lam. ii. 10. Joel i. 13. Amos viii. 10, etc.

Making bald is put for grieving. Micah i. 16.

Licking the dust is put for defeat and submission. Isa. xlix. 23. Ps. lxxii. 9.

Smiting the thigh is put for grief. Jer. xxxi. 19. So also is

Sitting on the ground. Lam. ii. 10.

Not discerning the right hand from the left is put for extreme youth. Jonah iv. 11.

(*a*). The whole utterance, which may consist of admonition, instruction, etc., sometimes consists of sign or symbol, and the signs are thus put for the things signified.

2 Kings iv. 29.—The instructions given by Elisha to Gehazi.

Jer. ix. 17, 18.—Jehovah to Jeremiah.

Jer. x. 18. And compare verses 9, 19, 20.

See also Jer. xlvi. 19, Ezek. xxxix. 9, 10. Isa. ii. 4. Amos v. 16. Matt. xxiv. 20. Luke xxii. 36, 38. 2 Cor. vii. 3.

vii. *The NAME of a person for the person himself; or the name of a thing for the thing itself.*

(1) The person, when that person is Divine. Deut. xxviii. 58. Ps. xx. 1 (2) ; cxv. 1. Prov. xviii. 10. Isa. xxx. 27. Jer. x. 25. Micah v. 4 (3). John i. 12 ; iii. 18 ; xvii. 6 ; xx. 31. Acts iii. 16 ; iv. 12 ; v. 41 ; x. 43. 1 John ii. 12, etc.

(2) When the person is human. Acts i. 15. Rev. iii. 4 ; xi. 13 (margin), etc.

(3) The name of a man for his posterity. Deut. xxv. 17. Ex. v. 2. Num. xxiii. 21 ; xxiv. 5, 17. Deut. xxxiii. 28. 1 Kings xviii. 17, 18. Ps. xiv. 7. Amos vii. 9, 16. Gen. ix. 27. Mal. i. 2, 3. Rom. ix. 13.

(4) The name of a thing for the thing itself. Eph. i. 21 : Dignities. Phil. ii. 9.

METALEPSIS; or, DOUBLE METONYMY.

Two Metonymies, one contained in the other, but only one expressed.

Met¹-a-lep¹sis, from μετά (*mĕta*), *behind*, and λείπω (*leipō*), *to leave, a leaving behind.*

The Figure is so called, because something more is deficient than in *Metonymy*, which has to be supplied entirely by the thought, rather than by the association or relation of ideas, as is the case in *Metonymy*.

This something more that is deficient consists of another *Metonymy*, which the mind has to supply. Hence *Metalepsis* is a double or compound *Metonymy*, or a *Metonymy* in two stages, only one of which is expressed.

Thus, for example, when we say that a man "drank his house," we do not mean that he drank the building of bricks and mortar with its contents, but we first use the word "house," and put it by *Metonymy* for the *money* it fetched when sold, and then, by a second *Metonymy*, the "money" is put for the *drink* it purchased, which was what the man actually drank.

So Virgil (Buc. Ecl. i. 70) speaks of Melibœus returning to hit home "after some ears of corn," where the "ears of corn" are first put (by *Metonymy* of Subject) for the *harvest-time*, and then the harvest-time is put mentally (by *Metonymy* of Adjunct) for a years So that what Melibœus means is that he will return *after some years*.

The Latins called the figure TRANSUMPTIO: *i.e., a taking across from one to another*. They sometimes called it TRANSLATIO, *a transferring across;* but this latter name is best reserved as representing *Metaphor* rather than *Metalepsis*.

We have one or two examples:—

Gen. xix. 8.—"Therefore came they under the shadow of my roof."

Here, "roof" is first put (by *Synecdoche*) for the whole house, of which it was a part: and then the house is put [for the protection it afforded.

Ecc. xii. 5.—The Heb. of this is literally "and the caper-berry shall be powerless."

Almost every part of the caper-berry plant was used to make condiments; but the berries were specially provocative of appetite,

ϙ 1

though not restricted to sexual desire. Hence it was called אֲבִיּוֹנָה (*aveeyōnah*), *desire* or *appetite*, from אָבָה (*avah*), *to desire.*

Here, then, we have first the plant or berry put for the condiments made from it, and then the condiments put for the desire they created. The meaning is that not only shall appetite or desire fail, but that condiments and stimulants shall be powerless to produce their usual effect.

The R.V. makes the sentence absurd by translating the figure literally : " The caper-berry shall fail." The A.V., with its elegant idiomatic version, much better conveys the essential meaning of the passage : " And desire shall fail."

Isa. xxxiii. 15.—" That stoppeth his ears from hearing of bloods." Here, " bloods " is first put for *blood-shedding*, and then *blood-shedding* is put for the murderers who shed it. See Prov. i. 11.

In the New Testament, the expression " the blood of Christ " is the figure *Metalepsis;* because first the " blood " is put (by *Synecdoche*) for blood-shedding : *i.e.*, the death of Christ, as distinct from His life ; and then His death is put for the perfect satisfaction made by it, for all the merits of the atonement effected by it : *i.e.*, it means not merely the actual blood corpuscles, neither does it mean His death as an act, but the merits of the atonement effected by it and associated with it.

Hos. xiv. 2 (3).—" So will we render the calves of our lips." Here, " calves " are put by *Metonymy* (of Subject) for sacrifices, and then, by another *Metonymy*, these sacrifices are put for the confession and praises rendered. See under *Metonymy*, pages 574 and 575.

Rom. iii. 25.—" Through faith in his blood " : *i.e.*, through faith in the merits of the atonement accomplished by it.

Rom. v. 9. — " Being now justified by his blood " : *i.e.*, his atonement.

Eph. i. 7.—" Redemption through his blood " : *i.e.*, through the merits of His atoning death.

Eph. ii. 13.—" But now in Christ Jesus ye who sometimes were far off are made nigh by the blood of Christ " : *i.e.*, by His death, not by His life : yet not by His death alone, but by the atonement made in His obedient act in dying for His people.

So Col. i. 14, 20. Heb. ix. 12, 14 ; x. 19 ; xii. 24 ; xiii. 12. 1 Pet. i. 2, 19.

1 John i. 7.—" The blood of Jesus Christ his Son cleanseth us from all sin." Here, when it is a question of "walking in the light," the saved sinner is reminded of that which put him there and which alone can keep him there. Whereas, in chapter ii. 1 where it is a question of *sin* (" If any man sin "), the sinful child is reminded, not of the blood, but of the Father, with whom Christ, the righteous One, is the Advocate, to show that relationship has not been broken.

Rev. i. 5.—" Unto him that loved us, and washed us from our sins in his own blood ": *i.e.*, loosed us from our sins by His atonement, which was accomplished by His death (reading λύσαντι (*lusanti*), *freed*, instead of λούσαντι (*lousanti*), *washed*, with all the Critical Texts and R.V.).

Here note that ἐν (*en*), whose first meaning is *in*, must not be so taken here, or in all the parallel passages ; we must take it as meaning *by* or *through*, a meaning which it frequently has: *e.g.*, Matt. ix. 34 : " He casteth out devils through (ἐν) the prince of the devils." Matt. v. 34, 35 : " Swear not at all, neither by (ἐν) heaven . . . nor by (ἐν) the earth." Gal. iii. 11 : " No man is justified by (ἐν) the law." 2 Tim. ii. 10 : " Salvation which is in (ἐν) Christ Jesus ": *i.e.*, by or through Him ; in virtue of His atoning death. In this very book (Rev. v. 9), it is rendered " by thy blood."

So, here, in Rev. i. 5, it must not be rendered " in his blood," which is not only contrary to Old Testament type (where nothing was ever washed *in* blood ! which would have defiled and made unclean instead of cleansing!) but is contrary to the letter as well as the spirit of the Word. Rev. i. 5 means washed us or loosed us from our sins by, or in virtue of, through the merits of, His atonement. So Rev. vii. 14.

So that such expressions are to be avoided, as " Washed *in* the blood of the Lamb " ; and the sentiment contained in the verse :—

> " There is a fountain filled with blood,
> Drawn from Immanuel's veins :
> And sinners plunged beneath that flood,
> Lose all their guilty stains."

All such expressions are contrary to physiology and common sense.

We lose nothing of the facts, but gain immensely as to their meaning, when we understand that, by *Metalepsis*, " blood " is put for *death*, and " death " for the atonement made by it and all its infinite merits.

In like manner "the Cross" is put first for the crucifixion as an act, or for Him who was crucified thereon : and then this is put for the resulting merits of His atonements procured thereby.

1 Cor. i. 17, 18.—" The preaching of the cross." Paul did not preach the cross, nor did he speak merely of the crucifixion (ii. 2), but of all the blessed results, not only of that death, but of the resurrection also.

Gal. vi. 14.—" God forbid that I should glory, save in the cross of our Lord Jesus Christ ": *i.e.*, not the wooden instrument of death, nor the act of crucifixion; but he gloried in all that this meant for him, all the precious merits of Christ's atonement and the blessings resulting from it.

Col. i. 20.—" And, having made peace through the blood of his cross." Here, again, " cross " is put for His death, and His death is put for all its meritorious results.

It is by forcing the word " cross " into a literal meaning in such passages as the above that the Church of Rome has appeared to have a Scriptural sanction for its reverence for and adoration of " the cross."

The reader may easily see where the word " cross " is used literally and historically and where it is used figuratively. If the latter be substituted for the former, not only shall we introduce much error, but we shall lose much of precious Scriptural truth and teaching.

SYNECDOCHÉ; or, TRANSFER.

The exchange of one idea for another associated idea.

Syn-ek'-do-kee. Greek, συνεκδοχή, from σύν (*sun*), *together with*, and ἐκδοχή, *a receiving from*. A figure by which one word receives something from another which is *internally* associated with it by the connection of two ideas: as when a part of a thing is put by a kind of Metonymy for the whole of it, or the whole for a part. The difference between *Metonymy* and *Synecdoché* lies in this; that in *Metonymy*, the exchange is made between *two related nouns;* while in *Synecdoché*, the exchange is made between *two associated ideas.*

Synecdoché of the Genus is where the genus is put for a species.

Synecdoché of the Species is where a species is put for the genus.

Synecdoché of the Whole is where the whole is put for a part: and

Synecdoché of the Part is where a part is put for the whole.

These four divisions may be further described and set forth as follows:—

I. SYNECDOCHÉ OF THE GENUS.

   i. All for the greater part.

   ii. Universal affirmative does not affirm particularly.

   iii. Universal negative does not deny particularly.

   iv. Universals for particulars.

   v. Wider meanings for narrower.

II. SYNECDOCHÉ OF THE SPECIES.

   i. Many for all.

   ii. Narrower meaning for wider.

   iii. Proper names for common.

   iv. A species put for whole genus.

   v. Verbs: special for general.

   vi. One example or specimen for all kinds.

III. Synecdoché of the WHOLE.

    i.   All or every for the whole.

    ii. Collective for the particular.

    iii. The whole for one of its parts.

    iv. A place for a part of it.

    v. Time for a part of it.

IV. Synecdoché of the PART.

    i.   An integral part of man (individually) for the whole man, etc.

    ii. An integral part of men (collectively) for the whole.

    iii. A part of a thing for the whole thing.

    iv. A part of a time for the whole time.

I. Synecdoché of the GENUS:

Where the genus is put for the species; or universals for particulars.

i. *All is put for the greater part.*

Ex. ix. 6.—" And all the cattle of Egypt died ": *i.e.*, all kinds of cattle, not all the individual animals of all species. The Heb. has no article.

The kinds of cattle are particularised in verse 3. This must be so, for no sane writer could stultify himself by meaning " all " in any other sense, when he goes on to speak of other beasts immediately after, in verse 10.

Ex. ix. 25.—" And the hail smote throughout all the land of Egypt," etc.: *i.e.*, all parts of it, or the greater part.

Ex. xxxii. 3.—" And all (*i.e.*, the greater part of) the people break off the golden earrings which were in their ears ": *i.e.*, that part of the people who wore them.

Verse 26: " And all the sons of Levi gathered themselves together unto him ": *i.e.*, all who had not joined in the idolatry, for see Deut. xxxiii. 9. There were some Levites who were not spared.

Deut. xxviii. 64.—" And the Lord shall scatter thee among all peoples ": *i.e.*, among all kinds of people, *i.e.*, all nations.

2 Sam. xvi. 22.—"In the sight of all Israel": *lit.*, for all Israel's eyes: *i.e.*, for anybody to see that chose.

2 Sam. xvii. 24.—"And Absalom ... and all the men of Israel": *i.e.*, the greater part of Israel.

1 Chron. xiv. 17.—"And the fame of David went out into all lands": *i.e.*, into lands in all parts of the world.

Ps. xxii. 7 (8).—"All they that see me laugh me to scorn": *i.e.*, the great majority; for there were many that believed.

Ps. cxviii. 10.—"All nations compassed me about": *i.e.*, a great many.

Isa. ii. 2.—"And all nations shall flow unto it": *i.e.*, many from all nations. See verse 3, and Micah iv. 1.

Jer. xxvi. 9.—"And all the people were gathered against Jeremiah in the house of the LORD": *i.e.*, a great many or most of the people. Not everyone; as is clear from verse 26, where "the princes and all the people" spake "unto the priests and to the prophets." So verse 18.

Hos. vii. 4.—"They are all adulterers": *i.e.*, most of them, or as a whole.

Hag. ii. 7.—"I will shake all (*i.e.*, people in all) nations, and the desire of all (*i.e.*, many in all nations) shall come."

Matt. iii. 5.—"Then went out to him Jerusalem and all (*i.e.*, people from all parts of) Judæa, and all the region round about Jordan."

Matt. viii. 34.—"And, behold, the whole (*i.e.*, nearly the whole) city came out to meet Jesus."

Mark i. 33.—"And all the city was gathered together at the door." Here "all" is put for the greater part.

Mark ix. 23.—"All things are possible to him that believeth": *i.e.*, all things comprehended in the promise. Not all things indiscriminately. *Faith always has respect to what is said or promised.*

John i. 16.—"And of his fulness have all we received": *i.e.*, "all" the "we" who have received grace. The "all" is thus defined and limited.

John x. 8.—"All that ever came before me are thieves and robbers": *i.e.*, all who did not enter in by the door, but climbed up some other way. See verse 1.

Other examples may be found in Matt. x. 22; xvi. 19; xviii. 18; xxi. 26; xxiv. 9. Luke xv. 1. 1 Cor. vi. 2; ix. 19, 22; xiii. 7. Phil. ii. 21; iv. 13. Col. i. 28. Heb. vi. 16.

ii. *When "all" and "every," as universal affirmations, extend not to all the individuals, but to all kinds; or all that are specified or implied.*

Gen. xxiv. 10.—"All the goods of his master were in his hand": *i.e.*, all that his master had given him. Compare verse 53.

2 Kings viii. 9.—"So Hazael went to meet him, and took a present in his hand (*Metonymy* for "with him") and every good thing in Damascus": *i.e.*, of every kind of, or all manner of good things. Hazael did not strip Damascus.

Joel ii. 28 (iii. 1).—"And it shall come to pass afterward that I will pour out my spirit upon all flesh": *i.e.*, upon all kinds of people out of all nations.

Here the figure is in the word ; "flesh," and the word "all" is therefore to be taken literally. The "all flesh" is used in distinction from "Israel": which before was the only People to enjoy the special gifts and calling of God.

Zeph. ii. 14.—"And flocks shall lie down in the midst of her, all the beasts of the nations": *i.e.*, all manner of beasts.

Matt. iv. 23.—"And healing every sickness": *i.e.*, as in A.V. and R.V., "all manner of disease."

Luke xi. 42.—"Ye tithe mint, and rue, and every herb, and pass over judgment and the love of God": *i.e.*, herb of every (tithable) kind, or, as in A.V., "all manner of herbs."

John i. 9.—We must take this with the R.V. margin. "This was the true light, which lighteth every man, coming into the world": *i.e.*, lighteth every man, now, *without distinction*, not without exception. Hitherto only Israel had the true light—the Shechinah or presence of Jehovah. Henceforth this distinction was to be done away: and every man (*i.e.*, all to whom the Son should reveal the Father, Matt. xi. 25, 26) would be thus enlightened. Every man who is enlightened, is enlightened by Christ.

John xii. 32.—"I, if I be lifted up from the earth, will draw all unto me": *i.e.*, all *without distinction*; clearly, not all without exception, as this would be contrary both to fact and experience. It must, therefore, be the figure *Synecdoché*; by which the genus is put for the species; and "all" means people of all sorts and conditions and nations and tongues, as distinguished from the one nation, Israel, which heretofore had been partaker of the Divine favour.

Acts x. 12.—"Wherein were all the quadrupeds of the earth": *i e.*, every kind, both clean and unclean; as it goes on to describe the species, for which the genus is thus put: *viz.*, "wild beasts and creeping things and fowls of the air." The A.V. correctly renders it "all manner of four-footed beasts," etc.

1 Tim. ii. 4.—"Who will have all men to be saved, and to come unto the knowledge of the truth."

Here the "all" is the same as in verse 1, and must mean all kinds of men, the genus being put for the species.

In verse 2, some of them are named: and this is in contradistinction to the former dispensation; when salvation was confined to the Jews (John iv. 22); but now it is extended to people out of all tongues, and nations, and peoples.

Heb. ii. 9.—"That he by the grace of God should taste death for every man": *i e.*, all manner of men, *without distinction*.

It cannot mean without exception, or else every man must be saved, and if it be taken as literally as that, then all women are excluded, for this word all is masculine. See below under *Synecdoché* of the Whole for part (Div. III. sec. iv.).

Heb. xiii. 4.—"Marriage is honourable in all": *i e.*, all kinds of degrees which the law of God allows, or all cases in which persons are entitled to marry. Otherwise it cannot be honourable.

2 Pet. iii. 9.—"Not willing that any should perish." Here, the word "willing" is βούλομαι (*boulomai*), *to be willing* or *disposed*, and not θέλω (*thelō*), as in 1 Tim. i. 4, which means *to purpose, determine*, or *design*. Hence, it means "is not disposed that any kind of person should perish, but that all *without distinction* should come to repentance."

"Whosoever" is to be taken in the same way; as meaning some out of all: the genus being put for the species: *i.e.*, *all* of a properly and carefully defined class or species. That is to say, "Whosoever" fulfils certain conditions: *i.e.*, "whosoever" believeth, "whosoever" willeth, etc. It means *all of these* without exception, all these as distinct from all the others who do not come within the specially described characters, or correspond with the specified conditions.

It does not mean all of all kinds indiscriminately without exception, but all without distinction.

The English word "whosoever" is not always the representative of the same Greek word.

It is most often used to translate the relative pronoun ὅς (*hos*), *he who*, and is sometimes followed by ἄν (*an*), or ἐάν (*ean*), *perchance*.

When it is not this word, then it represents one of these following :—

πᾶς (*pas*), *all*, *every* (sometimes with ἄν or ἐάν, *perchance*). See Matt. v. 22, 28. Luke vi. 47 ; xii. 10, 48 ; xiv. 11, 33 ; xvi. 18 (twice) ; xx. 18 (first). John iii. 15, 16 ; iv. 13 ; viii. 34 ; xi. 26 ; xii. 46 ; xvi. 2 ; xix. 12. Acts x. 43. Rom. ii. 1 ; ix. 33 ; x. 11. 1 John ii. 23 ; iii. 4, 6 (twice), 9, 10, 15 ; v. 1, 18. 2 John 9. Rev. xxii. 15.

πᾶς ὅς ἄν (*pas hos an*), *everyone who perchance*. Luke xii. 8. Acts ii. 21. Rom. x. 13.

ὅστις (*hostis*), *anyone who*. Matt. v. 39, 41 ; vii. 24 ; x. 32, 33 ; xii. 50 ; xiii. 12 (twice) ; xviii. 4 ; xxiii. 12. Mark viii. 34. Luke xiv. 27. Gal. v. 4, 10. Jas. ii. 10.

ὅσοι ἄν (*hosoi an*), *as many as perchance*. Luke ix. 6. Mark vi. 11.

ὅσπερ (*hosper*), *who indeed*. Mark xv. 6.

εἴ τις (*ei tis*), *if any*. Rev. xiv. 11 ; xx. 15.

ἐάν or ἄν τις (*ean* or *an tis*), *if perchance any*. John xiii. 20 ; xx. 23.

iii. *A universal negative does not deny particularly.*

Ex. xx. 10.—"The seventh day is the sabbath of the LORD thy God : in it thou shalt not do any work" : *i.e.*, work that is specifically forbidden : *viz.*, "servile" or mechanical work (Lev. xxiii. 7, 8. Num. xxviii. 18).

1 Sam. xx. 26.—"Nevertheless Saul spake not anything that day" : *i.e.*, concerning David or about his absence. He did speak, of course, but not specifically about the matter referred to.

Jer. viii. 6.—"No man repented him of his wickedness" : *i.e.*, scarcely any.

Matt. v. 34.—"Swear not at all" : *i.e.*, not lightly or thoughtlessly : the particulars are given in verses 35 and 36.

Matt. x. 26.—"For there is nothing covered, that shall not be revealed" : *i.e.*, no heavenly doctrine.

John iii. 32.—"And no man receiveth his testimony" : *i.e.*, no natural man receiveth it of himself; but only those to whom it is given of the Father. See Matt. xi. 25, 26 ; xvi. 17.

John xv. 5.—" Without me ye can do nothing " : *i.e.*, nothing that is good and true and right, or according to God ; but a great deal that is contrary to Him.

John xviii. 20.—" In secret have I said nothing " : *i.e.*, nothing seditious or criminal. In secret He had said many things, but nothing which they particularly meant.

Acts xxvii. 33.—" This day is the fourteenth day that ye have tarried and continued fasting, having taken nothing " : *i.e.*, no proper meal, or having declined to take anything beyond proper necessaries. It is μηδέν, not οὐδέν.

2 Thess. iii. 11.—" For we hear that there are some which walk among you disorderly, working not at all, but are busybodies." The negative does not deny working universally, but working of a particular kind : *i.e.*, not working officially, yet working officiously. This is a beautiful example of *Paregmenon (q.v.)* : " not *ergazomenous*, but *periergazomenous* " : *i.e.*, as we might put it, not *busy with their bodies*, but *busybodies*.

1 Tim. vi. 3, 4.—" If any man teacheth otherwise . . . he is proud, knowing nothing " : *i.e.*, nothing about what he professes to teach, " the doctrine which is according to godliness " : *i.e* , the Mystery, the truth which specially concerns the Church of God. See iii. 16 : " the great " Mystery of godliness.

iv. *Words denoting universality do not always affirm it of particulars.*

Mark xvi. 20.—" They went forth, and preached everywhere " : *i.e.*, everywhere where they went ; in every kind of place ; or everywhere where they were able to go.

Luke xviii. 1.—" And he spake a parable unto them to this end, that men ought always to pray, and not to faint " : *i.e.*, on all occasions ; or at every opportunity, and not to grow weary.

Luke xxiv. 54.—" And were continually in the temple " : *i.e.*, at every opportunity, at the proper and stated times for assembling there.

Acts xxviii. 22.—" As concerning this sect, we know that it is everywhere spoken against " : *i.e.*, everywhere where it is known and spoken about it is spoken against : as it is to this present day.

1 Cor. iv. 17.—" As I teach everywhere in every church " : *i.e.*, as I teach in every place where there is an assembly, or wherever I go.

v. *Words of a wider meaning are used in a narrower sense. The universal for the particular, but of the same kind.*

1. FLESH is put for *man* or *mankind.*

When the word "all" is used in connection with "flesh" (*i.e*, "all flesh"), it is literal, and the word "flesh" is the figure (*Synecdochê*). The literality of the word "all" is thus emphasized.

Gen. vi. 12.—"All flesh had corrupted his way upon the earth": *i.e.,* all mankind.

Ps. cxlv. 21.—"And let all flesh bless his holy name": *i.e.,* all men—all mankind (Heb.: "all flesh shall bless." See verse 10).

Isa. xl. 5.—"The glory of the LORD shall be revealed, and all flesh (*i.e.,* all people) shall see it together."

Isa. lxvi. 23.—"From one sabbath to another shall all flesh (*i.e.,* all men) come to worship before me, saith the LORD."

Luke iii. 6.—"And all flesh (*i.e.,* all people) shall see the salvation of God."

Rom. iii. 20.—"Therefore by the deeds of the law, shall no flesh be justified in his sight."

2. CREATURE is put for *man.*

Mark xvi. 15.—"Preach the gospel to every creature": *i.e.,* to all people. A precept fulfilled in

Col. i. 23.—"The Gospel . . . which was preached to every creature which is under heaven": *i.e.,* to every person without distinction.

1 Pet. ii. 13.—"Submit yourselves to every ordinance of man."
The Greek is "every human creation" or creature: ἀνθρωπίνη κτίσις (*anthrōpinee ktisis*): *i.e.,* institution.

3. DOMICILE is put for *prison.*

Acts xii. 7.—"And a light shone in the building (οἴκημα, *oikeema*)": *i.e.,* the prison, a particular kind of building defined by the context. It is called a building, for it was no longer a prison after the angel had entered it.

4. HOUSE is put for *temple.*

Luke xi. 51.—"From the blood of Abel . . . which perished between the altar and the House": *i.e.,* the temple building, as translated in A.V.

Acts vii. 47.—" But Solomon built him an house " : *i.e.*, a Temple, a kind of house.

5. MAN is put for *husband*.

Matt. xix. 10.—" If the case of the man (*i.e.*, a husband) be so with his wife," etc.

6. THE TONGUE is put for *the man*.

As man is fallen, it generally means *an evil-speaker !*

Ps. cxl. 11 (12).—" Let not a man of tongue (*i.e.*, an evil-speaker) be established in the earth."

Ps. ci. 5.—"Whoso privily slandereth his neighbour."
The Heb. is "the tongue (*i.e.*, the slanderer), in the secret places of his friend, him shall I cut off."

Ecc. x. 11.—"Surely the serpent will bite without enchantment, and a master of the tongue is no better " : *i.e.*, an adept in evil-speaking (which is a particular kind of use of the tongue). See A.V. margin.

7. CHANGE is put for *death*.

Job xiv. 14.—"All the days of my appointed time will I wait, till my change come " : *i.e.*, till I die : dying being one of many changes experienced by man.

Prov. xxxi. 8.—"Open thy mouth for the dumb in the cause of all the sons of change." Here, the A.V. renders it in the margin "sons of destruction," and in the Text : "such as are appointed to destruction."

8. QUADRUPEDS (τετράποδα, *tetrapoda*) is used for *tame* or *domestic animals*.

Acts x. 12.—"Wherein were all manner (*Synecdoche* of Genus) of four-footed beasts ": *i.e.*, tame or domestic animals which are classed off, as distinct from " wild beasts " which are also " four-footed."

9. STATUTE is put for *allowance*, or *necessary food.*

Gen. xlvii. 22.—"For the priests had a statute of (or from) Pharaoh, and did eat their statute which Pharaoh gave them : wherefore they sold not their lands ": *i.e.*, they ate, not the statute, but the food assigned to them by one of the statutes which Pharaoh gave them.

Ezek. xvi. 27.—"Behold, therefore, I have stretched out my hand over thee and have diminished thy statute ": *i.e.*, the food apportioned to thee.   A.V. : " ordinary food."

Prov. xxx. 8.—" Feed me with food of my statute": *i.e.,* my statutory food. See A.V. margin.

Job xxiii. 12.—" I have esteemed the words of his mouth more than my appointed portion": *i.e.,* my ordinary allowance. The R.V. has in the margin, literally, *my own law.* But the meaning is that the Lord's word was valued by him more than his daily bread. The A.V. catches the spirit of the words and the meaning of the figure beautifully: "my necessary food."

10. THE BOWELS are put for *the heart.*

Ps. xl. 8 (9).—"Thy law is in the midst of my bowels": *i.e.,* " in my heart," as in A.V. (but see the margin). Compare verse 10.

11. THE LIVING are put for *men.*

Gen. iii. 20.—" And Adam called his wife's name Eve ; because she was the mother of all living": *i.e.,* of all living beings, or of all people who should live hereafter.

Ps. cxliii. 2.—" In thy sight will no living (*i.e.,* person) be justified." The A.V. inserts the word " man": *e.g.,* " no man living."

12. A COMMON NAME is sometimes put for a *proper* one.

A name common to many is used of one *par excellence*: as, when God is called " *El,*" " *The Strong* " or " *the Mighty One,*" it is because, though others are strong, He is stronger than all. Gen. xiv. 22; xxi. 33. Ps. v. 4 (5); xxii. 1 (2), etc.

So Christ is called "the *Lord.*" Matt. xxi. 3. John xi. 3, 12, etc. " *The Teacher.*" Matt. xxii. 24. John xi. 28. " *The Angel.*" Gen. xlviii. 16. Ex. xxiii. 20, or " *the Angel of the Lord.*" Ex. iii. 2. Judges vi. 11. So Christ is " *the seed of the woman.*" Gen. iii. 15. All others are seed of some woman, but Christ is *the* seed.

Moses is called " *the Prophet.*" Hos. xii. 13 (14). Deut. xxxiv. 10, 11, 12.

The Euphrates is called " *the river,*" because of its magnitude. Gen. xxxi. 21. Josh. xxiv. 2, where the A.V. has " flood." Ps. lxxii. 8; lxxx. 11 (12). Micah vii. 12.

So the Emperor Nero is called *lord.* Acts xxv. 26.

13. The PLURAL NUMBER is put for the *singular.*

This is not *Enallage*; because this singular must be and is one of the same kind. As when Sarah said: " Sarah should have given children suck ? " Here, though the plural is used, it is used of her only son : as she goes on to say : " for I have born him a son in his old age."   Gen. xxi. 7.

Gen. xlvi. 7.—" His daughters " : *i.e.*, his one daughter " Dinah." See verses 15, 17.

Verse 23 : " The sons of Dan, Hushim " : *i.e.*, his one son.*

1 Chron. i. 41.—" The sons of Anah ; Dishon."*

1 Chron. ii. 7.—" The sons of Carmi ; Achar."*

Verse 8 : " The sons of Etham ; Azariah."*

Verse 31 : " The sons of Appaim ; Ishi. And the sons of Ishi ; Sheshan. And the children of Sheshan ; Ahlai." This Ahlai was a daughter (see verse 34) !

1 Chron. vii. 12.—" Hushim, the sons of Aher."

2 Chron. xxiv. 25.—" For the blood of the sons of Jehoiada the priest " : *i.e.*, Zechariah his son. See verses 20, 21.*

Mark i. 2. John vi. 45. Acts vii. 42.—The word " *prophets* " is put for the singular, because in only one prophet is the prophecy " *written* " (Mal. iii. 1). But the case is different with Matt. ii. 23. " That it might be fulfilled which was spoken by the prophets, He shall be called a Nazarene." A difficulty is created by supposing that Nazarene is from *netzer*, a branch (a word used of Christ only in Isaiah).

But apart from the most improbable, if not impossible etymology, it does not say it was *written*. It says it was *spoken* ; and who will deny that many prophets may have spoken and prophesied of this Branch ? Some prophecies were written and not spoken ; some were spoken and not written ; while others were both spoken and written. The same explanation may be given of Matt. xxvii. 9 and Acts xiii. 40 : where the preposition " in " means " by."

II. SYNECDOCHE OF THE SPECIES.

This is when the Species is put for the Genus (the opposite of the above), or when particulars are put for universals.

i. *Many is sometimes put for all.*

Isa. liii. 12.—" And he bare the sin of many." Yes, " many," but for *all His own people* according to verse 6, Heb. ix. 28, and Matt. i. 21.

---

* In these passages there is a reading called *Sevir*, and in some MSS., which has the *singular* number.

Dan. xii. 2.—" And many of them that sleep in the dust of the earth shall awake " : *i.e.*, *all* to whom the prophecy refers. See John v. 28. But "every man in his own order"; or rank and time and according to the Dispensation.

Rom. viii. 29.—" That he might be the first-born among many brethren" : *i.e.*, many relatively to others ; but *all* with respect to his own brethren.

John vi. 50.—" This is the bread which cometh down from heaven, that anyone may eat thereof, and not die " : *i.e.*, everyone who does eat of it.

ii. *Words of a limited and special sense are used with a wider and more universal meaning.*

1. MAN is used for *both sexes*, men and women.

See Ps. i. 1 ; xxxii. 1 ; cxii. 1. Jer. xvii. 5, 7, and so frequently as not to need further citation, or to be given in full.

2. One RELATIONSHIP is put for, and includes others.

Ps. xxii. 4 (5).—" Our fathers trusted in thee " : *i.e.*, all who had lived before them and trusted in God are included.

Ps. cvi. 6.—" We have sinned with our fathers " : *i.e.*, with all who have gone before.

2 Sam. ix. 7.—" And David said unto him, Fear not, for I will surely show thee kindness for Jonathan thy father's sake, and will restore thee all the land of Saul thy father" : *i.e.*, thy grandfather.

2 Sam. xix. 28.—Mephibosheth said to David, " All of my father's house were but dead men before my lord the king": he means his father's father.

Dan. v. 2, 11.—In verse 18 Daniel, speaking to Belshazzar, calls Nebuchadnezzar (by *Synecdoché*) his father, whereas he was his grandfather. See the margin of verse 2, 11. Daniel made no mistake, but he makes use of a common and well known figure of speech.

1 Kings xv. 10, 13.—Asa's grandmother is called his " mother." See margin of verse 10.

Judges ix. 1.—" Brethren " is put for other relations. So also

Gen. xiii. 8 ; xxxi. 23 ; 1 Chron. xii. 29, where it is rendered " kindred." See margin.

Jerome classifies four kinds of " brethren ":—" brethren " by

    1. Nature.   Gen. xxvii. 1.
    2. Nation.   Deut. xv. 3.
    3. Kindred.   Gen. xiii. 8.
    4. Affection.   Ps. cxxxiii. 1, etc., etc.

Ex. i. 7.—"Sons" are put for posterity. So also Jer. xxxi. 29.

Gen. xxix. 5.—Laban the " son " of Nahor is put for his grandson.

Gen. xxiv. 48.—Rebecca called Abraham's " brother's daughter," when she was the daughter of Bethuel and granddaughter of Nahor, not of Abraham.

2 Sam. xix. 24.—Mephibosheth is called " the son of Saul." " Son " is here put (by *Synecdoché*) for his grandson.

Josh. vii. 24.—Achan is called " the son of Zerah," which is put for great grandson. See verse 1. So

Matt. i. 1.—Christ is called " the Son of David " in a like way. The word "son" being used in a wide signification. So Matt. ix. 27; xii. 23; xv. 22; xx. 30, 31; xxi. 9, 15; xxii. 42. Mark xii. 35. Luke xviii. 38, 39. Compare Rom. i. 3. 2 Tim. ii. 8. Rev. xxii. 16.

Hence David is called his father (Luke i. 32).

Zacchæus is in the same way called a " son of Abraham " (Luke xix. 9). Compare Luke xiii. 16.

All the Jews called Abraham their " father " (Luke i. 73. John viii. 39, see verse 56. Acts vii. 2. Rom. iv. 1).

The Samaritans called Jacob their " father " (John iv. 12).

iii. *A proper name is put for a common; an individual is put for many; and the particular is put for the universal.*

Isa. lxiii. 16.—" Thou art our father, though Abraham be ignorant of us, and Israel acknowledge us not."

Here, the individuals are put for the great majority of the People of Israel. For the patriarchs named were long since dead.

1 Cor. iii. 6.—" Apollos " is put for any minister.

1 Cor. vii. 16.—" Wife " and " man " are put for all wives and all husbands.

iv. *A species of a thing is put for the whole genus.*

    1. Bow, Spear, etc., are put for all kinds of *arms*.

Ps. xliv. 6 (7).—" I will not trust in my bow, neither shall my sword save me ": *i.e.*, I will not trust in any weapons or in any human means

R 1

of defence, but in God alone, see verse 7 (8). This may be also *Metonymy* of the adjunct. So Zech. x. 4.

Ps. xlvi. 9 (10).—" He maketh wars to cease unto the end of the earth : he breaketh the bow, and cutteth the spear in sunder ; he burneth the chariot in the fire ": *i.e.*, if all wars are to cease, all kinds of implements of war must be included and represented in the few species named.

2. The Ass is put for all kinds of *animals* not sacrificed.

Ex. xiii. 13.—" And every firstling of an ass thou shalt redeem with a lamb." The firstborn of all unclean beasts, which might not be sacrificed, had to be redeemed (see Num. xviii. 15), but only one species is named here, and in xxxiv. 20.

3. Gold is put for *gifts*.

Ps. lxxii. 15.—" To him shall be given of the gold of Sheba." Here, the principal gift is put for all other kinds of gifts. See Isa. lx. 5-7.

4. Stones are put for whatever is hurtful to the *soil*.

Job v. 23.—" For thou shalt be in league with the stones of the field : and the beasts of the field shall be at peace with thee."

5. Lion is put for all kinds of *wild beasts*.

Isa. xv. 9.—" I will bring more upon Dimon, lions upon him that escapeth of Moab."

6. Commandment is put for all *commandments* and *doctrines*.

2 Pet. ii. 21.—" It had been better for them not to have known the way of righteousness, than, after they had known it, to turn from the holy commandment delivered unto them." So chap. iii. 2.

7. Honey is put for whatever is *sweet* and *delicious*.

Ex. iii. 8, 17.—" A land flowing with milk and honey ": *i.e.*, filled with all satisfying and delightful things, sweet and good : *i.e.*, a region irrigated and fruitful, abounding with pasture and fruits of all kinds. See Ex. xiii. 5 ; xxxiii. 3. Lev. xx. 24. Num. xiii. 27 ; xiv. 8 ; xvi. 13. Deut. vi. 3 ; xi. 9 ; xxvi. 9, 15 ; xxvii. 3 ; xxxi. 20. Josh. v. 6. Jer. xi. 5 ; xxxii. 22. Ezek. xx. 6, 15.

Sometimes " oil " is added, or " figs," etc. Deut. viii. 8 ; xxxii. 13. 2 Kings xviii. 32. Ezek. xvi. 13, 19.

Sometimes "butter." Job. xx. 17.

8. BREAD is put for all kinds of *food*, including fish.

It is often translated "food." Gen. iii. 19 ; xviii. 5 ; xxxix. 6 ; xliii. 25, 31 ; xlix. 20. Lev. iii. 11 (food) ; xxi. 6,* 8.* Num. xxviii. 2. Judg. xiii. 16. 1 Sam. xiv. 24 (food) ; xx. 27 (meat) ; xxviii. 20. Job. vi. 7 (meat) ; xx. 14 (meat) ; Ps. xli. 9 (10) ; cii. 4 (5) ; cxxxvi. 25 ; cxlvi. 7. Ecc. ix. 11 ; x. 19 (feast). Isa. iii. 1 ; lviii. 7. Jer. lii. 33 ; Dan. v. 1 (feast). Hos. ix. 4. Mal. i. 7. Matt. vi. 11 ; xv. 2, 26. Luke xiv. 1 : etc., etc.

Hence to " break bread " or to " eat bread " means to *partake of a meal*. It is the common Hebrew idiom to this day. Just as among the Arabs, " salt " (one particular and important kind of food) is put universally for the whole meal and for all kinds of food, and " to take salt " with anyone means to partake of his hospitality. So " to break bread " means not to partake of the Lord's supper, but to partake of an ordinary meal with others. By *Synecdoche* " bread " (one kind of food) is put for all kinds of food (or meat), and the *breaking* of it is merely equivalent to carving or cutting it up. See under *Idiom*.

When " water " is added (*i.e.*, " bread and water "), it is meant to include all kinds of solid and liquid food necessary to eat and to drink. See Isa. iii. 1 ; xxxiii. 16, etc.

9. PEACE is used for *plenty, and happiness ;* and of all kinds of *earthly good and blessing.*

Gen. xliii. 23.—" Peace be to you " : *i.e.*, peace and all blessings.

Num. vi. 26.—" The LORD . . . give thee peace."

Ps. cxix. 165.—" Great peace (*i.e.*, every blessing) have they which love thy law."

Rom. ii. 10.—" But glory, honour, and peace (*i.e.*, every earthly blessing) to every man that worketh good," etc. See this passage under the figure of *Ellipsis*. So also Jas. iii. 18.

PEACE is also used of all *heavenly and spiritual blessing*.

Isa. lvii. 19.—" I create the fruit of the lips ; peace, peace, to him that is far off," etc. See under *Epizeuxis*.

John xiv. 27.—" Peace I leave with you, my peace I give unto you " : *i.e.*, not peace alone, which is only one species of heavenly gifts, but all kinds of blessings. So John xx. 19, 21, 26.

Rom. i. 7.—" Grace to you, and peace."

---

* " Bread of thy God " : *i.e.*, food which God gives.

Rom. v. 1.—"Therefore having been justified by faith (*ἐκ πίστεως, ek pisteōs, on faith-principle,* as opposed to *law-principle*) we have peace with God through our Lord Jesus Christ"; and with it every heavenly blessing, as verse 2 goes on to show: "By whom we have obtained access also by faith into this grace wherein we stand." So also Rom. xiv. 17, etc., etc.

10. PREY (טֶרֶף, that which is taken in hunting: *i.e.*, one kind of food) is put for *any and all kinds of food*.

Ps. cxi. 5.—"He hath given prey (so margin: *i.e.*, meat) unto them that fear him": *i.e.*, those who fear God will not have to hunt in vain for their food! He will give it to them. See Ps. cxlvii. 9.

Prov. xxxi. 15.—"She riseth also while it is yet night, and giveth prey to her household": *i.e.*, finds and prepares their food.

Mal. iii. 10.—"Bring ye all the tithes into the storehouse, that there may be prey in mine house."

11. BLOOD (Heb. often BLOODS) is put for *murder* or *cruelty*; or death generally.

Deut. xix. 12.—"The avenger of blood": *i.e.*, murder.

Ps. ix. 12 (13).—"When He maketh inquisition for blood": *i.e.* for the shedding of blood.

So Hos. i. 4; iv. 2. Matt. xxiii. 35; xxvii. 24.

12. BLOOD is also put for *guilt*.

Lev. xx. 9.—"His blood shall be upon him": *i.e.*, his guilt or punishment, etc., etc.

Deut. xix. 10.—"And so blood (*i.e.*, guilt) be not upon him."

Deut. xxi. 8.—"And the blood (*i.e.*, the guilt) shall be forgiven them." So in the next verse the A.V. actually supplies the words: "So shalt thou put away the *guilt of* innocent blood from among you."

2 Kings xxiv. 4.—"He filled Jerusalem with innocent blood." "Blood" (*i.e.*, murder and the guilt of it) is here put as the gravest sin, for all the other kinds of sins which Jehoiakim committed in Jerusalem.

Ps. li. 14 (16).—"Deliver me from bloods, O God": *i.e.*, (as in A.V.), "from blood-guiltiness."

Isa. i. 15.—"Your hands are full of blood": *i.e.*, of murders and blood-guiltiness.

13. CLOTHING is put for *all necessary things.*

Isa. iii. 6.—" When a man shall take hold of his brother of the house of his father, saying, Thou hast clothing, be thou our ruler ": *i.e.,* thou art well dressed and therefore hast other good things beside.

14. WIDOWS AND FATHERLESS are put for *all kinds of afflicted.*

Ex. xxii. 21.—" Ye shall not afflict any widow, or fatherless child." Surely it does not follow that they might afflict all others. No ! one kind or class is put for all similar kinds of helpless people.

Deut. x. 18.—" He doth execute the judgment of the fatherless and widow."

Deut. xxvii. 19.—" Cursed be he that perverteth the judgment of the stranger, fatherless, and widow." So also Ps. cxlvi. 9. Prov. xxiii. 10. Isa. i. 17, 23. Jer. vii. 6; xxii. 3. Ezek. xxii. 7.

Jas. i. 27.—" Pure religion and undefiled before God and the Father is this, To visit the fatherless and widows in their affliction," etc. : *i.e.,* all in distress or trouble of any kind. This refers to " religion " which in itself is nothing. All who are " in Christ " will surely manifest such evidence as this and much more. But for those not " in Christ," all the visiting of all the widows and fatherless in the world will never accomplish the stupendous miracle of Divine grace ; for we are saved by grace and not by works.

v. *Verbs having a special meaning are used in a more general sense.*

1. " TO ASCEND " is used for *to come,* or *to enter into the thoughts, or the mind.*

2 Kings xii. 4.—" All the money that ascendeth upon the heart of a man ": *i.e.,* as in A.V., " that cometh into any man's heart " (*i e.,* thoughts, his thoughts or mind).

Jer. vii. 31.—" To burn their sons and daughters in the fire ; which I commanded them not, neither did it ascend upon my heart ": *i.e.,* come into my mind.

Ezek. xxxviii. 10.—" At the same time shall things ascend upon thine heart ": *i.e.,* as in A.V., come into thy mind.

1 Cor. ii. 9.—" Neither have ascended upon the heart of man ": *i.e.,* as in A.V., " Neither have entered into the heart of man." Here the idiom is Hebrew, though the language is Greek.

2. To MAKE (with time) is used for *to continue* or *abide*.

Acts xv. 33.—"And, having made a time, they were let go ": *i.e.*, as in A.V., " After they had tarried there a space."

Acts xviii. 23.—"And having made or done some time, he departed ": *i.e.*, as in A.V., " After he had spent some time there."

Acts xx. 3.—" And having done three months there ": *i.e.*, as in A.V., " And there abode three months."

2 Cor. xi. 25.—" A night and a day have I done or made in the deep ": *i.e.*, I have passed or been in the deep.

Jas. iv. 13.—" Go to now, ye that say, To-day or to-morrow we shall go into such a city, and shall do a year there ": *i.e.*, as in A.V., continue there a year.

So Latin, *agere vitam* (to live), and *agere poenitentiam* (to repent) which Rome, translating literally in all her versions, renders " *do penance*."

3. To GO OUT and COME IN is used of *official actions* or of *life in general*.

Num. xxvii. 16, 17.—". . . set a man over the congregation, Which may go out before them, and which may go in before them, and which may lead them out, and which may bring them in ; that the congregation of the LORD be not as sheep which have no shepherd."

So verse 21. 2 Chron. i. 10. Ps. cxxi. 8. Isa. xxxvii. 28. John x. 9. Acts i. 21.

4. To FIND is used for *to receive, to obtain*.

Gen. vi. 8.—" Noah found grace in the eyes of the LORD ": *i.e.*, received grace from the LORD.

Gen. xxvi. 12.—" Then Isaac sowed in that land, and found (*i.e.*, received, as A.V., see margin) in the same year an hundredfold : and the LORD blessed him."

Luke i. 30.—" Fear not, Mary : for thou hast found favour with (*i.e.*, received grace from) God."

Rom. iv. 1.—" What shall we say then that Abraham our father, as pertaining to the flesh, hath found ? " *i.e.*, received or obtained.

Heb. ix. 12.—" By his own blood he entered in once into the holy place, having found (*i.e.*, *obtained*, as in A.V.) eternal redemption for us."

5. To FIND is also used of *to have,* or *to be present with.*

1 Sam. xiii. 15.—" And Saul numbered the people that were found (*i.e.,* were present) with him, about six hundred men."

Luke ix. 36.—" And when the voice was past Jesus was found (*i.e.,* was present) alone."

Rom. vii. 18.—" For I know that in me (that is, in my flesh) there does not dwell any good thing : for to will is present with me , but *how* to perform that which is good I find not (*i.e ,* is not present with me)."

Phil. ii. 8.—" And being found (*i.e.,* present) in fashion as a man he humbled himself."

Phil. iii. 9.—"And be found (*i.e.,* be present) in him."

Heb. xi. 5.—" By faith Enoch was translated that he should not see death ; and was not found (*i.e.,* present), because God had translated him."

6. To CALL UPON THE LORD is used of *Divine worship.*

A special act is put for the general act of worship.

Gen. iv. 26.—" Then began men to call upon (*i.e.,* to worship) the name of the LORD " : *i.e.,* Jehovah. See under *Metonymy.*

Isa. xliii. 22.—" But thou hast not called upon me (*i.e.,* worshipped me), O Jacob."

So the Greek προσκυνέω (*proskuneō*), *to do homage by kissing the hand,* the general word for reverence is put for the special act of worship.

John iv. 23, 24.—" The hour is coming and now is, when the true worshippers will worship the Father in spirit and in truth : for the Father seeketh such to worship him. God is a spirit ; and they that worship him must worship him in spirit and in truth." See also under *Hendiadys* below.

7. To PASS THE NIGHT is used for *abiding.*

Ps. xlix. 12.—" Man being in honour, abideth not : he is like the beasts that perish."

Isa. i. 21.—" Righteousness lodged in it ; but now murderers."

8. To PLACE is put for *to make.*

Rom. iv. 17.—" I have placed thee (*i.e.,* made thee) a father of many nations."

Heb. i. 2.—" Whom he hath placed (*i.e.,* appointed) heir of all things."

9. To MEET (κατανπάω, *katantaō*) is used of arriving at so as *to touch*.

Acts xvi. 1.—" Then came he to (*i.e.*, and he arrived at) Derbe and Lystra," etc.

Eph. iv. 13.—" Till we shall all have come into (*i.e.*, arrived at) the unity of the faith," etc.

Phil. iii. 11.—" If by any means I might attain unto (*i.e.*, arrive at) the out-rising, that one from among the dead."* Paul is saying this from his point of view as a Jew, and not that of a saint. He is speaking of what he formerly counted as his gains (verse 7), and which he now " counted loss for the knowledge of Christ . . . that I may be found in him . . . that I may know him . . . if by any means I might arrive at the out-rising from among the dead."

This was not spoken as a Christian, as though he might attain something that other Christians could not attain ; but it was spoken as a Jew, that he might attain (in Christ) a resurrection *from among* the dead, which other Jews could not hope for. The Jews looked for a resurrection, but it was only τῶν νεκρῶν (*tōn nekrōn*), *of dead persons*, while Paul was willing to give up this and all his other supposed " gains " for the blessed hope of an out-rising, ἐκ τῶν νεκρων (*ek tōn nekrōn*), *from among the dead*.

1 Thess. iv. 17.—" Then we which are alive and remain shall be caught away together with them in clouds for a meeting of the Lord, into the air, and thus, always with the Lord shall we be."

Here, the meeting involves actual arrival at the meeting-place of the Lord, and actual presence there with him.

10. To DRINK is used of *partaking of food and drink of all kinds*.

1 Cor. iii. 2.—" I gave you milk to drink and not meat ": *i.e.*, as in A.V., I have fed you. See under *Zeugma*.

11. To ANSWER, or OPEN THE MOUTH is put for *speaking*.

Job iii. 1.—" After this Job opened his mouth, and cursed his day ": *i.e.*, Job said, etc.

Ps. cxix. 172.—" My tongue shall respond to thy word ": *i.e.*, speak of it, as in A.V.

And so, very frequently, this Hebrew idiom is used in the New Testament.

---

* καταντήσω εἰς τὴν ἐξανάστασιν τὴν ἐκ νεκρῶν. LTTr.WH. and R.V. read τὴν ἐκ for τῶν, as rendered above.

Matt. xi. 25.—"At that time Jesus answered (*i.e.*, spake), and said: I thank Thee Father, . . . Even so, Father, for so it seemed good in thy sight." Thus our attention is called to what He said; for the answer was to the circumstances of "that time." What were they? John had questioned (verses 2-6). The people had spurned both John and Himself (16-19). His mighty works had been fruitless (20-24). And, then, "at that time," when all *seemed* to end in failure, the Lord Jesus found *rest* in submission and resignation to the Father's will, and, then, turning to all His servants—"weary and heavy laden" with their burden and toil—He graciously invites them to find *rest* where He had found it, saying: "Come unto me . . . and I will give you rest. Take my yoke upon you, and learn of me ; . . and ye shall find rest."

Mark xi. 14.—" And Jesus answered and said unto it " (the fig-tree, which had not spoken), *i.e.*, spake and said.

So Luke vii. 40, etc.

12. To Sit is used of a *permanent condition* in which one is *placed*.

Isa. xlii. 7.—" Them that sit in darkness," quoted in Matt. iv. 16.

Acts xviii 11.—" And he sat there a year and six months teaching the word of God among them ": *i.e.*, he continued there, but the verb "sat" is used in order to be in harmony with his act of teaching. See under *Metonymy*.

13. To Sit Down and Rise Up is used for *all the ordinary acts of life which come between them.*

Ps. cxxxix. 2.—" Thou knowest my downsitting and mine uprising."

14. To Come, בּוֹא (*bō*), ἔρχεσθαι (*erchesthai*), is used of *going as well as coming.*

Jonah i. 3.—" But Jonah . . . found a ship coming (*i.e.*, going) to Tarshish."

Mark xvi. 2.—" They came (*i.e.*, went) unto the sepulchre."

John vi. 17.—" And (they) entered into a ship, and came (*i.e.*, went) over the sea toward Capernaum. And it was now dark, and Jesus was not come (*i.e.*, gone) to them.

John xi. 29.—" As soon as she heard that, she arose quickly, and came (*i.e.*, went) unto him."

Acts xxviii. 17.—" And so we came (*i.e.*, went, as in A.V.) towards Rome."

Rev. vi. 1, 3, 5, 7.—In these verses, the verb "and see "goes out, according to the R.V. and all the Critical Texts. In this case the verb "come " is used in the sense of "go," as a command from the throne to the horsemen, *e.g.*, " I heard as it were the noise of thunder, one of the four living creatures, saying, Go! and I saw and behold a white horse. . . and he went forth." So in each of the other cases.

vi. *One example or specimen is put for all kinds of similar things.*

1. In human actions.

Deut. xix. 5.—One kind of *homicide* is mentioned as an example of every kind.

Ps. cxii. 5.—"Lending" is put as one kind of favour which a good man sheweth. The most rare is given as an example of all kinds of merciful works.

Prov. xx. 10.—" Divers ephahs " are put for all kinds of measures.

Prov. xxvii. 14.—" Blessing " a friend with a loud voice,- is put for all kinds of flattery.

Jer. xv. 10.—" Lending on usury " is put for all kinds of business transactions and contracts which are liable to gender strife.

Zech. v. 3.—" Stealing " and " swearing "—two of the commonest kinds of sin—are put for other kinds.

Matt. v. 22.—" Raca " is put for all kinds of opprobrious terms, etc.

Matt. vi. 1.—" Take heed that ye do not your righteousness." The figure here led to an early corruption of the text. One kind of righteous acts, alms-giving, is put for all kinds. Hence ἐλεημοσύνην (*elëeemosuneen*), *alms*, was put for δικαιοσύνην (*dikaiosuneen*), *righteousness*.

Matt. vi. 5.—Prayer is only one of many things which are not to be done as the hypocrites do them.

Matt. vi. 16.—So with *fasting*.

Mark xi. 23.—Removing mountains—one kind of impossible thing, is put for all kinds that are " impossible with men." So Luke xvii. 6. Matt. xvii. 20: in which latter place the word " nothing " shows that removing mountains is only one of a class of impossibilities. It is not in the nature of things for a *word* to pluck up a mountain. See 1 Cor. xiii. 2.

Job ix. 5.—" Which removeth mountains, and they know not." This is only one kind of things which are possible with God, though impossible with men (Luke xviii. 27).

Heb. xiii. 9.—" It is a good thing that the heart to be established with grace, not with meats, which have not profited them that have been occupied therein." Here " meats," one of the things about which people are occupied, is put for all kinds of divers and strange doctrines which do not profit those who are occupied with them.

2. In Divine Precepts, etc.

Ex. xx. 12.—" Honour thy father and thy mother ": *i.e.*, all who stand in the place of parents.

Ex. xxiii. 4.—The " ox and ass " are mentioned only as examples, for surely a horse, or camel, or child, etc., would be included in the command.

Prov. xxv. 21. Rom. xii. 20.—Surely the two things mentioned are only examples of many ways in which love may be shown to our enemies.

Luke iii. 11.—One kind of vestment is put for any kind.

1 Tim. vi. 8.—" Food and raiment " are put by example for this world's goods. See 1 John iii. 17.

John xiii. 14.—" Washing the feet " is only one kind or one example of humble service which one may do for another. So 1 Sam. xxv. 41. 1 Tim. v. 10.

III. SYNECDOCHE OF THE WHOLE.

Synecdoche of the whole is when the whole is put for a part. This is a closer connection than that of mere genus or species. It is when the one is not merely of the same *kind* as the other, but actually a part or member of it.

i. *The whole is put for every part of it.*

Num. xvi. 3.—" Ye take too much upon you, seeing all the congregation are holy, every one of them, and the LORD is among them ": *i.e.*, the whole congregation having been *separated* to the Lord from the other nations, each person was also included.

1 Kings vi. 22.—" The whole house he overlaid with gold ": and therefore every part of it.

Matt. iii. 5.—"Then went out to him Jerusalem, and all (πᾶσα, *pasa*) Judæa, and all the region round about Jordan :" the words Jerusalem, Judæa, and region, being used by *Synecdoché* of the genus for the people in them. The word "all" is literal, and means the whole as including every *part*. So that "all Judæa" means people from *every part* of Judæa. So Mark i. 5. Acts i. 8.

Matt. xxvii. 45.—"There was darkness over all the land (ἐπὶ πᾶσαν τὴν γῆν, *epi pasan teen geen*)" : *i.e.*, the whole Land, as in Mark xv. 33 (ὅλην, *holeen*).

Eph. ii. 21.—"In whom all the building, fitly framed together, groweth unto an holy temple in the Lord" : *i.e.*, the whole building; πᾶσα (*pasa*), *every* being put for every part of it.

Eph. iii. 15.—"Of whom the whole family in heaven and earth is named." Here, the R.V. has rendered the figure literally "every family," which is not sense, but in the margin has put "Gr. *father-hood.*" "Every" here is used for "the whole," and means every part or member of the whole : *i.e.*, the whole family as made up of every principality, and power, and angel, and archangel "in heaven" (verse 10), and of Israel and the Church on earth. All are of or from one Creator and Source (Heb. ii. 11). See *Ellipsis.*

Col. ii. 9.—"For in him dwelleth all the fulness of the Godhead bodily" : *lit.*, *every* : *i.e.*, *every part of*; meaning the whole fulness of the Godhead in bodily form.

2 Tim. iii. 16.—"All Scripture is given by inspiration of God" : *i.e.*, the whole Scripture; not "every Scripture," as in the R.V., but every part of Scripture. See under *Ellipsis*, page 44.

Acts iv. 10.—"Be it known to you all, and to all the people of Israel" : *i.e.*, the whole of Israel.

Rom. iv. 16.—"To the end the promise might be sure to all the seed" : *i.e.*, the whole seed.

2 Thess. i. 10.—"When He shall have come (ἔλθῃ, *elthee*) to be glorified in his saints, and to be admired in all them that believe . . . in that day" : *i.e.*, the whole body of believers.

In like manner "every" (*i.e.*, "all") is used for *the whole* in Matt. xxvi. 59. Mark i. 33; xiv. 55. Acts ii. 47; vii. 10; xv. 22. Phil. i. 13.

ii. *The Collective is put for the particular.*

What is said of the whole, collectively, is sometimes said (by *Synecdoche*) only of a part; and not of all the parts, precisely and singularly.

Gen. vi. 12.—" All flesh." This did not include Noah. See verse 9.

Gen. xxxv. 26.—" These are the sons of Jacob, which were born to him in Padan-Aram." This does not include Benjamin. See verses 24 and 16.

Matt. xix. 28—" Ye which have followed me . . . when the Son of man shall sit on the throne of his glory, ye also shall sit upon twelve thrones, judging the twelve tribes of Israel." The "ye" does not include Judas Iscariot.

Heb. xi. 13.—" These all died in faith." This does not include Enoch (see verse 5), but only all who died.

1 Cor. xv. 22.—" For as in Adam all die, even so in Christ shall all be made alive." But all will not die (see verse 51). Those who are " alive and remain " to the coming of the Lord will not die at all, but be changed. Therefore it means—that, as, in Adam, all who are in him die, so in Christ also, all who are in Him shall be made alive. The "all" in the first clause clearly does not include the all who shall be " alive and remain," and cannot therefore include the "all" in the second clause.

iii. *The whole is put for one of its parts.*

Gen. viii. 13.—"And Noah removed the covering of the ark," *i.e.*, not the whole roof, but the covering of the aperture which was made in it as a part of it : see vi. 16.

Ex. xxii. 13.—" If it be torn in pieces, then let him bring it (*i.e.*, one of the pieces) for witness."

1 Sam. v. 4.—"And when they arose early on the morrow morning, behold, Dagon was fallen upon his face to the ground before the ark of the LORD ; and the head of Dagon, and both the palms of his hands were cut off upon the threshold : only Dagon was left to him, *i.e.*, only the body was left. So the A.V. puts in italics "only *the stump of* Dagon was left."

Ps. cii. 5 (6).—" My bones cleave to my flesh," *i.e.*, " my skin," as in A.V., see margin.

1 Sam. xix. 24.—" Naked " for scantily clad. So also Isa. xx. 2, 3. Micah i. 8. John xxi. 7. Job xxii. 6 ; xxiv. 10. Matt. xxv. 36, 43. Jas. ii. 15. 1 Cor. iv. 11. In all these cases " naked " is put for being scantily clothed, or poorly clad.

Acts xxvii. 33.—" And continued fasting." *Fasting*, the whole, is put for the part ; *i.e.*, from real nourishment, or regular meals.

iv. *A place is put for a part of it.*

1. THE WORLD is put for *persons in all parts of it.*

John iii. 16.—"God so loved the world": *i.e.,* people and
kindred and tongues in all parts of the world. Not, as heretofore,
only Israel. This love was confined to Israel, accordiug to Duet.
xxxiii. 3: "Yea, he loved the people": *i.e.,* Israel (chap. vii. 6-8, etc.).
But now His love was to go out beyond Israel to people of all nations
of the world, without any such distinction. It is not the world without
exception, but without distinction.

John xii. 19.—"Behold, the world is gone after him": *i.e.,* multitudes of people of all sorts. *Synecdoche* here is preferable to *Hyperbole*
(*q.v.*).

Rom. i. 8.—"Your faith is spoken of throughout the whole
world": *i.e.,* in all parts of the world.

1 John ii. 2.—"Not for ours only, but also for the whole world":
i.e., for all people, without distinction. See *Metonymy* of the Subject.

2. "THE WORLD" is put for *a primary part of it.*

Isa. xiii. 11.—"And I will punish the world for their evil": *i.e.,*
Babylon (see verse 1). So xiv. 17.

Luke ii. 1.—"There went out a decree from Cæsar Augustus,
that all the world (*i.e.,* the civilised world, or Roman Empire) should
be taxed."

3. ALL THE EARTH is put for *the greater part of its inhabitants*

Gen. xli. 57.—"In all lands": *i.e.,* in many neighbouring countries.

2 Sam. xv. 23.—"All the country": *i.e.,* all the country round
him.

Isa. xiii. 5.—"The whole land": *i.e.,* all the land of Chaldæa.

4. THE EARTH is put for *the land of Judæa.*

Hos. i. 2.—Rendered "land." So iv. 1. Joel i. 2, etc.

5. THE LAND ($\gamma\hat{\eta}$) is put for *city.*

Matt. ii. 6.—"And thou, Bethlehem, land (*i.e.,* city) of Juda."
Not seeing the figure, the A.V. interpolates the word "*in*" in italics.

6. The East is put for *Persia, Media, and other countries east of Jerusalem.*

Ezek. xxv. 4. 1 Kings iv. 30. Isa. ii. 6. Matt. ii. 1, etc.

7. The South is put for *Egypt*, with respect to Palestine.

Jer. xiii. 19. Dan. xi. 5, etc.

8. The South is put for *the Negev,* or *the hill country of Judæa,* with respect to Jerusalem.

Gen. xii. 9; xiii. 1, 3. Ezek. xx. 46, 47.

9. The North is put for *Chaldæa and its chief city Babylon,* because all armies from beyond the Euphrates crossed high up and entered Palestine from the North.

Jer. i. 13-15; xiii. 20; xlvii. 2. Zeph. ii. 13.

10. The North is put for *Media and Persia*, with respect to Babylon.

Jer. vi. 1 (compare li. 11 and 27, 28); l. 3, 41.

11. The Temple is put for *certain of the parts comprehended in it.*

Luke ii. 46. John xviii. 20.

v. *Time is put for a portion of time.*

לְעֹלָם (*l'ohlam*), *for ever*, used in various limited significations.

Ex. xxi. 6.—"And he shall serve him for ever" : *i.e.*, as long as he lives. So Deut. xv. 17, and Philem. 15.

Lev. xxv. 46.—"They shall be your bondmen for ever": *i.e.*, as long as they live.

1 Sam. i. 22.—"That he (Samuel) may appear before the Lord, and there abide for ever" : *i.e.*, as long as he lives.

1 Chron. xv. 2.—"For them (the Levites) hath the Lord chosen to carry the ark of God, and to minister unto him for ever": *i.e.*, without change.

2 Sam. xii. 10.—"Now therefore the sword shall never (*lit.*, not for ever) depart from thine house" : *i.e.*, while David or his family lived.

Jer. v. 15.—The Babylonians are called "a nation from eternity": *i.e.*, very ancient (compare Gen. x. 10).

Jer. xvii. 4.—" Ye have kindled a fire in mine anger, which shall burn for ever" : *i.e.*, until all is consumed.

Jer. xxv. 9.—" Eternal desolations." Here it is rendered " perpetual " to soften it down, as the period is distinctly defined in verse 11 to be " seventy years." After which Babylon is to become eternal desolation (verse 12), until it shall be rebuilt according to many prophecies. Verses 9 and 12 clearly mean, therefore, that the desolations shall be complete and continuous during the whole period referred to.

Dan. ii. 4 ; vi. 21 (22), etc.—" O King, live for ever " : *i.e.*, a long time : as we say, " Long live the king."

So in Luke xx. 9, " a long (a sufficient) time " (χρόνος, *chronos*) : *i.e.*, a year ; till the next season.

IV. Synecdoche of the PART.

Synecdoche of the Part is when a part is put for the whole. The connection between the part and the whole is closer also than that between the species and the genus ; inasmuch as the part is actually a member of the whole, and not merely a species or specimen of it.

In *Synecdoche* of the Part, one part or member is put for, and includes, every part or member.

i. *An integral part of man (individually) is put for the whole man.*

1. The Soul (נֶפֶשׁ, *nephesh*, and ψυχή, *psychee*) is put for the *whole person.*

Gen. xii. 5.—" The souls (*i.e.*, the persons) that they had gotten in Haran."

Gen. xiv. 21.—" And the king of Sodom said unto Abram, Give me the souls (*i.e.*, the persons) and take the goods to thyself."

Gen. xvii. 14.—" That soul (*i.e.*, that person) shall be cut off from his people."

So Gen. xlvi. 15, 26, 27. Ex. xii. 19 ; xvi. 16 (marg.) Lev. v. 2, 4. Josh. xx. 3. Ezek. xviii. 4, 20. Acts ii. 41, 43 ; vii. 14. Rom. xiii. 1. 1 Pet. iii. 20. Luke vi. 9, " to save a soul " : *i.e.*, a man.

In this sense we must take Rev. vi. 9 and xx. 4 : " the souls of them that were slain or beheaded " : *i.e.*, the persons. John saw the dead persons. They could not reign till they were made alive, hence in xx. 4, we read that " they lived." Moreover, how could " souls " cry " How long ? " or, as such, wear " white robes," which " were given unto every one of them " (vi. 11) ?

2. The expression MY SOUL, HIS SOUL, etc., becomes by *Synecdoché* the idiom for *me, myself, himself*, etc. See under *Idiom*.

Num. xxiii. 10.—" Let my soul die the death of the righteous ": *i.e.*, let me die, as in A.V. See the margin.

Judges xvi. 30.—"And Samson said, Let my soul (*i.e.*, me, as in A.V., see margin) die with the Philistines."

Job xxxvi. 14.—"Their soul dieth (*i.e.*, they die, as in A.V.) in youth."

Ps. iii. 2 (3).—"Many there be which say of my soul (*i.e.*, of me), There is no help for him in his God." So Ps. xi. 1.

Ps. xvi. 10.—" Thou wilt not leave my soul (*i.e.*, me) in Hades ": *i.e.*, the grave.

Ps. xxv. 13.—" His soul (*i.e.*, he) shall dwell at ease."

Ps. xxxv. 13.—" I humbled my soul (*i.e.*, myself) with fasting."

Ps. ciii. 1.—"Bless the LORD, O my soul ": *i.e.*, O myself. So in verses 2, 22, and Ps. civ. 1, 35.

Isa. lvii. 5.—" Is it such a fast that I have chosen ? a day for a man to afflict his soul ? " *i.e.*, himself.

Luke xii. 19.—" I will say to my soul " : *i.e.*, myself, etc.

Acts ii. 31.—"His soul (*i.e.*, He) was not left in Hades (the grave), neither his flesh did see corruption."

Rom. xvi. 4.—" Who have for my soul (A.V., life) laid down their own necks": *i.e.*, who have laid down their own necks for me.

1 Pet. i. 9.—" Receiving the end of you faith, even the salvation of your souls " : *i.e.*, of yourselves.

3. SOUL (נֶפֶשׁ, *nephesh*) is also used of *animals;*

and when joined with the word " living" (*khayah*), means "living creature," as translated in Gen. i. 20, 21, 24, 30. So also Rev. xvi. 3, as well as of man in Gen. ii. 7, where it is rendered "living soul."

4. THE BODY is put for *the person himself*.

Just as we say, " a hand " for a workman.

Ex. xxi. 3.—" If he (*i.e.*, the Hebrew servant) came in with his body (*i.e.*, by himself, as in A.V.) " : *i.e.*, alone, without a wife, as the rest of the verse explains it.

Rom. xii. 1.—" I beseech you therefore . . . that ye present your bodies (*i.e.*, yourselves) a living sacrifice," etc.

s 1

1 Cor. vi. 15.—" Know ye not that your bodies (*i.e.*, ye) are the members of Christ?"

Jas. iii. 6.—" So is the tongue among our members, that it defileth the whole body " : *i.e.*, the whole being.

5. THE FLESH, *an integral part* of man, is put for *the whole*.

Gen. xvii. 13.—" My covenant shall be in your flesh ": *i.e.*, in your body, on your person.

Ps. xvi. 9.—" My flesh also shall rest in hope ": *i.e.*, my body will rest in hope.   See Acts ii. 26-31.

Prov. xiv. 30.—" A sound heart is the life of the flesh " : *i.e.*, of the body.

2 Cor. vii. 1.—" Let us cleanse ourselves from all filthiness of the flesh (*i.e.*, of the body) and spirit."

6. THE FLESH is put for *the whole person*.

Gen. vi. 12.—" All flesh had corrupted his way upon the earth." Here " flesh," being the figure for *people*, the word " all " is literal : *i.e.*, all people, every person.   But even this excepts Noah.   See above.

Ps. lvi. 4 (5).—" I will not fear what flesh (*i.e.*, man) can do unto me."   See verse 11 (12).

Ps. lxv. 2 (3) —" O Thou that hearest prayer, unto Thee shall all flesh come " : *i.e.*, all people.

Ps. cxlv. 21.—" Let all flesh (*i.e.*, let all people) bless his holy name for ever " : *lit.*, " all flesh shall bless," as in verse 10.

Isa. xl. 5.—" The glory of the LORD shall be revealed, and all flesh (*i.e.*, all people) shall see it together."   See Luke iii. 6.

Isa. xl. 6.—" All flesh is grass."   See *Metaphor*.

Matt. xix. 5.—" And they twain shall be one flesh " : *i.e.*, one person, not a soulless body !

John vi. 51.—" My flesh ": *i.e.*, myself.

Rom. iii. 20.—" By the deeds of the law there shall no flesh (*i.e.*, not a single person) be justified."   Here, the " flesh " being figurative, the negative denies literally.   So

1 Cor. i. 29.—" That no flesh (*i.e.*, not a single person) should glory in his presence."

1 Pet. i. 24.—" All flesh (*i.e.*, every one) is as grass."

7. FLESH is put for *the whole, and true, humanity of Christ.*

John i. 14.—" The Word was made flesh ": *i.e.,* man, a human being.

John vi. 51-56.—Here, "flesh" and "blood," (see below) are jointly as well as severally put for *humanity* as distinct from *Divinity.* There are other figures in this passage; but the word " flesh " is put, not for the " body " of Christ, but for Himself in His true humanity.

1 Tim. iii. 16.—" Manifest in the flesh ": *i.e.,* in human beings. The "mystery" was manifest. The reading ὁ (*ho*), *which*, corresponds best with the context, and agrees with the neuter word Μυστήριον, mystery. This mystery is Christ Mystical (not personal): *i.e.,* Christ the head of the Body in glory and His members here upon earth. Otherwise the last three facts at the end of the verse are quite out of order. They describe the order as to Christ Mystical, but not as to Christ personal.*

1 Pet. iii. 18.—" Being put to death as to the flesh (*i.e.,* as to his human nature), but quickened (*i.e.,* raised from the dead) as to his spirit (*i.e.,* his resurrection or spiritual body)." There is no article with either word: only the dative case, describing what happened as to the body. This is the usage of the words " flesh " and " spirit " in 1 Cor. xv.† See also chap. iv. 1.

Heb. x. 20.—" By a new and living way, which he hath consecrated (marg., *new made*) for us, through the veil, that is to say, his flesh ": *i.e.,* his human nature, Himself as truly and really man.

1 John iv. 2.—" Every spirit that confesseth that Jesus Christ is come in the flesh (*i.e.,* in His real human nature) is of God." Note the three forms of the verb ἔρχομαι. Here, it is the perfect participle, ἐληλυθότα (*eleeluthota*), "being come." In chap. v. 6, it is the aorist participle, ὁ ἐλθὼν (*ho elthōn*), "this is He that came." While in 2 John 7, it is the present participle, ἐρχόμενον (*erchomenon*), " who confess not that Jesus Christ is coming in the flesh ": *i.e.,* in his human nature, the same Jesus, in like manner as he went into heaven (Acts i. 11).

8. FLESH is put for *all living beings.*

Gen. vi. 13.—" The end of all flesh is come before me ": *i.e.,* the end of every living creature. Here, the " all " is literal, because " flesh " is figurative.

---

* See *The Mystery*, by the same author and publisher.
† See *The Spirits in Prison*, by the same author and publisher.

Gen. vi. 17.—"I . . . bring a flood of waters upon the earth to destroy all flesh" : *i.e.*, every living thing.

Ps. cxxxvi. 25.—"Who giveth food to all flesh" : *i.e.*, to every living thing.

9. THE FLESH is put for *the animal lusts, and the evil desires of the Old nature : and for the Old nature itself.*

In Rom. i. 16-viii. 39, there are many examples. See

Rom. viii. 4.—"Who walk not after the flesh" : *i.e.*, the Old nature. This is not the same as in verse 3.

Rom. viii. 13.—"If ye live after the flesh, ye shall die" : *i.e.*, if ye live and are ruled by the principles of the Old nature. So in verse 12, and frequently.

See articles on Romans in *Things to Come*, 1898 and 1899.

Gal. v. 6.—"Walk in the spirit (*i.e.*, in the New nature), and ye shall not fulfil the lust of the flesh (*i.e.*, of the old man)."

10. BLOOD is put for *man*, as we say "poor blood" for "poor fellow."

Ps. xciv. 21.—"They gather themselves together against the soul of the righteous (*i.e.*, against the righteous man), and condemn the innocent blood" : *i.e.*, the innocent man.

Prov. i. 11.—"Let us lay wait for blood" : *i.e.*, for some man whom we may kill.

Matt. xxvii. 4.—"I have sinned in that I have betrayed the innocent blood" : *i.e.*, the innocent man.

Acts xvii. 26.—God "hath made of one blood all nations of men for to dwell on all the face of the earth" : *i.e.*, out of one man God hath made many different nations. Man is the same all over the world ; and, though there are different nations and races all over the world, they are all descended from one man.

11. FLESH AND BLOOD is put for the *human* nature as distinct from the Divine Nature : or for the body of man as animal, mortal, and corruptible.

Matt. xvi. 17.—"Blessed art thou Simon Bar-jona : for flesh and blood hath not revealed it unto thee, but my Father which is in heaven." Here, the Lord uses Peter's human name "Simon" and his human parentage, and "flesh and blood" in order to contrast and emphasize the distinction between these and the Divine origin of the communication and revelation. The figure of *Synecdoché* here puts the emphasis on man and humanity: "No human being revealed this unto thee."

1 Cor. xv. 50.—" Flesh and blood cannot inherit the kingdom of God ": *i.e.*, no mortal human being can enter there. Man must be " born again," and " born of the Spirit," and raised from the dead, or " changed " before he can find entrance into that kingdom. See the rest of the verse, and compare verses 42-49.

Gal. i. 16.—" I conferred not with flesh and blood ": *i.e.*, with no human being in contrast with God, Who alone revealed to him the Gospel which he was to preach.

Eph. vi. 12.—"We wrestle not against flesh and blood ": *i.e.*, against human beings, in contrast with wicked spiritual beings.

See under *Metonymy* of Adjunct.

Heb. ii. 14.—" Forasmuch then as the children are partakers of flesh and blood, he also himself likewise took part of the same ": *i.e.*, He became flesh, and took part in a true and perfect human body.

12. The Head is put for *the man himself.*

We use the figure when we reckon anything at so much " per *head*."

Judges v. 30.—" To the head of a man, a damsel, two damsels ": *i.e.*, one or two damsels per head, or for each man.

Here, there is a double *Synecdoché*, " a womb " being put for " a damsel." See below.

2 Kings ii. 3.—" Knowest thou that the Lord will take away thy master from thy head (*i.e.*, from thee) to-day ? "

Ps. iii. 3 (4).—" The lifter up of mine head ": *i.e.*, of me : " my head " meaning the same as " my soul."

Ps. vii. 16 (17).—" His mischief shall return upon his own head " : *i.e.*, upon his own self.

Ps. lxvi. 12.—" Thou hast caused men to ride over our heads " : *i.e.*, over us.

Prov. x. 6.—" Blessings are upon the head of the just " : *i.e.*, upon the man himself.

Isa. xxxv. 10.—" With songs, and everlasting joy upon their heads ": *i.e.*, upon them, themselves.

So " blood " is said to be upon the head of anyone, *i.e.*, where " blood " is put for the guilt of blood-shedding (*Metonymy* of the effect) and " head " is put (by *Synecdoché*) for the person himself.

2 Sam. i. 16.—" And David said unto him, Thy blood be upon thy head ": *i.e.*, thyself.

So 1 Kings ii. 37. Ezek. xxxiii. 4. Acts xviii. 6.

Matt. xxvii. 25.—" His blood (*i.e.*, the guilt of his blood-shedding, by *Metonymy* of the effect) be on us, and on our children."

13. The SKULL, as a part of the man, is put for the *man himself.*

Ex. xvi. 16.—" An omer a skull ": *i.e.*, an omer per head, or, as in A.V., an omer " for every man." See A.V. margin.

And many other plăces.

14. THE FACE is put for the *whole man, especially marking and emphasizing his presence.*

See under *Pleonasm.*

Gen. iii. 19.—" In the sweat of thy face shall thou eat bread."

When the face perspires, the person himself perspires : but, as it is only the face that is seen, it is that which is mentioned, and is thus put for the whole man.

" Bread," we have seen, is put by *Synecdoché* for food in general.

Gen. xix. 21.—" See, I have accepted thy face (*i.e.*, thee) concerning this thing also." See A.V. margin.

Gen. xxxii. 20 (21).—" And afterward I will see his face ": *i.e.*, himself. There are three instances here.

2 Sam. xvii. 11.—Hushai says to Absalom, " I counsel . . . that thy face (*i.e.*, thou thyself) go to battle."

There can be but little doubt, as Dr. Ginsburg points out in his *Introduction to the Hebrew Bible* (page 169), that the word בַּקְרָב (*baccrav*) rendered *to the battle*, is an abbreviation in the MSS. for בְּקִרְבָּם (*b'cheerbam*), which means *in the midst of them.* And so the Septuagint and the Vulgate translate it. Besides, קְרָב (*ch'rab*) is never used in Samuel for battle. It is always מִלְחָמָה (*milchamah*). So that the passage should read: " I counsel . . . that thou go in the midst of them in thine own person."

1 Kings ii. 20.—" And the king said unto her, Ask, my mother; for I shall not turn back thy face ": *i.e.*, as in A.V., " I will not say thee nay," with the emphasis on " thee."

1 Kings x. 24.—" And all the earth sought the face of Solomon " : *i.e.*, his presence, so as to see him and to speak with him personally.

Job xi. 19.—"Many shall intreat thy face": *i.e.*, as in A.V., "will make suit unto thee." See A.V. margin.

Ps. xlii. 5 (6).—" I shall yet praise Him for the salvations (*Heterosis* (*q.v.*) of number: *i.e.*, *the great salvation*) of His countenance": *i.e.*, which He (*i.e.*, His presence) shall give me.

So verse 11 (12): " I shall yet praise Him who is the salvations (*i.e.*, the great salvation) of my countenance (*i.e.*, me myself), and my God." So Ps. xliii. 5.

Ps. cxxxii. 10.—" For thy servant David's sake turn not away the face of thine anointed."

Here the figure emphasizes the last words, meaning not his face merely, but David himself.

Prov. xxviii. 21.—" To have respect of faces is not good ": *i.e.*, as in A.V , " persons," so as to be influenced by personal appearance rather than by justice and right.

Ecc. viii. 1.—" A man's wisdom maketh his face to shine (*i.e.*, the man himself), and his hardness is changed." See under *Metonymy*.

Isa. iii. 15.—" What mean ye that ye . . . grind the faces of the poor ? " So xxxvi. 9 : " Turn away the face of one captain."

Lam. v. 12.—" Princes are hanged up by their hand : the faces (*i.e.*, persons) of elders were not honoured."

15. The EYE is put for the *man himself, in respect to his vision, mental or physical.*

Matt. xiii. 16.—" Blessed are your eyes (*i.e.*, ye), for they (*i.e.*, ye) see." So Luke x. 23.

1 Cor. ii. 9.—" Eye hath not seen ": *i.e.*, no one hath seen. And many other passages.

16. The EYE lifted up is put for *a proud man, and his high looks.*

Ps. xviii. 27 (28).—" Thou wilt save the afflicted people : but wilt bring down high looks (Heb., soaring eyes) " : *i.e.*, proud people.
So Prov. vi. 17 (margin).

17. The MOUTH is put for *the whole man, in respect of his speaking.*

Prov. viii. 13.—" The froward mouth (*i.e.*, person) do I hate."

18. The BELLY is put for *man, in respect of his eating.*

Rom. xvi. 18.—" For they that are such serve not our Lord Jesus Christ, but their own belly" : *i.e.*, their own selves.

Phil. iii. 19.—" Whose God is their belly " : *i.e.*, themselves, and what they can get.

Tit. i. 12.—" Slow bellies " : *i.e.*, slow persons, who by reason of large eating, have grown stout and move slowly.

19. The Womb is put for *a female, in respect to her being marriageable.*

Judges v. 30.—" A womb—two wombs for each man." The A.V. renders the figure here by the word " damsel."

20. The Heart is put for *the whole man, in respect to his knowledge or affection.*

Gen. xxxi. 20.—" And Jacob stole away the heart of Laban " : *i.e.*, Jacob baffled Laban's knowledge by hiding his intentions. So in verse 26, where the A.V. renders it " unawares," but see the margin on verse 26; and in verse 27, " secretly."

2 Sam. xv. 6.—" So Absalom stole the hearts of the men of Israel " : *i.e.*, gained them through getting their affection.

Luke xxi. 34.—" Take heed to yourselves, lest at any time your hearts (*i.e.*, ye) be overcharged with surfeiting," etc.

21. The Feet are put for *the whole man, in respect to carefulness, quickness, etc.*

Prov. i. 16.—" Their feet (*i.e.*, they) run to evil."

Prov. vi. 18.—" Feet (*i.e.*, persons) that be swift in running to mischief." So Isa. lix. 7.

Isa. lii. 7.—" How beautiful upon the mountains are the feet of him that bringeth good tidings " : *i.e.*, how beautiful or pleasant is the coming of him who brings good news. So Rom. x. 15.

Rom. iii. 15.—" Their feet (*i.e.*, they) are swift to shed blood."

ii. *An integral part of men (collectively) is put for the whole, or others associated with them.*

Ex. xii. 40.—One person is mentioned; but with him are comprehended his father Isaac, and his grandfather Abraham.

" Now the sojourning of the children of Israel, who dwelt in Egypt, was four hundred and thirty years."

Note that it does not say that Israel's descendants dwelt in Egypt 430 years, as the commentators assume, but that their " sojourning " lasted that time; reckoning from Abraham (who is included by *Synecdoché*, as is Isaac also).

Four hundred and thirty years was the whole duration of the sojourning; as is stated also in Gal. iii. 16, 17.   While the 400 years' sojourning is dated from Abraham's "seed" (Isaac), who was born thirty years later.   See Gen. xv. 18 and Acts vii. 6.   There are two reckonings, starting from two different points, and both ending at the Exodus.

Ex. xvii. 8, 13.—Amalek (in verse 8) is put for him and his whole army. So Josh. x. 28, 40. 1 Sam. xviii. 7, etc.

Deut. xxxiii. 7.—Only "Judah" is named in the blessing, but in company with him Simeon is understood.   For their inheritance and blessing was one.   Josh. xix. 1 and Judges i. 3.

"And this for Judah," etc.

1 Kings viii. 66.—"David" is named, but Solomon, his son, is understood together with him; see 2 Chron. vii. 10, where it is expressly added; and 1 Kings x. 9.

1 Kings x. 11.—"The navy of Hiram" is named, but *Solomon* is included; see ix. 26, 27.

1 Kings xi. 32.—"One tribe" is mentioned; but, by *Synecdoché*, Simeon and Benjamin are included, as well as the Levites and others who joined the tribe.   See 2 Chron. xv. 9. 1 Kings xii. 23. 2 Chron. xi. 13.   All these are included, by *Synecdoché*, in 1 Kings xii. 20.

2 Kings xvii. 18.—The Levites and Benjamites, etc., are included.

Job xxxii. 4.—Job is named, but the others are included.

Isa. vii. 2, 5, 8, 9, and ix. 9.—"Ephraim" is named, because in that tribe was Samaria, the royal city ; and because out of that tribe was Jeroboam, the first king of Israel.   But by *Synecdoché* all the ten tribes are included.

Ps. lxxx. 2.—"Ephraim"* includes the ten tribes, while "Benjamin" includes Judah ; and "Manasseh" includes the two-and-a-half tribes.

Ps. lxxx. 1 (2).—"Joseph" (whose son Ephraim was) is put for all Israel.

Amos v. 15 and vi. 6.—"Joseph" is put for the ten tribes or the kingdom of Israel.

Jer. vi. 1.—"Benjamin" is put for all Judah, on account of their close connection with the Gibeathites (see Judges xix. 16. Hos. ix. 9 ; x. 9).

---

* One of the ancient readings called *Severin* has this: "For the sons of Ephraim," etc.

iii. *A part of a thing is put for the whole of the thing.*

1. A FIELD (שָׂדֶה, *sadeh*) is put for *a country or region.*

Gen. xiv. 7.—" And they smote the whole field (*i.e.*, country) of the Amalakites."

1 Sam. xxvii. 7.—" David dwelt in the field (*i.e.*, country) of the Philistines."

2. CORNER is put for *tower*, which was usually placed at the corner.

Zeph. i. 16.—" A day of trump and alarm against the fenced cities, and against the high corners": *i.e.*, towers (with A.V.). The word is so translated in margin of chap. iii. 6.

3. The BAPTISM OF JOHN is put for *his ministry.*

Not everywhere, but in a few passages.

Acts i. 22.—" Beginning from the baptism (*i.e.*, the ministry) of John, unto that same day that he (Christ) was taken up from us."
So Acts x. 37.

4. STONES is put for *the restored buildings.*

Ps. cii. 14 (15).—"Thy servants take pleasure in her stones."

5. WALL is put for *the whole city encompassed by it.*

Amos i. 7.—" I will send a fire on the wall of Gaza (*i.e.*, I will burn the city of Gaza with fire, as the rest of the verse declares), which shall devour the palaces thereof." So i. 10, 14; compare verse 12; and ii. 2, 5, etc.

6. In like manner GATE is put for *the whole city.*

Gen. xxii. 17.—" Thy seed shall possess the gate (*i.e.*, the cities) of his enemies."
The phrase "within thy gates" means within thy cities. See Ex. xx. 10. Deut. xii. 12; xiv. 27; xvi. 5.

Ps. lxxxvii. 2.—" The LORD loveth the gates (*i.e.*, the city) of Zion more than all the dwellings of Jacob."

Jer. xv. 7.—" And I will fan them with a fan in the gates (*i.e.*, cities) of the land."

7. GATE is also put for *the inhabitants of the city, or for the people who assemble at its gates.*

This may also be considered as *Metonymy* of the Subject.

Ruth iii. 11.—" All the gate (*i.e.*, the people assembling there) of my People doth know that thou art a virtuous woman."

Ruth iv. 10.—" That the name of the dead be not cut off . . . from the gate of his place ": *i.e.*, from his own city and People.

The two are combined in Isa. xiv. 31 : " Howl, O gate ; cry, O city." In neither case could the gate or the city cry or howl.

Two classes of people are addressed : first "gate" (a part of the whole) is put, by *Synecdoché*, for those who assemble there ; and then " city" is put, by *Metonymy* of the Subject, for all the inhabitants of the city.

8. The DEATH of Christ is put for *the atonement and its results* (and see under *Metalepsis*).

Rom. v. 10.—" We were reconciled to God by the death of his Son ": *i.e.*, not by the act or article of death only, but by the atonement of which it formed only a part.

So 1 Cor. xi. 26. Col. i. 22.

Heb. ii. 14.—" That through death he might destroy him that had the power of death."

Here, the first time the word " death " is used, it is put for the atonement associated with it ; and the second time it means literally the article of death. See under *Antanaclasis*.

9. The KNOB of the Roll is put for the *MS.* or *book itself.*

Heb. x. 7.—" In the volume of the book it is written of me."

Here ἐν κεφαλίδι βιβλίου (*en kephalidi bibliou*), *in the head of the book* (κεφαλίς, *kephalis*, head), is not a synonym for *roll*, as some try to show ; but it is the *head* or *knob* of the cylinder on which the manuscript was rolled, and which is put, by *Synecdoché*, for the roll and volume itself. It thus corresponds with the Hebrew in Ps. xl. 7 (8) : בִּמְגִלַּת סֵפֶר (*Bimegillath sepher*), *in the scroll of the book*, and is not a paraphrase, but gives the correct sense.

In Heb. x. 7 this book may be taken as referring to Ps. xl. 7 (8) ; but what about Ps. xl. 7 (8), where the same phrase occurs ? What is the book referred to there ? Surely it must be the book of the eternal covenant referred to in Ps. cxxxix. 16.

iv. *A part of time is put for the whole time.*

1. A YEAR is put for *time, definite and indefinite.*

Isa. lxi. 2.—" To proclaim the acceptable year of the LORD " : *i.e.*, the time of Christ's coming.

Isa. lxiii. 4.—" The year of my redeemed is come."

Jer. xi. 23.—" I will bring evil upon the men of Anathoth, even the year of their visitation."

2. IN THE DAY is put for an *indefinite time.*

Gen. ii. 4.—" When they were created,
" In the day that the LORD God made the earth and the heavens."

Here " in the day " in the second line answers to " when " in the first line.

Gen. ii. 17.—" In the day that thou eatest thereof thou shalt surely die." בְּיוֹם (*b'yōm*), *in the day*.

A noun with the preposition followed by the verb in the infinitive, as here, becomes an adverb of time, and means simply *when*, or *after then*, or *after that*.

Lev. xiii. 14.—" In the day that raw flesh appear " : in A.V., " when," and in R.V., " whensoever."

Lev. xiv. 57.—" To teach in the day of the unclean, and in the day of the clean."

Both A.V. and R.V. renders this : " To teach when it is unclean and when it is clean " (see A.V. margin).

Deut. xxi. 16.—" In the day that (*i.e.*, when) he maketh his sons to inherit that which he hath."

2 Sam. xxi. 12.—" In the day that (*i.e.*, when) the Philistines had slain Saul in Gilboa."

1 Kings ii. 37.—" It shall be that, on the day thou goest out, and passest over the brook Kidron, thou shalt know for certain that thou shalt surely die."

Then, after Shimei had gone out, and been to Gath to seek his servants, who had run away, and had come back again, " it was told Solomon that Shimei had gone from Jerusalem to Gath, and was come again " (verse 41). The king sent for Shimei ; and said : " Did I not make thee to swear by the LORD, and protested unto thee, saying,

Know for a certain, on the day thou goest out, and walkest abroad any whither, that thou shalt surely die?"

After all this, Solomon proceeded to make Shimei "know for certain that he should surely die."

In this case Shimei had been not merely outside his house, but far away to Gath, one of the royal cities of the Philistines; and had not only consumed some time on his journeys out and home, but, after he got there, he had to seek his lost servants out and find them. Therefore " on the day " could neither be intended nor taken in its literal meaning; but, by *Synecdoché*, for any indefinite yet certain time. It was so taken by Solomon here: and it is perfectly certain that it is to be so understood in Gen. iii. for in verse 19 the LORD distinctly says: " In the sweat of thy face shalt thou eat bread, till thou return unto the ground; for out of it wast thou taken: for dust thou art, and unto dust shalt thou return."

Not " in the day " that Adam ate of the forbidden fruit; for the Lord contemplates him as living on, and he did live for nine hundred and thirty years (Gen. v. 5). The interest of the passage in 1 Kings ii. is that the words are used in exactly the same connection, and with the corresponding figure, *Polyptoton* (*q.v.*), " *dying* thou wilt die," מוֹת תָּמוּת (*mōth tamuth*).

Those who see and understand the figure *Synecdoché*, here employed, need not trouble themselves to invent some new and strange and unscriptural theories as to *death*; or resort to strained interpretations in order to explain a self-created difficulty.

2 Kings xx. 1.—" In those days (*i.e.*, the days of Sennacherib's invasion) Hezekiah was sick unto death, and the prophet Isaiah came unto him."

Ps. xviii. 18 (19).—" They prevented me in the day of my calamity " : *i.e.*, when I was in trouble.

Isa. xi. 16.—" Like as it was to Israel in the day that he came up out of the land of Egypt " : *i.e.*, not the actual day (for it was dark), but at the time or on the occasion when he came up, etc.

Jer. xi. 3, 4.—" Cursed be the man that obeyeth not the words of this covenant, which I commanded your fathers in the day that I brought them forth out of the land of Egypt."

And in verse 7: " I earnestly protested unto your fathers in the day that I brought them up out of the land of Egypt."

Now the commands and protest referred to are written in Deut. xxvii., and were given some forty years after the Exodus. It is clear from this that בְּיוֹם (*beyōm*) is not to be taken literally, and that "in the day" is put by *Synecdoche* for the whole time covered by the events referred to. See Jer. xxxi. 32; xxxiv. 13. Ezek. xx. 5, 6.

Ezek. xxxvi. 33.—"Then saith Adonai Jehovah: In the day that I shall have cleansed you from all your iniquities, I shall also cause you to dwell in the cities, and the wastes will be builded."

It is clear that all this building will not be done in a day, but it will all be done when the time comes for the Lord's word to be fulfilled.

Ezek. xxxviii. 18.—"And it shall come to pass in the day of Gog's coming against the land of Israel," etc.

Here, the A.V. renders בְּיוֹם (*b'yōm*), *at the same time*; and the R.V., *in that day.*

And more generally DAYS are used for *time.*

Ps. cii. 11 (12).—"My days are like a shadow that declineth": *i.e.*, my life.

Ps. ciii. 15.—"As for man, his days are as grass": *i.e.*, he himself, or his life.

Isa. iv. 1.—"And in that day (*i.e.*, at that time) seven women shall take hold of one man," etc.

Isa. ix. 4 (3).—"Thou hast broken the yoke of his burden . . . as in the day of Midian": *i.e.*, at the time when Midian was broken.

Hos. ix. 9.—"As in the days of Gibeah": *i.e.*, at the time when the sons of Belial sinned at Gibeah (Judges xix. 22-25).

Matt. ii. 1.—"In the days (*i.e.*, in the reign) of Herod the king."

Acts v. 36.—"For before these days": *i.e.*, before this time.

The plural DAYS is put for *a full year.*

Gen. xxiv. 55.—"Let the damsel abide with us days at the least ten; after that she shall go." This is, according to the A.V. margin, "a full year or at least ten months."

Gen. xl. 4.—"And they continued days (*i.e.*, a year) in ward."

Ex. xiii. 10.—"Thou wilt therefore keep this ordinance at its appointed season: from days to days": *i.e.*, from year to year.

Lev. xxv. 29.—"If a man sell a dwelling house in a walled city, then he may redeem it within a whole year after it is sold; *within* days (*i.e.*, a full year) may he redeem it." Or as in R.V., "for a full year shall he have the right of redemption."

Judges xi. 40.—"The daughters of Israel went from days to days (*i.e.*, "yearly," as in A.V.) to talk with the daughter of Jephthah the Gileadite four days in the year." The verb תָּנָה (*tahnah*) occurs only twice : here and in chap. v. 11. It means *to rehearse, to talk with* or *of*.

Judges xvii. 10.—"I shall give thee ten *shekels* of silver for the days " : *i.e.*, by the year, as in A.V.

1 Sam. i. 3.—"And this man (Elkanah) went up out of his city from days to days (*i.e.*, from year to year, A.V. margin and R.V. ; or, yearly, A.V.) to worship and to sacrifice."

In verse 7, the Hebrew word " year " is used literally.

1 Sam. xxvii. 7.—"And the time that David dwelt in the country of the Philistines was days and four months ": *i.e.*, a full year and four months.

1 Kings xvii. 7.—"And it came to pass at the end of days that the brook dried up, because there had been no rain in the land." The A.V. and R.V., " after a while " is not far out. It may mean a full year ; but it evidently must include a whole season during which rain might have been expected.

In chap. xviii. 1, " many days " include the whole three years.

Amos iv. 4.—"Bring . . . your tithes after three of days " : *i.e.*, in the third year (according to the Law, Deut. xiv. 28).

3. The Sabbath is sometimes put for *the full week.*

Matt. xxviii. 1.—"In the end of the sabbaths " : *i.e.*, at the close of the week.

Luke xviii. 12.—"I fast twice in the sabbath ": *i.e.*, in the week.

1 Cor. xvi. 1.—"On the first of the sabbath ": *i.e.*, on the first day of the week.

4. The Morning is put for *a more lengthened period or continuous time.*

Job vii. 17, 18.—"What is man . . . that thou shouldest visit him every morning ? " *i.e.*, continually.

Ps. lxxiii. 14.—"All the day long have I been plagued and chastened every morning ": *i.e.*, continually.

Ps. ci. 8.—"At morn I will destroy the wicked of the land." Not " early," as in A.V. ; nor, " morning by morning," as in R.V., as though in millennial days each morning would commence with, and each day begin with, executions ! It means more than that. It means *continually ;*

so that all through the millennium all workers of iniquity will be continually cut off.

Ecc. xi. 6.—" In the morning sow thy seed ": *i.e.,* early and continuously.

Isa. xxxiii. 2. — " Be thou their arm every morning ": *i.e.,* continually.

Lam. iii. 23.—The LORD's mercies and compassions are " new every morning ": *i.e.,* always and continually new.

5. EVENING AND MORNING are put for *the full day ; or, the whole of a day and night.*

Gen. i. 5, 8, 13, 19, 23, 31.

6. HOUR is put for *a special time or season.*

John iv. 23.—" The hour cometh, and now is, when the true worshippers shall worship the Father in spirit and in truth." See this passage and verse 24, under *Hendiadys* below.

John v. 25.—" The hour is coming, and now is, when the dead shall hear the voice of the Son of God ; and they that hear shall live." Note that in this almighty act Christ's title is " Son of God " ; while, in verse 27, He executes judgment in the earth because He is the " Son of man." So John v. 28 ; xvi. 2 (A.V., " time ") ; xvii. 1. 1 Thess. ii. 17 (A.V., " time "). Philem. 15 (A.V., " season "). 1 John ii. 18, twice (A.V., " time ").

7. In CHRONOLOGY a part of a time or period is sometimes put for *the whole of such period.*

1 Kings ii. 11.—" Seven years " is put for seven years and a half. Compare 2 Sam. ii. 11.

2 Kings xxiv. 8.—" Three months " is put for three months and ten days. Compare 2 Chron. xxxvi. 9.

HENDIADYS; or, TWO FOR ONE.

Two words used, but one thing meant.

Hen-dī´-a-dÿs, from ἕν (*hen*), *one*, διὰ (*dia*), *by*, δίς (*dis*) *two* (from δύο, *two*). Lit., *one by means of two*. Two words employed, but only one thing, or idea, intended. One of the two words expresses the thing, and the other (of synonymous, or even different, signification, not a second thing or idea) intensifies it by being changed (if a noun) into an adjective of the superlative degree, which is, by this means, made especially emphatic.

The figure is truly oriental, and exceedingly picturesque. It is found in Latin as well as in Hebrew and Greek, and is very frequently used in both Old and New Testaments.

The two words are of the same parts of speech : *i.e.*, two nouns (or two verbs) always joined together by the conjunction " and." The two nouns are always in the same *case*.

An example or two from the Latin will serve to explain the true nature of this figure, which is one of the most important in the Bible.

TACITUS (*Ann.* i. 49. 5) says, "*ultio et satietas*," lit., a revenge and a sufficiency. Here we have not two things, but only one, though there are two words. The latter noun becomes a very strong adjective, which may be well and excellently expressed by our English idiom : " a revenge, yes—and a sufficient revenge too ": *i.e.*, *a sufficient revenge*, with strong emphasis on the word " sufficient," from its being thus changed from a noun to an adjective of superlative degree. Had the mere adjective been used, the emphasis would then have been on " revenge," thus naturally qualified.

TACITUS, again (*Ann.* i. 61), speaks of one who was slain, "*infelici dextera et suo ictu*," by his hapless right hand, and his own blow : *i.e.*, " by his hapless right hand, yes—a blow dealt by his own hand too."

TACITUS (*Ann.* ii. 82. end) : "*tempore et spatio*," time and space. Here we have not two things, but one : *i.e.*, " time, yes—and a long-extended time too."

TACITUS (*Ann.* iii. 65. 1) : "*posteritate et infamia*," posterity and infamy : *i.e.*, " posterity, yes—and an infamous posterity too."

VIRGIL (*Aen.* vii. 15): "*gemitus iraeque,*" roars and angers: *i.e.*, " roars, yes—and angry roars too."

VIRGIL (*Aen.* vii. 772): "*medicinae et artis,*" medicine and art, or healing and skill: *i.e.*, " healing, yes—and skilful healing too," or skill (and great skill too) in healing.

HORACE (*Od.* i. 35. 33): "*cicatricum et sceleris . . . fratrumque,*" scars and crime and brothers: *i.e.*, " scars and crime (*i.e.*, criminal scars), yes—and criminal scars inflicted by brethren too." This is a case of *Hendiatris* (see below).

CÆSAR (B. G. iv. 18): "*vi et armis,*" by force and arms: *i.e.*, " by force, yes—and armed force too."

Many more examples could be given of this figure which is so commonly used in Latin.

The Greek Classics also abound in examples :

SOPHOCLES (Ajax 145): βοτὰ καὶ λείαν (*bota kai leian*), cattle and plunder: *i.e.*, " cattle, yes—and plundered cattle too."

Hendiadys always raises the qualifying word to the superlative degree.

But we are not to suppose that whenever we find two words joined together by the word "and" we have the figure of *Hendiadys.* It may be *Epitheton.*

It does not follow that in every case where two nouns are thus joined we have only one idea. In the first place, there must be something to attract our attention, something out of the ordinary usage, and sometimes not strictly according to the *letter*.

And occasionally, even in an undoubted *Hendiadys*, the two words may be equally true when taken separately and severally, as when joined together in one. In these cases both letter and figure are correct, and the passage gains considerable additional light and force.

Another point to be remembered is that the two words must have a certain *relation* to each other: one must indicate a property of the other, or be associated in some way with it.

There cannot be a *Hendiadys* where the two words are opposed in any way in their signification; nor even when there is no real connection between them.

For example : Phil. i. 25, " I know that I shall *abide* and *continue* with you all for your *furtherance* and *joy* of faith." Here, in each case, there are two distinct ideas : the abiding in life, and continuing with the Philippian saints ; also, their " furtherance " was one thing, and their " joy " another.

On the other hand, verse 11 may be taken in both ways: " Being filled with the fruits of righteousness, which are by Jesus Christ, unto the glory and praise of God." This may be two things: either, to the glory of God, and the praise of God; or it may be only one: " Unto the praise, yes—the glorious praise, of God."

So Rom. xv. 4 : " Whatsoever things were written aforetime were written for our learning, that we through *patience* and *comfort* of the Scriptures might have hope."

Here there are two things, not one, because *comforting* is not a proper qualification of patience.

In reading this verse, therefore, a pause must be made after the word " patience " (which we possess), so as to distinguish it from the "comfort" (which the Scriptures give).

In most cases, the context and the analogy of Scripture will decide the doubt.

Some of the examples we present more by way of suggestion than actual illustration. About most of them there can be no doubt: but a few (such as Gen. ii. 9) may be open to question; and these are submitted for the judgment and consideration of the reader.

1. NOUNS.

Gen. i. 26. — " Let us make man in our **image**, after our **likeness** ": *i.e.*, in the likeness of our image.* Not two things but one, though two words are employed.

Gen. ii. 9.—" The tree of knowledge of **good** and **evil** ": *i.e.*, of evil enjoyment.

Gen. iii. 16.—" Multiplying I will multiply (*i.e.*, " I will greatly multiply," see *Polyptoton*) thy **sorrow** and thy conception ": *i.e.*, thy sorrow, yes—and thy conceiving sorrow too: [*for*] " in sorrow thou shalt bring forth children."

Gen. iv. 4.—" And Abel, he also brought of the **firstlings** of his flock and of the **fat** thereof": *i.e.*, *he brought the firstlings of his flock, yes—and the fattest ones too*, or the fattest firstlings of his flock, with the emphasis on " fattest."

Gen. xix. 24.—" Then the LORD rained upon Sodom and upon Gomorrah **brimstone** and **fire** from the LORD out of heaven ": *i.e.*,

---

* " Image " is צֶלֶם (*tzelem*), εἰκών (*eikōn*), 1 Cor. xi. 7; Col. iii. 10. " Likeness " is דְּמוּת (*d'mūth*), ὁμοίωσις (*homoiōsis*), Jas. iii. 9.

brimstone, yes—and burning brimstone too; or, simply "burning brimstone" with emphasis on "burning."

1 Sam. xvii. 40.—"And put them in his **shepherd's vessel** and in his **leather bag**": *i.e.*, *in his shepherd's leather bag.* This is the "scrip" of Matt. x. 10. Mark vi. 8. Luke xxii. 35, 36.

1 Sam. xxviii. 3.—They "buried him in **Ramah** and his own **city**": *i.e.*, *in Ramah, yes—even in his own city;* or, in his own city, Ramah.

2 Sam. xx. 19.—"Thou seekest to destroy **a city** and **a mother** in Israel": *i.e.*, *a city, yes—and a mother city too*;* or, a metropolitan city. Neither the A.V. nor R.V. sees the figure here; but both translate the words literally, though the figure is obvious.

1 Kings xx. 33.—"Now the men **divined** and **hasted**": *i.e.*, divined, yes—and quickly too; or, as in A.V., "diligently observed," with the emphasis on the word diligently. See Ginsburg's *Introduction*, page 438.

1 Chron. xxii. 5.—"**Of fame** and **of glory**"; *i.e.*, of glorious fame.

2 Chron. ii. 9.—"The house which I am about to build, shall be **great** and **wonderful**." (Heb., see margin).

Here, the A.V. sees the figure, and translates it accordingly: "shall be wonderful great." The exact sense, however, is "shall be great, yes—and wonderfully great too."

2 Chron. xvi. 14.—"**Sweet** odours and **divers** kinds": *i.e.*, sweet odours, yes—and of all manner of kinds.

Job x. 17.—"**Changes** and **war** are against me": *i.e.*, changes, yes—and warlike ones too—are against me: *i.e.*, successive changes of attack. Or it may be read: "changes, aye—a host of them."

Job x. 21.—"Before I go whence I shall not return, even to the land of **darkness** and the **shadow** of death": *i.e.*, the land of darkness, yes—and the darkness of death's shadow too. Compare Ps. xxiii. 4; and see under *Periphrasis*.

Ps. lxxiv. 16.—"Thou hast prepared the **light** and the **sun**": *i.e.*, sunlight.

Ps. xcvi. 7.—"Give unto the LORD **glory** and **strength**": *i.e.*, glory, yes—and great glory too. See under *Metonymy*.

---

* In the same way "villages" are called *daughters* (Num. xxi. 25, 32; xxxii. 42. Josh. xvii. 11. Judges xi. 26.

Ps. cxvi. 1.—" I love the LORD, because he hath heard my **voice** *and* my **supplications** ": *i.e.*, my supplicating voice, with emphasis on " supplicating."

Ps. cxix. 138.—" Thy testimonies that thou hast commanded are righteous and very faithful." So the A.V. correctly according to the figure. But, literally, this verse reads : " Thou hast commanded the righteousness of thy **testimonies** and **faithfulness** exceeding " (see A.V. margin) : *i.e.*, thy testimonies, yes—thy exceeding faithful testimonies.

Isa. i. 13.—" I am not able [*to endure*] your **iniquity** and **assembly** ": *i.e.*, your iniquity, yes—your iniquitous assemblies, or your festal iniquity.

See R.V., and margin, and also A.V., for the confusion and obscurity through failing to see the combined figures of *Ellipsis* and *Hendiadys* in this sentence.

Jer. xxii. 3.—" Execute ye **judgment** and **righteousness** ": *i.e.*, execute ye judgment, yea—and righteous judgment too.

Jer. xxii. 15.—" And do **judgment** and **justice** ": *i.e.*, execute judgment, yes—and righteous judgment too.

Jer. xxix. 11.—" I know the thoughts that I think toward you, saith the LORD, thoughts of peace, and not of evil, to give you **an end** and **expectation**."

Here the A.V. gives this in the margin, and translates it " to give you an expected end." The R.V. renders it " to give you hope in your latter end," and puts in the margin " Heb., *a latter end and hope.*"

All this is a recognition of the difficulty, without grasping or catching the spirit of the figure : " to give you the end, yes—the end you hope for ": *i.e.*, the end which I have promised and on which I have caused you to hope and depend. All this, and more, is contained in and expressed by the figure *Hendiadys.*

Jer. xxxvi. 27.—" Then the word of Jehovah came to Jeremiah after that the king had burned **the roll** and **the words** which Baruch wrote ": *i.e.*, the roll, yes—and the roll that contained the words of Jehovah too.

Dan. viii. 10.—" It cast down some **of the host** and **of the stars** ": *i.e.*, *of the starry host.* Only one thing, not two.

Zeph. i. 16.—" A day of **trumpet** and **alarm** ": *i.e.*, of the trumpet, yes—and an alarming trumpet too.

Matt. iii. 11.—" He shall baptize with the Holy Ghost and with fire."

First observe that there are no articles. It is ἐν πνεύματι ἁγίῳ καὶ πυρί (*en pneumati hagiō kai puri*), *with Holy Spirit and fire : i.e.,* with Holy Spirit, yes—and burning purifying spirit too. Not two things, but one thing : Judgment !

The contrast is with John's baptism, which was with *water* which mingled together the chaff and the wheat (as the water sign has done in all ages). But the new baptism of Christ should not be like *that.* It would separate the chaff from the wheat by burning it up, as the Baptist goes on to declare, without a break in his words : " whose fan is in his hand, and he will throughly purge his floor, and gather his wheat into his garner: but he will burn up the chaff with unquench- able fire." The " fire " in verse 11 is different from the " fire " in verse 12. In verse 11 it is a figure for purifying and cleansing ; and in verse 12 it is a literal fire that is meant. But the effect of its operations are the same in each case.

The Baptist is speaking, not of the Church, but of Christ and His kingdom, as was prophesied in Isa. iv. 3, 4 : "And it shall come to pass that he that is left in Zion, and he that remaineth in Jerusalem, shall be called holy, even every one that is written among the living in Jerusalem : when the Lord shall have washed away the filth of the daughters of Zion, and shall have purged the blood of Jerusalem from the midst thereof by **the spirit of judgment** and by **the spirit of burning** " : *i.e.,* by spirit of judgment—His consuming.

This is the purging of the floor, and the burning up of the chaff, which the Baptist speaks of in verse 12. John only foretold it ; but Christ shall do it in the day referred to in Isa. iv.

"The Spirit" is the Worker, and "the fire" denotes His operations, searching, consuming, and purifying. The day of the Lord's coming will be " like a refiner's fire . . . And he shall sit as a refiner and purifier of silver: and he shall purify the sons of Levi, and purge them as gold and silver" (Mal. iii. 1-4). That day " shall burn as an oven ; and all the proud, yea, and all that do wickedly, shall be stubble (as in Matt. iii. 12) : and the day that cometh shall burn them up, saith the Lord of hosts." Mal. iv. 1 (iii. 19).

That future judgment is referred to, and not any ecclesiastical ordinance, is clear from verse 10.

When the future baptism of the members of Christ's mystical body with the Holy Spirit is spoken of there is no mention of or reference to fire.

Christ "fans" to get rid of the chaff. Satan "sifts" to get rid of the wheat (Luke xxii. 31).

Matt. iv. 16.—"In a **region** and **shadow** of death." This does not denote two places, but one : in a region, yes—in death's dark region too, as is clear from Isa. ix. 1, 2 (viii. 23-ix. 1).

Matt. xxiv. 30.—"They shall see the Son of man coming in the clouds of heaven with **power** and **great glory**": *i.e.,* with power, yes—with great and glorious power.

Matt. xxiv. 31.—"And he shall send his angels with a great sound of a trumpet." In the margin we learn that the Greek is "with **a trumpet** and **a great voice**." Here, it is clear that we have not two things but one : "a trumpet, yes—and a great sounding trumpet too."

Both the A.V. and R.V. recognize the Figure *Hendiadys* here. But the A.V. gives the literal Greek (according to one reading) in the margin ; while the R.V. gives as an alternative rendering, " Or, *a trumpet of great sound* "; which represents the change of the second noun into an adjective in a different way.

Luke i. 17.—"He shall go before Him in the **spirit** and **power** of Elijah ": *i.e.,* in spirit, yes—in Elijah's powerful spirit too.

Luke xxi. 15.—"For I will give you a **mouth** and **wisdom** ": *i.e., a mouth (Metonymy,* for speech), *yes — and a wise mouth. too ;* such wisdom of speech that "all your adversaries shall not be able to gainsay nor resist."

John i. 17.—"The law was given by Moses, but **grace** and **truth** came by Jesus Christ." This must be the figure *Hendiadys,* because otherwise the words taken literally would not be true to fact.

Was there no " grace " in the Law ? How came only Israel to have it and not the Babylonians, Egyptians, Philistines, Assyrians, etc. ? Yes ; it was all grace : as God asks and tells them so earnestly and so often ; in Deut. iv. 32-40, and other places.

And was there no " truth " in the Law ? Yes ; surely, every word was truth.

But, in John i. 17, the contrast is between one thing that was given by Moses, and another and a different thing that came by Jesus Christ.

The figure *Hendiadys* explains the difficulty and sheds light on the verse.

The Law was given by Moses, and there was grace in it; and moreover it was truth itself :. " but grace, yes—and true grace too (the real thing) came by Jesus Christ.

John iii. 5.—This is literally, " Except a man shall have been begotten of water and spirit." There is no article to either of the two nouns.

That only one thing is meant by the two words is clear from verses 6 and 8, where only the Spirit (the one) is mentioned.

The Lord is speaking to Nicodemus of "earthly things" (see verse 12). And as "a master in Israel," he knew (or ought to have known) perfectly well the prophecy of Ezek. xxxvi. 25-27 concerning the kingdom (not the Church). Concerning Israel, in the day of their restoration to their own land, Jehovah had declared : " Then will I sprinkle clean water upon you, and ye shall be clean . . . And I will put my spirit within you," etc.

The cleansing of that day is not to be with literal water, as in the ceremonial cleansings of the Law, but with the Spirit of God.

Hence only one thing is meant :—" Except a man be begotten of water, yes—and spiritual water too, he cannot enter into the kingdom of God." That spiritual water stands, by another figure (*Metonymy*), for the Holy Spirit Himself: as is clear from John vii. 38, 39: " water— (But this spake He of the Spirit, which they that believe on Him should receive . . .)."

Hence there is no reference here to ceremonial or ecclesiastical water—but to that baptism of the Spirit which is the one indispensable condition of entering into the kingdom of God ; a moral sphere, which includes and embraces the Church of God, here and now, as well as the future kingdom foretold by God through the prophets.

John iv. 21-24.—The one subject of these verses is—What is true *worship* ? its nature and its character. It was the sixth word of the Lord Jesus to the woman of Samaria : " Woman, believe me, the hour cometh, when ye shall neither in this mountain, nor yet at Jerusalem, worship the Father. Ye (*Samaritans*) worship ye know not what: we (*Jews*) know what we worship : for salvation is of (*i.e.*, proceeds from) the Jews. But the hour cometh, and now is, when the true worshippers shall worship the Father in spirit and in truth : for the Father seeketh such to worship Him. God *is* a spirit (*i.e.*, a Spiritual Being) : and they that worship him must worship *him* in spirit and in truth."

Here, notice first that there is only one preposition (ἐν, *en*), " in," for the two nouns. It is not to be repeated as in the A.V. It is " in spirit and truth." Moreover, one of the usages of this preposition with the noun turns it into an adverb: so that " in spirit " means " spiritually ": *i.e.*, in accordance with another of its meanings, with the spirit, or with our spirits. Then, the figure *Hendiadys* comes in to strengthen this. " God is a Spirit : and they that worship Him must worship Him spiritually, yes—in a truly spiritual manner too."

Observe, further, that the Lord says, " MUST " ! There is nothing left to our choice or taste in the matter. This " great rubrick " over-rides all others : so that it is of no use for anyone to say : " I like this form of service," or " I prefer that kind of service." It says, " MUST " ! God is a Spirit, and therefore He cannot be worshipped by the flesh : *i.e.*, by means of any of our *senses*, which are essentially of the flesh. We cannot worship God with our *eyes*, by looking at decorations, however beautiful ; we cannot worship Him with our *ears*, by listening to music, however ravishing ; we cannot worship Him with our *noses*, by the smelling of incense, however sweet ; no ! not by any separately or by all of them together can we worship a Spiritual Being. All such things are, really, only hindrances ; which are destructive of all true spiritual worship. We, who cannot pray or listen to a prayer without wandering thoughts, need no such temptations to attract or distract our spirits from doing that which God can alone accept. It is a positive cruelty to professing worshippers to present anything to their senses. It is a device of the devil to destroy spiritual worship, and to render obedience to this great rubric impossible. Hence this impressive figure used here, in conjunction with the word " MUST." It is the same word as in chap. iii. 7 : " Ye MUST be born again " ; and chap. iii. 14 : " The Son of man MUST be lifted up." So here, in the next chap., iv. 24 : " They that worship God, who is a spirit, MUST worship Him with the spirit, yes—really and truly with the spirit." See further under *Hyperbaton ;* which is used in this verse in order to enchance and enforce this interpretation of these words.

Acts i. 25.—" That he may take part of this ministry and apostleship, from which Judas by trangression fell ": *i.e ,* this ministry, yes—this apostolic ministry, with emphasis on the adjective " apostolic," which is obtained by exchange for the noun.

Acts iii. 14.—" But ye denied the **Holy One** and the **Just**." Here, it is perfectly clear that only One Person is meant, though two are apparently described : *i.e.*, " ye denied the Holy One, yes—the righteous Holy One, and desired a murderer (an unrighteous criminal) to be granted unto you." By the use of this figure here the contrast between that " righteous " one and the criminal is strongly marked and emphasized.

Acts xiv. 13.—" Then the priest of Jupiter which was (*i.e.*, whose statue stood) before their city, brought **oxen** and **garlands** unto the gates, and would have done sacrifice."

In the heathen worship, the victim to be sacrificed was always decorated with a garland immediately before the sacrifice took place, as may be seen to-day in pictures and sculptures. There were two things then brought by the priest, but there is only one idea ; and the figure tells us and shows us that every arrangement had been made, and that all was ready ; nothing hindered the immediate offering of the sacrifice. " The priest . . . brought oxen, yes—and they had their garlands on too." All this gives a vivid picture ; and the whole scene is presented to our minds by the employment of this simple yet beautiful and expressive figure, " oxen and garlands."

Acts xxiii. 6.—" Of the **hope** and **resurrection** of the dead I am called in question " : *i.e., of the hope, yes—the resurrection hope* . . . am I called in question.

Rom. i. 5.—" By whom we have received **grace** and **apostle-ship** " : *i.e.*, grace, yes—and apostolic grace too.

Rom. ii. 27.—" **Letter** and **circumcision.**" See under *Ellipsis,* page 23.

Rom. xi. 17.—" And with them partakest of the **root** and the **fatness** of the olive tree " : *i.e.*, the root, yes—and the fat or prolific root ; or the rich blessings which come forth from that root.*

1 Cor. ii. 4.—" In demonstration of the **Spirit** and of **power** " : *i.e.*, of the Spirit, yes—of the power of the Spirit too.

1 Cor. xi. 7.—" Forasmuch as he is the **image** and **glory** (*i.e.*, the glorious image) of God."

Eph. iv. 11.—" And he gave some, apostles ; and some, prophets ; and some, evangelists ; and some, **pastors** and **teachers** " : *i.e.*, pastors (or shepherds), yes—shepherds who should feed too ; or teachers, yes—teachers who should shepherd too. Not two classes of persons, but one ; implying that a shepherd who did not feed would fail in his duty ; and so would a teacher who failed to be a pastor.

---

* See Article on " The Fig, the Olive, and the Vine " in *Things to Come* for July, 1899.

Eph. v. 5.—" Hath any inheritance in the kingdom **of Christ and of God**": *i.e.*, the kingdom of Christ, yes—of Christ who is truly God.

Eph. vi. 18.—" Praying always with all **prayer** and **supplication** in the Spirit, and watching thereunto with all **perseverance** and **supplication** for all saints ": *i.e.*, praying with all prayer (this is *Polyptoton, q.v.*) and supplication : *i.e.*, prayer, yes—with supplicating prayer too ; and watching thereunto with every kind of supplication, yes, with persevering supplication too.

Col. ii. 8.—" Beware lest any man spoil you through **philosophy** and **vain deceit.**"

Here, we have not two things, but one : through philosophy, yes —a vain, deceitful philosophy too.

Col. ii. 18.—" Let no man beguile you of your reward in a voluntary **humility** and **worshipping** of angels, intruding into those things which he hath not seen, vainly puffed up by his fleshly mind."

The marginal notes in A.V. and R.V. show the difficulties created by not seeing the *Hendiadys* here.

It is certain that θρησκεία (*threeskeia*) means *religion* (not *worship*), and is so rendered in all the other places where it occurs (see Acts xxvi. 5. Jas. i. 26, 27). It must be so rendered here : " **humility** and **religion** " : *i.e.*, humility, yes—the religious humility of angels.

If we observe this figure, it throws all the other words into their right places, and enables us to give them their right meanings. This gives sense also to the reading of all the Textual Critics, and with the R.V. in omitting the negative μή (*mee*) before the word " seen." It also saves our having to condemn these Colossian saints for angelworship ! Surely there is nothing in this epistle to warrant the conclusion that they had fallen as low as that ! The passage is a warning to the saints who had been well-instructed as to their standing in Christ that they were not to forget in their worshipping the Father that they had a higher standing than that of angels, even that of beloved sons, in the acceptance of " the Beloved One." They had " boldness of access " as sons, and not merely that which pertained to " angels " as messengers.

We cannot think that this is a mere warning not to make angels an object of worship. Such a thought is far below the whole scope and teaching of the epistle.

The verse then will read : " Let no one deprive you of your prize, having pleasure in (so Lightfoot) the religious humility of angels, taking his stand upon (so R.V. margin) the things which he hath seen, vainly puffed up by the mind of his flesh (*i.e.*, by his old nature) and not holding the head," etc.

If we hold the great truth of the " Mystery " concerning the Head and members of the Body of Christ, we shall understand and take our proper standing before God, which He himself has given us.

To cease from " holding the Head " is to lose practically all our special privileges as members of His Body. It is to take up an attitude before God, in our access to Him, below that in which His love and grace has set us. It is to take the place of religious humility as the angels, as servants instead of sons—even the sons of God. It is to worship with veiled faces at a distance, instead of with unveiled faces, beholding the glory of the Lord. It is a feigned humility, not apprehending the exceeding riches of the grace of God toward us in Christ Jesus; which is sure to issue in a regard for visible things and religious ordinances which are the natural objects of the fleshly mind (the Old nature), the only things which it can comprehend or understand. Hence the theme of ordinances being done away in Christ follows in verses 11-15. " Which sort of things have indeed an appearance of wisdom in self-devised religious observances and humiliation (of mind) and discipline (of the body); yet are not really of any value to remedy indulgence of the flesh* (*i.e.*, the Old nature)."

The exhortation is plural; but the warning is directed against some individual, who, puffed up and led by his Old nature, would fain teach them that as angels in their worship "veiled their faces " and take the most humble place, therefore it was only becoming that they should do the same. These were the only things which the " flesh " could see; this was the standing that the flesh would fain take! But they were not to be thus defrauded of that high calling and standing which they had in Christ, and which enabled them to draw near with boldness to the throne of grace.

1 **Thess. ii. 12.**—" That ye would walk worthy of God, who hath called you unto his **kingdom** and **glory** ": *i.e.*, his kingdom, yes—his glorious kingdom too; or, his glorious kingdom, with emphasis on the word " glorious."

1 **Tim. iii. 15.**—" The Church of the living God, the **pillar** and **ground** of the truth."

---

* See R.V. and Lightfoot (*Com. in loco*) for this beautiful and happy rendering.

This is spoken of "the truth"—"the mystery of the faith" (verse 9), and "the mystery" which is "confessedly great" (verse 16). This is the pillar, yes—the great foundation pillar of the truth: *i.e.*, Christ Mystical, as set forth in verse 16.*

2 Tim. i. 10.—"Our Saviour Jesus Christ, who hath abolished death and hath brought **life** and **immortality** to light": *i.e.*, life, yes —and immortal life too.

2 Tim. iv. 1, 2.—This verse requires re-translating; owing to the Figures, and the older readings witnessed to by the Critical Texts and the R.V.

" I adjure thee, therefore, before God, yes—Christ Jesus, I mean (1 Tim. v. 21), who is about to judge the living and dead; and [*I adjure thee*] by His appearing, yes—and His royal appearing too, Preach the Word." For this judgment shall be when He "shall sit upon the throne of His glory," not in the act of His first shining forth at His *epiphaneia*. The adjuration is similar to Deut. iv. 26; xxx. 19; xxxi. 28, and is called forth by the fact that the Scriptures are God-breathed and profitable. " Therefore " it is that " I adjure thee " to preach the word. The solemn adjuration is needed, because of the fact that "the time will come when they will not endure sound teaching." This is no reason why preachers should seek for something that men will endure, but it is given as the very reason why the word of God and that alone should be persistently proclaimed and taught. It is a reason so strange that the charge has to be set in the full view of coming judgment. Hence, in verses 1 and 8, the fact of judgment is twice stated. The charge is beset with judgment before and behind.

The figure *Hendiadys*, which the Spirit twice employs to enhance the force of the words, the enemy uses to obscure it; trading by his devices on the ignorance of those who profess to be preachers of this Word.

Titus ii. 13.—" Looking for that blessed **hope** and the glorious **appearing**." Not two things but one : our hope is the glorious appearing !

The latter clause is also *Hendiadys* : One Person being meant, not two : the appearing of the great God, yes—even our Saviour Jesus Christ : *i.e.*, our Divine Saviour.

Jas. iii. 9.—"Therewith bless we God, even the Father." Lit., the **God** and **Father**: *i.e.*, *God, yes—even that God who is our Father.*

---

* See *The Mystery*, by the same author and publisher. Price sixpence.

2 Pet. i. 3.—" Through the knowledge of him who hath called us to **glory** and **virtue**."

But the Greek is " by," as stated in the margin, διά (*dia*) with the genitive, denoting the cause or instrument. The R.V. renders it " by his own glory and virtue" (and tells us, in the margin, that " some ancient authorities read *through glory and virtue*"), translating the figure literally, and (like the A.V.), missing the force of it.

But it is one thing, not two.

Note that the Critical Texts read ἰδίᾳ (*ideā*), *his own*, instead of διά (*dia*), *through*, the dative case denoting the agency, *by*.

Note also that ἀρετή (*aretee*) means *goodness, excellence in art or workmanship ; goodness*, as shown by the possession of reputation for bravery and merit. This is what God has called His people by : His own goodness, will and power, yes—His glorious power too ; His own excellent workmanship, His own gracious dealing.

2 Pet. i. 16.—" When we made known unto you the **power** and **coming** " : *i.e.*, either the coming power, or the powerful coming, or both.

2 Pet. i. 17.—" For he received from God the Father **honour** and **glory** " : *i.e.*, honour, yes—and glorious honour too.

Christ received this glorious honour, which was put upon Him, " on the holy mount " of transfiguration.

The wondrous act which there took place was the official anointing, appointing, and consecrating of Christ for His Priestly office and sacrificial work. The only subject spoken of on that mount was " the Exodus which He should accomplish at Jerusalem " (Luke ix. 31). Not the death to which man should put Him, but " which He should accomplish" Himself. Heb. ii. 9 distinctly tells us *why* Christ was thus crowned : 2 Pet. i. 17, 18, tells us *where*.

It tells us that He was made a little lower than the angels for the suffering of death ; crowned with glory and honour, that He, by the grace of God, should taste death for every man " (see *Synecdoché*).

This is confirmed by Exod. xxviii. 2, where we are distinctly told that, when Aaron was consecrated to his priestly office, " that he may minister unto me in the priest's office," " thou (Moses) shalt make holy garments for Aaron thy brother, for glory and for beauty." Here are the same two words, τιμὴ καὶ δόξα (*timee kai doxa*), for honour, yes—and for glorious honour too !

Can we resist the conclusion that on the Holy Mount the Lord Jesus was thus consecrated for His (Melchisedekian) priesthood. True,

Moses was there, and Elijah ; but this glorious honour with which
Christ was clothed and crowned was put upon Him by no earthly
hands. It came " from the excellent glory."*

Rev. v. 10.—Here we must adopt the rendering of the R.V. :
" And madest them to be unto our God a **kingdom** and **priests,** and
they reign upon the earth " : *i.e.*, a kingdom, yes—and a great priestly
kingdom too, the plural " priests " being put by *Heterosis* for the
singular, denoting the greatness.

2. VERBS.

Matt. xiii. 23.—The *Hendiadys* is disguised in the A.V. through
the separation of the two words : " He that was sown upon the good
ground, this is he who **hears** and **understands** the word." The
person who heareth and understandeth is one. One act is meant, and
not two. All hear, but this one heareth, yes—and understandeth it too.

Luke vi. 48.—" He is like a man . . . who **dug** and **deepened,**
and laid the foundation on the rock."

Here, the A.V. renders it : " and digged deep." The R.V. : " who
digged and went deep."

It is clear that we have the figure *Hendiadys* in the two
verbs : the man digged, yes—and very deep ; deeper and deeper
indeed till he got to the rock itself.

Acts ix. 31.—" Then . . . the churches . . . were **edified** and
walking in the fear of the Lord . . . were multiplied.

Here, in the Received Text, the verbs are not in the same inflection.
But the Critical Texts (L.T.Tr.A.WH., and R.V.) read : οἰκοδομουμένη
καὶ πορευομένη (*oikodomoumenee kai poreuomenee*), *being* **built up** *and*
progressing : *i.e.*, being built up, yes—and increasingly so too.

Note also that the Critical Texts read : ἐκκλησία (*ecclesia*)
assembly (instead of plural) ; and ἐπληθύνετο (*epleethuneto*), *was
multiplied* (instead of plural).

Acts xiii. 41.—" Behold, ye despisers, and **wonder** and **perish** :
i.e., perish, yes—and perish wonderfully too.

1 Thess. iv. 1.—" As ye have received of us how ye ought **to
walk** and **to please** God " : *i.e.*, how ye ought *to walk, yes—and how
to please God in your walk*, with emphasis on the verb *to please.*

---

* For further elucidation of the Transfiguration and its objects, see *Christ's
Prophetic Teaching*, by the same author and publisher.

2 Pet. iii. 12.—" Looking for and hasting unto the coming of the day of God." Here, " looking for" is προσδοκάω (*prosdokaō*),* and " hasting" is σπεύδω (*speudō*), *to hasten.* Everywhere else† the latter verb is intransitive; but here it is *transitive* to correspond with " looking for," and means *to be eager* or *earnest for a thing.* It qualifies the " looking for" and not the " coming" itself: *i.e.,* looking for, yes—and earnestly looking for that coming too.

We cannot hasten that day, which is fixed in the counsels of God, but we can be more eager and earnest in our looking for it. The R.V. has " earnestly desiring the coming." This is better; but it is stronger when we recognize the figure—*looking for* and *being earnest for*, which is the figure *Hendiadys ; earnestly looking for*, with the emphasis on earnestly.

Rev. xx. 4.—" And they lived and reigned with Christ a thousand years ": *i.e.*, they lived, yes—and they reigned too.

Rev. xxii. 17.—" And let him that is athirst come. And whosoever willeth, let him take." Not two classes of persons, but one. Not thirsty ones who do not will ; or willing ones who do not thirst ; but *willing thirsty ones*, let them come: See under *Epistrophe.*

---

* Matt. xi. 3 ; xxiv. 50. Luke i. 21 ; iii. 15 ; vii. 19, 20 ; viii. 40 ; xii. 46. Acts iii. 5 ; x. 24 ; xxvii. 33 ; xxviii. 6 (twice). 2 Pet. iii. 12, 13, 14.

† Luke ii. 16 ; xix. 5, 6. Acts xx. 16 ; xxii. 18.

HENDIATRIS ; or, THREE FOR ONE.

Three words used, but one thing meant.

THOUGH the Greeks did not name such a figure, it is clear that it is employed in Scripture. For we sometimes find three nouns instead of two, and in these cases there are two nouns exalted to the place of emphatic adjectives, which are thus raised to equal importance with the subject itself.

Jer. iv. 2.—" And thou shalt swear, The LORD liveth, in **truth**, in **judgment**, and in **righteousness** ": *i.e.*, thou shalt swear, in truth (*i.e.*, truly, yes—justly and righteously).

In swearing by Jehovah in truth, justice and righteousness is included ; not only that people swear the truth (Lev. xix. 12. Num. xxx. 3. Jer. v. 2. Matt. v. 33), but also that they swear by Jehovah alone (*i.e.*, justly and righteously), and not by idols also, as, according to Zeph. i. 5, they did in his day.*

Dan. iii. 7.—" All the **people**, the **nations**, and the **languages** fell down and worshipped the golden image that Nebuchadnezzar the king had set up."

Now " languages " do not fall down ; neither do they worship ; Therefore the words are used as a figure, and the figure is *Hendiatris* : All the people, yes—and people of all nations and languages, fell down and worshipped.

Matt. vi. 13.—" For thine is the **kingdom**, and the **power**, and the **glory** " : *i.e.*, for thine is the kingdom, yes—and the powerful and glorious kingdom too.

John xiv. 6.—" I am the **way**, and the **truth**, and the **life**." This is hidden in the A.V. which ignores the first " and."

The whole subject of conversation here is Christ as " the way." See the context. We have here therefore another example of *Hendiatris* : " I am the way, yes—the true and living way ; for no man cometh unto the Father, but by me."

Of course, Christ is the " truth," as He is also the " life " : but this is not what is stated in this verse. Here, only one subject is in question : *viz.*, " the way " ; and the other two nouns are used to define its true nature and character.

---

* Scott, *Com. in loco.*

CATACHRESIS; or, INCONGRUITY.

One word changed for another only remotely connected with it.

Cat'-a-chree-sis. Greek, κατάχρησις, from κατά (*kata*), *against*, and χρῆσθαι (*chreesthai*), *to use.* Hence, *misuse.*

Catachresis is a figure by which one word is changed for another, and this against or contrary to the ordinary usage and meaning of it. The word that is changed is transferred from its strict and usual signification to another that is only remotely connected with it. Hence called by the Latins ABUSIO, *abuse.*

In METONYMY there is a *relation* between the two words. In SYNECDOCHE there is some *association* between them. In HENDIADYS there is a real *connection* between them. But in CATACHRESIS all this is wanting, and the two words or meanings, though they may have between them something remotely akin or analagous, yet have no real or strict relation; and the connection is often incongruous.

When man uses this figure, it may often be from ignorance or through carelessness, but often with good effect. Attention is sometimes arrested by a delightful incongruity, as when Young writes:

" Her voice was but the *shadow* of a sound ":

where the sense is very forcibly conveyed by changing the ordinary usage of the word " shadow."

" Sorrow was *big* at her heart."

Or when we say that a thing is " beautiful to the ear," or " melodious to the eye "; or, when we apply the word " sweet" to things other than articles of food which we taste.

But, when the Holy Spirit uses this figure, it is in order to arrest us; and to attract our attention, by the apparent incongruity, and thus fix it on what He says.

Sometimes the translators introduce a *Catachresis*, where there is none in the Original: *e.g.*, in Ex. xxxviii. 8, they say: " Moses made the laver of brass, and the foot of it of brass out of the looking-*glasses* of the women." (But see margin.) The R.V. avoids this by rendering the word correctly " mirrors."

The figure does not mislead; it merely acts as spice or condiment does to food.

Catachresis is of three kinds :—

i. Of two words, where the meanings are remotely akin.

ii. Of two words, where the meanings are different.

iii. Of one word, where the Greek receives its real meaning by permutation from the Hebrew, or some other language, or foreign usage.

i. *Of two words, where the meanings are remotely akin.*

Lev. xxvi. 30.—" I will cast your carcases upon the carcases of your idols."

Here the word " carcase " is changed from its strictly correct application to flesh and blood, and its use applied to the fragments of wood or stone of an idol.

Num. ix. 18.—" At the mouth of Jehovah."

Here it is translated " commandment " : but the figure arrests us ; and points us to the *Divine* Source of the command as opposed to any human injunction. See *Epistrophe.*

Deut. xvi. 7.—" And thou shalt cook and eat it in the place which the LORD thy God shall choose."

Both A.V. and R.V. render it " roast." The latter however puts *seethe* in the margin. " Seethe " is sometimes used for *cook :* and thus there is a remote connection with *roast*, as commanded, in Exod. xii. 8, 9. So 1 Sam. ii. 15. Compare Joel iii. 13 (iv. 13).

Deut. xxxii. 14.—" Thou didst drink the pure blood of the grape."

Here " blood " is used by *Catachresis.* For, as " blood " is that which comes from man, so the juice is that which comes from the grape. There is an incongruity, because the two are only remotely akin. But our attention is attracted to what is being said.

2 Sam. xxiii. 17.—" Is not this the blood of the men that went in jeopardy of their lives ? "

The water which the three mighty men brought to David is called their blood : and thus, in one incongruous word, is eloquently expressed the shedding of their own blood, which the men had risked for David's sake.

Job iv. 12.—" Now a word was brought by stealth to me."

This is a most unusual way of describing an angelic communication.

Ps. lxxiv. 1.—" Why doth thine anger smoke against the sheep of thy pasture ? "

Ps. lxxx. 4 (5).—" How long wilt thou smoke against the prayer of thy people ? " (margin).

Used by *Catachresis* for the heat of anger.

Ps. lxxxviii. 5.—" Free among the dead " : *i.e.*, set at liberty is put by *Catachresis* for cast off, deserted.

Isa. lxii. 5.—" For as a young man marrieth a virgin, so shall thy sons marry thee."

To speak of sons marrying their mother is incongruous, and yet what else could be said ? How else could it be expressed ? But בָּעַל (*baal*) means not only *to marry*, but *to possess;* or as we express it " *to have and to hold* " in possession. This is the primitive and proper meaning of the word, and *to marry* is only a secondary usage. It means *to have, own, possess.* See 1 Chron. iv. 22, " who *had the dominion* in Moab " ; Isa. xxvi. 13, " other lords beside thee have *had dominion over* us."

It is from not seeing the beautiful figure *Catachresis* here, by which, through what looks like an incongruity, that Bishop Lowth and others suggest an emendation of the Hebrew Text, by reading בֹּנָיִךְ (*bonahyik*), *thy builders*, for בָּנָיִךְ (*bahnayik*), *thy sons*. The change is plausible ; but it is destitute of any MS. or other ancient authority ; and such arbitrary alterations of the Text are to be deprecated, being purely conjectural. Moreover, it is unnecessary, for the builder is not necessarily the possessor or the owner. The apparent incongruity of the figure arrests our attention ; and, when we give the attention which is thus demanded, we find the passage means that as a young man marries a virgin, so shall Zion's sons hold her in sure and happy possession.

Hos. xiv. 2 (3).—" So will we render the calves of our lips " : *i.e.*, our lips as sacrifices. See under *Metonymy ;* and compare Heb. xiii. 15.

Matt. xii. 5.—" On the sabbath days the Priests in the temple profane the sabbath, and are blameless." It sounds incongruous to state this as a fact : but it expresses what was true according to the mistaken notions of the Pharisees as to manual works performed on the sabbath.

Rom. vii. 23.—" I see another law in my members." He means that he sees *sin :* which, through the authority with which it rules his members, he calls, by *Catachresis*, " law." See under *Antanaclasis*.

I Cor. i. 25.—" The foolishness of God is wiser than men ; and the weakness of God is stronger than men." It is incongruous to speak of " foolishness " or " weakness " with respect to God. So we are arrested by the use of this figure *Catachresis*.

Col. iii. 5.—" Mortify therefore your members which are upon the earth." The members which commit the sins are put by a forcible *Catachresis* for the sins themselves. For the sins are immediately enumerated, not the members. See chap. ii. 11.

ii. *Of two words, where the meanings are different.*

Exod. v. 21.—" Ye have made our savour to stink in the eyes of Pharaoh."

Here " stink " and " eyes " are incongruously conjoined to call our attention to the highest degree of abhorrence.

Exod. xx. 18 (15).—" And all the people saw the thunderings."

Here seeing is joined to what was only heard. But see under *Zeugma*, by which one verb is made to go with two different nouns. (See Rev. i. 12 below).

Mark vii. 21, 22.—" Out of the heart proceed evil thoughts . . . an evil eye."

Here the *Catachresis* is only in appearance, as " an evil eye " is put by *Metonymy* for *envy*, which does proceed out of the heart.

Compare Matt. xx. 15, and see further under *Asyndeton*.

I Tim. vi. 19.—" Laying up in store for themselves a good foundation against the time to come, that they may lay hold on eternal life."

Here the " laying up treasure " is joined with " foundation," and " laying hold " is joined with the house which is from heaven. 2 Cor. v. 2.

Rev. i. 12.—" And I turned to see the voice that spake with me."

Here " voice " is put by *Metonymy* (*q.v.*), for the person speaking. Apart from this, there is a *Catachresis; seeing* being joined with that which is *invisible* and only heard. (See Ex. xx. 18.)

iii. *Of one word, where the Greek receives its real meaning by permutation from another language, or foreign usage.*

Matt. viii. 6. Acts iv. 27.—Where παῖς (*pais*), *a child*, is used of *a servant*, from the Hebrew נַעַר (*nahar*), which has both meanings. The A.V. renders it " servant " in Matt., and " child " in Acts; while

the R.V. renders it " servant " in both places, spelling it in Acts
" Servant."

Matt. xi. 25; Luke x. 21; Rom. xiv. 11; Heb. xiii. 15.—
ὁμολογεῖν (*homologein*), *to confess*, is used of *to praise* or *celebrate*, like
the Hebrew הוֹדָה (*hōdah*) which has both meanings. See Gen. xlix. 8·
2 Sam. xxii. 50.

Matt. xxiv. 29.—"And the powers of the heavens shall be shaken."
Here, δυνάμεις (*dunameis*), *powers*, means really *armies*, from the
Hebrew הַיִל (*chayeel*) which has both meanings.

Matt. xxviii. 1.—μία (*mia*), *one*, is the Greek cardinal numeral, but
it is used here for the ordinal, *first*, like the Hebrew אֶחָד (*echad*), which
has both meanings. See Gen. i. 5, etc. (See Mark xvi. 9.)

Luke i. 37.—" For with God nothing shall be impossible." Here,
ῥῆμα (*rheema*), *word* or *saying*, is used for *thing*, the Hebrew דָּבָר (*davar*)
having both meanings. The R.V. renders ῥῆμα literally ; at the expense
of forcing the word ἀδυνατήσει (*adunateesei*), *shall be impossible ;* which
it renders " shall be void of power."

Luke xvi. 17.—" It is easier for heaven and earth to pass than
one tittle of the law to fail." Here, πίπτειν (*piptein*), *to fall* or *fail*, is
used for *not to be fulfilled*, or *to be of no effect* (Rom. ix. 6. 1 Sam. iii. 19).
The Hebrew נָפַל (*naphal*) has both meanings. See Josh. xxiii. 14.
Est. vi. 10.

The reference to the " tittle " is interesting, and very beautifully
includes both the meanings.

The קֶרֶן (*cheren*), *horn*, is called in the Greek κεραία (*keraia*), *little
horn* (Matt. v. 18 and Luke xvi. 17). Another, and commoner Hebrew
name is תָּאָבִים (*taageem*), *little crowns.**

The Massorah explains that the *little horn* or *crown* is an ornament
or little flourish (something like a tiny fleur-de-lis, of various forms, or
a mere hair-line flourish) placed above certain letters and coming out
from their top, according to certain definite and prescribed rules.
Thus the common fancy, which is as old as Jerome, is exploded : which
explained the " tittle " as being the difference between two similar
letters : *e.g., Daleth* (ד) and *Resh* (ר) ; *Beth* (ב) and *Kaph* (כ), etc.

The meaning of the passage is that it is easier for heaven and
earth to pass away, than for one of these *Taagim*, or *little crowns* to
fall, or for the minutest word of God not to be fulfilled.

---

* The plural of קֶרֶן (*cheren*), *horn*, is קְרָנוֹת (*ch'rahnoth*), *horns.*

Acts x. 22. Luke i. 6; ii. 25.—δίκαιος (*dikaios*), which is an adjective, and means strictly *righteous*, is used generally for *a good man*, like the Heb., צַדִּיק (*tzaddeek*), which has both meanings.

Acts xiii. 34.—" The sure mercies of David."

Here the words τὰ ὅσια (*ta hosia*), *holy* or *just things*, are used for *promises* made, and *mercies* vouchsafed, in pure grace; the Heb. חֲסָדִים (*chasadeem*) having both meanings. The quotation is from Isa. lv. 3; and the reference is to Jehovah's unconditional covenant made with David in 2 Sam. vii. The passage means " I will give to you the faithful promises made to David."

The A.V. gives an unusually long marginal note; and the R.V. renders it " I will give you the holy and sure *blessings* of David"; which is very laboured and obscure, compared with the simplicity of meaning conveyed and brought out by the figure *Catachresis*, which shows that 2 Sam. vii. was in question, and the *holy things*, *i.e.*, the *promises*, there made in grace to David.

1 Cor. ii. 6.—" Howbeit we speak wisdom among them that are perfect."

Here the word τέλειος (*teleios*) receives its true meaning, *initiated*, from the Greek mysteries, where it was used of one who had been *initiated* into them.

1 Cor. xv. 54.—" Death is swallowed up in victory ": *i.e.*, for ever, as the Heb. נֶצַח (*netzach*) means, as well as *victory*, when it has the *Lamed* (ל) prefixed. See Isa. xxv. 8 (R.V.). Amos i. 11 (both A.V. and R.V.). Also Ps. xiii. 1 (2). Prov. xxi. 28.

2 Cor. vi. 12; vii. 15. Luke i. 78. Col. iii. 12. Phil. i. 8.— σπλάγχνα (*splangna*), *bowels*, is used for *mercy*, like the Heb., רחמים (*rachameem*), which has both meanings.

See Gen. xliii. 30. Ps. li. 1 (3). Prov. xii. 10. When used with the word " mercies " itself, it denotes *tender mercies*.

Gal. ii. 21.—" I do not frustrate (or esteem at a small price) the grace of God : for if righteousness come by the law, then Christ is dead (*i.e.*, died) in vain." Here, δωρεάν (*dōrean*), *a free gift*, is put for μάτην (*mateen*), *in vain;* and the A.V. so translates it. The R.V. renders it " for nought." But, like the Heb. חִנָּם (*chinnam*), μάτην means *in vain*, while δωρεάν means *without a cause*. See Ps. cix. 3.

1 Thess. iv. 4, and 1 Pet. iii. 7, where σκεῦος (*skeuos*), *a vase* or *utensil*, is used for the Heb. כְּלִי (*k'lee*), which has a wider meaning, *instrument* or *weapon*. See Hos. xiii. 15, and 1 Sam. xxi. 3-6.

Heb. xi. 31; Jas. ii. 25.—"The harlot Rahab": where πόρνη (*pornee*), *a harlot*, receives its true meaning from the Heb. זוֹנָה (*zōnah*) which means a *female hostess*, or *landlady*, as well as *harlot*.

1 Pet. iii. 14.—δικαιοσύνη (*dikaiosunee*), *righteousness*, is used of ordinary *piety*, *kindness*, etc. So 2 Cor. ix. 9. Matt. vi. 1 according to one reading (see *Metonymy* and *Synecdoche*).

Rev. ii. 7; xxii. 2, 14.—"The tree of life." In the Greek ξύλον (*xylon*) means *wood*; but receives its meaning of "tree" from the Heb. עֵץ (*eytz*), *tree*, which is frequently rendered ξύλον (*xylon*) in the LXX.

Rev. xiv. 8; xviii. 3.—"She hath made all nations drink of the wine of the wrath of her fornication." Here, θυμός (*thumos*), *wrath*, means *heat*, as well as *anger*; like the Heb. חֵמָה (*cheymah*), *heat*, *venom*, or *poison*. See Job vi. 4, where the LXX. renders it θυμός (*thumos*), *evil* or *affliction*, as Matt. vi. 34. So that the meaning is "the heating or poisonous wine of her fornication."

METALLAGE; or, A CHANGING OVER.

A different subject of thought substituted for the original subject.

Me-tal'-la-gee. Greek μεταλλαγή, from μετά (*meta*), *beyond*, or *across ;* and ἀλλαγή (*allagee*), *a change*, *exchange* (from ἀλλάσσω, *allasso*). Hence, *Metallage* means a taking over in exchange.

In this figure the word taken over is exchanged for a separate object of thought.

The Latins called it SUPPOSITIO, *substitution*, and MATERI-ALIS, *the mother stuff : i.e.*, one material out of which something else is made. The figure *Metallage* is used when a word is taken as the material, and out of it another object of thought is made and substituted.

Brydane exclaims, " O frightful and terrible *perhaps !* " Whitefield speaks of " Judas accosting his glorious Lord with a ' Hail, Master ! ' "

Hos. iv. 18.—" Their drink is sour : they have committed whoredom continually : her rulers with shame do love, ' Give ye.' "

ANTONOMASIA ; or, NAME-CHANGE.

Change of proper name for appellative ; or vice versa.

An ·-to-no-mā'-si-a. Greek, ἀντονομασία, *a different name*, from ἀντονο-μάζειν, *to name instead* ; and this from ἀντί *(anti), instead,* and ὀνομάζειν *(onomazein), to name* (from ὄνομα *(onoma), a name*).

This figure is so called because a proper name is put for a common or appellative noun ; or because, on the contrary, an appellation derived from some attribute is put for a proper name. As when a name of some office, dignity, profession, science, or trade, is used instead of the proper name of the person : *e.g.*, when we speak of the Queen as *Her Majesty*, or of a nobleman as *his lordship ;* or when a wise man is called *a Solon*, or *a Solomon*, etc.

When we speak of David as "the Psalmist," or of Paul as "the Apostle," we use the figure *Antonomasia.*

Gen. xxxi. 21.—The Euphrates is called "the river" on account of its greatness. See also Josh. xxiv. 2. Ps. lxxii. 8 ; lxxx. 11 (12), where also "the sea" is put for "the Great Sea," which is another *Antonomasia* for the Mediterranean. See also Mic. vii. 12.

1 Sam. iv. 21.—"And she named the child ' In-glorious ' (*i.e., I-chabōd*), saying, ' The glory is departed,' " *I-chabōd* meaning *there is no glory.* The name occurs once more, in chap. xiv. 3.

Isa. lxii. 4.—
"Thou shalt no more be termed ' Forsaken ' ;
    Neither shall thy land any more be termed ' Desolate ' :
But thou shalt be called ' Hephzi-bah ' (*i.e., my delight is in her*),
    And thy land ' Beulah ' (*i.e., married*)."

Here note that the four lines are alternate : the subject of the first and third being the *People*, while that of the second and fourth is the Land.

Hos. i. 6.—"And He said unto him, Call her name ' Not-having-obtained-mercy (*i.e., Lo-ruhamah*)."

Hos. xii. 13 (14).—Moses is called "a Prophet," because he was *par excellence* the prophet. See Deut. xxxiv. 10, 11, 12.

Mark viii. 20.—"And when [*I brake*] the seven among four thousand " : *i.e.*, the seven loaves.

Acts iii. 14.—" But ye denied the Holy One and the Just ": *i.e.*, the Lord Jesus Christ. See *Hendiadys*.

Acts xxii. 14.—" The God of our fathers hath chosen thee, that thou shouldest know his will, and see that Just (or Righteous) One ": *i.e.*, the Lord Jesus. Thus was Paul led of the Spirit to avoid the use of any word which would excite and inflame them. By this means he obtained audience, until, in verse 21, he had to use the word "Gentiles" ("I will send thee far hence unto the Gentiles"), when we read: "And they gave him audience unto this word."

Acts xxv. 26.—The Roman Emperor is called "my lord."

The Divine Names and Titles are sometimes the attributes of God used as proper names:—

God is called *the Strong One* (*El*); or, *the Most High* (*Elyōn*). Ps. v. 4 (5); xxii. 1 (2), etc.

Christ is in the same way called *the Lord*. Matt. xxi. 3. John xi. 3, 12, etc.

The Teacher or *Master*. Matt. xxvi. 18. John xi. 28.

The Son of man (see under *Synecdoche*). Matt. viii. 20; ix. 6; x. 23; xi. 19; xii. 8, etc.

The Angel. Gen. xlviii. 16. Ex. xxiii. 20.

The Angel of the Lord. Ex. iii. 2. Judges vi. 11

So also other appellatives are used: *e.g.*, "The Seed of the woman," "The Messiah," "The Servant of Jehovah," "The Messenger of the Covenant," "The Prophet," etc.

EUPHEMISMOS; or, EUPHEMY.

Change of what is unpleasant for pleasant.

Eu¹-phee-mis¹-mos. Greek, εὐφημισμός, from εὐφημίζειν *(euphemizein), to use words of good omen,* from εὐ *(eu), well,* and φημί *(pheemi),* to speak Hence, Eng., *Euphemy.*

Euphemy is a figure by which a harsh or disagreeable expression is changed for a pleasant and agreeable one; or, where an offensive word or expression is changed for a gentle one; or an indelicate word for a modest word.

This figure is not, strange to say, generally used as with us of the ordinary functions of nature, which are often exaggerated by civilization and fashion into a false modesty. The Scriptures use very plain language on plain subjects: but there are beautiful *Euphemies* used where really delicate feelings or sentiments are affected.

Indeed, we may say that the contrast between the Hebrew and other languages in this respect is one of the greatest proofs of Inspiration. Other languages abound in terms of indecency and immorality, which are a corrupt reflex of the corrupt mind of fallen man. But "the words of Jehovah are pure words."

As to our "uncomely parts," as the Holy Spirit terms them, there is actually no word in the Hebrew for the female, and for the male a *Euphemy* is employed.

We may contrast with this the tendency of man, not only downward in this direction, but in his vain attempts to cover his sin and to make himself appear better than he is. Examples abound in every day life. "A love-child" covers illegitimacy; "a free life" glosses a debauchee; "a gentleman of the road" covered a highway robber. So the Romans called a thief "a man of three letters," because the Latin word for thief is "*fur.*" On the other hand, among ourselves, "the hydraulic van" has superseded the water-cart; the shop has become an "establishment" or "emporium"; the butcher has blossomed into "a purveyor of meat"; the hair-dresser is "an artist" or "professor," etc., etc.

But the *Euphemisms* of the Bible are not like these! Sin is not glossed over or "wrapped up," but spoken of plainly in all its abomination. Man is not deceived by coloured and pretty ornaments of speech.

Compare, again, man's *Euphemies* of " life " and " death " ; and note the false teaching conveyed by them, when compared with those used in the word of God. Man calls " death " a friend, and speaks of " joining the majority " : but God speaks of it as a terrible calamity, and calls it " the enemy " ; " the last enemy," " the king of terrors," etc., though, in the case of His own people, He speaks of their being " put to sleep by Jesus " (1 Thess. iv. 14). It is only a " sleep " ; because the Lord Himself will come to wake them.

The change in *Euphemy* is necessarily obtained by using several words for one, and is therefore a special kind of *Periphrasis : i.e.*, a *Periphrasis* used with a special object.

Hence it was called also PERIPLOCE (*Per-i-plok'-ee*), from περί (*peri*), *around*, and πλοκή (*plokee*), *a folding* ; a figure by which the unpleasantness of a thing is wrapped round and made to appear agreeable.

CHROMA (*Chro'-ma*) was another name given to the figure, from χρῶμα (*chrōma*), *a colouring*, an *ornament*, or *embellishment.*

The Latins called it also INVOLUTIO : *i.e.*, an *involution*.

In English we might call it " a smooth handle " : *i.e.*, a polite expression for a rough or unpleasant one.

Gen. xv. 15.—" Thou shalt go to thy fathers " : *i.e.*, shalt die.

Gen. xlii. 38.—" Then shall ye bring down my gray hairs with sorrow to the grave " : *i.e.*, ye will kill me.

Judges iii. 24.—" Surely he covereth his feet in his summer chamber." When an Eastern stoops down, his garments fall over and cover his feet. Hence the *Euphemy*, the meaning of which is given in the margin. See also 1 Sam. xxiv. 3.

2 Sam. xviii. 32.—David enquired of Cushi : " Is the young man Absalom safe ? And Cushi answered, The enemies of my lord the king, and all that rise against thee to do thee hurt, be as that young man is."

Thus, by two beautiful *Euphemisms*, Cushi reminded David of Absalom's treason and its deserts, while he also intimated that he had been slain.

Ruth iii. 9.—" Spread . . . thy skirt over thine handmaid " : *i.e.*, receive me in the way of marriage.

2 Kings xxii. 20.—" I will gather thee unto thy fathers (*i.e.*, thou shalt die), and thou shalt be gathered into thy grave (*i.e.*, be buried) in peace."

Neh. iv. 23 (17).—"None of us put off our clothes, *saving that* every one put them off. for washing." (Margin, *every one* went *with his weapon for water.*)

The R.V. is no clearer : " None of us put off our clothes, every one *went with* his weapon *to* the water "; and puts it in the margin : " The text is probably faulty " ! This is like man ; who always thinks the *fault* is in the Text instead of in himself. When he meets with a difficulty, it never dawns on him that the difficulty lies in his own head, or is of his own creating !

The Hebrew is literally : " None of us put off our clothes ; each man went with his weapon (or tool) and water " : *i.e., he discharged his water as he was* (or *as he stood*): *i.e.*, there was neither time nor opportunity for retiring and for that laborious arrangement of the clothes which an Eastern requires. And thus the simple *Euphemy* is most expressive, and explains, instead of needing an explanation (which after all does not explain) !

Glassius would treat the word " water" as a *Synecdoche* by which " water," the most important part of a man's ration, is put for all of it. "This would require the translation : " Each one went with his sword *and* water": *i.e.*, one single weapon and one measured ration, " water " being used alone for a measured ration, as it was a very important part of the rations served out. Just as " salt " was served and measured out to the Roman soldiers, and afterwards was used by *Synecdoche* of the whole ration of which it was a part. Hence our term " salt-money "; and the Latin, *salarium*, and English, *salary*. When we say " a man is not worth his salt," we preserve this *Synecdoche ;* and, putting a part for the whole, we mean that he is not worth his salary.

So it may be here in Neh. iv. 23. The A.V. and R.V., with these marginal renderings, clearly show that something more is meant than what is said. But we believe that the figure of *Euphemy* sufficiently and satisfactorily explains it.

There is, however, something to be said for Glassius's suggestion as to *Synecdoche*.

One thing is clear, which makes either figure explain or express the one fact that is specially emphasized : *viz.*, that Nehemiah and his companions were building the wall with a trowel in one hand and a sword in the other (iv. 17 (11), etc). So exigent were the circumstances that they worked all night, and could take with them no armour or supplies of food. A single weapon and a single ration were all they could take.

Or so exigent were the circumstances that there was not even the usual opportunity for performing the functions of nature in the ordinary way. In either case the figure read in the light of the context shows the urgency of the circumstances.

Job x. 21, 22.—Here, we have two beautiful *Periphrases*: " Before I go whence I shall not return (*i.e.*, before I die), even to the land of darkness and the shadow of death ": *i.e.*, the grave, etc.   So xvi. 22.

Job xviii. 13. — " The first-born of death shall devour his strength ": *i.e.*, the cruellest and most calamitous death shall destroy him.

Job xviii. 14.—Death is called " the king of terrors ": *i.e.*, the terrible king who claims so many subjects.

Ps. xciv. 17.—" Unless the LORD had been my help, my soul had almost (marg., *quickly*) dwelt in silence ": *i.e.*, I should soon have been dead and buried.

Isa. xxxviii. 10.—" I shall go to the gates of the grave (*Sheol*) ": *i.e*, I shall die.   This explains Matt. xvi. 18; where the corresponding word (*Hades*) is used, and in the same sense: *i.e.*, death shall not prevail against the accomplishment of God's purposes.

Ecc. iii. 21.—See Appendix E, and *Erotesis*.

Ecc. xii. 1-7.—We have a series of connected *Periphrases* and *Euphemisms*.

One of them is worthy of a longer notice:—

Ecc. xii. 5. — " And desire shall fail."   We have already considered this under *Metalepsis* (*q.v.*), because there is a double *Metonymy*.   But there is a beautiful latent *Euphemy* as well.   The " *caper-berry* " is put for the *condiment* made from it, and then the condiment is put for the *appetite* or desire created by it.

But as this condiment was supposed specially to create sexual desire, the *Euphemy* is elegantly expressed in the A.V. (" and desire shall fail ").   The sense is absurdly lost in the R.V.; while to make the obscurity caused by the literal translation still greater, it is suggested in the margin that " fail " may mean " burst."

This is certainly one of the many passages in which the A.V. far exceeds the R.V. in beauty as well as accuracy, and shows that the A.V. is a *Version*, while the R.V. is a *Translation*.

Matt. viii. 11.—" Many shall come from the east and west, and shall sit down with Abraham, and Isaac, and Jacob, in the kingdom of heaven."

This was a beautiful *Euphemism*; to avoid giving offence (at that stage of Christ's ministry) to the Jews, who grudged the blessings being extended to Gentiles.

Matt. xi. 19 and **Luke vii. 35.**—" But wisdom is justified of (or on the part of) her children." By this *Euphemy* the Lord Jesus condemns those who received Him not.

True wisdom was shown in submitting to the Son of God : " Be wise now therefore, O ye kings : be instructed, ye judges of the earth." These words were written (Ps. ii. 10) with special reference to the reception of the Messiah : and all who were truly wise submitted themselves. Those who did not are thus rebuked.

John ii. 25.—" He knew what was in man." This is a solemn condemnation of man; and shows something of his true nature and character.

John xi. 11.—" Our friend Lazarus sleepeth (*i.e.*, is dead) ; but I go, that I may awake him out of sleep ": *i.e.*, raise him from the dead.

Acts ii. 39.—" For the promise is unto you, and to your children, and to all that are afar off " : *i.e.*, to the Gentiles. Peter did not wish at that time to give unnecessary offence.

There are many other *Euphemisms* which require no explanation, and which the student will now readily note and mark for himself.

AMPLIATIO; or, ADJOURNMENT:
i.e., AN OLD NAME FOR A NEW THING.

*A retaining of an old Name after the reason for it is
passed away.*

Am'-pli-a'-ti-o is a figure discovered and named by the Latins. It is
from *am'-pli-o*, *to fill out, extend*; hence, its more special and technical
sense, *to adjourn*: *i.e.*, *to extend the time.* So that *Ampliatio* means an
adjournment: and the name is given to this figure, because a name or
epithet is used of a subject either (1) before it has acquired the reason
for giving the name, or (2) after the reason has ceased.

In the latter case "the wolf" is still spoken of as the wolf in
Millennial days, when its wolf's nature has been changed (Isa. xi. 6):
and in the former the Saviour is so called by the angels while still an
infant (Luke ii. 11). This use of the figure is of the nature of
Prolepsis (*q.v.*).

Ampliatio thus differs from *Amplificatio* (*q.v.*), though the two
words are from the same root. The former has reference to a *change*
which has taken place; while in *Amplificatio* the sense of a word or
expression is made wider and expanded by a *repetition* of the words in
another form, in order to enlarge a narrative, and to heighten or
intensify what has already been said.

Ampliatio is thus a form of *Epitheton* (*q.v.*). The original meaning
of the figure is what is called *permansive*: *i.e.*, the name lives through
the change which has taken place, and is still used, though in a new
sense.

There is a form of *Prolepsis* which is distinguished from *Ampliatio*,
(as opposed to *Occupatio*), but only as to *time*. It is a statement of
future things as though present, the real interpretation of them being
adjourned.

See under *Prolepsis* § 4 and § 6 of the last subdivision of Figures
involving Change.

Gen. ii. 23.—"This is now bone of my bones, and flesh of my
flesh."

Though the bone and flesh of Adam were changed and made into
Eve, yet the name of the original source, " bone," etc., is retained.

Ex. vii. 12.—The rod of Aaron, when changed into a serpent, is
still called " a rod " by way of *Ampliatio*.

1 **Sam. xxx. 5.** **2 Sam. iii. 3.**—Abigail is still called, by way of *Ampliatio*, " the wife of Nabal the Carmelite," though Nabal was dead, and she was the wife of David. Compare Matt. i. 6.

Isa. xi. 6.—The term " wolf" is used, by *Ampliatio*, of the animal in Millennial days, though his nature will have then been so changed that he shall dwell with the lamb, which formerly he devoured, and be no more really a wolf.

Amos vi. 8.—" I abhor the excellency of Jacob " : *i.e.*, that which was once so called, but was no longer worthy of the name, if this were the Temple, it is so called by *Ampliatio*.

Matt. x. 3.—" Matthew the Publican " is still so called, though he had ceased to be a *publicanus*, or tax-farmer : *i.e.*, " Matthew, who had formerly been a publican."
See *Epitheton*.

Matt. xi. 5.—The blind are said to see, and the lame to walk after they are restored. Thus, by the figure *Ampliatio*, the *Epithet* still clings to them.

Matt. xxvi. 6.—" Simon the leper " is so called after he was healed. The *Epithet* still clings to him.

Luke ii. 11.—" Unto you is born this day in the city of David a Saviour." He is so called proleptically, by way of *Ampliatio*. His saving work, which gives Him this title, had then yet to be accomplished.

John ix. 17.—The *Epithet* "blind man " is still used of the man after his sight was restored. Compare verses 13 and 24.

John x. 16.—" Other sheep I have." They are so called, though they were not yet in existence, except in the purpose of the Father.

Rom. iv. 5.—" The ungodly " is so called after he is justified. The *Epithet* is still used by way of *Ampliatio*.

1 **Cor. xv. 5.**—" The twelve " are so-called after Judas's death, by way of *Ampliatio*, because they were formerly twelve : although there were only eleven after, until Matthias was appointed.
So Acts i. 21, 22.

2 **Cor. iv. 3.**—" The perishing " are those who shall hereafter be destroyed, and who were then or are now on their way to destruction.

Heb. xi. 31 and **Jas. ii. 25.**—Rahab is still called " the harlot." The term remains as an *Epithet*. But see under *Catachresis*.

ANTIPHRASIS; or, PERMUTATION:
i.e., A NEW NAME FOR THE OLD THING.

A new and opposite Name for a thing after the original Meaning has ceased.

An-tiph¹-ra-sis. Greek, ἀντίφρασις, from ἀντιφράζειν (*antiphrazein*), *to express by antithesis or negation;* from ἀντί (*anti*), *against,* and φράζειν (*phrazein*). Hence, φράσις (*phrasis*), *a way of speaking.* The figure is so called, because a word or phrase is used in a sense opposite to its original and proper signification; the figure is thus one of change : the name of a thing or subject being changed to the opposite, in order to emphasize some important fact or circumstance, as when a court of justice was once called "*a court of vengeance.*"

It thus partakes of, and is indeed a species of, *Irony (q.v.).* The difference is that *Antiphrasis* is used only of single words or phrases, while *Irony* is used of connected sentences. Another difference is that *Antiphrasis* affects rather the *meaning* of words, while *Irony* affects the *application* of words.

Hence *Antiphrasis* is called, by the Latins, PERMUTATIO, or *permutation,* because of this change of meaning.

Gen. iii. 22.—" Behold, the man is become as one of us " : *i.e.,* he had become, not necessarily or really "a God," but what the tempter promised him ; and now he will get the Tempter's doom and be cast out from God's presence.

Isa. xliv. 25.—" That turneth wise men backward " : *i.e.,* those who are accounted wise by themselves or others. Not those who are truly and really wise in God's sight. So the word " knowledge " is used in the next sentence by *Antiphrasis.*

II. *AFFECTING THE ARRANGEMENT AND ORDER OF WORDS.*

1. Separate Words.

HYPERBATON; or, TRANSPOSITION.

The placing of a Word out of its usual order in a Sentence.

Hy-per'-ba-ton. Greek, ὑπέρβατον, from ὑπέρ (*hyper*), *over*, and βαίνειν (*bainein*), *to step.* Hence ὑπερβατός and *Hyperbaton, a stepping over, transposition.*

The figure is so called because the words of a sentence are put out of their natural and usual grammatical order.

All words are arranged in a sentence according to certain laws, which have been acquired by usage. These laws are not the same in all languages, but each language has its own peculiar laws, called *Syntax*, which merely means *a putting together in order.* Even in one language this order may vary in different stages of its history and development.

Hyperbaton is a putting together of words in a way contrary to or different from the usual order. Hence, what is *Hyperbaton* in one language may not be *Hyperbaton* in another.

In English, the arrangement of words in a sentence usually follows the order of thought. Hence, naturally, the *subject* (with all that pertains to it) comes first: *i.e.*, the thing spoken of; then follows the *copula*: *i.e.*, the verb, and all words connected with it; and then the *predicate*: *i.e.*, something said about the subject, called the object, with its adjuncts.

In an inflected langnage (like the Greek, for example) it is not so necessary to keep to the formal arrangement of the words in a sentence, the grammatical dependence of words being sufficiently indicated by the inflections. Consequently there is great room for a variety of arrangements, when a particular word has to be emphasized.

It is hopeless to attempt to give an adequate idea of the nature and extent of the beautiful and subtle shades of meaning and thought produced by these unusual collocation of words called *Hyperbaton*. So delicate are they, at times, that it is scarcely possible to reproduce them in a translation.

In the Greek language, the object usually follows the governing verb; but it sometimes comes before it. The predicate usually comes after the object; but sometimes it stands first. The adjective usually follows the noun which it qualifies; but sometimes it stands before its noun: etc, etc.

The most emphatic position for these transposed words is at the beginning of a clause; but sometimes it is at the end; in which case the word is held back, and kept in suspense, while the attention is kept up, and the hearer or reader has nothing for it but to listen to the close for fear of losing the whole. When it is put out of its place, and stands out at the beginning, it thrusts itself upon our notice, and compels us to give all our attention, and see what it is that is going to be said about it.

In the old Hebrew Syntax, the subject usually precedes the predicate, the adjective the substantive, pronouns the nouns, the genitive the nominative, and the nominative the verb: *e.g.*, Judges i. 7 : " seventy kings thumbs of their hands and feet cut off, were."

In more modern Hebrew Syntax, the adjective follows the substantive; pronouns follow nouns; while the genitive follows the nominative which has a special form called the " construct."

In Chaldee, the verb is placed after the subject, and the article after the noun.

It has been said that " proper words in proper places is the true definition of style." But an intentional deviation from the ordinary " style " for the purpose of attracting attention and expressing the emphasis is the definition of *Hyperbaton*.

We may illustrate its use in this way. A person has a particular chair in his room, which he wishes his friends to notice. They continue to call, but do not notice it. It is in the usual place where chairs ought to be, and so does not attract any special attention. But one day he places this chair upon the table. Who can then fail to observe it, the moment the room is entered ?

This is exactly what takes place with words, in the figure *Hyperbaton*. Special attention is desired for some particular word. Placed in its ordinary and usual position, it may not be noticed. But, put out of its usual order and place at the beginning instead of at the end of a sentence, it is impossible for the reader not to be arrested by it.

If we say, for example, " The mystery of godliness is great," that is the natural order of the English words. But if we say, " Great is the mystery of godliness," we see at once that all the emphasis is to be placed on the word " great."

This figure has also been called SYNCHYSIS, *Syn'-chy-sis :* Greek, σύγχυσις, from συγχεῖν (*synchein*), *to mix up*, which is from σύν (*sun*), *together*, and χεῖν (*chein*), *to pour.* Hence, χύσις (*chysis*), *a pouring*, and *Synchysis*, *a mixing up*, as of words in a sentence.

We now give a few examples :—

Isa. xxxiv. 4.—" And the heavens shall be rolled together as a scroll." Here, (in the Heb.) the word "heavens" is emphasized by being, by *Hyperbaton*, put last : " And they shall be rolled together as a scroll—**the heavens.**"

Jer. xiv. 1.—" The word of the LORD that came to Jeremiah concerning the dearth." Here, by *Hyperbaton*, it is **That which was the Word of the LORD** came, etc.

Jer. xvii. 3.—" I will give thy substance and all thy treasures to the spoiler." Here, the verb is emphasized by being put last : " All thy substance and all thy treasures to the spoiler—**will I give.**"

Matt. v. 3-11.—In these verses, called the " Beatitudes," the participle is put out of its usual place, and made to begin the sentences instead of ending them : thus calling attention to the emphasis placed upon it.

Matt. vii. 13.—" Enter ye in at the strait gate."

Here the adjective is placed before the noun to call attention to its narrowness. So with the adjectives " wide " and " broad," which are both to be emphasized.

Luke xvi. 11.—" Who will commit to your trust the true riches."

The *Hyperbaton* (in the Greek) shows where the emphasis is to be placed : " The true riches—who will entrust them to you."

John i. 1.—Here the subject, " the Word," being defined by the article which is prefixed to it, can be placed at the end of two of the clauses : " In the beginning was **the Word**, and God **the Word** was": *i.e.*, in plain cold English, " The Word was in the beginning . . . and the Word was God."

The A.V. preserves the *Hyperbaton* in the first clause, but not in the last, because the English idiom will not bear it. But in each case we are to put the stress on " **the Word.**"

See under *Climax.*

John iv. 19.—The order of the words is, "Saith to him, the woman, Sir, I perceive that a prophet art thou " : thus emphasizing both the words " **thou** " and " **prophet,**" which should be greatly emphasized in reading.

John iv. 24.—" A Spirit is God."

The true emphasis is to be placed on the word " **Spirit,**" through its being placed (in the Greek) at the beginning of the sentence. In the ordinary order, it would be placed after the subject. The two words are transposed to call our attention to this great fact ; as being the basis of the Great Rubric which emphasizes the absolute necessity of our worship being truly spiritual.

See under *Hendiadys.*

John vi. 60.—" **Hard** is this saying."

Here again the predicate is put first, and the object last, in order to emphasize both.

John vii. 4.—" For no one in secret doeth anything and [*at the same time*] seeketh for it **in public** to be."

John ix. 31.—" Now we know that sinners—God **does not hear.**"

John xvii. 5.—" And now glorify **me, Thou, Father,** with Thyself, with the glory which I had, before the world was, **with Thee.**" Here, the mysterious depths of the words are forced upon our attention by the *Hyperbaton.*

The force of it is weakened by the literalness of the A.V. and R.V.

Acts xvii. 23.—The true emphasis is here brought out by the *Hyperbaton:* " For passing through and beholding the objects of your worship, I found an altar also, on which stood inscribed, ' To an unknown God.' What therefore, unknowing, ye reverence, this I— even **I, announce to you.**"

Rom. i. 3.—" Concerning His Son, Jesus Christ our Lord." Here, the A.V. entirely loses the emphasis of the *Hyperbaton,* by which the words " Jesus Christ our Lord " in sense follow the words " His Son," but are held back in suspense to the very end of the clause.

The R.V. restores it, but we give our own rendering of this difficult passage (verses 1-4) :—

" Paul, a servant of Jesus Christ, by Divine calling an apostle (see *Ellipsis*), separated unto God's Gospel which He promised in former times through His prophets in Holy Scriptures: *viz., the Gospel* concerning His Son, who was of David's seed according to the flesh, but was powerfully (ἐν δυνάμει) demonstrated *to be* God's Son with respect to His holy spiritual nature, by His resurrection from the dead * (Ps. ii. Acts ii.), even Jesus Christ our Lord."

Rom. v. 8.—Here the words are out of the natural order to excite our attention. The Greek is: "But commends His own love to us—God." The nominative is put last, and the verb first, to emphasize both.

Rom. viii. 18.—"Not worthy are the sufferings of the present time [*compared with*] the coming glory, to be revealed."

Here, the emphasis is placed on the non-worthiness of the sufferings, and the nearness of the revelation of the glory.

Rom. xi. 13.—"For to you I speak, to you Gentiles, inasmuch as I am of Gentiles the apostle."

Here the shades of emphasis can be traced in the unusual order of the words in which fleshly wisdom can discern only "bad grammar"! The first and last words are seen to be very emphatic.

Rom. xii. 19.—How unusual to commence like this: "Not yourselves avenging (or, be no self-avengers), beloved, but give place to [*Divine*] wrath," thus emphasizing "yourselves."

Rom. xiv. 1.—"Him that is weak in the faith receive ye, but not for disputings of doubts": *i.e.*, doubtful disputations, with emphasis on doubtful.

1 Cor. iii. 9.—"For God's fellow-workers, God's husbandry, God's building ye."

The emphasis is on "God's"; and it is to be noted that it is we who are fellow-workers with one another; not with God, as though He were one like ourselves. We are the fellow-workers with one another, and we belong to God and work for Him. We work, and He it is who giveth the increase.

1 Cor. xiii. 1.—"If with the tongues of men I speak and of angels."

Eph. vi. 8.—"Whatsoever thing each may have done that is good."

Here the adjective is held over to the last in order to emphasize it.

1 Tim. i. 15; iii. 1; iv. 9. 2 Tim. ii. 11. Tit. iii. 8.—"πιστὸς ὁ λόγος: Faithful the saying."

---

* Or "by a resurrection of dead persons": *viz.*, that referred to in Matt. xxvii. 52, 53. See under *Hysteresis* and *Heterosis.*

How much more emphatic than the ordinary coldness of the natural order : "The saying *is* faithful."

1 Tim. iii. 16.—"**Great** is, of godliness, **the mystery.**"

How wonderful is the emphasis thus placed on the word "great," put as it is before the subject, which is kept back and put as the very last word in the sentence (in the Greek).

See under *Synecdoche, Hendiadys,* and *Synonymia.*

1 Tim. vi. 5.—"Supposing that gain is **godliness.**"

Here the principal word is put out of its place, at the end, to call our attention to it. The emphasis is thus put on the word "godliness," "Supposing that godliness is gain."

1 Tim. vi. 12.—"Keep on struggling the fine **good** struggle of the Faith, lay hold on the life eternal, unto which life thou wast called also, and didst confess the fine confession before many witnesses."

Here the adjective "fine" (or "good") is greatly emphasized in each case.

Heb. vi. 16.—"For with men it is the Greater by whom they swear, and of all dispute they have a decisive settlement **the oath.**"

Heb. vii. 4.—"To whom, even a tenth, Abraham gave out of the spoils, **the patriarch.**"

Notice how the subject of the verse is kept back to the last, in order to call attention to the fact that, if Abraham—the patriarch himself—gave the tithe, He to whom he gave them must of necessity be greater, even than Abraham.

Heb. x. 30.—"To me vengeance belongeth, **I** (even I) will recompense, saith the Lord": emphasising the pronouns very strongly.

1 Pet. ii. 7.—"To you therefore is the preciousness—[*unto you*] **who believe.**" The subject is put last in order to emphasize the fact that the Lord Jesus is precious only to believers and to none else.

1 Pet. iii. 21.—The order and emphasis of the Greek is:—

"Which [*water*]—in the antitype—now saves you also—namely, **baptism**: not a putting away of bodily defilement, but an appeal of **a good conscience to God,** through the resurrection of Jesus Christ": *i.e.,* that while it was water which was the instrumentality through which Noah was brought safely through, it is the Holy Ghost who is now the antitype of this, which we have through the resurrection of Christ.

It was often declared that He should thus baptize : " I baptize with water : but He shall baptize you with the Holy Ghost."

1 John ii. 24.—Here again the peculiarity of the *Hyperbaton* attracts our attraction, and causes us to reflect on the words. " Ye, then, what ye heard from the beginning (or primitively), in you let it abide: if in you shall have abode what from the beginning ye heard, ye also, in the Son, and in the Father, shall abide."

So verse 27 : " And you, the anointing, which ye received from Him, in you abideth; and no need have ye that anyone should teach you : but, as the same anointing teacheth you concerning all things, and is true, and is not a lie, and even as it [*first*] taught you, ye will abide in Him."

Rev. xiii. 8.—" Whose names are not written in the book of life, of the Lamb slain, **from the foundation of the world.**"

The last sentence is put by *Hyperbaton* out of its place, at the end, so as to call our attention to it. It is a question whether it does not belong to the writing of the names and not to the slaying of the Lamb:—" Whose names are not written from the foundation of the world in the book of life of the Lamb slain." As in xvii. 8. Compare Dan. xii. 1. Ps. lxix. 28 and Isa. liii. 7.

ANASTROPHE ; or, ARRAIGNMENT.

The position of One word changed so as to be set over against the Other.

A-nas'-tro-phee. Greek, ἀναστροφή, from ἀνά (*ana*), *back again*, and στρέφειν (*strephein*), *to turn, a turning back*.

The figure is so-called because one word is turned, or turned back out of its proper or usual position in a sentence.

Hence it is a kind of *Hyperbaton ;* but affecting only one word, instead of several words, in a sentence.

It is called also PARALLAGE, *Par-al'-la-gee.* Greek, παραλλαγή, from παραλλάσσω (*parallasso*), *to make things alternate.* Hence *Parallage* means a *deviation, a turning aside, variation.* And SYNCATEGOREMA, *syn-cat'-ee-gor-ee'-ma,* from σύν (*syn*), *together with,* and κατηγόρημα, *an arraignment.* Hence the figure is so called because one word is set over against or arraigned against another. *Reversal* would be a good English name for this figure.

The Latins called it TRAJECTIO : *i.e., a crossing over, a transposition* or *trajection* of words. And INVERSIO, *a turning about, an inversion* of words.

The word thus put out of its usual place receives great emphasis.

We have many examples in English :—

The Verb before its Noun.

" Burns Marmion's swarthy cheek like fire."—*Scott.*

Adjective after its Noun.

" He ceased ; and death involved him dark around."—*Cowper.*

Objective before the Verb.

" Me didst thou constitute a priest of thine."—*Wordsworth.*

Preposition before the Participle.

" Into what pit thou seest, from what height fallen."—*Milton.*

Preposition after the Noun.

" It only stands our lives upon, to use
Our strongest hands."—*Shakespeare.*

Noun at end of sentence.

" Ape-born, not God-born, is what the atheists say of—man."

Deut. xxii. 1.—" Thou shalt not see thy brother's ox or his sheep go astray, and hide thyself from them."

Here, the *negative* is put with "see" instead of with "hide," in order to emphasize the command, which would otherwise tamely read:—
"If thou shalt see . . . thou shalt not hide," etc.   See under *Metonymy.*

Micah vi. 10.—"Are there yet the treasures of wickedness in the house of the wicked?"   In the Hebrew, the verse begins with the adverb: "Still are there *in the* house of the wicked man treasures of wickedness?"

Acts vii. 48.—In the English, the negative is joined with the verb, with which it is to be read: but in the Greek, the negative is put at the beginning of the clause, and the verb at the end, which greatly intensifies the force of the word "not."

"But not the Most High in hand-made temples dwelleth."

SYLLEPSIS; or, CHANGE IN CONCORD.

Grammatical Syllepsis, by which there is a change in the Ideas rather than in actual words, so that the concord is logical rather than grammatical.

Syl-lep'-sis. Greek, σύλληψις, from σύν (*sun*), *together with*, and λῆψις (*leepsis*), *a taking*.

It is a figure by which one word, or the meaning of one word, is *taken with another;* or, when one word is used, and another idea is meant. When involving *addition* of words, or sense, it has already been described in Div. II.

It is a kind of *Enallage*, or *Heterosis*; in that there is an exchange of genders, of numbers, or of both. But it differs from *Enallage*, in that the change takes place rather in the idea than in the actual words.

It is a kind of *Zeugma*, in that one adjective or verb belonging to two or more nouns of different genders, persons, or numbers, agrees with one rather than with another.

Syllepsis therefore depends on a change or disturbance in the *concord* of parts of speech; in making a *logical* rather than a *grammatical* concord.

John xvi. 13, 14.—"When he, the Spirit of truth, is come, he will guide you unto all truth," etc.

Here, though the word πνεῦμα (*pneuma*), *Spirit*, is neuter, the word ἐκεῖνος (*ekeinos*), *He*, is masculine; agreeing with the Divine Person rather than with the actual word "Spirit."

John xxi. 12.—"And none (*sing.*) of the disciples durst ask him Who art thou? knowing (*pl.*) that it was the Lord."

The figure points out that *not one* asked; for *all* knew.

2 Cor. v. 19.—"God was in Christ, reconciling the world (*sing.,*) unto himself, not imputing their trespasses unto them (*pl.*)."

Here, the figure *Metonymy*, by which the "world" is put for its *inhabitants*, is interpreted by the use of the plural, "them."

TMESIS; or, MID-CUT.

A Change by which one Word is cut in two, and another Word put in between.

Tmē¹-sis. Greek, τμῆσις, *a cutting*, from τέμνειν (*temnein*), *to cut*.

It is a figure by which a compound word or connected phrase is separated, and the position of its syllables changed, by the intervention of one or more words.

Each of the syllables thus cut off is a separate and complete word. Thus in "to us ward," the word "toward" is, by the figure *Tmesis*, cut in two: and the word "us" is put in between the two separated words, "to us ward." So also we say "to heaven ward," or "what condition soever."

The figure is also called DIACOPE, *Di-ac¹-o-pee*. Greek, διακοπή, *a cutting in two*.

DIÆRESIS, *Dī-æ¹-re-sis*. Greek, διαίρεσις (*diairesis*), *a dividing through*.

DIASTOLE, *Di-as-to-lee*. Greek, διαστολή, *a separating through*.

ECTASIS, *Ec¹-ta-sis*. Greek, ἔκτασις, *a stretching out*.

DIALYSIS, *Di-al¹-y-sis*. Greek, διάλυσις, *a dissolving* or *parting asunder*.

DIVISIO, Division.

There is an example of it in Eph. vi. 8 : ὅ τι ἐάν (*ho ti ean*), three words, which usually go together in this order, are divided : and the last is put in between the other two, so that it reads "what soever thing," instead of "what thing soever."

Our English *Tmesis* here better expresses the Greek, than the A.V. which neglects the Greek *Tmesis*.

Through not seeing the figure in this passage, there are several various readings created in order to explain it.

HYSTERON-PROTERON ; or, LAST-FIRST.

The Second of two things put First.

Hys¹-te-ron - Prot¹-e-ron, from ὕστερος (*hysteros*), *the latter*, and πρότερος (*proteros*), *the former*.

A figure in which the word that should be the latter of two words comes first.

It is, therefore, a kind of *Hyperbaton :* where 'the cart is put before the horse.' It occurs in most languages; but it is a question whether in this sense it occurs in the Bible, as the figure is considered rather a blemish than an ornament. If it is used, it is certainly for unusual emphasis.

Phil. iii. 19 has been cited : " Whose end is destruction, whose God is their belly, and whose glory is in their shame, who mind earthly things."

Here, the " end " is put first : in order that the mind may dwell with the greater horror on the things which lead to it.

The structure of these verses (18, 19) throws more light on them, and shows that after the words " many walk " there is a parenthetical break, which is resumed at the end of verse 19, to show who these " walkers " are, *viz.*, " the earthly minded."

a | " For many are walking

   b | Whom I often told you, and do tell you now—even weeping, *calling them* the enemies of the cross of Christ,

   b | Whose end—destruction ; whose god—the belly ; and their glory—in shame.

a | Such [*namely*] as are minding earthly things."

Here, in " a " and " *a* " we have the walkers ; while in " b " we have their walk, and in " *b* " their end. Hence their walk ends in destruction, their worship ends in their belly, and their glory ends in shame.

Heb. iii. 8.—" Harden not your hearts, as in the provocation, in the day of temptation in the wilderness."

The provocation of God followed the temptation in the wilderness ; but is here put first to mark out the special temptation referred to.

Heb. iv. 2.—" For unto us was the Gospel preached, as well as unto them." Here, the order of time is inverted, to agree with the order of thought, and for emphasis.

But, as we have said, it is a question whether we have any real examples of this figure in the Bible.

HYSTEROLOGIA; or, THE FIRST, LAST.

The First of two things put Last : or, the opposite of Hysteron-Proteron.

Hys'-ter-o-log'-i-a. Greek, ὑστερολογία, from ὕστερος (*hysteros*), *last*, and λόγος (*logos*), *speech, discourse.*

A figure by which that which is put last, ought, according to the usual order, to come first.

It is the opposite of *Hysteron-Proteron*; except that it refers to a transposition of connected events, rather than of words.

It differs from *Hysteresis* (*q.v.*).

Gen. x. and xi.—In chapter x. the dispersion of the nations is put before the cause of it, which is recorded in chap. xi.

Gen. xii. 1.—Here, the call of Abraham is put, by *Hysterologia*, after the obedience to it (or to a previous call) in chap. xi. 31, 32.

Abraham and Terah came out of Haran in consequence of this call; which is not recorded till afterward.

The figure thus emphasizes the fact that God had called them out of " Ur of the Chaldees" (see chap. xv. 7) " into a land that I will show thee " (chap. xii. 1): while the history shows that the obedience, from some cause, was not complete, for "they came unto Haran, and dwelt there." The Divine comment in Acts vii. 2-4 reveals the secret to us: " From thence (*i.e.*, from Haran) when his father was dead, he removed him into this land," showing that Terah, his father, was the hindrance to Abram's complete obedience.

The figure thus calls attention to the fact that in his day, as well as in our own, family ties often hinder full obedience to God.

The two calls are still further marked by the contrasted expressions in chaps. xi. 31 and xii. 5.

In chap. xi. 31, we read : "They went forth . . . from Ur of the Chaldees, to go into the land Canaan; and they came unto Haran, and dwelt there."

In chap. xii. 5, we read, as to Haran, that " they went forth to go into the land of Canaan; and into the land of Canaan they came."

Gen. xxx. 22-24.—The birth of Joseph is described by *Hysterologia*. For it happened, really, after the birth of the sixth son of Jacob (Naphtali) and during the first seven years of his servitude. It was after the birth of Joseph that Jacob wished to go away and leave Laban. In the

Y 1

first seven years were born Reuben, Simeon, Levi, Judah, Dan, Naphtali, and Joseph. Then he served seven more years (chap. xxxi. 41), and in these were born Gad, Asher, Issachar, Zebulun, and Dinah.

So Joseph's birth, which took place after Naphtali's, is recorded, by *Hysterologia* : after Dinah's.

Gen. xxxviii.—The history of Judah in this chapter is put by *Hysterologia*, for the greater part of it took place before the selling of Joseph, which is recorded in chap. xxxvii.

Judges xx. and xxi.—These chapters describe the Benjamite war; which must have taken place many years before; indeed soon after Joshua's death, though recorded here. For Phinehas, the grandson of Aaron, was high priest (chap. xx. 28): and Jonathan, the grandson of Moses, was the first idolatrous priest to the tribe of Dan!*

Moreover, Jebus or Jerusalem was still in the hands of strangers (chap. xix. 10-12), whereas chap. i. 8, 21 describes its capture and firing by the tribe of Judah.

I Sam. xvi.-xviii.—Here, four events in the history of Saul and David are transposed, by *Hysterologia*, in order to bring together certain facts relating to each; and especially to the Spirit of God in relation to each. In chap. xvi. 1-13, David is anointed, and the Spirit of God comes upon him. Then, in order to contrast the Spirit of the Lord departing from Saul, a *later* fact is brought forward here (chap. xvi. 14-23), which, in the history, really follows chap. xviii. 9. So that chaps. xvii.-xviii. 9 record an earlier event in David's life, which is brought in here parenthetically, describing one of the illustrations of chap. xiv. 52, that, when Saul saw any strong man or any valiant man, he took him unto him. Chaps. xvii.-xviii. 9 go on to give an instance of this with David, and tell how Saul thus found David. Then (after chap. xviii. 9) we have to go back again to prior events (recorded in chap. xvi. 14-23); while, in chap. xviii. 10-30, we have further facts concerning Saul's "evil spirit" and other events of David's life.

The whole section is beautifully constructed; and the parentheses between the different members are clearly seen: each member being parenthetical to the other two, between which it is placed:—

---

* See pamphlet on *The Massorah*, by the same author and publisher.

A | xvi. 1-13. DAVID anointed. The Spirit of the Lord comes upon him.

    B | 14-23. SAUL rejected. The Spirit of the Lord departs from Saul, and an evil spirit troubles him.

A | xvii. 1-xviii. 9. DAVID. An earlier incident in his life.

    B | 10-30. SAUL. The Spirit departed, and evil spirit troubling him.

So that, while *Saul* and *David* alternate, we see why the special arrangement is made; so as to bring out into contrast the facts recorded in each pair of corresponding members, which are not recorded in their historical order, but in the order of the spiritual instruction which is to be conveyed. The *historical* order is obtained by reading on from A to *A* (treating B as being in a parenthesis); and then from B to *B* (treating *A* as though it were in a parenthesis); while the logical sequence of the *spiritual* order is obtained by reading straight on, as the history is written in the Text.

2 Sam. xxiii. and xxiv.—The latter chapter is put after chapters xxii. and xxiii., which contain David's "last song" and "last words," while the events really follow chap. xxi. The "song" and the "words" follow more appropriately, immediately after the record of David's mighty acts, instead of after David's sin in numbering the People.

Isa. xxxviii. 21, 22.—Here, the sign which Hezekiah had asked for, in verse 22, is described in verse 21, beautifully emphasizing the Divine over-ruling of the history.

Amos vi. 2.—The cities are put according to logical emphasis, rather than geographical sequence.

Matt. xxvii. 52, 53.—Here, the events which took place later, are recorded in their consequential order, rather than in the actual historical order.

At the moment when the Lord Jesus "yielded up His Spirit . . . the earth was shaken, and the rocks were rent, and the tombs were opened [and now comes, (by *Hysterologia*) "many bodies of the saints who had fallen asleep, arose, and, coming forth out of the tombs after His resurrection, entered into the holy city, and appeared privately* to many]. Now the centurion, and those with him, keeping guard over Jesus—seeing the earthquake, and the things that were taking place—feared greatly, saying, 'Truly, God's Son this Man was.'"

---

* This seems to be the meaning of ἐμφανίζειν (*emphanizein*), see its only other occurrences: Heb. ix. 24 and xi. 14.

It is a question whether it be not this which is referred to in Rom. i. 4 : where the Lord Jesus is said to have been marked out as " God's Son . . . as the result of raising (or rising) again of dead persons." For it is not ἐκ τῶν νεκρῶν, *from among the dead*, but simply νεκρῶν, *of dead people.* That He was so marked out is described in the history by the exclamation of the Centurion. In both cases we have υἱὸς θεοῦ (without articles), " *God's Son.*"

Some have suggested that we have this figure in the record of the temptation (Luke iv. 5, 9), where the temptation which seems to come first in order of events is put last. Compare Matt. iv. 5, 8.

Rev. xii.—In this chapter, we have the prophetic record of events, which shall take place before chapter vi., and lead up to what is recorded in chapters vi.-xi.

Chapters vi.-xi. give the *exoteric* view of the future history, which ends with the judgment (chap. xi. 18). Chap. xi. 18 therefore brings us parallel to chap. xx. The Beast and false prophet are upon the earth during this period, and their actions are seen in chaps. ix. and xi., though they are not named, and their actual coming is not described, till chap. xiii.

But chapter xii. gives the *esoteric* view of the same period, and takes us back to a point prior to chap. vi., and shows us the causes which shall lead to the rising up of the Beast and the false prophet.

First, the war takes place in heaven, and the Devil is cast out into the earth.

Then " he " stands upon the sand of the sea (chap. xiii. 1, R.V.) ; and John sees these two awful beings coming up, the one from the sea and the other from the earth. There is no record of their doings, except what is recorded in chaps. vi.-xi., and in xiii.

See further under *Ellipsis.*

HYSTERESIS; or, SUBSEQUENT NARRATION.

A subsequent Narration of prior Events.

Hys¹-ter-ee-sis. Greek, ὑστέρησις, from ὑστερέω (*hystereō*), *to come later.* Hence, *a coming after or later.*

This is a special form of *Hysterologia*, and does not refer to connected records or events, but gives, long afterwards, further details of some long prior events ; or, gives events never before recorded.

When a record, written much later, gives supplemental or new particulars, quite *disconnected* from the original historical record, it is called *Hysteresis :* and hence has been called

HISTORICAL HYSTERESIS,

by which the Holy Spirit, in later and subsequent Scriptures, adds supplementary details which were not given in the history itself ; and sometimes even historical facts, of which no mention had before been made.

Man often does, and is allowed to do, this in human literature : but God may not ! and so man cavils at this beautiful figure, and sees in it only " discrepancy " ; instead of delighting in these subsequent supplementary facts thus revealed to us by the Holy Spirit, and such as none but He could give.

Gen. xxxi. 7, 8.—Jacob mentions later, certain facts in his history which had taken place before.

1 Sam. xii. 12.—A prior event is here recorded, not mentioned in the earlier narration.

1 Sam. xxii. 9-16.—Certain supplementary details are given here which are not recorded in the account as narrated in chap. xxi. 1-9.

Ps. cv. 18.—" Whose feet they hurt with fetters." This, by *Hysteresis*, is mentioned here, though not recorded in the history of Joseph in Genesis.

Hos. xii. 3-5 gives further particulars supplementing the history in Gen. xxxii. 24, etc. ; xxviii. 12-19, and xxxv. 9-15.

Amos i. 1.—A particular earthquake is here mentioned, of which no historical record is given. It is possibly the earthquake mentioned in Zech. xiv. 5. Amos is said to have prophesied " in the days of

Uzziah . . . and Jeroboam"; and it is added, "two years before the earthquake." Now, in Zechariah, we have no mention of Jeroboam. Hence it is very possible that, by the time the earthquake took place, he was dead. How Amos came to be "among the herdmen from Tekoa"; or, why these men migrated, as it may seem, into Israelite territory, we are not told. But if we take the mysterious "it,"* which the Lord, by Amos, says, He will not "avert," to be this very earthquake, we avoid a very puzzling *Ellipsis*, and shall very likely be correct.

Amos ii. 1.—Moab is here said to have "burned the bones of the king of Edom into lime," a fact of which we have no historical mention. Mesha, king of Moab, evidently was a cruel man. In his superstitions he offered his own son upon the wall, and turned the tide of battle.

See further information concerning this in the history of *The Moabite Stone*.

Amos v. 25, 26.—Here we learn the names of certain of the gods which the Children of Israel worshipped in the wilderness. See also Ezek. xx. 6, 7, 18, 22, etc.

Zech. xiv. 5.—See above under Amos i. 1.

Matt. ii. 23.—"And he came and dwelt in a city called Nazareth : that it might be fulfilled which was spoken by the prophets, He shall be called a Nazarene."

Through missing this *Hysteresis*, the commentators have created a difficulty of their own.

First, they cannot find such a prophecy in any of the prophets.

Then, they try and make a connection between *netzer*, a branch, and *Nazarene ;* and, as there is none, the difficulty is only increased.

Even if the connection could be established, the difficulty would not be removed: for it says "prophets" (*plural*), and the word *netzer* is used of Christ in only one prophet, Isaiah. So the difficulty is further increased.

But there is really no difficulty at all. It is absolutely created. It is assumed from the outset that it says "which was *written*." But it does not say so! It says "which was SPOKEN." The fact is, some prophecies were written down and never spoken ; some were both written and spoken ; while others were spoken and never written. This is one of the latter class : and there is all the difference in the

---

* Which is *masc.* in all the eight occurrences: and *always* followed by the great pause.

world between τὸ ῥηθέν (to rheethen), *which was spoken*, and ὃ γέγραπται (ho gegraptai), *which standeth written !*

Thus, this beautiful *Hysteresis* reveals to us the historical fact that several prophets had declared by the Holy Spirit that the Messiah should be called a Nazarene. But for this *Hysteresis* we should never have known it.

Matt. xxiii. 35, 36.—"That upon you may come all the righteous blood shed upon the earth, from the blood of righteous Abel unto the blood of Zacharias son of Barachias, whom ye slew between the temple and the altar." etc.

Now, from failing to see the historical *Hysteresis* here, it has been hastily assumed that the reference is to 2 Chron. xxiv. 20, 21, where we read, "The Spirit of God came upon Zechariah the son of Jehoiada the priest . . . And they conspired against him, and stoned him with stones at the commandment of the king in the court of the house of the LORD."

By this inaccurate reference, the Lord Jesus Christ, the Son of God, is charged with making a serious mistake.

But note that when the Lord says that Zachariah was "the son of Barachias," He could not possibly have been speaking of "the son of Jehoiada" as the same man.

If He began with Abel, the first martyr, it is not probable He would end with a murder which took place 870 years before he spoke the words, when there were many more during those 870 years.

How much more probable that he referred to Zechariah the (last but one) prophet (and the one of whom he is speaking, verse 31), who lived only 450 years before the Lord spoke the words? Moreover, he is expressly called "the son of Berechiah" in Zech. i. 1, and i. 7.

It is remarkable that there was another Zechariah, the son of Baruch, who was martyred some 36 years afterward (A.D. 69), immediately before the destruction of Jerusalem, as recorded by Josephus (*Wars*, iv. 5, 4).

Matt. xxvii. 9, 10.—See under *Gnome*.

Acts ix.; xxii.; xxvi.—In the three accounts of the conversion of Saul, we have supplementary facts, disconnected from the historical event.

2 Tim. iii. 8.—"Jannes and Jambres" are named as two of the Egyptian wise men; whose names are not given in Exodus, but are supplied here by the Holy Spirit.

Heb. ix. 19.—The sprinkling of the book is supplementary information which is not given in Ex. xxiv.

Heb. xi. 21.—Here we have an additional fact, which at once explains and amplifies Gen. xlviii. 12, and is not in discrepancy with Gen. xlvii. 31, as is commonly supposed.

We must give the whole of this verse, because of the controversies which have raged around it : " By faith, Jacob, when he was a dying, blessed both the sons of Joseph; and worshipped, *leaning* upon the top of his staff."

The marginal reference in the A.V. is Gen. xlvii. 31 ; but this, though followed by every one, is certainly not correct. The circumstance in Heb. xi. 21 is Jacob's blessing of the sons of Joseph, which is set in company with Isaac's blessing of his own sons. The two together giving the beautiful lesson that Isaac's blessing was given contrary to *the will of the flesh* (*i.e.*, his own will), while Jacob's blessing was given contrary to *the will of man* (*i.e.*, Joseph's will) (Heb. xi. 20, 21).

It is clear, therefore, that the whole emphasis of the reference is to the occasion of *the blessing :* of which there is not a word in Gen. xlvii. 31, and to which it does not refer.

In Gen. xlvii. 31, Jacob was causing Joseph to swear that he would bury him not in Egypt, but in the land of Canaan, and " Israel bowed himself upon the bed's head."

But it was "after these things" (Gen. xlviii. 1), that the blessing of Joseph and his sons took place. And, then, we have, in chap. xlviii. 12, the *worship* of Jacob who " bowed himself with his face to the earth." Jacob must, therefore, have been in a sitting posture ; for, in verse 2, we read that when they told him that Joseph was approaching, " Israel strengthened himself, and sat upon the bed " ; and, from verse 12, when he embraced Ephraim and Manasseh, he took them "between his knees." It was then, we gather that, in the blessing of his own sons (for chaps. xlviii. and xlix. are continuous), that he " leaned on the top of his staff." And this inspired addition to the information is given us in Heb. xi. 21, to enhance and emphasize his faith, and to indicate Israel's extreme infirmity, for it was his last dying act (chap. xlix. 33).

There is no necessity, therefore, for us to discuss the question of the various reading involved in the Hebrew מִטָּה (*mittah*), *the bed*, and the LXX. and Syriac rendering, *the staff,* which would require the Hebrew to be pointed מַטֶּה (*matteh*). Had the word been used in the

Hebrew of Gen. xlviii., the true pointing would have been there decided.*
But the point is decided for us in Heb. xi. 21; which clearly states
that it was his "staff" that Israel leaned upon while worshipping God
and blessing "by faith" the sons of Joseph. We must, however, point
out "the incalculable quantity of idolatrous nonsense," to use the words
of Dean Alford (*in loco*), which (he says) "has been written on these
words by Roman Catholic commentators, taking as their starting point
the rendering of the Vulgate: *et adoravit fastigium virgae ejus* [*and
worshipped the top of his staff*], and thence deriving an argument for
the worship of images"! This corruption of the Vulgate is perpetuated in all the Romish translations of it; and all therefore come under
the Dean's vigorous condemnation.

Heb. xii. 21 gives a particular which we do not find recorded
in Ex. xix. and xx.

Jas. v. 17. — The earnest prayer of Elijah is not recorded in
1 Kings xvii. 1.

Jude 9 mentions by the Holy Spirit the contention of Satan about
the body of Moses; and, in verse 14, some words of a prophecy of
Enoch. Trading on this reference, men have forged "the book of
Enoch" evolving its fancies and trivialities out of this historical
Hysteresis.

---

* Had a *staff* been intended in Gen. xlvii. 31, it would probably have been
מַקֵּל (*makkail*), as in chaps. xxx. 37; xxxii. 10, etc.

SIMULTANEUM; or, INSERTION.

A parenthetic Insertion between the record of two simultaneous Events.

Si'-mul-ta'-ne-um. Latin, from *simul, at the same time, together.*

This figure is used when, in a description of events, properly belonging to the same time, one is changed and put out of its historical place, and put in between two others, which is thus divided so as to take us by surprise.

It is, therefore, a kind of historical *parenthesis*, or logical *Tmesis* (*q.v.*).

Mark xv. 12, 13, 14.—Where Pilate's words (verses 12, 14) are interrupted by the shouts of the People (verse 13). The events took place literally in this order: but, instead of describing the two events separately, Pilate's words and the People's are described at one and the same time.

Rev. xvi. 13, 14, 15, 16.—Here the description (14, 16) of the work of the three unclean spirits in gathering together the kings of the earth to Armageddon is interrupted by verse 15; which is an injunction specially referring to that same time, and is therefore introduced there, by *Simultaneum*, for the sake of emphasis.

ANTITHESIS ; or, CONTRAST.

A setting of one Phrase in Contrast with another.

An-tith'-e-sis. Greek, ἀντίθεσις, from ἀντί (*anti*), *against*, and θέσις (*thesis*), *a setting*, from τιθέναι (*tithenai*), *to set* or *place.*

It is a figure by which two thoughts, ideas, or phrases, are set over one against the other, in order to make the contrast more striking, and thus to emphasize it.*

The two parts so placed are hence called in Greek *antitheta*, and in Latin *opposita* and *contraposita.* For example :

" When our vices leave us, we flatter ourselves we leave them."

" Curved is the line of beauty,
Straight is the line of duty."

"The prodigal robs his heir, the miser robs himself."

"God demands man's homage; man offers Him his patronage."†

Man often misuses this figure, for the mere fancy of balancing sentences ; and thus often falsely exaggerates a contrast which lies more in the words than in the thoughts. When this is the case it is called *Antimetabole, Parison, Annominatio*, etc. (*q.v.*).

It is called also CONTENTIO : *i.e., comparison*, or *contrast.*

When this contrast is made by affirmatives and negatives, it is called *Enantiosis*, see below.

The Book of Proverbs so abounds in such *Antitheses* that we have not given any examples from it.

Isa. i. 21.—Of Jerusalem it is said " Righteousness lodged in it ; but now murderers [*lodge in it*].

Isa. lix. 9.—
" We wait for the light, but behold obscurity ;
For brightness, but we walk in darkness."

Isa. lxv. 13, 14.—Where we have many beautiful *Antitheses.* See also under *Symploce.*

Lam. i. 1.—" How doth the city sit solitary that was full of people ! "

---

* When this consists of *words* rather than of sentences, it is called *Epanodos*, and *Antimetabole* (*q.v.*).

† Dr. Robert Anderson in *The Silence of God.*

Luke ii. 14.—" Glory in the highest to God, and on earth peace." And then, after these two *Antitheta*, a third fact is stated as resulting from them when coming together:—" Good will toward men." *

See under *Ellipsis*.

Rom. v. 18.—" Therefore as through one offence judgment came upon all men to condemnation, even so too, through the righteous act (δικαίωμα, not δικαιοσύνη) of one, the free gift came upon all men unto a justifying (δικαίωσις, spoken only of God's activity in justifying us) of life " (or, a life-long justifying).†

Rom. v. 19.—" For as by one man's disobedient *act* many were made sinners, so by the obedient *act* of one (*i.e.*, His death) shall many be made righteous."

See also *Paronomasia* and *Paregmenon*.

Rom. vi. 7, 8.—" For he that died, has been justified from sin. Now, if we died with Christ, we believe that we shall live also with him."

Rom. viii. 5.—" For they that are (or live) after (or according to) flesh (the Old nature) do mind the things of the flesh; but they that are (or live) after (according to) spirit (the New nature) [*do mind*] the things of the spirit " : *i.e.*, the things that belong to the New nature. See under *Metonymy*.

Rom. viii. 13.—" For if ye live according to flesh, ye shall die : but if ye through spirit (the New nature) do mortify the deeds of the body (*i.e.*, by reckoning that it died with Christ, Rom. vi. 11), ye will live."

Rom. xv. 12.—" There shall be a root of Jesse, and he that shall rise [*and raise His banner*] to reign over the Gentiles; in him shall the Gentiles trust." The reference is to Isa. xi. 10 : where נֵס (*neys*), *a banner*, which is raised aloft, is put in contrast with the " *root* " which is the lowest point. So Messiah rises from the lowest to the highest.

2 Cor. iv. 17, 18 contains several beautiful *Antitheses*.

---

* Is it not clear that εὐδοκία (*eudokia*) refers to *Divine complacency*, and that we find the explanation in the εὐδόκησα (*eudokeesa*) of Matt. iii. 17 ; xii. 18 ; xvii. 5. Mark i. 11. Luke iii. 22. 2 Pet. i. 7 ? With these, contrast God's side (Heb. x. 6, 8, 38); and on man's side (2 Thess. ii. 12. How scholars can tolerate the Revisers' reading εὐδοκίας (*eudokias*) is a marvel. Can a parellel be produced ?

† See articles on Romans in *Things to Come*, Vol. V.

2 Cor. vi. 8-10 contains a series of beautiful *Antitheses*.

In verses 4 and 5-, we have a seven-fold *passive experience* :—

    patience,
    afflictions,
    necessities,
    distresses,
    stripes,
    imprisonments,
    tumults.

In verses -5, 6-, we have a seven-fold *self-denial* :—

    labours,
    watchings,
    fastings,
    pureness,
    knowledge,
    longsuffering.
    kindness.

In verses -6, 8-, we have a seven-fold means to *endure* :—

    the Holy Ghost,
    love unfeigned,
    the word of truth,
    the power of God,
    the armour of righteousness,
    honour and dishonour,
    evil report and good report.

In verses -8-10, we have a seven-fold *result* in the following *Antitheses* :—

    deceivers, and yet true ;
    unknown, yet well-known ;
    dying, yet living ;
    chastened, yet not killed ;
    sorrowful, yet alway rejoicing ;
    poor, yet enriching others ;
    having nothing, yet possessing all things.

Phil. iii. 7.—" But what things were gain to me, those I counted loss for Christ."

Note that, by *Antithesis*, our attention is called to the fact that Paul is here speaking, by the Spirit, of his " gains," not of his *sins*. Of his gains, as a man and an Israelite ; which included the hope of resurrection as well as righteousness, of course : but he was willing to give them all up for that righteousness which he had in Christ, and for that "out-rising from among the dead," which he should have at Christ's appearing.

He does not, in verse 11, speak of something which he could attain to as a Christian more than other Christians ; but he is *contrasting* his "gains," as a Jew, and putting them in *Antithesis* with his greater gains as a Christian.

2 Pet. ii. 19.—" While they promise them (*i.e* their dupes) liberty, they themselves are the servants of corruption."

ENANTIOSIS; or, CONTRARIES.

Affirmation or Negation by Contraries.

E-nan-ti-ō'-sis. Greek, ἐναντίωσις, from ἐναντίος (*enantios*), *opposite*. The figure *Antithesis* is called *Enantiosis* when the contrast is expressed by *affirmatives* and *negatives*. What is stated affirmatively is meant negatively, or *vice versa*. When it is stated both ways, it is a kind of *Pleonasm* (*q.v.*). The difference being that *Pleonasm* refers to any statement, while *Enantiosis* refers to affirmation by contraries.

Ps. i. 1.—We have here a beautiful series of affirmation by contraries.

Isa. xlv. 22.—" I am God, and there is none else."

Luke vii. 44-46.—The difference between reality and formality is beautifully shown by a series of contrasts which are affirmatives by contraries.

Rom. viii. 15.—" For ye have not received the spirit of bondage again to fear; but ye have received the spirit of adoption (or a sonship-spirit), whereby we cry, " Abba, Father."

Phil. iii. 9.—" And be found in him (Christ), not having mine own righteousness, which is of the law, but that [*righteousness*] which is through the faith of Christ, the righteousness which is of God by faith." See under *Synecdoche*.

ANACOLUTHON ; or, NON-SEQUENCE.

A breaking off the sequence of Thought.

An¹-a-co-lū¹-thon.   Greek, ἀνακόλουθον, from ἀ or ἀν, *negative*, and ἀκόλουθος (*akolouthos*), *following* : *i.e.*, *not following*, want of sequence or connection in a sentence, the latter part of which does not follow on or correspond with the former part.

This figure is so-called, because the construction with which a proposition begins is abandoned ; and, either for the sake of perspicuity, emphasis, or elegance, the sentence proceeds in a manner, different from that in which it set out.

Human writings of deep thought or feeling or argument frequently have the figure *Anacoluthon*, which in these cases is mere irregularity attributable to inadvertence, arising from the negligence or carelessness of the writer.

But, in the case of the Scriptures, where the Holy Spirit is the Author, and all is perfect, the figure not only imparts grace, but strength and force to the language, and is intended to catch and fix the attention of the reader.   In this case, of course, what is abandoned is not further necessary.   It has served its purpose in arresting, and so the argument passes on to that to which the attention is to be given.

1. Sometimes the accusative stands alone at the beginning of a sentence.

This is not an " accusative absolute," but is to be rendered " as for " or " as to."

Luke xxi. 6.—Here, the Lord says : " These things which ye behold " : and then He turns off, and says : " There will come days." So that we must supply the words " *As to* " these things, etc.

Acts x. 36.—Here, again, the sentence begins with the accusative : " The word which He sent unto the children of Israel."   Some MSS., not understanding the *Anacoluthon*, omit the relative pronoun " which." But the sense is " *As touching* the word which He hath sent," etc.   Or it may depend on οἴδατε, *ye know*, in the next verse : " Ye know the word which He sent," etc.

Rom. viii. 3.—" For what the law could not do, in that it was weak through the flesh."   Here, the argument breaks off to speak of what God has done : " God (by sending His own Son in the likeness of sinful flesh and *as an offering* for sin) did : namely, " He condemned sin in the flesh in order that the righteous-requirement (δικαίωμα, *dikaiōma*) of the Law might be fulfilled in us who walk not according to flesh (*i.e.*, the Old nature), but according to spirit (*i.e.*, the New nature)."

The figure requires the conclusion—this thing was impossible for the Law *to do*, because it was weak through the flesh : *i.e.*, man, owing to the corruption of his nature, could not keep the Law ; and the Law was powerless, because it could neither pardon the trangressor, nor alter his nature. This defect was overcome by God, Who condemned sin in the death of His Son (who was the sin-offering personified). His People, therefore, having died with Him, are discharged from the claims of the Law ; and, being now " in Christ," fulfil in Him all its righteous requirements.

2. Sometimes the leading proposition is interrupted by a parenthesis, and, when the subject is resumed, the grammatical connection is changed.

John vi. 22-24.

Gal. ii. 6, 7.

3. Sometimes the construction suddenly changes (without a parenthesis) by a change of persons ; or, from participles to finite verbs ; or, from singular to plural, and *vice versa*.

Mark vi. 11.—" And whosoever shall not receive you . . . shake off the dust of your feet against them."

Here, the *Anacoluthon* is seen only when we take the Critical Text approved by T.Tr.A. WH., and R.V. *viz.*, ὃς ἄν τόπος (*hos an topos*), *whatsoever place* (singular), instead of ὅσοι ἄν (*hosoi an*) *whosoever* or *as many as* (plural). So that the *Anacoluthon* is : " And whatsoever **place** (sing.) will not receive you . . . shake off the dust of your feet against **them**."

Luke xi. 11.—" From which of **you**, the father, shall his son **ask** bread ? Will **he** give him a stone ? "

Here the plural "you" is broken off for the singular " he."

1 Cor. vii. 13.—" And the **woman** which hath an husband that believeth not, and if **he** be pleased to dwell with her," etc.

Here the break is from the feminine to the masculine.

2 Cor. v. 6, 8.—Here the change is from participles to finite verbs :

z 1

" **Being** confident then always, and conscious that **being** at home [here] in the body, we are from home, away from the Lord (for by faith we are walking, not by sight). We are confident, however, and are content rather **to be** from home [*here*] out of the body, and **to be** at home with the Lord [*there*] ."

These words are usually misquoted " absent from the body, present with the Lord," as though it meant that the moment we are absent from the body we are present with the Lord. But this is exactly what it does not say : and the *Anacoluthon* calls our attention to this.

The whole subject is resurrection, starting from iv. 14. Our two bodies are contrasted in v. 1-5 : viz. : " the earthly house of this tabernacle (*i.e.*, this mortal body) " is contrasted with " our οἰκητήριον (*oikeeteerion*), our *spiritual* or resurrection body " (see Jude 6): *viz.* : " our house which is from heaven," the future body of glory being called a " house," as compared with the present body in which we groan, which is called a " tabernacle " or tent.

The argument is that, while we are in this " tabernacle " we cannot have that " house "; and that while we are in this tent we are away from our real eternal home, which is with the Lord.

There is no thought (here or elsewhere) of our being at home, or " with the Lord," apart from resurrection and our resurrection bodies.

Gal. vi. 1.—" Brethren, if a man be overtaken in a fault, **ye** which are spiritual, restore such an one in the spirit of meekness ; considering **thyself**, lest **thou** also be tempted."

Here the abrupt transition from the plural to the singular, which is a kind of *Enallage* (*q.v.*), makes the general precept applicable to each individual, in order to emphasize the absolute necessity of the " spirit of meekness" which is enjoined.

The figure calls our attention also to the fact that *restoration* is the object, and not *judgment*. Experience would lead us to believe that the text read : " Ye which are spiritual *judge* such an one in the spirit of bitterness and harshness, not considering thyself !" Hence the use of this figure to arrest our attention, and correct our error.

Eph. i. 20.—" **Having** raised him . . . he **set** him."

Col. i. 26.—" The secret which had been lying hid from the ages and from the generations, but lately **was** made manifest to his saints."

Other examples may be found, *e.g.* :—

Change from *first* person to the *second* : Gal. iii. 25, 26 ; iv. 5, 6, 20.

Change from *second* person to the *first* : Eph. ii. 2, 3, 13, 14 ; iv. 31, 32 ; v. 2 (textual reading). Col. i. 10-13; iii. 3, 4. 1 Thess. v. 5.

Change from second person *plural* to *singular :* Rom. xii. 16-19, 20. 1 Cor. iv. 6, 7. Gal. iv. 6, 7.

Change from *third* person to *second :* Jas. ii. 16.

4. Sometimes the construction is broken off altogether, and is not completed at all.

Mark xi. 32.—" But if we shall say, Of men ;—they feared the people."

Here, the reasonings of the rulers are broken off, and the sense must be supplied by *Ellipsis* (*q.v.*).

Rom. v. 12.—This is usually given as an example of what appears to be an *Anacoluthon ;* because the sense seems broken off at the end of verse 12 : but the structure of the passage shows us the connection, and where the sense or argument is resumed. Many suppose that this is verse 15 ; but the Correspondence of subjects shows that it must be verse 18.

The section to which verse 12 belongs is that from verse 12 to 21, and is as follows :—

THE STRUCTURE OF ROM. V. 12-21.

A | a | 12. By one man, sin : then, death upon all.
b | 13. Sin not imputed where no Law exists.
c | 14. The reign of death.

B | 15. Not as the offence, so the gracious gift.

B | 16, 17. Not as by one person, so the gift.

A | *a* | 18, 19. By one man's offence, all men under condemnation ; by one man's disobedient act the many were constituted sinners; and the counterpart.
b | 20. The offence abounded when Law came—and the counterpart.
c | 21. The reign of sin—and the counterpart.

Here, we see that verse 12 corresponds with verses 18, 19, and consequently all between (*viz.*, verses 13-17) is practically in a parenthesis. Moreover, note that the three members of *A* are stated *with their counterparts*, and are thus distinguished from the three in A.

1 Tim. i. 3, 4.—Here, the A.V. supplies the sense by adding " *so do.*" The R.V. adds " *so do I now.*"

5. Sometimes the change consists of a sudden transition from the *indirect* to the *direct* form of speech.

Mark vi. 9.—" But **being shod** with sandals ; and **put not on** two coats.

Luke v. 14.—" He charged him **to tell** no man, but **go and show** thyself," etc.

This may be explained by the *Ellipsis* of the verb " say," " but [*he said*] go and show thyself," etc.

John v. 44.—" How can ye believe, **receiving** honour one from another ? and the honour that is only from God, **ye seek** not."

Acts i. 4.—" **Wait** for the Father's promise which **ye heard** of me." The A.V. and R.V. treat this as *Ellipsis*, supplying the words " which [*saith* or *said he*] ye have heard of me."

Acts xvii. 3.—" **Opening and alleging**, that Christ must needs have suffered and have risen from among the dead, and that this is the Christ whom **I announce** to you." The R.V. (and A.V. margin) treat this as *Ellipsis*, " whom [*said he*] I preach," etc.

6. Sometimes the change is from the *direct* form, which passes into the *indirect*.

John xiii. 29.—" **Buy** those things that we have need of against the feast; or, that **he should give** something to the poor."

Acts xiv. 22. — " **Establishing** the souls of the disciples, **exhorting** them to continue in the faith, and that through many tribulations **must we** enter into the Kingdom of God."

See under *Ellipsis*.

Acts xxiii. 23.—" **Get ready** two hundred soldiers that **they may** go to Cæsarea." The natural sequence would have been " and go."

7. Sometimes two equivalent constructions are united in the same proposition.

It is scarcely necessary to present these in full. The student can readily search them out for himself.

See Mark vi. 7 ; xii. 38. Rom. xii. 4. 1 Cor. xiv. 5. Eph. v. 27, 33. And in the Old Testament the following may be noticed :—

Gen. xxxv. 3. Josh. xxiii. 16. Judges xvi. 24. Neh. x. 30.

III. *AFFECTING THE APPLICATION OF WORDS.*

We now come to the last class of the three great divisions of figurative language, *viz.*, figures which involve the *Application* of words rather than their *Meaning* or *Order*.

These we propose to consider under those that have to do with *change*; not that there is any real or absolute change; but because there is a deviation or change from the *literal*, or from the more ordinary and usual *application* of words. This change is brought about and prompted by some internal action of the mind, which seeks to impress its intensity of feeling upon others. The *meaning* of the words themselves continues to be literal: the figure lies in the *application* of the words. This *application* arises from some actual resemblance between the words, or between two or more mental things which are before the mind.

When the literal application of the words is contrary to ordinary plain human experience, or to the nature of the things themselves, then we are compelled to regard the *application* as figurative, though the words themselves still retain their literal *meaning*; otherwise, the application would lose all its force and all its point.

The first three important figures in this class should be studied together : *viz.*: *Simile* (comparison by *Resemblance*), *Metaphor* (comparison by *Representation*), and *Hypocatastasis* (comparison by *Implication*), because they are like three degrees of comparison in the emphasis conveyed by the inter-relation of words and their application. They are the positive, comparative, and superlative degrees of relation between words and thoughts.

In conforming to the order in which we are presenting these Figures of language, we lose much that would elucidate and bring out the beauties of these three. They would each gain in force and emphasis if we were to combine them in one chapter and under one head.

Even if we could present the passages out of the order of the books of the Bible, one could be made to lead on and up to another, so as to enhance the general effect and force of the subject.

But we proceed on the lines we have laid down, and consider the *Application* of words :

SIMILE ; or, RESEMBLANCE.

*A Declaration that one Thing resembles another ; or, Comparison by
Resemblance.*

Sim'-i-le. This is the Latin name of the figure; from *similis, like,
similar, resembling closely,* or *in many respects.*

This figure has no corresponding Greek name. Indeed it can
hardly be called a figure, or an unusual form of expression, seeing it is
quite literal, and one of the commonest forms of expression in use.
It is a cold, clear, plain statement as to a *resemblance* between words
and things. The whole application of the figure lies in this *Resemblance,*
and not in *Representation,* as in *Metonymy ;* or in *Implication,* as in
Hypocatastasis ; or, in *Association,* as in *Synecdoche.*

Accordingly, when this resemblance is not apparent, or is counter
to our ordinary perception of things, it jars upon the ear. Such *Similes*
abound in human writings. Hence the pleasure of studying the use of
them in the Word of God, where we have the Holy Spirit's own perfect
work.

Many examples could be given of false, or incongruous *Similes* in
human writings. Take, for example, Montgomery's poem on Satan : *

> " Lo ! the bright dew-bead on the bramble lies,
> Like liquid rapture upon Beauty's eyes."

We fail to see any resemblance between beauteous eyes and a
bramble ; or, any meaning at all in " liquid rapture."

So Mrs. Browning :

> " Then the bitter sea
> Inexorably pushed between us both ;
> And sweeping up the steep with my despair,
> Threw us out as a pasture to the stars."

We fail to see any resemblance between a ship and a pasture ;
and why stars go out to grass ; or, when they do, why they should feed
on ships and their passengers !

No such inexplicable similes as these can be found in the
Scriptures.

---

* Quoted in Macbeth's *Might and Mirth of Literature.*

When one is used there, it is "for our learning;" and the more we study it the more we may learn.

They are usually marked by the *Caph* (כ) in Hebrew ; and in the Greek by ὡς (*hōs*), *as ;* καθώς (*kathōs*), *like as ;* or, by some seventeen other kindred words *; and the English : "*as*," "*like as*," "*even as*," "*like*," etc.

Simile differs from Comparison, in that comparison admits of dissimilitudes as well as resemblances.

Simile differs from *Allegory* (*q.v.*) in that allegory names only one of the two things and leaves us to find, and make the resemblance with the other, ourselves.

Simile differs from *Metaphor* (*q.v.*), in that it merely states resemblance, while *Metaphor* boldly transfers the *representation*.

Simile differs from *Hypocatastasis* (*q.v.*), in that the latter only *implies* the resemblance, while *Simile* states it.

Simile, therefore, is destitute of feeling. It is clear, beautiful, gentle, true to fact, but cold and too deliberate for passion.

All this will be seen as the Similes are studied. They require no explanation. They explain and are intended to explain themselves. It is scarcely necessary to give any examples. They abound throughout the Scripture, and impart to it much of its beauty and force.

Ps. i. 3.—" He shall be **like** a tree planted by the rivers of water." Here, the similitude tells us that the man who meditates in God's word is planted and protected, just as a tree in a garden is cared for as a " tree of the field " is not.

See under *Ellipsis*, page 97.

Ps. i. 4.—" The ungodly are not so : but are **like** the chaff which the wind driveth away." The contrast between the driven chaff and the " planted " tree is most striking and solemn.

The two comparisons are the great features of the Psalm, the structure of which is as follows :—

A | a | 1. The godly blessed in not standing among the ungodly.
      b | 2, 3-. Comparison (כי אם). " Like a tree."
        c | -3. Prosperity.

A   c | 4-. The Contrary : " not so."
       b | -4. Comparison (כי אם). " Like the chaff."
  a | 5. The ungodly punished in not standing among the godly.

---

* See under the word "AS" in *A Critical Lexicon and Concordance*, by the same author. Longman and Co., 15s.

Then the last verse stands out alone in solemn grandeur as giving the reason for the whole.

Ps. v. 12 (13).—"With favour wilt thou compass him as with a shield." And why is His "favour" (*i.e.*, His grace, which is favour to the unworthy) like a shield? Because "in his favour is life," Ps. xxx. 5 (6); because in His favour there is mercy (Isa. lx. 10); because in His favour there is preservation (Ps. lxxxvi. 2, margin); because in His favour there is security, Ps. xli. 11 (12): and therefore the prayer of all such favoured ones will ever be Ps. cvi. 4.

Ps. xvii. 8.—" Keep me as the apple of the eye [*is kept*]."

Ps. cxxxi. 2.—" I have behaved and quieted myself, as a child that is weaned of his mother : my soul is even as a weaned child."

Matt. vii. 24-27.—Here we have a magnificent and extended *Simile*, almost amounting to a parable. It is too long to quote, and too plain to need elucidation. It explains to us very clearly and forcibly its own powerful lesson.

Matt. ix. 36.—"They . . . were scattered abroad as sheep having no shepherd.

1 Pet. ii. 25.—"Ye were as sheep going astray; but are now returned unto the Shepherd and Bishop of your souls."

Here we have *Simile*, which stands in marked contrast to the *Proverb* in 2 Pet. ii. 22, as to the " sow." Both the stray sheep and the washed sow " return." But the one returns to the shepherd, and the other to the mire. We may note also that the verb " returned " as used of the " sheep " is the *passive* form ; while, as used of the " sow," it is the *active* form. Showing that the " sheep " is made to return by a constraining power, while the " sow " returns of its own act and free-will. See under *Parœmia*.

Sometimes a *Simile* is really used as a figure, implying not merely a resemblance but the actual thing itself.

Gen. xxv. 31.—" Sell me as on this day (כַּיּוֹם, *kayyōm*) " : *i.e.*, on this very day. See, too, verse 33.

Num. xi. 1.—The Heb. reads : " And when the People was as murmurers, it was evil in the ears of Jehovah."

Here the resemblance was real : *i.e.*, they *were* murmurers.

Neh. vii. 2.—" I gave my brother Hanani . . . charge over Jerusalem : for he acted as a faithful man (כְּאִישׁ), etc." : *i.e.*, he *was* a faithful man.

Isa. i. 7.—" It is desolate as the overthrow of strangers." See A.V. margin.

See under *Antimereia*, and compare Isa. xiii. 6.

Isa. i. 9.—" Except the LORD of hosts had left unto us a very small remnant, we should have been as Sodom, and we should have been like unto Gomorrah."

Here the words of the godly remnant declare the resemblance; and in the next verse Jehovah endorses it as true; addressing the ungodly but most religious nation actually as " the rulers of Sodom " and " the people of Gomorrah."

Ps. cxxii. 3.—" Jerusalem is builded as a city that is compact together " : *i.e.*, it *was* a city so built.

Hos. v. 10.—" The princes of Judah were like them that remove the bound " : *i.e.*, they actually committed this sin, the greatness of which is seen from Deut. xix. 14 ; xxvii. 17.

Matt. xiv. 5.—" Because they counted him as a prophet " : *i.e.*, as actually a prophet.

Luke xxii. 44.—" His sweat was as it were great drops of blood " : *i.e.*, it was.

John i. 14.—" And we beheld his glory, the glory as of the only begotten of the Father " : *i.e.*, the glory of Him who was really the only begotten Son of the Father.

Rom. ix. 32.—" Wherefore ? Because they sought it not by faith, but as it were (*i.e.*, actually) by the works of the law."

2 Cor. ii. 17.—" We are not as many, which corrupt the word of God : but as of sincerity, but as of God, in the sight of God speak we in Christ " : *i.e.*, we speak really and truly sincere, pure, and Divine words.

2 Cor. iii. 18.—" We are all with unveiled face beholding as in a mirror (κατοπτριζόμενοι, *katoptrizomenoi*) the glory of the Lord, are transfigured to the same image, from glory to glory, **even as** from the Lord—the Spirit " : *i.e.*, really by the actual operation of the Holy Spirit. His office is to glorify Christ; and those who are led by the Spirit do occupy themselves with Christ—the heavenly object, and thus become like Him, heavenly, and that without an effort. Indeed, the measure in which we are " filled with the Spirit " is the measure in which we are thus occupied with Christ.

Sometimes the word " **as** " is followed by the word " **so**," to
strengthen and heighten the comparison, and make
it more clear : as in

Isa. xxiv. 2.—" And it shall be
  As with the people,
    So with the priest ;
  As with the servant,
    So with his master ;
  As with the maid,
    So with her mistress ;
  As with the buyer,
    So with the seller ;
  As with the lender,
    So with the borrower ;
  As with the taker of usury,
    So with the giver of usury to him."

And all this to show the universality of the judgment which
shall make the land empty and desolate.

This is a combination of *Syncrisis* with this form of *Simile*.

Isa. lv. 10, 11.—

a | " **As** the rain cometh down, and the snow

  b | From heaven,

    c | And returneth not thither, but watereth the earth, and
      | maketh it bring forth and bud,

      d | That it may give seed to the sower, and bread to the
        | eater.

a | **So** shall my word be that goeth forth

  b | Out of my mouth :

    c | It shall not return unto me void,

      d | But it shall accomplish that which I please, and it
         | shall prosper in the thing whereto I sent it."

Here, in this beautiful comparison, we have in a and *a* the two
things compared, the Word resembling the rain and snow ; in b and *b*
we have their *source ;* in c and *c*, their *destiny*, not returning void ;
and in d and *d*, their *end* prospering, and the accomplishment of their
mission.

" AS " and " SO."

We have collected a number of these examples of the use of " as "
and " so " together ; and arranged them, not in the sequence of the

books of the Bible, or in full ; but we have numbered them and placed them so as to illustrate the ways of God in grace :—

(1) Sin and death (Rom. v. 12). These words explain the mystery of the first and last Adam, and the first and second man : their temptation and its results as shown in Gen. iii., Matt. iv., and Rom. vi. 23. This explains

(2) Offence and righteousness : judgment and free gift (Rom. v. 18) ; also

(3) Disobedience and obedience : sinners and righteous (Rom. v. 19). Hence the eternal results of

(4) Sin and death : grace and eternal life (Rom. v. 21).

Now we pass from sin and its entrance and consequences to

(5) its remedy. The Serpent and the Son of Man (John iii. 14). Note the two "musts" (verses 7 and 14) ; and the parabolic miracle of Num. xxi. 5-9. Note the "lifting up" spoken of in John xii. 32. The "all" means all *without distinction* (no longer the *one* People of Israel) not "all" *without exception.*

In due time Christ came to be thus "lifted up," and

(6) do the Father's will, and Commandment, and He did (John xiv. 31), and

(7) suffered; Lamb dumb, and so He; etc. (Isa. liii. 7). Hence

(8) Once to die, and once offered (Heb. ix. 27, 28).

Then

(9) they are sent, "Sent Me" and "sent them" (John xvii. 18)

(10) to bear testimony of His grace : "Believed" and "done" (Matt. viii. 13),

(11) yea, of His life-giving grace : Life (John v. 26).

(12) God reveals *Himself* : Heaven and earth; ways and thoughts (Isa. lv. 9), and

(13) man, *morally* : Foolish as a beast (Ps. lxxiii. 22).

(14) Fathers and sons, etc., ye (Acts vii. 51) ; and

(15) *physically*, the Flower that flourisheth (Ps. ciii. 15).

Then He reveals

(16) His *mercy* : Heaven high and mercy great (Ps. ciii. 11),

(17) His *forgiveness* : East from west and trangressions removed (Ps. ciii. 12),

(18) His *pity* : A father and the Lord (Ps. ciii. 13), and

(19) His *love* : The Father and I (John xv. 9).

Then He reveals

(20) our relationships and duties : Many members and one body (Rom. xii. 4 ; see 1 Cor. xii. 12, 13).

(21) Mutual forgiveness : Christ forgave and do ye (Col. iii. 13),

(22) Christ-like walk : Received and walk ye (Col. ii. 6).

(23) Divine consolations : Sufferings and consolation (2 Cor. i. 5, 7).

(24) Missionary work : Received and minister (1 Pet. iv. 10) ; with

(25) the Divine promise, Rain and snow : the word of God (Isa. lv. 10, 11) ; and

(26) the Divine support, Thy days and thy strength (Deut. xxxiii. 25).

Oh may our desire to do His will be according to,

(27) The hart panting, and the soul longing (Ps. xlii. 1 (2)).

THE JEW.

(28) All blessing based on God's original covenant-promise; Stars and seed (Jer. xxxiii. 22), see especially Gen. xv. 5, and Rom. iv. 18. The covenant of works they brake, see Ex. xxiv. 3, 7 and Jer. xxxi. 32, and are now suffering the consequences.

(29) The future blessing of Israel will be under the original covenant of grace : as Mother comforteth, so will I comfort (Isa. lxvi. 13).

(30) Bridegroom and thy God (Isa. lxii. 5).

(31) The waters of Noah, and wrath (Isa. liv. 9, 10).

(32) Shepherd seeking and I will seek (Ezek. xxxiv. 12).

THE GENTILE. We must not separate what God has joined together, nor join together what God has separated (Matt. xix. 6). The Jew, the Gentile, and the Church of God, are distinct in their calling, standing, hope, and destiny (1 Cor. x. 32). The preaching of the Gospel is not to convert the world, but to take out a People (Acts xv. 14); while the world will get worse and worse until Christ suddenly comes.

(33) Lightning, and coming (Matt. xxiv. 27).

(34) The days of Noah, and the coming of the Son of Man (Matt. xxiv. 37-39).

THE CHURCH OF GOD. Christ's advent will wear a different aspect to the Church. Not like the lightning or a thief, but

(35) "this same Jesus." As ye have seen Him go will so come (Acts i. 11). Christ's *resurrection* is the type and pledge of ours.

(36) As all in Adam die, so all in Christ made alive (1 Cor. xv. 22). Note the "order" (verses 23 and 24).

SYNCRISIS; or, REPEATED SIMILE.

Repetition of a number of Resemblances.

Syn'-cri-sis. Greek, σύγκρισις, from σύν (*sun*), *together with*, and κρίσις (*crisis*), *a judging* or *deciding*.

Hence, *Syncrisis* is *the judging* or *comparing* of one thing with another; and is used of the figure which consists of a repeated *Simile*, or of more than one, or of a number of separate comparisons used together.

Another name for this figure is PARATHESIS (*Pa-rath'-e-sis*), Greek, παράθεσις, *a putting beside*; from παρά (*para*), *beside*, and τιθέναι (*tithenai*), *to place*.

It was called by the Latins COMPARATIO: *i.e., a bringing together and comparing.*

Isa. i. 18.—

"Though your sins be as scarlet,
   They shall be as white as snow;
Though they be red like crimson,
   They shall be as wool."

Isa. xxxii. 2.—"And a man shall be as an hiding place from the wind, and a covert from the tempest; as rivers of water in a dry place, as the shadow of a great rock in a weary land."

Isa. lxvi. 12.—"For thus saith the LORD, Behold, I will extend peace to her like a river, and the glory of the Gentiles like a flowing stream."

METAPHOR ; or, REPRESENTATION.

*A Declaration that one Thing is (or represents) another ;
or, Comparison by Representation.*

Met'-a-phor. Greek, μεταφορά (*metaphora*), *a transference*, or *carrying over or across.* From μετά (*meta*), *beyond* or *over*, and φέρειν (*pherein*), *to carry.* We may call the figure "Representation" or "Transference."

Hence, while the *Simile* gently states that one thing is like or resembles another, the *Metaphor* boldly and warmly declares that one thing IS the other.

While the *Simile* says "All flesh is AS grass" (1 Pet. i. 24), the *Metaphor* carries the figure *across* at once, and says "All flesh IS grass" (Isa. xl. 6). This is the distinction between the two.

The *Metaphor* is, therefore, not so true to *fact* as the *Simile*, but is much truer to *feeling.*

The *Simile* says "All we **like** sheep," while the *Metaphor* declares that "we **are** the sheep of His pasture."

While, therefore, the word "resembles" marks the *Simile :* "represents" is the word that marks the metaphor.

We have recourse to Metaphor when we say of a picture, "This is my father," or "This is my mother." The verb "is" means in this case *represents ;* there may not be the least *resemblance !* The verb "is" always has this meaning and no other when used as a *metaphor.* No other verb will do.

Few figures are more misunderstood than the *Metaphor.* It is one of the few whose names are well known, and hence it has become. a general term *for any figure ;* and any figurative language is commonly called "metaphorical."

Few figures have been more variously defined. But all the differences of opinion arise from not separating the figure *Hypocatastasis* (*q.v.*) on the one hand, or distinguishing *Simile* on the other. The same confusion is seen with reference to *Allegory* (*q.v.*).

Let it then be clearly understood that a *Metaphor* is confined to a distinct affirmation that *one thing is another thing*, owing to some association or connection in the uses or effects of anything expressed or understood. The two nouns themselves must both be mentioned, and are always to be taken in their absolutely literal sense, or else no one can tell what they mean. The figure lies wholly in the verb, or

copula, which, in English, must always be expressed, and never
understood by *Ellipsis.*

For example, " All flesh **is** grass." Here " flesh " is to be taken
literally as the subject spoken of, and " grass " is to be taken equally
literally as that which *represents* " flesh." All the figure lies in the
verb " is." This statement is made under strong feeling, the mind
realising some point of association; but, instead of using the more
measured verb " resembles," or " is like "; which would be truer to
fact, though not so true to feeling; the verb "**is**" is used, and the
meaning of one thing is *carried across* and *transferred* to the other. It
is not, as some might think, a mere Hebrew idiom to use " is " for
" represents "; but it is a necessity of language arising from the actual
condition and character of the human mind.

We must, therefore, banish the common and loose way in which
the words " metaphor " and " metaphorical " are used, and confine the
figure strictly and exclusively to this, its one true and proper signification : that of *representation.*

The Representation referred to in the figure may not lie upon the
surface, and may not be at all apparent in the language itself. It may
be in the uses of the thing represented, or in the effects which it
produces. In this case the *Metaphor* often comes as a surprise, by the
discovery of a point in which two apparently unrelated objects have
some point in which they really agree. Hence the same thing may be
used, by a *Metaphor*, to represent two totally different objects by some
different quality or character which may be referred to : *e.g.,* a lion is
used both of Christ and of the devil. We are to " cease from man " as
opposed to trust in God ; we are exhorted to " quit " ourselves like men
as opposed to all that is effeminate.

The Latins * called the figure TRANSLATIO : *i.e., Translation,*
thus denoting the same fact : *viz., the translation* or *carrying across* of
one thing and applying it to another which *represents* it, just as what is
meant in one language is carried across and expressed or *translated* in
the words of another language.

It should be observed that the Hebrew has no verb substantive or
copula answering to the Greek and English verb " *to be.*" Consequently
the A.V. generally puts in italics the verbs " *is,*" " *are,*" " *were,*" etc.
The verb " to be," though it is not necessary to be expressed in Hebrew,
is yet so really there that the R.V. has abandoned the use of italic
type with regard to it in the Old Testament, and so the Revisers

---

* Cicero. *Orat.* xxvii.

state it in their preface. We prefer the practice of the translators of the A.V., and believe it is more correct.

In the Greek, as we shall see below, whenever a *Metaphor* is intended, the verb substantative must be used; otherwise it is often omitted according to the Hebrew usage (see the Beatitudes, etc.). It is, therefore, more easy to discern a *Metaphor* in the New Testament than in the Old. In the latter we have to be guided by what is true to *fact* and what is true only to *feeling*. If we distinguish between these, we shall not fail to see what is a statement of fact, and what is a *Metaphor*.

Ps. xxiii. 1.—"The LORD *is* my Shepherd." Here, we have a *Metaphor;* and in it a great and blessed truth is set forth by the representation of Jehovah as a Shepherd. It is He who tends his People, and does more for them than any earthly shepherd does for his sheep. All His titles and attributes are so bound up with this care that in this Psalm we have the illustration of all the Jehovah-titles :—

In verse 1. " I shall not want," because He is JEHOVAH-JIREH (Gen. xxii. 14), and will provide.

In verse 2. " He leadeth me beside the waters of quietness (margin), because He is JEHOVAH-SHALOM (Judges vi. 24), and will give peace.

In verse 3. " He restoreth my soul," for He is JEHOVAH-ROPHECHA (Ex. xv. 26), and will graciously heal.

In verse 3. He guides me " in the paths of righteousness," for He is JEHOVAH-TZIDKENU (Jer. xxiii. 6), and is Himself my righteousness, and I am righteous in Him (Jer. xxxiii. 16).

In verse 4. In death's dark valley "Thou art with me," for thou art JEHOVAH-SHAMMAH (Ezek. xlviii. 35), and the LORD is there.

In verse 5. " Thou preparest a table before me in the presence of mine enemies," for Thou art JEHOVAH-NISSI (Ex. xvii. 15), my banner, and will fight for me, while I feast.

In verse 5. " Thou anointest my head with oil," for Thou art JEHOVAH-MEKADDESCHEM (Ex. xxxi. 13, etc.), the LORD that sanctifieth me.

In verse 6. " Surely " all these blessings are mine for time and eternity, for He is JEHOVAH-ROHI (Ps. xxiii. 1), Jehovah my Shepherd, pledged to raise me up from the dead, and to preserve and bring me "through" the valley of death into His glorious kingdom (John vi. 39).

Ps. lxxxiv. 11 (12).—" The LORD God *is* a Sun and Shield." Here, the *Metaphor* is taken from the uses and effects of the two things mentioned. He is my light and my defence. See P.B.V.

Ps. xci. 4.—" His truth *is* a shield and a buckler " (R.V.). Here, we have the *Metaphor*, by which the one thing is *carried over* and *stated* as being the other. In Ps. v. 12, we have the same fact stated literally as a *Simile*. See page 728 above.

Metaphors are so numerous in the Old Testament, that it is impossible to give more than these few to serve as specimens and examples. We add a few from the New Testament.

Matt. v. 13.—" Ye are the salt of the earth ": *i.e.*, ye are (or *represent*) with regard to the earth what salt is to other things, preserving it from total corruption and destruction ; just as the few righteous in Sodom would have preserved that city.

When the Lord Jesus shall have returned and caught up His People (the salt) to meet Him in the air and to be for ever with Him, then the corruption will proceed apace, and the harvest of the earth speedily be ripened for judgment.

Matt. xxvi. 26.—" This is my body " (τοῦτό ἐστι τὸ σῶμά μου, *touto esti to sōma mou*).

Few passages have been more perverted than these simple words. Rome has insisted on the literal or the figurative sense of words just as it suits her own purpose, and not at all according to the laws of philology and the true science of language.

Hence the Latin idiom, " *agere pænitentiam*," *repent*, has been rendered literally in all her versions from the Vulgate, in various languages, " do penance," except when God is said to repent ! Rome dared not translate *agere pænitentiam* literally in these cases, which proves her design in thus systematically perverting the Word of God : and the false doctrine is thus *forced* into the words under a show or semblance of literal translation.* So the *Metaphor*, " This is my body," has been forced to teach false doctrine by being translated literally.

No perversion of language has been fraught with greater calamity to the human race. Tens of thousands have suffered martyrdom at the hands of Rome rather than believe the " blasphemous fable " forced

---

* Rome would not dare to translate the same Latin idiom " *agere vitam*," *to do life*, though the expression has passed into slang. It means simply *to live*, as the other idiom means *to repent*.

into these words. The exquisite tortures of the Inquisition were invented to coerce the consciences of men and compel them to accept this lie!

Luther himself was misled, through his ignorance of this simple law of figurative language. In his controversy with Zwingle, he obstinately persisted in maintaining the *literal* sense of the figure, and thus forced it to have a meaning which it never has. He thus led the whole of Germany into his error! For, while his common sense rejected the error of "Transubstantiation," he fell into another, and invented the figment of "Consubstantiation," and fastened it upon the Lutheran Church to this day.

What a solemn and instructive lesson as to the importance of a true understanding of the figures of language!

The whole figure, in a metaphor, lies, as we have said, in the verb substantive "IS"; and not in either of the two nouns; and it is a remarkable fact that, when a *pronoun* is used instead of one of the nouns (as it is here), and the two nouns are of different genders, the pronoun is always made to agree in gender with that noun to which the meaning is carried across, and not with the noun from which it is carried, and to which it properly belongs. This at once shows us that a figure is being employed; when a pronoun, which ought, according to the laws of language, to agree in gender with its own noun, is changed, and made to agree with the noun which, by *Metaphor, represents* it.

Here, for example, the pronoun, "this" (τοῦτό, *touto*), is *neuter*, and is thus made to agree with "body" (σῶμά, *sōma*), which is *neuter*, and not with bread (ἄρτος, *artos*), which is *masculine*.*

This is always the case in *Metaphors*, and a few examples may be cited here, instead of in their natural order and place.

In Zech. v. 8, "This is wickedness." Here, "this" (*fem.*) does not agree with "ephah" (to which it refers), which is *neuter* (LXX.), but with "wickedness," which is *feminine*.

In Zech. v. 3, "This is the curse." "This" (*fem.*) agrees with "curse," which is *feminine*, and not with "flying roll," which is *neuter*, (to which it refers), (δρέπανον, *drepanon*, LXX.).

In Matt. xiii. 38, "The good seed are the children of the kingdom." Here, "these" (*masc.*) (οὗτοι, *houtoi*),† agrees with "children of the kingdom" (*masc.*), and not with seed (σπέρμα, *sperma*), which is *neuter*.

---

* In violation of this law, a recent revision of the Marathi Prayer Book has deliberately changed the gender of the pronoun and made it to agree with the word for "bread"!

† This pronoun is omitted in the English of the A.V. and R.V.

Luke viii. 14, "These are they which having heard," etc. Here, "these" (*masc.*) (οὗτοι, *houtoi*) agrees with the participle (οἱ ἀκούσαντες, *hoi akousantes*), "they which having heard," which is *masculine*, and not with the seed, (to which it refers), which is *neuter*.

All this establishes our statement that, in a *Metaphor*, the two nouns (or pronoun and noun) are always literal, and that the figure lies only in the *verb*. Another remarkable fact is that in the vast number of cases where the language is literal, and there is no metaphor at all, the verb is omitted altogether.* Even when a *Metaphor* has been used, and the language passes suddenly from figurative to literal, the verb *is at once dropped*, by *Ellipsis*, as not being necessary for the literal sense, as it was for the previous figurative expression: *e.g.*, in 1 Cor. xii. 27, "Ye ARE the body of Christ." Here is a metaphor, and consequently the verb is used. But in verse 29, which is literal, the change is at once made, and the fact is marked by the omission of the verb, " [*Are*] all apostles? [*are*] all prophets? [*are*] all teachers? [*are*] all workers of miracles?"

Next compare other examples of *Metaphors* which are naturally used in the explanations of Parables. Note the Parables of the Sower, and of the Tares (Matt. xiii. 19-23, and 37-43).

> "He that soweth the good seed is (*i.e.*, represents) the Son of man."
>
> "The field is (*i.e.*, signifies) the world."
>
> "The good seed are the children of the kingdom."
>
> "But the tares are the children of the wicked one."
>
> "The enemy that sowed them is the devil."
>
> "The harvest is the end of the age."
>
> "And the reapers are the angels."

In all these (as in every other *Metaphor*) the verb means, and might have been rendered, "*represents*," or "*signifies*."

The Apocalypse is full of metaphors, *e.g.*:

> "The seven stars are (*i.e.*, represent) the angels of the seven churches."
>
> "And the seven candlesticks which thou sawest are the seven churches" (i. 20).

The odours " are the prayers of the saints " (v. 8).

"They are the spirits of demons" (xvi. 14).

> "The seven heads are (*i.e.*, represent) seven mountains (xvii. 9): etc., etc.

---

* This rule does not apply to the Hebrew, of course, as we have said above: because it has no verb " *to be*."

So in the very words that follow " this **is** (*i.e.,* represents or signifies) my body," we have an undoubted *Metaphor.* " He took the cup . . . saying . . . this **is** my blood." *Here,* thus, we have *a pair* of metaphors. In the former one, " this " refers to " bread," and it is claimed that " **is** " means *changed into* the " body " of Christ. In the latter, " this " refers to " the cup," but it is not claimed that the cup is changed into " blood." At least, we have never heard that such a claim has been put forward. The difference of treatment which the same figure meets with in these two verses is the proof that the former is wrong.

In 1 Cor. xi. 25 we read " this cup **is** the new covenant." Will Romanists, in and out of the Church of England, tell us how this " cup " becomes transubstantiated into a " covenant " ?

Is it not clear that the figure in the words, " This **is** my body," is *forced* into a literal statement with the set purpose and design of making it teach and support erroneous doctrine ?

Other examples of *Metaphor* in this immediate connection are :

1 Cor. x. 16.—" The cup of blessing which we bless, **is** it not (*i.e.,* does it not represent) the communion of the blood of Christ." through which all blessing comes to us ?

" The bread which we break, **is** it not (*i.e.,* does it not represent) the communion of the body of Christ ? " *i.e.,* does it not signify the fellowship of all the members of Christ's mystical body, who, being many, **are** one body (1 Cor. xii. 12) ? " For we being many **are** one bread, and one body," as 1 Cor. x. 17 declares.

It is because those who eat of that bread do not " discern " or discriminate that " one body " (*i.e.,* Christ mystical) that they are said to eat to their own condemnation ; for they witness to the fact of that " great Mystery " and yet are ignorant of its truth ! And hence they condemn themselves.

Further, the verb, εἰμι (*eimi*), *I am,* or the *infinitive* of it, *to be,* means *to be* in the sense of *signifying, amounting to.* And that this is one of its primary senses may be seen from the following passages, where it is actually translated " *to mean,*" and not merely *to be :*—

" But go ye and learn what that **is** " (*i.e., meaneth,* as in A.V.), Matt. ix. 13.

" But if ye had known what that **is** " (A.V., *meaneth*), Matt. xii. 7.

" He asked what these things **were** " (A.V., *meant*), Luke xv. 26.

" What **is** this ? " (A.V., " What meaneth this ? ") Acts ii. 12.

" Now, while Peter doubted in himself what this vision **was** which he had seen " (A.V., " What this vision should mean "), Acts x. 17, etc., etc., etc.

On the other hand, if an *actual* change is meant, then there must be a verb which shall plainly and actually say so : for the verb " *to be* " never has or conveys any idea of such change.

The usual verb to express such a change is γίνομαι (*ginomai*), which means *to be* or *become*.   Mark iv. 39, " There *was* (*i.e.*, there became) a great calm," and the storm was changed (or turned into) into calm.

Luke iv. 3, " Command this stone that it *be made* (*i.e.*, changed into) bread."

John ii. 9, " When the ruler of the feast tasted the water that *was made* (*i.e.*, changed into) wine."

John xvi. 20, " Your sorrow *shall be turned* into joy."   This was a real transubstantiation.

Acts xxvi. 28, Agrippa said, " Almost thou persuadest me *to be* (*i.e.*, to become) a Christian.".

Rev. viii. 8, " The third part of the sea *became* blood," and in verse 11, " Many men died of the waters, because they were *made* bitter."

In all these cases (but the last) the verb is γίνομαι (*ginomai*), *to become :* and, if the Lord had meant that the bread *became* His body, that is the verb He would have necessarily used.   The fact that He did not use it, but used the simple verb, εἰμι (*eimi*), instead, *i.e.*, " is," proves conclusively that no *change* was meant, and that only *representation* was intended.

Just as when we are looking over a map and say, " This is England," " This is America," " This is Palestine," etc., we do not mean that that piece of paper is England, but we mean that those marks upon it *represent* those respective countries.

From all this it is philologically, philosophically, and scientifically clear that the words, " This is my body," mean " This [*bread*] represents my body."   And as Professor Macbeth has put it, " We trample on the laws of nature, and we trample on the laws of language when we force the verb ' is ' to mean *what it never does mean.*"

And, besides all this, to pass from the use made of this perversion, suppose for a moment that we grant the claim, and the words mean that the Lord Jesus then and there did transmute the bread into *His own body* (if we can imagine such an impossibility !), what then ? Where is there a breath about His giving that power to any one else ? Where is there one word about such gifts being conferred ?   And, if it be claimed, as it is by some traitors in the Church of England, that the words, " Do this," convey that power and authority, it could have been conveyed only to the eleven that were present. Where is there a breath about not only giving them power, but delegating it to them to give to others, and these to others again indefinitely? There is not one single word expressed or implied that conveys the idea that one iota of such power was conferred or delegated. So that the whole fabric of transubstantiation rests on absolutely no foundation whatsoever! There is a "missing link" which is fatal to the whole position.

And this, on the assumption which we have only for the moment granted. But, when it is seen that not only is there this link missing, which can never be supplied: but that there is also this claim which can never be substantiated; we have an explanation of the *Metaphor* which sweeps the dogma out of the Scriptures, and proves it to be a fiction which is the outcome of ignorance, and this by arguments that cannot be overthrown, and facts that cannot be denied.

John vi. 35. " I am the bread of life" : *i.e.*, what bread does in supporting natural life is a *representation* of what Christ does in supporting and nourishing the new, Divine, spiritual life.

John viii. 12.—" I am the light of the world."

John x. 9.—" I am the door": *i.e.*, I am what a door is. I am the entrance to the sheepfold, and to the Father. Yes, a door, and not a flight of steps. A door, through which we pass in one movement from one side to the other.

John xv. 5.—" I am the true vine."

Here the word ἀληθινός (*aleethinos*) helps the figure, for it means *true* as regards the reality in relation to shadows or representations. Not "true" as opposed to what is false, but the " *very* " vine : the vine all earthly vines represent, and to which they point in such Scriptures as Isa. v. and Ps. lxxx.*

Gal. iv. 24.—" Which things **are** an allegory : for these **are** the two covenants," etc.

---

* See an Article, by the same author, in *Things to Come* for July, 1899.

HYPOCATASTASIS ; or, IMPLICATION.

A Declaration that implies the Resemblance or Representation ;
or Comparison by Implication.

Hy¹-po-cat-as¹-ta-sis. Greek, ὑποκατάστασις, *substitution* or *implication ;* from ὑπό *(hypo)*, *underneath*, κατά *(kata)*, *down*, and στάσις *(stasis)*, *a stationing.* Hence, *a putting down underneath.*

As a figure, it differs from *Metaphor*, because in a metaphor the two nouns are *both* named and given ; while, in *Hypocatastasis*, only *one* is named and the other is implied, or as it were, is *put down underneath* out of sight. Hence *Hypocatastasis* is implied resemblance or representation : *i.e.*, an implied *Simile* or *Metaphor*. If *Metaphor* is more forcible than *Simile*, then *Hypocatastasis* is more forcible than *Metaphor*, and expresses as it were the superlative degree of resemblance.

For example, one may say to another, " You are like a beast." This would be *Simile*, tamely stating a fact. If, however, he said, " You are a beast " that would be *Metaphor*. But, if he said simply, " Beast ! " that would be *Hypocatastasis*, for the other part of the *Simile* or *Metaphor* (" you "), would be *implied* and not stated.

This figure, therefore, is calculated to arouse the mind and attract and excite the attention to the greatest extent.

So well known was it to the ancients, that it received this significant name. But it is, to-day, unmentioned by literary men, though it is often unconsciously used by them. Thus, their language is enriched by its use, while the figure is unknown, even by name !

What a proof of the sad neglect into which this great subject has fallen ; and what an example of the consequent loss which has ensued.

This beautiful and far-reaching figure frequently occurs in Scripture. The Lord Jesus Himself often used it, and that with wonderful effect.

Its beauty and force will be at once seen, if we compare one or two passages.

When, in Jer. xlix. 19, we read of the king of Babylon coming up against Edom, it says : " Behold, he shall come up like a lion . . . against the habitation of the strong ": etc. Here, we have a *Simile*, and the feelings are unmoved, as it is only against EDOM that the assault is made.

But it is a very different case in Jer. iv. 7, where the same king of Babylon is spoken of as coming up against Zion. In the heat of excited feeling he is not named, but only *implied.*

" The lion is come up from his thicket."

So, in all the other cases, it will be well to contrast every example of *Hypocatastasis* with both *Simile* and *Metaphor*, in order to gather the full force of its meaning and the reason for its use instead of either of the other two.

Ps. xxii. 16 (17).—" Dogs have compassed me about."

Here He does not say that his enemies were **like** dogs, or that they were dogs; no: the word *" enemies "* is not mentioned. It is implied: and by a kind of *Prosopopoeia*, they are spoken of as " dogs." It means of course, " mine enemies have compassed me about" as the next sentence goes on to explain. See also under *Paronomasia.*

Matt. xv. 13.—" Every plant, which my heavenly Father hath not planted, shall be rooted up." This is *Hypocatastasis*, bordering on Allegory. Persons are implied, though only plants are named. The solemn lesson of this implication is, that unless the work in the heart be that of God Himself, all is vain. It is useless therefore to attempt to effect conversion or to impart a new nature by personal appeals, persuasions, or excitement. This is only to make the flesh religious, and " that which is born of the flesh is flesh."

Matt. xvi. 6.—" Beware of the leaven of the Pharisees, and of the Sadducees." There the word " doctrine " is implied. Had the Lord said, " the doctrine of the Pharisees is **like** leaven," that would have been *Simile*, and a cold, bare statement of fact; but He did not say so. Had He said " the doctrine of the Pharisees is leaven," that would have been *Metaphor*; much bolder, much more forcible, but not so true to fact though much truer to truth. But He did not say so. He took the word " doctrine " and *put it down underneath*, and did not mention it at all. He only *implied* it: and this was *Hypocatastasis.*

No wonder then that the attention of the disciples was excited and attracted. No wonder their interest was aroused: for this was the Lord's object.

" They reasoned among themselves, saying, It is because we have taken no bread. Which when Jesus perceived, he said unto them, O ye of little faith, why reason ye among yourselves, because ye have brought no bread? Do ye not yet understand? . . . How is it that ye do not understand that I spake not to you concerning bread, that ye should beware of the leaven of the Pharisees and of the Saducees ? Then understood they how that he bade them not beware of the leaven of bread, but of the doctrine of the Pharisees and of the Sadducees" (verses 6-12). This example is remarkable when we compare it with another, in the previous chapter, which we give next ; and out of its textual order for the purpose of contrast.

Matt. xv. 26.—" It is not meet to take the children's bread, and to cast it to dogs." Here, the Lord Jesus, did not say to the woman of Canaan, *Thou art a dog of the Gentiles* (which would have been *Metaphor*), but He left out all reference to her, and only referred to her by *implication,* substituting a " dog " for herself. The woman, unlike the disciples (in chap. xvi.), at once saw and understood what the Lord *implied,* viz., that it was not meet to take that which belonged to Israel and give it to a Gentile (or a dog of a Gentile as they were called by the Jews), " And she said, Truth, Lord." What she felt is clear : " It is quite true ; Thou art perfectly right ; I called Thee ' the Son of David,' and deserved no answer; I pleaded for ' help ' and said : ' Lord, help me ' ; but I made no confession as to who the ' me ' was : no acknowledgment of my unworthiness and unmeetness as ' a dog of the Gentiles.' " " Truth, Lord : yet the dogs eat of the crumbs which fall from their master's table. Then Jesus answered and said unto her, O woman, great is thy faith."

So, it is " great faith " to understand what the Lord *implied* by the use of this beautiful figure, and it is " little faith " not to understand it! even though the former was spoken of a Gentile woman, and the latter of the apostles of the Lord. See also under *Synecdoche* and *Meiosis.*

John ii. 19.—" Destroy this temple, and in three days I will raise it up." The Lord Jesus did not say that His body was like the temple (that would have been *Simile*), or that it **was** His body (that would have been *Metaphor*). He merely *implied* the word *body,* as ver. 21 plainly declares : " He spake of the temple of his body."

Here was neither " great faith " nor " little faith," but wilful unbelief of His words. His disciples remembered them *after* He was raised from the dead, and believed. His enemies remembered them *before* and perverted them : " This fellow said, I am able to destroy the temple of God, and to build it in three days " (Matt. xxvi. 61). He said no such thing. What He foretold was that they would destroy " this temple " of His body, and that He should raise it again from the dead in three days, and build it again. See also under *Heterosis.*

Other examples are :—

Matt. iii. 10.—Where, by the axe being laid to the root of the trees, etc., is *implied* the result of the ministry of John the Baptist. The same is the case with ver. 12.

Matt. v. 29, 30.—May also be explained by this figure better than by *Hyperbole* (*q.v.*). The right eye, etc., is compared *by implication* to the most highly prized possession.

Matt. vii. 3-5.—The mote and beam refer by *implication* to anything that perverts the vision.

Matt. vii. 6.—Here " dogs " and " swine " are compared by *implication* to persons.

Mark i. 17.—" I will make you to become fishers of men." The Lord does not say *like* fishers, nor does He use direct *metaphor*. The resemblance is only by *implication*.

Acts xx. 29.—" I know this, that after my departing shall grievous wolves enter in among you, not sparing the flock."

Thus does the Holy Spirit inform us, by *Implication*, as to the true character of " apostolic succession," in order to impress the solemn fact on our minds.

ALLEGORY ; or, CONTINUED METAPHOR AND HYPOCATASTASIS.

Continued Comparison by Representation or Implication.

Al'-le-go-ry. Greek, ἀλληγορία, from ἄλλος (*allos*), *another*, and ἀγορεύειν (*agoreuein*), *to speak* or *make a speech in the agora* (*i.e.*, assembly).

Few figures have been the subject of greater controversy than *Allegory ;* or, have been more variously defined. One class of Rhetoricians declare that it is a continued metaphor : and another class declare that it is not. But, as is often the case under such circumstances, neither is quite correct, because both have a part of the truth and put it for the whole. Neither of the contending parties takes into consideration the existence of *Hypocatastasis.* And this fact accounts for the confusion, not only with regard to *Allegory*, but also with regard to *Metaphor.*

All three figures are based on *comparison.* *Simile* is comparison by *resemblance ; Metaphor* is comparison by *representation ; Hypocatastasis* is comparison by *implication.*

In the first the comparison is *stated ;* in the second it is *substituted ;* in the third it is *implied.*

Thus *Allegory* is a continuation of the latter two, *Metaphor* or *Hypocatastasis ;* while the *Parable* (*q.v.*) is a continuation of the *Simile.*

This definition clears the whole ground, and explains the whole of the difficulties, and reconciles the different schools.

The *Allegory*, therefore, is of two kinds ; one in which it is *continued Metaphor* (as in Ps. xxiii.), where the two things are *both* mentioned (Jehovah, and the Shepherd's care), and what is asserted belongs to the principal object ; the other, in which it is *continued Hypocatastasis* (Ps. lxxx. 8-15), where only one thing is mentioned (the vine), and what is asserted belongs properly to the secondary object ; *viz.*, to *Israel.* Israel whom it really refers, is not mentioned, but only implied.

Isa. v. 1-6.—This is an *Allegory* which combines both forms. "Judah and Jerusalem " (concerning whom Isaiah prophecies i. 1) are again represented as a vine, and the Allegory commences by *implying* them, and afterwards proceeds to *substitute* them (vers. 3-7).

Allegory thus differs from *Parable*, for a *parable* is a *continued Simile.* It never departs from the simple statement that one thing resembles another. While the allegory *represents*, or *implies*, that the one thing is the other. As in the allegory of the Pilgrim's Progress : What is spoken of one person refers to another person in similar circumstances and experiences. In Ps. lxxx. and Isa. v., what is spoken of a Vine refers to Israel : but, in Genesis, what is stated of Israel and Ishmael, Sarah and Hagar is all true history, yet in Gal. iv. it is made to speak of and set forth other truths, and hence *there* it is, and is called an " *Allegory* " (Gal. iv. 24).

No figure requires more careful discrimination than *Allegory*. And it would be safer to say that there are no allegories in Scripture than to follow one's own judgment as to what is allegory, and what is not.

At any rate, we have only one which is distinctly declared to be such ; and that is Gal. iv. 22, 24. " It is written, that Abraham had two sons, the one by a bondmaid, the other by a free woman. But he who was of the bond-woman was born after the flesh ; but he of the free-woman was by promise. Which things are an Allegory " : or, which things teach or tell us something beyond what is said.

The modern and common usage of the word *allegoria* is thus quite different from this Scriptural definition. According to the modern sense it is taken to mean a fictitious narrative which has another and deeper meaning than that which is expressed.

An allegory *may* sometimes be fictitious, but Gal. iv. shows us that a true history may be allegorized (*i.e.*, be shown to have further teaching in that which actually took place) *without detracting from the truth of the history*. Here note this important fact : that, in either case, *Allegory* is always stated in the *past* tense, and *never in the future*. Allegory is thus distinguished from Prophecy. The *Allegory* brings other teaching out of past events, while the prophecy tells us events that are yet to come, and means exactly what is said.

Gen. xlix.—The prophetical blessing of Jacob is mixed. Part of it is *Simile* (verse 4). Some is *Metaphor* (verse 9). In some parts the *Metaphors* are repeated, in which case we have *Allegory*.

Judges ix. 7-15.—This is not a parable, as the A.V. chapter-heading calls it ; because there is no similitude, by which one thing is likened to another. It is a continued *Hypocatastasis*, only one of the two things being plainly mentioned. Were it not for the interpretation given in verses 16-20, there would be nothing beyond what is implied.

It is interesting to note that the four trees referred to—the Fig-tree, the Olive, the vine, and the Bramble—are the four which are used to combine the whole of Israel's history.

The FIG-TREE represents the *National position* of Israel, from which we learn (in the Synoptic Gospels) that it withered away and has been cut down.

The OLIVE TREE represents the *Covenant privileges* of Israel (Rom. xi.): which are now in abeyance.

The VINE represents Israel's *Spiritual blessings*, which henceforth are to be found only in Christ, the True Vine (John xv.).

The BRAMBLE represents the Antichrist, in whose shadow they will yet trust, but who will be to Israel a consuming fire in the day of " Jacob's trouble "—" the great Tribulation."*

Isa. xxviii. 20 is *Allegory : i.e.*, repeated *Hypocatastasis*, only one part of the figure being mentioned : *viz.*, the bed and its covering, and not the people to whom it refers. The prophet is speaking of the great fear which ought to agitate the people of Judea at the speedy coming of Sennacherib ; but they preferred to be left in their false security. By this beautiful allegorical illustration they are informed that their rest should be restless, and their sleep should be soon disturbed.

Matt. iii. 10, 12 is repeated *Hypocatastasis*, and therefore *Allegory*.

Matt. v. 13 is the same, following on " Ye **are** the salt of the earth," which is *Metaphor*.

Matt. vii. 3-5 is the same ; only one thing, the mote and the beam, being named. What they mean is only implied.

Matt. ix. 15 is the same, the meaning being implied.

Matt. ix. 16, 17. — The " old piece " on the new implies the solemn lesson as to the impossibility of reforming the Old nature.

Matt. xii. 43-45.—" When the unclean spirit is gone out of a man," etc. This is an *Allegory*. It is to be interpreted of the Jewish nation, as verse 45 declares. By *application* also it teaches the unclean spirit's *going out* of his own accord, and not being " cast out " (verse 28, 29). When he is " cast out," he never returns ; but when he " goes out," he comes back ; and finds only a " reformed character," instead of the Holy Spirit indwelling in the one who is born again.

Luke ix. 62.—" No man having put his hand to the plough, and looking back, is fit for the kingdom of God." This is a brief allegory.

For other examples, see John iv. 35. Rom. xi. 16-18, etc. ; xiii. 11, 12. 1 Cor. iii. 6-8, 12-15 ; v. 7, 8. 2 Cor. iii. 2, 3 ; v. 1, etc. ; x. 3-5 ; xi. 2. Gal. vi. 8. Eph. vi. 11, etc.

---

* See *Things to Come* for July, 1899. A. Holness, 14 Paternoster Row.

PARABOLA ; or, PARABLE :
i.e., CONTINUED SIMILE.

Comparison by continued Resemblance.

Par-ab'-o-la. Greek, παραβολή (*pa-rab'-o-lee*), *a placing beside* for the purpose of comparison, from παρά (*para*), *beside*, and βάλλειν (*ballein*), *to throw* or *cast.*

The classical use of the word was for one of the subdivisions of παράδειγμα (*paradeigma*), *an example, viz.,* a presentation of an analogous case by way of illustration.

In the LXX. it occurs about thirty times as the translation of מָשָׁל (*mahshal*), and of no other word : and, if we look at some of the sayings to which the word "parable" is applied, the meaning which was attached to it will be clearly seen.

1 Sam. x. 12 : We read of "the proverb," "Is Saul also among the prophets ?" So xxiv. 14 (13): Of "the proverb of the ancients," "Wickedness proceedeth from the wicked." Compare Ezek. xii. 22; xvi. 44 ; xviii. 2. Deut. xxviii. 37. 2 Chron. vii. 20. Ps. xliv. 14 (15). Jer. xxiv. 9. But see below under *Parœmia.*

Growing out of this came a later meaning of מָשָׁל (*mahshal*) as used of any saying which required an explanation. We see this as early as in Ezek. xx. 47-49.

In the New Testament instances of the word, it is used of a story with a hidden meaning, without pressing, in every detail, the idea of a comparison.

As the name of a Figure of Speech, it is limited to what we may describe as repeated or *continued Simile*—an illustration by which one set of circumstances is likened to another. It consists in *likeness*, not in representation, and therefore is not a continued *Metaphor*, as some have said ; but a *repeated Simile.*

This likeness is generally only in some special point. One person may be like another in appearance, but not in character, and *vice versa* ; so that when resemblance or likeness is affirmed it is not to be concluded that the likeness may be pressed in all points, or extended to all particulars.

For example, a lion is used as a resemblance of Christ, on account of his strength and prowess. The Devil is likened to "a lion" because

of his violence and cruelty.   Christ is compared to a thief, on account
of his coming, being unexpected ; not on account of dishonesty.

The resemblance is to be sought for in the scope of the context,
and in the one great truth which is presented, and the one important
lesson which is taught : and not in all the minute details with which
these happen to be associated.

The *interpretation* of the parable must be further distinguished
from any *application* which may be made of it.   For example : in the
Parable of the "Ten Virgins" (Matt. xxv. 1-12), the *interpretation* belongs
to some special point of time immediately preceding the return of the
Lord to the earth.   This is indicated by the word " Then," with which
it commences, and by its place in relation to the context.   Any lesson
for ourselves, as to watchfulness on our part, must come as an *application* of it to present circumstances.

So with the parable of the Great Supper (Luke xiv. 16-24).   The
application to the present time must not blot out the *interpretation* of
it, which refers to the successive ministries connected with the invitations to " the great supper."

(1) " A certain man " sends " his servant " to those who had been
previously "bidden."   This was Peter's first ministry (Acts ii.-vii.).   All
excuse themselves.

(2) The " master of the house " sends him again to " the streets
and lanes of the city."   This is Peter's second ministry (Acts x.-xii.).

(3) Then " the lord " sends out another servant to " the highways
and hedges."   This is Paul's ministry to the great Gentile world (Acts
xiii.-xxviii.)

Parables are used from the resemblance of one thing to another.
The thing, or history, or story may be true or imaginary ; but the events
must be possible, or likely to have happened ; at any rate those who
hear must believe that they are possible events, though it is not
necessary that the speaker should believe them.

Where they are impossible, such as trees or animals speaking and
reasoning, we have *Fable* ; and if the Fable is explained, then we have
Allegory (*q.v.*).   See Judges ix. 8-15, where we should have *Fable*, but for
the application of it, which we have in verse 16, which renders it
Allegory.

We do not propose to give even a list of the parables of Scripture,
as they can be so easily and readily found by the reader.

One word of caution, however, we must give : and that is concerning
the object of parables.   The common idea is that they are intended to
make things clear and plain.   Hence every young minister and

Sunday-school teacher turns to the parables as though they were the simplest things in the world. Whereas they were spoken that the truth might be veiled from those who " seeing, see not : and hearing, hear not." See Matt. xiii. 10-17. Hence they are among the most difficult portions of God's Word.

Without wearying the student with all the varying definitions and explanations which Rhetoricians and Divines have given, we add what is perhaps the best classification of Similitudes, *viz.:* that by P. Rutilius Lupus.

I. PARADEIGMA.

 1. Persons without words.

 2. Words without persons.

 3. Both persons and words.

II. PARABOLA or PARABLE.

 1. *Icon.* Simile forming a complete image.

 2. *Homœon.* Simile founded on certain points only.

 3. *Epagoge.* Argument from induction.

APOLOGUE; or, FABLE.

A Fictitious Narrative used for Illustration.

Ap'-o-logue. Greek, ἀπόλογος, from ἀπό (*apo*), *from*, and λόγος (*logos*), *speech* (from λέγειν, *to speak*), *a story*, *tale ;* and especially *a fable*. Latin, FABULA, *a fable*.

An *Apologue* (or Fable) differs from a *Parable*, in that the Parable describes what is likely or probable, or at any rate what is believed by the hearers as probable, while the Fable is not limited by such considerations, and is used of impossiblities, such as trees, or animals, and inanimate things talking and acting.

The *Fable*, therefore, is a fictitious narrative intended to illustrate some maxim or truth.

Judges ix. 8-15 would be a Fable, were it not explained in verse 16.

As it is, there are no examples of *Fable*, as such, in the Word of God.

PARŒMIA ; or, PROVERB.

A wayside-saying in common use.

Par-oi'-mi-a. παροιμία, a way-side; from παρά (para), beside, and οἶμος (oimos), a way or path. Hence Parœmia is a way side saying, a trite expression, or common remark, a proverb. As we say " a saw " or adage.

Like Parable, Parœmia is used in the Septuagint Version to translate the Hebrew word מָשָׁל (mahshal). Now this noun מָשָׁל (mahshal) belongs to the verb מָשַׁל (mahshal), which means to rule, control, to have, or exercise control.

Hence it is plain that there must be a close connection between " a rule " and " a proverb." This connection may be illustrated by our phrase " a ruling principle "; and by the fact that we might term what we call 'the Proverbs of Solomon' 'Solomon's Rules'; since that is just what they are: rules for guiding life. Indeed, if we ask what is the derivation of the word " Maxim," we may find its history not unlike that of παροιμία in Greek. It would seem to mean 'a saying most widely used,' 'most in vogue,' in the market, by the roadside, and in ordinary life generally. By degrees, usage separated the words Parable and Parœmia ; and Parable was limited to an illustration ; while Parœmia was confined to what we now call a proverb.

The figure is used, therefore, of any sententious saying, because these are generally such as control and influence life.

The word Parœmia is used in the New Testament (John x. 6), where it is rendered " parable "; and in xvi. 25 (twice), 29, and 2 Pet. ii. 22, where it is rendered " Proverb."

The Latin name for the figure is PROVERBIUM, Proverb. Hence, the name given to the book of Proverbs,* which consists of collections of such brief sentertious sayings which govern the life and control the walk.

Parœmiæ or Proverbs occuring in Scripture may be divided into three classes :—

(1) Those that are quoted as being already in use as such.

(2) Those which, though not quoted as such, were very probably already in use as proverbial expressions.

---

* See The Names and Order of the Books of the Old Testament, by the same author and publisher. Price fourpence.

(3) Those which appear for the first time in Scripture; but which, owing to their fulness of meaning and their wide application, have since passed into general use as proverbial sayings.

1. *Parœmiæ which are quoted as being already in use as such.*

Gen. x. 9.—" He was a mighty hunter before the LORD: wherefore it is said, ' Like Nimrod a mighty hunter before the LORD' " (R.V.).

Num. xxi. 27.—" Wherefore they that speak in proverbs say, ' Come into Heshbon, Let the city of Sihon be built and prepared,' " etc.

Three strophes are given from a popular poem, introduced by the word " wherefore."

The *first* (-27, 28) is an ironical call to the Amorites to rebuild their city Heshbon, which Israel had destroyed (see verses 25, 26).

The *second* (verse 29) is a prophecy of Moab's ruin.

The *third* (verse 30) is the justification of the woe pronounced in verse 29.

Verse 30 is obscure, because of the reading of the letter ר in אֲשֶׁ֖ר which, according to Massorah, is one of the fifteen cases in which words, etc., are dotted. The letter (ר) ought, therefore, to be cancelled. In this case אִשׁ (*ish*), *man*, is put for אִישׁ (*ish*), *men*, and וַנַּשִּׁים (*vannashsheem*), *we have laid them waste*, would then be the plural of אִשָּׁה (*isshah*) : *women*.

The strophe would then read :—

" We have shot at them,
      Heshbon is destroyed even unto Dibon,
   The women also even unto Nopha,
         And the men even unto Medeba."*

1 Sam. x. 12.—" Therefore it became a proverb: ' Is Saul also among the prophets?' "

1 Sam. xxiv. 13. — " As saith the proverb of the ancients, ' Wickedness proceedeth from the wicked: but mine hand shall not be upon thee.' "

2 Sam. xx. 18.—" They were wont to speak in old time, saying, ' They shall surely ask *counsel* at Abel ': and so they ended *the matter*."

---

* See Ginsburg's *Introduction* to the Hebrew Bible, pp. 326-328.

Jer. xxxi. 29.—" In those days they shall say no more, ' The fathers have eaten a sour grape, and the children's teeth are set on edge.' "

This is what they did once say. See Ezek. xviii. 2, 3.

Ezek. xvi. 44.—" Behold, every one that useth proverbs shall use this proverb against thee, saying: ' As is the mother, so is her daughter.' " See xix. 2, 3.

Luke iv. 23.—" Ye will surely say unto me this proverb: ' Physician, heal thyself.' "

This was a well known proverb. It may be found in the Talmud, " Physician, heal thine own lameness." *

John i. 46 (47).—" Can there any good thing come out of Nazareth ? "

This appears from vii. 41, 42, 52, to have been a proverb already in use.

John iv. 37.—" And herein is that saying true; ' One soweth, and another reapeth.' "

2 Pet. ii. 22.—" But it is happened unto them according to the true proverb (Prov. xxvi. 11):

" The dog is turned to his own vomit again ;
And the sow that was washed to her wallowing in the mire."

When we contrast this with 1 Pet. ii. 25, we see how forcible is the difference between the *saved sinner* and the " reformed character." The saint may go astray, and the ungodly may reform; but they both turn again, the one to his Shepherd, and the other to his mire ! There is all the difference in the world between a dirty sheep and a washed sow ! It is not that which goeth into the mouth that defileth the man, but that which cometh out of the heart (Matt. xv. 17-20).

The mouth, dish, or sepulchre, may be cleansed or whitened without, but within it is all uncleanness (Matt. xxiii. 25-28).

" Man looketh on the outward appearance, but the LORD looketh on the heart " (1 Sam. xvi. 7).

Truly " the Lord seeth not as man seeth."

How many hirelings are there who are engaged in merely washing sows and amusing goats, instead of seeking out and feeding Christ's harassed and scattered and famishing sheep, who are at their wits' end

---

* Beresh. rab. sect. 23, and in Tanchuma, fol. 4. 2.

to know where to find a little green grass, or fresh water, which has not been trodden down with the feet of the goats, or defiled with the " vomit " of the dogs ?

2. *Parœmiæ which, though not quoted as such, were very probably already in use as proverbial expressions.*

" Like to a grain of mustard seed " (Matt. xiii. 31, 32 ; xvii. 20. Luke xvii. 6). This was doubtless a proverbial saying among the Hebrews (not the Greeks), to indicate a very small thing: as we say, of rent, etc., " a peppercorn." See Buxtorf *Lex. Talmud*, under the word חרדל, and above, under *Ellipsis* and *Synecdoche.*

" As the sand of the sea," or " as the sand." This was used proverbially, in order to express a vast multitude that could not be numbered.

See Gen. xxii. 17 ; xxxii. 12 ; xli. 49. Josh. xi. 4. Judges vii. 12. 1 Sam. xiii. 5. 2 Sam. xvii. 11. 1 Kings iv. 20, 29 (v. 9). Job xxix. 18. Ps. lxxviii. 27 ; cxxxix. 18. Isa. x. 22 ; xlviii. 19. Jer. xv. 8 ; xxxiii. 22. Hos. i. 10 (ii. 1). Hab. i. 9. And in the New Testament—Rom. ix. 27. Heb. xi. 12 ; and Rev. xx. 8. See under *Hyperbole.*

" As the dust of the earth," or " dust," is used proverbially, by *Metonymy (q.v.)*, for an innumerable multitude.

See Gen. xiii. 16 ; xxviii. 14. Num. xxiii. 10.* 2 Chron. i. 9. Job xxii. 24 ; xxvii. 16. Ps. lxxviii. 27. Zeph. i. 17. Zech. ix. 3. See under *Hyperbole.*

" As the stars of heaven," or " as the stars," is used proverbially to indicate a vast number that could not be counted.

See Gen. xv. 5 ; xxii. 17 ; xxvi. 4. Ex. xxxii. 13. Deut. i. 10 ; x. 22 ; xxviii. 62. 1 Chron. xxvii. 23. Neh. ix. 23. Jer. xxxiii. 22. Nah. iii. 16.

" It is easier for a camel to go through the eye of a needle " (Matt. xix. 24. Mark x. 25. Luke xviii. 25). This was a proverbial

---

* Num. xxiii. 10. The A.V. renders this " Who can count the dust of Jacob, and the number the fourth part of Israel." The R.V. renders the second line, " Or number the fourth part of Israel " ; and in the margin says, " Heb. Or, *by number.*" But Dr. Ginsburg points out in his *Introduction* to the Hebrew Bible (p. 168), that the word וּמִסְפָּר (*umispahr*), rendered " *and the number,*" is obscure, because the first two letters וּמ were originally a separate word, being the abbreviation of the first word of the first line, viz.: וּמ for וּמִי, *and who.* Thus the two lines (dividing the word into two) are now seen to be a beautiful parallel :—

" Who can count the dust of Jacob ?
And who can number the fourth part of Israel ? "

expression for a thing very unusual and very difficult. Lightfoot (*Horæ Hebraicae*) quotes several examples: from the Talmud,* where, concerning dreams, it says "They do not show a man a palm-tree of gold, nor an elephant going through the eye of a needle." The gloss is, "A thing which he was not wont to see, nor concerning which he had ever thought." Another example is given,† where Rabbi Sheshith answered R. Amram, disputing with him, and asserting something that was incongruous of him, and said, "Perhaps thou art one of these Pombeditha, who can make an elephant pass through the eye of a needle": *i.e*, as the *Aruch* interprets it, "Who speak things that are impossible."

"That strain out a gnat, and swallow a camel" (Matt. xxiii. 24). Not "straining at a gnat." See Buxtorf in *Lex. Talmud*, under סכן.

"With what measure ye mete, it shall be measured to you again" (Matt. vii. 2). This was a very common proverb among the Jews. See Bab. *Sanhedrim*, fol. 100, 1, and the Tract *Sotah* cap. 1, quoted by Lightfoot.

"Let me pull out the mote out of thine eye," etc. (Matt. vii. 4). Lightfoot quotes from the *Baba Bathra*, fol. 15, 2, a well known proverb : "It is written in the days when they judged the judges (*i e.*, in the generation which judged their judges), When any [*judge*] said to another ' Cast out the mote out of thine eye,' he answered, ' Cast you out the beam out of your own eye,' " etc.

"There shall not an hair of your head perish," etc. (Luke xxi. 18. Acts xxvii. 34; and, in the Old Testament, 1 Sam. xiv. 45. 2 Sam. xiv. 11. 1 Kings i. 52. Compare also Matt. x. 30.

"Whosoever shall exalt himself shall be abased : and he that shall humble himself shall be exalted" (Matt. xxiii. 12. Luke xiv. 11). Many similar sayings might be quoted from the Talmud. See *Erubim*, cap. i. Indeed, it was very ancient. See Job v. 11; xxii. 29. Ps. xviii. 27 (28) ; cxiii. 6 (7). Prov. xxix. 23, and the song of Hannah (1 Sam. ii. 6-8), and of Mary (Luke i. 52, 53).

"Shake off the dust of your feet" (Matt. x. 14. Mark vi. 11. Luke ix. 5. And Acts xiii. 51). The schools of the Scribes taught that the dust of heathen lands caused defilement.‡ The shaking off

---

* Babyl. *Berachoth*. fol. 55, 2.

† *Baba Mezia*, fol. 38, 2.

‡ *Tosaph. ad Kelim*, cap. 1. Bab. *Sanhedr.*, fol. 12. 1. Bab. *Shabb*, fol. 15. 2. Gloss in *Sanhedr.*, fol. 5. 2. *Tosaph. in Sanhedr.*, cap. 1, article 30, quoted by Lightfoot.

of the dust of the feet, therefore, was a sign that, though the place might be in the land of Israel, it was as though it were a heathen and profane and defiled place.

" It is enough for the disciple that he be as his master, and the servant as his lord," etc. (Matt. x. 25. Luke vi. 40. John xiii. 16).*

" Every kingdom divided against itself is brought to desolation," etc. (Matt. xii. 25. Mark iii. 24, 25. Luke xi. 17. (See Buxtorf. *Lex. Talmud*, under חיב).

"To remove mountains" (Matt. xxi. 21. 1 Cor. xiii. 2) was a Hebrew proverb, as may be seen in Buxtorf. *Lex. Talmud*, under עקר. It was common to say of a great teacher that he was " a rooter up of mountains." (See Bab. *Berachoth*, fol. 64. 1; *Erubim*, fol. 29. 1; *Sanhedrim*, fol. 24. 1; *Baba Bathra*, fol. 3. 2). And thus what they foolishly said of the learning of their wisest men, Christ said of His humblest disciple. In 1 Cor xiii. 2, knowledge and faith are combined by this *Parœmia.*

" Whatsoever ye would that men should do to you, do ye even so to them : for this is the Law and the Prophets " (Matt. vii. 12. Luke vi. 31. (See Talmud, Bab. *Sabbath*, fol. 31. 1, and Buxtorf. *Lex. Talmud*, under נגם).

" To unloose the shoe-latchet " (Matt. iii. 11. Mark i. 7. Luke iii. 16) was a proverb connected with the buying of a servant : the loosening of the shoe being a token of purchase. See Ruth iv. 7, 8; and Bab. *Kiddushin*, fol. 22. 2, cap. 1.

" If they do these things in a green tree, what shall be done in the dry ? " (Luke xxiii. 31), or better (comparing Matt. iii. 10 : " Now, also the axe is laid unto the root of the trees.")

" If to a green tree, these things they are doing ;
   To the dry *tree*, what shall happen ? " †

I.e., if they deal thus with Me, a green and flourishing Tree, what shall happen to the nation—a dry and sapless trunk, when the Romans shall presently lay their axe to it? (See Ps. i., and Jer. xvii. 5-8).

" It is hard for thee to kick against the pricks " (Acts ix. 5; xxvi. 14.

This was a proverb common among the Greeks as well as the Hebrews.

---

* See the Talmud. *Berachoth*, cap. 9 and *Chusar*, cap. 20. Also Aben Ezra on Hos. i. 2.

† Talmud *Sanhedrim*, quoted by Drusius.

3. *Parœmiæ which appear for the first time in Scripture; but, which, owing to their fulness of meaning and their wide application, have since passed into general use as proverbial sayings.*

Gen. xxii. 14.—"As it is said to this day, 'In the mount of the LORD it shall be seen.'"

Deut. xxv. 4 is a Scripture which afterward became a proverb, because it is a brief sententious saying with many applications. "Thou shalt not muzzle the ox when he treadeth out the corn (marg., Heb. *thresheth*). See 1 Cor. ix. 9 and 1 Tim. v. 18.

1 Kings viii. 46. 2 Chron. vi. 36.—"For there is no man that sinneth not." This became a proverb on account of its great truth, as may be seen from Prov. xx. 9. Ecc. vii. 20. Jas. iii. 2. 1 John i. 8, 10.

1 Kings xx. 11.—This also has come down to, and is used by posterity as a proverb, full of meaning, and with many applications :

> "Let not him that girdeth on his harness
> Boast himself as he that putteth it off."

Job vi. 5.—"Doth the wild ass bray when he is at grass ? or loweth the ox over his fodder ? " (See A.V. margin).

Job xiv. 19.—"The waters wear the stones."

Job xxviii. 18.—"The price of wisdom is above rubies."

Ps. lxii. 9.—"Surely men of low degree are vanity, and men of high degree are a lie : to be laid in the balance they are altogether lighter than vanity."

Ps. cxi. 10.—"The fear of the LORD is the beginning of wisdom." So Deut. iv. 6. Job xxviii. 28. Prov. i. 7 : ix. 10. Ecc. xii. 13. Probably the first use is in Job xxviii. 28, but it passed into a common proverb.

Prov. i. 17.—"Surely in vain the net is spread in the sight of any bird."

Prov. i. 32.—"The prosperity of fools shall destroy them."

Prov. iii. 12.—"For whom the LORD loveth He correcteth : even as a father the son in whom he delighteth." Here we have a *Simile* as well. It is referred to in Heb. xii. 5, 6. See also Job v. 17. Ps. xciv. 12, and Rev. iii. 19.

Prov. vi. 6.—"Go to the ant, thou sluggard : consider her ways and be wise." Compare Job xii. 7.

Prov. vi. 27.—" Can a man take fire in his bosom, and his clothes not be burned?" This is doubtless a saying arising from common observation of daily life.

Prov. x. 5.—" He that gathereth in summer is a wise son."

Prov. x. 13.—"A rod is for the back of him who is void of understanding." So xxvi. 3.

Verse 19: "In the multitude of words there wanteth not sin."

Prov. xi. 15.—" He that is surety for a stranger shall smart for it." Heb. *shall be sore broken* (so A.V. margin). The common experience of this fact has made this a common proverb; but they are blessed indeed who learn and know from a happy experience that when Christ became Surety for His People, who were "strangers," He smarted for it, and was "sore broken" that they might be for ever blessed.

Prov. xxii. 6.—" Train up a child in the way he should go."

Few proverbs have passed more into common use than this. Mr. C. H. Spurgeon once put it, "in the way you wish you had gone yourself." See under *Pleonasm* and *Metonymy*.

Prov. xxvi. 11.—"As a dog returneth to his vomit, so a fool returneth to his folly."

This is also a simile, which passed into a proverb. See 2 Pet. ii. 22, quoted and referred to above.

Prov. xxvii. 6.—" Faithful are the wounds of a friend."

Verse 7: "The full soul loatheth the honeycomb."

Verse 17: "As iron sharpeneth iron," etc.

Prov. xxviii. 21.—"To have respect of persons is not good."

See *Synecdoche*, and Prov. xviii. 5, and xxiv. 23.

Ecc. i. 15.—"That which is crooked cannot be made straight." So vii. 13. Job. xii. 14. Isa. xiv. 27.

This perhaps gave rise to another expressive Hebrew proverb: " You cannot straighten a pig's tail."

Ecc. i. 18.—" For in much wisdom is much grief." So xii. 12.

Ecc. ix. 4.—" For a living dog is better than a dead lion."

Ecc. x. 1.—" Dead flies cause the ointment of the apothecary to send forth a stinking savour."

See under *Ellipsis*.

Ecc. xi. 6.—" In the morning sow thy seed, and in the evening withhold not thine hand."

Jer. xiii. 23.—" Can the Ethiopian change his skin, or the leopard his spots ? "

Jer. xxiii. 28.—" What is the chaff (Heb., straw) to the wheat ? "

Hab. ii. 6.—" Shall not all these take up a parable against him, and a taunting proverb against him, and say, ' Woe to him that increaseth that which is not his !   How long ? and to him that ladeth himself with thick clay ' " (see R.V.).

Mal. ii. 10.—" Have we not all one father ? "   The Jews used this proverb in their controversy with the Lord in John viii. 33, 39, etc.

Matt. v. 13.—" If the salt have lost his savour (or taste) where-with shall it be salted ? "

Matt. v. 14.—" A city that is set on a hill cannot be hid."

Matt. vi. 3.—" Let not thy left hand know what thy right hand doeth."

Matt. vi. 21.—" Where your treasure is, there will your heart be also."   Greek, " there will your heart also be," with emphasis on " heart."   (See *Metonymy*).

Matt. vi. 24.—" No man can serve two masters."   See *Hermeneia.*

Verse 34 : " Sufficient unto the day is the evil thereof."

Matt. vii. 16.—" Ye shall know them by their fruits."

These words were first used by the Lord concerning *false teachers.* But to-day the saying has passed into general use, and is spoken (not so correctly) of every one.

Matt. ix. 12.—" They that be whole need not a physician."

Matt. x. 10.—" The workman is worthy of his meat."   So Luke x. 7. 1 Cor. ix. 7, etc.

Verse 22 : " He that endureth to the end shall be saved."   This *Parœmia* is further used Dan. xii. 12. Matt. xxiv. 13. Mark xiii. 13, etc. and refers to the faithful remnant of Jews enduring to the end of the coming " great tribulation."   The τέλος (telos), *end*, should be distinguished from the συντέλεια (*sunteleia*), which is also translated *end*.

The latter word is used of *the time of the end*, while the former (*telos*) is used of the end or crisis of the *sunteleia*.   The *sunteleia* refers to the consummation of all the ages and dispensations; a joining together of the ages, or ends, as it were, and is used of the whole time of the " great tribulation " ; while the *telos* is the point of time at the end of it. It is of this point that this saying is used: " He that endureth to the end (*telos*) shall be saved (or delivered)."

The word συντέλεια (*sunteleia*) occurs only in Matt. xiii. 39, 40, 49; xxiv. 3; xxviii. 20, and Heb. ix. 26. It will be easy, therefore, for the student to distinguish it from τέλος (*telos*), which is used in the other passages.

Matt. xii. 34.—" For out of the abundance of the heart the mouth speaketh."

Matt. xiii. 57.—" A prophet is not without honour, save in his own country and in his own house."

Matt. xv. 14.—" If the blind lead the blind, both shall fall into the ditch."

Matt. xxiv. 28.—" For wheresoever the carcase is, there will the eagles be gathered together." The word " for " introduces the *Parœmia*, which is from Job xxxix. 30. " Her young ones suck up blood: and where the slain are, there is she." Had this *Parœmia* been understood, and the title " Son of Man" noticed as referring to Christ's title as exercising dominion in the Earth,* these words would never have been interpreted of the church as the " Body" of Christ. Luke xvii. 37 clearly shows that it is a time of judgment (see verses 24-37); and that the *taking* and the *leaving* refer to judgment, and not to the Rapture of 1 Thess. iv. 17; which was a subsequent revelation, and ought not to be read into the Gospels, which are perfectly clear without it.

Mark ix. 50.—See Matt. v. 13.

Luke xvii. 37.—See Matt. xxiv. 28 above.

Acts ix. 5.—" It is hard for thee to kick against the pricks " : *i.e.*, the goads.

Acts xx. 35.—" It is more blessed to give than to receive." This is one of the un-recorded *Parœmiæ* or *Logia* of Christ. But it does not follow that a papyrus which professes, some centuries later, to give other *Parœmiæ* is genuine and authentic.

---

* See *The Divine Names and Titles,* by the same author and publisher. One shilling.

1 **Cor. v. 6.**—" A little leaven leaveneth the whole lump." Leaven is always used in a bad sense. Even in the case of one of the two wave-loaves, leaven was to be used because that loaf represented human nature; while the other loaf which represented Christ's perfect nature had no leaven.

See other examples of such Proverbs in Prov. xi. 27; xii. 11, 15; xv. 2, 33; xvii. 1, 10, 19, 28; xix. 2, 24; xx. 4, 11, 14, 21, 25; xxii. 13; xxv. 11, 16, 27; xxvi. 4, 5 (see under *Ellipsis*), 14; xxvii. 8, 10, 22; xxx. 15, etc., etc. Ecc. iv. 5, 12; v. 2, 6, 8, 9, 10; vi. 9; ix. 18; x. 2, 8, 9, 15, 19, 20; xi. 3, 4, 7; xii. 12. Micah vii. 5, 6. Matt. v. 15; vii. 2, 5; ix. 16; x. 24, 26; xiii. 12. Luke ix. 62; xii. 48; xxiii. 31. 1 Cor. x. 12; xv. 33. 2 Cor. ix. 6, 7. 2 Thess. iii. 10. Tit. i. 15

NON-CANONICAL, or, SUPPOSED SCRIPTURE, PROVERBS.

There are many common sayings which are supposed to be in Scripture, even by those who should know better; and pass current among those who are ill-informed. For example—

" *God tempers the wind to the shorn lamb.*"

This is not in the Bible; but is taken from Laurence-Sterne's *Sentimental Journey*. And he took it probably from the French of Henri Etienne, *Dieu mesure le froid à la brebis tondue.* And both may have been acquainted with Isa. xxvii. 8: " He stayeth his rough wind in the day of his east wind."

" *Spare the rod and spoil the child.*"

Many use this, thinking it is Scripture. Even Butler, in his *Hudibras*, says: " That may be heard ten times to one quotation of Solomon." And yet Solomon said: " He that spareth the rod hateth his son " (Prov. xiii. 24).

" *A word to the wise is sufficient.*" (Sometimes " *for them* " is added, whereas it is singular, not plural).

This has been quoted as Scripture. But it is from the Latin of Terence*; who himself is misquoted; for he said : " *Dictum sapienti sat est,*" not *Verbum sat sapienti.*

It is said that the celebrated Robert Hall once planned a sermon on the words

" *In the midst of life we are in death,*"

But he abandoned it, we are told, when he found that it was not to be found in the Bible; but only in the Prayer-book.

---

* *Phormio*, Ac. iii. sc. 3. v. 8. In Parry's edition of Terence, he says in a note that the Proverb is found in Plautus *Persa* iv. 7. 18.

It appears to have come from a monk of St. Gall, named Notker, in the tenth century, whose Latin hymn contained the line : " *Media vita in morte sumus.*"

MISQUOTED PROVERBIAL SAYINGS.

Even in quoting common sayings from Scripture and the Prayer Book, which have passed into Proverbs, there is an habitual misquotation which has become practically universal. It may not be out of place to give one or two examples by way of warning.

" *Man is prone to sin as the sparks fly upward.*" But Job v. 7 says : " Man is born unto trouble," etc.

" *A still small voice* " is generally quoted as " *the* still small voice " (1 Kings xix. 12).

" *A merciful man is merciful to his beast.*" But Prov. xii. 10 has it : " A righteous *man* regardeth the life of his beast."

" *The truth as it is in Jesus* " is almost invariably thus quoted. The Scripture says (Eph. iv. 21): "As the truth is in Jesus," which is a very different thing. The former implies that there is truth apart from Him. But the latter implies that the truth is in Jesus, and nowhere else.

" *A nation shall be born in a day.*" No concordance will give this passage. Isa. lxvi. 8 asks : " Shall the earth be made to bring forth in one day ? or shall a nation be born at once ? "

" *So plain that he who runs may read.*" On the contrary. So plain was to be the written vision that he who reads it may run, and flee from the coming judgments (Hab. ii. 2).

" *My time is in thy hand.*" Thank God, He said " times " (Psa. xxxi. 15 (16)). Yes, " My times are always in thy hand." All my times : my times of sorrow and of joy ; of trouble and of danger. All are in the hand of my God.*

" *Let him cast the first stone.*" But John viii. 7 says : " He that is without sin among you, let him first cast a stone."

---

* Shakespeare is misquoted in the other direction. He said : "The time is out of joint," not *the times are out of ·joint.* The next line would set people right, for he says :—

　　" The time is out of joint ;—O cursed spite !
　　That I was born to set it right."
　　　　　　　　(*Hamlet*, Act i. sc. 4, at the close).

So Cowper : " The cups that cheer," not *cup.* (See his *Task*, iv. 39, 40).

"*How great a fire a little matter kindleth.*" But in Jas. iii. 5 it is written : " Behold, how great a matter a little fire kindleth."

The Apostolic benediction (2 Cor. xiii. 14) suffers from various changes : fellowship, instead of communion ; or, in addition to it, as though they were two different things : rest upon and abide ; be and abide : for ever ; now, henceforth, and for ever ; now and for ever. And these are supposed to improve the words of the Holy Spirit! That such attempted improvement of Scripture meets with no check is a sad sign of the low regard in which its accuracy is held.

TYPE.

A figure or ensample of something future and more or less prophetic, called the " Antitype."

Type. Greek, τύπος (*typos*). The verb τύπτειν (*tuptein*), *to strike, make an impress.* Hence *Type* means primarily *a blow*; then, the *impress* or *mark left by a blow*; then, a *mark, print,* or impress of any kind.

In the New Testament the word occurs in several of these senses. It is rendered:—

1. *A print* or *mark* (John xx. 25).*
2. *Figure* (Acts vii. 43. Rom. v. 14).
3. *Form* (Rom. vi. 17).
4. *Fashion* (Acts vii. 44).
5. *Manner* (Acts xxiii. 25).
6. *Pattern* (Tit. ii. 7. Heb. viii. 5).
7. *Ensample* (1 Cor. x. 11. Phil. iii. 17. 1 Thess. i. 7).†
   2 Thess. iii. 9. 1 Pet. v. 3
8. *Example* (1 Cor. x. 6. 1 Tim. iv. 12).

The Greeks used it of the *symptoms* of a disease. Galen wrote a medical work entitled περὶ τῶν τύπων, concerning *symptoms.* In a Legal sense it was used of what we technically cite as a "*case.*"

It will thus be seen that the special and technical sense which has been given to it by Theologians is not exactly equivalent to any of these usages : the nearest being Rom. v. 14, where Adam is spoken of as a *type* of the Coming One.

The theological use of the word agrees more with what in the New Testament is called σκιά (*skia*), *a shadow* (Heb. x. i. Col. ii. 17).

There is, therefore, not much profit in following out what have been called types by men. Many are merely *illustrations;* and it would be better so to call them ; inasmuch as they did not and do not of themselves *teach* the truths, but only *illustrate* those truths which are elsewhere clearly revealed. We should never have called them *types* but for such subsequent revelation ; and therefore they are only illustrations so far as their teaching agrees with clear revelation afterward made.

---

* The second occurrence in this verse is read τόπος, *the place,* by Lachmann, Tischendorf, Tregelles (margin).

† According to the best texts, this is singular, as in R.V., not plural.

SYMBOL.

A material Object substituted for a moral or spiritual Truth.

Greek, σύμβολον (symbolon), from σύν (syn), together, and βάλλειν (ballein), to cast; hence a casting together. Used by the Greeks, much in the same way as we use the word "coupon," where one part corresponded with or represented another part. Hence, in language, the use of one thing to represent another; or, the use of a material object to represent a moral or spiritual truth.

The word does not occur in the New Testament, and nothing is said in Scripture as to one thing being so used. The assertion as to anything being a symbol of another rests entirely on human authority, and depends for its accuracy on its agreement with the teaching of Scripture.

The nearest word to symbol is *mystery*; and, by the Fathers, μυστήριον was used as being synonymous with σύμβολον.

Μυστήριον (mysteerion) means *secret*;* and later it came to mean a *secret sign* or *symbol*. Justin Martyr (A.D. 148) says † that in all false religions the serpent was represented as "a great *symbol* and *mystery*."

Speaking of Isa. vii. 14, "Behold, a virgin shall conceive and bear a son," he says, "since this refers to the house of David, Isaiah has explained how that which was spoken by God to David, ἐν μυστηρίῳ (en mysteerio), *in a mystery*, would actually come to pass. Perhaps," he adds, "you are not aware, my friends, of this—that there were many sayings written ἐπικεκαλυμμένως (epikekalummenōs), *obscurely*; or, ἐν παραβολαῖς (en parabolais), *in parables*; or, μυστηρίοις (mysteeriois), *in secret signs*; or, ἐν συμβόλοις (en symbolois), *in symbols*; which the prophets, who lived after the persons who said or did them, expounded." ‡

Thus it will be seen that *symbol* is practically synonymous with the latter use of *mystery* as meaning *a secret sign*. It is only two or three times so used in Scripture:—In Rev. i. 20, the stars which John saw were *a mystery*: i.e., secret sign (or symbol); and in Rev. xvii. 5, 7, Babylon is said to be a *mysteerion* (or symbol): i.e., a secret sign of something spiritual and moral which it represented.

---

* See *The Mystery*, by the same author and publisher.

† *Apology*, i. 27.

‡ *Trypho*, c. 68.

Eph. v. 32 shows us that it was also synonymous with the Latin *sacramentum*, which is there used to represent the Greek *mysteerion*. So that the *sacramentum* of the Latin Vulgate meant simply a symbol.

Sacramentum is said to have reference to a military oath, but it must have been only because of some *secret sign* used in connection with the administration of the oath. From this it is clear that "the sacrament" so called is only a secret sign or symbol of spiritual truths and acts or events which it is used to commemorate.

Doubtless there are many *symbols* in the Scriptures, but great care and caution must be exercised in their interpretation. The different interpretations which have been given to the same so-called symbol, are sufficient to serve as a warning.

All *Metonymies* (*q.v.*) are, in a certain sense, symbols. When, for example, "cup" is used, by *Metonymy*, for blessing (Ps. xvi. 5; cxvi. 13); or, "clay" for man (Isa. lxiv. 8 (7)); or, "gate" for entrance, etc., the one is practically a symbol of the other: and when by repeated and constant use the one gets to be more and more closely associated with the other, it is then used as a symbol of it and is substituted for it. The transition stage is *Hypocatastasis* (*q.v.*) or *Implication*.

The stages by which a symbol is reached, therefore, are: (1) either by *Metonymy* or *Metaphor*, one thing is used to *represent* another; then (2) the one is used to *imply* the other; and finally (3) it becomes permanently *substituted* for it as a *symbol* of it.

Thus, with regard to "leaven," we have first the thing itself causing fermentation, and therefore forbidden to be used in connection with any sacrifice or offering to the Lord. Then it is used by *Metonymy* for that which is corrupt (1 Cor. v. 6-8). Then by *Implication* for corrupt or evil doctrine (Matt. xvi. 6). And finally it is used as the permanent *symbol* of it (Matt. xiii. 33). Indeed, "leaven" is always used in a bad sense, and of that which is corrupt. In the case of the two wave-loaves, where leaven was to be put into one and not into the other, the exception is significant, and proves the rule. For one represented Christ, and the other His People.

In the same way, "key" is used as a symbol of power and authority, and especially the power of opening and closing (Rev. i. 18; iii. 7. Isa. xxii. 22). In Matt. xvi. 19, the power and authority of opening the doors of the kingdom were committed to Peter, and he exercised that commission in making the final offer of the Messiah to the nation of Israel (Acts ii.-viii., and x.). Observe, that they were the keys of the *Kingdom*, not of the church; and that he was altogether incompetent and unable to transfer that power and authority to others.

It is scarcely necessary for us to attempt to say more with regard to symbols. The subject would form a work by itself; and, indeed, many works have been written upon it. We can only repeat our caution as to their use.

ÆNIGMA ; or, DARK SAYING.

A Truth expressed in obscure Language.

E-nig'-ma. Greek, αἴνιγμα (*ai-nig-ma*), from αἰνίσσεσθαι (*ainissesthai*), *to tell a strange tale,* then *to speak darkly* or *in riddles.* Hence an *enigma* is *a dark* or *obscure saying,* a *puzzling statement* or *action.* A statement of which the meaning has to be searched for in order to be discovered.

Enigma thus differs from *Parable,* in that the latter is generally explained. When a Parable is without any explanation, it may be called an Enigma, *i.e., a dark* or *obscure saying.*

See Ps. lxxviii. 2 quoted in Matt. xiii. 35. The " dark saying " of the Old Testament is חִידָה (*cheedah*); from חוּד (*chood*), *to tie in a knot, to twist : a knotty* or *intricate saying.*

It is rendered *dark saying* three times (Ps. xlix. 4 (5) ; lxxviii. 2. Prov. i. 6) ; *dark sentence,* once (Dan. viii. 23) ; *dark speech,* once (Num. xii. 8) ; *hard question,* twice (1 Kings x. 1. 2 Chron. ix. 1) ; *proverb,* once (Hab. ii. 6) ; *riddle,* nine times (Judges xiv. 12, 13, 14, 15, 16, 17, 18, 19. Ezek. xvii. 2).

When the saying is very obscure indeed, it is called

HYPÆNIGMA, *i.e.,* the same word, with the preposition ὑπό (*hypo*) prefixed, meaning *under, i.e.,* a saying *deep* as well as *dark.*

Also HYPÆNIXIS, from ὑπό (*hypo*), *under,* and αἰνίσσομαι (*ainissomai*), *to speak darkly.* Hence, *a speaking beneath : i.e.,* having another meaning beneath what is actually said.

When the Enigma is connected with the names of persons or places, it is known by the name *Polyonymia.* (See the next Figure).

There are sayings dark and deep in the Scriptures beside those that are actually so designated.

Gen. xlix. 10 is in the form of *Enigma.* " The sceptre shall not depart from Judah, nor a lawgiver from between his feet, until Shiloh come; and unto him shall the gathering of the people be." See under *Metonymy.*

Judges xiv. 14.—Samson's *Enigma* is well known.

" Out of the eater came forth meat,
And out of the strong came forth sweetness."

The answer is given in verse 18, in the form of another question (See *Anteisagoge*):

> " What is sweeter than honey ?
> And what is stronger than a lion ? "

This is a saying both "dark" and "deep": for there is precious truth hidden in that darkness and those depths, which neither the Philistines nor the natural man can understand or receive.

The Living Word (Christ) is stronger than the strong man armed (Matt. xii. 29. Mark iii. 27. Luke xii. 21, 22). For the Lion means in Hebrew *the strong one*.

The Written Word (the Scriptures of truth) are sweeter than honey (Ps. cxix. 103 ; xix. 10 (11). Jer. xv. 16).

All who know this blessed deliverance which the great Deliverer brings, cry out in the words of Ps. xxxv. 10, " LORD, who is like unto thee, which deliverest the poor from him that is too strong for him, yea, the poor and needy from him that spoileth him ? " (See *Erotesis* and *Prosopopœia*).

THE LAW was a strong Lion (Gal. iii. 10) : but the honey is found in verse 13.

SIN is a strong Lion (Rom. v. 21) : but the honey is found in Rom. vi. 6 ; vii. 18-25. And 1 Cor. xv. 56, 57.

THE WORLD is a strong Lion (Luke viii. 14. Gal. v. 21): but the honey is found in John xvi. 33.

AFFLICTION is a strong Lion (Job v. 6, 7 ; xiv. 1, 2. Acts xiv. 22): but the honey is found in Ps. cxix. 67, 71 ; xxxiv. 19 (20). Rom. viii. 35-39. Heb. xii. 11.

DEATH is a strong Lion (Rom. v. 12. Heb. ix. 27): but the honey is found in 2 Tim. i. 10. Hosea xiii. 14, and 1 Cor. xv. 54, 55.

The answer to these *Enigmas* is found in Ps. lxxiii. 16, 17, " When I thought to know this it was too painful for me; Until I went into the sanctuary of God. Then understood I."

Isa. xi. 1 is a dark saying, and has to be interpreted by what follows.

Isa. xxi. 11, 12, is another dark saying.

Ezek. xvii. 2-10 gives a prophecy concerning the King of Babylon's coming to Jerusalem, and leading it into captivity, under the Enigma of two Eagles.

Dan. v. 25-28.—The handwriting on the wall is given in the form of an *Enigma*, in which the immediate fall of Babylon was announced.

Three words were written, the first twice (by *Epizeuxis, q.v.*), for emphasis.

מְנֵה, *M'neh.* NUMBERED.

תְּקֵל, *T'kel.* WEIGHED.

פְּרֵס, *P'res.* DIVIDED.

These three words are interpreted by Daniel in verses 26-28, and the fulfilment of them follows in verses 30, 31. See under *Paronomasia.*

POLYONYMIA; or, MANY NAMES.

An Application of Ænigma to the Names of Persons or Places.

Pol'-y-ō-nym'-i-a. Greek, πολυωνυμία, *having many names*, or *more than one name*: from πολύς (*polys*), *many*, and ὄνομα (*onoma*), *a name*.

It is not uncommon for persons or places to be known by different names.

In Matt. xv. 39, for example, there is no Enigma, but merely a case of two names for the same place: "The coasts of Magdala." In Mark viii. 10, it is called "The parts of Dalmanutha," DALMANUTHA being the name of the region, and MAGDALA of the city. The former was general, the latter was special.

In Matt viii. 28, the people are called *Gergesenes*; and in Luke viii. 26, and Mark v. 1, *Gadarenes*. Some suppose that these were either different names of the same place, or two places forming one larger place. It is a question also as to whether precisely the same event is described in these places, or whether two similar events took place at two different times.

So with the names of Esau's wives, which have formed a great subject for the attention of infidels.

It is clear from a comparison of Gen. xxvi. 34 and xxviii. 9, that Esau's wives were three in number:

1. "The daughter of Elon the Hittite"; called ADAH (xxxvi. 2); but she also had another name, BASHEMATH (xxvi. 34).

2. "The daughter of Anah the daughter of ZIBEON the Hivite"; called AHOLIBAMAH (xxxvi. 2); but not the Aholibamah of verse 25, who was her aunt (compare verses 2 and 25). She was called also JUDITH, and in xxvi. 34 this Judith is said to be the daughter of BEERI the Hittite. But there is no contradiction in this, for ANAH appears to have been called BEERI, or *the Spring-man*, because he discovered the "hot-springs" (see xxxvi. 24)*; not "mules," as in A.V.

---

* So the R.V., הַיֵּמִם (*Hay-ye-meem*), from הוּם (*Hoom*), *to put in commotion*, *agitate* (Deut. vii. 23. Micah ii. 12. Ps. lv. 3). The Syriac has "waters." "Mules" are always פְּרָדִים (*Pharahdeem*), (2 Sam. xiii. 29; xviii. 9. 1 Kings x. 25. 2 Kings v. 17. Ps. xxxii. 9, etc.). The A.V. Translators followed an error of the Talmud. Moreover, מָצָא (*matzah*), *to find*, means *to happen on*, not *to invent*.

It is true that in xxxvi. 2, Anah, alias Beeri, is called " the Hivite," while in xxvi. 34, he is called " the Hittite." The latter is *history*, and is therefore general ; the former is *genealogy*, and is therefore more precise. " Hittite " is the general term; " Hivite " is the special and more particular term (compare Josh. i. 4. 1 Kings x. 29. 2 Kings vii. 6 ; and Gen. xxviii. 8, when Esau's Hittite wives are spoken of as " daughters of Canaan ").

3. The third wife was " the daughter of Ishmael," and was called BASHEMATH (xxxvi. 2), and MAHALATH (xxviii. 8).

When three persons are so carefully and minutely described, it is preposterous for anyone to create a difficulty about the similar names, when down to our own day precisely the same phenomenon constantly occurs.

But this feature of *Polyonymia* is not what we are describing and discussing here. There is no Enigma in these common *aliases*.

It is only when another name is given, because of some special meaning, " dark " or " deep " in it, that it becomes a Figure, being used in a figurative sense, having some important signification beyond what appears upon the surface.

Gen. x. 10 ; xi. 2.—" The Land of Shinar" is another name for Babel or Babylon. Babylon must be intended by " the land of Shinar" in the prophecy of the " Ephah" (Zech. v. 11). Had the name Babylon been used here it might have been urged that it was put by *Enigma* for some other place; but, when "the land of Shinar " is used for Babylon it can hardly be that, after this, Babylon can be used for some other name by a double use of the figure.

Deut. i. 2, 44 ; ii. 8, etc.—Edom is called Seir, and this was afterwards known in the Jerusalem Targum as גְּבְלָא, *Gabla* or *Gebal*.

We have the name in Psalm lxxxiii. 6 (7). " Gebal, and Ammon, and Amelek " : *i.e.*, Edom, Ammon, and Amelek—three of Israel's greatest enemies at critical moments in the history of the Nation.

2 Kings xxiii. 13.—The Mount of Olives is called " the mount of corruption," because of the idolatries connected with it.

Ps. lxxxvii. 4 ; lxxxix. 10 (11). Isa. li. 9.—Egypt is called Rahab on account of its pride (רַהַב, *Rachab*, having this signification). This judgment of Egypt is in Isa. xxx. 1-14.

Isa. xiv. 4.—The Antichrist is called " the King of Babylon," because he is the end and final outcome of Babel.

Isa. xxix. 1.—Jerusalem is called Ariel, which means *the Lion of God*. It is so called to denote its greatness, glory, and strength (cf. 2 Sam. xxiii. 20. 1 Chron. xi. 22), and is thus put in contrast with the woe here pronounced against it. (See under *Ellipsis*, page 5).

Jer. xxv. 26.—"And the king of Sheshach shall drink after them." Here Sheshach is put for Babylon.

The subject is the cup of the fury of the God of Israel (verse 15). Four classes of nations were to drink of it, and all at one time. (1) Jerusalem and the cities of Judah (18). (2) Egypt, etc. (19). (3) The mingled nations (20-22), and (4) the nations further off (23-25), and, finally, "the king of Sheshach." In Jeremiah "the times of the Gentiles" are not within the scope of his prophecy. Nor in Ezekiel. Daniel, on the other hand, fills in these present times, and makes but little reference to what goes before or comes after, as in Jeremiah and Ezekiel.

The point is that the judgment of these nations takes place all at the same time with that of "the king of Sheshach," and that time is veiled in the *Enigma* contained in this peculiar name. Babylon is meant; and, according to the ancient *Kabbalah*, the last letter of the alphabet was put for the first, and the penultimate for the second, and the antepenultimate for the third, and so on. By which Enigma the word "Sheshach" (שֵׁשַׁךְ) spells *Babel* (בָּבֶל). So that the final judgment upon the nations is yet future, when Babylon shall have been restored, and when "Great Babylon" "comes into remembrance." See further under *Paronomasia* and *Amphibologia*.

Ezek. xxiii. 4.—Jerusalem is called "AHOLIBAH": *i.e.*, *my tabernacle is in her*. While Samaria (Israel) is called AHOLAH: *i.e.*, *his (own) tabernacle*. There is a depth of meaning, therefore, in each name.

Hos. iv. 15; x. 5.—Bethel (*the house of God*, Gen. xxviii. 19, 22) was made, by Jeroboam, a house of his idol (1 Kings xii. 29). Hence, God gives it another name, and calls it *Beth-Aven*: *i.e.*, *the house of vanity*.

GNOME ; or, QUOTATION.

Gnō¹-mee. Greek, γνώμη, *knowledge, understanding ;* also *a means of knowing.* From γνῶναι *(gnōnai), to know.*

Hence, the term Gnome is given to the citation of brief, sententious, profitable sayings expressive of a universal maxim or sentiment which appertains to human affairs, cited as well-known, or as being of general acceptance, but without quoting the author's name.

In Prov. i. 2, they are called "words of understanding." The Scriptures, as Bengel remarks, are so "full of the best things, that these constitute, as it were, certain continued sentiments openly set forth in the form of *gnomes.*"

When these are applied to a certain person, time, or place ; or to individual cases ; or are clothed with circumstantial particulars, the figure is called NOEMA, νόημα *(no-ee-ma),* (plural, NOEMATA), *i.e., sense, thought, that which is thought,* from νοεῖν, *to perceive.*

When the author's name is given, the figure is called CHREIA, χρεία, *chree¹-a, use, usage,* or *usance,* (from χράομαι, *chraomai, to use).*

For the Greek name of the figure *Gnome* the Latins substituted SENTENTIA *(sen-ten¹-ti-a), sentiment,* or *a sententious saying ;* a *philosophic aphorism, maxim,* or *axiom,* which is quoted on account of its application to the subject in hand.

These are exactly what are referred to in Ecc. xii. 11.

> " The words of the wise
> Are as goads ;
> And as tent-pegs well fixed are
> [*The words*] of the masters of assemblies.*

A *Gnome,* however, differs from a Proverb in this : that every Proverb is a *Gnome,* but every *Gnome* is not necessarily a Proverb. A *Gnome* is, properly speaking, a quotation: and therefore this figure opens up the whole question of the Quotations from the Old Testament in the New.

This is a large subject, many volumes having been written upon it, both in ancient and in recent times.

---

* See under *Ellipsis,* page 74.

It is also a difficult subject, owing to certain phenomena which lie upon its surface.

It is a fact that there are variations between the quotations and the Text quoted from.

Sometimes they agree with the Septuagint translation, and differ from the Hebrew, and *vice versa ;* and sometimes they differ from both.

Sometimes they are direct quotations; at other times they are composite quotations of several passages joined in one ; while others are mere allusions.

Consequently it is difficult for anyone to make a list or table of such quotations which shall agree with those made by others.

The general fact seems to be that there are 189 separate passages quoted* in the New Testament, according to Spearman's reckoning :† *i.e.,* counting a passage only once, though it may be quoted several times. Including the whole, there are, according to Bishop Wetenhall's method, 244 : of which 147 agree with the LXX, and 97 differ from it.

Reckoning according to Spearman, we find, out of the 189 passages quoted, 105 that agree with the Septuagint, 21 that differ from it, 45 that differ from both it and the Hebrew, and 18 neutral.

These may be exhibited in the following table :—

---

* If it is merely a *reference* or *allusion*, as distinct from a *quotation*, then there are many more, of course. The Lord Jesus Himself referred to 22 out of our 39 Old Testament books.

In Matthew there are references to 88 passages in 10 Old Testament books. In Mark to 37 passages in 10 books. In Luke to 58 passages in 8 books. In John to 40 passages in 6 books.

Deuteronomy and Isaiah, the two books most assailed by the Higher Critics, are referred to more often than any other Old Testament books. While Revelation contains no less than 244 references to 25 Old Testament books.

In Romans there are 74 references. Corinthians, 54. Gal., 16. Eph., 10. Heb., 85.

In all, out of 260 chapters in the New Testament, there are 832 quotations, or references, or allusions to the Old Testament Scriptures.

Every Old Testament book is referred to with the exception of Ezra, Neh. Est., and Canticles.

The Apocryphal books are not referred to at all.

† *Letters to a friend.* Edinburgh, 1759.

No. of Quotations in	Total.	Acc. to LXX.	Differ from LXX.	Differ from both.	Neutral.
Matt.	38	25	4	8	1
Mark	3	1	—	2	—
Luke	5	—	—	3	2
John	11	3	2	5	1
Acts	19	11	1	7	—
Rom.	51	30	4	5	12
1 Cor.	11	4	2	5	—
2 Cor.	8	4	1	1	2
Gal.	4	3	1	—	—
Eph.	2	—	1	1	—
Hebrews	22	15	3	4	—
1 Peter	7	6	—	—	1
Jude	1	1	—	—	—
Rev.	7	2	2	3	—
	189	105	21	44	19

It will thus be seen that by far the larger number of quotations correspond with the Septuagint translation.

Now, all the difficulties have been caused by thinking and speaking only of the instrument or the agent employed : instead of having regard to the great and important fact that the Bible has only One Author, and that " Holy men of God spake as they were moved by the Holy Ghost " (2 Pet. i. 21).

Our studies will certainly be incomplete if we do not observe the manner in which the Holy Spirit quotes in the New Testament those Scriptures which He had before inspired in the Old. Notice, then, the following examples :—

Mark xii. 36.—" David himself *said by the Holy Ghost.*" This was the introduction to a quotation from Psa. cx. 1.

Matt. xv. 4.—Referring to Ex. xx. 12, our Lord says, " *God commanded*, saying," etc.

Heb. iii. 7.—Referring to Ps. xcv. 7-11. " Wherefore *as the Holy Ghost saith*," not " as David saith," or " as the Psalmist saith."

Heb. ix. 8.—Referring to Ex. xxv.-xl. (concerning the Tabernacle and its teaching), " *The Holy Ghost this signifying*," etc.

Heb. x. 15.—Quoting Jer. xxxi. 33, 34, "Whereof *the Holy Ghost is a witness* to us."

Acts i. 16.—Peter, quoting Ps. xli. 9 (10), says, "This Scripture must needs have been fulfilled, which *the Holy Ghost*, by the mouth of David, *spake* before concerning Judas." Observe, that while David *spake*, the words were not his, but "the words of the Holy Ghost."

Acts iii. 18.—Peter, referring to the Old Testament prophecies of Christ, says, "Those things, which *God before had showed* by the mouth of all his prophets, that Christ should suffer, he hath so fulfilled."

Acts xxviii. 25.—Paul, quoting Isa. vi. 9, exclaims, "Well *spake the Holy Ghost* by Isaiah the prophet unto our fathers.

Old Testament passages are introduced in various ways:

1. γέγραπται (*gegraptai*), *it standeth written*. Matt. iv. 4-10. Luke iv. 4, 8. Rom. i. 17; iii. 4, 10; x. 15. 1 Cor. i. 19, 31. 1 Pet. i. 16, etc.

2. λέγει γὰρ ἡ γραφή (*legei gar hee graphee*), *for the Scripture saith*. Rom. ix. 17 (Ex. ix. 16). Rom. x. 11 (Isa. xxviii. 16). 1 Tim. v. 18 (Deut. xxv. 4).

3. ὁ νόμος (*ho nomos*) *The Law*. John xv. 25, from Ps. xxxv. 19; lxix. 4 (5), emphasizes the fact that the Sacred Writings of the Old Covenant, viewed as a whole, constituted the Law of Israel. The pronoun "their" shows this. John x. 34 (from Ps. lxxxii. 6) is written in Ex. xxi. 6; xxii. 8, 9 (7, 8). And 1 Cor. xiv. 21 (from Isa. xxviii. 11, 12) has a reference to Deut. xxviii. 49. Thus the reference is carried back, not only to the passage quoted, but to the one still earlier, in which it had its origin.

In the New Testament eight men are specified as the *agents* employed by the Holy Spirit: Moses, 13 times; David 7; Elijah, once; Isaiah, 12; Joel, once; Hosea, once; Jeremiah, twice; Daniel, once.

In Matthew an agent is named 13 times (Jeremiah, Isaiah, Moses, David, and Daniel).

In Mark, 7 (Moses, Isaiah, David, Daniel).

In Luke, 6 (Moses, Isaiah, David).

In John, 4 (Isaiah, Moses).

In Acts, 10 (David, Joel, Moses, Isaiah).

In Rom., 10 (David, Hosea, Isaiah, Moses, Elijah).

In 1 Cor., (Moses) once.

In Hebrews, 3 (David, Moses).

In Rev., (Moses) once.

Thus, 14 passages are ascribed to the agency of Moses ; 8 to that of David ; 13 of Isaiah; 2 of Hosea; 2 of Jeremiah ; 1 of Daniel ; 1 of Joel; 1 of Elijah.

These facts are deeply instructive ; because, for example, while the modern critics divide the book of Isaiah into two authorships, the New Testament ascribes *six* out of the thirteen passages to Isaiah in the first part of the prophecy (chaps. i.-xxxix.), and *seven* out of the last part (chaps. xl.-xlvi.). The recognition of this one simple fact demolishes completely the hypothesis of the Higher Critics, and will cause us to prefer the statements of God to the imagination of men.

In making a quotation from the Old Testament in the New, surely the Holy Spirit is at liberty to do what any and every *human* writer may do, and frequently does, in his own works. Human writers and speakers constantly repeat, refer to, and quote what they have previously written and spoken, introducing the words in new senses, in different connections, with varied references, and in fresh applications.

This is the case with the quotations in the Bible, and this one consideration explains all the so-called difficulties connected with the subject.

Our work, then, in considering these differences, becomes totally different in character from that which treats them merely as dis- crepancies, arising from human infirmity or ignorance. These differ- ences become all important, because they convey to us Divine comments, and reveal to us new truths.

In quoting, or using again, words and expressions which the Holy Spirit has before used, we may note the following interesting ways in which He varies the sense or the words in order to convey to us new truths and lessons by the new application.

In referring to these by way of illustration we have not classified them according to these definitions and divisions, as the student can determine each case for himself. But we have followed the arrange- ment of Glassius in his chapter on *Gnomes.**

I. As to their INTERNAL form (*i.e.*, the *sense* as distinct from the *words*).

    1. Where the sense originally intended is preserved.

    2. Where the sense is modified.

    3. Where the sense is accommodated (ACCOMMODATIO)

---

* Which Keach translates almost verbatim, without any acknowledgment.

II. As to their EXTERNAL form (*i.e.*, the *words* as distinct from the *sense*).

 1. Where the words quoted are the same as the Hebrew or the Septuagint.

 2. Where the words are varied as to omission, position, or addition.

 3. Where words are changed :
  (*a*) by a reading :
  (*b*) by an inference :
  (*c*) in number :
  (*d*) in person :
  (*e*) in mood or tense.

 4. Where several citations are amalgamated (composite quotations).

 5. Where the quotations are made from books other than the Bible.

We will now consider these forms of Quotation in order :—

I. As to their INTERNAL FORM, *i.e.*, the sense as distinct from the words.

In the consideration of Quotations, care must be taken to note what is said to be "*spoken*," and what is said to be "*written*." Some prophecies were written and never spoken ; some were spoken by the Prophet and afterwards written down in his "prophecies"; others were "spoken" and never written down at all, and when, therefore, a passage is quoted as having been "*spoken*," we may or may not find it written down in the Old Testament Scriptures. But when it is said to have been "*written*," then we shall find it surely written down in the Scriptures of truth.

Surely there is all the difference in the world between τὸ ῥηθέν (*to rheethen*), *that which was spoken*, and ὁ γέγραπται (*ho gegraptai*), *that which standeth written*.

There is a further consideration which will help us when the quotations are *prophecies*. Prophecy is the utterance of the LORD— Jehovah : He Who was and is and is to come. His words, therefore, may often have a *past*, *present* and *future* reference.

Prophecy frequently has all three : (1) the reference to the events at the time of its utterance ; (2) a subsequent reference to some great crisis ; and (3) a final consummation, which shall fulfil and exhaust it.

When a prophecy is said, therefore, to be "fulfilled," that exhausts it. In other cases, where that final fulfilment is still future, the quotation is general—"as it is written," or some such indefinite reference.

The mistake made by most students of prophecy consists in this: that they do not bear in mind this threefold aspect of prophecy; but take one *part*, and put it for the *whole*.

For example, with regard to the prophecy in Dan. xi. There was a reference to Antiochus Epiphanes, now *past*; but this neither fulfilled nor exhausted the prophecy; which waits for the yet *future* revelation of one who shall fill it full: while there may be a *historical* reference to the course of events between. Each is true as *part* of the general fulfilment; but neither contains the *whole* truth embodied in the fulness of the prophetic record.

An example of this may be seen in the very first recorded fulfilment of prophecy in the New Testament (Matt. i. 23 below). We there see how the same Holy Spirit who first inspired that prophecy afterwards Himself interprets and applies it.

1. *Where the sense originally intended by the Holy Spirit is preserved, though the words may vary.*

Matt. i. 23.—"Behold a virgin shall be with child and shall bring forth a son, and they shall call his name Emmanuel."

This prophecy was "spoken" by Isaiah to Ahaz (Isa. vii. 13, 14), and afterwards written down. It was first spoken with special reference to Ahaz and the circumstances then existing; but was afterwards fulfilled and quoted with reference to the event which the prophet, who was merely "the mouth," did not understand, but which the Lord really intended. The *words* differ from both the Heb. and the LXX., but the sense is the same.

It never had or could have a proper fulfilment, except in Christ, for no virgin ever conceived and bore a child. In the days of Isaiah a certain woman, who was a virgin at the time when the prophecy was uttered, afterwards brought forth a son, whom they were told to name "Emmanuel"; and, before that child was old enough to know how to refuse the evil and choose the good, the deliverance promised to King Ahaz was wrought for him. But this prophecy did not have its complete and proper fulfilment in the days of Ahaz, because a real virgin did not conceive and bring forth a real Emmanuel.

This is not a prophecy, therefore, where the original sense is modified; for this was the sense in which it was originally intended, although there was a preliminary and partial fulfilment at the time.*

Matt. ii 6.—Quoted from Mic. v. 2 (1). The words differ from the Heb. and LXX, but the sense originally intended is preserved.

Matt. xi. 10.—(Mark i. 2, etc.). Quoted from Mal. iii. 1. Here the words differ from the Heb. and the LXX, though the original sense intended is preserved.

Matt. xii. 17, etc.—Quoted from Isa. xlii. 1-4. The words differ from the LXX, but the original sense is preserved.

Matt. xiii. 14, 15.—(Mark iv. 12. Luke viii. 10. John xii. 40. Acts xxviii. 26, 27). Quoted from Isa. vi. 9, 10, agreeing with the LXX.

Matt. xxi. 5.—(John xii. 14, 15). Quoted from Isa. lxii. 11 and Zech. ix. 9, agreeing with LXX.

Matt. xxi. 16.—" Have ye never read, Ps. viii. 2 (3), ' Out of the mouth of babes and sucklings thou hast perfected (or prepared) praise,' " which agrees with the LXX.

Matt. xxi. 42.—(Mark xii. 10. Acts iv. 11. 1 Pet. ii. 7). Quoted from Ps. cxviii. 22, 23 (LXX).

Matt. xxii. 44.—(Mark xii. 36. Luke xx. 42, 43. Acts ii. 34, 35. 1 Cor. xv. 25. Heb. i. 13). Quoted from Ps. cx. 1 (LXX).

Matt. xxvi. 31.—Quoted from Zech. xiii. 7. Though the words differ both from the Heb. and the LXX, the sense originally intended is preserved.

Matt. xxvii. 35.—(John xix. 24). Quoted from Ps. xxii. 18 (19) (LXX).

Luke iv. 18, 21.—Quoted from Isa. lxi. 1, 2. The words differ both from the Heb. and LXX, though the original intention is preserved.

John xix. 37.—Quoted from Zech. xii. 10. The words differ from the LXX, but the sense is the same.

Acts iii. 22, 23.—Quoted from Deut. xviii. 15-19 (LXX).

Acts xiii. 33.—Quoted from Ps. ii. 7 (LXX).

Acts xv. 16, 17.—Quoted from Amos ix. 11, 12. The words differ from the Heb. and LXX., though the sense is preserved.

Rom. xiv. 11.—Quoted from Isa. xlv. 23. The words differ both from the Heb. and the LXX, but the original sense is preserved.

Rom. xv. 3.—Quoted from Ps. lxix. 9 (10) (LXX).

---

* See *Number in Scripture* (page 63) by the same author and publisher.

Rom. xv. 12.—Quoted from Isa. xi. 1, 10 (LXX).

Eph. iv. 8.—Quoted from Ps. lxviii. 18 (19). Here the original sense is preserved, though the words differ both from the Heb. and the LXX.

Heb. i. 8, 9.—Quoted from Ps. xlv. 6, 7 (7, 8), etc. (LXX).

Heb. i. 10-13.—Quoted from Ps. cii. 25 (26), etc. (LXX).

Heb. v. 6 and vii. 17.—Quoted from Ps. cx. 4.

Heb. x. 5, 6.—Quoted from Ps. xl. 6-9 (LXX). Here the words differ from the Hebrew (see below page 793), though the original intention and scope of the words is preserved.

1 Pet. ii. 6.—Quoted from Isa. xxviii. 16 (LXX).

2. *Where the original sense is modified in the quotation
or reference.*

Matt. xii. 40.—Where, in the reference to Jonah i. 17 (ii. 1), the words are used with a new and different application.

John iii. 14, 15, where the words respecting the brazen serpent, though not directly quoted, are modified in their new application.

John xix. 36.—"A bone of him shall not be broken." Quoted from Ex. xii. 46, where we have the words, "Neither shall ye break a bone thereof." That "another Scripture saith" this, is perfectly true, but not in the same sense. It was said of the passover lamb, and it is here modified and applied to Christ. (See 1 Cor. v. 7.)

Eph. v. 31, 32.—Where, in the reference to Gen. ii. 23, 24, the words are used with a new application.

3. *Where the sense is* ACCOMMODATED, *being quite different from that
which was first intended, and the sense is accommodated by
analogy to quite a different event or circumstance.*

Hence this particular form of the figure is called ACCOM-MODATIO.

Matt. ii. 15.—"Out of Egypt have I called my son," which agrees with the Hebrew of Hos. xi. 1, and not with the LXX, which has "have I sent for his (*i.e.*, Israel's) children."

Matt. ii. 17, 18.—From Jer. xxxi. 15: but differs both from the Heb. and the LXX (xxxviii. 15). The sense of each is given, but is accommodated to the new circumstances.

Matt. viii. 17.—Quoted from Isa. liii. 4, but differing from the LXX, and exactly answering to the Hebrew. The sense is accommodated; for, whereas the Spirit in Isaiah uses the words of Christ bearing our spiritual infirmities and sins in His passion and death (as shown in 1 Pet. ii. 24, 25), the same Spirit uses them in Matthew, and accommodates them to other circumstances, *viz.*, to Christ's healing people of their bodily sicknesses (Matt. viii. 16). But this only shows the wonderful fulness of the Divine words.

Matt. xiii. 35.—Quoted from Ps. lxxviii. 2 : but the sense in which Christ used them was different from that in the Psalm, where they are used of the past history of Israel : here they are accommodated by Christ, the Speaker, to the present circumstances. The words are said to be " fulfilled," because, though the agent or speaker knew not of this ultimate use of the words, the Holy Spirit, Who spake by him, foreknew it. The words are said to be " spoken by the prophet," and so they were (see Ps. lxxviii. 1, 2), though they were afterwards written down.

The actual words differ both from the Heb. and the LXX, as well as from the sense which is accommodated to them.

Christ was making known concerning that Kingdom certain things which would happen on its rejection. These things were not the subject of Old Testament prophecy, but had been " kept secret," and are therefore called " the mysteries of (or secrets concerning) the kingdom."

Matt. xv. 8, 9.—Quoted from Isa. xxix. 13, according to the Septuagint, but accommodated to different circumstances from those to which the words referred when first spoken.

Matt. xxvii. 9, 10.—" Then was fulfilled that which was spoken by Jeremiah the prophet, saying, And they took the thirty pieces of silver, the price of him that was valued, whom they of the children of Israel did value ; And gave them for the potter's field, as the Lord appointed me."

In the margin the reference given is Zech. xi. 12, 13 : but the words differ so widely both from the Heb. and the Septuagint that it is more than doubtful whether this can be the passage which is said to be fulfilled.

As no such passage is found in Jeremiah, the difficulty is supposed to be very great. As an example of misapplied ingenuity, we give the various attempts which have been made by way of evading the difficulty :

1. It was a mistake of Matthew's memory.　This was Augustine's opinion, followed by Alford, who says: " The citation is not from Jeremiah, and is probably quoted from memory and unprecisely."

2. The reading, " Jeremiah " is spurious.　(Rupert von Deutz and others).

3. It occurs in a work of Jeremiah's which has been lost.　(Origen and others).

4. It was in Jeremiah, but the Jews have expunged it. (Eusebius).

5. That, Because Jeremiah, in the Talmud, and some MSS., commences the " latter " prophets, his name is put for the whole body of their writings which would include Jeremiah.　(Lightfoot, Adam Clark, Scrivener, and others).

6. Wordsworth boldly asserts that the mistake was purposely made ; the name Jeremiah being substituted for Zechariah in order to teach us not to depend on the prophets who were merely channels and not the sources of Divine Truth.

Concerning this Alford says : " I put it to any faithful Christian to say, whether of the two presents the greater obstacle to his faith, the solution given above (see No. 1 above), or that given in Wordsworth's note."

7. Others again think Matthew's mistake arose from the Jewish tradition " *Zechariam habuisse spiritum Jeremiæ* " (" Zechariah had the spirit of Jeremiah ").

Need we say, with regard to these seven, that

1. Is improbable : inasmuch as he quotes Zechariah elsewhere (xxi. 5, xxvi. 31).

2. Is devoid of MS. authority, which is essential in a case of this kind.　Origen and Eusebius suspect it, but only conjecturally.

3. This, too, is only a conjecture.

4. So with this.

5. This has more weight, but is unlikely and unsatisfactory: so evidently a make-shift.

6. We admire Wordsworth's faith in the accuracy of the Bible more than Alford's free handling of the Word : but it is, after all, a wild conjecture.

7. The same is the case with this.

Now these are just the sort of explanations which do more harm than all the assaults of the enemies of the Bible.　But they serve to prove the truth of inspiration, in that the Bible still stands in spite of all the defences of its friends!

If it be a quotation from Zechariah, it can be so only by *accommodation*, or by *composition* (see below page 797, "composite quotations"), in which case it combines four different quotations:—

(*a*) "They took the thirty pieces of silver," which is derived from the narrative, with special reference to Zechariah;

(*b*) "The price of him that was valued," also after Zechariah.

(*c*) "Whom they bought of the children of Israel" (A.V. marg.) as Joseph was bought and sold. After Gen. xxxvii. :

(*d*) "And gave them for the potter's field," the narrative of the text, with a special reference to Zechariah.

(*e*) "As the Lord appointed me," which is from Jer. xxxii. 6, 8, and connects the transaction in Matthew with that in Jer. xxxii. A field was bought in each case; and the latter, like the former, has special reference to the future. Thus they treasured up a witness against their own perfidy, while Jeremiah witnessed to the Lord's faithfulness.

But in reality, all these so-called explanations are utterly beside the point, and are not only unnecessary, but absolutely worthless. The mention of them here would be a waste of paper and printer's ink, except that they testify to the fact that, like most other difficulties, this one is first invented and put into the text, and then it is wrestled with, and the text wrested.

There is not a word about the prophecy being *written* in Jeremiah at all. It says τὸ ῥηθέν (*to rheethen*) "that which was SPOKEN" : but these clever critics practically take the trouble to exchange these two words, and put in two others ὃ γέγραπται (*ho gegraptai*), or ἦν γεγραμμένον (*een gegrammenon*), "that which is *written.*" And then, having made the assertion that it was *written* in Jeremiah, they have to show cause why it cannot be found there.

Some prophecies were written and never (so far as we know) spoken at all; others were both spoken and written; while some were spoken and never written.

It says: "That which was SPOKEN by Jeremiah the prophet." Surely it is neither suspicion nor conjecture, nor "unprecise" to maintain that it was thus "spoken." Who can prove that it was not "spoken by Jeremiah?"

True, Zechariah may have written down similar words, though not referring to the same circumstances; but it ought never to have occurred to anyone to say that Matt. xxvii. 9, 10 was quoted from what is *written by Zechariah*, when it positively states that it was "*spoken by Jeremiah.*"

Acts xiii. 40, 41.—Quoted from Hab. i. 5, according to the LXX, but accommodated to another set of circumstances, and to the Romans rather than to the Chaldeans.

Rom. ix. 27, 28.—Quoted from Isa. x. 22, 23, nearly according to the LXX.

Rom. ix. 29.—Quoted Isa. i. 9, according to the LXX.

Rom. x. 6-8.—Where what the Scripture (or, rather, "the righteousness which is of faith) "saith" (Deut. xxx. 12-14) is accommodated to different circumstances—verses 6 and 8 agreeing with the LXX, and verse 7 differing from it.

1 Cor. i. 19, 20.—Quoted from Isa. xxix. 14 and xxxiii. 18, and differing from the LXX, as well as accommodated to other circumstances.

1 Cor. x. 6, 11. — "These things happened unto them for ensamples." Where the events cited are used and accommodated to our sins and infirmities.

Rev. i. 7.—An allusion to Zech. xii. 10.

Rev. i. 17.—An allusion to Isa. xli. 4 and xliv. 6, but differing from the LXX.

Rev. xi. 4.—Quoted from Zech. iv. 14, differing both from the Heb. and the LXX, and accommodated to different circumstances.

II. As to their EXTERNAL form (*i.e.*, the words, as distinct from the sense).

1. *Where the words are from the Hebrew, or from the Septuagint.*

Matt. ii. 15, from Hos. xi. 1 ; **Matt. ii. 6,** from Mic. v. 2 (1) ; **Matt. xii. 18-21,** from Isa. xli. 1-4. These and other passages are from the Hebrew and not from the LXX.

Luke iv. 18 quoted from the LXX. of Isa. lxi. 1, 2. We have already instanced this as a citation in which the original sense is preserved. But we repeat it here because the *words* are varied.

"The Spirit of the Lord (Heb., Adonai Jehovah) is upon me because he (Heb., Jehovah) hath anointed me to preach the Gospel to the poor; he hath sent me to heal the broken-hearted, to preach deliverance to the captives, and recovering of sight to the blind."

Thus far we have the words of the LXX. The last sentence " the recovering of sight to the blind," not being in the Hebrew Text *; while the last sentence in the Hebrew is not in the LXX. But the two words in the Hebrew contain both senses. פָּקַח (*pahkach*) means simply *to open*. Spoken once of the ears (Isa. xlii. 20) ; and often of the eyes (2 Kings iv. 35; vi. 17, 20; xix. 16. Dan. ix. 18. Job xxvii. 19. Prov. xx. 13. Jer. xxxii. 19. Isa. xlii. 7). Hence the first of the two words means to open the eyes of: and the other word means *prison*. Thus, in reading, the sense of the first word was expanded and given in the words of Isa. xlii. 7; while that of the second word was expanded and given in the words of Isa. lviii. 6—the two together meaning that the eyes of the prisoners should be opened on being released from the darkness of their prison. Or, to open [*their eyes*, and *open or release*] the prisoners. The explanation lies in the fact that the *eyelids* were called "*the doors*" of the eyes (עַפְעַפִּים, *aphappayim*) (Ps. cxxxii. 4. Prov. vi. 4. Job xvi. 16, etc.). Hence the term "to open" applies equally to the eyes and to prison doors.

2. *Where the words are varied by omission, addition, or transposition.*

Matt. iv. 10 and Luke iv. 8.—"Thou shalt worship the Lord thy God," from Deut. vi. 13 and x. 20; and then the Lord added His own Divine conclusion from this: "And Him only shalt thou serve."

The Heb. and the LXX. have "fear": but the fear of God includes the *worship* of God ; and as worship was the matter in question (see Matt. iv. 9), the φοβηθήσῃ (*phobeetheesee*), *thou shalt fear*, of the LXX. is changed by the Lord to προσκυνήσεις (*proskuneeseis*), *thou shalt worship*.

Matt. iv. 15, 16, from Isa. ix. 1, 2 (viii. 23; ix. 1). Here, the quotation differs both from the Hebrew and from the LXX. But this is partly an accommodation; because in Isaiah (LXX) it is *prophecy*, while in the Gospel it is *fulfilment* that is in question.

Matt. v. 31, from Deut. xxiv. 1 : but here it is not given as an exact quotation. It introduces the words by the simple formula: " It hath been said," implying that those who thus said, put their own meaning on what the Law said.

Matt. xii. 18-21, from Isa. xlii. 1-4. Here, the Gospel differs from the LXX, scarcely a word being the same till we come to the

---

* See Ginsburg's Hebrew Bible, which gives two readings.

last clause. It differs, too, from the Hebrew in the last clause, because it records the act of "fulfilment," and not merely the words of the *prophecy*. The words, therefore take the form of a Divine comment or re-statement.

Matt. xix. 5.—"And they twain" (οἱ δύο, *hoi duo*). These words are added to the usual text of Gen. ii. 24 : and yet the sense is the same, for only of two were these words spoken. The quotation agrees with the LXX.

Matt. xxii. 24.—From Deut. xxv. 5, 6. But here it is the Sadducees, who do not quote, but merely give the substance of the matter under the loose formula "Moses said."

Rom. xi. 3, 4.—From 1 Kings xix. 10, 14, 18. Here neither the Heb. nor the LXX is followed, but the facts are recorded ; while the destruction of the altars and the killing of the prophets are transposed.

1 Cor. ii. 9.—From Isa. lxiv. 4 (3). It is clear from this that the formula, "As it is written," refers to the *sense* rather than to the *words ;* and that the Divine Author, in repeating the words, sometimes varied them, as He does here ; first, by transposing the *hearing* and the *seeing ;* and then, by adding "neither have entered into the heart of man," thus varying both from the Heb. and the LXX.

Moreover, He employs the general sentiment in a particular case. For what is said in the abstract, and universally, in Isaiah, is here put in contrast to some particular things which are revealed. See verse 10.

1 Cor. xiv. 21.—From Isa. xxviii. 11, 12. Here the quotation differs both from the Heb. and the LXX : and is accommodated to the new circumstances by the omission of the middle passage, which was not relevant.

1 Pet. i. 24, 25.—From Isa. xl. 6-8. Here the words are not introduced by any formula as a quotation. Isa. xl. is referred to ; and certain words are used again by the same Author : and, therefore, some are omitted ; as not being relevant, or necessary for the purpose in hand.

3. *Where the words are changed by a reading, or an inference ; or in number, person, mood, or tense.*

We all constantly thus quote the Scriptures : and, in adapting them by application to some special circumstance, we depart from the original interpretation as to the special circumstances connected with them, and do not hesitate to change a tense, or number, or person, etc.

It is no less authoritative, as Scripture, nor does it alter the word of God.

(a) By a different reading.

Heb. x. 5 (7).—"A body hast thou prepared me."

These words are like the LXX of Psalm xl. 6 (xxxix. 6), and differ from the Hebrew, which is, " Mine ears hast thou opened."

But this is not given as a quotation. It does not say, " as it is written "; but it gives the words which " he saith," "*when he cometh into the world.*" What he then said in the accomplishment of a prophecy must certainly differ from the form in which the event was foretold and written centuries before.

What we have here is an adaptation or accommodation (see above page 786) of a prophecy ; and the words are changed to make it suit the actual fulfilment of the prophecy.

It consists of four lines arranged alternately :—

a | " Sacrifice and offering thou didst not desire ;

   b | Mine ears hast thou opened :

a | Burnt offering and sin offering hast thou not required ;

   b | Then said I, Lo, I come . . . to do thy will, O my God."

Here in a and *a* we have *sacrifices* ; while in b and *b* we have *obedience.*

This is another statement of the truth in 1 Sam. xv. 22 :

   a | " To obey

      b | Is better than sacrifice,

   a | And to hearken

      b | Than the fat of rams."

Here, again, we have *obedience* and *sacrifice* set in contrast. And that is exactly what we have in Heb. x. 5, except that the *obedience* is differently expressed.

In Ps. xl 6, the symbol is the opening or boring of the ears, which is in harmony with Isa. l. 5 ; xlviii. 8 ; and an allusion to Ex. xix. 5 ; xxi. 5, 6 ; and Deut. xv. 16, 17 ; while the contrast is in harmony with 1 Sam xv. 22 and Jer. vii. 22. The boring of the ears signifies the voluntary acceptance of bond-service, and the promise to perform it. But in Heb. x. 5 we have not the promise (as in Ps. xl. 6), but the actual *performance*, and therefore the words are changed by the One who came to do that will of God. Surely He had the right to change them, and to state as a fact, " A body hast thou prepared me " in which to obey, and by that perfect obedience unto death to do that which is "better than sacrifice." The "great delight" (1 Sam. xv. 22) of the Father is expressed in Matt. iii. 17, as well as foretold in Isa. xlii. 1.

Heb. xi. 21.—This is not a quotation; but, as it is generally treated as such, and as being in discrepancy with Gen. xlvii. 31, we refer the reader to *Hysteresis* (*q.v.*).

(b) By an *inference*.

Matt. ii. 6.—Here we have several changes by way of inference and explanation, bringing out more of the meaning of the words in the prophet. Micah v. 2 (1) reads (R.V.) : " But thou Bethlehem Ephrathah, which art little to be among the thousands of Judah, out of thee shall One come forth unto me that is to be ruler in Israel."

In Matt. ii. 6 we have " land of Judah " instead of Ephrathah, which was its ancient name (see Gen. xxxv. 16, 19 : xlviii. 7), as being better understood by Herod.

Instead of the positive " art little," we have the negative, " art in no wise least," because, though little in the time of Micah, yet now, after the birth of the Messiah (Matt. i.), it could no longer be so called, in view of the event which had given the city true greatness.

Instead of " thousands," we have the *Metonymy* (*q.v.*), properly translated " princes," because Messiah was the Prince of princes.

Instead of " be ruler," we have " be shepherd of " (A.V. rule, margin *feed*). This explanation brings in the next verse but one in Micah (" He shall stand and shall feed.")

Finally, the words of the prophet, " unto me," are omitted, because the emphasis is now on the *fact* rather than the *purpose* (though both were true) ; and hence the *reason* is given in the word " for," and the fact is added in the words, " my people."

Acts vii. 43.—Here the citation differs both from the Hebrew and LXX (Amos v. 25-27) in words ; but, by Divine inference other facts and truths are referred to.

Instead of using the Hebrew name " Chiun," in Amos v. 26, the Greek equivalent, " Remphan," is used.*

Instead of saying " the figures which ye made for yourselves," the *object* for which they were made is given by Him, who knew their

---

* Just as " Ethiopia " is used for the Hebrew " *Koosh* " ; " Egypt " for " *Mizraim* " ; " Syria " and " Mesopotania " for the Hebrew " *Aram*."

hearts—" figures which ye made to worship them," thus bringing out and emphasising their idolatry.

Instead of saying "beyond Damascus," Stephen says: "beyond Babylon." But this is no " scribal error," or " inadvertence," as critics assert.

Even the stoutest defenders of verbal inspiration read both Amos and Acts, as though they both " referred to the Babylonian exile," and do not appear to notice that it says " beyond " Babylon.

The fact is that it is "the house of Israel" as distinct from Judah that is spoken of in Acts vii. 42, and in Amos; and, while Judah was taken away *to* Babylon, Israel was taken " beyond " Babylon. Amos speaking before either captivity (about 780 B.C.) says: " beyond Damascus "; or, beyond where Damascus will go captive. See Amos i. 5.

In other words, in the Old Testament the Holy Spirit alludes to the country, and refers to *Assyria*, and says " beyond Damascus "; while speaking by Stephen, in the light of all the past history, He alludes to the fact that Israel was removed farther than Judah, for while Judah was taken away *to* Babylon, Israel was removed " beyond " it.

Rom. ix. 27.—" Though the number of the children of Israel be as the sand of the sea " (so LXX). In Isa. x. 22 it is, " Though thy People Israel be as the sand of the sea," etc. Here, by way of inference, the same people are mentioned in other words.

Rom. ix. 29 is referred to as a difference in *reading*. " Except the Lord of Sabaoth had left us a seed " (σπέρμα, *sperma*). In Isa. i. 9 it is " Except the LORD of hosts had left unto us a *remnant* (שָׂרִיד, *sareed*), but *sareed* means the same thing exactly, though the words differ. The seed that is left will form the remnant, and the " remnant " that is left will consist of the " seed."

Rom. ix. 33.—" Whosoever believeth on him shall not be ashamed." This, in Isa. xxviii. 16, is " He that believeth shall not make haste."

The Hebrew (חוּשׁ, *chūsh*), means *to flee, flee away*, hence, of the feelings, *to be excited*. Rom. ix. 33 is the Divine inference from this, for he who really believes has no need for fleeing or for excitement; but can patiently wait for and expect the fulfilment of the Divine promises. Hence, he will have no ground for that shame which causes others to run away.

Eph. iv. 8.—This is supposed to be a case where there is a difference of reading. The English is: "and gave gifts unto men." But the Hebrew of Ps. lxviii. 18 (19) is: "Thou hast received gifts for men."

In the Psalm we have the prophecy "that Jah Elohim might dwell among them"; while in the Epistle we have the fulfilment in the gifts *received* being "actually" *given*, and the Lord God dwelling in the midst of His People by the Holy Spirit. But apart from this it ought to be noted that the Hebrew לָקַח (*lakach*) has the double and beautiful sense of first *receiving* and then *giving*: *i.e.*, *receive* and *give what is received*. Hence it is often rendered "to *fetch*." See Gen. xviii. 5; xxvii. 13; xlii. 16. Ex. xxvii. 20 "bring." Lev. xxiv. 2 "bring." 2 Kings ii. 20 "bring."

We ought, however, to note that in the Psalm we have בָּאָדָם (*baadam*) with the article: *i.e.*, *in the man*. So that we may render it: "Thou didst receive gifts in human nature": *i.e.*, as "the Son of man" (compare Matt. xxviii. 18. John xiii. 3). He did give gifts to men.

(*c*) In number.

Matt. iv. 7.—"Thou shalt not tempt the Lord thy God." In Deut. vi. 16 it is: "Ye shall not tempt." If the command is given to all in general, then surely it applies to each individual in particular: and so the Lord applied it in reply to the Tempter.

Rom. iv. 7.—"Blessed are they whose iniquities are forgiven." In Ps. xxxii. 1 it is in the singular number: "Blessed is he," etc.

But this is not a direct quotation. It is introduced by the words: "David also describeth the blessedness of the man unto whom God imputed righteousness without works [*saying*] Blessed are they whose iniquities are forgiven, and whose sins are covered. Blessed is the man to whom the Lord will not impute sin."

But in the Hebrew the word "man" (אָדָם) does not occur until verse 2. In verse 1 it is literally "O the happinesses of the forgiven of transgression: the covered of sin." And this singular may be used of a forgiven People collectively, and be Divinely expanded according to its sense: "Blessed are they."

In both places the plural is meant, the singular being put for it in the former case only by *Synecdoche* (*q.v.*).

Rom. x. 15.—"How beautiful are the feet of them that preach the Gospel of peace."

In Isa. lii. 7 the Heb. is "the feet of him," the singular being put by *Synecdoche* for the plural, just as "the feet" are put (the part for the whole) for the person who preaches.

(*d*) In person.

Examples of this may be found under *Heterosis* of Person.   See above, where one person is put for another.

(*e*) In mood and tense.

Examples of this may be found under *Heterosis* of the Verb.   See above.

One illustration may be given in Matt. xiii. 14, 15, where (in the quotation of Isa. vi. 10) the *indicative* mood is put by *Heterosis* for the *imperative*.

4.   *Where several citations are amalgamated.* *Composite quotations.*

Sometimes a number of separate sentences are drawn from different passages and presented as one connected passage.

This is a common use practised generally in all literature.   Dr. Franklin Johnson * gives some interesting examples from various authors.

Plato, in his *Ion* (p. 538), quotes two lines from Homer pieced together by Plato himself, the first from *Iliad* xi., line 638; and the second, line 630, col. 629.

Xenophon (*Memorabilia*, bk. I., ch. 2, sec. 58) quotes connectedly as one passage, two passages from Homer (*Iliad* ii., 188 sqq. and 198 sqq.

Lucian, in his *Charon* (sec. 22), runs five lines together from Homer.   But Jacobitz † shows that they are brought together from different passages : *viz.* : *Iliad* ix. 319, 320, and *Odyssey* x. 521 ; xi. 539.

Plutarch, in his treatise on *Progress in Virtue*, treats two separate lines of Homer as a single sentence, *viz.*, *Odyssey* vi. 187 and xxiv. 402.

Cicero, in *De Oratore*, book II., sec. 80, quotes from the *Andria* of Terence, making up in two lines parts of Terence's lines 117, 128 and 129.

---

* *The Quotations of the New Testament from the Old considered in the light of general literature*, pp. 92-102.

† *Lucian* i., p. 39.

Philo, in his treatise, *Who is the heir of divine things ?* sec. 5, quotes, as one address of Moses, parts of two, viz., Num. xi. 13 and 22, but both refer to the same matter.

In the same treatise (sec. 46) he runs together parts of Gen. xviii. 14 and xvii. 19.

Conybeare and Howson (Life and Epistles of St. Paul, vol. I., p. 54) quote, as one passage, parts of Ps. cxxii. 4 ; lxviii. 27 (28) ; cxxii. 5, 2, 6, 7 ; and lxviii. 35 (36). And these are not accompanied by any references or explanation.

Ruskin, in his *Modern Painters*, vol. V., p. 146, quotes as one passage : "How I love thy law ! It is my meditation all the day. Thy testimonies are my delight and my counsellors; sweeter also than honey and the honeycomb." All these four sentences are from the Psalms. The first two are from Ps. cxix. 97, 24 and xix. 10 (11).

All these composite quotations are made up of sentences that relate to the same subject. And this is always true of those which we find in the Scriptures.

Not so when man quotes the Scriptures in this manner. When he thus strings texts together it is a very different matter; and, though sometimes harmless, it is often dangerous, and is a practice greatly to be deprecated. By a system, which may be called text-garbling, he is able to support his own theories and views.

We recently saw two texts (quotations) thus connected in order to support Fasting, though they relate to totally distinct subjects : " The Lord Jesus fasted forty days and forty nights. Do this in remembrance of Me." This is a flagrant example, but less likely to harm than many others which are less glaring and more specious.

Quite different are those examples in which the Holy Spirit Himself takes His own words and thus links them together, making one subject of them, even though that subject cannot be discerned by us in the separate passages.

The following are examples :—

Matt. xxi. 5.—" Tell ye the daughter of Sion, Behold, thy king cometh unto thee," etc.

This is a composite quotation, the first sentence, " Tell ye," etc., being taken from Isa. lxii. 11, and the latter contracted from Zech. ix. 9.

In **Matt. xxi. 13** (Mark xi. 17, and Luke xix. 46), the Lord exclaimed : " It is written, My house shall be called the house of prayer ; but ye have made it a den of thieves." The first half of this is from

Isa. lvi. 7, and the second slightly altered from Jer. vii. 11. In both passages (which agree with the LXX) the subject is the same; viz., the Temple, and the right use of it.

Mark i. 2, 3.—"As it is written in the prophets, Behold," etc. The prophets quoted are Mal. iii. 1, and Isa. xl. 3.

Luke i. 16, 17 is from Mal. iv. 5, 6 (iii. 23, 24) and iii. 1.

Acts i. 20 is made up from Ps. lxix. 25 (26), and cix. 8, and differs both from the Heb. and the LXX.

Rom. iii. 10-18 is a long quotation made up of the following passages, which all refer to the same subject. They are composed of two classes, the general and the particular ; verses 10-12 are taken from Ecc. vii. 20. Ps. xiv. 2, 3 ; and liii. 2, 3 (3, 4), which speak generally of the universality of sin ; while the second kind, verses 13-18, taken from Ps. v. 9 (10). Isa. lix. 7, 8, and Ps. xxxvi. 1 (2) proves the same thing ; being the manifestations of sin in particular cases. Thus two methods of proof by induction are employed : and yet some, "forgetting their logic" (as Dr. Franklin Johnson says), see a difficulty in this simple method of proof which is common to all writers of all ages, and of various languages.

It should be noted that in these cases the reasoning is always correctly from the general to the particular ; and not, as is so often the case with man, from the particular to the general : which is false in logic and fatal as to the argument.

Rom. ix. 33 is made up from Isa. xxviii. 16 and viii. 14. Varied both from the Heb. and the LXX.

Rom. xi. 8 is made up from Isa. xxix. 10 and Deut. xxix. 4.

Rom. xi. 26, 27 is made up from Isa. lix. 20, 21 and xxvii. 9, and agreeing with the LXX.

1 Cor. xv. 54, 55 is made up from Isa. xxv. 8, and Hos. xiii. 14, and varied both from the Heb. and the LXX.

2 Cor. vi. 16 is made up from Lev. xxvi. 11, 12 and Ezek. xxxvii. 27, and is varied from the LXX.

Gal. iii. 8 is made up from Gen. xii. 3 and xviii. 18.

Heb. ix. 19, 20 is made up from Ex. xxiv. 6, 7, 8, and Num. xix. 6.

1 Pet. ii. 7 is made up from Ps. cxviii. 22 and Isa. viii. 14.

Objectors have made a difficulty of these composite quotations, as though the Holy Spirit, the Author of the words as well as of the Word, may not repeat, vary, or combine His words in any way He pleases : and as though He were to be denied the right claimed and practised by writers in all ages.

So far from seeing a difficulty in this, we may learn many important lessons from these variations, which are nothing less than Divine Comments on the Divine Word by the Divine Author.

5. *Where quotations are from secular works, or books other than the Bible.*

Sometimes the Holy Spirit quotes words from secular and human writings, and either thus endorses the truth of the statement, or uses it against those who believed it and accepted it as truth.

Not all, however, that are generally considered as quotations are really so. For example : " As Jannes and Jambres withstood Moses " (2 Tim. iii. 8) is said to be a quotation from the Targum of Jonathan ben Uzziel upon Ex. vii. 11. But the Holy Spirit may give this independently, as a fact, quite apart from the Targum altogether ; while many believe the Targum to be of a later date.

So, too, the prophecy of Enoch in Jude 14, 15 may just as well be the foundation on which the so-called. " Book of Enoch " was afterwards made up, as a quotation made from that book. We certainly prefer to believe that the book of Enoch was originated from Jude 14, 15 ; and, taking this as the starting point, other prophecies were concocted and added by some old and unknown writer.

The same applies to Jude 9 concerning the controversy between Michael and the Devil about the body of Moses. This Scriptural statement was the original centre round which numberless fancies and fictions subsequently gathered, and from which the traditions started.

On the other hand, there are three certain undoubted quotations from secular writings. We will give them all.

The first is :—

Acts xvii. 28.—" For in him we live, and move, and have our being ; as certain also of your own poets have said, ' *For we are also his offspring* ' (τοῦ γὰρ καὶ γένος ἐσμέν, *tou gar kai genos esmen*)." This is an exact quotation from ARATUS, a native of Tarsus ; who, being a poet, had been requested by ANTIGONUS GONATAS, son of DEMETRIUS, and King of Macedonia (273-239 B.C.), to put into poetry an astronomical work of EUDOXUS (an astronomer of Cnidus, 403-350 B.C.), called *Phainomena*. This he did about 270 B.C., and he called his work *Diosemeia* (*i.e.*, *the Divine signs*), being a description and explanation of the signs of the Zodiac, and the Constellations, as the Greeks then understood, or rather misunderstood, them.* The poem opens with praise of God (*Zeus* or Jupiter), and these words occur in the fifth line :—

> " From Zeus we lead the strain ; He whom mankind
> Ne'er leave unhymned ; of Zeus all public ways,
> All haunts of men, are full ; and full the sea,
> And harbours ; and of Zeus all stand in need.
> *We are his offspring ;* and he, ever good to man,
> Gives favouring signs, and rouses us to toil," etc., etc.

Similar words, ἐκ σοῦ γὰρ γένος ἐσμέν (*ek sou gar genos esmen*) are used by KLEANTHES (*Hymn in Jov.* 5), who was born at Assos in Troas about 300 B.C. Also in *The Golden Verses* of Pythagoras.

In Acts xvii. 28, the word " poets," being in the plural, may refer to both of them, while the article in both cases refers to ZEUS, or JUPITER. The statement of the quotation was believed by the Greeks, and it is used here as an *argumentum ad hominem.* For it could never be that Zeus is really Jehovah, or that Jehovah is the " father " of everyone. The " universal fatherhood of God "—the Devil's lie—was the belief of the heathen, as well as of most modern " Christian " teachers. But both are wrong : for God is " the Father of our Lord Jesus Christ," and of those only who are " in Christ." It is to " as many as received Him, to them [and to none other] gave He authority to be called the sons of God " (John i. 12).

1 Cor. xv. 33.—" Evil communications (or companionships) corrupt good manners."

φθείρουσιν ἤθη χρήσθ' ὁμιλίαι κακαί (*phtheirousin eethee chreesth' homiliai kakai*). The words occur in this form, according to Jerome,† in the *Thais* of Menander. Dr. Burton thinks Menander may have quoted it from Euripides. Meyer quotes Plato (*Rep.* viii. 550B).

These various opinions show that the words were current as a common place quotation (*Parœmia, q.v.*), and are quoted as such here.

Tit. i. 12.—" One of themselves, *even* a prophet of their own, said, ' The Cretians *are* alway liars, evil beasts, slow bellies ' (*i.e.*, liars, evil wild-beasts, gluttons, lazy). This involves another figure called *Oxymoron* (*q.v.*). Jerome‡ says that the poet was Epimenides, and that the words occur in his work called *de Oraculis* (*i.e., of Oracles*), whence he is called a " prophet," either by way of irony, or because of

---

* See *The Witness of the Stars*, by the same author and publisher.

† In his *Epistle to the Orator Magnus.*

‡ Com. *in loco.*

the title of his work. Callimachus (a poet of Cyrene) makes use of
these words in a hymn to Jupiter, and satirizes the Cretans for their
boast that Jupiter was buried in Crete, whereas he maintains (of
course) that Jove was immortal. It was from this that Ovid said ' *Nec
fingunt omnia Cretes* ' (The Cretans do not always lie*).

The origin of all this was that the Cretans had a certain sepulchre
with this epitaph : " Here lies one whom they call Jupiter."

Because of this, the " Poet " charges them with a lie, saying :
" the Cretans are alway liars, evil beasts, slow-bellies ; therefore (O
Jupiter) they have built a Sepulchre for you. But thou hast not died,
. . . thou always livest," etc.

But it has been pointed out (by Archbishop Whately, we believe),
that if the Cretans are always liars, this was said by a Cretan, therefore he must have been a liar, and what he said could not be true !
But all this reasoning is set at rest by the Holy Ghost, who says :
" This testimony is true ! "

In **Acts xvii. 22, 23**, we have not, indeed, a quotation, but a reference to a matter on which contemporary and later writers give confir-
matory and interesting evidence. " I perceive that in all things ye are
unusually religious. For, as I passed by and carefully observed your
objects of worship, I found an altar also with this inscription ;
'Αγνώστῳ θεῷ (*Agnostō theō*) ' *to an unknown God.*' Whom therefore,
not knowing, ye reverence, him I make known to you."

Jerome† says (speaking of St. Paul) ; " He learned of the true
David to snatch the sword from the enemy's hand, and cut off his
head with his own weapon."

Ludovicus Vives says‡ that " in the Attic fields there were very many
altars dedicated to unknown Gods," and that " Pausanias in his *Attics*,
speaks of *The Altars of Unknown Gods*, which altars were the invention
of Epimenides, the Cretan. For, when Attica was visited with a
sore plague, they consulted the Delphian Oracle, whose answer was
reported to be : That they must offer sacrifices, but named not the
god to whom they should be offered. Epimenides, who was then at
Athens, commanded§ that they should send the beasts intended for the

---

* See Ovid, A. iii. 10, 19. Ellicott refers to Ovid, de A. A., i. 298. This says
" quamvis sit mendax, Creta negare potest."

† *Epist. ad Magnum Oratorem Romanum.* Vol. III. Operum, f. 148.

‡ *De Civit, Dei.* Book VII., cap. 17.

§ Hence called ' a prophet ' in Tit. i. 12. See *The Man of God*, by the same
author and publisher.

sacrifice through the fields, and that the sacrificers should follow the beasts with this direction : that, wherever they should stand, there they must be sacrificed to the unknown god, in order to pacify his wrath. From that time, therefore, to the time of Diogenes Laertius these altars were visited.*

Col. ii. 21.—" Touch not ; taste not ; handle not." These ordinances of men were probably prescribed in these words, and are referred to as well known. We know them also to-day; for man is the same, and human nature is not changed.

---

* For further information on this subject, see Sixtus Senensis, book 2, *Biblioth Tit. Aræ Athenensis Inscriptio.* Also Wolfius, Vol. I., *Lectionum Memorabilium*, p. 4, v. 20, etc.

AMPHIBOLOGIA ; or, DOUBLE MEANING.

A Word or Phrase susceptible of two Interpretations.

Am-phib-o-log'-i-a, from the Greek ἀμφί (*amphi*), *on both sides*, βόλος (*bolos*), *a throw*, and λόγος (*logos*), *a word ;* hence ἀμφιβολογία is a word or phrase susceptible of two interpretations. It is not synonymous with what we speak of as ambiguous ; which means that which is uncertain or equivocal.

A statement which is amphibological has two meanings, both of which are absolutely true. (An *equivocation* has two meanings also, but only one of them is true.) There are several such statements in Scripture, and indeed all prophecies are more or less of this character. They are the words of Jehovah, who was, and is, and is to come ; hence His words have a fulness of reference and meaning which one interpretation often fails to· exhaust. A prophecy may have a reference to something at the time of its utterance. It may wait for its final fulfilment in the remote future. And there may be an application to the time between these two limits. Hence the Futurist and Præterist interpretations are both true, in so far as they are each a part of the truth. But they are each wrong when the one is put for the other, and a part is put for the whole.

A beautiful example of *Amphibologia* is furnished in

2 Kings v. 18.—"Go in peace." This was Elisha's answer to Naaman, who wished to know whether the LORD would pardon if, when he went with his master, the king of Syria into the temple of Rimmon, he bowed himself there.

Elisha's answer was an *Amphibologia :* "Go in peace." If he had said, "Yes ; you may bow," that would have been to sanction idolatry. And if he had said, "No ; you must not bow," that would have been to put Naaman's conscience under a yoke of bondage to Elisha.

Ezek. xii. 13.—The term *Amphibologia*, however, refers more especially to a prophecy like that concerning Zedekiah, king of Judah, in Ezek. xii. 13 : "I will bring him to Babylon to the land of the Chaldeans ; yet shall he not see it, though he shall die there." This prophecy, by itself, is almost in the form of an *Ænigma (q.v)* : for it is capable of two interpretations, both of which are true. The other is in Jer. xxxiv. 3 : "Thine eyes shall behold the eyes of the king of

Babylon, and he shall speak with thee mouth to mouth, and thou shalt go to Babylon."

Zedekiah, in his unbelief and perverseness, determined not to believe either of these prophecies, because he could not understand them. So Josephus tells us. Yet both were perfectly true, as the fulfilment proved.

Zedekiah had his eyes put out by the king of Babylon at Riblah (2 Kings xxv. 7. Jer. xxxix. 7; lii. 11). He spoke to the king of Babylon, and saw him ; and he was afterwards taken to Babylon, but did not see it, though he died there (Ezek. xvii. 16).

John xix. 22.—"What I have written I have written." Pilate said this to convey two meanings. First, to state a matter of fact ; and second, to dismiss an inconvenient subject ; implying that he did no wish to alter what he had written, and yet did not declare that he would not. The history seems to imply that he did afterwards either alter it or permit it to be altered. For

(1) The inscription in John xix. 19 was written (probably in Latin) and put on the cross before it left Pilate's presence.

(2) The inscription in Matt. xxvii. 37 was written probably in Hebrew, and placed over his head, not by the soldiers who nailed him to the cross, but by the persons, " they," who crucified him. This was not so placed until after the garments had been divided, and the soldiers had " sat down to watch him there."

(3) The inscription in Luke xxiii. 38 appears to have been of Hebrew origin (the *Hebrew* being put last, whereas in Pilate's (John) the *Latin* was last). It was not seen till near the sixth hour, and was apparently the cause of the reviling which followed, "Jesus" being omitted from Matthew's, which seems to have been intermediate between John's and Luke's, while Mark's was probably the same as that to which Luke refers and gives merely another translation of the Hebrew.

It is impossible for us, now, to know what discussion went on during the day. All that we know is, from John xix., that the Jews earnestly desired to have it altered, and that Pilate did not decidedly refuse at the time. So that it is probable that the discussions continued, and these different inscriptions are the evidence of it, put up in different terms, and at different times : or it may be that it was the various translations that were so put up.

From these considerations we would suggest that the difficulty felt as to the variations in the wording of the inscriptions may be removed more easily and satisfactorily by believing that there were at least three inscriptions put up at different times during the day, and that these, being changed, differed from each other. If this be not the explanation then another series of difficulties is created—as to the sequence of the events recorded in the different gospels.

Our present suggestion meets both sets of difficulties at once.

Acts xvii. 22 is another example. "Ye men of Athens, in all things I perceive that ye are very religious." (See R.V. margin, *somewhat religious*).

This has two interpretations: for they were truly very "religious," and yet knew nothing of true Christianity.

We thus learn that Christianity is religion; but religion is not necessarily Christianity.

To say that a person is religious tells us nothing : for he may be a Buddhist, a Mahommedan, a Roman Catholic, or a votary of any other religious system; but it does not follow that such an one is " in Christ," and therefore a Christian.

EIRONEIA ; or, IRONY.

The Expression of Thought in a form that naturally conveys its opposite.

I'-ron-y. Greek, εἰρωνεία *(eirōneia), dissimulation.* Hence, *a dissembling, especially in speech, from* εἴρειν *(eirein), to speak.*

The figure is so called when the speaker intends to convey a sense contrary to the strict signification of the words employed : not with the intention of concealing his real meaning, but for the purpose of adding greater force to it. There are not many examples of this figure in Scripture. *Irony* haš too much of contempt in it to suit the pity which is rather the spirit of the Scriptures.

And, moreover, *Irony* in the Scriptures is generally connected with serious words which make its use perfectly patent and clear.

There are three classes of *Irony :*—

1. ANTIPHRASIS, *an-tiph'-rasis,* from ἀντί *(anti), against* or *opposite,* and φράσις *(phrasis), a way of speaking* (from φράζειν, *phrazein, to speak*). This name is given to *Irony* when it consists of one word or a single expression. As when "a court of justice" is called "a court of *vengeance.*"

2. PERMUTATIO or *permutation,* when the *Irony* consists of phrases, and sentences, or longer expressions.

3. SARCASMOS, *sar-cas'-mos.* Greek, σαρκασμός ; (Latin, *sarcasmos*), from σαρκάζω *(sarkazō), to tear flesh as dogs do ;* hence, a rending or tearing or wounding with cutting words ; sarcasm. *Irony* is so called when it is used as a taunt or in ridicule.

We have not arranged our examples in these three divisions, but have combined these together in five other divisions more simply, thus :—

I. DIVINE IRONY. Where the speaker is Divine.

II. HUMAN IRONY. Where the speaker is a human being.

III. PEIRASTIC IRONY. Where the words are not spoken *ironically* in the ordinary sense, but *peirastically :* i.e., by way of trying or testing (PEIRASTIKOS).

IV. SIMULATED IRONY. Where the words are used by man in dissimulation or hypocrisy.

V. DECEPTIVE IRONY. Where the words are not only hypocritical, but false and deceptive.

I. DIVINE IRONY:

Where the speaker is Divine.

Gen. iii. 22.—" And the LORD God said : Behold the man is become as one of us, to know good and evil."

Man had not become " as one of us." He had become a wreck and a ruin, even as man. These words call our attention to verse 5, and show how false was the Serpent's promise.

Deut. xxxii. 37.—" And he shall say : Where are their gods, their rock in whom they trusted, Which did eat the fat of their sacrifices, and drank the wine of their drink-offerings ? let them rise up and help you, and be your protection."

This is Divine Sarcasm ; for their gods were no rock or defence, neither did they accept offerings or give help.

Judges x. 14.—" Go and cry unto the gods which ye have chosen ; let them deliver you in the time of your tribulation." This was Divine Sarcasm, for those gods could neither hear nor deliver.

Job xxxviii. 4.—" Where wast thou when I laid the foundations of the earth ? " Verse 5. " Who hath laid the measures thereof, if thou knowest ? or who hath stretched the line upon it ? " So throughout this chapter.

This is the Divine Sarcasm on all scientists who profess to understand and tell us all about the earth, its size, and its shape, and its weight, etc., etc.

Considering the various changes which have taken place during the centuries in what is called " science," we may well lay this question to heart, emphasised as it is by being Divine Irony.

Ps. lx. 8 (10).—" Philistia triumph thou over me." This is said ironically ; for the truth is put literally in Ps. cviii. 9 (10) : " Over Philistia will I triumph." See margin and compare Exodus viii. 9 (5).

Ecc. xi. 9 is generally considered to be Irony, but we can hardly so regard it. It is almost too solemn to be Irony. It says : Do it ; do all this : " but know thou that for all these things God will bring thee into judgment."

Isa. ii. 10.—" Enter into the rock, and hide thee in the dust, for fear of the LORD and for the glory of his majesty." This is *Irony :* to show that neither rocks nor any other shelter can save man from the judgments in " the day of the LORD."

Isa. viii. 9, 10.—This *Irony* is meant to emphasise the fact that; however much men may unite together against God, it will all come to naught. These are the words of God in the mouth of the prophet.

Isa. xvii. 3.—" They shall be as the glory of the children of Israel " : *i.e.,* the glory of Damascus and Syria shall fade as the glory of Israel had passed away. The word " glory " is thus marked by *Antiphrasis* to point us to that which had been lost, and the height from which Israel had fallen.

Isa. xxi. 5.—This is God's message to Babylon : to show that all her preparation for defence would not prevent the ultimate cry : " Babylon is fallen, is fallen." See verses 6-9.

Isa. xxix. 1.—" Woe to ˙Ariel, to Ariel (*i.e., the lion of God*), the city where David dwelt ! " This glorious title is put by *Metonymy* (*q.v.*) for Jerusalem : and, is used here in order to emphasise, by *Irony*, the depth to which the City had fallen from the height of its past glory.

Isa. l. 11.—This is Divine Irony to show the vanity of striving for light and happiness apart from God. It is a solemn warning for all those to-day who are seeking to bring about a millennium without Christ.

Isa. lvii. 12.—" I will declare thy righteousness and thy works." These words were addressed, by sarcasm, to an apostate and wicked People. The word " righteousness," by *Antiphrasis*, marks the fact, which is clear from the words which follow : " For they shall not profit thee." Had the works been really righteous, they would have profited.

Isa. lvii. 13.—" When thou criest, let thy companies deliver thee." To show that the abundance of riches or people cannot deliver in the day of trouble.

Jer. vii. 21.—" Thus saith the LORD God of hosts, the God of Israel : Put (or add) your burnt offerings unto your sacrifices and eat flesh." That this was *Irony* is clear from what follows. They were the sacrifices of hypocrites which Jehovah would not accept.

Jer. xi. 15.—" What hath my beloved to do in mine house ? " What follows clearly shows what is meant by the *Antiphrasis* in the word " beloved."

Jer. xxii. 20.—" Go up to Lebanon, and cry ; and lift up thy voice in Bashan, and cry from the passages." This is *Irony*, or Sarcasm, addressed to the family of Jehoiakim, who looked to Egypt for help against the king of Babylon : but 2 Kings xxiv. 7 tells us that " the king of Egypt came not again any more out of his land ; for the king of Babylon had taken from the river of Egypt unto the river Euphrates all that pertained to the king of Egypt." It was no use, therefore, for Jehoiakim to go up to the passes of Lebanon or Bashan and cry out for those who before had helped.

Jer. xlvi. 9.—The words of God to Egypt. Shown to be *Irony* by verse 10.

Jer. xlvi. 11.—" Go up into Gilead, and take balm, O virgin, the daughter of Egypt." This is shown to be *Irony* by the words that follow : " In vain shalt thou use many medicines ; for thou shalt not be cured."

Jer. li. 8.—" Howl for her (Babylon) ; take balm for her pain, if so be she may be healed." But the context shows that it was destruction, and not healing, that awaited her. So verse 11.

Lam. iv. 21.—" Rejoice and be glad, O daughter of Edom," etc. This is *Irony ;* for judgment is announced in verse 22. The meaning simply is, that, however much Edom might rejoice, the punishment of her iniquity should be accomplished.

Ezek. iii. 24.—" Go, shut thyself within thine house." But the 25th verse shows that however closely he might shut himself up his enemies should find him and bind him.

Ezek. xx. 39.—" As for you, O house of Israel, thus saith the Lord God ; Go ye, serve ye every one his idols," etc.

It is impossible that Adonai Jehovah should command idolatry. It is *Irony*, as is clear from the context.

Ezek. xxviii. 3.—" Behold, thou art wiser than Daniel ; there is no secret that they can hide from thee."

God thus ironically addresses the king of Tyre. Daniel, on account of Divine gifts, was esteemed most wise. But the king of Tyre was a mere man, as verse 2 declares.

Amos iv. 4, 5.—" Come to Bethel and transgress ; at Gilgal multiply transgression ; and bring your sacrifices every morning, and your tithes after three years : And offer a sacrifice of thanksgiving with leaven, and proclaim and publish the free offerings : for this liketh you (*i.e.*, you love to do this), O ye children of Israel."

That this is *Irony* and sarcasm is clear from the conclusion of the address in verse 12. Deut. xiv. 28 and Lev. vii. 13 are the passages referred to.

Nahum iii. 14.—"Draw thee waters for the siege, fortify thy strongholds": etc.: *i.e.,* prepare as you will, but all your labour will be in vain. (See under *Heterosis*).

Zech. xi. 13.—"A goodly price."

The word "goodly" is used by *Antiphrasis*, to denote the opposite.

Mal. i. 9.—"And now, I pray you, beseech God (El) that he will be gracious unto us."

These words are put by God in the mouth of the priests, and His answer is given in what follows.

Mark vii. 9.—Here the *Irony* is beautifully brought out by translating καλῶς (*kalōs*) "full well." καλῶς means *with propriety, suitably, becomingly*. It suited the people to set aside the commandment of God, and make void the Word of God by their tradition. This exactly suited and corresponded to the action of those who washed the outside but were defiled within.

See the whole context, which applies with force, to-day, to all mere philanthropists and reformers, who preach a "social" Gospel, in order to raise the ungodly in the social scale, but leave the masses short of that which God requires.

"Well do ye reject." No, ye do evil!

Luke xi. 41.—"But rather give alms of such things as ye have; and, behold, all things are clean unto you." It is *Irony*. It was what the Pharisees taught, but it was not true.

Luke xiii. 33.—"I must walk to-day, and to-morrow, and the day following: for it cannot be that a prophet perish out of Jerusalem."

This is a message to Herod, whom He calls (by *Hypocatastasis*) "that fox" (or that vixen), and the last words are Ironical, as is clear from the solemn exclamation which follows in the next verse.

The sense of the whole passage seems to be:—We are still three days' walk from Jerusalem. To Jerusalem I must get: to die there: for Jerusalem is become the natural place for prophets to perish in. So you need not threaten me with death from Herod. It is not within his jurisdiction—(see xxiii. 7: "As soon as he knew that He *belonged* to Herod's jurisdiction")—that I must die.

John iii. 10.—"Art thou a master of Israel, and knowest not these things?" This is a species of mild *Irony*.

John vii. 28 is *Irony*, and refers back to verse 27. "Whom ye know not" points to the fact that they knew not God, and, therefore, they knew not Christ.

1 Cor. vi. 4.—"Set them to judge who are least esteemed in the church."

The next verse shows clearly that this is *Irony*, and a condemnation of what they had really done. For he asks, "Is it so that there is not a wise man among you? No; not one that shall be able to judge between his brethren?"

2 Cor. v. 3.—"If so be that being clothed we shall not be found naked."

Here, the *Irony* being missed, the text has been altered in some MSS. (περ, *as I suppose*, for γε, *at least*). There is no sense unless the *Irony* is seen. "If indeed being clothed also, we shall not be found naked," as some of you believe who say "that there is no resurrection of the dead" (1 Cor. xv. 12), and therefore no resurrection body for us to be clothed-upon with.

2 Cor. xiii. 5.—"Examine yourselves, whether ye be in the faith; prove your own selves."

The *Hyperbaton* (*q.v.*), by which the pronoun ἑαυτούς (*heautous*), *yourselves*, is placed at the beginning of the sentence, (the object before the subject), shows the emphasis which is to be placed upon it, and tells us that this is the serious *irony* of a grieved heart, and not a general command. These Corinthian saints, having been beguiled by the Jewish enemies of the apostle to question his apostleship, actually sought a proof of Christ speaking in him! So he meets their questionings with another question: "Since ye seek a proof of Christ speaking in me . . . YOURSELVES examine ye, if ye are in the faith; YOURSELVES prove ye. Know ye not that Jesus Christ is in you except ye be reprobates?"

The answer to this question, thus ironically put, would prove them to be the seals of his ministry, and the real proof of his apostleship.

Here is no command for the saints to-day, no admonition to practise continual self-examination and introspection, to see whether they are in the faith; for Christ is in them. Read the words in connection with the context, and the force of this solemn *Irony* will be at once seen: and it will be used no more to vex and perplex God's dear children, by taking words which refer to their *state* to upset their *standing*, which is perfect and complete "in Christ."

II. Human Irony:

Where the speaker is a human being.

1 Sam. xxvi. 15.—The words of David to Abner: "Art thou not a valiant man?   And who is like to thee in Israel?"

This sarcasm was used to show how Abner had neglected his duty.

1 Kings xviii. 27.—The words of Elijah to the prophets of Baal were sarcasm of the severest kind.

1 Kings xxii. 15.—The words of the prophet Micaiah to Ahab and Jehoshaphat: "Go, and prosper"; to show by *Irony* the false prophecies of Ahab's own prophets.

2 Kings viii. 10.—The words of Elisha to Hazael: "Go, say unto him (*i.e.*, the king of Syria), Thou mayest certainly recover: howbeit the Lord hath shewed me that he shall surely die."

By the Irony in the first clause, Elisha stated a fact, that there was no reason why Benhadad should not recover.   In the latter clause he revealed to Hazael that he knew he meant to murder him, as it came to pass.   Compare verses 11, 14 and 15.

Job xii. 2.—"No doubt but ye are the people, and wisdom shall die with you."   This powerful *Irony* is meant to emphasise the fact that Job's friends had no more knowledge than he: and may be used with great truth of many who arrogate to themselves the right to sit in judgment on their sinful fellow-servants.

Job xxvi. 2, 3.—The words of Job to his friend: "How hast thou helped him that is without power," etc.

Matt. xi. 19.—"A friend of publicans and sinners."   This was said in *Irony*, but it expresses a blessed fact for all Divinely-convicted sinners.

Luke xv. 2.—"This man receiveth sinners, and eateth with them."   This was said in *Irony*, but it expresses a most blessed truth for all who know and feel themselves to be sinners.

John xviii. 38.—"Pilate saith unto him, What is truth?"

By his not waiting for the answer it seems that the question was not seriously put.   (See under *Erotesis*).   So, his words in

John xix. 14.—"Behold your king," were also *Irony*.

1 Cor. iv. 8.—This verse is true *Irony*.   But other figures are involved.   See under *Asyndeton*, *Anabasis*, and *Metonymy* (of the subject).

2 Cor. x. 12.—In the words, "we dare not," the Apostle intimates, by *Irony*, that he was far beyond those who thought themselves to be somebodies.

2 Cor. xi. 19.—"Ye suffer fools gladly, seeing ye yourselves are wise."

2 Cor. xii. 13.—"Forgive me this wrong."

III. PEIRASTIC IRONY:

By way of trying or testing.

This third kind of *Irony* is where the words may not mean exactly what they seem to say, but are used *by way of trial* to the persons to whom they were spoken, not sarcastically, but *peirastically :* i.e., by way of *trying* and *testing*. The Greeks called this PEIRAS-TIKOS, πειραστικός, *fitted for trying and testing ;* from πειράζω (*peirazō*), *to make proof or trial.*

Gen. xix. 2.—The angels said to Lot, "Nay; but we will abide in the street all night." This was said to try Lot, to see what he would do ; for they were not sent to abide in Sodom at all.

Gen. xxii. 2.—God said to Abraham, "Take now thy son, thine only son, Isaac, whom thou lovest, and get thee into the land of Moriah ; and offer him there for a burnt offering upon one of the mountains which I will tell thee of." God said this (it distinctly says) to try him (not tempt, in our modern use of the word).

Verse 12 farther shows that God never intended that the sacrifice should actually take place. Abraham thought He did, and believed that, if Isaac had been offered, God would have raised him from the dead. See Heb. xi. 17-19.

It seems very probable that this was the spot where the altar of burnt offering was afterwards erected. Compare 1 Chron. xxi. 26, 28 ; xxii. 1, and 2 Chron. iii. 1.

Matt. xv. 24.—Jesus said to the disciples what was perfectly true as a matter of fact, and as though to endorse their position, "I was not sent except to the lost sheep of the house of Israel." But it was said by way of trial to the woman's faith.

So also in verse 26, when He said to her : "It is not meet to take the children's bread (with emphasis on children, by *Antimereia*, q.v.), and to cast it to the little dogs," meaning herself (by *Hypocatastasis*, q.v.). See also this verse under *Meiosis* and *Synecdoche.*

IV. Simulated Irony:

*Where the words in question are used by man either in
dissimulation or hypocrisy.*

Gen. xxxvii. 19.—Joseph's brethren said : " Behold this dreamer cometh." The Heb. is stronger than this, as is partly shown in the margin : " Behold that Master of the dreams, there he comes." They did not mean this, for see verses 5 and 11.

2 Sam. vi. 20.—Michal to David : " How glorious was the king of Israel to-day ! "

That this was hypocritical is shown by verse 16 : " She despised him in her heart." And so David understood it (verses 21, 22). Note that the *uncovering* of which Michal spoke referred only to his royal robes ; as is clear from 1 Chron. xv. 27, which tells us what he was " clothed " with.

Ps. xxii. 8 (9).—" He trusted in the LORD that he would deliver him."

Most true, but not meant as truth in the lips of His enemies, as is clear from Matt. xxvii. 43. See also under *Heterosis*.

Isa. v. 19.—These words are used hypocritically, as is clear from the " Woe " pronounced on the speakers in verse 18.

Matt. xxii. 16.—The disciples of the Pharisees, and the Herodians say to Christ : " Master, we know that thou art true," etc.

Matt. xxvii. 29.—" Hail, King of the Jews ! " So also verses 40, 42 and 43 ; Mark xv. 29, etc.

V. Deceptive Irony:

Where words are clearly false as well as hypocritical.

Gen. iii. 4, 5.—Words clearly false, for Satan knew the opposite : and Eve ought to have known the same, as they flatly contradicted the words of the LORD God.

Matt. ii. 8.—Herod says to the wise men : " Go and search for the young child ; and when ye have found him, bring me word again, that I may come and worship him also " (or that I also may come and worship him).

This was false, for Herod wanted to slay Him, and not to worship Him.

OXYMORON ; or, WISE-FOLLY.

A Wise saying that seems Foolish.

Ox'-y-mō'-ron. Greek, ὀξύμωρον, from ὀξύς (*oxus*), *sharp, pointed*, and μωρός (*mōros*), *dull, foolish.*

This is a figure, in which what is said at first sight appears to be foolish, yet when we come to consider it, we find it exceedingly wise.

It is a smart saying, which unites words whose literal meanings appear to be incongruous, if not contradictory; but they are so cleverly and wisely joined together as to enhance the real sense of the words. The Latins called it ACUTIFATUUM (*a-cu'-ti-fat'-u-um*), from *acutus, sharp* or *pointed* (English, *acute*), and *fatuus, foolish, fatuous,* or *simple.*

Examples from General Literature are common :—

Cicero says to Catiline :—

> "Thy country, silent, thus addresses thee."

Milton shows to Despair :—

> "In the lowest depth a lower depth."

Examples abound in common use: *e.g.,* "cruel kindness"; "*Festina lente*" (hasten slowly) ; "cruel love"; "blessed misfortunes."

Many Americanisms are *Oxymorons: e.g.,* "powerful weak," "cruel easy," etc., etc.

The Scriptures have many examples: which are very instructive, because God's wisdom is esteemed foolish by man, and is yet so wise as to be far beyond his comprehension. This affords a wide field for the use of this most expressive figure.

Job xxii. 6.—"And stripped the naked of their clothing."

Here the figure *Synecdoche* (*q.v.*) turns the phrase into a powerful *Oxymoron.*

Isa. lviii. 10.—"Thy darkness shall be as the noon-day." See under *Antimetathesis.*

Jer. xxii. 19.—"He shall be buried with the burial of an ass": *i.e.,* not buried at all; he shall have an unburied burial! Compare 2 Chron. xxxvi. 6, and Jer. xxxvi. 30; and see under *Enallage.*

Matt. vi. 23.—"If therefore the light that is in thee be darkness, how great is that darkness."

How can light be darkness ? The *Oxymoron* arises from the *Metonymy* by which "light" is put for the human wisdom of the natural man, which is darkness (Eph. iv. 18).

Matt. xvi. 25.—" Whosoever will save his life shall lose it : and whosoever will lose his life for my sake shall find it."

So Mark viii. 35.

Acts v. 41.—" Rejoicing that they were counted worthy to suffer shame for his name."

This may sound folly to the natural man, but those who have been "made wise" understand it. The two contrary Greek words mark the *Oxymoron* more emphatically :—καταξιοῦσθαι (*kataxiousthai*), *to be accounted very worthy*, and ἀτιμασθῆναι (*atimastheenai*), *to be treated as unworthy*, or with indignity. (See under *Metonymy*).

1 Cor. i. 25.—" The foolishness of God is wiser than men ; and the weakness of God is stronger than men."

See under *Parechesis*, *Metonymy* (of Adjunct), and *Catachresis*.

1 Cor. i. 27-29 is a beautiful and elaborate *Oxymoron*; in order to enhance the conclusion "that no flesh should glory in his presence."

1 Cor. ix. 17.—" If I do this thing willingly (ἑκών, *without wages*), I have a reward (μισθόν, *wages*)."

See under *Paronomasia* and *Meiosis*.

2 Cor. vi. 4, 8-10.—"Approving ourselves as the ministers of God . . .

> As deceivers, and yet true ;
> As unknown, and yet well-known ;
> As dying, and, behold, we live ; . . . .
> As chastened, and not killed ;
> As sorrowful, yet alway rejoicing ;
> As poor, yet making many rich ;
> As having nothing, and yet possessing all things."

2 Cor. viii. 2.—" Their deep poverty abounded unto the riches of their liberality."

This is a most elegant *Oxymoron*.

2 Cor. xii. 10.—" When I am weak, then am I strong."

This is folly to the natural man, but blessed truth to those who know by experience the true wisdom.

2 Cor. xii. 11.—" In nothing am I behind the very chiefest apostles, though I be nothing."

Eph. iii. 8.—" Less than the least of all saints." This pleasing *Oxymoron* emphasises the apostle's growth in grace (*i.e.*, in his knowledge of what grace was to him, and what it had done for him). Before this, (in A D. 60), he said: "I was not behind the very chiefest apostles" (2 Cor. xi. 5) In A.D. 62, he could say that he was "less than the least of all saints," while, later than this, (A.D. 67), his knowledge of God's grace made him see himself as "the chief of sinners" (1 Tim. i. 15, 16). See under *Meiosis.*

1 Tim. v. 6.—" She that liveth in pleasure is dead while she liveth."

This *Oxymoron* arises from a latent *Ploce* (*q.v.*), the word "dead" denoting the absence of spiritual life: " dead in trespasses and sins."

IDIOMA; or, IDIOM.

The peculiar usage of Words and Phrases.

Id-i-ō'-ma. Greek, ἰδίωμα, *a peculiarity,* from ἴδιος (*idios*), *one's own,** and ἰδιωτισμός (*id-i-o-tis'-mos*), *the common manner of speaking.* Whence the Latin name for the figure IDIOTISMUS. The English name for it is IDIOM.

The word is used in three significations:

(1) The language peculiar to the vulgar, as opposed to what is classical.

(2) The language peculiar to one nation or tribe, as opposed to other languages or dialects.

(3) The language peculiar to any particular author or speaker.

It is in the second of these senses that it becomes important as a figure of speech.

The fact must ever be remembered that, while the language of the New Testament is Greek, the agents and instruments employed by the Holy Spirit were Hebrews. God spake " by the mouth of his holy prophets." Hence, while the "mouth" and the throat and vocal-chords and breath were human, the *words* were Divine.

No one is able to understand the phenomenon ; or explain how it comes to pass: for Inspiration is a fact to be believed and received, and not a matter to be reasoned about.

While therefore, the *words* are Greek, the *thoughts* and *idioms* are Hebrew.

Some, on this account, have condemned the Greek of the New Testament, because it is not classical; while others, in their anxiety to defend it, have endeavoured to find parallel usages in classical Greek authors.

---

* Hence ἰδιώτης (*idiōtees*), our English *idiot : i.e., a private person,* as opposite to one, engaged in public affairs. Hence, a civilian as opposed to a military man; a layman, as opposed to a cleric or lawyer ; an amateur, as opposed to a professional ; a prose-writer, as opposed to a poet ; an ignorant person, as opposed to a learned person. Hence, again, anyone unskilled or unpractised in any particular art or science ; the opposite of expert. Thus, as knowledge and learning became more common, the term *idiot* came to be limited to one who is ignorant and unable to understand much.

Both might have spared their pains by recognising that the New Testament Greek abounds with *Hebraisms: i.e.,* expressions conveying Hebrew usages and thoughts in Greek words.

It will be seen at once that this is a subject which has a large and important bearing on the interpretation and clear understanding of many passages in the New Testament.

Much is said in favour of a literal translation. But in many cases this makes no sense whatever, and would sometimes make nonsense. What is wanted is an *idiomatic* version: *i.e.,* the exact reproduction, not of the words, but of the thought and meaning of the phrase. It is in this that the difference is seen between the Authorized Version and the Revised. The former is a *Version,* while the latter is a *translation.* Hence the A.V. is English, while the R.V. often is not.

This refers to words as well as to phrases. To bring the matter home, imagine an Englishman and an American translating from the French:—*Gare,* the one would render "Station," and the other "Depôt": *Wagon de marchandises* would be in English "Goods-Truck"; and in America, "Freight Car": *Bureau (de billets)* would be "Booking Office" and "Ticket Office" respectively; *En Voiture* would be, in English, "Take your seats": and in America, "All abroad."

Fancy rendering *Mont de piété,* literally *mountain of piety,* instead of "pawn-shop"! or *Commissionaire de Piété,* literally *Commissionaire of Piety,* instead of "Pawnbroker"! or *Faire des châteux en Espagne,* literally *to make castles in Spain* instead of "to build castles in the air"!

Or *Tomber dans l'eau,* literally *to fall into the water,* instead of "to fall to the ground," or more colloquially "to fall through"!

On the other hand, what would a Frenchman understand if "How do you do?" were rendered literally, instead of idiomatically: "How do you carry yourself,"* or "the water of life," Eau de vie! instead of "Eau vive."

All this makes it perfectly clear that, unless the translation be idiomatic, there must be grave mistakes made; and that, if a translation be absolutely literal, it will be a fruitful source of errors.

The importance of this fact can hardly be over-rated; and, considering the way in which many talk of, and insist on, a "literal"

---

* Or the German: How goes it? wie gehts?

translation, it is necessary to press the point and enforce it by examples from the Scriptures.

Idiom, however, is not generally classed among *Figures* in the technical sense of the word. But, as the words do not mean *literally* what they say, and are not used or combined according to their literal signification, they are really Figures; and we have, therefore, included them here.

We will consider them under the following divisions: giving only a few examples under each by way of illustration:—

I.   Idiomatic usage of VERBS.

II.   Special idiomatic usages of NOUNS and VERBS.

III.   Idiomatic DEGREES OF COMPARISON.

IV.   Idiomatic use of PREPOSITIONS.

V.   Idiomatic use of NUMERALS.

VI.   Idiomatic forms of QUOTATION.

VII.   Idiomatic forms of QUESTION.

VIII.   Idiomatic PHRASES.

IX.   Idioms arising from OTHER Figures of Speech.

X.   Changes in usage of WORDS in the Greek language.

XI.   Changes in usage of WORDS in the English language.

I. VERBS IN GENERAL.

i. *Idiomatic usages of Verbs.*

1. The Hebrews used active verbs to express the agent's design or attempt to do anything, even though the thing was not actually done.

Exod. viii. 18 (14).—" And the magicians did so (*i.e.*, attempted to do so) with their enchantments, to bring forth lice, but they could not."

Deut. xxviii. 68.—" Ye shall be sold (*i.e.*, put up for sale) unto your enemies . . . and no man shall buy you."

Ezek. xxiv. 13.—" Because I have purged thee (*i.e.*, used the means to purge, by instructions, reproofs and ordinances, etc.), and thou wast not purged."

We have the same usage in the New Testament.

Matt. xvii. 11.—" Elijah truly cometh first, and restoreth all things ": *i.e.*, shall begin to restore or design or attempt to do so, for

Christ will be the real Restorer of all things.　The contrast here, however, is between Elijah and John, as brought out by the μὲν and the δέ.　" Elijah, indeed (μὲν, *in one respect*) cometh, and will restore all things, but (δέ, *in another respect*) I say unto you that Elijah is come already," etc.

Gal. v. 4.—" Whosoever of you are justified (*i.e.*, seek to be justified) by the law; ye are fallen from grace": for chap. iii. 11 distinctly declares that " no man is justified by the law in the sight of God."

Phil. iii. 15.—"As many as be (*i.e.*, would be, or try to be) perfect."

1 John i. 10.—" We make him (*i.e.*, we attempt so far as in us lies to make him) a liar."　(See also chapter v. 10).

1 John ii. 26.—" These things have I written unto you concerning them that seduce (or deceive) you ": *i.e.*, that would, or that try to, deceive you.

2. *Active Verbs* are sometimes used to denote the effect of the action expressed.

Isa. lxv. 1.—" I am sought of them that asked not for me ": *i.e.*, I am found of them that sought me not, as in Rom. x. 20.

John xvi. 5.—" None of you asketh me whither goest thou ": *i.e.*, none of you knoweth or hath discovered; for Peter had asked that question in xiii. 36.　Lit., None is enquiring.

3. Active Verbs are used to declare that the thing has been or shall be done, and not the actual doing of the thing said to be done.

The Priest is said to cleanse or pollute according as he declares that the thing is clean or polluted.　See Lev. xiii. 6, 8, 11, 13, 17, 20, etc., where it is actually translated " pronounce."　See under *Metonymy* (of the subject) and *Synecdoche*.

Acts x. 15.—" What God hath cleansed (*i.e.*, declared to be clean) do not thou pollute (*i.e.*, as in A.V. " call common ")."

Isa. vi. 10.—" Make the heart of this people fat, and make their ears heavy," *i.e.*, declare, or foretell that the heart of this people will be fat, etc. (See *Metonymy*).　In Matt. xiii. 15, this idiomatic use of the verb is not literally translated, but is idiomatically rendered " the heart of this people is waxed gross."　So in Acts xxviii. 27.　While, in John

xii. 40, it is rendered literally according to the Hebrew idiom: " He hath blinded," etc.; but who hath done so is not said.

Jer. i. 10.—" I have this day set thee over the nations and over the kingdoms, to root out, and to pull down," etc.: *i.e.*, to declare or prophesy concerning the nations that they shall be rooted out, etc.

The Anglo-Israelites, wrongly taking this literally, declare that Great Britain is now literally fulfilling this prophecy!

Ezek. xliii. 3.—"According to the vision that I saw when I came to destroy the city," etc.: *i.e.*, when I came to prophesy or declare that it should be destroyed.

Ezek. xxii. 2.—"Son of man, wilt thou judge, wilt thou judge the city of bloods (*i.e.*, of great bloodshedding)?" This is explained in the words that follow: " Yea, thou shalt shew her (Heb., make her know) all her abominations." See under *Heterosis*.

4. Active verbs were used by the Hebrews to express, not the doing of the thing, but the *permission* of the thing which the agent is said to do. Thus:

Gen. xxxi. 7.—Jacob says to Laban: "God did not give him to do me evil ": *i.e.*, as in A.V., God suffered him not, etc.

Ex. iv. 21.—" I will harden his heart (*i.e.*, I will permit or suffer his heart to be hardened), that he shall not let the people go." So in all the passages which speak of the hardening of Pharaoh's heart. As is clear from the common use of the same *Idiom* in the following passages,

Ex. v. 22.—" Lord, wherefore hast thou so evil entreated this people? " *i.e.*, suffered them to be so evil entreated.

Ps. xvi. 10.—"Thou wilt not give thine Holy One (*i.e.*, suffer Him) to see corruption." So the A.V.

Jer. iv. 10.—" Lord GOD, surely thou hast greatly deceived this people ": *i.e.*, thou hast suffered this People to be greatly deceived, by the false prophets, saying: Ye shall have peace, etc.

Ezek. xiv. 9.—" If the prophet be deceived when he hath spoken a thing, I the LORD have deceived that prophet ": *i.e.*, I have permitted him to deceive himself.

Ezek. xx. 25.—" Wherefore I gave them also statutes that were not good": *i.e.*, I permitted them to follow the wicked statutes of the surrounding nations, mentioned and forbidden in Lev. xviii. 3.

Matt. vi 13.—" Lead us not (*i.e.*, suffer us not to be led) into temptation."

Matt. xi 25.—" I thank thee, O Father . . . because thou hast hid (*i.e.*, not revealed) these things," etc.

Matt. xiii. 11.—" It is given to know unto you," etc. (*i.e.*, ye are permitted to know . . . but they are not permitted to know them.

Acts xiii. 29. — " When they (*i.e.*, the rulers, verse 27) had fulfilled all that was written of him, they took him down from the tree, and laid him in a sepulchre " : *i.e.*, they permitted Joseph of Arimathea and Nicodemus to do so.

Rom. ix. 18.—" Whom he will he hardeneth " : *i.e.*, he suffereth to be hardened. Not that this in any way weakens the absolute sovereignty of God.

Rom. xi. 7.—" The rest were hardened " : *i.e.*, were suffered to become blind (as in A.V. marg.).

Rom. xi. 8.—" God hath given them the spirit of slumber " : *i.e.*, hath suffered them to fall asleep.

2 Thess. ii. 11.—" For this cause God shall send them strong delusion, that they should believe a lie " : *i.e.*, God will leave them and suffer them to be deceived by the great Lie which will come on all the world.

5. Active verbs are used to express, not the doing of a thing, but the occasion of a thing's being done.

Gen. xlii. 38.—" If mischief befall him by the way . . . then shall ye bring down (*i.e.*, ye shall be the occasion of bringing down) my gray hairs," etc.

1 Kings xiv. 16.—Jeroboam " made Israel to sin " : *i.e.*, was the cause of Israel's sin by setting up the two calves in Bethel and Dan.

Acts i. 18.—" This man purchased a field " (*i.e.*, caused the field to be purchased), as is plain from Matt. xxvii. 7.

6. Two imperatives are sometimes united, so that the first expresses a *condition* or *limitation* in regard to the second; by which the latter becomes a future.

This idiom was also used by the Latins " *Divide et impera*," not divide and govern, but *divide and thou wilt govern*.

John vii. 52.—" Search and look " : *i.e.*, search and thou wilt see.

1 **Cor. xv. 34.**—" Awake to righteousness, and sin not " : *i.e.*, and then ye will not sin.

1 **Tim. vi. 12.**—" Fight the good fight of faith, lay hold of eternal life " : *i.e.*, thou shalt lay hold of, etc.

Sometimes the future is used literally instead of the idiomatic second imperative. See John ii. 19. Jas. iv. 7. In Eph. v. 14, we have two imperatives and then the future.

ii. *Special idiomatic usages of Nouns and Verbs.*

(1) Noun (*in regimen*) for Adjective. See under *Heterosis*.

(2) Noun (a second) for Adjective. See *Hendiadys*.

(3) Plural Nouns for emphatic singular. See *Heterosis*.

(4) Certain Adjectives or Nouns used in the New Testament, according to Hebrew idiom, in a sense peculiar to themselves :—

" **Able**," when applied to God or Christ, denotes both *willingness* and *ability*. Rom. iv. 21 ; xi. 23 ; xiv. 4 ; xvi. 25. Heb. ii. 18.

" **All** " often denotes the greater part. 1 Cor. viii. 1, for see verse 17. 1 Cor. xi. 2.

" **All** " often means the greatest degree or quality of that to which it is applied. 1 Cor. xiii. 2. 2 Tim. i. 15. Jas. i. 2.

" **All** " signifies some of every kind. Matt. iv. 23. Acts x. 12. See further for the usage of the word " *all*," under *Metonymy* and *Synecdoche*.

" **A blessing** " signifies a gift.

Gen. xxxiii. 11.—Jacob says to Esau: " Take, I pray thee, my blessing (*i.e.*, my gift and present) that is brought to thee; because God hath dealt graciously with me, and because I have enough (Heb., *all things*). And he urged him, and he took it " : *i.e.*, everything.

1 **Sam. xxv. 27.**—" This blessing (*i.e.*, gift ; margin, *present*) which thine handmaid hath brought."

Rom. xv. 29.—" I shall come in the fulness of the blessing (*i.e.*, the gift) of the Gospel of Christ."

2 **Cor. ix. 5.**—" That they would go before unto you, and make up beforehand your blessing " : *i.e.*, your gift to the saints (see A.V. marg.).

" **Doctrine** " (διδαχή, *didachee*) means the thing taught; but it is used idiomatically and by *Metonymy* (*q.v.*), for the discourse in which it is taught.

This is because it denotes more than διδασκαλία (*didaskalia*), for it has to do with the *style* of teaching; the *manner* as well as the thing taught. See, *e.g.*, Matt. vii. 28, 29.

Mark iv. 2.—" He taught them many things by parables, and said unto them in his doctrine " : *i.e.*, his teaching or discourse. So chap. xi. 18 ; xii. 38.

Acts ii. 42.—" And they continued stedfastly in the apostles' doctrine " : *i.e.*, they regularly attended at the teaching of the apostles : *i.e.*, when they taught.

1 Cor. xiv. 26.—" Every one of you hath a psalm, hath a doctrine, etc. " : *i.e.*, a discourse to give.

" To eat or drink."—As the Hebrews used the nouns *meat* and *drink* of knowledge (by *Metonymy*, *q.v.*), so they naturally used the verbs *eating* and *drinking* to denote the operation of the mind in receiving, understanding, and applying doctrine or instruction of any kind, as we speak of " digesting " what is said, or of " inwardly digesting " it.

It thus marks a very intimate and real partaking of the benefits of that which we receive through our minds.

Jer. xv. 16.—" Thy words were found, and I did eat them." The rest of the verse explains the figure.

Ezek. iii. 1.—" Son of man . . . eat this roll, and go speak unto the house of Israel": *i.e.*, consider it, and get the contents of this roll by heart, and then go and speak it to the house of Israel, as is clear from verse 4 : " Speak with my words unto them."

John vi. 51.—" I am the living bread which came down from heaven : if any man eat of this bread, he shall live for ever": *i.e.*, just as the body lives temporally by eating bread, so the new life is nourished by feeding upon Christ in our hearts by faith.

So, verse 53 : " Except ye eat the flesh of the Son of man, and drink his blood, ye have no life in you " : *i.e.*, except you feed on Christ in your hearts and partake of His life (for the blood is the life), ye have no life in you. That this cannot refer to the Lord's supper is clear from the fact that it was not then instituted, and the words could not have been understood (as they were) ; and, further, that it would shut out all who, from age and infirmity or other cause, had not partaken of that supper.

It cannot refer to the Mass, as there is no *drinking* at all in the Mass.

By comparing verses 47 and 40 with verses 53 and 54, it will be seen that *believing on Christ* is exactly the same thing as eating and drinking of His flesh and blood.

1 Cor. xii. 13.—"And have been all made to drink into one spirit": *i.e.*, receive. Compare Luke xiii. 15.

"**Not to be**" is a Hebraism for *to be abject* and *vile*, *to be nothing* (1 Cor. i. 28); while on the other hand,

"**To be**" means to be in high esteem, or of great value (1 Cor. i. 28). God hath chosen "things which are not, to bring to nought things that are." So also

2 Sam. xix. 6 (9).—"Thou regardest neither princes nor servants." Here, the figure is *translated*; for the Heb. is (as in the margin: "that princes and servants are not to thee.") R.V.: "Are nought unto thee."

"**To permit.**" Heb. vi. 3: "This will we do, if God permit": *i.e.*, if God so orders it, and gives the needed grace and strength.

"**To seek.**" Matt. vi. 32: "After all these things do the Gentiles seek": *i.e.*, they put them in the first place, and are over-anxious, with excessive solicitude. So Luke xii. 30.

"**To salute.**" Acts xviii. 22: "And when he had . . . gone up, and saluted the church": *i.e.*, and had held familiar intercourse with them. Compare xx. 1. See also xxi. 7, 19; xxv. 13. This is shown from the opposite; 2 Kings iv. 29: "Salute him not": *i.e.*, do not stop to talk with him. So Luke x. 4.

"**To touch**" for to hurt or to do any harm to. Gen. xxvi. 29. Ruth ii. 9. Job i. 11; ii. 5; xix. 21. Ps. cv. 15. Jer. xii. 14. Ezek. xvii. 10. Zech. ii. 8. Heb. xi. 28. 1 John v. 18.

Also, "*to touch*" is used for cohabitation. Gen. xx. 6. Prov. vi. 29. 1 Cor. vii. 1.

Also, for *detention*, or for diverting from any purpose. John xx. 17.

"**To come**": where the simple verb is used for all that pertains to Christ's advent. Matt. xi. 3. 1 John iv. 2, 3; v. 6.

"**To see another**" is used for making war with him, or of meeting him in battle. 2 Kings xiv. 8, 11; xxiii. 29, etc.

"**To build**" is used for restore anything to all its former glory. Ezek. xxvi. 14.

"**To walk**" is used for proceeding happily and prosperously. Hos. xiv. 9.

"**To hear**" is used of understanding and obeying.   John viii. 47. Luke viii. 15.

"**To confess**" is used of abiding in the faith, and walking according to truth. 1 John iv. 15. Rom. x. 9, 10.   So also Matt. x. 32.

"**Able to say**" is used of being able really and truly to affirm from the heart.   Prov. xx. 9.

1 Cor. xii. 3.—"No man can say that Jesus is the Lord, but by the Holy Ghost." Any one can utter the words ; but no one can truly, with the whole heart, own Jesus as his Lord, and take Him for his Master, but by the Holy Ghost.

"**To eat and drink**" is a Hebraism used not merely for chewing food or swallowing any liquid, but for good living and drinking wine; Matt. xi. 18, 19 with Luke vii. 33, 34 and Prov. xxxi. 4.

"**To do**" for to bring to pass, do a very great deal, do all.   So it is translated in Ps. xxxvii. 5. Dan. ix. 19.

"**To do** (*i.e.*, commit) **sin**" means to sin wilfully and willingly. 1 John iii. 9. See i. 8, 10 ; v. 18. John viii. 34.

"**To do justice** or **righteousness**" is used for willingly, earnestly and joyfully walking and living as one whom God has justified. 1 John iii. 7.

"**To work**" is used of seeking to gain salvation by human merit. Rom. iv. 4, 5, as opposed to grace (chap. xi. 6).

"**To give account**" means not simply to render a mere account, but to suffer all the consequences of unrighteousness. 1 Pet. iv. 5. Matt. xii. 36.

"**To will**" is used for to wish to do anything speedily and spontaneously. 2 Cor. viii. 11. The figure is well translated "to be forward" (verse 10)—as being greater even than the actual doing.

Also for eager desire (Mark x. 35; xii. 38), where the figure is well translated "which love to go in long clothing," etc. Gal. iv. 21, where it is well rendered "desire." "Tell me, ye that desire (love) to be under the law." So it ought to be rendered in 1 Tim. vi. 9: "They that will to be rich": *i.e.*, love to be rich.

"**To look**" or "**to see**" is often used (*a*) implying the *delight* or *pleasure* felt by the beholder (whether it be sinful or innocent): Ps. xxii. 17 (18) ; xxxv. 21 ; lix. 10 (11).   (*b*) Sometimes also as implying *sorrow* *and grief:* Gen. xxi. 16; xliv. 34. John xix. 37 (compare Zech. xii. 10-14. Rev. i. 7). (*c*) And sometimes implying *attention and provision:* 2 Kings x. 3. Matt. vii. 5. 1 Cor. x. 12 (where the figure is well translated " take heed," as it is also in Col. iv. 17).

" **To live** " is used not merely of being alive, or having life, but of having all that makes life worth living, flourishing and prospering. 1 Sam x. 24, where the figure is rendered " God save," " God save the king." The Heb. is " Let the king live." So also 1 Kings i. 25. In 1 Sam. xxv. 6, it is rendered " That liveth *in prosperity.*" Ps. xxii. 26 (27); lxix. 32 (33). Ecc. vi. 8. 1 Thess. iii. 8. (The opposite of this is 1 Sam. xxv. 37: " his heart died within him ").

The word " life " has also the same usage, Ps. xxxiv. 12 (13). 1 Pet. iii. 10, as it has also in our English idiom.

" **To hear.**" The verb ἀκούειν (*akouein*), *to hear,* is used idiomatically when followed by the *accusative* case. It then means, not only to hear the voice of the person speaking (which is indicated by the *genitive* case following), but to *understand, to receive, to believe,* etc., what is said, having regard, not to the speaker, but to the subject-matter.

The apparent discrepancy between Acts ix. 7 and Acts xxii. 9 is explained by this idiomatic use of ἀκούειν (*akouein*). In the former passage it is followed by the *genitive* case, and means that they heard *the sound* of the voice; while in the latter passage, it is followed by the *accusative* case, and means that they did not hear the subject-matter: *i.e.,* they heard the sound of the voice, but did not *understand* what was said.

John viii. 43.—" Why do ye not understand my speech ? even because ye cannot hear (*i.e.,* receive) my word."

John ix. 27.—" I have told you already, and ye did not hear (*i.e.,* believe). Why again do ye desire to hear ? " In the latter clause it is used in its ordinary sense ; in the former idiomatically.

1 Cor. xiv. 2.—" He that speaketh in an unknown tongue speaketh not to men, but to God, for no one heareth (*i.e.,* understandeth) him." The A.V. so renders it, and puts " *heareth* " in the margin.

Gal. iv. 21.—" Ye, that desire to be under law, do ye not hear (*i.e.,* understand) the Law ? "

1 Cor. v. 1.—" It is commonly heard (*i.e.,* understood) that there is fornication among you." The A.V. has " reported."

" **Hearing** " ἀκοή (*akoee*) is used, not merely of the act of hearing, but of what is heard: *a narration, report, fame.* This is a kind of *Metonymy* (*q.v.*).

Matt. xiv. 1.—" Herod the tetrarch heard the hearing (*i.e.*, the fame) of Jesus."

John xii. 38.—" Who hath believed our hearing ? " (*i.e.*, our report).

" **Called.** " *To be called* is used of being *acknowledged, accounted*, or simply of *being*.

1 John iii. 1.—" That we should be called the sons of God."

" **Holy** " means primarily that which is ceremonially clean and free from defilement.

Deut. xxiii. 14.—" Therefore shall thy camp be holy: that he see no unclean thing."

Hence it means *separated from a common to a sacred or special use.* For places and inanimate things can clearly be *holy* only in this special sense, and not as regards intrinsic moral purity.

The word *Holy* in Hebrew sometimes means *bountiful, merciful, beneficent.* And so may have the same meaning in some passages of the New Testament. See Titus i. 8. Heb. vii. 26, etc.

" **Honour** " has a wide range of meaning in Hebrew, and is used of *nourishment, maintenance.*

Matt. xv. 6.—" And shall not honour (*i.e.*, support) his father or his mother."

1 Cor. xii. 26.—" Or one member be honoured (*i.e.*, nourished) all the members rejoice with it."

1 Tim. v. 3.—" Honour widows that are really widows," : *i.e.*, maintain them out of the funds of the church, as is clear from verse 4.

1 Tim. v. 17.—" Let the elders that rule well be counted worthy of double honour " : *i.e.*, of a liberal (see *Metonymy*) maintenance."

1 Pet. iii. 7.—" Giving honour unto the wife as unto the weaker vessel " : *i.e.*, nourishing and supporting her, etc.

" **Hand.** " For various idiomatic phrases in connection with the word " hand," see under *Metonymy*.

" **Living** " was used by the Hebrews to express the *excellency* of the thing to which it is applied. In some cases the A.V. has " lively."

John iv. 10, 11.—"Living water."

Acts vii. 38.—" Living oracles."

Heb. x. 20.—" Living way."

1 Pet. ii. 4, 5.—" Living stones."

Rev. vii. 17.—" Living fountains."

" Riches " denotes not merely money, but an *abundance* of that to which it is applied ; as our English word " wealth " is used of things other than money.

Rom. ii. 4.—" Or despisest thou the riches (*i.e.*, the greatness) of his goodness ? " *i.e.*, His abounding goodness, or wealth of goodness.

Eph. i. 7.—" According to the riches (*i.e.*, the great abundance or wealth) of his grace."

Eph. iii. 8.—" The unsearchable (or the untrackable) riches (*i.e.*, wealth or greatness) of Christ." This greatness consisting of all God's purposes in Christ as set forth in this epistle ; which the Old Testament saints could not trace out or understand. See 1 Pet. i. 10, 11.

Col. i. 27.—" What is the riches (*i.e.*, the great abundance) of the glory of this Mystery."

Col. ii. 2.—" All riches of the full assurance of understanding " : *i.e.*, the abundant or fullest assurance of knowledge.

" To sanctify " often means to make *ceremonially clean : i.e.*, to cleanse a thing from those defilements which made it unfit for sacred uses. Hence, it means simply *to set apart, fit*, or *prepare* for a particular purpose.

Jer. xii. 3.—"Sanctify (*i.e.,prepare*) them for the day of slaughter."

1 Cor. vii. 14.—" For the unbelieving husband is sanctified by the wife, and the unbelieving wife is sanctified by the husband" : each (though one be an unbeliever) is fitted to perform the respective duties as husband and wife. So with the *children*, " now are they holy " : *i.e.*, they were to be no longer reckoned as idolators, but were separated from heathen associations, and ceremonially free from such defilement. See under " holy " above.

How can we " sanctify God," as in Isa. viii. 13. Matt. vi. 9. 1 Pet. iii. 15, except by setting Him high above and apart from every other object of respect and veneration ?

" Spirit " was used in various combinations by the Hebrews to denote the greatest degree of any mental quality. As we speak of the spirit or essence of any person or thing!

Luke x. 21.—" Jesus rejoiced in spirit " : *i.e.*, exceedingly.

Acts xviii. 25.—" Being fervent in spirit " means exceedingly zealous. So Rom. xii. 11.

Acts xix. 21.—" Paul purposed in spirit " : *i.e.*, firmly resolved.

Acts xx. 22.—" Behold, I go bound in the spirit unto Jerusalem " : *i.e.*, with a fixed determination and settled purpose.

Rom. i. 9.—" Whom I serve with my spirit " : *i.e.*, with the most fervent zeal.

" **Walk** " is used of one's continued course of action and life : *i.e.*, the habitual habit and manner of life.

Gen. v. 22, 24.—" Enoch walked with God."

Rom. viii. 1.—" Who walk not after the flesh," etc.

2 Cor. v. 7.—" We walk by faith, not by sight."

" **Word** " (λόγος, *logos*) in the New Testament follows the Hebrew idiom ; and signifies not merely *a word*, but *speech*, which is the outcome of words.   Hence, it is used of any *matter*, *thing*, or *affair* of any kind.

Luke i. 2.—" Were eye witnesses and ministers of the Word " : *i.e.*, the Living Word, the Lord Jesus Christ.

Acts vi. 2.—" It is not reason that we should leave the word of God (*i.e.*, the preaching and ministry of the Gospel), and serve tables."

Acts x. 44.—" The Holy Ghost fell on them that heard the word " : *i.e.*, the Gospel which Peter preached.

Matt. xxi. 24.—" I also shall ask you one word " : *i.e.*, one thing, or a question as to one matter.

Acts x. 29.—" I ask therefore for what word (*i.e.*, as in A.V., for what intent) ye have sent for me."

Acts xix. 38.—" Have a word."   The A.V. has *a matter ;* but according to the Heb. idiom, *an accusation.*

1 Cor. xv. 2.—" If ye keep in memory by what word I preached unto you " : *i.e.*, what was the subject-matter of my preaching.

Thus the word must take its colouring from the context. In Ex. xxxiv. 28, it means the ten *commandments*. So in Rom. xiii. 9.

In 1 Cor. xiv. 19, it means *sentences*.

The word " **son** " was used, not only by *Synecdoche* (*q.v.*), but idiomatically, and not according to Greek usage.

" A son of death " (1 Sam. xx. 31) means *devoted to death*, and is rendered in A.V. : " he shall surely die." So xxvi. 16, and Ps. cii. 20 (21).

This idiom means that the persons thus spoken of belong very emphatically to that which they are thus said to be " sons of."

" Sons of the bride-chamber." Matt. ix. 15. Luke v. 34.

A " son of hell." Matt. xxiii. 15.

" Sons of the wicked one." Matt. xiii. 38.

" Son of the devil." Acts xiii. 10.

" Sons of disobedience." This is very much stronger than the mere tame expression disobedient children. It means that they pertain to and belong to Satan in a special manner ; are those in whom he works (Eph. ii. 2), and on whom the wrath of God comes (Eph. v. 6). It does not say that God's children *were* such, but only that we had our conversation " among " them. We were, by nature, " sons of wrath " (Eph. ii. 3) : *i.e.*, those deserving of God's wrath; but, through His grace another has borne that wrath, as verses 4-7 goes on to say.

" The son of perdition " (2 Thess. ii. 3. John xvii. 12) is one who is lost in a very emphatic and terrible sense.

See under *Synecdoche.*

iii. *Idiomatic Degrees of Comparison.*

In the Hebrew there are several idiomatic ways of emphasizing adjectives, and making them superlative.

1. Preposition after Adjective.

By the use of the preposition " **in** " or " **among** " after a simple adjective, as Prov. xxx. 30, " a lion, strong among beasts " : *i.e.*, the strongest of beasts.

The New Testament has the same *Idiom.*

Luke i. 42.—" Blessed art thou among women " : *i.e.*, the most blessed of women.

2. Noun (in regimen) for Adjective.

By using a noun (by *Enallage*) instead of an adjective, and putting it *in regimen :* as " angels of might," which is stronger than simply using the ordinary adjective " mighty." " Kingdom of Heaven " : *i.e.*, God's kingdom, as greater and better than all kingdoms which are " of " (ἐκ) this world. See for examples under *Enallage.*

3. Noun repeated in Genitive Plural.

By repeating the same noun in the genitive plural, as " Heaven of heavens " : *i.e.*, the highest heaven. See under *Polyptoton*.

4. " Of God " as Adjective.

By using the words " of God " instead of an adjective, *e.g.*,

1 Sam. xiv. 15.—" Tremblings of God " : *i.e.*, great or very mighty tremblings, meaning an earthquake.

Ps. xxxvi. 6 (7).—" Mountains of God " : *i.e.*, the loftiest or grandest mountains. See under *Enallage*.

5. Duplication of Noun as Adjective.

By the repetition of the same word, as " peace, peace " : *i.e.*, perfect peace. So

Matt. xxiii. 7 : " Rabbi, Rabbi " : *i.e.*, most excellent Rabbi.

Matt. vii. 21.—" Not every one that saith unto me, Lord, Lord " : *i.e.*, most gracious Lord.

Mark xiv. 45.—" Master, master " : *i.e.*, most excellent Master. See further under *Epizeuxis*.

6. Two Nouns conjoined.

By using a noun instead of an adjective, not in regimen, but (by *Hendiadys*) in the same case and number, and joined to the other noun by a conjunction.

2 Sam. xx. 19.—" A city and a mother " : *i.e.*, a metropolitan city.

Acts xiv. 13. — " Oxen and garlands " : *i.e.*, oxen — yes, and garlanded oxen too. See under *Hendiadys*.

7. Plural Noun for Singular Adjective.

By using the plural instead of the singular.

Ps. li. 17 (19).—" The sacrifices of God are a broken spirit," etc. : *i.e.*, the great sacrifice which God requires is a broken spirit and a contrite heart. See under *Heterosis*.

8. Verb and Cognate Noun.

Even *a verb* can be exalted to a superlative degree, as well as an adjective, by using with it a cognate noun : *e.g.*,

Luke xxii. 15.—"With desire I have desired ": *i.e.,* I have greatly desired.

Acts iv. 17.—" Let us threaten them with a threat ": *i.e.,* let us threaten them very severely.

Acts v. 28.—" Did we not charge you with a charge ": *i.e.,* did we not straitly charge you. See under *Polyptoton.*

9. Verb and its Participle.

A verb can also be emphasized superlatively by combining with it its participle : *e.g.,* "Seeing I have seen ": *i.e.,* I have surely seen. " Dying thou wilt die ": *i.e.,* thou wilt surely die. See under *Polyptoton.*

iv. *Idiomatic Use of Prepositions.*

Prepositions are used in the New Testament not according to the Greek idiom, but to the Hebrew. The Greeks had many prepositions, but the Hebrews had very few. Consequently, used according to the Hebrew Idiom, the manifold relations cannot be expressed with great definiteness.

The few Hebrew prepositions are used in the Old Testament with various meanings which can be easily gathered from the context. For example, the Hebrew ב (*beth*) means primarily *in* ; but it also frequently means *by* (with reference to the instrument used), or *among ;* or *at,* or *near ;* also *upon,* and *with.* Now the Greeks have, and would have used, a different preposition for each of these.

It is a great mistake, therefore, always to translate ἐν (*en*), *in,* as is too frequently done in the New Testament. It must be taken with all the shades and breadth of meaning which the Hebrew *beth* (ב) has. When the Greek of the New Testament is put into Hebrew, this fact is at once clearly seen.

For example :—

Matt. iii. 11.—John said, " I indeed baptize you *with* water."

Matt. vii. 2.—" *With* what judgment ye judge . . . *with* what measure ye meet."

Matt. vii. 6.—" Lest they trample them *with* (A.V., under) their feet."

Mark iii. 22.—" *By* the prince of the devils."

Luke xi. 20.—"*With* the finger of God."

Luke xxii. 49.—" Shall we smite *with* the sword."

Rev. i. 5.—"Washed us from our sins *by* (or *through*) his own blood," not *" in,"* as A.V. The R.V. renders this " by," and puts in the margin, " Greek, *in.*"

Rev. v. 9.—Here the A.V. renders it properly "*by.*"

v. *Idiomatic Use of Numerals.*

1. According to the Hebrew idiom, the numeral εἷς (*heis*), *one,* is used instead of the ordinary pronoun.

Matt. viii. 19.—"One scribe said to him ": *i.e.,* one of the scribes, or a certain particular scribe.

See also ix. 18; xvi. 14; xviii. 24, 28; xxi. 19; xxvi. 69. Mark x. 17; xii. 42. Luke v. 12, 17. John vi. 9; vii. 21; xx. 7. Rev. viii. 13, etc.

2. Sometimes, following the Hebrew idiom, the negative is joined with the verb instead of with the predicate : *e.g.,*

Matt. x. 29.—"One of them shall not fall." The ordinary Greek idiom would be, " not one (οὐδείς) of them shall fall." Luke xii. 6.

3. The adjective πᾶς (*pas*), *every* or *all* is frequently so used.

The Hebrews would say *everything is not,* and this is put instead of the ordinary Greek idiom, *nothing is.*

Ps. ciii. 2.—" Forget not all his benefits ": *i.e.,* forget not any.

Luke i. 37.—" Every thing will not be impossible with God ": *i.e.,* nothing is impossible.

So Matt. xxiv. 22. Mark xiii. 20. John iii. 15, 16; vi. 39; xii. 46. Rom. iii. 20. 1 Cor. i. 29. Gal. ii. 16. 1 John ii. 21. Rev. xviii. 22.

4. In Hebrew the numeral is doubled to express distribution.

We find this in the New Testament, instead of the Greek idiom which expresses it by the preposition ἀνά (*ana*). We find the Hebrew idiom, *e.g.,* in Mark vi. 7, "He sent them two two " (*i.e.,* two and two together): *i.e.,* in pairs. Compare the Greek idiom in Luke x. 1.

This idiom is not confined to numerals, for we find it with other nouns : *e.g.,*

Mark vi. 39, by companies (so Ex. viii. 14 (10), LXX).

In **Mark vi. 40,** both the Hebrew and Greek idioms are used. Compare Luke ix. 14. 2 Cor. iv. 16.

vi. *Idiomatic forms of Quotations.*

In quotations the Hebrews generally omitted the word " *saying*," whenever the words of another speaker were quoted. They very frequently stand alone without the verb " *saying*." Hence it is often supplied by *italics*. See Ps. ii. 2, but sometimes even italics are omitted, and the passage is most obscure.

Ps. cix.—" *Saying* " should be added in italics at the end of verse 5; all the words down to the end of verse 19 being the words of David's adversaries which they spake against David. See this passage under *Ellipsis* (page 33).

Ps. cxliv. 12 should begin with the word " *saying* "; verses 12 to the middle of verse 15 being the " vanity " and the " falsehood " which the " strange children " spake (verses 8, 11).

See this passage also under *Ellipsis* (page 33).

From this usage another idiom followed, in the asking of a question.

vii. *Idiomatic Forms of Question.*

In Hebrew a question often begins with " *if* ": *i.e.*, " *if* this be done " means " tell me whether this is done." But the Greeks never used the " if " in this sense in order to ask a question. In Greek it always expresses a condition. Yet, following the Hebrew idiom, we have:

Luke xxii. 49.—" *If* we shall smite with sword " : *i.e.*, shall we smite, etc.

viii. *Idiomatic Phrases.*

1. " **Answered and said** " was used by Hebrew idiom of whatever kind of speech is in question.

It should therefore not be rendered literally, " *Answered and said*," but translated so as to express whatever may be the particular kind of speech referred to in the verb " said "; *e.g.* :

Matt. xi. 25.—" At that time Jesus answered and said, I thank thee, O Father," etc.

This should be, " At that time Jesus *prayed* and said," etc.

Mark xii. 25.—" At that time Jesus answered and said, while he taught in the temple, How say the scribes that Christ, etc."

Here it should be " *Asked* and said." So Mark xiii. 2, etc.

Mark xi. 14.—" And Jesus answered and said unto it, No man eat fruit of thee hereafter for ever."

It is clear that this cannot be literally meant, for the tree had said nothing. It should be " Jesus *addressed* the tree, and said to it."

2. My soul, your soul, their souls, is the Hebrew idiom for *myself, yourself, yourselves,* etc.

See Num. xxiii. 10. Judges xvi. 30. Ps. lix. 3 (4) ; xxxv. 13 ; ciii. 1 ; cxxi. 7. Jer. xviii. 20 (cf. ẍxxviii. 16).

Ps. xvi. 10.—" Thou wilt not leave my soul (*i.e., me*) in Sheol (or *Hades*, the grave). This is explained in the next line as meaning " thou wilt not suffer thine Holy One to see corruption."

So Acts ii. 27, 31 ; xiii. 35.

It is resurrection from the grave which is taught and referred to here, as is clear from Ps. xlix. 15 (16), where *Sheol* is properly translated " grave." See under *Synecdoche.*

3. " Out of the Way."

ἐκ μέσου (2 Thess. ii. 7) must not be translated literally, arise or become developed " out of the midst," as is done by a certain school of prophetic students ; because it is a Greek idiom for being *out of the way,* and always implies decisive action, either of the person's own will or of force on the part of others.

Plutarch (*Timol.* 238. 3) says : " He determined to live by himself, having *got himself out of the way* " (*i.e.,* from the public).

Herodotus (3. 83 and 8. 22). The speaker (in 8. 22) exhorts some, and says : " Be on our side, but if this is impossible, then sit down *out of the way,*" or as we should say in our idiom " stand aside " (not " arise out of the midst " !)

The same idiom is found in Latin. Terence (*Phorm.* v. 8. 3) says : " She is dead, she is gone from among us " (*i.e.,* forced or torn away by the cruel hand of death, " *e medio abiit* ").

The opposite expression shows the same thing.

In Xenophon (*Cyr.* v. 2. 26), some one asks : " What stands in the way of your joining us ? " (ἐν μέσῳ ἐστί) : *i.e.,* your standing in with us.

The same *idiom* is found in the Scriptures.

Matt. xiii. 49.—The wicked are " severed *from among* the just " : (*i.e.,* taken away by force).

Acts xvii. 33.—" Paul departed *from among* them."

Acts xxiii. 10.—Paul was taken " by force from among them."

1 Cor. v. 2 is very clear : where the complaint is made that they had not mourned that " he that hath done this deed might be taken away *from among* you."

2 Cor. vi. 17.—" Wherefore come out from among them, and be ye separate."

Col. ii. 14.—We read of the handwriting of ordinances which was against us. Christ " took it out of the way."

We have the same *idiom* in the Septuagint.

Isa. lii. 11.—" Depart ye . . . go ye out of the midst of her," and

Isa. lvii. 1 (lxx. 2).—" The righteous is taken away from the evil to come."

It is thus perfectly clear that, in 2 Thess. ii. 7, where it says that he who now holds fast [*to his position*] will continue to do so until he is cast out, the " he " is Satan, who is holding on to his position in the heavenlies, until the great war shall take place (Rev. xii.), and he be cast out into the earth.

Then it is that (Rev. xiii. 1) " he stands (R.V.) on the sand of the sea," and as the result of this the two beasts rise up. They cannot, therefore, " arise " till Satan is cast out. This is the teaching of 2 Thess. ii. See further under *Ellipsis*.

4. " Breaking of Bread."

" *To break bread*," κλάσαι ἄρτον (*klasai arton*), is the literal rendering of the Hebrew idiom פָּרַס לֶחֶם (*paras lechem*), and it means *to partake of food*, and is used of eating as in a meal.* The figure (or idiom) arose from the fact that among the Hebrews bread was made, not in loaves as with us, but in round cakes about as thick as the thumb. These were always *broken*, and not cut. Hence the origin of the phrase *to break bread*. Indeed so close is the connection that we sometimes have the word " break " without " bread." So clear is the meaning that there may be the *Ellipsis* of the latter word.

See examples of this Hebrew idiom in Jer. xvi. 7 (see A.V. margin) " Neither shall men break bread for them," as in Ezek. xxiv. 17. Hos. ix. 4. See Deut. xxvi. 14, and Job xlii. 11.

Isa. lviii. 7.—" Is it not to break thy bread to the hungry ? "

---

* Just as among the Arabs to-day, the *Idiom*, *to eat salt*, means partaking of a meal.

Lam. iv. 4.—" The young children ask bread, and no man breaketh it unto them."

Ezek. xviii. 7.—" Hath broken (A.V. given) bread to the hungry."

We have the same Hebrew idiom in the Greek words of the New Testament, and the readers could have had no other idea or meaning in their minds (Matt. xiv. 19). He took the five loaves, and blessed, and brake, and gave the loaves to his disciples, etc. This was in connection with ordinary eating. See Matt. xv. 36; Mark viii. 6, 19; xiv. 22.

Luke xxiv. 30.—" And it came to pass, as he sat at meat with them, he took bread, and blessed it, and brake, and gave to them."

In verse 35, they speak of how Christ " was known of them in breaking of bread," *i.e.*, as He *sat at meat with them.*

Acts. xxvii. 33-36.—" This day is the fourteenth day that ye have tarried and continued fasting,* having taken nothing. Wherefore I pray you take some meat : for this is for your health : . . . And when he had thus spoken, he took bread, and gave thanks to God in presence of them all ; and when he had broken it, he began to eat. Then were they all of good cheer, and they also took some meat."

It is perfectly clear that in all these cases the " breaking of bread " is the ordinary Hebrew idiom for eating as in a meal. The bread could not be eaten till it was broken, hence the idiom which is used by Hebrews down to the present day.

It is also evident that the Passover was a meal, and it was at this meal, and of it, that the idiom is used in Matt. xxvi. 26. Mark xiv. 22 Luke xxii. 19. 1 Cor. xi. 24.

In Acts ii. 46, their breaking bread at home (margin) is mentioned to emphasise the fact that they no longer offered sacrifices, and therefore could not eat of them in the Temple. So that though they went to the Temple to worship, they ate their meat at home in their private houses.

It is incredible, therefore, that in Acts xx. 7, the idiomatic expression can mean in any sense the Lord's supper, as is clear also from verse 11.

The one solitary passage left is 1 Cor. x. 16, " The bread which we break." This is referred by some to the Lord's supper in ignorance of the prevailing custom of the early Christians when meeting together on

---

* See under *Synecdoche.*

the first day of the week. Assemblies were few, and the members were scattered. Many came from long distances, and food had to be brought for the day's sustenance. The early fathers tell us that the people brought from their own homes hampers filled with cooked fowls, and geese, etc., meat, loaves of bread, with skin-bottles of wine, etc. The rich brought of their abundance, and the poor of their poverty. These Sunday feasts acquired the ecclesiastical name, *agapai* or "love-feasts" (from ἀγάπη, *brotherly love*, see Jude 12), because the richer brethren made them for the benefit of the poor.

It is easy to see how this would in time become a feast; and how, though all partook of the common food, some would have too much, and some too little; and, as it is written, some would be hungry, and others drunken (1 Cor. xi. 21).

This looks as though the feast or meal itself came to be spoken of as "the Lord's supper," from the fact that each received an equal portion, as on that night when the Lord Himself presided, and received it as from Himself and not merely from one another.

But in process of time, a special ordinance was added at the close of these feasts, at the end of the assembly, and at the end of the day. to which the name, "the Lord's supper," was afterwards confined, Up to the time of Chrysostom it followed the feast; but, as superstition increased, it preceded the feast; but for 700 years after Christ they accompanied each other: and the Lord's supper was unknown as a separate ordinance !

As late as A.D. 692 the close of the Lenten fast was celebrated by an *agapee*, or feast, as the anniversary of the institution of the Lord's supper; and in England the day was called Maunday Thursday, from the *maunds*, *i.e.*, the baskets or hampers in which the provisions were brought. No one but Royalty now keeps up this ancient custom. It fell into desuetude from the superstition of "fasting communion;" which had been brought in (though Chrysostom wished himself *anathema* if he had been guilty of it !).

The "breaking of bread" therefore was used of the love-feast, and never, until recent years, used of the Lord's supper as a separate ordinance.

The error has arisen from the misunderstanding of the Hebrew idiom; and, from translating *literally* that which is used as a *figurative* expression.

Rome has done exactly the same, though in another direction. Rome forces the words "to break bread," to prove its practice of withholding the cup from the laity, or of communion in one kind ! Rome argues that as it only says "bread," and *wine* is not mentioned; therefore the "wafer" is sufficient!

Had Gentiles been acquainted with the Hebraism, neither malice nor ignorance could have diverted the words from their simple and only meaning.

5. To "**Take the Sword**" is used for rashly usurping magisterial power instead of giving obedience and subjection to God.

Matt. xxvi. 52.

6. To "**Open the Mouth**" is a Hebraism, used for speaking at length or with great solemnity, liberty, or freedom.

Judges xi. 35, 36. Job iii. 1 ; xxxiii. 2. Ps. lxxviii. 2. Prov. xxxi. 26. Ezek. xxiv. 27. Dan. x. 16. Matt. v. 2, with xiii. 35. Luke i. 64. Acts viii. 35 ; x. 34. 2 Cor. vi. 11. Rev. xiii. 6.

So the opposite, "*not to open the mouth*," is a Hebraism for silence :—Ps. xxxviii. 13 (14) ; xxxix. 9 (10). Prov. xxiv. 7. Isa. liii. 7. Acts viii. 32.

7. To "**Taste Wine**" is a Hebraism for drinking with others to indulgence.

Dan. v. 2.

So also to "*drink wine.*" Prov. xxxi. 4.

8. "What to me and to thee ?"

τί ἐμοὶ καὶ σοί (*ti emoi kai soi*) which is rendered, "What have I to do with thee ?" means what is there between thee and me : *i.e.*, what have we in common.

2 Sam. xvi. 10; xix. 22. 1 Kings xvii. 18. 2 Kings iii. 13. Matt. viii. 29. Mark i. 24. Luke iv. 34. John ii. 4.

9. "The Son of Man."

Under *Synecdoche* we have considered the ordinary meaning of "Son of Man"; but, with the definite article, the phrase appears to have a special idiomatic usage of its own. No one was ever so called, but Christ Himself. He first thus calls Himself in John i. 51 (52). The reference is to the first occurrence of the phrase in Ps. viii., where the title is seen to involve universal dominion in the earth. Dominion was given to the first man, Adam, and lost. It is to be restored in "the Son of man," "the second man," "the Lord from Heaven."

From John xii. 34 (cf. viii. 28), the Jews rightly inferred that the title involved His Messiahship.

That the title has to do with dominion in the earth is clear from the fact that it does not occur in the Epistles, and does not, therefore, pertain to Christ in relation to the Church—the Body of which He i; the Head, though it occurs constantly in the Gospels, as well as in the Apocalypse (but here only twice : i. 13, and xiv. 14).*

10. " Turn to Ashes."

Ps. xx. 3.—This was the Hebrew idiom for God's acceptance of offerings by fire : *i.e.*, He accepted them by causing fire to fall from heaven and consume the sacrifice. No fire having its origin in this world ever consumed the sacrifices which God accepted.

The sacrifices of the heathen were wholly independent of and apart from God. He neither commanded them, nor accepted them. It is even so with all worship now that is not the fruit of the Holy Spirit (who is symbolized by burning fire). For the flesh to offer worship is the offering of " strange fire."

The fire which kindled the incense on the Golden Altar of worship within the Holy Place was the same fire which had consumed the sacrifice on the Brazen Altar. This tells us that there can be no incense of prayer ascending to heaven that is not based on and does not proceed from the blood of atonement.

That this fire from heaven was the essential part of God's acceptance of the offering may be seen from the fact that the fire of God fell from heaven at the first (Lev. ix. 24) (at the Tabernacle), and again at the Temple (2 Chron. vii. 1), and that fire was kept continually burning.

Whenever God accepted an offering away from the one place which He had appointed the fire fell especially upon that occasion only. See Gideon, Judges vi. 21 ; Manoah, Judges, xiii. 15-23 ; David, 1 Chron. xxi. 26 ; and Elijah, 1 Kings xviii. 38.

This, therefore, is what is meant in Gen. iv. 4, when " the LORD had respect unto Abel and to his offering," because it was what He had ordered. But to Cain and his offering God " had not respect," because it was not what He had appointed. " The way of Cain " (Jude 11) is therefore human inventions in Divine worship !

This is how Abel " obtained witness that he was righteous." This is how " God testified of his gifts." This is how Abel " being dead,

---

* See *The Divine Names and Titles*, by the same author and publisher.

yet speaketh" (Heb. xi. 4), but few hear his voice. Few understand the great fact that God left nothing for man's imagination when He made known how He would be approached, and how He would be worshipped. In the last chapter of Exodus (xl.), we have fourteen times "thou shalt" (2-15), in the directions given to Moses ; and eight times the significant words that all was done " as the LORD commanded Moses." Then Leviticus, the book of worship, opens with the words : " And the LORD called unto Moses . . . out of the Tabernacle of the congregation (for Moses was not able to enter in, Ex. xl. 35), saying . . . If any man of you bring an offering unto the LORD, ye shall bring," etc.

Thus it is the Lord who dictates the particulars as to how He will be approached. And, if He does not accept the sacrifice by *turning it to ashes,* in vain would they worship Him.

It is the same to-day. The true worshippers, who worship God, do so in spirit, and through that sacrifice which God has accepted, even Christ our substitute, on whom the Divine judgment fell instead of on His People. " BY HIM " it is that we offer the sacrifice of praise to God continually, that is the fruit of our lips giving thanks to His name (Heb. xiii. 15).

There is no other worship now which He accepts, and no other worshippers whom the Father seeks to worship Him (John iv. 23).

11. " The Sons of God " (*Sons of Elohim*).

This is the Hebrew idiomatic expression for angels. In every place where the expression occurs, angelic beings are to be understood. It occurs in :

Gen. vi. 2, 4. Job i. 6 ; ii. 1.—Where it is בְּנֵי־הָאֱלֹהִים (*benai ha-Elohim*), *sons of the Elohim.*

Job xxxviii. 7.—Where it is without the article, " *Sons of Elohim.*"

Ps. xxix. 1 ; lxxxix. 6 (7).—Where it is בְּנֵי אֵלִים (*benai Eyleem*), *sons of Eyleem.*

Dan. iii. 25.—Where it is singular, " A son (Chald., בַּר) of God."

Seven times in all, and in each case it means angels.*

It is clear, therefore, that *angels* are meant in Gen. vi. 2, 4, and their " sin " is there recorded. How it was committed we are not

---

* In Hos. i. 10 (ii. 1), it is a different form בְּנֵי אֵל הָי (*Benai El hai*), *sons of the living God.* The context leaves us in no doubt that this is used of men, and not angels, for it is put in contrast with עַמִּי (*ammai*), *my people.*

told. In 2 Pet. ii. 4, 9 and Jude 6, it is further described, and is spoken of in connection with Noah. Is it not strange that in 1 Pet. iii. 18, 19, where exactly the same connections occur (*i.e.*, " Noah," and " chains," and " prison "), they should be taken for *men !* Especially when we recall the statement that " He maketh His angels spirits " (Ps. civ. 4. Heb. i. 7), and that man is never spoken of as a " spirit." He is said to have a spirit, but not to be one.

In Gen. vi. 4, the progeny of these fallen angels is called *Nepheleem :* i.e., *the fallen ones* (from נָפַל, *naphal, to fall*) : and so awful were the consequences that all flesh was corrupt, and Noah was the only one who was not tainted.*

All the race, therefore, had to be destroyed. Noah's sons' wives were tainted, and this may be the solution of the Ethnological problem as to the different races. There were *Nepheleem* in the days of Moses (Num. xiii. 33), because it appears from Gen. vi. 4 that there was another irruption " after that " : *i.e.*, after the days of Noah. It was for the extermination of this awful breed of beings that Israel was used : and yet there are Christians with an excess of (false) charity who deplore the slaughter effected by Israel, forgetting the necessity for the destruction.

It was to these fallen angels, "reserved" and " in prison " in Tartarus (the utmost bounds of creation) that the triumph of Christ reached and was proclaimed—an encouragement to those who now " suffer "—bidding them too, to look forward to the " glory " which shall surely follow.†

12. " Three days and three nights."

Jonah i. 17 (ii. 1), quoted in Matt. xii. 40.

The expression, "three days and three nights," is an *idiom* which covers any parts of three days and three nights.

In 1 Sam. xxx. 11 (12), it is said that a certain Egyptian had not eaten bread and drunk water for " three days and three nights," and yet it was only three days since he fell sick (ver. 13), not four days.

In Est. iv. 16, Esther says she and her maidens will fast " three days and three nights," and yet it was on " the third day " that Esther

---

* The two words " generations " are not the same in Gen. vi. 9. The first is *Toledoth*, meaning *the offspring* in succession, while the second is *Dorothai*, which has respect to *breed* (Isa. liii. 8).

† See *The Spirits in Prison*, by the same author and publisher.

went in to the king; not the *fourth* day, which it must have been if the expression were literally understood.

It may seem absurd to Gentiles and to Westerns to use words in such a manner, but that does not alter the fact.

Now the New Testament is for the most part Hebrew in *idiom,* but Greek in *language.* This is the simple explanation of the difference between it and classical Greek. Moreover, there is reason to believe that the First Gospel, as we have it, is a translation from a Hebrew Original. This is one of the idioms. It is used in Jonah i. 17 (ii. 1), and by our Lord in Matt. xii. 40. And yet many Scriptures say that He should rise, and did actually rise on " the third day." This could not have been if the expression were used in its literal sense. It must have been the *fourth* day and not the " third."

The fact is that the *idiom* covers any part of " three days and three nights." This method of Hebrew reckoning is as distinct from Gentile reckoning, as their commencing the day at sunset and our commencing it at midnight. All these different modes of reckoning are peculiar to the respective peoples and languages and must be duly taken into account.

The Lord's words in Matt. xii. 40 do not disagree with the Scripture assertion that He should rise on " the third day."

We have the expression " after three days " once (Matt. xxvii. 63), and " in three days " once (John ii. 19). But the common expression is " on the third day," and it occurs ten times. But if the expression be literal and not an *idiom,* all these passages should say the *fourth* day ! Paul preached the resurrection on " the third day " according to the Scriptures (1 Cor. xv. 4), and this is the great Scriptural fact which we cannot get away from.

Neither can we alter the fact that He rose on " the first day of the week."

Neither can we alter the history which records His death and burial as taking place the day before the Sabbath. " The sabbath drew on " (Luke xxiii. 54. Matt. xxvii. 62) ; "the day before the sabbath " (Mark xv. 42) ; and yet the two disciples going to Emmaus on the first day of the week say, " This is the third day (not the fourth) since these things were done " (Luke xxiv. 21).

From all this it is perfectly clear that nothing is to be gained by forcing the one passage (Matt. xii. 40) to have a literal meaning, in the face of all these other passages which distinctly state that the Lord died and was buried the day before the Sabbath and rose the day after it, *viz.,* on the first day of the week. These many statements are literal and are history: but the *one* passage is an *idiom* which means any part of "three days and three nights." The one complete day and night (24 hours) and the parts of two nights (36 hours in all) fully satisfy both the *idiom* and the history.

It may be added that we have a similar usage in English. When a person is sentenced to "three days' imprisonment," it may be late in the evening of the first day when he arrives at the prison, but when the doors open on the morning of the third day (not the fourth) he walks out a free man. In other words, if a person is commited to prison for three days—and he reaches it on Monday night—he leaves it the first thing on Wednesday morning.

See *The Coming Prince*, by Dr. Robert Anderson, C.B.

On the other hand,

"**Thou sayest**" is not, as is generally supposed, an idiomatic expression, conveying merely a simple affirmation or consent.

The fact is that εἶπας (*eipas*) already means "thou saidst," for the pronoun is included in and forms part of the verb. If therefore the pronoun σύ (*su*), *thou*, is used as well, it makes it very emphatic; and indeed it places all the emphasis upon the pronoun (*thou*) instead of on the verb (*sayest*) and causes the phrase to mean "*thou* (and not I) hast said it," or *It is thou that madest the statement*; or *Thou hast said it thyself.* So clear is this emphasis that the words "*and not I*" are often added.* So, too, σὺ λέγεις (*su legeis*), *thou thyself dost allege*.

See, *e.g.*, Matt. xxvi. 25: "Then Judas, which betrayed him, answered and said, Master, is it I? He said unto him, *Thou* hast said it thyself," not I. Thou hast taken the fatal word "traitor" on thine own lips.

So, in Matt. xxvi. 63, 64, the High Priest (before whom Jesus had held his peace) asked, "Tell us whether thou be the Christ, the Son of God." Jesus saith unto him, "*Thou* hast said it thyself," not I. I neither affirm it nor deny it. *Thou* hast spoken the word. But then not to leave the matter in further suspense. Jesus says: "Only, I tell you, hereafter ye will see the Son of Man sitting on the right hand of Power, and coming upon the clouds of heaven."

It has been suggested that σὺ εἶπας (*su eipas*), *thou saidst*, should be read in the text of Matt. xvi. 18, instead of σὺ εἶ Πέτρος (*su ei Petros*), *thou art Peter.*

---

* Euripides and Sophocles both have examples. See Wetstein. And compare Matt. xxvii. 11. Mark xv. 2. Luke xxii. 70; xxiii. 3. John xviii. 37; (and Sept. Exod. x. 29).

But this is merely an invention to get out of a supposed difficulty. It is based on the fact that in the most ancient MSS. there were no divisions between the words, and hence it has been suggested that the three words

ΣΥ ΕΙ ΠΕΤΡΟΣ (*su ei Petros*)
thou art Petros (*i.e.*, Peter, or a stone)

might originally have been written as one word,

ΣΥΕΙΠΣ (*sueips*),

and could be differently divided into two words, thus:—

ΣΥ ΕΙΠΣ (*su eips*, abbr. of *eipas*)
thou saidst.

But against this are to be placed the following objections:

1. There are the *Palæographical* objections as to the suggested abbreviations (*a*) of *eips* for *eipes* or *eipas*; (*b*) of *ps* for *petros*. The only known ancient abbreviation of *Petros* or *Peter* is in one of the Vienna Papyrus Fragments from Fayûm, where it is written ΠΕΤ. (*pet.**), *i.e.*, the first three letters instead of the first and the last.

2. There is the objection arising from the absence of definite MS. authority, which makes the evidence conjectural rather than documentary.

3. There is the objection arising from the actual context, which is unquestioned; the two words "thou sayest" do not follow at all. Try it: "And I say to thee, That *thou saidst*, and upon this rock I shall build My Church." It will be seen at once that the difficulty is increased instead of being removed! Had the words been in the previous verse, the case would be different; but, coming after the declaration in verse 17, and especially after the formula, "And I also say to thee," the words "*thou saidst*" seem to be quite impossible.

The best exposition of the passage is that which distinguishes between the two words *petros*, *a stone*, *a* rolling *stone*, *a stone* for throwing; and *petra*, *a rock*, or *cliff*, which cannot be moved.

Thou art a *petros* (a vacillating, unstable man, no one can build on thee), but upon this *petra* (this rock which flesh and blood cannot reveal, but which is revealed only by God Himself, upon Christ as "the Son of God"), I shall build My Assembly.

And so it came to pass. For in Gal. i. 15, 16 Paul says, "When it pleased God . . . to *reveal* His Son in me, that I might preach him among the Gentiles; immediately I conferred not with flesh and blood": *i.e.*, I conferred not with those who know not all the truth

---

* See the *Supplementum Nov. Test. Græci*, 1896, p. 67. By Ed. Nestlé, of Ulm.

involved in preaching Christ as "the Son of God." For all such are born of blood, or of the will of the flesh, and they learn these truths only by Divine *revelation*. We have the same word "reveal" in Matt. xvi. 17 (as we have also "flesh and blood") and Gal. i. 16, which is most significant. Paul was the wise master-builder. Paul was the first to preach Christ as "the Son of God," as declared in Acts ix. 20. This therefore was the *petra*—the rock foundation of the Church of the living God; and no mere *petros* or unstable man. Thus we have the contrast between the two, the *petros* and the *petra*, the stone and the ROCK.

ix. *Idioms arising from other Figures of Speech.*

Certain idiomatic phrases arise out of other Figures of Speech, and they will be found, as scattered examples, throughout this work.

For example, *Pleonasm* gives rise to a few; but the following are important, from *Anthropopatheia*. They will be found under that figure :

> " To hide from one's eyes.
> To swear by one's soul.
> To hide one's face.
> To hide one's eyes.
> To spare with the eyes.
> To stretch forth the hand.
> To put forth the hand.
> To shake the hand.
> To make the hand heavy.
> To make the hand light.
> To withdraw the hand.
> To turn the hand upon.
> To lift up the hand.
> To spread forth the hand.
> To turn the hand back.
> To smite or clap the hands.
> To open the hand,"
> > etc. etc.

Synecdoche and *Metonymy* also give rise to the peculiar usage of certain words in certain phrases: and these Figures must be referred to, as it is unnecessary to repeat them here.

x. *Changes of Usage of Words, in the Greek Language.*

These may be added as another class : where the meanings of words change in the course of centuries, even among the same people.

The Greek of the New Testament is, as we have seen, full of the idioms of another language (Hebrew). But there is more than this. Greek is a language which was spoken and used by different races under different conditions at different times and in different countries.

In the interpretation of Scripture, we have to take into account the fact that Greek was a living language, and was consequently marked by constant gradual changes. The New Testament Greek is four centuries later than Attic Greek. It is, therefore, impossible for us to depend solely on Attic Greek for its understanding and meaning.

Examples could be given of these changes :—

ζωοποιεῖν (*zōŏpoiein*) which meant in classical Greek *to produce live offspring*, had changed to *preserve alive* or *make alive, to quicken.*

πάροικος (*paroikos*) which meant *neighbour*, had come to mean *sojourner.*

πράκτωρ (*praktōr*) which meant *tax-gather*, had come to mean *jailor* (Matt. v. 25. Luke xii. 58). We learn this from the use of the word in the recently discovered Papyri.

On the other hand, Modern Greek exhibits similar changes of New Testament Greek : *e.g.,*

χρόνος which meant *time*, is used to-day in Greece of *a year.*

καιρός which meant *season*, is to-day in Greece used of *weather.*

It is clear therefore that any correct interpretation of New Testament Greek must take into account, not only particular usages, but also *changes* of usage. This properly comes under *Idiom*, and forms one of its most interesting and important branches. Biblical Greek occupies an unique position, and has never yet secured the attention and study which it demands. It is a neglected study, and is destitute alike of Lexicon and Grammar.*

We can, here, give only a few examples of the idiomatic usage of certain important Greek words in the New Testament, which had been changed from their original classical meaning, and were used in a different Biblical sense. It is clear that many words which had been used

---

* The late Professor Hatch, of Oxford, has shown the importance of this branch of Biblical study, and laid the foundations for it in his *Essays in Biblical Greek*. Clarendon Press, 1889.

by heathens could not possibly be brought into use in the sphere of spiritual and Divine truths without considerable modifications, and, in some cases, important changes.

The same phenomenon is encountered to-day, wherever the attempt is made to translate the Bible into a heathen language.

The knowledge of these changes as they affect the more important theological words is absolutely necessary to the correct interpretation of the New Testament Scriptures.

Dr. Hatch gives (among others) the following instructive examples :—

ἀγγαρεύειν (*angareuein*). In classical Greek it was used with strict reference to the Persian system of mounted couriers (Herod. 8. 98. Xen. *Cyr.* 8. 6, 17).

But the customs of other countries changed the meaning to the forced transport of military baggage (Jos. *Ant.* 13. 2, 3. Epictetus, *Diss.* 4. 1, 79).

In the New Testament, therefore, it is used of being compelled to carry the load or baggage of another person. See Matt. v. 41 ; xxvii. 32. Mark xv. 31. Compare Luke iii. 14.

ἀναγινώσκειν (*anaginōskein*) meant originally *to persuade* ; then, *to know well, to gather exact knowledge of*, hence *to read*.

But later usage extended the reading to *reading aloud with comments* so as to persuade others. (See Epictetus, *Diss.* 3. 23, 20 and 1. 10, 8).

So in the New Testament (Matt. xxiv. 15. Mark xiii. 14), "Let him that readeth" means let him who reads and comments on these words in the assembly take care to understand them.

It explains also 1 Tim. iv. 13.

ἀποστοματίζειν (*apostomatizein*). Its classical use was to dictate to a pupil what he was to learn by heart and afterwards recite.

But its later use was widened to the examination by questioning as to what had been already taught (Pollux 2. 102).

Hence in Luke xi. 53, where it is rendered "provoke him to speak," it means they began to put questions to Him as if they were questioning a pupil.

ἀρετή (*aretee*) in classical Greek meant *excellence* of any kind, especially of manly qualities. Hence, Latin, *vir-tus, manhood, valour, prowess, skill*.

In the LXX it is used for the translation of הוֹד (*hōd*), *glory*. Hab. iii. 3. Zech. vi. 13.

Also of תְּהִלָּה (*t'hillah*), *praise*. Isa. xlii. 8, 12 ; xliii. 21 ; lxiii. 7.

In the New Testament, therefore, it must have one of these two senses. See Phil. iv. 8 (virtue). 1 Pet. ii. 9 (praises). 2 Pet. i. 3 (virtue) ; i. 5 (virtue).

γλωσσόκομον (*glōssokomon*) was the *case* in which the *tongues* (γλῶσσαι) of musical instruments were kept (*tongue-case*).

All trace of this vanishes in later Greek, and it was used of any *chest*, especially of what we should call *the strong-box*, or *coffer*.

In the LXX it is used in 2 Chron. xxiv. 8, 10, 11. See 2 Kings xii. 9, etc., where we have κιβωτός (*kibōtos*), of what we should call *the money-box*.

Hence its meaning and use in John xii. 6 ; xiii. 29.

δεισιδαίμων (*deisidaimōn*) and δεισιδαιμονία (*deisidaimonia*) were used of *religion* or *religiousness* in a good sense.

But in later Greek they were used in a bad sense ; and this is the sense in Acts xvii. 22 ; xxv. 19.

διάβολος (*diabolos*) was used of *slanderous* or *malicious accusation*.

In the LXX it is used with or without the article of a single person, like the Heb. שָׂטָן, *Satan* ; and צַר, *Tsar*. See 1 Chron. xxi. 1. Est. vii. 4 ; viii. 1. Ps. cix. 6 (LXX, cviii. 6). (See Num. xxii. 22, where *opposition* is the meaning without implying accusation of any kind.)

In the New Testament it is used as a proper name, except in 1 Tim. iii. 11. 2 Tim. iii. 3. Tit. ii. 3, where it is used as an adjective, and in its ordinary sense of *malicious accuser*.

διαθήκη (*diatheekee*). In classical Greek it had two meanings : (1) *a last will* or *testament*, and (2) very rarely, of *a covenant*.

In the LXX it is used 280 times, and always of *a covenant*. This is its only use in the New Testament, and though it is translated "testament" several times, it should always be *covenant*. For Heb. ix. 16, 17, see under *Ellipsis*.

Dr. Hatch observes that "the attempt to give it in certain passages its classical meaning of 'testament' is not only at variance with its use in Hellenistic Greek, but is probably also the survival of a mistake : in ignorance of the philology of later and vulgar Latin, it was formerly supposed that 'testamentum,' by which the word is rendered in the early Latin versions as well as in the Vulgate, meant 'testament' or 'will,' whereas in fact it meant also, if not exclusively, 'covenar.t.'"

θρησκεία (*threeskeia*) was used (in the pl.) by Herodotus (2. 37) of *external ceremonies* of the Egyptian priests.

In Biblical Greek it is not used of these, but is transferred to any similar *ceremonial observances* and to these only : not of Christianity, but of that which has its origin in feelings or experiences, or of piety. This is its meaning in Acts xxvi. 5 (" religion "). Col. ii. 18 ("worshipping "). Jas. i. 26, 27 (" religion ").

μυστήριον (*musteerion*) always rendered or rather transliterated "mystery "; but meaning *a secret*. See a pamphlet on *The Mystery*, by the same author and publisher.

οἰκονόμος was used of *managing a household*, hence *manager*.

But in later Greek it was specially used of a slave who gave the other slaves their rations. So Luke xii. 42. Gal. iv. 2. Also of a land-steward, or as we should say an " agent." Luke xvi 1, 3, 8. Rom. xvi. 23.

πειράζειν (*peirazein*) usually translated *to tempt* : and πειρασμός (*peirasmos*), *temptation*.

The classical use of the verb was to *make proof* or *trial of* (Homer, *Od.* 16. 319; 23. 114 ; 9. 281). *To make an attempt* (Polyb. *Fr. hist.* 60).

In the LXX the meaning was extended to the *mode of trial* : viz., by affliction or disaster. Hence " *trial* " came to mean trouble : as being that which most effectually tries anyone.

In the New Testament there are several passages where this sense of *tribulation*, *trouble*, and even *chastisement* and *persecution* are the more suitable renderings :—

Luke viii. 13 (Matt. xiii. 21. Mark iv. 17).

Matt. vi. 13 (Luke xi. 4) Bring us not into trial, but deliver us from him, or that, which does the mischief.

Matt. iv. 1 (Mark i. 13. Luke iv. 2) to be tried or afflicted by the devil (hence Heb. iv. 15).

Acts xx. 19—" Perils " : *i.e.*, hardships through the plots and conspiracies of the Jews (2 Cor. xi. 24, 26). Heb. ii. 18. 1 Pet. i. 6 ; iv. 12. Rev. iii. 10.

πονηρός (*poneeros*) is defined by Aristotle as being only *weak*, having a good-will, and therefore only " half-wicked," because what is done is not done from malice.

On the contrary in the LXX, the meaning seems to point to the activity of mischief : of wild beasts (Gen. xxxvii. 20. Ezek. xiv. 15) : of the plagues of Egypt (Deut. vii. 15) : of blood-shedding (Isa. lix. 7) : of violence and mischief (Isa. xxxv. 9 ; x. 1).

So in the New Testament, *active harmfulness* and *mischievousness* are the prevailing meaning. Matt. v. 11, 39; vi. 13; xxii. 18 (Mark xii. 15. Luke xx. 23). Matt. xii. 45 (Luke xi. 26).

In some of the apocryphal books, the sense seems to be that of *grudging* (Sir. xiv. 4, 5; xxxi. 23). See Prov. xxiii. 6. Deut. xxviii. 56. In the New Testament this seems to be the sense in Matt. vi. 19-24; vii. 11 (Luke xi. 13); Matt. xx. 15.

παράκλητος (*parakleetos*) meant in classical Greek merely *called to one's aid*, *assisting*, especially in a court of justice. Hence *a legal adviser* or *helper*.

But this falls short of the meaning it afterwards obtained: *viz.*, not only of helping another to do a thing, but to help him *by doing it for him*. It is used only in John of the Holy Spirit's help (by Christ) in xiv. 16, 26; xv. 26; xvi. 7. And of Christ's help (by the Holy Spirit) in 1 John ii. 1.

πίστις (*pistis*), *faith*. In classical Greek, it meant, psychologically, *conviction*: rhetorically, *proof* which brings about the conviction; and morally, *good-faith* or *mutual trust*.

In Biblical Greek, there is added a fourth usage, which is, theologically, an *ideal virtue: viz*, *a full assurance* (Rom. iv. 20, 21). And, since it believes that, what God has said He will surely bring to pass, therefore, its objects are also objects of hope as well as faith (Heb. xi. 1).

συκοφαντεῖν (*sukophantein*). This word meant originally an *informer*, and was used of one who gave information against persons who exported figs from Attica. Literally, a *fig-shewer*. Hence *a common informer; especially* with the view of extorting money, *a black-mailer* (Xenophon, *Mem.* 2. 9, 4-6).

Hence in Biblical Greek it comes to have a wider range of meaning, and is used for Hebrew words which mean *to oppress;* and thus passed from black-mailing the rich, to the oppression of the poor to extort money, etc.

So Gen. xliii. 18. (See Gen. xxvi. 20. Lev. vi. 2. Deut. xxiv. 14. Job x. 3; xxxv. 9. Ps. lxxii. 4; cxix. 122, 134. Prov. xiv. 31; xxii. 16; xxviii. 3, 16. Ecc. iv. 1; v. 7; vii. 8. Ezek. xxii. 12, 29. Jer. vi. 6.)

In the New Testament it is used only in Luke iii. 14; xix. 8.

The distinction between the following words in classical and Septuagint and New Testament Greek is not observed in the Translations :—

πένης *(penees)* is *poor,* as opposed to rich : one who has to work for his living.

πτωχός *(ptōchos)* is *destitute,* and in want : *a pauper,* or *beggar.*

πραΰς *(praus)* is *easy-tempered,* as opposed to ὀργίλος *(orgilos),* *passionate ;* and πικρός *(pikros), bitter* or *sour.*

ταπεινός *(tapeinos)* is *dejected* as well as *lowly.*

In the LXX these words are used interchangeably to represent the same Hebrew words, and do not denote inferiority in morals, but only in outward condition : *viz.,* the peasantry *(fellahin),* who lived quiet, peaceful lives, and were the victims of lawless and powerful oppressors, who plundered and ill-treated them.

See Ps. x. 9 ; xii. 5 (6) ; xxxiv. 6 ; xxxv. 10 ; xxxvii. 14 ; xl. 17 (18) ; lxxii. 4, 13 ; lxxvi. 9 (10) ; cxlvii. 6.

This is the sense underlying these words in the New Testament.

Professor Deissmann* has recently illustrated many New Testament idiomatic usages and expressions from the collections of *papyri* at Berlin and Vienna. They were recently discovered in Egypt, and are of the age of the Ptolemies. They consist of petitions, letters, receipts, accounts, divorces, bribes, etc. His contention is that these contain marks, not of what is called "New Testament Greek," but of the vernacular usage of words at that time : *e.g.,* he shows that νεόφυτος *(neophytos) novice* (1 Tim. iii. 6) is used in the *papyri* of *newly planted palm trees.*

ἀθέτησις *(atheteesis), disanulling* (Heb. vii. 18 and ix. 26) is used as a technical legal expression, and is often found with ἀκύρωσις *(akurōsis) a depriving of authority,* and in *Antithesis* to βεβαίωσις *(bebaiōsis), a confirming,* or *establishing.*

ἀναπέμπω *(anapempō), to send up* (Luke xxiii. 7, 11, 15. Acts xxv. 21) is used of sending up to a superior authority.

ἀπέχω *(apechō), to have in full* (Matt. vi. 2, 5, 16. Luke vi. 24) is used in two Fayûm receipts dated respectively : Dec. 29th, 44 A.D., and Sept. 6th, 57 A.D., of *giving a discharge for an account.* This gives an ironical turn to these passages. See also Phil. iv. 18.

ἐπίσκοποι *(episcopoi), overseers* (A.V., bishops), is used of civil functionaries in Rhodes, in the first centuries, both B.C. and A.D. ; and also of an official in the temple of Apollo.

πρεσβύτεροι *(presbyteroi), elders,* is used of civil functionaries in Egypt, and also of temple officials, in the Fayûm *papyri.*

---

* *Bibelstudien,* Marburg, 1895, and *Neue Bibelstudien,* 1897.

σφραγίζω (*sphragizō*), *to seal*, is used of *certifying as correct*. This may explain Rom. xv. 28. John iii. 33. 2 Cor. i. 22. Eph. i. 13; iv. 30.

ἀμετανοητος (*ametanoeetos*), *impenitent* (Rom. ii. 5) occurs in a *papyrus* record of a sale, denoting that there was to be no change in it.

βιάζομαι (*biazomai*), *suffer violence* (Matt. xi. 12), is usually taken as passive, but a Lycian inscription uses it as a deponent: *i.e.*, the kingdom of God *presses itself* on the notice of men.

δοκίμιον (*dokimion*), *the trying* (1 Pet. i. 7). This usage would render Jas. i. 3, "What is genuine in your faith."

ἀρετή (*aretee*), 1 Pet. ii. 9, "That ye should show forth the *praises* of him who hath called you." And 2 Pet. i. 3, "Him that hath called us to glory and *virtue*."

Inscriptions are quoted from the Egyptian *papyri*, which show that ἀρετή was used at that time in the sense of *a display of power*. And this is exactly what it means in the above passages; for God's wondrous power is displayed and manifested forth in His calling of His People. See Eph. i. 18, 19. (See above, page 851).

xi. *Changes of Usage of Words in the English Language.*

It is most important that these should be carefully noticed: otherwise many words and expressions in the English of the A.V. cannot be understood.

It is most instructive to observe the evidence afforded by many of these changes as to the constant effect of fallen human nature; which, in its use of words, is constantly lowering and degrading their meaning:

" All to brake " (Judges ix. 53). This is an old Anglo-Saxon word *tobrecan*, from which the prefix " *to* " has got separated. It means altogether or completely smashed. (See Spenser's *Faerie Queene*: iv. 7. 66; Milton's *Comus* 379, " all to ruffl'd." So that "all to " meant " altogether ").

" And if" (Matt. xxiv. 48. 1 Cor. vii. 11). " But and if": *i.e.*, *but even if*.

" A work " (2 Chron. ii. 18).

" A fishing " (John xxi. 3). The " a " is a softening down of the Anglo-Saxon " on ": " on sleep " (Acts xiii. 36).

" Away with " (Isa. i. 13) meant *to tolerate*.

"**By and by**" (Luke xxi. 19) meant *immediately*.

"**Come at**" (Num. vi. 6) meant to *come near*, as in R.V.

"**Company with**" (1 Cor. v. 9. Compare *v.* 11) meant *to have company with*, as in R.V : *i.e.*, to associate with.

"**Do to wit**" (2 Cor. viii. 1) meant *make to know* (see "Wit" below) : *to certify*.

"**Fetched a compass**" (2 Kings iii. 9) meant *to make a circuit*, or round-about course (as in R.V.). So Acts xxviii. 13.

"**For to do**' (Deut. iv. 1) Here, the "for" was used in the sense of "*in order that*" : *i.e.*, that ye may do.

"**Full well**" (Mark vii 9): *i.e., with full knowledge.*

"**Go to**" (Jas. iv. 13) meant *come now*.

"**On sleep**" (Acts xiii. 36). The "on" has now become softened in modern usage to "a"—asleep.

"**Presently**" (1 Sam. ii. 16. Prov. xii. 16. Matt. xxi. 19; xxvi. 53. Phil. ii 23) meant *immediately*.

"**Prevent**" (Ps. lix. 10 (11); lxxix. 8; lxxxviii. 13 (14); cxix. 148. 1 Thess. iv. 15) meant *to go or come before*, *precede*. See under *Ellipsis*, Ps. xii. 6 (7).

"**Strike hands**" (Job xvii. 3) meant *to conclude a bargain* by shaking hands.

"**Trow**" (Luke xvii. 9) meant *to suppose* or *imagine* (A.S., *treowian, to believe*).

"**Wit**" or "**to wit**" (Gen. xxiv. 21. Ex. ii. 4) meant *to know*. Hence it came to mean any special cleverness (as a noun), and then humour. So "*wot*" meant *to know* (Acts iii. 17. Rom. xi. 2, etc.), and "*witty*" (Prov. viii. 12) meant simply *skilful* or *clever*, and "*wittingly*" (Gen. xlviii. 14) knowingly, skilfully.

"**Wist**" (Mark xiv. 40) is the past tense of *wit*, knew. "*Unwittingly*" (Josh. xx. 3) meant *unknowingly*. R.V. margin, *through error*.

"**Whit**" (1 Sam. iii. 18. 2 Cor. xi. 5). This is the Anglo-Saxon, *wiht*, a person or thing; hence "*not a whit*" meant not at all.

"**Very**" (Gen. xxvii. 21. Prov. xvii. 9. John vii. 26; viii. 4) meant *true, real*.

So there are certain words which have changed their meaning in the course of years :—

"**Advisement**" (1 Chron. xii. 19) meant *deliberation :* from the Latin *ad*, to, and *visum*, seemed good).

"**Adventure**" (Deut. xxviii. 56. Acts xix. 31) meant *to venture to go.*

"**Artillery**" (1 Sam. xx. 40). This meant (from the Low Latin *artillaria*, any warlike weapons, hence) *bows and arrows.* To-day we confine the word to quite another class of weapon.

"**Assay**" (Job. iv. 2) meant *to attempt, to try.*

"**Beeves**" (Num. xxxi. 33, etc.) was the plural of "beef": the Norman-French for ox.

"**Bonnet**" (Ex. xxviii. 40) was at one time used of a man's head-dress: and is still so used in Scotland.

"**Brigandine**" (Jer. xlvi. 4; li. 3) was *a coat of mail.* Now we use the word *brigand* in a special sense.

"**Carriages**" (Acts xxi, 15). From the three voices of the Greek Verb we have *Carriage* (passive: *i.e.*, that which I carry): *Carry* (middle: *i.e.*, how I carry myself); *Carriage* (active: *i.e.*, that which carries me). The former of these uses of the word (from the Passive) is now obsolete.

"**Clouted**" (Josh. ix. 5) meant *patched.* And "**Clouts**" (Jer. xxxviii. 11, 12).

"**To ear**" (1 Sam. viii. 12. Isa. xxx. 24) meant to *plough* (from Anglo-Saxon *erian*, to plough). So the R.V. now renders it; in 1 Sam. viii. 12, spelling it "plow," but in Isa. xxx. 24, "till." Compare Gen. xlv. 6, "Neither earing nor harvest." Ex. xxxiv. 21. Deut. xxi. 4.

"**Earing**" (Gen. xlv. 6. Ex. xxxiv. 21) meant, as in R.V., *plowing.*

"**Eared**" (Deut. xxi. 4) meant *ploughed.*

"**Earnest**" (2 Cor. i. 22. Eph. i. 14) meant a *pledge ;* but differing from an ordinary *pledge* in this, that while a *pledge* might be of a different kind, the *earnest* was a pledge of the same kind.

"**Fast**" (Ruth ii. 8) was used in the sense of *close, near.*

"**Fat**" (Joel ii. 24. Mark xii. 1) was used for a *Vat*, from Anglo-Saxon *faet*, which was pronounced *vat.*

"**Goodman**" (Matt. xx. 11) meant *householder* (as in R.V.).

"**Libertines**" (Acts vi. 9), a class of *freedmen* amongst the Romans.

"**Lusty** " (Judges iii. 29) meant merely *vigorous ;* and *Lust* meant simply pleasure or desire generally, as Ex. xv. 9. Deut. xii. 15, etc. 2 Tim. iv. 3 John viii. 44. 1 John ii. 16. Now we use it of one special form of desire.

"**Mote** " (Matt. vii. 3) is the Anglo-Saxon *mot, i.e.,* a particle of dust.

"**Naughty** " (Prov. vi. 12 ; xvii, 4. Jer. xxiv. 2) meant *worth naught, worthless.* Now we use it of any evil, and sometimes of some special form.

"**Nephew** " (Judges xii. 14. Job xviii. 19) meant *a grandson.* See Isa. xiv. 22. 1 Tim. v. 4 from the Latin *nepos.*

"**Occupy** " (Luke xix. 13) meant *to carry on business, to trade,* from the Latin *occupare, to lay hold of.* Hence our word "occupation."

"**Outgoings**," Josh. xvii. 9. Ps. lxv. 8 (9), meant *utmost limits.*

"**Penny** " (Matt. xx. 2) was used of *any piece of money.* Even silver money used to be so called. Hence the phrase : "to turn a penny." In Icelandic, *peningr* means *cattle,* as well as money. Now it is limited to a particular coin, which we represent by "d " (the initial of *denarius*). "A penny a day " was the idiom for the ordinary wage for such labour. In Luke x. 35, the "two pence " equalled two days' wages or double pay.

"**Publican** " (Matt. ix. 10, etc., etc.) was the Latin *Publicanus,* a *tax-collector.* Now the usage is changed to *a Vintner.*

"**Quick** " (Lev. xiii. 10, 24. Num. xvi. 30. Ps. lv. 15 ; cxxiv. 3. Isa. xi. 3. Acts x. 42. 2 Tim. iv. 1. Heb. iv. 12. 1 Pet. iv. 5) is the Anglo-Saxon *cwic, alive,* as opposite to dead. Now we use it in the sense of *lively* as opposite to sluggish. So

"**Quicken** " means *to make alive* (Ps. lxxi. 20 ; lxxx. 18 ; cxix. 25, 37, 40, 88, 107, 149, 154, 156, 159 ; cxliii. 11. Rom. xiii. 11).

"**Quickened**," *made alive* (Ps. cxix. 50, 93. 1 Cor. xv. 36. Eph. ii. 1, 5. 1 Pet. iii. 18.

"**Quickeneth**," *maketh alive* (John v. 21 ; vi. 63. Rom. iv. 17. 2 Cor. iii. 6 (marg.). 1 Tim. vi. 13.

"**Quickening**," *making alive* (1 Cor. xv. 45).

' **Silly** " (Job. v. 2. Hos. vii. 11. 2 Tim. iii. 6) meant, originally, as Anglo-Saxon, *saelig, timely,* then, *happy,* and *innocent.* But now, because a person who acts thus is supposed by the world to be foolish, so it has come to be used. The same is the case with the word

" **Simple**," which meant, originally, *without guile, open, artless.* But now, because a person who acts thus, is considered devoid of all sense, it has come to mean foolish. In the Bible the word is used in its original sense, as the usage had not then changed. See Ps. xix. 7 (8); cxvi. 6 ; cxix. 130. Prov. i. 4, 22, 32 ; vii. 7; viii. 5 ; ix. 4, 13 ; xiv. 15, 18 ; xxi. 11 ; xxii. 3. Ezek. xlv. 20. Rom xvi. 18, 19.

" **Simplicity** " is used in the corresponding sense : 2 Sam. xv. 1 . Prov. i. 22. Rom xii. 8. 2 Cor. i. 12 ; xi. 3.

" **Sottish** " (Jer. iv. 22) meant *stupid, dull, heavy.* Now, because a person is made so by drink, its use is limited to stupidity thus induced.

" **Vagabond** " (Gen. iv. 12, 14. Acts xix. 13. Ps. cix. 10) meant originally, *a wanderer,* from Latin *vagari, to wander.* But, because those who thus wander, are generally compelled to do so on account of their worthless character, so the word came to be limited to this special sense.

PROSOPOPŒIA ; or, PERSONIFICATION.

Things represented as Persons.

Pros'-ō-po-poe'-i-a (*i.e., pros'-o-po-peé-ya*). Greek, προσωποποιΐα, from πρόσωπον (*prosopon*), *face* or *person*, and ποιεῖν (*poiein*), *to make.*

A figure by which things are represented or spoken of as persons ; or, by which we attribute intelligence, by words or actions, to inanimate objects or abstract ideas.

The figure is employed when the absent are spoken of (or to) as present; when the dead are spoken of as alive; or when anything (*e.g.*, a country) is addressed as a person.

Personification is the English name for the figure.

The Latins called it PERSONIFICATIO, or PERSONÆ FICTIO, *the making* or *feigning of a person.* Also CONFORMATIO, *a conforming* or *fashioning, delineation, conception.*

The figure of *Personification* may be divided into the following six classes or groups :—

    I.   The members of the Human body.

    II. Animals.

    III. The products of the earth.

    IV. Inanimate things.

    V.   Kingdoms, countries, and states.

    VI. Human actions, etc., attributed to things, etc.

i. *The members of the human body.*

Gen. xxxi. 35.—Heb., Let not the eyes of my lord kindle with anger.

So xlv. 5 margin : and compare Isa. iii. 8.

Gen. xlviii. 14.—" He made his hands to understand " (שִׂכֵּל, *sikkeyl*), *skilful.*

Deut. xiii. 8.—" Neither shall thine eye pity him."

1 Kings xx. 6.—" Whatsoever is pleasant (or *desirable*, marg.) in thine eyes " : *i.e.*, pleases thine eyes. So Ezek. xxiv. 16 (see under *Periphrasis* and *Metonymy*), 21 (see *Paronomasia*). 1 John ii. 16.

Job xxix. 11.—"When the ear heard me, then it blessed me and when the eye saw me, it gave witness to me." How beautiful is this *Prosopopœia*. It is more than putting the "eye," by *Metonomy*, for any one who used the eye and saw. It is the actual personification of the eye; and, therefore, much more expressive.

Job xxxi. 7.—"If . . . mine heart walked after mine eyes," *i.e.*, if I covet that which I have seen. Compare 1 John ii. 16.

Ps. xxxv. 10.—"All my bones shall say, LORD, who is like unto thee," etc.

When it is written "All my bones," it is the figure *Synecdoche*, by which a part or some of the members are put for the whole being or person. When it is written "shall say," that is *Prosopopœia*, because they are represented as speaking.

This is a Psalm of David: and it is therefore true of David's Son, and David's Lord, as well as of David himself.

David could say that he, with all his members and powers, used these words and said, "Jehovah! Who is like unto thee," etc.

The Lord Jesus could use them in like manner of Himself. But there is a further *application* to Christ mystical: a truth not then revealed. All the members of Christ's body now say exactly the same thing. In Ps. cxxxix. 16 we see the formation of those members (1 Cor. xii.). We see how they are placed in the Body.

They are "vexed." Ps. vi. 2 (3).

They are "sundered" (Ps. xxii. 14 (15), margin), but never "broken" (Ps. xxxiv. 20 (21). Ex. xii. 46): therefore Christ's literal bones were not to be broken (John xix. 33, 37).

Their "hearts" are broken, as His was (Ps. lxix, 20). See Ps. xxxiv. 18 (19), (and cf. verse 20), but they themselves, never!

They all are "poor and needy," and they all say one thing. They all own Jesus as "the Lord"; and all confess that there is none like Him. Sometimes they ask the question (Ps. lxxxix. 6 (7); lxxi. 19. Ex. xv. 11), and sometimes they answer it (Deut. xxxiii. 26, 27. 1 Sam. ii. 2).

They thus confess Him as beyond compare, because He delivers the "poor and needy" from the strong spoiler.

From the *Law* which was too strong (Gal. iii. 10 and 13).

From *Sin* which is too strong (Rom. vii. 23, 24; v. 21).

From the *World* which is too strong (John xvi. 33), and

From *Death* (2 Cor. i. 10. 2 Tim. i. 10. Hos. xiii. 14).

Ps. lxviii. 31 (32).—" Ethiopia shall soon stretch out her hands unto God." Here, Ethiopia is first put, by *Metonymy* (of subject), for the inhabitants who lift up their hands. Otherwise, it is a *Prosopopœia*, for Ethiopia has no hands ! This will be fulfilled in the day of Ps. lxxii. 15.

Ps. lxxiii. 9.—" Their tongue walketh through the earth." It is the wicked who walk through the earth, using their tongues against God.

Ps. ciii. 1.—" All that is within me, bless his holy name." See also *Synecdoche* and *Idiom*.

Ps. cxix. 82.—" Mine eyes fail for thy word": *i.e.*, mine eyes are consumed in looking for the fulfilment of Thy Word: *i.e.* (by *Synecdoche*) I am consumed. So verse 123.

Ps. cxxxvii. 5 (6).—" If I forget thee, O Jerusalem, let my right hand forget." The A.V. and R.V. supply *" her cunning "* in italics. This is usually treated as an *Ellipsis*, but by some as a *Prosopopœia*. But it is neither. When the correct reading of the Hebrew is understood, we have here a beautiful *Paronomasia* (*q.v.*), and the reading is " let me forget my right hand."

Ps. cxlv. 15.—" The eyes of all wait (marg., *look unto*) thee."

Prov. x. 32.—" The mouth of the just bringeth forth wisdom."

Isa. xiii. 18.—" Their eye shall not spare children."

Ezek. xx. 7.—" Cast ye away every man the abominations of his eyes." See under *Enallage*.

Matt. vi. 3.—" Let not thy left hand know," etc. See *Parœmia*.

2 Pet. ii. 14.—" Having eyes full of an adulteress." (See A.V. margin.)

1 Cor. xii. 15, 16.—" If the foot shall say, Because I am not the hand, I am not of the body ; Is it therefore not of the body ? And if the ear shall say, Because I am not the eye, I am not of the body ; Is it therefore not of the body ? "

ii. *Animals.*

Gen. ix. 5.—" At the hand of every beast will I require it." Beasts are thus spoken of as intelligent and responsible. How much more man !

Job xii. 7.—" Ask now the beasts, and they shall teach thee : and the fowls of the air, they shall tell thee." Compare verses 8, 11, etc.

Job xli. 29 (21).—" He (leviathan) laugheth at the shaking of a spear.

Joel i. 6.—" A nation is come up upon my land . . . whose teeth are the teeth of a lion, and he hath the cheek teeth of a great lion." So verse 4.

Animals are represented as doing what the hostile nation had done.

See further illustrations under *Allegory*.

iii. *The products of the earth*.

Lev. xix. 23.—" Ye shall count the fruit thereof as uncircumcised." For three years the fruit of a young tree was not to be eaten, but in the fourth year it " shall be holiness of praises to Jehovah " : *i e.*, it shall be counted holy to the great praise and glory of Jehovah. See *Heterosis*. In the fifth year it might be eaten.

Joel i. 10.—" The land mourneth—the oil languisheth." So Isa. xvi. 8. Nahum i. 4.

Hab. iii. 17 (margin).—" The labour of the olive shall lie." So Hos. ix. 2.

iv. *Inanimate things*.

Gen. iv. 10.—" The voice of thy brother's blood crieth unto me from the ground." See under *Heterosis*.

So in verse 11. The earth is represented as opening her mouth to receive the blood of Abel.

Gen. xlii. 9, 12.—" The nakedness of the land."

Gen. xlvii. 19.—Desolation is spoken of as the death of the land.

Ex. xix. 18.—" Mount Sinai quaked as though with fear."

Lev. xviii. 25, 28.—" The land itself vomiteth out her inhabitants." " It spued out the nations."

Deut. xxxii. 42.—Arrows are said to be made drunk ; and the sword is said to devour. Compare Isa. xxxiv. 5, 6. Jer. xlvi. 10.

The four lines are as follows :—

> a | I will make mine arrows drunk with blood,
>   b | And my sword shall devour flesh ;
> a | *drunk* with the blood of the slain and of the captives,
>   b | from the hairy head of the enemy (R.V. marg).

Here *a* refers to the arrows mentioned in a : while *b* refers to the work of the sword mentioned in b.   See under *Parallelism.*

Josh. xxiv. 27.—" This stone shall be a witness unto us; for it hath heard all the words of the LORD which he spake unto us."

Judges v. 20.—" The stars in their courses fought against Sisera.'' See under *Homœopropheron.*

2 Kings iii. 19.—Here, the figure is translated :—" And shall mar every good piece of land with stones " The Heb. is *grieve.* (See A.V. marg.)

Job iii. 9.—Let the night " look for light, but have [or *see*] none ; neither let it see the dawning of the day." Heb., *the eyelids of the morning.* (See A.V. marg. and R.V. text). So xli. 18 (10).

Job xxviii. 22.—" Destruction and death say, We have heard of the fame thereof with our ears."

Job xxxi. 38.—" If my land cry against me, or that the furrows likewise thereof weep." (A.V., complain. Marg., *weep*).

Job xxxviii. 7.—" When the morning stars sang together, and all the sons of God (*i.e.,* the angels) shouted for joy." The stars are also called on to praise God in Ps. cxlviii. 3.

Ps. xix. 1 (2).—" The heavens declare the glory of God." *

Ps. lxxvii. 16 (17).—" The waters saw thee, O God, the waters saw thee ; they were afraid : the depths also were troubled." (See under *Epizeuxis*). Thus is the history of Ex. xiv., powerfully and beautifully expressed.

Ps. xcvi. 11, 12 ; xcviii. 7, 8 are beautiful examples of *Prosopopœia.* It is a figure of speech : but it emphasises the rejoicing of the whole creation of God, when Christ shall return to remove its curse, and cause its groanings to cease.

Ps. ciii. 16.—" The place thereof shall know it no more."   Compare Job vii. 10 ; viii. 18, etc.

Ps. civ. 19.—" The sun knoweth his going down." So

Song i. 6.—" The sun hath looked upon me."

Isa. iii. 26.—" Her gates shall lament and mourn ": *i.e.,* after the eastern custom. See Job i. 20 ; ii. 13.

---

* See on the whole of this wondrous Psalm, *The Witness of the Stars,* by the same author and publisher. Pages 1-6.

Isa. v. 14.—" Sheol hath enlarged herself, and opened her mouth without measure ": and this, to show the great mortality of that day.

Isa. xiv. 8.—" The fir-trees rejoice at thee."

Isa. xiv. 9-11.—Dead people in the grave are represented as speaking. And *Sheol* or the grave (margin) is represented as being moved and stirred. That it is the grave is clear from the reference to the " worms."

Isa. xxiv. 4.—" The earth mourneth." (See under *Paronomasia*). Similar examples are seen in verse 7 ; xxxiii. 9. Jer. iv. 28 ; xii. 4. Lam. ii. 8. Hos. iv. 3. Joel i. 10. Amos i. 2, etc.

Isa. xxiv. 23.—" Then the moon shall be confounded, and the sun ashamed," etc. And this, in order to emphasise the glory of the presence of the Lord.

Jer. li. 48.—" Then the heaven and the earth, and all that is therein, shall sing for Babylon " : *i.e.*, the joy over her fall shall be great and universal.

Isa. lv. 12.—" The mountains and the hills shall break forth before you into singing, and all the trees of the field shall clap their hands." And thus is emphasised the universal joy of Israel in the coming day of her glory, when Jehovah shall comfort her. So xlix. 13.

Jer. xxxi. 15.—Rachel, long since dead, is represented as weeping. So Matt. ii. 18.

Lam. i. 4.—" The ways of Zion do mourn," etc. This most elegant *Prosopopœia* graphically describes the desolation.

Ezek. xxxii. 21, 22.—Dead people are represented as speaking out of *Sheol* : *i.e.*, the grave, as is clear from the whole context.

Verses 22-32 are about those who have been slain with the sword, and are fallen and lying in their graves.

Hos. ii. 22 (24).—See also this verse under *Anaphora*, *Climax*, and *Polysyndeton ;* and compare Deut. xxviii. 23. Jer. xiv. 22, where the heavens and the earth are said to give their substance, or withhold it, by the hand of God. So Jonah i. 4.

Rom. viii. 19.—" For the earnest expectation of the creature waiteth for the manifestation of the sons of God." See under *Metonymy* (of Adjunct), *Ellipsis*, and *Epitrechon*.

Rom. ix. 2c.—" Shall the thing formed say to him that formed it, Why hast thou made me thus ? "

Rom x. 6-8.—"The righteousness which is of faith speaketh on this wise," etc.

Rev. vi. 9, 10.—The dead are represented as speaking, notwithstanding it says that they had been slain.

For, after the Church shall have been taken away, the Remnant of Israel will be dealt with and go through a "great tribulation" and suffer great persecution. Many will be martyred and "beheaded for the witness of Jesus and for the word of God which had not worshipped the beast, neither his image, neither had received his mark upon their foreheads or in their hands" (Rev. xx. 4).

In Rev. vi. 9, this time of persecution is not yet over, and those who have been slain are represented, by *Prosopopœia*, as speaking and asking, How long it would be before the earth should be judged, and their blood avenged. That this is not the language of the Church is clear; for they address the Lord as Δεσπότης (*Despotees*): *i.e.*, *Despot, Master*, esp., *a master of slaves. Despot* (see Luke ii. 29. Acts iv. 24. 2 Pet. ii. 1. Jude 4). And not as Κύριος (*Kurios*), *Lord*, as the Church always does.

They have "white robes" given to them, thus keeping up the *Prosopopœia*.

The word "souls" is put for persons by *Synecdoche* (*q.v.*).

Moreover the dead do not speak.

See Ps. cxv. 17; cxlvi. 4, etc.

v. *Kingdoms, Countries, and States.*

1. A whole people as an individual man.

Isa. i. 5, 6.—"Why should ye be stricken any more? ye will revolt more and more: the whole head is sick, and the whole heart faint. From the sole of the foot even unto the head there is no soundness in it; but wounds, and bruises, and putrifying sores." (See under *Hypotyposis*). Thus the whole Jewish nation is elegantly addressed as one man. See verses 7-9.

Careful students of the Old Testament, especially in the original, will find abundant instances of this Figure. See Isa. vii. 20; xxx. 28, etc.

2. A whole Nation is spoken of as a Man.

Lam. iii. 1 (2).—"I am the man that hath seen affliction . . . He hath led me," etc.

This is generally but wrongly taken of Christ. It is the figure by which a People is personified.

Dan. ii. 31.—"This great image . . . stood before thee."

3. A whole People or State as a Woman.

Isa. xxxii. 9-11.—" Rise up, ye women that are at ease ; " etc.

Here the whole People is addressed as a class of women. So chap. iii. 18-26. Micah vii. 8-10, etc.

Idolatrous Israel is spoken of, and to, as an adulterous woman : Jer. iii. 1, 3, 4 ; iv. 30. Ezek. xvi. and xxiii. Hos. ii. etc. This is based on such passages as Ex. xxxiv. 15, 16. Deut. xxxi. 16. Judges ii. 17. Isa. i. 21 ; lvii. 3. Nah. iii. 4. Isa. xxiii. 15-17.

4. A City spoken of as a Mother (*i.e.*, a metropolitan city).

2 Sam. xx. 19. See under *Hendiadys.*

See also for a city or People spoken of as a mother, Isa. l. 1. Hos. ii. 2. Ezek. xxiii. 2. Gal. iv. 26.

5. Cities and Villages are spoken of as Daughters.

Josh. xvii. 16. Num. xxi. 25. Judges xi. 26, etc. See esp. Josh. xv. 45, 47 ; xvii. 11, 16, 17. 1 Chron. vii. 28, 29 ; xviii. 1, 2 ; xiii. 19 ; xxviii. 18, etc.

Ps. xlv 12 (13).—" The daughter of Tyre " : *i.e.*, as explained by *Epexegesis* (*q.v.*), the rich among the peoples.

Ps. cxxxvii. 8.—The " daughter of Babylon." It is possible that the " little ones " of verse 9 may be small offshoots of Great Babylon, and not literal infants.

Lam. i. 6 ; ii. 1, etc.—The " daughter of Zion."

Lam. ii. 2.—The " daughter of Judah."

Zech. ix. 9.—" Daughter of Zion," " Daughter of Jerusalem." And elsewhere often. See Isa. i. 8 ; x. 32 ; xvi. 1 ; xxxvii. 22. Jer. iv. 31 ; vi. 2. Micah iv. 10, 13. Zeph. iii. 10, 14.

Jer. xxxi. 4, 21.—" Virgin of Israel."

So chap. xviii. 13, and Amos v. 2.

Sometimes " virgin " and " daughter " are combined. Isa. xxiii. 12 ; xxxvii. 22 ; xlvii. 1. Jer. xlvi. 11. Lam. ii. 13.

vi. *Human Actions attributed to Things, etc.*

Called SOMATOPŒIA (*Sō¹-mat-o-pœ¹-ia*). Greek σωματοποιΐα, from σωμα (*sōma*), *a body,* and ποιεῖν (*poiein*), *to make.* Hence, *to make like a body or person,* as we speak of *embodying.*

Gen. iv. 7.—" Sin lieth at the door."

See *Metonymy*, by which " sin " is put for *sin-offering*, and this sin-offering is a live animal represented as a person waiting at the door. The Hebrew רָבַץ (*rahvatz*) is specially used of animals.

Gen. xviii. 20.—" The cry of Sodom and Gomorrah is great." This is *Prosopopœia*, whereas in Jas. v. 4 we have it literally.

Gen. xxx. 33.—" So shall my righteousness answer for me in time to come."

See under *Antimereia* (of Adv.).

Ex. xviii. 8.—" All the travail that had found them."

So Gen. xliv. 34. Num. xx. 14. Deut. xxxi. 17, 21, 29. Job. xxxi. 29. Ps. cxvi. 3 ; cxix. 143.

Job xvi. 8.—" My leanness rising up in me beareth witness to my face."

Ps. lxxxv. 10 (11).—" Mercy and truth are met together; righteousness and peace have kissed each other."

Isa. lix. 12.—" Our sins testify against us."

Isa. lix. 14.—" Judgment is turned away backward, and justice standeth afar off."

Jer. xiv. 7.—" Our iniquities testify against us."

1 Cor. xiii. 4, 5, 6, 7.—Human actions are attributed to charity.

Jas. i. 15.—" When lust hath conceived, it bringeth forth sin." See under *Climax*.

Rev. xviii. 5.—" Her sins have reached unto heaven."

ANTIPROSOPOPŒIA;
or, ANTI-PERSONIFICATION.

The opposite of Prosopopœia ; Persons represented as inanimate things.

An'-ti-pros-o'-po-pœ-ia. This is the name of the former figure with ἀντί (*anti*), *opposite*, prefixed. The name is given to this figure because it is the opposite of the other: *persons being represented as things,* instead of things as persons.

2 Sam. xvi. 9.—"Then said Abishai the son of Zeruiah unto the king, Why should this dead dog curse thy lord, the king? let me go over, I pray thee, and take off his head."

A dog does not curse; still less does a "dead dog": but the vivid figure is eloquent, and stands for a whole paragraph which would be required to express literally all that the figure implies.

ANTHROPOPATHEIA;
or, CONDESCENSION.

The Ascribing of Human Attributes, etc., to God.

An-thrōp'-o-path-ei'-a. Greek, ἀνθρωποπάθεια, from ἄνθρωπος (*anthropos*), *man*, and πάθος (*pathos*), *affections* and *feelings*, etc. (from πάσχειν, *paschein*), *to suffer*).

This figure is used of the ascription of human passions, actions, or attributes to God.

The Hebrews had a name for this figure, and called it דֶּרֶךְ בְּנֵי אָדָם (*Derech Benai Adam*), *the way of the sons of man.*

The Greeks had another name for it: SYNCATABASIS (*Syn'-cat-ab'-a-sis*), from σύν (*syn*), *together with*, κατά (*kata*), *down*, and βαίνειν (*bainein*), *to go* : *a going down together with* : *i.e.*, God, by using this figure, condescends to the ignorance and infirmity of man.

Hence, the Latin name for it was CONDESCENSIO, *condescension*.

The following are the divisions in which the various uses of this figure may be presented :—

I. HUMAN AND RATIONAL BEINGS.

    1. Parts and Members of Man.
    2. The Feelings of Men.
    3. The Actions of Men.
    4. Circumstances:

        (*a*) Negative.
        (*b*) Positive.
        (*c*) Of Place.
        (*d*) Of Time.
        (*e*) Of Person.

II. IRRATIONAL CREATURES.

    1. Animals.
    2. The Actions of certain Animals.
    3. Parts or Members of certain Animals.
    4. Plants :

        (*a*) Of Genus.
        (*b*) Of Species.

III. Inanimate Things.

1. Universals.
2. Particulars.
3. The Elements.
4. The Earth.

I. Human and Rational Beings.

1. *Parts and Members of Man ; or, of the Human Body.*

A Soul is attributed to God

in condescension, so that we may understand His essence and will : *i.e.*, God Himself.

Lev. xxvi. 11.—" And I will set my tabernacle among you : and my soul shall not abhor you " : *i.e., I myself* (see under *Idiom* and *Synecdoche*).

So Ps. xi. 5. Isa. i. 14 ; xlii. 1. Jer. v. 9, 29 ; xv. 1 (rendered " mind "). Matt. xii. 18. Heb. x. 38.

Hence the expression " *to swear by one's soul*," Jer. li. 14. (See A.V. marg.) Amos vi. 8, where it is rendered, " by himself."

Lam. iii. 20.—" And thy soul will condescend to me."

This was the primitive text, and we find here one of the eighteen emendations of the Sopherim, who altered it to, " My soul is humbled in me." (See Appendix E).

Jerusalem, personified, speaks, and says (verses 19, 20) addressing God :

" Remember my misery and my forlorn state,
   The wormwood and the gall.
 Yea, verily, Thou wilt remember,
   And Thy soul will mourn over me.
 This I recall to my heart,
   Therefore I have hope."

A Body is used of Christ.

Col. ii. 17.—" Which are a shadow of things to come : but the body of Christ *is the substance* " : *i.e.*, Christ Himself, either personally (verse 9) or mystically.*

See under *Ellipsis*, and compare 1 Tim. iii. 16. Eph. i. 22, 23 ; iv. 12, 15, 16.

---

* See *The Mystery*, by the same author and publisher.

The HEAD is spoken of Christ.

1 Cor. xi. 3.—"The head of Christ is God." This is in respect to His human nature, and is spoken of Christ as man. John xiv. 28. Rom. viii. 29.

So Christ is said to be head of the Body : *i.e.*, the Mystical Body. Eph. i. 22 ; iv. 15. Col. i. 18. See 1 Cor. xii. Hence ἀνακεφαλαιώσασθαι *(anakephalaiōsasthai), to reduce to one head,* or to *head up* in Eph. i. 10.

The FACE, to signify presence.

It is used of the Divine presence in happiness and of Divine favour. Ps. xvi. 11 : " In thy face (*i.e.*, presence) is fulness of joy." So Ps. xvii. 15.

Ex. xxxiii. 20, 23.—Compare 1 Cor. xiii. 12. Jonah i. 3. Ps. li. 11 (13).

Ps. xxxi. 20 (21).—"Thou wilt hide them in the secret of thy face ": *i.e.*, of thy presence, in Divine grace and favour.

Ps. xvii. 2.—" Let my sentence come forth from thy face " : *i.e.*, Thy presence or Thyself, in righteousness and truth.

Ps. lxxxix. 15 (16).—" They will walk, O LORD, in the light of thy face ": *i.e.*, in the light of Thy presence, enjoying Thy favour and blessing.

1 Chron. xxix. 12.—" Riches and honour come from thy face " : A.V., " of Thee ": *i.e.*, from Thy grace and favour.

So Num. vi. 25, 26. Ps. iv. 6 (7); xxxi. 16 (17) ; lxxx. 3, 7, 19 (4, 8, 20). Dan. ix. 17.

Matt. xviii. 10.—" Their angels do always behold the face of my Father ": *i.e.*, enjoy or stand in His presence, which is explained by 2 Kings xxv. 19. Est. i. 14.

Hence the *hiding of God's face* meant the withholding of His grace and favour.

Ps. xiii. 1 (2) : xxvii. 9 ; xxx. 7 (8). Ezek. xxxix. 24.

It is used of the Divine presence in anger and judgment.

Ps. ix. 3 (4).—" They shall fall and perish from thy face " (*i.e.*, at Thy presence manifested in judgment).

Ps. xxi. 9 (10).—" Thou shalt make them as a fiery oven in the time of Thy face " (*i.e.*, Thy presence in judgment).

The A.V. actually renders this " anger " : but not in

Ps. xxxiv. 16.—" The face of the LORD is against them that do evil " (*i.e.*, the anger of the Lord, as in xxi. 9 and Lam. iv. 16. See A.V. marg.)

2 Thess. i. 9.—" The face of the Lord." Here, it is rendered " presence." See under *Ellipsis.* So 1 Pet. iii. 12.

It is used of Jehovah Himself, for emphasis.

Ex. xxxiii. 14, 15, as is explained in verse 16, and Isa. lxiii. 9. Ex. xxiii. 20, etc., where doubtless Christ is meant by " the angel."

So **Ex. xxiii. 15 :** " None shall appear before my face (*i.e.*, Me) empty."

Lev. xvii. 10.—" I will set my face (*i.e* , myself) against that soul." So Jer. xxi. 10.

Hence the shewbread was called *the bread of the presence* (*lit.*, the *bread of the faces*), because it was in the holy place in the manifested presence of God.

Ex. xxv. 30.—" Thou shalt set upon the table the bread of the faces (פָּנִים, *pahneem*) before me (לְפָנַי, *l'phahnai*) alway." Observe the *Paronomasia* (*q.v,*).

Ps. xxvii. 8.—" Seek ye my face ": *i.e.*, seek me.

Ps. c. 2.—" Come before his face (*i.e.*, before Him) with singing."

Ps. cv. 4.—" Seek his face (*i.e.*, Himself) evermore." So 2 Sam. xxi. 1 : " And David enquired of the Lord " : *lit., sought the face of the* LORD. (See A.V. marg.)

Ps. cxxxix. 7.—" Whither shall I flee from thy face ? " (A.V., presence) : *i.e.*, from Thee.

2 Chron. vii. 14.

Hence " *Face to face* " means great intimacy. Deut. v. 4 ; xxxiv. 10. Num. xii. 6, 7, etc., which is explained by Ex. xx. 18-21. In Num. xii. 8 we have " *mouth to mouth* " for the first time. See below.

EYES are attributed to God.

2 Sam. xvi. 22.—" The LORD will behold with his eye." This was the primitive text ; and is one of the eighteen passages altered by the Sopherim (see Appendix E) to " mine eye," which has been taken (by *Metonymy*) to stand for tears or affliction.

Zech. ii. 8 (12).—" He that toucheth you toucheth the apple of my eye." So the primitive Hebrew text read, but was altered by the Sopherim to " his eye." See Appendix E.

Eyes are used of God's observation.

Ps. xi. 4.—" His eyes behold, his eyelids try, the children of men ": *i.e.*, the Lord observeth and noteth and understandeth the acts and ways of men. See Job. xxxiv. 21 : " His eyes are upon the ways of man, and he seeth all his goings." So Isa. i. 16. Heb. iv. 13.

Hos. xiii. 14.—" Repentance shall be hid from mine eyes ": *i.e.*, I will not repent. So Rom. xi. 29.

Hence the phrase *to* " *hide from one's eyes* " means not to look upon or regard. See Isa. lxv. 16. Amos ix. 3.

Eyes are used of God's grace and favour.

Deut. xi. 12.—" The eyes of the Jehovah thy God, are always upon it ": *i.e.*, regarding the Land with Divine benevolence. So 1 Kings ix. 3. 2 Chron. xvi. 9.

Ps. xxxii. 8.—A.V.: " I will guide thee with mine eye." R.V.: " I will counsel thee with mine eye upon thee." *Lit., I cause mine eye to take counsel concerning thee: i.e.*, I will cause My Spirit to graciously to inform thee and lead thee in the right way. (See A.V. marg.)

So 1 Pet. iii. 12. See above.

Hence the phrases, " Mine eye spared them " (Ezek. xx. 17): *i.e.*, I was propitious toward them, and showed them My favour. So Ezek. v. 11 ; vii. 4.

" I am cut off from before thine eyes" (Ps. xxxi. 22): *i.e.*, I have lost Thy favour.

" To keep as the apple of the eye " (Deut. xxxii. 10).

Ears are attributed to God.

Ps. x. 17.—" Thou wilt cause thine ear to hear."

Ps. xxxi. 2 (3).—" Bow down thine ear to me."

Ps. xl. 6 (7).—" Mine ears hast thou opened or bored ": *i.e.*, Christ says, " A servant for ever hast thou made me." See margin, and compare Ex. xxi. 6 and Deut. xv. 17 ; and see under *Metonymy*.

Ps. lv. 1 (2).—" Give ear to my prayer, O God."

Ps. lxxi. 2.—" Incline thine ear unto me and save me."

Ps. cxxx. 2.—" Lord, hear my voice : let thine ears be attentive to the voice of my supplications."

Ezek. viii. 18.—" Though they cry in mine ears with a loud voice, yet will I not hear them."

Jas. v. 4.—"The cries of them which have reaped are entered into the ears of the Lord of sabaoth."

See also Isa. 1. 4, 5, where Messiah speaks.

NOSTRILS are attributed to God.

Ex. xv. 8.—"With the blast of thy nostrils the waters were gathered together."

Job iv. 9.—"By the breath of his nostrils are they consumed." The A.V. margin says "That is, *by his anger*," as Isa. xxx. 33. See Ex. xv. 8.

Deut. xxxiii. 10.—"They shall put (or let them put) incense to thy nose." A.V. and R.V., "before thee." (But see A.V. marg.)

Ps. xviii. 15.—"At the blast of the breath of thy nostril."

Ezek. viii. 17.—"Lo, they put the branch (the Asherah) to my nose." So the Heb. Text originally read, but was altered by the Sopherim, "to their nose." See Appendix E.

A MOUTH and LIPS and a TONGUE are attributed to God,
in connection with His will, His word,
His commands, etc.

Num. xii. 8.—"With him (Moses) will I speak mouth to mouth": *i.e.*, familiarly, and with really audible words.

Deut. viii. 3.—"By every word that proceedeth out of the mouth of Jehovah doth man live." So Matt. iv. 4.

Josh. ix. 14.—"And the men took of their victuals, and asked not counsel at the mouth of the LORD."

Job xi. 5.—"Oh that God would speak and open his lips against thee."

Isa. xi. 4.—"He shall smite the earth with the rod of his mouth, and with the breath of his lips shall he slay the wicked." This is quoted of Christ in 2 Thess. ii. 8.

Isa. xxx. 27.—"His lips are full of indignation, and his tongue as a devouring fire."

Isa. lv. 11.—"So shall my word be that goeth forth out of my mouth."

A VOICE is attributed to God.

Isa. xxx. 30.—"Jehovah shall cause the glory of His voice to be heard": *i.e.*, as in A.V. and R.V., "his glorious voice," thus interpreting and rendering the *Hypallage* (*q.v.*). See Ps. xxix.

ARMS are attributed to God, to indicate His strength and power, which in men lies so largely in the arms.

Ex. xv. 16. Job xl. 9.—"Hast thou an arm like God?"

Ps. lxxvii. 15 (16).—"Thou hast with thine arm redeemed thy people." (So Ex. vi. 6. Deut. ix. 29. Ps. cxxxvi. 12).

Ps. lxxix. 11.—"According to the greatness of thine arm." Here, the A.V. and R.V. both actually render it "thy power' (marg. *thine arm*).

Ps. lxxxix. 10 (11).—"Thou hast scattered thine enemies with the arm of thy strength." So R.V. But A.V., "with thy strong arm" (see margin).

Isa. li. 9.—"Awake, awake, put on strength, O arm of the LORD." See also under *Epizeuxis*.

Isa. lix. 16.—"Therefore his arm brought salvation." So lxiii. 5.

Isa. lxii. 8.—"Jehovah hath sworn by his right hand, and by the arm of his strength": *i.e.*, by His strong arm, or, His strength.

Luke i. 51.—"He hath shewed strength with his arm."

Ps. lxxxix. 13 (14).—"Thou hast an arm with might" (see A.V. and R.V. margin).

Here A.V. and R.V. both render it "a mighty arm."

Isa. xxx. 30.—Jehovah "shall shew the lighting down of his arm." Here His voice is used of thunder, and His arm denotes His lightning.

The ARM of the Lord not only denotes power, but power executed in judgment.

See Ps. cxxxvi. 12.

The ARM of the Lord is also used of the making known of His grace in wondrous power.

Isa. lii. 10.—"Jehovah hath made bare His holy arm in the eyes of all the nations." Verses 7, 8 clearly show that this was His power manifested in grace to Israel.

Isa. liii. 1.—"Who hath believed our report (see *Metonymy* of Adjunct)? and to whom is the arm of Jehovah revealed?"

Compare John xii. 38 and Rom. i. 16.

A HAND is attributed to God, by which various powers and actions are indicated

POWER AND MIRACULOUS OPERATION.

Num. xi. 23.—"Is Jehovah's hand waxed short?" *i.e.*, has His power got less? So Isa. lix. 1.

Job x. 8.—"Thine hands have made me and fashioned me."

Job xii. 9.—"The hand of Jehovah hath wrought this."

Job xii. 10.—"In whose hand is the life of every living thing."

Ps. viii. 6 (7).—"Thou madest him to have dominion over the works of thy hands."

Ps. xcv. 5.—"His hands formed the dry land."

Isa. xi. 11.—"The Lord (Adonai) shall set His hand again the second time to recover the remnant of His People."

PURPOSE.

Acts iv. 28.—"To do whatsoever thy hand and thy counsel determined before to be done."

PROTECTION, gracious deliverance, and security.

Ps. xxxi. 5 (6).—"Into thine hand I commit my spirit."

Ps. cxliv. 7.—"Send thine hand from above: rid me, and deliver me out of great waters." See under *Heterosis*.

John x. 28.—"Neither shall any pluck them out of my hand."

John x. 29.—"None can pluck them out of my Father's hand."

Acts iv. 30.—"By stretching forth thine hand to heal."

PROVIDENCE.

Ps. civ. 28.—"Thou openest thine hand, they are filled with good."

Ps. cxlv. 16.—"Thou openest thine hand, and satisfiest the desire of every living thing."

PROSPERING.

Neh. ii. 8.—"The king granted me, according to the good hand of my God upon me."

Neh. ii. 18.—"Then I told them of the hand of my God which was good upon me."

So Ezra vii. 6, 9, 28 ; viii. 18.

PRESERVATION.

John x. 28.—"Neither shall any man pluck them out of my hand." And verse 29 : "No man is able to pluck them out of my Father's hand."

PUNISHMENT.

Ex. ix. 3.—"Behold the hand of the LORD is upon thy cattle," etc.

Job xix. 21.—"The hand of God (Eloah) hath touched me." (See under *Tapeinosis*).

Ps. xxi. 8 (9).—"Thine hand shall find out all thine enemies," etc.

Ps. xvii. 14.—"From men which are thy hand, O Jehovah " (marg., *from men by thine hand.* Compare R.V.) : *i.e.*, "from the men who are instruments in Thy hand, O Jehovah."

Ps. xxxviii. 2 (3).—"Thy hand presseth me sore."

Acts xiii. 11.—"And now, behold, the hand of the Lord is upon thee."

Ezek. xxxix. 21.—"All the heathen shall see my judgment that I have executed, and my hand that I have laid upon them."

So Job (xxiii. 2) uses the word "hand," by *Metonymy*, for his punishment. "My hand (*i.e.*, punishment) is heavier than my groaning." (See A.V. marg.).

See xxvii. 11. Hence the

IDIOMATIC EXPRESSIONS.

" *To stretch forth the hand* " : *i.e.*, to send judgments upon. Ex. vii. 5. Ps. cxxxviii. 7. Isa. v. 25 ; ix. 12, 17, 21 ; x. 4 ; xiv. 27 ; xxxi. 3. Jer. vi. 12. Ezek. xvi. 27 ; xxv. 7. Zeph. i. 4 ; ii. 13.

" *To put forth the hand* ": *i.e.*, to inflict punishment. Job i. 11 ; ii. 5.

" *To shake the hand.*" Isa. xix. 16.

" *To make the hand heavy* " : *i.e.*, to make the chastisement severe. Ps. xxxii. 4.

" *To make the hand light* ": *i.e.*, to reduce the chastisement. 1 Sam. vi. 5.

" *To withdraw the hand* " : *i.e.*, to take away the punishment. Ezek. xx. 22.

"*To turn the hand upon* " : *i.e.*, to repeat the punishment. Isa. i. 25.

Jehovah asks why this should be in verse 5.

" *To lift up or spread out the hand* " : *i.e.*, to call for the receiving of mercy, or invite to receive. Prov. i. 24. Isa. xlix. 22 ; lxv. 2.

" *To open the hand* " : *i.e.*, to bestow or give bountifully. See Ps. civ. 28 ; cxlv. 16 above.

"*To clap or smite the hands together* " : *i.e.*, to express derision or disdainful anger Ezek. xxi. 17 ; xxii 13.

" *To lift up the hand* " : *i.e.*, to swear solemnly.

Ex vi. 8 (margin). Deut. xxxii. 40. Ezek. xx. 5, 6 ; xxxvi. 7, etc. (See also Gen. xiv. 22). This explains the difficult verse Ex. xvii. 16. See the Text and margins of A.V. and R.V. There is the *Ellipsis* of the verb which is clearly understood from the idiom, thus " Surely the hand is [lifted up] on the banner of Jehovah." So that the A.V. is quite correct in sense : " The LORD hath sworn." (See Ginsburg's *Introduction to the Hebrew Bible*, page 382, 383).

" *The hand of the Lord upon* " a man denoted also the power of the prophetic spirit.

1 Kings xviii. 46. 2 Kings iii. 15. Ezek. i. 3 ; viii. 1 ; xxxiii. 22.

A RIGHT HAND is attributed to God ; to denote the highest power, and most Divine authority.

Ex. xv. 6, 12. Ps. lxxvii. 10 (11) ; cxviii. 15, 16 ; cxxxix. 10. Isa. xlviii. 13.

It denotes also His grace and mercy in delivering and saving His people.

Ps. xviii. 35 (36) ; xx. 6 (7) (margin) ; xliv. 3 (4) ; lxiii. 8 (9) ; lxxx. 15, 17 (16, 18).

It is used also of the place accorded to Christ in His human nature as now exalted.

Ps. cx. 1. Matt. xxvi. 64. Mark xvi. 19. Acts ii. 33, 34 ; vii. 55, 56. Rom. viii. 34. Col. iii. 1, etc. Eph. i. 20-22. Heb. i. 3, 4 ; viii. 1.

So Christ's dignity is further described by the figure THEOPREPŌS, *worthy of a god.* 1 Cor. xv. 25. Eph. iv. 10, etc.

A FINGER is attributed to God, to denote the putting forth of
His formative power, and the direct and immediate
act of God.

Ex. viii. 19; xxxi. 18. Ps. viii. 3 (4). So Luke xi. 20, by which,
according to Matt. xii. 28, the Spirit of God is meant.

Isa. xl. 12 (a span of the fingers). See xlviii. 13.

A HEART is attributed to God.

Gen. vi. 6; viii. 21. Jer. xix. 5 (6). 1 Sam. xiii. 14: "A man after
his own heart": *i.e.*, His own Divine and eternal purpose; having
regard, not to David's worthiness or unworthiness, but to *God's* own
will. So Acts xiii. 22. See also Jer. xxxii. 41.

BOWELS are attributed to God; to denote His mercies and
His pity.

All these figures of *Anthropopatheia* are figures of *Metonomy*, by
which one thing is put for another. Here, because, when a person is
much moved by deep feeling, there is a movement of the bowels, so
they are put, by *Metonymy*, for the feeling itself.

Isa. lxiii. 15.—"Where is thy zeal and thy strength, the
sounding of thy bowels and of thy mercies towards me?" So Jer.
xxxi. 20.

Luke i. 78.—"Through the bowels of the mercy of our God."
(See A.V. margin). Here it is translated, "through the tender mercy
of our God."

Matt ix. 36.—"He was moved with compassion": *lit.*, his bowels
moved. So xiv. 14; xv. 32. Mark i. 41; vi. 34, etc. (See also Gen.
xliii. 30. 1 Kings iii. 26. And compare this as attributed to God,
Ps. li. 1 (3): "The multitude of thy tender mercies.") So Isa. lxiii. 7.

A BOSOM is attributed to God; to denote comfort and rest.

Ps. lxxiv. 11 (the hand in the bosom denoting ease, according to
Prov. xix. 24 and xxvi. 15).

Isa. xl. 11. John i. 18 ("In the bosom of the Father"). Num. xi.
12.

FEET are attributed to God; to denote His presence in the earth,
in power, in universal dominion.

Isa. lxvi. 1. Ps. lxxiv. 3; cx. 1. Isa. lx. 13. In this respect the
earth is spoken of as His "footstool."

Footsteps are also attributed to God.

Ps. lxxvii. 19 (20) ; lxxxix. 51 (52).

2. Human Affections *and* Feelings *are attributed to God.*

Human affections and feelings are attributed to God : not that He has such feelings ; but, in infinite condescension, He is thus spoken of in order to enable us to comprehend Him.

Rejoicing is attributed to God.

Ps. civ. 31.—" The Lord shall rejoice in his works." So Isa. lxii. 5. Deut. xxviii. 63 ; xxx. 9. Jer. xxxii. 41, etc.

Sorrow and Grief are attributed to God.

Gen. vi. 6.—" It grieved him at his heart."

Judges x. 16.—" His soul was grieved for the misery of Israel."

Ps. lxxviii. 40.—" How oft did they provoke him in the wilderness, and grieve Him in the desert ! "

Isa. lxiii. 10.—" They rebelled, and vexed his holy Spirit." So Eph. iv. 30.

See Zech. xi. 8. Ezek. vi. 9.

Repentance is attributed to God.

Gen. vi. 6.—" It repented Jehovah that he had made man on the earth."

So Ex. xxxii. 12, 14. 2 Sam. xxiv. 16. Ps. cvi. 45. Jer. xviii. 8 ; xxvi. 3. Hos. xi. 8. Amos vii. 3, 6. Joel ii. 13, 14.

Anger, Vengeance, and Hatred are attributed to God.

Ex. xv. 7.—" Thou sentest forth thy wrath."

Ps. v. 5 (6).—" Thou hatest all workers of iniquity."

Isa. i. 14.—" Your new moons and your appointed feasts my soul hateth."

Isa. i. 24.—"I will . . . avenge me of mine enemies."

Jer. ix. 9.—" Shall not my soul be avenged on such a nation as this ? "

Nah. i. 2.—" God (El) is jealous, and Jehovah revengeth ; the Lord revengeth, and is furious : the Lord will take vengeance on his adversaries, and he reserveth wrath for his enemies."

So Ezek. v. 13.   Ps. ii. 12 ;   lxxxv. 5 (6).   Deut. i. 37 ;   xxxii. 16. 1 Kings xi. 9.

COMFORT is spoken of God.

Isa. lvii. 6.—" Should I receive comfort in these ? "

Ezek. v. 13.—" And I will be comforted."

JEALOUSY.

Ex. xx. 5.—" For I the LORD thy God am a jealous* God (*El*)."

Num. xxv. 11.—" That I consumed not the children of Israel in my jealousy."

Deut. xxxii. 16.—" They provoked him to jealousy with strange gods."   So in verse 21, and in 1 Kings xiv. 22.   Isa. ix. 7 (6).   Ezek. viii. 3. Joel ii. 18.

Zech. i. 14.—" I am jealous for Jerusalem and for Zion with a great jealousy."   See also under *Polyptoton*.

ZEAL.

Isa. ix. 7 (6).—" The zeal of the Lord of hosts will perform this."

DISPLEASURE.

Zech. i. 15.—" I am very sore displeased with the heathen that are at ease : for I was but a little displeased, and they helped forward the affliction."

PITY.

Joel ii. 18.—" Then will Jehovah . . . pity His People."

3. HUMAN ACTIONS *are attributed to God.*

KNOWING.   Not actual knowledge as such, but the acquiring of knowledge as though before ignorant.

Gen. xviii. 21.—" I will go down now, and see whether they have done altogether according to the cry of it,† which is come unto me; and if not, I will know."

---

* It is noteworthy that קָבָא (*kabah*) out of its six occurrences, is, in five, connected with אֵל (*El*), *God*.

† The *Severus Codex* reads ם for ה : *i e., their cry*, instead of " the cry of it." See Ginsburg's *Introduction to the Hebrew Bible*, page 412.

Gen. xxii. 12.—" Now I know that thou fearest God, seeing thou hast not withheld thy son, thine only son from me."

God, of course, knew it already; but, in wondrous condescension, He stoops to make Abraham understand.

Deut. viii. 2.—" The LORD thy God led thee, etc. . . . to know what was in thine heart." So xiii. 3 (4). The Lord knew already : " For He knoweth the way of the righteous " (Ps. i. 6; xxxi. 7 (8). 2 Tim. ii. 19).

Ps. xiv. 2.—" The LORD looked down from heaven upon the children of men, to see (*i e.*, to know) if there were any that did understand," etc.

So Ps. liii. 2 (3). (See also this verse under *Epanadiplosis*).

The very action of our prayer to God involves an *Anthropopatheia*. God knows all our petitions before we pray. And yet we have to pray as though we were making them known to Him. Phil. iv. 6.

NOT KNOWING, the opposite of knowledge, is attributed to God.

Gen. iii. 9.—" The LORD God called unto Adam, and said unto him, Where art thou?" This implies ignorance. The Lord knew ; but the question is put to make Adam know and realise his changed condition.

Gen. iv. 9.—" Where is Abel thy brother ? "

These first two Divine questions in the Bible are very significant. See under *Erotesis*.

Num. xxii. 9.—" What men are these with thee ? "

1 Kings xix. 9, 13.—" What doest thou here, Elijah ? " So 2 Kings xx. 14, 15. Isa. xxxix. 3, 4.

To this figure must be referred the passages which represent God as doubting, or having to wait to see certain results.

Ezek. xx. 8. Hos. xi. 8, 9.

Also when God tries, or proves, or searches, it is not that He does not know, but that He may make others know.

Ps. vii. 9 (10).—" The righteous God trieth the hearts and reins." (See *Metonymy* of subject).

So Jer. xi. 20. Rev. ii. 23. 1 Cor. ii. 10.

So Christ declares that He will say :

Matt. vii. 23 : " I never knew you "; xxv. 12 : " I know you not." Luke xiii. 25, 27.

The questions of Christ in the New Testament are to be referred to the same Figure.

Matt. xxii. 20.—" Whose is this image and superscription ? "

Also verse 45 : " If David then call him Lord, how is he his son ? "

Luke viii. 45.—" Who touched me ? "

REMEMBERING.

Gen. viii. 1.—" And God remembered Noah." So xxx. 22. 1 Sam. i. 11, 19.

Gen. ix. 15, 16, and **Ex. vi. 5,** where God speaks of remembering His covenant. So Ps. cv. 8, 42 * ; cvi. 45 : " He remembered for them His covenant," though " they (verse 13) soon forgat His works," and (verse 21) " they forgat God their saviour."

It denotes specially a remembrance for good. As in Ps. xxv. 6, 7 ; lxxviii. 39; cxv. 12; cxix. 49 ; cxxxvi. 13. Isa. xliii. 25. Rev. xviii. 5.

Ex. ii. 24.—" And God remembered his covenant with Abraham, with Isaac, and with Jacob." See this passage under the figures *Synonymia, Anaphora, Polysyndeton,* and *Metonymy* (of the Cause).

1 Sam. i. 11.—" If thou wilt . . . remember me and not forget thine handmaid." See under *Pleonasm.*

1 Sam. i. 19.—" And the LORD remembered her." There is *Hypocatastasis* here ; for it is implied that He heard Hannah's prayer (verse 9), and did according to her request.

Ps. lxxviii. 39.—" He remembered that they were but flesh." This stands in solemn contrast with verse 42 : " They remembered not His hand."

Ps. ciii. 14.—" He knoweth our frame; he remembereth that we are dust." This is the one thing that man will not do: he will not remember our *infirmities.* Man will remember our *sins ;* but these are the very things that God will not remember (Isa. xliii. 25). Infinite in power, He remembers our weakness. Perfect in holiness, He will not remember our sins.

This remembrance, though in mercy to His people, involves the punishment of their enemies.

See Ps. cxxxvii. 7. Rev. xviii. 5.

---

* See the Structure of this Psalm in *A Key to the Psalms,* by the same author and publisher.

Forgetting and Not Forgetting is also attributed to God.

Ps. ix. 18 (19).—" For the needy shall not alway be forgotten."

Ps. xiii. 1 (2).—" How long wilt thou forget me, O Jehovah."

Ps. xlii. 9 (10).—" I will say unto God (El) my rock, Why hast thou forgotten me ? "

Isa. xlix. 15.—" Yet will I not forget thee."

Jer. xxiii. 39.—" I, even I, will utterly forget you, and I will forsake you " : *i.e.*, the false prophets, who would say " the burden of the Lord."

Hos. iv. 6.—" I will also forget thy children." (See under *Metonymy* of Cause.)

Luke xii. 6.—" Not one of them is forgotten before God."

When God says He will not forget His enemies, it means that their punishment is certain, and will not be indefinitely deferred.

Job xi. 6.—" Know therefore that God causeth to be forgotten for thee of thine iniquity."

The A.V. and R.V. both render this " God exacteth of thee *less* than thine iniquity *deserveth* " : where two words have to be supplied through not seeing the Figure, which denotes that " God (Eloah) causeth the punishment of thine iniquity to be deferred." The Heb. is : " He constantly lendeth to thee " : *i.e.*, crediteth thee like a lenient creditor.

Ps. lxxiv. 23.—" Forget not the voice of thine enemies " : *i.e.*, do not defer their punishment.

Amos viii. 7.—" I will never forget any of their works " : *i.e.*, I will surely remember them and punish them for them.

Thinking.

Gen. 1. 20.—" Ye thought (*i.e.*, devised) evil against me : but God thought it for good."

Ps. xl. 5 (6).—" The thoughts which are to usward : they cannot be reckoned up in order unto thee."

Ps. xcii. 5 (6).—" O Lord, how great are thy works ! and thy thoughts are very deep."

Ps. cxxxix. 17.—" How precious also are thy thoughts unto me, O God " (El).

Isa lv. 8.—These words may be presented according to their structure. (See under *Epanodos*).

a | For my thoughts are not
    b | your thoughts, neither are
    b | your ways
a | My ways, saith the LORD (Jehovah).

Jer. xxix. 11.—" I know the thoughts that I think toward you, saith Jehovah, thoughts of peace, and not of evil, to give you an expected end." (See this verse also under *Metonymy* of Adjunct and *Hendiadys*).

So Jer. li. 12 ; iv. 28, etc.

HISSING.

Isa. v. 26.—" He will lift up an ensign to the nations from far, and will hiss unto them from the end of the earth." (See under *Hypotyposis*).

Isa. vii. 18.—" Jehovah shall hiss for the fly that is in the uttermost parts of the rivers of Egypt," etc.

Zech. x. 8.—" I will hiss for them ; and gather them, for I have redeemed them."

BREATHING.

Gen. ii. 7.—" The LORD God formed man of the dust of the ground, and breathed into his nostrils the breath of life ; and man became a living soul."*

Compare Ezek. xxi. 31 (36), and John xx. 21.

LAUGHING.

Ps. ii. 4.—" He that sitteth in the heavens shall laugh: the Lord (Adonai†) shall have them in derision."

Ps. xxxvii. 13.—" Adonai† shall laugh at him : for he seeth that his day is coming." (See under *Metonymy* of Adjunct).

CRYING OUT.

Isa. xlii. 13.—" He shall cry, yea, roar; he shall prevail against his enemies." And verse 14 : " Now will I cry like a travailing woman."

Compare Ps. lxxviii. 65.

---

* Or " living creature," as in chap. i. 20, 21, 24, 30.

† Or " Jehovah," according to another reading.

SPEAKING, by way of discourse or command.

See Gen. i. 3; ii. 16; iii. 9; vi. 13, to Noah. Gen. xii. 1; xiii. 14; xv.-18, to Abraham. Ex. iii. 4, 5, etc., to Moses.

These instances occur so frequently that a great part of the Bible would have to be transcribed if we gave them all.

STANDING.

Gen. xviii. 22.—" But the LORD stood yet before Abraham."

This was the primitive Text; but it is one of the eighteen passages altered by the *Sopherim* to remove the harshness of the *Anthropopatheia*. (See Appendix E).

SITTING.

Mal. iii. 3.

SEEING.

Gen. i. 4, 10, 12, 18, 21, 25; xvi. 13: Ex. ii. 25; xxxii. 9. 1 Sam. xvi. 8. Ps. xi. 4.

HEARING.

Gen. xvi. 11. Ex. ii. 24. So Ps. iv. 3; v. 1, 2, 3: x. 17; lxvi. 18; cxxx. 2. Isa. lxv. 24. 1 John v. 14.

SMELLING.

Gen. viii. 21. Ex. xxix. 18, 25, 41. Lev. i. 9; ii. 12; iii. 16; viii. 21. Num. xxviii. 2. Ezek. xx. 28, 41, etc. So New Test.: 2 Cor. ii. 15. Eph. v. 2. Phil. iv. 18.

TASTING and TOUCHING.

Ps. civ. 32; cxliv. 5. Hos. ix. 4. Jer. i. 9. John iv. 32, 34.

WALKING.

Lev. xxvi. 12, 24, 28. Deut. xxiii. 14 (15). 2 Cor. vi. 16.

RIDING.

Deut. xxxiii. 26. Ps. xviii. 10 (11); lxviii. 33 (34). Isa. xix. 1.

MEETING.

Num. xxiii. 4, 16.

RETURNING.

Hos. v. 15.

Rising up.

Num. x. 35. Ps. xii. 5 (6); xliv. 26 (27); lxviii. 1 (2); cii. 13 (14). Isa. ii. 19, 21; xxxiii. 10.

Passing through.

Ex. xii. 12, 23. Amos v. 17.

Begetting.

Ps. ii. 7. Heb. i. 5. So, those who believe, are said to be begotten by God. Ps. xxii. 31 (32); lxxxvii. 4-6. See especially 1 John ii. 29; iii. 9, etc.

Washing.

Ps. li. 2 (4). Isa. iv. 4. Ezek. xxxvi. 25.

Hiding,

for protection and defence. Ps. xxxi. 20 (21) (See *Metonymy*); lxiv. 2 (3); xci. 1.

Wiping,

in judgment. 2 Kings xxi. 13 (See *Polyptoton*); and in mercy, Isa. xxv. 8. Rev. vii. 17.

Girding.

Ps. xviii. 32 (33); xxx. 11 (12); xlv. 3 (4).

Building.

Gen. ii. 22 (marg.). Ps. xxviii. 5: "Because they regard not the works (פֹּעַל *poal* = *contrivance*) of Jehovah, nor the operation (מַעֲשֵׂה *ma'aseh* = *the actual execution*) of his hands."
So Jer. xlii. 10. 2 Sam. vii. 27.

Binding up.

Job v. 18. Ps. cxlvii. 3. Isa. lxi. 1. Hos. vi. I.

Opening doors, windows, etc.

Ps. lxxviii. 23. Deut. xxviii. 12. Mal. iii. 10.

Proving and Trying.

Ps. xvii. 3; lxvi. 10. Zech. xiii. 9. Mal. iii. 3 (compare Ezek. xxii. 18-22).

Breaking.

Ps. ii. 9; iii. 7 (8). Isa. xxxviii. 13 (compare Ps. xxii. 16 (17) under *Paronomasia*); xlv. 2.

Sifting.

Amos ix. 9.

Blotting out.

Ex. xxxii. 32, 33 (compare under *Aposiopesis*). Ps. li. 1 (3).

Eating, or Swallowing.

Ex. xv 7. Isa. xxv. 7, 8 (compare 1 Cor. xv. 54).

Enlarging.

Gen. xxvi. 22. Ps. iv. 1 (2).

Making a straight way.

Ps. v. 8 (9). Isa. xlv. 2, 13 (marg.).

Pouring out.

Ps. lxxix. 6. Ezek. ix. 8; xx. 13, 21, 33. Hence the pouring out (*i.e.*, giving the gifts of) the Spirit in abundant measure. Joel ii. 28, 29 (iii. 1, 2). Zech. xii. 10. Acts ii. 17, 18, 33. Rom. v. 5. Tit. iii. 5, 6.

Loosening the loins.

Isa. xlv. 1.

Wounding the head.

Ps. cx. 6.

Breaking forth.

2 Sam. v. 20; vi. 8.

Shooting with arrows.

Ps. lxiv. 7 (8) (compare verses 3, 4 (4, 5)).

Writing.

Ex. xxxi. 18. xxxii. 16. Deut. ix. 10. Isa. iv. 3. Dan. xii. 1. So Jer. xxxi. 33. Heb. viii. 10.

Fanning.

Jer. xv. 7. So Matt. iii. 12. Luke iii. 17.

Sweeping.

Isa. xiv. 24.

Cutting off the Spirit.

Ps. lxxvi. 12 (13).

ANOINTING.

Ps. xxiii. 5 : xcii. 10 (11). 2 Cor. i. 21.

4. CIRCUMSTANCES *are attributed to God.*

Circumstances are attributed to God, and may be divided into five classes :—

(*a*) *Negative* (when, by *Anthropopatheia*, He is represented as not being able to do anything),

(*b*) *Positive*,

(*c*) As to *place*,

(*d*) As to *time*, and

(*e*) As to *person*.

(*a*) *Negative*.

Gen. xxxii. 28 (29).—"As a prince hast thou power with God . . . and hast prevailed." So Hos. xii. 3, 4 (4, 5).

Ex. xxxii. 10. " Now therefore let me alone, that my wrath may wax hot against them."

Isa. i. 13.—"I am not able to endure " (A.V., " I cannot away with.") See under *Ellipsis* and *Idioma*.

Ps. cvi. 23.—" He said that he would destroy them, had not Moses his chosen stood before him in the breach, to turn away his wrath, lest he should destroy them."

Ezek. xxiii. 18.—" Like as my mind was alienated from her sister."

(*b*) *Positive*.

When God or Christ is spoken of as a HUSBANDMAN (*i.e.*, by *Synecdoche*), or a VINEDRESSER. See Isa. v. 1-9. John xv. Matt. xx. 1-16, etc.

As a BUILDER. Heb. ii. 4 ; xi. 10.

As a WARRIOR. Ex. xv. 3. Ps. xlv. 3-5 (4 6) ; xlvi. 8, 9 (9, 10) ; lxxvi., etc.

As a COUNSELLOR. Isa. ix. 6 (5).

As a PHYSICIAN. Ex. xv. 26. Ps. cxlvii 3.

As a SHEPHERD. Ps. xxiii. Ezek. xxxiv. 23 ; xxxvii. 24. Micah v. 4 (3) ; vii. 14. Zech. xiii. 7. John x. 11. Heb. xiii. 20. 1 Pet. ii. 25 ; v. 4.

As a FATHER.   Deut. xxxii. 6.   Ps. lxviii. 5, 6.   Isa. lxiv. 8 (7).
Matt. vi. 1, 6, 8, 9.   Rom. viii. 15.   Heb. xii. 5-10.

As a KING, PRINCE, etc.   Isa. ix. 6 (5); lv. 4; xxxii. 1; xxxiii. 22,
etc.

As a SPOUSE.   Matt. ix. 15; xxv. 1.   Mark ii. 19.   Luke v. 34.
John iii. 29.

As a WITNESS.   Isa. xliii. 10; lv. 4.   Jer. xxix. 23.   Mal. iii. 5.
Rev. i. 5; iii. 14.   John xviii. 37.

(c) As to *Place.*

When God is spoken of being in circumstances which have to do
with *Place* and *Time* as men are—

Heaven is his dwelling place.   1 Kings viii. 39, 43, etc.   Ps. ii. 4;
xxiv. 3.   Isa. xxvi. 21.   Micah i. 3.

He *returns* to his place.   Hos. v. 15.

He sits on *a throne.*   Ps. xi. 4; xlvii. 8 (9); ciii. 19.   Isa. lxvi. 1.
Jer. xiv. 21.   Matt. v. 34.

Christ, also in the dignity of His human nature, is spoken of as
having a throne.   Ps. xlv. 6.   Isa. xvi. 5.   Matt. xix. 28.   Heb. i. 8;
iv. 16; viii. 1.   Rev. iii. 21.

Also as having a *footstool*—the earth.   Isa. lxvi. 1.   Matt. v. 35,
etc.   The Ark of the Covenant is spoken of as His footstool.
1 Chron. xxviii. 2.   Ps. xcix. 5; cxxxii. 7.   Lam. ii. 1.

Also as having all enemies under His feet.   Ps. cx. 1.   1 Cor. xv.
25.   Heb. i. 13, denoting the completeness of their subjection.
Ps. viii. 6 (7).   Eph. i. 22.   Heb. ii. 8, etc.

As *standing afar off.*   Ps. x. 1.

As *standing at the right hand of His People.*   Ps. xvi. 8.   Acts ii. 25.

As *sitting upon the flood,* or at the flood.   Ps. xxix. 10.

As *sitting upon the Cherubim.*   Ps. lxxx. 1 (2); xcix. 1.

As *sitting* upon the circle (*i.e.,* the horizon) of the earth, and the
arch of heaven, as it appears to us.   Isa. xl. 22: *i.e.,* high above all.

As *dwelling in the sanctuary.* · Ps. lxviii. 17 (18).   Lit., according to
the primitive orthography: "The Lord hath come from Sinai into the
Sanctuary."   In *Zion,* Ps. cxxxii. 13, 14; cxxxv. 21.   In *the humble
and contrite heart,* Isa. lvii. 15.   *With His People,* Ezek. xxxvii 27.
John xiv. 23.   2 Cor. vi. 16.   In *the thick darkness,* 1 Kings viii. 12.

In the *Shechina*, Lev. xvi. 2. Ex. xiii. 21, 22 ; xvi. 10. Num. ix. 15. Isa. vi. 4. Matt. xvii. 5.

(*d*) As to *Time*.

Years are attributed to God. Ps. cii. 24, 27 (25, 28). (Heb. i. 12). Job xxxvi. 26.

Days. Dan vii. 9. Mic. v. 2 (1) (see the Heb.). 2 Pet. iii. 18 (see the Greek). Heb. xiii. 8.

Christ is said to be the "*first-born*" as to time. Rom. viii. 29. Col. i. 15, 18. Heb. i. 6.*

(*e*) As to *Circumstances* connected with the person.

Arms are attributed to God : *i.e.*, weapons of war. Ps. xxxv. 2, 3. Isa. lix. 17, 18. Jer. l. 25 ; li. 20.

Bow and Arrow. Ps. xxi. 12 (13). Lam. ii. 4 ; iii. 12, 13. Deut. xxxii. 23, 42. Job vi. 4. Ps. xxxviii. 2 (3) ; lxiv. 7 (8). Zech. ix. 14.

The Arrows of God. Ps. xviii. 14 (15) ; cxliv. 6. Hab. iii. 11.

Sword. Deut. xxxii. 41. Judges vii. 20. Ps. xvii. 13. Isa. xxvii. 1 ; xxxiv. 5, 6. Ezek. xxi. 9 (14). Zech. xiii. 7.

Spear. Hab. iii. 11.

Shield or Buckler. Gen. xv. 1. Deut. xxxiii. 29. Ps. iii. 3 (4) ; xviii. 2 (3) ; xxviii. 7 ; lxxxiv. 11 (12). (See under *Metaphor*.)

Chariots are attributed to God. Ps. lxviii. 17 (18). 2 Kings vi. 16, 17.

Clouds are represented as His chariots. Ps. xviii. 10, 11 (11, 12) ; civ. 3. Isa. xix. 1.

Riches. Prov. viii. 18. Rom. ii. 4 ; ix. 23 ; x. 12 ; xi. 33. 2 Cor. viii. 9. Eph. i. 7, 18 ; ii. 4, 7 ; iii. 8, 16. Col. i. 27. Phil. iv. 19.

An Inheritance is attributed to God. Deut. xxxii. 9. Jer. ii. 7 ; xii. 7, 8.

A Book is attributed to God.

> *A book of providence and of grace* (Ps. cxxxix. 16) which may be applied to the new birth of the members of the body of Christ.

A Book of Life. Ex. xxxii. 32, 33 (compare verse 10). Num. xi. 15. Ps. lvi. 8 (9) ; lxix. 28 (29). Isa. iv. 3. Dan. xii. 1. Mal. iii. 16. Phil. iv. 3. Rev. iii. 5 ; xiii. 8 ; xvii. 8 ; xx. 12, 15 ; xxi. 7.

---

* See article, "Word," in Bullinger's *Lexicon and Concordance*. Longmans.

A Book of Judgment. Dan. vii. 10. Rev. xx. 12.

Oil or *Anointing* is attributed to God (Ps. xlv. 7 (8). Heb. i. 9) which may apply to the Holy Spirit. Isa. lxi. 1. Acts x. 38 The word "Christ" means *anointed*, both in its Hebrew form מָשִׁיחַ, *Messiah,* and its Greek form χριστός, *christos.* See Ps. ii. 2. Dan. ix. 25, 26. John i. 41 (42); iv. 25.

"Christians" are therefore only those who are thus anointed by the Holy Spirit. 2 Cor. i. 21. 1 John ii. 20, 27. Acts xi. 26.

Bread is attributed to God. Num. xxviii. 2 (see *Synecdoche*). John vi. 35, 48.

A Seal is attributed to God. Jer. xxii. 24. Hag. ii. 23.

Treasure is attributed to God. In a good sense, Deut. xxviii. 12; and in judgment, Deut. xxxii. 34, 35, which is referred to in Rom. ii. 5, 9, 10.

Out of this He brings *Arms,* Jer. l. 25; and *Winds,* Ps. cxxxv. 7. Jer. x. 13; li. 16.

Spiritual blessings are also said to be in the Divine treasuries. Isa. xxxiii. 6. Matt. vi. 20; xix. 21. Mark x. 21. Luke xii. 33; xviii. 22. 2 Cor. iv. 7.

Raiment is attributed to God. Ps. xciii. 1; civ. 1, 2. Isa. li. 9; lix. 17.

A Banner or *Flag* is attributed to God. Ex. xvii. 15 (16). Ps. lx. 4 (6). Cant. ii. 4. Isa. v. 26; xi. 10 (12); lix. 19.

A Rod, Staff or *Sceptre* is attributed to God or Christ. Ps. xxiii. 4, and, by *Metonymy,* is put for His power and authority. Ps. ii. 9; xlv. 6 (7); cx. 2. Heb. i. 8.

II. God is figured by an IRRATIONAL CREATURE.

1. ANIMALS.

Christ is called *a Lamb.* John i. 29. 1 Cor. v. 7. 1 Pet. i. 19. Rev. v. 6; xiii. 8.

Christ is called *a Lion.* Rev. v. 5.

2. *The* ACTIONS *of* CERTAIN *Animals are attributed to God.*

To bellow or *roar.* Isa. xlii. 13, etc. Jer. xxv. 30. Hos. xi. 10. Joel iii. 16. Amos i. 2.

Thunder is called the voice of the Lord. Ps. xxix. 3, 9: The cry of Christ is called *roaring.* Ps. xxii. 1 (2) (see Heb. v. 7). Ps. xxxviii. 8 (9).

To fly. 2 Sam. xxii. 11. Ps. xviii. 10 (11).

To brood or *incubate.* Gen. i. 2.

3. PARTS *or* MEMBERS *of* CERTAIN ANIMALS *are attributed to God.*

A horn. 2 Sam. xxii. 3. Ps. xviii. 2 (3). Messiah is so called. Luke i. 69 (Hence it is used, by *Metonymy,* for strength and power. Ps. lxxv. 10 (11); cxii. 9. Lam. ii. 3)

Wings and *Feathers* are attributed to God. Ps. xci. 4. Hence "the shadow of his wings" denotes His care. Ps. xvii. 8; xxxvi. 7 (8); lvii. 1 ; lxiii. 7 (8). And "the covert of His wings" denotes protection. Ps. lxi. 4 (5). Compare Deut. xxxii. 11. Isa xxxi. 5. Matt. xxiii. 37.

4. CERTAIN PLANTS *are used as figures of God.*

(*a*) *Genus.*

A Branch or *Sprout.* Isa. iv. 2; xi. 1. Jer. xxiii. 5 ; xxxiii. 15. Zech. iii. 8 ; vi. 12.

The Fruit of the Earth. Isa. iv. 2.

Wood (green or living). Luke xxiii. 31.

A Root. Isa. xi. 10. Rom. xv. 12. Rev. v. 5 ; xxii. 16.

(*b*) *Species.*

A Cedar. Ezek. xvii. 22, 23.

A Vine. John xv. 1-5.

III. INANIMATE THINGS are sometimes used as figures of God.

1. *Universals.*

The heights of heaven. Job xi. 7, 8. Eph. iii. 18.

Magnitude or *greatness* is attributed to God. Ex. xv. 16 ; xviii. 11. Num. xiv. 19. Deut. iii. 24. Ezra v. 8. Ps. xlviii. 1 (2) ; xlvii. 2 (3). Jer. xxxii. 17, 18, 19. Dan. ii. 45. Mal. i. 14, etc.

Comparison is used of God.

> *Greater than man.* Job xxxiii. 12.
>
> *Greater than our heart.* 1 John iii. 20.
>
> *Greater than all.* John x. 29.

Multitude or *fulness* is attributed to God. Ps. lxxxvi. 15 ; ciii. 8 ; cxxx. 7.

In spite of all this condescension, it is impossible to convey to human understanding, the greatness, vastness, illimitable perfection and infinity of God. Ps. xxxvi. 5-8 (6-9). Rom. xi. 33. 1 Cor. ii. 10, etc.

2. *Particulars.*

God is spoken of as Light. 1 John i. 5. It would require a volume to investigate and carry out all that is taught by this wondrous *Metaphor.* First, we should have to understand what Light itself is, and science was never more baffled than to-day in defining it or explaining it. So is God incomprehensible. A little while ago they thought they knew. Professor Röntgen has now shown that they do not yet know.

Lights. Jas. i. 17. " The Father of lights " : *i.e.*, the source, not only of light itself, but of all light producers and light-bearers and light givers : *viz.*, the sun, moon, stars, planets, and all the fountains of light contained in earthly substances producing electricity, gas, and light of all kinds.

Ps. xxvii. 1.—" The LORD is my light ": *i.e.*, the source and origin of my life and grace and salvation, etc., etc. Compare Num. vi. 25. Ps. xxxvi. 9 (10); xliii. 3, etc.

3. CERTAIN ELEMENTS *are used as emblems of God.*

God is spoken of as a Fire. Deut. iv. 24 ; ix. 3 ; xxxii. 27. Isa. x. 17. Hence the smoke of fire denotes His anger. Ps. lxxiv. 1 ; lxxx. 4 (5) (margin). Deut. xxix. 20.

God is spoken of as a Lamp. 2 Sam. xxii. 29. Ps. xviii. 28 (29). Hence His word is so called. Ps. cxix. 105. Prov. vi. 23. 2 Pet. i. 19.

God is spoken of as Air or Wind, and *breath* is attributed to Him. Job iv. 9. Ps. xviii. 15 (16). Isa. xxx. 33.

God is spoken of as Water. Jer. ii. 13 ; xvii. 13. Ps. xxxvi. 8, 9 (9, 10). John vii. 37-39. The gift of the Holy Spirit pertains to this figure. Isa. xliv. 3. Joel ii. 28, 29 (iii. 1, 2). Zech. xii. 10. Acts ii. 17, 18, 33. Tit. iii. 5, 6. The blessings and merits of Christ are called the water of life. John iv. 10, 14. Compare Isa. lv. 1. Ezek. xxxvi. 25. Zech. xiv. 8.

God is figured by things which pertain to the EARTH.

A Stone. Ps. cxviii. 22. Matt. xxi. 42. Acts iv. 11. 1 Pet. ii. 7.

A corner-stone, Eph. ii. 20, 21 ; and *foundation and stumbling stone,* Isa. viii. 14 ; xxviii. 16.   Zech. iii. 9.   Luke ii. 34.   Rom. ix. 32, 33. 1 Pet. ii. 4, 6, 7, 8.

A rock (*in situ*).   Deut. xxxii. 31.   Ps. xviii. 2 (3) ; xxxi. 2, 3 (3, 4); xlii. 9 ; lxxiii. 26 (margin).   Isa. xxvi. 4 (margin).

So Christ is thus spoken of Matt. xvi. 18.   (See under *Paregmenon* and *Syllepsis*).

So, in relation to the earth, God is spoken of as

A hiding-place, etc.   Ps. xci. 1 ; cxix. 114.   Isa. iv. 6.

A fortress.   Ps. xxxi. 2, 3 (3, 4) ; lxxi. 3 ; xci. 2 ; cxliv. 2.   Zech. ii. 5.

A tower of strength.   Ps. lxi. 3 (4).   Prov. xviii. 10.   2 Sam. xxii. 51.

A Temple, Rev. xxi. 22 ; and Christ is the *Way* thither, John xiv. 6.

A Shade or Shadow.   Ps. cxxi. 5.   Ps. xci. 1.   Isa. li. 16 ; xlix. 2. Compare Luke i. 32, 34, 35.   This shadow is called the " back-parts." Compare Ex. xxxiii. 20-23.

ANTIMETATHESIS; or, DIALOGUE.

A Transference of Speakers.

An-ti-me-tath'-e-sis, from ἀντί (*anti*), *against*, or *opposite to*, and μετάθεσις (*metathesis*), *a placing differently* (and this from μετά (*meta*), *beyond*, or *over*, and τιθέναι (*tithenai*), *to place* or *set*.

So that *Antimetathesis* is a figure by which there is *a transposition* of one thing over against another, especially of one person over against another; as when the writer or speaker addresses the reader or hearer in the second person as if he were actually present.

Hence the figure is called also POLYPROSOPON, *pol'-y-pros-ō'-pon*, from πολύς (*polus*), *many*, and πρόσωπον (*prosōpon*), *a person*. Hence *many persons*, or more than one person.

Sometimes the address is simple; sometimes it is continued, in which case it is called a *Dialogue*.

In Romans ii. the Gentile is personified, and by *Antimetathesis* is addressed personally instead of being described as in chapter i.

"Therefore thou art inexcusable, O man, whosoever thou art that judgest" (ii. 1, etc.).

Then, after describing and defining a true Jew, and distinguishing him from one who is not, we have apparently a dialogue in chapter iii., as Macknight has pointed out. Thus:—

Jew. "What advantage then hath the Jew? or what profit is there of circumcision?"

Apostle. "Much every way: chiefly, because that unto them were committed the oracles of God."

Jew. "But what if some have not believed? Will not their unbelief make void the faithfulness of God [*who promised to be the God of Abraham's seed*]?"

Apostle. "Far be it: No, let God prove true [*to His covenant*], though every man *be* a liar [*in denying that Jesus is the Messiah*]: as it is written, 'That thou mayest be justified in thy words [*of threatening*] and mayest overcome when on thy trial.'"

Jew. "But if our unrighteousness [*in rejecting Christ*] establisheth the righteousness of God [*in casting us off*], what shall we say? God is not unrighteous who visiteth us with his anger, is He? (*I say this in the character of an unbeliever*)."

Apostle. " By no means : otherwise how shall God judge the world ? "

Jew. " [*This is hardly satisfactory*] ; for, if the truth of God [*in visiting His nation with His wrath*] hath redounded unto His glory through my lie [*in affirming that Jesus is not the Messiah*], why am I also [*as an individual*] still further judged as a sinner ? "

Apostle. " And why not add, (as we are slanderously reported *to practise*, and as some affirm that we say), ' Let us do evil that good may come ' ?   Of these the condemnation is just."

Jew. " Well, then ; Do we *Jews* excel *the Gentiles* ? "

Apostle. " Not at all ; for we have already proved both Jews (ii. 21-24) and Gentiles (i. 18-32) to be all under sin.   Even as it standeth written (in various Scriptures, which are selected and quoted from Ps. liii. 1-3 ; xiv. 1-3, etc.)."

Thus the figure *Antimetathesis*, or Dialogue, helps to clear the sense and to indicate the manner in which certain words and expressions should be translated.

Rom. xi. 18.—" Boast not against the branches.   But, if thou boastest [*know thou that*] thou bearest not the root, but the root [*beareth*] thee."

Here the apostle is addressing " you Gentiles " as such : not the saints of God.

Rom. xi. 19.—" Thou wilt plead then, The branches were broken off, that I might be graffed in."

This was true as to the *effect*, but not as to the *cause*.   It was what a Gentile, as such, would say, but not what the Holy Spirit said.   No ! On the contrary, it was " Because of unbelief they were broken off."

And so he goes on to speak of the Gentiles by *Antimetathesis*, greatly enhancing and intensifying the argument.

Rom. xiv. 15.—" But, if thy brother is grieved with thy meat." Here, the change of persons emphasises the point that it is " thy brother " in Christ.   Not merely a fellow-man, but thy brother's Christian conscience, which is stumbled at thy eating that which has been offered to idols.

1 Cor. vii. 16.—Here, the individual husband and wife are singled out and addressed, as though they were present.

1 Cor. xv. 35.—Here, an objector is singled out : perhaps the actual words of a known person are quoted and dealt with.

ASSOCIATION; or, INCLUSION.

When the Writer or Speaker associates himself with those whom he addresses.

THIS name is given to the Figure because the writer or speaker turns, and (1) includes himself in what he says for others : (2) or, *vice versa*, includes others in what he says of himself; (3) or, includes many in what he says of one.

We have examples in

Acts xvii. 27.—"That they should seek the Lord, if haply they might feel after him, and find him, though he be not far from every one of **us**."

Eph. ii. 1-3.—"And you hath he quickened, who were dead in trespasses and sins; Wherein in time past ye walked according to the prince of the power of the air, the spirit that now worketh in the children of disobedience: Among whom also **we all** had our conversation in times past," etc.

Tit. iii. 1-3.—After speaking of the exhortations to be given to others, the apostle includes himself when he comes to speak of the state and condition of every sinner by nature. "For **we ourselves** also were sometimes foolish," etc.

Heb. iii. 6.—"But Christ as a son over his own house: whose house are **we**."

Heb. x. 25.—"Not forsaking the assembling of **ourselves** together, as the manner of some is."

Sometimes this turning to include others is only apparent. That is to say, there may be a change from the immediate context, but not from the *real* continuation as shown by the structure.

See Heb. i. and ii. :—

A | i. 1, 2-. God speaking to "us."

    B | -2-14. The Son (God) "better than the angels" ("them").

A | ii. 1-4. God speaking to "us."

    B | 5-18. The Son (man) "lower than the angels" ("them").

Here ii. 1 is the real continuation of i. 2-, and not of i. 14; while ii. 5 is the real continuation of i. 14, and not of ii. 4.

So that the change of persons here is only apparent, and does not arise from the Figure *Association*.

3. As to Subject-Matter.

APOSTROPHE.

A Turning Aside from the direct Subject-Matter to address others.

A-pos'-tro-phe. Greek, ἀποστροφή, *a turning away from,* from ἀπό (*apo*), *away from,* and στρέφειν (*strephein*), *to turn.*

The figure is so called when the speaker turns away from the real auditory whom he is addressing, and speaks to an imaginary one. It is a sudden breaking off in the course of speech, diverting it to some new person or thing.

It is called also PROSPHONESIS (προσφώνησις, *pros-phō-nee'-sis*), *an addressing one's self to:* from πρός (*pros*), *to,* and φωνεῖν (*phōnein*), *to speak.*

Also by the Latins, AVERSIO, *aversion,* or *a turning from.*

The examples of the use of this figure may be arranged as follows :—

APOSTROPHE ADDRESSED

    I. To God.

    II. To Men.
        1. Definite.
        2. One's self.
        3. Indefinite.
        4. In prophecies.

    III. To Animals.

    IV. To Inanimate Things.

I. Apostrophe to GOD.

Neh. iv. 4 (iii. 36).—Nehemiah turns from his description of the opposition of his enemies to address God (by *Apostrophe*) in prayer : "Hear, O our God; for we are despised: and turn their reproach upon their own head," etc.

There is another beautiful and sudden *Apostrophe* in

Neh. vi. 9.—" For they all made us afraid, saying, Their hands shall be weakened from the work, that it be not done. **Now, therefore, O God, strengthen my hands.**"

Ps. xxxiii.—After addressing us concerning God in the third person, the Psalmist suddenly turns away, and concludes (verse 22) with a brief *Apostrophe* addressed to God,

" **Let thy mercy, O LORD, be upon us, according as we hope in thee.**"

Ps. lxxxii.—After speaking of God (verse 8) and the wickedness of man (verses 1-7), he suddenly concludes with the *Apostrophe*,

" **Arise, O God, judge the earth ; for thou shalt inherit all nations.**"

Ps. civ. 24.—After enlarging on the wonderful works of God, he exclaims, " **O LORD, how manifold are thy works ! in wisdom hast thou made them all : the earth is full of thy riches.**"

Ps. cix.—After describing how his enemies had rewarded him evil for good, and spoken evil against him (verses 6-20), he suddenly turns aside in verse 21, and prays, " **But do thou for me, O GOD the Lord** (Jehovah Adonai), **for thy name's sake : because thy mercy is good, deliver thou me,**" etc.

II. APOSTROPHE TO MEN : EITHER LIVING OR DEAD.

1. *To certain definite persons.*

2 Sam. i. 24, 25.—In David's lament over Saul and Jonathan, he suddenly turns, and, (in verse 24), addresses the daughters of Israel. And in verse 25 he turns from these to dead Jonathan.

2 Sam. vii. 23.—In the midst of David's beautiful prayer, he suddenly turns from addressing Jehovah as to what He had done, and speaks to the people " **to do for you great things and terrible.**"

Ps. ii. 10-12.—After speaking of what God will do, the Psalmist suddenly turns, and addresses the kings and judges of the earth (10-12).

Ps. vi. 8 (9).—He turns from his prayer in trouble to address those who had brought the trouble upon him. " **Depart from me, all ye workers of iniquity,**" etc.

Isa. i. 4, 5.—The prophet turns from the third person to the second, " they have provoked the Holy One of Israel unto anger, they are gone away backward. " **Why should ye be stricken any more ?** " etc.

Jer. v. 10 is an *Apostrophe*, addressed to the enemy who should fulfil the prophecy which was being delivered.

Jer. xi.—After prophesying the evils to come upon the houses of Israel and Judah, he breaks off in verse 18, and speaks of himself.

"And the LORD hath given me knowledge of it, and I know it: then thou shewedst me their doings."

Acts xv. 10.—After speaking to the apostles and elders as to what God had been doing, Peter suddenly turns and addresses them as to what they proposed to do.

Rom. xi. 13, 14.—He turns and addresses "you Gentiles" in the midst of his revelation concerning the past and future of Israel.

Jas. iv.—He has been addressing the poor and oppressed: but, in verses 1-6 he turns away, and apostrophizes the rich oppressors, returning to his former subject in verse 7.

2. *To one's own self.*

This is done by the common Hebrew idiom, by which one's "soul" is put (by *Synecdoche*) for *one's self.*

Ps. xlii. 5, 11 (6, 12).—"Why art thou cast down, O my soul."

See also under *Cycloides, Heterosis, and Synecdoche.*

Ps. ciii. 1, 22.—"Bless the LORD, O my soul."

So Ps. civ. 1 ; cxlvi. 1, etc.

3. *To some second person or persons indefinite* (put, by *Synecdoche*, for anyone).

Ps. xxvii. 14.—After prayer to God for himself, David turns and addresses anyone who is in like circumstances, and exhorts him. "Wait on the LORD: be of good courage, and he shall strengthen thine heart: wait, I say, on the LORD."

See also under *Epanadiplosis.*

Ps. xxxiv. 12 (13).—He suddenly turns from the plural to the singular, and addresses some undefined individual: "Keep thy tongue from evil, and thy lips from speaking guile," etc.

Gal. vi. 1.—"Brethren, if a man be overtaken in a fault, ye which are spiritual restore such an one in the spirit of meekness; [now comes the *Apostrophe*, to some, or rather each, individual] considering thyself, lest thou also be tempted."

See also Rom. ii. 17 (" thou "); ix. 19 (" Thou "), 20 (" O man "); xii. 20 (" thine "); xiii. 3 (" thou "); xiv. 4 (" thou "), 10 (" thou "). 1 Cor. vii. 16 (" O wife," " O man "). See under *Antimetathesis* and *Metonymy.* Gal. iv. 7 (" thou ").

4. *In Prophecies.*

In certain solemn prophecies, the Prophet is told what to say directly (instead of indirectly or obliquely).

Isa. vi. 9.—" And he said, **Go, and tell this people, ' Hear ye indeed, but understand not,' "** etc.

(See under *Polyptoton,* and compare Matt. xiii. 14. Acts xxviii. 26, 27, etc.)

Isa. xxiii. 16.—Tyre is addressed as a person, after a prophecy concerning the city.

See also xlvii. 1.

III. APOSTROPHE TO ANIMALS.

Ps. cxlviii. 7 (dragons), **10** (beasts).

Joel ii. 22.—" **Be not afraid, ye beasts of the field,**" etc.

IV. APOSTROPHE TO INANIMATE THINGS.

Deut. xxxii. 1.—" **Give ear, O ye heavens, and I will speak : and hear, O earth, the words of my mouth.**"

Thus solemnly and emphatically opens this " Song of Moses " (which describes the whole history of Israel from the beginning to the end) and call us to give our attention to it and to consider it.

As every Israelite was expected to learn and study it (see verses 44-47) its importance to the interpreter of prophecy must be very great indeed. It is the key to Israel's history—past, present, and future.

Its structure may be seen under *Correspondence* (page 375).

2 Sam. i. 21.—" **Ye mountains of Gilboa.**"

1 Kings xiii. 2.—" And he cried against the altar in the word of the LORD and said, **O altar, altar, thus saith the LORD,** etc."

Ps. cxiv. 5.—" What ailed thee, O thou sea, that thou fleddest ? thou Jordan, that thou wast driven back ? Ye mountains that ye skipped like rams ? and ye little hills, like lambs ? Tremble, thou earth, at the presence of the Lord (Adon), at the presence of the God (Eloah) of Jacob."

Ps. cxlviii. 3-5.—" Praise ye him, sun and moon ; praise him, all ye stars of light. Praise Him, ye heavens of heavens, and ye waters that be above the heavens," etc.

Isa. i. 2.—" Hear, O heavens, and give ear, O earth ; for the Lord hath spoken."

These words were chosen for, and invariably put in, the title-page of the early printed editions of the English Bible.

Jer. ii. 12.—" Be astonished, O ye heavens, at this," etc.

Jer. xxii. 29.—"O earth, earth, earth, hear the word of the LORD." See *Epizeuxis*.

Jer. xlvii. 6.—" O thou sword of the LORD, how long will it be ere thou be quiet ? " See Ezek. xxi. 16.

Ezek. xiii. 11.—After saying that an overflowing storm shall burst upon the work of the false prophets, he turns away and addresses the hailstones. "**And ye, O great hailstones, shall fall ; and a stormy wind shall rend it.**"

Ezek. xxxvi. 4, 8.—" Ye mountains of Israel," compare verse 1.

Hos. xiii. 14.—" O death, I will be thy plagues ; O grave, I will be thy destruction." See 1 Cor. xv. 55.

Joel ii.—After prophesying concerning the land, he turns away and addresses it in verse 21. "**Fear not, O land ; be glad and rejoice :** for the LORD will do great things."

Micah vi. 2.—" Hear ye, O mountains, the LORD's controversy," etc.

Zech. xi. 1.—" Open thy doors, O Lebanon," etc.

Verse 2.—" Howl, fir-tree " ; etc. " howl, O ye oaks of Bashan."

PARECBASIS; or, DIGRESSION.

A temporary Turning Aside from one Subject to another.

Par-ek'-ba-sis. Greek, παρέκβασις, *a digression*, from παρά (*para*), *beside*, ἐκ (*ek*), *out of*, or *from*, and βάσις (*basis*), *a stepping* (from βαίνειν (*bainein*), *to step*).

A figure by which the speaker or writer *steps from beside* his subject, and makes a digression, changing his subject-matter, and adding something beyond the scope of his subject, though necessary to it. Sometimes this digression is mentioned, and a promise given to return to it again.

The figure was hence called by the Latins DIGRESSIO, or *digression*, and was known by other names among the Greeks:—

PARABASIS (*par-ab'-a-sis*), from the above roots, *a stepping aside*.

ECBOLE. Greek, ἐκβολή (*ec'-bo-lee*), *a throwing out*, from ἐκ (*ek*), *out*, and βάλλειν (*ballein*), *to throw* : hence, *a digression* in which a person is introduced speaking (or *throwing out*) his own words.

APHODOS. Greek, ἄφοδος (*aph-od'-os*), *a going away from*, from ἀπό (*apo*), *away from*, and ὅδος (*hodos*), *a way*.

The nature of this figure therefore is clear; and examples are not wanting in Scripture.

It is more than a mere *Parenthesis* (*q.v.*) : being a digression to quite a different subject.

A parenthesis is really part of the same subject, but *Parecbasis* is a stepping aside to another.

Gen. ii. 8-15, is a *Parecbasis* : *i.e.*, a digression, or change of subject-matter, by which the provision made by God for man's habitation is described.

The original subject is then resumed in verse 16, from verse 7.

Gen. xxxvi. is a *Parecbasis*, a turning aside from "the generations of Isaac" (xxv. 19—xxxv. 29) to "the generations of Esau" (xxxvi. 1-8), and "the generations of Esau, in Mount Seir," etc. (9-43) before continuing "the generations of Jacob" in xxxvii.

Gen. xxxviii. is a *Parecbasis*, a stepping aside from the history of Joseph in order to introduce an episode in the life of Judah. So that Joseph's life, which began in xxxvii., is not resumed till xxxix.

Rom. i.—The opening verses of this Epistle form a beautiful *Parecbasis.* It is caused by the structure of the Epistle: in which i. 2-6 has for its subject "God's Gospel," which was never hidden, but was always revealed (corresponding with xvi. 25-27, the subject of which is "the Mystery," which was never revealed, but always hidden).

Chap. i. 1 is, therefore, properly part of the epistolary subject, which is resumed in verse 7 and continued to verse 15 (corresponding with the Epistolary portion at the end, xv. 15-xvi. 24): and chap. i. 2-6 is, therefore, a *Parecbasis*, and is thus made to correspond with the closing chap. xvi. 25-27 *; while verse 7 is the continuation of verse 1, and not of verse 6.

Such digressions as this often arise out of, and form part of, the *Structures* or Correspondences of which the Scripture is made up : and the figure *Parecbasis* must be studied in connection with them.

---

* See the structure of the whole Epistle under *Correspondence* (page 385).

METABASIS; or, TRANSITION.

A passing from one subject to another.

Me-tab'-a-sis. Greek, μετάβασις, from μετά (*meta*), *beyond* or *over*, and βαίνειν (*bainein*), *to step* or *go*, *a stepping from one thing to another.*

Hence, called by the Latins, TRANSITIO, *transition*, and INTERFACTIO, *a doing or putting a thing in between*, as in passing from one thing to another.

The figure is used when the speaker or writer passes from one thing to another by reminding his hearers or readers of what has been said, and only hinting at what might be said, or remains to be said.

Sometimes, however, it is used of an abrupt transition.

1 Cor. xi. 16, 17.—In verse 16, Paul only hints at the contentions, of others; and then passes on, in verse 17 to the subject of the Lord's Supper.

1 Cor. xii. 31.—Having hinted at the best spiritual gifts, Paul suddenly makes the transition to one which is more excellent than all: *viz.*, Divine love, which becomes the subject of chapter xiii.

1 Cor. xv.—The apostle hints at the subject matter of his former preaching among the Corinthians; but, in verse 12, he passes on to discuss the great subject of the resurrection of the dead.

Heb. vi. 1-3.—In verse 1, the "first principles" are mentioned; and, these having been briefly hinted at, the transition is at once made to the subject in hand.

EPANORTHOSIS; or, CORRECTION.

A Recalling of what has been said, in order to correct it as by an Afterthought.

Ep'-a-nor-thō-sis. Greek, ἐπανόρθωσις, from ἐπί (*epi*), *upon*, ἀνά (*ana*), *up* or *again*, and ὀρθοῦν (*orthoun*), *to set straight* (from ὀρθός *(orthos)*, *straight*).

Hence *Epanorthosis* means a setting upright again.

The figure is so called when a writer or speaker has said something, and immediately recalls it in order to substitute something better, or stronger, or weightier, in its place, thus correcting what has been said. Hence the Latins called this figure CORRECTIO, *correction*.

The Greeks had other names for it, owing to its beauty and power, and also to the frequency of its employment. They called it

DIORTHOSIS (*di-or-thō'-sis*), from διά (*dia*), *through*, and ὀρθοῦν (*orthoun*), *to set straight*.

EPIDIORTHOSIS (*ep'-i-di-or-thō'-sis*). The above name with ἐπί (*epi*), *upon*, prefixed.

METANŒA (*met'-a-nœ'-a*), *an after-thought*, from μετανοέω (*metanoeō*), *to change one's mind.*

Epanorthosis is of three kinds :

1. Where the retraction is *absolute*.

2. Where it is *partial* or *relative*.

3. Where it is *conditional*.

1. WHERE THE RETRACTION IS ABSOLUTE.

Mark ix. 24.—" Lord, I believe ; [but, remembering his weakness, the speaker immediately corrects this great profession of faith, and says] **help thou mine unbelief.**"

John xii. 27.—The Lord Jesus prays as perfect man, " Father, save me from this hour : [and then, remembering, as perfect God, the work which He had come to do, He adds] **but for this cause came I unto this hour.**"

See under *Metonymy*.

Rom. xiv. 4.—"Who art thou* that judgest another man's servant? to his own master he standeth or falleth. [And then, remembering the blessed fact of the security of such an one, and the provision made for all his need, the Apostle adds] **Yea, he shall be holden up: for God is able to make him stand.**"

2. WHERE IT IS PARTIAL OR RELATIVE.

This phase of the figure has been called COLLATIO, *Collation*.

Prov. vi. 16.—"These six things doth the LORD hate: **yea, seven are an abomination unto him.**" See chap. xxx. 15, 18.

Matt. xi. 9.—"But what went ye out for to see? A prophet? (and then, as though correcting it and them, the Lord adds), **yea, I say unto you, and more than a prophet.**"

John xvi. 32.—"Behold, the hour cometh, **yea, is now come,** that ye shall be scattered, every man to his own home." (See A.V. margin.)

Then another *Epanorthosis* immediately follows:—

"and shall leave me alone; [with respect to men, but not with respect to God. Therefore we have the *Epanorthosis*], **and yet I am not alone, because the Father is with me.**"

Acts xxvi. 27.—"King Agrippa, believest thou the prophet? **I know that thou believest.**"

1 Cor. vii. 10.—"And unto the married I command: **yet not I but the Lord.**"

See also under *Zeugma*.

1 Cor. xv. 10.—"I laboured more abundantly than they all: **yet not I, but the grace of God which was with me.**"

Gal. i. 6.—"I marvel that ye are so soon removed . . . unto another (ἕτερος, *a different*) Gospel. **Which is not another** (ἄλλος, another of the same kind)."

Gal. ii. 20.—"Nevertheless I live: **yet not I, but Christ liveth in me.**"

See under *Zeugma*, *Epanadiplosis*, and *Polyptoton*.

Gal. iv. 9.—"But now, after that ye have known God: **or rather are known of God.**"

---

* See under *Apostrophe*.

2 **Tim. iv. 8.**—" Henceforth there is laid up for me a crown of righteousness, which the Lord, the righteous judge, shall give me at that day : [then comes a beautiful *Epanorthosis*] **and not to me only, but unto all them also that love his appearing.**"

1 **John ii. 2.**—" And he is the propitiation for our sins: [then comes the *Epanorthosis*, pointing out that He was the Propitiation for Gentiles as well as Jews, so John adds], **and not for our's only, but also for the whole world.**"

See especially under *Synecdoche* and *Metonymy*.

3. WHERE IT IS CONDITIONAL.

Gal. iii. 4.—" Have ye suffered so many things in vain ?—If it be yet in vain."

AMPHIDIORTHOSIS ; or, DOUBLE CORRECTION.

A setting both Hearer and Speaker right by a Correction which acts both ways.

Am¹-phi-di-or-thō¹-sis. From ἀμφί (*amphi*), *about, on both sides,* διά (*dia*), *through,* and ὀρθοῦν (*orthoun*), *to set straight* (from ὀρθός *(orthos)*, *straight*).

The figure is so called because, like the former Figure, *Epanorthosis,* it is a recalling or correction of what has been said, yet not merely with reference to the meaning of the speaker, but also as to the feeling of the hearer. So that the correction is *on both sides.* When this, or rather a similar figure, is used in *Argumentation,* it is called *Prodiorthosis* ; and in *Prodiorthosis* it is not so much are calling, so that there may be no shock at all (as in *Amphidiorthosis*), but a preparing for a shock that does actually come.

Some have confounded these two figures, but this is the distinction between them.

1 Kings xiv. 14.—". . . that day : but what ? even now "; as if the prophet meant (being led of the Spirit) to say, first, " that day "; and then to add shock upon shock by going on, " But what am I saying ? ' that day ? ' even now."

See also under *Ellipsis* and *Aposiopesis.*

1 Cor. xi. 22.—" What am I to say to you ? Commend you herein ? No, indeed."

ANACHORESIS; or, REGRESSION.

A Return to the Original Subject after a Digression.

An-a-cho¹-ree-sis. Greek, ἀναχώρησις, *a going* or *drawing back*, from ἀνά (*ana*), *back*, and χώρησις (*choreesis*), *a withdrawing* or *retiring* (from χωρέω, *choreō, to retire, withdraw*).

This figure is *a return* from a digression which has been made. Hence called by the Latins, REGRESSIO, *a regression*, and RECESSIO, *a receding* or *recession*.

The Greeks had another name for it, calling it EPANACLESIS, *Ep-an-a-clee-sis*, from ἐπί (*epi*), *upon*, ἀνά (*ana*), *back*, κλῆσις (*kleesis*), *a calling* (from καλέω (*kaleō*), *to call*), *a calling back upon*, or *recalling*, in the sense of returning from a digression.

See Eph. iii. 14, where the subject commenced in verse 1 is resumed.

Rom. i. 7, where the subject (the salutation) commenced in verse 1 is resumed.

Further examples will easily be found by the observant reader.

PROLEPSIS (AMPLIATIO); or, ANTICIPATION.

An Anticipation of some future Time which cannot yet be enjoyed: but has to be deferred.

Pro-leep-sis. Greek, πρόληψις, *a taking beforehand, anticipation.*

The Figure is so called when we anticipate what is going to be done, and speak of future things as present.

The name is also given to the Figure when we anticipate what is going to be said, and meet an opponent's objection. But that *Prolepsis* is distinguished by the further description "*Occupatio*"; because, in that case, the opponent's objection is not only anticipated, but *seized* and *taken possession of* (as the word means).

Whereas *Prolepsis*—when it anticipates *time* which it cannot *hold* or *keep possession* of, but has to *defer* it, after having anticipated it— is distinguished from the other by the word "*Ampliatio*," which means *an adjourning*.

God Himself used the figure in Gen. i. 28, when he spoke to both our first parents as then already present, though the building of Eve did not take place till the time spoken of in chap. ii. 20-23.

Ex. x. 29 is proleptic of the final departure of Moses from Pharaoh; as Moses did speak to him again. See xi. 4-8.

1 Kings xxii. 50 (51).—Jehoshaphat's death is spoken of pro-leptically. See 2 Kings iii.

Isa. xxxvii. 22 beautifully speaks of the then future rejoicing of Jerusalem at her deliverance from Sennacherib, as already present: "The virgin, the daughter of Zion, hath despised thee, and laughed thee to scorn"; etc.

Isa. xlviii. 5-7.—Jehovah describes how He had from the beginning spoken of future things in this way, and why He had done so.

Luke iii. 19, 20.—The imprisonment of John is recorded by *Prolepsis*. Compare Matt. xi. 2, etc.

Heb. ii. 8.—"Thou hast put all things in subjection under his feet."

This is said by *Prolepsis*, as it is distinctly declared that "We see not yet all things put under him."

In like manner we are to understand those Psalms which are written for use in millennial days; especially those commencing "the

LORD reigneth." The Lord does not now reign in the special sense and manner definitely spoken of and described in these and similar Psalms. We use them now (by way of application and) by *Anticipation* or *Prolepsis*. But the day is coming when they will be used literally, and be true by a real interpretation to the very letter.

There are three Psalms that commence " The LORD reigneth " : *viz.*, Pss. xciii., xcvii., and xcix. ; and it is remarkable that they each end with a reference to *holiness*. This is because, when the Lord does actually reign, as here described, all will be holy. His name will be " hallowed " on earth as it is in heaven. " In that day shall there be upon the bells (or bridles) of the horses, HOLINESS UNTO THE LORD ; and the pots in the LORD's house shall be like the bowls before the altar. Yea, every pot in Jerusalem and in Judah shall be holiness unto the LORD of hosts " (Zech. xiv. 20, 21). And it is written in Isa. xxiii. 18 : " Her merchandise and her hire shall be holiness to the LORD."

This is why also, the four living creatures who call for judgments (Rev. vi.) which shall issue in the Lord's reign on earth, do so with the three-fold cry of these three Psalms. " Holy, holy, holy " (Rev. iv. 8).

This is why their cry is foretold in Isa. vi. 3 in connection with Adonai upon his " throne, high and lifted up " (verse 1).

The songs and words of the Apocalypse, though then (and for the most part, if not all, now) future, are spoken of as present. In other words they are *proleptic*, being given to us under the figure *Prolepsis*.

Only by the use of this figure can we sing many of the hymns which are put into our mouths, when they speak of future heavenly realities as though resurrection had already taken place ; which it has not.

5. As to Feeling.

PATHOPŒIA; or, PATHOS.

The Expression of Feeling or Emotion.

Path'-o-pœ-i-a. Greek, παθοποιΐα, from πάθος (*pathos*), *a feeling* or *passion*, and ποιεῖν (*poiein*), *to make.*

This figure is so called, because the writer or speaker manifests some *pathos* or *emotion*: or betrays some strong and excited condition of mind.

It is of four kinds :—

Two arising out of pleasure : *love* and *joy*. And
Two arising out of pain : *hatred* and *sorrow*.

Examples, which are too many and too long to be quoted in full, may be found in Isa. xxii. 4 ; xlix. 15. Jer. ix. 1, 2 ; xxiii. 9, 10 ; xxxi. 20. Hos. xi. 8, 9. Mark iii. 5 ; vii. 34 ; x. 14, 21. Luke xix. 41, 42. Acts vii. 54, 57. 2 Cor. ii. 4. Gal. iv. 19, 20. 2 Tim. i. 16-18.

ASTEÏSMOS; or, URBANITY.

An Expression of Feeling by way of Politeness.

As-te-is'-mos. Greek, ἀστεϊσμός, *refined* or *polite talk*; *clever*, *witty*, or *pleasing language*; *graceful* or *happy* turn of phrase.

It is from ἀστεῖος *(asteios)*, *of the town* (from ἄστυ *(astu)*, *city*): *i.e.*, the polite and genteel expressions of society: Urbanity as opposed to Rusticity.

It is used as a *change* involving the *application* of words by way of expression of feeling.

Sometimes *Asteïsmos* is used as an *addition* affecting the sense of words by way of reasoning. For this, see page 488.

ANAMNESIS; or, RECALLING.

An Expression of Feeling by Way of Recalling to Mind.

An'-am-nee'-sis. Greek, ἀνάμνησις, *a calling to remembrance*, from ἀνά (*ana*), *again*, and μιμνήσκειν (*mimneeskein*), *to put in mind.*

This figure is used when the course of the direct statement is changed, to recall something to mind; and the matter, instead of being stated as a fact, as it might have been, is mentioned by way of calling it to memory.

It is a very effective method of emphasising what we wish to impress on another.

The Latins called it RECOLLECTIO, *recollection.*

Rom. ix. 3 is an interesting example; which has been already referred to under *Epitrechon* and *Hyperbole* (*q.v.*).

We should note that the verb is in the imperfect tense ηὐχόμην (*eeuchomeen*), and has the sense of *I used to wish.* And it may refer to his former condition as a Jew, and to his old hatred of the very name of Christ.

It occurs as the opening of the Dispensational part of the Epistle to the Romans. See under *Correspondence.*

BENEDICTIO; or, BLESSING.

An Expression of Feeling by Way of Benediction or Blessing.

Ben¹-e-dic¹-ti-o. English, *benediction*: and it means both *the act of blessing*, and the *blessing* itself.

The latter is called a *beatitude* or *blessing*.

A large field of study is here opened out before us. It is unnecessary for us to exhaust it. The student will find much spoil in searching out and classifying the various blessings and beatitudes which come under this figure.

See, for example, Deut. xxviii. 3-6. Ecc. x. 17. Isa. xxx. 18. Eph. i. 3.

Then they may be considered collectively.

The three blessings at the creation. Gen. i. 22, 28; ii. 3.

The *blessings* in the book of Psalms (i. 1; ii. 12; xxxii. 1, 2; xxxiii. 12; xxxiv. 8 (9); xl. 4 (5); xli. 1 (2); lxv. 4 (5); lxxxiv. 4, 5, 12 (5, 6, 13); lxxxix. 15 (16); xciv. 12; cvi. 3; cxii. 1; cxix. 1, 2; cxxvii. 5; cxxviii. 1 (2); cxxxvii. 8, 9; cxliv. 14, 15; cxlvi. 5).

The *seven blessings* in the Apocalypse. Rev. i. 3; xiv. 13; xvi. 15; xix. 9; xx. 6; xxii. 7, 14.

EUCHE; or, PRAYER.

An Expression of Feeling by way of Prayer, Curse, or Imprecation.

Eu¹-chee. Greek, εὐχή, *a prayer, wish,* or *vow.* Latin VOTUM.

This includes a *prayer,* or *wish*; also *a prayer* for evil; hence *curse, imprecation.*

This figure is a change by which a statement is expressed as a prayer, instead of as a matter of fact. And where the prayer comes in by way of parenthesis caused by the sudden change.

Its use arises from and betokens an excited condition of feeling.

The Scriptures abound with examples of all kinds, which may be sought out and studied for instruction and example.

See Deut. xxviii. 67. Isa. lxiv. 1, 2 (lxiii. 19; lxiv. 1). Acts xxvi. 29. Rom. ix. 3.

The subject to which this figure introduces us may be treated of quite separately: as the prayer may be introduced as an ejaculation, as a parenthesis, or as an addition or conclusion, etc.

Ps. cxviii. 25.—"Save now, I beseech thee, O LORD: O LORD, I beseech thee, send now prosperity."

PARÆNETICON; or, EXHORTATION.

An Expression of Feeling by way of Exhortation.

Par'-æ-net'-i-con. Greek, παραινετικός, *hortatory*, from παραινέω (*paraineō*), *to recommend, advise, exhort.*

This figure is employed when a direct statement is changed, and put into the form of exhortation.

The Scriptures abound with examples, which the reader may easily find and note for himself.

ŒONISMOS; or, WISHING.

An Expression of Feeling by way of wishing or hoping for a thing.

Œ'-ō-nis'-mos. Greek, οἰωνισμός, *a divining by the flight of birds, divination*. Then, because these diviners generally saw what they wished to see, it came to mean *a looking for*, especially in the sense of *a foreboding*.

The Latins named the figure OPTATIO, a *hoping for*, or *wishing*. By this figure, what is said is changed from a plain statement to the expressing of it *as a hope*, or an ardent desire, or lively anticipation, often introduced by the words " O that," etc. See Deut. v. 29 (26). Num. xiv. 2.

See Deut. xxxii. 29 : " O that they were wise, that they understood this, that they would consider their latter end ! "

Ps. lv. 6. (7).—" Oh ! that I had wings like a dove ! "

Ps. lxxxi. 13 (14).—" Oh that my people had hearkened unto me, and Israel had walked in my ways! " etc.

Isa. xlviii. 18.—" O that thou hadst hearkened to my commandments ! then had thy peace been as a river, and thy righteousness as the waves of the sea."

Isa. lxiv. 1 (lxiii. 19).—" Oh that thou would rend the heavens, that thou wouldst come down, that the mountains might flow down at thy presence." See also under *Euche*.

There are many examples, which the Bible student will call to mind or search out for himself.

Gal. v. 12.—" I would that they were even cut off which trouble you."

THAUMASMOS; or, WONDERING.

An Expression of Feeling by way of Wonder.

Thau-mas'-mos. Greek, θαυμασμός, *a marvelling.* The figure is used when, instead of describing or stating a thing as a matter of fact, it is expressed in the form of marvelling at it, either directly or by implication.

When the wonder is expressed as an exclamation, it combines with it the character of *Ecphonesis* (see below).

Num. xxiv. 5.—"How goodly thy tents, O Jacob."

Matt. viii. 10.—"When Jesus heard it, he marvelled, and said to them that followed, Verily I say unto you, I have not found so great faith, no, not in Israel."

Rom. xi. 33.—"O the depth of the riches both of the wisdom and knowledge of God! how unsearchable are his judgments, and his ways past finding out!"

This is a proper *Ecphonesis*, except that it expresses wonder and astonishment, so that it is combined with *Thaumasmos*.

Gal. i. 6.—"I marvel that ye are so soon removed from him that called you into the grace of Christ unto another (ἕτερον *(heteron)*, *different*) Gospel."

A simple statement would have expressed the fact, "Ye are soon removed," etc., but thus solemnly is our attention called to the whole subject-matter of the epistle.

See under *Correspondence* (the order of the seven Pauline Epistles).

PÆANISMOS; or, EXULTATION.

An Expression of Feeling by calling on Others to Rejoice.

Pæ-an'-is'-mos. Greek, παιανισμός, *the chanting of the pæan.* The παιάν (*pæan*) was a term first applied to a *physician*, then generally of any *saviour*, or *deliverer.* Then it was used of a *song of deliverance,* or *of triumph* after victory, and even before it, as a war-song. Then it was used of *any solemn song of triumph.**

So that the figure consists of *a calling on others to rejoice* over something, instead of merely stating the thing as a matter of fact; thus emphasizing and calling attention to it.

Deut. xxxii. 43.—The song of Moses, having commenced with an *Apostrophe* (q.v.), and carried us through the whole history of Israel (see under *Correspondence,* page 375), ends with a glorious and triumphant *Pæanismos,* in which Jehovah calls on all the nations to rejoice with His People for His judgment on their enemies, and the cleansing of His People and His land: thus carrying us right on to the glory of millennial days.

The fourth book of the Psalms anticipates this time of rest and peace for the earth. Hence all are called on to rejoice now (by *Prolepsis*) in view of that glorious time.

---

* This is also written παιωνισμός ; as the name from which it is derived is also written παιών. Indeed, according to the 1890 edition of Liddell and Scott, the " ω " in these words and their derivatives would seem to have been the Attic form. Moreover, according to L. and S., παιάν, παιήων (whence perhaps the Attic form) was, originally, the name of "*the physician of the gods*"!! In this character, they tell us, "he cures the wounded Hades and Ares" (see Hom. *Il.* v. 401 and 899). From him, it seems, the name came to be applied to human physicians. After Homer, L. and S. tell us, "the name and office of healing were transferred to Apollo." And from his son, Esculapius (Asclepius, in its more Greek form), physicians got another of their titles. So, then, παιάν meant a choral song, of which the main burden was ἰή (contracted from ἰήἰε, apparently, which would seem to be connected with ἰάομαι, "*I heal*") or ἰώ, παιάν, sung in commemoration of deliverance from some evil—[a *pestilence*, perhaps, originally] —and hence a song of triumph generally. Such a song would be sung *before* as well as *after* battle. Thence, again, any solemn song or chant; often sung, as an omen of success, *before* an undertaking.

A xcv. Exhortation for His People and sheep (verse 1), " to come before His presence with thanksgiving " (verse 2). For the LORD is " great " (verse 3).

> B a xcvi. A summons to sing the " New Song," " for he cometh."
>
> > b xcvii. The New Song, " The LORD Reigneth."
>
> B a xcviii. A summons to sing the " New Song " " for he cometh."
>
> > b xcix. The New Song, " The LORD Reigneth."

A c. Exhortation for His People and sheep (verse 3), to " come before his presence with singing " (verse 2), for the Lord is " good " (verse 5).

Isa. xliv. 23.—" Sing, O ye heavens; for the LORD hath done it, Shout," etc.

Zeph. iii. 14.—" Sing, O daughter of Zion ; shout, O Israel ; be glad and rejoice with all the heart, O daughter of Jerusalem."

Then follows the reason to the end of the prophecy.

Zech. ix. 9.—" Rejoice greatly, O daughter of Zion ; shout, O daughter of Jerusalem : behold thy King cometh unto thee : " etc.

Luke x. 21.—" In that hour Jesus rejoiced in spirit, and said, I thank thee, O Father, Lord of heaven and earth, that thou hast hid these things from the wise and prudent, and hast revealed them unto babes."

See under *Catachresis.*

Phil. iv. 4.—" Rejoice in the Lord alway : and again I say, Rejoice."

See under *Epanadiplosis.*

Jas. i. 9.—" Let the brother of low degree rejoice in that he is exalted."

The Scriptures abound with beautiful examples. See Ps. lvii. 8 (9), Isa. xlii. 10 ; xlix. 13. Jer. li. 48. Rev. xviii. 20, etc.

ASTERISMOS; or, INDICATING.

The Calling Attention to by making a Star or Mark.

As¹-ter-is¹-mos. Greek, ἀστερισμός, *a calling of attention to a thing by making an asterisk* (from ἀστήρ, *asteer, a star*). A marking by *putting a star* (* or *.*), in order to direct particular attention to a passage or statement. Hence the figure is used when we employ (not an asterisk) but some word, which answers the same purpose, in directing the eye and the heart to some particular point or subject, such as " Lo ! " " Behold ! "

As a concordance will furnish a complete list of these, it is not necessary for us to give examples. We will only note that the word "behold" is not a mere interjection, but is really a verb, telling us actually to look and see, and observe and note attentively.

" Behold " seems to be specially the word used by the Holy Spirit as the Inspirer of Scripture : while " **Verily** " (amen) is the word used by the Lord Jesus ; and " **Yea** " is the word of God the Father.

Ps. cxxxiii. 1.—" **Behold,** how good and how pleasant it is for brethren to dwell together in unity ! "

ECPHONESIS; or, EXCLAMATION.

An Expression of Feeling by way of Exclamation.

Ec'-phō-nee'-sis. Greek, ἐκφώνησις, *a crying out, an exclamation,* from ἐκ (*ek*), *out,* and φωνεῖν (*phonein*), *to speak,* from φωνή (*phōnee*), *voice or sound.*

The figure is used when, through feeling, we change our mode of speech; and, instead of merely making a statement, express it by an *exclamation.* So that *Ecphonesis* is an outburst of words, prompted by emotion, and is not used as though any reply were expected.

It was called also ANAPHONESIS, *an'-a-phō'-nee'-sis,* the same word, with ἀνά (*ana*), *up,* prefixed instead of ἐκ (*ek*), *out, a lifting up of the voice.*

The exclamation itself is called ANAPHONEMA (*An'-a-phō-nee'-ma*).

The Latins called it EXCLAMATIO, *exclamation.*

But note that, when the exclamation occurs at the end of a sentence, as an *addition* by way of conclusion, it is called *Epiphonema* (see page 464).

When the *Ecphonesis* is an exclamation thrown in parenthetically, it is called *Interjectio* (see page 478).

Josh. vii. 7.—"And Joshua said, Alas, O Lord God (Adonai Jehovah), wherefore hast thou at all brought up this people over Jordan," etc.

1 Chron. xi. 17.—"And David longed, and said, Oh that one would give me drink of the water of the well of Bethlehem, that is at the gate!" This would come also under the figure *Œonismos* (*q.v.*).

Ps. xxii. 1 (2).—"My God (Eli), my God (Eli), why hast thou forsaken me?" (Matt. xxvii. 46. Mark xv. 34). See under *Epizeuxis.*

Ps. lvii. 7 (8) is also a beautiful *Ecphonesis.*

Ps. lxxxiv. 1 (2). — "How amiable (*i.e.,* How lovely, or How delightful) are thy tabernacles, O Lord of hosts," etc.

Isa. i. 4.—"Ah sinful nation, a people laden with iniquity, a seed of evil-doers, children that are corrupters."

See under *Synonymia* and *Anabasis.*

Isa. vi. 5.—"Then said I, Woe is me! for I am undone"; etc. This is the true *Ecphonesis* of a convicted soul. A confession, not of what he has done, but of what he IS; as to nature, condition, and deserts. Of such an exclamation the result is ever (as recorded in the next verse) " THEN flew," etc.

Ezek. ix. 8.—" I fell upon my face, and cried, and said, Ah Lord God (Adonai Jehovah)!" etc.

Hos. xiii. 9.—" O Israel, thou hast destroyed thyself; but in me is thine help."

Matt. xv. 28.—" Then Jesus answered and said unto her, O woman, great is thy faith: be it unto thee even as thou wilt."

Matt. xvii. 17.—"Then Jesus answered and said, O faithless and perverse generation," etc.

Acts vii. 51 is also an *Ecphonesis.*

Rom. vii. 24.—" O wretched man that I am! who shall deliver me from this body of death?" (marg.). See *Hypallage, Ellipsis,* and *Metonymy.*

This is a true *Ecphonesis*; but, as concluding the whole of the chapter, it is also in that respect a kind of *Epiphonema* (*q.v.*).

This verse expresses the continuous experience of every true child of God, who understands the conflict between the two natures :—the old man and the new man: the flesh and the spirit, the old nature and the Divine nature implanted within him by the Holy Spirit.

This conflict is the one thing of which a merely *religious* person is destitute. It is the one thing that cannot be imitated by the hypocrite. He never has an abiding sense of inward corruption and of the conflict with it; because he has not the New nature by which alone it is manifested and brought to light. He has no standard within him to detect it, or by which to try it.

Until the truth of the abiding conflict between the two natures is seen no spiritual peace can be enjoyed.

The *fruits* of the old tree are dealt with in the former portion of this Doctrinal part of the Epistle (Rom. i. 16 to v. 11): and then the *old tree itself* is dealt with in chap. v. 12 to viii. 39, and is shown to be (in God's sight) as dead, having been crucified with Christ. Thus, the conflict goes on till this body of death (*i.e.*, until this dying body). either dies, or is " changed" at Christ's appearing.

Then the longing desire will be realised, and faith will be rewarded, as expressed in the words that follow, where the *Ellipsis* must be supplied :—" I thank God—*He will deliver me*—[and reckoning myself even now as already having died with Christ (vi. 11)—I thank God, that He will deliver me] through Jesus Christ our Lord."

APORIA; or, DOUBT.

An Expression of Feeling by way of Doubt.

A-pō'-ri-a. Greek, ἀπορία, *a being in doubt,* or *at a loss,* from ἄπορος (*aporos*), *without a passage* (ἀ, *privative,* and πόρος *(poros),* *a passage*).

The figure is used when the speaker expresses himself as though he were at a loss what course to pursue ; or when we express a doubt as to what we ought to think or say or do.

It was also called DIAPORESIS (*Di'-a-po-ree'-sis*). Greek, διαπόρησις, from διά (*dia*), *through,* and ἀπόρησις (*aporeesis*), *a being without passage* or *resource.*

The Latins called it DUBITATIO, *a wavering, a doubting, uncertainty, doubt,* and ADDUBITATIO, the former word with *ad, to,* denoting *the beginning* of the *hesitation* or *doubting.*

Hos. vi. 4.—" O Ephraim, what shall I do unto thee ? O Judah, what shall I do unto thee ? "

See under *Erotesis.*

Hos. xi. 8.—" How shall I give thee up, Ephraim ? how shall I deliver thee, Israel ? " etc.

See under *Anthropopatheia.*

Matt. xxi. 25, 26. — " The baptism of John, whence was it ? from heaven, or of men ? And they reasoned with themselves, saying, If we shall say, From heaven ; he will say unto us, Why did ye not then believe him ? But if we shall say, Of men ; we fear the people ; for all hold John as a prophet."

Luke xvi. 3.—" Then the steward said within himself, What shall I do ? for my lord taketh away from me the stewardship : I cannot dig ; to beg I am ashamed."

EPITIMESIS; or, REPRIMAND.

An Expression of Feeling by way of Censure, Reproof, or Reproach.

Ep'-i-ti-mee'-sis. Greek, ἐπιτίμησις, *reproof, reprimand,* from ἐπιτιμάω (*epitimao*), *to put a price upon,* from τιμή (*timee*), *worth* or *value.*

It is also called EPIPLEXIS, *ep'-i-pleex'-is.* Greek, ἐπίπληξις, *chastisement, punishment, blame.*

The figure is used, where a rebuke, reproof, or reproach is conveyed.

Seeing that God's ways and thoughts are the opposite of man's, it is impossible that God should speak to man without many rebukes and reproaches.

These are of various kinds; and some have their own special names, as will be seen below.

We give merely one or two by way of example, and as showing what we may learn from them.

Luke ix. 55.—"He turned, and rebuked them (James and John), and said, Ye know not what manner of spirit ye are of." etc.

Luke xxiv. 25.—"Then he said unto them, O fools, and slow of heart to believe all that the prophets have spoken."

This was the rebuke for Jewish disciples, but Christians to-day need it as much: for both believe and receive *some* Scriptures, but not "ALL."

The Jews received the passages which spoke of Christ's "glory," but rejected those that told of His "sufferings": and Christians to-day are guilty of the opposite folly.

The Jews thought the Lord Jesus was not good enough for the world, and so they cast Him out. Christians, to-day, think they have not yet made the world good enough for Christ, and so would fain keep Him out.

Both take a part of the truth, and put it for the whole; and both, therefore, come under this solemn rebuke.

The correction for the folly of both is given in the words which follow, "Ought not Christ to have suffered these things, AND to enter into his glory?" The Jews thought the former humiliating; and Christians call the latter "carnal": and so Jews reject the Scriptures which testify of the sufferings, and Christians neglect the Prophecies which speak of Christ's coming glories.

The Holy Spirit saith (2 Pet. i. 19), concerning these prophecies, 'The world is a dark place; and ye do well to take heed to the only light in it.' Christians, to-day, say that prophecy is a dark place, and ye do well to avoid it!

Rom. ix. 20.—" Nay but, O man, who art thou that repliest against God? Shall the thing formed say to him that formed it, Why hast thou made me thus?" etc. See this passage also under *Apostrophe* and *Prosopopœia.*

ELEUTHERIA; or, CANDOUR.

An Expression of Feeling by way of bold Freedom of Speech in Reprehension.

El-eu'-ther-i'-a. Greek, ἐλευθερία, *liberty* or *licence.* Hence, ἐλευθέριος, (*eleutherios*), *speaking* or *acting like a free man, frank.*

The figure is so called, because the speaker or writer, without intending offence, speaks with perfect freedom and boldness.

Eleutheria is therefore the bold reprehension of *free speech.*

It is called PARRHESIA (*Par-rhee'-si-a*). Greek, παρρησία, *free spokenness, openness, boldness, frankness.*

The Latins called it LICENTIA, *licence.*

The words of Elihu (Job xxxii.-xxxvii.) are a beautiful example of this figure.

Luke xiii. 32.—" Go ye, and tell that fox," was a very frank and fearless message to Herod.

John viii. 44.—" Ye are of your father the devil, and the lusts of your father ye will do. He was a murderer from the beginning, and abode not in the truth, because there is no truth in him." etc.

See under *Idiom* and *Metonymy.*

1 John iii. 10.—" In this the children of God are manifest, and the children of the devil."

This is free-speaking indeed; too free for the false toleration and charity-mongering of the present day; but these are the words of the God of love, through John the apostle of love.

The following places where the word *Parrhesia* is used in the New Testament will furnish many interesting examples.

The word is translated:

" Boldness of speech," 2 Cor. vii. 4.

" Plainness of speech," 2 Cor. iii. 12 (marg. *boldness*).

" Boldness," Acts iv. 13, 29, 31. Eph. iii. 12. Phil. i. 20. 1 Tim. iii. 13. Heb. x. 19 (marg. *liberty*). 1 John iv. 17.

" Be much bold," Philem. 8 (πολλὴν . . . παρρησίαν ἔχων).

" With . . . confidence," Acts xxviii. 31. Heb. iii. 6 ; x. 35. 1 John ii. 28 ; iii. 21 ; v. 14.

Dative: " Boldly," John vii. 26. " Openly," Mark viii. 32. John vii. 13 ; xi. 14 ; xvi. 25, 29.

With ἐν (*en*) *in* or *with*, " boldly," Eph. vi. 19. " Openly," John vii. 4. Col. ii. 15.

With μετά (*meta*), *with*, " boldly," Heb. iv. 16. " Freely," Acts ii. 29.

AGANACTESIS; or, INDIGNATION.

An Expression of Feeling by way of Indignation.

Ag'-an-ak-tee'-sis. Greek, ἀγανάκτησις, *physical pain* and *irritation ;* hence *vexation, indignation.*

The figure is used when an exclamation proceeds from the deep feeling of indignation.

See Gen. iii. 13 ; iv. 10 ; xx. 9 ; xxxi. 26.

Acts xiii. 10.—Here we have a forcible example of Paul's indignation at the opposition of Elymas the Sorcerer.

APODIOXIS; or, DETESTATION.

An Expression of Feeling by way of Detestation.

Ap'-o-di-ōx'-is.   Greek, ἀποδίωξις, *a chasing away*; from ἀπό (*apo*), *away from*, and διώκειν (*diōkein*), *to pursue.*

The figure is so called, because the speaker or writer repels something, and spurns it as absurd or wicked.

The Latins called it REJECTIO, *a rejecting* or *rejection*; DETESTATIO, *a detesting* or *detestation*; and ABOMINATIO, *an abominating* or *abomination*.

Ps. l. 16.—" But unto the wicked God saith, What hast thou to do to declare my statutes, or that thou shouldest take my covenant in thy mouth ? "

Isa. i. 12-15 is a solemn expression of Jehovah's detestation of religion, *per se*, such as existed among, and was manifested by, the Jews at Christ's first coming. This passage describes the most minute attention to every religious observance, which only heightens the indignation with which the Lord repudiates it all, because it does not proceed from the heart.

See this passage also under *Ellipsis, Anthropopatheia, Synathrœsmus,* and *Hypotyposis.*

Jer. ix. 2 (1).—We have Jeremiah's detestation of Israel's idolatry.

Matt. iv. 10.—" Get thee hence, Satan :" etc.

Matt. xvi. 23.—" He . . . said unto Peter, Get thee behind me, Satan : thou art an offence unto me : for thou savourest not the things that be of God."

The fact of this repulsion following so closely upon the other words addressed to Peter in verses 17, 18, should have for ever precluded the Romish perversion of them.

Acts viii. 20-23.—Peter repels with horror the thought of Simon Magus that the gift of the Holy Ghost could be purchased with money.

DEPRECATIO; or, DEPRECATION.

An Expression of Feeling by way of Deprecation.

Dep-re-ca'-ti-o. The name of this figure is from the Latin, and means literally *a praying against, an act of deprecation.*

The figure is used in three senses :—

(1) A praying against evil, so as to avert or prevent its results : as when an Advocate pleads former good character, etc., on behalf of the accused person.

(2) Where the speaker prays against others, that evil may fall upon them ; or even against himself. This is properly IMPRECA-TION.

(3) When the ejaculatory prayer is for the prevention or removal of any evil generally.

We have an example in the *Deprecation* of Moses :—

Ex. xxxii. 32.—"Blot me, I pray, thee out of thy book."
See this passage under *Aposiopesis* and *Anthropopatheia.*

DIASYRMOS; or, RAILLERY.

An Expression of Feeling by way of tearing away Disguise.

Di'-a-syrm-os. Greek, διασυρμός, *a tearing in pieces,* from διασύρειν (*diasurein*); and this from διά (*dia*) and σύρειν (*surein*), *to drag, to force away.*

Twice the word is used in connection with Paul: Acts viii. 3, " haling " ; and Acts xiv. 19, " drew."

This figure is so called, because it tears away the veil, or whatever may be covering the real matter in question, and shows it up as it really is. Hence, *raillery* which tears away all disguise.

Matt. xxvi. 50.—" Friend, wherefore art thou come ? "

John vii. 4.—The Lord's brethren seek to reflect upon Him, as if He were mismanaging His affairs. But, in this case, the *Diasyrmos* proceeded from their own mistake as to what His mission really was. " There is no man that doeth anything in secret, and he himself seeketh to be known openly."

CATAPLEXIS; or, MENACE.

An Expression of Feeling by way of Menace.

Cat'-a-pleex'-is. Greek, κατάπληξις, *a striking down, terrifying menace.*

This figure is used where the speaker or writer employs the language of menace.

EXOUTHENISMOS; or, CONTEMPT.

An Expression of Feeling by way of Contempt.

Ex¹-ou-then-is¹-mos.   Greek, ἐξουθενισμός, *scorn, contempt,* or *disparagement.*

The figure is used where a speaker or writer expresses *contempt* of anything.

See 2 Sam. vi. 20. Job xxvi. 2. Jer. xxii. 23.

MALEDICTIO ; or, IMPRECATION.

Expression of Feeling by way of Malediction or Execration.

Mal'-e-dic'-ti-o. This is the Latin name, and means *denunciation, cursing, imprecation,* or *execration.*

Hence the other Latin names, IMPRECATIO and EXECRATIO, COMMINATIO. Also ARA, *an altar,* by which, and at which, oaths and execrations were pronounced.

The Greeks called it APEUCHE, *ap-eu-chee,* from ἀπεύχομαι, *to pray a thing away, to pray that a thing may not be,* and MISOS, *mi-sos,* Greek μῖσος, *hate, hatred, a hateful object* or *thing.*

See 1 Sam. iii. 17. Ruth i. 17.

Ps. cix. 6-19, where we have the *Imprecation* of David's enemies for evil to come upon him. See under *Ellipsis.*

Ezek. xxxiv. 2.—" Woe be to the shepherds of Israel that do feed themselves ! "

A woe that comes upon all shepherds to-day who do not " feed the flocks."

See the whole chapter for the reasons for this solemn " Woe."

A concordance will enable students to find the examples for themselves, as they begin with " Woe," such as those in Deut. xxviii. 11-19. Isa. iii. 11. Jer. xlviii. 46. Matt. xi. 21.

DEASIS ; or, ADJURATION.

An Expression of Feeling by Oath or Asseveration.

De¹-a-sis, from Greek, δέησις, *an entreating, obtestation,* or *calling to witness.*

The Latins called it OBSECRATIO, *a beseeching, imploring,* and OBTESTATIO, *an adjuring,* or *calling of God to witness.*

The figure is used when the speaker or writer calls God or heaven to witness to the truth of what is said, or to the facts which he states. Apart from this *calling to witness,* the figure is of the nature of *Apostrophe (q.v.).*

For examples, see Deut. iv. 26; xxx. 19. 2 Sam. xx. 20. Job xxvii. 5. Isa. xiv. 24; lxii. 8. Jer. xxii. 5; xxvii. 5. Ezek. v. 11; xxxiii. 11; xxxiv. 8. Acts xx. 26.

It is exemplified in such phrases as : " Be it far from me " ; " The LORD do so unto me," if I do or do not, etc. ; " As the LORD liveth, and as thy soul (thy own self) liveth."

" Be it far from me " seems to mean " profane be it to me " : *i.e.,* be it as far from me as I could wish a profane thing to be.

CHLEUASMOS ; or, MOCKING.

An Expression of Feeling by Mocking and Jeering.

Chleu-as'-mos. Greek, χλευασμός, *mocking, scoffing, sneering, jeering,* from χλεύη (*chleuee*), *a jest,* and χλευάζω (*chleuazō*), *to make a jest of, scoff at.*

EPICERTOMESIS, Greek, ἐπικερτόμησις (*Ep-i-ker-to-mee-sis*), *a sneering* or *jeering.*

MYCTERISMOS, Greek, μυκτηρισμός (*muk-teer-is-mos*), *a turning up of the nose at, sneering,* or *snuffing,* from μυκτήρ (*mukteer*), *the nose, snout, nostrils.*

The figure is used when the speaker or writer excites laughter by a jeer or sneer; or excites ridicule by turning up the nose.

This is exactly what the Holy Spirit says the Pharisees did at the Lord's teaching in Luke xvi. 14, and which led Him to rebuke them, and put them to shame and silence by a parable similar to those they were fond of using (See Lightfoot).

It is also what Jehovah will do, in return, to those who have thus treated His Anointed.

Ps. ii. 4.—"He that sitteth in the heavens shall laugh: the Lord shall have them in derision."

Prov. i. 24-33.—This is a solemn example of the figure.

See also Isa. xiv. 4, 12. Micah ii. 4.

5. As to Argumentation.

We now come to the last part of the third great branch of Figures involving Change, and to the last division of these, affecting the application of words as to Argumentation.

It is neither the smallest division, nor is it the least in importance.

The application of words is so wide that it is difficult to separate every Figure, and say that one belongs to a certain class; because they frequently overlap, and belong to more than one class.

For example: we have put in this last section, *Argumentation*, *Erotesis*, or Interrogating; but interrogation is not always used by way of argument. In like manner we have included *Dialogismus*; but as it represents two or more persons speaking, it might have been classed under the use " as to *Persons*."

So that, while each figure cannot be arbitrarily arranged under the separate heads, we have placed them in the order which seemed to be most proper to themselves, and most instructive and helpful to the Bible student.

Under this last division, *Argumentation*, we have put no less than nineteen figures; and first, as being one of the most important, *Erotesis*.

Separate works have been published on this figure alone; and it would form the subject of years of fruitful study by itself.

————

EROTESIS; or, INTERROGATING.

The Asking of Questions without waiting for the Answer.

Er'-ō-tee'-sis.   Greek, ἐρώτησις, *interrogation* (from ἐρωτᾶν, *to ask, to enquire, to question* : also *to request*).

This figure is used when a speaker or writer asks animated questions, but not to obtain information. Instead of making a plain and direct statement, he suddenly changes his style, and puts what he was about to say or could otherwise have said, into the form of a question, without waiting for an answer. Instead of declaring a conviction, or expressing indignation, or vindicating authority, he puts it in the form of a question without expecting any reply

The figure is so important that not only is it of frequent occurrence, but it has several other names. It is called

PEUSIS (*peu'-sis*). Greek, πεῦσις, *an asking, inquiry* (from πεύθομαι (*peuthomai*) : poetic present of πυνθάνομαι (*punthanomai*), *to ask, inquire*).

PYSMA (*pys'-ma*). Greek, πύσμα (*pusma*), *what is learnt by the interrogation* (from the same root).

The Latins called it PERCONTATIO, *an asking, inquiring after ;* and INTERROGATIO, *an interrogating.*

While these names are all used of the act of interrogation, the question itself is called EROTEMA (*er'-o-tee'-ma*).

There are questions in the Hebrew which are not reproduced in the English; and some are given below, though the labour of making an exhaustive list would be too great.

But, counting the questions as they appear in the English Bible, the importance of this figure *Erotesis*, or *Interrogating*, will be seen when we state that, in the 1,189 chapters into which the Bible is divided, there are no less than 3,298 questions. It is clear, therefore, that it is impossible for us here to quote, or even to give, all the references. Out of the 1,189 chapters of the Bible there are only 453 which are without a question.

These are divided as follows:—The 929 chapters of the Old Testament contain 2,274 questions; while the 260 chapters of the New Testament contain no less than 1,024. The average of questions in the New Testament is much higher, per chapter, than that in the Old Testament. For, while the average of the whole Bible is 2.75 (*i.e.*, 2¾ questions for every chapter), the Old Testament average is 2.3 (or 2⅓), and the New Testament nearly twice as much : *viz.*, 3.9 (or nearly 4).

This is how the Bible is affected as a whole. When we come to the separate Books, we find that Job stands first with 329 questions; while Jeremiah comes next with 195.

In the New Testament, the Gospel of Matthew stands first with 177 questions; then John's Gospel with 167 : etc.

When we come to separate chapters, Job xxxviii. stands first with 40 questions; then 2 Sam. xix., with 22 questions. In the New Testament, 1 Cor. ix. stands first, with 20 questions; followed closely by John vii., which has 19.

These facts are interesting, but are not important, as to the chapters ; inasmuch as these are only human in their origin, and are often very incorrectly divided. As to the two Testaments and the separate books, however, they serve to show us the relative distribution of this beautiful figure *Erotesis.*

With regard to the questions themselves, their classification is another matter altogether. Some are *searching*, causing the mind to pause, wonder, and admire. Some are *revelations* of the attributes of God, and of the depravity of man. The very first Divine question of the Old Testament reveals the condition of man by nature: " WHERE ART THOU ? " It comes from God to the sinner, now " far off " (Eph. ii. 13), from God. While the first question in the New Testament reveals the effect of this on the sinner's heart, causing him to turn to that Saviour whom the New Testament reveals, and cry, " WHERE IS HE ? "

The questions of the Bible, whether God addresses them to man; or whether man turns to God; or whether he questions himself; contain a mine of truth and teaching; while the heart is awakened, and the attention is aroused to seek out the answer, which is ever fraught with deep and blessed instruction.

We have only to reflect on the interesting fact that the figures used most frequently by the Lord Jesus are *Interrogation* and *Implication* (*Erotesis* and *Hypocatastasis*). The very first thing that is mentioned concerning Him as the first act of His life, is that He was found " in the temple, sitting in the midst of the doctors, both hearing them, and *asking them questions* " (Luke ii. 46).

Doubtless He could teach them much that would astound them, by the use of this Figure, in spite of the disparity of age. For a child of twelve years of age may *question*, when he may not *teach ;* and yet, by this simple means, teach more effectively than the greatest of teachers. No wonder that " all that heard him were astonished."

All writers and speakers have always drawn largely on this Figure, and many interesting examples might be given from general literature.

Science lifts its head against the word of God as though all were uncertainty outside of its own proud boastings. And yet a few questions soon prick and burst the bubble.

Scientia means real or intuitive *knowledge*, as does its Greek representative γνῶσις (*gnōsis*). (Hence our words " know " and "knowledge"). Neither of these words means *acquired* knowledge. But beyond a very few facts and the small circle of mathematical demonstrations: How little is really *known !* What is matter ? What is mind ? What is life ? What is light ? What is electricity ? What is gravitation ? or, Is there any such thing at all ? What is the history of our own earth geologically ? Who can tell us this ? So long ago as 1806, the French

o 2

Institute tabulated more than eighty geological theories, and how many have there been since then ?

We merely give this as illustrating how we may ourselves, by a few questions, dispose of the giants who would demolish us and rob us of the Inspired Word of God, which comes to us in all its blessed and Divine certainty.

We turn, then, to its questions ; and our best course will be to indicate certain divisions into which they may be classified ; so that the Bible-searching student may have somewhere to place the questions, as he seeks them out and finds them.

Several classifications have been attempted by various writers from Glassius downwards, and probably none is either correct or complete. The subject is too large, and its divisions over-lap too much, to allow of too minute an arrangement.

We might classify them under their subject matter, or under the words with which they commence ("Who," "How," "Why," "Whether," etc.).

If we used both these divisions they would get mixed up, and many questions would appear in each. So that we present the following, as embracing practically all the divisions into which the questions of the Bible may be classified.

1. In positive affirmation.
2. In negative affirmation.
3. In affirmative negation.
4. In demonstration.
5. In wonder and admiration.
6. In rapture.
7. In wishes.
8. In refusals and denials.
9. In doubts.
10. In admonition.
11. In expostulation.
12. In prohibition or dissuasion.
13. In pity and commiseration.
14. In disparagement.
15. In reproaches.
16. In lamentation.
17. In indignation.
18. In absurdities and impossibilities.
19. Double questions.

1. In Positive Affirmation.

Where the answer must be in the affirmative.

"Wilt not thou deliver my feet from falling ? " (Ps. lvi. 13 (14)). [Yes, thou wilt]. Here the *present* comes in between the *past* (" thou hast delivered my soul from death ") and the *future* (" that I may walk before God in the light of the living."

" These two things are come unto thee ; who shall be sorry for thee ? [Every one]. Desolation and destruction, and the famine, and the sword : by whom shall I comfort thee ? " (Isa. li. 19) : *i.e.*, by every one.

" Which of you shall have an ass or an ox fallen into a pit, and will not straightway pull him out on the sabbath day ? " (Luke xiv. 5). [No one].

2. In Negative Affirmation.

Where the question is put in the negative form, and the answer must be in the affirmative, and very emphatically so ; the truth being thus much more forcibly brought out by the question than by a mere cold and formal statement of the fact.

" Is not the whole land before thee ? " (Gen. xiii. 9) : *i.e.*, yes, it is.

" Do not thy brethren feed in Shechem ? " (Gen. xxxvii. 13). [Yes, they do.] Here, in A.V. and R.V., the words " the flock " are inserted (in the latter not in italics). This is because of the words " their father's flock," which occur in the previous verse. But this is one of the fifteen dotted words in the Hebrew Text, which means that they had got into the Text at a very early date ; and the scribes, not liking actually to remove them from the Text, put a row of small dots along the top to show that the word or words ought not to be in the Text, though they had not been taken out. As the words " the flock " are dotted in the Hebrew, verse 12, means that they had gone to feed *themselves* in Shechem ! (Compare Ezek. xxxiv. 2, 8, 10, and Isa. lvi. 11, 12).

" Is not Aaron the Levite thy brother, whom I know to be eloquent ? " (Ex. iv. 14) : *i.e.*, I know that he is so.

" Are they not on the other side Jordan ? " etc. (Deut. xi. 30).

" Shall I not seek rest for thee ? " etc. (Ruth iii. 1).

" Is it not I that commanded the people to be numbered ? " (1 Chron. xxi. 17 ; compare 2 Sam. xxiv. 17).

" Is there not a warfare to man upon the earth ? " (Job vii. 1, R.V.) ; marg., *a time of service.* (See the A.V. margin).

" Do not all go to one place ? " (*i.e.*, to *Sheol*, or the grave) (Ecc. vi. 6). The answer is : Yes, they do !

" Is my hand shortened at all, that it cannot redeem ? or have I no power to deliver ? " (Isa. l. 2). Here, we have a combined affirmative and negative :—No ; my hand is not shortened. I can redeem ; and, I have power to deliver. Compare lix. 1.

" Do not I fill heaven and earth ? saith the LORD " (Jer. xxiii. 24). Yes. The previous question is positive.

" Is not the meat cut off before our eyes ? " (Joel i. 16).

" Is it not even thus, O ye children of Israel ? saith the LORD" (Amos ii. 11).

" Shall not the day of the LORD be darkness, and not light ? " (Amos v. 20). See under *Metonymy* and *Pleonasm.*

" Lord, Lord, have we not prophesied in thy name ? and in thy name have cast out devils ? and in thy name done many wonderful works ? " (Matt. vii. 22). See under *Epizeuxis.*

" Do ye not therefore err, because ye know not the Scriptures, neither the power of God ? " (Mark xii. 24). Here, the " not " is μή (*mee*) which denies subjectively, and implies not merely negative ignorance, but positive unwillingness to know the Scriptures. See Matt. xxii. 29.

" The cup of blessing which we bless, is it not the communion of the blood of Christ ? " (1 Cor. x. 16). Yes, it is the fellowship of the members of the one Body in partaking of all the merits of Christ's blood. " The bread which we break, is it not the communion (or fellowship) of the Body of Christ ? "

The next verse makes it perfectly clear that the Body here mentioned is Christ Mystical, because the Holy Spirit goes on to give the reason—" For we being many are one bread, and, one Body." See 1 Cor. xii. 12.

" Are they not all ministering spirits, sent forth to minister for them who shall be heirs of salvation ? " (Heb. i. 14).

So Obad. 5, 8. Jonah iv. 11. John iv. 35 ; vi. 70 ; xi. 9.

Sometimes the negative is omitted by *Ellipsis* (*q.v.*).

2 Sam. xv. 27.—" The king said also unto Zadok the priest, *Art not* thou a seer ? "

Here the negative is supplied in italics. But not in

Ezek. viii. 6.—" Son of man, seest thou what they do ? " : *i.e.*, seest thou not ?

So 1 Sam. ii. 27, and especially Jer. xxxi. 20, where it should be " *Is not* Ephraim my dear son ? *Is he not* a pleasant child ? " as is clear from what follows.

3. IN AFFIRMATIVE NEGATION.

This is a very important division, because some of the weightiest truths are conveyed by this form of question : *i.e* , where the question is put in the affirmative, and the answer to be supplied by the mind is a very emphatic negative.

" Is anything too hard for the LORD ? " (Gen. xviii. 14). No! there is nothing too hard for Him, for compare Jer. xxxii. 17. Zech. viii. 6. Matt. iii. 9 ; xix. 26. Luke i. 37.

" Shall I hide from Abraham that thing which I do ? " (Gen. xviii. 17).

" How can I dispossess them ? " (Deut. vii. 17) : *i.e.*, I cannot do it.

" Who is like unto thee ? " is the cry of all the " poor and needy " ones whom Jehovah has delivered. (Ps. xxxv. 10). See Ex. xv. 11. Deut. xxxiii. 26, 27. 1 Sam. ii. 2. Ps. lxxi. 19; lxxiii. 25 ; lxxxix. 6 (7) ; cxiii. 5.

" Shall they escape by iniquity ? " (Ps. lvi. 7 (8)). No, they shall not.

" Who will rise up for me against the evildoers ? or who will stand up for me against the workers of iniquity ? " (Ps. xciv. 16) : *i.e.*, there is no one to do this but God ; as verse 17 clearly shows.

" Who can utter the mighty acts of the LORD ? who can show forth all his praise ? " (Ps. cvi. 2). The answer is that no one can.

Ps. ix. 14 (15) does not conflict with this : for there it is a prayer for Jehovah's mercy, so that he " may show forth " all His praise. Compare Ps. xl. 5 (6) ; cxxxix. 17, 18.

Ecc. iii. 21.—Here, we must take the question " who know . . . whether," etc., as requiring a negative answer. See under Appendix E.

" Can any hide himself in secret places that I shall not see him ? saith the LORD " (Jer. xxiii. 24). No, none can so hide. The following question is negative.

" How shall then his kingdom stand ? " (Matt. xii. 26) : *i.e.*, it is impossible.

" Which of you convicteth me of sin ? " (John viii. 46). ἐλέγχω (*elengcho*) does not mean *to convince*, but *to convict by bringing in guilty*, *lay bare, expose*. No one could ever bring Christ in guilty of sin. This explains John xvi. 8. See *Prosapodosis*.

" What if some did not believe ? Shall their unbelief make the faith of God without effect ? " (Rom. iii. 3). See under *Tapeinosis*.

" If God be for us, who can be against us ? "

" Who shall lay anything to the charge of God's elect ? "

" Who is he that condemneth ? "

" Who shall separate us from the love of Christ ? " (Rom. viii. 31-35). See under *Epistrophe*, *Anaphora*, *Ellipsis*, which are all employed in these verses.

" Who hath known the mind of the Lord ? or who hath been his counsellor ? Or who hath first given to him, and it shall be recompensed unto him again ? " (Rom. xi. 34, 35).

" Who goeth a warfare any time at his own charges ? " etc. (1 Cor. ix. 7).

" Unto which of the angels said he at any time, Thou art my Son ? " (Heb. i. 5) : *i.e.*, to none of them, but to the Son only. These words, " Thou art my Son," appear to be the Divine formula for the anointing of Christ : Matt. iii. 17, for His office of *prophet* ; Matt. xvii. 5, for His office of *priest*,* and Ps. ii. 7 (cf. Heb. i. 5), for His office of *king*.

" To which of the angels said he at any time, Sit on my right hand, until I make thine enemies thy footstool ? " (Heb. i. 13), *i.e.*, He never said this to any created angelic being.

See, for other instances, Gen. l. 19. 1 Sam. ii. 25. Job xl. 2, etc. Isa. xl. 13, 14. Joel i. 2, etc., and many other places.

> Sometimes the negative in the answer is not absolute,
> but only relative.

" Who knoweth the power of thine anger ? " (Ps. xc. 11). Not every one. See verses 13 and 16.

See also under *Metonymy*.

" Who can find a virtuous woman ? " (Prov. xxxi. 10) : *i.e.*, not that there are absolutely none, but that they are relatively few. See the structure under *Acrostichion*.

---

* See *Christ's Prophetic Teaching*, by the same author and publisher.

"Who hath believed our report?" (Isa. liii. 1). Not, no one, but those to whom it is given—the Remnant. See under *Hypotyposis* and *Metonymy*.

"Who is wise, and he shall understand these things? prudent, and he shall know them?" (Hos. xiv. 9 (10)) : *i.e.*, not that no one is wise, but that such are relatively few.

4. IN DEMONSTRATION.

Sometimes a question is used to make an affirmation as to a certain subject, demonstrating a fact or proving a truth.

"What man is he that feareth the LORD?" (Ps. xxv. 12). This is to call attention to the demonstration in the next verse.

"Son of man, seest thou [*not*] what they do?" (Ezek. viii. 6). We have already had this under a negative affirmation, but its object was to say, Behold, thou art a witness of their abominable idolatry.

"What went ye out into the wilderness to see?" This question is three times repeated: to demonstrate to the People the greatness of John the Baptist (Matt. xi. 7, 8, 9).

So Ps. xxxiv. 12, 13 (13, 14). Jer. ix. 12 (11). Hos. xiv. 9 (10) might also be put under this head. Prov. xxii. 29 ; xxix. 20.

5. IN WONDER AND ADMIRATION.

"Shall a child be born unto him that is an hundred years old? And shall Sarah, that is ninety years old, bear?" (Gen. xvii. 17), in wonder at the Divine power. See Rom. iv. 17-21. Abraham laughed for *joy*, for he fell upon his face in reverence (John viii. 56. Gen. xxi. 8). Sarah laughed from *incredulity* (xviii. 12). Contrast Martha and Mary in John xi. 21 and 32. Mary "fell down at his feet."

"How is it that thou hast found it so quickly, my son?" (Gen. xxvii. 20).

"What is this that God hath done unto us?" (Gen. xlii. 28).

"How good and how pleasant it is for brethren to dwell together in unity!" (Ps. cxxxiii. 1). See under *Asterismos*.

"Who is this that cometh from Edom, with dyed garments from Bozrah?" (Isa. lxiii. 1, 2). See under *Prosopopœia*.

This refers not to Christ's work of redemption for His People, but to the day of His vengeance and judgment on His enemies; as the context clearly shows.

" How weak is thine heart, saith the Lord GOD (Adonai Jehovah) ? "
(Ezek. xvi. 30).

" How soon is the fig-tree withered away ? " (Matt. xxi. 20). Or
better—How can the fig-tree have withered by this time ?

So also Mark vi. 37.

See also 1 Sam. ix. 21. Hab. iii. 8.

6. IN RAPTURE OR EXULTATION.

" Oh how great is thy goodness ! " (Ps. xxxi. 19 (20)).

" How precious also are thy thoughts unto me, O God (El) !
How great is the sum of them ! " (Ps. cxxxix. 17). See *Anthropopatheia.*

" What is man, that thou art mindful of him ? " (Ps. viii. 4 (5) ;
cxliv. 3. Job vii. 17. Heb. ii. 6), to magnify the grace of God in lifting up
such an one from the dunghill to make him inherit the throne of glory
(1 Sam. ii. 8). See Ps. cxiii. 7, 8.

" Who am I, O Lord GOD (Adonai Jehovah) ? " (2 Sam. vii. 18).

It was the revelation of the greatness of God's grace that enabled
David thus to take the place of a true worshipper.   In verse 1, David
" sat in his house," and before himself ; then his thought was to build
a house for God ; but, when he learnt that God was going to build him
a house, then he went in, and " sat before the LORD."

" Is this the manner of man, O Lord GOD (Adonai Jehovah) ? "
(2 Sam. vii. 19).   The margin of the R.V. reads " *Is this the law of
man, O Lord GOD,*" and the A.V. margin says, " Heb. *law.*"   But
idiomatically it means, " Is this the law for humanity ? " : *i.e.,* the
promise to David embraced blessing for the whole of humanity, and
David by faith saw it, and exulted in it.

7. IN WISHES.

" Who will give me drink of the water of the well of Bethlehem,
which is by the gate ? " (2 Sam. xxiii. 15, Heb.).   See under *Œonismos.*

" Whom shall I send, and who will go for us ? " (Isa. vi. 8).

" Who shall deliver me from this body of death ? " (Rom. vii. 24
(marg.)).   See under *Ecphonesis, Metonymy, Hypallage,* and *Ellipsis.*   By
these figures is this height of Christian experience emphasised : *i.e.,*
the knowledge of the fact as to what God had done with " sins " (Rom.
i. 16-v. 11), and also as to what He had done with " sin " (v. 12-viii. 39) ;
so that, although the *fruits* of the old tree are still seen and mourned

over, there is the blessed knowledge that God reckons it as dead—as having died with Christ, and that we are to reckon the same.

8. In Refusals and Denials.

"How shall I curse, whom God (EL) hath not cursed? or how shall I defy, whom the Lord (Jehovah) hath not defied?" (Num. xxiii. 8): *i.e.*, I neither can nor dare do so.

"What have I to do with thee?" (John ii. 4). See under *Idiom.* Also Judges xi. 12. 2 Sam. xvi. 10. 1 Kings xvii. 18. 2 Kings iii. 13. Matt. viii. 29. Mark v. 7. Luke viii. 28.

9. In Doubts.

"Therefore Sarah laughed within herself, saying, After I am waxen old shall I have pleasure?" (Gen. xviii. 12). See above.

"O Ephraim, what shall I do unto thee? O Judah, what shall I do unto thee?" (Hos. vi. 4). See under *Aporia.* So Hos. xi. 8.

"Wherewith shall I come before the Lord, and bow myself before the high God?" (Micah vii. 6).

"But the righteousness which is of faith, speaketh on this wise, Say not in thine heart, Who shall ascend into heaven?" (Rom. x. 6, 7). See under *Epitrechon.* These doubts, raised by self-righteousness, are seen to be removed only by the imputation of a Divine righteousness.

10. In Admonition.

"Hearest thou not, my daughter?" (Ruth ii. 8): *i.e.*, diligently hearken. "Go not to glean in another field."

"Who hath warned you (with the emphasis on the "you") to flee from the wrath to come?" (Matt. iii. 7).

11. In Expostulation.

"Where art thou?" (Gen. iii. 9). To show Adam where he really was, and the condition into which he had fallen, having lost fellowship and communion with God.

"What is this that thou hast done unto me?" etc. (Gen. xii. 18, 19).

"What is that betwixt me and thee?" (Gen. xxiii. 15).

"Who am I that I should go into Pharaoh?" (Ex. iii. 11).

" What could have been done more to my vineyard, that I have not done in it? wherefore, when I looked that it should bring forth grapes, brought it forth wild grapes ? " (Isa. v. 4).

" Wherefore, have we fasted, *say they*, and thou seest not ? wherefore have we afflicted our soul, and thou takest no knowledge ? " (Isa. lviii. 3).

So Gen. xxxi. 26, 27 ; xliv. 4, 15. Ps. xi. 1 ; l. 16 (see *Apodioxis*). Ezek. xii. 22 ; xviii. 1 (2). Dan. iii. 14 ; and many examples in the prophecy of Malachi.

12. IN PROHIBITIONS.

" Why should I be deprived also of you both in one day ? " (Gen. xxvii. 45).

" Why should I kill thee ? " (1 Sam. xix. 17) : *i.e.*, let me not have. to kill thee.

" Wherefore should the heathen say," etc. ? (Ps. lxxix. 10) : *i.e.*, let not the heathen say.

" Wherefore should God be angry at thy voice, and destroy the work of thine hands ? " (Ecc. v. 6).

" Why shouldest thou die before thy time ? " (Ecc. vii. 17).

" Why will ye die, thou and thy people, by the sword ? " (Jer. xxvii. 13). So verse 17, " Wherefore should this city be laid waste ? " *i.e.*, Do not die. Do not let this city be laid waste.

" Why will ye die, O house of Israel ? " (Ezek. xxxiii. 11) : *i.e.*, Turn from your ways, so that ye die not. See under *Epizeuxis* and *Obtestatio*.

So 2 Sam. ii. 22. 2 Chron. xxv. 16. Dan. i. 10, etc.

13. IN PITY AND COMMISERATION.

" How doth the city sit solitary, that was full of people ? " (Lam. i. 1 ; see ii. 1, etc.). See under *Antithesis* and *Ellipsis*.

" How often would I have gathered thy children, etc. ? " (Matt. xxiii. 37).

There are many examples in the Book of Lamentations.

14. IN DISPARAGEMENTS.

" Cease ye from man, whose breath is in his nostrils : for wherein is he to be accounted of ? " (Isa. ii. 22).

" What cities are these which thou hast given me, my brother ? "
(1 Kings ix. 13).

15. In Reproaches.

" When this people, or the prophet, or a priest, shall ask thee,
saying, What is the burden of the Lord ? thou shalt then say unto
them, What burden ? I will even forsake you, saith the Lord " (Jer.
xxiii. 33. So 35, 36).

"What is truth ? " (John xviii. 38).   See *Irony.*

16. In Lamentation.

" Lord, how are they increased that trouble me ! " (Ps. iii. 1 (2)):
i.e., how come mine enemies to be so many ?

" Why hast thou forsaken me ? " (Ps. xxii. 1 (2)).

" Will the Lord cast off for ever ? and will he be favourable no
more ?   Is his mercy clean gone for ever ?   Doth his promise fail for
evermore ?   Hath God forgotten to be gracious ?   Hath he in anger
shut up his tender mercies ?" (Ps. lxxvii. 7-9 (8-10)). These lamentations
arise from *self-occupation* (see verses 1-6).   It is our natural " infirmity "
(verse 10), that leads us into it.   The only remedy is to cease from
self-occupation, and look away from ourselves to God (verses 10-20):
then happiness and praise take the place of lamentation.

Compare Ps. lxxiii. ; where the same experience is gone through,
only then the trouble arises from *looking around* instead of *looking
within*.   But the remedy for this " foolishness " (verse 22) is the same
as for the " infirmity ": *viz.*, *looking up* (verses 17 and 23-28).

The lesson from questions in these two Psalms (lxxvii. and lxxiii.)
is this.   If we want to be *miserable*, all we have to do is to look within.
If we want to be *distracted*, all we have to do is to look around.   But
if we would be *happy*, we must look up, away from ourselves and others,
to God.*

" How is the faithful city become an harlot ! " (Isa. i. 21).   Or,
" How is it that the loyal city has turned harlot ? "   See under
Synecdoche and *Antithesis.*

" Shall the women eat their fruit, and children of a span long ?
Shall the priest and the prophet be slain in the sanctuary of the
Lord ? " (Lam. ii. 20).

---

* See *Things to Come* for Oct., 1899.

17. In Indignation.

"Why do the heathen rage? and [*why do*] the people imagine a vain thing?" (Ps. ii. 1).

"How long shall I be with you? How long shall I suffer you?" (Matt. xvii. 17). See *Ecphonesis.*

18. In Absurdities and Impossibilities.

"Who can bring a clean thing out of an unclean?" (Job xiv. 4).

"Shall mortal man be more just than God? or shall a man be more pure than His Maker?" (Job iv. 17).

"Can the Ethiopian change his skin, or the leopard his spots? then may ye also do good, that are accustomed to do evil" (Jer. xiii. 23). See *Parœmia.*

"How can a man be born when he is old?" etc. (John iii. 4).

"How can this man give us his flesh to eat?" (John vi. 52). It was "a hard saying" (verse 60), and hence they thought it absurd.

"Have any of the elders or of the Pharisees believed on him?" (John vii. 48). This question forms, from that day to this, the excuse for not acknowledging the claims of God or His Truth, unless the great and the influential of the Church receive them. It is the putting of man before God, instead of studying to show ourselves approved only to God.

"Who is this Son of man?" (John xii. 34). This was the expression of the absurdity on the part of Christ's enemies.

19. Double Questions.

Sometimes double questions are employed, repeating the same question in different words so as to express the fact more emphatically.

See Job iv. 17; vi. 5, etc.; viii. 3; x. 4, etc.; xi. 2, 7; xxii. 3. Isa. x. 15. Jer. v. 9, 29.

DIALOGISMOS; or, DIALOGUE.

Dī'-al-o-gis-mos. Greek, διαλογισμός, *conversation, arguing,* from δια-
λογίζεσθαι (*dialogizesthai*), *to converse, argue.*

This figure is used when we represent one or more persons as
speaking about a thing, instead of saying it ourselves : *Dialogue.*

The persons speak in a manner suitable to their character or
condition.

When there are not two persons represented, but the objecting
and answering is done by the one speaker, the figure is called
LOGISMUS, and what is stated is said to be *in dialogismo,* or *in
logismo.*

Sometimes the speaker brings forward another as speaking, and
uses his words, adapting them to the object in view.

The Latins called this figure SERMOCINATIO, which means the
same thing.

Isa. xiv. 16-19.—"They that see thee shall narrowly look upon
thee, and consider thee, saying,

> Is this the man that made the earth to tremble, that did
> shake kingdoms? etc.,

But thou art cast out of thy grave like an abominable branch," etc.

Isa. lxiii. 1-6.—" Who is this that cometh from Edom, with dyed
garments from Bozrah ? This that is glorious in his apparel, travelling
in the greatness of his strength ?

> I that speak in righteousness, mighty to save.

Wherefore art thou red in thine apparel, and thy garments like him
that treadeth in the winefat ?

> I have trodden the winepress alone ; and of the people there
> was none with me ; for I will tread them in mine anger, and
> trample them in my fury ; and their blood shall be sprinkled
> upon my garments, and I will stain all my raiment. For
> the day of vengeance is in mine heart, and the year of my
> redeemed is come." etc.

Thus, vividly and powerfully, is the day of vengeance, and of
judgment, described. And yet there are persons who take this passage
as treating of Christ's past work of grace on Calvary !

Micah ii. 4.—" In that day shall one take up a parable against you, and lament with a doleful lamentation, and say, We be utterly spoiled: " etc. (See under *Polyptoton*).

Zech. viii. 20-23.—" It shall yet come to pass that there shall come people, and the inhabitants of many cities : And the inhabitants of one city shall go to another, saying,

> Let us go speedily to pray before the LORD, and to seek the LORD of hosts : I will go also.

Yea, many people and strong nations shall come," etc. See *Polyptoton*.

Some think that Paul, when he says, in

1 Cor. ix. 24, " So run, that ye may obtain," does not directly exhort the Corinthians himself ; but by a *Sermocinatio*, brings forward and uses that incitement which the trainers and spectators in the public contests usually employed.

Other examples may be found under *Antimetathesis*, and in Matt. xxv. 37-39. Luke xiii. 6-9 ; xv. 20-32.

DIANŒA ; or, ANIMATED DIALOGUE.

Di'-a-næ'-a. Greek, διάνοια, *a revolving in the mind.* This Figure is employed when the speaker uses animated questions and answers in developing an argument. ——

The Latins called it SUBJECTIO, *a substituting*, RESPONSIO, *a responding.*

It is a form of *Dialogismos (q.v.).*

AFFIRMATIO; or, AFFIRMATION.

Spontaneous Affirmation.

Affirmation becomes a Figure when it is used otherwise than in answer to a question ; or, instead of a bare statement of the fact.

It emphasizes the words thus to affirm what no one has disputed.

The Apostle uses it in Phil. i. 18, " What then ? notwithstanding, every way, whether in pretence, or in truth, Christ is preached ; and I therein do rejoice, yea, and will rejoice."

NEGATIO; or, NEGATION.

Spontaneous Negation.

Negation is used in a similar way as a Figure, when it is a *denying* of that which has not been affirmed : *i.e.*, when, instead of merely making a statement, it is put in the form of a denial.

Paul uses it in Gal. ii. 5, " To whom we gave place by subjection, no, not for an hour." (See *Synecdoche*).

When the negation is very important, the negative is repeated, or combined with another negative to increase its emphasis. See *Repeated Negation*.

ACCISMUS; or, APPARENT REFUSAL.

Ac-cis'-mus, a cutting all but through, from the Latin, *accido*. This Figure is so named because it is an apparent or assumed refusal.

Matt. xv. 22-26.—When the woman of Canaan cried "Have mercy on me, O Lord, thou Son of David," the Lord did not intend to reject her : but, having no claim (as a Gentile) on Christ as the " Son of David," He uses the figure *Accismus*, and apparently refuses her request by saying, " I am not sent but unto the lost sheep of the house of Israel."

"Then came she and worshipped him, saying, Lord help me." But again, there was no confession as to the "me." It was not like the Publican, " God be merciful to me—A SINNER." It might have been a self-righteous " me."

So the Lord again uses the Figure *Accismus*, but He now combines it with *Hypocatastasis*; and says :

> " It is not meet to take the children's bread, and to cast it to dogs."

Now came the confession—she saw the point. She admitted the fact as to her condition as " *a dog of the Gentiles*," and said, " Truth, Lord : " and received the blessing which had been determined for her.

Matt. xxi. 29 is sometimes given as an example ; but this was a real refusal, altered by after repentance.

ÆTIOLOGIA; or, CAUSE SHOWN.

The rendering a Reason for what is said or done.

Ae¹-ti-o-log¹-ia (Aetiology). Greek Αἰτιολογία, *rendering a reason*, from αἰτία *(aitia), a cause,* and λόγος *(logos), a description.*

The figure is used when, either directly or indirectly, the speaker or writer renders a reason for what he thinks, says, or does.

The figure was also called APODEIXIS (*Ap-o-deix¹-is*). Greek, ἀπόδειξις, *full demonstration,* from ἀποδεικνύναι *(apodeiknunai), to point out, demonstrate.*

The Latins called it CAUSÆ REDDITIO: *rendering a reason,* or *showing the cause.*

Rom. i. 13.—"Now I would not have you ignorant, brethren, that oftentimes I purposed to come unto you, (but was let hitherto,) that I might have some fruit among you also, even as among other Gentiles."

Verses 15, 16: "I am ready to preach the Gospel to you that are at Rome also. For I am not ashamed of the Gospel of Christ; for it is the power of God unto salvation."

So Rom. iii. 20; iv. 14, 15, and all other passages where the word "For" points out the reason, or "Therefore" shows the cause.

These are too numerous to be quoted; but their significance should always be noted.

ANTEISAGOGE ; or, COUNTER-QUESTION.

The Answering of one Question by asking another.

An-teis'-a-gō'-gee. Greek, ἀντεισαγωγή, *a bringing in instead ;* from ἀντί (*anti*), *against* or *instead ;* εἰς (*eis*), *in ;* ἄγειν (*agein*), *to lead* or *bring.*

The figure is so called, because a question is answered by asking another.

It is called also ANTICATALLAXIS (*an'-ti-cat'-al-lax'-is*). Greek, ἀντικατάλλαξις, *a setting off* or *balancing of one thing against another* (as in trade).

The Greeks called it also ANTHUPOPHORA (*an'-thu-poph'-o-ra*). Greek, ἀνθυποφορά, *a reply to an objection ;* from ἀντί (*anti*), *against,* ὑπό (*hupo*), φέρειν (*pherein*), *to bring.*

Hence the Latin names of the Figure : COMPENSATIO, *compensation,* and CONTRARIA ILLATIO, *a bringing in against.*

Judges xiv. 8.—The answer to Samson's " riddle " is given in the form of a question, and is thus an *Anteisagoge.* See under *Enigma.*

A beautiful example is furnished in

Matt. xxi. 23-25 ; where, when the chief priests and elders asked Christ by what authority He acted ; He said, " I also will ask you one thing, which if ye tell me, I in like wise will tell you by what authority I do these things." He then goes on, in verse 25, to answer the question by asking another.

In the answer of His enemies we have the Figure *Aporia* (*q.v.*).

Rom. ix. 19, 20.—" Thou wilt say then unto me, Why doth he yet find fault ? For who hath resisted his will ? "

" Nay but, O man, who art thou that repliest against God ? " See below, under *Prolepsis.*

ANTISTROPHE; or, RETORT.

A turning the Words of a Speaker against himself.

An-tis¹-tro-phee. Greek, ἀντιστροφή, *a turning about*, from ἀντί (*anti*), *against,* and στρέφω (*strepho*), *to turn.*

The figure is so called because the words of a speaker are turned against himself in Retort.

When the retort is violent, it is called BIÆON (*Bi-ae¹-on*), Greek, Βίαιον, *forcible, violent, compulsory.*

Hence the Latin, VIOLENTUM, *violent,* and INVERSIO, *inversion, a turning against.*

Matt. xv. 26, 27.—The woman of Canaan used this figure in her reply to Christ. He had said " It is not meet to take the children's bread, and to cast it to dogs." And she said, "Truth, Lord; yet the dogs eat of the crumbs which fall from their master's table," and thus turned His words against Himself.

2 Cor. xi. 22.—" Are they Hebrews ? so am I. Are they Israelites ? so am I. Are they the seed of Abraham ? so am I." See also under *Epiphoza.*

When the words thus turned against the speaker are an *accusation*, then the figure is called

ANTICATEGORIA; or, TU QUOQUE.

The use of a Counter-Charge, or Recrimination.

An¹-ti-cat¹-ee-gor¹-i-a. Greek, ἀντικατηγορία, *a counter-charge :* from ἀντί (*anti*), *against*, and κατηγορέω, *to speak against :* hence, *to recriminate, to accuse in turn.*

The figure is used when we retort upon another the very insinuation or accusation which he has made against us. It differs from *Antistrophe* (see above); in that it has to do, not with any general kind of words, but with a particular *accusation*.

It is what the Latins called a TU QUOQUE; or, ACCUSATIO ADVERSA, *an opposite accusation*, or *an accusation turned against* another; or, TRANSLATIO IN ADVERSARIUM, *a transferring against an adversary.*

Ezek. xviii. 25.—"Yet ye say, The way of the Lord is not equal. Hear now, O house of Israel; Is not my way equal? are not your ways unequal?" So verse 29, and xxxiii. 17.

This would be *Anteisagoge*, were it a simple question instead of an accusation.

METASTASIS; or, COUNTER-BLAME.

A transferring of the Blame from one's self to another.

Me-tas¹-ta-sis. Greek, μετάστασις, from μετά *(meta)*, *beyond, over,* and στάσις, a *standing* or *placing* (from ἱστάναι *(histanai), to put* or *place).*

Hence, *Metastasis* means a placing beyond: *i.e.,* a transferring.

Hence called by the Latins TRANSLATIO, *a translating.*

The Figure is so called because it is a transferring of blame from one person or thing to another.

Elijah used the figure in his answer to Ahab in

1 Kings xviii. 17, 18.—" When Ahab saw Elijah, that Ahab said unto him, Art thou he that troubleth Israel? And he answered, I have not troubled Israel; but thou, and thy father's house," etc.

2 Kings ix. 19.—" Is it peace? . . . What hast thou to do with peace?" This is also the Figure *Anteisagoge (q.v.).*

Rom. vii. 14.—" We know that the law is spiritual: but I am carnal, sold under sin."

ANACŒNOSIS ; or, COMMON CAUSE.

An Appeal to others as having interests in Common.

An¹-a-cœ-nō¹-sis. Greek, ἀνακοίνωσις (*anakoinosis*), from ἀνακοινοῦν (*ana-koinoun*), *to communicate ;* from ἀνά (*ana*), *up,* and κοινοῦν (*koinoun*), *to make common* (from κοινός, *koinos, common*).

A Figure by which a speaker appeals to his opponents for their opinion, as having a common interest in the matter in question : as, " If the case were yours, how would you act ? " or " What do you think about it ? " or " What would you say ? "

The Greeks also called it SYMBOULESIS (*sym-boul-ee¹-sis,* συμ-βούλησις, *a counselling together :* from σύν (*sun* or *syn*), *together,* and βουλή, *a counselling.* Hence, βουλεύεσθαι (*bouleuesthai*), *to deliberate.*

The Latins called it COMMUNICATIO, *a making common.*

The figure is an appeal to the feelings or opinions of others, which they have in common with ourselves, and to which we submit the matter.

When this is done by way of *question*, it is a form of *Erotesis* (*q.v.*).

Isa. v. 3, 4.—" And now, O inhabitants of Jerusalem, and men of Judah, judge, I pray you, betwixt me and my vineyard. What could I have done more to my vineyard, that I have not done in it ? " etc.

Mal. i. 6.—" If then I be a father, where is mine honour ? and if I be a master, where is my fear ? saith the LORD of hosts unto you, O priests, that despise my name."

Luke xi. 19.—" If I by Beelzebub cast out devils, by whom do your sons cast them out ? therefore shall they be your judges."

Acts iv. 19.—" But Peter and John answered and said unto them, Whether it be right in the sight of God to hearken unto you more than unto God, judge ye."

1 Cor. iv. 21.—" What will ye ? Shall I come unto you with a rod, or in love, and in the spirit of meekness ? "

1 Cor. x. 15.—" I speak as to wise men ; judge ye what I say."

1 Cor. xi. 13, 14.—" Judge in yourselves : is it comely that a woman pray unto God uncovered ? Doth not even nature itself teach you, that, if a man have long hair, it is a shame unto him ? "

Gal. iv. 21.—" Tell me, ye that desire to be under the law, do ye not hear the law ? "

See also Jer. xxiii. 23. Gal. iii. 1, 2, 5, etc.

SYNCHORESIS; or, CONCESSION.

Making a Concession of one Point to gain another.

Syn'-chō-ree'-sis. Greek, συγχώρησις, *concession, acquiescence, consenting,* from συγχωρέω (*synchoreō*), *to come together, agree.*

The figure is used when we make a *concession* of one point in order to gain another. In this case the concession or admission is made, and may be rightly made, in order to gain a point.

It thus differs from *Epitrope* (see below), where we admit something that is wrong in itself for the sake of argument.

Synchoresis, therefore, is *concession*, while *Epitrope* is *admission* or *surrender.*

The Latins called it CONCESSIO, *concession,* while the Greeks had another name for it, EPICHORESIS (*Ep'-i-chō-ree'-sis*), *an agreement upon* a point.

Jer. xii. 1.—" Righteous art thou, O LORD, when I plead with thee : yet let me talk (marg. *reason the case*) with thee of thy judgments : Wherefore doth the way of the wicked prosper ? wherefore are all they happy that deal very treacherously ? "

Hab. i. 13.—"Thou art of purer eyes than to behold evil, and canst not look on iniquity ; wherefore lookest thou upon them that deal treacherously, and holdest thy tongue when the wicked devoureth the man that is more righteous than he ? " etc.

Rom. ii. 17-20.—All these claims of the Jew are admitted for the sake of argument, in order to emphasize the weighty reproof in verse 21, " Thou therefore, which teachest another, teachest thou not thyself ? " etc., to the end of verse 23.

1 Cor. iv. 8.—He concedes the point as to their desire to reign, but ironically adds, " I would to God ye did reign, that we also might reign with you."

2 Cor. x. 1.—He concedes the point that he was base among them : but verses 2 and 11 show that he does so only to gain another point. So in xii. 16.

Gal. iv. 15.—The apostle grants the fact, which was indisputable, as to the great friendship and love that existed between himself and the Galatian saints ; in order to gain another point, and add to his argument, when he asks in the next verse, " Am I therefore become your enemy because I tell you the truth ? "

Jas. ii. 19.—" Thou believest that there is one God ; thou doest well : the devils also believe, and tremble."

EPITROPE; or, ADMISSION.

Admission of Wrong in order to gain what is Right.

E-pit'-ro-pee. Greek, ἐπιτροπή, *reference, arbitration*, from ἐπιτρέπειν, *to turn over, surrender*, (from ἐπί *(epi)*, *upon*, and τρέπειν *(trepein)*, *to turn*).

The Figure is used when we surrender a point which we feel to be wrong, but we admit it for the sake of argument. In *Synchoresis (q.v.)*, we concede what is right in itself; but, in *Epitrope*, we admit what is wrong, giving way to the feelings or unreasonableness of another, in order that we may more effectually carry our point.

The Latins called it PERMISSIO, *a giving up, unconditional surrender.*

The figure sometimes approaches to *Irony (q.v.)*; when "what is admitted" is not *really* granted, but only apparently so for argument's sake.

1 Kings xxii. 15.—" Go, and prosper : for the LORD shall deliver it into the hand of the king." Micaiah (by *Epitrope* and *Irony*) admitted what was in Jehoshaphat's heart, and thus exposed and condemned it.

Ecc. xi. 9.—" Rejoice, O young man, in thy youth ; and let thy heart cheer thee in the days of thy youth, and walk in the ways of thine heart, and in the sight of thine eyes : but know thou, that for all these things God will bring thee into judgment."

Jer. ii. 28.—" But where are thy gods that thou hast made thee ? " Here, the admission as to these gods is made ; but only for the sake of exposing, by *Irony*, the fact that they were no gods. So vii. 21, and Ezek. xx. 39.

Amos iv. 4, 5.—See under *Irony*.

Matt. xxiii. 32.—" Fill ye up then the measure of your fathers." Christ was not inciting to murders and martyrdoms ; but, using the figure *Epitrope*, He granted their position, and ironically told them to act accordingly.

John xiii. 27.—" That thou doest, do quickly." The Lord is not sanctioning the evil, but permitting it.

Rom. xi. 19, 20.—" Thou (Gentile, verse 13) wilt say then, The branches were broken off, that I might be graffed in. Well ; because of unbelief they were broken off, and thou standest by faith.   Be not highminded, but fear."

Here, it is not *Synchoresis*, *i.e.*, a concession of what is right, but an admission of what is wrong, for the sake of argument.   Indeed, it is a mixture of the two, for there are two propositions.   "The branches were broken off": *i.e.*, the Jews were cast off for a time (though not cast away, verse 1), that is true.   That point is conceded; but "that I might be grafted in"?   No! that was not the object: that is what you Gentiles will say, "Thou wilt say."   It is not what the Holy Spirit says.   That was not the cause why the Jews were broken off.   It was "because of unbelief"!   That was the true reason!

PAROMOLOGIA; or, CONFESSION.

A Concession in Argument to gain Favour.

Par-o-mo-log'-i-a. Greek, παρομολογία, *confession*, from παρά (*para*), *by*, or *near*, and ὁμολογεῖν (*homologein*), *to confess.*

This Figure is used when we acknowledge some fault or wrong with a view to gain favour. Hence the Latins called it CONFESSIO, *confession, acknowledgment.*

PROTHERAPEIA; or, CONCILIATION.

The securing of Indulgence for what is about to be said.

Pro-ther-a-pei-a. Greek, προθεραπεία, *previous care* or *treatment*, from πρό (*pro*), *before*, and θεραπεία (*therapeia*), *service*.

The Figure is used when, by way of precaution, we secure indulgence, or conciliate others, with reference to something we are about to say.

It is called also PROEPIPLEXIS, *pro¹-ep-i-pleex¹-is*, from πρό (*pro*), *before*, and ἐπίπληξις, *blame*, *a blaming* (of one's self) *beforehand*: *i.e.*, in order to secure the attention or favour of another.

When it is added at the end of what is said, it is called *Epitherapeia* (*q.v.*).

John iii. 2.—"Rabbi, we know that thou art a teacher come from God," etc.

Matt. xix. 16.—"And, behold, one came and said unto him, Good Master." See under *Synocæosis*. So Mark x. 17. Luke xviii. 18.

Acts xvii. 22.—"Ye men of Athens, I perceive that in all things ye are very religious." This is the meaning of the word (see R.V. margin) δεισιδαιμονέστερος (*deisidaimonesteros*), *careful in the discharge of religious services*. For religion in itself is nothing. It depends entirely on what the religion is, whether true or false.

There are only two religions in the world; and there never have been more from Gen. iv. to the present day. They are put in the fore-front of Revelation. Abel's and Cain's; God's way and man's way; God's way, and man's attempted improvement on it.

All kinds of false religion agree in one thing. They are all alike, and all at one in demanding that the sinner must do *something*, be *something*, give, pay, feel, experience, or produce *something*, to merit God's favour. They quarrel bitterly as to what that something is to be. Controversies rage concerning it; the blood of martyrs has been shed; battles have been fought; but yet they are all agreed that the sinner must say, "Something in my hand I bring."

Whereas the one and only true religion is expressed in the words,

"NOTHING in my hand I bring."

So that a man may be " very religious," and yet be unsaved, and " far off " from God (Eph. ii. 13).

Acts xxvi. 2, 3 is another beautiful example of true *Protherapeia.* See also xxii. 3-6, etc.

PRODIORTHOSIS; or, WARNING.

Something said to prepare for a shock.

Pro¹-di-or-tho¹-sis. Greek, προδιόρθωσις, *a preparatory apology,* from πρό (*pro*), *before,* and διόρθωσις (*diorthosis*), *a making straight, putting right*; from διορθόω (*diorthoō*), *to make straight, set straight.*

This is the previous Figure of *Protherapeia* used to prepare the hearers or readers for what might otherwise shock or offend them.

PALINODIA; or, RETRACTING.

Approval of one Thing after reproving for another Thing.

Pal'-i-nōd'-i-a. Greek, παλινῳδία, *a song repeated a second time*; hence a *retracting* of a former one.

The Figure is used when, having spoken against or reproved any person or thing, we speak well of him or it.

Examples may be found in some of the Epistles to the Seven Churches.

EPHESUS: Rev. ii. 6, after the reproof of verses 4 and 5.

SARDIS: Rev. iii. 4 and 5, after the reproof of verse 1.

In the Old Testament, examples may be seen in 2 Chron. xv. 17; xix. 3. Ps. lxxxix. 33; cvi. 8, 44.

PROLEPSIS (OCCUPATIO) ; or, ANTICIPATION.

The answering of an Argument by anticipating it before it is used.

Pro-leep¹-sis. Greek, πρόληψις, *a taking beforehand,* from πρό (*pro*), *beforehand,* and λαμβάνειν (*lambanein*), *to take* or *receive.*

This is a beautiful figure; by which we *anticipate* objections to what we are stating.

The other general names of this figure are :

PROCATALEPSIS (*Pro¹-cat-a-leep¹-sis*). Greek, προκατάληψις, *a seizing beforehand, pre-occupation.*

APANTESIS (*Ap¹-an-tee¹-sis*). Greek, ἀπάντησις, *a meeting;* hence *a meeting* of an objection by anticipation.

The Latins called it:

OCCUPATIO, *anticipation.*

ANTEOCCUPATIO, *anticipation beforehand.*

PRÆMONITIO, *a defending beforehand, obviating objections.*

All these different names show us the importance of the figure in argumentation.

There is another kind of *Prolepsis,* which has to do only with *time.* It is distinguished from our present figure in that while it anticipates and speaks of future things as present it really *adjourns* the application of the words, and is called AMPLIATIO, or *adjournment.* (See pages 689 and 914).

The form of *Prolepsis* which we are considering is an anticipation which has to do with *Argumentation ;* and hence is distinguished from the other by the word OCCUPATIO: *i.e.,* we not only anticipate what is coming, but *occupy and deal with it,* instead of adjourning or putting it off. See Section 4, above.

Prolepsis, as relating to Argumentation is of two kinds : (i.) *Tecta,* or, *closed ;* and (ii.) *Aperta,* or, *open.*

I. *Tecta,* or Closed *Prolepsis,* is where the anticipated objection is merely stated or implied, not answered; or answered, but not plainly stated.

II *Aperta,* or Open *Prolepsis,* is where the anticipated objection is both answered and stated.

We will consider these in order with the different names which have been given to them.

I. Tecta:

From the Latin *tego, to roof* or *cover*. The *Prolepsis* is so called when it anticipates the objection, but confines itself merely to stating it. It is called HYPOPHORA, *hy-poph¹-o-ra*. Greek, ὑποφόρα, *a holding under, putting forward ;* then, *that which is held forth, an objection.*

Sometimes the objection is not stated, but is implied by the answer which is given.

Rom. ix. 6.—" Not as though the word of God hath taken none effect. For they are not all Israel which are of Israel."

The objection which is met is this : If Israel be rejected and cast off for a time (as is going to be shown), then the Word of God has failed, and is ineffectual. No ! For they are not all Israel which are of Israel. And there is to be a People taken out from among the Gentiles for His name, as well as a remnant of Israel, according to the election of grace.

Rom. x. 18.—" But I say, Have they not heard ? (Anticipating the objection that they have not heard.) Yes verily," etc.

Rom. xi. 1.—" I say then, Hath God cast away his people ? " (Anticipating the objection, which many make even until to-day.) To which he replies, " God forbid," etc.

Rom. xi. 11.—" I say then, Have they stumbled that they should fall [*for ever*] ? " (Thus anticipating the objection that they had done so, and meeting it in the words that follow), or, " Their falling away was not the object (or purpose) of their stumbling, was it ? "

II. Aperta.

Latin, *aperta, open.* This use of the figure is so called, because not only is the objection anticipated ; but it is stated, and the answer also is given.

The names for this variation are ANTHYPOPHORA, *an¹-thy-poph¹-o-ra.* Greek, ἀνθυποφόρα, *a reply to an objection ;* from ἀντί (*anti*), *against,* ὑπό (*hypo*), *under,* and φορέω (*phoreō*), *to bring* or *put under.* Hence, *a substitution by stealth.* The figure being so called because, by stealth, we take our opponent's objection, and substitute it for our own.

It was also called

SCHESIS, *schee¹-sis.* Greek, σχῆσις, ‑ *a checking;* because, by anticipating the objection, we check the opponent, and keep him from speaking or replying.

ANASCHESIS, *an-a¹-sche-sis¹.* Greek, ἀνάσχεσις, *a taking on one's self.*

PROSAPODOTON, *pros-a-pod¹-o-ton.* Greek, προσαπόδοτον, *a giving back to* or *besides.*

HYPOBOLE, *hy-pob¹-o-lee.* Greek, ὑποβολή, *a throwing under.*

Isa. xlix. 14.—Zion's objection is not merely anticipated in this verse, but is answered in the next.

" But Zion said, The LORD hath forsaken me, and my Lord hath forgotten me."

" Can a woman forget her sucking child, that she should not have compassion on the son of her womb ? yea, they may forget, yet will I not forget thee."

Matt. iii. 9.—"Think not to say within yourselves, We have Abraham to our father: for I say unto you, that God is able even of these stones to raise up children unto Abraham." See under *Parechesis.*

Rom. iii. 1-10.—Under the figure *Antimetathesis,* we have shown how the objections of an imaginary Jewish opponent are here stated and met. See section 2, above : " As to *persons.*"

Rom. iv. 1-3.—The objection is met, that Abraham was justified by works—his faith being a work. This is shewn in verse 4 and the following verses to be impossible, as denying the very first principles of grace.

Rom. vi. 1, 2.—" What shall we say then ? Are we to continue in sin that grace may abound ? God forbid. How shall we, who have died to sin, live any longer therein ? "

That is to say : If those who are " in Christ " died in God's purpose when Christ died, how can they live in sin ?

Rom. vii. 7.—" What shall we say then ? that the Law is sin ? God forbid. Nay, I had not known sin, but by the Law."

Rom. ix. 14, 15.—" What shall we say then ? Is there unrighteousness with God ? God forbid. For," etc.

Rom. ix. 19.—See above under *Anteisagoge.*

Rom. xi. 20, 21.—See above under *Epĭtrope.*

 1 Cor. xv. 35, 36.—"But some man will say, How are the dead raised up? and with what body do they come? Thou foolish man! that which thou sowest is not quickened, except it die."

———————————

APPENDICES.

———

APPENDIX A

ON

THE USE OF DIFFERENT TYPES IN THE ENGLISH VERSIONS.

ON page 2, under the figure *Ellipsis*, we have referred to the way in which this was indicated in the English Versions.

It may be well to add, by way of Appendix, some brief account of the use of different types.

The practice of indicating, by different types, words and phrases which were not in the original Text was, it is believed, first introduced by Sebastian Münster, of Basle, in a Latin Version of the Old Testament, published in 1534. The first of the "Former Translations" that used a different type, or what was then called "a small letter in the Text," was Cranmer's Bible (1539). But this was with quite a different object: *viz.*, to distinguish clauses from the Latin which were not in the Hebrew or Greek: *e.g.*, Matt. xxv. 1, "and the bride."

Subsequent Translations disregarded the Vulgate more, and reverted to the original purpose in the employment of *italic type*.

The English New Testament (published at Geneva, 1557) and the Geneva Bible (1560) "put in that word, which, lacking, made the sentence obscure, but set it in such letters, as may easily be discerned from the common text." The example was followed and extended in the Bishops' Bible (1568, 1572); and the *Roman* and *Italic* * types of these Bibles (as distinguished from the *black letter* and *Roman* type of previous Bibles) were introduced into the A.V. (1611).

The italics were used very loosely and inconsistently in the A.V. These inconsistencies were manifest on the same page and in the same verse.

The Cambridge Bibles of 1629 and 1639 made a great reform; which was extended by Dr. Paris in 1762 and Dr. Blayney in 1769. In these two Bibles, the number of words in italics was largely increased, though their use and application is far from being consistent.

The following seem to have been the principles guiding the translators of the A.V.

---

* The word *Italic* means *relating to Italy*, and is used of a kind of type dedicated to the States of Italy, by Aldus Manutius, about the year 1500.

1. To supply the omissions under the figure *Ellipsis*, or what they considered to be Ellipsis.

2. To supply the words necessary to give the sense, when the figure called *Zeugma* is employed (a kind of *Ellipsis*).

3. Once, at least, to indicate a word or words of doubtful MS. authority. 1 John ii. 23 (first introduced in Cranmer's Bible—doubtless from the Vulgate). Perhaps also Judges xvi. 2 and xx. 9.

4. Where the English idiom differs from that of the Originals, and requires essential words to be added, which are not necessary in the Hebrew or Greek.

When we speak of the *Authorized Version* of the English Bible (published in 1611), we are immediately confronted with the fact that two editions were published in that same year ; and that they differ in many material points, the one from the other. Both are in the British Museum.* Many subsequent editions followed, which contain very many not unimportant changes. Some of these may be attributed to oversight arising from human infirmity; but most of them are changes, deliberately made and introduced without any authority, by men whose names are for the most part unknown.

Some of these emendations have been discarded in later editions, and also some notable misprints, but many have been retained.

The Cambridge folio editions of 1629 and 1638 appear to have been a complete revision ; but, though wholly unauthorised, it cannot be doubted that the work was well done, and moreover was greatly needed on account of the corrupt state of the then current editions. The parallel textual references in the margin were greatly increased in these editions, and have been still further extended in those published subsequently.

Some of its emendations have dropped out in later editions, while some of its mistakes have been perpetuated ! Among the former the word " and " in John xiv. 6 (" and the truth ") was correctly inserted, but disappeared again in editions since 1817. Among the latter, Jer. xxxiv. 16 : " He had set," instead of " ye had set," as in 1611.

Ezek. xviii. 1 : " The word of the LORD," instead of " And the word," as in 1611.

---

* Press marks :—3050 g. 2 and 3050 g. 1 respectively. There can be no doubt as to which of these is the original edition, as one of them contains a serious printer's error in Exodus, which in the other is corrected : this must therefore have been printed subsequently, *though in the same year.*

Hos. xiii. 3 : "The whirlwind," instead of " A whirlwind," as in 1611.

Acts vi. 3 : "Whom ye may appoint," instead of " we may appoint," as in 1611. This mistake continued down to 1646.

An edition published in 1660, by Hills and Field, is remarkable for certain marginal notes then added ; and subsequently increased in a Cambridge Bible of 1682 with a great number of fresh textual references, probably by Dr. Scattergood.

An edition of 1701 first contained the marginal dates, which were chiefly those of Archbishop Ussher. There were also tables of Scripture measures, weights, and coins ; tables of kindred and of time, etc. Additional references were also given. This was the work of William Lloyd at the request of Convocation. But Lloyd exercised his own judgment in the insertion of Archbishop Ussher's dates. Ussher (in 1580-1656) had given 455 B.C., as the date of the Decree given to Nehemiah (in Neh. ii.) ; but Lloyd altered this to 445 B.C., as it now stands in our English Bibles ! This was done to suit his own theories, and is of no value as against Ussher's elaborate calculations.

The editions of Dr. Paris, in 1762, and of Dr. Blayney, which superseded it in 1769, contained additions in the use of italic type, marginal notes, dates, and textual references. These versions modernised the diction, and made many emendations of the Text ; some of them very needless ; and also introduced errors of their own, not always those pertaining to the printer.

Since that date controversies have been carried on ; and attempts have been made to effect a revision of the A.V., with the view to provide an edition which should prove to be a standard Text. But all efforts came to nothing ; and a new Revised Version was issued instead in 1881. The remarks of the revisers in their preface, as to the use of italic type, should be carefully studied ; inasmuch as they reviewed the whole subject and adopted certain principles which tended " to diminish rather than increase the amount of italic printing."

The Old Testament Company in their preface (1884) state that they have " departed from the custom of the Authorised Version, and adopted, as their rule, the following resolution of their Company :—

" ' That all such words, now printed in italics, as are plainly implied in the Hebrew and necessary in the English, be printed in common type.

" ' But where any doubt existed as to the exact rendering of the Hebrew, all words which have been added in order to give completeness to the English expression are printed in italic type,' " etc.

The use of large capital letters for certain words and phrases originated with the Authorised Version. None of the previous or "former translations" have them.

The revisers abandoned this practice, but have not been consistent in the plan they substituted for it. In most of the cases they have used small capital letters instead of the large capitals; but, in three cases (Jer. xxiii. 6 and Zech. iii. 8; vi. 12), they have used ordinary Roman type.

The use of the large capitals by the translators of the A.V. are destitute of any authority, and merely indicate the importance which they attached to such words and phrases thus indicated.

The following is a complete list :—

Large capitals in A.V.　Small capitals in R.V.

Ex. iii. 14 : " I am that I am."

Ex. iii. 14.—" I am."

Ex. vi. 3 : " Jehovah."

Ex. xxviii. 36; xxxix. 30: "Holiness (R.V., "HOLY") to the Lord."

Deut. xxviii. 58 : " The Lord thy God."

Ps. lxviii. 4 : " Jah."

Ps. lxxxiii. 18 : " Jehovah."

Isa. xxvi. 4 : " Jehovah."

Dan. v. 25-28 : " Mene, Mene, Tekel, Upharsin " (verse 28, Peres).

Zech. xiv. 20 : " Holiness (R V., " holy ") unto the Lord ."

Matt. i. 21 : " Jesus."

Matt. i. 25 : " Jesus."

Matt. xxvii. 37 : The inscriptions on the Cross. Also Mark xv. 26. Luke xxiii. 38. John xix. 19.

Luke i. 31 ; ii. 21 : " Jesus."

Acts xvii. 23 : " To the (R.V., " an ") unknown God."

Rev. xvii. 5 : " Mystery, Babylon the Great, the Mother of (R.V., " the ") Harlots and (R.V., " of the ") Abominations of the Earth."

Rev. xix. 16 : " King of kings, and Lord of lords."

Large capitals in A.V.　Small Roman letters in R.V.

Jer. xxiii. 6 : " The Lord our Righteousness."

Zech. iii. 8 : " Branch."

Zech. vi. 12 : " Branch."

APPENDIX B

ON

THE USAGE OF THE GENITIVE CASE.

WE have observed, on page 497, under the figure of *Antimereia*, that while a noun *in regimen* (*i.e.*, governed by another noun, and thus placed in the genitive case) is used instead of an adjective, it is not *always* that the genitive case thus used stands for an adjective. The word "of" therefore does not carry with it a uniform signification.

It is used in many ways: and it is ever the business of the student to stop whenever the word "of" is met with, and ask, "What is the meaning of it?" in each case.

Grammarians differ widely as to the mode of classifying the various usages of the genitive case. They differ both as to the classes themselves; the number of their varieties; and the names by which they are called. We therefore present our own.

The name of the case in which the latter of these two nouns is placed is called the genitive, from γενική (*genikee*), because it designates the *genus* to which anything is referred, or from which it is *generated*.

It is, therefore, what we may call *the birth-case: i.e.*, the case of birth or origin, and from that primal sense all its other meanings may be drawn. Our English word "of" is, properly speaking, a preposition governing the objective case; and is thus very often, but by no means always, a representative or substitute for the true genitive. There is therefore a danger in supposing that "of" in English always represents a genitive case in Hebrew or other languages.

The genitive case, of itself, answers the question, *Whence?* and as the answers to the question may be various in kind, so are the classifications of the nature of the genitive case (in *Antimereia* of the noun) of various kinds also.

It is sometimes difficult to decide to which class an example particularly belongs. It might often be quite correct to place it under more than one head.

It is for the student, whenever he finds the word "of" as the sign of the genitive, to consider and decide to which of these classes it belongs; and to test it by trying it under each until he can determine the head under which it is to be placed.

We give the examples as they stand in the original, with the interpretation; and the reader must see for himself how it is rendered in the A.V. and the R.V.

The examples given are by no means exhaustive. Ample scope is thus left for further investigation on the part of those who desire to pursue this study.

We have classified them thus:—

THE GENITIVE OF

    1. Character.

    2. Origin and efficient cause.

    3. Possession.

    4. Apposition.

    5. Relation.

    6. Material.

    7. Contents.

    8. Partition.

    9. Two Genitives depending one on the other.

1. *The Genitive of* CHARACTER.

This is more purely *adjectival* than the others, and is always emphatic. The emphasis is always to be placed on the adjective thus formed, and not on the noun thus qualified by it. We have given examples under the figure of *Antimereia*; where they will be found on pages 498-506.

2. *The Genitive of* ORIGIN AND EFFICIENT CAUSE.

This usage marks the source from which anything comes or is supplied; or from which it has its origin. With this we may group the examples denoting the efficient cause producing or effecting, and thus originating, whatever is spoken of.

Num. xxiv. 4, 16.—" Words of God ": *i.e.*, from El, and " the vision of the Almighty" : *i.e.*, from El Shaddai.

Deut. xxxii. 19.—" He abhorred them because of the provoking of his sons and of his daughters": *i.e.*, because of the provocation produced by the conduct of His People.

Ezra iii. 7.—" The grant that they had of Cyrus king of Persia ": *i.e.*, from him.

Job xiv. 1.—" Man that is born of a woman " : *i.e.*, woman-born.

Ps. xxxvii. 22.—" For such as be blessed of him shall inherit the earth ; and they that be cursed of him shall be cut off " : *i.e.*, by Him, in each case : *i.e.*, His blessed ones, His cursed ones.

Isa. i. 7.—" As the overthrow of strangers " : *i.e.*, as overthrown by strangers. Or, it may be possessive, as strangers' overthrow : *i.e.*, like Sodom's and Gomorrah's overthrow (see verse 9).

Isa. ix. 6.—" Prince of Peace." The Prince who makes and gives peace, and brings " peace on earth."

Isa. xi. 2.—" The spirit of wisdom and understanding," etc. : *i.e.*, who gives wisdom, etc.

Isa. liii. 4.—" Smitten of God " : *i.e.*, by God.

Isa. liii. 5.—" The chastisement of our peace " : *i.e.*, which pro-cured and gives us peace.

Isa. liv. 13.—" All thy children shall be taught of the LORD " : *i.e.*, by Jehovah.

Ezek. i. 1.—" Visions of God " : *i.e.*, from God.

Hag. i. 13.—" Haggai, the LORD'S messenger " : *i.e.*, the messenger from Jehovah.

Matt. iii. 2, etc.—" The kingdom of the heavens " : *i.e.*, the kingdom which has its origin and source from the heavens. It might be taken as the genitive of character, " heavenly kingdom " ; but still only in the above sense, as the words of the Lord teach in John xviii. 36 : " My kingdom is not of this world." The word " of " there is not the sign of the genitive case, but is the preposition ἐκ *(ek)*, *out of*, *from*, as to its origin. The kingdom depends on the Person of the King. It is the king that makes a kingdom, and not the kingdom the king. It is king-dom, the termination *dom* denoting jurisdiction. *Dom* is an abbreviation of *doom* or judgment. Hence it denotes the *sphere* in which anything is exercised, as earl-dom, wis-dom, Christen-dom. Hence a king-dom is the sphere where a king exercises his rule and jurisdiction. In his absence, therefore, there can be no kingdom. When the Lord said to His enemies, " The kingdom of God is among you " (Luke xvii. 21, margin), He meant in the person of the king. He could not mean that it was " within " the hearts of His enemies, who rejected the King and sought His life.

The kingdom for which we pray, therefore, is not " from hence," but from heaven.

The word " heaven," here, is used, by *Metonymy*, for " God." See further under the Figure *Metonymy*.

Luke i. 69. — "An horn of salvation": *i.e.*, which worketh salvation.

The word "horn" is used, by *Metonomy* (*q.v.*), for Christ—as being strong and powerful, and able to procure, and bring salvation.

John vi. 29.—"This is the work of God": *i.e.*, which God effects.

John xii. 43.—"They loved the praise of men (*i.e.*, that came from men) more than the praise of God (*i.e.*, that comes from God)."

Rom. i. 5.—"The obedience of faith" (see margin). Here, the words correspond with the same expression in xvi. 26.

In the former (in connection with the Gospel which was promised from of old), we have the apostolic grace committed to the apostle of the Gentiles with a view to (εἰς) [*procuring*] obedience produced by faith among all the Gentiles.

In the latter (in connection with the Mystery which was kept secret from of old), we have the apostolic commission committed to the same apostle with the same object unto all the Gentiles.

It is possible that the words "faith" in these two places may be the *Antimereia* of the noun, and denote *faith-obedience: i.e.*, obedience on faith-principle as distinct from law-principle.

Rom. i. 17.—"For therein (*i.e.*, in the Gospel, the good news concerning Christ, verse 16) is the righteousness of God (*i.e.*, which has its source and origin in God) revealed," and is imputed to man on the principle of faith.

Rom. iv. 11.—"The righteousness of faith": *i.e.*, which comes from God as its source, and is enjoyed instrumentally by faith.

Rom. iv. 13.—"The righteousness of faith": *i.e.*, imputed on the principle of faith as distinct from law.

Rom. v. 18.—"Justification of life": *i.e.*, which gives life.

Rom. xv. 4.—"Comfort of the Scriptures": *i.e.*, the comfort which the Scriptures supply. The word "patience" is better taken by itself, as being patience exercised by us, and combined here with "the comfort" which the Scriptures give.

2 Cor. xi. 26.—"Dangers of rivers": dangers occasioned by rivers.

Eph. ii. 8.—"The gift of God": *i.e.*, which God gives.

Eph. iv. 18.—"Being alienated from the life of God": *i.e.*, destitute of the life which God gives.

Phil. iv. 9.—"The God of peace ": *i.e.*, the God who has made peace and gives peace.

This differs from "the peace of God." See below under the genitive of *Possession*.

Col. i. 23.—"The hope of the Gospel ": *i.e.*, produced by it.

Col. ii. 12.—"Faith of the operation of God ": *i.e.*, faith effected, originated and produced by Almighty power.

1 Thess. i. 3.—"Work of faith ": *i.e.*, work produced by or proceeding from and having its origin in their faith, when they "turned to God from idols " (verse 9).

"Labour of love ".: *i.e.*, the labour or service proceeding from love, as manifested in a desire "to serve the living and true God" (verse 9).

"Patience of hope ": *i.e.*, patience which was the outcome of the hope, while they waited for God's "Son from heaven " (verse 10).

Heb. i. 3.—"By the word of his power." This is hardly His powerful word; but the word which is the instrument, by which His power is carried out.

After certain verbs of *sense* or *feeling*, the genitive is used to indicate the *source* or *origin* from which the sense or the affection proceeds.

E.g., the verb *to hear* :—

The source or person from whom the sound of the voice comes, is expressed by the genitive; while the words or that which the voice speaks is put in the accusative case.

In John x. 27, "My sheep hear of my voice " (gen.): *i.e.*, they hear and recognize that which comes *from Me*, as being Mine; while Matt. vii. 24, "Whosoever heareth my words " (acc.), the words, sayings, facts, truths, or commands which I utter.

In Acts i. 4, we have both in one verse, "the promise which (acc.) ye heard of me " (gen.).

This explains two otherwise difficult and apparently contradictory statements :—

In Acts ix. 7, "Hearing a voice " (gen.): *i.e.*, the sound, or the person who was the source of the words; but, in Acts xxii. 9, "They heard not the voice " (acc.): *i.e.*, what was actually said.

3. *The Genitive of* Possession.

This is perhaps the most common and frequent use of the genitive case. Its fundamental meaning denoting *Whence ?* is clear.

R 2

From the origin and source naturally flows *Possession*, especially in the use of the personal pronouns: "the daughter of me": *i.e.*, my daughter; "the disciples of Him": *i.e.*, His disciples. Hence, after the words "son," "brother," "wife," "house," etc.

We can give only a few of the more difficult and important examples:

Luke ii. 49.—"The business of my Father": *i.e.*, His "will," which Christ came to do, and of which at the close He could say, "It is finished." Note these first and last words uttered by the Lord Jesus, teaching us that the *will of God* was the source of our salvation, the *work of Christ* the channel of it, and the *witness of the Holy Spirit* the *power of it*. See Heb. x. 7, 12, 15.

Eph. vi. 16.—"The shield of faith": *i.e.*, faith's shield. The shield which faith possesses and uses: *viz.*, Christ (Gen. xv. 1. Ps. lxxxiv. 11 (12)). It is not the genitive of *Apposition*, which would regard faith itself as the shield; but, as in the next verse:—

Eph. vi. 17.—"The sword of the Spirit": *i.e.*, the Spirit's sword, "which is the word of God."

Phil. iv. 7.—"The peace of God": *i.e.*, God's peace; the peace which reigns in His presence, where the end is known from the beginning, producing a peace which nothing can therefore disturb.

It is the unknown future which disturbs our peace; but if our requests are made known to God, we need not be full of care about anything; and something of God's peace will keep and guard our hearts and minds.

Col. i. 13.—"The power of darkness": *i.e.*, the power belonging to Satan.

2 Thess. iii. 5.—"The patience of Christ" (margin, and R.V.): *i.e.*, Christ's patient waiting; for this is the meaning of ὑπομονή (*hypo-monee*), which always has the idea of endurance and waiting.

2. Tim. iii. 17.—"The man of God": *i.e.*, God's man. This was the popular name of a prophet, for in him the People recognised God's spokesman.*

Heb. v. 6.—"The order of Melchisedek": *i.e.*, Melchisedek's order.

Rev. xiv. 12.—"The patience of the saints": *i.e.*, possessed and manifested by the saints. Compare xiii. 10.

---

* See *The Man of God*, by the same author and publisher.

4. *The Genitive of* APPOSITION.

Sometimes the genitive is put by way of *Apposition*, in which case some such words as these have to be supplied: "*that is to say*," "*which is*," etc.

Isa. xiv. 14.—"The heights of the clouds": the height, *that is to say* the clouds.

John ii. 21.—"He spake concerning the temple of the body of him": which means the temple, *that is to say*, His body.

Rom. iv. 11.—"A sign of circumcision": *i.e.*, circumcision was itself the sign.

Rom. iv. 13.—"Through righteousness of faith." There is no article, and the genitive "of faith" is in Apposition: *i.e.*, through "faith-righteousness": *i.e.*, righteousness on the principle of faith, or on faith-principle.

So verse 18: "Justification of life": a life-justification (δικαίωσις).

Rom. viii. 23.—"The firstfruits of the Spirit": *i.e.*, the first-fruits [*of our inheritance*], *that is to say*, the Spirit.

2 Cor. v. 1.—"The house of our tabernacle": *i.e.*, the house, *that is to say*, our tabernacle.

2 Cor. v. 5.—"The earnest of the Spirit": *i.e.*, the earnest, *which is* the Spirit. So i. 22.

Eph. iv. 3.—"The bond of peace": *i.e.*, the bond, *which is* peace.

Eph. iv. 9.—"The lower parts of the earth": *i.e.*, the lower parts, *that is to say*, the earth. Compare Isa. xiv. 14.

Eph. vi. 14.—"The breastplate of righteousness." Here, it is not the genitive of possession as in verses 16 and 17, but of apposition, Christ's righteousness being our breastplate.

Heb. vi. 1.—"The foundation of repentance": *i.e.*, the foundation, *that is to say*, repentance, etc.

2 Pet. ii. 6.—"The cities of Sodom and Gomorrha": *i.e.*, the cities, *that is to say*, Sodom, etc.

5. *The Genitive of* RELATION AND OBJECT.

This is perhaps the most interesting of all the usages. It offers a great variety in the manner of expressing the peculiar *relation* intended; and this relation can be gathered only from the context, and from the general analogy of Scripture truth.

It must be borne in mind that it is often impossible to define and determine the exact sense, in which the genitive case is used. And very frequently it may be used in more senses than one. For example, " the Gospel of Christ " may either refer to *origin*—the Gospel which has Christ for its author—or *relation*, which has Christ for its subject. Both in Hebrew and Greek great attention must be paid to the presence or absence of the article, in judging of the sense.

Each example must be interpreted by the context.

Gen. ii. 9.—" The tree of life ": *i.e.*, which preserved life.

Gen. iii. 24.—" The way of the tree ": *i.e.*, " the way pertaining (or leading) to the tree of life."

Gen. l. 4.—" The days of his mourning ": *i.e.*, of mourning (lit., weeping) with respect to him or for him.

Judges xiii. 12.—" What shall be the manner (or ordering) of the child, and of his work": *i.e.*, what shall be the ordering of the child, and what shall we do with reference to him.

2 Sam. vii. 19.—" And is this the manner of man, O Lord God ? " The Heb. is : " And this is a law of humanity " (תּוֹרַת הָאָדָם): *i.e.*, the law for, or relating to, or extending to all mankind. Thus is indicated the fact that the blessing given in grace to David was to embrace the whole world in its scope.

Ps. iv. 1 (2).—" O God of my righteousness." This may be, by *Antimereia*, my righteous God. But it is this, and more : for it is the God who justifies and who defends my righteous cause. All, in fact, that has relation to my righteousness is included.

Ps. xliv. 22 (23).—"As sheep of slaughter ": *i.e.*, destined for slaughter.

Ps. cii. 20 (21).—" The children of death ": *i.e.*, persons destined to die.

Ps. cxlix. 6.—" The exaltations of God are in their throat ": *i.e.*, their praises, exalting God.

Prov. i. 7.—" The fear of the Lord ": *i.e.*, the fear which is felt with reference to the Lord, as is so beautifully expressed in Ps. v. 7 (8).

Prov. xxx. 24.—" Little of the earth ": *i.e.*, the least in the earth : or, earth's little ones.

Isa. iii. 14.—" The spoil of the poor ": *i.e.*, which they have taken from the poor. Observe that " poor" is singular :—the poor one.

Isa. xxxiv. 5.—"The people of my curse": *i.e.,* the people devoted to destruction.

Isa. lv. 3.—"The sure mercies of David": *i.e.,* pertaining to David, which Jehovah promised to him in 2 Sam. vii. Compare Acts xiii. 34.

Jer. l. 28.—"The vengeance of his temple": *i.e.,* the vengeance of God connected with His temple, avenging its destruction on those who had destroyed it.

Ezek. xx. 7.—"The abominations of his eyes": *i.e.,* pleasing in his eyes.

Joel iii. (iv.) 19.—"On account of the violence of the sons of Judah": *i.e.,* the violence *against* them, as in A.V. This is described in Hab. ii. 8.

Zech. ix. 1.—"The eyes of man." One sense of the Heb. may be "For Jehovah hath an eye of man": *i.e.,* with respect to man. So that it may be rendered, "For the LORD hath respect to men, and to all the tribes of Israel," and thus we have a *Periphrasis* (*q.v.*) for the Divine providence and care.

Matt. iii. 8.—"Fruit meet of repentance": *i.e.,* fruit worthy with respect to repentance.

Matt. iv. 23; xxiv. 14.—"The gospel of the kingdom": *i.e.,* the good news connected with, or relating to the coming kingdom.

It is often erroneously said that there can be only one "gospel"; but gospel means "good news," and this good news may be concerning "Christ," or "the Kingdom," or "the grace of God," or "the glory." And, if words are used to reveal God's mind and thoughts, we must not confuse or join together things which he has separated.

The "Gospel (or good news) of the Kingdom" was preached when the King appeared; but after His rejection that good news is necessarily in abeyance; and, in its stead, the "Gospel (or good news) of the grace of God" is preached to sinners, both of Jews and Gentiles, until the time of the King's second appearing shall come, when the good news of the coming King and Kingdom will be again preached. This is the preaching which is referred to in Matt. xxiv. 14, after the Church of God shall have been "caught up to meet the Lord in the air."

Matt. vi. 26.—"Fowls of the air": *i.e.,* which fly in the heaven or sky.

Matt. vi. 28.—"Lilies of the field": *i.e.,* which grow in the field.

Matt. x. 1.—" Power of unclean spirits " : *i.e.*, with reference to or over them.

Matt. xiv. 1.—" The fame of Jesus " : *i.e.*, in connection with, or concerning Jesus.

Mark i. 4.—" Baptism of repentance " : *i.e.*, which had reference to, or stood in connection with it.

Mark xi. 22.—" Have faith of God " : *i.e.*, with respect to God, toward Him, such faith as his faithfulness demands and warrants. Compare Col. ii. 12.

Luke xxi. 4.—" The gifts of God " : *i.e.*, pertaining to God, and which He accepts. This is quite different from Eph. ii. 8, which is the genitive of *origin*.

John ii. 17.—" The zeal of thy house " : *i.e.*, with respect to it, for or concerning it.

John v. 29.—" Resurrection of life " : *i.e.*, with a view to life. " Resurrection of damnation " : *i.e.*, for the purpose of judgment.

John vii. 35.—" The dispersion of the Gentiles " : *i.e.*, among. The dispersed people (of the Jews) among the Greeks (Gentiles).

John xvii. 2.—" Power of all flesh " : *i.e.*, over all flesh. See other examples with ἐξουσία (*exousia*), *power :* Matt. x. 1. Mark vi. 7. 1 Cor. ix. 12.

Acts iv. 9.—" A good work of an impotent man " : *i.e.*, as in the A.V., " the good deed done to " him.

Acts xxiii. 6 and all other passages where we have the expression " resurrection of (the) dead," it means the resurrection of dead bodies : *i.e.*, the resurrection connected with dead bodies as such. Acts xxiv. 15, 21. Rom. i. 4. 1 Cor. xv. 13. Heb. vi. 2. 1 Pet. i. 3. But when the resurrection of Christ, or that of His People is spoken of, the preposition ἐκ (*ek*), *out of* or *from among*, is always used. See Acts iv. 2. 1 Cor. xv. 8, etc.

With regard to Phil. iii. 11 : " The resurrection of the dead," there is more than one thing to remark. First, note that the word " resurrection " here is not the ordinary word. It is ἐξανάστασις (*exanastasis*), *out-resurrection*. *Secondly*, that the reading τὴν ἐκ (*teen ek*), *which is from* or *out of*, must be inserted in the Text, according to the R.V. and all the Critical Greek Texts. So that the words read : " If by any means I may arrive at the out-resurrection, that which is from among the dead." We must note, further, that Paul's stand-point here is that of a Jew. He has been showing all through the chapter what was his standing in the flesh, and what his gains were as a Jew. He is willing, he says, to give up all that he once counted "gain" as a Jew, that he might attain to this blessed and new revelation of a resurrection from among the dead, which was a secret not before revealed—brought to light by Christ and His Gospel (see 1 Cor. xv. 51). It is not that he, as a Christian, having this hope, desired to attain to something higher, which other Christians (or all of them) would not enjoy; but that he, as a Jew, counted his gains but loss, that he might enjoy this blessed hope of the *out-resurrection* at Christ's appearing.

Rom. iii. 22.—" By faith of Jesus Christ ": *i.e.*, faith which has respect to, or which embraces or rests on Him. Some take it as the genitive of *Origin*, faith which is the gift of Jesus Christ, according to Eph. ii. 8.

Compare Gal. iii. 22 and Rev. xiv. 12.

Rom. viii. 17.—" Joint-heirs of Christ ": *i.e.*, in relation to Christ, and hence partaking with Christ.

Rom. viii. 36.—" Sheep of slaughter ": *i.e.*, sheep devoted to slaughter. See Ps. xliv. 22 (23) above.

Rom. ix. 9.—" For, of promise is this word ": *i.e.*, this word is relating to the promise (*i.e.*, the promise made to Sarah). Lit , " For, of promise, the word is this."

Rom. x. 2.—" They have a zeal of God ": *i.e.*, a zeal for God, or with respect to Him.

A person may have this ; and yet be destitute of God's righteousness, which He has provided for us, and which is in Christ only, apart from all our zeal and all our " works of righteousness which we have done."

Rom. xiii. 3.—" Not a terror of good works ": *i.e.*, in respect to them.

Rom. xvi. 2.—" Worthily of the saints ": *i.e.*, in connection with, or in a manner becoming to the saints. A.V.: " As becometh saints."

2 Cor. x. 5.—" Obedience of Christ ": *i.e.*, rendered to the Christ : *i.e.*, loyalty to Him.

Eph. iv. 16.—" Every joint of the supply": *i.e.*, every joint or sensation for the purpose of supply, or with a view to supply.

Col. i. 24.—" The afflictions of Christ": *i.e.*, the afflictions pertaining to Christ Mystical, the apostle having an abundant measure of

them as a member of that Body of Christ. So that, if other members
had fewer afflictions, Paul made up any deficiency by having more
than the average share.

Col. ii. 18.—" Worship of angels." Here, the word rendered
" worship " is θρησκεία (*threeskeia*) which never means *worship*, but
always *religion*, or religious ritual. See Acts xxvi. 5. Jas. i. 26, 27 (its
only occurrences in the New Testament), and Wisd. xiv. 16, 18,
27 in the Septuagint.

Then, the Greek reads : " Humility and religion," which, by
Hendiadys (*q.v.*), means *religious humility* (with emphasis on religious).
So that the genitive, here, means *pertaining to : i.e.,* the religious
humility pertaining to, or entertained by angels in their access to God.

The context teaches that this is not proper *Christian* standing,
which is that of " sons," not of servants (which angels are. See Heb.
i. 14 ; ii. 5 ; and 1 Cor. vi. 3).

Verses 18, 19 may thus be rendered :—" Let no one defraud you
of your prize, having pleasure in the religious humility entertained by
angels, taking his stand upon the things which he hath seen, vainly
puffed up by the mind of his flesh (*i.e.*, his Old nature), and not holding
fast the Head," etc.

Tit. ii. 14.—" Zealous of good works " : *i.e.*, with respect to good
works.

Heb. iii. 12.—" An evil heart of unbelief " : *i.e.*, an evil heart in
respect to unbelief.

Heb. v. 13.—" Unskilled of the word of righteousness " : *i.e.*, in
respect of the word of righteousness.

Heb. ix. 21.—" Vessels of the ministry " : *i.e.*, pertaining to the
ministering.

Heb. xi. 26. — " The reproach of Christ " : *i.e.*, reproach in
connection with Christ.

Jas. i. 13.—" Cannot be tempted of evil (marg., *evils*) " : *i.e.*,
is not to be tempted with respect to evil things.

1 Pet. ii. 19.—" Conscience of God " : *i.e.*, conscience toward
God.

1 John ii. 5.—" The love of God " : *i.e.*, either our love which
goes out to God ; or, His love with regard to us (cf. especially John
xiv. 23).

Rev. iii. 10.—" The word of my patience " : *i.e.*, My word, which
enjoins a patient waiting.

Rev. xix. 10.—"The testimony of Jesus": *i.e.*, the testimony concerning Jesus.

6. *The Genitive of the* MATERIAL.

Denoting that of which anything is made.

Gen. iii. 21.—" Coats of skins ": *i.e.*, made out of skins.*

Gen. vi. 14.—"An ark of gopher wood ": *i.e.*, made out of that kind of wood.

Judges vii. 13.—"A cake of barley bread ": *i.e.*, bread made out of barley.

Ps. ii. 9.—"A rod of iron ": *i.e.*, made of iron.

This might be placed under *character*, " an iron rod " being put by another figure (*Metonymy*) for a powerful rule.

2 Sam. vii. 2.—"A house of cedar": *i.e.*, built of cedar-wood.

Dan. ii. 38.—"Thou art this head of gold ": *i.e.*, represented by the head of the image, which was made of gold.

7. *The Genitive of the* CONTENTS.

Denoting that with which anything is *filled*.

1 Sam. xvi. 20.—"And Jesse took an ass of bread, and a bottle of wine ": *i.e.*, an ass *laden with* bread, and a bottle *filled with* wine."

Matt. x. 42.—"A cup of cold water ": *i.e.*, filled with.

Matt. xxvi. 7.—"An alabaster box of very precious ointment ": *i.e.*, filled with it, or containing it.

John i. 14.—" Full of grace and truth ": *i.e.*, filled with grace and truth (See under *Hendiadys*).

John ii. 7.—Lit., " Fill the waterpots of water ": *i.e.*, full with water.

Acts vii. 16.—"A sum of money."

8. *The Genitive of* PARTITION, SEPARATION, *or* ABLATION.

This is closely connected with the fundamental idea of the genitive, which answers the question, *Whence ?* This genitive denotes *a part taken from the whole*, and is so easily recognised that we need add only a very few examples by way of illustration.

---

* The word for " of skins " is to be omitted according to the class of readings called *Severin.* See Ginsburg's *Introduction to the Hebrew Bible.*

Luke xx. 35.—Lit., " To attain of that world " : *i.e.,* to have part in it.

1 Cor. xv. 9.—" The least of the apostles."

1 Pet. i. 1.—" Elect sojourners of the dispersion " : *i.e.,* sojourners, being a part of the *Diaspora,* or " Scattered Nation."
Rendered by the A.V., " strangers scattered."

9. Two Genitives depending on each other.

Lev. vii. 35.—" This is of the anointing (*partition*) of Aaron (*possession*) and of the anointing (*partition*) of his sons (*possession*) " : *i.e.,* this is *part of* the perquisites of the anointing.

John vi. 1.—" The sea of Galilee (*relation*) of Tiberias (*apposition*) " : *i.e.,* the sea pertaining to Galilee ; *that is to say,* Tiberias (as the Gentiles call it).

Acts v. 32.—" We are witnesses of him (*possession*) of these things (*relation : i.e.,* with respect to)."

Acts xx. 24 and **1 Thess. ii. 9.**—" The gospel of the grace of God " : *i.e.,* the Gospel of (or concerning, gen. of *relation*) God's grace (gen. of *origin* or *possession*).

2 Cor. v. 1.—" The earthly house of us (*possession,* our) of the tabernacle " : *i.e.,* our earthly house, *that is to say,* our tabernacle.

Phil. ii. 30.—" The lack of you (*possession,* your) of service (*relation : i.e.,* in respect of service)."

Eph. i. 18.—" And what the riches of the glory of his inheritance in the saints " : *i.e.,* and what the rich, or exceeding rich glory (*Hypallage*), pertaining to or in (gen. of *relation*) the saints. If it is *Enallage,* it will mean *the glorious riches,* etc.

APPENDIX C

ON

HOMŒOTELEUTA IN THE MSS. AND PRINTED TEXT OF THE HEBREW BIBLE.

As a Figure of Speech, *Homœoteleuton* is applied to certain words which occur together, and have a similar termination. See page 176, where the figure is described and illustrated by examples.

But the term *Homœoteleuton* is used of a certain class of mistakes made by copyists in the transcription of the sacred text.

A Scribe, in copying a MS., would come to a certain word; and, having written it, he would sometimes carry his eye back, not to the word which he had just copied, but to the same or a similar word, or a word with the same termination occurring in the immediate context, and thus omit a few words or a whole sentence.

A number of examples are given by Dr. Ginsburg in his *Introduction to the Hebrew Bible;* where a whole chapter (Part II. chap. vi.) is devoted to this subject, which is there treated of for the first time. It is there shown that, while the Septuagint preserves *Homœoteleuta* which are omitted in the present Hebrew text, there are examples of *Homœoteleuta* in the LXX itself, arising from the same cause. The printed Hebrew text also exhibits *Homœoteleuta*, as compared with the MS. text. One or two examples may be quoted by way of explanation :—

Josh. ii. 1.—" And they went, and came [*to Jericho, and they* came] into an harlot's house," etc.

Josh. ix. 27 (26).—"And Joshua made them that day hewers of wood and drawers of water for the congregation, and for the altar of the LORD [*and the inhabitants of Gibeon became hewers of wood, and drawers of water for* the altar of the LORD] even unto this day." (This is preserved in the LXX).

Josh. x. 12.—" Then spake Joshua to the LORD in the day when the LORD delivered up the Amorites before the children of Israel, [*when they destroyed them in Gibeon, and they were destroyed from before the children of* Israel,] and he said in the sight of Israel," etc. (This is preserved in the LXX).

In **Josh. xxi.**, verses 36 and 37 are not in our ordinary printed Hebrew text at all, and they are omitted in most MSS. The LXX preserves them : and they are inserted in the A.V. without a word of explanation.   The R.V. calls attention to them in a marginal note.

Judges xvi. 13 (14).—" If thou weavest the seven locks of my head with the web, **and fastenest them with a pin** [*then shall I be weak as another man. And it came to pass, when he was asleep, that Delilah took the seven locks of his head, and wove them with a web,* and fastened them with a pin], and said unto him," etc.

1 Kings viii. 16.—" Since the day that I brought forth my people Israel out of Egypt, I chose no city out of all the tribes of Israel to build an house, that my name might be therein ; but **I chose** [*Jerusalem that my name might be there, and* **I chose**] David to be over my people Israel."   (The LXX in some MSS. preserves this).

We must refer the reader to Dr. Ginsburg's work for further examples.

Some various readings in the Greek New Testament are doubtless due to a similar cause.

APPENDIX D

ON

HEBREW HOMONYMS.

Hom'-o-nym, from the Greek ὁμός (*homos*), *the same*, and ὄνομα (*onoma*), *name*.

This term is given to words which are spelt exactly alike, but have different meanings.

The term is sometimes used for words which are not spelt alike, but only pronounced alike, as *bear* and *bare*. But this is properly *Paronomasia* (*q.v.*), and not a *Homonym*. The essential peculiarity of *Homonyms* is that the *spelling* is precisely the same in each case though the meaning is quite different.

Neither is it the same word used in two different senses. The words sometimes are from entirely different roots.

For example, we have many in English, such as

BASTE.	1. To beat.
	2. To pour fat over meat.
	3. To sew slightly.
BID.	1. To pray.
	2. To command.
	3. To make an offer at a sale.
BLOW.	1. To puff.
	2. To bloom.
	3. A stroke or hit.
BRAY.	1. To bruise or pound.
	2. To make a harsh noise as an ass.
COURT.	1. A yard.
	2. A royal palace.
	3. A place of justice.
	4. To woo or seek favour.

LEASE.	1. To let tenements.
	2. To glean.
	3. To lie.*
LET.	1. To permit.
	2. To hinder.
	3. To give a house for hire.
LIE.	1. To rest.
	2. To speak falsely.
LIGHTEN.	1. To illuminate.
	2. To alleviate.
	3. To flash.
LIKE.	1. Similar.
	2. To be pleased with.
MAIL.	1. Steel net-work.
	2. A letter-bag.
REPAIR.	1. To renew.
	2. To resort.
REST.	1. Repose.
	2. To remain.
TEND.	1. To move towards.
	2. To care for.
TIRE.	1. To fatigue.
	2. To deck or dress.
	3. An iron hoop.
	4. To tear a prey.
	5. A train of a dress.
WELL.	1. Excellently.
	2. A spring or fountain.
	3. To spring up as water.
WILL.	1. To be willing.
	2. Desire.

---

* In Old English. See A.V., Ps. iv. 2 ; v. 6.

These are examples merely of *English* Homonyms; but the fact of the existence of similar Homonyms in Hebrew has not been sufficiently investigated. Very often, assuming the existence of only one word, great ingenuity has been exercised in endeavouring to explain how the same word can possibly have such different meanings; or, how it can be used in such opposite senses.

And, often, through not observing this difference, difficulties have been introduced into Translations and into Interpretations; and passages have been sometimes obscured by a forced accommodation of the context to the *one* sense through not seeing the *Homonym*, or word with another sense.

We give a few examples * :—

עָזַב (*azav*). 1. To leave or *forsake*.
2. To *help* or *restore*; hence, to *strengthen* or *fortify*.

1. It means *to leave* or *forsake*.

Gen. ii. 24.—" Therefore shall a man leave his father and his mother."

Gen. xxxix. 6.—"And he left all that he had in Joseph's hand."

Neh. v. 10.—" I pray you, let us leave off this usury."

Ps. xlix. 10 (11).—They " leave their wealth to others."

Mal. iv. 1 (iii. 19).—" It shall leave them neither root nor branch."

2. It means *to restore, repair,* or *fortify*.

Neh. iii. 8 is clear upon this point: and both versions agree in so rendering it in this verse. " They fortified Jerusalem unto the broad wall." But, having thus rendered it *fortify* in the text, both versions suggest in the margin the word "*left*" as an alternative rendering.

Another similarly interesting example is

Ex. xxiii. 5.—" If thou see the ass of him that hateth thee lying under his burden, and wouldest forbear to help him, thou shalt surely help with him."

Both A.V. and R.V. take the right sense of the word "*help*" in the text; but, apparently repenting of it, the A.V. substitutes the sense of *leave* in the margin. They were compelled to render it "help" in the former clause (in the margin as well as in the text), for they could

---

* Those who wish to study this subject further, may consult *Die gegensinnigen Wörter im Alt-und Neuhebräischen*, by Dr. E. Landau, Berlin, 1896.

not well say "and wouldest forbear to forsake him." But, having thus used "help," the A.V. suggests (as one alternative) for the latter clause:

"*And wouldest cease to leave* thy business *for him : thou shalt surely leave* it to join *with him.*"

Young's "literal translation" is worse : "then thou hast ceased from leaving *it* to *it*: thou dost certainly leave *it* with him." This renders the obscurity more obscure.

The R.V. seeks to escape from the difficulty by using the neutral term "*release*" in the margin : "*And wouldest forbear to release* it *for him, thou shouldest surely release* it *with him.*"

But the supposed difficulty does not really exist : for, when the *Homonym* is observed, the italics so plentifully suggested are wholly unnecessary.

The word here is עָזַב (*azav*) in the sense of *to raise up* or *help ;* and the verse reads :—" If thou see the ass of him that hateth thee lying under his burden, and wouldest forbear from helping him, thou shalt surely help him."

That "help" is the real and only meaning of the word in the passages before us is evident from Deut. xxii. 4, where we have the synonym הָקֵם תָּקִים עִמּוֹ (*hakem takeem immo*),* raising thou shalt raise it up with him. This is used in Deut. xxii. 4 for עָזֹב תַּעֲזֹב עִמּוֹ (*azov tazov immo*),* helping thou shalt help with him, as in Ex. xxiii. 5.

Having thus established the meaning of *azav*, *to help, restore, strengthen,* or *fortify*, we have now sufficient authoritative information to enable us to elucidate the otherwise unintelligible expression, "shut up and left" which really means *shut in and fortified,* or *strengthened and defended.* The following are the passages :—

Deut. xxxii. 36.—" For the LORD shall judge his people, and repent himself for his servants, when he seeth that their power is gone, and there is none shut in or fortified ": *i.e.,* sheltered or protected.

"Shut up or left" makes no sense whatever. Nor is the R.V. any better, " And there is none *remaining*, shut up or left at large."

1 Kings xiv. 10.—" I will bring evil upon the house of Jeroboam, and will cut off from Jeroboam . . . him that is strengthened and fortified (*i.e.,* all the men and the men in the strongholds), and will take away the remnant of the house of Jeroboam as a

---

* Here we have *Paronomasia* (*q.v.*), as well as *Polyptoton* (*q.v.*).

man taketh away dung, till it be all gone." So chap. xxi. 21, and 2 Kings ix. 8.

2 Kings xiv. 26.—" For the LORD saw the affliction of Israel, that it was very bitter: for there was not any shut up, nor any left, nor any helper for Israel."

This yields no sense whatever! Nor is the R.V. any better. Not seeing the *Homonym*, they keep to the meaning *left*, and add " none shut up nor left at large "! But the sense is, "for there was not any strong man nor any fortified place," or, "not any place strengthened, nor any fortified " : *i.e.*, they were weak and defenceless.

In all these passages the R.V. seeks to avoid the difficulty by rendering עָזוּב *left at large ;* in spite of the fact that in Ex. xxiii. 5, and Deut. xxii. 4, it is rendered *help*, and not " and wouldest forbear to leave him at large "!

Jer. xlix. 25 is also spoiled in both versions. Damascus is mourned over because of its emptiness and desolation. And the lament is " How is the city of renown become unfortified ? " : *i.e.*, unprotected.

Whereas the A.V. renders it, " How is the city of praise not left "; and the R.V., " How is the city of praise not forsaken ? " But this was the very thing that is the subject of the lamentation! It was left and forsaken, and had become defenceless.

חֶסֶד (*chesed*). 1. *Mercy, goodness,* or *grace.*
　　　　　　　2. *Shame, disgrace,* or *blasphemy.*

1. *Mercy, kindness, goodness,* or *loving kindness.*

These are the common renderings given. See Gen. xxiv. 12. 2 Sam. vii. 15. 1 Chron. xix. 2. 2 Chron. vi. 14. Job xxxvii. 13. Ps. ciii. 4, 8, 11, 17, etc.

But there is a *Homonyn* which means

2. *Shame, disgrace, reproach, blasphemy,* etc.

Lev. xx. 17. — Where the A.V. renders it " a wicked thing," and the R.V. " a shameful thing."

Job xxxvii. 13.—" He causeth it to come (*i.e.*, the thick cloud and lightning, verse 11, R.V.) whether it be for correction (marg. *a rod*) or for his land, or for chastisement." The A.V. and R.V. here render this last word " mercy : " but " lightning " is not for mercy, but for judgment.

Both versions are compelled to recognise the *Homonym* in Lev. xx. 7, and in the passage to be next quoted, but they miss it in Jonah ii. 8.

Prov. xxv. 10.—Where the A.V. renders it, "put thee to shame," and R.V. "revile thee."

Jonah ii. 8 (9).—"They that observe lying vanities do not heed their correction," or chastisement. A.V. and R.V.: "forsake their own mercy."

נֶשֶׁף (*nesheph*). 1. *Darkness.*
2. *Daylight.*

Not seeing the *Homonym*, the renderings are confused, and the difficulties are evaded by the rendering *twilight*.

1. *Darkness.*

Job xxiv. 15.—"The eye also of the adulterer waiteth for the darkness"; not "twilight," as in A.V. and R.V., which mars the sense and destroys the parallelism of the next verse. So

Prov. vii. 9, where the whole context requires intense darkness; yet it is rendered "twilight."

2 Kings vii. 5, 7; where it is again rendered "twilight," and should be *darkness*.

Isa. v. 11.—The A.V. and R.V. render it *night*.

Isa. xxi. 4.—The A.V. renders it "night"; and R.V., "twilight."

Isa. lix. 10.—The A.V. renders it "night," and R.V. renders it "twilight."

Jer. xiii. 16. — The A.V. renders it "dark"; and R.V., "dark," and gives in margin: "Heb. *mountains of twilight*." So Job iii. 9, etc.

2. *Daylight.*

Job vii. 4.—"I am full of tossings to and fro unto the daylight." The A.V. and R.V. render it, here, "dawning of the day."

The introduction of the word "dawning" shortens the period of the tossings, which the context requires to be extended into the *broad* daylight.

1 Sam. xxx. 17.—"And David smote them from the daylight (or morning) unto the evening." Here, the A.V. and R.V. both say, "from the twilight to the evening of the next day."

Ps. cxix. 147.—Here, both A.V. and R.V. are compelled to recognise the *Homonym*, and render it "morning." "I anticipated the advent of the daylight."

גָּאַל (*gaal*).   1. *To redeem or save.*
2. *To reject or defile.*

1. *To redeem or save.*

Ex. vi. 6.—" I will redeem you with a stretched out arm.'   So Isa. xlviii. 17. Ps. lxxii. 14, etc.

2. *To reject or defile.*

Ezra ii. 62.—"Therefore were they rejected from the priesthood." The A.V. renders this : "Therefore were they, as polluted, put from the priesthood." The R.V., " deemed polluted and put from." They have, to make sense, mixed up גָּעַל (*gaal*) which sometimes does mean *polluted*. The context clearly shows that the simple meaning is *rejected*.

So also Neh. vii. 64 ; xiii. 29. Isa. lix. 3. Lam. iv. 14. Zeph. iii 1. Mal. i. 7.

תָּאַב (*taav*).   1. *To desire or long for.*
2. *To abhor*

1. *To desire or long for.*

Ps. cxix. 20, 40, 174.

2. *To abhor.*

Amos vi. 8, where the parallelism of the two lines is noticeable : " I abhor the excellency of Jacob, and hate his palaces."

Both versions recognize this *Homonym*.

נָכַר (*nachar*).   1. *To mistake*
2. *To acknowledge.*
3. *To deliver.*

1. *To mistake.*

Deut. xxxii. 27.—"Lest their adversaries mistake it, lest they say, Our hand is high, and the LORD hath not done all this." Here, the A.V. renders it " should behave themselves strangely " ; and the R.V., " misdeem."

2. *To acknowledge.*

Job xxxiv. 19.—"Nor regardeth the rich more than the poor." So R.V. thus admitting the *Homonym.*

3. *To deliver.*

1 Sam. xxiii. 7.—"And Saul said, God hath delivered him (David) into mine hand."

R.V. margin : " Heb. *alienated him* " !

———

אָסַף (*asaph*). 1. *To protect*, or *heal*, or *recover.*
 2. *To snatch away* or *destroy.*

1. *To protect* or *heal.*

Num. xii. 14, 15.—" Let her be shut out from the camp seven days, and after that let her be recovered again." A.V., " received in," and " brought in "; R.V., " brought in." So verse 15.

2 Kings v. 6.—" To recover him of his leprosy." So A.V. and R.V.

Ps. xxvii. 10.—" When my father and my mother forsake me, then the Lord will take me up." A.V. margin : " Heb. *will gather me.*" But the *Homonym* is : " Then Jehovah will become my protector."

2. *To snatch away*, or *destroy.*

Ps. xxvi. 9.—" Snatch me not away with sinners " ; *i.e.,* destroy me not with them. Here, the A.V. and R.V. render it, by the neutral term, " gather not "; and margin, " Or, *Take not away.*"

Jer. xvi. 5.—" I have snatched away my peace from this People." Here, both A.V. and R.V. recognize the *Homonym*, and render it " taken away."

———

פָּחַד (*pachad*). 1. *To fear.*
 2. *To rejoice.*

1. *To fear.*

Deut. xxviii. 66.—" Thou shalt fear day and night." So A.V. and R.V.

Job xxiii. 15.—" When I consider, I am afraid of him."

2. *To rejoice,* or *praise.*

Isa. lx. 5.—"Then thou shalt see, and flow together, and thine heart shall rejoice and be enlarged."

A.V., " Thine heart shall fear " !

R.V., " Thine heart shall tremble " !

Hos. iii. 5.—"Afterward shall the children of Israel return, and seek the Lord their God, and David their king; and shall praise the Lord and His goodness in the latter days."

The A.V. renders this, "And shall fear the Lord and His goodness." (R.V., " come with fear unto.") But the context leaves us in no doubt as to the *Homonym.*

אָוֶן (*avōn*). 1. *Might, strength.*

2. *Suffering, pain.*

1. *Might, strength.*

Gen. xlix. 3.—" Reuben, thou art my first-born, my might, and the beginning of my strength."

Deut. xxi. 17.—" He is the beginning of thy strength."

Job xxxi. 25.—" My wealth was great, and because mine hand had gotten much.

2. *Suffering, pain,* and *sorrow.*

Gen. xxxv. 18.—" She called his name Ben-oni " : *i.e.,* according to the margin of A.V. and R.V., " *The son of my sorrow.*" Thus both versions recognise this *Homonym,* as they do also in the other two passages:—

Deut. xxvi. 14.—" I have not eaten thereof in my mourning."

Hos. ix. 4.—" The bread of mourners." So A.V. and R.V.

צִוָּה (*tzivvah*). 1. *To command.*

2. *To forbid.*

1. *To command.*

This is the general rendering of the verb; but, in two other places, we have the *Homonym.*

2. *To forbid.*

Deut. iv. 23.—" Take heed unto yourselves, lest ye forget the covenant of the Lord your God, which he hath made with you, and

make you a graven image, or the likeness of any thing, which the
Lᴏʀᴅ thy God hath forbidden thee." So A.V. and R.V. ; but, in

Judges xiii. 14 where the same *Homonym* occurs, both Versions
translate it " commanded " instead of *forbidden.*

פָּרַץ (*paratz*).   1. *To increase* or *enlarge.*
2. *To break up.*

1. *To increase* or *enlarge.*

Gen. xxx. 43.—" And the man increased exceedingly."*

Ex. i. 12.—"The more they afflicted them, the more they
multiplied and grew " : *i.e.,* increased.

2. *To break up.*

2 Chron. xx. 37. — " Because thou hast joined thyself with
Ahaziah, the Lᴏʀᴅ hath broken thy works." Both the A.V. and R.V.
recognise the *Homonym* in this verse, and do not render it " increase."

---

* See this passage under *Epizeuxis.*

REDUCED *FAC-SIMILE* OF MS. (OR. 4445) IN THE BRITISH
MUSEUM LIBRARY

(Showing *two* lines of the Massorah at the top of the page, *four* at the bottom, and *two* at the side)

(Lev. xi. 4-21).

APPENDIX E

ON

"THE EIGHTEEN EMENDATIONS OF THE SOPHERIM."

The *Massorah*,* *i.e.*, the small writing in the margins of the Standard Hebrew Codices, as shown in the accompanying plate, consists of a concordance of words and phrases, etc., safe-guarding the sacred text.

A note in the *Massorah* against several passages in the manuscripts of Hebrew Bible states : " *This is one of the Eighteen Emendations of the Sopherim*," or words to that effect.

Complete lists of these emendations are found in the Massorah of most of the model or standard Codices of the Hebrew Bible, and these are not always identical; so that the total number exceeds eighteen. From which it would appear that these examples are simply typical.

The *Siphri†* adduces seven passages; the *Yalkut*,‡ ten; the *Mechiltha*,‖ eleven; the *Tanchuma*,§ seventeen; while the St. Petersburg Codex gives two passages not included in any other list (Mal. i. 12, and iii. 9 (see below).

These emendations were made at a period long before Christ, before the Hebrew text had obtained its present settled form, and

---

* For full particulars of *The Massorah*, see Dr. Ginsburg's *Introduction to the Hebrew Bible*, Part II., chap. xi., published by the Trinitarian Bible Society. Also a popular pamphlet, called *The Massorah*, by Dr. Bullinger, published by Eyre and Spottiswoode, price 1s.

† An ancient commentary on Leviticus (circa A.D. 219-247).

‡ A *Catena* of the whole Hebrew Scriptures, composed in cent. xi. from ancient sources by R. Simeon.

‖ An ancient commentary on Exodus, compiled about A.D. 90 by R. Ishmael b. Elisa.

§ A commentary on the Pentateuch, compiled from ancient sources by Tanchuma b. Abba, about 440 A.D.

before the Text passed out of the hands of the *Sopherim** into the hands of the Massorites,† and was handed on to the *Nakdanim*‡.

We cannot call these emendations a corruption of the text; because a note was placed in the margin, in order to call attention to the fact that these were emendations, and not part of the primitive text.

Moreover, most of the emendations were made by the simple change of *one letter*, so that in the Hebrew the alteration is not so great as it appears to be in the English.

An examination of the various passages and emendations will show that the only object was, from a mistaken sense of reverence, to remove from the text certain *Anthropomorphisms* (*q.v.*), so that expressions supposed to be derogatory to God should not be pronounced with the lips in reading aloud, while the true and primitive text was preserved by the note in the margin.

As, however, since the invention of printing, Hebrew Bibles have presented the text *without the Massoretic notes which were intended to safeguard it,* the knowledge of these emendations, together with the vast mass of information enshrined in the Massorah, have been lost to the students of the Hebrew Bible.‖

As these emendations affect the figure *Anthropopatheia* (*q.v.*), we here give a complete list of them, for the benefit of English Bible students.

1.   **Gen. xviii. 22.**—"But Abraham stood yet before the LORD." The primitive text was " *The LORD stood* yet before Abraham." It was felt to be derogatory for the Lord to stand and wait Abraham's pleasure; and so the text was altered, as we have it in the present Hebrew Bible and all its versions.

2.   **Num. xi. 15.**—"Kill me, I pray thee, out of hand, if I have found favour in thy sight; and let me not see my wretchedness," *lit.*, my evil.

The primitive text was " *Thy evil* " : " evil " being put by *Metonymy* (*q.v.*) for the punishment or evil which God would inflict on the People.

---

* The original editors of the then current text.

† The authoritative custodians and preservers of the sacred texts.

‡ The official copyists of the standard codices.

‖ Dr. Ginsburg has put the whole world of Bible students under a lasting obligation by his edition of the *Massorah* in three folio volumes, and by the fourth volume (in English), now in the press (1899), which will complete this great work

3. **Num. xii. 12.**—Here the original reading was "our flesh," and "our mother's."

This was changed to "the flesh," and "his mother," as being derogatory to the dignity of the great law-giver, Moses.

4. **1 Sam. iii. 13.**—"Because his sons made themselves vile (marg., Or, *accursed*), and he restrained them not (marg., Heb. *frowned not upon them*)."

The R.V. renders it: "Because his sons did bring a curse upon themselves, and he restrained them not."

The primitive Text read: "Because his sons *cursed God*"; but אֱלֹהִם, *God*, was changed to לָהֶם, *them*.

The translators of the Septuagint must have been aware of the emendation; for they render it "spake evil of God"; and it was this that influenced the marginal note of the A.V., and the rendering of the R.V., though the revisers did not altogether depart from the *Textus Receptus*.

5. **2 Sam. xvi. 12.**—David said, "It may be that the Lord will look on mine affliction" (marg., "Or, *tears* ; Heb. *eye*).

The R.V. renders it: "It may be that the Lord will look on the wrong done unto me" (marg., "Some ancient Versions read, *my affliction*").

The primitive Text was, "It may be that the Lord will behold *with His eye.*" בְּעֵינוֹ, *b'ayno, His eye*, one letter being altered: viz., ו to י, making it *my eye* (בְּעֵינִי, *b'ayni*). The LXX, Syriac, Vulgate, A.V., and R.V. translate the *kethiv*, and render it *affliction* ; which was a later emendation of the text doubtless with a view of making it clearer.

6. **2 Sam. xx. 1.**

7. **1 Kings xii. 16.**

8. **2 Chron. x. 16.**

"Every man to his tents, O Israel."

The primitive Text was "to his gods."

The emendation was made by transposing the ה and the ל. לאלהיו being changed into לאהליו.

9. **Jer. ii. 11.**—"But my people have changed their glory." (See Nos. 11 and 15).

This was originally *My glory* (כְּבוֹדִי, *kevodee*, being changed into כְּבוֹדוֹ, *kevodō*).

10. **Ezek. viii. 17.**—"They put the branch to their nose."

This was originally *to My nose* (אַפִּי, *appai*, being changed to אַפָּם, *appam*).

The primitive Text which was thus toned down set forth the awful extent of Judah's sin. The "branch" referred to was the *Asherah* (the *phallus* as an object of worship: the trees being cut into this shape in the "groves," where the worship was carried on). This worship had been actually introduced into the Temple and its courts; and the evil is spoken of as putting the *Asherah* to the nose of Jehovah Himself, by the figure *Anthropopatheia* (*q.v.*).

11. **Hos. iv. 7.**—"I will change their glory into shame." (See Nos. 9 and 15).

The primitive Text was "My glory they have turned into shame."

12. **Hab. i. 12.**—"Art thou not from everlasting, O LORD, my God, mine Holy One? we shall not die."

This latter clause originally read, "*Thou diest not.*"

Strange to say, the R.V. calls attention to only this one of their emendations, and puts in the margin, "According to an ancient Jewish tradition, *thou diest not.*" The R.V. takes no notice of any of the other emendations.

13. **Zech. ii. 8 (12).**—"He that toucheth you toucheth the apple of his eye": *i.e.*, of his own eye.

But the primitive text was "My eye."

14. **Mal. i. 13.**—"Ye have snuffed at it."

The original text was "*at Me,*" (אוֹתִי, *ōthee*, being changed to אוֹתוֹ, *ōthō*).

15. **Ps. cvi. 20.**—"They changed their glory."

This was originally "*My glory,*" (כְּבוֹדִי, *kevodee*, being changed to כְּבוֹדָם, *kevodam*). See Nos. 9 and 11.

16. **Job vii. 20.**—"Why have I become a burden to myself."

This was originally "*unto Thee,*" (עָלֶיךָ, *alecha*, being changed to עָלַי, *alai*).

17. **Job xxxii. 3.**—"And yet had condemned Job."

The primitive text was, "and because they had condemned *God*" (אֱלֹהִים, *Elohim*, being changed to אִיּוֹב, *Job*).

18. **Lam. iii. 20.**—"And my soul . . . is humbled in me."

This was originally "*And thy soul will mourn over me*" (or condescend to me). (נַפְשֶׁךָ, *naphshecha*, being changed to נַפְשִׁי, *naphshi*).

The R.V. reads, " My soul . . . is bowed down within me."

The following passages are noted by the Massorah, though they are not included in any of the special lists.

2 Sam. xii. 14.—" Thou hast given great occasion *to the enemies* of the LORD to blaspheme."

The received text really reads, " Thou hast greatly blasphemed the enemies of the LORD," but this is not sense. Hence the A.V. and R.V. have wrongly taken the Piel, נֵאֵץ, as causative; a sense which it never has.

The primitive text was, " *Thou hast greatly blasphemed the LORD.*" This was altered; to soften the sin of David; and gave rise to the difficulties of translators.

Ps. x. 3.—" The wicked boasteth of his heart's desire, and blesseth the covetous, whom the LORD abhorreth (margin, *the covetous blesseth* himself, *he abhorreth the LORD*)."

The R.V. is no clearer. " And the covetous renounceth, yea contemneth the LORD " (and gives in the margin, " Or, *the covetous blesseth* himself, *he abhorreth the LORD* ").

The primitive text was, " *And the covetous blasphemeth, yea abhorreth the Lord.*"

Here, as well as in 1 Kings xxi. 10, 13. Job i. 5, 11 ; ii. 5, 9, the word which was in the primitive Text was קָלַל (*kalal*), *to curse*, or גָּדַף (*gadaph*), *to blaspheme*, and to avoid having to pronounce these words in connection with God, the word ברך (*berech*), *to bless*, was substituted, and a note to this effect was put in the margin. The meaning, however, is so transparent that the translators have rendered it *curse*, instead of the printed Hebrew Text, which is *bless;* and commentators, ignorant of the real fact of the emendation, have laboured to prove that ברך (*berech*) means both *to bless* and *to curse*, which is not the case.

Ecc. iii. 21.—This is one of the emendations of the Sopherim, though it is not included in the official lists.

It is without a doubt that the primitive Text read and punctuated the ה as an interrogative: *i.e.*, Who knoweth whether the spirit of man goeth upward, and whether the spirit of the beast goeth downward to the earth ? " (The answer being *no one knows.*) The Chaldee, the Septuagint, the Syriac, the Vulgate, Luther, the Geneva (English) Version, and the Revised Version follow this reading.

But the A.V. follows Coverdale and the Bishops' Bible in adopting the reading of another school of editors; who, out of respect to the sensitiveness of some who listened to the public reading of the passage, endeavoured to remove the appearance of scepticism, or the psychological problem raised by the question, by punctuating the ה as the article pronoun, " that goeth upward . . . and that goeth downward ": thus, by the Figure *Euphemy*, avoiding and evading the supposed difficulty.*

---

* See Ginsburg's *Introduction to the Hebrew Bible*, pp. 461-2.

INDEXES.

I.

INDEX OF FIGURES.

PROPER NAMES.*

---

* For Analytical List see Table of Contents. For English Equivalents see Index II.

II.

INDEX OF FIGURES.

ENGLISH EQUIVALENTS.

III.

INDEX OF TEXTS AND PASSAGES ILLUSTRATED.*

* This index does not contain the passages that are merely *referred* to; but only those actually *used in illustration* of the Figures of Speech.

Numbers.

xxxiii.

3, 4	...	252

DEUTERONOMY.

i.

2, 44	...	776
4 ...	...	81
10 ...	...	758
26, 43	...	545
28 ...	...	423
37 ...	...	883

ii.

18 ...	...	776

iii.

4 ...	...	548
18 ...	...	504
24 ...	...	895

iv.

1 ...	...	857
12 ...	...	132
23 ...	...	1013
24 ...	...	896
26 ...	...	941
32 ...	594,	598

v.

4 ...	...	874
29 ...	...	922

vii.

17 ...	...	949

viii.

2 ...	...	884
3 ...	...	876
8 ...	...	626
17 ...	...	590

ix.

1 ...	570,	582
2 ...	...	409
3 ...	...	896
10 ..	...	890

x.

8 ...	...	605
17 ...	...	283

Deuteronomy.

x.

18 ...	...	629
22 ...	..	758

xi.

12 ...	...	875
30 ...	...	947

xii.

3 ...	...	535
12 ...	...	650
15 ...	...	859

xiii.

3 ...	...	884
4 ...	...	325
8 ...	...	861
13 ...	...	503
15 ...	...	407

xv.

5, 6	...	303
12 ...	...	61
17 ...	...	639
18 ...	...	585

xvi.

3 ...	...	586
5 ...	...	650
7 ...	...	675

xvii.

6 ...	...	545

xviii.

19 ...	...	413

xix.

5 ...	...	634
10 ...	...	628
12 ...	...	628

xx.

3 ...	...	326
19 ...	...	529

xxi.

4 ..	...	858
8 ...	...	628
10 ...	...	529
16 ...	...	652
17 ...	...	1013
22, 23	...	559

Deuteronomy.

xxii.

1 ...	605,	699
4 ...	...	1008
11 ...	...	895
15, 17	...	586

xxiii.

14 ...	830,	888
24 ...	...	545

xxiv.

5 ...	...	545
6 ...	...	563
19 ...	...	597

xxv.

4 ...	...	761
13 ...	...	559
17 ...	...	608

xxvi.

14 ...	...	1013

xxvii.

15-26	...	241
19 ...	...	629

xxviii.

1, 2	...	303
1-14	...	445
3-6	199,	919
5 ...	...	573
8 ..	...	602
11-19	...	941
12 ...	889,	894
13 ...	...	416
15-45	...	445
33 ...	...	551
43 ...	...	192
49-68	...	445
50 ...	...	606
53 ...	...	30
58 ...	608,	858
62 ...	...	758
63 ...	...	882
64 ...	...	614
66 ...	...	1013
67 ...	...	920
68 ...	...	821

Isaiah.		
vii.		
15 ...	...	533
18 ...	...	887
20 ...	...	867
23 ...	...	413
viii.		
9, 10	...	809
10 ...	...	514
12 ...	262,	277
13 ...	570,	601
14 ...	...	897
19, 20	...	85
ix.		
2 ...	...	518
4 ...	...	654
6 ...	891, 892,	991
7 ...	...	883
9 ...	..	649
10 ...	...	353
12, 17, 21	...	879
12, 17, 21 and x. 4		343
x.		
4 ...	...	879
14 ...	...	590
15 ...	...	956
16 ...	...	313
17 ...	...	896
22 ...	...	758
23 ...	...	412
27 ...	...	590
28-32	...	453
32 ...	...	868
xi.		
1 ...	...	773
2 ...	...	991
3 ...	...	859
4 ...	359,	876
6 ...	...	690
10 ...	894,	895
11 ...	...	878
15 ...	...	156
16 ...	...	653
xiii.		
4 ...	...	313
5 ...	598,	638
6 ...	313,	594

Isaiah.		
xiii.		
9 ...	...	30
11 ...	...	638
18 ...	...	863
xiv.		
4 ...	...	776
4, 12	...	942
6 ...	...	161
8 ...	34,	866
9-11	...	866
9-12	...	453
13 ...	...	425
14 ...	426,	995
15 ...	...	420
16-19	...	957
17 ...	...	638
21 ...	...	407
22 ...	...	859
24 ...	890,	941
26, 27	...	353
27 ...	762,	879
31 ...	579,	651
xv.		
9 ...	313,	626
xvi.		
1 ...	...	868
5 ...	...	892
9 ...	...	596
xvii.		
1 ...	...	313
2 ...	...	313
3 ...	...	809
5 ...	...	597
7, 8	...	354
xviii.		
2 ...	...	34
6 ...	...	354
xix.		
7 ...	888,	893
8 ...	...	407
11 ...	...	105
16 ...	...	879
xx.		
2, 3	...	637
5 ...	...	600

Isaiah.		
xxi.		
1 ...	...	584
2 ...	...	313
4 ...	...	1010
5 ...	...	809
7 ...	...	496
9 ...	...	194
11 ...	...	148
11, 12	...	773
xxii.		
4 ...	450,	916
13 ...	...	34
17 ...	...	277
18 ...	...	313
22 ...	...	606
xxiii.		
1 ...	...	577
3 ...	...	592
12 ...	...	868
16 ...	...	904
xxiv.		
1-3 ...	...	435
2 ...	...	730
3 ...	...	313
4 ...	314,	866
4, 5	...	254
14, 15	...	35
16 ...	...	280
17, 18	...	313
18 ...	...	413
23 ...	495,	866
xxv.		
1 ...	...	314
6 ...	...	314
7, 8	...	890
8 ...	...	889
xxvi.		
1 ...	...	6
3 ...	194,	497
4 ...	...	897
9 ...	...	541
21 ...	...	892
xxvii.		
1 ...	...	893

x 2

JOEL.

i.
```
2   ...   638, 950
3, 4      ...  257
4   ...   ...  864
6   ...   ...  864
10  ...   ..   864
13  ...   ...  607
15  ...   317, 595
16  ...   ...  948
17  ...   ...  493
```
ii.
```
1    ...   ...  595
1-11       ...  452
3    ..    ...  454
13   ...   ...  296
13, 14     ...  882
18   ...   303, 883
21   ...   303, 905
22   ...   ...  904
24   ...   ...  858
26, 27     ...  242
28   ...   ...  616
28, 29    890, 896
31   ...   303, 595
```
iii.
```
6    ...   ...  409
13   ...   ...  597
15   ...   ...  413
16   ...   ..   894
19   ...   ...  997
```

AMOS.

i.
```
1    ...   ...  709
2  ' ...   ...  894
7    ...   ...  650
10, 14     ..   650
```
ii.
```
1    ...   ...  710
2, 5       ...  650
11   ...   ...  948
```
iii.
```
2    ...   ...  554
8    ...   ...  402
11   ...   ...  29
12   ...   ...  75
```

Amos.

iv.
```
4    ...   ...       655
4, 5       810, 972
6    ...   ...       606
6, 8, 9, 10, 11      343
```
v.
```
2    ...   ...       868
8    ...   . .       407
11   ...   407, 601
15 and vi 6  ...     649
16   ...   ...       608
17   ...   ...       889
20   ...   418, 595, 948
25, 26     ...       710
```
vi.
```
2    ...   ...       707
6    ..    ...       649
8    ...   690, 872, 1011
12   ...   ...       85
```
vii.
```
3, 6       ...       882
9    ...   ..        544
9, 16      ...       608
17   ...   ...       548
```
viii.
```
1    ...   ...       596
1, 2       ..        317
3    ...   ...       588
5    ...   ...       592
7    ...   ...       886
10   ...   ...       607
```
ix.
```
2, 3       ...       433
9    ...   ...       890
13   ...   ...       426
14   ...   ...       317
```

OBADIAH.

```
1    ...   ...       599
4    ...   ...       427
5    ...   ...       948
8    ..    ..        948
12   ...   ...       595
```

JONAH.

i.
```
3    ...   ...       633
4    . .   ...       866
10   ...   ...       277
17   ...   ...       845
```
ii.
```
2    ...   ...       400
3    ...   400, 529
6    ..    . .       544
7    ..    ...       555
8    ...   ..        1010
9    ...   ..        464
```
iii.
```
3    ...   ...       503
5    . .   ...       527
9    ...   ...       122
```
iv.
```
6    . .   ...       317
11   . .   608, 948
```

MICAH.

i.
```
3    ...   ...       892
4    ...   ...       576
5    ...   ...       565
8    ...   ...       637
10   ...   ...       317
16   ...   ...       607
```
ii.
```
4    ...   278, 284
                942, 958
5    ...   ...       548
11   ...   ...       451
```
iii.
```
12-iv. 2   ...       303
```
iv.
```
10, 13     ...       868
```
v.
```
2    ...   ...       893
4    ...   409, 608, 891
9-13       ...       201
```
vi.
```
2    ...   ...       905
```

Matthew.

xv.
```
2    ...    ...    627
4    ...    ...    780
6    ...    ...    830
8, 9    ...    787
13    ...    ...    745
14    ...    ...    764
18-20    ...    401
22    ...    ...    625
22-26    ...    962
24    ...    ...    814
26    ...    156, 500
            617, 746
26, 27    ...    965
28    ...    ...    928
32    ...    ...    881
39    ...    ...    775
```

xvi.
```
6    ...    ...    745
7    ...    ...    51
14    ...    ...    836
17    ...    ...    644
18    ...    504, 687
            847, 897
19    ...    520, 569, 572
            606, 616
22    ...    ...    6, 339
23    ...    ...    935
25    ...    544, 817
28    ...    ...    340
```

xvii.
```
5    ...    464, 893
11    ...    521, 821
17    ...    928, 956
18    ...    ...    606
20    ...    ...    758
```

xviii.
```
1    ...    294, 527
4    ...    ...    618
8    ...    ...    526
10    ...    ...    873
11    ...    ...    534
12    ...    ...    655
14    ...    ...    156
18    ...    572, 616
24, 28    ...    836
```

Matthew.

xix.
```
1    ...    ...    413
5    ...    642, 792
10    ...    ...    621
12    ...    ...    270
13    ...    ...    18
16    ...    ...    975
17    ...    ...    21
16, 17    ...    294
21    ...    ...    894
24    ...    ...    758
28    ...    500, 637, 892
```

xx.
```
1-16    ...    891
2    ...    ...    859
11    ...    ...    858
15    ...    ...    854
16    ...    ...    464
23    ...    ...    123
28    ...    ...    544
30, 31    ...    625
```

xxi.
```
3    ...    622, 683
5    ...    785, 798
6    ...    ...    785
7    ...    ...    18
9, 15    ...    625
13    ...    426, 798
19    ...    531, 836, 857
20    ...    ...    952
21    ...    ...    760
22    ...    ...    48
23-25    ...    964
24    ...    ...    832
25    ...    ...    581
25, 26    ...    929
26    ...    ...    616
29    ...    ...    962
41    ...    ...    318
42    ...    534, 785, 896
```

xxii.
```
3    ...    157, 319
16    ...    ...    815
18    ...    ...    854
22    ...    ...    885
24    ...    622, 792
29    ...    ...    339
```

Matthew.

xxii.
```
42    ...    ...    625
44    . .    7, 785
45    ...    ...    885
```

xxiii.
```
2    ...    520, 604
7    ...    ...    837
12    ...    618, 759
15    ..    ...    833
24    ...    ...    759
29    ...    ...    111
32    ...    ...    972
35    ...    ...    628
35, 36    ...    711
37    ...    190, 197, 580
            895, 954
39    ...    ...    340
```

xxiv.
```
    ...    452
2    ...    ...    340
6    ...    ...    599
7    ...    ...    319
9    ...    ...    616
15    ...    ...    851
20    ...    166, 608
21    ...    ...    340
22    ...    ...    836
28    ...    464, 764
29    ...    ...    678
29-31    ...    218
30    ...    ...    663
31    ...    592, 598, 663
34    ...    ...    340
35    ...    ...    340
45    ...    ...    569
48    ...    ...    856
```

xxv.
```
1    ...    ...    892
9    ...    ...    49
10    ...    ...    592
12    ...    ...    884
16    ...    ...    557
21, 23    ...    592
36, 43    ...    637
37-39    ...    958
```

xxvi.
```
1    ...    ...    413
5    ...    ...    30
```

Luke.

xix.
41	...	... 450
41, 42	...	... 916
42	...	153, 552, 595
44	...	... 67
46	...	... 798

xx.
9	...	67, 640
18	...	... 618
23	...	... 854
34	...	... 504
35	...	... 1002
36	...	... 504
42	...	... 7
42, 43	...	... 785

xxi.
		... 452
4	...	593, 998
6	...	... 720
15	...	... 663
18	...	341, 759
19	...	... 857
24	...	... 407
28	...	... 606
34	...	... 648
35	...	407, 421
38	...	... 67

xxii.
8	...	... 596
11	...	... 596
15	...	278, 596, 835
17, 20	...	577
19	...	... 522
21	...	... 41
22	...	... 522
31	...	... 190
36	...	... 106
36, 38	...	608
37	...	85, 522
41	...	... 441
44	...	... 729
49	...	835, 837
67, 68	...	341

xxiii.
7, 11, 15	...	855
21	...	... 198
31	...	760, 765, 895
38	...	... 805

Luke.

xxiii.
| 46 | ... | ... 523 |

xxiv.
25	...	... 930
27	...	... 133
40	...	... 18
49	...	... 522
54	...	... 619

JOHN.

i.
1	...	... 694
1, 2	...	... 257
3	...	... 418
4	...	... 518
4, 5	...	... 258
5	...	178, 322
9	...	421, 576, 616
10	...	290, 576
11	...	284, 290
12	...	410, 520, 608
13	...	... 531
14	...	643, 729, 1001
15	...	518, 528
16	...	... 615
17	...	... 663
18	...	101, 881
20	...	... 418
22	...	... 415
23	...	... 67
24	...	... 459
25	...	... 494
28	...	... 459
29	...	... 894
46	...	534, 757
51	...	198, 842

ii.
4	...	... 842
7	...	... 1001
9	...	... 473
17	...	... 998
18	...	... 49
19	...	514, 746, 825
21	...	... 995
23	...	... 410
23, 24	...	290
25	...	... 688

John.

iii.
2	...	54, 975
4	...	... 956
5	...	... 664
6	...	534, 541
8	...	... 248
10	...	... 811
11	...	... 525
13	...	22, 281
		519, 521
14, 15	...	786
15	...	... 418
15, 16	...	618, 836
16	...	518, 576, 638
17	...	... 576
18	...	339, 410
		557, 608
19	...	556, 565
24	...	... 459
26	...	... 426
27	...	... 581
28	...	... 892
31	...	... 290
32	...	... 618
33	...	... 856
34	...	... 540

iv.
6	...	... 456
7-9	...	... 473
10, 11	...	... 831
10, 14	...	... 896
12	...	... 625
13	...	... 618
14	...	... 341
19	...	... 695
21-24	...	... 664
23	...	656, 844
23, 24	...	... 631
24	...	41, 695
31, 32	...	... 290
32, 34	...	... 888
35	...	750, 948
37	...	... 757
38	...	... 519

v.
| 7 | ... | ... 52 |
| 8-11 | ... | ... 377 |

z 2

	John.		Jonn.		ACTS.

John.

xiii.
- 6 ... 522
- 7 ... 270, 305
- 8 ... 339
- 10 ... 271
- 14 ... 635
- 16 ... 760
- 18 ... 50
- 27 ... 522, 972
- 29 ... 724, 852
- 34 ... 462
- 37, 38 ... 544

xiv.
- 1-4 ... 263
- 3 ... 522
- 6 ... 673, 897
- 10 ... 112
- 11 ... 254
- 16 ... 854
- 17 ... 302, 576
- 18 ... 161, 522
- 19 ... 522
- 23 ... 892
- 26 ... 854
- 27 ... 627
- 30 ... 577
- 31 ... 576

xv.
- ... 891
- 1-5 ... 895
- 2 ... 13, 305
- 4 ... 85
- 5 ... 495, 743, 619
- 6 ... 12, 520
- 8 ... 513
- 13 ... 544
- 16 ... 302
- 18 ... 528
- 20 ... 157
- 22 ... 527
- 25 ... 50
- 26 ...
- 27 ... 50

xvi.
- 2 ... 618, 656
- 5 ... 822
- 7 ... 854
- 8 ... 950

Jonn.

xvi.
- 8-11 ... 395
- 11 ... 577
- 12-15 ... 263
- 13, 14 ... 701
- 16 ... 522
- 27 ... 518
- 32 ... 910

xvii.
- 1 ... 656
- 2 ... 998
- 3 ... 441, 553
- 565, 695
- 6 ... 608
- 11 ... 522
- 12 ... 833
- 21 ... 577
- 26 ... 112, 271

xviii.
- 18 ... 455, 456
- 20 ... 619, 639
- 24 ... 520
- 37 ... 255, 892
- 38 ... 813, 955

xix.
- 12 ... 618
- 14 ... 813
- 19 ... 805
- 22 ... 805
- 36 ... 786
- 37 ... 785, 829

xx.
- 7 ... 836
- 17 ... 518, 522
- 19, 21, 26 ... 627
- 23 ... 589, 572
- 25 ... 340
- 30 ... 468

xxi.
- 3 ... 856
- 7 ... 637
- 12 ... 701
- 15-17 ... 401
- 24 ... 525
- 25 ... 428

ACTS.

i.
- 4 ... 602, 724, 993
- 5 ... 542
- 6 ... 522
- 7 ... 531
- 8 ... 223, 636
- 11 ... 569
- 15 ... 473, 608
- 16 ... 781
- 18 ... 562, 824
- 20 ... 799
- 21 ... 630
- 21, 22 ... 690
- 22 ... 650
- 24 ... 569
- 25 ... 665

ii.
- 3 ... 107
- 4 ... 546
- 6 ... 413
- 8-11 ... 476
- 11 ... 546
- 15 ... 455
- 17, 18, 23 ... 896
- 17, 18, 33 ... 890
- 21 ... 618
- 23 ... 332
- 25 ... 892
- 26-31 ... 642
- 27, 31 ... 545, 838
- 29 ... 41
- 31 ... 641
- 33, 34 ... 880
- 34 ... 7
- 34, 35 ... 785
- 39 ... 688
- 41, 43 ... 640
- 42 ... 826
- 47 ... 636

iii.
- 6 ... 559
- 14 ... 665, 683
- 16 ... 608
- 17 ... 857
- 18 ... 781
- 19 ... 407
- 22, 23 ... 785
- 23 ... 413

Romans.

xi.

22 395
23 825
26, 27 ... 799
29 875
33 ... 175, 893, 923
34, 35 ... 950
36 282

xii.

1 ... 531, 641
2 594
3 ... 126, 305
4 724
6-8 ... 57
8 860
11 ... 76, 418, 832
13, 14 ... 291
14 418
15 ... 177, 274, 516
16-19, 20 ... 723
19 ... 23, 696
20 ... 635, 904

xiii.

1 ... 462, 640
3 ... 562, 904, 999
4 604
5 550
6-8 ... 57
7 58
8 322
9 832
10 163
11 ... 30, 859
11, 12 ... 750

xiv.

1 696
2 23
3 557
4 ... 825, 904, 910
5 23
8 250
10 904
11 ... 607, 678, 785
15 ... 562, 899
17 628
20 24
21 62
23 24

Romans.

xv.

3 785
4 ... 323, 659, 992
12 ... 786, 895
19 537
24 569
26 578
28 ... 13, 856
29 825

xvi.

2 999
3, 7 ... 569
4 641
16 62
18 647
18, 19 ... 860
23 853
25 825

I CORINTHIANS.

1 Corinthians ... 387

i.

1 125
2 125
10 ... 418, 518
16 574
17 507
17, 18 ... 612
19, 20 ... 790
21 ... 507, 597
23, 24 ... 179, 323
24, 25 ... 361
25 ... 597, 677, 817
26 58
27, 28 ... 496, 534
27-29 ... 817
28 827
29 ... 642, 836
30 224

ii.

2 512
4 666
6 679
9 ... 629, 647, 792
10 884
11 76

I Corinthians.

ii.

12 ... 31, 545
13 ... 76, 284
14 ... 163, 270, 339

iii.

1 13
2 ... 36, 133, 632
6 ... 512, 625
6-8 750
7 527
9 ... 202, 696
12, 13 ... 141
12-15 ... 750

iv.

3 595
4 79
6, 7 ... 723
8 .. 148, 431
813, 970
9 579
11 637
11, 13 ... 206
15 ... 87, 427
17 619
19 554
20 31
21 968
30 528

v.

1 829
3, 4, 5 ... 541
4, 5 ... 109
6 765
7 894
7, 8 ... 750
9 857
13 523

vi.

2 ... 271, 616
4 ... 513, 812
5 529
11 202
12 ... 109, 203
13 41
15 642
20 541

HEBREWS.

i., ii.	...	367, 900
i.		
1	...	175
2	...	594, 631
3	...	993
3, 4	...	880
5	...	889, 950
6	...	493, 893
8	...	892, 894
8, 9	...	786
9	...	894
10-13	...	786
13	...	7, 785
		892, 950
14	...	422, 948
ii.		
3	...	47
4	...	891
6	...	952
7	...	519
8	...	892, 914
9	...	470, 617
11	...	80
12	...	412
14	...	293, 645, 651
15	...	492
16	...	127, 521
18	...	825, 853
iii.		
6	...	900
7	...	780
8	...	703
12	...	1000
14	...	519
15	...	91
iv.		
1	...	493
2	...	704
7	...	91
10	...	91
12	...	859
13	...	875
15	...	18, 853
16	...	892
v.		
3	...	69

Hebrews.

v.		
6	...	786, 994
7	...	69
8	...	319
13	...	1000
vi.		
1	...	566, 995
1-3	...	908
3	...	827
12	...	408
14	...	274
16	...	616, 697
17	...	496, 508
vii.		
3	...	521
4	...	80, 697
7	...	534
8	...	92, 521
17	...	786
18	...	855
26	...	830
viii.		
1	...	110, 880, 892
10	...	890
ix.		
1	...	8
8	...	780
10	...	501
12	...	157, 531, 630
12, 14	...	610
15	...	509, 537
16, 17	...	69, 533, 852
17	...	493
19	...	712
19, 20	...	799
21	...	1000
23	...	531, 537
26	...	855
28	...	551
x.		
5	...	509, 793
5, 6	...	786
7	...	651
11	...	518
13	...	7
15	...	781

Hebrews.

x.		
19	...	610
20	...	643, 831
21	...	527
23	...	70
25	...	900
28	...	531
30	...	697
34	...	306
37	...	198, 272
38	...	872
39	...	504
xi.		128
1	...	854
4	...	844
5	...	631
7	...	574
10	...	891
12	...	427, 758
13	...	603, 606, 637
15	...	555
16	...	164
20, 21	...	50
21	...	712, 794
22-38	...	148
26	...	1000
31	...	680, 690
32	...	438, 484
34	...	407
39	...	468
xii.		
1	...	593
2	...	1127
5, 6	...	761
5-10	...	892
9	...	501
11	...	497
18	...	493
18-29	...	477
20	...	113
20, 21	...	474
21	...	713
22	...	520
24	...	610
25	...	92
27	...	494

IV.

INDEX OF STRUCTURES.

V.

INDEX OF SUBJECTS.

VI.

INDEX OF HEBREW WORDS EXPLAINED.

VII.

INDEX OF GREEK WORDS EXPLAINED.